Managerial Accounting

An Introduction to Concepts, Methods, and Uses

Managerial Accounting

An Introduction to Concepts, Methods, and Uses

Michael W. Maher

University of California—Davis

Clyde P. Stickney

Dartmouth College

Roman L. Weil

University of Chicago

The Dryden Press

Harcourt Brace College Publishers

Fort Worth   Philadelphia   San Diego   New York   Orlando   Austin   San Antonio
Toronto   Montreal   London   Sydney   Tokyo

Acquisitions Editor Tim Vertovec
Developmental Editor Craig Avery
Project Editor Jim Patterson
Production Manager Kelly Cordes
Art Director Guy Jacobs
Permissions Editor Shirley Webster
Publisher Elizabeth Widdicombe
**Director of Editing,
Design, and Production** Diane Southworth
Copy Editor Karen Carriere
Indexer Cherie B. Weil
Compositor York Graphic Services, Inc.
Text Type 10/12 Times

Requests for permission to make copies of any part of the work should be mailed to: Permissions Department, Harcourt Brace & Company, 8th Floor, Orlando, Florida 32887.

Address for Editorial Correspondence
The Dryden Press, 301 Commerce Street, Suite 3700, Fort Worth, TX 76102

Address for Orders
The Dryden Press, 6277 Sea Harbor Drive, Orlando, FL 32887
1-800-782-4479, or 1-800-433-0001 (in Florida)

ISBN: 0-03-098202-2

Library of Congress Catalog Card Number: 93-73779

Printed in the United States of America

3 4 5 6 7 8 9 0 1 2 039 9 8 7 6 5 4 3 2 1

The Dryden Press
Harcourt Brace College Publishers

For our students, with thanks.

Whatever be the detail with which you cram your students, the chance of their meeting in after-life exactly that detail is almost infinitesimal; and if they do meet it, they will probably have forgotten what you taught them about it. The really useful training yields a comprehension of a few general principles with a thorough grounding in the way they apply to a variety of concrete details. In subsequent practice the students will have forgotten your particular details; but they will remember by an unconscious common sense how to apply principles to immediate circumstances.

Alfred North Whitehead
The Aims of Education and Other Essays

The Dryden Press Series in Accounting

Introductory

Bischoff *Introduction to College Accounting* Second Edition

Principles

Hanson, Hamre, and Walgenbach *Principles of Accounting* Sixth Edition

Hillman, Kochanek, and Norgaard *Principles of Accounting* Sixth Edition

Morgenstein *Career Accounting Fundamentals*

Computerized

Bischoff and Wanlass *The Computer Connection: General Ledger and Practice Sets to Accompany Introductory Accounting* Second Edition

Brigham and Knechel *Financial Accounting Using Lotus 1-2-3*

Wanlass *Computer Resource Guide: Principles of Accounting* Fourth Edition

Yasuda and Wanlass *The Real Time Advantage*

Financial

Backer, Elgers, and Asebrook *Financial Accounting: Concepts and Practices*

Beirne and Dauderis *Financial Accounting: An Introduction to Decision Making*

Hanson, Hamre, and Walgenbach *Financial Accounting* Seventh Edition

Kochanek, Hillman, and Norgaard *Financial Accounting* Second Edition

Stickney and Weil *Financial Accounting: An Introduction to Concepts, Methods, and Uses* Seventh Edition

Managerial

Ketz, Campbell, and Baxendale *Management Accounting*

Maher, Stickney, and Weil *Managerial Accounting: An Introduction to Concepts, Methods, and Uses* Fifth Edition

Intermediate

Williams, Stanga, and Holder *Intermediate Accounting* Fourth Edition

Advanced

Huefner and Largay *Advanced Financial Accounting* Third Edition

Pahler and Mori *Advanced Accounting* Fifth Edition

Financial Statement Analysis

Stickney *Financial Statement Analysis: A Strategic Perspective* Second Edition

Auditing

Guy, Alderman, and Winters *Auditing* Third Edition

Rittenberg and Schwieger *Auditing: Concepts for a Changing Environment*

Theory

Belkaoui *Accounting Theory* Third Edition

Bloom and Elgers *Accounting Theory & Policy: A Reader* Second Edition

Taxation

Duncan *Essentials of U.S. Taxation*

Everett, Raabe, and Fortin *Income Tax Fundamentals 1994*

Sommerfeld, Madeo, Anderson, and Jackson *Concepts of Taxation*

Quattrochi *Federal Tax Research*

Reference

Miller and Bailey *Miller Comprehensive GAAS Guide* College Edition

Williams and Miller *Miller Comprehensive GAAP Guide* College Edition

Governmental and Not-for-Profit

Douglas *Governmental and Nonprofit Accounting: Theory and Practice* Second Edition

Ziebell *Management Control Systems in Nonprofit Organizations*

The Harcourt Brace College Outline Series

Campbell, Grierson, and Taylor *Principles of Accounting I* Revised Edition

Emery *Principles of Accounting II*

Emery *Intermediate Accounting I* Second Edition

Emery *Intermediate Accounting II*

Frigo *Cost Accounting*

Poteau *Advanced Accounting*

If we were to place managerial accounting textbooks on a continuum from managerial orientation at one end to procedural cost accounting orientation at the other end, *Managerial Accounting: An Introduction to Concepts, Methods, and Uses,* would be on the managerial end of the continuum. We have always assumed that most students using this book will be *users,* not producers, of accounting information. We want these students to understand the relevance of accounting information in marketing, production, systems design, engineering, management, and other non-accounting activities. Consequently, we focus on managerial accounting concepts and applications, not procedures.

Users and reviewers of previous editions have generally regarded *Managerial Accounting* as nurturing and stretching the critical thinking skills of students. A *critical thought approach* views accounting as a process of reporting information for people to use in decision making, as opposed to a view of accounting as a set of rules or procedures to follow. Both producers and users of accounting information must make many judgments based on the usefulness of information. We convey this idea throughout the book in text and assignment materials. Indeed, we have devoted an entire chapter (Chapter 16, *Getting the Most from Managerial Accounting*) to critical thinking about the accounting process.

In building on the book's enduring strengths—user orientation, conceptual focus, and critical thinking approach—we have thoroughly revised the Fifth Edition to make the book even more useful for current and future managers. Among other changes, we include a new chapter on activity-based management and costing (Chapter 6). We have rewritten chapters to make the concepts and applications clearer and more understandable at first reading. We have moved the Problems for Self Study to strategic points in the text for more immediate feedback. By significantly increasing the number of real-company references and illustrations, we have made the material more relevant for emerging managers.

Major Features of the Book

The Fifth Edition contains many features that differentiate it from other textbooks in the field.

Conceptual Approach

We present managerial accounting concepts to prepare students to focus on relevant issues. *This preparation is more important than ever with the increased emphasis on developing critical thinking skills in current curricula.* The Accounting Education Change Commission argues for a more conceptual approach to accounting education. We agree, and provide it in this book. Methods follow concepts, so students start with the big picture before they learn specific procedures. The book supports this conceptual approach with numerous examples and many short exercises.

For example, our presentation of variances starts with a "big picture" comparison of budgeted and achieved results in Chapter 12, then presents variance calculations in Chapters 13 and 14 as a more detailed presentation of the budget-versus-achieved comparison. This approach has two advantages. First, it keeps the larger view and the purpose of variance calculations in students' minds; they do not lose sight of their overall objectives as they analyze detailed variances. Second, students find the approach intuitive. They may forget how to compute particular variances, but they will remember the overall model, which will enable them to reconstruct variance analysis later.

Managerial Applications

Students are more highly motivated to learn the material if they see its application to real-world problems, particularly ones they believe they will face. These Managerial Applications allow the student to explore actual company practices that illustrate concepts discussed in the text without disrupting the flow of the concepts. Students often remember these real-company illustrations long after classes are over.

Extensive Use of Nonmanufacturing Applications

We have included numerous examples and applications to nonmanufacturing settings. Traditionally, accountants have considered certain topics, like cost accumulation and variance analysis, to be the domain of manufacturing. Our chapters on these topics show how to use the concepts in nonmanufacturing organizations.

Integrated Self-Study Problems and Solutions

Self-study problems are a vital part of the Fifth Edition. Integrated into the chapters, they give students instant feedback and critical thinking exposure at the points in the text where students need it most. (Solutions precede the assignment material.) Many chapters have three or four self-study problems.

Solutions to Even-Numbered Exercises

We have included Suggested Solutions to Even-Numbered Exercises at the end of every chapter with exercises. These fully annotated solutions give students even more feedback on their understanding of the text.

Chapter 16: "Getting the Most from Managerial Accounting"

Chapter 16 uniquely challenges students to analyze the uses of accounting critically. This chapter also discusses fraudulent financial reporting. Students can read this chapter anytime after Chapter 3.

Variety and Depth of Assignment Materials

Accounting instructors know the need for accurate and interesting assignment materials. We have class-tested the assignment material and worked every question, exercise, problem, and case at least twice in preparing this book.

The variety and quantity of assignment materials in the Fifth Edition allow the book to be used in various levels of courses. To help the instructor assign homework and select items for class presentation, we have divided the assignment materials into four categories:

1. *Questions* include both straightforward questions about key concepts and thought-provoking questions about the challenging issues that managers and accountants face. Questions are particularly good for written essays and class discussions.
2. *Exercises* reinforce key concepts in the chapter, often referring the student to a particular illustration. Exercises typically deal with a single topic and are particularly useful for classroom demonstration.
3. *Problems* challenge the student to apply and interpret the material in the chapter, many with thought-provoking discussion or essay questions. (Instructors also can easily add additional essay and critical thought questions.) Problems generally require students to think about managerial issues as well as accounting issues.
4. *Cases* encourage students to apply concepts from multiple chapters and their other courses to deal with complex managerial issues. Cases are particularly good for advanced students and graduate students with some previous background in managerial accounting.

Major Changes in This Edition

Increased Managerial Orientation

Although previous editions had a strong managerial orientation, we made the Fifth Edition even more managerial in both the text and assignment materials. We have reduced preparer-based requirements and added a managerial decision context to many assignment items. In Chapters 1 through 6, we have increased the emphasis on product costing and cost management for decision making and reduced the emphasis on costing for inventory values in external financial statements. The new chapter on activity-based costing and management (Chapter 6) focuses on managers' problems in managing activities and includes a discussion of strategic uses of activity-based costing and management.

New Chapter on Activity-Based Costing and Management

Chapter 6 is a new chapter on activity-based costing and management (ABCM). We added this chapter to alert students to current developments and opportunities for improvement in management accounting. This chapter takes a management orientation to activity and product costing using ABCM by emphasizing choices among accounting alternatives, benefits of activity management, and strategic opportunities provided by ABCM. Topics include applying cost-benefit tests to ABCM, the process of accounting system change, the use of ABCM to eliminate non-value-added costs, the use of ABCM in marketing, and opportunities to improve ABCM in practice.

Additional Discussion of New Production Methods Throughout the Text

In addition to the new chapter on activity-based costing and management, we have incorporated additional discussion of new production methods throughout the book. (We call these new ''production'' methods while others call them new ''manufacturing'' methods. We prefer the term ''production'' to ''manufacturing'' to recognize the importance of these new methods in producing services, not just goods.) Here are some examples:

- Chapter 1: Sections on activity-based costing and management, lean production, and quality.
- Chapter 3: Discussion of alternative cost drivers used to apply overhead to products.
- Chapter 4: Section on just-in-time and backflush costing; discussion of use of just-in-time to achieve lean production; discussion of difficulties in implementing just-in-time methods.
- Chapter 6: New chapter on activity-based costing and management.
- Chapter 7: Section on use of regression to identify cost drivers for activity-based costing including discussion of empirical research in identifying cost drivers.
- Chapter 9: Discussion of flexible manufacturing methods.
- Chapter 13: Section on nonfinancial performance measures emphasizing quality. Managerial Application on Texas Instruments' cost of quality program. Section on variance analysis when activity-based costing is used to derive standard costs.
- Chapter 14: Managerial Application on quality management and the Baldrige Award.

New Coverage of Ethical Issues That Affect Managers and Accountants

Our students face a future of increasing concern about the accountability of accountants and managers for their actions. This edition contains discussions of ethics that demonstrate the types of complex ethical choices students are likely to encounter during their careers. While the discussions focus on managerial accounting issues, inevitably the situations evoke organizational and managerial issues, corporate accountability, the role of internal and external auditors, and societal expectations for accountability.

Following is a sample of the new ethics materials in this edition:

- Chapter 1: Ethical implications of accounting choices and discussion of corporate codes of ethics such as the Johnson & Johnson Credo.
- Chapter 3: Ethical issues in increasing production to increase profits under full-absorption costing.
- Chapter 4: Improprieties in assigning costs to jobs, especially on government contracts.
- Chapter 12: Ethical issues in budgeting, including discussion of General Electric's attempts to deal with conflicts between behaving ethically and meeting performance standards.
- Chapter 16: Management ethics and financial fraud including discussion of actual financial fraud situations. This material provides students with a conceptual framework for evaluating situations conducive to fraud, including concepts drawn from work by the Treadway Commission. The assignment material has been class-tested; undergraduates, MBA students, and executives have found it interesting.

New Material: Chapter by Chapter

All Chapters

- Added *learning objectives* to each chapter to give students a better sense of what they can expect to learn from the chapter.
- Integrated *self-study questions* in the chapters so students can test their knowledge for immediate feedback on their understanding of the material as they read the chapter. (Solutions to self-study questions are at the end of the chapter.)
- Increased the number of references to actual companies to make the material more interesting and relevant to students. (The Index highlights real-company references.)
- Revised odd-numbered exercises and many problems.
- Rewrote text material for increased accessibility and to focus on use by managers.
- Revised problems to make them more straightforward.

Chapter 1   Added material on ethics, including Johnson & Johnson Credo and assignment materials, to help students see the ethical implications of management and accounting decisions. Added materials on the new production environment to emphasize the importance of lean production, quality, and activity-based management and costing.

Chapter 3   Added discussion of ethical issues in increasing production to increase profits under full-absorption costing.

Chapter 4   Revised the chapter for a more managerial and less procedural emphasis. Expanded coverage of alternative production methods to include operations, in addition to jobs and continuous processes. Expanded discussion of backflush costing in just-in-time settings. Added discussion of lean production methods and the use of just-in-time to achieve lean production. Expanded discussion of just-in-time, including implementation difficulties. Discussed improprieties in assigning costs to jobs, particularly on government contracts.

Chapter 5   Added classic dialog between a small business owner and his consultant (''Joe vs. The Efficiency Expert'') to demonstrate inherently controversial aspects of cost allocation about cost allocation issues. Simplified department allocation example.

Chapter 6   Added new chapter on activity-based costing and management (ABCM). This chapter reflects the authors' views that activity-based costing provides an important new concept in management by focusing on managing activities. Major features include:

- Dialog among company managers discussing inadequacies in the company's traditional accounting system in providing the information needed for the company to remain competitive.
- Cost-benefit considerations in choosing among plantwide allocation, department allocation, and ABC.
- Description of the steps involved in ABC, including identifying activity centers and cost drivers, and assigning costs to products.
- Use of ABC to eliminate non-value-added costs.
- Use of ABC in analyzing marketing costs.
- Strategic opportunities with ABC.
- Real-world application discussing use of ABC in managing health care costs.
- Opportunities to improve ABC in practice, including the hierarchy of costs approach proposed by Cooper and Kaplan.

Chapter 7   Added discussion of the use of regression to identify cost drivers for ABC; includes discussion of empirical research in identifying cost drivers.

Chapter 8   Added Managerial Application on breaking even in the auto industry. Demonstrated how computer spreadsheets are used in cost-volume-profit analysis.

Chapters 10 and 11   Simplified discussion of capital budgeting and added more basic exercises.

Chapter 12   Combined conceptual and analytical elements of Chapters 11 and 12 from the previous edition to provide a more logical flow and focus on operating budgets. Added discussion of ethical issues in budgeting, including managerial application discussing conflict between ethical issues and meeting performance standards at General Electric. Added Managerial Application on the State of California's problems in balancing its budget.

Chapter 13   Added section on nonfinancial performance measures. Added Managerial Application on Texas Instruments' cost of quality program. Added discussion of variance analysis when activity-based costing is used to derive standard costs.

Chapter 14   Added Managerial Application on quality management and the Baldrige Award.

Chapter 15   Added section on transfer pricing practices in the U.S., Canada, and Japan. Added discussion of multinational transfer pricing, including a Managerial Application of a transfer pricing dispute between U.S. tax authorities and a Japanese company.

Chapter 16   Added section on fraudulent financial reporting and added considerable assignment material on financial fraud. Text describes actual financial fraud situations and discusses ways to prevent and detect fraud. Features include:

- Common types of fraud, such as early revenue recognition and inventory overstatement.
- Motives and opportunities to commit fraud.
- The importance of the "tone at the top."
- Analysis of actual case studies of financial fraud.

Organization and Use of This Book

We divided the book into five major parts, as follows: Part One, Fundamental Concepts, Chapters 1–2; Part Two, Cost Methods and Systems, Chapters 3–6; Part Three, Managerial Decision Making, Chapters 7–11; Part Four, Managerial Planning and Performance Evaluation, Chapters 12–15; and Part Five, Special Topics, Chapters 16–18.

Part One   covers fundamental concepts and provides an overview of managerial accounting. Instructors may cover the other parts in any sequence, or omit them, after Part One, as the diagram below shows:

```
                    ┌→ Part Two  → Part Three → Part Four
                    ├→ Part Three → Part Two  → Part Four
        Part One ───┤
                    ├→ Part Two  → Part Four → Part Three
                    └→ . . .
```

Part Two describes cost methods and systems companies use. Chapter 3 discusses alternative methods of measuring product costs. Chapter 4 shows how accounting is done in alternative production settings. Chapter 5 discusses cost allocation. Chapter 6 discusses activity-based management and costing.

Part Three discusses concepts and methods useful for managerial decision making. Chapter 7 discusses methods of estimating cost behavior. Chapters 8 and 9 discuss the use of accounting data in short-run decision making, where capacity is held constant. Chapters 10 and 11 discuss the use of accounting in long-run decision making involving capital budgeting.

Part Four discusses managerial planning, control, and internal performance evaluation. Chapter 12 provides an overview of planning and control, and discusses development of budgets as tools for planning and control. Chapters 13 and 14 deal with variances. Chapter 13 presents the fundamental cost variance model that applies to any type of manufacturing or nonmanufacturing cost and includes a discussion of nonfinancial performance measures. Chapter 14 provides more detailed variance analysis. Chapter 15 focuses on performance evaluation in decentralized operations.

Part Five deals with special topics. Chapter 16 describes situations where managers may have incentives to take actions that do not serve the best interests of the firm but that make them look good to reviewers of accounting reports. The text and assignment material include coverage of financial fraud. Chapters 17 and 18 present an overview of financial accounting. For readers familiar with financial accounting, these chapters will serve as a review. Readers who have not studied financial accounting can use these chapters as an introduction to financial accounting concepts, methods, and uses. These chapters are independent of the rest of the book and students may read them at any time.

The Appendix to the book discusses compound interest calculations used in discounted cash flow analysis. It is also independent of the rest of the book. The glossary defines comprehensively the concepts and terms used in managerial accounting.

Instructors can cover any of the above chapters out of sequence or omit them, with two exceptions: Chapter 11 should follow Chapter 10 and Chapter 14 should follow Chapter 13.

Related Materials Accompanying the Text

Instructor's Manual by Anne J. Rich and Kathleen Simione

The Instructor's Manual includes sample course outlines, assignments, additional writing questions, ethical issues, chapter overviews, lecture notes, short progress tests to be given at the beginning or end of class, and other instructor help. A master list of Check Figures is available. Professors Anne J. Rich and Kathleen Simione both teach at Quinnipiac College.

Solutions Manual by the authors

This manual contains responses to questions and solutions to all exercises, problems, and cases. We have checked these solutions to eliminate errors.

Test Bank by Anne J. Rich

The test bank contains multiple choice questions and exercises for examinations. It also features a new Matching Section and short essay questions with suggested responses. Topical heads have been added for easier test creation, and all solutions are fully annotated.

Computerized Test Bank

The test bank is available in EXAMaster+ computerized format for most DOS-based and Macintosh personal computers.

RequesTest

Call (800) 447-9457 toll-free to order test masters through the HB RequesTest service. Allow 48 hours for compiling the test in addition to first-class mail delivery (fax delivery available). RequesTest service and software support are available Monday through Friday, 9 A.M. to 4 P.M. (Central Time) for questions, guidance, or other help.

Study Guide by Anne J. Rich

For each chapter and the appendix, the Study Guide includes

1. A brief summary of the chapter.
2. An outline of the chapter with emphasis on key points.
3. Several self-test and practice exercises, with answers or suggested solutions. Included are matching exercises and short problems.
4. A study plan designed to help students solve the problems in the text. Included here are references to text exhibits for review and coverage of those text problems solvable using the spreadsheet templates available to adopters.
5. Instructions on how to use the student software (see the following for more details).

Management Templates

Professors Anne J. Rich and David Cadden (both of Quinnipiac College) have prepared this supplement to give students experience in solving management accounting problems using electronic spreadsheets. This supplement enables students to solve selected problems from this text using the templates provided. Professor Rich provides notes and comments on using the software for students in the *Study Guide* and for the instructor in the *Instructor's Manual.* Requires Lotus® 1-2-3 (DOS version) or Microsoft Excel® (Macintosh version). End-of-chapter items workable using the templates are identified with a disk icon in the margin.

Transparencies

Acetate transparencies of 100 of the exhibits from the textbook are available to enhance classroom instruction. In addition Transparencies are now available for numerical solutions to all Exercises, Problems, and Cases found in the Solutions Manual.

Acknowledgments

We gratefully acknowledge the helpful criticisms and suggestions from the following people who reviewed the Fourth Edition at various stages: Paul K. Chaney, Vanderbilt University; Stephen V. Senge, Western Washington University; Philip H. Vorherr, University of Cincinnati; and Roland M. Wright, Belmont College. We further acknowledge the reviewers of the third edition, whose comments guided some of our efforts in this edition as well: Jane Reimers, Florida State University; Fred J. Croop, Wilkes College; Dennis C. Daly, University of Minnesota; Michael Haselkorn, Bentley College; Ilene Kleinsorge, Oregon State University; Larry Lewis, Gonzaga University; Eric W. Noreen, University of Washington; Denis Raihall, Drexel University; Michael F. van Breda, Southern Methodist University; and S. Mark Young, University of Colorado.

We thank those reviewers of the Fifth Edition who have given invaluable advice: Kevin Devine, Xavier University; Dileep Dhavale, Clark College; Robert Greenberg, Washington State University; In-Mu Haw, Texas Christian University; A. Ronald Kucic, University of Denver; Laureen A. Maines, Duke University; Ella Mae Matsumura, University of Wisconsin, Madison; Rafael Munoz, University of Texas at Austin; Eileen Peacock, Oakland University; Karl Putnam, University of Texas at El Paso; Anne J. Rich, Quinnipiac College; Edward L. Summers, University of Texas at Austin; Jim Voss, Pennsylvania State University.

We also thank Ann O'Brien, Mohanas Dissanayake, and Mary Lou Poloskey (all of the University of Texas at Austin) for their help in examining the problem material.

Thomas Horton and Daughters, Inc., has given us permission to reproduce material from *Accounting: The Language of Business.* The following have consented to let us use problems or cases they prepared: Case Clearing House, David O. Green, David Solomons, George Sorter, James Reece, Gordon Shillinglaw, Jean Lim, David Croll, Robert Colson, and Edward Deakin. Material from the Uniform CPA Examinations and Unofficial Answers, copyright by the American Institute of Certified Public Accountants, Inc., is adapted with permission. Permission has been received from the Institute of Management Accountants to use questions and unofficial answers from past CMA examinations.

We thank the following people for their help in preparing this book: Vanetta Van Cleave, Erin Kahn, and Katherine Xenophon-Rybowiak. Cherie Weil prepared the index. Rick Antle, Bob Colson, Peter Easton, Timothy Farmer, Robert Lipe,

M. Laurentius Marais, Harry Newman, Mark Penno, and Katherine Schipper, have all provided particularly thought-provoking comments.

We thank Tim Vertovec, Craig Avery, Jim Patterson, Kelly Cordes, Guy Jacobs, Shirley Webster, and Diana Farrell for their assistance in the preparation of this book.

Finally, Sidney Davidson. What can we say? He taught us and guided us and wrote with us. Thank you.

M.W.M.

C.P.S.

R.L.W.

Brief Contents

Contents

Chapter 9   **Analyzing Costs for Pricing and Short-Run
                        Decisions   331**

Chapter 10   **Capital Budgeting and Discounted Cash Flow
                        Analysis for Long-Run Decisions   381**

Chapter 11   **A Closer Look at Capital Budgeting   423**

PART FOUR   **Managerial Planning and Performance Evaluation 457**

Chapter 12   **Planning and Budgeting   459**

Chapter 13   **Evaluating Peformance 511**

Chapter 14   **Variance Analysis: Additional Topics 549**

Chapter 17   **Overview of Financial Statements   667**

Chapter 18   **Introduction to Financial Statement Analysis   731**

PART ONE

Fundamental Concepts

The noted management writer Peter Drucker has called accounting the most intellectually challenging and turbulent area in the field of management. We hope the ideas in this book will help you meet those challenges and deal with that turbulence throughout your career.

Part One has two chapters that lay the foundation for the rest of the book. Chapter 1 provides an overview of managerial accounting and shows how decision makers use managerial accounting information. Chapter 2 discusses cost behavior and the major cost concepts that we use in the book.

Managerial Uses of Accounting Information

1. Gain an overview of the use of managerial accounting information.
2. Compare and contrast managerial and financial accounting.
3. Understand the role of managerial accountants in organizations.
4. Gain an exposure to ethical issues and insight on what to do about ethical dilemmas.
5. See how managerial accounting supports the new production environment (total quality management, just-in-time methods, lean production).
6. Understand the importance of effective communication between accountants and managers.
7. (Appendix 1.1) Understand ethical standards as expressed in the Institute of Management Accountants' Code of Ethics.

Accounting affects virtually everyone. Workers in fast-food restaurants may not use accounting themselves, for example, but their managers use it in deciding whether to increase or decrease employees' hours. Decisions to close a factory, to expand a business, to offer a new product all involve the use of accounting information.

Adequate accounting information is fundamental to business survival. About 80 percent of new businesses fail within five years of opening their doors. Often they fail because management does not have adequate accounting information to make good decisions, plan for growth, and forecast cash needs. Organizations with poor accounting systems have difficulty obtaining financing from banks and shareholders.

Accounting touches our lives more than we may think. If you have observed Wal-Mart opening a new store, USAir or Southwest Airlines offering discounted airline fares, or employee hirings to help with seasonal increases in activity at ski resorts or department stores, you have seen the results of decisions that use accounting information.

Comparing Financial and Managerial Accounting

Exhibit 1.1 shows that accounting is part of an organization's information system, which includes both financial and nonfinancial data. Accounting commonly divides into financial accounting and managerial accounting. **Financial accounting** deals with preparing general purpose reports for people outside an organization to use. Such users include shareholders (owners) of a corporation, creditors (those who lend money to a business), financial analysts, labor unions, government regulators, and the like. External users wish primarily to review and evaluate the operations and financial status of the business as a whole.

Managerial accounting, on the other hand, deals with providing information that managers inside the organization will use. For example, a production manager wants a report on the cost of products to evaluate workers' performance. A sales manager wants a report showing the relative profitability of two products in order to focus selling efforts.

Although financial accounting reports of publicly held companies are readily available in libraries or from the companies themselves, firms do not widely distribute managerial accounting reports externally. Managerial accounting reports often contain confidential information. Consequently, we have relied on research and consulting experience to develop actual managerial accounting examples for this book.

Exhibit 1.1

Accounting as Part of the Information System

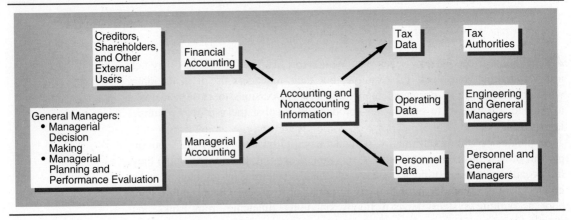

We assume that all of the readers of this book will use accounting data in their careers, though some readers will also be accounting professionals. Consequently, we take a user's perspective of accounting—we want you to understand accounting systems so you can effectively use the information they provide.

Uses of Accounting Information

Accounting provides information for three general uses: (1) managerial decision making; (2) managerial planning, control, and internal performance evaluation; and (3) financial reporting for external performance evaluation by shareholders and creditors. This book concentrates on the first two uses. Financial accounting books and courses focus on the third use.

Relations among Three Uses of Accounting

Exhibit 1.2 illustrates the relations among the three principal uses of accounting information discussed in this section. Note the close relation between the managerial decision-making process and the managerial planning and control process. In making a decision, management forms expectations about hypothetical performance if everything goes according to plan. The results of the internal performance evaluation in one period become inputs into the planning and decision-making process of the next period.

Managerial Decision Making

The decision-making process includes the following steps, as the first three boxes in Exhibit 1.2 show:

1. Identify a problem requiring managerial action.
2. Specify the objective or goal to be achieved (for example, maximize return on investment).
3. List the possible alternative courses of action.
4. Gather information about the consequences of each alternative.
5. Make a decision by selecting one of the alternatives.

Managerial accounting plays a critical role in step **4** of the decision-making process.

Example A health maintenance organization is considering adding dental care to the services it provides. Management wishes to predict the expected costs of operating the proposed dental care service. The managerial accountant must obtain cost data from the records of costs incurred in the past for providing similar types of services. Management and the accountants would then use these data to help project the costs they expect to incur from the proposed dental care service.

Exhibit 1.2

Managerial Processes and Accounting Information

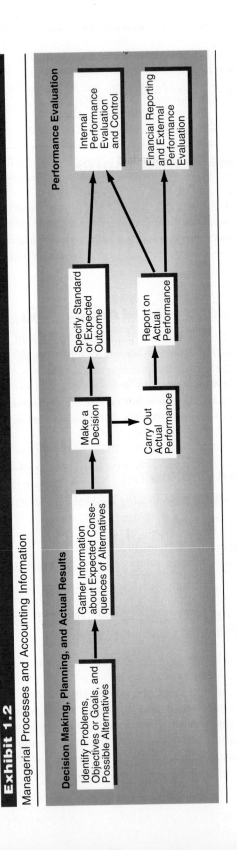

Decision Making, Planning, and Actual Results

Identify Problems, Objectives or Goals, and Possible Alternatives

Gather Information about Expected Consequences of Alternatives

Make a Decision

Specify Standard or Expected Outcome

Carry Out Actual Performance

Report on Actual Performance

Performance Evaluation

Internal Performance Evaluation and Control

Financial Reporting and External Performance Evaluation

Managerial Planning, Control, and Internal Performance Evaluation

The planning and control process includes the following steps:

1. Decide on a standard or budget specifying what actual performance should be.
2. Measure the results of actual performance.
3. Compare actual performance with the standard or budget. This evaluation helps management assess actions already taken and decide which courses of action it should take in the future.

Managerial accounting plays an important role in the planning and control process. The information generated in the decision-making process helps establish expectations of performance. In addition, accounting provides actual results to compare with expectations.

Example Assume the health maintenance organization in the previous example decided to add the dental care service. An important input to that decision was that management expected the first year's operating costs to be $5 million. This $5 million cost projection could serve as the budget or standard for evaluating the performance of the dental service managers.

If the costs varied significantly from $5 million, management would make an effort to find the cause of the difference, or *variance,* as accountants call it, between anticipated and actual costs. If factors or conditions that the dental service managers could not control caused the variance, management probably would not hold them responsible for it. For example, a dental technicians' strike might cause a labor shortage, thereby resulting in a loss in patient revenue that managers could not control. Similarly, management might not hold the dental service managers responsible for an unanticipated increase in the cost of materials used for dental work.

Financial Accounting: External Financial Reporting and Performance Evaluation

In contrast to managerial accounting reports prepared for internal use, the financial reports prepared for users external to publicly held firms must follow certain specified formats and measurement rules. For example, publicly held firms like Ford, Pillsbury, Coca-Cola, and The Limited must present statements of financial position, net income, and cash flows each year in accordance with generally accepted accounting principles.

Misuse of Accounting Information

Firms often mistakenly use data for one purpose that were intended for another. For example, many companies use the LIFO (last-in, first-out) inventory cost flow assumption and accelerated depreciation for tax purposes; however, these data are not necessarily appropriate for managerial uses.

Further, most managerial decisions require more detailed data than external financial reports provide. For instance, in General Electric's external financial statements, the balance sheet shows a single amount for inventory valuation and the income statement shows a single amount for cost of goods sold expense summarized for all product lines. For managerial purposes, however, management wants detailed data about the cost of each of several hundred products. The company's external financial statements provide some revenue and profit data for each major business segment, but managerial purposes would require more detailed information about the cost of operating each plant, department, and division.

Managers sometimes assume that they must use the same accounting data for their decision making, planning, and other managerial activities as presented in tax returns and external financial statements. That is simply not true. If the firm thoughtfully designs its information system, accountants can adapt the data to meet multiple needs.

Accountants currently face the challenge of designing systems with sufficient flexibility to provide information for multiple purposes. Managers face the challenge of understanding accounting well enough to know what information to request and to expect from accountants.

Differences between Financial and Managerial Accounting

Managerial and financial accounting differ fundamentally as shown below:

Financial Accounting	Managerial Accounting
Users	
External users of information—usually shareholders, financial analysts, and creditors.	Internal users of information—usually managers.
Generally Accepted Accounting Principles	
Compliance with generally accepted accounting principles.	Need not comply with generally accepted accounting principles.
Future versus Past	
Uses historical data in evaluating performance of the firm and its managers by outsiders.	Uses estimates of the future for decision making and historical data for internal performance evaluation.
Reporting Requirements	
Regulations often specify how much information is enough.	Internal cost/benefit evaluation dictates how much information is enough.
Detail Presented	
Presents summary data.	Presents more detailed information about product costs, revenues, and profits.

Problem 1.1 for Self-Study

Differences between financial and managerial accounting. What are the differences between financial and managerial accounting?

The solution to this self-study problem is at the end of this chapter on page 18.

Organizational Environment

Who manages the accounting function in organizations? In most corporate organizations, the **controller** is the chief accounting officer. Recognizing the importance of this function, many organizations place the controller in the same organization rank as corporate vice presidents. In other organizations, the controller and the treasurer may both report to a financial vice president, who is responsible for both the accounting and financial affairs of the corporation. (The activity that we call "managerial accounting" is known as "finance" in many organizations.) Exhibit 1.3 shows how the finance and accounting functions fit into a typical organization chart, in this case, an abbreviated version of Du Pont's organization chart.

Controller

As the chief accounting officer, the controller has authority both for accounting within the organization and for external reporting. Internally, the controller oversees providing information to managers. If you have a career in marketing, production, or general management, then you will have a lot of dealings with controllers. The controller usually oversees the company's internal control system.

External reports include reports to taxing authorities and regulatory bodies such as the Securities and Exchange Commission, as well as the financial statements for shareholders. The controller sometimes supervises data-processing operations, but frequently data processing is an independent department. The noted management author Peter Drucker recommends that companies bring together their computer-based data-processing and accounting systems in the future.[1]

Internal Audit

The **internal audit** department provides a variety of auditing and consulting services in many organizations, including auditing internal controls and assisting external auditors in their audit of an organization's external financial reports. In some organizations, internal auditors are internal consultants who provide an independent perspective on managers' problems. Such auditors are called "operational auditors." Many auditors in the federal government are operational auditors.

The internal audit manager sometimes reports directly to the controller. Some companies recognize the possibility for conflicts between the controller's record-keeping role and the audit function, however, so they have the internal audit supervisor report directly to the controller's superior. Also, top management usually gives the internal audit director authority to communicate directly to the audit committee of the board of directors.

Treasurer

The corporate **treasurer** is the manager in charge of raising cash for operations and managing cash and near-cash assets. The treasurer handles credit reviews and sets

---

[1]Peter Drucker, "Be Data Literate—Know What to Know," *The Wall Street Journal*, December 1, 1992, p. A16.

Exhibit 1.3

Organization Chart
E.I. du Pont de Nemours & Company

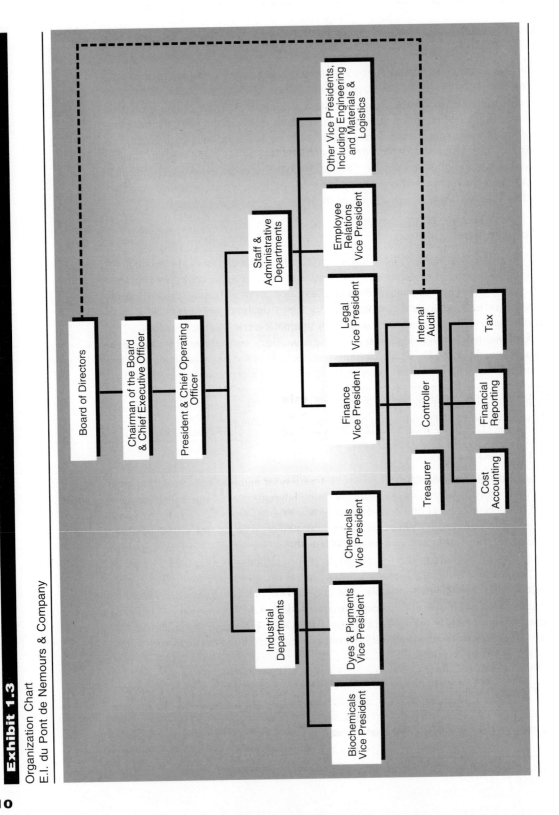

policy for collecting receivables. The treasurer normally handles relations with banks and other lending or financing sources, including public issues of shares or debt.

Professional Environment

Accountants are not only part of the management team, they are also professionals. Their professional environment influences the types of reports and data bases they develop in companies.

Accounting Authorities

Throughout this book we refer to the **generally accepted accounting principles (GAAP)** that govern financial accounting. Firms use these accounting principles in preparing their external financial statements. Although managerial accounting does not have to follow generally accepted accounting principles or other rules (such as the income tax laws), the fact that the accounting system must produce reports conforming with those regulations has implications for managerial accounting. The following organizations are important regulatory agencies that contribute to generally accepted principles of accounting.

Securities and Exchange Commission The U.S. Congress has granted the **Securities and Exchange Commission (SEC)** the legal authority to prescribe accounting principles that most corporations must follow. The SEC has used its power sparingly, however.

Institute of Management Accountants The **Institute of Management Accountants (IMA)** has thousands of members who work in management accounting. It publishes the journal *Management Accounting,* numerous policy statements, and research studies on accounting issues. It also sponsors the Certified Management Accountant (CMA) program that includes an examination and certification.

Institute of Internal Auditors The **Institute of Internal Auditors** is an organization of internal auditors. It publishes a periodical called the *Internal Auditor* and numerous research studies on internal auditing. It also sponsors the Certificate in Internal Auditing program.

The Association of Government Accountants The **Association of Government Accountants** is an organization of federal, state, and local government accountants. It publishes the *Government Accountant's Journal.*

Financial Accounting Standards Board Since 1973, the **Financial Accounting Standards Board (FASB)** has been the highest nongovernmental authority on generally accepted accounting principles. The FASB issues *Statements* *of Financial Accounting Standards* (and *Interpretations* of these statements) from time to time, establishing or clarifying generally accepted accounting principles.

American Institute of Certified Public Accountants   The American Institute of Certified Public Accountants (AICPA) is the national organization of certified public accountants. Its publications and committees influence the development of accounting principles and auditing practices. It actively promulgates standards of ethics.

Internal Revenue Service   Income tax legislation and administration have influenced the practice of accounting, although income tax requirements in themselves do not establish principles and practices for external or internal reporting. The *Internal Revenue Code* (passed by Congress), the *Regulations* and *Rulings* (of the Internal Revenue Service), and the opinions of the U.S. Tax Court form the basis for income tax reporting rules.

Cost Accounting Standards Board   In 1970 the U.S. Congress established the **Cost Accounting Standards Board (CASB)** to set accounting standards for contracts between the U.S. government and defense contractors like Boeing, Raytheon, and General Dynamics. The diversity in defense contractors' cost accounting systems makes it difficult for the U.S. government to evaluate proposals and to figure out the payments due contractors. The CASB attempts to set standards to achieve uniformity and consistency in contract proposals and cost reporting. Most of the work of the CASB does not directly affect the form of financial statements, but its requirements carry considerable weight in many areas of practice, especially those dealing with cost allocation. Accountants apply its standards to many transactions between defense contractors and the U.S. government.

Certifications

Certified Public Accountant   The designation **certified public accountant (CPA)** indicates that an individual has qualified to be registered or licensed as a certified public accountant by passing a written examination and satisfying audit experience requirements. The CPA examination includes questions on managerial accounting.

Certified Management Accountant   The **certified management accountant (CMA)** program recognizes educational achievement and professional competence in management accounting. The examination, educational requirements, and experience requirements are similar to those for the CPA examinations, but they aim at the professional in management and cost accounting. We have included many questions from CMA examinations in this book.

Canadian Certifications   Two Canadian organizations provide designations similar to the CPA designation in the United States. The Canadian Institute of Chartered Accountants provides the chartered accountant (CA) designation, and the

Certified General Accountants Association of Canada gives the certified general accountant (CGA) designation. The Society of Management Accountants in Canada gives a certified management accountant (CMA) designation similar to the CMA in the United States.

Ethical Issues

Management accounting information can have a major impact on people's careers. Companies hold managers accountable for achieving financial performance targets. Failure to achieve these targets can have serious negative consequences for managers. If a division or company is having trouble achieving financial performance targets, managers may be tempted to manipulate the accounting numbers.

For example, some companies have recorded sales before they earned the revenue. This early revenue recognition would occur just before the end of the reporting period, say, in late December for a company using a December 31 year-end. Management might rationalize the early revenue recognition because the firm would probably make the sale in January anyway; this practice just moved next year's sale (and profits) into this year. Nevertheless, this would be an example of fraudulent financial reporting.

We include discussions of ethical issues throughout this book. We hope these discussions will help alert you to potential problems that you and your colleagues will face in your careers. Many accountants and businesspeople have found themselves in serious trouble because they did many small things, none of which appeared seriously wrong, only to find that these small things added up to a major problem. If you know the warning signs of potential ethical problems, you will have a chance to protect yourself and set the proper ethical tone for your workplace at the same time.

Most large organizations have a corporate code of conduct. Because the code developed by Johnson & Johnson is particularly impressive, we have reprinted it in Exhibit 1.4. The Institute of Management Accountants (IMA) has also developed a code of conduct, called "Standards of Ethical Conduct for Management Accountants," that we have reproduced in the Appendix to this chapter. The IMA's code requires that management accountants have a responsibility to maintain the highest levels of ethical conduct.[2]

The IMA standards recommend that people faced with ethical conflicts first follow the company's established procedures that deal with such conflicts. These procedures include talking to an ombudsman, who keeps the names of those involved confidential. If this does not resolve the conflict, accountants should consider discussing the matter with superiors, potentially as high as the audit committee or the board of directors. In extreme cases, the accountant may have no alternative but to resign. (The IMA offers an 800-number hotline for its members to discuss the ethical problems they encounter.)

---

[2]See *Standards of Ethical Conduct for Management Accountants* (Montvale, N.J.: National Association of Accountants [now called the Institute of Management Accountants], June 1, 1983.)

Exhibit 1.4

Johnson & Johnson Code of Conduct

Our Credo

We believe our first responsibility is to the doctors, nurses and patients,
to mothers and all others who use our products and services.
In meeting their needs everything we do must be of high quality.
We must constantly strive to reduce our costs
in order to maintain reasonable prices.
Customers' orders must be serviced promptly and accurately.
Our suppliers and distributors must have an opportunity
to make a fair profit.

We are responsible to our employees,
the men and women who work with us throughout the world.
Everyone must be considered as an individual.
We must respect their dignity and recognize their merit.
They must have a sense of security in their jobs.
Compensation must be fair and adequate,
and working conditions clean, orderly and safe.
Employees must feel free to make suggestions and complaints.
There must be equal opportunity for employment, development
and advancement for those qualified.
We must provide competent management,
and their actions must be just and ethical.

We are responsible to the communities in which we live and work
and to the world community as well.
We must be good citizens—support good works and charities
and bear our fair share of taxes.
We must encourage civic improvements and better health and education.
We must maintain in good order
the property we are privileged to use
protecting the environment and natural resources.

Our final responsibility is to our stockholders.
Business must make a sound profit.
We must experiment with new ideas.
Research must be carried on, innovative programs developed
and mistakes paid for.
New equipment must be purchased, new facilities provided
and new products launched.
Reserves must be created to provide for adverse times.
When we operate according to these principles,
the stockholders should realize a fair return.

Managerial Accounting in the New Production Environment

Many companies have recently installed computer-assisted methods of manufacturing, merchandising, or providing services. These new technologies have changed managerial accounting. For example, where robots and computer-assisted manufacturing methods have replaced people, labor costs have shrunk from 20–40 percent of product costs to less than 5 percent. Accounting in traditional settings required more work to keep track of labor costs than do current systems. On the other hand, in highly automated environments, accountants have had to become more sophisticated in finding causes of costs because labor no longer drives many cost transactions.

Just-in-Time Methods

The development of **just-in-time (JIT)** production and purchasing methods also affects cost accounting systems. Firms using just-in-time methods keep inventories to a minimum. If inventories are low, accountants can spend less time on inventory valuation for external reporting. For example, a Hewlett-Packard plant eliminated 100,000 journal entries per month after installing just-in-time production methods and adapting the cost accounting system to this new production method. JIT thus freed accounting and finance people to work on managerial problems instead of recording accounting data.

Lean Production

Just-in-time production is a part of a ''lean production'' philosophy that has been credited for the success of many Japanese companies and such U.S. companies as General Electric, Lincoln Electric, and Harley-Davidson. Lean production eliminates inventory between production departments, making the quality and efficiency of production the highest priority. Lean production requires the flexibility to change quickly from one product to another. It emphasizes employee training and participation in decision making.

Quality

Additionally, many companies have adopted the concept of total quality management. **Total quality management (TQM)** means the organization is managed to excel on all dimensions, and quality is ultimately defined by the customer. Customers determine the company's performance standards according to what is important to them (not necessarily what is important to product engineers, accountants, or marketing people). This exciting and sensible idea affects accounting performance measures. Under TQM, performance measures are likely to include things like product reliability and service delivery, as well as traditional measures like profitability. We discuss these issues further in later chapters.

Activity-based Costing

Industries like the computer business, where competition is keen and direct labor costs are low, increasingly use activity-based costing. **Activity-based costing (ABC)** is a costing method that assigns the indirect costs of making a product, such as quality testing, machine repairs, and product engineering, to the activities that are needed to make a product, then sums the cost of those activities to determine the cost of making the product. This costing method is more detailed and complicated than conventional costing methods, but it can provide more useful information. Companies like Intel and Hewlett-Packard have been leaders in implementing activity-based costing.

We devote an entire chapter to activity-based costing and management later in the book; also, we discuss the topic in several other chapters. Those of you who plan careers (or already have careers) in consulting and industry are likely to have an opportunity to help companies develop and install activity-based costing systems, even if you do not plan to be accountants.

Problem 1.2
for Self-Study

How does the new production environment affect managerial accounting?

The solution to this self-study problem is at the end of this chapter on page 18.

Costs and Benefits of Accounting

A national steel company installed an accounting system that cost several million dollars. How did the managers justify such an expenditure? They believed that better management of information about costs would result in improved cost control and efficiency that would save the company enough to justify the cost of the system.

Managers should answer the question "How much information is enough?" for their purposes on a cost/benefit basis, much like the questions "How much advertising is enough?" or "Should we install a computerized inventory system?" Only if the benefits of the information exceed its costs should a firm generate accounting information for managerial purposes.

In practice, measuring the costs and benefits of accounting is difficult. The analysis of costs and benefits requires considerable communication and cooperation between users and accountants. Users are more familiar with the benefits of information, whereas accountants are more familiar with its costs. As Exhibit 1.5 shows, users identify their needs based on the decisions they make and request data from accountants, who develop systems to supply information when a **cost-benefit criterion** justifies it. If accountants and users interact, they eventually settle on a cost-benefit–justified supply of accounting data that meets users' needs.

The Value of Information for Particular Decisions

Deriving the value of information is important in many managerial settings. For example, should the firm undertake an additional marketing study that involves expanded sampling of a new product by consumers? Should the company discontinue its marketing tests and proceed directly to full-scale production? Should a doctor order laboratory tests before taking action in an emergency situation? Should a production manager stop production to test a sample of products for defects, or allow production to continue? Managers solve such problems conceptually by comparing the cost of information with the benefits of better decisions.

Managerial Application

The Increasing Importance of Cost Analysis

Note to Readers: We have included ''managerial applications'' of managerial accounting issues and practices in actual business settings in this and many later chapters. These applications are based on research into actual practice or on articles by practitioners who describe their experiences. We hope you will find these applications useful in thinking about real-world managerial accounting issues.

Nissan, Toyota, and other automobile companies are looking for ways to reduce costs. Domino's Pizza nearly went bankrupt until the owner discovered that the company was losing money on 6-inch pizzas; the company dropped the product line and went on to become a multibillion-dollar company. Many hospitals that thrived when insurers fully reimbursed health care costs are now facing large deficits.

What do all of these situations have in common? They all represent situations in which a better understanding and management of product costs is important for the organization to succeed. In general, an organization's ability to manage its costs becomes more important as the environment becomes more competitive. Hospitals, manufacturing companies, airlines, and many other organizations face increasingly stiff competition in the 1990s. As a result, they are seeking better ways of measuring productivity and product costs, which creates many new opportunities for experts in managerial accounting.[a]

[a]For more extensive reading, see Thomas H. Johnson and Robert S. Kaplan, *Relevance Lost: The Rise and Fall of Management Accounting* (Boston: Harvard Business School Press, 1987); and Robert S. Kaplan, ed., *Measures for Manufacturing Excellence* (Boston: Harvard Business School Press, 1990).

Exhibit 1.5

Supply and Demand for Accounting Information

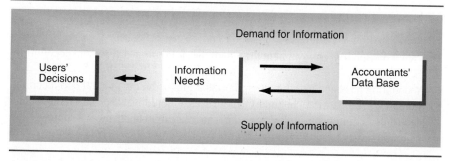

Demand for Information

Users' Decisions ⟷ Information Needs → Accountants' Data Base

Supply of Information

Both users and accountants recognize that information is not free. Management must take into account the costs and benefits of information in deciding how much accounting is enough.

Organization of the Book

Part One of this book (Chapters 1 and 2) provides background concepts for later use. Part Two (Chapters 3 through 6) provides an overview of cost systems to help you understand how accounting systems are designed and how you can use the information they provide. Parts Three and Four cover the two major uses of managerial accounting information: Part Three (Chapters 7 through 11) discusses the use of accounting for managerial decision making, and Part Four (Chapters 12 through 15) discusses the use of accounting for managerial planning and performance evaluation. Part Five (Chapters 16 through 18) presents a synthesis of the book and a discussion of financial fraud (Chapter 16), and a review of key financial accounting topics (Chapters 17 and 18).

Summary

Accounting comprises financial accounting and managerial accounting. Financial accounting refers to the preparation of general-purpose reports for external users; managerial accounting refers to the provision of information to managers inside the organization. This book concentrates primarily on the use of accounting for managerial decision making and planning and performance evaluation. Enjoy!

Solutions to Self-Study Problems

Suggested Solution to Problem 1.1 for Self-Study

Managerial accounting is the preparation and use of accounting information for *managers inside organizations* in making decisions and evaluating performance. Financial accounting is the preparation and use of accounting information for *outsiders,* such as investors and creditors.

Suggested Solution to Problem 1.2 for Self-Study

The new production environment has had the following effects on accounting:

- Accounting has become more computerized, thus reducing manual bookkeeping.
- Increased competition in many industries, including the automobile and electronic equipment industries, has increased management's interest in managing costs.

- Deregulation in industries like banks, airlines, and health care has also increased management's interest in managing costs.
- Developments of more highly technical production processes has reduced emphasis on labor and increased emphasis on overhead cost control.
- Developments in new management techniques have affected accounting. For example, by reducing inventory levels, just-in-time (JIT) methods have reduced the need to compute costs of inventory. Total quality management (TQM), which strives for excellence in business, requires new measurements of performance as defined by the customers. Activity-based costing (ABC) assigns indirect costs to products on the basis of the activities that caused the cost and the amount of the activity that the product consumed.

Appendix 1.1:
Institute of Management Accountants' Code of Ethics

Management accountants have an obligation to the organizations they serve, their profession, the public, and themselves to maintain the highest standards of ethical conduct. In recognition of this obligation, the Institute of Management Accountants has promulgated the following standards of ethical conduct for management accountants. Adherence to these standards is integral to achieving the *Objectives of Management Accounting.*[3] Management accountants shall not commit acts contrary to these standards nor shall they condone the commission of such acts by others within their organizations.

Competence

Management accountants have a responsibility to do the following:

- Maintain an appropriate level of professional competence by ongoing development of their knowledge and skills.
- Perform their professional duties in accordance with relevant laws, regulations, and technical standards.
- Prepare complete and clear reports and recommendations after appropriate analyses of relevant and reliable information.

Confidentiality

Management accountants have a responsibility to do the following:

- Refrain from disclosing confidential information acquired in the course of their work except when authorized, unless legally obligated to do so.

---

[3]Reprinted with the permission of the Institute of Management Accountants.

- Inform subordinates as appropriate regarding the confidentiality of information acquired in the course of their work and monitor their activities to assure the maintenance of that confidentiality.
- Refrain from using or appearing to use confidential information acquired in the course of their work for unethical or illegal advantage either personally or through third parties.

Integrity

Management accountants have a responsibility to do the following:

- Avoid actual or apparent conflicts of interest and advise all appropriate parties of any potential conflict.
- Refrain from engaging in any activity that would prejudice their ability to carry out their duties ethically.
- Refuse any gift, favor, or hospitality that would influence or would appear to influence their actions.
- Refrain from either actively or passively subverting the attainment of the organization's legitimate and ethical objectives.
- Recognize and communicate professional limitations or other constraints that would preclude responsible judgment or successful performance of an activity.
- Communicate unfavorable as well as favorable information and professional judgments or opinions.
- Refrain from engaging in or supporting any activity that would discredit the profession.

Objectivity

Management accountants have a responsibility to do the following:

- Communicate information fairly and objectively.
- Disclose fully all relevant information that could reasonably be expected to influence an intended user's understanding of the reports, comments, and recommendations presented.

Resolution of Ethical Conflict

In applying the standards of ethical conduct, management accountants may encounter problems in identifying unethical behavior or in resolving an ethical conflict. When faced with significant ethical issues, management accountants should follow the established policies of the organization bearing on the resolution of such conflict. If these policies do not resolve the ethical conflict, management accountants should consider the following courses of action:

- Discuss such problems with the immediate superior except when it appears that the superior is involved, in which case the problem should be presented initially to the next higher managerial level. If satisfactory resolution cannot be achieved when the problem is initially presented, submit the issues to the next higher managerial level.

If the immediate superior is the chief executive officer, or equivalent, the acceptable reviewing authority may be a group such as the audit committee, executive committee, board of directors, board of trustees, or owners. Contact with levels above the immediate superior should be initiated only with the superior's knowledge, assuming the superior is not involved.

- Clarify relevant concepts by confidential discussion with an objective advisor to obtain an understanding of possible courses of action.
- If the ethical conflict still exists after exhausting all levels of internal review, the management accountant may have no other recourse on significant matters than to resign from the organization and to submit an informative memorandum to an appropriate representative of the organization.

Except where legally prescribed, communication of such problems to authorities or individuals not employed or engaged by the organization is not considered appropriate.

Key Terms and Concepts

Certified public accountant
  (CPA)
Certified management
  accountant (CMA)
Just-in-time (JIT)

Total quality management
  (TQM)
Activity-based costing (ABC)
Cost-benefit criterion

Questions, Problems, and Cases

Questions

1. Review the meaning of the concepts and terms introduced in this chapter.
2. Generally accepted accounting principles are the methods of accounting publicly held firms use in preparing their financial statements. A principle in physics, such as the law of gravity, serves as a basis for developing theories and explaining the relations among physical objects. In what ways are generally accepted accounting principles similar to and different from principles in physics?
3. "Managerial accounting is not important in nonprofit organizations, such as agencies of the federal government and nonprofit hospitals, because they do not have to earn a profit." Do you agree with this statement? Why or why not?
4. What are the steps involved in the managerial decision-making process? What role does accounting play in that process?

5. What are the steps involved in the managerial planning, control, and internal performance evaluation process? What role does accounting play in that process?

6. Distinguish between internal performance evaluation and external performance evaluation.

7. Who in the organization is generally in charge of managerial accounting?

8. ''It is important for managerial accountants to understand the uses of accounting data and for users of data to understand accounting. Only in this way can accountants provide the appropriate accounting data for the correct uses.'' Do you agree with this statement? Why or why not?

9. A student planning a career in management wondered why it was important to learn about accounting. How would you respond?

10. ''The best management accounting system provides managers with all of the information they would like to have.'' Do you agree with this statement? Why or why not?

11. What are the two major uses of managerial accounting information?

12. What is meant by total quality management (TQM)? What performance measures are likely to be included under TQM?

13. What is just-in-time (JIT)? How does JIT help accountants serve managers better?

14. What is activity-based costing (ABC)? Under an ABC system, is the amount of information available to managers likely to be higher or lower than compared to traditional costing systems? Why?

15. The Johnson & Johnson credo in Exhibit 1.4 is quite detailed. Is all of this detail necessary? Why?

16. (Appendix) Do you think that an accountant working at Johnson & Johnson would have any conflicts working under both the company credo and the Institute of Management Accountants' code of conduct? Why?

17. An accounting employee notices that an employee in purchasing has been accepting tickets to sporting events from a company supplier, which is against company policy. According to the Institute of Management Accountants' code of conduct, what steps should the accounting employee take to stop the practice?

Problems

18. **Ethics and altering the books** (adapted from CMA exam). Alert, a closely held investment services group, has been successful for the past three years. Bonuses for top management have ranged from 50 percent to 100 percent of base salary. Top management, however, holds only 35 percent of the common stock, and recent industry news indicates that a major corporation may try to acquire Alert. Top management fears that they might lose their bonuses, not to mention their employment, if the takeover occurs. Management has told Roger Deerling, Alert's controller, to make a few changes to several accounting policies and practices, thus making Alert a much less attractive acquisition. Roger knows that these ''changes'' are not in accordance with Generally Ac-

cepted Accounting Principles. Roger has also been told not to mention these changes to anyone outside the top-management group.

a. From the viewpoint of the "Standards of Ethical Conduct for Management Accountants," what are Roger Deerling's responsibilities?

b. What steps should he take to resolve this problem?

19. **Responsibility for ethical action** (adapted from CMA exam). Jorge Martinez recently joined GroChem, Inc., as assistant controller. GroChem processes chemicals for use in fertilizers. During his first month on the job, Jorge spent most of his time getting better acquainted with those responsible for plant operations. Jorge asked the plant supervisor what the procedure was for the disposal of chemicals. The response was that he (the plant supervisor) was not involved in the disposal of waste and that Jorge would be wise to ignore the issue. Of course, this just drove Jorge to investigate the matter further. Jorge soon discovered that GroChem was dumping toxic waste in a nearby public landfill late at night. Further, he discovered that several members of management were involved in arranging for this dumping. Jorge was, however, unable to determine whether his superior, the controller, was involved. Jorge considered three possible courses of action. He could discuss the matter with his controller, anonymously release the information to the local newspaper, or discuss the situation with an outside member of the board of directors whom he knows personally.

a. Does Jorge have an ethical responsibility to take a course of action?

b. Of the three possible courses of action, which are appropriate and which are inappropriate?

20. **Ethics and inventory obsolescence** (adapted from CMA exam). The external auditors of HHP (Heart Health Procedures) are currently performing their annual audit of the company with the help of assistant controller Linda Joyner. Several years ago Heart Health Procedures developed a unique balloon technique for opening obstructed arteries in the heart. The technique utilizes an expensive component that HHP purchases from a sole supplier. Until last year, HHP maintained a monopoly in this field.

During the past year, however, a major competitor developed a technically superior product that uses an innovative, less costly component. The competitor was granted FDA approval, and it is expected that HHP will lose market share as a result. HHP currently has several years' worth of expensive components essential for the manufacturing of its balloon product. Linda Joyner knows that these components will decrease in price due to the introduction of the competitor's product. She also knows that her boss, the controller, is aware of the situation. The controller, however, has informed the chief financial officer that there is no obsolete inventory nor any need for reductions of inventories to market values. Linda is aware that the chief financial officer's bonus plan is tied directly to the corporate profits.

In signing the auditor's representation letter, the chief financial officer acknowledges that all relevant information has been disclosed to the auditors and that all accounting procedures have been followed according to generally accepted accounting principles. Linda knows that the external auditors are unaware of the inventory problem, and is unsure what to do.

    a. Has the controller behaved unethically?

    b. How should Linda Joyner resolve this problem? Should she report this inventory overevaluation to the external auditors?

Cases

21. **Value of information: nonbusiness setting.** Consider the value of the following information in a medical context.

Suppose that a patient visits a doctor's office and that the doctor decides on the basis of the signs that the patient's appendix should be removed immediately. Meanwhile the doctor orders a white blood cell count. The doctor decides that the appendix must be removed no matter what the blood count happens to be.

    a. What is the value to the doctor of the information (in the cost-benefit sense discussed in this chapter) about the blood cell count?

    b. Why might the doctor order the test anyway?

22. **Objectives and uses of financial statements** (adapted from CMA exam). Financial statements are an important means that firms use to communicate economic information to interested parties. The objectives of financial reporting have received the attention of the accounting profession, the business community, the government, and the general public at various times and in varying degrees for many years.

During the past 5 years concern and intensive study of financial reporting objectives have increased. The objectives recommended range from ''the statements are the management's report on its stewardship of the investors' capital'' to ''the statements provide information to investors for predicting, comparing, and evaluating the economic activities of an enterprise.''

The objectives established for financial reporting will depend on whether management or some other party prepares the reports, what the firm intends the reports to represent (results of past activities or predictions of future actions), for whom the firm intends the statements, and how those parties will use the statements.

    a. Discuss management's responsibilities for the business entity's financial reporting.

    b. Does management prepare financial reports to reflect past performance of the business entity or to help predict the future performance of the entity? Discuss briefly.

    c. Discuss briefly how investors can use financial reports in making investment decisions.

Chapter 2

Cost Concepts for Managerial Decision Making

Learning Objectives

1. Master the concept of *cost*.

2. Know what costs are required to make products.

3. Understand the difference between fixed and variable costs.

4. Use differential cost analysis for making decisions.

5. Know the meanings and computations of gross margins, contribution margins, and profit margins.

6. Compare and contrast income statements prepared for external reporting to those prepared for managerial use.

Chapter 1 indicated that managerial accounting deals with the information managers need for making decisions and for planning and performance evaluation. Managers primarily need information about the *costs* of carrying out the organization's activities.[1]

Chrysler Corporation needed information about the costs of producing the Jeep Grand Cherokee in its Detroit plant when it started the Grand Cherokee product line. Sears needed to know its cost savings before it decided to eliminate its financial services, real estate, and other businesses. Administrators at the University of California at Los Angeles needed to know the cost savings of dropping certain sports from its intercollegiate sports program. This chapter introduces important cost concepts that you will use throughout your career.

---

[1] A glossary of accounting terms and concepts appears at the back of this book to facilitate finding definitions. See especially the cost definitions under *cost terminology*.

Fundamental Cost Concepts

In principle, a cost is a sacrifice of resources. For example, if you purchased an automobile for a cash payment of $12,000, the cost to purchase the automobile would be $12,000.

Although this concept is simple, it can be difficult to apply. For example, what does a student sacrifice to obtain a college education? A student sacrifices cash to pay for tuition and books. What about cash paid for living costs? If the student would incur these costs whether or not the student attended college, the student should not consider them to be costs of getting a college education.

Students sacrifice not only cash. They also sacrifice their time. Placing a value on that time is difficult; it depends on the best forgone alternative use of the time. For students who sacrifice high-paying jobs to attend college, the total cost of college may be much greater than the cash sacrificed. Other students may not sacrifice as much in terms of forgone alternatives, so their college costs would be lower. In each case, costs are sacrifices of resources. The most important resources sacrificed to attend college are time and money.

The term *cost* is meaningful only if it is used in some particular context. To say ''the cost of this building is $1 million'' is ambiguous unless the context of the cost is identified. Does cost mean the original price the current owner paid, the price that the owner would pay to replace it new, or the price to replace it today in its current condition? Is it the annual rental fee paid to occupy the building? Is it the cash forgone from not selling it? Is it the original price paid minus accumulated depreciation? You need to know the context in which the term *cost* is used to reduce its ambiguity.

Many disputes arise over the definition of cost. The Managerial Application ''Cost and Profit Concepts at Ford in Dispute over Patent Value'' describes how a dispute over costs and profits ended up in court. We devote much of this chapter to describing how different contexts affect the meaning of costs.

Opportunity Costs

The definition of a cost as a ''sacrifice'' leads directly to the **opportunity cost** concept. If a firm uses an asset for one purpose, the opportunity cost of using it for that purpose is the return forgone from its best alternative use.

The opportunity cost of a college education includes forgone earnings during the time in school. Some other illustrations of the meaning of opportunity cost follow:

1. The opportunity cost of funds invested in a government bond is the interest that an investor could earn on a bank certificate of deposit (adjusted for differences in risk).
2. The opportunity cost of using a plant to produce a particular product is the sacrifice of profits that the firm would make by producing other products.
3. Proprietors of small businesses often take a salary. But the opportunity cost of their time may be much higher than the nominal salary recorded on the books. A proprietor can work for someone else and earn a wage. The highest such wage

Cost and Profit Concepts at Ford in Dispute over Patent Value*

A court found Ford Motor Company guilty of infringing a patent issued to Robert Kearns, who had invented a special circuit to operate intermittent windshield wipers (IWW). Kearns argued that he was entitled to receive a share of Ford's profits on the IWW options it installed in cars. Kearns pointed to some Ford documents showing contribution margin (revenues less variable material, labor, and marketing costs), which Ford called "economic profit," and profit margin ("economic profit" less certain fixed costs and allocated portions of administrative costs), which Ford called "accounted profit." Kearns asked for royalties amounting to about one-third of Ford's internally reported "economic profit," an amount equal to about $300 million.

Ford argued that even "accounted profit" did not accurately reflect the profits on IWW options because that measure fails to account for interest and income taxes. Moreover, Ford argued, if Kearns should receive a share of its profits, then the profits on an IWW option considered alone are irrelevant. Ford can't sell an IWW option without selling a car, and Ford can't sell an individual car without satisfying federal standards for fuel efficiency of the entire fleet that it sells. Ford argued that it prices its car fleets and the options on the cars to meet competition and to satisfy the federal requirements. Therefore the relevant profit figure would be the profit rate on the entire fleet of cars it sells.

More importantly, Ford argued, Kearns should not be entitled to recover any of Ford's profits, but only a portion of Ford's opportunity costs in using the Kearns patent. Because Ford could install IWW options using electrical circuits other than Kearns' invention, Ford should pay no more than the extra cost of the alternative circuit. Ford suggested that a competitor, the Amos circuit, cost only $.10 more each to produce than the Kearns circuit. Ford argued that if it gave Kearns the full $.10 per IWW produced, it should pay only $2 million.

The court ordered Ford to pay Kearns about $6 million in damages.

*Based on the authors' research.

(adjusting for differences in risk and nonpecuniary costs or benefits of being a proprietor) is the opportunity cost of being a proprietor. Entrepreneurs like Bill Gates at Microsoft and Phil Knight at Nike have become rich developing their enterprises. Depending on their personalities, they might also have become wealthy as executives in established companies.

Costs and Expenses

We distinguish *cost,* as used in managerial accounting, from *expense,* as used in financial accounting. A cost is a sacrifice of resources. An expense is the historical cost of the goods or services a firm uses in a particular accounting period.

Managerial accounting deals primarily with costs, not expenses. Generally accepted accounting principles and regulations such as the income tax laws specify when the firm can or must treat costs as expenses to be deducted from revenues. We shall reserve the term *expense* to refer to expenses for external reporting as defined by generally accepted accounting principles.

Concepts and Definitions

Accounting is the language of business. You need to know the basic concepts of accounting to communicate. This section defines and discusses those basic concepts.

Direct and Indirect Costs

Accountants make a distinction between direct and indirect costs. Costs that relate directly to a cost object are **direct costs.** Those that do not are **indirect costs.** A **cost object** is any item for which the manager wishes to measure cost. Departments, stores, divisions, product lines, or units produced are typical cost objects. The cost object establishes the context for labeling a cost as direct or indirect.

Example Electron, Inc., produces calculators. It buys the components from outside suppliers, assembles the components, and inspects the product for defects in workmanship. The company rents its factory facilities. If the cost object is a calculator, the materials and labor that the firm traces directly to the production of each calculator are direct costs. Electron considers the components to be direct materials, and workers' time to assemble and inspect the calculator to be direct labor.

In this example, when the cost object is a calculator, the factory rent is indirect. Now suppose that the purpose of calculating costs is to evaluate the performance of the factory manager. In that case, the cost object is the entire factory, not a unit produced, so factory rent would be a direct cost. Factory rent is direct to the factory but indirect to a calculator produced. The distinction between direct and indirect costs is meaningful only when applied to a particular cost object.

Common Costs Indirect costs are common to, or shared by, two or more cost objects, so accountants also call them **common costs.** A common cost results from the common use of facilities (for example, building or equipment) or services (for example, data processing or the legal staff) by several products, departments, or processes.

Examples of common costs include the following:

1. The factory rent Electron, Inc., pays is common to departments within the factory.

2. The cost of buildings that house a business school are usually common to each of the departments (accounting, finance, marketing, and so forth) within the school.

3. The cost of a computer is common to its various uses, such as payroll, accounts payable, and production scheduling.

The allocation of common costs involves assigning these costs to cost objects. Cost allocation pervades both internal and external accounting reports. The subject of cost allocation will come up in numerous places in this text, where we discuss it in the context of managerial decision making and performance evaluation.

Manufacturing Costs

The type of organization and the nature of its activities affect costs. The most complex organization, in terms of costs, is the manufacturing firm. Its activities include acquisition, production, marketing, administration, and service. If you understand the cost structure of a manufacturing organization, you will understand the cost structure of all types of organizations.

Manufacturing involves the transformation of materials into finished goods using labor and capital invested in machines and production facilities. **Manufacturing costs** comprise three elements: direct materials, direct labor, and manufacturing overhead.

Direct materials (also called *raw materials*) are those the firm can trace directly to a unit of output. They can range from natural materials, such as iron ore to make steel and logs to make lumber, to more synthetic materials, such as electronic chips used in making calculators and plastics used in making toys.

The adjective *direct* is important for classifying materials in this category. Accountants cannot associate many manufacturing materials with particular units of output. Examples of these **indirect materials** include lubricants for machines, lightbulbs, welding rods, cleaning materials, and the like. Accounting classifies indirect materials as part of overhead, which we describe below.

Direct labor represents the wages of workers who transform raw materials into finished products. Examples of direct labor costs are the wages of assembly-line workers who make automobiles, construction workers who build houses, and others whose labor the firm can trace directly to particular units of a product.

Labor costs that the firm cannot trace directly to the creation of products, yet the production process requires, are known as **indirect labor.** Examples include wages of maintenance personnel, supervisors, materials handlers, and inventory storekeepers. Like indirect materials, accounting classifies indirect labor costs as overhead. The sum of direct material and direct labor is called **prime cost.**

The third major category of manufacturing costs—**manufacturing overhead**—includes all manufacturing costs that the firm cannot trace to particular units of product as either direct material or direct labor. These costs include indirect materials, indirect labor, utilities, property taxes, depreciation, insurance, rent, and other costs of operating the manufacturing facilities. Manufacturing overhead and direct labor are the costs of converting raw materials into final products. Thus accountants call them **conversion costs.** Exhibit 2.1 diagrams the relation between the full ab-

Exhibit 2.1

Components of Manufacturing Product Costs

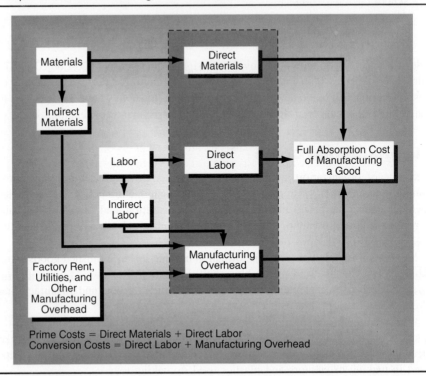

Prime Costs = Direct Materials + Direct Labor
Conversion Costs = Direct Labor + Manufacturing Overhead

sorption cost of manufacturing a good and the materials, labor, and manufacturing overhead required to produce it.

How indirect can a cost be to the manufacturing activity and still be part of manufacturing overhead? For example, are the costs of operating a factory employee cafeteria, or the plant manager's salary, or the cost of employing the plant's accounting staff part of manufacturing costs? In practice it is difficult to distinguish between such manufacturing and nonmanufacturing costs, so firms typically set their own guidelines and follow them consistently from period to period.

Although we use the term *manufacturing overhead,* accountants use many synonyms in practice, including *overhead, burden, factory burden, factory overhead,* and *factory expense.* The term *manufacturing overhead,* as we use it, refers only to manufacturing costs, not to nonmanufacturing marketing and administrative costs.

Nonmanufacturing Costs

Nonmanufacturing costs have two elements: marketing costs and administrative costs. **Marketing costs** are those the firm requires to obtain customer orders and to distribute goods to customers. These include advertising, sales commissions, and shipping, among others. (These costs are also known as *marketing and distribution costs.* We refer to these costs as simply *marketing* costs.) **Administrative costs** are those the firm requires to manage the organization, including executive and clerical salaries. Administrative costs also include staff support, such as legal, data processing, and accounting services.

Problem 2.1
for Self-Study

Computing categories of unit costs. After the death of his Uncle Sven early this year, Peter Sorenson left his $40,000-a-year job at an electronics company to assume control of Klogs, Inc., a manufacturer of quality clogs. His $28,000 salary at Klogs was substantially less than what he had earned in his previous job as a sales manager, but a sense of family duty persuaded him to head the ailing company.

Klogs produced and sold 70,000 pairs of clogs last year. At capacity, Klogs could manufacture 100,000 pairs of clogs. Peter obtained the following breakdown of last year's costs.

Item	Cost
(a) Sandpaper, Nails, and Varnish....................................	$ 8,400
(b) Leather	140,000
(c) Factory Rent—10 Years Remaining on Lease.........................	12,000
(d) Labor—Cutting	210,000
(e) Supervisor's Salary..	15,000
(f) Maintenance and Depreciation (fixed)	2,000
(g) Utilities—Factory (fixed)	6,000
(h) Sven's Salary..	28,000
(i) Labor—Assembling	175,000
(j) Sales Commission to Dealers ($0.15 per unit).......................	10,500
(k) Shipping Costs ($0.10 per unit).................................	7,000
(l) Administrative Manager's Salary	20,000
(m) Office Supplies	100
(n) Administrative Secretary's Salary	10,000
(o) Wood	70,000
(p) Advertising (fixed)	1,000

a. Ignoring any noneconomic value of self-employment, what is Peter Sorenson's opportunity cost of working for Klogs? $40,000
b. Identify the following costs, using last year's figures.
   (1) Unit direct materials costs.   b, o
   (2) Unit direct labor costs.   d, i
   (3) Unit manufacturing overhead. a, c, e, f, g
   (4) Unit marketing costs.   j k p
   (5) Unit administrative costs. h l n m

The solution to this self-study problem is at the end of this chapter on page 47.

Cost Concepts for Managerial Decision Making

In this section, we discuss concepts managers use to make decisions.

Cost Behavior: Fixed and Variable Costs

Managers must know cost behavior. Do total costs vary with activity (for example, production volume)? If so, they are **variable costs.** Costs that do not vary with activity are **fixed costs.**

Example   Electron, Inc., has received a special order for 10,000 calculators. The company must decide whether to accept or reject the order. Past experience enables management to predict that each calculator made to fill the special order will require $6.00 of direct materials, $1.00 of direct labor, and $1.00 of variable manufacturing overhead. (In some manufacturing settings firms include the direct labor costs in overhead. The accounting system at Electron separates direct labor from overhead.)

In this example variable manufacturing overhead includes indirect materials, power to run machines, and indirect labor required to handle materials. These are the only variable costs in manufacturing each calculator. In addition, each calculator requires $1.00 variable marketing and administrative costs. Hence, the total variable cost per unit to make and sell each calculator is $9.00. Knowing which costs vary with volume permits Electron to estimate the amount of costs incurred if it accepts the special order. The cost of accepting the special order is 10,000 units times $9.00 or $90,000.

Electron, Inc., rents its factory facilities for $10,000 per month. The rental fee is the same regardless of activity level—it is a fixed cost. Knowing that rent is a fixed cost for any level of activity permits Electron to exclude rent from the analysis of costs that will be affected by the special order. Whether or not Electron accepts the order it will pay $10,000 per month in rent. Other examples of fixed costs at Electron are property taxes, utilities to heat and light buildings, and marketing and administrative personnel costs (excluding commissions). In total, fixed costs are $110,000 per month composed of $50,000 manufacturing and $60,000 marketing and administrative costs.

The breakdown of the costs for Electron, Inc., into fixed and variable components appears in Exhibit 2.2. For a volume of up to 40,000 calculators per month, the accountants assume fixed costs will remain constant. The accountants also assume total variable costs will increase at the constant rate of $9.00 per calculator made and sold, which is the slope of the variable cost line. Note that the slope of the total cost line is $9.00—the variable cost per unit—and the intercept of the total cost line (that is, where it intersects the vertical axis) is $110,000—the fixed cost per month. Cost behavior is expressed by the following equation:

$$TC = F + VX$$

where TC refers to total cost for a particular period of time, F refers to the fixed costs for the period, V refers to the variable cost per unit, and X refers to the volume for the period in units. For Electron, Inc.,

$$TC = \$110,000 + \$9.00X.$$

If the volume was 30,000 for a month, the total cost would be

$$TC = \$110,000 + (\$9.00 \times 30,000 \text{ units}) = \$380,000.$$

Cost-Volume-Profit Relations

If we include the average sales price (P) per calculator in the equation, we can derive the profit equation. Assume the price is $25 per calculator.

$$\frac{\text{Operating}}{\text{Profit}} = \frac{\text{Total}}{\text{Revenue}} - \frac{\text{Total Variable}}{\text{Costs}} - \frac{\text{Fixed}}{\text{Costs}}$$

$$\pi = PX - VX - F$$

$$\pi = \$25X - \$9X - \$110,000$$

If the volume was 30,000 units, the profit would be

$$\pi = (\$25 \times 30,000) - (\$9 \times 30,000) - \$110,000$$

$$\pi = \$750,000 - \$270,000 - \$110,000$$

$$\pi = \$370,000.$$

Exhibit 2.3 shows these relationships. The **breakeven point** is the point at which the total cost and total revenue lines intersect. At volumes below this point, total cost exceeds total revenue; at volumes above this point, total revenue exceeds total cost. You can find the breakeven point by setting π in the profit equation equal to zero and solving for the breakeven volume, as follows:

$$\pi = PX - VX - F$$

$$0 = \$25X - \$9X - \$110,000$$

$$(\$25 - \$9)X = \$110,000$$

$$X = \frac{\$110,000}{\$16}$$

$$X = 6,875 \text{ units.}$$

(You can prove this result by computing total revenue and total cost at a volume of 6,875 units. You will find that total revenue and total costs both equal $171,875.)

Contribution Margin   The unit **contribution margin** is the excess of the unit selling price over the unit variable cost; that is, $P - V$. The contribution margin is the amount each unit contributes toward covering fixed costs and earning a profit. For Electron, Inc., the contribution margin is $16 (= $25 − $9). Many managerial decision models use the unit contribution margin. For example, linear programming models use it to compute optimal product mix. The contribution margin is such an important concept that it appears throughout this book in many contexts.

Change in Fixed Costs   Fixed costs will not necessarily remain at the same level, even with no inflation. For example, suppose Electron, Inc., can produce

Exhibit 2.2

ELECTRON, INC.
Fixed and Variable Costs

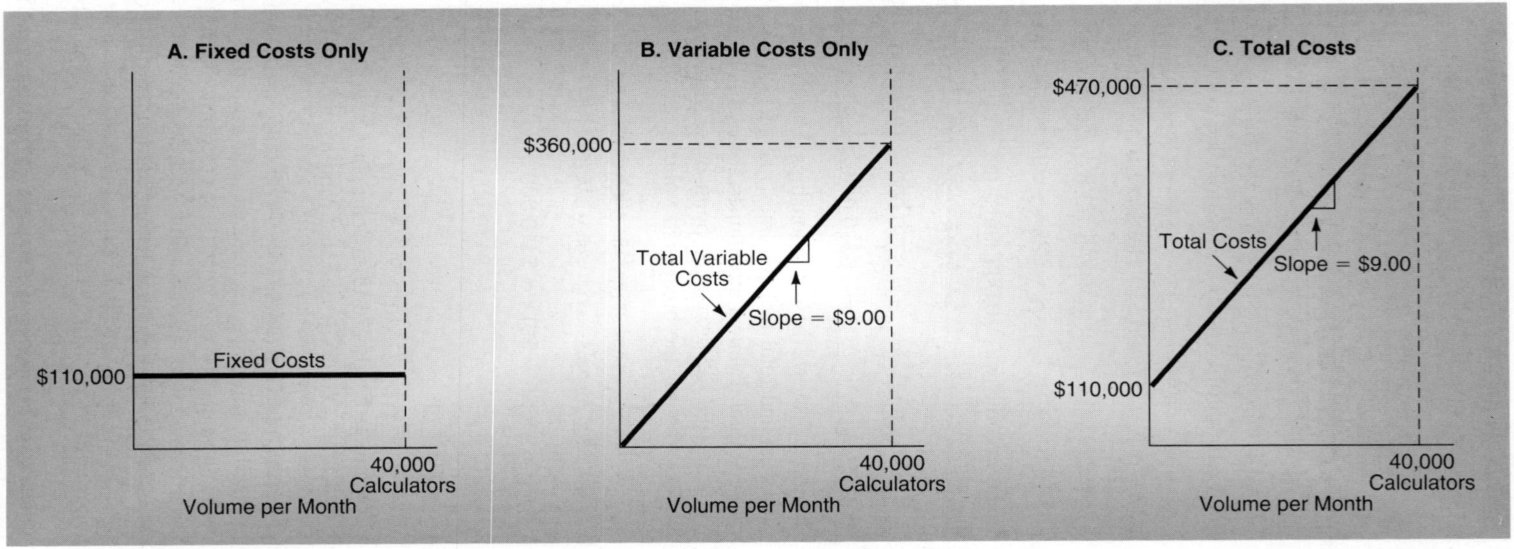

A. Fixed Costs Only

$110,000

Fixed Costs

40,000
Calculators

Volume per Month

B. Variable Costs Only

$360,000

Total Variable
Costs

Slope = $9.00

40,000
Calculators

Volume per Month

C. Total Costs

$470,000

$110,000

Total Costs

Slope = $9.00

40,000
Calculators

Volume per Month

Exhibit 2.3

Cost-Volume-Profit Relations

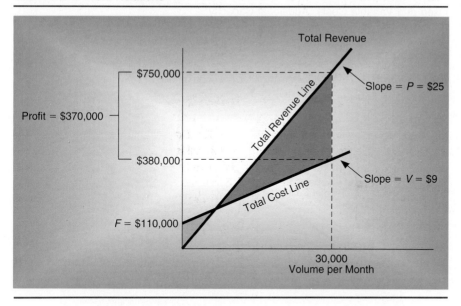

a maximum of 40,000 calculators per month with its present facilities. Assume that management wants to increase production and sales volume beyond 40,000 units per month. Now, the firm will have to acquire additional facilities, will incur additional utilities costs, and will have to hire more administrative and marketing personnel. Assume that adding facilities to expand capacity by 35,000 calculators per month would add $40,000 per month to fixed costs. Thus, for an additional capacity of 35,000 calculators, fixed costs would increase from $110,000 per month to $150,000 per month. Exhibit 2.4 illustrates this cost behavior.

In a sense, the marginal cost of the 40,001st calculator is $40,009.00 (that is, $40,000 additional fixed cost for the additional capacity plus $9.00 variable cost for the calculator). Of course, accounting would not charge such a cost to that particular calculator. Instead, the firm considers the $40,000 to be a *capacity cost,* that is, a cost of providing the additional capacity to produce and sell up to 75,000 calculators. If capacity is less than 40,000 calculators per month, fixed costs are $110,000 per month. If capacity is increased to a maximum of 75,000 calculators per month, fixed costs are $150,000 per month.

Long-Run Nature of Fixed Costs Decisions to increase or decrease capacity are usually long-term decisions. Firms decide to increase capacity assuming they will need additional capacity for a long time, say, several years. The length of the commitment to a particular level of capacity varies. An airplane manufacturer might commit for decades. A consulting firm might commit to the shortest lease available for office space.

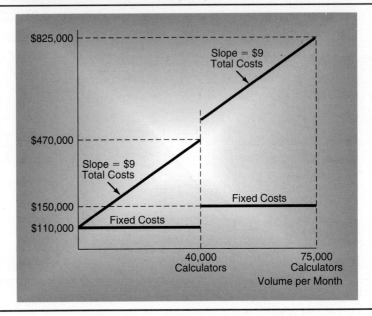

Exhibit 2.4

ELECTRON, INC.
Fixed and Variable Costs, Additional Capacity

Fixed costs are not fixed forever; they can change due to capacity changes. When the demand for Yamaha motorcycles decreased, for example, Yamaha reduced the volume of motorcycles but did not reduce the fixed costs of operating the factory for more than a year. We define fixed costs as those that remain the same for a given level of capacity. This definition is consistent with that used by economists, who say that fixed costs do not vary in the short run and that the short run is the period over which capacity remains unchanged. For practical purposes, we usually define the short run to be about 1 year.

Comparison of Direct Costs with Variable Costs   We often use the terms *direct* and *variable* interchangeably in the business world, because many costs that firms can directly trace to a unit are variable. Costs of direct materials are usually variable costs, for example. Variable manufacturing overhead costs, however, are *variable but not direct* if the implied cost object is a unit produced. A comparison of variable/fixed and direct/indirect costs for Electron's manufacturing costs appears in Exhibit 2.5. (This example assumes that the company has not added additional capacity.)

Differential Cost Analysis

In making decisions, managers often want to know how taking a certain action would affect costs. These costs are **differential costs;** that is, the costs that *differ*

Exhibit 2.5

ELECTRON, INC.
Comparison of Direct Costs with Variable Costs

	Direct versus Indirect Cost		Assumed Cost Behavior	
	Direct[a]	Indirect	Variable	Fixed
Manufacturing Costs:				
Direct Materials	X		X	
Direct Labor	X		X or X	
Variable Manufacturing Overhead (e.g., indirect materials, power to operate machines).....................		X	X	
Fixed Manufacturing Overhead (e.g., factory rent, property taxes)		X		X

[a]Direct means traceable directly to the production of a unit, in this case.

---

because of an action. We also call them *incremental costs.* Differential costs include both incremental costs (cost increases) and decremental costs (cost decreases).

If the contemplated action increases or decreases volume with no change in capacity, differential costs will be variable costs. In the Electron example, recall that management was considering filling a special order of 10,000 calculators. It assumed only variable costs would be affected. To be specific, an increase in costs of $90,000 (that is, 10,000 calculators times $9.00 per-unit variable cost) was expected. These are the differential costs of the special order.

Differential costs need not all be variable costs, however. If an action affects fixed costs, then those costs are differential. Virtually any long-run action involving changes in capacity causes fixed costs to differ. Consider the case in which Electron increased capacity. The additional fixed costs (of $40,000) would be differential costs of the additional capacity.

The differential concept is important in using accounting information for managerial decision making. A question uppermost in the minds of decision makers is "How are costs affected by the actions we are contemplating?" An understanding of how to use accounting data to estimate these differential costs is such an important part of decision making that we devote much of Chapters 7 through 10 to it.

Sunk Costs

Sunk costs result from past expenditures. Decisions made now do not affect such costs. Many decision makers have difficulty understanding this concept. Some managers, in an effort to overcome the results of unwise decisions in the past, will attempt to "recover their investment" by including sunk costs. The following example demonstrates how such behavior often leads to incorrect decisions.

Example The buyer for a sporting goods store purchased 200 pairs, at $20 per pair, of a new type of sandal called jog sandals (sandals used for jogging). "These are the coming thing!'' claimed the buyer. Unfortunately, in a year the store sold only two pairs at the retail price of $40 per pair and three pairs more at a reduced price of $25 per pair.

When the store manager suggested selling all the jog sandals at $10 per pair at a local running club, ''just to get rid of the things,'' the store's merchandise buyer questioned, ''How can we make a profit when we buy at $20 and sell at $10?'' The store manager believed the buyer's argument and held the price at $25 per pair. After another year without a single sale, the manager threw away the shoes, stating, ''It's unfortunate that these jog sandals didn't sell better, but at least we didn't sell them at a loss.'' Thus the manager missed an opportunity to recover $1,950 (= 195 pairs at $10 each).

Past expenditures are generally sunk costs and are irrelevant for decisions. Common examples of sunk costs include the past cost of inventory, whether bought or produced, the past cost of long-term assets (including residential homes), nonrefundable tuition paid for college, and the cost of a large dinner. (Moral: Don't feel obligated to eat all of your dinner just because you paid for it.)

The fact that past expenditures are sunk costs does not mean that information about past amounts spent is totally irrelevant. Managers can use information about the past to help predict differential costs of future actions. Further, managers often compare past expenditures with current expenditures for performance evaluation.

Problem 2.2 for Self-Study

Using differential cost analysis in making decisions. Refer to the discussion in Problem 2.1 for Self-Study. Peter discovered that Klogs had conducted very favorable marketing tests on a new clog, and he predicted that Klogs could expect to sell 40,000 pairs of this new product line. Peter collected the following facts and figures:

Cost of Producing 40,000 New Klogs	
Leather	$100,000
Wood	48,000
Nails, Varnish, and Sandpaper	1,000
Labor—Cutting	140,000
Labor—Assembling	120,000
Shipping Costs	4,000
Sales Commission to Dealers	6,000

Additionally, Klogs has spent $3,000 in the development of New Klogs and $2,000 in a market survey of retail outfits.

Assuming that Klogs continues to produce 70,000 pairs of traditional Klogs, the Klogs factory will have to operate on Saturdays to meet the additional capacity requirements. The additional costs of operating on Saturday follow:

Supervisor's Overtime Salary	$4,000
Utilities	1,200

What are the differential costs if Klogs wishes to produce an additional 40,000 new clogs?

The solution to this self-study problem is at the end of this chapter on page 48.

Period and Product Costs

Firms eventually expense all costs that they incur. If a firm does not expense a cost immediately, but adds it to an inventory account on the balance sheet until it sells the goods, that cost is said to be "inventoriable." We call inventoriable costs **product costs.** We call those that are not inventoriable **period costs,** because the firm expenses them in the period incurred.

Generally accepted accounting principles and income tax regulations require that firms treat all manufacturing costs as product costs for external financial reporting using full absorption costing (sometimes called absorption costing). Using **full absorption costing,** the firm assigns a unit's variable manufacturing cost plus a share of fixed manufacturing costs to each unit produced. Thus the total of units produced "fully absorbs" manufacturing costs.

For example, assume ConAgra, the large food producer, is making Banquet meals. Using full-absorption costing, ConAgra would assign materials, labor, and manufacturing overhead to each Banquet meal produced. Each meal would receive a share of fixed manufacturing costs (for example, rent, building depreciation, plant administrative salaries) under full-absorption costing.

By contrast, the **variable costing** method includes only each unit's variable manufacturing cost. Firms using variable costing treat fixed manufacturing costs as period costs. Using variable costing, ConAgra would not assign any of its fixed manufacturing costs to Banquet meals, but would expense fixed manufacturing costs as period costs.

Firms treat all nonmanufacturing costs as period costs, and therefore nonmanufacturing costs are not inventoriable under either method.

Components of Product Costs

The diagram in Exhibit 2.6 illustrates components of a product cost for one unit. We use the facts for the Electron, Inc., example to make the comparisons concrete. We can compute unit fixed costs only if we specify a particular volume. For this example, we assume a volume of 10,000 units for the month.

The diagram shows several important distinctions. First, note the difference between the full cost of making and selling the product and the full absorption cost inventory value. The full cost of making and selling the product includes marketing and administrative costs, but the full absorption cost inventory value does not. Managers who ask accountants for unit costs sometimes find to their surprise that the accountants have provided full absorption inventory costs when the managers wanted full costs.

Second, note the difference between unit variable costs, which include variable marketing and administrative costs, and variable manufacturing costs, which do not. Neither full absorption nor variable costing inventory values include marketing and administrative costs.

Exhibit 2.6

ELECTRON, INC.
What Makes Up a Product's Cost

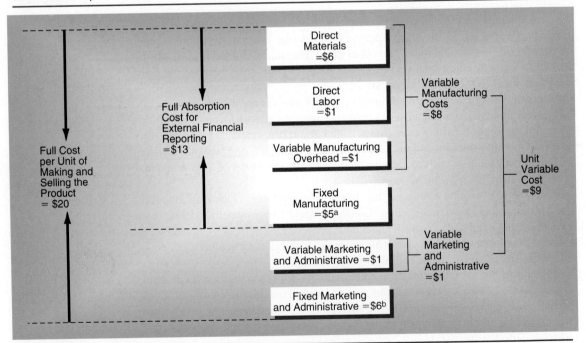

ᵃFixed manufacturing costs per unit = $50,000/10,000 units.
ᵇFixed marketing and administrative costs per unit = $60,000/10,000 units.

Exhibits 2.7 and 2.8 illustrate gross margin, contribution margin, and profit margin computations. Recall that the unit selling price for Electron, Inc., is $25.00. Using the information in Exhibits 2.6, 2.7, and 2.8, we find:

$$\text{Unit } \textbf{Profit Margin} = \frac{\text{Unit Selling}}{\text{Price}} - \frac{\text{Full Cost per Unit of Making}}{\text{and Selling the Product.}}$$

For Electron, Inc., the unit profit margin is $5 = $25 - $20.

$$\text{Unit } \textbf{Gross Margin} = \frac{\text{Unit Selling}}{\text{Price}} - \frac{\text{Unit Full Absorption Cost of}}{\text{Making the Product.}}$$

For Electron, Inc., the unit gross margin is $12 = $25 - $13.

$$\text{Unit } \textbf{Contribution Margin} = \frac{\text{Unit Selling}}{\text{Price}} - \frac{\text{Unit Variable Cost of Making}}{\text{and Selling the Product.}}$$

For Electron, Inc., the unit contribution margin is $16 = $25 - $9.

Gross margin and contribution margin are different concepts despite their similar-sounding names. Firms routinely report total gross margins on external financial statements. Many internal decisions involve choosing among products based on

Exhibit 2.7

ELECTRON, INC.
Gross Margin

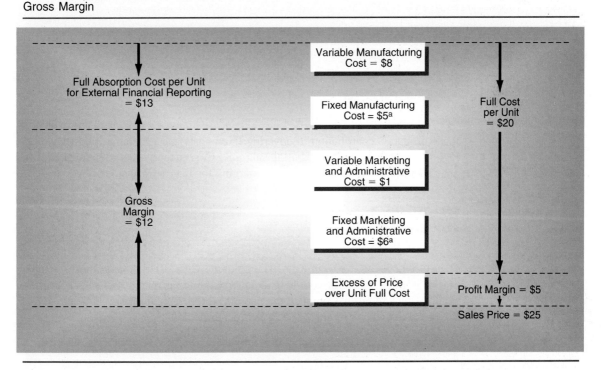

^aUnit fixed costs based on volume of 10,000 units.

Exhibit 2.8

ELECTRON, INC.
Contribution Margin

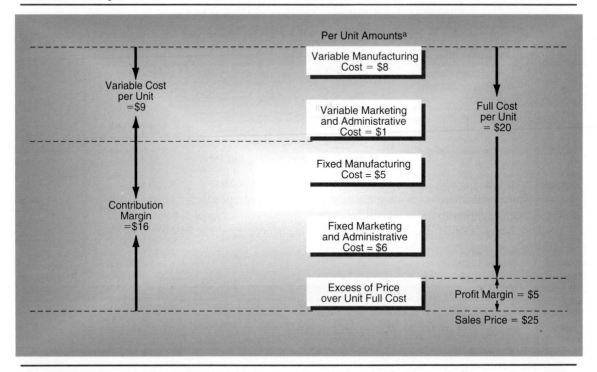

Per Unit Amounts[a]

Variable Manufacturing
Cost = $8

Variable Cost
per Unit
=$9

Variable Marketing
and Administrative
Cost = $1

Full Cost
per Unit
= $20

Fixed Manufacturing
Cost = $5

Contribution
Margin
=$16

Fixed Marketing
and Administrative
Cost = $6

Excess of Price
over Unit Full Cost

Profit Margin = $5

Sales Price = $25

[a]Unit fixed costs based on volume of 10,000 units.

those products' contribution to covering fixed costs and generating profits, which requires knowledge of contribution margins. Consequently, contribution margins are generally more useful than gross margins for internal decisions.

Problem 2.3
for Self-Study

Relation between Contribution Margin and Cost. Tori Adams makes exotic clocks. Tori has asked for your help in understanding the relation between contribution margin and costs. Complete the diagram for Tori by inserting amounts, given the data (after the diagram) about a particular clock:

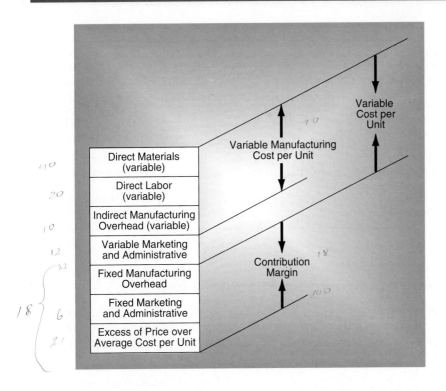

Price per Unit	$	100
Contribution Margin per Unit		18
Gross Margin for 1,000 Units		21,000
Variable Manufacturing Costs per Unit		70
Direct Materials per Unit		40
Direct Labor per Unit		20
Fixed Marketing and Administrative Costs per Unit		6

Complete the diagram for Tori by placing amounts per unit in the boxes.
The solution to this self-study problem is at the end of this chapter on page 48.

Costs Reported on Income Statements

This section compares the way accounting would present costs for two types of income statements: (1) external financial reporting and (2) managerial decision making.

Exhibit 2.9 shows the assumed facts for Electron, Inc., for the month of February.

Exhibit 2.9

ELECTRON, INC.
Facts

Units Produced and Sold in February	10,000 Units
Sales Price per Unit	$25 per Unit
Variable Manufacturing Cost per Unit:	
Direct Materials	$6 per Unit
Direct Labor	$1 per Unit
Variable Manufacturing Overhead	$1 per Unit
Fixed Manufacturing Costs:	
Fixed Manufacturing Overhead:	
Rent	$10,000 per Month
Other Manufacturing Overhead	$40,000 per Month
Marketing and Administrative:	
Fixed Costs	$60,000 per Month
Variable Costs	$1 per Unit

Income Statement for External Reporting

The income statement for external reporting appears in Exhibit 2.10. To comply with income tax regulations and generally accepted accounting principles using full absorption costing, Electron allocates fixed manufacturing costs to each unit produced, as follows:

$$\text{Fixed Manufacturing Cost per Unit} = \frac{\text{Fixed Manufacturing Costs}}{\text{Units Produced}}$$

$$= \frac{\$50,000}{10,000 \text{ Units}}$$

$$= \$5 \text{ per Unit.}$$

Exhibit 2.10

ELECTRON, INC.
Income Statement for External Financial Reporting
for the Month Ending February 28

Sales Revenue	$250,000[a]
Less Cost of Goods Sold	130,000[b]
Gross Margin	$120,000
Less Marketing and Administrative Expenses	70,000[c]
Net Income before Taxes	$ 50,000

[a]$250,000 = $25 × 10,000 Units.

[b]$130,000 = ($8 Variable Manufacturing Cost × 10,000 Units) + 50,000 Fixed Manufacturing Cost.

[c]$70,000 = ($1 Variable Marketing and Administrative Cost × 10,000 Units) + $60,000 Fixed Marketing and Administrative Costs.

Adding this $5 per unit to the $8 variable manufacturing cost per unit makes the full absorption cost of manufacturing a unit $13. Hence, the cost of goods sold is $130,000 (= $13 × 10,000 units).

Income Statement for Managerial Decision Making

The income statement for external reporting does not show actual manufacturing cost behavior because it "unitizes" fixed manufacturing costs to assign a share of these costs to each unit produced. The income statement in Exhibit 2.11, as prepared for managerial use, will help management do its job because it represents cost behavior.

Note the difference between the *gross margin* and the *contribution margin,* as shown in Exhibits 2.10 and 2.11. The gross margin is the difference between revenue and cost of goods sold, whereas the contribution margin is the difference between revenue and variable costs, including variable marketing and administrative costs. We use the term *operating profit* at the bottom of income statements prepared for managerial use to distinguish it from net income used in external reporting.

Income statements such as the one shown in Exhibit 2.11 use variable costing. Recall that, using variable costing, accounting assigns each unit of a good produced the unit's variable manufacturing cost for inventory valuation. Accounting treats fixed manufacturing costs as period costs; the firm does not assign them to units for inventory valuation. (The firm does not assign nonmanufacturing costs to units for inventory valuation under either variable or full absorption costing.) Firms often use variable costing for internal reporting because it reflects cost behavior better than full absorption costing does.

Exhibit 2.11

Income Statement for Managerial Decision Making: Contribution Margin Format for the Month Ending February 28

Sales Revenue		$250,000
Less Variable Costs:		
Variable Cost of Goods Sold	$80,000[a]	
Variable Marketing and Administrative Costs	10,000[b]	
Total Variable Costs		90,000
Contribution Margin		$160,000
Less Fixed Costs:		
Fixed Manufacturing Costs	$50,000	
Fixed Marketing and Administrative Costs	60,000	
Total Fixed Costs		110,000
Operating Profit		$ 50,000

[a]$80,000 = 10,000 Units × $8 Variable Cost.
[b]$10,000 = 10,000 Units × $1 Variable Cost.

Summary

Knowledge of cost concepts is important for external reporting, managerial decision making, and planning and performance evaluation. In concept, a cost is a sacrifice of resources. An opportunity cost is the best alternative use of resources forgone because of some action.

Distinguishing between costs and expenses is important. Costs are a sacrifice of resources. Expenses are costs that the firm uses up (and matches against revenues) in a particular accounting period for external reporting purposes.

Manufacturing costs consist of direct materials, direct labor, and manufacturing overhead. Accounting attributes direct materials and direct labor (which are some-

---

Exhibit 2.12

Summary of Definitions

Concept	Definition
Nature of Cost	
Cost	A sacrifice of resources.
Opportunity cost	The return that one could realize from the best forgone alternative use of a resource.
Expense	The cost charged against revenue in a particular accounting period. We use the term *expense* only when speaking of external financial reports.
Cost Concepts for Cost Accounting Systems	
Product costs	Costs that firms can more easily attribute to products; costs that are part of inventory.
Period costs	Costs that firms can more easily attribute to time intervals.
Full absorption costing method	A method of inventory valuation in which firms use all manufacturing costs—both fixed and variable—in computing a unit cost.
Variable costing method	A method of inventory valuation in which firms use only variable manufacturing costs in computing a unit cost.
Cost object	Any item for which the manager wishes to measure cost (e.g., product, department).
Direct costs	Costs directly related to a cost object.
Indirect costs	Costs not directly related to a cost object.
Common costs	Costs two or more cost objects share.
Additional Cost Concepts Used in Decision Making	
Variable costs	Costs that vary with the volume of activity.
Fixed costs	Costs that do not vary with volume of activity in a specified time span.
Differential costs	Costs that change in response to a particular course of action.
Sunk costs	Costs that result from an expenditure made in the past and that present or future decisions cannot change.

times called prime costs) directly to each unit produced, whereas it does not attribute manufacturing overhead directly to units. Accounting usually classifies nonmanufacturing costs as either administrative or marketing.

For decision making, cost behavior classifications become important. Activity levels affect variable costs but not fixed costs. This classification is meaningful only over a specified range of activity levels for a specified time interval. Other important cost concepts for decision making are differential costs and sunk costs. Differential costs differ because of an action. Sunk costs are past expenditures irrelevant for future decisions.

We have introduced many concepts and terms in this chapter that you will use throughout the book. You should find it helpful to refer back to these concepts and terms, particularly to Exhibit 2.12, as you proceed through the book.

Solutions to Self-Study Problems

Suggested Solution to Problem 2.1 for Self-Study

a. Opportunity cost = $40,000.

b. **(1)** Items **(b)** and **(o)**:

$$\frac{\$140,000 + \$70,000}{70,000 \text{ units}} = \frac{\$210,000}{70,000} = \$3.00$$

(2) Items **(d)** and **(i)**:

$$\frac{\$210,000 + \$175,000}{70,000 \text{ units}} = \$5.50$$

(3) Items **(a)**, **(c)**, **(e)**, **(f)**, and **(g)**:

$$\frac{\$8,400 + \$12,000 + \$15,000 + \$2,000 + \$6,000}{70,000 \text{ units}} = \$.62$$

(4) Items (j), (k), and (p):

$$\frac{\$10,500 + \$7,000 + \$1,000}{70,000 \text{ units}} = \$.264 \text{ (rounded)}$$

(5) Items **(h)**, **(l)**, **(m)**, and **(n)**:

$$\frac{\$28,000 + \$20,000 + \$100 + \$10,000}{70,000 \text{ units}} = \$.83$$

Suggested Solution to Problem 2.2 for Self-Study

Differential costs:

Direct Materials ($100,000 + $48,000)	$148,000
Direct Labor ($140,000 + $120,000)	260,000
Variable Manufacturing Overhead	1,000
Variable Marketing ($4,000 + $6,000)	10,000
Supervisor's Overtime	4,000
Utilities	1,200
Total	$424,200

The $3,000 spent on development and $2,000 spent on the survey of retail outlets are sunk costs and no longer differential. While the costs of the survey are sunk, and should not be considered when deciding the fate of New Klogs, the knowledge gained from the development and survey remains useful and should be considered.

Suggested Solution to Problem 2.3 for Self-Study

Diagram for Problem 2.3 for Self-Study is below. Computations appear on the next page.

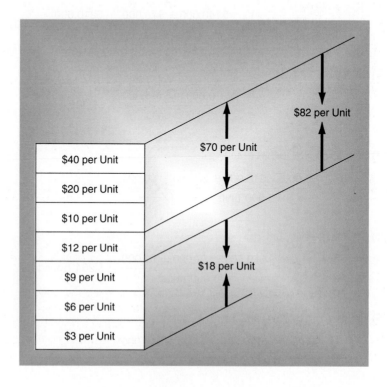

Variable Manufacturing Cost per Unit	$70 per Unit
Direct Materials	$40 per Unit
Direct Labor	$20 per Unit
Variable Manufacturing Overhead = $70 − ($40 + $20) = ...	$10 per Unit
Variable Costs per Unit = Price − Unit Contribution Margin = $100 − $18 = ...	$82 per Unit
Variable Marketing and Administrative Costs = $82 − $40 − $20 − $10 = ...	$12 per Unit

Fixed Manufacturing Costs per Unit = Manufacturing Costs per Unit
   − Variable Manufacturing Costs per Unit = (Price
   − Gross Margin per Unit) − Variable Manufacturing Costs per Unit
   $= \left(\$100 - \dfrac{\$21{,}000}{1{,}000 \text{ Units}}\right) - \$70 =$ ....
	$9 per Unit

Fixed Marketing and Administrative Cost per Unit = ...	$6 per Unit
Excess of Price over Average Cost of Each Unit = $100 − ($40 + $20 + $10 + $12 + $9 + $6) = ...	$3 per Unit

Key Terms and Concepts

Opportunity cost
Direct versus indirect costs
Cost object
Common costs
Manufacturing costs
Direct versus indirect materials
Direct versus indirect labor
Prime cost
Manufacturing overhead
Conversion costs
Nonmanufacturing costs
Marketing costs

Administrative costs
Variable versus fixed costs
Breakeven point
Contribution margin
Differential costs
Sunk costs
Product versus period costs
Full absorption costing
Variable costing
Profit margin and gross margin
Contribution margin

Questions, Exercises, Problems, and Cases

Questions

1. Review the meaning of the concepts or terms given above in Key Terms and Concepts.
2. ''The cost of my trip to Hawaii was $3,000.'' Using the concept of cost developed in this chapter, explain why this statement is ambiguous.
3. Zappa, a mechanic, left his $25,000-a-year job at Joe's Garage to start his own body shop. Zappa drew an annual salary of $15,000. Identify his opportunity costs.

4. People often use expenses and costs interchangeably, yet the terms do not always mean the same thing. Distinguish between the two terms.

5. Identify and describe the three elements that make up manufacturing costs.

6. Compare and contrast prime costs and conversion costs.

7. Firms usually classify nonmanufacturing costs as either marketing costs or administrative costs. How do these two types of costs differ?

8. "Since fixed manufacturing overhead costs such as factory rent or property taxes are independent of the number of units produced, we should treat them as period costs rather than product costs." Comment.

9. In financial accounting, accountants always treat manufacturing costs as product costs, and nonmanufacturing costs as period costs. Is this a hard-and-fast rule in managerial accounting? Explain.

10. Can costs that we normally consider to be fixed costs actually change?

11. "Only variable costs are differential costs." Comment.

12. Mark Burchinshaw, a member of the Shaughnessy Heights Country Club, paid $400 for unlimited tennis court time for the entire summer because he anticipated spending many hours improving his game. In early June, Mark slipped on a wet floor at work, severely wrenching his ankle. Mark's ankle was put in a cast for 8 weeks. With 3 weeks left on his summer tennis deal, Mark was back on the courts the moment his cast came off, despite his doctor's advice to avoid strenuous exercise for a month. "This summer's tennis court time cost me $400," Mark said. "I have to get my money's worth." Given your understanding of cost concepts, comment.

13. "This is an excellent feasibility study of our new product, Hughes. But why haven't you included the cost of the test marketing we carried out last month in the analysis?" How should Hughes reply?

14. What do managerial accountants mean when they speak of cost behavior? Why is it important in managerial decision making?

15. Refer to this chapter's Managerial Application, "Cost and Profit Concepts at Ford in Dispute over Patent Value." Why did Ford argue that "accounted profit" did not accurately reflect profits?

16. "Fixed costs are really variable. The more you produce, the smaller the unit cost of production." Is that statement correct? Why or why not?

17. You are to match each of the listed items that follow with one of the numbered terms that *most specifically* identifies the cost concept indicated parenthetically.

Terms

(1) Fixed cost.
(2) Differential cost.
(3) Opportunity cost.
(4) Prime cost.

(5) Sunk cost.
(6) Full absorption costing.
(7) Variable costing.

Items

a. The management of a corporation is considering replacing a machine that operates satisfactorily with a more efficient new model. Depreciation on the cost of the existing machine is omitted from the data used in judging the proposal, because it has little or no significance with respect to such a decision. Ignore tax effects. *(The omitted cost.)*

(continued)

    b.   A company declined an offer to rent one of its warehouses and elected to use the warehouse for storage of extra raw materials to ensure uninterrupted production. Accounting has charged storage cost with *the monthly amount of the rental offered. (This cost is known as?)*

    c.   A manufacturing company excludes all "fixed" costs from its valuation of inventories, assigning to inventory only applicable portions of costs that vary with changes in volume. *(The term accounting employs for this costing procedure.)*

    d.   The sales department urges developing a new product and, as part of the data presented in support of its proposal, indicates the total additional cost involved. *(The increase in total cost.)*

    e.   The "direct" production cost of a unit includes those portions of *labor* and *materials* obviously traceable directly to the unit. *(The term used to specify the sum of the two named components.)*

---

18. Assuming no income taxes, how should management use each of the following costs in a decision to replace old equipment?

    a.   Book value of old equipment.

    b.   Disposal value of old equipment.

    c.   Cost of new equipment.

19. USAir announced a substantial reduction in airfares to increase the number of passengers. What might be the differential costs of this decision?

20. Classify each of the following costs as variable or fixed or a combination of the two. For each fixed cost, attempt to judge the time period over which the cost is fixed.

    a.   Depreciation of an office building.

    b.   Costs of raw materials used in producing a firm's products.

    c.   Leasing costs of a delivery truck, which is $950 per month and $.38 per mile.

    d.   Costs of internal programs for teaching recent business school graduates about the operating procedures and policies of the firm.

    e.   Local property taxes on land and buildings.

    f.   Compensation of sales staff on straight commission.

    g.   Compensation of sales staff on salary plus commission.

21. A medical doctor (pathologist) and several laboratory technicians staff the pathology laboratory at Presbyterian University Hospital. The lab contains equipment of two basic kinds: microscopes and the like for doing individual tests and sophisticated testing equipment for doing 12 tests simultaneously on batches of specimens from several patients. A list of costs follows.

    a.   Salary of the pathologist.

    b.   Hourly wages of the lab technicians.

    c.   Depreciation of a microscope.

    d.   Supplies for tests.

    e.   Fees paid to a local university professor of accounting who has been helping the hospital director understand the causes of total costs shown for each month.

    (1) In your judgment, are these costs variable, fixed, or a combination of these?

    (2) For each cost with a fixed component (all but strictly variable), attempt to judge the time period over which the cost is fixed.

Exercises

Solutions to even-numbered exercises are at the end of this chapter after the cases.

22. **Opportunity cost analysis.** Geoff Parkhurst operates a covered parking structure that can accommodate up to 300 cars. Geoff charges $2 per hour for parking. Parking attendants are paid $7.00 an hour to staff the cashier's booth at Parkhurst Parking. Utilities and other fixed costs average $1,000 per month.

    Recently, the manager of a nearby Marriott Hotel approached Geoff concerning the reservation of 50 spots over an upcoming weekend for a small convention party for a lump sum of $600. Normally, Geoff welcomed such opportunities, but this particular weekend was a football weekend. Because of the structure's proximity to the football stadium, all available spots would be taken 2 hours before game time on football Saturdays, and the structure would stay full until after the game, 6 hours later. What is the opportunity cost of accepting the offer?

23. **Manufacturing cost concepts.** Bubba Brothers, a toy manufacturer, produces a variety of inflatable plastic toys. One day, the owner (Bubbles, as he is affectionately known to his employees) decided to take a look at the manufacturing costs of Squeaky Duck, a product the company introduced 2 years ago. Squeaky Duck is an inflatable plastic duck with a whistle attached to its beak. During the last 6 months, Bubba Brothers produced 10,000 Squeaky Ducks and incurred the following manufacturing costs:

Plastic	$4,000
Labor—Cutting	2,000
Labor—Assembling	10,000
Whistles	6,000
Supplies	1,000
Machine Cost (Variable Overhead)	4,000
Fixed Manufacturing Overhead	6,000

    Bubbles wants to know the prime cost and the conversion cost of each Squeaky Duck. What are the prime costs per unit and the conversion costs per unit?

24. **Manufacturing costs.** Whizz Incorporated produced 3,000 Kiddy Kars in May. The Whizz plant incurred the following costs for that month:

Variable Costs					
Cutting		**Fabrication**		**Assembly**	
Wood	$3,000	Labor	$6,000	Paint and	
Labor	4,500	Nails	500	miscellaneous	
		Sandpaper	100	supplies	$ 900
				Labor	7,500
				Wheels	12,000
				Axles	6,000

(continued)

Fixed Costs

Plant Supervisor's Salary	$3,000
Utilities (heat and light)	400
Depreciation—Machinery	1,000
Plant Rent	1,600

Management wants to know the following costs of each Kiddy Kar:

a. Direct materials cost.

b. Direct labor cost.

c. Variable manufacturing overhead.

d. Fixed manufacturing overhead.

Calculate these costs per unit.

25. **Nonmanufacturing costs.** Trailblaster, a tent manufacturer, sold 10,000 tents last year and reported the following financial results:

Sales Revenue (10,000 units)		$750,000
Less Cost of Goods Sold		300,000
Gross Margin		$450,000
Less:		
Advertising (fixed costs)	$1,500	
Sales Commissions to Dealers	6,000	
Office Rent	7,200	
Office Supplies	300	
Depreciation—Office Equipment	150	
Sales Promotion (fixed cost)	4,000	19,150
Operating Profit		$430,850

Management asks you to classify costs other than Cost of Goods Sold into the following three categories:

a. Variable marketing costs.

b. Fixed marketing costs.

c. Administrative costs.

26. **Product and period costs.** Refer to Trailblaster in Exercise 25. Suppose that the Cost of Goods Sold could be broken down into the following costs:

Variable Costs:	
Direct Materials	$ 50,000
Direct Labor	100,000
Variable Overhead	80,000
Fixed Overhead	70,000

a. What would be the product costs and period costs using full absorption costing?

b. Management wants to make decisions requiring variable manufacturing costs to be product costs (that is, variable costing). What would be the product costs and period costs using variable costing?

27. **Differential cost analysis.** Eat Right, Inc., is considering a contract to supply a government agency with 10,000 meals per year for senior citizens. Each meal has a variable cost of $5. Eat Right would sell each meal to the government agency for $6. An opponent of this contract has stated that Eat Right should not accept the contract because the cost per meal would be $7, including fixed costs of $20,000 per year allocated to the meals. The total fixed costs in the company would be $1,000,000 whether or not it accepts this contract.

   What is the differential cost per year to Eat Right if the contract is accepted? Assuming $6 per meal is the highest price the government agency will pay, should Eat Right accept the contract?

28. **Differential costs.** Assume Nike Shoes has a plant capacity that can produce 2,500 units per week (each unit is a pair of shoes). Its predicted operations for the week follow:

Sales (2,000 units at $40 each)	$80,000
Manufacturing Costs:	
Variable	$24 per Unit
Fixed...	$17,000
Marketing and Administrative Costs:	
Variable (sales commissions)	$2.50 per Unit
Fixed...	$2,500

   Should Nike accept a special order for 400 units at a selling price of $32 each? Assume these units are subject to half the usual sales commission rate per unit, and assume no effect on regular sales at regular prices. How will the decision affect the company's operating profit?

29. **Components of full costs.** The following data apply to the cost of producing a particular model snowboard. Using these data, put amounts beside each label in Exhibit 2.6 in the text.

Price per Unit	$150
Fixed Costs:	
Marketing and Administrative	$24,000 per Period
Manufacturing Overhead	$40,000 per Period
Variable Costs:	
Variable Marketing and Administrative	$5 per Unit
Direct Materials	$30 per Unit
Direct Labor	$20 per Unit
Variable Manufacturing Overhead	$10 per Unit
Units Produced and Sold	1,000 per Period

30. **Cost and margin relations.** Refer to the data in Exercise 29. Compute the profit margin and gross margin.

31. **Cost and margin relations.** You and a friend are considering manufacturing a new type of skateboard. Based on industry publications and other research, you have collected the following data:

Sales Price	$200 per Unit
Fixed Costs:	
Marketing and Administrative	$30,000 per Period
Manufacturing Overhead	$33,600 per Period
Variable Costs:	
Marketing and Administrative	$6 per Unit
Manufacturing Overhead	$9 per Unit
Direct Labor	$30 per Unit
Direct Materials	$60 per Unit
Units Produced and Sold	1,200 per Period

    a. How much are each of the following unit costs (see Exhibit 2.6)?
      (1) Variable manufacturing cost.
      (2) Variable cost.
      (3) Full absorption cost.
      (4) Full cost.
    b. How much *per unit* are each of the following margins (see Exhibits 2.7 and 2.8)?
      (1) Profit margin.
      (2) Gross margin.
      (3) Contribution margin.
    c. How much *per unit* are each of the following costs (see Exhibit 2.1)?
      (1) Prime costs.
      (2) Conversion costs.

32. **Product and period costs.** Under full absorption costing, all costs of manufacturing the product are product costs (that is, they are inventoriable). Using the data from Exercise 31, what are the following?
    a. Product cost *per unit,* using full absorption costing.
    b. Period costs for the *period,* using full absorption costing.

33. **Cost-volume-profit relations.** Given the data in Exercise 31:
    a. Graph total revenue and total cost lines (as in Exhibit 2.3).
    b. Compute the breakeven point.

Problems

34. **Alternative concepts of cost: George Jackson** (adapted from CMA exam). George Jackson operates a small machine shop. He manufactures one standard product available from many other similar businesses and he also manufactures products to customer order. His accountant prepared the following annual income statement:

	Custom Sales	Standard Sales	Total
Sales.........................	$50,000	$25,000	$75,000
Material	$10,000	$ 8,000	$18,000
Labor	20,000	9,000	29,000
Depreciation	6,300	3,600	9,900
Power........................	700	400	1,100
Rent	6,000	1,000	7,000
Heat and Light	600	100	700
Other.........................	400	900	1,300
Total Costs	$44,000	$23,000	$67,000
Operating Profit	$ 6,000	$ 2,000	$ 8,000

The depreciation charges are for machines used in the respective product lines. The rent is for the building space, which Mr. Jackson has leased for 10 years at $7,000 per year. The accountant apportions the rent and the heat and light to the product lines based on amount of floor space occupied. Material, labor, power, and other costs are variable costs that are directly related to the product line causing them.

A valued custom parts customer has asked Mr. Jackson to manufacture 5,000 special units. Mr. Jackson is working at capacity and would have to give up some other business in order to take this business. He must produce custom orders already agreed to, but he could reduce the output of his standard product by about one-half for 1 year and use the freed machine time normally used for the Standard product to produce the specially requested custom part. The customer is willing to pay $9.00 for each part. The material cost will be about $3.00 per unit and the labor will be $3.60 per unit. Mr. Jackson will have to spend $2,000 for a special device that he will discard when the job is done. The new job will also require additional power costing $300.

a. Calculate and present the following costs related to the 5,000-unit custom order:

   (1) The differential cash cost of filling the order, considering both the cost of the order and the costs saved by reducing work on Standard products.

   (2) The opportunity cost of taking the order.

b. Should Mr. Jackson accept the order? Explain your answer.

35. Fixed and variable cost analysis (adapted from a problem by D. O. Green). The sales representatives of the Piney Paper Company have secured two special orders, *either* of which, in addition to regular orders, will keep the plant operating at capacity through the slack season. Hence, the company can accept one order or the other, or neither. One order is for 20 million printed placemats and the other is for 30 million sheets of engraved office stationery. The proposed prices are $.0070 per mat for the placemats and $.0062 per sheet for the stationery. Cost estimates follow:

	Mats (cost per 100 mats)	Stationery (cost per 100 sheets)
Direct Materials	$0.3550	$0.2775
Labor Costs:		
Variable	0.1100	0.0993
Fixed	0.0300	0.0089
Manufacturing Overhead Costs:		
Variable	0.0430	0.0330
Fixed	0.0370	0.0523
Variable Marketing and Administrative Cost (already incurred to procure order)	0.0900	0.0912
Fixed Marketing and Administrative Cost (already incurred to procure order)	0.0950	0.0878
Total Cost per 100 items	$0.7600	$0.6500
Selling Price per 100 items	$0.7000	$0.6200

After reviewing these figures, management decides to reject the orders on the basis that "we cannot make much money if it costs more than we can sell it for."

Is management correct? Based on the data in the table, prepare a schedule to show which alternative Piney Paper should accept, if either.

36. **Cost data for multiple purposes: Omega Auto Supplies** (contributed by J. Lim). Omega Auto Supplies manufactures an automobile safety seat for children that it sells through several retail chains. Omega makes its sales exclusively within its five-state region in the Midwest. The cost of manufacturing and marketing children's automobile safety seats at the company's normal volume of 15,000 units per month follows:

Variable Materials	$300,000	
Variable Labor	150,000	
Variable Overhead	30,000	
Fixed Overhead	180,200	
Total Manufacturing Costs		$660,200
Variable Nonmanufacturing Costs	$ 75,000	
Fixed Nonmanufacturing Costs	105,000	
Total Nonmanufacturing Costs		180,000
Total Costs		$840,200

The following questions refer only to the data given here. Unless otherwise stated, assume that the situations described in the questions are not connected; treat each independently. Unless otherwise stated, assume a regular selling price of $70 per unit. Ignore income taxes and other costs that we do not mention in the data or in a question itself.

a. In any normal month, what would be the inventory value per completed unit according to generally accepted accounting principles?

b. On April 1, a nonprofit charitable organization offers Omega Auto Supplies a special-order contract to supply 2,000 units to several orphanages for delivery by April 30. Production for April was initially planned for 15,000 units, and Omega can easily accommodate this special order without any additional capacity costs. (Thus Omega would produce a total of 17,000 units.) The special-order contract will reimburse Omega for all manufacturing costs plus a fixed fee of $25,000. (Omega would incur no variable marketing costs on the special order.) Write a short report to management indicating whether management should accept the special order.

Cases

37. **Differential analysis: Justa Corporation** (adapted from CMA exam). The Justa Corporation produces and sells three products. The company sells the three products, A, B, and C, in a local market and in a regional market. At the end of the first quarter of the current year, Justa has prepared the following income statement:

	Total	Local	Regional
Sales....................................	$1,300,000	$1,000,000	$300,000
Cost of Goods Sold..................	1,010,000	775,000	235,000
Gross Margin	$ 290,000	$ 225,000	$ 65,000
Marketing Costs	$ 105,000	$ 60,000	$ 45,000
Administrative Costs	52,000	40,000	12,000
Total Marketing and Administrative Costs	$ 157,000	$ 100,000	$ 57,000
Operating Profit	$ 133,000	$ 125,000	$ 8,000

Management has expressed special concern with the regional market because of the extremely poor return on sales. Justa entered this market a year ago because of excess capacity. The firm originally believed that the return on sales would improve with time, but after a year Justa sees no noticeable improvement from the results as reported in the quarterly statement.

In attempting to decide whether to eliminate the regional market, management has gathered the following information:

	Products		
	A	**B**	**C**
Sales.....................................	$500,000	$400,000	$400,000
Variable Manufacturing Costs as a Percentage of Sales	60%	70%	60%
Variable Marketing Costs as a Percentage of Sales	3%	2%	2%

(continued)

	Product	Sales by Markets	
		Local	Regional
A	....	$400,000	$100,000
B	....	300,000	100,000
C	....	300,000	100,000

All administrative costs and fixed manufacturing costs are common to the three products and the two markets, and are fixed for the period. Remaining marketing costs are fixed for the period and separable by market. All fixed costs are based on a prorated yearly amount.

a. Prepare the quarterly income statement showing contribution margins by markets.

b. Assuming that Justa has no alternative uses for its present capacity, would you recommend dropping the regional market? Why or why not?

c. Prepare the quarterly income statement showing contribution margins by products.

d. Management believes that it can have a new product ready for sale next year if it decides to continue the research. Justa can produce the new product simply by converting equipment presently used in producing product C. This conversion will increase fixed costs by $10,000 per quarter. What must be the minimum contribution margin per quarter for the new product to make the changeover financially feasible?

38. **Estimating cash flows for decision making—sensitivity analysis.** An automobile dealer sells its Excalibre model in two versions—one with a gasoline engine and one with a diesel engine. It sells the gasoline version for $12,500 and the diesel version for $13,900. Assume for the purposes of this problem that the dealer actually charges the list prices in purchase transactions. According to federal EPA mileage tests, the gasoline version gets, on average, 23 miles per gallon of gasoline, which costs $1.50 per gallon. The diesel version gets, on average, 30 miles per gallon of diesel fuel, which costs $1.40 per gallon. Assume that a purchaser had decided to acquire one of these two cars and that other operating costs of the two models of cars are identical. The purchaser expects to drive 12,000 miles a year for 5 years before disposing of the car. Experts expect the gasoline version to have a resale value 5 years hence of $2,500, and the diesel a resale value of $2,600.

Assume that analysts expect costs per gallon of gasoline and diesel fuel to remain constant over the 5 years.

a. What cash flows for each year are relevant to the purchaser who wants to decide which of the two models of Excalibre to buy?

b. Assume that the customer can purchase each of the cars for a 10-percent discount from list price. Repeat the instructions in part **a.**

c. Assume that fuel costs increase at the rate of 10 percent per year and that the customer pays the full list price. Repeat part **a.**

Suggested Solutions to Even-Numbered Exercises

22. **Opportunity cost analysis.**

    On football Saturdays, the opportunity cost is

$$50 \text{ Spots for Cars} \times 6 \text{ Hours} \times \$2 = \underline{\underline{\$600}}.$$

    All other costs are not differential.

24. **Manufacturing costs.**

    a. Direct materials cost:

Wood	$ 3,000
Wheels	12,000
Axles..	6,000
	$21,000

    Unit direct materials cost = $7.00.

    b. Direct labor cost:

Labor—Cutting	$ 4,500
Labor—Fabrication	6,000
Labor—Assembly..	7,500
	$18,000

    Unit direct labor cost = $6.00.

    c. Variable manufacturing overhead:

Nails	$ 500
Sandpaper..	100
Paint and Miscellaneous Supplies	900
	$ 1,500

    Unit variable overhead = $0.50.

    d. Fixed manufacturing overhead:

Plant Supervisor's Salary	$ 3,000
Utilities	400
Depreciation	1,000
Plant Rent	1,600
	$ 6,000

    Unit fixed overhead = $2.00.

26. **Product and period costs.**

    a. Product costs are all manufacturing costs using full absorption costing. Therefore,

$$\text{Product Costs} = \$300,000.$$

Period costs are all nonmanufacturing costs. Therefore,

$$\text{Period Costs} = \$19{,}150.$$

b. Only *variable* manufacturing costs are treated as product costs using variable costing. Therefore,

$$\text{Product Costs} = \$50{,}000 + \$100{,}000 + \$80{,}000$$

$$= \$230{,}000.$$

All nonmanufacturing costs and fixed manufacturing costs are treated as period costs. Therefore,

$$\text{Period Costs} = \$70{,}000 + \$19{,}150$$

$$= \$89{,}150.$$

28. **Differential costs.**
Accept the order.

Special-Order Sales (400 × $32)		$12,800
Less Variable Costs:		
Manufacturing (400 × $24)	$(9,600)	
Sales Commissions (400 × $1.25)....................	(500)	(10,100)
Addition to Company Profit		$ 2,700

30. **Cost and margin relations.**

$$\text{Profit Margin} = \text{Price} - \text{Full Cost}$$

$$= \$150 - \$129$$

$$= \$21.$$

$$\text{Gross Margin} = \text{Price} - \text{Full Absorption Cost}$$

$$= \$150 - \$100$$

$$= \$50.$$

32. **Product and period costs.**
a. Product cost per unit:

$$\$60 + \$30 + \$9 + (\$33{,}600/1{,}200) = \underline{\$127}.$$

b. Period costs:

$$\$30{,}000 + (\$6 \times 1{,}200) = \underline{\$37{,}200}.$$

PART TWO

Cost Methods and Systems

Each organization has a unique accounting system. As a user of accounting information, you will need to understand differences in accounting systems. Various accounting systems measure costs differently; without knowing the type of system that generated the cost, you will not know whether you have the cost number suited to your purpose.

Chapter 3 presents alternative methods of computing product costs. Chapter 4 describes different accounting systems used in service and manufacturing organizations, as well as accounting in just-in-time production environments. It also shows how cost systems in organizations that focus on jobs, such as construction and consulting, differ from cost systems in organizations with a process orientation, such as producers of steel, cereals, and most consumer products.

Chapter 5 discusses cost allocation, including the rationale for cost allocation, cost allocation methods, and pitfalls of misusing cost allocation in decision making. Chapter 6 discusses a new development in managerial accounting—activity-based management and costing.

Chapter 3

Product Costing

1. Contrast product costing for external reporting to product costing for managerial purposes.
2. Distinguish variable costing from full absorption costing.
3. Know how accountants apply overhead to products using predetermined rates.
4. Compare and contrast normal costing to actual costing.
5. Understand how improving technology has affected costing methods.
6. Understand the difference between fixed and variable costs.
7. Analyze differential costs in making decisions.
8. Compare and contrast gross margins, contribution margins, and profit margins.
9. Contrast income statements prepared for external reporting to those prepared for managers to use.

Chapter 2 emphasized that no single measure of cost is correct for all contexts or relevant for all decisions. Different costs are relevant for different purposes. For example, if we manage a coffee shop and are trying to decide whether to lower prices to increase our volume, we need to know which costs are fixed and which are variable. If we are preparing financial statements for reporting to shareholders, we need full absorption costing for inventory costs and cost of goods sold. The theme of "different costs for different purposes" appears throughout this book.

Chapter 2 introduced product costing using the actual costing method. This chapter describes alternatives to actual costing, namely, normal costing and standard costing. The chapter shows how different methods of measuring product costs can have a big impact on reported operating profit and on managers' decisions. When people use accounting data, they should be certain that they have the right data for their purposes.

Product Costing for Managerial Purposes versus Product Costing for External Financial Reporting

Organizations measure the costs of producing a good in many different ways. Users of accounting information should know the alternative ways of measuring unit costs. Otherwise, they may inappropriately use costs for one purpose that accountants intended for another. Users of accounting can also put their knowledge of alternative product costing methods to good use by providing ideas to the designers of accounting systems.

A former student in an MBA class provided a good example of the need to understand product costing methods. The student, who worked as an industrial engineer for a large automobile company, told of an assignment to operate a computerized model to find the optimal product mix for the company. This model required the *variable cost* of each product as input. When the firm first implemented the model, the former student asked plant managers and their accountants for the unit cost of each product produced in each plant.

The plant managers and accountants did not realize that the model specifically required *variable* unit costs. They provided data on the unit costs used for finished goods inventory valuation, which were *full absorption* costs. (Recall from Chapter 2 that full absorption unit costs include unit variable manufacturing costs *plus* a share of fixed manufacturing costs.)

Without realizing that the unit costs provided by the accountants were inappropriate for the model, the company's industrial engineers computed the product mix. It should come as no surprise that the results were wrong. Management eventually tracked down and corrected the problem, but not without some lost profits and embarrassment to those involved.

Cases like this one commonly occur in practice. They lead us to emphasize the importance of better communication between accountants and the users of accounting information.

Overview of the Alternatives

The 2×3 matrix in Exhibit 3.1 shows the six fundamentally different ways to measure a product's unit cost based on the following questions:

1. *Cost inclusion.* What costs will the firm include in per-unit costs? For manufacturing costs, the choices are *variable costing* and *full absorption costing*.
2. *Cost measure.* How will the firm measure costs? The choices are *actual costing, normal costing,* and *standard costing.*

For now, we limit our discussion to the cost of producing the product and exclude marketing and administrative costs.

Exhibit 3.1

Alternative Cost Measures

Cost Inclusion	Cost Measure		
	Actual Costing	**Normal Costing**	**Standard Costing**
Variable Costing	X	X	X
Full Absorption Costing	X	X	X

Cost Inclusion: Variable versus Full Absorption Costing

Variable Costing

Chapter 2 introduced the difference between variable costing and full absorption costing. Using a **variable costing** system, the unit manufacturing costs for inventory valuation are the variable manufacturing costs. We assume that direct materials, direct labor, and variable manufacturing overhead are variable costs unless we state otherwise.

Full Absorption Costing

When an organization uses **full absorption costing,** the product "fully absorbs" all manufacturing costs, including both variable and fixed manufacturing costs. External financial reporting holds these costs in inventory on the balance sheet until the firm sells the units and then matches the costs against revenue as an expense on the income statement.

Since fixed manufacturing costs are total costs, not unit costs, accounting uses the following formula to convert them to unit costs:

$$\text{Unit Fixed Manufacturing Cost} = \frac{\text{Total Fixed Manufacturing Costs for the Period}}{\text{Activity for the Period}}$$

Note how full absorption costing "unitizes" fixed costs. Accounting converts a total fixed cost to a "unit" cost by allocating the total fixed cost equally to the units produced.

Full absorption unit costing information is readily available in companies, because external financial reporting requires these data under generally accepted accounting principles and income tax regulations. Managers find it easy to misuse this information for managerial decisions because firms may not have variable costs per unit as readily available. Consequently, managers mistakenly use unitized full absorption costs when they should have used variable costs.

Profit Effects of Variable versus Full Absorption Costing

In this section we examine the profit effects when an organization uses variable compared to full absorption costing for inventory valuation. Assume the following facts for Electron, Inc., for one month (based on the example in Chapter 2):

1. Electron produced 10,000 units.
2. Variable manufacturing costs are $8 per unit produced, made up of $6 for materials, $1 for direct labor, and $1 for variable overhead. Fixed manufacturing overhead is $50,000 per month and $5 per unit (= $50,000 cost at 10,000 units). Unit full absorption cost at 10,000 units is $13 (= $8 variable plus $5 fixed).
3. Selling price is $25 per unit.
4. Variable marketing costs are $1 per unit sold.
5. Fixed marketing and administrative costs are $60,000 per month.

Comparison of Variable and Full Absorption Costing: Production Is Greater Than Sales

We first examine the reported profit effects when production exceeds sales and inventories increase.

During a particular month, Electron produced 10,000 units, incurring the manufacturing costs noted above, and sold 9,000 units. Assume Electron had no beginning inventory. Ending finished goods inventory comprised 1,000 units (= 10,000 units produced − 9,000 units sold) valued as follows:

	Total (1,000 units)	Per Unit
Variable Costing	$ 8,000	$ 8.00
Full Absorption Costing	$13,000	$13.00

Sales revenue was $225,000 (= 9,000 units sold × $25), and variable marketing costs were $9,000 (= 9,000 units sold × $1.00).

Exhibit 3.2 shows the comparative income statements with an increase in inventory. Profits differ because of the different treatment of fixed manufacturing overhead.[1] Under variable costing, Electron expenses all of the fixed manufacturing overhead, $50,000 for the month. Under full absorption costing, some of the period's fixed manufacturing overhead remains in ending inventory. To be precise,

---

[1]We use the term *operating profits* to describe the bottom line of the income statement. We use that term whenever a firm prepares the income statement for internal use. We also distinguish operating profits from an economic notion of profits. Economic profits are sales revenue minus the sum of operating costs recorded in the accounting records *and* implicit opportunity costs, which are not recorded in the accounting records. Operating profits are sales revenue minus only the operating costs recorded in the accounting records.

Exhibit 3.2

Variable and Full Absorption Costing:
Comparative Income Statements with Production (10,000 units) Greater
Than Sales (9,000 units)

Variable Costing

Sales Revenue (9,000 units sold @ $25.00)		$225,000
Variable Cost of Goods Sold:		
Beginning Inventory	$ –0–	
Add Current Month's Production (10,000 units @ $8.00)	80,000	
	$ 80,000	
Subtract Ending Inventory (1,000 units @ $8.00)	8,000	
Variable Cost of Goods Sold		72,000
Variable Marketing Costs		9,000[a]
Contribution Margin		$144,000
Fixed Manufacturing Costs		50,000
Fixed Marketing and Administrative Costs		60,000
Operating Profit		$ 34,000

Full Absorption Costing

Sales Revenue (9,000 units sold @ $25.00)		$225,000
Cost of Goods Sold:		
Beginning Inventory	$ –0–	
Add Current Month's Production (10,000 units @ $13.00)	130,000	
	$130,000	
Subtract Ending Inventory (1,000 units @ $13.00)	13,000	
Cost of Goods Sold		117,000
Gross Margin		$108,000
Variable Marketing and Administrative Costs		9,000[a]
Fixed Marketing and Administrative Costs		60,000
Operating Profit		$ 39,000

[a]$1 × 9,000 units.

Electron expenses only $45,000 of fixed manufacturing overhead under full absorption costing, computed as follows:

$45,000 expensed = 9,000 units sold × $5 per unit of fixed manufacturing cost.

Under full absorption costing, fixed manufacturing overhead costs expensed are $5,000 lower, and therefore profits are $5,000 higher, as the following computations show:

Difference in Fixed Manufacturing Overhead Expensed = $50,000 (variable costing) − $45,000 (full absorption costing)	$5,000
Difference in Profits = $39,000 Profit under Full Absorption Costing − $34,000 Profit under Variable Costing	$5,000

Comparison of Variable and Full Absorption Costing: Production Is Less Than Sales

In the previous example, Electron, Inc., had no beginning inventory, produced 10,000 units, and sold 9,000 units, leaving an ending inventory of 1,000 units. Now assume it is the next month, with the following facts.

Electron, Inc., had 1,000 units in beginning inventory, valued as follows (this is the previous month's ending inventory):

	Total (1,000 units)	Per Unit
Variable Costing	$ 8,000	$ 8.00
Full Absorption Costing	$13,000	$13.00

During the month, Electron produced 10,000 units, incurring the production costs noted in the previous example, and sold 11,000 units. Ending inventory was zero (= 1,000 units + 10,000 produced − 11,000 units sold). Sales revenue was $275,000 (= 11,000 units sold × $25), and variable marketing costs were $11,000 (= 11,000 units sold × $1.00).

Exhibit 3.3 shows comparative income statements with a decrease in inventory. Full absorption costing shows a lower profit than variable costing. Using variable costing, Electron expenses only the $50,000 fixed manufacturing overhead cost incurred during the period. Using full absorption costing, Electron expenses $55,000 fixed manufacturing overhead, computed as follows:

1.	Electron sold 1,000 units from beginning inventory. Fixed manufacturing overhead in this 1,000 units (1,000 × $5.00 fixed overhead per unit)	$ 5,000
2.	Electron produced 10,000 units sold this period. Fixed manufacturing overhead in the 10,000 units (10,000 × $5.00 fixed overhead per unit)	$50,000
	Total fixed manufacturing overhead expensed under full absorption costing.	$55,000

Comparison

We recap manufacturing overhead expensed and operating profit for the two months from Exhibits 3.2 and 3.3 in Exhibit 3.4. It presents some interesting comparisons. First, the operating profit for the two-month period is the same under either method—$100,000. That is because the total fixed manufacturing costs expensed for the two months, $100,000, are the same under both methods.

Second, operating profits are higher under full absorption costing in the first month because units produced exceed units sold (so some fixed costs that Electron expensed under variable costing are not expensed under full absorption costing). The reverse is true in the second month.

Third, the difference in monthly operating profits between the two costing methods equals the *difference in inventory change* between the two methods. In general,

Exhibit 3.3

Variable and Full Absorption Costing:
Comparative Income Statements with Production Less Than Sales

Variable Costing

Sales Revenue (11,000 units sold @ $25.00)		$275,000
Variable Cost of Goods Sold:		
Beginning Inventory (1,000 units @ $8.00)	$ 8,000	
Add Current Month's Production (10,000 units @ $8.00)	80,000	
	$ 88,000	
Subtract Ending Inventory	–0–	
Variable Cost of Goods Sold		88,000
Variable Marketing Costs		11,000[a]
Contribution Margin		$176,000
Fixed Manufacturing Costs		50,000
Fixed Marketing and Administrative Costs		60,000
Operating Profit		$ 66,000

Full Absorption Costing

Sales Revenue (11,000 units sold @ $25.00)		$275,000
Cost of Goods Sold:		
Beginning Inventory (1,000 units @ $13.00)	$ 13,000	
Add Current Month's Production (10,000 units @ $13.00)	130,000	
	$143,000	
Subtract Ending Inventory	–0–	
Cost of Goods Sold		143,000
Gross Margin		$132,000
Variable Marketing and Administrative Costs		11,000[a]
Fixed Marketing and Administrative Costs		60,000
Operating Profit		$ 61,000

[a]$1 × 11,000 units.

Exhibit 3.4

Profit Effects of Variable versus Full Absorption Costing

	First Month	Second Month	Total
Variable Costing Income Statement			
Operating Profit	$34,000	$66,000	$100,000
Fixed Manufacturing Cost:			
Incurred	$50,000	$50,000	$100,000
Expensed	50,000	50,000	$100,000
Full Absorption Costing Income Statement			
Operating Profit	$39,000	$61,000	$100,000
Fixed Manufacturing Cost:			
Incurred	$50,000	$50,000	$100,000
Expensed	45,000	55,000	$100,000

we can trace differences in profits that arise when firms use alternative product costing methods to differences in inventories.

Fourth, the difference in monthly operating profits equals the difference in fixed manufacturing costs expensed under the two systems. When the amount of fixed manufacturing costs in the beginning inventory under full absorption costing equals the amount in ending inventory for a period, the fixed manufacturing costs expensed and operating profits are equal under both methods. A good rule of thumb is that *when the cost of inventory for manufactured goods does not change from the beginning of the period to the end of the period,* operating profits are *identical using either costing method.*

Our example assumes that only the fixed manufacturing cost is a portion of manufacturing overhead. If other manufacturing costs, such as direct labor, are fixed, accounting treats them as *product* costs under full absorption and *period* costs under variable costing, just like fixed manufacturing overhead in our example.

The difference between full absorption profits and variable costing profits results from the different treatment of *fixed manufacturing costs,* which are the only fixed costs inventoried. It does *not* result from any portion of marketing and administrative costs. These costs are period costs, and therefore the firm cannot inventory them as product costs under either variable or full absorption costing.

Summary: Variable versus Full Absorption Costing

The variable costing method measures unit costs using only variable manufacturing costs. The variable costing method treats variable costs as *unit* costs and fixed costs as *period* costs. Managers usually find the variable costing method more useful than the full absorption costing method for managerial decision making, planning, and performance evaluation.

Full absorption costing adds fixed manufacturing costs to variable manufacturing costs to arrive at a unit product cost. Thus, units fully absorb all manufacturing costs. External financial reporting requires using the full absorption method. Virtually all manufacturing companies use full absorption costing for external reporting, but many also use variable costing for management purposes.

Problem 3.1
for Self-Study

Comparison of variable to full absorption costing. Chelsea Corporation manufactures a single product with the following costs:

Selling Price	$8.00 per Unit
Variable Manufacturing Costs (direct materials and direct labor) . . .	$4.80 per Unit
Fixed Manufacturing Overhead (all manufacturing overhead is fixed)	$160,000 per Month
Marketing and Administrative Costs (all fixed)	$80,000 per Month

(continued)

Beginning Inventory (in those situations in which the
  company has beginning inventory)
Variable Manufacturing Costs .... $4.80 per Unit
Fixed Manufacturing Costs .... $1.60 per Unit
    Total .... $6.40 per Unit

Chelsea has no work-in-process inventories and uses the FIFO inventory cost flow assumption.

    The president of Chelsea wants to analyze the effects of three different variations in sales and production units. To help you, accounting has included the following charts. Complete the charts and comment on the differences in operating profits.

Units (in thousands)	(1)	(2)	(3)
Sales	100	115	90
Production	100	100	100
Beginning Inventory	0	15	0
Ending Inventory	0	0	10

Full Absorption Costing	(1)	(2)	(3)
Revenue	800,000	920,000	720,000
Cost of Goods Sold	(640,000)	96,000 (640,000) (=736,000)	640,000 576,000 -64,000
Gross Margin	160,000	184,000	144,000
Marketing and Administrative	(80,000)	(80,000)	(80,000)
Operating Profit	80,000	104,000	64,000
Beginning Inventory	0	96	0
Ending Inventory	0	0	64,000

Variable Costing	(1)	(2)	(3)
Revenue	800,000	920,000	720,000
Variable Cost of Goods Sold	480,000	72,000 480,000 (=552,000)	480,000 (432,000)
Contribution Margin	320,000	368,000	288,000
Fixed Manufacturing Costs	160,000	160,000	160,000
Fixed Marketing and Administrative	80,000	80,000	80,000
Operating Profit	80,000	128,000	48,000
Beginning Inventory	0	72	0
Ending Inventory	0	0	48,000

The solution to this self-study problem is at the end of this chapter on page 89.

Cost Measure: Actual or Normal Costing

Normal Costing

Our previous comparison of variable and full absorption costing methods assumed that firms measure product costs using actual costs incurred. We call this **actual costing.** This section describes a commonly-used alternative to actual costing, known as **normal costing.** Normal costing uses *actual* direct material and direct labor costs, plus an amount representing "normal" manufacturing overhead.

Under normal costing, a firm derives a rate for applying overhead to units produced before the production period. The firm uses this rate in applying overhead to each unit as the firm produces it. We first discuss the rationale for using normal manufacturing overhead costs; then we show how normal costing works.

Using normal overhead costs has advantages over using actual costs. First, actual total manufacturing overhead costs may fluctuate because of seasonality (the cost of utilities, for example), recording adjustments (compare actual with accrued property taxes, for example), or other reasons that are not related directly to activity levels. Also, if production is seasonal and overhead costs remain unchanged, the per-unit costs in low-volume months will exceed the per-unit costs in high-volume months, as the following example shows:

	Production	Total Monthly Fixed Manufacturing Overhead	Per-Unit Overhead Cost
January	1,000 Units	$20,000	$20
July	2,000 Units	20,000	10

Normal costs enable companies to smooth, or normalize, these fluctuations. The *per-unit* overhead cost would be the same throughout the year, regardless of month-to-month fluctuations in actual costs and activity levels.

Accounting systems can provide actual direct material and direct labor cost information quickly in firms that use perpetual inventory systems and a computerized payroll system. In contrast, the same firm may take a month or more to learn about the actual overhead costs for the same units. For example, often 2 weeks to a month (or longer) will elapse after the end of an accounting period before the firm receives invoices for utilities. The firm will not know the cost of supplies used until the end of a quarter or year when it takes an inventory of supplies. Thus firms frequently use a **predetermined overhead rate** to estimate the cost before the actual cost is known. (We use the terms *predetermined* rate and *normal* rate interchangeably.)

Applying Overhead Costs to Production

Apply overhead costs to production using these four steps:

1. Select a **cost driver,** or **allocation base,** for applying overhead to production. Cost drivers are factors that cause an activity's costs. For example, machine

hours could be the factor that causes energy and maintenance costs for a machine. For an automobile, miles driven would be a cost driver.

2. Estimate the amount of overhead and the level of activity for the period (for example, 1 year).
3. Compute the predetermined (that is, normal) overhead rate from the following formula:

$$\text{Predetermined Manufacturing Overhead Rate} = \frac{\text{Estimated Manufacturing Overhead}}{\text{Normal (or Estimated) Activity Level}}.$$

4. Apply overhead to production by multiplying the predetermined rate, computed in step **3,** times the actual activity (for example, the actual machine hours used to produce a product).

The first three steps take place before the beginning of the period. For example, a firm could complete these steps in November of Year 1 if it plans to use the predetermined rate for Year 2. Step **4** is done during Year 2.

Next we discuss these steps in more detail and show how a firm would apply them in the Electron example.

Example In the previous year, Electron's total variable manufacturing overhead cost was $95,000 and the activity level was 50,000 machine hours. The company expects the same level of activity for this year and that variable manufacturing costs will increase to $100,000 because of inflation. Therefore, the company's accountants compute the predetermined rate to be $2.00 per machine hour, as follows:

$$\text{Predetermined Variable Manufacturing Overhead Rate} = \frac{\$100,000}{50,000 \text{ Machine Hours}} = \$2.00 \text{ per Machine Hour}.$$

We compute the fixed manufacturing overhead rate in a similar fashion. Electron estimates manufacturing overhead cost to be $600,000 for this year and the activity level to be 50,000 hours. The company's accountants computed the following rate:

$$\text{Predetermined Fixed Manufacturing Overhead Rate} = \frac{\$600,000}{50,000 \text{ Machine Hours}} = \$12.00 \text{ per Machine Hour}.$$

The predetermined overhead rates mean that for each hour a machine operates, the accountants charge the product with $2.00 for variable manufacturing overhead cost and $12.00 for fixed manufacturing overhead.

Assume that Electron actually used 4,500 machine hours for the month. Electron applied the following overhead to production:

Variable Manufacturing Overhead: 4,500 Hours at $2.00	$ 9,000
Fixed Manufacturing Overhead: 4,500 Hours at $12.00	54,000

Problem 3.2 for Self-Study

Normal costing. Pete Petezah, manager of the local Pizza Shack, has asked for your advice about product costs. Pete wants you to compute the cost of making a pizza. Pete provides the following information to you.

1. Late last year, Pete made the following estimates for the Pizza Shack for this year:

(1)	Estimated Variable Overhead	$108,000
(2)	Estimated Fixed Overhead	$120,000
(3)	Estimated Labor Hours	12,000 hours
(4)	Estimated Labor Dollars per Hour	$20
(5)	Estimated Output	120,000 pizzas

2. You learn the following facts for March of this year:

Variable overhead = $9/hr = 108,000/12,000
Fixed overhead = $10/hr = 120,000/12,000

(1)	Actual Direct Labor Hours	1,100 hours
(2)	Actual Number of Units Produced	10,000 pizzas
(3)	Actual Labor Dollars per Hour	$21
(4)	Actual Direct Labor Cost per Pizza	$2.31
(5)	Actual Direct Materials Cost per Pizza	$1.10

Variable Manufact overhead = ($9 x 1,100 hrs)/10,000 pizza = $.99/pizza
Fixed Manufact Overhead = ($10 x 1,100 hrs)/10,000 pizza = $1.10/pizza

VC
Actual DM $1.10
" DL $2.31
Variable OH $.99
$4.40

Full
Actual DM $1.10
" DL $2.31
Ovhd $2.09
$5.50

Compute the unit cost per pizza for the month of March using (1) normal, variable costing, and (2) normal, full absorption costing. Apply overhead to pizzas using direct labor hours as the allocation base.

The solution to this self-study problem is at the end of this chapter on page 90.

Cost Flows through Accounts

We now demonstrate how the overhead would appear in the accounts. We use the example for Electron in which production exceeded sales volume. (See Exhibit 3.2 for actual variable and full absorption costing.) The facts are the same except we now assume Electron uses normal costing. We restate the facts here for your convenience.

Actual costs:	
Direct Materials	$ 60,000
Direct Labor	10,000
Variable Overhead...	10,000
Fixed Overhead	50,000
Variable Marketing Costs	9,000
Fixed Marketing and Administrative Costs	60,000
Total	$199,000
Sales Revenue for 9,000 Units Sold	$225,000

Flows of manufacturing costs through T-accounts using full absorption, normal costing and variable, normal costing appear in Exhibits 3.5 and 3.6. The debits to Work-in-Process Inventory assign costs to production. Electron computes overhead by multiplying the predetermined rate times the actual machine hours worked and applies it to production as work is done.

Electron, Inc., records actual overhead with a debit to the Overhead accounts and credits to accounts such as Accounts Payable for the cost of utilities or Accumulated Depreciation for depreciation of manufacturing equipment.

As goods are finished, accounting credits the actual materials and labor costs and the applied overhead to Work-in-Process Inventory and debits them to Finished Goods Inventory. Accounting bases the credit to Finished Goods Inventory and debit to Cost of Goods Sold on the first-in, first-out cost flow assumption.

Note that actual overhead costs do not flow through the inventory accounts if the firm uses normal costing. The firm records actual overhead costs in the Overhead accounts as information becomes available. After the end of the accounting period, when the firm knows the actual costs, accounting closes the Overhead account and debits or credits an amount to the Overhead Adjustment account. We compute the overhead adjustment as follows:

$$\text{Overhead Adjustment} = \text{Actual Overhead} - \text{Applied Overhead}.$$

For Electron, Inc. assume the overhead costs are: Variable overhead—$10,000 actual, $9,000 applied; fixed overhead—$50,000 actual, $54,000 applied.

$$\frac{\text{Variable Overhead}}{\text{Adjustment}} = \$10,000 - \$9,000 = \$1,000 \text{ (underapplied).}$$

$$\frac{\text{Fixed Overhead}}{\text{Adjustment}} = \$50,000 - \$54,000 = \$4,000 \text{ (overapplied).}$$

These adjustments appear in entries (3) and (4) in Exhibit 3.5. Entries (3) and (4) close the Overhead accounts and set up the adjustment accounts.

Some firms debit or credit the Cost of Goods Sold account instead of Overhead Adjustment accounts. We use the Overhead Adjustment account in this book to separate the overhead adjustment from the cost of goods sold before the adjustment.

Exhibit 3.5

Electron, Inc.
Cost Flows: Full Absorption, Normal Costing

Work-in-Process Inventory				Finished Goods Inventory				Cost of Goods Sold	
Beginning Balance	0			Beginning Balance 0					
Materials	60,000								
Labor	10,000	133,000 ⟶		133,000	119,700 ⟶			119,700	
					(9,000 units)				
Variable Overhead **(1)**	9,000								
Fixed Overhead **(2)**	54,000								
Ending Balance	0			13,300ª					

Variable Manufacturing Overhead				Variable Overhead Adjustment	
Actual	10,000	Applied		**(3)** 1,000ᵇ	
		$9,000 **(1)** = $2 × 4,500 Actual			
		1,000ᵇ **(3)** Machine Hours			

Fixed Manufacturing Overhead				Fixed Overhead Adjustment	
Actual	50,000	Applied			4,000ᶜ **(4)**
(4)	4,000ᶜ	$54,000 **(2)** = $12.00 × 4,500			
		Actual Machine Hours			

ªUnit cost = $133,000/10,000 units = $13.30. Total inventory value = 1,000 units × $13.30 = $13,300.
ᵇEntry to close variable overhead cost account and set up variable overhead adjustment account.
ᶜEntry to close fixed overhead cost account and set up fixed overhead adjustment account.

A firm could allocate or prorate the overhead adjustment to units in inventory and to those sold. In practice, firms typically expense the overhead adjustment as a period cost, just as if it were part of Cost of Goods Sold. In practice, prorating the overhead adjustment between units in inventory and units sold is difficult because overhead costs are inherently common to several product lines (for example, the

Exhibit 3.6

Electron, Inc.
Cost Flows: Variable, Normal Costing

Work-in-Process Inventory			Finished Goods Inventory			Cost of Goods Sold
Beginning Balance	0		Beginning Balance	0		
Materials	60,000					
Labor	10,000	79,000 ⟶	→ 79,000	71,100 ⟶	→ 71,100	
				(9,000 units)		
Variable Overhead **(1)** 9,000						
Ending Balance	0			7,900ᵃ		

Variable Manufacturing Overhead						Variable Overhead Adjustment
Actual	10,000	Applied $9,000 **(1)** = $2 × 4,500 Actual				**(2)** 1,000ᵇ
		1,000ᵇ **(2)** Machine Hours				

Fixed Manufacturing Overhead

50,000	

ᵃUnit cost = $79,000/10,000 units. Total inventory value = 1,000 units × $7.90 = $7,900.
ᵇEntry to close variable overhead account and set up variable overhead adjustment account.

department manager's salary is common to all the products made in the department). It is difficult, if not impossible, to know which product line is responsible for differences between actual and applied overhead costs when actual costs are common to numerous different products.

Exhibit 3.7 shows the income statements for variable, normal costing and full absorption, normal costing and compares them to corresponding actual costing statements. Note that under variable, normal costing, firms can expense the actual fixed manufacturing overhead as a period cost.

Exhibit 3.7

Electron, Inc.
Comparative Income Statements for the Month

A. Actual/Full Absorption Costing

Sales Revenue	$225,000
Less Cost of Goods Sold	117,000
Gross Margin	$108,000
Less Marketing and Administrative Costs	69,000
Operating Profits	**$ 39,000**

B. Actual/Variable Costing

Sales Revenue	$225,000
Less:	
Variable Cost of Goods Sold	72,000
Variable Marketing and Administrative Costs	9,000
Contribution Margin	$144,000
Less Fixed Manufacturing Costs	50,000
Less Fixed Marketing and Administrative Costs	60,000
Operating Profits	**$ 34,000**

C. Normal/Full Absorption Costing

Sales Revenue	$225,000
Less Cost of Goods Sold (normal)	119,700
Add Overapplied Overhead	3,000
Gross Margin	$108,300
Less Marketing and Administrative Costs	69,000
Operating Profits	**$ 39,300**

D. Normal/Variable Costing

Sales Revenue	$225,000
Less:	
Variable Cost of Goods Sold (normal)	71,100
Underapplied Overhead	1,000
Variable Marketing and Administrative Costs	9,000
Contribution Margin	$143,900
Less Fixed Manufacturing Costs	50,000
Less Fixed Marketing and Administrative Costs	60,000
Operating Profits	**$ 33,900**

Comparative Income Statements

Management has more potential use for the variable costing reports shown in parts B and D of Exhibit 3.7 than the corresponding full absorption statements in parts A and C, because the variable costing statements present more information about cost behavior. Firms must use one of the full absorption statements, A or C, for external reporting, however.

Problem 3.3 ▮▮▮▮▮▮▮▮▮▮▮▮▮▮▮▮▮▮▮▮
for Self-Study

Cost flows through accounts. Refer to the information in Self-Study Problem 3.2. Show the flow of costs through T-accounts using (1) normal, variable costing and (2) normal, full absorption costing. (See Exhibits 3.5 and 3.6 for examples to help you.) Use the following accounts: Variable Overhead, Fixed Overhead, Work-in-Process Inventory, and Cost of Goods Sold. You should also have Variable Overhead Adjustment and Fixed Overhead Adjustment accounts, as needed. You do not need a Finished Goods Inventory account because each pizza is sold as soon as it is made (which is fortunate for consumers).

For the month of March, actual variable overhead was $10,000 and the actual fixed overhead was $10,500.

The solution to this self-study problem is at the end of this chapter on page 91.

Cost Measure: Standard Costing

Using **standard costing,** firms develop a standard or predetermined cost for each unit. In most cases, management establishes these costs as the expectation. In that sense, they are the costs that the firm "should" incur to produce each unit. Firms develop standards for each input—for example, direct materials, direct labor, and manufacturing overhead in manufacturing companies and direct labor and overhead in service organizations.

Why Do Companies Use Standard Costs?

- Standards are benchmarks for performance. By comparing the actual costs against the standards, companies can measure how well they control costs.
- Planning and decision making require estimates of what costs would be if a firm takes a proposed action. The firm can use standard costs as those estimates.
- Firms also use standard costs in inventory valuation for financial reporting. Firms can reduce much of the clerical work needed to accumulate costs and allocate them to each unit produced if they use standard costing systems.

In short, firms can use standard costs for all three purposes of accounting information: managerial decision making, planning and performance evaluation, and external reporting.

Standard Costing Methods

Next we describe how we developed and used standard costs for the Electron, Inc., example. We describe an approach similar to one that many companies follow.

Example   Electron, Inc., computed the standard cost of each calculator as follows. (Like many companies, Electron, Inc., revises its standards yearly.)

Direct Materials   Based on engineering studies of the amount of direct materials required to make a calculator and the estimated costs of those materials, Electron set the standard as follows:

Direct Materials	$6.50 per Calculator

Direct Labor   Based on studies of the time required to make a calculator and inevitable idle time, Electron set the standard direct labor time at 0.06 hour per calculator. Electron estimated labor costs, including fringe benefits and employer-paid payroll taxes, to be $20.00 per hour. The direct labor cost follows:

Direct Labor (0.06 hour at $20.00)	$1.20 per Calculator

Variable Manufacturing Overhead   The standard variable overhead *rate* is the same as the predetermined rate under normal costing. Accounting multiplies that rate ($2.00 per machine hour) by standard machine hours per unit, which Electron set at 0.5 hour per unit, to give the standard variable manufacturing overhead cost per unit:

Variable Manufacturing Overhead Cost (0.5 hour at $2.00)	$1.00 per Calculator

Fixed Manufacturing Overhead   The standard fixed overhead *rate* is also the same as the predetermined rate for normal costing. The account system multiplies that rate ($12.00 per machine hour) by the standard machine hours per unit to give the standard fixed manufacturing overhead cost per unit:

Fixed Manufacturing Overhead Cost (0.5 hour at $12.00)	$6.00 per Calculator

Exhibit 3.8 shows the standard cost per calculator.

Exhibit 3.8

Electron, Inc.
Standard Costs

Direct Materials	$ 6.50
Direct Labor (0.06 labor hours × $20.00)	1.20
Variable Manufacturing Overhead (0.5 machine hours × $2.00)	1.00
Total Standard Variable Unit Cost	$ 8.70
Fixed Manufacturing Overhead (0.5 machine hours × $12.00)	6.00
Total Standard Full Absorption Unit Cost	$14.70

The flow of standard costs through T-accounts requires an understanding of variances between actual and standard costs. We cover this material in detail in Chapter 14.

Comparison of Product Costs

Exhibit 3.9 summarizes the six combinations of product costing methods we have discussed to this point and warrants special study. Note that full absorption unit costs systematically exceed variable costing unit costs because variable costing excludes fixed manufacturing overhead from product costs. This relation holds as long as fixed manufacturing overhead costs are greater than zero.

Exhibit 3.9

Electron, Inc.
Comparison of Product Costs

Cost Inclusion	Cost Measure		
	Actual Costing[a]	Normal Costing[a]	Standard Costing[b]
Variable Costing:			
Direct Materials	Actual = $6.00	Actual = $6.00	Standard = $6.50
Direct Labor	Actual = $1.00	Actual = $1.00	Standard = $1.20
Variable Manufacturing Overhead	Actual = $1.00	Normal = $ .90	Standard = $1.00
Fixed Manufacturing Overhead	—	—	—
Total Product Cost	$8.00	$7.90	$8.70
Full Absorption Costing:			
Direct Materials	Actual = $6.00	Actual = $6.00	Standard = $6.50
Direct Labor	Actual = $1.00	Actual = $1.00	Standard = $1.20
Variable Manufacturing Overhead	Actual = $1.00	Normal = $ .90	Standard = $1.00
Fixed Manufacturing Overhead	Actual = $5.00	Normal = $5.40	Standard = $6.00
Total Product Cost	$13.00	$13.30	$14.70

[a]We give materials and labor costs in the text. Overhead costs are computed as follows:

Actual Costing	**Normal Costing**
Variable Manufacturing Overhead:	Variable Manufacturing Overhead:
$\dfrac{\$10{,}000\ \text{Actual Costs}}{10{,}000\ \text{Units Produced}} = \$1.00\ \text{per Unit.}$	$\dfrac{\$2 \times 4{,}500\ \text{Hours}}{10{,}000\ \text{Units Produced}} = \dfrac{\$9{,}000\ \text{Applied}}{10{,}000\ \text{Units Produced}}$
	$= \$.90\ \text{per Unit.}$
Fixed Manufacturing Overhead:	Fixed Manufacturing Overhead:
$\dfrac{\$50{,}000\ \text{Actual Costs}}{10{,}000\ \text{Units Produced}} = \$5.00\ \text{per Unit.}$	$\dfrac{\$12 \times 4{,}500\ \text{Hours}}{10{,}000\ \text{Units Produced}} = \dfrac{\$54{,}000\ \text{Applied}}{10{,}000\ \text{Units Produced}}$
	$= \$5.40\ \text{per Unit.}$

[b]From Exhibit 3.8.

Variable versus Full Costs in Banking[a]

American National Bank in Chicago offered a check processing service for smaller banks in the Chicago area. Small banks accumulated and sent their checks to American National, which presented them to the banks on which the checks were drawn. The major direct costs of this service were the costs of processing checks and the costs of outside vendor charges, such as the use of the Federal Reserve clearinghouse. In addition, indirect costs were added to the direct costs of each product line. The sum of the direct and indirect costs were the full costs that covered all costs of running the bank, including general and administrative costs.

Several other financial institutions in Chicago also offered this service. Although American National relied on its excellent reputation for quality service to justify charging a higher price than its competitors, it nevertheless had dropped its prices in recent years to remain competitive. At one point its prices were less than 80 percent of the full cost per unit. It appeared that the bank could not justify continuing to offer the service based on a comparison of prices and full costs.

Several executives believed the full cost numbers developed for monthly financial reporting purposes were not appropriate for the decision to drop this service, however. Their analysis indicated that the bank would save few, if any, of the indirect costs allocated to the product lines if it dropped this service. Further, some of the processing costs included depreciation and other costs that would not reduce cash outlays if the bank discontinued the service. Their differential analysis indicated that the bank could lose several million dollars in contribution margin if it dropped the service. Based on their analysis, the bank decided against dropping the check processing service.

[a]Based on the authors' research.

Managers must keep this relation in mind when making decisions. Recall that firms use full absorption unit costs in inventory valuation for external financial reporting, whereas they use variable costs for many internal decisions. If decision makers mistakenly use full absorption costs when they think they are using variable costs, they will systematically overstate unit cost estimates and probably make incorrect decisions.

Example Electron receives a special order for 100 calculators. Filling this order will affect only variable manufacturing costs. Revenue from the order would be

$1,000, that is, $10 per calculator. The company's best estimate of the unit cost for this order is the normal cost.

A manager at Electron argues: "We cannot accept this order. Each unit costs $13.30 (using full absorption, normal cost), and the per-unit price is only $10."

The manager's error, of course, is that the appropriate per-unit cost is only $7.90 (using variable, normal cost), not $13.30. In fact, since each unit has a contribution margin of $2.10 (=$10–$7.90), the order contributes $210 (=100 calculations × $2.10) toward covering fixed costs and making profits. This order would not affect fixed costs. The confusion between full absorption and variable unit costs can lead to systematic errors in cost estimation and wrong decisions.

Problem 3.4 ▮▮▮▮▮▮▮▮▮▮▮▮▮▮▮▮▮▮▮▮▮▮▮▮▮▮▮▮▮▮▮
for Self-Study

Impact of cost reduction on various measures of product cost. Assume the management of Electron has found a way to reduce variable overhead. The predetermined rate (also the standard rate) would go down to $1.00 per machine hour. The actual variable overhead would go down to $5,000 for the month.

Management wants to know how this reduction in variable overhead would affect the production costs reported in Exhibit 3.9. Reconstruct Exhibit 3.9 with this new information about variable overhead.

The solution to this self-study problem is at the end of this chapter on page 93.

Alternative Cost Drivers for Applying Overhead

Here are some typical cost drivers for applying overhead to products:

Cost Driver	Predetermined Rate
Direct Labor Hours	Dollars per Direct Labor Hour
Machine Hours	Dollars per Machine Hour
Pounds of Direct Materials Used	Dollars per Pound
Number of Parts in a Product	Dollars per Part
Units of Output	Dollars per Unit of Output

Companies with only one product generally apply overhead using the "units of output" cost driver because it is easiest to use. Output is difficult to measure, however, in companies with multiple products. Consider a company such as General Motors that manufactures numerous types of automobiles, engines, auto parts, and other products. With multiple products, companies look for a common denominator to measure their activity. Companies typically use some input measure as a common denominator, such as direct labor hours or machine hours.

Nonmanufacturing Applications

Firms can adapt these bases to nonmanufacturing applications. For example, a hospital could use hours of nurse time as cost driver or a CPA firm could use hours of audit staff time. Passenger miles (or simply miles) may serve as an application of machine hours for transportation firms such as United Airlines, Amtrak, or Yellow Cab Company.

Overhead Application in High-Technology Companies

The cost driver management chooses for applying overhead is developing into an important issue for managerial accounting, particularly for manufacturing companies that are changing their production technologies. Before the introduction of machine-intensive manufacturing methods, direct labor costs usually made up about 30 to 40 percent of the cost of making a product, overhead represented about 10 to 30 percent, and material costs made up the rest. After introducing more machine-intensive methods, many companies have found that their direct labor costs now comprise 5 percent or less of manufacturing costs, whereas overhead has increased to 40 percent or more. As a result, predetermined overhead rates in excess of $100 per labor hour (which itself costs only $10 to $30 per hour) are not unusual, yet due to changes in technology, overhead may be virtually unrelated to direct labor.

Suppose management selects direct labor hours as the basis for allocating overhead to products and computes a predetermined rate per direct labor hour. The accounting system charges every direct labor hour that is worked on a job not only with an amount for wages but also with an amount for overhead. Recall that overhead costs are indirect costs by definition, so any activity base that management selects is a somewhat arbitrary allocator for overhead.

Suppose overhead actually represents machine-related costs such as machine repairs and power to operate machines. Using direct labor hours as the activity base makes the cost of using direct labor hours appear to be higher than it really is. In this case, the overhead application overstates the cost of direct labor hours and understates the cost of machine hours worked on the job. Thus a manager who wants to reduce the costs of production may mistakenly look for ways to reduce labor time instead of machine time spent on the job.

The Ethics of Increasing Production to Increase Profits under Full Absorption Costing

Nonaccountants generally do not understand that full absorption costing enables companies to increase profits just by increasing production. It is easy for people who understand that fixed costs can be inventoried instead of expensed under full absorption costing to mislead nonaccountants.

While studying accounting practices in a large Fortune 100 company, we encountered a case in which a division manager decided to increase production so some of his division's fixed manufacturing costs would be inventoried instead of expensed. This manager knew the fixed manufacturing costs would be expensed in the future when the inventory was sold. This manager figured the future expense to be someone else's problem because he expected to be transferred to another division the following year. Further, if his division's profits were high enough this year, he would be promoted to a better position in the company.

Increasing production to defer recognizing fixed manufacturing did not conflict with the company's accounting policies. Nor would it conflict with generally accepted accounting principles. Nevertheless, this manager's actions were intended to deceive his superiors. Was this manager's action ethical?

We believe this manager's action was unethical if the purpose of his action to increase production was to deceive his superiors and if he did not fully disclose how he increased profits. While his superiors *could* have discovered that the increase in profit was correlated with an increase in ending inventory, it is unlikely they would have made that connection unless they had accounting expertise or advice.

Are Some Accounting Methods Systematically Better Than Others?

Managers frequently ask, "What is the best accounting system?" The answer is usually, "It depends." It depends on the intended use of the accounting system.

In some cases, however, firms can rank accounting systems for managerial purposes. For example, if two accounting systems are equally costly, the system that is more detailed is more desirable than one that is less detailed. Suppose that System 1 contains all of the data that System 2 contains and more. For example, suppose that we compare cost data about a product from two accounting methods: one that separates fixed and variable manufacturing costs (System 1) and one that does not (System 2):

	System 1	System 2
Direct Materials	$ 4.00	$ 4.00
Direct Labor	3.00	3.00
Variable Manufacturing Overhead	1.00	
Unit Variable Cost	$ 8.00	
Total Manufacturing Overhead		3.00
Fixed Manufacturing Overhead Allocated to Each Unit..	2.00	
Total Unit Cost	$10.00	$10.00

System 1 divides manufacturing overhead into variable and fixed elements, whereas System 2 shows only the sum. System 1 contains at least as much information as System 2 and possibly more. We would prefer System 1 to System 2 if the systems were equally expensive to develop and operate.

Exhibit 3.10

Summary Comparison of Full Absorption and Variable Costing in Manufacturing Companies

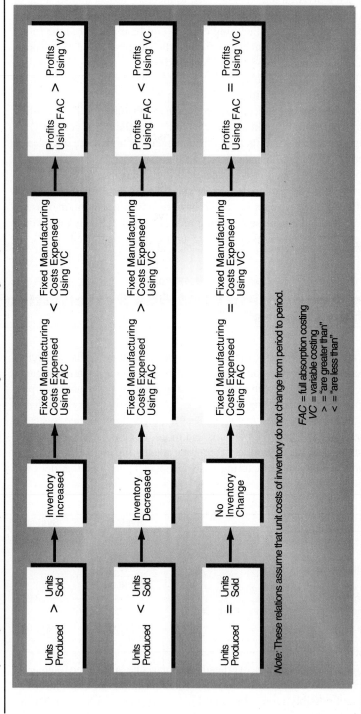

Units Produced > Units Sold → Inventory Increased → Fixed Manufacturing Costs Expensed Using FAC < Fixed Manufacturing Costs Expensed Using VC → Profits Using FAC > Profits Using VC

Units Produced < Units Sold → Inventory Decreased → Fixed Manufacturing Costs Expensed Using FAC > Fixed Manufacturing Costs Expensed Using VC → Profits Using FAC < Profits Using VC

Units Produced = Units Sold → No Inventory Change → Fixed Manufacturing Costs Expensed Using FAC = Fixed Manufacturing Costs Expensed Using VC → Profits Using FAC = Profits Using VC

Note: These relations assume that unit costs of inventory do not change from period to period.

FAC = full absorption costing
VC = variable costing
> = "are greater than"
< = "are less than"

Summary

This chapter analyzes alternative product costing methods manufacturing companies typically use. You should understand these costing methods in order to know which cost to use in decision making, particularly when choosing between unit costs under full absorption and variable costing. Decision makers frequently use full absorption unit costs when variable costing unit costs would be appropriate for the decision.

Full absorption and variable costing differ significantly in their treatment of fixed manufacturing costs—full absorption costing "unitizes" them and allocates them to products; variable costing treats them as period expenses. This difference implies that operating profits will differ under each method if units produced and sold differ, as Exhibit 3.10 shows.

Under *normal* costing, accounting charges direct materials and direct labor to products at actual costs, but uses a *predetermined rate* for variable and fixed manufacturing overhead. The total variable and total fixed overhead charged to products for the period is the predetermined rate times a measure of *actual* activity (for example, direct labor hours). The unit variable overhead and unit fixed overhead is the total normal cost divided by the actual number of units produced.

Note that the direct materials and direct labor costs charged to production departments are identical for each method. The choice of product costing method does not affect revenues, marketing costs, or administrative costs.

Solutions to Self-Study Problems

Suggested Solution to Problem 3.1 for Self-Study

The following data are used in the solution.

Current Period Unit Costs	(1)	(2)	(3)
Full Absorption Unit Manufacturing Cost[a]	$6.40	$6.40	$6.40
Variable Costing Unit Manufacturing Cost	4.80	4.80	4.80

[a] $6.40 = $4.80 + $\dfrac{\$160,000}{100,000 \text{ units produced}}$.

Full Absorption Costing[a]	(1)	(2)	(3)
Revenue (at $8 per unit)	$800	$920	$720
Cost of Goods Sold[b]	640	736	576
Gross Margin	160	184	144
Marketing and Administrative	80	80	80
Operating Profit	80	104	64
Beginning Inventory	0	96	0
Ending Inventory	0	0	64

[a]All dollar amounts in thousands.
[b]$640,000 = 100,000 units sold × $6.40
$736,000 = 115,000 units sold × $6.40
$576,000 = 90,000 units sold × $6.40

Variable Costing[a]	(1)	(2)	(3)
Revenue	$800	$920	$720
Variable Cost of Goods Sold[b]	480	552	432
Contribution Margin	320	368	288
Fixed Manufacturing Costs	160	160	160
Fixed Marketing and Administrative	80	80	80
Operating Profit	80	128	48
Beginning Inventory	0	72	0
Ending Inventory	0	0	48

[a]All dollar amounts in thousands.
[b]$480,000 = 100,000 units sold × $4.80
$552,000 = 115,000 units sold × $4.80
$432,000 = 90,000 units sold × $4.80

When units produced equal units sold, operating profits are the same under both variable costing and full absorption costing. When units sold exceed units produced, operating profits reported are higher under variable costing. Conversely, when units produced exceed units sold, operating profits are higher under full absorption costing. This difference in operating profits occurs because accounting carries fixed manufacturing costs in inventory under full absorption costing, whereas it expenses fixed manufacturing costs as period costs under variable costing.

Suggested Solution to Problem 3.2 for Self-Study

1. Compute the predetermined overhead rates as follows.
   The base is direct labor hours.
   Variable Overhead:

$$\text{\$9 per hour} = \$108,000/12,000 \text{ hours}$$

Fixed Overhead:

$10 per hour = $120,000/12,000 hours

2. Compute the overhead costs per pizza as follows:
The base is direct labor hours:
Variable Manufacturing Overhead:

$0.99 per pizza = ($9 × 1,100 hours)/10,000 pizzas

Fixed Manufacturing Overhead:

$1.10 per pizza = ($10 × 1,100 hours)/10,000 pizzas

3. Compute the unit cost using normal, variable costing:

Actual Direct Materials	$1.10
Actual Direct Labor	2.31
Variable Overhead	0.99
Total	$4.40

4. Compute the unit cost using normal, full absorption costing:

Actual Direct Materials	$1.10
Actual Direct Labor	2.31
Overhead ($0.99 VOH + $1.10 FOH)	2.09
Total	$5.50

Suggested Solution to Problem 3.3 for Self-Study

(1) Pizza Shack
Cost Flows: Variable, normal costing

Work-in-Process Inventory		**Cost of Goods Sold**	
Beginning Balance 0	44,000 ──────────→ 44,000		
Materials 11,000			
Labor 23,100			
Variable **(1)** 9,900			
OH			
Ending Balance 0			

Variable Manufacturing Overhead

Actual	Applied
10,000	$9,900 **(1)** = $0.99 × 10,000 Actual Pizzas
	100 **(2)**[a]

Variable Overhead Adjustment

(2) 100[a]

Fixed Manufacturing Overhead

10,500

[a]Entry to close variable overhead account and set up variable overhead adjustment account.

(2) Pizza Shack
Cost Flows: Full absorption, normal costing

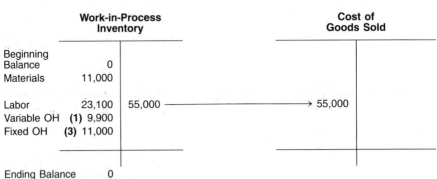

Work-in-Process Inventory

Beginning Balance	0	
Materials	11,000	
Labor	23,100	55,000
Variable OH **(1)**	9,900	
Fixed OH **(3)**	11,000	
Ending Balance	0	

Cost of Goods Sold

55,000

Variable Manufacturing Overhead

Actual	Applied
10,000	$9,900 **(1)** = $0.99 × 10,000 Actual Pizzas
	100 **(2)**[a]

Variable Overhead Adjustment

(2) 100[a]

Fixed Manufacturing Overhead		Fixed Overhead Adjustment	
Actual	Applied		
10,500	$1.10 × 10,000 Actual Pizzas = $11,000 **(3)**	500[a] **(4)**	
(4) 500[a]			

[a]Entries to close overhead accounts and set up overhead adjustment accounts.

Suggested Solution to Problem 3.4 for Self-Study

Electron, Inc.
Comparison of Product Costs

	Cost Measure		
Cost Inclusion	**Actual Costing[a]**	**Normal Costing[a]**	**Standard Costing**
Variable Costing:			
Direct Materials	Actual = $6.00	Actual = $6.00	Standard = $6.50
Direct Labor	Actual = $1.00	Actual = $1.00	Standard = $1.20
Variable Manufacturing Overhead	Actual = $0.50	Normal = $0.45	Standard = $0.50[b]
Fixed Manufacturing Overhead	—	—	—
Total Product Cost	$7.50	$7.45	$8.20
Full Absorption Costing:			
Direct Materials	Actual = $6.00	Actual = $6.00	Standard = $6.50
Direct Labor	Actual = $1.00	Actual = $1.00	Standard = $1.20
Variable Manufacturing Overhead	Actual = $0.50	Normal = $0.45	Standard = $0.50[b]
Fixed Manufacturing Overhead	Actual = $5.00	Normal = $5.40	Standard = $6.00
Total Product Cost	$12.50	$12.85	$14.20

[a]Actual and normal variable overhead costs are computed as follows:

Actual Costing	**Normal Costing**
Variable Manufacturing Overhead:	

$$\frac{\$5,000 \text{ Actual Costs}}{10,000 \text{ Units Produced}} = \$0.50 \text{ per Unit.}$$

$$\frac{\$1 \times 4,500 \text{ Hours}}{10,000 \text{ Units Produced}} = \frac{\$4,500 \text{ Applied}}{10,000 \text{ Units Produced}}$$

$$= \$.45 \text{ per Unit.}$$

[b]$.50 = $1.00 per machine hour (the new rate) times 0.5 machine hours per unit.

Key Terms and Concepts

Variable costing
Full absorption costing
Actual costing
Normal costing

Predetermined overhead rate
Cost driver
Standard costing

Questions, Exercises, Problems, and Cases

Questions

1. Review the meaning of the concepts or terms given above in Key Terms and Concepts.

2. Distinguish between full absorption costing and variable costing. Which method of costing would a firm use to evaluate the effects of decreasing production by 5 percent if it is currently producing at close to capacity?

3. How does accounting treat marketing and administrative costs under variable costing? Under full absorption costing?

4. Under what circumstances do operating profits under variable costing equal full absorption costing profits? When are variable costing profits smaller? When are they greater?

5. How can a company using full absorption costing manipulate profits without changing sales?

6. True or false: The dollar value of inventory change is greater under variable costing than under full absorption costing when sales volume exceeds production volume.

7. Does variable costing imply that inventory cost reflects every variable cost associated with a product?

8. "A 15-percent price increase to cover rising costs!" fumed an angry customer. "I know for a fact that materials cost has not increased, and the company has not increased its workers' pay. I bet the owner is lining his pockets!" Suppose that the company uses actual costs to measure the cost of its products. Give possible explanations for the increase in costs.

9. How does normal costing differ from actual costing?

10. How does standard costing differ from normal costing?

11. Refer to Exhibit 3.9 that compares the six alternative product costs. Explain the differences in (i) full absorption and variable costs, (ii) normal and actual costs, and (iii) normal and standard costs.

12. Refer to this chapter's Managerial Application: "Variable versus Full Costing in Banking." Why did the bank decide not to drop the check processing service?

13. Refer to the discussion about the ethical issues of increasing profits under full absorption costing by increasing production. Do you think it is ethical to increase profits by increasing production when no increase in sales is anticipated?

14. You have been offered a job in a company with rising profits. You are concerned that profits are increasing because the company is increasing production and inventorying fixed manufacturing costs under full absorption costing. What facts would help you learn whether your suspicions were true?

Exercises

Solutions to even-numbered exercises are at the end of this chapter after the cases.

15. **Computing product costs for variable and full absorption costing.** The Happy Health Center performed 60,000 tests for a particular disease. The center incurred the following testing costs:

Direct Materials Used in Tests...............................	$ 800,000
Direct Labor for Physician, Nurse, and Technician Time..............	900,000
Variable Overhead for Miscellaneous Supplies	100,000
Fixed Overhead	550,000
Total..	$2,350,000

The Center's administrator has asked you for the cost per test:

a. Calculate the unit variable cost per test.

b. Calculate the unit full absorption cost per test.

16. **Computing inventory value using variable costing and full absorption costing.** The following data are for Martha and Jane's Ice Cream Company in Year 1 and Year 5.

	Year 1	Year 5
Beginning Inventory in Units	0	7,000
Units Produced	50,000	48,000
Units Sold..	48,000	50,000
Fixed Overhead Production Costs	$12,000	$13,000
Variable Overhead Production Costs	12,000	14,000
Fixed Marketing Costs................................	10,000	10,000
Direct Labor (variable)..............................	36,000	40,000
Direct Materials	48,000	55,000

Martha and Jane's has no work-in-process inventories, and uses a FIFO inventory cost flow assumption.

a. Compute the dollar value of ending finished goods inventory in Year 1 under actual full absorption costing.

b. Compute the dollar value of ending finished goods inventory in Year 1 under actual variable costing.

c. Which method, full absorption or variable costing, implies larger reported operating profit for Year 1?

17. **Computing inventory value using variable costing and full absorption costing.** Refer to the data in the preceding problem for Martha and Jane's Ice Cream Company.

a. Compute the dollar value of ending finished goods inventory in Year 5 under actual full absorption costing.

b. Compute the dollar value of ending finished goods inventory in Year 5 under actual variable costing.

c. Which method, full absorption or variable costing, implies larger reported operating profit for Year 5?

18. **Computing allocated overhead and finished goods value.** The Singapore Boat Company allocates factory overhead to jobs on a direct labor hour basis at the rate of $3 per hour.

    a. Job 745 for four sailboats required a total of $8,400 of direct materials and $10,000 of direct labor at an average rate of $4 per hour. What was the total cost shown for job 745?

    b. Job 305 for a small trawler required $6,300 of direct materials and $20,000 of direct labor at an average rate of $5 per hour. Job 305 sold for $40,000. What was the gross margin on this sale? (Gross margin is revenue less total manufacturing costs for the goods sold.)

19. **Applied overhead in a bank.** Banco Nacional uses machine time as the basis for allocating overhead to its check processing activities. On January 1, Banco Nacional estimated that production for the coming year would equal 800 million units. It also estimated that total overhead for the same year would equal $2,000,000 and that estimated machine time would equal 50,000 hours. The units produced and machine time for the four quarters follow:

Quarter	Actual Units of Production (in millions)	Actual Machine Time
1st	300 Checks	16,000 Hours
2nd.	300 Checks	15,000 Hours
3rd	200 Checks	9,000 Hours
4th	100 Checks	6,000 Hours

    a. Compute the predetermined overhead rate for applying overhead on the basis of machine hours.

    b. Compute the amount of total overhead applied under normal costing for each quarter.

    c. Compute the overhead cost per unit (that is, per check processed) for each quarter using normal costing.

20. **Comparison of full absorption and variable costing in income statement formats.** Consider the following facts for the Celtics Shoe Company:

	Year 1	Year 2
Beginning Inventory	–0–	?
Sales Volume	70,000 Units	130,000 Units
Production Volume	100,000 Units	100,000 Units
Selling Price.	$20 per Unit	$20 per Unit
Variable Manufacturing	$13 per Unit	$13 per Unit
Fixed Manufacturing.	$340,000	$340,000
Nonmanufacturing Costs (all fixed)	$150,000	$150,000

    Prepare income statements under variable costing and full absorption costing for each year.

21. **Actual costs and normal costs under variable and full absorption costing.** Rockies Company uses a predetermined rate for applying overhead to produc-

tion using normal costing. The rates for Year 1 follow: variable, 200 percent of direct labor dollars; fixed, 300 percent of direct labor dollars. Actual overhead costs incurred follow: variable, $40,000; fixed, $50,000. Actual direct materials costs were $10,000, and actual direct labor costs were $18,000. Rockies produced 20,000 units in Year 1.

   a. Calculate actual unit costs using (1) variable costing and (2) full absorption costing.

   b. Calculate normal unit costs using (1) variable costing and (2) full absorption costing.

22. **Comparison of standard costing to actual and normal costing.** Refer to Exercise 21. Assume unit standard costs are materials, $.45; labor $.95; and variable overhead and fixed overhead use the rates indicated in Exercise 21 times the standard labor cost per unit. Prepare an exhibit like Exhibit 3.9 in the text.

Problems

23. **Computing applied manufacturing overhead from two different activity bases.** The Tall Texas Company makes a single product: Lone Star belt buckles. Management has asked you to compute the cost of belt buckles. You have the following information available about this product for January of Year 2:

Belt Buckles	
Actual Volume: Units	4,200 Buckles
Direct Labor Hours	3,300 Hours
Normal (estimated) Volume: Units	4,000 Buckles
Direct Labor Hours	3,000 Hours
Predetermined Average Wage Rate	$20 per Hour
Actual Average Wage Rate	$19 per Hour
Actual Manufacturing Overhead	$92,000
Actual Direct Materials Cost per Unit......................	$5 per Buckle
Normal (estimated) Manufacturing Overhead:	
Fixed Portion	$66,000
Variable Portion.......................................	$8 per Labor Hour

(Round all calculations to the nearest cent.)

   a. Compute unit manufacturing costs for belt buckles under (1) variable, normal and (2) full absorption, normal costing. Assume that Tall Texas applies fixed and variable manufacturing overhead using actual direct labor hours as the basis and that the predetermined manufacturing overhead rates are per direct labor hour.

   b. Repeat part **a**, except assume that Tall Texas applies manufacturing overhead as a predetermined percentage of direct labor cost. The predetermined rates are: variable overhead—40% of actual labor cost; fixed overhead—110% of actual labor cost.

24. **Computing product costs using direct labor dollars and labor hours for manufacturing overhead application.** The Kool Kentuckian Company makes a single product: leather cowboy hats. Management wants various measures of product costs for pricing purposes. You have the following information available about this product for January of Year 3:

Cowboy Hats	
Actual Volume: Units	2,100 Hats
Direct Labor Hours	1,100 Hours
Estimated Volume: Units	2,000 Hats
Direct Labor Hours	1,000 Hours
Predetermined Average Wage Rate	$20 per Hour
Actual Average Wage Rate	$19 per Hour
Actual Manufacturing Overhead	$33,000
Actual Direct Materials Cost per Unit	$15 per Hat
Estimated Manufacturing Overhead:	
Fixed Portion	$25,000
Variable Portion	$8 per Labor Hour

(Round all calculations to the nearest cent.)

a. Compute unit manufacturing costs for cowboy hats under (1) variable, normal and (2) full absorption, normal costing. Assume that Kool Kentuckian applies fixed and variable manufacturing overhead using direct labor hours as the basis and that the predetermined manufacturing overhead rates are per direct labor hour.

b. Repeat part **a**, except assume that Kool Kentuckian applies manufacturing overhead as a predetermined percentage of direct labor cost. The predetermined rates are: variable overhead—40% of actual direct labor cost; fixed overhead—125% of actual direct labor cost.

25. **Computing overhead using normal costing** (contributed by Robert H. Colson). The Smokey Mountain Production Corporation uses machine time as the basis for allocating manufacturing overhead to products. On January 1, Year 2, Smokey Mountain's production superintendent estimated that Smokey Mountain would produce 900,000 units in Year 2, requiring 45,000 hours of machine time. The controller estimated that total manufacturing overhead cost for Year 2 would equal $2,500,000.

Smokey Mountain collected the following records of the actual overhead costs, units produced, and machine time on a quarterly basis in Year 2:

Quarter	Actual Overhead Costs	Actual Units Produced	Actual Machine Time
1st	$800,000	333,333	17,000 Hours
2nd	900,000	333,333	18,000 Hours
3rd	500,000	222,223	11,000 Hours
4th	500,000	111,111	5,000 Hours

Compute the amount of overhead under normal costing for each quarter. (Round the application rate to two decimal places.) How close is the applied overhead to the actual overhead?

26. **Preparing income statements using variable and full absorption costing.** The Semi-Fixed Costs Company operates for two months: Month 1 and Month 2. It produces 20,000 tons in Month 1 and none in Month 2. It sells 10,000 tons of product each month at a selling price of $30 per ton. Its manufacturing costs are $7 per ton plus $210,000 per month. The fixed costs of $210,000 per month occur whether or not the plant produces any tons of product. Selling and administrative costs are $40,000 per month.

   a. Prepare income statements for each of the 2 months, using full absorption costing.

   b. Prepare income statements for each of the 2 months, using variable costing.

   c. Which costing method is management likely to prefer? Why?

27. **"I enjoy challenges."** (This problem is based on actual circumstances in a large manufacturing company. We have seen similar management actions in many other companies. All names have been changed.) E-Z Company uses an actual cost system to apply all production costs to the units produced. Although production has a maximum production capacity of 40 million units, E-Z produced and sold only 10 million units during Year 5. It had no beginning or ending inventories.

E-Z COMPANY
Income Statement for the Year Ending December 31, Year 5

Sales (10,000,000 units each $3.00)		$ 30,000,000
Less Cost of Goods Sold:		
Variable (10,000,000 each $1)	$(10,000,000)	
Fixed.	(24,000,000)	(34,000,000)
Gross Margin		$ (4,000,000)
Less Marketing and Administrative Costs		
(all fixed)		(5,000,000)
Operating Profit (Loss)		$ (9,000,000)

This loss concerns the board of directors. A consultant approached the board with the following offer: "I agree to become president for no fixed salary. But I insist on a year-end bonus of 10 percent of operating profit (before considering the bonus)." The board of directors agreed to these terms and hired the consultant.

The new president promptly stepped up production to an annual rate of 30,000,000 units. Sales for Year 6 remained at 10,000,000 units.

The resulting E-Z Company income statement for Year 6 follows:

E-Z COMPANY
Income Statement for the Year Ending December 31, Year 6

Sales (10,000,000 units each $3.00)		$ 30,000,000
Less Cost of Goods Sold:		
Cost of Goods Manufactured:		
Variable (30,000,000 each $1)	$(30,000,000)	
Fixed	(24,000,000)	
Total Cost of Goods Manufactured	$(54,000,000)	
Ending Inventory:		
Variable (20,000,000 each $1)	$ 20,000,000	
Fixed ($\frac{20}{30}$ × 24,000,000)	16,000,000	
Total Inventory	$ 36,000,000	
Cost of Goods Sold		(18,000,000)
Gross Margin		$ 12,000,000
Less Marketing and Administrative Costs		
(all fixed)		(5,000,000)
Operating Profit before Bonus		$ 7,000,000
Less Bonus		(700,000)
Operating Profit after Bonus		$ 6,300,000

The day after the statement was verified, the president took his check for $700,000 and resigned to take a job with another corporation. He remarked, ''I enjoy challenges. Now that E-Z Company is in the black, I'd prefer tackling another challenging situation.'' (His contract with his new employer is similar to the one he had with E-Z Company.)

a.   As a member of the board of directors, comment on the Year 6 income statement.

b.   Using variable costing, what would operating profit be for Year 5? For Year 6? What are the inventory values at the end of Year 6?

c.   Assuming production was 30,000,000 units, at what sales level would the president be indifferent to the product costing approach used to calculate his bonus? Why?

28.   **''I enjoy challenges''** using normal costing. Recompute the operating profit before bonus for Year 6 in Problem 27, based on the following assumptions:

(1)   All manufacturing overhead is fixed.

(2)   E-Z applied overhead based on units of output.

(3)   The predetermined overhead rate for Year 6 is $2.40 per unit (= $24,000,000/10,000,000 estimated units).

Why are operating profits computed here different than those computed for Year 6 in Problem 27?

29.   **Department versus plant-wide overhead rates.** Trekkie Industries, Inc., had a contract to produce a machine for the R2D2 Company. Departments A, B, and C would produce the machine. The three departments incurred the following costs on the R2D2 job:

	Dept. A	Dept. B	Dept. C
Materials Used	$6,200	$7,000	0
Direct Labor Cost	$3,500	$6,000	$8,000
Direct Labor Hours	1,000	1,500	2,000
Machine Hours	100	50	500
Overhead Allocation to the R2D2 Job .	$8 per Direct Labor Hour	150 Percent of Direct Labor Cost	$14 per Machine Hour

The complexities of this departmental overhead allocation method and the impact of different cost allocations on the computed job costs concerned management. The estimated total overhead in each department and the estimated total overhead bases for this year follow:

	Dept. A	Dept. B	Dept. C
Estimated Overhead	$640,000	$330,000	$140,000
Direct Labor Cost	$280,000	$220,000	$120,000
Direct Labor Hours......................	80,000	55,000	30,000
Machine Hours	10,000	1,500	10,000

One member of management suggested that Trekkie establish a plant-wide overhead rate based on direct labor cost. Another stated that plant-wide rates are not very useful.

a. Compute plant-wide rates based on
   (1) Direct labor cost.
   (2) Direct labor hours.
   (3) Machine hours.
b. Calculate the costs of the R2D2 job using
   (1) Overhead as initially allocated.
   (2) Overhead based on plant-wide direct labor costs.
   (3) Overhead based on plant-wide direct labor hours.
   (4) Overhead based on plant-wide machine hours.
c. Write a short report indicating whether the plant-wide or departmental method is better.

Cases

30. Applying overhead under normal costing using multiple bases (adapted from CMA exam). The Herbert Manufacturing Company manufactures custom-designed restaurant and kitchen furniture. The company applies the actual overhead costs incurred during the month to the products on the basis of actual direct labor hours required to produce the products. The overhead consists primarily of supervision, employee benefits, maintenance costs, property taxes, and depreciation.

Herbert Manufacturing recently won a contract to manufacture the furniture for a new fast-food chain that is expanding rapidly in the area. In general, this furniture is durable but of a lower quality than Herbert Manufacturing normally manufactures. To produce this new line, Herbert Manufacturing must purchase more molded plastic parts for the furniture than for its current line. The firm's innovative industrial engineering department has developed an efficient manufacturing process for this new furniture that requires only a minimal

Exhibit 3.11

Herbert Manufacturing Company
(all dollar amounts in thousands)

	Fast-Food Furniture	Custom Furniture	Consolidated
Nine Months Year-to-Date			
Sales............................	—	$8,100	$8,100
Direct Material	—	$2,025	$2,025
Direct Labor:			
Forming	—	758	758
Finishing.......................	—	1,314	1,314
Assembly	—	558	558
Manufacturing Overhead	—	1,779	1,779
Cost of Sales	—	$6,434	$6,434
Operating Profit	—	$1,666	$1,666
Operating Profit Percentage	—	20.6%	20.6%
October			
Sales............................	$400	$ 900	$1,300
Direct Material	$200	$ 225	$ 425
Direct Labor:			
Forming	17	82	99
Finishing.......................	40	142	182
Assembly	33	60	93
Manufacturing Overhead	60	180	240
Cost of Sales	$350	$ 689	$1,039
Operating Profit	$ 50	$ 211	$ 261
Operating Profit Percentage	12.5%	23.4%	20.1%
November			
Sales............................	$800	$ 800	$1,600
Direct Material	$400	$ 200	$ 600
Direct Labor:			
Forming	31	72	103
Finishing.......................	70	125	195
Assembly	58	53	111
Manufacturing Overhead	98	147	245
Cost of Sales	$657	$ 597	$1,254
Operating Profit	$143	$ 203	$ 346
Operating Profit Percentage	17.9%	25.4%	21.6%

capital investment. Management is optimistic about the profit improvement the new product line will bring.

At the end of October, the start-up month for the new line, the controller prepared a separate income statement for the new product line. On a consolidated basis the gross profit percentage was normal; however, the profitability for the new line was less than expected.

At the end of November, the results improved somewhat. Consolidated profits were good, but the reported profitability for the new product line was less than expected. John Herbert, president of the corporation, is concerned that knowledgeable shareholders will criticize his decision to add this lower-quality product line at a time when profitability appeared to be increasing with the standard product line.

The results as published for the first 9 months, for October, and for November are presented in Exhibit 3.11.

Mr. Jameson, cost accounting manager, has stated that the overhead allocation based on only direct labor hours is no longer appropriate. On the basis of a recently completed study of the overhead accounts, Mr. Jameson believes that the company should allocate only supervision and employee benefits on the basis of direct labor hours and the balance of the overhead on a machine hour basis. In his judgment, the increase in the profitability of the custom-designed furniture results from a misallocation of overhead in the present system.

The following exhibit shows the actual direct labor hours and machine hours for the past 2 months.

	Fast-Food Furniture	Custom Furniture
Machine Hours		
October:		
Forming......................	660	10,700
Finishing	660	7,780
Assembly	—	—
	1,320	18,480
November:		
Forming......................	1,280	9,640
Finishing	1,280	7,400
Assembly	—	—
	2,560	17,040
Direct Labor Hours		
October:		
Forming......................	1,900	9,300
Finishing	3,350	12,000
Assembly	4,750	8,700
	10,000	30,000
November:		
Forming......................	3,400	8,250
Finishing	5,800	10,400
Assembly	8,300	7,600
	17,500	26,250

The actual overhead costs for the past 2 months follow:

	October	November
Supervision	$ 13,000	$ 13,000
Employee Benefits	95,000	109,500
Maintenance	50,000	48,000
Depreciation	42,000	42,000
Property Taxes	8,000	8,000
All Other	32,000	24,500
Total	$240,000	$245,000

a. Based on Mr. Jameson's recommendation, reallocate the overhead for October and November using direct labor hours as the allocation base for supervision and employee benefits. Use machine hours as the base for the remaining overhead costs.

b. Support or criticize Mr. Jameson's conclusion that the increase in profitability of custom-designed furniture results from misallocation of overhead. Use the data developed in part **a** to support your analysis.

c. Mr. Jameson has also recommended that the company consider using predetermined overhead absorption rates calculated on an annual basis rather than allocating actual cost over actual volume each month. He stated that this is particularly applicable now that the company has two distinct product lines. Discuss the advantages of using annual predetermined overhead rates.

 31. **Problems in deriving product costs for multiple products.** The Fleetwood Mac Manufacturing Company makes three types of compact discs: X1, X2, and X3. The predetermined overhead rates are $36 per labor hour or 180 percent of direct labor costs.

Activity measures for January, Year 3, follow:

	X1	X2	X3
Normal (estimated) Volume per Month, in Units	1,000 Units	1,000 Units	2,000 Units
Normal (estimated) Volume per Month, in Direct Labor Hours	1,000 Hours	1,500 Hours	4,000 Hours
Actual Volume for January, Year 3, in Units	800 Units	1,200 Units	1,500 Units
Actual Volume for January, Year 3, in Direct Labor Hours	900 Hours	1,700 Hours	3,200 Hours

The company has not kept past records of manufacturing overhead for each product, nor has it broken down manufacturing overhead into fixed and variable components. Here are the available data about actual costs in January, Year 3:

Actual Direct Materials Costs:	
X1	$17,600
X2	28,800
X3	46,500
Actual Manufacturing Overhead	$232,000
All Other Costs (marketing and administrative)	$100,000

Actual labor rates averaged $21 per hour.

The company is experimenting with normal costing, using the following two methods of applying manufacturing overhead:

(1) Predetermined rate times actual direct labor hours.

(2) Predetermined percentage times actual direct labor costs.

a. Calculate the normal product cost for each of the three products for January, Year 3, using both methods of applying manufacturing overhead.

b. Given the data provided, can you compare the January, Year 3, actual product cost for Product X3 with the normal product cost for Product X3? If so, compare the two. If not, state why you cannot compare the two.

c. Your superior wants to know how much the variable costs of producing Product X2 were in January, Year 3. What would you say?

32. **Interpreting product cost numbers.** The Hawks Company, which started business on January 1, Year 1, manufactures a single product. The company management experimented with the use of three costing systems, including full absorption, normal costing with a predetermined overhead rate (for both fixed and variable overhead) based on labor hours; variable, actual costing; and full absorption, actual costing. Management provides the following information about the Hawks Company:

- The number of units produced exceeded the numbers of units sold.
- Hawks applies overhead on the basis of direct labor hours if it uses normal costing. Estimated direct labor hours for Year 1 were 100,000 hours. Actual direct labor hours worked were 120,000 hours.
- Hawks had no beginning inventories and no ending Work-in-Process Inventory for Year 1. It had an ending Finished Goods Inventory on December 31, Year 1.

The following data are available for the results of the experiment.

	Actual Costing		Normal Costing
	Variable Costing	Full Absorption Costing	Full Absorption Costing
Sales	$2,250,000	$2,250,000	$2,250,000
Operating Profit (before taxes)	438,000	461,000	466,200
Underapplied (Overapplied) Overhead			(52,000)
Actual Materials and Labor Costs Incurred in Production	1,280,000	1,280,000	1,280,000
Marketing and Administrative Costs (all fixed).......................	295,000	295,000	295,000
Number of Units Sold	180,000	180,000	180,000
Ending Finished Goods Inventory (cost per unit)	$7.15	$8.30	$8.56

a. Prepare income statements for each of the three product costing methods.

b. How many units are in ending finished goods inventory?

c. How much overhead is in the ending finished goods inventory (per unit) for each product costing method?

  d. What is the overhead application rate per labor hour under full absorption costing?

  e. What is the actual total variable overhead incurred in Year 1?

  f. How much overhead did Hawks expense on the income statement for each of the three product costing methods?

  g. Why does using full absorption, actual costing result in $23,000 more profit than using variable, actual costing?

  h. Why does using full absorption, normal costing result in $5,200 more profit than using full absorption, actual costing?

Suggested Solutions to Even-Numbered Exercises

16. **Computing inventory value using variable costing and full absorption costing.**

	a Full Absorption Costing	b Variable Costing
Direct Materials	$ 48,000	$48,000
Direct Labor	36,000	36,000
Variable Overhead	12,000	12,000
Fixed Overhead	12,000	—
Total Production Costs	$108,000	$96,000

$$\text{Ending Inventory Costs} = \frac{2,000}{50,000} \text{ of the Costs of Units Produced.}$$

$$\frac{2,000}{50,000} \times \$108,000 = \$4,320 \text{ Full Absorption Costing Ending Inventory}$$

$$\frac{2,000}{50,000} \times \$96,000 = \$3,840 \text{ Variable Costing Ending Inventory.}$$

  c. Inventory increased, so under full absorption costing a portion of the fixed costs is included in ending inventory. Total costs expensed will be less under full absorption costing and income will be larger.

18. **Computing allocated overhead and finished goods value.**

  a. Job 745:

Direct Materials	$ 8,400
Direct Labor	10,000
Overhead ($10,000/$4 × $3)	7,500
Total Manufacturing Costs	$25,900

b. Job 305:

Revenue....................................		$ 40,000
Less: Direct Materials	$ (6,300)	
Direct Labor	(20,000)	
Overhead ($20,000/$5 × $3)	(12,000)	(38,300)
Gross Margin		$ 1,700

20. **Comparison of full absorption and variable costing in income statement formats.**

Variable Costing
(all dollar amounts in thousands)

	Year 1	Year 2	Total[a]
Sales	$ 1,400	$ 2,600	$ 4,000
Variable Cost of Goods Sold:			
Beginning Inventory	$ 0	$ (390)	$ 0
Current Period Manufacturing Costs	(1,300)	(1,300)	(2,600)
Less Ending Inventory....................	390[b]	(0)	(0)
Variable Cost of Goods Sold	$ (910)	$(1,690)	$(2,600)
Total Contribution Margin	$ 490	$ 910	$ 1,400
Fixed Manufacturing Costs..................	(340)	(340)	(680)
Nonmanufacturing Costs....................	(150)	(150)	(300)
Operating Profits...........................	$ 0	$ 420	$ 420

Full Absorption Costing
(all dollar amounts in thousands)

	Year 1	Year 2	Total[a]
Sales	$ 1,400	$ 2,600	$ 4,000
Full Absorption Cost of Goods Sold:			
Beginning Inventory	$ 0	$ (492)	$ 0
Current Period Manufacturing Costs	(1,640)	(1,640)	(3,280)
Less Ending Inventory....................	492[c]	0	0
Full Absorption Cost of Goods Sold..........	$(1,148)	$(2,132)	$(3,280)
Gross Margin.............................	$ 252	$ 468	$ 720
Nonmanufacturing Costs....................	(150)	(150)	(300)
Operating Profits...........................	$ 102	$ 318	$ 420

[a]Not required.

[b]$390,000 = ($1,300,000/100,000 units produced) × 30,000 units in ending inventory.

[c]$492,000 = ($1,640,000/100,000 units produced) × 30,000 units in ending inventory.

22. **Comparison of standard costing to actual and normal costing.**

	Cost Measure		
	Actual Costing	Normal Costing	Standard Costing

Cost Inclusion

Variable Costing

	Actual Costing	Normal Costing	Standard Costing
Direct Materials	$ .50[a]	$ .50[a]	$ .45[g]
Direct Labor	.90[b]	.90[b]	.95[g]
Variable Manufacturing Overhead	2.00[c]	1.80[e]	1.90[h]
Fixed Manufacturing Overhead..............	—	—	—
Total Product Cost........................	$3.40	$3.20	$3.30

Full Absorption Costing

	Actual Costing	Normal Costing	Standard Costing
Direct Materials	$ .50[a]	$ .50[a]	$ .45[g]
Direct Labor	.90[b]	.90[b]	.95[g]
Variable Manufacturing Overhead	2.00[c]	1.80[e]	1.90[h]
Fixed Manufacturing Overhead..............	2.50[d]	2.70[f]	2.85[i]
Total Product Cost........................	$5.90	$5.90	$6.15

[a]$.50 = $10,000/20,000 units.

[b]$.90 = $18,000/20,000 units.

[c]$2.00 = $40,000/20,000 units.

[d]$2.50 = $50,000/20,000 units.

[e]$1.80 = 2 × $.90.

[f]$2.70 = 3 × $.90.

[g]Given in the exercise.

[h]$1.90 = 2 × $.95.

[i]$2.85 = 3 × $.95.

Chapter 4

Accounting in Alternative Production Settings

This chapter shows how the accounting system records and reports the flow of costs in organizations. The accounting system records costs to help managers answer questions such as these:

- What is the cost of a job at Kinko's copy shop or at the Deloitte & Touche public accounting firm?
- How much does it cost Levi Strauss to make a denim jacket? How does that cost compare to management's expectations?

- How much does it cost Chrysler Corporation to make the Jeep Grand Cherokee?
- How much does it cost the state of New York to provide an undergraduate education at one of the State Universities of New York?

This chapter provides an overview of the ways different types of organizations account for their production costs.

Recording Costs by Department and Assigning Costs to Products

As discussed in earlier chapters, experts must design a managerial accounting system to serve several purposes. For purposes of planning and performance evaluation, accountants record costs by departments or other *responsibility centers*. (A responsibility center is simply an organizational unit.) One or more managers are responsible for the activities in each responsibility center in a company. Divisions, territories, plants, and departments are all examples of responsibility centers.

Exhibit 4.1 shows the relation between recording costs by departments and assigning costs to products for a firm with two manufacturing departments, Assembling and Finishing. The accounting system records the costs of direct materials, direct labor, and manufacturing overhead incurred in production in separate accounts

Exhibit 4.1
Relation between Departmental and Product Costing

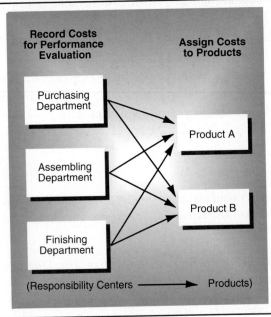

for the manufacturing departments, Assembly and Finishing. Management then compares these costs with the standard or budgeted amounts and investigates significant variances, as we will discuss later in Chapters 12 through 14. In recording costs by departments, the accounting system has served its function of providing data for departmental performance evaluation. The accounting system also assigns costs to products for managerial decision making, such as evaluating a product's profitability.

Nonmanufacturing Applications

You will also find this relation between recording costs by departments and assigning costs to products in nonmanufacturing settings. For example, accounting records the costs of performing surgery on a patient by department (for example, Surgery), then assigns these costs to a particular patient. In general, for the accounting system to provide product cost information, it must assign cost to products from responsibility centers.

Fundamental Accounting Model of Cost Flows

Exhibit 4.2 shows how firms transform materials into finished goods. Note that Work-in-Process is the account that both *describes* the transformation of inputs into outputs in a company and *accounts for* the costs incurred in the process.

In most companies, each department controls its costs (for example, the Assembly Department or the Finishing Department). Thus each department has a separate Work-in-Process account, as Exhibit 4.2 shows, which accumulates departmental costs. Management holds department managers accountable for the costs accumulated in their departments.

Companies that operate in competitive markets have little direct control over prices paid for materials or prices received for finished goods. Thus a key factor in a company's success is how well it controls the conversion costs (that is, direct labor and overhead). Companies closely monitor those costs in the Work-in-Process Inventory account.

In short, the accounting system serves two purposes in manufacturing and service companies: (1) to record costs by responsibility center (department) for performance evaluation and cost control and (2) to assign manufacturing costs to units produced for product costing.

Basic Cost Flow Equation

Accounting systems are based on the following basic **cost flow equation:**

$$\text{Beginning Balance} + \text{Transfers In} = \text{Transfers Out} + \text{Ending Balance}.$$

Or in symbols:

$$\text{BB} + \text{TI} = \text{TO} + \text{EB}.$$

Exhibit 4.2

Flow of Costs through the Accounts and Departments

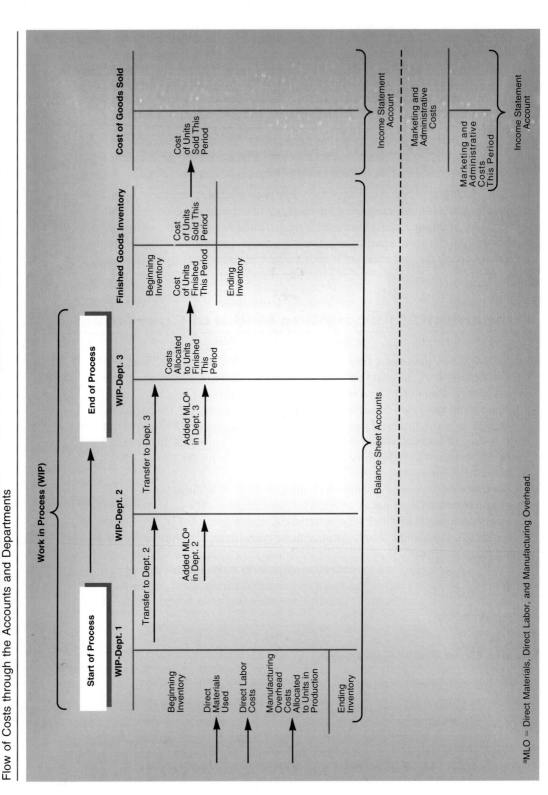

aMLO = Direct Materials, Direct Labor, and Manufacturing Overhead.

Managerial Application

Using the Basic Cost Flow Equation to Detect Fraud[a]

A top manager at Doughties Foods became curious about the high levels of inventory reported on the divisional financial statements of the Gravins Division. The amount of ending inventory at the Gravins Division seemed high compared to those of other divisions in the company. When asked about the high inventory levels, the division manager confessed that he had overstated the inventory numbers to overstate his divisional profits.

Overstating the ending balance of inventory understates cost of goods sold, which overstates gross margin and profits. In equation form,

$$BB + TI - (EB + F) = TO - F,$$

where F refers to the amount of overstatement from the financial fraud, EB is the correct ending inventory amount, and TO is the correct transfer out of inventory, which is also the correct Cost of Goods Sold. Thus, the reported Cost of Goods Sold was understated by the amount F. As the manager of the Gravins Division discovered to his dismay, the ending inventory for Period 1 is the beginning inventory for Period 2. Thus, the beginning inventory on the books carried an overstated amount, which had to be matched by an equal amount of overstatement at the end of Period 2.

The Gravins Division was a food distributor that kept some of its food inventory in freezers. The company's independent auditors were reluctant to go into the freezer, so the manager of the Gravins Division overstated his inventory by overstating the number of items in the freezer. As time passed, the Gravins Division manager continued to overstate inventory to continue looking good to his bosses. When confronted with the high inventory numbers, the Gravins Division manager confessed to the inventory overstatement, and handed over a notebook containing records of the overstated amounts. Then he resigned.

The Securities and Exchange Commission filed charges alleging financial fraud against the (former) manager of the Gravins Division and filed charges against the auditors for not complying with Generally Accepted Auditing Standards in conducting their audit.

[a]Based on the authors' research.

This equation is a fundamental equality in accounting. Transfers in to work in process represent the material, labor, and overhead used in production. In merchandising, transfers in to the inventory accounts represent the goods purchased.

Problem 4.1 for Self-Study

Using the basic cost flow equation. Fill in the missing item for each of the following inventory accounts:

	A	B	C
Beginning Balance	$40,000	?	$35,000
Ending Balance	32,000	$16,000	27,000
Transferred in	?	8,000	8,000
Transferred out	61,000	11,000	?

The solution to this question is at the end of this chapter on page 134.

Production Methods and Accounting Systems

Exhibit 4.3 shows how production methods vary across organizations, depending on the type of product. Companies that produce **jobs** include print shops, like Kinko's and R. R. Donnelly; custom construction companies, like Morrison-Knudsen; defense contractors, such as General Dynamics; and computerized machine manufacturers, like Cincinnati Milacron. These companies all produce customized products, which we call jobs. Companies producing customized products use **job costing** to record the cost of their products.

Many professional service organizations also use job costing, including public accounting and consulting firms, like Price Waterhouse and Andersen Consulting, and law firms, like Baker and McKenzie. These firms use job costing to keep track of costs for each client. Health-care organizations, like Kaiser and the Mayo Clinic, record the costs of each patient's care using job costing.

Exhibit 4.3

Production Methods and Accounting Systems

Type of Production	Accounting System	Type of Product
Job Shop (health care services, custom homes, CPA firm)	Job Costing	Customized
Operations (computer terminals, automobiles, clothing)	Operation Costing	Mostly Standardized
Continuous Flow Processing (oil refinery, soft drinks)	Process Costing	Standardized

Continuous flow processing is at the opposite end of the continuum from job shops. Companies using continuous flow processing mass-produce homogeneous products in a continuous flow. Companies with continuous flow processes use process costing to account for product costs. Coca-Cola and PepsiCo use process costing for making soft drink syrup. Dow Chemical uses process costing to record the costs of chemical production. AMOCO uses process costing for its oil refining, and Merck uses process costing to record costs of pharmaceutical manufacturing.

Many organizations use job systems for some products and process systems for others. A home builder might use process costing for standardized homes with a particular floor plan. The same builder might use job costing when building a custom-designed house for a single customer. Honeywell, Inc., a high-tech company, uses process costing for most of its furnace thermostats and job costing for customized aerospace contracting products.

Many companies use a hybrid of job and process costing, called operation costing. **Operations** are standardized methods of making a product that are performed repeatedly in production. Companies using **operation costing** produce products using standardized production methods, like process costing. Materials can be different for each product or batch of products like job costing. Companies in the apparel industry, like Liz Claiborne and Levi Strauss, computer companies, like IBM and Apple, and furniture manufacturers, like Herman Miller and La-Z-Boy Chair, use operations costing.

Nissan manufactures a variety of models of cars and trucks on one assembly line in its manufacturing plant near Nashville, Tennessee. Each car or truck goes through the same work stations; for example, every car and truck goes through the same painting work station where it is painted. Each model type has a different set of materials, however.

Job and Process Costing Systems

This section provides an overview of product cost accounting for the two major types of production operations: job operations and process operations.

In **job costing,** firms collect costs for each "unit" produced. Often each department collects costs for evaluating the performance of departmental personnel.

Example Unique Builders makes a customized product. In April, it started and completed three jobs (no beginning inventories). The manufacturing cost of each job follows:

Job No. 1001	$8,000
Job No. 1002	6,000
Job No. 1003	7,000

Unique Builders sold Job No. 1001. The flow of costs for this company appears in the top panel of Exhibit 4.4.

Exhibit 4.4

Flow of Costs, Job versus Process Costing

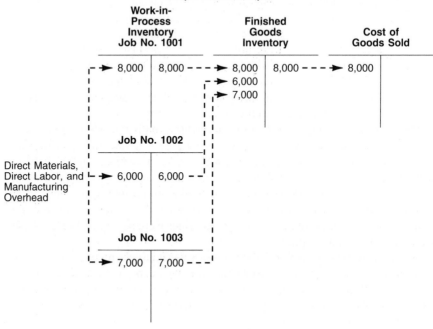

JOB COSTING

In **process costing,** firms accumulate costs in a department or production process during an accounting period (for example, a month), then spread those costs evenly over the units produced that month. The formula follows:

$$\text{Unit Cost} = \frac{\text{Total Manufacturing Costs Incurred During the Period}}{\text{Total Units Produced During the Period}}.$$

Example Standard Builders started and completed three homogeneous units in April (no beginning or ending inventories). Total manufacturing costs were $21,000, so Standard Builders assigned each unit a cost of $7,000. It sold one unit. This flow of costs appears in the bottom panel of Exhibit 4.4. Note how much more detail job costing would require for a large number (say, 10,000) of jobs or units.

We have presented an overview of job and process costing. Next, we examine managerial issues in choosing between job and process costing.

Job versus Process Costing: Cost-Benefit Considerations

Why do firms prefer one accounting system to another? Cost-benefit analysis provides the answer. In general, the costs of record keeping under job costing systems exceed those under process costing. Consider a house builder. Under job costing, the house builder must accumulate costs for each house. If a truck delivers lumber to several houses, it is not sufficient to record the total issued. The driver must keep records of the amount delivered to, and subsequently returned from, each house. If laborers work on several houses, they must keep track of the time spent on *each* house. Process costing, however, requires simply recording the total cost. For the house builder, process costing would report the average cost of all houses built. (In practice, house builders generally use job costing for custom-built houses and process costing for houses having a particular model type or floor plan.)

Under process costing, a firm does not report the direct cost incurred for a particular unit. If all units are homogeneous, this loss of information is probably minimal. Is it important for Kellogg's to know whether the cost of the 1,001st box of Raisin Bran differs from the 1,002nd box's cost? Not likely. The additional benefits from tracing costs to each box of Raisin Bran would not justify the additional record-keeping costs.

Although job costing provides more detailed information than process costing, it is a more expensive accounting system. Thus management and accountants must examine the costs and benefits of information and pick the method that best fits the organization's production operations.

Example In this example, a custom house builder explains the benefits of job costing for companies that make heterogeneous products.

We estimate the costs of each house for pricing purposes. Unless we know the actual costs of each house, we cannot evaluate our estimation methods. We use the information for performance evaluation and cost control, too. We assign a manager to each house who is responsible for seeing that actual costs don't exceed the estimate. If we come in less than 10 percent over estimate, the manager gets a bonus.

We need a job system to help us charge customers for any cost overruns, too. Usually, customers make changes as we build. If the changes have a small impact on costs, we absorb them. But if these changes add costs, we like to go to the customer with our tally of estimated and actual costs, and get an adjustment in the price of the house. Sometimes, we build on a cost-plus basis, in which case we *must* know and document costs for each house so we can collect from the customer.

Management generally finds that the comparative costs and benefits of job and process costing indicate matching the cost system to the production methods as follows:

Nature of Production	Costing System Used
Heterogeneous Units, Each Unit Large......................	Job Costing
Homogeneous Units, Continuous Process, Many Small Units....	Process Costing

Problem 4.2 for Self-Study

Classifying products as jobs or processes; diagraming cost flows through accounts.

a. Classify each of the following products as either a job or coming from a process:

- Work for a client on a lawsuit by lawyers in a law firm.
- Diet cola.
- Patient care in an emergency room for a college basketball player.
- House painting by a company called Student Painters.
- The paint used by Student Painters.

b. Diagram how costs would flow through T-accounts for house painting, assuming Student Painters has several jobs. (No numbers needed but feel free to use XXX's or make up your own numbers.)

The solution to this question is at the end of this chapter on page 134.

Just-in-Time (JIT) Methods

Many companies (Toyota, Hewlett-Packard, and Yamaha, to name a few) have adopted just-in-time methods for parts of their production activities. Management uses **just-in-time (JIT) methods** to obtain materials just in time for production and to provide finished goods just in time for sale. This practice reduces, or potentially eliminates, inventories and the cost of carrying them. Of particular importance, just-in-time requires that workers immediately correct a process making defective units because they have no inventory where they can hide defective units. Eliminating inventories exposes production problems. Consequently, just-in-time relies on high-quality materials and production.

Using a just-in-time system, production does not begin on an item until the firm receives an order. When an order is received for a finished product, people in production order raw materials. As soon as production fills the order, production ends. In theory, a JIT system eliminates the need for inventories because no production takes place until the firm knows that it will sell the item. As a practical matter, companies using just-in-time inventory usually have a backlog of orders or stable demand for their products to assure continued production.

Since just-in-time production responds to an order receipt, JIT accounting can charge all costs directly to cost of goods sold. When they need to report inventories in the financial statements, accountants ''back out'' the inventory amounts from the cost of goods sold account and charge them to inventory accounts.

Comparing JIT and Traditional Sequential Cost Flows at Hewlett-Packard

After installing a new production process, a Hewlett-Packard plant that makes printed circuit boards found that (1) it was able to reduce inventory levels significantly, (2) direct labor was only 3 to 5 percent of total product costs, and (3) most labor and overhead costs were fixed.[1] Consequently, H-P was able to use production methods that were almost ''just-in-time,'' which dramatically affected the plant's accounting methods.

Lower inventory levels and reduced time between production and delivery of finished product meant that accounting expensed virtually all of the overhead and direct labor incurred in the month in which it was incurred. Management decided to treat manufacturing overhead as an expense charged directly to cost of goods sold. Overhead remaining in work-in-process and finished goods was recorded using end-of-month adjusting entries.

Exhibit 4.5 compares the new method at the Hewlett-Packard plant with a traditional system. Accounting records only materials in inventory accounts; it expenses labor and overhead when incurred. Hewlett-Packard eliminated an estimated 100,000 journal entries per month by simplifying the accounting system because the new accounting system no longer allocated labor and overhead to each job.

The net result of these changes is that Hewlett-Packard realized significant savings in staff time and costs without any significant changes in costs reported in their financial statements, or costs used in planning and controlling production, or costs analyzed for pricing and make-or-buy decisions. Production line managers can now understand the simpler reports provided by the accounting department and actually use the information in those reports.[2]

Backflush Costing

What if a company's accountants record all manufacturing costs directly in Cost of Goods Sold, but at the end of the accounting period, the accountants learn that the

---

[1] R. Hunt, L. Garrett, and C. M. Merz, ''Direct Labor Cost Not Always Relevant at H.P.,'' *Management Accounting,* February 1985, pp. 58–62.

[2] Ibid., p. 61.

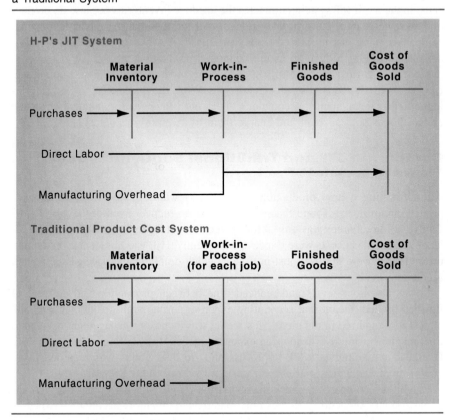

Exhibit 4.5

Comparing Cost Flows: H-P's JIT System and
a Traditional System

Source: Hunt, Garrett, and Merz, Figure 1, p. 60.

company has some inventory? (Despite using just-in-time production, companies
often find they have at least some inventory.) Companies that record costs directly
in Cost of Goods Sold can use a method called **backflush costing** to transfer any
costs back to the inventory accounts, if necessary.

Backflush costing is a method that works backward from the output to assign
manufacturing costs to work-in-process inventories. Companies have probably used
the term *backflush* because costs are "flushed back" through the production process
to the points at which inventories remain. Exhibit 4.6 compares the traditional
method of sequential costing with the backflush approach. Costs are initially recorded at the end of the production process, either in Finished Goods Inventory or in
Cost of Goods Sold, on the grounds that the company has little or no work-in-process
inventory. If the company has inventories at the end of a period, the accountants can
credit Cost of Goods Sold, as shown in Exhibit 4.6, and debit the inventory accounts
for the amount of inventory. (Backflush costing *looks* more complicated than traditional sequential costing, but it is simpler in practice.)

Example For example, Biotech Corporation uses JIT. Direct materials cost $1.50 per unit, and other manufacturing costs (including labor) are $.80 per unit. The company received an order for 10,000 units. Biotech incurred materials costs of $15,000 and other manufacturing costs of $8,000. The journal entries to record these events follow:

Cost of Goods Sold..	15,000	
Accounts Payable		15,000
To record materials.		
Cost of Goods Sold..	8,000	
Wages Payable and Manufacturing Overhead Applied		8,000
To record the other manufacturing costs.		

Accounting debits all of these costs directly to cost of goods sold.

Assume 1,000 completed units are left in Finished Goods Inventory when accounting prepares the financial statements. Accounting backs out 1,000 units from cost of goods sold based on a unit cost of $2.30, which is $1.50 for materials and $.80 for other manufacturing costs, for a total of $2,300 (= 1,000 units × $2.30 per unit). The journal entry to back out the inventory from cost of goods sold follows:

Finished Goods Inventory	2,300	
Cost of Goods Sold.......................................		2,300
To record inventory.		

Exhibit 4.7 shows these transactions in T-accounts.

If accounting charged the costs of these units to production using traditional costing methods, it would need to debit the materials costs to a direct materials account. As production used the materials, accounting would transfer their costs to Work-in-Process Inventory. Accounting would charge other manufacturing costs to Work-in-Process. As production completed goods, accounting would transfer their costs into Finished Goods and finally into Cost of Goods Sold.

Lean Production Methods

Just-in-time production is part of a "lean production" philosophy that has been credited for the success of many Japanese companies and such U.S. companies as Lincoln Electric. Lean production is characterized by eliminating buffers, such as inventory, placing the quality and efficiency of production at the highest importance, and providing the flexibility to change quickly from one product to another. Lean production emphasizes employee training, relating compensation to company and individual performance. Companies that do not have these characteristics find it difficult to implement just-in-time production methods because just-in-time requires each production step to be performed with no defects.

Many Japanese companies are presently using just-in-time inventory, including automobile manufacturers such as Nissan and Toyota and motorcycle manufacturers such as Yamaha. The new Saturn Corporation, General Electric, and General Motors use just-in-time methods.

Exhibit 4.6

Comparison of Backflush Costing with Traditional Sequential Tracking of Costs

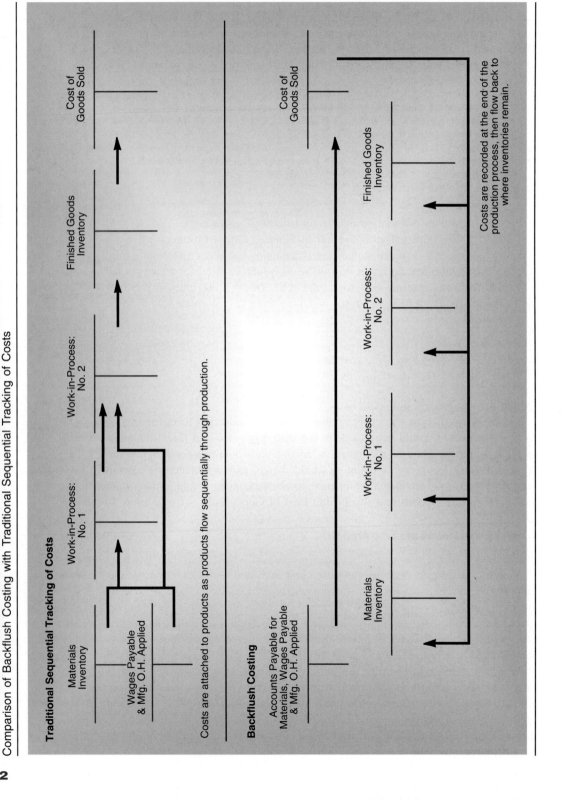

Traditional Sequential Tracking of Costs

Materials Inventory

Work-in-Process: No. 1

Work-in-Process: No. 2

Finished Goods Inventory

Cost of Goods Sold

Wages Payable & Mfg. O.H. Applied

Costs are attached to products as products flow sequentially through production.

Backflush Costing

Materials Inventory

Work-in-Process: No. 1

Work-in-Process: No. 2

Finished Goods Inventory

Cost of Goods Sold

Accounts Payable for Materials, Wages Payable & Mfg. O.H. Applied

Costs are recorded at the end of the production process, then flow back to where inventories remain.

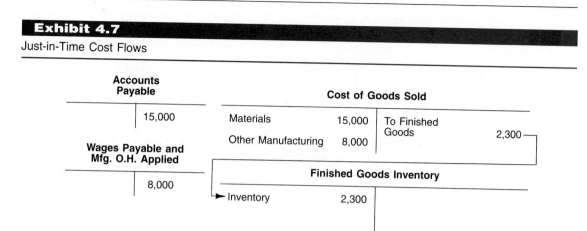

Exhibit 4.7

Just-in-Time Cost Flows

Just-in-Time Problems[3]

Although just-in-time has worked well in Japan where suppliers are clustered around their customers, JIT's reliance on reliable suppliers has created problems in the United States. For example, a United Auto Workers strike against a General Motors' parts plant resulted in a shutdown of the Saturn plant in Spring Hills, Tennessee. The Lordstown plant provided steel hoods, trunk lids, and roofs for the Saturn cars. The Saturn plant was forced to close within a few hours of the strike against the Lordstown plant because Saturn used just-in-time inventory and had only enough inventory for one or two shifts.

During the Persian Gulf War, the U.S. Army kept some of its Apache helicopters flying by grounding other helicopters to get parts. The army had spent about $12 billion on the Apache program but almost nothing for spare parts, according to a General Accounting Office study. Apparently the army would need six to twelve months before the next war started to provide enough lead time to acquire parts. Army officials argued that stockpiling parts would lead to criticisms that the army had excessive inventories.

GE Appliances found that low inventories of parts from its 75 suppliers prevented it from responding quickly to customer demands. By increasing its inventory 24 percent, the company reduced its response time for customer orders from 18 weeks to 3.6 weeks.

In general, companies have found they can use JIT if they can obtain materials rapidly from reliable suppliers and if customers are predictable in placing orders. Many companies that do not literally have ''just-in-time'' production have nevertheless significantly reduced their work-in-process inventories in an effort to lower inventory carrying costs, put emphasis on production efficiency, and simplify accounting for inventories.

---

[3]Based on articles in the *Washington Post,* September 6, 1992, the *Sacramento Bee,* April 27, 1991, and *The Wall Street Journal,* May 7, 1993.

International Applications of JIT

Toyota gets credit as the first large company to install JIT (although we suspect JIT has been used in some form for many decades, perhaps centuries, in various parts of the world). We now find JIT used in companies around the world. Countries like Japan that have a well-defined network of suppliers and manufacturers are particularly well-suited to JIT. JIT is more difficult to implement in countries like the United States that have dispersed suppliers and manufacturers. Efforts to increase international trade may increase the dispersion of suppliers, making JIT more difficult to implement.

Problem 4.3 for Self-Study

Traditional versus backflush cost flows. Influence "R" Us uses JIT production methods in making television commercials. For the month of January, the company incurred costs of $200,000 in making commercials. Twenty percent of January's costs was assigned to one commercial for a clothing store that was finished but not yet recorded in Cost of Goods Sold. Influence "R" Us has one materials account for film, one Work-in-Process account, one Finished Goods account, and one Cost of Goods Sold account.

Show the flow of costs through T-accounts using **(a)** traditional costing and **(b)** backflush costing. Assume that the credit entries for these costs when they were recorded were $10,000 to Accounts Payable for film, $90,000 to Accounts Payable for overhead, and $100,000 to Wages Payable for labor. The company had no beginning inventory on January 1.

The solution to this question is at the end of this chapter on page 135.

Service Organizations

The flow of costs in service organizations is similar to manufacturing. The service provided requires labor and overhead. Service organizations often collect costs by departments for performance evaluation.

In consulting, public accounting, and similar service organizations, the firm also collects costs by job or client. The accounting method is similar to that used in manufacturing job shops. As in manufacturing, the firm collects costs by job for performance evaluation, to provide information for cost control, and to compare actual with estimated costs for pricing of future jobs.

Service organizations differ from manufacturing or merchandising organizations in that service organizations do not show inventories (other than supplies) on the financial statements for external reporting. Service organizations often maintain

"Work-in-Process" in their internal records. This account shows the cost of service performed for a client but not yet billed, similar to the accumulation of unbilled costs for a special contract or job in a manufacturing job shop.

Example For the month of July, Strategic Action Group (SAG) has the following activity:

- Client A: 400 hours.
- Client B: 600 hours.
- Billing rate to client: $200 per hour.
- Labor costs (all consulting staff): $80 per hour.
- Total consulting hours worked in July: 1,200 hours. (SAG did not charge 200 hours to a client. The firm calls that time "direct labor—unbillable.")
- Actual overhead costs for July: $22,000. (Overhead includes travel, secretarial services, telephone, copying, supplies, and postage.)
- Accounting charges overhead to jobs based on labor hours worked using a predetermined rate of $20 per labor hour.
- Marketing and administrative costs: $12,000.
- All transactions are on account.
- Both jobs were billed to clients and the costs transferred from Work-in-Process to Cost of Services.

The entries to record these transactions are as follows:

(1)	Work in Process: Client A	32,000	
	Work in Process: Client B	48,000	
	Direct Labor—Unbillable	16,000	
	Wages Payable		96,000
	(Client A: 400 hours @ $80 = $32,000; Client B: 600 hours @ $80 = $48,000; Unbillable: 200 hours @ $80.)		
(2)	Work in Process: Client A	8,000	
	Work in Process: Client B	12,000	
	Overhead (applied)		20,000
	(Overhead applied to jobs at the rate of $20 per labor hour.)		
(3)	Overhead	22,000	
	Wages and Accounts Payable		22,000
	(Actual overhead: $22,000)		
(4)	Marketing and Administrative Costs	12,000	
	Wages and Accounts Payable		12,000
	(Actual cost: $12,000)		
(5a)	Accounts Receivable	200,000	
	Revenue		200,000
	(To record revenue at $200 per hour: 400 hours for Client A, 600 hours for Client B.)		
(5b)	Cost of Services Billed	100,000	
	Work in Process: Client A		40,000
	Work in Process: Client B		60,000
	(To record the cost of services billed to clients.)		

Note that 5a and 5b are really two parts of the same entry.

Exhibit 4.8

STRATEGIC ACTION GROUP
Flow of Costs in a Service Organization for July

Accounts and Wages Payable		Work in Process: Client A		Cost of Services Billed	
	96,000 **(1)**	**(1)** 32,000	40,000 **(5b)**	**(5b)** 100,000	
	22,000 **(3)**	**(2)** 8,000			
	12,000 **(4)**	Work in Process: Client B		Marketing and Administrative Costs	
		(1) 48,000	60,000 **(5b)**	**(4)** 12,000	
		(2) 12,000			

Accounts Receivable		Overhead		Direct Labor— Unbillable		Revenue	
(5a) 200,000		**(3)** 22,000	20,000 **(2)**	**(1)** 16,000			200,000 **(5a)**

Note: Numbers in parentheses correspond to journal entries in text.

Exhibit 4.8 shows the flow of costs through T-accounts. Exhibit 4.9 presents an income statement. Note that the unbilled labor and unassigned overhead are expensed with marketing and administrative costs. We use the full absorption costing format because some overhead is probably a fixed cost.

Exhibit 4.9

STRATEGIC ACTION GROUP
Income Statement for the Month Ending July 31

Revenue from Services	$200,000
Less Cost of Services Billed	100,000
Gross Margin	100,000
Less:	
Direct Labor—Unbillable	16,000
Overhead	2,000[a]
Marketing and Administrative Costs	12,000
Operating Profit	$ 70,000

[a]$2,000 = $22,000 incurred − $20,000 applied to jobs and expensed as part of cost of services billed.

Problem 4.4 ▮▮▮▮▮▮▮▮▮▮▮
for Self-Study

Cost flows in a service organization. For the month of September, Touche Andersen & Company, an accounting firm, worked 200 hours for Client A and 700 hours for Client B. Touche Andersen bills clients at the rate of $80 per hour, whereas the audit staff costs $30 per hour. The audit staff worked 1,000 total hours in September (100 hours were not billable to clients), and overhead costs were $10,000. (Examples of unbillable hours are hours spent in professional training and meetings unrelated to particular clients.) Accounting assigned overhead as follows: Client A $2,000, Client B $7,000, and $1,000 unassigned. In addition, Touche Andersen & Company spent $5,000 in marketing and administrative costs. All transactions are on account. The work done in September was billed to the clients.

a. Using T-accounts, show costs and revenue flows.
b. Prepare an income statement for the company for September.

The solution to this question is at the end of this chapter on page 136.

▮▮▮▮▮▮▮▮▮▮▮▮▮▮▮▮▮▮▮▮▮▮▮▮▮▮▮▮▮▮▮▮▮▮▮▮▮▮▮

Ethical Issues in Job Costing

Many organizations have been called to task for improprieties in the way they assign costs to jobs. For example, major defense contractors have come under fire for overstating the costs of jobs. Numerous universities have been accused of overstating the costs of research projects, the most famous case involving Stanford University. Improprieties in job costing generally are caused by one or more of the following actions: misstating the stage of completion of jobs, charging costs to the wrong jobs or categories (for example, charging the cost of university yachts to research projects), or simply misrepresenting the costs of jobs.

To avoid the appearance of cost overruns on jobs, job supervisors sometimes ask employees to charge costs to the wrong jobs. If you work in consulting or auditing, you may encounter cases where supervisors ask you to allocate your time spent on old jobs that are in danger of exceeding the cost estimate to other jobs that are in less danger of cost overruns. At minimum, this practice misleads managers who rely on accurate cost information for pricing, cost control, and other decisions. At worst, it also cheats people who may be paying for a job on a cost plus fee basis, where that job has not really cost as much as the producer claims.

People who supply the money for jobs often insist on audits of financial records to avoid such deception. Government auditors generally work on the site of defense contractors, universities, and other organizations that have contracts with the government for large jobs.

Summary

This chapter discusses accounting methods of recording and reporting cost flows in job shops, processes, operations, JIT settings, and service organizations. We start with the basic cost flow equation,

$$\underset{\text{Balance}}{\text{Beginning}} + \underset{\text{In}}{\text{Transfers}} = \underset{\text{Out}}{\text{Transfers}} + \underset{\text{Balance}}{\text{Ending}}$$

$$\text{BB} + \text{TI} = \text{TO} + \text{EB,}$$

which relates the flow of costs through accounts to beginning and ending inventory balances.

Companies use job costing when they produce unique jobs, particularly custom-designed jobs. Companies use processes when they make standardized products, particularly in a continuous flow. Operations are a hybrid of jobs and processes in which the materials are different for each product line (for example, compact cars and trucks), but products go through standardized operations (that is, both cars and trucks go through assembly operations, painting operations, and so forth).

Just-in-time production is part of the "lean production" philosophy that emphasizes quality, high worker skills, and eliminating inventory buffers. With just-in-time, companies have an opportunity to simplify accounting for inventories by bypassing inventory accounts and charging production costs directly to Cost of Goods Sold. If there are no inventories at the end of the period, accounting has been considerably simplified. If there are inventories at the end of the period, companies use "backflush costing" to back costs out of Cost of Goods Sold and account for inventories.

Appendix 4.1:
Computing Costs of Equivalent Production

This appendix describes product costing methods when a firm has only partially completed work on a product at the beginning or end of a period. For example, assume Davis Contractors, a house builder, is presently building several houses of a particular model. Davis had three partially built houses at the beginning of the second quarter of the year (April 1). Davis started four houses and completed five houses during the second quarter, and had two partially built houses at the end of the quarter (June 30). The contractor knows that she has spent $795,000 on construction materials, labor, and overhead for these houses during the second quarter and that the cost of the beginning work-in-process inventory for the three houses partially built on April 1 totals $42,000. The contractor wishes to know several other things, however, such as the cost of each house constructed in the second quarter, the cost of the ending work-in-process inventory, and the cost of the houses completed.

The contractor has several potential uses for the information about the cost of each house. First, the contractor had set prices based on market conditions and the estimate that each house would cost $145,000 to build. If she estimated incorrectly, the contractor would consider changing the prices on the houses or possibly would stop building this type of house if costs were so high that the contractor would make insufficient profits. Second, the contractor holds construction job supervisors responsible for managing and scheduling workers, for minimizing waste, and for other activities that affect construction costs. Product costs can provide feedback about their performance. Third, Davis Contractors prepares the external financial statements for its creditors that require ending inventory valuation and the cost of finished houses sold.

Procedure for Applying Costs to Units Produced

This section describes the five steps required to compute product costs, the cost of ending work-in-process inventory, and the cost of finished goods. Exhibit 4.10 presents the data required to do the analysis for the Davis Contractors example. Exhibit 4.10 shows that the contractor considered each of the three houses in the beginning work-in-process inventory to be 10-percent complete, on average, and the two houses in the ending work-in-process inventory each to be 30-percent complete, on average. Assume the first-in, first-out (FIFO) cost flow assumption for inventory, for now. (Later, we discuss the effects of using the weighted-average method.) Exhibit 4.11 summarizes the five steps in the process and presents the analysis for Davis Contractors.

Step 1: Summarize the Flow of Physical Units This appears in the top of the production cost report in Exhibit 4.11.

Step 2: Compute Equivalent Units Since the firm has some partially completed units at the beginning and end of the period, accounting must convert the work into equivalent (finished) units produced. **Equivalent units (E.U.)** represent the translation of partially complete work into equivalent whole units. For example, two units, each 50 percent complete, represent one equivalent unit. Three categories of work done require equivalent unit computations to derive the equivalent work done in a period:

1. **Equivalent units to complete beginning work-in-process inventory.** For Davis Contractors, the three houses in beginning work-in-process (WIP) inventory were 10-percent complete when the period started. Since Davis completed them during this period, as the bottom of Exhibit 4.10 shows, Davis did 90 percent of the work on these houses during the second quarter. Therefore, accounting required 2.7 equivalent units (= 3 houses × 90%) to complete the beginning inventory, as Exhibit 4.11 shows.

Exhibit 4.10

DAVIS CONTRACTORS
Cost of Houses Produced
Data for Second Quarter, April 1 through June 30

	Units[a]	Product Costs	Percent of Processing Completed
Beginning Work-in-Process Inventory, April 1	3	$ 42,000	10
Costs Incurred in Second Quarter...	—	795,000	—
Completed and Transferred Out to Finished Goods Inventory	5	?	100
Ending Work-in-Process Inventory	2	?	30

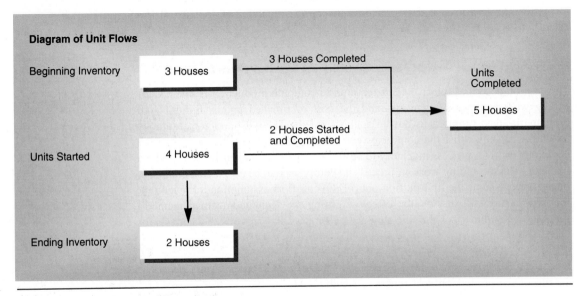

[a]Some of these units are only partially completed.

2. **Equivalent units for work started and completed during the period.** Exhibit 4.10 shows that Davis started and completed two houses during the period, representing two equivalent units produced, as shown in Exhibit 4.11.

3. **Units still in ending WIP inventory.** The ending WIP inventory represents the equivalent work done on units not completed and transferred out during the period. Two houses that Davis had 30-percent complete at the end of the period fit into this category, representing .6 equivalent units (= 2 houses × 30%).

The equivalent units produced for the second quarter are 5.3 units (= 2.7 + 2.0 + .6), as shown in Step 2 in Exhibit 4.11.

We base equivalent unit computations on the basic cost flow equation. If you know the equivalent work done in beginning and ending work-in-process inventories and the units transferred, you can derive the equivalent units produced during the period as follows:

$$\begin{matrix} \text{Equivalent Units} \\ \text{in the Beginning} \\ \text{Inventory} \end{matrix} + \begin{matrix} \text{Equivalent Units} \\ \text{of Work Done} \\ \text{This Period} \end{matrix} = \begin{matrix} \text{Equivalent Units} \\ \text{Transferred Out} \end{matrix} + \begin{matrix} \text{Equivalent Units} \\ \text{in Ending} \\ \text{Inventory.} \end{matrix}$$

In our example, to find the work done this period, use the following formula:

$$\begin{matrix} \text{Equivalent Units} \\ \text{of Work Done} \\ \text{This Period} \end{matrix} = \begin{matrix} \text{Equivalent Units} \\ \text{Transferred Out} \end{matrix} + \begin{matrix} \text{Equivalent Units} \\ \text{in Ending} \\ \text{Inventory} \end{matrix} - \begin{matrix} \text{Equivalent Units} \\ \text{in Beginning} \\ \text{Inventory} \end{matrix}$$

$$= 5.0 + .6 - (3.0 \times 10\%)$$
$$= 5.3 \text{ Equivalent Units of Work Done.}$$

Step 3: Summarize Costs to Be Accounted For

This step merely records the costs in beginning work-in-process inventory and the costs incurred during the period, as Step 3 of Exhibit 4.11 shows.

Step 4: Compute Unit Costs for the Current Period

Exhibit 4.11 shows that the cost per equivalent unit produced this period is $150,000. Note that this cost represents work done during this period only; it does not include costs in beginning inventory. Davis would use this unit cost to evaluate performance in controlling costs, and it would provide information to management about the cost of

---

Exhibit 4.11

DAVIS CONTRACTORS
Production Cost Report Using FIFO
Second Quarter, April 1 through June 30

	(Step 1) Physical Units	(Step 2) Compute Equivalent Units (E.U.)
Accounting for Units:		
Units to Account For:		
Beginning Work-in-Process (WIP) Inventory	3	
Units Started This Period....................	4	
Total Units to Account For...............	7	
Units Accounted For:		
Units Completed and Transferred Out:		
From Beginning Inventory	3	2.7[a] (90%)[b]
Started and Completed, Currently	2	2.0
Units in Ending WIP Inventory	2	0.6 (30%)[c]
Total Units Accounted For...............	7	5.3

(continued)

	Total Costs	Unit Costs
Accounting for Costs:		
(Step 3) Costs to Be Accounted For:		
Costs in Beginning WIP Inventory	$ 42,000	
Current Period Costs	795,000	
Total Costs to Be Accounted For	$837,000	
(Step 4) Cost per Equivalent Unit of Work Done This Period:		
$795,000/5.3 E.U.	=	$150,000 per E.U.
(Step 5) Costs Accounted For:		
Costs Assigned to Units Transferred Out:		
Costs from Beginning WIP Inventory	$ 42,000	
Current Costs Added to Complete Beginning WIP Inventory:		
2.7 E.U. × $150,000	= 405,000	
Current Costs of Units Started and Completed:		
2.0 E.U. × $150,000	= 300,000	
Total Costs Transferred Out	$747,000	$149,400 per Unit (= $747,000/5 Units Transferred Out)
Costs Assigned to Ending WIP Inventory:		
0.6 E.U. × $150,000	= 90,000	$150,000
Total Costs Accounted For	$837,000	

[a]Equivalent units required to complete beginning inventory. For example, 90 percent of 3 units must be added to the beginning inventory to complete it. Therefore, 2.7 (= 90% × 3) equivalent units are required to complete beginning inventory.

[b]Percent required to complete beginning inventory.

[c]Stage of completion of ending inventory.

building houses that Davis can use to assess prices and the profitability of continuing to build this type of house.

Step 5: Compute the Cost of Goods Completed and Transferred Out of Work-in-Process and the Cost of Ending Work-in-Process Inventory Exhibit 4.11 shows the cost of units transferred out, including the $42,000 from beginning inventory and the cost of the goods still in ending inventory, which accounting assigns a cost of $150,000 per equivalent unit.

Exhibit 4.12

DAVIS CONTRACTORS
Cost Flow through T-Accounts (FIFO)
Second Quarter

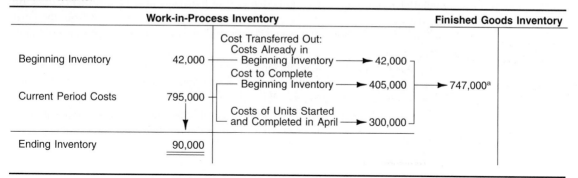

[a]Total costs transferred out of Work-in-Process Inventory

Flow of Costs through Accounts   Exhibit 4.12 presents the flow of costs through T-accounts.

Weighted-Average Method

The previous computations assumed FIFO, which means that accounting transferred out the cost of beginning inventory first and that the costs pertinent to ending inventory were the costs of goods produced during the current period.[4] If Davis used the weighted-average method instead of FIFO, accounting would assign the cost of goods transferred out and the cost of goods in ending inventory a weighted-average cost that considers both the current period cost and the beginning inventory cost. The weighted-average cost is $149,464 per unit, which equals the total costs Davis must account for, $837,000, divided by the total equivalent units, 5.6. The 5.6 equivalent units equal 5.3 equivalent units for the period plus .3 in beginning inventory. The 5.6 equivalent units also equal the 5.0 units transferred out plus .6 equivalent units in ending inventory. This result must be true because

$$BB + TI = TO + EB,$$

so

$$.3 + 5.3 = 5.0 + .6,$$

where TI is defined to be the equivalent units produced this period.

----

[4]This statement assumes that the firm completed the units in beginning WIP inventory during the period. If some of the units in beginning inventory were still in WIP inventory at the end of the period, the firm would carry some beginning inventory costs to the ending inventory.

Spoilage and Quality Production

Accounting typically includes the cost of normal waste in the cost of work done this period. If Davis Contractors incurs some normal wastage of lumber on a job, accounting would typically include that cost of materials in the cost of work done for the period. If the waste is not normal, accounting would remove it from the costs included in these computations and debit it to an account called "Abnormal Spoilage."

Companies concerned about quality production do not treat waste or spoiled goods as normal. Instead they remove waste and spoilage costs to avoid having waste costs buried in product costs. Some companies have been surprised to discover that, when they removed their waste and spoilage costs from other product costs, waste and spoilage costs were 20 to 30 percent of their total product costs.

Solutions to Self-Study Problems

Suggested Solution to Problem 4.1 for Self-Study

For each case, start with the formula:

$$BB + TI = TO + EB.$$

$$
\begin{aligned}
A: TI &= TO + EB - BB \\
&= \$61{,}000 + \$32{,}000 - \$40{,}000 \\
&= \$53{,}000.
\end{aligned}
$$

$$
\begin{aligned}
B: BB &= TO + EB - TI \\
&= \$11{,}000 + \$16{,}000 - \$8{,}000 \\
&= \$19{,}000.
\end{aligned}
$$

$$
\begin{aligned}
C: TO &= BB + TI - EB \\
&= \$35{,}000 + \$8{,}000 - \$27{,}000 \\
&= \$16{,}000.
\end{aligned}
$$

Suggested Solution to Problem 4.2 for Self-Study

a.
- Lawsuit—job.
- Diet cola—process.
- Emergency room care—job.
- House painting—job.
- Paint—process.

b.

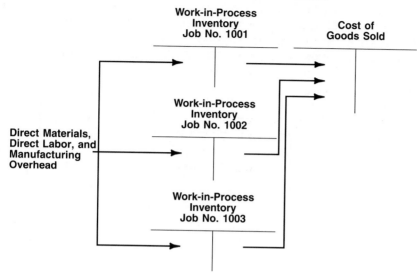

Job Costing
Student Painters

Work-in-Process
Inventory
Job No. 1001

Cost of
Goods Sold

Work-in-Process
Inventory
Job No. 1002

Direct Materials,
Direct Labor, and
Manufacturing
Overhead

Work-in-Process
Inventory
Job No. 1003

Suggested Solution to Problem 4.3 for Self-Study

a. **Traditional Costing**

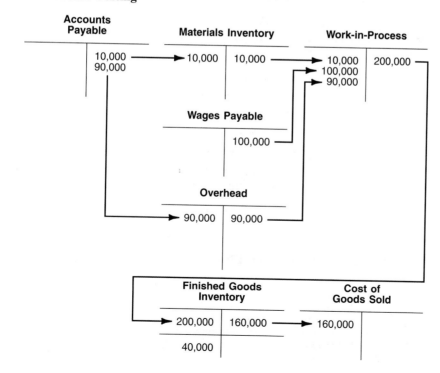

Accounts Payable		Materials Inventory			Work-in-Process	
	10,000	→ 10,000	10,000	→	10,000	200,000
	90,000			→	100,000	
				→	90,000	

Wages Payable	
	100,000

Overhead	
→ 90,000	90,000

Finished Goods Inventory		Cost of Goods Sold	
→ 200,000	160,000	→ 160,000	
40,000			

b. **Backflush Costing**

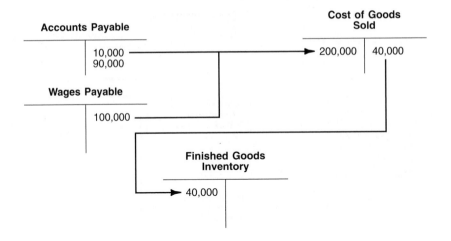

Suggested Solution to Problem 4.4 for Self-Study

a.

TOUCHE ANDERSEN & COMPANY
September

Accounts Receivable			Work in Process: Client A			Revenue	
(5a) 72,000		**(1)**	6,000	8,000 **(5b)**			72,000 **(5a)**
		(2)	2,000				

Wages and Accounts Payable			Work in Process: Client B			Cost of Services Billed	
	30,000 **(1)**	**(1)**	21,000	28,000 **(5b)**	**(5b)** 36,000	
		(2)	7,000			

Overhead				Direct Labor— Unbillable		
10,000 **(3)**	**(3)**	10,000	9,000 **(2)**	**(1)**	3,000	

		Marketing and Administrative Costs	
5,000 **(4)**		**(4)**	5,000

Entries: (1) Direct labor at $30 per hour. (2) Overhead as applied. (3) Actual overhead incurred. (4) Marketing and administrative costs. (5) Services billed.

b.

TOUCHE ANDERSEN & COMPANY
Income Statement for the Month Ended September 30

Revenue from Services	$72,000
Less Cost of Services Billed	36,000
Gross Margin	36,000
Less Other Costs:	
Direct Labor—Unbillable	3,000
Overhead	1,000[a]
Marketing and Administrative Costs	5,000
Operating Profit	$27,000

[a]Actual overhead $10,000 − $9,000 assigned to jobs.

Key Terms and Concepts

Cost flow equation

Jobs

Continuous flow processing

Operations

Operation costing

Job costing

Process costing

Just-in-time (JIT) methods

Backflush costing

Equivalent units (E.U.)

Questions, Exercises, Problems, and Cases

Questions

1. Review the meaning of the concepts or terms given above in Key Terms and Concepts.
2. Compare and contrast job costing and process costing systems.
3. Management of a company that manufactures small appliances is trying to decide whether to install a job or process costing system. The manufacturing vice president has stated that job costing gives the best control. The controller, however, has stated that job costing would require too much record keeping. What do you think of the manufacturing vice president's suggestion and why?
4. Why don't most service organizations have inventories (other than supplies)?
5. What is a production operation?
6. Why is operation costing called a hybrid costing method?
7. How does operation costing compare and contrast with job costing and process costing?
8. What types of savings can firms achieve with just-in-time methods compared to traditional production methods?

9. Explain the differences in accounting for the flow of costs using traditional accounting where accounting charges costs first to inventory accounts and using JIT.

10. What operating conditions of companies make just-in-time methods feasible?

11. Why must firms have reliable suppliers when using just-in-time methods?

12. Refer to the Managerial Application "Using the Basic Cost Flow Equation to Detect Fraud." How did the manager of the Gravins Division fraudulently increase profits? How was the fraud detected?

13. Refer to the discussion in the chapter about Hewlett-Packard's use of JIT ("Comparing JIT and Traditional Sequential Cost Flows at Hewlett-Packard"). What was the effect of JIT on the way accounting was done at Hewlett-Packard?

14. Refer to the discussion in the chapter about difficulties with JIT ("Just-in-Time Problems"). Why did JIT create a problem for GE Appliances and Saturn?

15. Given the experience with the Apache helicopters in the Persian Gulf War (discussed in "Just-in-Time Problems" in the chapter), should a military organization adopt JIT? (Imagine, if you will, a JIT war.)

16. Name three companies not mentioned in the text that make products using processes.

17. Name three companies not mentioned in the text that produce jobs.

Exercises

Solutions to even-numbered exercises are at the end of this chapter after the cases.

18. **Cost flow model.** Horace Zontal is trying to compute unknown values in inventory accounts in three of his department stores. Knowing of your expertise in cost flows, he asks for your help and provides you with the following information about each store:

	Store		
	Downtown	**Crossroads Mall**	**Northgate Mall**
Beginning inventory	$ 30,000	?	?
Transfers in to inventory accounts.	100,000	$200,000	$160,000
Transfers out of inventory accounts	110,000	180,000	150,000
Ending inventory	?	60,000	40,000

Tell Horace what the missing values are for each of his stores.

19. **Cost flow model.** A fire has destroyed the inventory of the Pyro Company. Before paying for damages, the Maniac Insurance Company wants to know the amount of ending inventory that is missing. You have been hired to dig through the ashes and find as much information as you can. You find the following information about four of Pyro's big-selling inventory items:

	Product			
	Hula Hoops	Motorized Skateboards	Dog-resistant Frisbees	Body-length T-shirts
Beginning inventory	$10,000	$ 40,000	$20,000	?
Transfers into inventory accounts	80,000	160,000	40,000	$60,000
Transfers out of inventory accounts	30,000	180,000	?	60,000
Ending inventory	?	?	?	?

Compute the ending inventory, which is the amount destroyed by the fire, for any of the products that you can. You may not be able to compute ending inventory for all products. If you cannot compute the ending inventory, state what additional information you need.

20. **Cost flow model.** A flood has destroyed the inventory of the Colorado Flash Company. Before paying for damages, the Just-Say-No Insurance Company wants to know the amount of ending inventory that is missing. You have been hired to search through the water-sodden mess to find as much information as you can. You find the following information about four of Colorado Flash's big-selling inventory items:

	Item			
	Rubber Rafts	Rubber Duckies	Galoshes	Diving Equipment
Beginning inventory	$20,000	$10,000	?	$40,000
Transfers into inventory accounts	80,000	30,000	$40,000	60,000
Transfers out of inventory accounts	90,000	25,000	50,000	80,000
Ending inventory	?	?	?	?

Compute the ending inventory, which is the amount destroyed by the flood, for any of the products that you can. You may not be able to compute ending inventory for all products. If you cannot compute the ending inventory, state what additional information you need.

21. **Cost flow model.** The law firm of Dewey, Cheathem & Howe has asked your help in computing damages in a lawsuit. The law firm's client claims an employee has stolen merchandise and is suspicious because this employee has just opened a discount electronics store. The law firm provides you with the following information from the accounting records:

	Product		
	Video-Cassette Recorders	Televisions	Compact-Disc Players
Beginning inventory	$40,000	$ 40,000	$30,000
Transfers into inventory accounts	80,000	100,000	40,000
Transfers out of inventory accounts from sales	70,000	110,000	50,000
Ending inventory	?	?	?

You physically counted the ending inventory and found it to be as follows: video-cassette recorders, $40,000; televisions, $10,000; and compact-disc players, $20,000. Compute the ending inventory according to the accounting records and compare it to the physical count. What discrepancy between the physical count and the accounting records could be attributed to the theft, if any?

22. **Cost flow model.** Kaasa, Rah & Associates, an auditing firm, is reconstructing the records of a client called Chips 'R Us, which is concerned that some of its inventory is missing. The accounting records provide the following information about Chips' inventories:

	Product		
	Computer Chips	Potato Chips	Poker Chips
Beginning inventory	$100,000	$ 40,000	$ 10,000
Transfers into inventory accounts	400,000	300,000	100,000
Transfers out of inventory accounts from sales	450,000	280,000	105,000
Ending inventory	?	?	?

You physically counted the ending inventory and found it to be as follows: computer chips, $50,000; potato chips, $20,000; and poker chips, $5,000. Compute the ending inventory according to the accounting records and compare it to the physical count. What discrepancy do you find between the physical count and the accounting records, if any?

23. **Just-in-time methods.** Lafayette Products uses a just-in-time system. To produce 2,000 units for an order, it purchased and used materials costing $25,000, and incurred other manufacturing costs of $15,000, of which $5,000 was labor. All costs were on account.

After Lafayette Products completed production of the 2,000 units and shipped 1,600 units, management needed the Finished Goods Inventory balance for the 400 units remaining in inventory for financial statement preparation. The firm incurred costs evenly across all products.

Show the flow of costs using journal entries and T-accounts using backflush costing.

24. **Just-in-time methods.** Austin Tech uses just-in-time production methods. To produce 1,200 units for an order, Austin purchased and used materials costing $10,000 and incurred other manufacturing costs of $11,000, of which $4,000 was labor. All costs were on account.

After Austin completed production and shipped 1,000 units, management needed the Finished Goods Inventory balance for the 200 units and $3,500 remaining in inventory for financial statement preparation.

Prepare journal entries and T-accounts for these transactions using backflush costing.

25. **Job costs in a service organization.** Nunez and Associates, a CPA firm, uses job costing. During April, the firm provided audit services for two clients and

billed those clients for the services performed. O'Brien Construction was billed for 2,000 hours at $100 per hour and Alamos Electronics was billed for 1,000 hours at $100 per hour. Direct labor costs were $60 per hour. Of the 3,200 hours worked in April, 200 hours were not billable. The firm assigns overhead to jobs at the rate of $20 per billable hour. During April, the firm incurred actual overhead of $70,000. The firm incurred marketing and administrative costs of $20,000. All transactions were on account.

a. Show how Nunez and Associates' accounting system would record these revenues and costs using journal entries.

b. Prepare an income statement for April.

26. **Job costs in a service organization.** Ads Unlimited, an advertising firm, uses job costing. During July, the firm provided advertising services for two clients and billed those clients for the services performed. MacLean River Soda was billed for $150,000 and Depardieu Productions was billed for $100,000. Direct labor costs were $80 per hour. Ads Unlimited worked 1,200 hours on the MacLean River Soda account and 900 hours on the Depardieu Productions account. The firm worked an additional 100 hours that it did not charge to either account. The firm assigns overhead to jobs at the rate of $30 per billable hour. During April, the firm incurred actual overhead of $70,000. The firm incurred marketing and administrative costs of $30,000. All transactions were on account.

a. Show how Ads Unlimited's accounting system would record these revenues and costs using journal entries.

b. Prepare an income statement for July.

27. **Job costs in a service organization.** Asymptotic Architects uses job costing. During September, the firm provided architect services for three clients and billed those clients for the services performed. Cadillac Construction was billed for 600 hours, Green Earth Homes was billed for 200 hours, Jane Fond-of-Turner was billed for 100 hours, all at $100 per hour. Direct labor costs were $50 per hour. Of the 1,000 hours worked in September, 100 hours were not billable. The firm assigns overhead to jobs at the rate of $30 per billable hour. During September, the firm incurred actual overhead of $40,000. The firm incurred marketing and administrative costs of $20,000. All transactions were on account.

a. Show how these revenues and costs would appear in T-accounts.

b. Prepare an income statement for September.

28. **Job costs in a service organization.** Creative Designs, a landscaping firm, uses job costing. During June, the firm provided landscaping services for two clients and billed those clients for the services performed. The city of Chicago was billed for $100,000 and Payfast Insurance was billed for $200,000. Direct labor costs were $50 per hour. Creative Designs worked 1,200 hours on the city of Chicago job, and 2,000 hours on the Payfast job. The firm could not charge 300 hours to either job. The firm assigns overhead to jobs at the rate of $20 per billable hour. During June, the firm incurred actual overhead of $70,000. The firm incurred marketing and administrative costs of $20,000. All transactions were on account.

a. Show the flow of these revenues and costs through T-accounts.

b. Prepare an income statement for June.

29. **Computing equivalent units** (Appendix 4.1). The Assembly Department had 30,000 units 60-percent complete in Work-in-Process Inventory at the beginning of May. During May, the department started and completed 80,000 units. The department started another 20,000 units and completed 30 percent as of the end of May. Compute the equivalent whole units of work performed during May using FIFO. Assume the department incurred production costs evenly throughout processing.

30. **Computing product costs with incomplete products** (Appendix 4.1). Refer to the data in Exercise 29. Assume that the cost assigned to beginning inventory on May 1 was $40,000 and that the department incurred $245,000 of production costs during May. Prepare a production cost report like the one shown in Exhibit 4.11.

Problems

31. **Job costing for the movies.** Movies and television shows are jobs. Some are successful, some are not. Studios must decide what to do with the cost of unsuccessful shows (''flops''). Some studios have been criticized for assigning the cost of flops to successful shows, which in turn reduces profits available under profit-sharing agreements with actors, actresses, directors, and others associated with the successful show.

    Studios point out that flops have to be paid for out of the profits from successful shows. For example, Orion Pictures, maker of the Academy Award-winning *Dances with Wolves,* was criticized for carrying the cost of flops in inventory, instead of writing them off, thereby overstating assets and overstating profits.

    a. How does carrying ''flops'' in inventory overstate assets and profits?
    b. When do you think the cost of a movie that turns out to be a flop should be written off (that is, expensed)?

32. **Comparing job costs to management's expectations.** Spoljaric Construction Company uses a job costing system. It applies overhead to jobs at a rate of 55 percent of direct labor cost.

    At August 1, the balance in the Work-in-Process Inventory account was $34,524. It had the following jobs in process at August 1:

Job No.	Materials	Direct Labor	Overhead	Total
478 (irrigation project)	$ 5,100	$ 9,620	$4,810	$19,530
479 (parking lot construction)	3,470	3,960	1,980	9,410
480 (street repair)........	4,120	976	488	5,584
Total.................	$12,690	$14,556	$7,278	$34,524

Selected transactions for the month of August follow:
(1) Materials issued: Job 480, $449; Job 481, $3,500; Job 482, $2,100; indirect materials, $390; total, $6,439.

(2) It assigned labor costs as follows: Job 478, $331; Job 479, $2,651; Job 480, $7,800; Job 481, $5,891; Job 482, $1,720; indirect labor, $853; total, $19,246.

(3) It applies overhead for the month to jobs using an overhead rate of 55 percent of direct labor costs.

(4) It completed Jobs 478 and 479 in August.

Management of Spoljaric Construction Company is concerned that costs are higher than anticipated. Management had expected the cost of completed jobs to be as follows:

Job 478 $20,000, when complete.
Job 479 $13,000, when complete.
Job 480 $15,000, as of August 31.
Job 481 $10,000 as of August 31.
Job 482 $4,000 as of August 31.

Compare the actual job costs to management's expected costs, and report your results.

33. **Analyzing costs in a job company.** On June 1, Springs Landscaping Company had two jobs in process with the following costs:

	Direct Materials	Direct Labor
Monument Valley	$500	$2,000
Arches	400	1,600

In addition, overhead is applied to these jobs at the rate of 150 percent of direct labor costs.

On June 1, Springs had materials inventory (for example plants and shrubs) totaling $1,000. During June, Springs purchased $2,000 of materials and had none left in materials inventory at the end of the month. (However, Springs had some materials in work-in-process inventory at the end of the month.)

During June, Springs completed both the Monument Valley and Arches jobs and recorded them as cost of goods sold. The Monument Valley job required no more materials in June, but it did require $600 of direct labor to complete. The Arches job required $200 in indirect materials and $1,000 of direct labor to complete.

Springs started a new job, Mesa Verde, during June and put $800 of direct labor costs into this job. Unfortunately, Springs lost the records of materials used on this job but knows all of the materials available in June went into either Arches or Mesa Verde. The Mesa Verde job is still in work-in-process inventory at the end of the month.

Springs needs to know the total cost of the Monument Valley and Arches jobs, and the cost to date for the Mesa Verde job, for billing purposes. (Otherwise, all the little Springs at home will go hungry in July.) Please provide the cost of direct materials, direct labor, and overhead (at 150 percent of direct labor cost) for the three jobs.

34. **Compare just-in-time to a traditional accounting system.** Illinois Precision Instruments produces heat measurement meters. The company received an order for 8,000 meters. The company purchased and used $240,000 of materials—purchased on account—for this order. The company incurred labor costs of $100,000 and other nonlabor manufacturing costs of $400,000.

    The accounting period ended before the company completed the order. The firm had 5 percent of the materials costs incurred still in Materials Inventory, 10 percent of the total costs incurred still in Work-in-Process Inventory, and 20 percent of the total costs incurred still in Finished Goods Inventory.
    a. Use T-accounts to show the flow of costs using backflush costing.
    b. Use T-accounts to show the flow of costs using a traditional costing system.

35. **Compare just-in-time to a traditional accounting system.** Vanessa's Video Productions received an order for 10,000 units. The company purchased and used $2,000,000 of materials—purchased on account—for this order. The company incurred labor costs of $900,000 and other nonlabor manufacturing costs of $1,500,000.

    The accounting period ended before the company completed the order. The firm had 10 percent of the materials costs incurred still in Materials Inventory, 5 percent of the total costs incurred still in Work-in-Process Inventory, and 20 percent of the total costs incurred still in Finished Goods Inventory.
    a. Use T-accounts to show the flow of costs using backflush costing.
    b. Use T-accounts to show the flow of costs using a traditional costing system.

36. **Computing equivalent units and cost flows under process costing** (Appendix 4.1). Denver Products Company has a process cost accounting system. Denver incurred material, direct labor, and manufacturing overhead costs evenly during processing. On September 1, the firm had 20,000 units in process, 40-percent complete, with the following accumulated costs:

Material	$78,000
Direct Labor	40,000
Manufacturing Overhead	30,000

During September, Denver started 110,000 units in process and incurred the following costs:

Material	$622,000
Direct Labor	490,000
Manufacturing Overhead	367,500

During September, Denver completed 90,000 units. The units in ending inventory were, on average, 40 percent complete.

Prepare a production cost report such as the one in Exhibit 4.11 using FIFO.

37. **Equivalent units—solving for unknowns** (Appendix 4.1). For each of the following independent cases, calculate the information requested, using FIFO costing.

a. Beginning inventory amounted to 1,000 units. The firm started and completed 4,500 units during this period. At the end of the period, the firm had 3,000 units in inventory that were 30 percent complete. Using FIFO costing, the equivalent production for the period was 5,600 units. What was the percentage of completion of the beginning inventory?

b. The ending inventory included $8,700 for conversion costs. During the period, the firm required 4,200 equivalent units to complete the beginning inventory and started and completed 6,000 units. The ending inventory represented 1,000 equivalent units of work this period. What was the total conversion cost incurred during this period?

Cases

38. **Completing missing data.** After a dispute concerning wages, Ernest Arson tossed an incendiary device into the Flash Company's record vault. Within moments, only a few readable charred fragments remained from the company's factory ledger, as follows:

Direct Materials Inventory		Manufacturing Overhead	
Bal. 4/1 12,000		Actual Costs for April 14,800	

Work-in-Process Inventory		Accounts Payable	
Bal. 4/1 4,500			Bal. 4/30 8,000

Finished Goods Inventory		Cost of Goods Sold	
Bal. 4/30 16,000			

Sifting through the ashes and interviewing selected employees generated the following additional information:

(1) The controller remembers clearly that the firm based the predetermined overhead rate on an estimated 60,000 direct labor hours to be worked over the year and an estimated $180,000 in manufacturing overhead costs.

(2) The production superintendent's cost sheets showed only one job in process on April 30. The firm had added materials of $2,600 to the job and expended 300 direct labor hours at $6 per hour.

(3) The accounts payable are for direct materials purchases only, according to the accounts payable clerk. He clearly remembers that the balance in the account was $6,000 on April 1. An analysis of canceled checks (kept

in the treasurer's office) shows that Flash made payments of $40,000 to suppliers during the month.

(4) A charred piece of the payroll ledger shows that the firm recorded 5,200 direct labor hours for the month. The employment department has verified that pay rates did not vary among employees (this infuriated Ernest, who thought that Flash underpaid him).

(5) Records maintained in the finished goods warehouse indicate that the finished goods inventory totaled $11,000 on April 1.

(6) From another charred piece in the vault you discern that the cost of goods manufactured (that is, finished) for April was $89,000.

Determine the following amounts:

a. Work-in-process inventory, April 30.
b. Direct materials purchased during April.
c. Overhead applied to work in process.
d. Cost of goods sold for April.
e. Over- or underapplied overhead for April.
f. Direct materials usage during April.
g. Direct materials inventory, April 30.

39. **Midwest Insurance Company: evaluating cost systems used in financial services companies.** John Frank, controller of Midwest Insurance Company, recently returned from a management education program where he talked to Peter Montgomery, his counterpart at Northern Insurance Company. Both companies had mortgage departments, but whereas Midwest gave loans only to businesses, Northern gave only home mortgage loans.

Peter Montgomery had described the use of standard costs at Northern as follows:

We have collected data over several years that give us a pretty good idea how much each batch of loans costs to process. We receive loans in three main categories: (1) FHA and VA mortgages, (2) conventional home mortgages, and (3) development loans. Banks and other financial institutions make these loans initially and banks then package the loans and offer them to us as a package. The Mortgage Division establishes terms for ascertaining whether we accept the mortgage and for legal work on the loan. We assume that each loan in a category costs about the same. To calculate how much processing loans costs, we periodically have people in the Mortgage Division keep track of their time on each package of loans. Our overhead is about 130 percent of direct labor costs, so we assign overhead accordingly to each package of loans. We don't keep track of the actual costs of processing each package of loans. What we lose in knowing the actual cost of processing each package of loans, we make up by saving clerical costs that we would incur to keep track of the time spent on each package of loans.

A cost statement for a recent month appears in Exhibit 4.13.

Montgomery's comment about saving clerical costs struck a respondent chord with John Frank. Midwest's accounting costs had reached alarming levels, according to the company president, and Frank was looking for ways to reduce costs. Midwest kept track of the following costs for each loan: labor; telephone costs; travel; and outside services, such as appraisals, legal fees, and

Exhibit 4.13

Northern Insurance Company
Mortgage Division
Loan Processing Costs
Month of October

Category of Loans	Labor	Overhead	Number of Loan Packages Processed
Standard Costs			
FHA and VA	$ 4,200	$ 5,460	14
Conventional	31,160	40,508	82
Development	20,440	26,572	73
Total	$55,800	$72,540	
Actual Costs	$58,172	$74,626	
Variance	$ 2,372	$ 2,086	
	Unfavorable	Unfavorable	

the cost of consultants. The costs of processing these loans often amounted to several thousand dollars. A sample of these loans and their processing costs appear in Exhibit 4.14.

When Frank told the Mortgage Division manager about the methods Northern used, the manager responded: ''That sounds fine for them because each package of loans in a category has about the same processing costs. The processing costs of each loan in our company vary considerably. I believe it would be invalid to establish standards for our loans.''

Frank thought the Mortgage Division manager's comments were reasonable, but he wanted to find some way to save clerical costs by not recording the costs of processing each loan. At the same time, he knew the firm would

Exhibit 4.14

Midwest Insurance Company
Mortgage Division
Loan Processing Costs
Month of July

Loan No.	Labor	Telephone	Travel	Outside Services		
				Appraisal	Legal	Other
A48-10136	$ 1,184	$ 113	$ 415	$ 1,500	—	—
A48-11237	3,631	42	—	2,300	—	—
B42-19361	814	78	—	—	$1,500	$ 150
C39-21341	4,191	240	110	—	2,200	—
•	•	•	•	•	•	•
•	•	•	•	•	•	•
•	•	•	•	•	•	•
Total	$47,291	$4,843	$2,739	$11,800	$9,950	$1,470

potentially benefit from having a standard against which to compare actual costs.

a. What would you advise Mr. Frank to do? Compare the advantages and disadvantages of the system each company uses.

b. Diagram the flow of costs for each company using the data available in Exhibits 4.13 and 4.14. Treat each loan or category of loans as a separate product in your diagram.

40. **Comprehensive job costing problem with equivalent units** (adapted from CPA exam). The Custer Corporation, which uses a job costing system, produces various plastic parts for the aircraft industry. On October 9, Year 4, Custer started production on Job No. 487 for 100 front bubbles (windshields) for commercial helicopters.

Production of the bubbles begins in the fabricating department, where fabricators melt down sheets of plastic (purchased as raw material) and pour the liquid into molds. The employees then place the molds in a special temperature and humidity room to harden the plastic. The fabricators remove the hardened plastic bubbles from the molds and handwork them to remove imperfections.

After fabrication, employees transfer the bubbles to the testing department, where each bubble must meet rigid specifications. Custer scraps bubbles that fail the tests with no salvage value.

Employees transfer bubbles that pass the tests to the assembly department, where other employees insert them into metal frames. The frames, purchased from vendors, require no work before installing the bubbles.

The assembly department then transfers the assembled unit to the shipping department for crating and shipment. Crating material is relatively expensive, and employees do most of the work by hand.

Management has the following information concerning Job No. 487 as of December 31, Year 4 (the information is correct as stated):

(1)   Direct materials charged to the job:

    (a)   Accounting charged 1,000 square feet of plastic at $12.75 per square foot to the fabricating department. This amount was to meet all plastic material requirements of the job at 10 square feet per bubble, assuming no spoilage.

    (b)   Accounting charged 74 metal frames at $408.52 each to the assembly department.

    (c)   Accounting charged packing material for 40 units at $75 per unit to the shipping department.

(2)   Direct labor charges through December 31 follow:

	Total	Per Unit
Fabricating Department	$1,424	$16
Testing Department	444	6
Assembly Department..............................	612	12
Shipping Department..............................	256	8
	$2,736	

(3) Differences between actual and applied manufacturing overhead for the year ended December 31, Year 4, were immaterial. Accounting charges manufacturing overhead to the four production departments by various allocation methods, all of which you approve.

Accounting allocates manufacturing overhead charged to the fabricating department to jobs based on heat-room hours; the other production departments allocate manufacturing overhead to jobs on the basis of direct labor dollars charged to each job within the department. The following reflects the manufacturing overhead rates for the year ended December 31, Year 4.

	Rate per Unit
Fabricating Department	$.45 per Hour
Testing Department	.68 per Direct Labor Dollar
Assembly Department.......................	.38 per Direct Labor Dollar
Shipping Department.......................	.25 per Direct Labor Dollar

(4) Job No. 487 used 855 heat-room hours during the year ended December 31.

(5) Following is a schedule of equivalent units in production by department for Job No. 487 as of December 31.

CUSTER CORPORATION
Schedule of Physical Activity in Production for Job No. 487
December 31

		Fabricating Department		
	Plastic (sq. ft.)	Bubbles (units)		
		Materials	Labor	Overhead
Transferred In from Direct Materials Inventory	1,000	—	—	—
Production to Date..............	(950)[a]	95[a]	89	95
Transferred Out to Other Departments	—	(83)	(83)	(83)
Spoilage......................	—	—	—	—
Balance at December 31	50	12	6	12

	Testing Department (units)		
	Bubbles		
	Transferred In	Labor	Overhead
Transferred In from Other Departments ..	83	—	—
Production to Date....................	—	74	74
Transferred Out to Other Departments ...	(61)	(61)	(61)
Spoilage............................	(15)	(6)	(6)
Balance at December 31	7	7	7

(continued)

	Assembly Department (units)			
	Transferred In	**Frames**	**Labor**	**Overhead**
Transferred In from Direct Materials Inventory	—	74	—	—
Transferred In from Other Departments	61	—	—	—
Production to Date.........	—	—	51	51
Transferred Out to Other Departments	(43)	(43)	(43)	(43)
Balance at December 31 ...	18	31	8	8

	Shipping Department (units)			
	Transferred In	**Packing Material**	**Labor**	**Overhead**
Transferred In from Direct Materials Inventory	—	40	—	—
Transferred In from Other Departments	43	—	—	—
Production to Date.........	—	—	32	32
Shipped	(23)	(23)	(23)	(23)
Spoilage.................	(1)	(1)	(1)	(1)
Balance at December 31 ...	19	16	8	8

[a]Custer produced 95 equivalent units requiring 950 square feet of plastic.

Prepare a schedule for Job No. 487 of ending inventory costs for work in process by department, and for cost of goods shipped. The firm charges all spoilage costs to cost of goods shipped.

Suggested Solutions to Even-Numbered Exercises

18. Cost flow model.

$$BB + TI = TO + EB.$$

Downtown: $30,000 + \$100,000 = \$110,000 + EB$

$EB = \$30,000 + \$100,000 - \$110,000$

$EB = \$20,000.$

Crossroads: $BB + \$200,000 = \$180,000 + \$60,000$

$BB = \$180,000 + \$60,000 - \$200,000$

$BB = \$40,000.$

Northgate: $BB + \$160,000 = \$150,000 + \$40,000$

$BB = \$150,000 + \$40,000 - \$160,000$

$BB = \$30,000.$

20. Cost flow model.

$$BB + TI = TO + EB.$$

Rubber rafts: $20,000 + $80,000 = $90,000 + EB
$$EB = $20,000 + $80,000 - $90,000$$
$$EB = $10,000.$$

Rubber duckies: $10,000 + $30,000 = $25,000 + EB
$$EB = $10,000 + $30,000 - $25,000$$
$$EB = $15,000.$$

Galoshes: Cannot compute because we do not have the beginning inventory amount.

Diving equipment: $40,000 + $60,000 = $80,000 + EB
$$EB = $40,000 + $60,000 - $80,000$$
$$EB = $20,000.$$

22. Cost flow model. Using the cost flow equation, $BB + TI = TO + EB$, to find what the ending inventory should be per the records:

Computer chips: $100,000 + $400,000 = $450,000 + EB
$$EB = $100,000 + $400,000 - $450,000$$
$$EB = $50,000.$$

No discrepancy between the records and the physical count.

Potato chips: $40,000 + $300,000 = $280,000 + EB
$$EB = $40,000 + $300,000 - $280,000$$
$$EB = $60,000.$$

There appears to be a $40,000 (= $60,000 - $20,000 physical count) discrepancy between records and actual chips in inventory.

Poker chips: $10,000 + $100,000 = $105,000 + EB
$$EB = $10,000 + $100,000 - $105,000$$
$$EB = $5,000.$$

No discrepancy in poker chips.

24. Just-in-time methods.

Journal Entries:

(1) Cost of Goods Sold	21,000	
Accounts Payable—Materials		10,000
Accounts Payable—Other Manufacturing Costs		7,000
Wages Payable		4,000
To record costs of production.		
(2) Finished Goods Inventory	3,500	
Cost of Goods Sold		3,500
To record inventory.		

T-accounts:

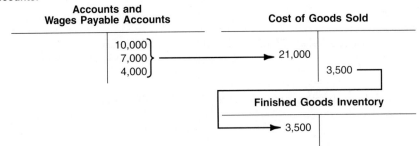

Accounts and Wages Payable Accounts / Cost of Goods Sold:
- 10,000
- 7,000
- 4,000
→ 21,000
- 3,500

Finished Goods Inventory → 3,500

26. Job costs in a service organization.

a. Journal entries

(1)	Work in Process: MacLean River Soda..........	96,000	
	Work in Process: Depardieu Productions	72,000	
	Direct Labor—Unbillable	8,000	
	Wages Payable		176,000
(2)	Work in Process: MacLean River Soda..........	36,000	
	Work in Process: Depardieu Productions	27,000	
	Overhead (applied).........................		63,000
(3)	Overhead	70,000	
	Wages and Accounts Payable		70,000
(4)	Marketing and Administrative Costs	30,000	
	Wages and Accounts Payable		30,000
(5a)	Accounts Receivable	250,000	
	Revenue		250,000
(5b)	Cost of Services Billed	231,000	
	Work in Process: MacLean River Soda........		132,000
	Work in Process: Depardieu Productions		99,000

b. Income statement.

ADS UNLIMITED
Income Statement
For the month ending July 31

Revenue from services......................................	$ 250,000
Less Cost of Services Billed	231,000
Gross margin	19,000
Less:	
Direct Labor—Unbillable	8,000
Overhead...	7,000[a]
Marketing and Administrative	30,000
Operating Profit (Loss)	$(26,000)

[a]$7,000 = $70,000 actual overhead incurred − $63,000 applied to jobs and expensed as part of the cost of services billed.

28. Job costs in a service organization.

a.

Wages and Accounts Payable		Work in Process: City of Chicago		Cost of Services Billed	
	175,000 (1)	(1) 60,000		(5b) 224,000	
	70,000 (3)		84,000 (5b)		
	20,000 (4)	(2) 24,000			

Overhead		Work in Process: Payfast Insurance		Marketing and Admin. Costs	
(3) 70,000	64,000 (2)	(1) 100,000		(4) 20,000	
			140,000 (5b)		
		(2) 40,000			

Accounts Receivable		Direct Labor—Unbillable		Revenues	
(5a) 300,000		(1) 15,000			300,000 (5a)

Entries:

(1) Labor costs at $50 per hour.
(2) Overhead at $20 per billable hour.
(3) Overhead actually incurred in June.
(4) Marketing and administrative costs.
(5) Services billed.

b. Income statement.

CREATIVE DESIGNS
Income Statement
For the month ending June 30

Revenue from Services	$300,000
Less Cost of Services Billed	224,000
Gross margin	76,000
Less:	
Direct Labor—Unbillable	15,000
Overhead..	6,000[a]
Marketing and Administrative	20,000
Operating Profit	$ 35,000

[a]$6,000 = $70,000 actual overhead incurred − $64,000 applied to jobs and expensed as part of the cost of services billed.

30. Computing product costs with incomplete products (Appendix 4.1).

	Physical Units	% Completed During Period	Equivalent Units
Units to account for:			
Beginning WIP	30,000	40	12,000
Started and Completed........	80,000	100	80,000
Ending WIP	20,000	30	6,000
Total	130,000		98,000

Costs to be accounted for:			
Beginning WIP	$ 40,000		
Current Period Costs ..	245,000		
Total costs to be accounted for	$285,000		
			Cost per Unit $2.50 per E.U.
Cost per E.U. done this period	$245,000 ÷ 98,000 E.U.		
Costs assigned to units transferred out:			
Costs from Beginning WIP.....................		$ 40,000	
Current costs added to complete beginning WIP ($2.50 × 12,000 E.U.)		30,000	
Current costs of units started & completed ($2.50 × 80,000)		200,000	
Total costs transferred out		$270,000	$2.45[a]
Costs assigned to Ending WIP: ($2.50 × 6,000 E.U.)		$ 15,000	
Total costs accounted for:		$285,000	

[a]$270,000 ÷ (30,000 units + 80,000 units).

Chapter 5

Cost Allocation

Learning Objectives

1. Understand the nature of common or indirect costs.
2. Know why companies allocate common costs to departments and products.
3. Allocate service department costs to production departments.
4. Allocate costs from production departments to the products they produce.
5. Know the net realizable value and physical units methods for allocating joint costs.
6. Understand the nature of by-products.
7. (Appendix 5.1) Allocate service department costs using the reciprocal method.

This chapter discusses concepts and methods of assigning indirect costs like overhead to departments. We call such cost assignment *cost allocation.*

The Nature of Common Costs

Accounting distinguishes between a **direct cost** and a **common cost.** (We also call common costs *indirect costs.*) A direct cost is one that firms can identify specifically with, or trace directly to, a particular product, department, or process. For example, direct materials and direct labor costs are direct with respect to products manufactured. A department manager's salary is a direct cost of the department, but common to the units the department produces.

A common or indirect cost, in contrast, results from the joint use of a facility or a service by several products, departments, or processes. For example, the cost of running a freight train for Union Pacific is common to the many cars on the train.

The cost of grounds keeping at a university is common to its various schools and colleges. Many costs are common to different products manufactured. To develop product cost information, firms must allocate these common costs. Examples include the following:

1. Firms allocate the costs of operating service departments (for example, computer services, maintenance department) to production departments for several purposes, discussed later in the chapter. We call this practice **service department cost allocation.**
2. Accounting allocates the costs incurred in a manufacturing process that jointly produces several different products simultaneously (for example, various wood products obtained from logs) to each of the products for inventory valuation. We call this practice **joint cost allocation.**

These examples illustrate the extent to which common cost allocations pervade accounting reports, both internal and external. To understand accounting reports and make appropriate interpretations, you must be familiar with the alternative allocation methods used and their effects on the resulting reports.

Purposes of Common Cost Allocations

Allocations in Contract Disputes

Example Two companies entered into a partnership and agreed to split the costs fifty-fifty. The partnership was to reimburse each partner for that partner's own costs and to give each partner an equal share of the profits. The first partner submitted an itemized list of costs chargeable to the partnership that included an allocation of $500,000 for his corporate headquarters' costs. The second partner argued that the first partner should not charge these costs to the partnership. The first partner asserted that without corporate headquarters, his company would not exist and, hence, they needed the costs of the headquarters for the operation of the partnership.

Should the partnership pay for a share of one partner's headquarters' costs? If so, what method should the partnership use to allocate those costs? Settling disputes such as these is seldom simple or straightforward. Indeed, the settlement process may involve costly litigation.

Cost Accounting Standards Board Sometimes companies in the defense industry contract with the U.S. government on a cost-plus-profit basis. These contracts require the companies to allocate costs between government and commercial work. A particular company may need further allocations among several contracts. Cost disputes are frequent enough that the Cost Accounting Standards Board (CASB) was formed in 1971 to establish standards for cost allocation to government contracts.

Misleading Cost Allocations

Example   Diversified Industries, Inc., is organized into 40 autonomous operating divisions. Corporate management uses the divisional rate of return on investment for evaluating the performance of the division managers. In calculating divisional net income, the accountants deduct an allocated share of central corporate expenses. The firm allocates expenses to divisions based on divisional sales. Division B increased its sales by 25 percent during the current year. Because of an increase in total central corporate expenses and an increase in the relative share of these expenses allocated to Division B, the 25-percent increase in sales resulted in only a 5-percent increase in Division B's operating profits.

Including a share of central corporate expenses in Division B's performance report can give a misleading picture of its operations. Allocation of these costs based on sales could lead division managers to reduce sales efforts, to the detriment of the company as a whole.

The message of this section should be fairly clear. Management must carefully interpret accounting data that include common cost allocations.

Use of Cost Allocation for Managerial Purposes

A firm may use full product costs, including indirect costs allocated to the product, for pricing and planning decisions. Such questions as, "Will the price received for product A cover all of its costs in the long run?" require knowledge of full product costs, including indirect costs allocated to the product. We discuss other managerial reasons for allocating indirect costs in the following sections.

Charging the Cost of Service Departments to Users   Virtually every organization has departments whose main job is to service other departments. These departments include the laundry in a hospital, the media services center in a university, maintenance in a factory, security in a retail store, and so forth. Because the firm does not sell the output of these departments to customers outside the organization, it must cover their costs by the contribution margins of revenue-generating departments. Thus organizations often allocate the costs of departments that do not generate revenue (which we call **service departments**) to revenue-generating departments as an attention-getting device. The allocation makes managers of user departments aware that just covering their own department's costs is not enough for the organization as a whole to break even or make a profit. The firm must cover indirect costs as well.

Example   Memorial Hospital did not allocate the costs of its computer department to user departments. In 1993, top management noted that computer department costs exceeded the costs in 1985 by 400 percent. Although top management acknowledged an increasing need for computer services, an increase of this magnitude far exceeded expectations. Top management learned upon investigation that the accounting department did not charge user departments for using the computer or computer department staff, so users treated the computer and computer staff as if they were free.

To deal with this problem, Memorial Hospital started allocating computer department costs to user departments using a rate per unit of the computer's time and space and a rate per unit of computer personnel time. As a result, user departments reduced their demand for the computer and related services to essential uses only. When computer personnel assisted a user department, the user department's manager monitored the computer personnel's work habits to avoid being charged for time inefficiently spent.

Preventing Users from Treating Services as Free   The previous example demonstrates how cost allocation gives users incentives to control the costs of services. In theory, the user should use a service as long as the marginal benefit of a unit of service exceeds its marginal cost. Thus the firm should charge the cost of supplying a unit of service to the user to induce the user to make the correct (economic) decision about how much of the service to use.

Cost allocation also encourages interdepartment monitoring. If the firm allocates the costs of a service department to user departments, managers of user departments have incentives to monitor the service department's costs. Presumably, the more efficient the service department is, the lower the costs that it will pass on to the user departments.

Problems with Allocating Fixed Service Department Costs

The allocation of fixed costs can have unintended effects, as the following example demonstrates.

Example[1]   The top administrators of California University observed that faculty and staff used the university's WATS (Wide Area Telephone Service) so much that the lines were seldom free during the day. WATS allowed the university unlimited toll-free service within the United States. The fixed cost of WATS was $10,000 per month; variable cost per call was zero.

The top administrators learned that the average usage was 50,000 minutes per month on the WATS line, so they initially allocated the $10,000 monthly charge to callers (that is, departments) at a rate of $.20 per minute (= $10,000/50,000 minutes). Now that they paid for phone calls, faculty and staff reduced their usage of WATS. Hence, the number of minutes used on WATS dropped to 25,000 per month, which increased the rate charged to $.40 per minute (= $10,000/25,000 minutes). The increase led to further reductions in usage until the internal cost allocation per minute exceeded the normal long-distance rates, and the use of WATS dropped almost to zero. California University's total telephone bill increased dramatically.

The top administrators subsequently compromised by charging a nominal fee of $.10 per minute. According to the university's chief financial officer, the $.10 per minute charge made users aware that the WATS service had a cost. The charge was sufficiently low, however, so as not to discourage bona fide use of WATS.

---

[1]This example is based on one given by Jerold L. Zimmerman, "The Costs and Benefits of Cost Allocations," *The Accounting Review,* vol. 54, no. 3, pp. 510–511.

Cost Allocation Practices[a]

Professors Fremgen and Liao studied cost allocation practices in 123 companies to see which indirect cost allocations businesses actually make and why.

These companies clearly distinguished between two basic types of indirect costs: (1) service department costs for the benefit of production departments (e.g., data processing, purchasing, accounting, and legal), and (2) corporate administrative costs (e.g., top management's salaries, the treasurer's functions, and public relations). Service department costs relate closely to particular production units, so firms can easily defend their allocation and can make them over quite specific allocation bases. Allocations of corporate administrative costs, on the other hand, are more arbitrary.

"Despite the many theoretical injunctions against indirect cost allocations, 84 percent of the companies participating in this survey reported that they do allocate at least some corporate indirect costs for some purposes."[b]

The most widely cited reason for allocations for purposes of performance evaluation was "simply to remind (department) managers that the indirect costs exist and had to be recovered by the (department's) earnings. . . . the real reason for the allocation is to influence managers' behavior in some positive way, not to measure some amount that will be regarded as uniquely 'correct.' Hence, the allocation may be regarded as good if it works, if it really has the intended effect, even though it is wholly arbitrary."[c]

[a]Based on J. M. Fremgen and S. S. Liao, *The Allocation of Corporate Indirect Costs* (Montvale, N.J.: National Association of Accountants, 1981).
[b]J. M. Fremgen and S. S. Liao, "The Allocation of Indirect Costs," *Management Accounting* (September 1981), p. 66.
[c]Fremgen and Liao, "The Allocation of Indirect Costs," p. 67.

Cost Allocation: A Note of Caution

Organizations commonly use cost allocations. Although allocations often have a purpose, they can easily mislead users of accounting information because users often do not appreciate how arbitrarily firms allocate most costs. We caution the reader to use allocated costs carefully.

Cost allocation is so prevalent that we often take it for granted. Companies must continually challenge the need for cost allocation and ask "Why allocate?" The Managerial Application for this chapter, "Cost Allocation Practices," presents some answers to the questions "Why allocate?"

The following discussion between the owner of a small restaurant, Joe, and his consultant, the "expert," shows some of the pitfalls of cost allocation. Joe has just bought a rack of peanuts to put on some unused space on the counter. The "expert" reacts as follows:[2]

Expert: Joe, you said you put in these peanuts because some people ask for them, but do you realize what this rack of peanuts is *costing* you?

Joe: It's not going to cost! It's going to be a profit. Sure, I had to pay $125 for a fancy rack to hold the bags, but the peanuts cost 30¢ a bag and I sell 'em for 50¢. Suppose I sell 50 bags a week to start. It'll take 12½ weeks to cover the cost of the rack. After that I have a clear profit of 20¢ a bag. The more I sell, the more I make.

Expert: That is an antiquated and completely unrealistic approach, Joe. Fortunately, modern accounting procedures permit a more accurate picture that reveals the complexities involved.

Joe: Huh?

Expert: To be precise, you must integrate those peanuts into your entire operation and allocate to them their appropriate share of business overhead. They must share a proportionate part of your expenditures for rent, heat, light, equipment depreciation, decorating, salaries for your waitresses, cook, . . .

Joe: The *cook?* What's he got to do with the peanuts? He doesn't even know I have them.

Expert: Look, Joe, the cook is in the kitchen, the kitchen prepares the food, the food is what brings people in here, and the people ask to buy peanuts. *That's* why you must charge a portion of the cook's wages, as well as a part of your own salary, to peanut sales. This sheet contains a carefully calculated cost analysis that indicates the peanut operation should pay exactly $6,320 per year toward these general overhead costs.

Joe: The peanuts? $6,320 a year for overhead? Nuts? The peanut salesperson said I'd make money—put 'em on the end of the counter, he said—and get 20¢ a bag profit . . .

Expert: (With a sniff) He's not an accountant. You must also raise your selling price. If you want a profit, you should charge $3 per bag.

Joe: (Flabbergasted) Nobody's that nuts about nuts! Who'd buy them?

Expert: That's a secondary consideration.

Joe: (Eagerly) Look! I have a better idea. Why don't I just throw the nuts out—put them in a trash can?

Expert: Can you afford it?

Joe: Sure. All I have is about 50 bags of peanuts—cost about fifteen bucks—so I lose $125 on the rack, but I'm out of this nutsy business and no more grief.

Expert: (Shaking head) Joe, it isn't quite that simple. You are *in* the peanut business! The minute you throw those peanuts out you are adding $6,320 of annual overhead to the *rest* of your operation. Joe—be realistic—*can you afford to do that?*

Joe: (Completely crushed) It's unbelievable! Last week I was making money. Now I'm in trouble—just because I think peanuts on a counter are going to bring me some extra profit—just because I believe 50 bags of peanuts a week is easy.

Expert: (With raised eyebrow) That is the object of modern cost studies, Joe—to dispel those false illusions.

---

[2]This piece is adapted from one that appeared in a Coopers and Lybrand publication.

What should Joe do? Clearly Joe should fire his "expert" and rely on his common sense. If the peanut rack does not *affect* any of the other costs of running the restaurant, then none of the costs should be allocated to the peanut rack.

General Principles of Cost Allocation

The cost allocation process involves three principal steps:

1. Recording the costs.
2. Identifying the recipient of the allocated costs (this recipient may be a product, department, or any other cost object).
3. Selecting a method or basis for relating the costs in step 1 with the cost object (or recipient) in step 2.

This third step is the most difficult, because you cannot associate common costs directly with a single product or department. You need to find an indirect relation that can serve as a meaningful **allocation base.** Follow some of these guidelines in selecting an allocation base:

1. Does an analysis of past cost behavior suggest a casual relation between the incurrence of the cost and an allocation base? (For example, costs of power could be related to machine usage.)
2. Does knowledge of operations suggest a logical relation between the incurrence of cost and an allocation base? (For example, maintenance costs could be related to square feet serviced.)
3. Can the parties affected accept arbitrary allocations? If not, perhaps the organization should not allocate the common costs at all.

Cost Allocation to Departments and Products

In the sections that follow, we illustrate allocation procedures for overhead and service department costs, joint product costs, and marketing and administrative expenses.

Allocating Overhead and Service Department Costs

The following illustration demonstrates how companies allocate costs. Management could apply these methods to both manufacturing and nonmanufacturing settings.

A division of Berdan Products Company has four departments. Departments A and B are production departments. Departments M (maintenance) and S (storeroom) are service departments (that is, they exist to provide support to the production departments). Berdan keeps records of the direct material and direct labor costs incurred in both production departments. Berdan considers all other manufacturing costs to be overhead. Exhibit 5.1 shows the relation among departments.

Exhibit 5.1

BERDAN PRODUCTS COMPANY
Organization Chart

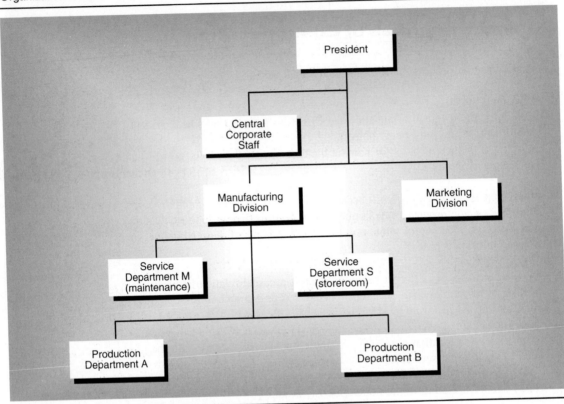

Stage 1: Cost Allocation to Production Departments

Column (1) of Exhibit 5.2 shows a list of the manufacturing overhead costs incurred during the month of March for Berdan Products Company.

1. The firm first allocates overhead costs that Berdan can attribute directly to one of the four departments. Costs in this category include salaries, labor costs, and supplies used. Exhibit 5.2 assigns these costs to the appropriate departmental columns.
2. Next the firm allocates manufacturing overhead costs that Berdan cannot attribute directly to one of the departments. These costs appear in column (6) of Exhibit 5.2 and include the payment to an outside security agency, property taxes, rent and utilities, and miscellaneous factory costs. At this stage Berdan must select a cost driver for each cost. Exhibit 5.3 shows the allocation of each

Exhibit 5.2

BERDAN PRODUCTS COMPANY
Manufacturing Overhead Costs for March

	Total (1)	Dept. A (2)	Dept. B (3)	Dept. S (4)	Dept. M (5)	Indirect Costs (6)
[a]Supervisor's Salary for Each Department	$11,930	$3,825	$4,300	$1,260	$2,545	
[a]Maintenance Labor—Dept. M	6,000				6,000	
[a]Storeroom Labor—Dept. S	1,000			1,000		
[a]Supplies Used	2,750	600	900	800	450	
Payment for Security	1,000					$1,000
Property Taxes	1,200					1,200
Rent and Utilities—Factory Building	1,440					1,440
Miscellaneous Factory Costs	600					600
Total	$25,920	$4,425	$5,200	$3,060	$8,995	$4,240

[a]Berdan can assign each of these items directly to a department.

Exhibit 5.3

BERDAN PRODUCTS COMPANY
Distribution of Various Overhead Costs for March

(1) Security Cost

Dept.	No. Visits	Percent[a]	Distribution of Security Cost to Department[b]
A	12	30	$300
B	12	30	300
S	16	40	400
M	0	—	—
Totals	40	100	$1,000

(2) Property Taxes

Dept.	Book Value of Assets	Percent	Distribution of Property Taxes to Department
A	$100,000	50	$ 600
B	70,000	35	420
S	26,000	13	156
M	4,000	2	24
Totals	$200,000	100	$1,200

(3) Rent and Utilities—Factory Building

Dept.	Square Feet of Floor Space	Percent	Distribution of Rent and Utilities to Department
A	15,000	37.50	$540
B	15,000	37.50	540
S	6,000	15.00	216
M	4,000	10.00	144
Totals	40,000	100.00	$1,440

[a]Percent equals number of visits to each department divided by the total visits in a typical night. For Dept. A, 30% = 12 visits/40 total visits.

[b]Distribution to department equals percent times total cost. For example, for Dept. A, $300 = 30% × $1,000.

of these costs to the four departments. Note the types of additional information that management must have to make these allocations, as shown below:

Cost	Cost Driver[a]	Allocation Appears in Exhibit 5.3 Section ( )
(1) Security	Number of Visits Made to Each Department	Section (1)
(2) Property Taxes	Book Value of Equipment and Inventory in Each Department	Section (2)
(3) Rent and Utilities—Factory Building	Floor Space Each Department Occupies	Section (3)
(4) Miscellaneous factory costs are distributed equally over the four production and service departments because the firm has no other logical basis for an allocation.		

[a]Managers and accountants selected these cost drivers as the bases to allocate security, property taxes, rent, and utilities.

Exhibit 5.4 shows the results of these allocations of overhead costs.

Allocating Service Department Costs to Production Departments

The next step is to allocate the service department overhead costs to the production departments. One logical method, where two or more service departments serve each other as well as the production departments, is the reciprocal method. The reciprocal method, which we discuss in Appendix 5.1, requires the use of matrix algebra.

Exhibit 5.4

BERDAN PRODUCTS COMPANY
Allocation of Overhead by Step Allocation Procedure
Overhead Allocation Schedule for Month Ending March 31

	Total	Dept. A	Dept. B	Dept. S Storeroom	Dept. M Maintenance	Reference[a]
Supervisors' Salaries..............	$11,930	$3,825	$4,300	$1,260	$2,545	★
Maintenance Labor	6,000	—	—	—	6,000	★
Storeroom Labor	1,000	—	—	1,000	—	★
Supplies Used	2,750	600	900	800	450	★
Security	1,000	300	300	400	—	(1)
Property Taxes	1,200	600	420	156	24	(2)
Rent and Utility—Factory Building	1,440	540	540	216	144	(3)
Miscellaneous Factory Costs[b]	600	150	150	150	150	
Totals	$25,920	$6,015	$6,610	$3,982	$9,313	

[a]Berdan allocates each item marked with a star directly to a department. The number in parentheses refers to a section of Exhibit 5.3.
[b]Allocated evenly to departments as indicated above.

A less exact but simpler solution is the **step method.** The step method allocates costs in steps as follows: We start with the service department that receives the smallest dollar amount of service from the other service departments. We allocate its costs to the other service and production departments. Next, we distribute the total costs of the service department receiving the next smallest amount of service from other service departments and so on until we have allocated all service department costs to the production departments. Once we have allocated a given service department's costs to other departments, we do not allocate any costs back to that given service department.

Assume Department M, the maintenance department, receives little or no service from Department S, the storeroom department. Therefore, we allocate Department M first, using the step method. Assume the cost driver for maintenance costs is the number of maintenance hours required in each department. Maintenance hours and our allocation appear below:

Department	Maintenance Hours	Percent[a]	Distribution of Dept. M Costs[b]
A	400 Hours	50	$4,657
B	200	25	2,328
S	200	25	2,328
Totals	800 Hours	100	$9,313

[a]50% = 400 hours/800 hours; etc.

[b]$4,657 = 50% × $9,313 cost of Maintenance Dept.; etc.

Since Department A has 50 percent of the maintenance hours, we allocate 50 percent of the maintenance department costs to it, and so forth for the remaining departments.

Assume the cost driver for the storeroom department's costs is the quantity of materials and supplies that Departments A and B requisition. Department A requisitioned 40 percent of the total materials and supplies and Department B the other 60 percent, so the firm allocates these departments 40 and 60 percent, respectively, of storeroom department costs. Exhibit 5.5 shows the allocation of maintenance and storeroom costs to the production departments.

Summary of Stage 1 Allocation Firms allocate of costs in three ways: (1) allocation of costs directly to departments for costs that are directly traceable to departments (managers' salaries at Berdan Products), (2) allocation of costs not directly traceable to departments using a reasonable method (security costs at Berdan Products), and (3) allocation of service department costs to the production departments using an arbitrary method (miscellaneous factory costs at Berdan Products). Thus Berdan allocated the total manufacturing overhead of $25,920 as $13,196 to Department A and $12,724 to Department B as shown in Exhibit 5.5.

| | | **Exhibit 5.5** | | | | |

Exhibit 5.5

BERDAN PRODUCTS COMPANY
Allocation of Service Department Costs to Production Departments

	Total	Dept. A	Dept. B	Dept. S	Dept. M
Total before Allocation	$25,920	$ 6,015	$ 6,610	$ 3,982	$ 9,313
		50%	25%	25%	
Allocation of Dept. M to Dept. A, B, and S	—	4,657	2,328	2,328	(9,313)
	$25,920	$10,672	$ 8,938	$ 6,310	
		40%	60%		
Reallocation of Dept. S to Dept. A and B	—	2,524	3,786	(6,310)	
Total Production Department Costs	$25,920	$13,196	$12,724		

Stage 2: Cost Allocation from Production Departments to Products

Berdan next allocates these amounts to the products manufactured in the two production departments. A firm usually bases this allocation on the number of units produced, machine hours, direct labor hours, direct labor cost, and/or some other activity base, as we discussed in Chapters 3 and 4.

Using a simple example, if a total of 10,000 machine hours were worked in Department A and 20,000 machine hours were worked in Department B during the month, the overhead rates per hour would be as follows:

$$\text{Department A: } \$1.3196 \text{ per Hour} = \frac{\$13,196}{10,000 \text{ Hours}}.$$

$$\text{Department B: } \$ .6362 \text{ per Hour} = \frac{\$12,724}{20,000 \text{ Hours}}.$$

If a particular job required 200 machine hours of work in Department A and 300 machine hours of work in Department B, the firm then would assign $454.78 of overhead to the job, computed as follows:

$$\$454.78 = 200 \text{ Hours in Department A} \times \$1.3196$$
$$+ 300 \text{ Hours in Department B} \times \$.6362.$$

This approach assumes only one cost driver, namely, machine hours. Many companies would use multiple cost drivers reflecting the various activities that cause product costs, which is known as **activity-based costing.**

Activity-based Costing

Consider allocating Department A's overhead of $13,196 using three cost drivers, instead of one as in the example above. (In practice, companies using multiple cost drivers often use many more than three cost drivers, but the principles are the same whether companies use three cost drivers or three hundred cost drivers. We use three cost drivers to make the point without burdening you with details.)

Assume Berdan Company's accountants find the following cost drivers affect Department A's overhead costs.

Cost Driver	Cost Category or "Pool"
Number of Different Parts in the Product	Cost to Purchase, Inspect, Handle, and Store the Parts
Machine Hours	Cost to Maintain Machines, Energy Costs to Operate Machines, Machine Depreciation, Wages of Machine Operators
Hours to Set Up a Job	Costs of Changing the Machines to Make Them Appropriate for a New Job, Including Wages of Production Workers, Engineers, and Computer Technicians

Assume the accountants divided Department A's overhead of $13,196 into these three categories, or "cost pools" as accountants commonly say. The accountants then measured the number of units of activity for each cost driver for the period, and derived the following overhead rates per activity unit for each cost driver:

Department A: Cost Driver (1)	Overhead in Each Pool (Total = $13,196) (2)	Units of Activity for Each Cost Driver for All Jobs (3)	Overhead Rate (2)/(3) (4)
Number of different parts in all products	$1,846	200 parts	$\dfrac{\$1,846}{200 \text{ parts}}$ = $9.23 per part in the product
Machine hours worked on all jobs	$6,150	10,000 machine hours	$\dfrac{\$6,150}{10,000 \text{ hours}}$ = $.615 per machine hour used to make the product
Hours required to set up all jobs	$5,200	200 setup hours	$\dfrac{\$5,200}{200 \text{ hours}}$ = $26.00 per setup hour used to set up the job

This information applies to all products manufactured during the period. Now assume Berdan's production managers inform the accountants that a particular job uses the following amounts of these activities in Department A:

1. twenty different parts in the job's product,
2. two hundred machine hours, and
3. ten hours to set up the job by changing machinery settings to make the equipment suitable for the job's products.

Using the overhead rates for all products and this information for a particular job, the accountants allocated Department A's overhead costs to the job as follows:

(20 parts × $9.23 per part) + (200 machine hours × $.615 per machine hour)
+ (10 setup hours × $26 per setup hour)
= $567.60.

This procedure allocates Department A's overhead, only. The accountants would use similar steps to compute overhead rates for Department B and to allocate Department B's overhead costs to this job.

You can imagine how complex and time-consuming this process can be if a company has numerous production departments, and if the accountants use many different overhead rates. Proponents of activity-based costing argue that it increases the accuracy of product costs which improves the quality of information available to management. Each company must ascertain how much benefit, if any, it obtains from activity-based costing and compare that benefit with the additional costs of developing and using a more complex and time-consuming cost allocation method. Chapter 6 discusses these issues further.

Problem 5.1 for Self-Study

Overhead allocation. The partially completed overhead distribution schedule for Merriam Company appears in Exhibit 5.6. Merriam Company allocates its costs on

Exhibit 5.6

MERRIAM COMPANY
Overhead Allocation Schedule for February

	Total	Dept. A	Dept. B	Dept. C	Dept. S Storeroom	Dept. M Maintenance	Indirect Costs
Maintenance Wages	$1,800					$1,800	
Storeroom Wages	1,000				$1,000		
(1) Janitor's Wages	1,000						$1,000
Supplies Used	1,400	$200	$300	$100	600	200	
(1) Rent—Factory Building	2,000						2,000
(2) Electricity, Gas, and Water	200						200
(2) Miscellaneous Factory							
Costs	600						600
Total	$8,000						

	Total	Dept. A	Dept. B	Dept. C	Storeroom	Maintenance
Floor Space (square feet)	50,000	16,000	11,000	20,000	2,000	1,000
Chargeable Maintenance Hours	500	150	200	100	50	—
Requisitions Drawn	200	140	40	20	—	—
Other Distribution Data:						
Electricity, Gas, Water, and Misc.	100%	30%	30%	20%	10%	10%

the following bases:

(1) Janitor's wages and rent of building on the basis of floor space.
(2) Electricity, gas, water, and miscellaneous factory costs on the basis of percentages given.
(3) Maintenance department costs on the basis of chargeable maintenance hours.
(4) Storeroom department costs on the basis of proportion of number of requisitions.

Management has hired you as a consultant to prepare a schedule of allocated costs. Use the step method to allocate service department costs to production departments, starting with the maintenance department.

The solution to this self-study problem is at the end of the chapter on page 179.

Joint Products

Suppose you get multiple products from a single production process. For example, Georgia-Pacific gets various wood products from its lumber mills. Dairy producers like Borden and Land O' Lakes get multiple products from milk.

In real estate a similar problem exists in the development of a subdivision. The total cost of developing the tract represents a joint cost for all of the lots that the developer will sell. The developer who wants to calculate a cost and profit for each lot must find some reasonable method of allocating this total figure among the lots.

Exhibit 5.7 presents the following information graphically. The firm initially introduces direct materials into processing. After incurring direct labor and manu-

Exhibit 5.7

Joint Production Process

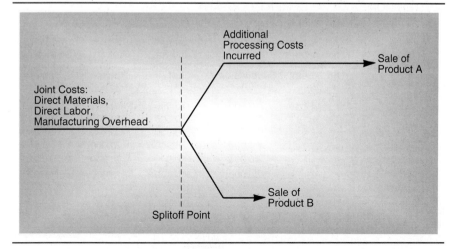

facturing overhead costs, two identifiable products, Product A and Product B, emerge from the production process. The firm processes Product A further, but sells Product B immediately. We call the point at which the identifiable products emerge the **splitoff point.** Costs incurred up to the splitoff point are the **joint costs.** We call costs incurred after the splitoff point **additional processing costs.**

Allocation of Joint Production Costs

Firms use one of two methods to allocate joint costs: the **net realizable value method** (also known as the relative sales value method) or the **physical units method.** We describe both in the following illustration based on a real estate development. Sorter Homes Development Company purchases a 2-acre tract of land adjoining a lake for $38,000 and spends $2,000 in legal fees to have the land subdivided into five lots. The company builds a house on each of the lots. Exhibit 5.8 shows the various costs and price data.

The different prices for the half-acre and quarter-acre lots result from differing proximity to the lake. The joint cost problem in this context is to allocate the $40,000 cost of the land to each of the five lots.

Net Realizable Value Method

Suppose that once Sorter subdivides the land it has a ready market for the lots without houses. The market prices for the five lots are shown in column **(3)** of Exhibit 5.8. Sorter Homes allocates the $40,000 joint cost to the lots in proportion to their relative net realizable values. Sorter Homes would assign each lot a cost in the proportion: net realizable value of the lot divided by the sum of net realizable values. It would allocate $8,000 to lot 1($8,000 = $16,000/$80,000 × $40,000). It would allocate the following costs to the other lots: lots 2 and 3, $12,500 each; lot 4,

Exhibit 5.8

SORTER HOMES DEVELOPMENT COMPANY
Data for Joint Cost Allocations

Lot Number (1)	Size (in acres) (2)	Resale Price after Subdivision (3)	Selling Price for House and Lot (4)	Cost to Build House (5)	Approximate Sales Value of Land at Splitoff (6)
1	½	$16,000	$ 75,000	$ 50,000	$ 25,000
2	½	25,000	80,000	50,000	30,000
3	½	25,000	80,000	50,000	30,000
4	¼	4,000	35,000	30,000	5,000
5	¼	10,000	40,000	30,000	10,000
	2	$80,000	$310,000	$210,000	$100,000

(3) market prices given.

(6) = (4) − (5).

$2,000; and lot 5, $5,000. Under this method, then, Sorter Homes assigns each lot a portion of the joint cost so that it yields a profit equal to 50 percent of selling price.

Approximate Net Realizable Value Method

To alter the illustration, suppose the information in column (3) of Exhibit 5.8, resale price after subdivision, is not available.

The only information Sorter Homes has is the selling price of the house and lot in column (4) and the cost to build a house in column (5). From the information in columns (4) and (5), we compute the approximate sales value of land in column (6).

Sorter Homes would not logically assign the land's cost on the basis of the information in column (4), because those prices include the value of the house as well as the land. For example, the selling price of lot-house combination 4 is $35,000, which is about 11 percent of the total selling price of $310,000. We can see from the information in column (3) that lot 4 represents only 5 percent (= $4,000/ $80,000) of the value of the total land package.

The diagram in Exhibit 5.9 can help you understand the nature of the problem. The splitoff point comes just before the firm incurs the costs of the individual houses. To use the **approximate net realizable value method,** the firm must derive the relative sales values at the splitoff, which appears in column (6) of Exhibit 5.8.

We define the approximate net realizable value of a joint product (lot) as the selling price of the final product (lot-house combination) less the cost to complete the final product (lot-house combination). The approximate net realizable value of lot 1 is $25,000, or the price of the lot-house combination, $75,000, less the cost of the house, $50,000.

Exhibit 5.9

Splitoff Point in Allocating Joint Costs

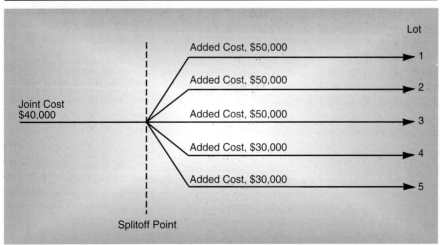

The sum of the approximate net realizable values of the lots at the splitoff point is $100,000. Sorter Homes would assign each lot a cost based on the ratio of the lot's approximate net realizable value to the sum of the approximate net realizable value. To Lot 1, for example, Sorter Homes would allocate $10,000 (= $25,000/ $100,000 × $40,000, where $25,000 and $100,000 are approximate net realizable values from column (6) of Exhibit 5.8). Allocations for the other lots appear in column (2) of Exhibit 5.10.

Physical Units Method

We do not base the physical units method on dollar costs but on some obvious physical measure. Here, the obvious measure is area in acres. In other contexts the obvious physical measure may be weight or volume. Because lots 1, 2, and 3 each contain ½ acre out of 2 acres, Sorter Homes would allocate each (.5/2) × $40,000, or $10,000. Sorter Homes would allocate each ¼-acre lot (.25/2) × $40,000, or $5,000.

Firms may easily apply the physical units method, but its results may not make good sense. For example, if a firm applies the physical units method using pounds of salable product to allocate the cost of beef cattle to cuts of meat, New York steak will carry the same allocated joint cost as hamburger. The net realizable value method will allocate more of the joint costs of beef cattle to a pound of steak than to a pound of hamburger.

Exhibit 5.10

SORTER HOMES DEVELOPMENT COMPANY
Joint Cost Allocation under Various Methods

| Lot Number | Joint Product Cost = $40,000 | | |
| | Basis of Allocation | | |
	Net Realizable Values (1)[a]	Approximate Net Realizable Values (2)[b]	Physical Units (3)[c]
1	$ 8,000	$10,000	$10,000
2	12,500	12,000	10,000
3	12,500	12,000	10,000
4	2,000	2,000	5,000
5	5,000	4,000	5,000
Total	$40,000	$40,000	$40,000

[a](1)Allocated based on resale price after subdivision.
[b](2)Allocated based on approximate sales value of land at splitoff (column (6), Exhibit 5.8).
[c](3)Allocated based on size.

Problem 5.2
for Self-Study

Allocating Joint Costs. Up to the point of separation of joint products X, Y, and Z, total production costs amount to $51,500. The firm produced the following quantities.

- Product X: 3,000 units with an estimated sales value of $3 per unit.
- Product Y: 4,500 units with an estimated sales value of $4 per unit.
- Product Z: 9,700 units with an estimated sales value of $5 per unit.

a. Prepare a schedule showing the allocation of production costs to the three joint products and the unit cost of each product, using the net realizable value method.
b. Repeat part **a** using the physical quantities method.

The solution to this self-study problem is at the end of the chapter on page 180.

By-Products

In accounting for jointly produced products, managers usually want to distinguish between by-products and joint products. A firm produces a **by-product** as the inevitable result of the production of a main product, and it is of relatively small value. For example, steel shavings in a machine shop and scraps of lumber in a furniture factory are typical instances of by-products. A **joint product** is one that firms treat as equally significant with other products that emerge from a process. The different grades of lumber in a lumber mill, milk and butter in dairy operations, and subdivision lots are examples of joint products. By-products and joint products differ in degree only; the dividing line is not distinct. For instance, a Consolidated Edison power plant that produces both electricity and steam may consider one or the other as a by-product or may treat them both as joint products.

In accounting for by-products, just as for joint products, firms assign no processing cost to the by-product until production separates it from the joint process. The by-product's net realizable value is its estimated selling price minus any costs the firm will incur for further processing, handling, and disposal. The firm then deducts the net realizable value assigned to by-products from the total accumulated joint costs, and the remaining joint costs become the cost of the main product or products. The net realizable value assigned to the by-products therefore reduces the cost of the main product or products.

To illustrate accounting for by-products, reconsider the Sorter Homes example. Suppose that at the time Sorter Homes arranged for legal subdivision of the land purchase, it also sold to the city the rights for the public to use the lake for $2,000. The firm should probably view the rights to the lake as a by-product in this case, so it would treat the rights as a reduction in the cost of the land. The firm would allocate only $38,000 to the joint costs of the five lots. Exhibit 5.11 summarizes the allocation of the remaining $38,000 joint costs.

An alternative method treats the net realizable value from the by-product as other income.

Problem 5.3 for Self-Study

Allocating By-Product Costs. At the conclusion of process 4, the total cost of processing 25,000 gallons of chemical product K is $362,000. At this point, 5,000 gallons of by-product Y emerge and the processing department transfers the remaining 20,000 gallons of K to process 5 for further work. The Y material will require further processing at an estimated cost of $1 per gallon, and then the firm can sell it for $3 per gallon. Calculate the cost per gallon of chemical product K transferred to process 5.

The solution to this self-study problem is at the end of the chapter on page 180.

Exhibit 5.11

SORTER HOMES DEVELOPMENT COMPANY
Joint Cost Allocation with By-Products

Lot Number	Net Realizable Values (1)[a]	Physical Units (2)[b]
	By-Product Value = $2,000 **Joint Product Cost = $38,000**	
	Basis of Allocation	
1	$ 7,600	$ 9,500
2	11,875	9,500
3	11,875	9,500
4	1,900	4,750
5	4,750	4,750
Total	$38,000	$38,000

[a](1)Proportion of resale price after subdivision times $38,000.

[b](2)Proportion of size in acres times $38,000.

Marketing and Administrative Expenses

Management often applies techniques similar to those employed in manufacturing cost analysis in allocating marketing and administrative costs. Macy's department store, for example, may wish to have its operating costs and cost of goods sold allocated to men's clothing, furnishings, teenwear, and other departments. A wholesaler of Honda motorcycles may wish to obtain information concerning the profitability of different territories and types of customers (such as senior citizens).

Allocating costs in service and merchandising is much the same as the allocation in manufacturing. Accountants can assign some items, such as salaries and commissions of salespeople, directly to departments.

Exhibit 5.12 shows some of the bases of allocation that firms have suggested for marketing and administrative costs. One striking aspect of the problem of such cost analysis is that firms must accumulate extensive data in addition to the regular accounting information.

Summary

Common cost allocations permeate accounting reports, both financial and managerial. Managers should read and interpret accounting reports carefully, taking into consideration the effects of common cost allocations. For most decision making, planning, and control purposes, accountants should base their reports on a minimum of cost allocations.

The cost allocation process involves (1) recording costs to be allocated, (2) identifying cost objects, and (3) selecting a basis for relating costs to cost objects.

Exhibit 5.12

Allocation Bases

For Allocation Of	Basis
1. Insurance	Average Value of Finished Goods
2. Storage and Building Costs	Floor Space
3. Cost of Sending Monthly Statements, Credit Investigations, Etc.	Number of Customers
4. Various Joint Costs Such as Advertising and Supervision of Selling Activities	Sales, Classified by Dealers, Territories, or Products
5. Credit Investigation, Postage, Stationery, and Other Such Expenses	Number of Orders Received
6. Handling Costs	Tonnage Handled
7. Salespersons' Expenses	Number of Salespersons' Calls
8. Order Writing and Filling	Number of Items on an Order
9. Stenographic Expense	Number of Letters Written
10. Automobile Operation, Delivery Expense, Etc.	Number of Miles Operated

External reporting standards require cost allocations (for example, to value inventory on external financial reports). Cost-plus contracts and cost-based rate regulations require allocations of common costs. Firms allocate service department costs for managerial purposes to charge users for the cost of services and to encourage users to monitor service department costs.

Appendix 5.1: Reciprocal Method for Allocation of Service Department Costs

How can accountants allocate service department costs to production departments when service departments *serve each other* in addition to servicing production departments? The text mentioned the **reciprocal method** for allocating service departments' costs to production departments, which algebraically solves the problem. This method normally uses matrix algebra.

Students unfamiliar with matrix algebra may skip this appendix without losing continuity with the rest of the book.

The data you need to use the **reciprocal method** for Berdan Products Company appear in Exhibit 5.13. The maintenance and storeroom service departments provide service to each other as well as to production departments A and B.

The service department costs requiring allocation are $9,313 in maintenance and $3,982 in the storeroom. The simplified procedure explained in the text in Exhibit 5.5 assumed that the storeroom directly serviced the two production departments. A more realistic treatment allocates the costs in proportion to the cost of factory supplies the storeroom issues to each department. The firm used $2,750 of factory

---

Exhibit 5.13

BERDAN PRODUCTS COMPANY
Fractions of Service Departments' Outputs Used by Service and Production Departments for March

	Services Performed By	
	Maintenance *(M)*	Storeroom *(R)*
Services Used By		
Service Departments		
Maintenance	0	.164
Storeroom	.25	.291
Production Departments		
A	.50	.218
B	.25	.327
	1.00	1.000
Costs to Be Allocated	$9,313	$3,982

Matrix **S** spans the Maintenance and Storeroom service department rows (.164/.291 with 0/.25). Matrix **P** spans the production department rows (.218/.327 with .50/.25).

supplies. Maintenance consumed $450, or 16.4 percent of that total. Exhibit 5.13 shows the fractions of storeroom services consumed by the four departments. The storeroom column contains the figure .164 to indicate the maintenance department's consumption. The other entries in the storeroom column, including self-service in the storeroom ($800/$2,750 = .291), result from dividing the factory supplies used in that department by the total factory supplies used, or $2,750. The basis for distributing maintenance department costs remains the same as the step procedure explained in the text because the maintenance department itself required no maintenance.

Notice that each column in the schedule adds exactly to 1.00. All departments together consume all of a service department's output. The top portion of the schedule shows the service department's use of service department outputs. Matrix **S** denotes that section of the schedule. Matrix element s_{ij} represents the fraction of service department j's output used by service department i. For example, $s_{MR} = .164$, or the maintenance department (M) uses 16.4 percent of the storeroom's (R) output. (We refer to the storeroom as R so you will not confuse it with **S**, which stands for the entire service department matrix.)

The bottom portion of the schedule shows the production department usage. Matrix **P** denotes that section of the schedule. Matrix element p_{ij} represents the fraction of service department j's output that production department i uses. To allocate the service department costs to production departments, we need an allocation matrix such as the one in Exhibit 5.14. In matrix **A**, a_{ij} represents the fraction of service department j's cost allocable to production department i after we take account of the use of the service department output by the service departments themselves.

The matrix **A** results from the matrix equation $\mathbf{A} = \mathbf{P}(\mathbf{I} - \mathbf{S})^{-1}$, where **I** is the identity matrix and $(\mathbf{I} - \mathbf{S})^{-1}$ means the inverse of the matrix $(\mathbf{I} - \mathbf{S})$. We can derive the equation for **A**. For example, a_{AM} represents the fraction of the maintenance department's (M) output allocable to product Department A. That fraction is

$$a_{AM} = p_{AM} + a_{AM}s_{MM} + a_{AR}s_{RM}$$

$$= .50 + a_{AM} \times 0 + a_{AR} \times .25,$$

Exhibit 5.14

BERDAN PRODUCTS COMPANY
Allocation Matrix for March

	Services Performed By	
	Maintenance *(M)*	Storeroom *(R)*
Service Costs Allocated To		
Production Departments		
A	.61	.45
B	.39	.55
	1.00	1.00

Matrix **A** brackets group the .61/.39 and .45/.55 pairs.

or the direct use of maintenance by Department A (p_{AM}) plus the fraction of maintenance costs used by maintenance allocable to Department A $(a_{AM}s_{MM})$ plus the fraction of maintenance costs used by the storeroom—that is, allocable to Department A $(a_{AR}s_{RM})$. Notice that the equation for a_{AM} shows both a_{AM} and other a_{ij} on the righthand side, so that a system of simultaneous equations for the a_{ij} results.

Consider another example, a_{BR}:

$$a_{BR} = p_{BR} + a_{BM}s_{MR} + a_{BR}s_{RR}$$

$$= .327 + a_{BM} \times .164 + a_{BR} \times .291.$$

The fraction of storeroom costs allocable to Department B equals the sum of the direct use of the storeroom by Department B (p_{BR}) plus the fraction of storeroom costs maintenance used allocable to Department B $(a_{BM}s_{MR})$ plus the fraction of storeroom costs the storeroom used allocable to Department B $(a_{BR}s_{RR})$.

Writing out a similar equation for each a_{ij}, where i represents production department A or B, and j represents service department M or R, yields a matrix equation for the entire system:

$$a_{ij} = p_{ij} + \sum_{k=M, R} a_{ik}s_{kj}$$

or

$$A = P + AS.$$

Rearranging terms yields

$$A - AS = P$$

or

$$A(I - S) = P.$$

Postmultiply both sides by $(\mathbf{I} - \mathbf{S})^{-1}$ to get[3]

$$A = P(I - S)^{-1}.$$

Once you compute the matrix **A,** to allocate service department costs to production departments is straightforward. The allocation appears in Exhibit 5.15, along with the allocation that the easier, but approximate, step procedure demonstrated earlier provides.

Observe that the matrix method gives different answers than the approximation method. The matrix method is cumbersome to carry out by hand when it involves more than two service departments and two production departments. The solution to the set of simultaneous equations (or the matrix inversion) is tedious, and except for small problems, you should do the calculations on a computer. If all entries in the **S**

---

[3]If the inverse of $(\mathbf{I} - \mathbf{S})$ does not exist, then a subset of the service departments completely uses the entire output themselves without providing any service to the other service departments or to production departments. If you eliminate the subset of service departments that mutually consume each other's output, then you can carry out the procedure.

Exhibit 5.15

BERDAN PRODUCTS COMPANY
Allocation of Service Department Costs to Production Departments, March

Production Department	Service Departments			
	Matrix Method			Step Approximation Method
	Maintenance	Storeroom	Total	
A	$5,681	$1,792	$ 7,473	$ 7,181
B	3,632	2,190	5,822	6,114
	$9,313	$3,982	$13,295	$13,295

matrix are zero (that is, when all service departments service only production departments), the matrix procedure and the approximate step procedure will give the same answer.

Solutions to Self-Study Problems

Suggested Solution to Problem 5.1 for Self-Study

MERRIAM COMPANY
Overhead Allocation Schedule for February

	Total	Dept. A	Dept. B	Dept. C	Dept. S Storeroom	Dept. M Maintenance
Maintenance Wages	$1,800	—	—	—	—	$1,800
Storeroom Wages	1,000	—	—	—	$1,000	—
(1) Janitor's Wages[a]	1,000[a]	$ 320	$ 220	$ 400	40	20
Supplies Used	1,400	200	300	100	600	200
(1) Rent—Factory Building[a]	2,000[a]	640	440	800	80	40
(2) Electricity, etc.[b]	200[b]	60	60	40	20	20
(2) Misc. Factory Costs[b]	600[b]	180	180	120	60	60
Total	$8,000	$1,400	$1,200	$1,460	$1,800	$2,140
Allocation of Maintenance Dept. Costs to Other Depts.[c]	—	642	856	428	214	(2,140)[c]
	$8,000	$2,042	$2,056	$1,888	$2,014	
Allocation of Storeroom Dept. Costs to Depts. A, B, and C[d]	—	1,410	403	201	(2,014)[d]	
Total Overhead in Depts. A, B, and C	$8,000	$3,452	$2,459	$2,089		

[a]Allocated based on the percentages shown in column (1) of Schedule A; 32% of the total cost to Dept. A, 22% to Dept. B, etc.

[b]Allocated based on the percentages shown in column (2) of Schedule A; 30% to Dept. A, 30% to Dept. B, etc.

[c]Allocated based on the percentages shown in column (3) of Schedule A; 30% to Dept. A, 40% to Dept. B, etc.

[d]Allocated based on the percentages shown in column (4) of Schedule A; 70% to Dept. A, etc.

Schedule A: Allocation Percentages

	(1) Floor Space	(2) Other	(3) Maintenance	(4) Requisitions
Dept. A..................	32%	30%	30%	70%
Dept. B..................	22	30	40	20
Dept. C..................	40	20	20	10
Dept. S.	4	10	10	—
Dept. M	2	10	—	—
Total	100.0%	100.0%	100%	100%

Suggested Solution to Problem 5.2 for Self-Study

a.

	Units	Unit Price	Total Sales Value	Percent of Value	Cost Allocation[a]	Unit Cost[b]
Product X	3,000	$3	$ 9,000	11.92%	$ 6,139	$2.046
Product Y	4,500	4	18,000	23.84	12,278	2.728
Product Z.....	9,700	5	48,500	64.24	33,083	3.411
Total			$75,500	100.00%	$51,500	

[a]$6,139 = 11.92% × $51,500; etc.

[b]$2.046 = $6,139/3,000 units; etc.

b.

	Units	Percent of Total	Cost Allocation[a]	Cost[b]
Product X	3,000	17.44%	$ 8,982	$2.994
Product Y	4,500	26.16	13,472	$2.994
Product Z	9,700	56.40	29,046	$2.994
Total........................	17,200	100.00%	$51,500	

[a]$8,982 = 17.44% × $51,500; etc.

[b]$2.994 = $8,982/3,000 units; etc.

Note the costs per unit are correlated with sales value using the net realizable method but not with the physical quantities method.

Suggested Solution to Problem 5.3 for Self-Study

The by-product has a net realizable value of $10,000 [= 5,000 gallons × ($3 − $1)]. Subtract this amount from the joint cost of $362,000. Allocate the remaining $352,000 to Product K. The cost per gallon, therefore, is $352,000/20,000 gallons = $17.60 per gallon.

Key Terms and Concepts

Direct cost
Common cost
Service department cost allocation
Joint cost allocation
Service departments
Allocation base
Step method
Activity-based costing
Splitoff point
Joint costs

Additional processing costs
Net realizable value method
Physical units method
Approximate net realizable
  value method
By-product
Joint product
Reciprocal (matrix allocation)
  method (appendix)

Questions, Exercises, Problems, and Cases

Questions

1. Review the meaning of the concepts or terms given above in Key Terms and Concepts.
2. When firms allocate service department costs to production departments, why do they first accumulate these costs at the service department level rather than assigning them directly to production departments?
3. Distinguish between a production department and a service department.
4. Refer to the Managerial Application, "Cost Allocation Practices." What was the most cited reason to allocate costs for performance evaluation?
5. Refer to the exchange in the chapter between Joe and his consultant-expert. Is the expert right? Should Joe have allocated costs to the peanut stand?
6. Why do firms allocate service department costs to production departments?
7. Distinguish between a joint product and a by-product.
8. Comment on the following statement: "The net realizable value method is the best method to use in decisions concerning whether a firm should sell a joint product at splitoff or process it further."
9. Name some of the costs and benefits of cost allocation.
10. A critic of cost allocation noted, "You can avoid arbitrary cost allocations by not allocating any costs." Comment.
11. Give the steps in the cost allocation process.
12. For each of the types of common cost in the first column, select the most appropriate allocation base from the second column:

Common Cost	Allocation Base
Building Utilities	Value of Equipment and Inventories
Payroll Accounting	Number of Units Produced
Property Taxes on Personal Property	Number of Employees
Equipment Repair	Space Occupied
Quality Control Inspection	Number of Service Calls

Exercises

Solutions to even-numbered exercises are at the end of the chapter after the cases.

13. **Allocating overhead to departments and jobs.** The accountants of Altman Films made the following estimates for a year:

	Filming Department	Editing Department	Printing Department
Estimated Overhead	$33,000	$50,000	$60,000
Estimated Direct Labor Cost ...	$60,000	$50,000	$75,000
Estimated Direct Labor Time...	11,000 Hours	12,500 Hours	15,000 Hours

a. Compute the overhead allocation rates for each department using direct labor hours as a basis.

b. Management wants to know how much the KRTV commercial job cost. The following table shows the materials and labor costs; you will have to add the overhead costs using direct labor hours as the allocation base.

	KRTV Commercial		
	Filming Department	Editing Department	Printing Department
Direct Material	$600	—	$80
Direct Labor Cost................	$1,500	$2,000	$200
Direct Labor Time	250 Hours	400 Hours	38 Hours

14. **Allocating overhead.** The George Hamilton Sunscreen Company has two production departments and a maintenance department. In addition, the company keeps other costs for the entire plant in a separate account. The estimated cost data for Year 1 follow:

Cost	Production Dept. 1	Production Dept. 2	Maintenance	General Plant
Direct Labor	$50,000	$30,000	—	—
Indirect Labor	28,000	14,000	$22,500	$20,000
Indirect Materials ...	9,000	7,000	900	8,000
Miscellaneous	3,000	5,000	1,600	5,000
	$90,000	$56,000	$25,000	$33,000
Maintenance	7,000 Hours	13,000 Hours	—	—

The general plant services the three departments in the following proportions: 50 percent (Department 1); 30 percent (Department 2); 20 percent (Maintenance). Allocate maintenance costs based on maintenance hours.

Allocate maintenance department and general plant costs to the production departments. Use the step method, starting with general plant costs.

15. **Allocating overhead to jobs.** Wong Inc., uses a job system of cost accounting. The data presented here relate to operations in its plant during January.

Wong, Inc., has two production departments and one service department. The actual factory overhead costs during the month are $4,000. At the end of the month Mr. Wong allocates overhead costs as follows: Department A, $2,100; Department B, $1,600; Department C, $300. He allocates the service department (Department C) overhead of $300 as follows: two-thirds to Department A, one-third to Department B.

Mr. Wong applies factory overhead to jobs at the predetermined rates of 50 percent of direct labor costs in Department A and 75 percent in Department B. The firm delivers the jobs upon completion. The firm completed job nos. 789, 790, and 791 in January. Jobs 788 and 792 are still in process on January 31.

a. Complete the job production record in the following table by filling in the appropriate amounts. Be sure to show supporting calculations. (Job 788 has been done for you.)

b. For Departments A and B, compute the difference between the applied overhead using the predetermined rates and the actual overhead after allocating Department C overhead to Departments A and B.

Job Production Record

Job Order No.	Jobs in Process, Jan. 1	Direct Labor Dept. A	Direct Labor Dept. B	Direct Matl. Dept. A	Direct Matl. Dept. B	Applied Overhead Dept. A	Applied Overhead Dept. B	Total Costs	Jobs in Process, Jan. 31	Completed Jobs
788	$1,200	$ 300	$ 200	$ 250	$ 150	$ 150	$ 150	$2,400	$2,400	$
789	850	600	300	450	300					
790		800	400	550	350					
791		1,000	600	600	450					
792		1,200	800	900	400					
Totals	$2,050	$3,900	$2,300	$2,750	$1,650	$	$	$	$	$

16. **Allocating service department costs using the step method.** Meridian Box Company has two service departments (maintenance and general factory administration) and two operating departments (cutting and assembly). Management has decided to allocate maintenance costs on the basis of the area in each department and general factory administration costs on the basis of labor hours the employees worked in each of their respective departments.

The following data appear in the company records for the current period:

	General Factory Administration	Maintenance	Cutting	Assembly
Area Occupied (square feet)	1,000	—	1,000	3,000
Labor Hours	—	100	100	400
Direct Labor Costs (operating departments only)			$1,500	$4,000
Service Department Direct Costs	$1,200	$2,400		

Use the step method to allocate service departments' costs to the operating departments, starting with maintenance.

17. **Using multiple cost drivers to allocate costs.** Assume Johnson Manufacturing uses three allocation bases to allocate overhead costs from departments to jobs: number of different parts, number of machine hours, and number of job setup hours. The information needed to compute the allocation rates follows.

	Department A		Department B	
	Costs	Units of Activity	Costs	Units of Activity
1. Number of Different Parts	$2,000	40 Parts	$400	10 Parts
2. Number of Machine Hours Worked	$100,000	16,000 Hours	$30,000	1,500 Hours
3. Number of Hours to Set up Jobs	$12,000	300 Hours	$4,000	100 Hours

Job 300ZX required the following activities:

Department A: 10 parts, 1,000 machine hours, 20 setup hours.
Department B: 2 parts, 200 machine hours, 10 setup hours.

Allocate overhead cost to Job 300ZX using the two stages described in the chapter.

18. **Allocating service department costs directly to operating departments.** Joyner's Jolly Burgers has a commissary with two operating departments: P1, food inventory control, and P2, paper goods inventory control. It has two service departments: S1, computer services, and S2, administration, maintenance, and all other. Each department's direct costs are as follows:

P1	$90,000
P2	60,000
S1	30,000
S2	40,000

P1, P2, and S2 use S1's services as follows:

P1	10 Percent
P2	10 Percent
S2	80 Percent

P1 and P2 use S2's services as follows:

P1	62.5 Percent
P2	37.5 Percent

Compute the allocation of service center costs to operating departments. Allocate directly to operating departments. Do not allocate costs from one service center to another.

19. **Allocating service department costs using the step method.** Using the data for Exercise 18, allocate service department costs using the step allocation method, in which the firm allocates service center costs to other service centers as well as to operating departments. Start by allocating S1 to S2, P1, and P2. Then allocate S1 to P1 and P2. See Exhibit 5.5 for an example.

20. **Joint cost allocations—net realizable value method.** Green Company processes Chemical XX-12 to produce two outputs, Al and Gore. The monthly costs of processing XX-12 amount to $45,000 for materials and $160,000 for conversion costs. This processing results in outputs that sell for a total of $455,000. The sales revenue from Al amounts to $273,000 of the total.

   Compute the costs the firm will assign to Al and Gore in a typical month using the net realizable value method.

21. **Joint cost allocations—approximate net realizable value method.** A batch of ore yields three refined products for Montana Mining: lead, copper, and manganese. The costs of processing the ore up to the splitoff point, including ore costs, are $55,000 per batch. Selling prices and additional processing costs after splitoff follow (per batch):

Product	Additional Processing Cost	Sales Price
Lead	$8,000	$20,000
Copper	5,000	45,000
Manganese	7,000	35,000

   Management wants to know the cost of these products after allocating joint costs. Use the approximate net realizable value method to allocate joint costs to the three refined products.

22. **Joint cost allocations using the physical quantities method—by-products.** The following diagram presents the facts for a group of products:

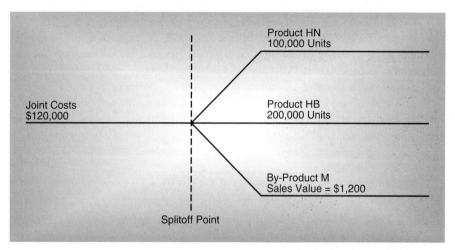

The firm uses by-product sales value to reduce joint product costs before allocation. The $120,000 is the joint cost before reduction for by-product sales value. Allocate joint costs.

Problems

23. **Joint costing—solving for unknowns** (adapted from CPA exam). O'Connor Company manufactures Product J and Product K from a joint process. O'Connor produced 4,000 units of Product J with a sales value at the splitoff point of $20,000. If O'Connor processed Product J further, the additional costs would equal $3,000 and the sales value would equal $25,000. O'Connor produced 2,000 units of Product K with a sales value at splitoff of $10,000. If O'Connor processed Product K further, the additional costs would equal $1,500 and the sales value would equal $14,000. Using the net realizable value at splitoff approach, the firm allocated $9,000 to the portion of the total joint product costs for Product J.

    Compute the total joint product costs.

24. **Joint costing—finding missing values.** Demski Enterprises makes stuffed animals, known as "Ralph" toys. From a joint process, Demski produces three toys, anteaters (A), bears (B), and camels (C). The company allocates joint costs based on relative sales value at splitoff. Additional data follow:

	Product			
	A	**B**	**C**	**Total**
Units Produced...............	8,000	4,000	2,000	14,000
Joint Costs	$ 72,000	a	b	$120,000
Sales Value at Splitoff........	c	$50,000	$30,000	200,000
Additional Costs to Process Further	14,000	$10,000	6,000	30,000
Sales Value If Processed Further	140,000	60,000	40,000	240,000

    Derive the values for the lettered items.

25. **Allocating overhead.** The APCO Company applies manufacturing overhead to the Melting and Molding departments. From the following data, prepare an overhead allocation schedule showing in detail the manufacturing overhead chargeable to each department. Some costs can be assigned directly (for example, indirect labor). Allocate machinery and equipment costs based on the cost of machinery and equipment, power based on horsepower rating, compensation insurance based on labor and indirect labor costs, and building related costs based on floor space. Round all decimals to three places and all dollars to whole dollars.

APCO COMPANY
Manufacturing Overhead Costs during the Month

Indirect Labor:
Melting .... $ 6,600
Molding... 3,600

(continued)

Supplies Used:

Melting	$ 1,500
Molding..	900
Taxes (machinery and equipment, $72; building, $144)	216
Compensation Insurance	906
Power..	300
Heat and Light	480
Depreciation: Building	384
Machinery and Equipment	360
Total	$15,246

Other Operating Data

	Floor Space (square feet)	Cost of Machinery and Equipment	Direct Labor per Month	Horsepower Rating
Department:				
Melting	2,000	$35,000	$ 2,000	120
Molding.............	6,000	25,000	10,000	180
Total	8,000	$60,000	$12,000	300

26. **Allocating unassigned costs to retail store departments.** The Kellermeyer Specialty Shop has two departments, Clothing and Accessories. The operating expenses for the year ending December 31 follow.

a. Prepare a three-column statement of operating expenses with column headings: Clothing, Accessories, Total. Begin with direct departmental expenses and show a subtotal. Then continue with the allocated expenses, assigning each item to the various departments. Round all values to the nearest dollar and all percentages to one decimal place.

b. Prepare a condensed income statement with columns for Clothing, Accessories, and Total. Show the total operating expenses calculated in part **a** as a single deduction from gross margin.

KELLERMEYER SPECIALTY SHOP

	Clothing	Accessories	Unassigned	Total
Salaries:				
Clerks	$78,240	$69,360	—	$147,600
Others.................			$48,000	48,000
Supplies Used	3,800	3,200	1,400	8,400
Depreciation of				
Equipment	1,600	4,800	—	6,400
Advertising...............	3,726	8,586	3,888	16,200
Building Rent			19,000	19,000
Payroll Taxes			12,300	12,300

(continued)

	Clothing	Accessories	Unassigned	Total
Worker's Compensation Insurance..............			2,080	2,080
Fire Insurance............			1,000	1,000
Delivery Expense..........			1,800	1,800
Miscellaneous Expenses..............	1,000	800	600	2,400

KELLERMEYER SPECIALTY SHOP

	Clothing	Accessories	Total
Sales...............................	$600,000	$400,000	$1,000,000
Cost of Goods Sold.................	$440,000	$240,000	$680,000
Equipment..........................	$10,080	$24,960	$35,040
Inventory (average).................	$100,800	$139,200	$240,000
Floor Space (square feet)...........	2,400	3,600	6,000
Number of Employees...............	10	15	25

KELLERMEYER SPECIALTY SHOP

Expense	Basis of Allocation
Salaries—Other......................	Gross Margin
Supplies Used (unassigned)...........	Sales
Advertising (unassigned)..............	Sales
Building Rent.......................	Floor Space
Payroll Taxes......................	Salaries (including both direct and other allocated salaries)
Worker's Compensation Insurance.......	Salaries (including both direct and other allocated salaries)
Fire Insurance......................	Cost of Equipment and Inventory
Delivery Expense....................	Sales
Miscellaneous Expenses (unassigned)...	Number of Employees

27. **Allocating service department costs.** The Schneider Spaghetti Company has two production departments, Tubing and Packing, and two service departments, Quality Control and Maintenance. In June, the Quality Control department provided 2,000 hours of service—995 hours to Tubing, 255 hours to Maintenance, and 750 hours to Packing. In the same month, Maintenance provided 2,700 hours to Tubing, 1,800 hours to Packing, and 500 hours to Quality Control. Quality Control incurred costs of $50,000, and Maintenance incurred costs of $105,000.

Use the step method to allocate service department costs sequentially based on hours of service provided. Start with Maintenance and then allocate Quality Control. Check your solution by making certain that the firm finally allocates $155,000 to the production departments.

28. **Sell or process further.** A joint production process results in the splitoff of three products, A, B, and C. Joint costs incurred total $100,000. At splitoff, 10,000 units of Product A, 10,000 units of Product B, and 20,000 units of Product C emerge.

    a. The firm can sell the units at splitoff at the following prices: Product A, $3 each; Product B, $6 each; Product C, $4.50 each. Using the net realizable value method, calculate the gross margin (= sales − allocated joint costs) of each product if the firm sells it at splitoff.

    b. By incurring additional processing costs of $1 per unit, the firm can sell Product A for $5 a unit. By incurring additional processing costs of $3 a unit, it can sell Product C for $8 a unit. Using the approximate net realizable value at splitoff method, calculate the net income of each product if additional processing takes place.

    c. Which products should the firm sell at splitoff and which products should it process further? Explain.

29. **Joint cost allocations with by-products** (adapted from CPA exam). Harrison Corporation produces three products, Alpha, Beta, and Gamma. Alpha and Gamma are main products, whereas Beta is a by-product of Alpha. Information on the past month's production processes follows:

    (1) Department I processed 110,000 units of raw material Rho at a total cost of $120,000. After processing, Department I transferred 60 percent of the units to Department II and 40 percent of the units (now unprocessed Gamma) to Department III.

    (2) Department II processed the materials received from Department I at a total additional cost of $38,000. Seventy percent of the units became Alpha and Department II transferred them to Department IV. The remaining 30 percent emerged as Beta and the firm sold them at $2.10 per unit. The selling costs for the Beta amounted to $8,100.

    (3) Department III processed Gamma at an additional cost of $165,000. A normal loss of units of Gamma occurs in this department. The loss equalled 10 percent of the units of good output. The firm sold the remaining good output for $12 per unit.

    (4) Department IV processed Alpha at an additional cost of $23,660. After this processing, the firm sold Alpha for $5 per unit.

    Prepare a schedule showing the allocation of the $120,000 joint cost between Alpha and Gamma using the net realizable value approach. Credit the net realizable value from sales of by-products to the manufacturing costs of the related main product.

30. **Allocating service department costs** (adapted from CPA exam). The Jurassic Company has three service departments (administration, maintenance, and computer support) and two production departments (creative and assembly). A summary of costs and other data for each department prior to allocation of service department costs for the year ended June 30, Year 1, follow:

	Administration	Maintenance	Computer Support	Creative	Assembly
Direct Material Costs.............	0	$65,000	$91,000	$3,130,000	$ 950,000
Direct Labor Costs...............	$90,000	82,100	87,000	1,950,000	2,050,000
Overhead Costs	70,000	56,100	62,000	1,650,000	1,850,000
Direct Labor Hours	31,000	27,000	42,000	562,500	437,500
Number of Computers	12	8	20	280	200
Square Footage Occupied........	1,750	2,000	4,800	88,000	72,000

Jurassic allocates the costs of the administration, maintenance, and computer services departments on the basis of direct labor hours, square footage occupied, and number of computers, respectively. Round all final calculations to the nearest dollar.

a. Assuming that Jurassic elects to distribute service department costs directly to production departments without interservice department cost allocation, what amount of maintenance department costs would Jurassic allocate to the creative department?

b. Assuming the same method of allocation as in part **a,** what amount of administration department costs would Jurassic allocate to the assembly department?

c. Assuming that Jurassic elects to distribute service department costs to other service departments (starting with the computer support department) as well as the production departments, what amounts of computer support department costs would Jurassic allocate to the maintenance department? (Note: Once the firm has allocated a service department's costs, no subsequent service department costs are allocated back to it.)

d. Assuming the same method of allocation as in part **c,** what amount of maintenance department costs would Jurassic allocate to the computer support department?

31. **Using matrix algebra for cost allocations** (Appendix 5.1). Refer to the problem data for Schneider Spaghetti Company, Problem 27.

a. Following the method outlined in Appendix 5.1, set up the full matrices of services output, **S,** and usage, **P,** based on the data given in Problem 27.

b. Express algebraically the fraction of the Maintenance department's output allocable to Tubing. Use the notation described in Appendix 5.1 for the Berdan Products example.

c. Express algebraically the fraction of the Quality Control department's output allocable to Packing. Use the notation described in Appendix 5.1 for the Berdan Products example.

d. Use matrices **S** and **P** to solve for matrix **A,** the allocation matrix.

e. Use the results of matrix **A** to allocate the service department costs.

32. **Cost allocations using the reciprocal method** (Appendix 5.1). The following data describe services that the four departments of the Oak Bank produced and consumed during October. Using these data, write the system of simultaneous equations describing the proper allocation of service department costs to the

production departments. Solve for the final allocation of costs with simultaneous equations or the matrix method explained in Appendix 5.1.

OAK BANK
Fractions of Service Departments' Output Used by Service and Production Departments for October

	Services Performed By	
	Personnel (*P*)	Administration (*A*)
Services Used By		
Service Departments		
Personnel (*P*)	—	.30
Administration (*A*)	.10	—
Production Departments		
Services (*S*)	.60	.20
Loans (*L*)	.30	.50
Costs to Be Allocated	$40,000	$60,000

33. **Cost allocations with matrices given** (Appendix 5.1). The Twin City Manufacturing Company derived the following allocation matrices (**A**) for April, May, and June:

TWIN CITY MANUFACTURING COMPANY
Allocation Matrices

	Services Performed by	
	Repairs (R)	Administration (A)
Services Used in April By		
Production Departments		
Cleaning (C)	.435	.343
Mixing (M)	.215	.358
Pouring (P)	.350	.299
	1.000	1.000
Costs to Be Allocated	$50,000	$60,000

	Services Performed By	
	Repairs (R)	Administration (A)
Services Used in May By		
Production Departments		
Cleaning (C)	.40	.30
Mixing (M)	.40	.20
Pouring (P)	.20	.50
	1.00	1.00
Costs to Be Allocated	$52,000	$58,000

(continued)

	Services Performed By	
	Repairs (R)	Administration (A)
Services Used in June By		
Production Departments		
Cleaning (C)	.45	.35
Mixing (M)	.25	.40
Pouring (P)	.30	.25
	1.00	1.00
Costs to Be Allocated	$55,000	$64,000

Use the allocation matrices to calculate how much Twin City should charge each production department for service costs for

a. April.

b. May.

c. June.

Cases

34. **Relating allocation methods to organizational characteristics for a retailer** (adapted from CMA exam). Columbia Company is a regional office supply chain with 26 independent stores. The firm holds each store responsible for its own credit and collections. The firm assigns the assistant manager in each store the responsibility for credit activities, including the collection of delinquent accounts, because the stores do not need a full-time employee assigned to credit activities. The company has experienced a sharp rise in uncollectibles the last 2 years. Corporate management has decided to establish a collections department in the home office that takes over the collection function company-wide. The home office of Columbia Company will hire the necessary full-time personnel. The firm will base the size of this department on the historical credit activity of all the stores.

Top management discussed the new centralized collections department at a recent management meeting. Management has had difficulty deciding on a method to assign the costs of the new department to the stores because this type of home office service is unusual. Top management is reviewing alternative methods.

The controller favored using a predetermined rate for charging the costs to the stores. The firm would base the predetermined rate on budgeted costs. The vice president for sales preferred an actual cost charging system.

In addition, management also discussed the basis for the collection charges to the stores. The controller identified the four following measures of services (allocation bases) that the firm could use:

(1) Total dollar sales.

(2) Average number of past-due accounts.

(3) Number of uncollectible accounts written off.

(4) One twenty-sixth of the cost to each of the stores.

The executive vice president stated that he would like the accounting department to prepare a detailed analysis of the two charging methods and the four service measures (allocation bases).

a. Evaluate the two methods identified—predetermined rate versus actual cost—that the firm could use to charge the individual stores the costs of Columbia Company's new collections department in terms of

   (1) Practicality of application and ease of use.

   (2) Cost control.

   Also indicate whether a centralized or decentralized organization structure would be more conducive for each charging method.

b. For each of the four measures of services (allocation bases) the controller of Columbia Company identified:

   (1) Discuss whether using the service measure (allocation base) is appropriate in this situation.

   (2) Identify the behavioral problems, if any, that could arise as a consequence of adopting the service measure (allocation base).

35. **Allocation for economic decisions and motivation** (adapted from CMA exam). Bonn Company recently reorganized its computer and data processing system. Bonn has replaced the individual installations located within the accounting departments at its plants and subsidiaries with a single data-processing department at corporate headquarters responsible for the operations of a newly acquired large-scale computer system. The new department has been operating for 2 years and regularly producing reliable and timely data for the past 12 months.

Because the department has focused its activities on converting applications to the new system and producing reports for the plant and subsidiary managements, it has devoted little attention to the costs of the department. Now that the department's activities are operating relatively smoothly, company management has requested that the departmental manager recommend a cost accumulation system to facilitate cost control and the development of suitable rates to charge users for service.

For the past 2 years, the department has recorded costs in one account. The department has then allocated the costs to user departments on the basis of computer time used. The schedule on the next page reports the costs and charging rate for Year 4.

The department manager recommends that the five activity centers within the department accumulate the department costs. The five activity centers are systems analysis, programming, data preparation, computer operations (processing), and administration. She then suggests that the firm allocate the costs of the administration activity to the other four activity centers before developing a separate rate for charging users for each of the first four activities.

After reviewing the details of the accounts, the manager made the following observations regarding the charges to the several subsidiary accounts within the department:

(1) Salaries and benefits—records the salary and benefit costs of all employees in the department.

Data Processing Department
Costs for the Year Ended December 31, Year 4

(1) Salaries and Benefits..	$ 622,600
(2) Supplies	40,000
(3) Equipment Maintenance Contract	15,000
(4) Insurance	25,000
(5) Heat and Air Conditioning..................................	36,000
(6) Electricity	50,000
(7) Equipment and Furniture Depreciation.......................	285,400
(8) Building Improvements Depreciation	10,000
(9) Building Occupancy and Security	39,300
(10) Corporate Administrative Charges	52,700
Total Costs..	$1,176,000
Computer Hours for User Processing[a]........................	2,750
Hourly Rate ($1,176,000/2,750)...............................	$428

[a]Use of available computer hours:

Testing and Debugging Programs	250
Setup of Jobs...	500
Processing Jobs...	2,750
Downtime for Maintenance	750
Idle Time	742
	4,992

(2) Supplies—records paper costs for printers and a small amount for other miscellaneous costs.

(3) Equipment maintenance contracts—records charges for maintenance contracts which cover all equipment.

(4) Insurance—records cost of insurance covering the equipment and the furniture.

(5) Heat and air conditioning—records a charge from the corporate heating and air conditioning department estimated to be the incremental costs to meet the special needs of the computer department.

(6) Electricity—records the charge for electricity based on a separate meter within the department.

(7) Equipment and furniture depreciation—records the depreciation charges for all equipment and furniture owned within the department.

(8) Building improvements—records the amortization charges for the building changes required to provide proper environmental control and electrical service for the computer equipment.

(9) Building occupancy and security—records the computer department's share of the depreciation, maintenance, heat, and security costs of the building; the firm allocates these costs to the department on the basis of square feet occupied.

(10) Corporate administrative charges—records the computer department's share of the corporate administrative costs. The firm allocates them to the department on the basis of number of employees in the department.

a. For each of the ten cost items, state whether or not the firm should distribute it to the five activity centers; and for each cost item that the firm should distribute, recommend the basis on which it should distribute it. Justify your conclusion in each case.

b. Assume that the costs of the computer operations (processing) activity will be charged to the user departments on the basis of computer hours. Using the analysis of computer utilization shown as a footnote to the department cost schedule presented in the problem, determine the total number of hours that should be employed to determine the charging rate for computer operations (processing). Justify your answer.

36. Differential cost analysis with joint products and by-products (contributed by M. L. Marais). KLEEN Chemical Company conducts comprehensive annual profit planning to estimate unit costs, to calculate pricing, and to plan production. One product group that KLEEN analyzes separately each year involves two joint products and two by-products.

The two joint products, specialty chemicals X and Y, emerge at the end of processing in Department A. KLEEN can sell both chemicals at this splitoff point: X for $25 per kilogram (kg) and Y for $20 per kg. By-product MUTIN-X also emerges at the splitoff point in Department A and KLEEN can sell it without further processing for $1.50 per kg.

In the past, KLEEN has sold chemical Y without further processing, but has transferred X to Department B for additional processing into a refined rodent-control chemical called RAT-BUST. Department B adds no additional raw materials. KLEEN sells RAT-BUST for $30 per kg. The additional processing in Department B creates the by-product MUTIN-Z and KLEEN sells it for $3 per kg.

Exhibit 5.16 presents a portion of the Year 2 budget established in September, Year 1. Shortly after the company compiled this information, it learned that another company was planning to introduce a chemical that would compete with RAT-BUST. The marketing department has estimated that for KLEEN to sell RAT-BUST in present quantities, it would have to permanently reduce prices to $27 per kg.

The introduction of this new chemical will not affect the market for chemical X. Consequently, the quantities of X that KLEEN usually processed into RAT-BUST can sell at the regular price of $25 per kg. Marketing estimates costs of $105,000 to market X. If KLEEN terminates the processing, it will have to dismantle Department B and will eliminate all costs except $115,000 of the company's administrative costs allocated to Department B.

a. What alternative actions can KLEEN Chemical's executives take? How will profits differ among these alternatives? What do you recommend?

b. During discussion of the possibility of dropping RAT-BUST, one person noted that the gross margin for chemical X would be more than 40 percent, whereas the gross margin for chemical Y would be negative. Firms normally mark up by 20 percent products sold in the market with X. For the Y portion of the line, firms normally mark up 25 percent. The person argued that the company's unit costs must be incorrect, because the margins differ from the typical rates. Briefly explain why the margins for KLEEN Chemical's products differ from the normal rates.

Exhibit 5.16

KLEEN CHEMICALS
Year 2 Profit Plan

	Production and Sales Schedule (kilograms)	
	Chemical Y	**Chemical X or RAT-BUST**
Estimated Sales and Production Units	60,000	40,000
By-Product Output:		
MUTIN-X		20,000
MUTIN-Z		10,000

Budgeted Production Costs	**Department A**	**Department B**
Raw Materials.	$1,300,000	—
Costs Transferred from Department A	(577,300)	$577,300
Direct Labor	195,000	75,000
Variable Overhead.	182,000	70,000
Fixed Overhead (includes corporate administrative costs allocated to departments)	250,000	190,000
	$1,349,700	$912,300

	Chemical Y	**RAT-BUST**
Budgeted Marketing Costs.	$196,000	$105,000

37. Cost-based reimbursement for hospitals.[4] The annual costs of hospital care under the Medicare program amount to $20 billion per year. In the Medicare legislation, Congress mandated that Medicare would limit reimbursement to hospitals to the costs of treating Medicare patients. Ideally, neither the patients nor the hospitals would bear the costs of the Medicare patients nor would the government bear costs of non-Medicare patients. Given the large sums involved, cost reimbursement specialists, computer programs, publications, and other products and services have arisen to provide hospital administrators with the assistance needed to obtain an appropriate reimbursement for Medicare patient services.

Accountants would divide hospital departments into two categories, revenue-producing departments and nonrevenue-producing departments. Accountants use this classification because the traditional accounting concepts associated with service department cost allocation, although appropriate to this context, lead to confusion in terminology. This confusion results because most people consider all of the hospital's departments to render services.

Accountants charge costs of revenue-producing departments to Medicare and non-Medicare patients on the basis of actual usage of the departments. Accountants can apportion these costs relatively simply. Accountants have more difficulty apportioning the costs of nonrevenue-producing departments.

---

[4]Copyright © 1989 by CIPT, Inc.

The approach to finding the appropriate distribution of these costs begins with the establishment of a reasonable basis for allocating nonrevenue-producing department costs to revenue-producing departments. Accountants must ascertain statistical measures of the relationships between departments. Medicare regulations have established the cost allocation bases listed in Exhibit 5.17 as acceptable for cost reimbursement purposes. Accountants must use the regulated order of allocation for Medicare reimbursement even though the general rule may call for another order.

A hospital may then use the step method to allocate costs. If the hospital uses the step method, it allocates costs to the departments in the same order as listed in Exhibit 5.17. Thus it allocates depreciation of buildings before depreciation of movable equipment. It must establish cost centers for each of these nonrevenue-producing costs that are relevant to a particular hospital's operations.

In the past year, the hospital reported the following departmental costs:

Nonrevenue-Producing:	
Laundry and Linen...	$ 250,000
Depreciation—Buildings	830,000
Employee Health and Welfare.................................	375,000
Maintenance of Personnel	210,000
Central Supply	745,000
Revenue-Producing:	
Operating Room..	$1,450,000
Radiology...	160,000
Laboratory	125,000
Patient Rooms	2,800,000

Exhibit 5.17

Bases for Allocating Nonrevenue Department Costs to Revenue-Producing Departments

Nonrevenue Cost Center	Basis for Allocation
Depreciation—Buildings	Square Feet in Each Department
Depreciation—Movable Equipment	Dollar Value of Equipment in Each Department
Employee Health and Welfare	Gross Salaries in Each Department
Administrative and General	Accumulated Costs by Department
Maintenance and Repairs	Square Feet in Each Department
Operation of Plant	Square Feet in Each Department
Laundry and Linen Service	Pounds Used in Each Department
Housekeeping	Hours of Service to Each Department
Dietary	Meals Served in Each Department
Maintenance of Personnel	Number of Departmental Employees Housed
Nursing Administration	Hours of Supervision in Each Department
Central Supply	Costs of Requisitions Processed
Pharmacy	Costs of Drug Orders Processed
Medical Records	Hours Worked for Each Department
Social Service	Hours Worked for Each Department
Nursing School	Assigned Time by Department
Intern/Resident Service	Assigned Time by Department

Percentage usage of services by one department from another department was as follows:

From	Laundry and Linen	Depreci- ation— Buildings	Employee Health and Welfare	Maintenance of Personnel	Central Supply
Laundry and Linen.....		.05	.10	0	0
Depreciation— Buildings	.10		0	.10	0
Employee Health and Welfare........	.15	0		.05	.03
Maintenance of Personnel..........	0	0	0		.12
Central Supply	.10	0	0	.08	

	Operating Rooms	Radiology	Laboratory	Patient Rooms
Laundry and Linen.............	.30	.10	.05	.40
Depreciation—Buildings	.05	.02	.02	.71
Employee Health and Welfare...	.25	.05	.04	.43
Maintenance of Personnel	.36	.10	.08	.34
Central Supply	.09	.04	.03	.66

The proportional usage of revenue-producing department services by Medicare and other patients was as follows:

	Medicare	Other
Operating Rooms.......................................	25%	75%
Radiology..	20	80
Laboratory	28	72
Patient Rooms	36	64

Ascertain the amount of the reimbursement claim for Medicare services using the step method of allocation.

Suggested Solutions to Even-Numbered Exercises

14. **Allocating overhead.**

	Department			
	No. 1	No. 2	Maintenance	General Plant
Charged Directly to Department:				
Indirect Labor	$28,000	$14,000	$22,500	$20,000
Indirect Material	9,000	7,000	900	8,000
Miscellaneous	3,000	5,000	1,600	5,000
	$40,000	$26,000	$25,000	$33,000

(continued)

	Department			
	No. 1	**No. 2**	**Maintenance**	**General Plant**
Allocations:				
General Plant	16,500	9,900	6,600	(33,000)
Maintenance[a]	11,060	20,540	(31,600)	
Total Overhead[b]	$67,560	$56,440	0	0

[a]Total costs to be allocated: $25,000 + $6,600 = $31,600. Allocate on the basis of maintenance hours.

[b]$67,560 + $56,440 = $40,000 + $26,000 + $25,000 + $33,000.

16. Allocating service department costs using the step method.

	General Factory Administration	**Maintenance**	**Cutting**	**Assembly**
Service Department Costs	$1,200	$2,400	NA	NA
Maintenance Allocation....	480(1/5)	(2,400)	$480(1/5)	$1,440(3/5)
General Factory Administration Allocation	(1,680)		336(1/5)	1,344(4/5)
Total Costs Allocated			$816	$2,784

18. Allocating service department costs directly to operating departments.

		To	
From		**P1**	**P2**
S1		$15,000[a]	$15,000[a]
S2		25,000[b]	15,000[b]
		$40,000	$30,000

[a]$15,000 = $\dfrac{.10}{.10 + .10}$ × $30,000. (The eighty percent of S1's costs used by S2 are ignored.)

[b]$25,000 = .625 × $40,000.

$15,000 = .325 × $40,000.

20. Joint cost allocations—net realizable value method.
Total joint costs are $205,000 (based on the $45,000 materials plus $160,000 conversion). The firm allocates these costs as follows:

To Output Al: $\dfrac{\$273,000}{\$455,000}$ × $205,000 = $123,000.

To Output Gore: $\dfrac{\$455,000 - \$273,000}{\$455,000}$ × $205,000 = $82,000.

22. **Joint cost allocations using the physical quantities method—by-products.**
Deduct the net realizable value of M ($1,200) from the total processing costs ($120,000) to obtain the net processing costs to be allocated ($118,800). Compute the allocation as follows:

$$\text{To HN: } \frac{100,000 \text{ Units}}{100,000 \text{ Units} + 200,000 \text{ Units}} \times \$118,800 = \underline{\$39,600}.$$

$$\text{To HB: } \frac{200,000 \text{ Units}}{100,000 \text{ Units} + 200,000 \text{ Units}} \times \$118,800 = \underline{\$79,200}.$$

Activity-Based Management and Costing

1. Understand the issues in allocating costs to products.

2. See the advantages and disadvantages of activity-based costing.

3. Compute product costs using activity-based costing.

4. Compare product costing using activity-based costing to traditional cost allocation methods.

5. See the impact of the new production environment on activity bases.

6. Understand how activity-based management and costing can be used to eliminate non-value added costs.

7. See opportunities to improve activity-based management and costing in practice.

8. Identify behavioral problems to be addressed in implementing activity-based costing.

Many companies, like Hewlett-Packard, Procter & Gamble, Boeing, Caterpillar, and IBM, have recently implemented new methods to improve the way they manage costs. These new methods have revealed startling new information about product profitability. For example, Tektronix, Inc., found, to the surprise of management, that one of its products, a printed-circuit board, was generating negative margins of 46 percent.[1]

This chapter deals with the allocation of indirect costs to products, and how this allocation affects managerial decisions. Indirect costs include overhead costs incurred to manufacture a good or provide a service, indirect costs to market a prod-

---

[1]"A Bean-Counter's Best Friend," *Business Week/Quality,* 1991, pp. 42–43.

uct, and indirect costs incurred to manage the company. Unlike direct materials and direct labor that accountants can trace directly to a product, accountants must *allocate* indirect costs to products.

Chapter 5 described how companies allocate costs to production departments. That allocation is the first stage in the two-stage cost allocation process. In Chapter 5, the **cost pools,** groupings (or aggregations) of costs, were departments. In general, cost pools group costs into either (1) plants, which are entire factories, stores, banks, and so forth, or (2) departments within plants, or (3) activity centers. This chapter discusses issues in establishing cost pools and the second stage of cost allocation: allocating costs from cost pools to products.

We use predetermined overhead rates throughout this chapter. Recall from Chapter 3 that use of predetermined rates normally results in over- or underapplied overhead. To keep the examples in this chapter from becoming too complex, we do not deal with the accounting disposition of over- or underapplied overhead.

Choosing the Cost Pool

Plantwide versus Departmental versus Activity Center

The simplest allocation method, **plantwide allocation,** uses the entire plant as a cost pool. Although accountants call this method the plantwide method, in fact, the ''plant'' need not refer to a manufacturing facility but can mean store, hospital, or other multidepartment segment of a company. A bank, for example, could apply overhead to different customer accounts, to different types of loans, and to other products using just one overhead rate for the entire bank.

Simple organizations having only a few departments and not much variety in activities in different departments might justify using the plantwide method.

When companies use the **department allocation method,** they have a separate cost pool for each department. The company establishes a separate overhead allocation rate or set of rates for each department. Recall from Chapter 5 that service departments provide services to production departments, and production departments produce goods and services. Each production department would be a separate cost pool.

Most complex organizations have moved from single, plantwide cost pools to multiple department cost pools. Some companies, such as Hewlett-Packard, Procter & Gamble, Caterpillar, and Chrysler among others, use even more cost pools, one each for numerous **activity centers.** Each company defines its own activity centers to be for parts of the company that perform some easily described activity.

For example, of a motorcycle plant that one of the authors studied defined the paint quality inspection activity in the Paint Department as an activity center. This activity center handled all paint-related quality inspections to see that the manufacturing had properly applied the paint, with no paint runs, splatters, splotches, oversprays, and the like. The detailed activity-based costing system in this motorcycle plant separated the paint inspection costs from the paint spraying costs. In contrast, a cost system based on department cost pools combines all Paint Department costs into a single pool, not separating paint spraying from the inspection of paint spraying. In contrast the plantwide allocation method would have a single cost pool for the entire motorcycle factory. The plantwide allocation method thus compiles no separate costs for the Paint Department, much less the quality inspection activity.

Choice of Cost Allocation Method: A Cost-Benefit Decision

Should managers use plantwide, departmental, or activity center cost pools? The choice requires managers to make cost-benefit decisions. Plantwide methods cost least but provide the least information. Maintaining cost pools by activity center costs most but provides the most information. Do the benefits justify the costs? If managers in the motorcycle plant have a use for information about which motorcycle types consume the most resources in paint quality inspection, they must think about the benefits of that information. Then they compare the benefits of separating quality inspection costs with the cost of collecting and processing more detailed data.

Selecting more cost pools, to provide more detail, requires more time and skill to collect and process accounting information. Increased benefits from improved decisions must justify the additional costs of getting better information from more detailed costing systems.

Activity-Based Costing

Activity-based costing (ABC) first assigns costs to activities, then to the products based on each product's use of activities. Activity-based costing rests on this premise: *Products consume activities; activities consume resources.*

If managers want their products to be competitive, they must know both (1) the activities that go into making the goods or providing the services, and (2) the cost of those activities. To reduce a product's costs, managers will likely have to change the activities the product consumes. A manager who announces, ''I want across-the-board cuts—everyone reduce costs by 20 percent,'' rarely gets the desired results. To make significant cost reductions, people must first identify the activities that a product consumes. Then they must figure out how to rework those activities to improve production efficiency.

Is activity-based costing a new idea or an old idea whose time has come? Some accounting experts argue that activity-based costing simply extends departmental allocation methods. Just as departmental allocation provides more detailed cost information than plantwide allocation, activity-based costing provides more detailed cost information than department allocation. According to this view, activity-based costing simply extends allocation methods that companies have used for years.

Does it matter? Many proponents of activity-based costing argue that ABC does not simply extend traditional departmental allocation. Instead, they argue, activity-based costing changes the way managers do their jobs. These proponents argue that people manage activities, not costs. Activity-based costing focuses attention on the things that management can make more efficient or otherwise change. We believe that ABC does alter management focus in sensible ways.

Strategic Use of Activity-Based Costing

Some companies use activity-based costing to plan their corporate strategies.[2] For example, some companies develop competitive advantages by becoming a low-cost producer or seller. Companies such as Wal-Mart in retailing, United Parcel in delivery services, and Southwest Airlines in the airline industry create a competitive advantage by reducing costs. Some companies have learned to use information from their cost systems to make substantial price cuts to increase sales volume and market share.[3]

Activity-based costing can help a company develop strategy, long-range plans, and subsequent competitive cost advantage by focusing attention on activities. To reduce costs generally requires changes in activities. Top management can beg or command employees to reduce costs, but implementation requires changes in activities. Anyone can cut costs—just close down the operation. Effective management cuts costs while maintaining quality and quantity of output.

Examples If you have been in school during a period of successful education cost-cutting, you saw that to achieve the cuts required some combination of canceling classes, increasing class sizes, and reducing services, such as library or computer center hours. Each of these involves focus on activities: setting numbers of classes in the schedule, setting class sizes and choosing classrooms for those classes, and the school-wide activity of setting hours for facility openings and closings. Focus on departments, such as on the English department or the Accounting Department or even on the Library or Computer Center will not so easily result in overall cost cuts.

For example, to cut overall costs with minor effects on quality of education might involve reducing hours in the labor-intensive library reference room while increasing the amount of software help installed in the Computer Lab's on-line library catalog services. Measuring the effect of changes in activities on costs requires cost information provided by activity-based costing. For example, costs gathered for departments, such as the whole Library (a large department) or even for the reference room (a smaller department), do not provide information on the costs to be be saved by closing the Library (or reference room) one hour earlier.

To take another example, consider the problem of supplying quiet study areas to students. Many colleges provide such space in libraries which have large heating

---

[2]See J. Shank and V. Govindarajan, *Strategic Cost Analysis* (Homewood, IL.: Irwin, 1989), for discussion of strategic uses of cost analysis.

[3]M. E. Porter, *Competitive Advantage* (New York: Free Press, 1985).

and cooling bills for stack areas and large security bills to help ensure that students don't steal books. Note that many students use the library as a study place, not as a place to refer to books. A cost-cutter knows that closing the library early will save costs, but will degrade services by reducing quiet study places. The cost-cutter wonders if providing quiet study places in cafeterias will give students the quiet study places while saving costs. To deal effectively with such questions requires cost data on the activities of keeping the cafeteria and the library open, rather than on the departmental costs of running the cafeteria and library. ABC will likely help such a cost-cutter more than a departmental cost system.

Implementing Activity-Based Costing

The following discussion considers the advantages of activity-based costing. This discussion takes place at the New Challenge Cycle Company that makes bicycles and small motorized scooters. The participants worry about the company's ability to compete; they believe the company's cost accounting system is inadequate.

Joan Sommers (President of the company) expresses her frustration: Ten years ago, we led the industry in market share and profits. In the last few years, our profits have shrunk to almost nothing. We can't even meet competitors' prices for the basic mountain bike, which has been our most important and highest-volume product.

Peter Kim (Vice-President of Marketing): I agree we don't match competitors' prices but our prices just barely cover costs now. I think the problem lies in production costs; our costs exceed our competitors' costs.

Andrea Gates (Vice-President of Production): I think we could reduce costs if our cost system better guided our efforts. I don't trust the cost numbers we get now. The accountants arbitrarily allocate our overhead, totalling almost half the cost of manufacturing, to our products. For us to reduce costs, we need better cost data than we get now. (Note, she doesn't know the aspect of the cost system causing her problem, only that the data don't help her.)

Kris Murphy (Controller) understands Andrea's concern: For several months, our staff has studied changes to our department cost allocation system. We learned that such companies as Ford, Deere & Company, and Hewlett-Packard discovered problems with their cost systems. Their problems appear similar to ours; namely, they believe they can't lower prices to be competitive on high-volume products and their profits shrink.

Joan: That sounds like us. What are they doing about it?

Kris: First, they're installing the new activity-based costing system, known for short as ABC. The system provides more detailed and, they believe, better estimates of product costs, which helps marketing staff set prices. Based on our analysis of their experiences I think activity-based costing could reveal that our mountain bike costs less than we thought. This means we could lower prices and still profit from sales of the mountain bikes.

Peter: That would be good news, but I thought costs were pretty cut-and-dried. How can a product's cost under one cost system be different than its cost under another cost system?

Kris: Peter, the product doesn't *actually* cost more or less, it just *appears to cost more or less.* No cost system can measure costs perfectly. We trace some costs, like materials, directly to the product. Overhead costs like the cost of electricity to run machines, salaries of product designers, quality control inspectors and machine operators, and machine maintenance costs are *allocated* to products using an allocation base like the number of machine hours. Products that require more machine hours are allocated more overhead costs, even if the overhead isn't related to machine hours.

For example, the salaries of inspectors are related to the number of inspections, which is related to the complexity of the welding and the quality of materials, not to the number of machine hours. If we change the allocation base, we change the *apparent* product cost.

Joan: I understand that overhead allocation is somewhat arbitrary. How will activity-based costing help?

Kris: Activity-based costing provides more accurate information because we identify the activities that cause costs, and we measure the cost of the activity. Activity-based costing identifies and measures costs of performing the activities that go into a product much better than traditional cost methods. For example, if a particular type of bike requires ten inspections for a production run of 1,000 units, which is a lot of inspections, then we assign the cost of ten inspections to those 1,000 units. Under our present cost system, we bury the cost of inspections in overhead and spread it over all the units—like spreading peanut butter on bread.

Andrea: How would activity-based costing help us cut production costs?

Kris: ABC identifies activities that cause costs, and computes the costs of those activities. Using this information, we can eliminate or modify costly activities. For example, if we find that motorized scooters require too many costly inspections, we could redesign the scooter to reduce the need for inspections. Under our current cost system, we don't know how many inspections each product requires, nor how much it costs to perform an inspection.

Joan: Kris, if activity-based costing is so great, why haven't you used it before?

Kris: Activity-based costing provides more information, but it takes more time and effort than traditional cost systems. New accounting methods sound great in theory, but they must provide enough benefits from improved management decisions to justify the additional work required to provide the numbers. Until now, I did not think activity-based costing would pass a cost-benefit test.

Joan: We could get a lot of benefits from activity-based costing. We could improve our pricing, we could design new production methods to reduce the use of high-cost activities, and we could identify which products should be dropped because they are costing more than we thought. As you all know, Univega, Trek, and the rest of the industry are very competitive. We have to provide new products in new markets where we are low-cost, low-price producers. We need the best cost information we can get to succeed in those markets. Kris, what do you need to get started developing an activity-based costing system?

Kris: Installing a new cost system requires teamwork among people who know about different parts of the business—management, accounting, marketing, engineering, production, purchasing, and many other areas. We accountants need to learn a lot about how the product is made and marketed. Furthermore, we need other people in the company to buy into the results of our efforts. To be effective, activity-based costing must provide accurate information that reflects the real consumption of resources. Otherwise, we will have simply replaced an old arbitrary cost allocation system with a new arbitrary cost allocation system.

Joan: Let's get to work, and make sure we develop this new cost system right.

To summarize, the preceding discussion made the following key points about activity-based costing:

1. Different cost allocation methods provide different estimates of how much it costs to make a product.
2. Activity-based costing provides more detailed measures of costs than plantwide or department allocation methods.
3. Activity-based costing provides more accurate product cost numbers for marketing decisions about pricing and about which products to keep or eliminate.
4. Activity-based costing helps production managers by providing better information about how much each activity costs. ABC identifies previously unknown cost drivers. To control production costs, production managers learn to control the cost drivers.
5. Activity-based costing provides more information about product costs, but requires more record keeping. Managers must decide whether the benefits of improved decisions justify the additional cost of activity-based costing compared to department or plantwide allocation.
6. Installing activity-based costing requires teamwork among accounting, production, marketing, management, and other nonaccounting people.

We next discuss the methods used for activity-based costing, followed by an example.

Activity-Based Costing Methods

Activity-based costing requires accountants to follow four steps.

1. Identify the activities that consume resources, and assign costs to those activities. Purchasing materials would be an activity, for example.
2. Identify the cost driver(s) associated with each activity. A **cost driver** is a factor that causes, or "drives," an activity's costs. For the activity "purchasing materials," the cost driver could be "number of orders." (Each activity could have multiple cost drivers.)
3. Compute a cost rate per cost driver unit. The cost driver rate could be the cost per purchase order, for example.

4. Assign costs to products by multiplying the cost driver rate times the volume of cost drivers consumed by the product. For example, the cost per purchase order times the number of orders required for Product X for the month of December would measure the cost of the purchasing activity for Product X for December.

Identifying the Activities That Consume Resources (Step 1)

This is often the most interesting and challenging part of the exercise because it requires people to understand all of the activities required to make the product. Managers attempt to identify those activities that have the greatest impact on costs.

A Deere & Company plant identified eight major activities required to produce one of its products, for example. The company used one cost driver for each activity. Then it developed two cost rates for each cost driver, one for variable costs and one for fixed costs. For the materials handling activity, Deere used the number of loads required to move parts around the plant as the cost driver. Most of the materials handling costs were for labor. The company had very little fixed cost associated with materials handling.[4] To reduce materials handling costs, Deere and Co. managers sought ways to reduce the number of loads required to move parts around the plant.

Complexity As an Activity That Consumes Resources

One of the lessons of activity-based costing has been that costs are a function not only of volume, but also of complexity.[5] Imagine you produce 100,000 gallons per month of vanilla ice cream and your friend produces 100,000 gallons per month of 39 different flavors of ice cream. Further, assume your ice cream is sold only in one-liter containers, while your friend sells ice cream in various sizes of containers. Your friend has more complicated ordering, storage, packing in containers, and product testing (one of the more desirable jobs, nevertheless). Your friend has more machine setups, too. Presumably, you can set the machinery to one setting to obtain the desired product quality and taste; your friend has to set the machines each time a new flavor is produced. Although both of you produce the same total volume of ice cream, you can easily imagine that your friend's overhead costs will be considerably higher.

In general, the number of cost drivers has increased as companies have become more highly automated and more complex. Cost systems based on a simple direct labor basis for allocating costs are generally inadequate in all but the simplest production or selling enterprise.

Department allocation rates based on volume, like direct labor hours or machine hours, have naturally allocated costs to products proportional to volume. Accountants have allocated a higher proportion of overhead costs to higher-volume products and a lower proportion of overhead costs to lower-volume products.

---

[4]See "John Deere Component Works," Harvard Business School, Case 187–107.

[5]R. D. Banker, G. Potter, and R. G. Schroeder, "An Empirical Analysis of Manufacturing Overhead Cost Drivers," Working paper, April 3, 1992; and G. Foster and M. Gupta, "Manufacturing Overhead Cost Driver Analysis," *Journal of Accounting and Economics,* January 1990.

After installing activity-based costing, managers have generally found that lower-volume specialty products should be allocated more overhead than previously assumed under traditional volume-based allocation methods. Low-volume products may be more specialized, requiring more drawings and specifications, and require more inspections.

Low-volume products often require more machine setups for a given level of production output because they are produced in smaller batches. In the ice cream example, one batch of 1,000 gallons of the low-volume 39th flavor might require as much overhead cost for machine setups, quality inspections, and purchase orders as one batch of 100,000 gallons of the highest-volume flavor. Further, the low-volume product adds complexity to the operation by disrupting the production flow of the high-volume items. (Consider this fact the next time you stand in line at the store, bank, fast-food restaurant, or student aid line when someone ahead of you has a special, complex transaction.)

When overhead is applied based on the volume of output, high-volume products are allocated relatively more overhead than low-volume products. In a sense, high-volume products "subsidize" low-volume products. The high costs of providing a large number of low-volume products are hidden by volume-based allocation methods. Many companies continue producing or selling products without realizing their cost. For example, Nissan, the Japanese automobile company, found it had 110 different types of radiators, 1,200 types of floor carpets, and 300 varieties of ashtrays in 2,200 different model variations. In profitable years, management believed it could afford the array of choices, but by the early to mid-1990s, the company's losses forced management to reduce the variety in its cars. The company reduced the number of model variations by 35 percent, and even cut the number of different screws and other fasteners from 6,000 to 3,000. Engineers at Nissan explained that using different types of screws required workers to change the heads on their power tools more often, thus increasing the cost of making cars.[6]

Identifying Cost Drivers (Step 2)

Exhibit 6.1 presents several examples of the kinds of cost drivers that companies use. Most cost drivers are related to either the volume of production or to the complexity of the production or marketing process.

How do managers decide which cost driver to use? Three criteria are used for selecting cost drivers.

1. *Causal relation.* Choose a cost driver that *causes* the cost. This is ideal but not always possible because indirect costs are generally not causally linked to cost objects.
2. *Benefits received.* Choose a cost driver so costs are assigned in proportion to benefits received. For example, if the Physics Department in a university benefits more from the university's supercomputer than does the History Depart-

---

[6]"A Slump in Car Sales Forces Nissan to Start Cutting Swollen Costs," *The Wall Street Journal,* March 3, 1993, pp. A1, A6.

Exhibit 6.1

Examples of Cost Drivers

Machine Hours	Computer Time
Labor Hours or Cost	Items Produced or Sold
Pounds of Materials Handled	Customers Served
Pages Typed	Flight Hours
Machine Setups	Number of Surgeries
Purchase Orders	Scrap/Rework Orders
Quality Inspections	Hours of Testing Time
Number of Parts in a Product	Number of Different Customers
Miles Driven	

---

ment, the university should select a cost driver that recognizes the benefits to Physics. For example, the number of faculty and/or students in each department who use the computer would relate the costs of the supercomputer to the benefits.

3. *Reasonableness.* Some costs cannot be linked to products based on causality or benefits received, so are assigned on the basis of fairness or reasonableness. We noted above that Deere & Company selected eight cost drivers for certain products. The cost of a ninth activity, general and administrative overhead, was allocated to products using the reasonableness approach; namely, these costs were allocated to products as a simple percentage of the costs of the other eight activities that had been allocated to products.

Computing a Cost Rate per Cost Driver Unit (Step 3)

In general, predetermined rates for allocating indirect costs to products are computed as follows:

$$\frac{\text{Predetermined}}{\text{indirect cost rate}} = \frac{\text{Estimated indirect cost}}{\text{Estimated volume of the allocation base}}.$$

This formula applies to all indirect costs, whether manufacturing overhead, administrative costs, distribution costs, selling costs, or any other indirect cost.

Companies using department rates compute the predetermined indirect cost rate for each department. Companies using activity-based costing compute the rate for each cost driver in each activity center. For example, accountants assign the costs of setting up machines to the activity center that sets up machines. Each activity center has just one cost driver in many companies, but it is possible to have more than one cost driver in an activity center.

If inspecting products for quality is the cost driver, for example, then the company must be able to estimate the inspection costs before the period. Ideally, the company would also keep track of the actual cost of inspections as these costs are incurred during the period to compare actual and applied inspection costs.

Assigning Costs to Products (Step 4)

Workers and machines perform activities on each product as it is produced. Costs are allocated to products by multiplying each cost driver's rate by the amount of cost driver activity used in making the product, as described in the illustration that follows.

Activity-Based Costing Illustrated

After discussing the merits of activity-based costing, the controller and the production vice-president at New Challenge Cycle Company, visited the company's factory in Ciudad Juarez to study the possibility of implementing activity-based costing. The Ciudad Juarez factory made two products—a mountain bike and a racing bike. The mountain bike was a high-volume product line in the plant, while the racing bike was a low-volume, specialized product.

At the time of the New Challenge managers' visit, the Ciudad Juarez factory allocated overhead to products at the rate of 500 percent of a product's direct labor costs. The direct materials costs were $100 and $200 per bike for the mountain and racing bikes, respectively; and the direct labor costs were $30 and $60 per bike for the mountain and racing bikes. Adding overhead at the rate of 500 percent of direct labor costs gave the following product costs per unit.

	Mountain Bikes	Racing Bikes
Direct Materials	$100	$200
Direct Labor	30	60
Manufacturing Overhead	150[a]	300[a]
Total	$280	$560

[a]Amount equals direct labor times 500 percent.

Assigning Costs Using Activity-Based Costing

The New Challenge managers decided to experiment with activity-based costing at the Ciudad Juarez factory. First, they identified four activities that were important cost drivers. These activities were (1) purchasing materials, (2) setting up machines to produce a different product, (3) inspecting products, and (4) operating machines.

The New Challenge managers estimated the amount of overhead and the volume of activity events for each activity. For example, they estimated the company would purchase 10,000 frames that would require overhead costs of $200,000 for the year. Salaries of people to purchase, inspect, and store materials are examples of these overhead costs. They assigned an overhead cost of $20 (=$200,000/10,000 frames) to each frame that the factory actually purchased for purchasing overhead. Machine operation requires energy and maintenance, which they estimated to cost $30 per machine hour. They estimated the rate for inspections to be $100 per hour in the

---

Exhibit 6.2

Predetermined Annual Overhead Rates for Activity-Based Costing

(1)	(2)	(3)	(4)	(5)
Activity	Cost Driver	Estimated Overhead Cost for the Activity	Estimated Number of Cost Driver Units for Year 2	Rate (Column 3/Column 4)
Purchasing materials	Number of frames purchased	$ 200,000	10,000 frames	$20 per frame
Machine setups	Number of machine setups	800,000	400 setups	$2,000 per setup
Inspections	Hours of inspections	400,000	4,000 hours	$100 per hour
Running machines	Machine hours	600,000	20,000 hours	$30 per hour
Total estimated overhead		$2,000,000		

---

inspection station and the machine setup rate to be $2,000 per setup. Exhibit 6.2 shows the predetermined annual rates computed for all four activities.

Picking the month of January for their study, the New Challenge managers collected the following information about the actual number of cost driver units for each of the two products:

	Mountain Bikes	Racing Bikes
Purchasing materials	1,000 frames	200 frames
Machine setups	13 setups	30 setups
Inspections	200 hours	200 hours
Running machines	1,500 hours	500 hours

During January, the factory produced 1,000 mountain bikes and 200 racing bikes.

Multiplying the actual number of cost driver units for each product times the predetermined rates computed above resulted in the overhead allocated to the two products shown in Exhibit 6.3.

Exhibit 6.3

Overhead Costs Assigned to Products Using Activity-Based Costing

Activity	Rate	Mountain Bikes Actual Cost Driver Units	Mountain Bikes Cost Allocated to Mountain Bikes	Racing Bikes Actual Cost Driver Units	Racing Bikes Cost Allocated to Racing Bikes
Purchasing materials	$20 per frame	1,000 frames	$ 20,000	200 frames	$ 4,000
Machine setups	$2,000 per setup	13 setups	26,000	30 setups	60,000
Inspections	$100 per inspection hour	200 hours	20,000	200 hours	20,000
Running machines	$30 per hour	1,500 hours	45,000	500 hours	15,000
Total cost allocated to each product			$111,000		$99,000
Total overhead			$210,000		

Unit Costs Recall the factory produced 1,000 mountain bikes and 200 racing bikes in January. The direct materials cost $100 per unit for mountain bikes and $200 per unit for racing bikes. Direct labor costs were $30 per unit for mountain bikes and $60 per unit for racing bikes. Based on the overhead costs computed for the two product lines, which appear in Exhibit 6.3, overhead per unit was $111 (=$111,000/1,000 units) for mountain bikes and $495 (=$99,000/200 units) for racing bikes. After putting together the data shown in the top panel of Exhibit 6.4, the New Challenge managers were surprised to find the product costs were a lot different using activity-based costing compared to the traditional approach. Using the traditional approach, they had computed numbers shown in the bottom panel of Exhibit 6.4. They had assigned *considerably* more overhead to racing bikes and less to mountain bikes using activity-based costing.

Analysis In analyzing the results, the New Challenge Cycle managers realized the racing bikes were allocated considerably more overhead per unit than the mountain bikes because the factory performed more machine setups for the racing bikes. Also, the factory had as many total inspection hours for the lower-volume racing bike, meaning the inspection hours per bike were greater for the racing bike.

Activity-based costing revealed two important facts. First, the mountain bikes were cheaper to make and the racing bikes more expensive to make than the company had realized. With this information, the New Challenge Cycle Company management lowered its price on the mountain bikes to make them more competitive.

Exhibit 6.4

Product Costs Using Activity-Based Costing

Activity-Based Costing

	Mountain Bikes	Racing Bikes
Direct Materials	$100	$200
Direct Labor	30	60
Overhead	111[a]	495[b]
Total Cost	$241	$755

Traditional Approach

	Mountain Bikes	Racing Bikes
Direct Materials	$100	$200
Direct Labor	30	60
Manufacturing Overhead	150	300
Total Cost	$280	$560

[a] $111 = overhead cost allocation to products using activity-based costing divided by number of units produced = $111,000/1,000 units.

[b] $495 = overhead cost allocation to products using activity-based costing divided by number of units produced = $99,000/200 units.

Second, management realized the Ciudad Juarez factory production methods were inefficient, so the company reworked the production process to reduce the number of setups, particularly on racing bikes.

Problem 6.1
for Self-Study

Compute product costs using activity-based costing. The following information is available for the month of December for the New Challenge Cycle Company:

Bikes Produced	
Mountain Bikes Produced	600
Racing Bikes Produced	200

	Cost Driver Units	
Activities	**Mountain Bikes**	**Racing Bikes**
Purchasing materials..................................	600 frames	200 frames
Machine setups	7 setups	24 setups
Inspections	100 hours	200 hours
Running machines.....................................	800 hours	600 hours

Compute the costs (1) in total and (2) per unit for both products using the activity-based costing rates. The actual cost driver units for December are given in this self-study problem. You should use the rates presented in the text. Assume the direct materials costs are $100 and $200 per unit for mountain bikes and racing bikes, respectively; and direct labor costs are $30 and $60 per unit for mountain bikes and racing bikes, respectively. Round unit costs to the nearest dollar. Recall that overhead allocated to products equals the cost driver rate (for example, $20 per frame for materials handled according to the schedule of rates in Exhibit 6.2) times the cost driver units (for example, 600 frames for mountain bikes in December).

The solution to this self-study problem is at the end of the chapter on page 223.

Impact of New Production Environment on Activity Bases

When cost systems were first developed in industry, companies were far more labor intensive than today. Much of the overhead cost was related to the support of labor, so it was logical for accountants to allocate overhead to products based on the amount of labor in the products.

Japanese Allocation Methods[a]

Managers in Japanese companies are known to prefer to allocate overhead to create particular incentive effects. Although world leaders in implementing new manufacturing technology, many Japanese companies still use direct labor as a basis for allocating overhead to products. For example, the Hitachi VCR plant is highly automated, yet it continues to use direct labor as a base for allocating overhead.

"Hitachi, like many large Japanese manufacturers, is convinced that reducing direct labor is essential for ongoing cost improvement. The company is committed to aggressive automation to promote long-term competitiveness. Allocating overhead based on direct labor creates the strong pro-automation incentives throughout the organization."[b]

Another Hitachi plant allocated overhead based on the number of parts in a product to create incentives to reduce the number of parts in the product. In a highly automated Japanese motorcycle plant studied by the authors, indirect costs are allocated to products based on the amount of direct materials and direct labor in each type of motorcycle, in part to create incentives to reduce labor costs.

[a]This discussion is based on the authors' research and Toshiro Hiromoto, "Another Hidden Edge—Japanese Management Accounting," *Harvard Business Review,* July-August, 1988.
[b]Ibid., p. 23.

Labor is still a major product cost in many companies, especially service organizations like public accounting firms. Many of these labor-intensive organizations still allocate overhead to products based on the amount of labor in the product.

Some companies have become more automated, making direct labor less appropriate for allocating overhead. Direct labor has shrunk to less than 5 percent of product costs in many companies. When labor is such a small part of product costs, there is little, if any, relation between labor and overhead. Further, small errors in assigning labor to products are magnified many times when overhead rates are several hundred percent of labor costs, or more.

Allocating overhead on the basis of direct labor creates incentives to reduce the labor content of products. This may be a desirable incentive in particular circumstances, as in the Hitachi plant discussed in the Managerial Application "Japanese Allocation Methods." In general, managers prefer the cost numbers not be overstated or understated because of an arbitrary cost allocation method, however.

Activity-Based Management and Costing in Marketing

Activity-based costing can also be applied to marketing or administrative activities. The principles and methods are the same as discussed above: (1) identify activities and cost drivers, (2) compute an indirect cost rate for each cost driver, and (3) allocate indirect costs by multiplying the rate for each cost driver by the number of cost driver units.

Instead of computing a cost of production, however, accountants compute a cost of performing an administrative or marketing service. Tissue products, for example, can be sold to grocery stores, convenience stores, and the industrial market, or through a number of other channels of distribution. Each channel has different activities. For example, consider the following:

- Convenience stores would require many shipments in small orders and considerable marketing support.
- Grocery stores would have relatively large shipments, a variety of products, and require considerable marketing support.
- Industrial users would require the use of brokers, minimum marketing support, and large orders.[7]

Marketing managers who make decisions about which channel to use need to know the cost of alternative channels of distribution. Cost drivers for distribution costs include the number of shipments per period, the size of shipment, and the number of products in a shipment.

Using Activity-Based Costing to Eliminate Non–Value Added Costs

Activity-based costing can be used to identify and eliminate activities that add costs but not value to the product. Non–value added costs are costs of activities that could be eliminated without reducing product quality, performance, or value. For example, storing bicycle frames until needed for production does not add to the finished bicycle's value. If management can find ways to eliminate storing bicycle frames, say by using just-in-time purchasing, the company could save money without reducing the quality of the finished product.

The following types of activities are candidates for elimination because they do not add value to the product.

1. *Storage.* Storage of materials, work-in-process, or finished goods inventories is an obvious non–value added activity. Many companies have applied the just-

---

[7]See J. M. Reeve, ''Cost Management in Continuous-Process Environments,'' in Barry J. Brinker, ed., *Emerging Practices in Cost Management* (Boston, MA: Warren, Gorham & Lamont, 1992), pp. F3-1–F3-13.

in-time philosophy to purchasing and production to reduce or even eliminate storage.

2. *Moving items.* Moving parts, materials, and other items around the factory floor is another activity that does not add value to the finished product. A steel mill in Michigan once had hundreds of miles of railroad tracks just to move materials and partially finished products from one part of the factory to another. Eliminating a hundred miles or so of track reduced both labor and overhead costs, and even eliminated some spoilage because products were sometimes damaged by train accidents.

3. *Waiting for work.* Idle time does not add value to products. Reducing the amount of time people wait to work on something reduces the cost of idle time.

4. *Production process.* Managers should investigate the entire production process including purchasing, production, inspection, and shipping to identify activities that do not add value to the finished product. In the New Challenge Cycle Company example, managers should ascertain whether the company needs as many setups, whether the cost of higher-quality materials and labor could be justified by a reduction in inspection time, whether the cost of ordering could be reduced, and so forth.

These are only a few examples of non–value added costs. If you observe activities in universities, health-care organizations, fast-food restaurants, construction sites, government agencies, and lots of other organizations, you will see many examples of non–value added activities.

Activity-based costing helps measure the costs of non–value added activities. For example, referring to Deere & Co. discussed previously, the company measured the variable cost of moving materials to be $293 per load, where a "load" was a movement of materials around the factory.[8] If the company could have eliminated 1,000 loads per year, it would have saved $293,000, all other things equal, without any reduction in the value of the finished product.

Opportunities to Improve Activity-Based Costing in Practice

The use of activity-based costing in industry is relatively new. Companies are continually encountering limitations and finding ways to improve activity-based costing. A philosopher once said that our knowledge is like a circle, the more we know the larger the circle. But the larger the circle, the greater its boundary and the more we realize the limits of our knowledge. Activity-based costing has shown managers they have much to learn about the cost of the activities required to make their products. We next discuss several of the problems managers face in trying to improve on the basic activity-based costing model presented in this chapter.

---

[8]"John Deere Component Works," Harvard Business School, Case 187-107.

Variable versus Fixed Costs

A major area of difficulty encountered by companies is how to deal with variable versus fixed costs at the unit level.[9] If the cost of a quality inspection is estimated to be $100 per inspection, for example, does that mean that eliminating one inspection will save the company $100? The answer is no if the $100 inspection costs include some of the inspector's salary, because the inspector's salary will not likely be reduced if one inspection is eliminated. If any costs that are fixed in the short run are included in the activity's cost, then those costs would not be affected by short-run changes in the volume of activity.

Companies could deal with this in several ways. First, companies could treat fixed costs as period costs and ignore them in computing product costs. Managers would then have only variable costs as their measure of product costs. This approach may be appropriate for short-run decisions, but it ignores costs that managers should take into account when making long-run decisions.

Deere & Company used another approach; it computed separate activity rates for variable and fixed costs.[10] Deere & Company's accountants computed two rates for each cost driver—one rate for variable costs and one rate for fixed costs. For example, accountants computed a total rate of $34 per hour for time to set up machines for production runs. The $34 rate was made up of $22 for variable overhead items and $12 for fixed cost items. By dividing the cost into fixed and variable rates, managers have cost information for short-term decisions in which only the variable costs change (for example, the cost increase for a temporary increase in volume).

Hierarchy of Overhead Costs

Allocating all costs to units is misleading if some costs do not vary with the volume of units. For example, machine setups are generally batch-related costs. A machine setup is required for each new batch of products whether the batch contains one unit or 1,000 units. The setup cost is not affected by the number of *units,* but rather by the number of *batches.*

Management can establish a hierarchy of expenses like that shown in Exhibit 6.5.[11] Strictly variable costs, such as energy costs to run machines, are affected by the volume of units produced. These costs would appear at the bottom of Exhibit 6.5 as a function of unit activities. Naturally, any variable costs such as direct materials are unit-level costs. At the other extreme, at the top of Exhibit 6.5, are capacity costs. These costs are essentially fixed by management's decisions to have a particular size of store, factory, hospital, or other facility. Although they are fixed with respect to volume, it would be misleading to give the impression that these costs cannot be changed. Managers can make decisions that affect capacity costs, it just requires a longer time horizon than decisions to reduce unit-level costs.

---

[9]E. Noreen and N. Soderstrom, ''Are Cost Drivers Strictly Proportional to Their Cost Drivers? Evidence from the Hospital Service Departments,'' June 1991, provides empirical evidence from hospitals that indirect costs are not proportional to the volume of activities.

[10]''John Deere Component Works,'' Harvard Business School, Case 187-107 and 187-108.

[11]R. Cooper and R. S. Kaplan, ''Profit Priorities from Activity-Based Costing,'' *Harvard Business Review,* May-June 1991, pp. 130–35.

Exhibit 6.5	

Hierarchy of Product Costs[a]

Activity Category	Examples
Capacity Sustaining Activities	Plant Management
	Building Depreciation and Rent
	Heating and Lighting
Product and Customer Sustaining Activities	Customer Records and Files
	Product Specifications
	Customer Service
Batch Activities	Machine Setups
	Quality Inspections
Unit Activities	Energy to Run Machines
	Direct Materials

[a]Adapted from R. Cooper and R. S. Kaplan, "Profit Priorities from Activity-Based Costing," *Harvard Business Review,* May-June 1991, p. 132.

The two middle categories of costs are affected by the way the company manages its activities. A company that makes products to order for a customer will have more product/customer-level costs than a company that provides limited choices. A company that schedules its work so that one product is made on Monday, a second product on Tuesday, and so on through Friday has lower batch-related costs than if it produced all five products on Monday, all five again on Tuesday, and so on through the week. In practice, many of the greatest opportunities for reducing costs are in these middle categories of product/customer and batch-related costs. Suppose management makes decisions that affect units, but not batches, products, or capacity. Using a hierarchy like this, management would focus on costs in the fourth category—costs of unit activities. If management makes decisions that affect capacity, however, all activities in the first through fourth categories would probably be affected, and costs in all four categories would be analyzed.

Cost of Activities When the Demand for Services Causes Congestion

Another opportunity to improve activity-based costing takes into account both the volume and the timing of the demand for an activity. If the demand for a product is uneven, then the demands on overhead activity are likely to increase. To see the point, imagine that a local McDonald's restaurant could serve 900 meals per day spaced evenly at the rate of one meal per minute. At that rate, the company would probably need only two people per day, each working an eight-hour shift. In fact, demand peaks at breakfast, again at lunch, and again at dinner. More than two people have to be hired to serve the 900 meals scheduled according to these demands at peak times, although for shorter work shifts. Hiring additional people to meet these peak demands increases the overhead costs of hiring and training additional people and of developing work schedules.

Managerial Application

Integrating Process Management and Activity-Based Costing to Reduce Health-Care Costs[a]

Health-care costs are now approaching 15 percent of gross national product and may increase as baby boomers age. Yet many people go untreated under the current United States health-care system. New medical technology will be required to improve the quality of health care while reducing costs.

Stuart Pharmaceuticals wanted to estimate the impact of a new anesthesia on health-care costs. This new drug had the potential to reduce the time that patients remained in the recovery room after surgery because they would awaken sooner with fewer side effects. Reducing the time patients spent in the recovery room could reduce the amount of time nurses needed to be present watching over patients, thereby reducing costs.

In a study of two outpatient surgery centers, one at the Methodist Memorial Hospital in Peoria, Illinois, and the other at Emory University Hospital in Atlanta, Georgia, physicians and researchers attempted to determine the potential reduction in recovery room costs using activity-based costing as a tool. Using such activities as patient minutes in recovery did not measure the potential cost savings. A reduction in patient minutes reduced the need for nursing time, but because nursing time is "purchased" in increments of several hour shifts, not minutes, there was no simple relation between reduction in the number of minutes a patient spent in the recovery room and a reduction in nursing costs.

To further complicate the analysis, enough nurses had to be on hand to deal with the times when the recovery room had the most patients. If the new drug reduced the number of patients in the recovery room at peak demand times, the cost savings would be greater than if the drug reduced demand in slack times.

To estimate the effects of the new drug on the need for nurses in the recovery room, the researchers and physicians collected data on two groups of patients, one group anesthetized with the new drug and one group with a traditional drug. Using these actual cases and a computer software package, the researchers simulated the running of the outpatient surgery centers as if patients had only the new drug and determined the number of nurses needed at each minute of the day. They did the same with the traditional drug. The research team found that the new anesthesia provided an opportunity to reduce the nursing staff 10 to 25 percent without reducing the quality of patient care.

[a]Based on the paper by M. L. Marais and M. W. Maher, "Process-Oriented Activity-Based Costing," Unpublished paper. University of California, Davis, January 1994.

Work on this problem is in the early stages. Some academics and practitioners have worked to develop computer models of companies' activities, like that discussed in the Managerial Application on health-care cost reduction. These models take into account both the volume of activity and the congestion that occurs when there are peaks and valleys in the demand for services.

Problem 6.2 for Self-Study

Classifying activities. Using the hierarchy of product costs in Exhibit 6.5, classify the following activities as either capacity sustaining activities, product or customer sustaining activities, batch activities, or unit activities.

1. Piecework labor
2. Long-term lease on a building
3. Telephone equipment
4. Engineering drawings for a product
5. Purchase order
6. Movement of materials for products in production
7. Change order to meet new customer specifications

The solution to this self-study problem is at the end of the chapter on page 223.

Behavioral and Implementation Issues

Accountants cannot implement activity-based costing without becoming familiar with the operations of the company. In identifying activities, accountants become part of a team with management and people from production, engineering, marketing, and other parts of the company who all work to identify the activities that drive the company's costs. This often creates discomfort at first as accountants are forced to deal with unfamiliar areas, but in the long run, their familiarity with the company's operating activities can improve their contribution to the company. Also, non-accountants believe the numbers reported by accountants are credible if accountants understand the business.

One of the problems encountered when implementing activity-based costing is the failure to get influential people in the organization to buy into the process. Accounting methods in companies are like rules in sports: people become accustomed to playing by the rules and oppose change to something unknown.

For example, two analysts at one company spent several months of their time and hundreds of hours of computer time to develop an activity-based costing system. Their analysis revealed several hundred products that were clearly unprofitable and should be eliminated. However, the key managers to make product elimination decisions agreed to eliminate only about 20 products. Why? The analysts had failed to talk to these key managers early in the process. When presented with the final results, these managers raised numerous objections that the analysts had not anticipated.

Moral: If you are involved in trying to make a change, get all of the people who are important to that change to buy into the process early.

Summary

This chapter deals with the allocation of indirect costs from plants, departments, or activity centers to products, and the management of activities for effective cost management. Product cost information helps managers make numerous decisions, including pricing, deciding whether to keep or drop a product, estimating the cost of making a similar product, and determining how to reduce the costs of making products.

Accounting for overhead is simple using *plantwide allocation.* All overhead costs are recorded in one cost pool for the plant without regard to the department or activity that caused them. An overhead rate, or set of rates, is used for the entire plant. Using *department allocation,* each production department would be a separate cost pool. The company establishes a separate overhead allocation rate, or set of rates, for each department. Activity-based costing is a costing method that assigns costs first to activities, then to the products based on each product's use of activities. Activity-based costing is based on the premise, ''Products consume activities; activities consume resources.''

The chapter discussion made the following important points about activity-based costing:

1. Different cost allocation methods result in different estimates of how much it costs to make a product.
2. Activity-based costing provides more detailed measures of costs than plantwide or department allocation methods.
3. Activity-based costing can help marketing managers by providing more accurate product cost numbers for decisions about pricing and which products to eliminate.
4. Activity-based costing helps production managers by providing better information about how much each activity costs. To manage costs, production managers learn to manage the activities that cause costs.
5. Activity-based costing provides more information, but requires more record keeping. Managers must decide whether the benefits of improved decisions justify the additional cost of activity-based costing.
6. Installing activity-based costing requires teamwork between accounting, production, marketing, management, and other nonaccounting people.

Solutions to Self-Study Problems

Suggested Solution to Problem 6.1 for Self-Study

Activity	Rate	Mountain Bikes		Racing Bikes	
		Actual Cost Driver Units	Costs Allocated to Mountain Bikes	Actual Cost Driver Units	Costs Allocated to Racing Bikes
Purchasing materials	$20 per frame	600 frames	$12,000	200 frames	$ 4,000
Machine setups	$2,000 per setup	7 setups	$14,000	24 setups	$48,000
Inspections	$100 per inspection hour	100 hours	$10,000	200 hours	$20,000
Running machines	$30 per hour	800 hours	$24,000	600 hours	$18,000
Total cost allocated to each product:			$60,000		$90,000

The costs of producing 600 mountain bikes and 200 racing bikes are as follows:

	Mountain Bikes	Racing Bikes
Direct Materials	$ 60,000 ($100 each)	$ 40,000 ($200 each)
Direct Labor	18,000 ($30 each)	12,000 ($60 each)
Overhead.........................	60,000 (see above)	90,000 (see above)
	$138,000	$142,000

	Unit Costs	
	Mountain Bikes	Racing Bikes
Direct Materials	$100	$200
Direct Labor	30	60
Overhead...	100[a]	450[b]
Total	$230	$710

[a]$100 = total allocation to products divided by number of units produced = $60,000/600 units.

[b]$450 = total allocation to products divided by number of units produced = $90,000/200 units.

Suggested Solution to Problem 6.2 for Self-Study

Activity	Category
1. Piecework labor	Unit
2. Long-term lease on a building	Capacity sustaining
3. Telephone equipment	Capacity sustaining
4. Engineering drawings for a product	Product sustaining
5. Purchase order	Batch
6. Movement of materials for products in production	Batch
7. Change order to meet new customer specifications	Customer sustaining

Key Terms and Concepts

Cost pools   Activity centers
Plantwide allocation method   Activity-based costing (ABC)
Department allocation method   Cost driver

Questions, Exercises, Problems, and Cases

Questions

1. Review the meaning of the concepts and terms given above in Key Terms and Concepts.
2. "Activity-based costing is great for manufacturing plants, but it doesn't really address the needs of the service sector." Do you agree? Explain.
3. If stage 1 of cost allocation is the allocation of costs to departments, what is stage 2 of cost allocation?
4. What basis or cost driver does a company using a single plantwide rate typically select for the allocation of indirect costs?
5. Explain the basic difference between plantwide and department allocation.
6. What exactly is a cost driver? Give three examples.
7. Martha Clark, the vice-president of marketing, wonders how products can cost less under one cost system than under another: "Aren't costs cut-and-dried?" How would you respond?
8. According to a recent publication, "Activity-based costing is the wave of the future. Everyone should drop their existing cost systems and adopt ABC!" Do you agree? Explain.
9. A drawback to activity-based costing is that it requires more record keeping and extensive teamwork between all departments. What are the potential benefits of a more detailed product cost system?
10. What are the four basic steps required for activity-based costing?
11. "One of the lessons learned from activity-based costing is that all costs are really a function of volume." True, false, or uncertain? Explain.
12. Allocating overhead based on the volume of output, such as direct labor hours or machine hours, seems fair and equitable. Why, then, do many people claim that high-volume products "subsidize" low-volume products?
13. Give three criteria for choosing cost drivers or allocation bases for allocating costs to products.
14. Give examples of two non–value added activities that may be found in each of the following organizations: (1) university, (2) restaurant, and (3) bicycle repair shop.
15. "The total estimated overhead for the year will differ depending on whether you use department allocation or activity-based costing." Do you agree? Explain.

16. Many companies have experienced great technological change resulting in potential for erroneous product cost figures, assuming traditional labor-based cost drivers are used to allocate overhead to products. What is that technological change?

17. See the Managerial Application "Japanese Allocation Methods" in the chapter. If the allocation of overhead based on direct labor can yield erroneous results, why do highly automated plants such as Hitachi continue this practice?

18. "Activity-based costing is for accountants and production managers. I plan to be a marketing specialist, so ABC won't help me." Do you agree with this statement? Explain.

19. What is the difference between a capacity-sustaining cost and a unit-level cost? How can managers use a hierarchy of overhead costs like the one presented in Exhibit 6.5?

20. Refer to the Managerial Application "Integrating Process Management and Activity-Based Costing to Reduce Health-Care Costs." If the new anesthesia reduces the number of minutes a patient stays in the recovery room after surgery, why wouldn't nursing costs necessarily be reduced proportional to the reduction in the number of minutes the patient stays in the recovery room?

Exercises

Solutions to even-numbered exercises are at the end of the chapter after the cases.

21. **Activity-based costing.** Sandy O'Neal has just joined the New Challenge Cycle Company (text example) as the new production manager. He was pleased to see the company used activity-based costing. O'Neal believes he can reduce production costs if he reduces the number of machine setups. He has spent the last month working with Purchasing and Sales to better coordinate raw material arrivals and the anticipated demand for the company's products. In March, he plans to produce 1,000 mountain bikes and 200 racing bikes. O'Neal believes that with his efficient production scheduling he can reduce the number of setups for both the mountain and racing bike products by 50 percent.

   a. Refer to Exhibit 6.2. Compute the amount of overhead allocated to each product line, mountain bikes and racing bikes, assuming a 50-percent annual reduction in setups. Assume all events are the same as in the text example except the number of machine setups in March are 6.5 setups for mountain bikes and 15 setups for racing bikes. (One setup for mountain bikes will be one-half done in March and one-half done in April.) Assume the overhead costs of setting up machines decrease proportionately with the reduction in the number of setups; thus, the setup rate remains at $2,000 per setup.

   b. What information did activity-based costing provide that enabled Sandy O'Neal to pursue reducing overhead costs? In general, what are the advantages of activity-based costing over the traditional volume-based allocation methods. What are the disadvantages?

22. **Activity-based costing.** The manager of Wildwater Adventurers uses activity-based costing to compute the costs of her raft trips. Each raft holds six paying customers and a guide. She offers two types of raft trips, 3-day float trips for beginners and 3-day whitewater trips for seasoned rafters. The breakdown of the costs is as follows:

Activities (with cost drivers)	Float Trip Costs	Whitewater Trip Costs
Advertising (trips)	$215 per trip	$215 per trip
Permit to Use the River (trips)	30 per trip	50 per trip
Equipment Use (trips, people).....	20 per trip + $5 per person	40 per trip + $8 per person
Insurance (trips)	75 per trip	127 per trip
Paying Guides (trips, guides)	300 per trip per guide	400 per trip per guide
Food (people)	60 per person	60 per person

a. Compute the cost of a four-raft 28-person (including four guides) float trip.

b. Compute the cost of a four-raft 28-person (including four guides) whitewater trip.

c. Recommend a minimum price per customer to the manager if she wants to cover her costs.

23. **ABC versus traditional costing.** Soundex Corporation produces two types of audio cassettes: standard and high-grade. The standard cassettes are used primarily in answering machines, and are designed for durability rather than accurate sound reproduction. The company only recently began producing the higher-quality high-grade model to enter the lucrative music recording market. Since the new product was introduced, profits have been steadily declining, although sales of the high-grade tape have been growing rapidly. Management believes the accounting system may not be accurately allocating costs to products.

Management has asked you to investigate the cost allocation problem. You find that manufacturing overhead is currently assigned to products based on the direct labor costs in the products. Last year's manufacturing overhead was $440,000 based on production of 320,000 standard cassettes and 100,000 high-grade cassettes. Selling prices last year averaged $2.30 per standard tape and $3.60 per high-grade tape. Direct labor and direct materials costs for last year were as follows:

	Standard	High-Grade	Total
Direct Labor	$174,000	$ 66,000	$240,000
Materials	125,000	114,000	239,000

Management believes the following three activities cause overhead costs. The cost drivers and related costs are as follows:

	Costs Assigned	Activity Level		
		Standard	High-Grade	Total
Number of Production Runs ...	$200,000	40	10	50
Quality Tests Performed.......	180,000	12	18	30
Shipping Orders Processed....	60,000	100	50	150
Total Overhead..............	$440,000			

a. How much of the overhead will be assigned to each product if the three cost drivers are used to allocate overhead? What would be the cost per unit produced for each product?

b. How much of the overhead would have been assigned to each product if direct labor cost had been used to allocate overhead? What would have been the total cost per unit produced for each product?

c. How might the results explain Soundex's declining profits?

24. Activity-based costing in a nonmanufacturing environment. Plantcare, Inc., is a garden care service. The company originally specialized in serving residential clients, but has recently started contracting for work on larger commercial clients. Ms. Plantcare, the owner, is considering reducing residential services and increasing commercial lawncare.

Five field employees worked a total of 10,000 hours last year, 6,500 on residential jobs and 3,500 on commercial jobs. Wages were $9 per hour for all work done. Direct materials used were minimal and are included in overhead. All overhead is allocated on the basis of labor hours worked, which is also the basis for customer charges. Because of greater competition for commercial accounts, Ms. Plantcare can charge $22 per hour for residential work but only $19 per hour for commercial work.

a. If overhead for the year was $62,000, what were the profits of commercial and residential service using labor hours as the allocation base?

b. Overhead consists of office supplies, garden supplies, and depreciation and maintenance on equipment. These costs can be traced to the following activities:

Activity	Cost Driver	Cost	Activity Level	
			Commercial	Residential
Office Supplies	Number of Clients Serviced	$ 8,000	15	45
Equipment Depreciation and Maintenance	Equipment Hours	18,000	3,500	2,500
Garden Supplies	Area Covered (computed as number of square yards of garden times number of times garden is serviced per year)	36,000	65,000	35,000
Total Overhead		$62,000		

Recalculate profits for commercial and residential services based on these activity bases.

c. What recommendations do you have for management?

25. **ABC versus traditional costing.** Dialglow Corporation manufacturers travel clocks and watches. Overhead costs are currently allocated using direct labor hours, but the controller has recommended an activity-based costing system using the following data:

Activity	Cost Driver	Cost	Activity Level	
			Travel Clocks	Watches
Production Setup	Number of Setups	$100,000	10	15
Material Handling and Requisition	Number of Parts	30,000	18	36
Packaging and Shipping	Number of Units Shipped	60,000	45,000	75,000
Total Overhead		$190,000		

a. Compute the amount of overhead allocated to each of the products under activity-based costing.

b. Compute the amount of overhead to be allocated to each product using labor hours as the allocation base. Assume 30,000 labor hours were used to assemble travel clocks and 90,000 labor hours were used to assemble watches.

c. Should the company follow the controller's recommendations?

26. **ABC versus traditional costing.** Vicki Greenshade, CPA, provides consulting and tax preparation services to her clients. She charges a fee of $100 per hour for each service. Her revenues and expenses for the year are shown in the following income statement:

	Tax	Consulting	Total
Revenue..............................	$80,000	$120,000	$200,000
Expenses:			
Filing, scheduling, and data entry	———	———	40,000
Supplies	———	———	36,000
Computer costs	———	———	20,000
Profit.................................	———	———	$104,000

Vicki has kept records of the following data for cost allocation purposes:

Expenses	Cost Driver	Activity Level	
		Tax Preparation	Consulting
Filing, scheduling, and data entry	Number of Clients	72	48
Supplies	Number of Hours Billed	800	1,200
Computer Costs	Computer Hours	1,000	600

a. Complete the income statement using Vicki's three cost drivers.

b. Recompute the income statement for using hours billed as the only allocation base.

c. How might Vicki's decisions be altered if she were to use only hours billed to allocate expenses?

27. **When do ABC and traditional methods yield similar results?** Refer to Exercise 26. In general, under what circumstances would the two allocation methods in parts **a** and **b** result in similar profit results?

Problems

28. **Comparative income statements and management analysis.** Fleetfoot, Inc., manufacturers two types of shoes: B-Ball and Marathon. B-Ball has a complex design that uses gel-filled compartments to provide support. Marathon is simpler to manufacture and uses conventional padding. Last year, Fleetfoot had the following revenues and costs:

Fleetfoot, Inc.
Income Statement

	B-Ball	Marathon	Total
Revenue..............................	$390,000	$368,000	$758,000
Direct Materials	110,000	100,000	210,000
Direct Labor	80,000	40,000	120,000
Indirect Costs:			
Administration........................	_____	_____	39,000
Production setup	_____	_____	90,000
Quality control.......................	_____	_____	60,000
Sales & marketing	_____	_____	120,000
Operating Profit	_____	_____	$119,000

Fleetfoot currently uses labor costs to allocate all overhead, but management is considering implementing an activity-based costing system. After interviewing the sales and production staff, management decides to allocate administrative costs on the basis of direct labor costs, but to use the following bases to allocate the remaining overhead:

		Activity Level	
Activity	**Cost Driver**	**B-Ball**	**Marathon**
Production Setup	Number of Production Runs	10	20
Quality Control	Number of Inspections	40	40
Sales and Marketing	Number of Advertisements	12	48

a. Complete the income statement using the activity bases above.

b. Write a brief report indicating how management could use activity-based costing to reduce costs.

c. Restate the income statement for Fleetfoot, Inc., using direct labor costs as the only overhead allocation base.

d. Write a report to management stating why product line profits differ using activity-based costing compared to the traditional approach. Indicate whether activity-based costing provides more accurate information and why (if you believe it does provide more accurate information). Indicate in your report how the use of labor-based overhead allocation could result in Fleetfoot management making suboptimal decisions.

29. **Comparative income statements and management analysis.** Magic Photography offers two types of services: Deluxe Portraits and Standard Portraits. Last year, Magic had the following costs and revenues:

Magic Photography
Income Statement

	Deluxe	Standard	Total
Revenue.	$360,000	$400,000	$760,000
Direct Materials	50,000	50,000	100,000
Direct Labor	180,000	120,000	300,000
Indirect Costs:			
Administration	————	————	50,000
Production setup	————	————	100,000
Quality control.	————	————	50,000
Sales and Marketing	————	————	40,000
Operating Profit	————	————	$120,000

Magic Photography currently uses labor costs to allocate all overhead, but management is considering implementing an activity-based costing system. After interviewing the sales and production staff, management decides to allocate administrative costs on the basis of direct labor costs, but to use the following cost drivers to allocate the remaining overhead:

		Activity Level	
Activity	**Cost Driver**	Deluxe	Standard
Production Setup	Number of Photo Sessions	150	250
Quality Control	Number of Customer Inspections	300	200
Sales and Marketing	Number of Advertisements	60	40

a. Complete the income statement using the cost drivers above.

b. Write a report indicating how management might use activity-based costing to reduce costs.

c. Restate the income statement for Magic Photography using direct labor costs as the only overhead allocation base.

d. Write a report to management stating why product line profits differ using activity-based costing compared to the traditional approach. Indicate whether activity-based costing provides more accurate information and why (if you believe it does provide more accurate information). Indicate in your report how the use of labor-based overhead allocation could result in Magic Photography management making suboptimal decisions.

30. **ABC and predetermined overhead rates.** Fashion-Eye Company makes three types of sunglasses: Nerds, Stars, and Fashions. Fashion-Eye presently applies overhead using a predetermined rate based on direct labor hours. A consultant recommended that Fashion-Eye switch to activity-based costing. Management decided to give ABC a try, and identified the following activities, cost drivers, and estimated costs for Year 2 for each activity center.

Activity	Recommended Cost Driver	Estimated Costs	Estimated Cost Driver Units
Production Setup	Number of Production Runs	$ 30,000	100
Order Processing	Number of Orders	50,000	200
Materials Handling	Pounds of Materials Used	20,000	8,000
Equipment Depreciation and Maintenance	Machine-Hours	60,000	10,000
Quality Management	Number of Inspections	50,000	40
Packing and Shipping	Number of Units Shipped	40,000	20,000
Total Estimated Overhead		$250,000	

The company estimated 5,000 labor hours would be worked in Year 2. Assume the following activities occurred in February of Year 2:

	Nerds	Stars	Fashions
Number of Units Produced	1,000	500	400
Direct Materials Costs	$4,000	$2,500	$2,000
Direct Labor-Hours	200	150	87
Number of Orders	8	8	4
Number of Production Runs	1	2	6
Pounds of Material	400	200	200
Machine-Hours	400	200	200
Number of Inspections	1	1	1
Units Shipped	1,000	500	300
Direct labor costs are $20 per hour.			

a. Compute an overhead allocation rate for each of the cost drivers recommended by the consultant and for direct labor.

b. Compute the production costs for each product for February using the cost drivers recommended by the consultant.

c. Management has seen your numbers and wants to know how you account for the discrepancy between the product costs using only direct labor hours as the allocation base and using activity-based costing. Write a brief response to management, including calculation of product costs using direct labor hours to allocate overhead.

31. **Choosing an ABC system.** Cyclaris Corporation manufactures three bicycle models: a racing bike, a mountain bike, and a children's model. The racing model is made of a titanium-aluminum alloy and is called the Aerolight. The mountain bike is called the Summit and is made of aluminum. The steel-framed children's bike is called the Spinner. Because of the different materials used, production processes differ significantly between models in terms of

machine types and time requirements. However, once parts are produced, assembly time per unit required for each type of bike is similar. For this reason, Cyclaris had adopted the practice of allocating overhead on the basis of machine-hours. Last year, the company produced 1,000 Aerolights, 2,000 Summits, and 5,000 Spinners and had the following revenues and expenses:

Cyclaris Corporation
Income Statement

	Aerolight	Summit	Spinner	Total
Sales..........................	$380,000	$560,000	$475,000	$1,415,000
Direct costs:				
Direct Materials	150,000	240,000	200,000	590,000
Direct Labor	14,400	24,000	54,000	92,400
Variable Overhead:				
Machine Setup	____	____	____	26,000
Order Processing	____	____	____	64,000
Warehousing Costs	____	____	____	93,000
Depreciation of Machines.........	____	____	____	42,000
Shipping........................	____	____	____	36,000
Contribution Margin	____	____	____	$ 471,600
Fixed Overhead:				
Plant Administration.............				88,000
Other Fixed Overhead				140,000
Operating Profit				$ 243,600

The CFO of Cyclaris had heard about activity-based costing and hired a consultant to recommend cost allocation bases. The consultant recommended the following:

		Activity Level		
Activity	**Cost Driver**	**Aerolight**	**Summit**	**Spinner**
Machine Setup	Number of Production Runs	11	17	22
Order Processing	Number of Sales Orders Received	200	300	300
Warehousing Costs	Number of Units Held in Inventory	100	100	200
Depreciation	Machine-Hours	5,000	8,000	12,000
Shipping...........................	Number of Units Shipped	500	2,000	5,000

The consultant found no basis for allocating the plant administration and other fixed overhead costs and recommended that these not be applied to products.

    a. Using machine-hours to allocate variable overhead, complete the income statement for Cyclaris Corporation. Do not attempt to allocate fixed overhead.

    b. Complete the income statement using the cost drivers recommended by the consultant.

c. How might activity-based costing result in better decisions by Cyclaris management?

d. After hearing the consultant's recommendations, the CFO decided to adopt activity-based costing, but expressed concern about not allocating some of the overhead to the products (administration and other fixed overhead). In the CFO's view, "Products have to bear a fair share of all overhead or we won't be covering all our costs." How would you respond to this comment?

32. **Benefits of activity-based costing** (CMA adapted). Many companies recognize that their cost systems are inadequate for today's global market. Managers in companies selling multiple products are making important product decisions based on distorted cost information. Most systems of the past were designed to focus on inventory valuation.

If management should decide to implement an activity-based costing system, what benefits should they expect?

33. **Benefits of activity-based costing** (CMA adapted). Moss Manufacturing has just completed a major change in the method it uses to inspect its products. Previously ten inspectors examined the product after each major process. The salaries of these inspectors were charged as direct labor to the operation or job. In an effort to improve efficiency, the Moss production manager recently bought a computerized quality control system consisting of a microcomputer, 15 video cameras, peripheral hardware, and software. The cameras are placed at key points in the production process, taking pictures of the product and comparing these pictures with a known "good" image supplied by a quality control engineer. This new system allowed Moss to replace the ten quality control inspectors with only two quality control engineers.

The president of the company is confused. She was told that the production process was now more efficient, yet she notices a large increase in the factory overhead rate. The computation of the rate before and after automation is as follows:

	Before	After
Budgeted Overhead	$1,900,000	$2,100,000
Budgeted Direct Labor	1,000,000	700,000
Budgeted Overhead Rate	190%	300%

How might an activity-based costing system benefit Moss Manufacturing and clear up the president's confusion?

Cases

34. **Distortions caused by inappropriate overhead allocation base.**[12] Steve Stanley, Inc. (SSI), manufactures creamy deluxe chocolate candy bars. The firm has developed three distinct products: Almond Dream, Krispy Krackle, and Creamy Crunch.

---

[12]Copyright © Michael W. Maher, 1993.

While SSI is profitable, Steve Stanley is quite concerned about the profitability of each product and the product-costing methods currently employed. In particular, Steve questions whether the overhead allocation base of direct labor-hours accurately reflects the costs incurred during the production process of each product.

In reviewing cost reports with the marketing manager, Steve notices that Creamy Crunch appears exceptionally profitable, while Almond Dream appears to be produced at a loss. This surprises both Steve and the manager, and after much discussion, they are convinced the cost accounting system is at fault and that Almond Dream is performing very well at the current market price.

Steve Stanley decides to hire Jean Sharpe, a management consultant, to study the firm's cost system over the next month and present her findings and recommendations to senior management. Her objective is to identify and demonstrate how the cost accounting system might be distorting the firm's product costs.

Jean Sharpe begins her study by gathering information and documenting the existing cost accounting system. The system is rather simplistic, using a single overhead allocation base, direct labor-hours, to calculate and apply overhead rates to all products. The rate is calculated by summing variable and fixed overhead costs and then dividing the result by the number of direct labor-hours. The product cost is determined by multiplying the number of direct labor-hours required to manufacture the product by the overhead rate and adding this amount to the direct labor and direct material costs.

SSI engages in two distinct production processes for each product. Process 1 is labor-intensive, using a high proportion of direct materials and labor. Process 2 uses special packing equipment which wraps each individual candy bar and then packs them into boxes of 24 bars. The boxes are then packaged into cases containing six boxes. The special packing equipment is used on all three products and has a monthly capacity of 3,000 cases, each containing 144 candy bars.

To illustrate the source of the distortions to senior management, Sharpe collects the cost data for the three products—Almond Dream, Krispy Krackle, and Creamy Crunch (see Exhibit 6.6).

SSI recently adopted a general policy of discontinuing all products whose gross profit margin [(gross margin/selling price) × 100] percentages were less than 10 percent. By comparing the selling prices to the firm's costs and then calculating the gross margin percentages, Sharpe could determine which products, under the current cost system, should be dropped. The current selling prices of Almond Dream, Krispy Krackle, and Creamy Crunch were $85, $55, and $35 per case, respectively.

a. Complete the following schedule (Exhibit 6.6) under the current cost system and determine which product(s), if any, would be dropped.

b. What characteristic of the product that would be dropped makes it appear relatively unprofitable?

c. Calculate the gross profit margin percentage for the remaining products. Assume SSI can sell all products it manufactures and that it will use the

Exhibit 6.6

	Almond Dream	Krispy Krackle	Creamy Crunch
Product Costs:			
Labor-Hours per unit[a]	7	3	1
Total units produced	1,000	1,000	1,000
Material cost per unit	$ 8.00	$ 2.00	$ 9.00
Direct labor cost per unit	$42.00	$18.00	$ 6.00
Labor-hours per product.....................	7,000	3,000	1,000

Total overhead = $69,500
Total labor-hours = 11,000
Direct labor costs per hour = $6.00
Allocation rate per labor-hour =   (a)

Costs of Products:			
Material cost per unit	$ 8.00	$ 2.00	$ 9.00
Direct labor cost per unit	42.00	18.00	6.00
Allocated overhead per unit (to be computed)	(b)	(c)	(d)
Product Cost............................	(e)	(f)	(g)

[a]A unit is one case.

excess capacity from dropping a product to produce more of the most profitable product. If SSI maintains its current rule about dropping products, which additional products, if any, would SSI drop under the existing cost system? Overhead would remain $69,500 per month under all alternatives.

d. Recalculate the gross profit margin percentage for the remaining product(s) and ascertain whether any additional product(s) would be dropped.

e. Discuss the outcome and any recommendations you might make to management regarding the current cost system and decision policies.

35. Refer to the previous case.[13]

Jean Sharpe decides to gather additional data to identify the cause of overhead costs and figure out which products are most profitable.

Jean Sharpe notices that $30,000 of the overhead originated from the equipment used. She decides to incorporate machine-hours into the overhead allocation base to see its effect on product profitability. For each unit produced, Almond Dream requires two hours of machine time. Krispy Krackle requires seven hours and Creamy Crunch requires six hours. Additionally, Jean notices that the $15,000 per month spent on the rental of 10,000 square feet of factory

---

[13]Copyright © Michael W. Maher, 1993.

space accounts for almost 22 percent of the overhead. Almond Dream is assigned 1,000 square feet. Krispy Krackle is assigned 4,000 square feet, and Creamy Crunch is assigned 5,000 square feet. Jean decides to incorporate this into the allocation base for the rental costs.

Since labor-hours is an important element of overhead, Jean decides she should use labor-hours to allocate the remaining $24,500.

SSI still plans to produce 1,000 cases each of Almond Dream, Krispy Krackle, and Creamy Crunch. Assume SSI can sell all products it manufactures and that it will use excess capacity, if it drops any products, to produce additional units of the most profitable product. Overhead will remain $69,500 per month under all alternatives.

a. Based on the additional data, determine the product cost and gross profit margin percentages of each product using the three allocation bases to determine the allocation assigned to each product.

b. Would management recommend dropping any of the products based on the criteria of dropping products with less than 10-percent gross profit margin?

c. Based on the recommendation you make in (**b**), recalculate the allocations and profit margins to determine whether any of the remaining products should be dropped from the product line. If any additional products are dropped, substantiate the profitability of remaining products.

Suggested Solutions to Even-Numbered Exercises

22. **Activity-based costing.**
    a. and b.
    Cost per trip:

Activities	Float Trips (3 day)	Whitewater Trips (3 day)
Advertise Trips	$215	$215
Permit to Use the River ..	$30	$50
Equipment Use	$160 [($5 × 28) + $20]	$264 [($8 × 28) + $40]
Insurance	$75	$127
Paying Guides	$1200 ($300 × 4 guides)	$1600 ($400 × 4 guides)
Food	$1680 ($60 × 28)	$1680 ($60 × 28)
Total	$3,360	$3,936

c. If the manager wants to cover her costs she should charge $140 per customer for the 3-day float trip ($3,360/24 paying customers) and $164 per customer for the 3-day whitewater trip ($3,936/24 paying customers).

24. **(Plantcare, Inc., activity based costing in a service-environment.)**
    a. *Using labor hours.*

	Commercial	Residential	Total
Revenue..........................	66,500[a]	143,000[b]	209,500
Direct labor	31,500[c]	58,500[d]	90,000
Overhead..........................	21,700[e]	40,300[f]	62,000
Profit	13,300	44,200	57,500

[a]$66,500 = 3,500 hours × $19 per hour
[b]$143,000 = 6,500 hours × $22 per hour
[c]$31,500 = 3,500 hours × $9 per hour
[d]$58,500 = 6,500 hours × $9 per hour
[e]$21,700 = ($62,000/10,000 hours) × 3,500 hours
[f]$40,300 = ($62,000/10,000 hours) × 6,500 hours

b. *Using the three cost drivers.*

	Rate	Commercial	Residential	Total
Revenue[a]..............		$66,500	$143,000	$209,500
Direct labor		31,500	58,500	90,000
Overhead				
Office supplies	$133.33[b]	2,000[e]	6,000	8,000
Equipment	3.00[c]	10,500[f]	7,500	18,000
Garden supplies	0.36[d]	23,400[g]	12,600	36,000
Total Overhead.........		35,900	26,100	62,000
Profit		$ (900)	$ 58,400	$ 57,500

[a]From part **a**
[b]$133.33 per client = $8,000/60 clients served
[c]$3.00 per hour = $18,000/6,000 equipment hours
[d]$0.36 per square yard = $36,000/100,000 square yards
[e]$2,000 = $133.33 × 15 commercial clients
[f]$10,500 = $3.00 × 3,500 equipment hours
[g]$23,400 = $0.36 × 65,000 square yards

c. Ms. Plantcare should reconsider reducing residential services in favor of
the commercial business. From the results in part **b**, commercial work is
losing money, while the residential business is making a profit. The cost
driver analysis shows that commercial work, which provides only about
30 percent of the revenues, incurs most of the equipment and garden
supplies overhead costs. Allocating overhead costs based on direct labor,
as in part **a**, implies commercial business incurs about 35 percent of the
total overhead, whereas the cost driver analysis in part **b** shows commercial business incurs more than one-half of the total overhead.

26. **(Vicki Greenshade; ABC versus traditional costing.)**

a.

Account	Rate	Tax	Consulting	Total
Revenue................		$80,000	$120,000	$200,000
Expenses				
Filing, scheduling, and data entry	$333.33[a]	24,000[d]	16,000	40,000
Supplies	18.00[b]	14,400[e]	21,600	36,000
Computer Costs	12.50[c]	12,500[f]	7,500	20,000
Profit		$29,100	$ 74,900	$104,000

[a]$333.33 per client = $40,000/120 clients
[b]$18 per hour billed = $36,000/2,000 hours billed
[c]$12.50 per computer hour = $20,000/1,600 hours
[d]$24,000 = $333.33 per client × 72 clients
[e]$14,400 = $18 per hour × 800 hours
[f]$12,500 = $12.50 per computer hour × 1,000 hours

b.

Account	Rate	Tax	Consulting	Total
Revenue.....................		$80,000	$120,000	$200,000
Expenses....................	$48[a]	38,400[b]	57,600	96,000
Profit........................		$41,600	$ 62,400	$104,000

[a]2,000 hours billed = $200,000 revenue/$100 per hour. $48 per hour = ($40,000 + $36,000 + $20,000)/2,000 hours.
[b]$38,400 = $48 per labor hour × 800 hours of labor

c.   The cost driver approach shows consulting generates 62% profit-to-revenue whereas tax generates only about 36%. Consulting appears to be more profitable. However, under labor-based costing in **b** consulting work appears relatively less profitable. Believing that to be the case, Vicki might erroneously concentrate more heavily in tax work.

PART THREE

Managerial Decision Making

At the beginning of this book, we described two major uses of managerial accounting information: managerial decision making and managerial planning, control, and performance evaluation. This part of the book, Chapters 7 through 11, deals with *managerial decision making*. This use of accounting information addresses questions like the following:

- What costs will the university save if it cuts enrollment?
- What is the minimum price that a coffee shop should charge for a cup of espresso?
- Should a hospital build a new wing?
- Is it cheaper for Nike to make shoes or to acquire them from external sources?

These are only a few of the many decisions managers make using accounting information. All of these decisions have one thing in common—they are future-oriented. Managers attempt to estimate the future costs and benefits of alternative operations. The data in the accounting records are, of course, data about the past. These data provide a potentially good source of information about the future when used wisely.

Chapter 7 presents methods of estimating cost behavior. We focus on *costs* because cost differences among options are particularly important and challenging to estimate. Chapter 8 shows the interrelations among selling prices, volume, costs, and profits. Chapters 9, 10, and 11 present applications of differential analysis to many important business decisions. Chapter 9 deals with short-term decisions, whereas Chapters 10 and 11 focus on long-term capacity decisions and on capital budgeting.

Chapter 7

Estimating Cost Behavior

1. Understand the nature of fixed and variable costs.
2. Recognize the effects of learning on costs.
3. Present graphs of semivariable and semifixed costs.
4. Understand how analysts estimate cost behavior using engineering methods and account analysis.
5. Visually fit cost curves to data.
6. Interpret the results of regression estimates.
7. See how regression can be used to estimate the effects of alternative cost drivers.
8. Understand the strengths and weaknesses of alternative cost estimation methods.
9. (Appendix 7.1) Know how learning curves are derived.

Chapter 2 discussed the fundamental distinction between fixed and variable costs. This chapter discusses methods of *estimating* or deriving the breakdown of costs into fixed and variable components. Some costs, such as rent, usually have only a fixed portion, whereas others, such as direct materials, usually have only a variable portion. Many costs, however, have both fixed and variable components. For example, automobiles incur both fixed costs per year (for example, license fees) and variable costs per mile.

We express the total costs of an item as follows:

$$\begin{array}{l} \text{Total} \\ \text{Cost} \\ \text{during} \\ \text{Period} \end{array} = \begin{array}{l} \text{Fixed} \\ \text{Cost} \\ \text{during} \\ \text{Period} \end{array} + \left(\begin{array}{l} \text{Variable} \\ \text{Cost per} \\ \text{Unit of} \\ \text{Activity} \end{array} \times \begin{array}{l} \text{Units of} \\ \text{Activity} \\ \text{during} \\ \text{Period} \end{array} \right)$$

or, using briefer notation:

$$TC = F + VX,$$

where *TC* refers to the total cost for a time period. *F* refers to the total fixed cost for the time period, *V* refers to the variable cost per unit, and *X* refers to the number of units of activity for the time period. Nearly all managerial decisions deal with choices among different activity levels; hence, the manager must estimate which costs will vary with the activity and by how much.

The process of cost estimation works as follows: Suppose management expects a temporary reduction in customers at a particular restaurant during the summer. Some costs will not decline, while others will. Management would estimate the relation between costs and meals served to ascertain which costs would vary. The average unit variable cost, *V*, multiplied by the reduced number of meals, *X*, provides the amount of cost savings, *VX*. This process estimates future costs because the decision involves reducing production in the future.

Because many costs do not fall neatly into fixed and variable categories, managers use statistics and other techniques for estimating **cost behavior.** These techniques break down costs to identify underlying cost behavior patterns.

The Nature of Fixed and Variable Costs

Short Run versus Long Run

Variable costs change as the level of activity changes, whereas **fixed costs** do not change with changes in activity levels. During short time periods, say 1 year, the firm operates with a relatively fixed sales force, managerial staff, and set of production facilities. Consequently, many of its costs are fixed. Over long time spans—many years perhaps—no costs are fixed because staff size can be changed and facilities sold.

This fact provides the basis for the distinction drawn in economics between the long run and the short run and in accounting between fixed costs and variable costs. To the economist, the **short run** is a time period long enough to allow management to change the level of production or other activity within the constraints of current total productive capacity. Management can change total productive capacity only in the **long run.**

To the manager, costs that vary with activity levels in the short run are variable costs: costs that will not vary in the short run, no matter what the level of activity, are fixed costs. The accounting concepts of variable and fixed costs are, then, short-run concepts. They apply to a particular period of time and relate to a particular level of productive capacity.

Consider, for example, the total costs (both variable and fixed) for the firm appearing in Exhibit 7.1. The graph on the left shows the total costs in the long run. If the productive capacity of the firm is 10,000 units per year, total costs will vary as on line *AB*. If the firm acquires new production facilities to increase capacity to 20,000 units, total costs will be as on line *CD*. An increase in capacity to 30,000

Exhibit 7.1

Long-Run versus Short-Run Nature of Costs

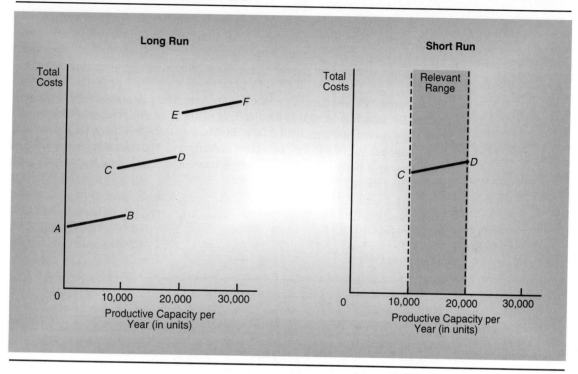

units will increase the total costs as on line *EF*. These shifts in capacity represent long-run commitments. Of course some overlap will occur; production of 10,000 units per year could be at the high-volume end of the *AB* line or at the low-volume end of the *CD* line.

In the short run, a firm has only one capacity level: namely, the capacity of the existing plant. The total costs in the short run appear at the right side of the graph in Exhibit 7.1 on the assumption that the capacity of the existing plant is 20,000 units per year. Note that line *CD* represents costs for the production level of approximately 10,000 units to 20,000 units only. Production levels outside of this range require a different plant capacity, and the total cost line will shift up or down.

Relevant Range

Managers frequently use the notion of relevant range in estimating cost behavior. The **relevant range** is the range of activity over which the firm expects a set of cost behaviors to hold. For example, if the relevant range of activity shown in Exhibit 7.1 is between 10,000 and 20,000 units, the firm assumes that certain costs are fixed while others are variable within that range. The firm would not necessarily assume that costs fixed within the relevant range will stay fixed outside the relevant range.

As Exhibit 7.1 shows, for example, costs step up from point D to point E when production increases from the right side of the 10,000 to 20,000 range to the left side of the 20,000 to 30,000 range.

Estimates of variable and fixed costs apply only if the contemplated level of activity lies within the relevant range. If the firm considers an alternative requiring a level of activity outside the relevant range, then the breakdown of costs into fixed and variable components requires a new computation.

Example Exotic Eats, a profitable restaurant, features a menu of Far Eastern dishes. Because it is located in the financial district of a city, management keeps it open only from 11:00 a.m. until 2:00 p.m., Monday through Friday, for lunch business. Although the restaurant can serve a maximum of 210 customers per day, it has been serving a daily average of 200 customers. The daily costs and revenues of operations follow:

Revenues...	$1,000
Less Variable Costs	(400)
Less Fixed Costs...	(350)
Operating Profits	$ 250

Exhibit 7.2

EXOTIC EATS
Analysis Ignoring Increase in Fixed Costs (which is incorrect)

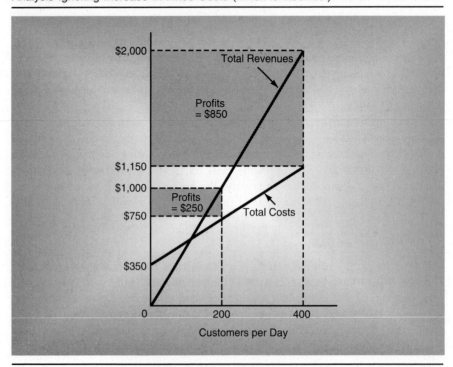

Based on this information, the restaurant's management considers doubling capacity. Cost behavior for doubling capacity is outside of the relevant range. Initial calculations indicate that the number of customers would double. Management wants to know whether operating profits would double. A simple extrapolation indicates that the operating profits would *more* than double, as Exhibit 7.2 shows, because total revenues would double whereas total costs would not.

This simple extrapolation assumes that the total revenues and total variable costs double to $2,000 and $800, respectively, whereas fixed costs remain constant at $350. When capacity changes, fixed costs will not likely remain constant, however. The management of Exotic Eats realizes that with additional capacity and increased customers, it must hire additional cooks, occupancy costs (for example, space rental) would increase, and other fixed costs would increase. The projected new volume is outside the relevant range of volume over which the originally assumed cost behavior pattern would hold. Therefore the original cost behavior pattern shown in Exhibit 7.2 would be invalid.

A revised, more realistic analysis of the cost behavior pattern estimates the unit variable cost of $2 per customer to be the same as before, but estimates fixed costs to increase from $350 to $550 per day. Fixed costs would not double because some fixed costs would not increase (for example, many of the administrative costs).

The revised cost behavior pattern appears in Exhibit 7.3. Exhibit 7.4 compares profits at the original activity level, 200 customers per day, with the projected

Exhibit 7.3

EXOTIC EATS
Increase in Fixed Costs Accompanying Expansion

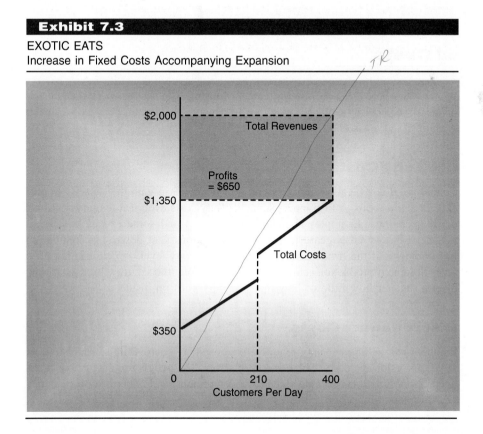

Exhibit 7.4

EXOTIC EATS
Comparison of Profits at Original and Projected Activity Levels

| | Status Quo: 200 Customers per Day | Alternative: 400 Customers per Day | |
		Incorrect Assumption That Fixed Costs Are Constant	Correct Assumption That Fixed Costs Will Change
Revenues..................	$1,000	$2,000	$2,000
Less Variable Costs	(400)	(800)	(800)
Total Contribution Margin	$ 600	$1,200	$1,200
Less Fixed Costs...........	(350)	(350)	(550)
Operating Profits	$ 250	$ 850	$ 650

increase to 400 per day. Management would use these cost estimates to decide whether or not to increase capacity. These decisions usually require discounted cash flow analysis in addition to the estimated change in cash flow discussed here. (Discounted cash flow analysis is discussed in Chapter 10.)

Types of Fixed Costs

In practice, where the short run stops and the long run starts is fuzzy. The accountant divides fixed cost into subclassifications to explain the relation between particular types of fixed costs and current capacity.

Capacity Costs

Certain fixed costs, called **capacity costs,** provide a firm with the capacity to produce or sell or both. A firm incurs some capacity costs even if it temporarily shuts down operations. Examples include property taxes and some executive salaries.

Other capacity costs cease if the firm's operations shut down, but continue in fixed amounts if the firm carries out operations at any level. A firm can lay off a security force if production ceases, but once employed, the security force guards the plant no matter how little or how much activity goes on inside.

Discretionary Costs

Productive or selling capacity requires fixed capacity costs. Companies also incur fixed **discretionary costs.** These costs are also called **programmed costs** or **managed costs.** Examples include research, development, and advertising to generate new business.

These costs are discretionary because the firm need not incur them in the short run to operate the business. They are, however, usually essential for achieving long-run goals. Imagine the long-run impact on Procter & Gamble of eliminating media advertising. Or consider the effects if Eastman Kodak were to drop research and development. Although these companies would survive for a time, after a while they would become different, and likely less profitable, companies.

Discretionary costs reflect top management's policies and commitments to partic-ular programs. When General Motors started thinking about building the Saturn automobile, the company incurred discretionary costs for the Saturn program. Once General Motors committed to building the Saturn plant, the company began incur-ring fixed capacity costs.

Other Cost Behavior Patterns

We have made the following distinction between fixed and variable costs: Total fixed costs remain constant for a period of time (the short run) over a range of activity level (the relevant range); total variable costs change as the volume of activity changes within the relevant range.

Curved Variable Costs

The straightforward linear fixed and variable cost behavior patterns, shown in Ex-hibits 7.2 and 7.3, do not always arise in practice. Total variable cost behavior may be curvilinear as Exhibit 7.5 shows with three different examples of variable cost behavior. **Curvilinear variable cost** functions indicate that the costs vary with the volume of activity, but not in constant proportion. For example, as volume in-creases, the unit prices of some inputs, such as materials and power, may decrease. Another example of curved cost behavior occurs when employees become more efficient with experience, as discussed below.

Learning Curves

Systematic learning from experience often occurs. As employees' experience in-creases, productivity improves and costs per unit decrease. This phenomenon fre-quently occurs when a firm initiates new products or processes or hires a group of new employees. Many high-tech companies, like National Semiconductor and Sun Microsystems, experience learning effects on costs. These companies compete by learning quickly so they can become low-cost producers and capture significant market share.

The effect of learning is often expressed as a **learning curve** (also known as an **experience curve**). The learning curve function shows how the amount of time required to perform a task goes down, per unit, as the number of units increases (see Exhibit 7.6).

Accountants model the nature of the learning phenomenon as a constant percent-age reduction in the *average* direct labor input time required per unit as the *cumula-*

Exhibit 7.5

Examples of Curvilinear Total Variable Cost Behavior

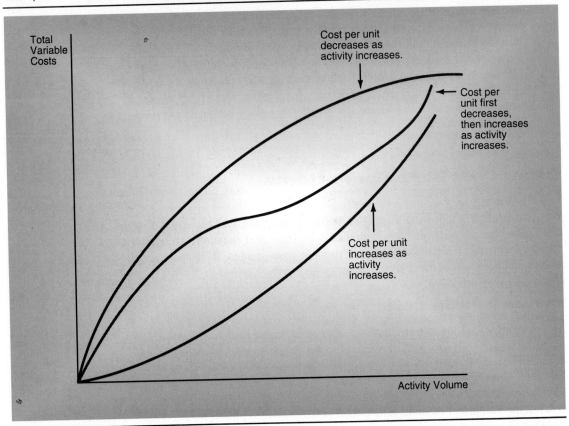

tive output doubles. For example, assume a time reduction rate of 20 percent (that is, an 80-percent cumulative learning curve). Assume also that the first unit takes 125 hours. The *average* for two units should be 100 hours per unit (= .80 × 125 hours), a total of 200 hours for both units. Four units would take an average of 80 hours each (= .80 × 100 hours), or a total of 320 hours. Appendix 7.1 presents the mathematical formula for the learning curve.

The results in this example follow:

Quantity		Time in Hours	
Unit	Cumulative Units	Cumulative	Average per Unit
First.............................	1	125	125
Second...........................	2	200	100 (= .80 × 125)
Third and Fourth	4	320	80 (= .80 × 100)
Fifth through Eighth...............	8	512	64 (= .80 × 80)

Exhibit 7.6 shows the relation between volume and *average* labor hours in graph A, between volume and *total* labor hours in graph B, and between volume and total labor costs in graph C. The labor cost is $20 per hour.

The possible consequences of learning on costs can affect decision making and performance evaluation. Suppose that you are trying to decide whether to make a

Exhibit 7.6

Impact of Learning Curves on Time and Cost Behavior

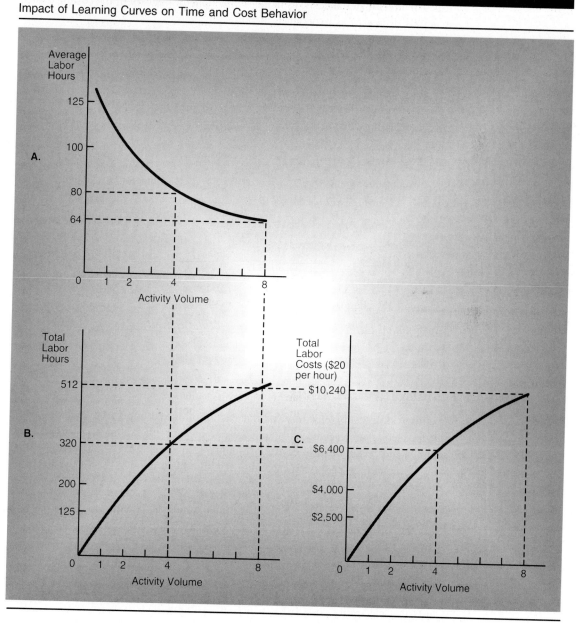

new product that would be subject to the 80-percent cumulative learning curve. Using the data in Exhibit 7.6, if you assumed that the product would require labor costs of $2,500 (= $20 × 125 hours) per unit for the first eight units made, you would seriously overstate the costs for the eight units. If you used the $2,500 per unit as a standard for judging actual cost performance, you would set too loose a standard for all but the first unit.

To what costs do learning curves apply? The learning phenomenon results in savings of time; any labor-related costs could be affected. The learning phenomenon can also affect material costs, as in the semiconductor industry, if the cost of wasted materials decreases as experience increases.

Problem 7.1 for Self-Study

Computing cost decreases because of learning. Bounce Electronics recently recorded the following costs, which are subject to a 75-percent cumulative learning effect.

Cumulative Number of Units Produced	Average Manufacturing Cost Per Unit	Total Manufacturing Costs
1	$1,333	$1,333
2	1,000	2,000
4	?	?
8	?	?
16	?	?

Complete the chart by filling in the cost amounts for volumes of 4, 8, and 16 units.

The solution to this self-study problem is at the end of the chapter on page 274.

Semivariable Costs

Semivariable costs refer to costs that have both fixed and variable components, such as those represented by lines *CD, CE,* and *CF* in Exhibit 7.7A. Repair and maintenance costs or utility costs exemplify semivariable cost behavior, like line *CE*. Minimum repair service capability within a plant requires a fixed cost (*C*) for providing service and an extra charge for uses of the service above some fixed amount. If the charge per unit of, say, electricity decreases at certain stages as consumption increases, the cost curve would look like line *CF*. If the per-unit charge increases at certain stages as usage increases, the costs would look like line *CD*. The term *mixed costs* often denotes semivariable costs.

Example   Mykrochip Corporation has an automated plant. The hours of electricity used varies directly with the number of units produced. Past experience suggests that electricity costs behave in a semivariable pattern as follows:

Exhibit 7.7

Patterns of Cost Behavior: Semivariable and Semifixed Costs

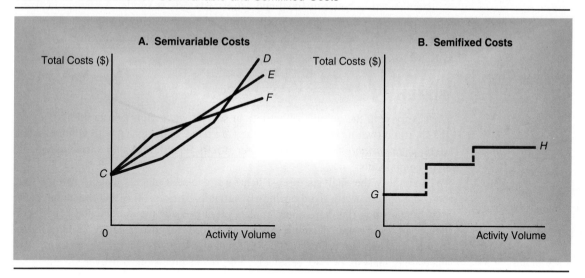

Up to 5,000 Units...	$300
Next 2,000 Units	$.06/Unit
Next 2,000 Units	$.05/Unit

Myckrochip Corporation expects to produce 6,500 units but is considering an order for 1,000 more units. The expected cash outflow for electricity is $390 [= $300 for the first 5,000 units + (1,500 units × $.06)]. If it accepts the order for 1,000 units, production will increase to 7,500 units (= 6,500 + 1,000). Electricity costs will therefore be $445 [= $300 for the first 5,000 units + (2,000 units × $.06) + (500 units × $.05)]. The incremental cash outflow for electricity from accepting this order is $55 (= $445 − $390).

Semifixed Costs

The term **semifixed costs** refers to costs that increase in steps, such as those shown by the broken line *GH* in Exhibit 7.7B. Accountants sometimes describe semifixed costs as *step costs*. If a quality-control inspector can examine 1,000 units per day, inspection costs will be semifixed, with a step up for every 1,000 units per day.

Example Radio House hires one quality-control inspector for each 25,000 toy robots produced per month. The annual salary is $30,000 per inspector. Production has been 65,000 units, so the company has three inspectors. If a special order increases volume from 65,000 to 75,000 units, the firm need hire no additional inspectors. If the special order increases production to a level greater than 75,000 units (say, to 85,000 units), the firm must hire a fourth inspector.

The distinction between fixed and semifixed costs is subtle. A change in fixed costs (other than for inflation or other price changes) usually involves a change in long-term assets, whereas a change in semifixed costs often does not.

Summary

Costs vary with the volume of activity in several ways. Some costs do not vary in the short run over a relevant range—they are *fixed*. Others vary with volume—that is, they are *variable*. Some costs, neither strictly fixed nor strictly variable, contain both components.

To simplify the analysis of cost behavior, decision makers usually assume that costs are either strictly fixed or linearly variable. The reason is that the incremental cost of analyzing the more complex data often exceeds the incremental benefits of doing so. The assumed simple linear variable-fixed cost behavior usually sufficiently approximates reality for decision-making purposes. Many cases require estimates and analysis of cost behavior with greater precision, however.

Problem 7.2 for Self-Study

Sketching cost graphs. Draw graphs of the following cost behaviors.

a. Costs of direct materials used in producing a firm's products.
b. Wages of delivery truck drivers. The firm requires one driver, on average, for each $1 million of sales.
c. Leasing costs of a delivery truck, which are $250 per month and $.18 per mile.
d. Fixed fee paid to an independent firm of CPAs for auditing and attesting to financial statements.
e. Compensation of sales staff with salary of $10,000 plus commission rates that increase as sales increase: 4 percent of the first $100,000 of annual sales, 6 percent of all sales from $100,000 to $200,000, and 8 percent for sales in excess of $200,000.
f. Cost of electricity, where the electric utility charges a flat rate of $50 for the first 5,000 units, $.005 per unit for the next 45,000 units, and $.004 per unit for all units in excess of the first 50,000 units.

The solution to this self-study problem is at the end of the chapter on page 274.

Cost Estimation Methods

In **cost estimation,** analysts break down total costs (TC) into fixed and variable components:

$$TC = F + VX,$$

F is total fixed costs during the period, V is variable cost per unit of activity, and X is the number of units of activity. For example, assume that analysts show the total cost of utilities per month to be \$400 plus \$.05 per kilowatt-hour used. If the firm expects to use 100,000 kilowatt-hours next month, it estimates utilities cost to be \$5,400 [= \$400 + (\$.05 per kilowatt-hour × 100,000 kilowatt-hours)].

The activity represented by X is often called the **independent variable** and the amount of total costs is the **dependent variable.** In some analyses, more than one activity or independent variable influences total cost. If so, such a relation may be expressed as

$$TC = F + V_1X_1 + V_2X_2 + \cdots + V_nX_n$$

F is total fixed cost per period. V_1 is the variable cost per unit of activity X_1 carried out. V_2 is the variable cost per unit of activity X_2 carried out, and so on. X_1 might be the number of automobiles produced in the Nissan plant in Tennessee and X_2 might be the number of trucks produced in the same plant, for example.

Next we discuss the major methods of estimating cost behavior. Each method attempts to estimate the equation $TC = F + VX$ for the particular cost item we are analyzing.

Engineering Method of Estimating Costs

Engineering estimates indicate what costs *should be*. The **engineering method of cost estimation** probably got its name because managers first used it in estimating manufacturing costs from engineers' specifications of the inputs required to manufacture a unit of output. The method is not, however, confined to manufacturing. Banks, McDonald's, the U.S. Post Office, hospitals, and other nonmanufacturing enterprises use time-and-motion studies and similar engineering methods to estimate what costs "should be" to perform a particular service.

Engineers study the physical relation between the quantities of inputs and output. The accountant assigns costs to each of the inputs (wages, prices of material, insurance costs, etc.) to estimate the cost of the outputs.

Estimating the indirect costs of production—the cost of utilities, supervision, maintenance, security—with the engineering method is difficult, however. The method is more reliable when costs vary directly with output (for example, direct labor and direct materials). The engineering method is surprisingly costly to use. Analysis of time, motion, materials, operating characteristics of equipment, and the abilities of workers with varying skills, requires experts. Expert engineers are expensive!

In short, the engineering method of estimating costs is most useful when input/output relations are well defined and fairly stable over time. For an aluminum manufacturer like ALCOA that has stable production methods over time, the engineering method results in good estimates of product costs, particularly for direct materials, direct labor, and certain overhead items like energy costs.

Account Analysis

In contrast to the engineering method, other methods of estimating cost behavior use actual accounting data. The **account analysis method** reviews each cost account and classifies it according to cost behavior. People familiar with the activities of the firm, and the way the firm's activities affect costs, do the classification.

Example The administrators of the Chicago Hospital want to classify operating room overhead costs into fixed and variable components. They will use the information to estimate the effects of increases or decreases in the number of operations performed on operating room overhead costs.

Exhibit 7.8 shows operating room costs coded according to cost behavior. Virtually all organizations have a chart of accounts that presents the numerical codes assigned to accounts. Exhibit 7.8 codes variable costs as V and fixed costs as F. If management wants a more complex classification of cost behavior, such as classification into semivariable costs semifixed, or discretionary fixed costs, the coding system can have additional symbols added.

The accountant assigned a code to each operating room overhead account for Chicago Hospital to indicate whether it was fixed or variable. The following table shows the sum of the amounts in the respective fixed and variable categories for a year. During the year the operating room was in service for 5,700 hours of surgery.

Exhibit 7.8

CHICAGO HOSPITAL
Cost Behavior
Account Analysis

	Account Codes	
Account	**Item[a]**	**Behavior[b]**
Supplies Directly Assigned to Particular Operations	101	V
Labor (physicians and nurses)	102	V
Operating Room Overhead:		
Indirect Supplies...	103	V
Indirect Labor (janitorial, supply room, personnel)	104	V
Utilities (heat, lights)	105	F
Insurance..	106	F

[a]Each account is assigned a different number.

[b]V = variable cost; F = fixed cost.

Note: Additional codes can be used to assign costs to departments or other responsibility centers.

Code	Cost Behavior	Amount
V	Variable	$3,990,000
F	Fixed	1,491,000
		$5,481,000

Dividing the fixed costs by 12 gives a monthly average of $124,250. Dividing the variable costs by the 5,700 operating room hours gives a variable cost rate per hour of operating room use: $700 per operating room hour. The following monthly estimated cost equation results:

$$TC = \$124,250 + (\$700 \times \text{Operating Room Hours Used during Month}).$$

Account analysis requires detailed examination of the data, presumably by accountants and managers who are familiar with the cost. Their expert judgments can uncover cost behavior patterns that other methods may overlook. Because account analysis is judgmental, different analysts are likely to provide different estimates of cost behavior.

Problem 7.3 for Self-Study

Estimating fixed and variable costs using the account analysis method. By the end of its second year of operations, Wonder Genetics had enough data for Naomi Ramos, the company's chief financial officer, to do a detailed analysis of its overhead cost behavior. Ms. Ramos accumulated monthly data that are summarized below as two-year totals.

Indirect Materials	$ 503,000
Indirect Labor	630,000
Lease	288,000
Utilities (heat, light, etc.) ..	206,000
Power to Run Machines ..	104,000
Insurance	24,000
Maintenance	200,000
Depreciation............	72,000
Research and Development	171,000
Total Overhead	$2,198,000
Direct Labor Hours.......	815,800 hours
Direct Labor Costs	$4,997,400
Machine Hours	1,022,700 hours
Units Produced	202,500 units

Ms. Ramos has asked you to prepare an analysis that, using the account analysis method, calculates the *monthly average* fixed costs and the variable cost rate per:

1. Direct labor hour.
2. Machine hour.
3. Unit of output.

You discuss operations with production managers who inform you that three costs are variable—indirect labor, indirect materials, and power to run machines. All other costs are fixed.

The solution to this self-study problem is at the end of the chapter on page 275.

Estimating Costs Using Historical Data

When a firm has been carrying out activities for some time and expects future activities to be similar to those of the past, the firm can analyze the historical data to estimate the variable and fixed components of total cost and to estimate likely future costs. The procedure for analyzing historical cost data requires two steps:

1. Make an estimate of the past relation for $TC = F + VX$.
2. Update this estimate so that it is appropriate for the present or future period for which management wants the estimate. This step requires adjusting costs for inflation and for changes that have occurred in the relation between costs and activity. For example, if a firm expects the production process to be more capital intensive in the future, the accountant should reduce variable costs and increase fixed costs.

Accountants use several methods to estimate costs from historical data; these range from simple ''eyeball estimates'' to sophisticated statistical methods. Before relying on cost estimates, the manager should take the following preliminary steps.

Preliminary Steps in Analyzing Historical Cost Data

Data analysts use the term ''garbage-in, garbage-out'' to indicate that the results of an analysis cannot be better than the input data. Before using cost estimates, the analyst should be confident that the estimates make sense and result from valid assumptions.

Keep in mind that we are trying to find fixed costs per period, F, and variable cost per unit, V, of some activity variable, X, in the relation

$$TC = F + VX.$$

Historical data comprise numerous observations. An observation is the total cost amount for a period and the level of activity carried out during that period. Thus we may have total labor costs by month (the dependent variable) and the number of units produced during each of the months, or the number of direct labor hours worked during each of the months (the independent variable). Exhibit 7.9 shows 12 observations, one for each month, for Chicago Hospital.

We should take the following steps in analyzing cost data:

1. **Review Alternative Cost Drivers (Independent Variable)** A **cost driver** ideally measures the activity that *causes* costs. The cost drivers, if not the sole cause of costs, should directly influence cost incurrence. Operating room hours is an example of a cost driver in a hospital; machine hours is an example in a manufacturing firm; labor hours is an example in a service firm.

2. **Plot the Data** One simple procedure involves plotting each of the observations of total costs against cost driver activity levels. Such plots can highlight an **outlier** observation—one unlike the others. Such outliers may indicate faulty data collection, incorrect arithmetic, or merely a time period when production was out of control. It may be sensible to omit the outlier observation in estimating the average relations among total, fixed, and variable costs. Moreover, plotting the data may make it clear that no relation or only a nonlinear relation exists between the chosen cost driver and actual costs.

3. **Examine the Data and Method of Accumulation** Do the time periods for the cost data and the activity correspond? Occasionally, accounting systems will record costs actually incurred late on a given day as occurring on the following day. Observations collected by the month may smooth over meaningful varia-

Exhibit 7.9

CHICAGO HOSPITAL
Operating Room Overhead Cost Data by Month

Month	Total Overhead Costs Incurred during Month	Operating Room Hours[a]
January	$ 558,000	600
February	433,000	550
March	408,000	350
April	283,000	300
May	245,500	250
June	308,000	200
July	358,000	400
August	445,500	450
September	533,000	500
October	658,000	650
November	558,000	700
December	693,000	750
	$5,481,000	5,700

[a]An operating room hour is one hour that one operating room is being used for surgery.

tions of the cost driver's activity level and cost that would appear if the accountant collected weekly data.

Be aware that a number of common recording procedures can make data appear to exhibit incorrect cost behavior patterns. Accounting systems often charge fixed manufacturing overhead to production on the basis of some activity measure, such as direct labor hours. This unitizing of fixed manufacturing costs makes these costs appear to be variable. Therefore, the manufacturing overhead cost observations should be *actual costs,* not *applied costs.*

Sometimes an inverse relation seems to appear between activity and particular costs—when activity is high, these costs are low; when activity is low, these costs are high. An excellent example is maintenance, which firms sometimes purposefully do only when activity is slow. High maintenance levels often occur during plant shutdowns for automobile model changes, for example. The analyst would be naive to infer that low activity levels cause high maintenance costs.

These examples are a few of the data-recording methods that could lead the analyst astray. In general, we should investigate cost allocations, accruals, correcting and reversing entries, and relations between costs and activity levels to ensure that costs match activities in the appropriate time period for estimating costs.[1] Invalid relations between activity and costs will invalidate the analysis.

Methods of Estimating Costs Using Historical Data

Having taken the preliminary steps to analyze the historical data, we can use several methods to estimate the historical relations between total costs and cost driver activity levels, that is, to estimate $TC = F + VX$.

This section discusses the estimation of variable and fixed overhead for the Chicago Hospital operating room. Keep in mind that the concepts apply to any type of organization. Also, we assume all data have been adjusted for the effects of inflation.

Total operating room overhead costs of the Chicago Hospital for each month during the previous year appear in Exhibit 7.9. Exhibit 7.10 plots them. The task is to estimate the relation between total overhead costs and activity. We expect that, of the possible activity bases, the number of operating room hours during the month primarily causes total overhead costs. Exhibit 7.9 shows total overhead costs and operating room hours each month.

The cost relation we will estimate is

$$\begin{array}{l} \text{Total Overhead} \\ \text{Costs per} \\ \text{Month} \end{array} = \begin{array}{l} \text{Fixed} \\ \text{Costs} \\ \text{per Month} \end{array} + \left(\begin{array}{l} \text{Variable Overhead} \\ \text{Cost per} \\ \text{Operating} \\ \text{Room Hour} \end{array} \times \begin{array}{l} \text{Operating Room} \\ \text{Hours} \\ \text{Used during} \\ \text{Month} \end{array} \right)$$

$$TC = F + VX.$$

---

[1]For an extension of these remarks, see W. E. Wecker and R. L. Weil, "Statistical Estimation of Incremental Costs from Accounting Data," Chapter 30 in P. Frank et al., eds., *Litigation Series Handbook* (New York: John Wiley & Sons, 1990).

Exhibit 7.10

CHICAGO HOSPITAL
Scatter Plot of Total Monthly Overhead Costs
and Operating Room Hours Used during Month

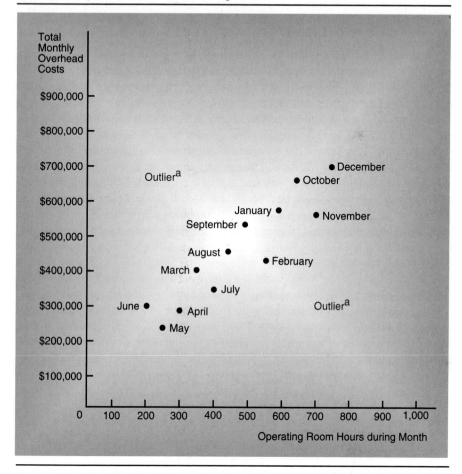

[a]Outliers are assumed and plotted for purposes of illustration. They do not appear in the data in Exhibit 7.9.

Before estimating the cost relation, we plot the data, as in Exhibit 7.10. No outliers are apparent for the 12 observation pairs taken from Exhibit 7.9. Two outliers appear on the plot so that you can see what we mean by an outlier.[2] If only one or two months had outliers such as those shown, we would investigate those months and

_____

[2]One of the outliers, the one corresponding roughly to 750 hours and $300,000 of total costs, has total costs much less than one's intuition says they should be. We suspect that the cause here is faulty data recording; but if not, we would want to know what happened that month. Investigation of outliers illustrates the concept called "management by exception." Understanding the cause of outliers is particularly important for managerial control, as we discuss in the topic of variance analysis in Chapter 13.

once we understood their cause, possibly discard the observations. If several months of a year have outliers, then we probably would not have a meaningful cost estimate.

Next, we illustrate two common methods of estimating the cost relationship, that is, identifying F and V in the preceding equation.

Visual Curve-Fitting Method

One method of estimating costs from data such as those in Exhibit 7.10 is visual curve fitting. Using the **visual curve-fitting method** we draw a straight line through the data points that seems to fit well. By "fit," we mean a straight line that goes through the middle of the data points as closely as possible.

To demonstrate the procedure to yourself, try drawing such a line to fit the observations in Exhibit 7.10. The line that we visually fit to these data intercepts the vertical axis of $100,000 and has a slope of $750 per hour, as shown in Exhibit 7.11. Chances are that the line you drew is not exactly the same as ours. Yours and ours may each give roughly the same estimate of total costs for activity ranging from 300 to 600 operating room hours per month, but would probably give significantly different estimates of total costs for 100 or 1,000 hours per month. You can understand the shortcoming of this method by noting the difference between your visually fit line and ours. The visually fit line is subjective, and different analysts may reach different conclusions from the same data.

Once you have drawn a line to fit the data, you have estimated the fixed cost component F as the total cost for a zero level of activity—the amount at the point where the line intercepts the vertical axis. This estimate of F is outside of the range of observations, so it should be viewed with some skepticism. The estimate of the variable cost per unit of activity is the slope of the line. You can derive it numerically by reading the numbers for any two points *on the line*. The relation is as follows, where subscripts 1 and 2 refer to the two points:

$$\begin{matrix} \text{Variable Cost} \\ \text{per Unit of} \\ \text{Base Activity} \end{matrix} = V = \frac{TC_1 - TC_2}{X_1 - X_2}$$

$$= \frac{\text{Change in Costs between Two Points}}{\text{Change in Activity between the Two Points}} =$$

$$\text{Slope of Total Cost Line.}$$

In our case, we use the following points:

- Point 1: 800 hours; $700,000 total costs.
- Point 2: 0 hours; $100,000 total costs.

Using the preceding formula, we find that

$$V = \frac{\$700,000 - \$100,000}{800 \text{ Hours} - 0 \text{ Hours}} = \frac{\$600,000}{800 \text{ Hours}} = \$750 \text{ per Hour.}$$

Thus we have estimated the total overhead cost relation as

$$\begin{matrix} \text{Total Overhead} \\ \text{Costs per Month} \end{matrix} = \$100,000 + \$750 \text{ per Operating Room Hour.}$$

Exhibit 7.11

CHICAGO HOSPITAL
Visual Curve-Fitting Method of Estimating Fixed Overhead Costs per
Month and Variable Overhead Costs per Operating Room Hour

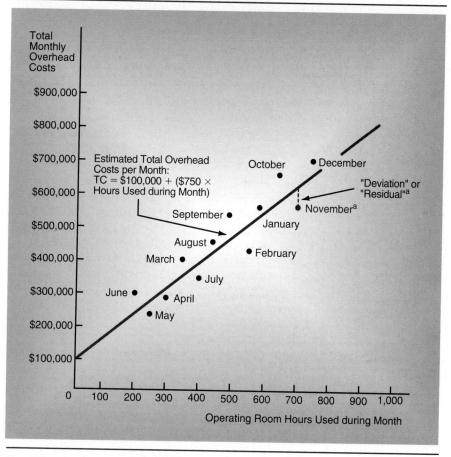

Note: This exhibit is based on data in Exhibit 7.9.

[a]The graph shows vertical distance between the line and the observation, called a *deviation or residual,* for
November. Because the November data point is below the line, the residual is negative.

Your estimate of the fixed and variable overhead costs will differ if the line you
drew differs from ours.

A variation of the visual curve-fitting approach is the *high-low method,* in which
you fit a curve to the highest and lowest total cost observations.

Regression Analysis

With computers widely available, you will find that generally the most cost-effective and accurate method for estimating cost relations is the statistical method
known as **regression analysis.** Rather than estimating the cost relation by the visual

United Airlines Uses Regression to Estimate Profit of Apollo[a]

In the 1970s United Air Lines (UAL) developed Apollo, a computer reservation system costing several hundred million dollars. UAL sold the right to install Apollo computers and communications equipment to travel agencies. These systems allow an agency to communicate directly with UAL and other airlines about reservations. In the late 1980s, UAL decided to sell part of its ownership interest in Apollo. In deciding on a sales price, UAL analyzed the profitability of Apollo. UAL suspected that one benefit of having Apollo is that some passengers who might not otherwise fly on UAL would do so. The travel agent, with an Apollo reservations system, may prefer making a reservation for its customers on a United flight, rather than some other airline's flight. The question arose, how much additional profit did UAL earn from these additional passengers? Some analysts thought UAL would earn a large profit from the extra passengers, because these passengers would fill otherwise empty seats. Others thought UAL would increase its capacity generating new costs, not just put extra passengers in empty seats.

Thus, UAL analysts undertook to ascertain the incremental costs of flying incremental revenue passenger miles. The analysts had quarterly data on UAL costs, classified into several hundred accounts, revenue passenger miles, and revenues. UAL analysts specified the regression model by regressing the change in total costs each period against the changes in revenue passenger miles and system-wide takeoffs. The analysts concluded that about 70 percent of UAL's costs varied with passenger traffic and takeoffs.

This result surprised other analysts who thought that UAL's costs must be mostly fixed. These skeptics observed that UAL averages 35 percent empty seats on its flights. They thought that when UAL carried a few extra passengers, these passengers would sit in the otherwise empty seats. Then, the only incremental costs would be about 25 percent of revenues for extra fuel, food, check-in agents, and baggage handling. The skeptics assumed UAL would not buy new airplanes and other major assets to handle the incremental passenger traffic.

The analysts who developed the regression estimates showed that, optimally, the airline responds to an increase in demand for seats by expanding its total airline capacity, not just planning to put the extra passengers in otherwise empty seats.

UAL sold about half the ownership interest in Apollo and related systems in 1989 for approximately $500 million.

[a]Based on the authors' research.

curve-fitting method, the regression analysis "fits" a line to the data by the method of least squares. The method fits a line to the observations to minimize the sum of the squares of the vertical distance of the observation points from the point on the regression line. (See November in Exhibit 7.11 for an illustration of the vertical distance.) The statistical regression locates the line that best goes through the data points using the least-squares criterion.

In our example, an observed actual value of total overhead cost is TC, and the line we fit by the least squares regression will be of the form

$$\hat{TC} = \hat{F} + \hat{V}X,$$

where the $\hat{}$ on $\hat{TC}$ indicates that we have estimated the value of TC. The right-hand side of the equation should already be familiar to you. Standard terminology designates the vertical distance between the actual and the fitted values, $TC - \hat{TC}$, as the *residual*. The method of least squares fits a line to the data to minimize the sum of all the squared residuals.

This text merely introduces the methods of regression analysis, but virtually every computer system and spreadsheet software package for personal computers can execute regression analysis. Furthermore, pocket calculators available for less than $50 will perform many of these calculations. Here we illustrate statistical methods and explain how to interpret the results. You should be aware that entire books are needed to explain these methods fully, however.

Running the data for TC and X in Exhibit 7.9 through a computer least-squares regression program gives the following results, which we explain later.

$$
\begin{array}{c}
\text{Estimated} \\
\text{Total} \\
\text{Overhead} \\
\text{Costs} \\
\text{per Month}
\end{array}
=
\begin{array}{c}
\$100,168 \\
(\$47,005)
\end{array}
+
\left(
\begin{array}{c}
\$751 \\
(\$93)
\end{array}
\times
\begin{array}{c}
\text{Operating Room Hours} \\
\text{Worked during Month}
\end{array}
\right)
$$

$$R^2 = 0.85.$$

Exhibit 7.12 presents the line implied by this equation.

By now, you should be able to interpret the $100,168 and $751 amounts. The first is the intercept, which estimates the fixed overhead cost per month, and the second estimates the variable overhead cost per unit of base activity, operating room hours worked during the month. The two numbers, $100,168 (for fixed costs) and $751 (for variable costs), are the *coefficients* of the regression equation, sometimes called the regression coefficients.

The previous discussion dealt only with one independent variable. *Multiple regression* has more than one independent variable.

Standard Errors of the Coefficients   The numbers shown in parentheses below the regression coefficients are the **standard errors of the coefficients.** The standard errors of the coefficients measure their variation and give an idea of the confidence we can have in the fixed and variable cost coefficients. The smaller the standard error relative to its coefficient, the more precise the estimate. (Such

Exhibit 7.12

CHICAGO HOSPITAL
Statistical (Least-Squares Regression) Method of Estimating
Fixed Overhead Costs per Month and Variable
Overhead Costs per Operating Room Hour

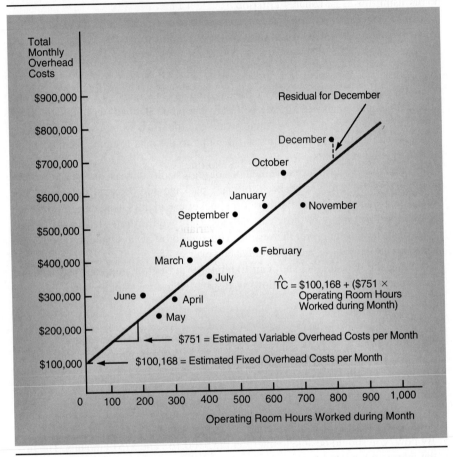

Note: This illustration is based on data in Exhibit 7.9.

computational precision does not necessarily indicate that the estimating procedure is *theoretically* correct, however.)

For example, the standard error of the fixed overhead cost per month is $47,005; the estimate of fixed costs of $100,168 is 2.13 (= $100,168/$47,005) times as large as the standard error. The ratio between an estimated regression coefficient and its standard error is known as the *t*-value or **t-statistic.** If the absolute value of the *t*-statistic is approximately 2 or larger, we can be relatively confident that the actual coefficient differs from zero.[3] The estimated variable cost coefficient is relatively large compared to the standard error of the variable cost coefficient in this example;

---

[3]Statistics books provide *t*-tables that make the analysis of *t*-statistics more precise.

the t-statistic is relatively large: $751/$93 = 8.08. We conclude, therefore, that a statistically significant relationship exists between changes in total overhead costs and changes in operating room hours: Larger amounts of operating room hours worked per month imply larger amounts of overhead costs.

In cases where the standard error of the cost coefficient is large relative to the coefficient (small t-statistic), the cost coefficient may not differ significantly from zero. If a variable cost coefficient has a small t-statistic, we may conclude that little, if any, relation exists between this particular activity (or independent variable) and changes in costs. If a fixed cost coefficient has a small t-statistic, we may conclude that these costs have little, if any, fixed cost component (which we would expect for operating room supplies or direct materials in manufacturing, for example).

R^2 The R^2 attempts to measure how well the line fits the data (that is, how closely the data points cluster about the fitted line). If all the data points were on the same straight line, the R^2 would be 1.00—a perfect fit. If the data points formed a circle or disk, the R^2 would be zero, indicating that no line passing through the center of the circle or disk fits the data better than any other.[4] Technically, R^2 is a measure of the fraction of the total variance of the dependent variable about its mean that the fitted line explains.[5] An R^2 of 1 means that the regression explains all of the variance; an R^2 of zero means that it explains none of the variance. R^2 is sometimes known as the "coefficient of determination."

Many users of statistical regression analysis believe that low R^2s indicate a weak relation between total costs (dependent variable) and the activity base (independent variable). A low standard error (or high t-statistic) for the estimated variable cost coefficient signals whether or not the activity base performs well as an explanatory variable for total costs. With a large number of data observations, both low R^2 and significant regression coefficients can occur. Exhibit 7.13 illustrates this possibility.

Using the Regression to Estimate Costs

The least-squares regression equation,

$$TC = \$100{,}168 + (\$751 \times \text{Operating Room Hours}),$$

appears as a heavy straight line in Exhibit 7.14 with the observations identified by month. The dashed line graphed on Exhibit 7.14 shows that these same data observations may result from a nonlinear relation between costs and activity that appears to be linear in the range of observations.

---

[4]Other situations can also lead to an R^2 of zero.

[5]Many books and computer outputs report both an adjusted and an unadjusted R^2. The adjustment takes into account the number of coefficients fit to the data—two in a linear regression of the kind illustrated here: one for the constant (fixed costs in our applications) and one for the coefficient of the activity variable. An adjusted R^2 measures better than an unadjusted R^2 because the mathematics penalizes the adjusted R^2 for the use of more independent variables. (If you used as many independent variables as you have observations, you would always get an unadjusted R^2 of 1.00.) The unadjusted R^2 for a simple linear regression is the square of the correlation coefficient between the independent and dependent variables.

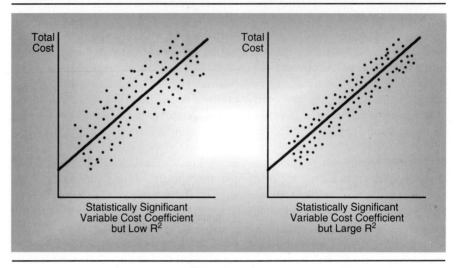

Exhibit 7.13

Relation between Statistical Significance of Variable Cost Coefficient and R^2

Total Cost

Total Cost

Statistically Significant
Variable Cost Coefficient
but Low R^2

Statistically Significant
Variable Cost Coefficient
but Large R^2

We should be wary of predicting total costs for operating room hours worked outside the range of observations, that is, less than about 200 per month or more than about 800 per month. We should be wary of our estimate of fixed costs, because it is outside the relevant range. We can check the regression estimate of fixed costs with the account analysis or other methods to be sure that it makes sense. If we made this check here, we might find that the dashed line in Exhibit 7.14, not the assumed straight line, represents the true relation between costs and activity.

Cautions When Using Regression

Computers easily perform statistical estimating techniques but often do not provide the necessary warnings. We conclude this section by providing several cautionary comments. A relation achieved in a regression analysis does not imply a causal relation; that is, a correlation between two variables does not imply that changes in one will cause changes in the other. An assertion of causality must be based on either *a priori* knowledge or some analysis other than a regression analysis.

Users of regression analysis should be wary of drawing too many inferences from the results unless they are familiar with such statistical estimation problems as *multicollinearity, autocorrelation,* and *heteroscedasticity* and how to deal with them. Statistics books deal with these statistical estimation problems.

Briefly, *multicollinearity* refers to the problem caused in multiple linear regression (more than one independent variable) when the independent variables are not independent of each other but are correlated. When severe multicollinearity occurs, the regression coefficients are unreliable. For example, direct labor hours worked during a month are likely to be highly correlated with direct labor costs during the

Exhibit 7.14

CHICAGO HOSPITAL
Comparison of Regression Estimate to Possible Nonlinear Relation

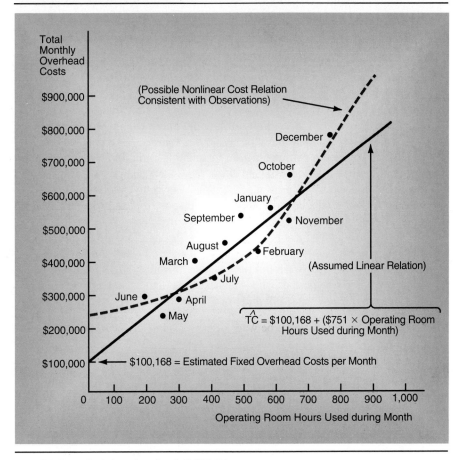

Note: This illustration is based on data in Exhibit 7.9.

month, even when wage rates change over time. If both direct labor hours and direct labor costs are used in a multiple linear regression, we would expect to have a problem of multicollinearity.

When cost drivers are multicollinear, the regression equation can have high adjusted R^2, but the regression coefficients will have low *t*-values.

Autocorrelation problems arise when the data represent observations over time. Autocorrelation occurs when a linear regression is fit to data where a nonlinear relation exists between the dependent and independent variables. In such a case, the deviation of one observation from the fitted line can be predicted from the deviation of the prior observation(s). For example, if demand for a product is seasonal and production is also seasonal, a month of large total costs will more likely follow another month of large total costs than a month of small total costs. In such a case,

Multicollinearity Defeats an Attempt to Estimate Costs

Hughes Tool Company produces equipment used in oil drilling. Hughes owns a patent on a seal used to keep mud out of the mechanism on bits used in drilling. A competitor, Smith International, wanted to license the patent to produce its own drill bits. Hughes needed to know how much incremental profit it earned on its drill bits so it could know what it would lose if Smith produced and sold the bits.

Hughes engaged a consultant from its auditing firm, one of the largest accounting firms. The consultant did a regression analysis on Hughes' costs, as reflected in its internal accounting records, to estimate the incremental costs of producing drill bits. Hughes planned to deduct the resulting cost estimate from the price of a drill bit to estimate potentially lost profit.

The oil drilling business is cyclical and the demand for various oil drilling equipment is highly correlated. That is, in a period when Hughes manufactures and sells many drill bits, it also manufactures and sells much drill pipe. Conversely, in periods when Hughes manufactures and sells few drill bits, it manufactures and sells little drill pipe.

Hughes' accounting data did not separate the costs of producing drill bits from the costs of producing the other oil-drilling equipment. Consequently, the consultant doing the regression analysis faced multicollinearity in the data. He estimated the incremental costs associated with an extra dollar of sales revenue, but he was unable to separate the incremental costs of drill bits from the incremental costs of the drill pipe.

Ultimately, Hughes relied on account analysis to estimate the incremental costs of drill bits.

we would have autocorrelation in the deviations of the data points from a fitted straight line.

Autocorrelation affects the estimates of standard errors of the regression estimates, and therefore it affects the t-statistics. If autocorrelation exists, the estimates of standard errors may be understated and the t-statistics may be overstated in the regression output.

Heteroscedasticity refers to the phenomenon that occurs when the average deviation of the dependent variable from the best-fitting linear relation is systematically larger in one part of the range of independent variable(s) than in others. For example, if the firm uses less reliable equipment and employs less skilled labor in months of large total production, variation in total costs during months of large total production is likely to be greater than in months of small total production. Heteroscedasticity affects the reliability of the estimates of standard errors of the regression coefficients (and therefore affects the reliability of the t-statistics).

Users of regression analysis should be aware of problems in the data base. This awareness comes from a thorough study of the activities that give rise to the data. For example, one should estimate operating room overhead costs only after studying the activities in the operating room that cause overhead costs to be incurred.

Using Regression Analysis to Identify Cost Drivers in Activity-Based Costing

Regression can be particularly helpful in activity-based costing because of the need to identify which of numerous possible cost drivers is related to overhead costs.[6] Use of activity-based costing would require increasing the number of cost drivers beyond the simple one- or two-independent-variable analysis discussed so far. The basic concepts for using regression analysis are the same, nevertheless, whether we use two independent variables (that is, cost drivers) or many independent variables.

People who have an understanding of regression and cost accounting, and who are able to use computer spreadsheets with regression functions, will have ample opportunities to help organizations understand their costs better. Of course, it is important to remember that statistical analysis merely aids our understanding of the relation between costs and causes of costs; it does not substitute for experience, good sense, and managerial judgment.

Where does one start in identifying possible cost drivers? The answer to that question is simple—start with people who are familiar with the day-to-day operations of the company, such as supervisors and department managers. Research to date has found overhead costs to be associated with cost drivers reflecting (1) complexity of operations (for example, the number of setups or the number of different products), (2) volume, and (3) capacity (for example, the value of buildings and equipment).

A study of 31 manufacturing plants in three industries—electronics, automobile components, and machinery—by researchers at the University of Minnesota used regression analysis to identify manufacturing overhead cost drivers. Their approach treated manufacturing overhead cost as the dependent variable and various possible cost drivers as independent variables.[7] Each plant was a separate data point, so there were 31 observations in total. The regression line appeared to be a good fit to the data, with an adjusted R^2 of .779; the coefficients on several independent variables (that is, cost drivers) had t-statistics greater than 2.0.

The researchers found a strong relation between overhead costs and both com-

---

[6]See the article by A. M. Novin, "Applying Overhead: How To Find the Right Bases and Rates," *Management Accounting,* March 1992, for a discussion of the use of Lotus 1-2-3® regression function to find cost drivers and overhead rates.

[7]See R. D. Banker, G. Potter, and R. G. Schroeder, "An Empirical Analysis of Manufacturing Overhead Cost Drivers," Carlson School of Management, University of Minnesota; presented at the American Accounting Association Annual Meetings, Washington, D.C., August 1992.

plexity-based cost drivers, like number of parts and number of setups, and volume-based cost drivers.[8]

The researchers also found that plants implementing new manufacturing methods—namely, just-in-time production, total quality management, and the use of work teams for problem solving on the shop floor—had lower overhead costs than those that had not implemented these new manufacturing methods, all other things equal. This result is particularly important in view of debates over whether improved quality increases or decreases costs.

Problem 7.4
for Self-Study

Interpreting regression output. The following computer output presents two regressions for Wonder Genetics—one using machine hours as the independent variable and the other using units produced as the independent variable. Each regression has one data point per month for two years. Which activity, units produced or machine hours, do you believe best explains the variation in overhead costs?

OUTPUT NO. 1:

Dependent variable = Overhead
Independent variable: Mach. hrs.
$R^2 = .863$ Adjusted $R^2 = .857$
24 observations

Variable	Estimated Coefficient	Standard Error	t-statistic
M-hrs.	4.9015	.41645	11.770
Intercept	−117.28	17.796	−6.5902

OUTPUT NO. 2:

Dependent variable = Overhead
Independent variable: Units Produced
$R^2 = .870$ Adjusted $R^2 = .864$
24 observations

Variable	Estimated Coefficient	Standard Error	t-statistic
Units produced	23.799	1.9610	12.136
Intercept	−109.22	16.597	−6.5805

The solution to this self-study problem is at the end of the chapter on page 276.

---

[8]A study by Foster and Gupta, using regression analysis, found a statistically significant relation between overhead costs and volume-based cost drivers but only a limited association between overhead costs and cost drivers based on the complexity of the production process. See G. Foster and M. Gupta, "Manufacturing Overhead Cost Driver Analysis," *Journal of Accounting and Economics,* vol. 12, no. 1.

Strengths and Weaknesses of Cost Estimation Methods

Each of the methods discussed has advantages and disadvantages. Probably the most informative estimate of cost behavior results from using several of the methods discussed, because each method has the potential to provide information not provided by the others. When deciding which to use in practice, compare the cost of each method with its benefits. Exhibit 7.15 summarizes the strengths and weaknesses of these methods.

Summary

Managers need estimates of cost behavior to apply manufacturing overhead to products, to estimate how decisions will affect costs, to plan, and to develop budgets.

Variable costs change with the level of activity, whereas fixed costs remain constant. These categories remain valid within some assumed time period (usually called the short run) and range of activity (the relevant range).

Many fixed costs are capacity costs. They will remain constant (in the absence of inflation) as long as the firm does not change capacity. Other fixed costs are discretionary costs. These costs include such things as advertising and research and development, which may not be absolutely essential for operating the business but are essential for achieving long-run goals.

Many costs are not simply fixed or variable. Variable costs may be curvilinear (curved) as well as linear. Curvilinear variable costs may occur in cases where

Exhibit 7.15

Strengths and Weaknesses of Cost Estimation Methods

Method	Strengths	Weaknesses
Engineering Method	Based on studies of what future costs should be rather than what past costs have been.	Not particularly useful when the physical relation between inputs and outputs is indirect. Can be costly to use.
Account Analysis	Provides a detailed expert analysis of the cost behavior in each account.	Subjective.
Visual Curve-Fitting Method	Uses all the observations of cost data. Relatively easy to understand and apply.	The fitting of the line to the observations is subjective. Difficult to do where several activity bases cause costs.
Regression Method	Uses all of the observations of cost data. The line is statistically fit to the observations. Provides a measure of the goodness of fit of the line to the observations. Relatively easy to use with computers and sophisticated calculators.	The regression model requires that several relatively strict assumptions be satisfied for the results to be valid.

learning reduces labor and labor-related costs per unit as workers gain experience with a new product or process. Costs also may be *semivariable,* having both fixed and variable components. *Semifixed* costs are those that increase in steps.

There are numerous methods for estimating cost behavior. Each method attempts to estimate *TC, F,* and *V* in the equation

$$TC = F + VX,$$

where *TC* is the total cost during the period. *F* is the fixed cost during the period, *V* is the variable cost per unit of activity, and *X* is the number of units of activity during the period.

The *engineering method* involves a study of the physical inputs required to produce each unit of output. This method forms the basis for estimating the costs of each unit of output. The *account analysis method* analyzes each cost account and classifies the account according to cost behavior—usually either fixed or variable.

Two methods, *visual curve fitting* and *regression analysis,* rely on historical data in the accounting records. The visual curve-fitting method estimates the relation between costs and activity from a line drawn to provide the best visual fit of the data. Regression analysis fits a line to the data to minimize the sum of the squares of the vertical distance of each observation point from the regression line.

The results of computerized regression analyses provide considerable data. *Standard errors of the coefficients* of the regression equation give an idea of the confidence we have in the coefficients—the smaller the standard error relative to its coefficient, the better. The R^2 attempts to measure how well the regression line fits the data. To use regression to estimate costs, (1) find a logical relation between the costs and the cost driver (independent variable), (2) examine the data base for problems induced by the accounting system, and (3) consider and deal with statistical estimation problems signalled by the regression outputs.

Appendix 7.1:
Deriving Learning Curves[9]

Mathematically, the learning curve effect is

$$Y = aX^b,$$

where

Y = average number of labor hours required per unit for *X* units
a = number of labor hours required for the first unit
X = cumulative number of units produced
b = index of learning equal to the log of the learning rate divided by the log of 2.

For the learning curve example in the text, $b = -.322$, which we derive as follows.

If the first unit takes *a* hours, then the average for 2 units is .8*a* hours according to the model. Because *X* = 2, the equation gives $.8a = a2^b$. Taking logs,

$$\log 0.8 + \log a = \log a + b \log 2.$$

---

[9]The learning curve derivation in this appendix is known as the cumulative-average-time learning model.

Simplifying,

$$b = \log 0.8/\log 2 = -.322.$$

Thus we can derive the average number of labor hours from the example in the text as follows:

X	Y	
1	125	
2	100	$Y = 125 \times (2^{-.322}) = 100$
3	88	$Y = 125 \times (3^{-.322}) = 88$
4	80	$Y = 125 \times (4^{-.322}) = 80$
.	.	
.	.	
.	.	
8	64	$Y = 125 \times (8^{-.322}) = 64$

The function

$$Y = aX^b$$

is curvilinear, as shown in the text. The function is linear when expressed in logs, because

$$\log Y = \log a + b \log X,$$

so the function is linear when plotted on log-log paper, as the following exhibit shows.

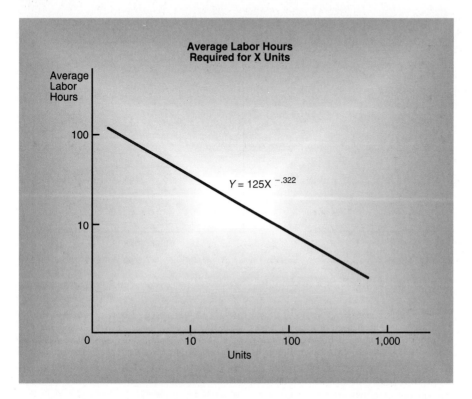

Average Labor Hours Required for X Units

$$Y = 125X^{-.322}$$

Operations management textbooks provide expanded discussions.[10]

Solutions to Self-Study Problems

Suggested Solution to Problem 7.1 for Self-Study

Cumulative Number of Units Produced	Average Manufacturing Cost Per Unit	Total Manufacturing Costs
1	$1,333	$1,333
2	1,000(= 75% × $1,333)	2,000
4	750(= 75% × $1,000)	3,000
8	562.50(= 75% × $750)	4,500
16	421.88(= 75% × $562.50)	6,750

Suggested Solution to Problem 7.2 for Self-Study

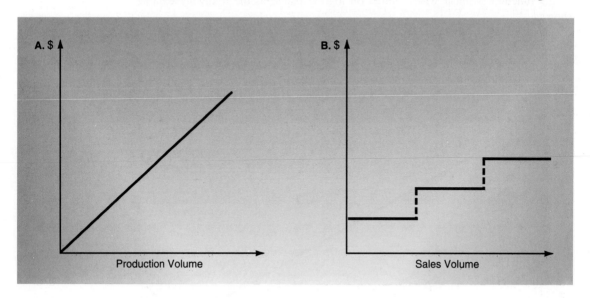

[10]For accounting application of learning curves, see J. Chen and R. Manes, "Distinguishing the Two Forms of the Constant Percentage Learning Curve Model," *Contemporary Accounting Research,* Spring 1985, pp. 242–252; and A. Belkaoui, *The Learning Curve: A Management Accounting Tool* (Westport, Conn.: Quorum Books, 1986).

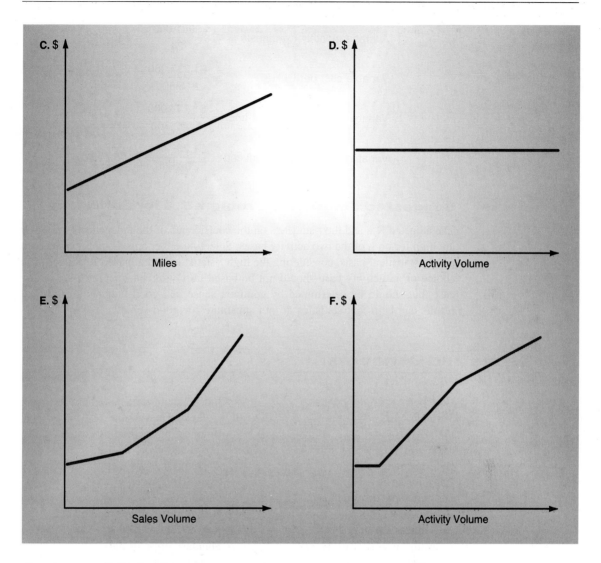

Suggested Solution to Problem 7.3 for Self-Study

Indirect Materials	$ 503,000
Indirect Labor	630,000
Power	104,000
Total Variable Costs	$1,237,000
Lease	$ 288,000
Utilities	206,000
Insurance	24,000
Maintenance	200,000
Depreciation	72,000
Research and Development	171,000
Total Fixed Costs	$ 961,000

$$\text{Average monthly fixed costs} = \frac{\$961,000}{24} = \$40,042$$

$$\text{Variable cost per DLH} = \frac{\$1,237,000}{815,800} = \$1.516$$

$$\text{Variable cost per machine-hour} = \frac{\$1,237,000}{1,022,700} = \$1.210$$

$$\text{Variable cost per unit produced} = \frac{\$1,237,000}{202,500} = \$6.109$$

Suggested Solution to Problem 7.4 for Self-Study

The adjusted R^2s and the t-statistics on the coefficients of the independent variables are high for both of the two activity bases. Selecting either appears appropriate on a purely statistical basis, considering the high t-statistics and adjusted R^2 values. The choice of an activity base should not be based purely on statistical results, in any case, but should be determined by common sense and good judgment. Statistical results can help, but statistics do not substitute for good sense.

Key Terms and Concepts

Cost behavior
Variable costs
Fixed costs
Short run versus long run
Relevant range
Capacity costs
Discretionary (programmed, managed) costs
Curvilinear variable costs
Learning (experience) curves
Semivariable costs
Semifixed (step) costs
Cost estimation

Independent variable versus dependent variable
Engineering method of cost estimation
Account analysis method
Cost driver
Outlier
Visual curve-fitting method
Regression analysis
Standard error of the coefficient
t-statistic
R^2

Questions, Exercises, Problems, and Cases

Questions

1. Review the meaning of the concepts or terms given above in Key Terms and Concepts.
2. "The concepts of short-run costs and long-run costs are so relative—Short run could mean a day, a month, a year, or even 10 years, depending on what you are looking at." Comment.

3. "My variable costs are $2 per unit. If I want to increase production from 100,000 units to 150,000 units, my costs should go up by only $100,000." Comment.

4. Describe the phenomenon that gives rise to learning curves. To what type of costs do learning curves apply?

5. "Simplification of all costs into just fixed and variable costs distorts the actual cost behavior pattern of a firm. Yet businesses rely on this method of cost classification." Comment.

6. Which method of cost estimation does not rely primarily on historical cost data? What are the drawbacks of this method?

7. "The account analysis method uses subjective judgment. So we cannot really consider it a valid method of cost estimation." Comment.

8. What methods of cost estimation rely primarily on historical data? Discuss the problems an unwary user may encounter with the use of historical cost data.

9. Why might the relevant range be limited to the range of observations in a data set?

10. If an analyst simply enters data into a program to compute regression estimates, what major problems might he or she encounter?

11. When estimating fixed and variable costs, it is possible to have an equation with a negative intercept. Does this mean that at zero production level the company has negative fixed costs?

12. Suggest ways that one can compensate for the effects of inflation when preparing cost estimates.

13. Refer to the Managerial Application "United Airlines Uses Regression to Estimate Profit of Apollo." What independent variables did the analysts use in the regression? What did the analysts who developed the regression conclude? Based on your experience, do you agree with their conclusions?

14. Refer to the Managerial Application "Multicollinearity Defeats an Attempt to Estimate Costs." Why wasn't the analyst able to estimate the costs of drill bits? How might account analysis be used to make the analysis of the cost of drill bits when regression failed?

15. How is regression used to identify what cost drivers might be used in activity-based costing?

16. Refer to the discussion under the heading "Using Regression Analysis to Identify Cost Drivers in Activity-Based Costing." What did the researchers find about the relation between complexity-based cost drivers and overhead costs? What about the relation between new production methods such as just-in-time and quality improvement and overhead costs?

Exercises

Solutions to even-numbered exercises are at the end of the chapter on page 288.

17. **Graphs of cost relations.** Sketch cost graphs for the following situations:
    a. A 20-percent increase in fixed costs will enable Twickenham Products to produce up to 50 percent more. Variable costs will remain unchanged.
    b. Refer to part **a**. What if Twickenham Products' variable costs double for the additional units it intends to produce?

    c.   Aerodyne's variable marketing costs per unit decline as more units are sold.

    d.   Richmond Paper pays a flat fixed charge per month for electricity plus an additional rate of $.15 per unit for all consumption over the first 2,000 units.

    e.   Indirect labor costs at National Bank consist only of supervisors' salaries. The bank needs one supervisor for every twenty clerks.

    f.   Petersham Plastics currently operates close to capacity. A short-run increase in production would result in increasing unit costs for every additional unit produced.

18. **Cost behavior in event of capacity change.** Muller's Gasthaus, a lodge located in a fast-growing ski resort, is planning to open its new wing this coming winter, increasing the number of beds by 40 percent. Although variable costs per guest-day will remain unchanged, fixed costs will increase by 25 percent. Last year's costs follow:

Variable Costs	$50,000
Fixed Costs	$30,000

    a.   Sketch the cost function.

    b.   Calculate the additional fixed operating costs that Muller's Gasthaus will incur next year.

19. **Cost behavior when costs are semivariable.** Data from the shipping department of Martinez Company for the last 2 months follow:

	Number of Packages Shipped	Shipping Department Costs
November	6,000	$9,000
December	9,000	12,000

    a.   Sketch a line describing these costs as a function of the number of packages shipped.

    b.   What is the apparent variable cost per package shipped?

    c.   The line should indicate that these shipping costs are semivariable. What is the apparent fixed cost per month of running the shipping department during November and December?

20. **Cost behavior when costs are semivariable.** Data from the shipping department of Pete's Coffee for the last 4 months follow:

	Number of Packages Shipped	Shipping Department Costs
May	0	$1,500
June	2,000	3,500
July	2,500	4,500
August	1,500	3,000

Are these costs fixed, semifixed, variable, or semivariable?

21. **Cost estimation using visual curve fitting.** The Lopez Accounting Company prepares tax returns for small businesses. Data on the company's total costs and output for the past 6 months appear in the table that follows.
    a. Estimate fixed costs per month and variable cost per tax return prepared from the data in the table, using a straight line visually fit to a plot of the data.
    b. Estimate total monthly costs for a month when 250 tax returns are prepared, using the estimates of fixed and variable costs from part **a**.

LOPEZ ACCOUNTING COMPANY

Month	Tax Returns Prepared	Total Costs
January	200	$160,000
February...	280	192,000
March	300	198,000
April..	260	180,000
May...	260	186,000
June	240	170,000

22. **Learning curve.** R&D Co. makes technical products for mysterious customers. To make Product RPE, the company recently recorded the following costs, which decline subject to a 75-percent cumulative learning curve.

Cumulative Number of Units Produced	Average Manufacturing Costs per Unit
1	$1,333
2	1,000
4	?
8	?
16	?

Complete the chart by filling in the cost amounts for volumes of 4, 8, and 16 units.

23. **Average cost calculations.** Slumber Beds has the following cost equation:

$$\text{Total Costs} = \$13,266 + \$75n,$$

where $n =$ units of output.
    a. Calculate Slumber's average fixed cost per unit when output is 500 units.
    b. Calculate the average variable cost per unit when output is 500 units.
    c. Calculate the average cost per unit when output is 500 units.

24. **Repair cost behavior.** The Baiman Company analyzed repair costs by month using linear regression analysis. The equation fit took the following form:

$$\begin{matrix} \text{Total} \\ \text{Repair} \\ \text{Costs} \end{matrix} = \begin{matrix} \text{Fixed} \\ \text{Costs} \end{matrix} + \left(\begin{matrix} \text{Variable Repair Costs} \\ \text{per Machine Hour Used} \\ \text{during Month} \end{matrix} \times \begin{matrix} \text{Machine Hours} \\ \text{Actually Used} \\ \text{during Month} \end{matrix} \right)$$

$$TRC = a + bx.$$

The results were (standard error of coefficients appear in parentheses)

$$TRC = \$20,000 - \$.75x$$
$$(\$7,000) \quad (\$.25)$$

The R^2 was 0.90.

Average monthly repair costs have been $18,800, and machine hours used have averaged 1,600 hours per month. Management worries about the ability of the analyst who carried out this work because of the *negative* coefficient for variable cost.

What is your evaluation of these results?

25. **Interpreting regression results.** The output of a regression of overhead costs on direct labor costs per month follows:

Regression Results:
Equation:
    Intercept... $15,500
    Slope 2.35
Statistical Data:
    R^2 .... .85

The company plans to operate at a level that would call for direct labor costs of $14,000 per month for the coming year.

a. Use the regression output to write the overhead cost equation.
b. Based on the cost equation, compute the estimated overhead cost per month for the coming year.
c. How well does this regression explain the relation between direct labor and overhead?

26. **Interpreting regression data.** A marketing manager of a company used a pocket calculator to estimate the relation between sales dollars for the past 3 years and monthly advertising expenditures (the independent variable). The regression results indicated the following equation:

Sales Dollars = $97,000 - (1.45 × Advertising Dollars)

Do these results imply that advertising hurts sales? Why would there appear to be a negative relation between advertising expenditures and sales?

27. **Cost estimation using visual curve fitting.** Kakimoto Beverages has observed the following overhead costs for the past 12 months:

Month	Overhead Costs	Gallons of Output
January	$22,800	9,000
February...........................	31,200	22,000
March	33,600	24,000
April...............................	24,000	11,000
May	28,200	18,000
June	31,200	21,000
July	26,400	15,000

(continued)

Month	Overhead Costs	Gallons of Output
August	$24,600	10,000
September	31,200	23,000
October	25,800	12,000
November	28,800	17,000
December	30,000	20,000

a. Prepare a scatter plot of the data.

b. By visual inspection, fit a line through the plotted points and calculate the approximate monthly fixed cost and unit variable cost.

Problems

28. Interpreting multiple regression results. To select the most appropriate activity base for allocating overhead, Mercury Gas, an oil refinery, ran a multiple regression of several independent variables against its nonmaintenance overhead cost. The results were as follows for 24 observations:

Variable Name	Coefficient	Standard Error	t-Statistic
Direct Labor Hours	.876	2.686	.326
Units of Output	10.218	5.378	1.900
Maintenance Costs	$(12.786)	$1.113	(11.488)
Cost of Utilities	.766	.079	9.696
Intercept	12.768	6.359	2.008
R^2 for the Multiple Regression = 0.90			

Discuss the appropriateness of each of these variables for use as an activity base. Which would you recommend selecting? Why?

29. Interpreting regression results (adapted from an example by G. Benston, *The Accounting Review* 41, pp. 657–672). The Benston Company manufactures widgets and digits. Benston assembles the widgets in batches, but makes digits one at a time. Benston believes that the cost of producing widgets is independent of the number of digits produced in a week. The firm gathered cost data for 156 weeks. The following notation is used:

C = Total manufacturing costs per week
N = Number of widgets produced during a week
B = Average number of widgets in a batch during the week
D = Number of digits produced during the week

A multiple linear regression fit to the observations gave the following results (standard errors of estimated coefficients are shown in parentheses under the coefficients):

$$C = \$265.80 + \$8.21N - \$7.83B + \$12.32D.$$
$$(\$110.80) \quad (\$.53) \quad (\$1.69) \quad (\$2.10)$$

The adjusted R^2 was .89.

a. According to the regression results, how much are weekly costs expected to increase if the number of widgets increases by 1?

b. What are the expected costs for the week if Benston produces 500 widgets in batches of 20 each and produces 300 digits during the week?

c. Interpret the negative coefficient $(7.83) estimated for the variable B.

30. **Regression analysis, multiple choice.** Armer Company estimated the behavior pattern of maintenance costs. Data regarding maintenance hours and costs for the previous year and the results of the regression analysis follow:

	Hours of Activity	Maintenance Costs
January	480	$ 4,200
February..........................	320	3,000
March	400	3,600
April.............................	300	2,820
May	500	4,350
June	310	2,960
July	320	3,030
August	520	4,470
September........................	490	4,260
October	470	4,050
November	350	3,300
December	340	3,160
Sum	4,800	43,200
Average	400	3,600

$$TC = F + VX$$
$$= 684.65 + 7.2884X$$
$$(49.515) \quad (.121)$$

Intercept..	684.65
V Coefficient	7.2884
Standard Error of the Intercept...................................	49.515
Standard Error of the V Coefficient	.121
R^2	.997
t-Statistic for the Intercept	13.827
t-Statistic for the V Coefficient	60.105

a. In the equation $TC = F + VX$, the best description of the letter V is as the
   (1) Independent variable.
   (2) Dependent variable.
   (3) Coefficient for the intercept.
   (4) Variable cost coefficient.

b. The best description of TC in the preceding equation is as the
   (1) Independent variable.
   (2) Dependent variable.
   (3) Constant coefficient.
   (4) Variable coefficient.

c. The best description of the letter X in the preceding regression equation is as the
   (1) Independent variable.
   (2) Dependent variable.

    (3) Coefficient for the intercept.

    (4) Variable cost coefficient.

d. Based on the data derived from the regression analysis, 420 maintenance hours in a month mean that the maintenance costs would be estimated at

    (1) $3,780.

    (2) $3,461.

    (3) $3,797.

    (4) $3,746.

    (5) Some other amount.

e. The percentage of the total variance that the regression equation explains equals

    (1) 99.7%.

    (2) 69.6%.

    (3) 80.9%.

    (4) 99.8%.

    (5) Some other amount.

31. Graphing costs and interpreting regression output (adapted from CMA exam). Management of Monahan's Pizza wants to estimate overhead costs accurately to plan the company's operations and its financial needs. A trade association publication reports that certain overhead costs tend to vary with pizzas made. Management gathered monthly data on pizzas and overhead costs for the past 2 years for 12 pizza restaurants. No major changes in operations were made over this time period. The data follow:

Month No.	Number of Pizzas	Overhead Costs
1	20,000	$84,000
2	25,000	99,000
3	22,000	89,500
4	23,000	90,000
5	20,000	81,500
6	19,000	75,500
7	14,000	70,500
8	10,000	64,500
9	12,000	69,000
10	17,000	75,000
11	16,000	71,500
12	19,000	78,000
13	21,000	86,000
14	24,000	93,000
15	23,000	93,000
16	22,000	87,000
17	20,000	80,000
18	18,000	76,500
19	12,000	67,500
20	13,000	71,000
21	15,000	73,500
22	17,000	72,500
23	15,000	71,000
24	18,000	75,000

An analyst entered these data into a computer regression program and obtained the following output:

Coefficient of Correlation	.9544
R^2	.9109
Coefficients of the Equation:	
Intercept..	$39,859
Independent Variable (slope).....................................	2.1549
Standard Error of the Independent Variable	.1437

    a. Prepare a graph showing the overhead costs plotted against pizzas.

    b. Use the results of the regression analysis to prepare the cost estimation equation and to prepare a cost estimate for 22,500 pizzas for one month.

    c. Evaluate how well the regression estimates overhead cost behavior.

32. Interpreting regression results (adapted from CMA exam). Horizon Company is making plans for the introduction of a new product that it will sell for $6 a unit. The following estimates have been made for manufacturing costs on 100,000 units to be produced the first year:

Direct materials	$50,000
Direct labor	$80,000 (the labor rate is $8 an hour × 10,000 hours)

Manufacturing overhead costs have not yet been estimated for the new product, but monthly data on total production and overhead costs for the past 24 months have been analyzed using regression. The following results were derived from the regression and will provide the basis for overhead cost estimates for the new product.

Regression Analysis Results	
Dependent variable—Factory overhead costs	
Independent variable—Direct labor-hours	
Computed values:	
Intercept..	$55,000
Coefficient of independent variable	$ 3.20
Coefficient of correlation.......................................	.953
R^2	.908

    a. What percentage of the variation in overhead costs is explained by the independent variable?

        (1) 90.8 percent.

        (2) 42 percent.

        (3) 48.8 percent.

        (4) 95.3 percent.

        (5) Some other amount.

    b. The total overhead cost for an estimated activity level of 20,000 direct labor-hours would be:

    (1) $55,000.
    (2) $64,000.
    (3) $82,000.
    (4) $119,000.
    (5) Some other amount.

c. What is the expected contribution margin per *unit* to be earned during the first year on 100,000 units of the new product? (Assume all marketing and administrative costs are fixed.)
    (1) $4.38.
    (2) $4.89.
    (3) $3.83.
    (4) $5.10.
    (5) Some other amount.

d. How much is the variable manufacturing cost per *unit,* using the variable overhead estimated by the regression (and assuming direct materials and direct labor are variable costs)?
    (1) $1.30.
    (2) $1.11.
    (3) $1.62.
    (4) $3.
    (5) Some other amount.

e. What is the manufacturing cost equation implied by these results, where x refers to *units* produced?
    (1) TC = $80,000 + 1.11x$.
    (2) TC = $55,000 + 1.62x$.
    (3) TC = $185,000 + 3.20x$.
    (4) Some other equation.

33. Effect of learning on cost behavior. Zipper Incorporated manufactures aircraft parts for various commercial airlines. One particular contract, resulted in the following labor costs:

Cumulative Number of Units Produced, X	Average Labor Costs (in real dollars), Y
1	$1,333
2	1,000
3	845
4	750
5	684
6	634
7	594
8	562

a. Sketch the relation between X and Y.
b. If there is a learning phenomenon, estimate the constant percentage reduction in labor costs, that is, the percent cumulative learning curve.

Cases

34. Learning curves (adapted from CMA exam). The Major Electric Company plans to manufacture a product called Electrocal, which requires a substantial amount of direct labor on each unit. Based on the company's experience with other products that required similar amounts of direct labor, management believes that learning affects the production process used to manufacture Electrocal.

Each unit of Electrocal requires 50 square feet of direct material at a cost of $30 per square foot for a total material cost of $1,500. The standard direct labor rate is $25 per direct labor hour. The accounting system assigns variable manufacturing overhead to products at a rate of $40 per direct labor hour. The company adds a markup of 30 percent to variable manufacturing cost in setting an initial bid price for all products.

Data on the production of the first two lots (16 units) of Electrocal follow:
(1) The first lot of 8 units required a total of 3,200 direct labor hours.
(2) The second lot of 8 units required a total of 2,240 direct labor hours.
Based on prior production experience, Major Electric anticipates that production time will not improve significantly after the first 32 units. Therefore, a standard for direct labor hours will be established based on the average hours per unit for units 17 through 32.
a. What is the basic premise of the learning curve?
b. Based on the data presented for the first 16 units, what learning rate appears to apply to the direct labor required to produce Electrocal? Support your answer with appropriate calculations.
c. Calculate the standard for direct labor hours that Major Electric Company should establish for each unit of Electrocal.
d. After Major Electric had manufactured the first 32 units, the customer asked Major Electric to submit a bid for an additional 96 units. What price should Major Electric bid on this order of 96 units? Explain your answer.
e. Knowledge of the learning curve phenomenon can be a valuable management tool. Explain how management can apply the learning curve in planning and controlling business operations.

35. Estimating health-care cost behavior. The health-care industry has been faced with increasing pressure to control costs. Health-care costs have increased substantially more rapidly than general inflation rates. At the same time, health care facilities face price competition for services because insurance companies and government-funded health programs are limiting opportunities for cost reimbursement.

To control costs, one must first relate the costs of providing services to the volume of activity. The first step is often to estimate a cost model, TC = F + VX, where X refers to the volume of activity. Examples of activity bases include patient days to estimate nurse staff costs or number of tests to estimate costs in a laboratory.

Although it may appear simple to estimate the relation TC = F + VX, analysts often find a lack of good data to make the estimates. For example, the cost of medical supplies shown in the accounting records is often the cost of *purchases,* not the cost of supplies *used.* Consequently, large purchases in one month followed by no purchases in the next month make these costs appear to behave in unrealistic ways.

Although recent pressures on health-care facilities to reduce costs have increased the incentives for administrators and doctors to improve recordkeeping, our research indicates the information needed to control costs is lacking in many health-care organizations. For example, hospitals often keep track of *charges* to patients but not the *costs* of the items being charged.

How would information that makes it possible to estimate the equation $TC = F + VX$ help health-care managers control costs?

36. **Learning curves, managerial decisions** (adapted from CMA exam). The Xyon Company purchases 80,000 pumps annually from Kobec, Inc. The price has increased each year and reached $68 per unit last year. Because the purchase price has increased significantly, Xyon management has asked its analyst to estimate the cost to manufacture the pump in its own facilities. Xyon's products consist of stampings and castings. The company has little experience with products requiring assembly.

The engineering, manufacturing, and accounting departments have prepared a report for management that includes the following estimate for an assembly run of 10,000 units. The firm would hire additional production employees to manufacture the subassembly. It would not need extra equipment, space, or supervision.

The report estimates total costs for 10,000 units at $957,000, or $95.70 a unit. The current purchase price is $68 a unit, so the report recommends continued purchase of the product.

Components (outside purchases)............	$120,000
Assembly Labor[a]	300,000
Factory Overhead[b]	450,000
General and Administrative Overhead[c].......	87,000
Total Costs	$957,000

Fixed Overhead	50 Percent of Direct Labor Dollars
Variable Overhead.......................	100 Percent of Direct Labor Dollars
Factory Overhead Rate	150 Percent of Direct Labor Dollars

[a]Assembly labor consists of hourly production workers.

[b]Factory overhead is applied to products on a direct labor dollar basis. Variable overhead costs vary closely with direct labor dollars.

[c]General and administrative overhead is applied at 10 percent of the total cost of material (or components), assembly labor, and factory overhead.

a. Was the analysis prepared by the engineering, manufacturing, and accounting departments of Xyon Company and the recommendation to continue purchasing the pumps that followed from the analysis correct? Explain your answer and include any supportive calculations you consider necessary.

b. Assume Xyon Company could experience labor cost improvements on the pump assembly consistent with an 80-percent learning curve. An assembly run of 10,000 units represents the initial lot or batch for measurement purposes. Should Xyon produce the 80,000 pumps in this situation? Explain your answer.

Suggested Solutions to Even-Numbered Exercises

18. **Cost behavior in event of capacity change.**

   a.

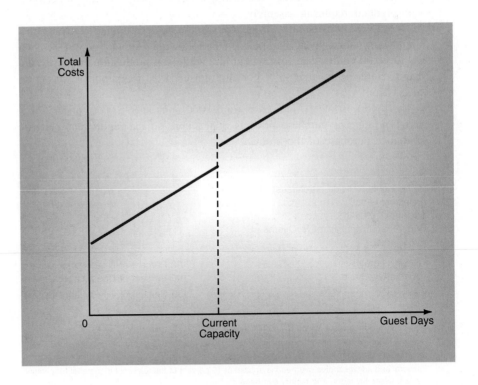

   b.   Additional Operating Costs = 0.25(30,000)
                                   = $7,500.

20. Cost behavior when costs are semivariable.

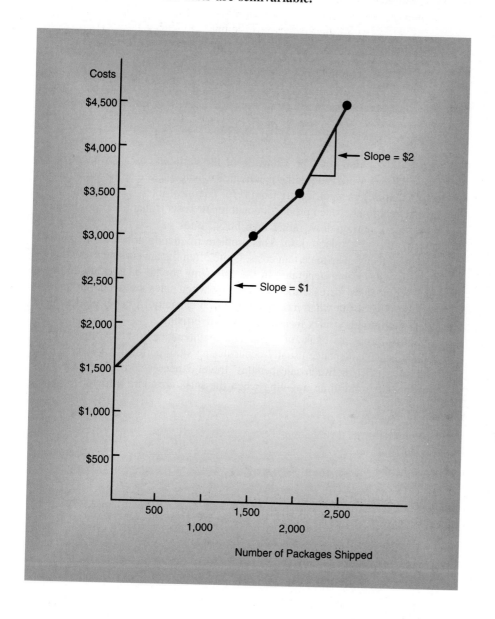

Plotting the data, these costs appear to be semivariable. The fixed-cost component estimate is $1,500, and the variable cost component is $1 per package up to 2,000 packages [$1 = ($3,500 − $1,500)/2,000 pkgs.]. With only four data points, you should view these estimates skeptically, however.

22. **Learning curve.**

Cumulative Number of Units Produced	Average Manufacturing Costs per Unit
1	$1,333
2	1,000 ($1,333 × 75%)
4	750 ($1,000 × 75%)
8	562.50 ($750 × 75%)
16	421.88 ($562.50 × 75%)

24. **Repair cost behavior.** The t-statistic of the variable cost coefficient is -3 ($= -.75/.25$), which should help convince management that the variable cost coefficient differs significantly from zero. The most likely explanation for the inverse relation between production and repair costs is that the firm schedules repair work during slow, rather than busy, times.

26. **Interpreting regression data.** This problem frequently arises when applying analytical techniques to certain costs. Quite often the advertising expenditures result in sales being generated in the following month or later. In addition, many companies increase their advertising when sales are declining and cut back on advertising when manufacturing is at capacity. A better model might relate this month's sales to last month's advertising.

Similar problems exist for repair and maintenance costs, because routine repairs and maintenance usually occur during slow periods. An inverse relation often exists between salespersons' travel expenses and sales, if the sales staff spends more time traveling when the sales are more difficult to make.

Chapter 8

Cost-Volume-Profit Analysis

1. Understand how costs, volume, and prices are interrelated.
2. Use the cost-volume-profit model to find breakeven and target-profit volumes.
3. Know how to compute the margin of safety.
4. Apply the cost-volume-profit model for multiple products.
5. Apply the cost-volume-profit model to managerial decisions, including using the model for sensitivity analysis.
6. Critically evaluate the cost-volume-profit model in view of its assumptions and simplifications.

Successful management requires understanding the relations among revenues, costs, volume, and profits. The cost-volume-profit model represents the firm's activities because virtually all decisions affect costs, volume, or profits. Managers can use it as a macro model to describe a firm's financial activities. For example, an automotive company executive stated that the company did not show a quarterly profit because, "Given the prices we can charge and the costs we incur, we simply did not have enough volume to break even last quarter."

A situation involving cost-volume-profit analysis follows. Suppose a student organization wants to show movies on campus. The organization can rent a particular movie for 1 weekend for $1,000. Rent for an auditorium, salaries to the ticket takers and other personnel, and other fixed costs would total $800 for the weekend. The organization would sell tickets for $4 per person. In addition, profits from the sale of soft drinks, popcorn, and candy are estimated to be $1 per ticket holder. How many people would have to buy tickets to break even, and therefore justify renting the movie? (The answer is 360.)

The analysis relies on concepts of fixed and variable cost behavior that Chapter 2 discussed. This chapter presents the cost-volume-profit model and demonstrates how managers can use (or misuse) it in a number of decision-making situations. The chapter focuses on short-run operating decisions, those which do not involve a change in capacity.

After reading this chapter, you should understand the nature of the cost-volume-profit model, applications of the model, and the model's limitations and assumptions.

The Cost-Volume-Profit Model

The **cost-volume-profit model** specifies a relation among selling prices, unit costs, volume sold, and profits. It starts with the basic equation relating profits to revenues less costs:

$$\pi = TR - TC,$$

where π = operating profit for the period, TR = total revenues for the period, and TC = total costs for the period.

The cost-volume-profit equation in more detail is

$$\pi = TR - TC$$
$$= PX - (F + VX),$$

where P = unit selling price, X = number of units sold in the period, F = fixed operating costs for the period, and V = unit variable costs.

Profits in managerial models or on internal reports differ from net income for external financial reporting under generally accepted accounting principles (GAAP). For example, the cost-volume-profit model treats fixed manufacturing overhead as a cost of the period (that is, the variable costing method), not as a unit cost as required for external reporting under GAAP (the full absorption method). The cost-volume-profit model also typically omits financing costs such as interest expense on long-term debt.

Example We base much of our discussion in this chapter on illustrative data for Baltimore Company, which makes a particular type of computer software known as BC-1234. These data appear in the top panel of Exhibit 8.1. The cost-volume-profit equation for Baltimore Company is

$$\pi = PX - (F + VX)$$
$$= \$30X - (\$4,800 + \$22X).$$

The bottom panel of Exhibit 8.1 presents two linear relations: total revenue, $TR = PX = \$30X$; and total cost as a function of units sold,[1] $TC = \$4,800 + \$22X$. Because the fixed costs are \$4,800 per month, the total cost line goes through the vertical axis at \$4,800. Because variable costs are \$22 per unit, the total cost line increases \$22 per unit for increases in units produced and sold during the month.

---

[1] We assume the firm produced and sold units in the same time period to keep the analysis from becoming unnecessarily complex.

Exhibit 8.1

BALTIMORE COMPANY
Cost-Volume-Profit Data

Selling Price per Unit $30

Cost Classification	Variable Cost (per unit)	Fixed Cost (per month)
Manufacturing Costs	$17	$3,060
Marketing and Administrative Costs..................	5	1,740
Total Costs	$22	$4,800

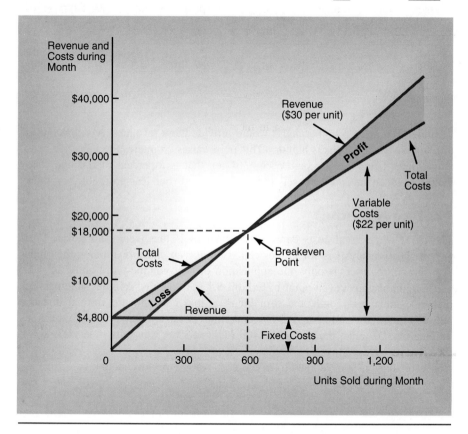

The Contribution Concept

Each unit sold contributes to fixed costs and the earning of profit. The **contribution margin per unit** is the excess of unit selling price over unit variable cost:

Contribution Margin per Unit = $P - V$.

For the Baltimore Company, the contribution margin is

$$\$8 = \$30 \text{ Selling Price per Unit} - \$22 \text{ Variable Cost per Unit}.$$

Using the Contribution Margin in Product Choice Decisions

The contribution margin has important applications in product choice decisions. Suppose that you have the opportunity to produce and sell one unit of either of the following products to a customer (not both):

	Price
Product A	$12
Product B	15

Which would you sell? Product B? Is it more profitable? We cannot tell which product is more profitable until we consider respective variable costs. Suppose that we find the following information:

	Price	Variable Cost	Contribution Margin
Product A.....................................	$12	$ 7	$5
Product B.....................................	15	11	4

Although B's price is higher and it would provide more revenues, A's contribution to fixed costs and profits is higher. (This point raises an interesting incentive problem if sales personnel are paid a commission that is a percent of revenue. They would have an incentive to sell the higher-priced, but less-profitable, product.)

Breakeven Point

The point where total costs equal total revenues is the **breakeven point.** Cost-volume-profit analysis is sometimes called *breakeven analysis.* Finding the breakeven point, however, is only one application of cost-volume-profit analysis.

The monthly breakeven point in Exhibit 8.1 is 600 units. At sales volumes less than 600 units per month, the firm incurs a loss equal to the vertical distance between the total cost line and the revenue line. For example, verify that at a sales volume of 300 units, the loss is $2,400 [$TR = \$30 \times 300$ units $= \$9,000$; $TC = \$4,800 + (\$22 \times 300) = \$11,400$.]

The breakeven point comes from the cost-volume-profit equation

$$\pi = PX - (F + VX).$$

At the breakeven point, profit, π, must be zero. In our example, we know that $P = \$30$, $F = \$4,800$, and $V = \$22$. Thus the breakeven sales volume, which is represented by X_b in the equation, is found as follows:

$$0 = \$30X_b - (\$4,800 + \$22X_b),$$

or

$$0 = \$8X_b - \$4,800$$
$$\$8X_b = \$4,800$$
$$X_b = \frac{\$4,800}{\$8}$$
$$= 600 \text{ Units.}$$

In general, the breakeven equation is

$$\text{Breakeven Point in Units} = \frac{\text{Fixed Costs per Period}}{\text{Contribution Margin per Unit}},$$

or, in symbols,

$$X_b = \frac{F}{P - V}.$$

Finding Target Profits

Managers frequently use the preceding equations to find the volume required for a target profit. For example, if Baltimore Company wants to know the amount of sales required in a month to achieve a profit of $5,000, it can solve the following:

$$\$5,000 = \$30X - (\$4,800 + \$22X)$$
$$\$5,000 = \$8X - \$4,800$$
$$\$8X = \$9,800$$
$$X = 1,225 \text{ Units per Month.}$$

The Profit-Volume Model

The **cost-volume-profit graph** in Exhibit 8.1 shows the breakeven point or provides a rough idea of profit or loss at various sales levels. However, because the profit or loss appears as the vertical distance between two lines, neither of which is horizontal, the graph does not conveniently depict the profit or loss as a function of sales volume. Consequently, accountants often express the relation between profit and volume with the profit-volume graph as in Exhibit 8.2.

The profit-volume relation derives from the cost-volume-profit equation. Start with the cost-volume-profit equation:

$$\pi = PX - (F + VX).$$

Rearrange terms to get

$$\pi = PX - F - VX,$$

and

$$\pi = -F + (P - V)X,$$

which is the **profit-volume equation.**

The vertical axis of the profit-volume graph shows the amount of profit or loss for the period—1 month in our example. At zero sales, the loss equals the fixed costs, F, of $4,800. At the breakeven point, 600 units in our example, the profit is zero. The slope of the profit line is equal to $P - V$ (the contribution margin per unit sold) $= \$30 - \$22 = \$8$.

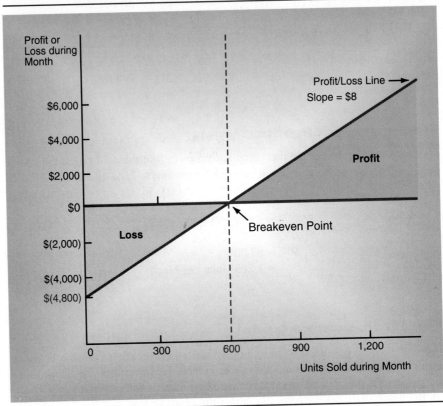

Exhibit 8.2

BALTIMORE COMPANY
Profit-Volume Graph

Applications of the Cost-Volume-Profit Model

In this section, we illustrate several uses of the cost-volume-profit model.

Example 1: Required Selling Price The management of Baltimore Company wants to know the price it must charge if sales are 800 units per month and the target profit is $4,000 per month. Fixed costs per month are $4,800 and unit variable costs are $22. We can solve for the required selling price as follows:

$$\text{Profit} = \text{Revenues} - \text{Costs}$$
$$\$4,000 = 800P - [\$4,800 + (800 \times \$22)]$$
$$800P = \$17,600 + \$4,800 + \$4,000$$
$$800P = \$26,400$$
$$P = \$33 \text{ Required Selling Price per Unit.}$$

Example 2: New Breakeven Point with an Increase in Fixed Costs

The manager of Baltimore Company wants to know how many units it must sell each month to break even under the following conditions: fixed costs increase to $5,600 per month, but variable costs remain at $22 per unit and selling price remains at $30 per unit. Solving for X, which represents the number of units produced and sold, we have

$$\text{Profit} = \text{Revenues} - \text{Costs}$$
$$\$0 = \$30X - (\$5,600 + \$22X)$$
$$\$8X = \$5,600$$
$$X = 700 \text{ Units Required to Break Even.}$$

Example 3: Sensitivity Analysis

One useful application of cost-volume-profit analysis, particularly for planning, is sensitivity analysis. **Sensitivity analysis** explores the impact of changes or variations in estimates of prices, costs, and volumes. It asks "what-if" questions and receives "if-then" answers. For example, the manager of Baltimore Company wants to know the impact of changing costs, prices, and volume on profits. Specifically, consider the following alternative cases ("what-ifs"):

- Costs:
  - **(1)** No change
  - **(2)** 10-percent increase.
- Price and volume:
  - **(1)** No change
  - **(2)** 10-percent price increase and 5-percent volume decrease.

Profit as a Function of Cost, Volume, and Price

Price and Volume		Costs	
		No Change	10-Percent Increase
No Change		Profit = ($30 × 800) − [$4,800 + ($22 × 800)] = **$1,600**	Profit = ($30 × 800) − [$5,280 + ($24.20 × 800)] = **($640)**
10-Percent Price Increase 5-Percent Volume Decrease		Profit = ($33 × 760) − [$4,800 + ($22 × 760)] = **$3,560**	Profit = ($33 × 760) − [$5,280 + ($24.20 × 760)] = **$1,408**

Exhibit 8.3

Comparison of Variable Company and Fixed Company

	Variable Company (1,000,000 units)	Fixed Company (1,000,000 units)
Sales	$1,200,000	$1,200,000
Variable Costs	750,000	250,000
Contribution Margin	$ 450,000	$ 950,000
Fixed Costs	250,000 ⎤ Total Costs = $1,000,000	750,000 ⎤ Total Costs = $1,000,000
Operating Profit	$ 200,000	$ 200,000

Breakeven Point:

Variable Company:
$$X_b = \frac{F}{P - V} = \frac{\$250,000}{\$1.20 - \$.75} = 555,556 \text{ Units}$$

Fixed Company:
$$X_b = \frac{F}{P - V} = \frac{\$750,000}{\$1.20 - \$.25} = 789,474 \text{ Units}$$

Margin of Safety (units):

Variable Company:
Sales Volume − Breakeven Volume
= 1,000,000 − 555,556
= 444,444 Units

Fixed Company:
Sales Volume − Breakeven Volume
= 1,000,000 − 789,474
= 210,526 Units

Margin of Safety as a Percentage of Forecast Sales Volume:

Variable Company:
$$\frac{444,444}{1,000,000} = 44 \text{ Percent}$$

Fixed Company:
$$\frac{210,526}{1,000,000} = 21 \text{ Percent}$$

The matrix on the preceding page shows the results (that is, the "if-thens") from applying the cost-volume-profit equation:

$$\text{Profit} = \text{Revenues} - \text{Costs}$$
$$\pi = PX - (F + VX).$$

The status quo (starting point) is

$$\$1,600 = (\$30 \times 800) - [\$4,800 + (\$22 \times 800)].$$

These results show the manager that a 10-percent cost increase, with no change in selling price or volume, produces a loss for the company. The results also show that if costs do not increase, but prices increase by 10 percent, causing volume to drop by 5 percent, profits more than double. You can easily perform a sensitivity analysis like this using a personal computer spreadsheet.

Example 4: Comparison of Alternatives   The manager of Baltimore Company is considering an alternative production method. With the current method, variable costs are $22 per unit and fixed costs are $4,800. The alternative would substitute machines for labor; variable costs would drop to $18 per unit, but the annual lease of the machines and machine maintenance would increase fixed costs to $6,000 per month. The alternative requires no new investment in the machines. Under both alternatives, the selling price will be $30 per unit and the company will sell 800 units each month. The expected profit under the status quo is

$$\begin{aligned}
\text{Profit} &= \text{Revenues} - \text{Costs} \\
&= (\$30 \times 800) - [\$4,800 + (\$22 \times 800)] \\
&= \$24,000 - \$22,400 \\
&= \$1,600.
\end{aligned}$$

The expected profit under the proposed alternative is

$$\begin{aligned}
\text{Profit} &= \text{Revenues} - \text{Costs} \\
&= (\$30 \times 800) - [\$6,000 + (\$18 \times 800)] \\
&= \$24,000 - \$20,400 \\
&= \$3,600.
\end{aligned}$$

The analysis indicates that the alternative will increase expected profits.

Margin of Safety

The **margin of safety** is the excess of projected (or actual) sales units over the breakeven unit sales level. The formula for margin of safety is

$$\text{Sales Units} - \text{Breakeven Sales Units} = \text{Margin of Safety}.$$

In our example, the level of activity is 800 units, whereas the breakeven point is 600 units. Therefore, the margin of safety is 200 units. Sales volume can drop 25 percent before the firm incurs a loss, other things held constant.

Companies that become more capital intensive, substituting fixed costs for variable costs, often find that their margin of safety declines. Exhibit 8.3 shows how two companies that are alike in every respect, except that 75 percent of Variable Company's total costs are variable, whereas 75 percent of Fixed Company's total costs are fixed at current volume levels.

Fixed Company has a lower margin of safety. It will incur losses sooner than Variable Company if sales volume decreases. Companies in capital-intensive industries like Ford Motor Company, IBM, and Bethlehem Steel have relatively high fixed costs. Such companies have found that small decreases in sales volume can result in losses.

Problem 8.1
for Self-Study

Identifying CVP relations on a graph. The graph in Exhibit 8.4 contains cost-volume-profit and profit-volume graph elements. Identify the concept from the list on the right on page 301 that corresponds to the line segment or relation on the left.

Exhibit 8.4
Graph for Problem 8.1 for Self-Study

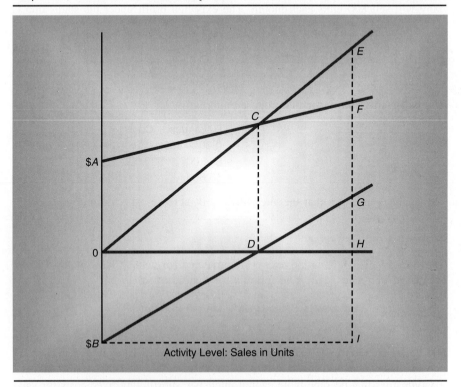

Activity Level: Sales in Units

Line Segment or Relation	Concept
a. *0A.*	**(1)** Variable Cost per Unit.
b. *IG.*	**(2)** Fixed Cost per Period.
c. *0D.*	**(3)** Revenue.
d. *B0.*	**(4)** Contribution Margin per Unit.
e. *0H − 0D.*	**(5)** Margin of Safety in Units.
f. *B0/0D.*	**(6)** Breakeven Sales in Units.
g. *HF + HG.*	**(7)** None of the Above.

Refer to the graph in Exhibit 8.4. Answer each of the following as True or False (holding everything else constant).

h. If revenue is *CD*, the margin of safety is zero.
i. If revenue is *HE*, the margin of safety is *D0*.
j. Total fixed costs could never be larger than total variable costs.
k. If selling price increases, breakeven sales in units would decrease.
l. If selling price increases, *HF* would increase.
m. *FE = HG.*

The solution to this self-study problem is at the end of this chapter on page 313.

Use of Spreadsheets in Cost-Volume-Profit Analysis

Computer spreadsheets, like Lotus® 1-2-3® and Excel®, provide you with considerable additional power in analyzing costs, volume, and profits. For example, Exhibit 8.5 presents a "what-if" analysis prepared using a computer spreadsheet based on data for Baltimore Company. Column E shows the operating profit computed by the spreadsheet program for each of nine different scenarios. Columns A and B show three different price-volume scenarios. Columns C and D show three different variable and fixed cost alternatives.

Once you have set up the basic CVP formula, you can see how easy it is to determine the effect if you change the values of prices, costs, and volume. Spreadsheet applications of CVP are particularly helpful in answering "what-if" questions in planning and decision making.

Exhibit 8.5

BALTIMORE COMPANY
Spreadsheet Results

	A	B	C	D	E
			Variable		
1			cost per	Fixed	Operating
2	Price	Volume	unit	costs	profits
3	$30	1000	$22	$4800	$3200
4	30	1000	24	4500	1500
5	30	1000	20	5100	4900
6	35	800	22	4800	5600
7	35	800	24	4500	4300
8	35	800	20	5100	6900
9	25	1200	22	4800	−1200
10	25	1200	24	4500	−3300
11	25	1200	20	5100	900

Using Sales Dollars as a Measure of Volume

Firms also measure volume in sales dollars. With this measure, the cost-volume-profit equation remains the same as before, except that PX is total revenue, not "price times quantity," and VX is total variable costs, not "unit variable cost times quantity." We substitute PX for X when solving for volume of activity. For example, the breakeven volume in units for Baltimore Company is

$$X_b = \frac{F}{P - V}$$

$$= \frac{\$4,800}{(\$30 - \$22)}$$

$$= 600 \text{ Units.}$$

With volume defined as PX, we multiply both sides of the breakeven formula by P to express volume in sales dollars:

$$PX_b = \left(\frac{F}{P - V}\right)P$$

$$= \frac{F}{(P - V)/P}$$

$$= \frac{\$4,800}{(\$30 - \$22)/\$30}$$

$$= \frac{\$4,800}{.26667}$$

$$= \$18,000.$$

Thus the breakeven volume expressed in sales *dollars* is $18,000. (You can verify that this result is the same as 600 units sold at $30 per unit.)

The term $(P - V)/P$ in the denominator of the breakeven equation is the **contribution margin ratio,** that is, the ratio of the unit contribution margin to unit price. Hence, the formula in words is

$$\text{Breakeven Sales Dollars} = \frac{\text{Fixed Costs}}{\text{Contribution Margin Ratio}}.$$

In the example, this ratio states that each dollar of sales generates $.26667 of contribution.

Income Taxes

You can include income taxes in the cost-volume-profit model as follows:

$$\text{After-Tax Profit} = \text{Before-Tax Profit} \times (1 - \text{Tax Rate}).$$

This means that the after-tax profit equals the before-tax profit minus taxes, where taxes equal the tax rate times the before-tax profit. If π_{at} designates after-tax profits, π_{bt} designates before-tax profits, and t designates the tax rate, we have

$$\pi_{at} = \pi_{bt}(1 - t)$$
$$= [(P - V)X - F](1 - t).$$

Example The management of Baltimore Company wants to know the volume of sales required to provide $1,920 profit *after taxes* in April. $P = \$30$, $V = \$22$, $F = \$4,800$, and $t = .40$ (that is, an average tax rate for April of 40 percent). We find the volume that provides an after-tax profit of $1,920 as follows:

$$\pi_{at} = \pi_{bt}(1 - t)$$
$$\$1,920 = [(P - V)X - F](1 - t)$$
$$= [(\$30 - \$22)X - \$4,800](1 - .40)$$
$$= [(\$8X - \$4,800)(.60)]$$
$$= \$4.8X - \$2,880$$
$$\$4,800 = \$4.8X$$
$$\frac{\$4,800}{\$4.8} = X$$
$$X = 1,000 \text{ Units.}$$

Problem 8.2
for Self-Study

Finding profits, break-even point, and quantities. Given the following information for Sara's Ice Cream Company for April:

Sales (20,000 units)	$180,000
Fixed Manufacturing Costs	22,000
Fixed Marketing and Administrative Costs	14,000
Total Fixed Costs	36,000
Total Variable Costs	120,000
Unit Price	$9
Unit Variable Manufacturing Cost	5
Unit Variable Marketing Cost	1

Compute the following:

a. Operating profit when sales are $180,000 (as above).
b. Breakeven quantity in units.
c. Quantity of units that would produce an operating profit of $30,000.
d. Sales dollars required to generate an operating profit of $20,000.

The solution to this self-study problem is at the end of this chapter on page 313.

Multiproduct Cost-Volume-Profit

Most companies produce or sell many products. Multiple products make using cost-volume-profit analysis more complex, as the following example shows.

Example Sport Autos, a sports car dealership, sells two models, Sleek and Powerful. The relevant prices and costs of each appear in Exhibit 8.6. Average monthly fixed costs of the new car department are $100,000.

We expand the cost-volume-profit equation presented earlier to consider the contribution of each product:

$$\pi = (P_s - V_s)X_s + (P_p - V_p)X_p - F,$$

Exhibit 8.6

SPORT AUTOS
Price and Cost Data

	Sleek		Powerful	
Average Selling Price per Car		$20,000		$30,000
Less Average Variable Costs:				
Cost of Car	$(11,000)		$(15,000)	
Cost of Preparing Car for Sale	(3,000)		(3,000)	
Sales Commissions	(1,000)	(15,000)	(2,000)	(20,000)
Average Contribution Margin per Car		$ 5,000		$10,000

Breaking Even in the Automobile Industry[a]

During the 1980s and first half of the 1990s, Chrysler, Ford, and General Motors found themselves, at various times, striving to reach the breakeven point. Chrysler was the first of the "Big Three" automobile companies to reach the brink of disaster. In the early 1980s, the company was forced to lay off employees to reduce fixed costs. In the mid-1980s, Ford found its most successful cars were still costing thousands of dollars more to manufacture than comparable cars made by Japanese companies. During the 1980s and early 1990s, Ford suffered losses, but retooled its manufacturing facilities, came out with new, popular designs, improved quality, and developed efficiencies that substantially cut costs.

General Motors was the last of the Big Three to see losses, possibly because its huge size enabled the company to make profits despite losing market share to Honda, Toyota, and other foreign imports. After management shake-ups in the first half of the 1990s that brought in more outside talent, the company increased its focus on improving production methods, improving quality, and reducing costs.

Perhaps because these three companies were so large—all three were among the top ten companies in the United States at one time—their managements became complacent about the need to improve quality, provide cars that appealed to younger customers, and reduce costs. Since the Japanese automobile industry became a competitive force in the United States, these three companies have been striving to find ways to be consistently above break even again.

[a]Based on the authors' research.

where the subscript s designates the Sleek model, and the subscript p designates the Powerful model. Based on the information for Sport Autos, the company's profit equation is

$$\pi = (\$20{,}000 - \$15{,}000)X_s + (\$30{,}000 - \$20{,}000)X_p - \$100{,}000$$
$$= \quad \$5{,}000X_s \quad + \quad \$10{,}000X_p \quad - \$100{,}000.$$

The complexity of analysis increases when the firm has more than one product, particularly when managers attempt to derive breakeven points or target volumes. For example, the chief executive of Sport Autos has been listening to a debate between two of the salespeople about the breakeven point for the company. According to one, "We have to sell 20 cars a month to break even." But the other one claims that 10 cars a month would be sufficient. The chief executive wonders how these two salespeople could hold such different views.

The breakeven volume is the volume that provides a contribution that just covers all fixed costs. For Sport Autos, that is

$$\$5,000X_s + \$10,000X_p = \$100,000.$$

The claim that 20 cars must be sold to break even is correct if the firm sells *only* the Sleek model, whereas the claim that only 10 cars need to be sold is correct if the firm sells *only* the Powerful model. In fact, Sport Autos has many possible product-mix combinations at which it would break even.

Exhibit 8.7 lists possible breakeven points for Sport Autos. Exhibit 8.8 presents graphically the possible breakeven volumes for the company. Profits are the same for any combination of product volumes on the line. (To see this, find a couple of breakeven points from Exhibit 8.7 on the breakeven line in Exhibit 8.8.) Any combination of product volumes to the right of the line provides a profit; any to the left results in a loss.

This simple example demonstrates how complex multiproduct cost-volume-profit analysis can become. In a company with many products, billions of combinations of product volumes can provide a specific target profit. To deal with this problem, managers and accountants can (1) assume that all products have the same contribution margin, (2) assume that a particular product mix does not change, (3) assume a weighted-average contribution margin, or (4) treat each product line as a separate entity. In addition to these simplifications, firms can conduct multiproduct analyses with a mathematical method known as *linear programming*, discussed in Chapter 9. We now look at each of these alternatives.

1. Assume the Same Contribution Margin The analyst can often group products so they have equal or nearly equal contribution margins. It does not matter whether the firm sells a unit of Product A or a unit of Product B if both have the same contribution margin. (This approach won't work for Sport Autos, because Sleeks and Powerfuls have different contribution margins.)

2. Assume a Fixed Product Mix Suppose the experience at Sport Autos is that Sleeks outsell Powerfuls at a rate of 2 to 1. Define a ''package sale,''

Exhibit 8.7

SPORT AUTOS
Combinations of Breakeven Quantities

Sleek Model		Powerful Model		Total	Fixed	
Quantity	Contribution	Quantity	Contribution	Contribution	Costs	Profit
20	$100,000	0	$ 0	$100,000	$100,000	$0
18	90,000	1	10,000	100,000	100,000	0
16	80,000	2	20,000	100,000	100,000	0
•	•	•	•	•	•	•
•	•	•	•	•	•	•
•	•	•	•	•	•	•
4	20,000	8	80,000	100,000	100,000	0
2	10,000	9	90,000	100,000	100,000	0
0	0	10	100,000	100,000	100,000	0

Exhibit 8.8

SPORT AUTOS
Possible Breakeven Volumes

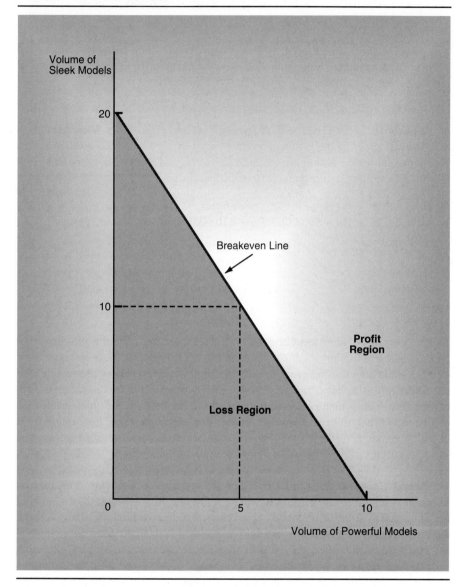

X^*, to be the sale of two Sleeks and one Powerful. The contribution from this package is as follows:

Sleek:	$2 \times \$5,000 =$	$\$10,000$
Powerful:	$1 \times \$10,000 =$	$10,000$
Total Package:		$\$20,000.$

The breakeven point is

$$X_b^* = \frac{\$100,000}{\$20,000}$$
$$= 5.$$

This equation shows that the sale of five packages, each comprising two Sleeks and a Powerful, contributes enough to break even. In other words, the breakeven volume for the month is 15 units—10 Sleeks and 5 Powerfuls.

3. Assume a Weighted-Average Contribution Margin
Another way of applying the assumed product mix is to use a weighted-average contribution margin. If we assume the product mix to be two Sleeks for every Powerful, the per-unit weighted-average contribution margin is

$$\begin{matrix} Sleeks & Powerfuls \\ (\tfrac{2}{3} \times \$5,000) + (\tfrac{1}{3} \times \$10,000) & = \$6,667. \end{matrix}$$

The breakeven point is

$$X_b = \frac{\$100,000}{\$6,667}$$
$$= 15 \text{ Cars},$$

of which ⅔, or 10, are Sleeks and ⅓, or 5, are Powerfuls, according to the above product-mix assumption.

What is the effect of incorrect assumptions in this analysis about product mix? If the actual mix is richer than assumed (more Powerfuls, in our example), the firm requires fewer units than predicted to break even. The firm requires more units than predicted to break even if the mix is poorer than assumed. (See, for example, the data in Exhibits 8.7 and 8.8.)

4. Treat Each Product Line as a Separate Entity
This method requires allocating fixed costs to product lines. To illustrate, we must allocate part of the Sport Autos' $100,000 monthly fixed costs that the two products share to Sleek automobiles and the rest to Powerfuls. The problem is to find a reasonable method of allocating costs. Often the product lines share these costs, so any allocation method is arbitrary. In such situations, companies often resort to allocating on the basis of relative sales dollars or on the basis of quantities of the product lines. Other allocation bases used include relative total contributions, relative direct costs, relative number of employees per product line (particularly to allocate labor-related costs), or relative square feet of space used by each product line (particularly to allocate space-related costs).

Suppose that of the $100,000 common costs, Sport Autos arbitrarily allocates 40 percent to Sleeks and 60 percent to Powerfuls. We can then do breakeven analysis and other cost-volume-profit analyses by product line, as follows:

For Sleeks:

$$\pi = (P - V)X - F$$
$$= (\$20,000 - \$15,000)X - \$40,000$$
$$X_b = \frac{\$40,000}{\$5,000}$$
$$= 8 \text{ Units.}$$

For Powerfuls:

$$\pi = (P - V)X - F$$
$$= (\$30,000 - \$20,000)X - \$60,000$$
$$X_b = \frac{\$60,000}{\$10,000}$$
$$= 6 \text{ Units.}$$

Allocating fixed costs to product lines facilitates product line cost-volume-profit analysis. But decision makers should be wary of any analysis that relies on arbitrary cost allocations. It would be a mistake to believe that Sleeks cause fixed costs of $40,000 and Powerfuls cause fixed costs of $60,000. The two product lines *combined* cause fixed costs of $100,000; the breakdown of those costs is arbitrary. Further, note that a change in the arbitrary allocation method changes the breakeven volumes. (For example, if we allocated the $100,000 as $20,000 to Sleeks and $80,000 to Powerfuls, breakeven requires the sale of 4 Sleeks [= $20,000/$5,000 per unit] and 8 Powerfuls [= $80,000/$10,000 per unit].)

Problem 8.3
for Self-Study

Finding breakeven points in units, sales. Triple X Company manufactures three different products with the following characteristics:

	Product I	Product II	Product III
Price per Unit	$5	$6	$7
Variable Cost per Unit......................	$3	$2	$4
Expected Sales (units)	100,000	150,000	250,000

Total fixed costs for the company are $1,240,000.

Assume that the product mix at the breakeven point would be the same as that for expected sales. Compute the breakeven point in

a. Units (total using weighted-average method and by product line).
b. Sales dollars (total using weighted-average method and by product line).

The solution to this self-study problem is at the end of this chapter on page 314.

Simplifications and Assumptions

The cost-volume-profit model simplifies costs, revenues, and volume to make the analysis easier. A more complete description of the economic relations than the model gives is possible but costly. The careful user of cost-volume-profit analysis should be aware of the following common assumptions and be prepared to perform sensitivity analysis to see how the assumptions affect the model's results.

Comparison with Economists' Profit Maximization Model

Textbooks in economics usually present nonlinear cost and revenue curves, as in Exhibit 8.9. Total revenue increases at a decreasing rate if the firm faces a downward-sloping demand curve. Total costs increase at an increasing rate as volume approaches capacity. In Exhibit 8.9, the economists' cost curve includes the opportunity cost of owners' invested capital, whereas the linear approximation from the accounting records typically does not. Neither the economists' nor the accountants' cost and revenue curves are correct in an absolute sense. Both approximate actual cost and revenue behavior.

Exhibit 8.9

Comparison of Economics and Accounting Assumptions about Cost and Revenue Behavior

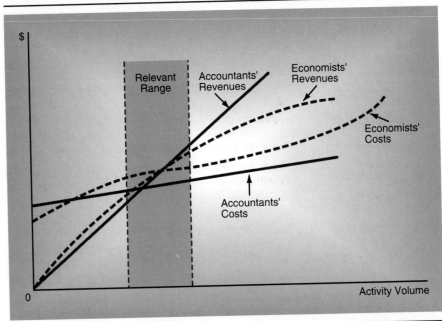

Basic Assumptions Required to Make the CVP Model Work

You can use the cost-volume-profit model most powerfully by analyzing how various alternatives affect operations. This analysis works because the model captures most of the important operating relations of the firm in a single equation. We can analyze the effects of changes in any of the following variables on the remaining variables: selling price, number of units sold, variable cost, fixed cost, sales mix, and production mix. The model requires the major assumption that *total costs have only fixed and variable components.*

Our illustrations in this chapter assumed a linear relation between revenues and volume and between costs and volume. You can, however, apply the model with nonlinear revenue and cost functions. Practice usually assumes cost and revenue curves to be linear over some **relevant range** of activity, as discussed in Chapter 7. Exhibit 8.9 presents an example where cost and revenue curves are reasonably linear within the relevant-range limits, even though the curves are nonlinear outside the relevant range.

We also implicitly assumed that the analyst can predict the variables in the model with certainty and that selling price per unit, total fixed costs, and variable costs per unit will not change as the level of activity changes. This assumption implies that prices paid and charged are constant, and workers' productivity does not change during the period. Finally to derive a unique breakeven point for multiple products, we require that the production mix and sales mix will not change as the level of activity changes.

Summary of Assumptions

1. We can divide total costs into fixed and variable components.
2. Cost and revenue behavior is linear throughout the relevant range of activity. This assumption implies the following:
   a. Total fixed costs do not change throughout the relevant range of activity.
   b. Variable costs *per unit* remain constant throughout the relevant range of activity.
   c. Selling price per unit remains constant throughout the relevant range of activity.
3. Product mix remains constant throughout the relevant range of activity.

Assumptions of the cost-volume-profit model make it easy to use, but they also make it unrealistic. Before criticizing the model for being unrealistic, however, you need to consider the costs and benefits of relaxing those assumptions to create more realism. Often the cost of more realism exceeds the benefits from improved decision making.

One method of dealing with the assumptions is to perform some sensitivity or "what-if" analyses. For example, the mean or expected value of Baltimore Company's variable costs per unit is $22. But suppose that a reasonable range of values is from $15 to $29; that is, management estimates a very small probability that variable costs are less than $15 or greater than $29. Managers would probably want a sensitivity analysis performed to ascertain whether decisions would change if variable costs were (say) $15 or $29 instead of $22 per unit.

Summary

The cost-volume-profit model shows relations among revenues, costs, volume, and profits. The manager can use it as an economic model to describe a firm's activities. The manager can use it also as an analytical model to derive, for example, a product line breakeven point, target profits for a store, or the impact of a change in volume on profits.

In equation form, the model is

$$\pi = TR - TC$$
$$= PX - (VX + F)$$
$$= (P - V)X - F,$$

where

$$\pi = \text{Operating Profit}$$
$$TR = \text{Total Revenues}$$
$$TC = \text{Total Costs}$$
$$P = \text{Selling Price per Unit}$$
$$V = \text{Variable Cost per Unit}$$
$$F = \text{Fixed Costs per Period}$$
$$X = \text{Volume per Period}$$
$$(P - V) = \text{Contribution Margin per Unit.}$$

Sensitivity analysis is one of the most useful applications of the cost-volume-profit model, particularly for planning. It enables managers to respond to "what-if" questions such as "If costs are 10 percent higher than expected, or if volume is 5 percent higher than expected, what will be the impact on profits?"

The simple cost-volume-profit model assumes a single product. Many organizations, however, have multiple products. This does not affect the usefulness of the model as a tool for descriptive work or sensitivity analysis, but makes deriving breakeven points more difficult. Some ways of dealing with this multiproduct problem follow:

(1) Assume that all products have the same contribution margin so that product mix does not affect the breakeven point.
(2) Assume a particular product mix.
(3) Assume a weighted-average contribution margin based on an assumed product mix.
(4) Treat each product as a separate product line, which usually requires an arbitrary allocation of common costs.

Users of the cost-volume-profit model recognize that it is merely a model, not a complete description of reality. The simpler the model, the greater its potential applications but the less realistic it is. Making the model more realistic is costly. For example, you can use a more realistic nonlinear model of cost behavior if the benefits of better decision making exceed the additional costs of building nonlinear relations into the model.

Solutions to Self-Study Problems

Suggested Solution to Problem 8.1 for Self-Study

a. $0A$.   (2) Fixed Cost per Period.
b. IG.   (7) None of the above.
c. $0D$.   (6) Breakeven Sales in Units.
d. $B0$.   (2) Fixed Cost per Period; also, Operating Loss When Sales Are Zero.
e. $0H - 0D$.   (5) Margin of Safety in Units.
f. $B0/0D$.   (4) Contribution Margin per Unit.
g. $HF + HG$.   (3) Revenue.
h. True.
i. False; if revenue is HE, the margin of safety is DH.
j. False.
k. True.
l. False.
m. True.

Suggested Solution to Problem 8.2 for Self-Study

a. Operating profit:

$$\pi = PX - VX - F$$
$$= \$180{,}000 - \$120{,}000 - \$36{,}000$$
$$= \$24{,}000.$$

b. Breakeven point:

$$X = \frac{F}{P - V} = \frac{\$36{,}000}{\$9 - 6}$$
$$= 12{,}000 \text{ units.}$$

c. Target volume:

$$X = \frac{F + \text{Target } \pi}{P - V}$$
$$= \frac{\$36{,}000 + \$30{,}000}{\$3}$$
$$= 22{,}000 \text{ units.}$$

d. Target volume in sales dollars:

$$\frac{\text{Contribution}}{\text{margin ratio}} = \frac{\$3}{\$9} = .333 \text{ (rounded).}$$
$$\text{Target volume} = \frac{\$36{,}000 + \$20{,}000}{.333}$$
$$= \$168{,}000.$$

Suggested Solution to Problem 8.3 for Self-Study

a. Compute weighted-average contribution margin:

	Product I	Product II	Product III
Product Mix	$\dfrac{100{,}000 \text{ Units}}{500{,}000 \text{ Units}}$ = .20	$\dfrac{150{,}000}{500{,}000}$ = .30	$\dfrac{250{,}000}{500{,}000}$ = .50
Weighted-Average Contribution Margin $(P - V)$	.20($2) +	.30($4) + = $3.10	.50($3)

Or

$$\frac{(100{,}000 \text{ Units})(\$2) + (150{,}000)(\$4) + (250{,}000)(\$3)}{500{,}000} = \$3.10$$

$$X = \frac{\$1{,}240{,}000}{\$3.10}$$

$$X = 400{,}000 \text{ Units.}$$

(See solution to **b** for product-by-product amounts.)

b. To compute breakeven sales dollars, find the weighted-average price and variable costs:

$$P = (.20)(\$5) + (.30)(\$6) + (.50)(\$7)$$
$$P = \$6.30$$
$$V = (.20)(\$3) + (.30)(\$2) + (.50)(\$4)$$
$$V = \$3.20$$

$$\text{Breakeven } PX = \frac{F}{\dfrac{P - V}{P}} = \frac{\$1{,}240{,}000}{\$3.10/\$6.30}$$

$$= \frac{\$1{,}240{,}000}{.492 \text{ (rounded)}}$$

$$= \$2{,}520{,}000.$$

(Check: 400,000 units $\times$ $6.30 = 2,520,000.)
    Product line amounts:

	Total (100%)	Product I (20%)	Product II (30%)	Product III (50%)
Units	400,000	80,000	120,000	200,000
Unit Price	$6.30	$5	$6	$7
Sales Dollars	$2,520,000	$400,000	$720,000	$1,400,000

Key Terms and Concepts

Cost-volume-profit model
Contribution margin per unit
Breakeven point
Cost-volume-profit graph
  (compared to profit-volume graph)

Profit-volume equation
Sensitivity analysis
Margin of safety
Contribution margin ratio
Relevant range

Questions, Exercises, Problems, and Cases

Questions

1. Review the meaning of the terms or concepts given above in Key Terms and Concepts.
2. Define the profit equation.
3. Define the term *contribution margin.*
4. How does the total contribution margin (unit contribution margin times total number of units sold) differ from the gross margin often seen on companies' financial statements?
5. Compare cost-volume-profit analysis with profit-volume analysis. How do they differ?
6. Is a company really breaking even if it produces and sells at the breakeven point? What costs may not be covered?
7. How do spreadsheets assist cost-volume-profit analysis?
8. How does the profit equation change when the analyst uses the multiproduct cost-volume-profit model?
9. Why does multiproduct cost-volume-profit analysis often assume a constant product mix?
10. When would the sum of the breakeven quantities for each of a company's products not be the breakeven point for the company as a whole?
11. Distinguish between economic *profits* and accounting *net income* or *operating profit.*
12. Name three common assumptions of a linear cost-volume-profit analysis.
13. Refer to the Managerial Application, "Breaking Even in the Automobile Industry." If the auto companies cannot raise prices, what must they do to break even?
14. Fixed costs are often defined as "fixed over the short run." Does this mean that they are not fixed over the long run? Why or why not?
15. Why do accountants use a linear representation of cost and revenue behavior in cost-volume-profit analysis? Justify this use.
16. What effect could the following changes, occurring independently, have on (1) the breakeven point, (2) the unit contribution margin, and (3) the expected total profit?
    a. An increase in fixed costs.
    b. A decrease in wage rates applicable to direct, strictly variable labor.

    c. An increase in the selling price of the product.

    d. An increase in production and sales volume.

    e. An increase in building insurance rates.

17. Assume the linear cost relation of the cost-volume-profit model for a single-product firm and use the following answer key:

    (1) More than double.

    (2) Double.

    (3) Increase, but less than double.

    (4) Remain the same.

    (5) Decrease.

Complete each of the following statements, assuming that all other things (such as quantities) remain constant.

    a. If price doubles, revenue will _____.

    b. If price doubles, the total contribution margin (contribution margin per unit times number of units) will _____.

    c. If price doubles, profit will _____.

    d. If contribution margin per unit doubles, profit will _____.

    e. If fixed costs double, the total contribution margin will _____.

    f. If fixed costs double, profit will _____.

    g. If fixed costs double, the breakeven point of units sold will _____.

    h. If total sales of units double, profit will _____.

    i. If total sales dollars double, the breakeven point will _____.

    j. If the contribution margin per unit doubles, the breakeven point will _____.

    k. If both variable costs per unit and selling price per unit double, profit will _____.

Exercises

Solutions to even-numbered exercises are at the end of the chapter on page 327.

18. **Breakeven and target profits.** Analysis of the operations of the Super Ski Wax Company shows the fixed costs to be $100,000 and the variable costs to be $4 per unit. Selling price is $8 per unit.

    a. Derive the breakeven point expressed in units.

    b. How many units must the firm sell to earn a profit of $140,000?

    c. What would profits be if revenue from sales was $1,000,000?

19. **Cost-volume-profit; volume defined in sales dollars.** An excerpt from the income statement of the Layton and Brown Company follows on the next page.

Estimated fixed costs in Year 1 are $660,000.

    a. What percentage of sales revenue is variable cost?

    b. What is the breakeven point in sales dollars for Layton and Brown Company?

LAYTON AND BROWN COMPANY
Income Statement
Year Ended December 31, Year 1

Sales...		$3,000,000
Operating Expenses:		
Cost of Goods Sold............................	$1,425,000	
Selling Costs.....................................	450,000	
Administrative Costs	225,000	
Total Operating Costs		2,100,000
Profit..		$ 900,000

    c. Prepare a cost-profit-volume graph for Layton and Brown Company.
    d. If sales revenue falls to $2,800,000, what will be the estimated amount of profit?
    e. What volume of sales produces a profit of $1,120,000?

20. **Cost-volume-profit graph.** Identify each item on the following graph:
    a. The total cost line.
    b. The total revenue line.
    c. Total variable costs.
    d. Variable cost per unit.
    e. The total fixed costs.
    f. The breakeven point.
    g. The profit area (or volume).
    h. The loss area (or volume).

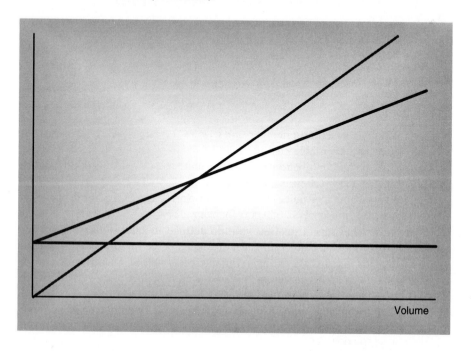
Volume

21. **Profit-volume graph.** Identify the places on the profit-volume graph indicated by the letters:

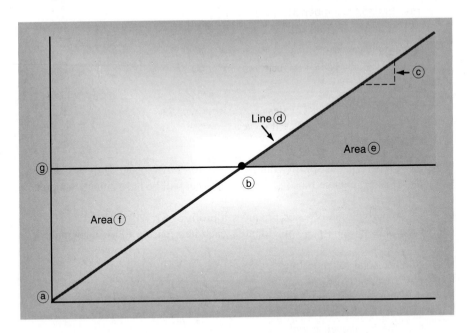

22. **Cost-volume-profit analysis.** Surf's Up Company produces one type of sunglasses with the following costs and revenues for the year:

Total Revenues	$5,000,000
Total Fixed Costs	$1,000,000
Total Variable Costs	$3,000,000
Total Quantity Produced and Sold	1,000,000 Units

    a. What is the selling price per unit?
    b. What is the variable cost per unit?
    c. What is the contribution margin per unit?
    d. What is the breakeven point?
    e. What quantity of units is required for Surf's Up Company to make an operating profit of $2,000,000 for the year?

23. **Breakeven and target profits; volume defined in sales dollars.** The manager of Lever Company estimates operating costs for the year will total $450,000 for fixed costs and that variable costs will be $3 per unit.
    a. Find the breakeven point in sales dollars at a selling price of $4 per unit, using the contribution margin ratio.
    b. Find the breakeven point in sales dollars at a selling price of $5 per unit.
    c. How many units must be sold at a price of $5 per unit to generate a profit of $150,000?

24. **CVP—sensitivity analysis.** Giovanni Kitchen Creations is considering introducing a new gourmet cooking seminar with the following price and cost characteristics:

Tuition..	$100 per Student
Variable Cost (supplies, food, etc.)	$60 per Student
Fixed Costs (advertising, instructor's salary, insurance, etc.)...	$200,000 per Year

   a. What enrollment enables Giovanni to break even?

   b. How many students will enable Giovanni to make an operating profit of $100,000 for the year?

   c. Assume that the projected enrollment for the year is 8,000 students for each of the following situations:

   (1) What will be the operating profit for 8,000 students?

   (2) What would be the operating profit if the tuition per student (that is, sales price) decreases by 10 percent? Increases by 20 percent?

   (3) What would be the operating profit if variable costs per student decrease by 10 percent? Increase by 20 percent?

   (4) Suppose that fixed costs for the year are 10 percent lower than projected, whereas variable costs per student are 10 percent higher than projected. What would be the operating profit for the year?

25. **Multiple product profit analysis.** Harry's Hamburgers produces two products, ½ pound burgers and ¾ pound burgers, with the following characteristics:

	½ pound Burger	¾ pound Burger
Selling Price per Unit	$4	$6
Variable Cost per Unit..................	$2	$3
Expected Sales (Units)	100,000	150,000

The total fixed costs for the company are $400,000.

   a. What is the anticipated level of profits for the expected sales volumes?

   b. Assuming that the product mix would be the same at the breakeven point, compute the breakeven point.

   c. If the product sales mix were to change to four ½ pound burgers for each ¾ pound burger, what would be the new breakeven volume?

26. **Multiple product profit analysis.** The Multiproduct Company produces and sells three different products. Operating data for the three products follow.

	Selling Price per Unit	Variable Cost per Unit	Fixed Cost per Month
Product P......................................	$3	$2	—
Product Q	5	3	—
Product R	8	5	—
Entire Company	—	—	$48,000

Define a unit as the sum of one unit of product R sold, two units of product Q sold, and three units of product P sold.

a. Draw a cost-volume-profit graph for the Multiproduct Company.

b. At what sales revenue does the Multiproduct Company break even?

c. Change the facts. Suppose a "unit" now consists of two units of product P for every two units of product Q and one unit of product R. At what sales revenue does Multiproduct break even?

Problems

27. **Explaining sales and cost changes.** You have acquired the following data for Years 1 and 2 for Metropolitan Art Institute:

	Year 1		Year 2		Dollar Increase
Revenue from Admissions ..	$750,000	100%	$840,000	100%	$90,000
Variable Costs of Operating the Institute	495,000	66	560,000	66⅔	65,000
Contribution Margin	$255,000	34%	$280,000	33⅓%	$25,000
Admission Price per Person	$10		$12		

Explain the increase in sales and cost of goods sold between Year 1 and Year 2.

28. **CVP—missing data.** Management of Fred's Frozen Foods has performed cost studies and projected the following annual costs based on 40,000 units of production and sales:

	Total Annual Costs (40,000 units)
Direct Material	$ 400,000
Direct Labor	360,000
Manufacturing Overhead	300,000
Selling, General, and Administrative	200,000
Total	$1,260,000

a. Compute Fred's unit selling price that will yield a projected profit of $100,000, given sales of 40,000 units.

b. Assume management selects a selling price of $30 per unit. Compute Fred's dollar sales that will yield a projected 10-percent profit on sales, assuming variable costs per unit are 70 percent of the selling price per unit and fixed costs are $420,000.

29. **CVP—sensitivity analysis.** Assume last year's sales of a Blockbuster Video store were $2,400,000, fixed costs were $800,000, and variable costs were $1,200,000.

a. At what level of sales revenue will the store break even?

b. If sales revenue increases by 15 percent but unit prices, unit variable costs, and total annual fixed costs do not change, by how much will profit increase?

c. Ignoring the sales increase in **b**, what if fixed costs decrease by 20 percent, by how much will profit increase?

d. Ignore the facts in **b** and **c**, what if variable costs decrease by 10 percent, by how much will profit increase?

30. **Solving for unknowns** (Problems 30 through 32 adapted from problems by D. O. Green). When Britain's auto business slumped in 1921, William R. Morris (the "Henry Ford of Britain") gambled on cost saving from his new assembly lines and cut prices to a point where his expected loss per car in 1922 would be $240 if sales were the same as in 1921, or 1,500 cars. However, sales in 1922 rose to 60,000 cars, and profits for the year were $810,000. For 1922, calculate:

a. Contribution margin per car.

b. Total fixed costs.

c. Breakeven point in cars.

31. **Solving for unknowns.** During the third quarter of a recent year, a division of an automobile company sold 45,000 cars for $250 million and realized a loss for the quarter of $24 million. The breakeven point was 60,000 cars. Calculate for the quarter:

a. Contribution margin per car.

b. Total fixed costs.

c. Profits had sales been twice as large.

32. **Solving for unknowns.** *Time* magazine reported that the future of the American Motors Company seemed so shaky that its creditors, a consortium of banks headed by Chase Manhattan, examined the books every 10 days. The new management trimmed fixed costs by $20 million to cut the breakeven point from 350,000 cars in one year to 250,000 cars for the next year. From this information, calculate:

a. Contribution margin per car (assumed constant for both years).

b. Fixed costs for each year.

c. Losses in the first year, assuming sales of 300,000 cars.

d. Profits in the second year, assuming sales of 400,000 cars.

33. **CVP—missing data; assumptions.** You are analyzing the financial performance of Western Agriculture Company based on limited data from a *Farm Journal* article. The article says that despite an increase in sales revenue from $4,704,000 in Year 8 to $4,725,000 in Year 9, the Western Agriculture Company recently reported a decline in net income of $129,500 from Year 8 to an amount equal to 2 percent of sales revenue in Year 9. The average total cost per bushel increased from $2.200 in Year 8 to $2.205 in Year 9.

a. Compute the changes, if any, in average selling price and sales in bushels from Year 8 to Year 9.

b. Can you compute the total fixed costs and variable cost per bushel during Year 9? If so, do so. If not, illustrate why with a graph and discuss any important assumptions of the cost-volume-profit model that this application violates.

34. **Alternatives to reduce breakeven sales.** The Sunnyside Fruit Farms operated near the breakeven point of $1,125,000 during Year 1, while incurring fixed costs of $450,000. Management is considering two alternatives to reduce the breakeven level. Alternative A trims fixed costs by $100,000 annually with no change in variable cost per unit; doing so, however, will reduce the quality of the product and result in a 10-percent decrease in selling price, but no change in the number of bushels sold. Alternative B substitutes mechanical fruit-picking equipment for certain operations now performed manually. Alternative B will result in an annual increase of $150,000 in fixed costs, but a 5-percent decrease in variable costs per bushel produced, with no change in product quality, selling price, or sales volume.

    a. What was the total contribution margin (contribution margin per unit times number of units sold) during Year 1?
    b. What is the breakeven sales in dollars under alternative A?
    c. What is the breakeven sales in dollars under alternative B?
    d. What should the company do?

35. **Solving for cost-based selling price.** Perot Instruments Corporation follows a cost-based approach to pricing. Prices are 120 percent of cost. The annual cost of producing one of its products follows:

Variable Manufacturing Costs	$40 per Unit
Fixed Manufacturing Costs	$100,000 per Year
Variable Selling and Administrative Costs	$10 per Unit
Fixed Selling and Administrative Costs	$60,000 per Year

    a. Assume that Perot produces and sells 10,000 units. Calculate the selling price per unit.
    b. Assume that Perot produces and sells 20,000 units. Calculate the selling price per unit.

36. **Solving for cost-based selling price.** Western Health Clinic follows a cost-based approach to pricing. It sets prices equal to 110 percent of cost. The clinic has annual fixed costs of $600,000. The variable costs of the clinic's services follow:

Treatment Type	Variable Cost per Procedure
A	$10
B	20
C	30

The clinic expects to provide 1,000 type A treatments, 4,000 type B treatments, and 1,000 type C treatments.

    a. Compute the price of each treatment if the clinic allocates fixed costs to services on the basis of the number of treatments.
    b. Compute the selling price of each treatment if the clinic allocates fixed costs to treatments on the basis of total variable costs.

37. CVP analysis with semifixed (step) costs. Mountaineer Co. has one product: dehydrated meals for backpacking. The sales price of $10 remains constant per unit regardless of volume, as does the variable cost of $6 per unit. The company is considering operating at one of the following three monthly levels of operations:

	Volume Range (production and sales)	Total Fixed Costs	Increase in Fixed Costs from Previous Level
Level 1	0–16,000	$40,000	—
Level 2	16,001–28,000	72,000	$32,000
Level 3	28,001–38,000	94,000	22,000

  a. Calculate the breakeven point(s).
  b. If the company can sell everything it makes, should it operate at level 1, level 2, or level 3? Support your answer.

38. CVP analysis with semifixed costs and changing unit variable costs. The Eades Company manufactures and sells one product. The sales price, $50 per unit, remains constant regardless of volume. Last year's sales were 15,000 units and operating profits were $200,000. Fixed costs depend on production levels, as the following table shows. Variable costs per unit are 40 percent *higher* for level 2 (two shifts) than for level 1 (day shift only). The additional labor costs result primarily from higher wages required to employ workers for the night shift.

	Annual Production Range (in units)	Annual Total Fixed Costs
Level 1 (day shift)	0–20,000	$100,000
Level 2 (day and night shifts)	20,001–36,000	164,000

Eades expects last year's cost structure and selling price not to change this year. Maximum plant capacity is 36,000. The company sells everything it produces.
  a. Compute the contribution margin per unit for last year for each of the two production levels.
  b. Compute the breakeven points for last year for each of the two production levels.
  c. Compute the volume in units that will maximize operating profits. Defend your choice.

39. CVP analysis with semifixed costs. Beverly Miller, director and owner of the Discovery Day Care Center, has a master's degree in elementary education. In the 7 years she has been running the Discovery Center, her salary has ranged from nothing to $20,000 per year. "The second year," she says, "I made 62 cents an hour." (Her salary is what's left over after meeting all other expenses.)

Could she run a more profitable center? She thinks perhaps she could if she increased the student-teacher ratio, which is currently five students to one teacher. (Government standards for a center such as this set a maximum of 10 students per teacher.) She refuses to increase the ratio to more than six-to-one. "If you increase the ratio to more than 6:1, the children don't get enough attention. In addition, the demands on the teacher are far too great." She does not hire part-time teachers.

Beverly rents the space for her center in the basement of a church for $900 per month, including utilities. She estimates that supplies, snacks, and other nonpersonnel costs are $80 per student per month. She charges $380 per month per student. Teachers receive $1,200 per month, including fringe benefits. She has no other operating costs. At present, she cares for 30 students and employs six teachers.

a. What is the present operating profit per month of the Discovery Day Care Center before Ms. Miller's salary?

b. What is (are) the breakeven point(s), before Ms. Miller's salary, assuming a student-teacher ratio of 6:1?

c. What would be the breakeven point(s), before Ms. Miller's salary, if the student-teacher ratio increased to 10:1?

d. Ms. Miller has an opportunity to increase the student body by six students. She must take all six or none. Should she accept the six students, if she wants to maintain a maximum student-teacher ratio of 6:1?

e. (Continuation of part **d.**) Suppose that Ms. Miller accepts the six children. Now she has the opportunity to accept one more, which requires hiring one more teacher. What would happen to profit, before her salary, if she accepts one more student?

40. **CVP with taxes** (adapted from CMA exam). R. A. Ro and Company, maker of quality, handmade pipes, has experienced a steady growth in sales for the past 5 years. However, increased competition has led Mr. Ro, the president, to believe that to maintain the company's present growth requires an aggressive advertising campaign next year. To prepare the next year's advertising campaign, the company's accountant has prepared and presented Mr. Ro with the following data for the current year, Year 1.

Cost Schedule

Variable Costs:	
Direct Labor	$ 8.00 per Pipe
Direct Materials	3.25
Variable Overhead	2.50
Total Variable Costs	$13.75 per Pipe
Fixed Costs:	
Manufacturing	$ 25,000
Selling	40,000
Administrative	70,000
Total Fixed Costs	$135,000
Selling Price, per Pipe	$25.00
Expected Sales, Year 1 (20,000 pipes)	$500,000.00
Tax Rate: 40 Percent	

Mr. Ro has set the sales target for Year 2 at a level of $550,000 (or 22,000 pipes).

a. What is the projected after-tax operating profit for Year 1?

b. What is the breakeven point in units for Year 1?

c. Mr. Ro believes that to attain the sales target requires an additional selling expense of $11,250 for advertising in Year 2, with all other costs remaining constant. What will be the after-tax operating profit for Year 2 if the firm spends the additional $11,250?

d. What will be the breakeven point in dollar sales for Year 2 if the firm spends the additional $11,250 for advertising?

e. If the firm spends the additional $11,250 for advertising in Year 2, what is the sales level in dollars required to equal Year 1 after-tax operating profit?

f. At a sales level of 22,000 units, what is the maximum amount that the firm can spend on advertising to earn an after-tax operating profit of $60,000?

Cases

41. Breakeven analysis for management education. The dean of the graduate school of management at the University of California at Davis was considering whether to offer a particular seminar for executives. The tuition was $650 per person. Variable costs, which included meals, parking, and materials, were $80 per person. Certain costs of offering the seminar, including advertising the seminar, instructors' fees, room rent, and audio-visual equipment rent, would not be affected by the number of people attending (within a "relevant range"). Such costs, which could be thought of as step costs, amounted to $8,000 for the seminar.

In addition to these costs, a number of staff, including the dean of the school, worked on the program. Although the salaries paid to these staff were not affected by offering the seminar, working on the seminar took these people away from other duties, thus creating an opportunity cost, estimated to be $7,000 for this seminar.

Given this information, the school estimated the breakeven point to be ($8,000 + $7,000)/($650 − $80) = 26.3 students. If the school wanted to at least break even on this program, it should offer the program only if it expected at least 27 students to attend.

Write a report to the dean that evaluates the quality of this analysis. In particular, focus on concerns about the accuracy of the data and the limitations of cost-volume-profit analysis.

42. Cost analysis for Chrysler Corporation.[a] Cost-volume-profit analysis showed how much Chrysler had to improve just to break even in 1979. In that year, the breakeven point was 2.2 million units, but the company was selling considerably fewer than 2 million units. Faced with a severe recession in the automobile industry, Chrysler had virtually no chance to increase sales enough to break even. Meanwhile, the company had received loan guarantees from the

---

[a]See R. S. Miller, "The Chrysler Story," *Management Accounting* (August 1983), pp. 22–27, and *Detroit Free Press*, June 6, 1982.

U.S. government, which evoked considerable criticism that the federal government was supporting a ''failing'' company.

By 1982, Chrysler reduced its breakeven point to 1.1 million units, and the company reported a profit for the first time in several years. The headlines read, '' 'We're in black,' Iacocca chortles.''[b] The turnaround came despite continued low sales in the automobile industry; it resulted primarily from severe cost cutting, which reduced fixed costs in constant dollars from $4.5 billion in 1979 to $3.1 billion in 1982. In addition, the company made improvements in its production methods, which enabled it to maintain its volume of output despite the reduction in fixed costs.

a. If Chrysler's breakeven volume was 1.1 million units and its fixed costs were $3.1 billion, what was its average contribution margin per unit?

b. Why do you think Iacocca concentrated on reducing fixed costs to put Chrysler above its breakeven point?

c. As a shareholder of Chrysler, what concerns might you have about the company's massive cost-cutting?

43. **CVP—partial data; special order.** Partial income statements of Ford Food Service for the first two quarters of Year 2 follow.

FORD FOOD SERVICE
Partial Income Statements for First and Second Quarters of Year 2

	First Quarter	Second Quarter
Sales at $3.60 per Meal (unit)	$ 36,000	$ 63,000
Total Costs	49,000	67,000
(Loss)	$(13,000)	$ (4,000)

Each dollar of variable cost per meal comprises 50 percent direct labor, 25 percent direct materials, and 25 percent variable overhead costs. Ford expects sales units, price per unit, variable cost per unit, and total fixed costs to remain at the same level during the third quarter as during the second quarter. Ford sold 17,500 meals in the second quarter.

a. What is the breakeven point in meals (units)?

b. The company has just received a special order from a government agency that provides meals for senior citizens for 7,500 meals at a price of $3.20 per meal (unit). If the company accepts the order, it will not affect the regular market for 17,500 meals in the third quarter. The company can produce the additional meals with existing capacity, but direct labor costs per meal will increase by 10 percent for *all* meals produced because of the need to hire and use new labor. Fixed costs will increase $3,000 per quarter if the company accepts the new order. Should it accept the government order?

c. Assume that the company accepts the order in part **b**. What level of sales to nongovernment customers provides third-quarter profit of $6,800? (The third quarter would be just like the second quarter if the company does not accept the government order.)

---

[6]*Detroit Free Press*, June 6, 1982.

Suggested Solutions to Even-Numbered Exercises

18. Breakeven and target profits.

    a. $\text{Contribution Margin (per unit)} = \text{Unit Selling Price} - \text{Unit Variable Cost}$

$$= \$8 - \$4$$
$$= \$4.$$

$$\text{Profit} = (\text{Contribution Margin per Unit} \times \text{Units}) - \text{Fixed Costs}$$
$$0 = (\$4 \times \text{Units}) - \$100{,}000$$
$$\text{Units} = 25{,}000.$$

    b.

$$\$140{,}000 = (\$4 \times \text{Units}) - \$100{,}000$$
$$\$240{,}000 = \$4 \times \text{Units}$$
$$60{,}000 = \text{Units}.$$

    c. $\text{Contribution Margin Percentage} = \dfrac{\text{Unit Selling Price} - \text{Unit Variable Cost}}{\text{Unit Selling Price}}$

$$= \frac{\$8 - \$4}{\$8} = \frac{\$4}{\$8} = 50\%.$$

$$\text{Profit} = (.5 \times \$1{,}000{,}000) - \$100{,}000$$
$$= \$400{,}000.$$

20. Cost-volume-profit graph.

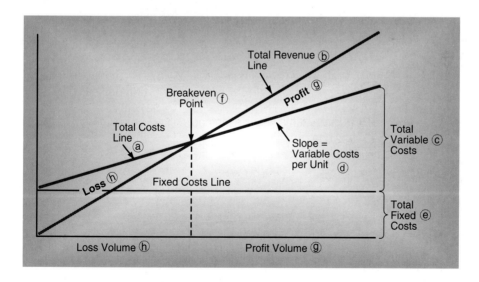

22. Cost-volume-profit analysis.

    a. $5,000,000/1,000,000$ Units = \$5 per Unit.

    b. $3,000,000/1,000,000$ Units = \$3 per Unit.

    c. $5 - \$3 = \$2$ per Unit.

d.
$$\pi = (\$5 - \$3)X - \$1,000,000.$$
Let $\pi = 0$.
$$0 = (\$5 - \$3)X - \$1,000,000.$$
$$X = \frac{\$1,000,000}{(\$5 - \$3)} = 500,000 \text{ Units.}$$

e.
Let $\pi = \$2,000,000$.
$$\$2,000,000 = (\$5 - \$3)X - \$1,000,000.$$
$$X = \frac{\$3,000,000}{(\$5 - \$3)} = 1,500,000 \text{ Units.}$$

24. **CVP—sensitivity analysis.**

a.
$$\pi = (P - V)X - F$$
$$0 = (\$100 - \$60)X - \$200,000$$
$$X = \frac{\$200,000}{(\$100 - \$60)} = 5,000 \text{ Students.}$$

b.
$$\$100,000 = (\$100 - \$60)X - \$200,000$$
$$X = \frac{\$300,000}{(\$100 - \$60)} = 7,500 \text{ Students.}$$

c. (1)
$$\pi = (\$100 - \$60)8,000 - \$200,000$$
$$= \$120,000.$$

(2) *10-percent price decrease. Now P = $90.*
$$\pi = (\$90 - \$60)8,000 - \$200,000$$
$$= \$40,000.$$

20-percent price increase. Now P = $120.
$$\pi = (\$120 - \$60)8,000 - \$200,000$$
$$= \$280,000.$$

(3) *10-percent variable cost decrease. Now V = $54.*
$$\pi = (\$100 - \$54)8,000 - \$200,000$$
$$= \$168,000.$$

20-percent variable cost increase. Now V = $72.
$$\pi = (\$100 - \$72)8,000 - \$200,000$$
$$= \$24,000.$$

(4)
$$\pi = (\$100 - \$66)8,000 - \$180,000$$
$$= \$92,000.$$

26. Multiple product profit analysis.

  a.

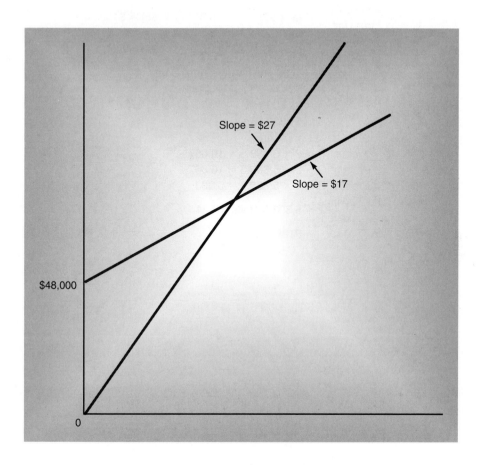

A unit = production of one product R, two product Qs, and three product Ps.

$$\frac{\text{Variable Cost}}{\text{per Unit}} = (3 \times \$2) + (2 \times \$3) + (1 \times \$5) = \$17.$$

$$\frac{\text{Revenue}}{\text{per Unit}} = (3 \times \$3) + (2 \times \$5) + (1 \times \$8) = \$27.$$

  b.

$$0 = \text{Total Revenue} - \text{Total Cost}$$
$$0 = \$27X - (\$17X + \$48,000)$$
$$\$10X = \$48,000$$
$$X = 4,800 \text{ Units.}$$

Product volume at breakeven point is

Product P = 3 × 4,800 = 14,400
Product Q = 2 × 4,800 = 9,600
Product R = 1 × 4,800 = 4,800.

$$\frac{\text{Total Revenue at}}{\text{Breakeven Level}} = 4,800 \text{ Units} \times \$27 = \$129,600.$$

c.
$$\text{A unit} = \text{two product Ps, two product Qs,}$$
$$\text{and one product R.}$$

$$\frac{\text{Variable Cost}}{\text{per Unit}} = (2 \times \$2) + (2 \times \$3) + (1 \times \$5) = \$15.$$

$$\frac{\text{Revenue}}{\text{per Unit}} = (2 \times \$3) + (2 \times \$5) + (1 \times \$8) = \$24.$$

$$0 = \text{Total Revenue} - \text{Total Costs}$$
$$0 = \$24X - (\$15X + \$48,000)$$
$$\$9X = \$48,000$$
$$X = 5,333.3 \text{ Units.}$$

Sales at breakeven point are

$$\text{Product P} = 2 \times 5,333.3 = 10,667$$
$$\text{Product Q} = 2 \times 5,333.3 = 10,667$$
$$\text{Product R} = 1 \times 5,333.3 = 5,333.$$

$$\frac{\text{Total Revenue}}{\text{at Breakeven}} = 5,333.3 \text{ Units} \times \$24$$

$$= \$128,000.$$

Chapter 9

Analyzing Costs for Pricing and Short-Run Decisions

1. Understand how managers use differential costs and revenues to make decisions.
2. Interpret cost data so that you use the relevant costs for decisions.
3. Make pricing decisions using differential cost information.
4. Decide whether to make or buy products using differential costs.
5. Decide whether to add or drop product lines based on differential cost and revenue information.
6. Choose the best mix of products to produce and sell.
7. Manage inventory using differential cost information.
8. (Appendix 9.1) Use linear programming to choose the optimal product mix.
9. (Appendix 9.2) Use the economic order quantity (EOQ) model to choose the optimal amount of goods to order.

This chapter deals with using accounting information to make decisions such as pricing, accepting special orders, making versus buying, choosing the optimal mix of products, and inventory management. We emphasize short-run decisions in this chapter. For example, the decision by USAir to cut fares in its Northeast market fits our short-run pricing concept. A decision by Nordstrom's to have a November sale is a short-run decision. A decision by Continental Airlines to buy 12 Boeing 767s, however, would be a long-run decision affecting the capacity of Continental Airlines. We discuss using accounting information in long-run decisions in Chapter 10.

Differential Analysis for Superstars[a]

When the Los Angeles Kings acquired Wayne Gretzky from the Edmonton Oilers for $15 million and other considerations, many hockey executives and analysts said it was a good deal for both sides. The different business situations for the two teams affected their differential cost analyses.

The Edmonton Oilers were an established NHL powerhouse with a captive sports audience. While fans initially criticized the trade of the national hero, attendance declined little.

The Oilers benefitted substantially. In addition to the fifteen million dollars received, the Oilers laid the foundation for the future by acquiring a young star and three number one draft picks over the next five years. If the competition for the Edmonton sports dollar became more intense, the Oilers would be able to maintain their fan loyalty by fielding a consistently good team. Finally, the Oilers would be reducing their payroll. For the Oilers, potential differential revenues lost in the short-run were less than the differential cost savings.

The differential analysis for the Los Angeles Kings was more complicated. The Kings needed a big draw to compete in a highly competitive sports market that included several professional teams as well as two major college sports powers. The Kings management hoped that Gretzky would provide star quality and the foundation for a winning franchise.

Before making the deal, the Kings estimated differential revenues and costs from increased concessions, television and radio rights, and ticket sales, and estimated additional revenues from ticket sales. Based on their analysis, they estimated an increased annual revenue of $10.5 million, increased additional payroll costs of $2 million per year, plus interest on the money borrowed to acquire Gretzky. The Kings concluded that they would recover their $15-million investment in less than three years. In view of their improved record, it appears the Kings' investment in Gretzky paid off, despite more recent injury problems.

[a]Based on the authors' research.

This chapter deals with several applications of one principle—**differential analysis,** the analysis of differences among particular alternative actions.[1] Owners typically judge management's performance on the basis of a firm's profitability. Thus

---

[1]Differential analysis is also known as *incremental analysis* or *marginal analysis.*

managers want to know the differential effect of various alternative actions on profits. As you go through each application of differential analysis, we encourage you to keep the following questions in mind: What differs among the alternatives? By how much?

Virtually all managers use differential analysis. We see differential analysis used by professional sports teams such as in the San Francisco Giants' acquisition of Barry Bonds and the Los Angeles Kings' acquisition of Wayne Gretsky (see the Managerial Application, ''Differential Analysis for Superstars.''

The Differential Principle

Managerial decision making is the process of choosing among alternatives. The differential analysis model, shown in Exhibit 9.1, extends the cost-volume-profit model discussed in Chapter 8. The first column represents the alternative being considered. The second column presents the **status quo,** or baseline. The third column shows the difference between the status quo and the alternative. If the difference is such that $\pi_1 > \pi_0$, the alternative is more profitable than the status quo. If $\pi_0 > \pi_1$, the status quo is more profitable. A *differential cost* is a cost that changes (differs) as a result of taking some action.

The following example illustrates differential analysis. To provide continuity, we use the facts from this example throughout the chapter. We use a manufacturing firm in this illustration because it is the most comprehensive and complex of any type of organization. The concepts apply as well to service, financial, merchandising, and other organizations.

Example Assume the following status quo data for Baltimore Company, a high-tech company that makes a particular type of computer software known as BC-1234.

Exhibit 9.1

Differential Analysis Model[a]

Revenue.....................................	P_1X_1	$- \quad P_0X_0$	$= \quad \Delta PX$
Less Variable Costs	V_1X_1	$- \quad V_0X_0$	$= \quad \Delta VX$
Total Contribution Margin	$(P_1 - V_1)X_1$	$- \quad (P_0 - V_0)X_0$	$= \Delta(P - V)X$
Less Fixed Costs	F_1	$- \quad F_0$	$= \quad \Delta F$
Operating Profit	π_1	$- \quad \pi_0$	$= \quad \Delta \pi$

[a]P = price per unit; X = volume per period; V = variable cost per unit; $P - V$ = contribution margin per unit; F = fixed costs per period; π = operating profit per period; Δ = amount of difference.

Units Made and Sold	800 Units Per Month
Maximum Production and Sales Capacity	1,200 Units per Month
Selling Price	$30

Cost Classification	Variable Cost (per unit)	Fixed Cost (per month)
Manufacturing Costs	$17	$3,060
Marketing and Administrative Costs.................	5	1,740
Total Costs	$22	$4,800

The management of the Baltimore Company believes that it can increase volume from 800 units to 900 units per month by decreasing the selling price from $30 to $28 per unit. Would the price reduction be profitable? The differential analysis for this example indicates that the alternative would not increase profits. Exhibit 9.2 shows the alternative's profit is only $600 whereas the status quo generates $1,600 in profits.

Relevant Costs

Note in Exhibit 9.2 that this particular decision does not affect all costs. Specifically, fixed costs in this example do not change. Thus only revenues and *total* variable costs are relevant to the analysis; fixed costs are not. We sometimes call differential analysis **relevant cost analysis** as it identifies the costs (or revenues) relevant to the decision. A cost or revenue is *relevant* if an amount appears in the Difference column; all others are irrelevant. Thus we could ignore fixed costs in this example. (This is not true in general. Fixed costs nearly always differ in long-run decisions involving changes in capacity, and they sometimes differ in short-run operating decisions, as we shall see later in this chapter.)

Exhibit 9.2

BALTIMORE COMPANY
Differential Analysis of a Price Reduction[a]

	Alternative P = $28 X = 900	−	Status Quo P = $30 X = 800	=	Difference
Revenue.....................................	$25,200[b]	−	$24,000[d]	=	$ 1,200
Less Variable Costs	(19,800)[c]	−	(17,600)[e]	=	(2,200)
Total Contribution Margin	$ 5,400	−	$ 6,400	=	$(1,000)
Less Fixed Costs	(4,800)	−	(4,800)	=	0
Operating Profit	$ 600	−	$ 1,600	=	$(1,000)

[a]Numbers within parentheses are costs or losses; numbers with minus signs are the result of row operations.
[b]$25,200 = $28 × 900 Units.
[c]$19,800 = $22 × 900 Units.
[d]$24,000 = $30 × 800 Units.
[e]$17,600 = $22 × 800 Units.

As you become familiar with differential analysis, you will find shortcuts by ignoring irrelevant costs (and revenues) from the outset of your work. For instance, you needed to work only with revenues and total variable costs in the previous example to get the answer.

Problems in Identifying Costs

Focus on Cash Flows

The most difficult part of decision making is estimating the benefits and costs of each alternative. Although benefits and costs have several dimensions, the most important dimensions for business decisions are the amounts and timing of **cash flows.** (Chapter 10 provides analytical methods of dealing with the *timing* of cash flows; this chapter deals only with the *amount* of cash flows.) The emphasis on cash flows is fundamental for two reasons:

1. Cash is the medium of exchange. The firm can use cash immediately to pay debts or dividends or to purchase equipment. The firm can eventually convert noncash assets into cash, but this step takes time and perhaps requires additional costs.
2. Cash serves as a common, objective measure of the benefits and costs of alternatives. If the analysis states one alternative in terms of units of inventory to be produced and another in terms of the number of machines to be acquired, it is not expressing the alternatives in a common measuring unit. Before the manager can compare these alternatives, the analysis must reexpress their benefits and costs in a common measuring unit. Cash flows are the common measuring unit because they represent the most objective and quantifiable measure of benefits and costs.

Consequently, differential analysis focuses mostly on differential cash flows. The previous example assumed both differential revenues and costs to be cash flows or near-cash flows (for example, it assumed that revenues and costs on account are cash flows). Managers who focus on cash flows alone, however, may overlook an additional cost: economic depreciation.

Economic Depreciation

Depreciation may create confusion in differential analysis. In financial accounting, depreciation allocates part of an asset's cost to time periods or to units of production. Differential analysis includes the change in the economic value of an asset because of its use. This change in value is **economic depreciation.** The cash outflow to acquire an asset less the cash inflow when the firm sells is a differential cost. Differential analysis, therefore, takes into account economic depreciation, which is the decline in value of an asset.

Example Management of Hertz rental car company is deciding between purchasing a fleet of Oldsmobile or Buick automobiles. All operating costs for both models are equal. However, economic depreciation differs. The Buicks cost $15,000 each and have a salvage value of $11,000 if sold after 6 months. The Oldsmobiles cost $15,000 each and have a salvage value of $12,000 if sold after 6 months. The following table shows that the Oldsmobiles have a lower economic depreciation in this case. Regardless of the depreciation recorded in the accounting records, the cash flows reflect economic depreciation.

	Alternative 1: Buick		Alternative 2: Oldsmobile		Difference (1 − 2)
Cost of Car (cash outflow).............	$(15,000)	−	$(15,000)	=	$ 0
Salvage Value after 6 months (cash inflow)........................	11,000	−	12,000	=	(1,000)
Economic Depreciation (decline in value)....................	$ (4,000)	−	$ (3,000)	=	$(1,000)

Uncertainty and Differential Analysis

Cost and revenue estimates for the status quo are usually more certain than estimates for alternatives. The status quo represents something known, whereas estimates for alternatives may be little more than educated guesses. Analysts may easily omit some critical aspect of the alternative.

Most managers are averse to risk and uncertainty unless they receive additional compensation to bear risk. They prefer the known to the unknown, all other things being equal. Consequently, we sometimes see managers rejecting, because of uncertainty, an alternative expected to be more profitable than the status quo. Managers often deal with uncertainty and differential analysis by setting high standards for the alternative. (For example, ''The alternative must increase profits by 25 percent before we will accept it.'')

Pricing Decisions

Decisions regarding the prices a firm charges for its products are complex, involving factors such as competitors' actions and market conditions. In many cases a firm will not be in a position to set prices. The more highly competitive the market, the more likely the firm must accept the market price as given. In some situations, however, firms do have some control over prices they charge; for example, companies like McDonnell Douglas and Aerojet sell to government agencies or other buyers with cost-plus-fixed-fee contracts. In this section, we consider pricing decisions to show that correct pricing decisions involve the principles of differential analysis.

Cost-Based Approach to Pricing

One approach to setting prices is to add a markup to the firm's costs. Suppose the management of the Baltimore Company has set a goal of reporting profits of $2,000 per month. If it estimated the volume to be 800 units per month, it would calculate the per-unit price as follows:

$$\pi = PX - (VX + F)$$

$$\$2,000 = (P \times 800) - [(\$22 \times 800) + \$4,800]$$

$$\$2,000 = (P \times 800) - \$22,400$$

$$\$24,400 = P \times 800$$

$$P = \frac{\$24,400}{800}$$

$$= \$30.50.$$

So it would set the unit price at $30.50.

If a firm is to remain in business in the long run, it must recover all of its accounting costs and provide an adequate return to its owners.[2] Basing prices on costs, however, has four shortcomings.

First Basing prices on costs ignores the relation between P (price) and X (quantity sold) in the market. If the Baltimore Company faces a downward-sloping demand curve, it may not be able to sell 800 units at a price of $30.50.

Second Cost-plus pricing is often simplistic, such as, "Add $2.50 to the total cost of producing and selling each unit to get the price." Basing prices on costs creates a circularity. The number of units produced critically affects the per-unit cost of a product. As the number of units increases, the amount of fixed cost allocated to each unit decreases. Thus the per-unit cost of a product if Baltimore Company produced 800 units is

$$\$22 + \frac{\$4,800}{800} = \$28.$$

If the company produces 1,000 units, the per-unit cost is

$$\$22 + \frac{\$4,800}{1,000} = \$26.80.$$

In the former case,

$$P = \$2.50 + \$28$$

$$= \$30.50,$$

---

[2]Accountants and economists realize that "an adequate return for owners" is an economic (opportunity) cost, but not an accounting cost (appearing in the financial statements).

whereas in the latter case,

$$P = \$2.50 + \$26.80$$

$$= \$29.30.$$

If management priced in this manner, it might drop prices when demand was stronger and raise them when it was weaker.

Moral: If managers base prices on per-unit total costs and per-unit total costs change with volume and volume depends on prices, then prices are highest when volume is lowest and vice versa.

Third   Accounting practices and conventions not appropriate for the decision may affect the costs attributable to a particular product. For example, accounting treats the acquisition cost of using a plant and machinery as a cost of these assets. The cost of using these assets is actually the opportunity cost of foregone use elsewhere or foregone cash from selling the assets. Accounting gives no recognition to the opportunity cost of using the plant and machinery in manufacturing the product. The allocation of various indirect costs to specific products is questionable also. Accounting practices for such costs raise questions about the validity of product cost amounts for decision-making purposes.

Fourth   Cost-based pricing can lead to incorrect decisions, particularly in the short run. For example, assume that the Baltimore Company has received a special order for 100 units for $25 per unit. This order will not affect the firm's regular market, and the company can fill the order with existing capacity. If the company uses a cost-based approach to pricing, it will probably reject this special order because the $25 price is less than the $28 per-unit full cost ($28 = $22 + $4,800/800). Exhibit 9.3 demonstrates that rejecting this order is incorrect, however. Applying the differential approach to pricing results in the correct decision to accept the order.

Exhibit 9.3

BALTIMORE COMPANY
Differential Analysis of a Special Order

	Alternative	−	Status Quo	=	Difference
Revenue..............................	$26,500[a]	−	$24,000	=	$2,500
Less Variable Costs	(19,800)[b]	−	(17,600)	=	(2,200)
Total Contribution.......................	$ 6,700	−	$ 6,400	=	$ 300
Less Fixed Costs	(4,800)	−	(4,800)	=	0
Operating Profit	$ 1,900	−	$ 1,600	=	$ 300

[a]$26,500 = $24,000 + ($25 × 100 Units).
[b]$19,800 = $17,600 + ($22 × 100 Units).

Differential Approach to Pricing

The differential approach to pricing presumes that the price must at least equal the **differential cost** of producing and selling the product. In the short run, this practice will result in a positive contribution to covering fixed costs and generating profit. In the long run, this practice will require covering all costs, because *both fixed and variable costs become differential costs in the long run*.

The differential approach particularly helps in making special-order decisions. Consider the special order discussed previously. Exhibit 9.3 presents an analysis of the effects of not accepting and of accepting the special order, assuming that the regular market is 800 units sold at a price of $30 a unit. Exhibit 9.3 demonstrates that Baltimore should accept the special order at $25 per unit, because that price permits the firm to cover the differential costs of $22 per unit and provide a contribution of $3 per unit toward covering fixed costs and earning profit. (A shortcut computes the per-unit contribution margin on the special order, $3, and multiplies it by the number of units, 100. This computation gives the additional total contribution from the special order, $300.)

The differential approach to pricing works well for special orders but some criticize it for pricing a firm's regular products. Critics suggest that following the differential approach in the short run will lead to underpricing in the long run, because the contribution to covering fixed costs or generating profits will be inadequate.

Others respond in two ways to this criticism. First, the differential approach does lead to correct short-run pricing decisions. Once the firm has set plant capacity and incurred fixed costs, the fixed costs become irrelevant to the short-run pricing decision. The firm must attempt to set a price at least equal to the differential, or variable, costs. Second, in both the short and long run, the differential approach provides only an indicator of the *minimum* acceptable price. The firm can always charge some higher amount, taking into consideration market demand, competitor's actions, and similar factors.

Consider the data for the Baltimore Company in Exhibit 9.4. The minimum acceptable price in the short run is the differential cost of $22 per unit. In the long run, the minimum acceptable price is $28 per unit, because the firm must cover both variable and fixed costs. A more desirable long-run price is the current price—$30,

Exhibit 9.4

BALTIMORE COMPANY
Data for Pricing

Short-Run Differential Costs (variable costs)	$22	= Short-Run Minimum Price
Fixed Cost	6[a]	
Long-Run Incremental Costs	$28	= Long-Run Minimum price
Expected Profits	2	
Target Selling Price	$30	= Long-Run Desired Price

[a]$6 = $4,800/800. This assumes a long-run volume of 800 units.

which includes a profit. Between the $22 short-run minimum price and the $30 long-run desired price lies the range of price flexibility for the firm. The firm may set a price slightly higher than the variable cost for a special order as long as excess capacity exists and doing so will not affect the firm's regular market.

If Baltimore Company faces a competing market for its regular product, it can set a price slightly higher than the $22 minimum. The firm hopes to underprice competitors and to capture a larger share of the market. The increase in quantity sold may more than offset the reduction in the contribution margin per unit from a lower selling price, resulting in a larger *total* contribution margin.

If a firm is the only supplier of this product, it can charge a price higher than $28. If the firm sets the price too high, however, it may earn high profits that induce other firms to enter the market. Thus, the pricing decision should include an analysis of short-run and long-run differential costs, market conditions, and competitors' actions.

Make-or-Buy Decisions

When a firm must decide whether to meet its needs internally or to acquire goods or services from external sources, it faces a **make-or-buy decision.** If Pillsbury grows its own farm products for its frozen foods, then it "makes." If it buys products from other farmers, then it "buys." If Weirton Steel mines its own iron ore and coal and processes it through to final product, then it "makes" the pig iron. If it purchases these raw materials, then it "buys." Housing contractors who do their own site preparation and foundation work "make," whereas those who hire subcontractors "buy." Professional baseball teams that rely on the draft and their minor league system "make," whereas those that trade for established players "buy."

Whether to make or to buy depends on cost factors and on nonquantitative factors such as dependability of suppliers and the quality of purchased materials. The decision may appear to be a one-time choice between making or buying, but managers usually base such decisions on the long-run reputation of suppliers.

Example The Baltimore Company has an opportunity to buy part of its product for $12 per unit. This purchase would affect prices, volume, and costs as follows:

	Alternative: Buy	Status Quo: Make
Unit Selling Price	$30	$30
Volume	800 per Month	800 per Month
Unit Variable Manufacturing Costs	$6	$17
Purchased Parts, per Unit	$12	$0
Unit Variable Marketing and Administrative Costs	$5	$5
Fixed Manufacturing Costs	$2,100	$3,060
Fixed Marketing and Administrative Costs	$1,740	$1,740

Exhibit 9.5

BALTIMORE COMPANY
Differential Analysis of Make-or-Buy Decision

	Alternative: Buy	_	Status Quo: Make	=	Difference
Revenue......................................	$24,000	–	$24,000	=	0
Less:					
Variable Costs to Produce and Sell........	(8,800)[a]	–	(17,600)	=	$8,800
Variable Costs of Goods Bought	(9,600)[b]	–	—	=	(9,600)
Total Contribution Margin...................	$ 5,600	–	$ 6,400	=	$ (800)
Less Fixed Costs.........................	(3,840)[c]	–	(4,800)	=	960
Operating Profit	$ 1,760	–	$ 1,600	=	$ 160

[a]$8,800 = ($6 + $5) × 800 units.
[b]$9,600 = $12 × 800 units.
[c]$3,840 = $2,100 + $1,740.

Exhibit 9.5 shows that the alternative to buy is more profitable. The $9,600 cost to buy is more than offset by the fixed and variable cost savings.

Problem 9.1
for Self-Study

Applying differential analysis. Boilermaker Technologies, Inc., produces a valve used in electric turbine systems. The costs of the valve at the company's normal volume of 5,000 units per month appear below. Unless otherwise specified, assume a selling price of $1,750.

Cost Data for Boilermaker Technologies

Unit Manufacturing Costs:		
Variable Materials	$250	
Variable Labor	175	
Variable Overhead...	75	
Fixed Overhead	150	
Total Unit Manufacturing Costs................................		$ 650
Unit Nonmanufacturing Costs:		
Variable	200	
Fixed..	175	
Total Unit Nonmanufacturing Costs		375
Total Unit Costs		$1,025

a. Market research estimates that a price increase to $1,900 per unit would decrease monthly volume to 4,500 units. The accounting department estimates total variable costs would decrease proportionately with volume and total fixed costs would be $1,617,500. Would you recommend that the firm take this action? What would be the impact on monthly revenues, costs, and profits?

b. An outside contractor proposes to make and ship 1,000 valves per month directly to Boilermaker Technologies' customers as Boilermaker's sales force receives orders. This proposal would not affect Boilermaker's fixed nonmanufacturing costs, but its variable nonmanufacturing costs would decline by 25 percent for the 1,000 units the contractor produced. Boilermaker's plant would operate at 80 percent of its normal level, and total fixed manufacturing costs would decline by 15 percent. How much would the firm be willing to pay the contractor?

The solution to this self-study problem is at the end of the chapter on page 353.

Adding and Dropping Parts of Operations

Managers must decide when to add or drop products from the product line and when to open or abandon sales territories. For example, Ernst & Young, a Big Six accounting firm, decided to shut down its litigation consulting group. K Mart decided to close certain stores. Sears decided to eliminate certain real estate and financial services operations.

These can be either long-run decisions involving a change in capacity or short-run decisions in which capacity does not change. This chapter deals with these as short-run decisions.

The differential principle implies the following rule. If the differential revenue from the sale of a product exceeds the differential costs required to provide the product for sale, then the product generates profits and the firm should continue its production. This decision is correct even though the product may show a loss in financial statements because of overhead costs allocated to it. If the product more than covers its differential costs, and if no other alternative use of the production and sales facilities exists, the firm should retain the product in the short run.

Example   Suppose that the Baltimore Company had three products, not just the one in the previous examples, and used common facilities to produce and sell all three. Neither product affects sales of the others. The relevant data for these three products follow:

	Product			
	A	B	C	Total
Sales Volume per Month	800	1,000	600	—
Unit Sales Price	$30	$20	$40	—
Sales Revenue	$24,000	$20,000	$24,000	$68,000
Unit Variable Cost	$22	$14	$35	—
Fixed Cost per Month	—	—	—	$13,600

Management has asked the accounting department to allocate fixed costs to each product so that it can evaluate how well each product is doing. Total fixed costs were 20 percent of total dollar sales, so the accountant charged fixed costs to each product at 20 percent of the product's sales. For example, Product C received $4,800 (= .20 × $24,000 sales) of fixed costs.

As the product-line income statements on the top panel of Exhibit 9.6 show, the report demonstrated an apparent loss of $1,800 for Product C. One of Baltimore's managers argued, "We should drop Product C. It is losing $1,800 per month." A second manager suggested performing a differential analysis on dropping Product C to see the costs saved and the revenues lost. The bottom panel of Exhibit 9.6, the differential analysis, shows dropping Product C makes the company less profitable.

Exhibit 9.6

BALTIMORE COMPANY
Differential Analysis of Dropping a Product

Income Statement Analysis

	Product			
	A	B	C	Total
Sales...........................	$24,000	$20,000	$24,000	$68,000
Less Variable Costs	(17,600)	(14,000)	(21,000)	(52,600)
Total Contribution Margin	$ 6,400	$ 6,000	$ 3,000	$15,400
Less Fixed Costs Allocated to Each Product.......................	(4,800)[a]	(4,000)[a]	(4,800)[a]	(13,600)
Operating Profit (Loss)	$ 1,600	$ 2,000	$ (1,800)	$ 1,800

Differential Analysis

	Alternative: Drop Product C	−	Status Quo	= Difference
Sales......................................	$44,000	−	$68,000 =	$(24,000)
Less Variable Costs	(31,600)	−	(52,600) =	21,000
Total Contribution Margin	$12,400	−	$15,400 =	$ (3,000)
Less Fixed Costs	(13,600)	−	(13,600) =	0
Operating Profit (Loss)	$ (1,200)	−	$ 1,800 =	$ (3,000)

[a]Fixed costs of $13,600 allocated in proportion to sales; 20 percent of sales dollars charged to each product as fixed costs.

The first manager incorrectly assumed that dropping the product would save fixed costs. The firm should investigate more profitable uses of the facilities used to produce and sell Product C, because its contribution margin appears to be the weakest of the three products. Until such alternatives emerge, however, producing and selling Product C is profitable.

Problem 9.2 for Self-Study

Product decisions. Assume Baltimore Company did not drop Product C, but Product B's revenue and variable costs dropped to 50 percent of their current levels, as shown in Exhibit 9.6. Should Baltimore drop Product B?

The solution to this self-study problem is at the end of the chapter on page 354.

Product Choice Decisions

Managers ask, "Which products should we sell?" Most firms can supply a number of different goods and services to the market, but manufacturing or distribution constraints limit what firms can do. Firms must choose among alternatives just as students must choose how to allocate their study time between accounting and finance, or their time between Question 1 and Question 2 on a final exam. Team salary caps limit the amount professional basketball teams can pay and therefore the number of top players each team can have. In its Detroit Jeep plant, Chrysler must decide how many Limiteds to make, how many Laredos, and how many other models. The Gap must decide how many items of which size to carry in its limited retail space.

We normally think of these product-choice problems as short-run decisions. With enough time, students can study for *both* accounting and finance. In the short run, however, capacity limitations require choices among options.

Example The Baltimore Company has just purchased one machine that can make Products L, M, and N. The market for these products will absorb all of them, or any combination. Management wants to pick the most profitable product, or combination of products, to produce. The firm has only 400 hours of time available on the machine each month.

The time requirements for each of the three products, their selling prices, and their variable costs appear in Exhibit 9.7. For this example, assume that all marketing and administrative costs are fixed. Also assume that fixed manufacturing, marketing, and administrative costs are the same (that is, are not differential) whichever product or combination of products the firm produces.

Exhibit 9.7

Rationing Scarce Capacity
(Machine is available only 400 hours per month.)

	Product		
	L	**M**	**N**
Time Required on the Machine per Unit Produced	0.5 Hour	2.0 Hours	4.0 Hours
Selling Price per Unit	$5.00	$12.00	$16.00
Less Variable Costs to Produce One Unit	(3.00)	(5.00)	(6.00)
Contribution Margin per Unit . . .	$2.00	$ 7.00	$10.00
Contribution Margin per Hour on the Machine (contribution margin per unit/time requirement in hours)	$4.00 per Hour[a]	$3.50 per Hour[b]	$2.50 per Hour[c]
Total Contribution from Using 400 Hours on the Machine . .	$1,600	$1,400	$1,000

[a]$4.00 per Hour = $2.00/0.5 Hour.
[b]$3.50 per Hour = $7.00/2.0 Hours.
[c]$2.50 per Hour = $10.00/4.0 Hours.

Even though Product N has a per-unit contribution of $10.00, whereas Product L has a per-unit contribution of only $2.00, Product L is still the best product to produce given the capacity constraint on the machine. Product L contributes $4.00 per hour (= $2.00 per unit/.5 hour per unit) of time on the machine, whereas Product N contributes only $2.50 per hour ($10.00 per unit/4 hours per unit) of time on the machine. Differential analysis indicates that the total contribution margin from using the machine to produce Product L is $1,600, whereas the contribution from producing Product M is $1,400 and that from producing Product N is $1,000.

If the machine time were unlimited, the Baltimore Company should produce and sell all three products in the short run because all have a positive contribution margin. But with constrained machinery time, the most profitable product is *the one that contributes the most per unit of time*. If you face time constraints on an examination and must choose between Question 1 and Question 2, and if working on Question 1 provides 1 point per minute and Question 2 provides 2 points per minute, then work on Question 2.

When there is only one scarce resource, the decision is easy: *Choose the product that gives the largest contribution per unit of the scarce resource used.* When each product uses different proportions of several scarce resources, the computational problem becomes more difficult. Appendix 9.1 describes linear programming, a mathematical tool for solving such multiple constrained decision problems. Textbooks on operations research and quantitative methods describe these techniques in more detail.

Incorrect Use of Accounting Data Many accounting systems routinely provide unit cost information that includes an *allocation* of fixed costs to each

Exhibit 9.8

Rationing Scarce Capacity by Incorrectly Using Full Absorption Unit Costs

	Product		
	L	M	N
(1) Time Required on the Machine per Unit Produced	0.5 Hour	2.0 Hours	4.0 Hours
(2) Selling Price per Unit	$5.00	$12.00	$16.00
Variable Costs to Produce One Unit:			
(3) Direct Materials	$1.00	$2.00	$2.50
(4) Direct Labor	1.50	2.00	2.50
(5) Variable Manufacturing Overhead	.50	1.00	1.00
(6) Total Variable Costs per Unit	$3.00	$5.00	$6.00
(7) Allocation of Fixed Costs at 100 Percent of Direct Labor	1.50	2.00	2.50
(8) Full Absorption Cost per Unit	$4.50	$7.00	$8.50
(9) Gross Margin per Unit [line (2) minus line (8)]	$ .50	$5.00	$7.50
(10) Gross Margin per Hour	$1.00 per Hour	$2.50 per Hour	$1.875 per Hour

unit. This is the full absorption method of product costing. We assume the variable costing method so far in this chapter. Full absorption unit costs for short-run decision making will lead to incorrect decisions as the following example demonstrates.

Example We have seen that production of Product L is optimal because its total monthly contribution is the highest of the three products. (Refer to Exhibit 9.7.) Suppose accountants have allocated fixed manufacturing costs in the amounts shown on line (7) of Exhibit 9.8. As line (10) of Exhibit 9.8 shows, full absorption cost may lead to an incorrect assessment that Product M is most profitable and Product L is least profitable per machine hour.

This example shows how the use of accounting data intended for one purpose may not be useful for other purposes. External reporting requires full absorption unit cost data. Most managerial decision models, on the other hand, assume *variable* unit costs.

Unsophisticated users of accounting data often incorrectly assume that any calculated unit cost is a variable cost. You should not *assume* that the unit cost reported by an accounting system is a variable cost. Those unit costs often contain unitized fixed costs.

Inventory Management Decisions

Inventory management affects profits in merchandising, manufacturing, and other organizations with inventories. Having the correct type and amount of inventory can prevent a production shutdown in manufacturing. In merchandising, having the correct type of merchandise inventory may mean making a sale. Inventories are costly to maintain, however. The costs include storage costs, insurance, losses from damage and theft, property taxes, and the opportunity cost of funds tied up in inventory. Key inventory management questions include the following:

1. How many units of inventory should be on hand and available for use or sale?
2. How often should the firm order a particular item? What is the optimal size of the order?

Differential Costs for Inventory Management

Inventory management decisions involve two types of opposing costs. The firm incurs differential costs each time it places an order or makes a production run (for example, the cost of processing each purchase order or the cost of preparing machinery for each production run). These are setup or order costs. The firm could minimize them by minimizing the number of orders or production runs.

By ordering or producing less frequently, however, each order or production run must be for a larger number of units. The firm will carry a larger average inventory. Larger inventories imply larger carrying costs for these inventories (for example, the cost of maintaining warehouse facilities).

Management would like to find the optimal trade-off between these two types of opposing costs, carrying costs and order costs. Refer to Exhibit 9.9, based on the

Exhibit 9.9

Inventory Costs

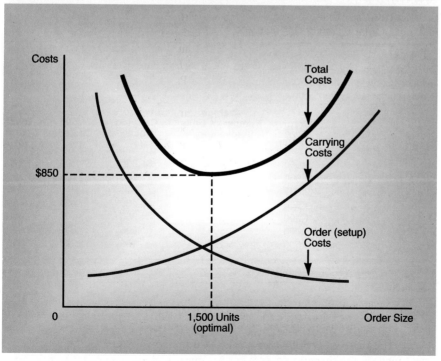

example below. (We refer to both order costs and setup costs as *order costs* for the rest of our discussion.) The problem is to calculate the optimal number of orders or production runs each year and the optimal number of units to order or produce. The optimal number of units to order or produce is the **economic order quantity (EOQ).**

Example California Merchandising sells 6,000 units of a product per year, spread evenly throughout the year. Each unit costs $2 to purchase. The differential cost of preparing and following up on an order is $100 per order. The cost of carrying a unit in inventory is 30 percent of the unit's cost. Thus, if the firm places one order for the year, it will purchase 6,000 units and have, *on average,* 3,000 units ($6,000) in inventory during the year. The carrying cost would be $1,800 (= $6,000 × .30) for the year. Exhibit 9.10 presents the inventory carrying costs, order costs, and total costs of the inventory. Note the trade-off between carrying costs and order costs: As one decreases, the other increases. The optimal number of orders per year is four, which has the lowest total costs [see column (6) in Exhibit 9.10].

A formal model (called the EOQ model) for deriving the optimal number of orders (or setups of production runs) and the optimal number of items in an order (or in a production run) appears in Appendix 9.2.

Exhibit 9.10

CALIFORNIA MERCHANDISING
Economic Order Quantity Calculation

Differential costs per order are $100.
Annual requirement is 6,000 units.
Inventory carrying costs are 30 percent per year.
Purchase cost per unit is $2.00.

Orders (1)	Order Size[a] (2)	Average Number of Units in Inventory[b] (3)	Inventory Carrying Costs[c] (4)	Order Costs[d] (5)	Total Costs[e] (6)
1	6,000	3,000	$1,800	$ 100	$1,900
2	3,000	1,500	900	200	1,100
3	2,000	1,000	600	300	900
4	1,500	750	450	400	850[f]
5	1,200	600	360	500	860
6	1,000	500	300	600	900
12	500	250	150	1,200	1,350

[a]6,000 units/number of orders from column (1).
[b]Column (2)/2.
[c]Amount in column (3) × $2 cost per unit × .30.
[d]$100 × number of orders from column (1).
[e]Amount in column (4) + amount in column (5).
[f]Lowest total cost. Optimal number of orders is four per year.

Estimating the Costs of Maintaining Inventory

Managers, industrial engineers, analysts, and others who attempt to derive optimal solutions to inventory management problems typically use costs the accounting system provides. An important but difficult task for management accountants is estimating inventory order costs and carrying costs. Keep in mind that only *differential* costs matter. For example, suppose that the firm uses one purchasing agent whether customers place one order or twelve orders per year, and the number of orders made does not affect the agent's salary. Assume that the opportunity cost of the agent's time equals zero. Therefore, the agent's salary does not differ, and it would not be part of the order costs.

Order Costs To estimate differential order costs, consider whether any salaries or wages differ because of the number of orders and whether there are opportunity costs of lost time. Production setups, in particular, usually result in lost time for production employees. Order costs should include differential costs of receiving and inspecting orders, costs of processing invoices from suppliers, and freight costs.

Example If freight costs are a constant amount (say $.10) per unit, they do not differ as the number of orders varies. If the firm pays freight charges per *shipment,* however (say, $50 per shipment), costs increase as the number of shipments increases. In this case, freight is a differential cost.

Carrying Costs Differential carrying costs include insurance, inventory taxes, the opportunity cost of funds invested in inventory, and other costs that differ with the number of units held in inventory. If the firm pays additional wages or leases additional warehouse space because inventory quantity increases, these costs are differential carrying costs. Carrying costs should not include an allocated portion of warehouse depreciation or rent if these costs do not vary with the number of units in inventory. Such depreciation and rent are not differential carrying costs.

Costs of Not Carrying Sufficient Inventory

Order costs and carrying costs are not the only inventory-related costs. Management must consider the costs of not carrying sufficient inventory. These costs include production shutdowns or customer ill will if inventory is unavailable for production or sale, as well as added freight and handling charges to expedite special handling. To manage inventory, management must consider this third category of cost.

Safety stocks are buffers against running out of inventory. Assume the optimal pattern of ordering and inventory depletion is as follows:

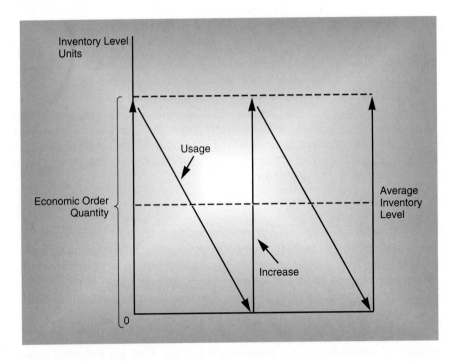

The model assumes replenishment just as inventory levels reach zero. Many events could result in a stock-out—a delivery truck delay, for example. The firm may have to stop production or sales to await the delivery of inventory. To prevent such a stock-out, management will provide a safety stock, as the following figure shows:

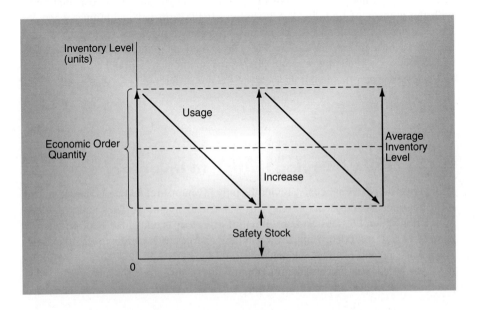

What is the optimal level of safety stock? The level depends on the trade-off between **stock-out costs** and holding costs. The higher the stock-out costs, the higher the safety stock of inventory. The higher the holding costs, the lower the safety stock of inventory.

Just-in-Time Inventory

Just-in-time inventory is a method of managing purchasing, production, and sales, where the firm attempts to produce each item only as needed for the next step in the production process, or where the firm attempts to time purchases so that items arrive just in time. This practice can reduce inventory levels virtually to zero.

Just-in-time inventory requires that production correct a process resulting in defective units immediately because the plan does not include accumulating defective units while they await reworking or scrapping. This turns out to be a major advantage of just-in-time and a major cost of carrying inventory. EOQ models that omit this cost of carrying inventory overstate the optimal level of inventory. Manufacturing managers find that eliminating inventories can prevent production workers from hiding production problems.

Innovations in Inventory Management and Flexible Manufacturing

Recent innovations in production could revolutionize both the production process and the accounting in manufacturing companies. The use of just-in-time inventory enables accountants to spend less time on inventory valuation for external reporting purposes and more time obtaining data for managerial decisions such as those discussed in this chapter.

Another innovation has the potential to reduce both setup costs and inventory levels. As this chapter discusses, reducing inventory levels means increasing the number of setups. Consider an automobile manufacturer that makes fenders for several models of cars. When it is time to change from left fenders to right fenders, or from fenders for cars to fenders for trucks, the production line stops while workers modify the machines to make the new fenders. Making only a few fenders of each type during a single production run requires many separate setups. Many companies are experimenting with flexible manufacturing methods that use computer-assisted machines to make these changeovers quickly, thereby reducing the cost of downtime in production.

The use of flexible manufacturing practices to reduce setup costs enhances companies' abilities to use just-in-time inventory. If setup costs are low, each production run can be small—perhaps just one unit. These innovations are likely to decrease the need for detailed record keeping for inventory valuation and to increase accountants' time spent on managerial activities.

Problem 9.3
for Self-Study

Inventory decisions. Compute the minimum total costs for JIT-not Incorporated, given the following facts:

Differential Costs per Order..	$41
Total Units Purchased per Year	40,000 Units
Differential Carrying Costs per Unit of Inventory.......................	$5.35 per Unit

Prepare a table like Exhibit 9.10, and find the minimum total costs of ordering and holding inventory. (Hint: Start with 50 annual orders.)

The solution to this self-study problem is at the end of the chapter on page 354.

Summary

This chapter considers *differential analysis:* that is, ascertaining *what* would differ and by *how much* if the firm takes an alternative action, rather than status quo. Differential analysis compares alternatives to the status quo, or present situation, as follows (where the terms have the same definitions as earlier):

	Alternative	−	Status Quo	=	Difference
Revenue.................................	P_1X_1	−	P_0X_0	=	ΔPX
Less Variable Costs	V_1X_1	−	V_0X_0	=	ΔVX
Total Contribution Margin	$(P_1 - V_1)X_1$	−	$(P_0 - V_0)X_0$	=	$\Delta(P - V)X$
Less Fixed Costs	F_1	−	F_0	=	ΔF
Operating Profit	π_1	−	π_0	=	$\Delta \pi$

We applied differential analysis to several short-run operating decisions, and we focused on identifying and measuring *differential costs*. These costs will differ because of an action. Identifying relevant costs is important for decision making. Costs that do not differ are not relevant for ascertaining the financial consequences of a contemplated action. Differential costs comprise differential cash flows.

Prices sometimes result from cost analysis as well as from market factors. Firms may enter into special cost-based contracts, such as those between government agencies and defense contractors. For any organization, prices must at least cover differential costs if the organization is to maximize its profit position. In the short run, this practice will result in a positive contribution toward covering fixed costs and generating a profit. In the long run, this practice will cover all costs, because both fixed and variable costs become differential in the long run.

In addition to pricing, differential analysis aids decisions to make or buy products, decisions to accept special orders, and decisions to add products or close parts of operations. Routine accounting reports rarely provide the relevant costs for these decisions. Special analysis of cost behavior is nearly always necessary. Choice of the optimal product mix when capacity limitations exist requires estimating not only differential cost (that is, variable cost) per unit but also differential cost per unit of scarce resource each product consumes.

Inventory management decisions require an estimate of differential order costs and differential inventory carrying costs. Part of the inventory management problem is finding the optimal trade-off between number of orders (or production runs) and the level of inventory so that total costs are minimized. In recent years, companies have emphasized reducing inventory levels using just-in-time and flexible manufacturing methods.

Solutions to Self-Study Problems

Suggested Solution to Problem 9.1 for Self-Study

a.

	Alternative	− Status Quo	= Difference
Price.	$ 1,900	$ 1,750	
Volume	4,500	5,000	
Revenue[a]	$8,550,000 −	$8,750,000	= $(200,000)
Variable Costs[b]	(3,150,000) −	(3,500,000) =	350,000
Contribution Margin	5,400,000 −	5,250,000 =	$ 150,000
Fixed Costs.	(1,617,500) −	(1,625,000) =	7,500
Operating Profit	$3,782,500 −	$3,625,000	= $ 157,500

[a]Number of units × sales price.

[b]Number of units × variable costs per unit. (Variable costs per unit = $700.)

Jackson Technologies should raise its prices to $1,900.

b.

	Alternative: Contract for 1,000 Units	− Status Quo: All Production In-House	= Difference
Revenue[a]	$8,750,000 −	$8,750,000	= $ 0
Variable Manufacturing Costs[b] . . .	(2,000,000) −	(2,500,000)	= 500,000
Variable Nonmanufacturing Costs[c]	(950,000) −	(1,000,000)	= 50,000
Contribution Margin	$5,800,000 −	$5,250,000	= $ 550,000
Fixed Manufacturing Costs[d]	(637,500) −	(750,000)	= 112,500
Fixed Nonmanufacturing Costs . .	(875,000) −	(875,000)	= 0
Payment to Contractor.	(X) −	0	= (X)
Operating Profit	$4,287,500 − X −	$3,625,000	= $662,500 − X

[a]Units × sales price.

[b]Units × variable costs per unit.

[c]Note the Alternative's variable cost is $200 for 4,000 units and $150 (25% lower) for 1,000 units.

[d]Fixed costs are 15% lower under the alternative.

Boilermakers would be willing to pay up to $662,500:

$$X = \$4,287,500 - \$3,625,000$$

$$= \$662,500 \text{ for } 1,000 \text{ Units,}$$

or $$\frac{\$662,500}{1,000} = \$662.50 \text{ per Unit.}$$

Suggested Solution to Problem 9.2 for Self-Study

Baltimore should not drop Product B in the short run because it continues to have a positive contribution margin.

Suggested Solution to Problem 9.3 for Self-Study

Annual Orders	Order Size[a]	Average Number of Units in Inventory	Inventory Carrying Costs[b]	Order Costs[c]	Total Costs
40	1,000	500	$2,675	$1,640	$4,315
•					
•					
•					
50	800	400	2,140	2,050	4,190
51	784	392	2,097	2,091	4,188
52	769	384.5	2,057	2,132	4,189
53	755	377.5	2,020	2,173	4,193
•					
•					
•					
60	667	333.5	1,784	2,460	4,244

[a]40,000 units/number of orders.
[b]Average units in inventory × $5.35.
[c]Number of orders × $41.

Minimum total costs are $4,188 at 51 orders per year.

Appendix 9.1: Linear Programming

Factors such as factory capacity, personnel time, floor space, and so forth constrain most managerial decisions. If the firm has enough time before implementing a decision, it can relax constraints by increasing capacity. In the short run, however, decision makers face a constrained amount of resources available to them. **Linear programming** solves problems of this type. We refer to linear programming as a *constrained optimization* technique, because it solves for the optimal use of scarce (that is, constrained) resources.

Two simple examples demonstrate how linear programming works. We solve these using graphs and simple algebra. More complex problems require some systematic procedure like the *simplex method,* described in textbooks on operations research and quantitative methods. Most linear programming problem solutions result from computer implementation of the simplex method or variations of it.

Profit Maximization

Example Moline Company produces two products, 1 and 2. The contribution margins per unit of the two products follow:

Product	Contribution Margin per Unit
1	$3
2	4

Fixed costs are the same regardless of the combination of products 1 and 2 the firm produces; therefore, the firm wants to maximize the total contribution per period of these two products.

Both products have a positive contribution margin. If Moline Company faced no constraints, it should make (and sell) both products, eliminating our problem. When production of a unit of each product consumes the same quantity of a scarce resource, managers solve the problem by making and selling only the highest contribution item. For our example, if Product 1 and Product 2 each require one hour of machine time, and the quantity of machine hours is finite, Moline would choose Product 2, all else being equal. Products usually do not consume equal amounts of scarce resources, however. So the problem is to find the optimal mix of products given the amount of a scarce resource each product consumes.

Moline Company uses two scarce resources to make the two products, labor time and machine time. Twenty-four hours of labor time and 20 hours of machine time are available each day. The amount of time required to make each product follows:

	Product	
	1	**2**
Labor Time	1 Hour per Unit	2 Hours per Unit
Machine Time................................	1 Hour per Unit	1 Hour per Unit

This problem formulation follows. (X_1 and X_2 refer to the quantity of Products 1 and 2 produced and sold.)

(1) Maximize: $\$3X_1 + \$4X_2 = $ Total Contribution
(2) Subject to: $X_1 + 2X_2 \leq 24$ Labor Hours
(3) $X_1 + X_2 \leq 20$ Machine Hours.

The first line, the **objective function,** states the objective of our problem as a linear equation. Here the objective is to maximize total contribution where each unit of Product 1 contributes $3 and each unit of Product 2 contributes $4. The lines that follow specify the parameters of the constraints. Line (2) is the labor time constraint, which states that each unit of Product 1 requires 1 labor hour and each unit of Product 2 requires 2 labor hours. Total labor hours cannot exceed 24 per period (that is, one day). Line (3) is the machine time constraint, which states that Product 1 and Product 2 each use 1 machine hour per unit, and total machine hours cannot exceed 20.

Exhibit 9.11 graphs the constraints. The shaded area shows feasible production; production does not use up more scarce resources than are available. The lowercase letters show the *corner points*. We find the optimal solution by deriving the total contribution margin at each point, using the following steps.

Step 1 Find the production level of Product 1 and Product 2 at each point. Points a and c are straightforward. At a, $X_1 = 20$ and $X_2 = 0$; at c, $X_2 = 12$ and $X_1 = 0$. Point b requires solving for two unknowns using the two constraint formulas:

$$\text{Labor Time:} \quad X_1 + 2X_2 = 24$$

$$\text{Machine Time:} \quad X_1 + X_2 = 20.$$

Exhibit 9.11

Linear Programming, Graphic Solution
Comparison of Corner and Noncorner Points

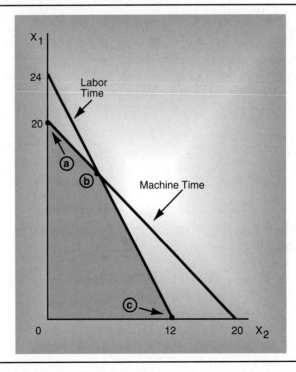

Setting these two equations equal, we have

$$X_1 = 24 - 2X_2$$

$$X_1 = 20 - X_2,$$

$$24 - 2X_2 = 20 - X_2$$

$$4 = X_2.$$

If $X_2 = 4$, then

$$X_1 = 20 - X_2$$

$$= 20 - 4$$

$$= 16.$$

At point b, Moline produces 16 units of Product 1 and 4 units of Product 2.

Step 2 Find the total contribution margin at each point. (Recall that the unit contribution margins of products 1 and 2 are $3 and $4.) Exhibit 9.12 shows the solution. It is optimal to produce at point b, where $X_1 = 16$ and $X_2 = 4$.

Why must the optimal solution be at a corner? If production moves away from the corner at point b in any feasible direction, total contribution will be lower. Exhibit 9.13 shows a movement away from point b in four feasible directions. Exhibit 9.14 compares contributions at those noncorner points with the contribution at corner point b. Although these examples show intuitively that the contribution margin declines away from the corner point, we can prove mathematically our assertion that the optimal solution always lies on a corner point.

Sensitivity Analysis

The contribution margins and costs in the objective functions are estimates, subject to error. Decision makers frequently need to know how much the estimates can change before the decision changes.

To demonstrate our point, we use our earlier profit-maximization problem for Moline Company, which we formulated as appears on the following page:

Exhibit 9.12

Optimal Product Mix

| | Production | | Contribution | | |
Point	X_1	X_2	1	2	Total
a	20	0	$60	$ 0	$60
b	16	4	48	16	64
c	0	12	0	48	48

Exhibit 9.13

Linear Programming, Graphic Solution
Comparison of Corner and Noncorner Points

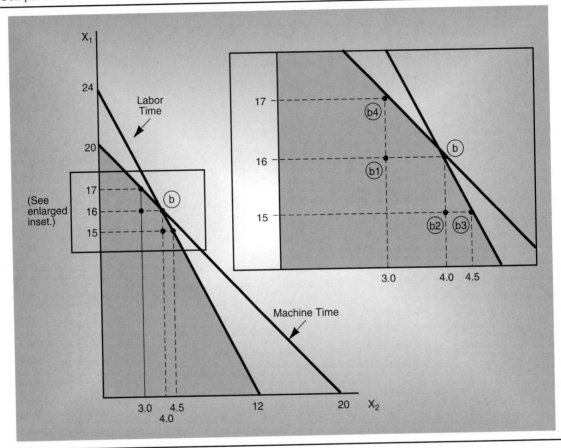

Maximize: $\$3X_1 + \$4X_2 =$ Total Contribution

Subject to: $X_1 + 2X_2 \leq 24$ Labor Hours

$X_1 + X_2 \leq 20$ Machine Hours.

Suppose that the variable cost estimate for Product 2 was $.50 per unit too low, so Product 2's unit contribution margin should have been $3.50 instead of $4.00. What effect would this have? We have calculated the new contributions in Exhibit 9.15. If you compare Exhibit 9.15 with Exhibit 9.12, you will see that the contribution for Product 2 changes; thus the total contribution changes. The optimal decision to produce 16 units of Product 1 and 4 units of Product 2 does not change, however. In spite of the change in costs and thus in contributions, the *decision* does not change. In this example, the unit contribution margin of Product 2 would have to drop to less

Exhibit 9.14

Comparison of Corner Point with Noncorner Points

	Production		Contribution		
Point	X_1	X_2	1	2	Total
b	16	4	$48	$16	$64
b1	16	3	48	12	60
b2	15	4	45	16	61
b3[a]	15	4.5	45	18	63
b4[b]	17	3	51	12	63

[a]Let $X_1 = 15$ and find X_2 as follows:

$$X_1 = 24 - 2X_2$$
$$15 = 24 - 2X_2$$
$$2X_2 = 9$$
$$X_2 = 4.5.$$

[b]Let $X_2 = 3$ and find X_1 as follows:

$$X_1 = 20 - X_2$$
$$= 20 - 3$$
$$= 17.$$

than $3 per unit before the optimal decision would change, assuming that all other things remained constant.

Most linear programming computer programs can provide this type of sensitivity analysis. With it, managers and accountants can ascertain how much a cost or contribution margin can change before the optimal decision will change.

Opportunity Costs

Any constrained resource has an opportunity cost, which is the profit forgone by not having an additional unit of the resource. For example, suppose that Moline Company in our previous example could obtain one additional hour of machine time.

Exhibit 9.15

Optimal Product Mix: Revised Cost Estimates

	Production		Contribution		
Point[a]	X_1	X_2	1	2	Total
a	20	0	$60	$ 0	$60
b	16	4	48	14[b]	62
c	0	12	0	42	42

[a]The graph in Exhibit 9.11 presents these points.

[b]Four units × $3.50 per unit.

With one more hour of machine time, the machine constraint would move out, as shown in Exhibit 9.16. We find the new production level at point b as follows:

$$X_1 = 24 - 2X_2$$

$$X_1 = 21 - X_2$$

$$24 - 2X_2 = 21 - X_2$$

$$X_2 = 3$$

$$X_1 = 18.$$

The new total contribution at point b would be $3(18) + $4(3) = $66, compared to $64 when machine time was constrained to 20 hours per day, as shown for point b in

Exhibit 9.16

Linear Programming, Graphic Solution
Increase in Machine Time from 20 to 21 Hours

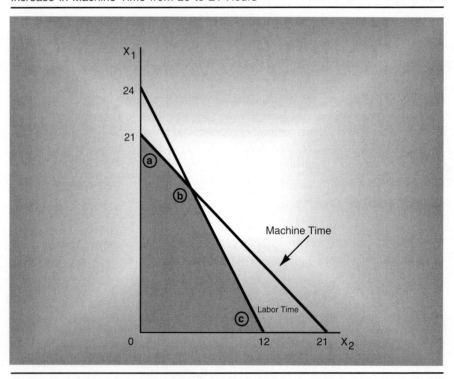

$^a X_1 = 24 - 2X_2$ and $X_1 = 21 - X_2$, so

$$24 - 2X_2 = 21 - X_2$$
$$X_2 = 3$$
$$X_1 = 21 - X_2$$
$$= 21 - 3$$
$$= 18.$$

Exhibit 9.14. Thus the opportunity cost of not having an extra hour of machine time is \$2 (= \$66 − \$64).

Linear programming computer programs regularly provide opportunity costs, called **shadow prices.** Opportunity cost data indicate the benefits of acquiring more units of a scarce resource. For example, if Moline Company could rent one more machine hour for less than \$2 per hour, the company would profit by doing so, all other things being equal.

Appendix 9.2: Economic Order Quantity Model

In our discussion of inventory management, we derived the optimal number of orders or production runs by trial and error. We also could derive the optimal number of orders or production runs per period from the following formula:

$$N = \frac{D}{Q},$$

where

$$Q = \sqrt{\frac{2K_0D}{K_c}}$$

N = the optimal number of orders or production runs for the period

Q = the economic order quantity, or the optimal number of items in an order or production run

D = the period demand in units

K_0 = the order or setup cost

K_c = the cost of carrying one unit in inventory for the period.

The formula $Q = \sqrt{2K_0D/K_c}$ results from using calculus to minimize total cost with respect to Q. The total cost (TC) formula is

$$\frac{\text{Total Cost}}{\text{per Period}} = \frac{\text{Carrying Costs}}{\text{per Period}} + \frac{\text{Order Costs}}{\text{per Period}}$$

$$TC = K_c\frac{Q}{2} + K_0\frac{D}{Q}.$$

Take the first derivative of TC with respect to Q, set it equal to zero, and solve for Q:

$$\frac{dTC}{dQ} = \frac{d}{dQ}\left(K_c\frac{Q}{2} + K_0\frac{D}{Q}\right)$$

$$= \frac{K_c}{2} - \frac{K_0D}{Q^2} = 0.$$

$$Q = \sqrt{\frac{2K_0D}{K_c}}.$$

Example The following facts for the California Merchandising example appeared in the text:

$$D = \text{period demand} = 6,000 \text{ units per year}$$

$$K_0 = \text{order cost} = \$100 \text{ per order}$$

$$K_c = \text{carrying cost} = 30 \text{ percent of the cost of inventory or}$$
$$\$.60 \text{ per unit } (\$.60 = 30 \text{ percent} \times \$2.00 \text{ per unit}).$$

Solving for Q (the optimal number of items in an order), we have

$$Q = \sqrt{\frac{2K_0 D}{K_c}}$$

$$= \sqrt{\frac{2 \times \$100 \times 6,000 \text{ Units}}{\$.60}}$$

$$= \sqrt{2,000,000 \text{ Units}}$$

$$= 1,414 \text{ Units per Order.}$$

$$N = \frac{D}{Q}$$

$$= \frac{6,000 \text{ Units}}{1,414 \text{ Units}}$$

$$= 4.2 \text{ Orders per Year.}$$

From these equations, we derived the optimal order size, 1,414 units, and the optimal number of orders per year, 4.2. This result is approximately the same one we derived by trial and error earlier. Using the economic order quantity model is usually more efficient for finding the least costly size and number of orders (or productions).

This is known as the **economic order quantity (EOQ) model.** Textbooks on operations research and quantitative methods present many variations and applications of this model.

Key Terms and Concepts

Differential analysis	Economic order quantity (EOQ)
Status quo	Safety stocks
Relevant cost analysis	Stock-out costs
Cash flows	Just-in-time inventory
Economic depreciation	Linear programming
Differential cost	Objective function
Make-or-buy decision	Shadow prices
Setup or order costs	Economic order quantity (EOQ)
Carrying costs	model

Questions, Exercises, Problems, and Cases

Questions

1. Review the meaning of the terms and concepts given above in Key Terms and Concepts.
2. "Users of differential analysis should use revenues and expenses of a particular period rather than cash flows, because they better represent a firm's performance during a given period." Comment.
3. "A proper evaluation of any project using differential analysis requires the consideration of all relevant costs—past, present, and future." Comment.
4. Assume that there are no income taxes. How should each of the following costs enter into a decision to replace old equipment?
    a. Book value of old equipment.
    b. Disposal value of old equipment.
    c. Cost of new equipment.
5. How significant are opportunity costs and economic depreciation in differential analysis? When will you use or not use these costs?
6. State and explain the shortcomings of using a cost-based approach to product pricing.
7. What is a common criticism made against the differential approach to product pricing based on variable costs? How can you refute this criticism?
8. Refer to the Managerial Application about the "Differential Analysis for Superstars." What analysis do you think a sports team uses before signing a player to estimate the player's economic value to the team?
9. You are asked to supply profit figures for a linear program your firm wishes to run. Do you give the gross margin per unit or contribution margin per unit? Why?
10. Inventory management problems usually involve two types of opposing costs. Describe these costs and sketch a graph showing how they change as order size changes. (Put order size on the horizontal axis.)

Exercises

Solutions to even-numbered exercises are at the end of this chapter on page 377.

11. **Special order.** Waterwear Products has the capacity to produce 4,000 swimsuits (units) per year. Its predicted operations for the year follow:

Sales (3,000 units @ $70)	$210,000
Manufacturing Costs:	
Variable	$50 per Unit
Fixed.	$22,000
Marketing and Administrative Costs:	
Variable	$3 per Unit
Fixed.	$6,000

Assume Lands' End is willing to purchase 300 swimsuits at a price of $55 each. Should Waterwear accept the special order for 300 units at a selling price of $55? Variable marketing and administrative costs for this order will be zero. Regular sales and fixed costs will not change. How will the decision affect the company's operating profit?

12. **Product choice.** Yuppie Enterprises renovated an old train station into warehouse space, office space, restaurants, and specialty shops. If used all for warehouse space, the estimated revenue and variable costs per year to Yuppie would be $960,000 and $40,000, respectively. If used all for office space, the revenue and variable cost per year would be $982,800 and $70,000. If used all for restaurants and specialty shops, the revenue and variable costs would be $1,101,100 and $95,000, respectively. Fixed costs per year would be $600,000 regardless of the alternative chosen.

To which use should Yuppie Enterprises put the old train station?

13. **Special order.** Anticipating unusually high sales for May, Mr. Twinkles, a breakfast cereal company, plans to produce 40,000 pounds of cereal, using all available capacity. Mr. Twinkles anticipates costs for May as follows:

Unit Manufacturing Costs per Pound:		
Variable Direct Materials Cost...............................	$0.14	
Variable Labor	0.04	
Variable Overhead...	0.03	
Fixed Overhead	0.11	
Total Manufacturing Costs per Pound......................		$0.32
Unit Marketing Costs per Pound:		
Variable	$0.03	
Fixed..	0.22	
Total Marketing Costs per Pound..........................		0.25
Total Unit Costs per Pound		$0.57
Selling Price per Pound		$0.84

On April 30, Mr. Twinkles received a contract offer from Feed the Hungry (FTH), a government agency, to supply 10,000 pounds of cereal for delivery by May 31. The FTH offer would reimburse Mr. Twinkles' share of both variable and fixed manufacturing costs (that is, $.32 per pound) plus a fixed fee of $4,000. Variable marketing costs would be zero for this order. None of the fixed costs would be affected by this order. Mr. Twinkles would lose 10,000 pounds of sales to regular customers in May, but this order would not affect sales in any subsequent months.

Prepare a differential analysis comparing the status quo for May with the alternative case in which Mr. Twinkles accepts the special order from the FTH. Write a brief report to Mr. Twinkles' management explaining why the company should or should not accept the special order.

14. **Make or buy.** Ol'Salt Enterprises produces 1,000 sailboats per year. Although the company currently buys sails for the sailboats (one set of sails per boat), it

is considering making sails in some space that it does not presently use. The company purchases each set of sails for $300. It could make the sails for variable costs of $250 per set, plus it would allocate $200,000 of fixed costs per year to the sail-making operation. However, this $200,000 is not a differential cost of making sails; it is part of the costs the company already incurs that it would allocate away from sailboat manufacture to sail making.

a. Prepare a differential analysis to show whether Ol'Salt Enterprises should make or buy the sails. What do you recommend to management? Explain why the $200,000 fixed costs allocated to sail making is or is not relevant to the decision.

b. If Ol'Salt buys the sails, then it would have unused factory space. Suppose Ol'Salt received an opportunity to rent out this unused factory space for $80,000 per year. Would that affect your recommendation in part **a**?

15. **Dropping a product line.** Coos Bay Wood Products currently operates at 75 percent capacity. Worried about the company's performance, the general manager segmented the company's income statement product by product and obtained the following picture:

	Product		
	A	**B**	**C**
Sales.....................................	$32,000	$42,000	$51,000
Less Variable Costs	(22,000)	(38,000)	(40,000)
Total Contribution Margin	$10,000	$ 4,000	$11,000
Less Fixed Costs	(4,000)	(5,000)	(7,000)
Net Operating Profit (Loss)	$ 6,000	$ (1,000)	$ 4,000

Should Coos Bay Wood Products drop Product B, if that would eliminate Product B's sales and variable costs and reduce the company's total fixed costs by $2,000?

16. **Dropping a product line.** Timeless Products, a clock manufacturer, operates at capacity. Constrained by machine time, the company decides to drop the most unprofitable of its three product lines. The accounting department came up with the following data from last year's operations.

	Manual	**Electric**	**Quartz**
Machine Time per Unit	0.4 Hour	2.5 Hours	5.0 Hours
Selling Price per Unit	$20	$30	$50
Less Variable Costs per Unit.............	(10)	(14)	(28)
Contribution Margin	$10	$16	$22

Which line should Timeless Products drop? (Hint: Compute the contribution per machine hour because machine time is the constraint.)

17. **Product choice using linear programming** (Appendix 9.1). Hernandez Corporation manufactures two products whose contribution margins follow:

Product	Contribution Margin
A	$10
B	13

Each month Hernandez Corporation has only 12,000 hours of machine time and 14,400 hours of labor time available. The amount of time required to make Products A and B follows:

	Product A	Product B
Labor Time	4 Hours per Unit	8 Hours per Unit
Machine Time	6 Hours per Unit	4 Hours per Unit

The firm sells all units produced. Management wants to know the number of units of each product the company should make.

Set up the problem in the linear programming format and solve for the optimal production mix.

 18. **Economic order quantity.** (Appendix 9.2). The Magee Foundry regularly uses 2,500 axles per year. It can purchase axles for $100 each. Ordering costs are $10 per order, and the holding costs of items in inventory are 20 percent of cost per year. Prepare an analysis for management that answers the following questions.

What is the economic order quantity and annual ordering costs, assuming that only lots of 1,000 items are available?

19. **Economic order quantity.** (Appendix 9.2). The purchasing agent responsible for ordering gortex gloves estimates that Arctic Handwear sells 5,000 pairs of gortex gloves evenly throughout each year, that each order costs $24 to place, and that holding a pair of gloves in inventory for a year costs $.24 per pair.
   a. How many pairs of gloves should Arctic Handwear request in each order?
   b. How many times per year should Arctic Handwear order gortex gloves?

20. **Product mix decisions** (Appendix 9.1; adapted from CPA exam). The Random Company manufactures two products, Zeta and Beta. Each product must pass through two processing operations. All materials enter production at the start of Process No. 1. Random has no work-in-process inventories. Random may produce either one product exclusively or various combinations of both products, subject to the following constraints:

	Process No. 1	Process No. 2	Contribution Margin per Unit
Hours Required to Produce One Unit of:			
Zeta...............................	1	1	$4.25
Beta	2	3	5.25
Total Capacity per Day in Hours	1,000	1,275	

A shortage of technical labor has limited Beta production to 400 units per day. The firm has *no* constraints on the production of Zeta other than the hour constraints in the preceding schedule. Assume that all relations between capacity and production are linear.

What is the total contribution from the optimal product mix?

21. **Product mix decisions** (Appendix 9.1). Use the information for the Random Company in Exercise 20 and assume that the present Process No. 1 already costs the company $1.65 for each unit of Zeta. What is the maximum price that Random would be willing to pay for additional Process No. 1 time to produce one more unit of Zeta?

22. **Finding most profitable price-quantity combination.** The Bulls Company is introducing a new product called Scottie Dolls and must decide what price should be set. An estimated demand schedule for the product follows:

Price	Quantity Demanded (in units)
$10	40,000
12	36,000
14	28,000
16	24,000
18	18,000
20	15,000

Estimated costs follow:

Variable Manufacturing Costs	$4 per Unit
Fixed Manufacturing Costs	$40,000 per Year
Variable Selling and Administrative Costs	$2 per Unit
Fixed Selling and Administrative Costs	$10,000 per Year

a. Prepare a schedule showing the total revenue, total cost, and total profit or loss for each selling price.

b. Which price provides the most profits?

23. **Dropping a product line.** Andersen & Waterhouse is a public accounting firm that offers three types of services; audit, tax, and consulting. The firm is concerned about the profitability of its consulting business and is considering dropping that line. If the consulting business is dropped, more tax work would be done. If consulting is dropped, all consulting revenues would be lost, all of the variable costs associated with consulting would be saved, and 50 percent of the fixed costs associated with consulting would be saved. If consulting is dropped, tax revenues are expected to increase by 40 percent, the variable costs associated with tax would increase by 40 percent, and the fixed costs associated with tax would increase by 20 percent. Revenues and costs associated with auditing would not be affected.

Segmented income statements for these three product lines appear as follows:

	Product		
	Consulting	**Tax**	**Auditing**
Revenue.....................	$300,000	$400,000	$500,000
Variable costs	250,000	300,000	350,000
Contribution margin	50,000	100,000	150,000
Fixed costs	50,000	60,000	80,000
Operating profit.............	$ –0–	$ 40,000	$ 70,000

Prepare a report to the management of Andersen & Waterhouse advising whether to drop consulting and increase tax. Assume tax would not be increased if consulting were kept. Include a differential analysis like that in the bottom part of Exhibit 9.6.

Problems

24. **Special order.** Southeastern Furniture Company has a capacity of 100,000 tables per year. The company is currently producing and selling 80,000 tables per year at a selling price of $400 per table. The cost of producing and selling one table at the 80,000-unit level of activity follows:

Variable Manufacturing Costs	$160
Fixed Manufacturing Costs	40
Variable Selling and Administrative Costs	80
Fixed Selling and Administrative Costs..............................	20
Total Costs	$300

The company has received a special order for 10,000 tables at a price of $260. Because it need not pay sales commission on the special order, the variable selling and administrative costs would be only $50 per table. The special order would have no effect on total fixed costs. The company has rejected the offer based on the following computations:

Selling Price per Table	$260
Variable Manufacturing Costs	(160)
Fixed Manufacturing Costs	(40)
Variable Selling and Administrative Costs	(50)
Fixed Selling and Administrative Costs..............................	(20)
Net Loss per Table	$ (10)

Management is reviewing its decision and wants your advice. Should Southeastern have accepted the special order? Show your computations.

25. **Special order.** Gates Electronics Company produces precision instruments for airplanes. It currently operates at capacity. It has received an invitation to bid

on a government contract for 1,000 specially designed precision instruments. The company has estimated its costs for the contract to be as follows:

Variable Manufacturing Costs	$40,000
Allocated Fixed Manufacturing Costs (not affected by the order)	15,000
Special Design and Production Setup Costs	10,000
Shipping Costs	5,000
Special Administrative Costs	5,000
Total Costs	$75,000
Cost per Precision Instrument ($75,000/1,000)	$ 75

If Gates accepts the government contract, it will have to forgo regular sales of 1,000 units. These 1,000 units would have a selling price of $100 each and variable costs of $60 each. The company's total fixed costs would not be affected by accepting the government contract offer. Management has asked your advice in answering the following questions:

a. What is the lowest per-unit price that Gates can bid on this contract without sacrificing profits?

b. Gates has learned that it will receive the contract if it bids $90 or less per unit. What action should Gates take?

26. **Dropping a machine from service.** The Central States Grain Company has four large milling machines of approximately equal capacity. Each was run at close to its full capacity during Year 5. Each machine is depreciated separately using an accelerated method. Data for each machine follow (X0 refers to Year 0):

	No. 1	No. 2	No. 3	No. 4
Date Acquired	1/1/X0	1/1/X1	1/1/X3	1/1/X4
Cost	$50,000	$60,000	$75,000	$80,000
Operating Costs, Year 5:				
Labor	$20,000	$18,000	$22,000	$21,500
Materials	5,000	6,000	4,500	3,000
Maintenance	1,000	1,000	700	500
Depreciation (a fixed cost)	3,000	5,000	11,000	15,000
Total	$29,000	$30,000	$38,200	$40,000

Central States expects activity in Year 6 to be less than in Year 5, so it will drop one machine from service. Management proposes that Central States drop No. 4 on the grounds that it has the highest operating costs. Do you agree or disagree with this proposal? Why or why not?

27. **Make or buy.** Austin Computers produces computer boards of which part no. 301 is a subassembly. Austin Computers currently produces part no. 301 in its own shop. The Silicon Chips Company offers to supply it at a cost of $400 per 500 units. An analysis of the costs of Austin Computers' producing part no. 301 reveals the following information:

	Cost per 500 Units
Direct (Variable) Material	$130
Direct (Variable) Labor	180
Other Variable Costs..	50
Fixed Costsᵃ	100
Total	$460

ᵃFixed overhead comprises largely depreciation on general-purpose equipment and factory buildings.

Management of Austin Computers needs your advice in answering the following questions:

a. Should Austin Computers accept the offer from Silicon Chips if Austin's plant is operating well below capacity?

b. Should the offer be accepted if Silicon Chips reduces the price to $340 per 500 units?

c. If Austin can find other profitable uses for the facilities it now uses in turning out part no. 301, what maximum purchase price should Austin pay for part no. 301?

28. **Accepting or rejecting an order.** The Milky Way Company produces a precision part for use in rockets, missiles, and a variety of other products. In the first half of the year, it operated at 80 percent of capacity and produced 160,000 units. Manufacturing costs in that period follow:

Direct Material	$430,000
Direct Labor	770,000
Other Variable Costs...	150,000
Fixed Costs..	450,000

The parts were all sold at a price of $14 per unit.

The AMF Aircraft Company offers to buy as many units of the part as the Milky Way Company can supply at a price of $10 per unit. Milky Way estimates that to increase operations to a 100-percent capacity level would increase office and administrative costs by $50,000 for a 6-month period. Management believes that sales to AMF at this price will not affect the company's ability to reach the previous level of sales at the regular price. There are no legal restrictions on selling at the lower price.

Present a schedule indicating whether Milky Way should accept the AMF offer.

29. **Cost estimate for bidding: consulting firm.** Clear Computer Consultants (CCC) operates a computer consulting firm. It has just received an inquiry from a prospective client about its prices for educational seminars for the prospective client's employees. The prospective client wants bids for three alternative activity levels: (1) one seminar with 20 participants, (2) four seminars with 20 participants each (80 participants total), or (3) eight seminars with 150 participants in total. The consulting firm's accountants have provided the following differential cost estimates:

Startup Costs for the Entire Job	$ 500
Materials Costs per Participant (brochures, handouts, etc.)	50
Differential Direct Labor Costs:	
One Seminar	900
Four Seminars	3,600
Eight Seminars	6,750

In addition to the differential costs listed above, CCC allocates fixed costs to jobs on a direct-labor-cost basis, at a rate of 80 percent of direct labor costs (excluding setup costs). For example, if direct labor costs are $100, CCC would also charge the job $80 for fixed costs. CCC seeks to make a profit of 10 percent of the bid price for each job. For this purpose, profit is revenue minus all costs assigned to the job, including allocated fixed costs. CCC has enough excess capacity to handle this job with ease.

a. Assume CCC bases its bid on the average total cost, including fixed costs allocated to the job, plus the 10-percent profit margin. What should CCC bid for each of the three levels of activity?

b. Compute the differential cost (including startup cost) and the contribution to profit for each of the three levels of activity.

c. Assume the prospective client gives three options. It is willing to accept either of CCC's bids for the one-seminar or four-seminar activity levels, but the prospective client will pay only 90 percent of the bid price for the eight-seminar package. CCC's president responds, "Taking the order for 10 percent below our bid would wipe out our profit! Let's take the four-seminar option; we make the most profit on it." Do you agree? What would be the contribution to profit for each of the three options? The differential cost?

30. **Differential cost analysis in a service organization** (contributed by Robert H. Colson). Top-Dogs Search, Inc., is a "head-hunting" firm that provides information about candidates for executive and cabinet-level positions. Major customers include corporations and the federal government.

The cost per billable hour of service at the company's normal volume of 8,000 billable hours per month appears below. (A billable hour is one hour billed to a client.)

TOP-DOGS SEARCH, INC.
Cost per Billable Hour of Service

Average Cost per Hour Billed to Client:		
Variable Labor—Consultants	$100	
Variable Overhead, Including Supplies and Clerical Support	20	
Fixed Overhead, Including Allowance for Unbilled Hours	80	
		$200
Marketing and Administrative Costs per Billable Hour (all fixed)		50
Total Hourly Cost		$250

Treat each question independently. Unless given otherwise, the regular fee per hour is $300.

a. How many hours must the firm bill per month to break even?

b. Market research estimates that a fee increase to $400 per hour would decrease monthly volume to 6,000 hours. The accounting department estimates that fixed costs would be $1,040,000 while variable costs per hour would remain unchanged. How would a fee increase affect profits?

c. Top-Dogs Search is operating at its normal volume. It has received a special request from a cabinet official to provide investigative services on a special-order basis. Because of the long-term nature of the contract (4 months) and the magnitude (1,000 hours per month), the customer believes a fee reduction is in order. Top-Dogs Search has a capacity limitation of 8,500 hours per month. Fixed costs will not change if the firm accepts the special order. What is the lowest fee Top-Dogs Search would be willing to charge?

31. **Comprehensive differential costing problem.** Hospital Supply, Inc., produces hydraulic hoists used by hospitals to move bedridden patients. The costs of manufacturing and marketing hydraulic hoists at the company's normal volume of 3,000 units per month follow:

HOSPITAL SUPPLY
Costs per Unit for Hydraulic Hoists

Unit Manufacturing Costs:		
Variable Materials	$100	
Variable Labor	150	
Variable Overhead	50	
Fixed Overhead	200	
Total Unit Manufacturing Costs		$500
Unit Nonmanufacturing Costs:		
Variable	$100	
Fixed	100	
Total Unit Nonmanufacturing Costs		200
Total Unit Costs		$700

Unless otherwise stated, assume that the situations described in the questions are not connected; treat each independently. Unless otherwise stated, assume a regular selling price of $1,000 per unit.

a. What is the breakeven volume in units? In sales dollars?

b. Market research estimates that volume could be increased to 3,500 units which is well within hoist production capacity limitations, if the firm reduces the price from $1,000 to $800 per unit. Total fixed costs will not change. Do you recommend that the firm take this action? What would be the impact on monthly sales, costs, and income?

c. On March 1, Hospital Supply receives a contract offer from the federal government to supply 500 units to Veterans Administration hospitals for delivery by March 31. Because of an unusually large number of rush orders from its regular customers, Hospital Supply plans to produce 4,000 units during March, which will use all available capacity. If it accepts the government order, it will lose to a competitor 500 units normally sold to regular customers.

The contract offered by the government would reimburse the government's share of March manufacturing costs, plus pay a fixed fee (profit) of $50,000. The offer does not specify how to measure "manufacturing costs." The firm would not incur any variable or fixed marketing costs on the government's units. What impact would accepting the government contract have on March income?

d. Hospital Supply can enter a foreign market in which price competition is keen. An attraction of the foreign market is that demand there is greatest when demand in the domestic market is low; thus the firm could use idle production facilities without affecting domestic business.

The firm received an order for 1,000 units at a below-normal price in this market. Shipping costs for this order will be $100 per unit; total costs of obtaining the contract (marketing costs) will be $10,000. This order will not affect domestic business. What is the minimum unit price Hospital Supply should consider for this order of 1,000 units?

e. An inventory of 230 units of an obsolete model of the hoist remains in the stockroom. If the firm does not sell these units through regular channels at reduced prices, the inventory will soon be worthless. What is the minimum acceptable price for selling these units?

32. **Make or buy with opportunity costs.** Refer to Hospital Supply in the previous problem.

a. Hospital Supply receives a proposal from an outside contractor who will make and ship 1,000 hydraulic hoist units per month directly to Hospital Supply's customers as Hospital Supply's sales force receives orders. The proposal would not affect Hospital Supply's fixed marketing costs, but its variable marketing costs would decline by 20 percent for these 1,000 units produced by the contractor. Hospital Supply's plant would operate at two-thirds of its normal level. Total fixed manufacturing costs would decline by 30 percent.

What in-house unit cost should the firm use to compare with the quotation received from the supplier? Should the firm accept the proposal for a price (that is, payment to the contractor) of $600 per unit?

b. Assume the same facts as in part a, except that the firm will use idle facilities to produce 800 modified hydraulic hoists per month for hospital operating rooms. It can sell these modified hoists for $1,200 each, while the costs of production would be $700 per unit variable manufacturing cost. Variable marketing costs would be $100 per unit. Fixed marketing and manufacturing costs will not change whether the firm manufactures the original 3,000 regular hoists or the mix of 2,000 regular hoists plus 800 modified hoists. What is the maximum purchase price per unit that Hospital Supply should be willing to pay the outside contractor? Should it accept the proposal for a price of $600 per unit?

33. **Product mix decision.** The Vancil Company has one machine on which it can produce either of two products, Y or Z. Sales demand for both products is such that the machine could operate at full capacity on either of the products and Vancil can sell all output at current prices. Product Y requires 2 hours of machine time per unit of output and Product Z requires 4 hours of machine time per unit of output. Vancil charges machine time (depreciation) to products at the rate of $8 per hour.

The following information summarizes the per-unit cash inflows and costs of Products Y and Z.

| | Per Unit | |
	Product Y	Product Z
Selling Price	$60	$110
Materials	$ 9	$ 11
Labor	3	5
Machine Depreciation[a]	16	32
Allocated Portion of Fixed Factory Costs[b]	12	20
Total Cost of Unit Sold	$40	$ 68
Gross Margin per Unit	$20	$ 42

[a]This item under these circumstances could be referred to as "variable factory costs."

[b]Allocated in proportion to (direct) labor costs.

Selling costs are the same whether Vancil produces Product Y or Z, or both. You may ignore them. Should Vancil Company plan to produce Product Y, Product Z, or some mixture of both? Why?

Cases

34. **Department closing.** Prior to last year, Kahn Wholesalers Company had not kept departmental income statements. To achieve better management control, the company decided to install department-by-department accounts. At the end of last year, the new accounts showed that although the business as a whole was profitable, the Dry Goods Department had shown a substantial loss. The income statement for the Dry Goods Department, shown here, reports on operations for last year.

KAHN WHOLESALERS COMPANY
Dry Goods Department
Partial Income Statement

Sales...	$500,000
Cost of Goods Sold............................	(375,000)
Gross Margin	$125,000

(continued)

Costs:

Payroll, Direct Labor, and Supervision	$(33,000)
Commissions of Sales Staff[a]	(30,000)
Rent[b]	(26,000)
State Taxes[c]	(3,000)
Insurance on Inventory	(4,000)
Depreciation[d]	(7,000)
Administration and General Office[e]	(22,000)
Interest for Inventory Carrying Costs[f]	(5,000)
Total Costs	(130,000)
Loss before Allocation of Income Taxes..............	$ (5,000)

Additional computations:

[a]All sales staff are compensated on straight commission, at a uniform 6 percent of all sales.

[b]Rent is charged to departments on a square-foot basis. The company rents an entire building, and the Dry Goods Department occupies 15 percent of the building.

[c]Assessed annually on the basis of average inventory on hand each month.

[d]Eight and one-half percent of cost of departmental equipment.

[e]Allocated on basis of departmental sales as a fraction of total company sales.

[f]Based on average inventory quantity multiplied by the company's borrowing rate for 3-month loans.

Analysis of these results has led management to suggest that it close the Dry Goods Department. Members of the management team agree that keeping the Dry Goods Department is not essential to maintaining good customer relations and supporting the rest of the company's business. In other words, eliminating the Dry Goods Department is not expected to affect the amount of business done by the other departments.

What action do you recommend to management of Kahn Wholesalers Company in the short run? Why?

35. **Product choice with constraints** (Appendix 9.1; adapted from CMA exam). Leastan Company manufactures a line of carpeting that includes a commercial carpet and a residential carpet. Both types of carpeting use two grades of fiber—heavy-duty and regular. The mix of the two grades of fiber differs in each type of carpeting, with the commercial grade using a greater amount of heavy-duty fiber.

Leastan will introduce a new line of carpeting in 2 months to replace the current line. The new line cannot use the fiber now in stock. Management wants to exhaust the present stock of regular and heavy-duty fiber during the last month of production.

Data regarding the current line of commercial and residential carpeting follow:

	Commercial	Residential
Selling Price per Roll	$1,000	$800
Production Specifications per Roll of Carpet:		
Heavy-Duty Fiber.............................	80 Pounds	40 Pounds
Regular Fiber	20 Pounds	40 Pounds
Direct Labor Hours	15 Hours	15 Hours

(continued)

Standard Cost per Roll of Carpet:

Heavy-Duty Fiber ($3 per pound)................	$240	$120
Regular Fiber ($2 per pound)	40	80
Direct Labor ($10 per direct labor hour)	150	150
Variable Manufacturing Overhead (60 percent of direct labor cost)	90	90
Fixed Manufacturing Overhead (120 percent of direct labor cost)	180	180
Total Standard Cost per Roll.................	$700	$620

Leastan has 42,000 pounds of heavy-duty fiber and 24,000 pounds of regular fiber in stock. Leastan will sell all fiber not used in the manufacture of the present types of carpeting during the last month of production for $.25 a pound.

A maximum of 10,500 direct labor hours are available during the month. The labor force can work on either type of carpeting.

Sufficient demand exists for the present line of carpeting so that the firm can sell all quantities produced.

a. Calculate the number of rolls of commercial carpet and residential carpet Leastan Company must manufacture during the last month of production to exhaust completely the heavy-duty and regular fiber still in stock.

b. Can Leastan Company manufacture these quantities of commercial and residential carpeting during the last month of production? Explain your answer.

36. **Sell or process further** (adapted from CMA exam). The management of Bay Company is considering a proposal to install a third production department within its existing factory building. With the company's present production setup, 200,000 pounds per year of direct materials are passed through Department I to produce Materials A and B in equal proportions. Material A is then passed through Department II to yield 100,000 pounds of Product C. One hundred thousand pounds of Material B is presently being sold "as is" at a price of $20.25 per pound.

The costs for the Bay Company are as follows:

	Department I (Materials A and B)[a]	Department II (Product C)[a]	(Material B)[a]
Prior department costs	$ —	$33.25	$33.25
Direct materials	20.00	—	—
Direct labor	7.00	12.00	—
Variable overhead	3.00	5.00	—
Fixed overhead:			
Direct (Total = $675,000)	2.25	2.25	—
Allocated (2/3, 1/3)	1.00	1.00	—
	$33.25	$53.50	$33.25

[a]Cost per pound.

The fixed costs were developed by using the production volume of 200,000 pounds of direct materials as the volume. Common fixed overhead costs of $300,000 are allocated to the two producing departments on the basis of the space used by the departments.

The proposed Department III would process Material B into Product D. One pound of Material B yields one pound of Product D. Any quantity of Product D can be sold for $30 per pound. Costs under this proposal are as follows:

	Department I (Materials A and B)	Department II (Product C)	Department III (Product D)
Prior department costs	$ —	$33.00	$33.00
Direct materials	20.00	—	—
Direct labor	7.00	12.00	5.50
Variable overhead	3.00	5.00	2.00
Fixed overhead:			
Direct (Total = $850,000) ..	2.25	2.25	1.75
Allocated (½, ¼, ¼)	.75	.75	.75
	$33.00	$53.00	$43.00

If sales and production levels are expected to remain constant in the foreseeable future, these cost estimates are expected to be true, and there are no foreseeable alternative uses for the available factory space, should Bay Company produce Product D? Show calculations to support your answer.

Suggested Solutions to Even-Numbered Exercises

12. **Product choice.**

- Alternative 1: Warehouse.
- Alternative 2: Office space.
- Alternative 3: Restaurants and specialty shops.

	Alternative		
	1	2	3
Revenue...........................	$960,000	$982,800	$1,101,100
Less Variable Costs	40,000	70,000	95,000
Total Contribution Margin...............	$920,000	$912,800	$1,006,100
Less Fixed Costs.....................	600,000	600,000	600,000
Operating Profit	$320,000	$312,800	$ 406,100

Yuppie Enterprises should choose alternative 3.

14. **Make or buy.**

a.

	Buy	−	Make	=	Difference
Variable costs	$300,000	−	$250,000	=	$50,000

Ol' Salt should make the sails. The fixed costs are not relevant to the discussion.

b.

	Buy	−	Make	=	Difference
Variable costs	$300,000	−	$250,000	=	$50,000
Revenue	(80,000)	−	0	=	(80,000)
Net effect	$220,000	−	250,000	=	$(30,000)

Ol' Salt should buy. (The rental opportunity makes buying the sails more attractive.)

16. **Dropping a product line.**

	Manual	Electric	Quartz
Machine Time per Unit	0.4 Hours	2.5 Hours	5.0 Hours
Contribution Margin	$10.00	$16.00	$22.00
Contribution Margin per Machine Hour	$25.00[a]	$6.40[b]	$4.40[c]

[a]$25 = $10/0.4 hrs.
[b]$6.40 = $16/2.5 hrs.
[c]$4.40 = $22/5 hrs.

Timeless Products should drop the quartz line.

18. **Economic order quantity.**

$$D = 2,500 \text{ axles per year}$$

$$K_o = \$10$$

$$K_c = 0.20 \times \$100 = \$20$$

$$Q = \sqrt{\frac{2 \times \$10 \times 2,500}{\$20}} = \underline{\underline{50}}$$

$$N = \frac{D}{Q} = \frac{2,500}{50} = \underline{\underline{50}}$$

Annual ordering costs = $\underline{\$500}$ (= 50 × $10).

20.   Product mix decisions.

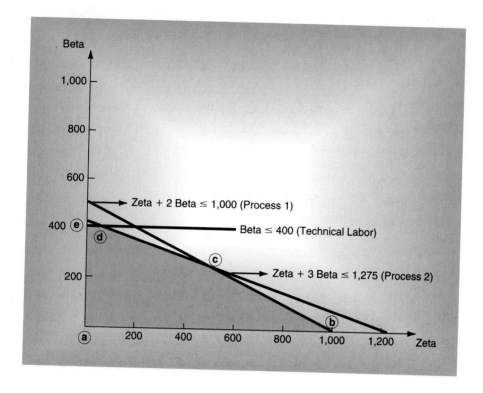

Problem Formulation:

Maximize Total Contribution Margin = 4.25 Zeta + 5.25 Beta.

Subject to:

Process 1 Constraint: Zeta + 2 Beta ≤ 1,000

Process 2 Constraint: Zeta + 3 Beta ≤ 1,275

Technical Labor Constraint: Beta ≤ 400.

Critical Points	Produce and Sell Zeta	Beta	Total Contribution Margin[a]
a	0	0	0
b	1,000	0	$4,250.00*
c	450[b]	275[b]	$3,356.25
d	75[c]	400[c]	$2,418.75
e	0	400	$2,100.00

*Optimal solution.

[a]Total Contribution Margin = $4.25 Zeta + $5.25 Beta.

[b]Zeta + 2 Beta = 1,000 (Process 1 Constraint).

Zeta + 3 Beta = 1,275 (Process 2 Constraint).

Solving simultaneously:

$$(1,000 - 2 \text{ Beta}) + 3 \text{ Beta} = 1,275$$

$$\text{Beta} = \underline{\underline{275}}.$$

$$\text{Zeta} + 2(275) = 1,000$$

$$\therefore \text{Zeta} = \underline{\underline{450}}.$$

[c]Zeta + 3 Beta = 1,275

Beta = 400.

Solving simultaneously:

$$\text{Zeta} + 3(400) = 1,275$$

$$\text{Zeta} = \underline{\underline{75}}.$$

22. **Finding most profitable price-quantity combination.**

a.

Price (1)	Quantity Demanded (2)	Revenues (3)	Total Variable Manufacturing Costs[a] (4)	Total Variable Selling and Administrative Costs[b] (5)	Total Costs[c] (6)	Total Profit[d] (7)
$10	40,000	$400,000	$160,000	$80,000	$290,000	$110,000
12	36,000	432,000	144,000	72,000	266,000	166,000
14	28,000	392,000	112,000	56,000	218,000	174,000
16	24,000	384,000	96,000	48,000	194,000	190,000
18	18,000	324,000	72,000	36,000	158,000	166,000
20	15,000	300,000	60,000	30,000	140,000	160,000

[a]Quantity demanded × $4.

[b]Quantity demanded × $2.

[c]Columns (4) + (5) + $50,000 (fixed manufacturing + administrative costs).

[d]Column (3) − (6).

b. Select a price of $16, because it results in the most profit.

Chapter 10

Capital Budgeting and Discounted Cash Flow Analysis for Long-Run Decisions

1. Note the separation of the investing and financing aspects of making long-term decisions.
2. Practice the steps of the net present value method for making long-term decisions using discounted cash flows.
3. Construct cash flows pertinent for discounted cash flow analysis. Observe the effect of income taxes on cash flows. Master the difference between depreciation, which does not affect cash flows, and the depreciation tax shield, which does.
4. Distinguish between the cost of capital (driven by characteristics of assets) and its measurement (often carried out on components of liabilities and owners' equity).
5. Understand the components of observed interest rates and the implications for choosing a discount rate.

Earlier chapters applied the differential principle to several kinds of short-run operating decisions. In each case, the firm's capacity was fixed. The manager must decide how best to use that fixed capacity in the short run. For example, how many units should we produce this month? Should a management consulting firm accept a one-time consulting assignment?

This chapter shifts attention to the long run. We focus on decisions to change operating capacity. Should Weyerhaeuser build a larger plant to manufacture paper? Should NBD Bank open a new branch? Should Nordstrom's expand? Should Boston Consulting Group hire more staff consultants on long-term employment contracts? Should a job shop acquire new machinery to replace older, less efficient machinery? Should Track Auto acquire new technology that will perform services currently performed by workers? No decision affects the long-run success of a firm more than deciding which investment projects to undertake.

Short-run operating decisions and long-run capacity decisions both rely on a differential analysis of cash inflows and cash outflows. Long-run capacity decisions involve cash flows over several future periods, whereas typical operating decisions involve only short-range cash flows. When the cash flows extend over several future periods, the analyst must use some technique to make the cash flows comparable, because the value of one dollar received now exceeds that of one dollar received several years from now. Present value analysis, sometimes called discounted cash flow (or DCF) analysis, provides the technique. The appendix at the back of this book further illustrates present value techniques. You should be familiar with its contents before studying this chapter.

Capital Budgeting: Investment and Financing Decisions

Capital budgeting involves deciding which long-term investments to undertake and how to finance them. A firm considering acquiring new plant or equipment must decide (1) whether to acquire the new asset (the investment decision) and (2) how to raise the funds required to obtain the new asset (the financing decision). The firm may raise funds through borrowing, from curtailing dividends, or by issuing additional capital stock.

Fundamental to the theory of financial economics is the principle that a firm should make the **investment decision** independently of the **financing decision.** In other words, the firm should generally make the investment decision first, and only after a project gets the go-ahead, should management begin to consider how to finance it.

Separating the investment and financing decisions results from the premise that all of a firm's equities (that is, liabilities plus owners' equity) finance all of a firm's assets. Acquiring a new asset will involve investing funds, but once the firm adds the asset to its portfolio of assets, all of the firm's equities finance that asset. Specific equities generally do not finance specific assets.

The capital budgeting decision involves estimating future cash flows, deciding on an appropriate interest rate for discounting those cash flows, and, once the firm makes a decision to undertake a project, deciding on how to finance that project. This text focuses on the first of these three issues. Although we discuss the last two, we leave their details to corporate finance courses.

Discounted Cash Flow Methods

If you have an opportunity to invest $1 today in return for $2 in the future, your evaluation of the attractiveness of the opportunity depends, in part, on how long you have to wait for the $2. If you must wait only 1 week after making the initial investment, you are much more inclined to accept the offer than if you have to wait 10 years to receive the $2. **Discounted cash flow (DCF) methods** aid in evaluating investments involving cash flows over time where the time elapsing between cash payment and receipt is significant. The two discounted cash flow methods are the net present value (NPV) method and the internal rate of return (IRR) method. This chapter discusses the net present value method. Chapter 11 discusses the internal rate of return method.

The Net Present Value Method

The net present value method involves the following steps:

1. Estimate the amounts of future cash inflows and future cash outflows by date for each alternative under consideration.
2. Discount the future cash flows to the present using the project's cost of capital. The **net present value of cash flows** of a project is the present value of the cash inflows minus the present value of the cash outflows.
3. Accept or reject the proposed project or select one from a set of mutually exclusive projects.

If the present value of the future cash inflows exceeds the present value of the outflow for a proposal, the firm should accept the alternative. If the net present value of the future cash flows is negative, the firm should reject the alternative. If the firm must choose one from a set of mutually exclusive alternatives, it should select the one with the largest net present value of cash flows.

This three-step procedure summarizes a complex process involving many estimates and projections. Later discussion treats these complexities. For now, however, we examine two illustrations of the net present value method, the first ignoring income taxes and the second considering income taxes.

Illustration Ignoring Income Taxes

The example in this section illustrates the steps of the net present value method. After we introduce the basics here, we make the example more realistic in a later section. Finally, Problem 10.2 for Self-Study shows a more complicated example.

JEP Realty Syndicators, Inc., contemplates the acquisition of computer hardware that will allow it to bring a new variety of real estate investment partnerships to the market. The hardware and software cost $100,000 and will last 5 years before becoming obsolete. Exhibit 10.1 shows the cash inflows and cash outflows expected

Exhibit 10.1

JEP REALTY SYNDICATORS, INC.
Cash Flows Associated with New Real Estate Investment Products
(ignoring income taxes)[a]

Cash Flow Analysis

End of Year (1)	Cash Inflows (2)	Cash Outflows (3)	Net Cash Inflow (Outflows) (4)	Present Value Factor at 20 Percent (5)	Present Value of Cash Flows (6)
0	—	$100,000	$(100,000)	1.00000	$(100,000)
1	$120,000	70,000	50,000	0.83333	41,667
2	80,000	40,000	40,000	0.69444	27,778
3	60,000	30,000	30,000	0.57870	17,361
4	50,000	25,000	25,000	0.48225	12,056
5	40,000	25,000	15,000	0.40188	6,028
Total	$350,000	$290,000	$ 60,000		$ 4,890

Accounting Income Data

Year (7)	Revenues – (8)	Other Expenses – (9)	Depreciation = (10)	Net Income (11)
0	—	—	—	—
1	$120,000	$ 70,000	$ 20,000	$30,000
2	80,000	40,000	20,000	20,000
3	60,000	30,000	20,000	10,000
4	50,000	25,000	20,000	5,000
5	40,000	25,000	20,000	(5,000)
Total	$350,000	$190,000	$100,000	$60,000

[a]Amounts in columns are derived as follows:

(2), (3), (8), (9): given.

(4) = (2) − (3).

(5) taken from Table 2 of the Compound Interest and Annuity Tables at the back of the book.

(6) = (4) × (5).

(10) = $100,000/5.

(11) = (8) − (9) − (10).

from this investment during each of the 5 years of its useful life. At the end of Year 0 (that is, at the start of the project), the firm purchases the computer system for $100,000. The decreasing pattern of cash inflows over the 5 years results from the expected reaction of other real estate syndicators, who will copy the investment instrument and force down the commissions and underwriting fees.

The cash outflows for each of the 5 years are for programmers, sales staff, and supplies. We have assumed that the hardware has zero salvage value at the end of 5 years. Column **4** shows the net cash flow for each year.

The cash flow related to the computer equipment in column (3) represents the initial outlay for its acquisition. Distinguish cash flows from accounting costs, such as for depreciation. Depreciation appears in the financial statements, as in column (10) in the bottom panel of Exhibit 10.1. Depreciation allocates costs to periods of benefit. Although the acquisition has no immediate impact on income, it does require an expenditure or cash outflow at the time of acquisition. (In practice, a cash inflow can occur upon disposal of the asset at the end of the project's life.)

Cash flow data show the timing of cash flows, not accrual accounting data. Hence, cash flows enable decision makers to compute the time value of money as needed for investment decisions. Use cash flow data, not accrual accounting data, for making investment decisions. In accrual accounting, over long-enough time spans, income equals cash in minus cash out. Thus, the equality of the sums in columns (4) and (11) is not a coincidence. The timing of accounting income differs from the timing of cash flows. Note that JEP Realty Syndicators must spend the $100,000 early in the project's life but those amounts become accounting expenses over a 5-year period. Analysis of accounting expenses, rather than cash flows, makes the costs seem less burdensome than they are: $100,000 spent today is more costly than $20,000 per year for 5 years. DCF analysis focuses on cash flows, not accounting income.

Because you can invest cash over time to earn interest, cash you receive or pay today has a higher present value than cash you receive or pay at some time in the future. To put the cash flows in column (4) on an equivalent basis, we discount them to their present value. This illustration uses a 20-percent discount rate for the proposed project. (We discuss the selection of an appropriate discount rate later.) If the firm can invest cash to earn 20 percent, the right to receive $90,000 at the end of Year 1 is equivalent to receiving $75,000 (= $90,000/1.20) today. Column (5) shows the discount factors for the present value of $1 for various periods at 20 percent. (These discount factors appear in the tables following the appendix at the back of the book. Some calculators or computer spreadsheet programs contain functions to provide these factors.) Column (6) shows the present value of each cash flow.

This project results in a positive net present value of $4,890; that is, the present value of the net future cash inflows exceeds the initial investment by $4,890. JEP should, therefore, accept this project because its net present value is greater than zero. A decision to accept positive net present value projects will increase the value of the firm when the discount rate is the firm's opportunity cost of capital, as discussed later.

Illustration Considering Income Taxes

Income taxes affect both the *amounts* of cash flows and the *timing* of cash flows, and, consequently, the firm must consider them in making investment decisions.

Reconsider the proposed computer acquisition by JEP Realty. In this case, assume a combined federal and state income tax rate of 40 percent. The discount rate for after-tax cash flows is 12 percent [= .20 × (1 − .40)], because the project's pretax cost of capital is 20 percent and the tax rate is 40 percent. Also assume that the firm uses straight-line depreciation. The top panel of Exhibit 10.2 shows the calculation of the proposed project's net present value, assuming that the firm depreciates the

Exhibit 10.2

JEP REALTY SYNDICATORS, INC.
Cash Flows Associated with New Real Estate Investment Products
(considering income taxes)[a]

End of Year (1)	Cash Inflows (2)	Cash Outflows (3)	Pretax Net Cash Flow (4)	Depreciation Deduction (5)	Taxable Income (6)	Income Tax Payable (7)	Net Cash Inflow (8)	Present Value Factor at 12 Percent (9)	Present Value of Cash Flows (10)
A. Straight-Line Depreciation Method									
0	—	$100,000	$(100,000)	—	—	—	$(100,000)	1.00000	$(100,000)
1	$120,000	70,000	50,000	$ 20,000	$30,000	$12,000	38,000	0.89286	33,929
2	80,000	40,000	40,000	20,000	20,000	8,000	32,000	0.79719	25,510
3	60,000	30,000	30,000	20,000	10,000	4,000	26,000	0.71178	18,506
4	50,000	25,000	25,000	20,000	5,000	2,000	23,000	0.63552	14,617
5	40,000	25,000	15,000	20,000	(5,000)	(2,000)[b]	17,000	0.56743	9,646
Total	$350,000	$290,000	$ 60,000	$100,000	$60,000	$24,000	$ 36,000		$ 2,208
B. Accelerated Cost Recovery Method									
0	—	$100,000	$(100,000)	—	—	—	$(100,000)	1.00000	$(100,000)
1	$120,000	70,000	50,000	$ 20,000	$30,000	$12,000	38,000	0.89286	33,929
2	80,000	40,000	40,000	32,000	8,000	3,200	36,800	0.79719	29,337
3	60,000	30,000	30,000	19,000	11,000	4,400	25,600	0.71178	18,222
4	50,000	25,000	25,000	14,500	10,500	4,200	20,800	0.63552	13,219
5	40,000	25,000	15,000	14,500	500	200	14,800	0.56743	8,398
Total	$350,000	$290,000	$ 60,000	$100,000	$60,000	$24,000	$ 36,000		$ 3,105

[a]Amounts in columns are derived as follows:

(2), (3): given.
(4) = (2) − (3).
(5) Panel A = $100,000/5.
(5) Panel B: $100,000 × .20 = $20,000.
        $100,000 × .32 = $32,000.
        $100,000 × .19 = $19,000.
        $100,000 × .145 = $14,500.
        $100,000 × .145 = $14,500.

(6) = (4) − (5).
(7) = .40 × (6).
(8) = (4) − (7).
(9) Taken from Table 2 of the Compound Interest and Annuity Tables at the back of the book.
(10) = (8) × (9).

[b]Assumes that in Year 5 there is sufficient otherwise-taxable income that the tax loss in Year 5 will reduce income taxes otherwise payable.

equipment using the straight-line method for income tax purposes. Although depreciation for tax purposes is not itself a cash flow, it does represent a deductible expense. Hence, **depreciation affects cash flows** by its effect on taxable income and the income taxes paid. Using a 12-percent discount rate, the project has a positive net present value of $2,208 and the firm should accept it.

Accelerated Cost Recovery   One of the most important effects of income tax laws on investment decisions arises from the firm's ability to use accelerated depreciation methods, called the **modified accelerated cost recovery system** or **MACRS**, in the income tax laws. MACRS generally shifts depreciation deduc-

Managerial Application

DCF Analysis in Plant Expansion and Dispute Resolution

Union Carbide decided in the mid-1980s that the market for polycrystalline silicon (polysilicon), a key ingredient in the manufacture of computer chips, was about to expand rapidly. It entered into an agreement with a Japanese manufacturer, Komatsu, under which it would expand its polysilicon plant and manufacture large quantities of polysilicon that Komatsu would purchase. The agreement specified that Carbide and Komatsu would submit to arbitration any disputes arising between them.

Before entering the agreement, Carbide gathered data on plant expansion technologies, the expected cash flows for each, and the size of the projected market. It performed a discounted cash flow analysis both to decide whether the expansion would be profitable and to choose the preferred method of expanding. In carrying out the DCF analysis, Carbide used its cost of capital, estimated at about 23 percent per year. Ultimately, Carbide invested $80 million in expanding its polysilicon manufacturing plant in the state of Washington.

After Carbide completed the plant expansion, Komatsu began building its own plants to produce polysilicon. Carbide viewed Komatsu's doing so as breach of the agreement. Carbide invoked the arbitration clause of the agreement and asked Komatsu for compensation for damages caused by the alleged contract breach. Komatsu argued that any damages Carbide may have suffered resulted from the collapse of the market for computer chips, not from Komatsu's actions. In settling the dispute between Carbide and Komatsu, Carbide produced copies of its earlier DCF analysis to show that it had undertaken the expansion only after careful planning. Carbide and Komatsu settled their dispute prior to formal arbitration, but the terms are confidential.

tions from later to earlier years as compared to the straight-line method. This practice delays taxable income and tax payments from earlier to later years. Although accelerated cost recovery does not change the total tax liability generated by a project over its life, it does influence the desirability of the project by affecting the timing of cash flows.

The lower panel of Exhibit 10.2 shows the calculation of the net present value of the project assuming that the firm uses MACRS for tax reporting. Assume that tax law requires equipment with a 5-year life, such as the computer JEP Realty acquires, to be depreciated over 5 years for tax purposes under MACRS: 20 percent in the first year, 32 percent in the second, 19 percent in the third, and 14.5 percent in both the fourth and fifth years. Note that the total depreciation expense in column **(5)** is

$100,000 under both straight-line and MACRS. In the latter case, however, the deductions occur sooner; they are more *accelerated*. The net cash flows in column **(8)** total $36,000 in both cases, but they occur in a different pattern. The net present value of the project is $897 (= $3,105 − $2,208) greater if the firm uses accelerated cost recovery, rather than straight-line, for tax calculations.

Identifying Cash Flows

In practice, analysts consider a variety of cash flows. Later sections explain and illustrate some of the more difficult steps in the detailed checklist below. The cash flows associated with an investment project divide into those at the inception of the project (the initial cash flows), those occurring during the life of the project (the periodic cash flows), and those occurring at the conclusion of the project (the terminal cash flows). This three-way classification of cash flows follows:

Initial Cash Flows

1. Asset cost—outflow.
2. Freight and installation costs—outflow.
3. Salvage or other disposal value of existing asset—inflow.
4. Income tax effect of gain or loss on disposal of existing asset—outflow (if gain) or inflow (if loss).
5. Investment tax credit, if any, on new asset—inflow.[1]

Periodic Cash Flows

1. Receipts (*not* revenues, which generally precede receipt of cash) from sales—inflow.
2. Lost ''other'' inflows caused by undertaking this particular project, if any—outflow. (For example, the new equipment for JEP Realty allows the company to market a new investment package. If this decreases the sales of other packages, there would be lost ''other'' inflows.)
3. Expenditures for fixed and variable production costs—outflow (at time of incurrence, which generally precedes date of sale.)
4. Savings for fixed and variable production costs, if any—inflow.
5. Selling, general, and administrative expenditures—outflows.
6. Savings in selling, general, and administrative expenditures, if any—inflows.
7. Income tax effects of flows **1** through **6**—which are opposite in sign to the cash flow that generates the tax consequences. For example, extra cash inflow from customers' payments results in extra cash outflows for income taxes. Extra cash outflow for computer programmers results in savings in cash outflows for income taxes. The tax effect may occur in a period different from the preceding items. For example, the tax-reducing effect of deducting cost of

---

[1] As this book goes to press, the U. S. income tax rules do not provide for an investment tax credit, but the rules have granted such credit at various times, in varying amounts, over the past several decades.

goods manufactured and sold occurs for the period of sale, which generally follows the period of cash outflow to purchase raw materials and manufacture the goods.

8. Savings in taxes caused by deductibility of depreciation on tax return (sometimes called "depreciation tax shield")—inflow.

9. Loss in tax savings from lost depreciation, if any—outflow. Conversely, any gain in tax savings from additional depreciation deductions on the tax return is an inflow.

10. Do *not* count noncash items such as financial accounting depreciation expense or allocated items of overhead not requiring differential cash expenditures.

Terminal Cash Flows

1. Proceeds of salvage of equipment—inflow.
2. Tax on gain (or loss) on disposal, if any—outflow (or inflow).

Problem 10.1 for Self-Study

Cash Flow Analysis. Kary Kinnard has an opportunity to open a franchised pizza outlet. He can lease the building, so he needs to invest only in equipment, which he estimates will cost $60,000. He will depreciate the equipment over 6 years using MACRS percentages of 20, 32, 19.2, 11.5, 11.5, and 5.8. For financial reporting, he will depreciate the equipment over 6 years using the straight-line method. For purposes of this analysis, assume the equipment will last for 6 years, after which Kinnard will sell it for $6,000. He will pay taxes at 40 percent on the taxable gain on the disposal at the end of Year 6.

Kinnard estimates the following revenues, variable costs, and fixed costs from operations for the 6-year period. He has included expected inflation in these estimates. Assume end-of-year cash flows.

	1	2	3	4	5	6
Revenues............	$30,000	$36,000	$41,000	$45,000	$48,000	$50,000
Variable Costs	12,000	14,400	16,400	18,000	19,200	20,000
Fixed Costs (includes depreciation of $10,000 per year) ...	15,000	15,200	15,500	15,900	16,400	17,000

Use an after-tax cost of capital of 12 percent per year and an income tax rate of 40 percent for this analysis. The $60,000 outlay for the equipment will be made at the beginning of Year 1.

Prepare an analysis of all cash flow. Should Kinnard make the investment?

The solution to this self-study problem appears at the end of the chapter on page 401.

The Cost of Capital—An Opportunity Cost

Financial economics suggests that the discount rate appropriate for use in evaluating investment projects of average risk is the firm's cost of capital. The cost of capital (or the normal rate of return or the hurdle rate) is the opportunity cost of funds. The **opportunity cost of capital** used for an investment is the income the owner could have earned if the owner invested the funds elsewhere in a project of comparable risk. The term **cost of capital** means the minimum rate of return required by the owner of an asset to justify using it.

Measuring the Cost of Capital

Often, firms measure the cost of capital by computing the cost of all of the liabilities and owners' equity on the balance sheet. All of a corporation's funds raised from various sources finance all its assets. When financial markets are in equilibrium, one can compute the rates of return required on the assets from the cost of raising the funds used to acquire assets. Measuring the cost of capital as the weighted average of the sources of funds is often useful, but it confuses some people into thinking that the average cost of liabilities and owners' equity is the cost of capital. It is not; the cost of capital is the **required rate of return** on the assets themselves.

Cost of capital is a notion about assets; the measurement just described concerns liabilities and other equities. Take an extreme example to cement this concept.[2] Suppose that we have $10,000 cash to invest. Assume that the highest risk-free interest that we can earn from using that cash fixes the required rate of return on that asset. If this rate is 9 percent per year, then the cost of capital for projects of such risk is 9 percent per year. Notice that the derivation of the required rate of return, the cost of capital, does not require knowing how we raised the asset, $10,000 cash. If we earned the $10,000 by hard physical labor, or won it in a lottery, or even found it in the street, its cost of capital is 9 percent. No matter the origin of the funds, the cost of capital—the rate of return required on the asset cash—is 9 percent. Note that the cost of capital does not depend on the source of funds used to acquire those assets. It does depend on the risk characteristics of the alternative investments: the riskier the project, the higher the cost of capital for the assets used to carry out the project.[3]

---

[2]Professor Ezra Solomon of Stanford University, to our knowledge, first suggested this example.

[3]Because we separate the investment and financing decisions, we expect each investment project (with risk equal to the average for the firm) to earn a rate of return equal to at least the *average* cost of capital for the firm.

Assume that the market value of a firm's shares is the present value of the net cash flows to be earned by the firm. Corporate finance texts provide insight into why this assumption is generally valid. See, for example, J. Fred Weston and Eugene F. Brigham, *Essentials of Managerial Finance,* 9th ed. (Hinsdale, Ill.: The Dryden Press, 1990), or J. Fred Weston and Thomas E. Copeland, *Managerial Finance,* 8th ed. (Hinsdale, Ill.: The Dryden Press, 1989). If an investment project earns just the cost of capital (that is, the project has a zero net present value), the market value of the firm's shares will remain unchanged as a result of it. If a project has a positive net present value, the market value of the firm's shares should increase when the firm undertakes that project. The shares increase in value because the firm is able to generate a higher rate of return than the average rate required by the suppliers of capital. Because the returns to creditors and preferred shareholders are fixed, this excess return accrues to the benefit of the common shareholders.

One may choose to *measure* the cost of capital by looking at the cost of liabilities and owners' equity, but one should not confuse that measure of the cost of capital with the actual cost of capital, which is the rate of return required on assets of comparable risk.

Sensitivity of Net Present Value to Estimates

The calculation of the net present value of a proposed project requires three types of projections or estimates:

1. The amount of future cash flows.
2. The timing of future cash flows.
3. The cost of capital rate.

Some error is likely in the amount predicted or estimated for each of these three items. The net present value model exhibits different degrees of sensitivity to such errors.

Amounts of Future Cash Flows

Errors in predicting the amounts of future cash flows will likely have the largest impact of the three items. Exhibit 10.2 indicated that the proposed project for JEP Realty had a net present value (using the straight-line depreciation method) of $2,208 based on the cash flows initially predicted. Suppose that these predictions err by 10 percent and that the estimate of future cash flows (excluding the initial $100,000 outlay) each year should have been 10 percent less than the amounts appearing in column **(8)** of Exhibit 10.2. The net present value of the proposed project using the same 12-percent discount rate is a negative $8,013.[4] The total error in present value dollars is $10,221 (= $2,208 + $8,013), which is about 10 percent of the initial investment of $100,000. Given the sensitivity of the net present value to errors in the projections of cash flows, the manager will want accurate projections. Statistical techniques have recently been developed for dealing with the uncertainty inherent in predictions of cash flows.[5]

Timing of Future Cash Flows

The degree of sensitivity of the net present value model to shifts in the pattern, but not in the total amount, of cash flows depends on the extent of the shifting. Column **(8)** of Exhibit 10.2 shows net cash flows for Years 1 through 5 of $38,000, $32,000, $26,000, $23,000, and $17,000, or $136,000 in total, assuming the straight-line

---

[4]Note that ($100,000) + .90 × [$33,929 + $25,510 + $18,506 + $14,617 + $9,646] = ($8,013).

[5]Interested readers might consult the following book for additional discussion of capital budgeting under uncertainty: Harold Bierman, Jr., and Seymour Smidt, *The Capital Budgeting Decision,* 7th ed. (New York: Macmillan, 1988). See also the computer spreadsheet add-on program, At Risk.

depreciation method. Suppose that the pattern of cash flows will be relatively stable, as follows: $28,000, $27,000, $27,000, $27,000, and $27,000 again totaling $136,000. Then, net present value will be *minus* $1,778, compared to $2,208 in Exhibit 10.2.[6] The error is $3,986 (= $2,208 + $1,778) in present value terms, or about 4 percent of the initial investment. We could construct other examples that would result in a different percentage effect. Errors in predicting the amount of cash flows tend to be more serious than in predicting their pattern.

Calculation of Cost of Capital

A third uncertain factor in the net present value calculation is the cost of capital. The difficulty here lies not in predicting a future cash flow but in estimating returns to alternative uses of capital. Financial economists have not yet developed foolproof techniques for empirically verifying a firm's estimate of its cost of capital rate.

What loss does a firm suffer if it incorrectly calculates its cost of capital? Using the 12-percent aftertax cost of capital for JEP Realty in Exhibit 10.2 results in a net present value of $3,105 for the proposed project using MACRS depreciation. If the after-tax cost of capital is 15 percent, the net present value of this project is about minus $3,047. Management miscalculated the cost of capital by one-fourth [= (.15 − .12)/.12]. That large error resulted in a faulty estimate of the net present value by about $6,152 (= $3,105 + $3,047), or about 6 percent of the initial investment. In general, if a project appears marginally desirable for a given cost of capital, it will ordinarily not be grossly undesirable for slightly higher rates. If a project is clearly worthwhile when analysts use a cost of capital of 12 percent, for example, it is likely to be worthwhile even if they should have used a cost of capital of 15 or 18 percent.

Using Spreadsheet Features to Deal with Uncertain Estimates

Personal computer spreadsheet programs, such as Lotus 1-2-3 and Microsoft Excel, have become the preferred tool for analysts carrying out DCF computations. Refer to rows 1 through 5 of Exhibit 10.2. Note that although the numbers differ from one row to the next, the formulas for each of the numbers in a given column, except column **(5)**, are the same for each row. In fact, the notes at the foot of the exhibit give those formulas. The personal computer spreadsheets allow the analyst to replicate the computations required to derive the periodic cash flows from repetitive computational structures. The analyst will write the formulas once, for row 1, say, and then with a few key strokes, copy the structure of those formulas to rows 2 through 5.

An even more useful feature of the spreadsheet programs helps the user see the effect on the net present value of changes in assumptions and estimates. Thoughtful design of a computer spreadsheet enables the user to change assumptions (such as for growth rates in sales, tax rates, discount rates) with a few key strokes. The net present value changes as the assumptions change and the process takes only a few

---

[6]$(100,000) + [$28,000 × .89286] + [$27,000 × .79719] + [$27,000 × .71178] + [$27,000 × .63552] + [$27,000 × .56743] = $(1,778).

seconds. This method is the best way to study the sensitivity of DCF analyses to assumptions.

Exhibit 10.6 accompanying the Solution to Problem 10.2 for Self-Study shows part of a computer spreadsheet for a complex DCF analysis.

Complications in Computing Periodic Cash Flows

Previous sections have described and illustrated the steps for using the net present value method. In practice, decision makers sometimes have difficulty computing the periodic after-tax cash flows. Some of the difficulty results from confusion between accounting data and cash flow data. Other difficulty stems from an inability to identify the differential cash flows. This section describes and illustrates a number of such potential difficulties. Problem 10.2 for Self-Study contains a comprehensive example.

New Asset Acquisition: Deriving the Net Proceeds When the Firm Retires Assets

Often, when a firm undertakes a new investment, it already owns a product line which it must, or can, discontinue and already owns assets which it can sell or retire. Treating the proceeds from selling off such assets requires clear thinking. These cases represent **mutually exclusive investments** because selecting any one alternative precludes selecting all others. The best strategy to deal with this potential confusion constructs a series of mutually exclusive investment alternatives, evaluates each, and chooses the best.

Example A kitchen appliance manufacturer currently makes food blenders. The manufacturer is considering producing a more versatile and complex food processor. If the manufacturer continues to make and sell blenders, the existing product line of blenders will generate net cash flows of $200,000 at the end of each of the next 10 years. The firm can sell today the currently owned blender equipment for $1,000,000. This equipment will last 10 more years; by then it will have no salvage value. New equipment for manufacturing food processors will cost $5,000,000 but will generate net cash flows of $900,000 at the end of each of the next 15 years. After 15 years, it will have no salvage value. Ignore tax considerations. The two cases that follow illustrate the construction of the mutually exclusive alternatives.

Case A If the firm markets food processors, it will have no further market for blenders. Although you can find the right answer in several ways, you can easily err if you try to combine the cash flow implications of the various strategies. The three mutually exclusive alternatives and their cash flows are as follows:

1. Sell the existing blender equipment and get out of the business. This implies cash flow of $1,000,000 today, a net present value of $1,000,000 at any discount rate.

Investing in Improved Technology

Boston Metal Products, a small manufacturer in Medford, Massachusetts, considered buying a robot. The company controller calculated whether the $200,000 investment made financial sense. The controller found that "[I]t didn't even come close. It was hard to scrape together enough to convince us it was a reasonable risk, let alone a positive investment. There was no way an M.B.A. would have justified it."[a]

The company bought the robot anyway, because the president wanted to inject new technology into the company's manufacturing operations. According to company management, "the robot's prowess in welding has speeded up deliveries, allowing the company's sales of steel shelving for supermarket refrigerators to grow fourfold in three years. The investment has paid off. What standard accounting procedures failed to see were some of the intangibles in such an investment—improved quality, greater flexibility, and lower inventories."[b]

Many apparently worthwhile investments in improved technology do not show a positive net value when management uses traditional investment analysis. Technological innovations usually have a high investment outlay and a long time period before the project returns cash inflows. It is not unusual for an investment in automated equipment to take two or three years (or more) before it is fully operational. In companies with high discount rates, cash flows received or cash savings several years in the future have low present values. Further, as noted in the Boston Metal Products example, technological improvements usually provide benefits that are not easily quantified, so the analyst often omits them from the cash flow projections.

[a]From *The New York Times*, Business Section, Tuesday, October 14, 1986, p. 1.
[b]*New York Times*, October 14, 1986, p. 1.

2. Stay in the blender business. This implies net cash flows of $200,000 at the end of each of the next 10 years.
3. Sell the blender equipment and purchase the processor equipment. This implies cash flow of ($4,000,000) [= ($5,000,000) for new + $1,000,000 from selling old] today and $900,000 at the end of each of the next 15 years.

Using the cost of capital, one computes three net present values and chooses the alternative with the largest one. If alternative **1** is not a realistic alternative, ignore it.

Case B The manufacturer has the alternative of keeping the blender business while adding the processor business. For simplicity, however, we assume that the net cash flow for the first 10 years is $1,050,000 if the firm markets both blenders and processors. In this case, a fourth mutually exclusive project results:

4. Stay in the blender business and add the processor business. This implies cash flow of ($5,000,000) today, $1,050,000 per year at the end of the next 10 years, and $900,000 per year at the end of the following 5 years.

Depreciation and Cash Flow

Depreciation expense reduces income, but does not use cash. The cash effects occur in the year the owner acquires the asset. Depreciation itself does not affect cash flows for net present value analysis. Insofar as depreciation is deductible on the tax return, however, it shields otherwise taxable income from taxation. The analyst must be careful to focus on the tax shield provided by depreciation while recognizing that depreciation itself does not affect cash.

Example A firm will depreciate an automobile costing $15,000 over 5 years using the straight-line method for financial reporting. On the tax return, the firm will depreciate the automobile over 5 years using MACRS: 20 percent in the first year, 32 percent in the second, 19 percent in the third, 14.5 percent in the fourth, and 14.5 percent in the fifth. The firm's current and expected future combined federal and state income tax rate is 40 percent of taxable income. The company has sufficient other taxable income that the depreciation deductions can reduce taxable income dollar for dollar. The cash flows relevant for a net present value analysis are ($15,000) today followed by $1,200 (= $15,000 × .20 × .40) tax saving at the end of the first year, $1,920 (= $15,000 × .32 × .40) at the end of the second year, $1,140 (= $15,000 × .19 × .40) at the end of the third year, and so on. (Of course, the automobile must produce other positive cash inflows or savings in outflows to be worthwhile.)

Salvage Value of Equipment

When a firm acquires an asset for a specific project, the asset's cost will be a cash outflow at the start of the project. At the end of the project, the firm will scrap or sell the asset or possibly convert it to another use. The firm must include in the DCF analysis the cash flow impact of the disposal and any tax implications thereof. Typically, that cash flow occurs in the last period.

Example The firm expects the food-processing equipment described earlier to have a fair market value of $400,000 at the end of the 15-year period of production of food processors. At that time, the manufacturer plans to sell the equipment to a distributor of spare parts. The DCF analysis should increase the cash flows for the fifteenth year by $400,000. (Tax consequences may affect the calculation.)

Impact on Working Capital

Ordinarily, when a firm starts a new business, it expects to tie up cash in inventories, accounts receivable, and bank accounts. Eventually it sells these inventories for cash, collects the accounts receivable, and uses the cash. Cash flows out in the early periods but flows back in the later periods, usually much later. The cash spent to acquire inventories, the cash not immediately received from customers who purchase on account, and the ultimate cash flow require no special treatment. The analyst needs to show all cash outlays in the period when they occur and all cash inflows in the period collected, which may differ from the period of sale.[7]

Effects of Inflation on the Cost of Capital and Cash Flows

Cost of Capital The cost of capital or discount rate used in computing net present values reflects, at least in part, current market interest rates. Recall that the cost of capital is an opportunity cost, and one alternative opportunity available to all investors is the purchase of relatively risk-free bonds issued by the federal government and by some low-risk corporations. Market interest rates, a factor determining the cost of capital, reflect three separate phenomena:

1. A *pure* or *real* rate of interest reflecting the productive capability of capital assets. (Economists debate the results of empirical research, but most would agree that the pure rate of interest generally lies between 0 and 5 percent per year.)
2. A risk factor reflecting the likelihood of default of the particular borrower. (The federal government has the lowest probability of default, so government bonds usually have the lowest risk premiums.)
3. A premium reflecting inflation expected to occur over the life of the loan. (A lender lends out dollars with a particular purchasing power and receives at maturity dollars with a smaller purchasing power if inflation has occurred during the loan term. As the expected rate of inflation increases, the lender will charge a higher interest rate to compensate for the correspondingly larger expected decline in the purchasing power of the dollars lent.)

If the pure rate of interest is p, the risk premium is r, and the expected inflation is e, then the market rate of interest i satisfies the equations on the following page:

---

[7]Some textbooks on managerial finance, in treating the subject of working capital requirements for investments projects, show explicit investments in working capital at the start of the project and a specific recovery of it sometime later. This special treatment of the investment in working capital is more likely to confuse than to help. Why should DCF analysis treat this particular investment differently from any other? We prefer to show all cash inflows and outflows in parallel, not treating any of them differently from the others. The important point is, in constructing a dated schedule of cash flows (for example, for sales), to use the time of collection of cash from a sale, not the time of the sale.

$$(1 + i) = (1 + p)(1 + r)(1 + e),$$

or

$$i = (1 + p)(1 + r)(1 + e) - 1.$$

The market rate is sometimes called the *nominal* rate.

Example   Assume a pure rate of interest of 3 percent, a risk premium for the IBM Corporation of 2 percent, and an expected rate of inflation for the next year of 4 percent. The market rate of interest i for IBM is

$$i = (1.03)(1.02)(1.04) - 1$$

$$\cong .093 \text{ or } 9.3 \text{ percent.}$$

Effect of Inflation on Cash Flows   In times of expected general inflation, interest rates exceed those in times of lower expected general inflation. High costs of capital, other things being equal, reflect high expected inflation.[8] Decision makers using market interest for net present value computations are reflecting anticipated inflation in the discounting process. Such decision makers would be inconsistent if they did not also reflect the effects of anticipated future inflation on cash flows.

Consider the following points in carrying out a capital budgeting analysis:

1.   If forecasts of future cash flows involve nominal (that is, actual) dollar amounts, discount nominal dollar cash flows at a rate that includes anticipated inflation. If forecasts involve real dollar cash flows, discount using a rate that excludes anticipated inflation.
2.   If you expect general inflation, but no change in relative prices, you need not forecast anticipated inflation. Discounting of real cash flows will provide correct results. If you expect relative prices to change significantly and you can forecast these relative changes, then forecast nominal dollars and discount rate with a nominal cost of capital.
3.   Because you compute the depreciation tax shield from the acquisition cost of the equipment, its amount is fixed, even when you anticipate inflation in the nominal cash flows. The value, but not the amount, of the depreciation shield will fall as anticipated inflation increases.
4.   If you anticipate significant inflation, you may need larger amounts of cash to provide for increased investments in inventories (or, as some might say, to provide working capital).

Example   An owner of a plot of land zoned for commercial use considers renting the land to the operator of a supermarket. The landlord/owner will base rental charges on a percentage of retail sales. Analysis projects that, given the traffic patterns in the area, 4,000 families per week will do their shopping in this store.

---

[8]Compare, for example, the rate of interest and rates of inflation in the early 1980s to those of the mid 1990s.

Because of competing stores in nearby neighborhoods and the lack of room for further real estate development in the market area of the proposed supermarket, the owner is fairly sure that the number of families using the store will not change substantially over time. The owner's after-tax cost of capital is 15 percent per year. The owner can easily estimate the rental payments for the first year.

Given an estimate that the number of families shopping will not increase over time, the analyst might project level cash flows for the 10-year proposed lease term. Assume, for example, that the rental terms propose a payment by the supermarket to the lessor of $100,000 at the end of the first year. If the owner projects rental payments of $100,000 each year for 10 years and discounts them at 15 percent per year, the present value of the cash flows is $501,877 (= $100,000 × 5.01877; see Table 4 at the back of the book, 10-period row, 15-percent column). An after-tax cost of capital of 15 percent per year is so high for projects of this risk that the cost of capital appears to anticipate substantial general inflation over the life of the lease. To be consistent, the analysis should anticipate that such inflation will also increase disposable incomes of shoppers and prices of the merchandise they purchase in the store.

Thus, careful analysis will probably project price increases for the items sold in the stores, in the net sales of the store, and in the rental revenues to the owner. If, for example, sales prices increase at the rate of 6 percent per year, the stream of rental payments will be $106,000 (= $100,000 × 1.06) at the end of the first year, $112,360 (= $100,000 × 1.06^2) at the end of the second year, . . . , $179,085 (= $100,000 × 1.06^{10}) at the end of the tenth year. The net present value of that stream of payments discounted at 15 percent per year is $656,411.[9] This figure is almost one-third larger than the net present value assuming no increase in selling price and rentals.

Problem 10.2 for Self-Study

Data Analysis. This comprehensive problem illustrates the analysis of accounting data to derive cash flows for an investment decision and the choice among mutually exclusive alternatives. The last section of the answer to this problem presents a computer spreadsheet application.

---

[9]Note that

$$\sum_{i=1}^{10} \frac{\$100,000 \times (1.06)^i}{(1.15)^i} = \sum_{i=1}^{10} \frac{\$100,000}{(1.15/1.06)^i}.$$

Because $1.15/1.06 - 1 = 8.49$ percent (rounded), the computation is equivalent to computing the present value of a level annuity of $100,000 per year discounted at 8.49 percent per year.

Problem Data

Magee Company considers undertaking a new product line. If it does so, it must acquire new equipment with a purchase price of $140,000 at the beginning of Year 1. The equipment will last for 5 years and Magee expects to sell it at the end of the fifth year for its salvage value of $2,500 if there is no inflation. Magee forecasts equipment prices, including prices of used equipment of this sort, to rise at an annual rate of 12 percent, so the actual salvage expected to be realized at the end of the fifth year is $4,406 ($= \$2,500 \times 1.12^5$). Magee will pay taxes on any gain on disposal at 40 percent at the end of Year 6.

Magee Company owns old manufacturing equipment with both book and market value of $18,000 that it must retire, independent of whether it acquires the new machine.

Magee will depreciate any new equipment over 5 years for tax purposes using the following MACRS cost percentages: 20, 32, 19, 14.5, and 14.5.

Salvage value does not affect MACRS deductions for tax purposes but does affect depreciation computed for financial reporting purposes. Magee will depreciate the equipment for financial reporting over 5 years using the straight-line method. (These combinations result from the rules of generally accepted accounting principles and the income tax law, not from our wish to make the example complicated.)

Magee makes the following forecasts and projections:

1. Sales volume will be 15,000 units each year.
2. Sales price will be $7.00 per unit during Year 1, but will increase by 10 percent per year, to $7.70 in Year 2, $8.47 in Year 3, and so on.
3. Variable manufacturing costs are $3.00 per unit in Year 1, but will increase by 8 percent per year, to $3.24 in Year 2, and so on.
4. Selling costs are $5,000 per year plus $.50 per unit in Year 1. Variable selling costs per unit will increase by 10 percent per year to $.55 in Year 2, $.61 in Year 3, and so on.
5. Income tax rates will remain at 40 percent of taxable income each year.
6. The after-tax cost of capital is 15 percent per year.

Magee makes the following assumptions about the timing of cash flows:

7. It will pay all variable manufacturing costs in cash at the beginning of each year.
8. It will pay all selling costs, fixed and variable, in cash at the end of each year.
9. It will collect cash from customers at the end of each year.
10. It will pay income taxes for each year's operations at the end of the year.

Magee makes the following assumptions about its operations and accounting:

11. Although it may deduct selling costs on the tax return in the year incurred, it may not deduct manufacturing costs until it sells the goods.
12. It will have sufficient other taxable income that losses on this project in any period will offset that income, saving $.40 in income taxes for every $1.00 of operating loss.
13. It must produce enough each year to meet each year's sales, except that it must produce 20,000 units in Year 1 to provide a continuing supply of inventory of 5,000 units. It need produce only 10,000 units in Year 5, so that ending inventory will be zero.
14. It will use a LIFO cost flow assumption for inventories.
15. It will charge all depreciation for a year to the cost of units it produces that year.
    a. List the mutually exclusive alternatives that Magee Company faces.
    b. Construct a schedule of cash flows for acquiring the new asset.
    c. Analyze the alternative and suggest a decision to management of Magee Company.

The solution to this self-study problem appears at the end of the chapter on page 401.

Exhibit 10.3

Operating Cash Flow Analysis
(Problem 10.1 for Self-Study)

	1	2	3	4	5	6
Cash Inflows	$30,000	$36,000	$41,000	$45,000	$48,000	$50,000
Less Variable Costs Cash Outflows	12,000	14,400	16,400	18,000	19,200	20,000
Less Fixed Cost Cash Outflows	5,000	5,200	5,500	5,900	6,400	7,000
(1) Cash Flow before Taxes and Depreciation	$13,000	$16,400	$19,100	$21,100	$22,400	$23,000
Depreciation (MACRS).....................	12,000	19,200	11,520	6,900	6,900	3,480
Taxable Income	$ 1,000	$(2,800)	$ 7,580	$14,200	$15,500	$19,520
(2) Tax (40% rate).........................	400	(1,120)	3,032	5,680	6,200	7,808
(3) Cash Flows from Operations = (1) − (2)	12,600	17,520	16,068	15,420	16,200	15,192
(4) Present Value Factors (12%)	.89286	.79719	.71178	.63552	.56743	.50663
Present Value .... $63,343 =	$11,250	$13,967	$11,437	$ 9,800	$ 9,192	$ 7,697

	Present Value at Beginning of Year 1
Analysis of All Cash Flows	
Operating Cash Flows	$ 63,343
Cash Outlay for Machinery	(60,000)
Salvage Proceeds from Selling Machinery—Year 6, $6,000 × .50663	3,040
Taxes on Gain of $6,000 (= $6,000 Proceeds − $0 Tax Basis); Year 6, $6,000 × .40 × .50663	(1,216)
Net Present Value	$ 5,167

Summary

In deciding whether to invest cash today in return for cash payoffs in the future, the decision maker should take into account the time value of money using a discounted cash flow (DCF) method.

The net present value method involves making forecasts of future cash inflows and outflows for the proposed project. Making effective investment decisions requires careful analysis of accounting data to derive cash flows, which do not equal revenues less expenses in any given period. The DCF analysis discounts estimated cash flows to present value with a rate equal to the required rate of return on assets. The required rate of return is the cost of capital or the hurdle rate. Analysts often measure the cost of capital by taking a weighted average of the equities that provide a firm's financing, even though the cost of capital reflects the opportunity cost of the assets to be committed to the proposed project.

Solutions to Self-Study Problems

Suggested Solution to Problem 10.1 for Self-Study

Depreciation Schedule; MACRS Basis Is $60,000

Year	Rate	Depreciation
1	.200	$12,000
2	.320	19,200
3	.192	11,520
4	.115	6,900
5	.115	6,900
6	.058	3,480
		$60,000

See Exhibit 10.3 for cash flow analysis. Kinnard should undertake the project, because it has positive net present value.

Suggested Solution to Problem 10.2 for Self-Study

a. **Alternatives**
   (1) Sell the old equipment and do not acquire the new.
   (2) Sell the old equipment and purchase the new.
   Note that this problem does not have an alternative to retain the old equipment and continue using it, which would be possible in many situations.

b. **Acquiring the New Asset** Exhibit 10.4 derives the operating cash flows, including income tax effects. Exhibit 10.5, discussed later, combines operating

Exhibit 10.4

MAGEE COMPANY
Analysis of Cash Flow Data by Year[a]
(Part b of Problem 10.2 for Self-Study)

		1	2	3	4	5	
Production and Selling Costs during Year							
(1)[a]	Number of Units Produced	20,000	15,000	15,000	15,000	10,000	
(2)	Variable Manufacturing Cost per Unit	$ 3.00	$ 3.24	$ 3.50	$ 3.78	$ 4.08	
(3)	Total Variable Costs (at the beginning of year) = (1) × (2)	$ 60,000	$ 48,600	$ 52,500	$ 56,700	$ 40,800	
(4)	Depreciation Charge for Year for Taxes . . .	28,000	44,800	26,600	20,300	20,300	
(5)	Total Manufacturing Costs for Taxes = (3) + (4)	$ 88,000	$ 93,400	$ 79,100	$ 77,000	$ 61,100	
(6)	Manufacturing Cost per Unit for Taxes = (5)/(1)	$ 4.40	$ 6.23	$ 5.27	$ 5.13	$ 6.11	
(7)	Variable Selling Cost per Unit	$ .50	$ .55	$ .61	$ .67	$ .73	
Revenues, End of Year							
(8)	Number of Units Sold	15,000	15,000	15,000	15,000	15,000	
(9)	Selling Price per Unit	$ 7.00	$ 7.70	$ 8.47	$ 9.32	$ 10.25	
(10)	Total Revenues = (8) × (9)	$105,000	$115,500	$127,050	$139,800	$153,750	
Tax Return for Year							
(11)	Revenues = (10)	$105,000	$115,500	$127,050	$139,800	$153,750	
(12)	Less Manufacturing Costs of Sales	66,000	93,400	79,100	77,000	83,100	
(13)	Less Selling Expenses	12,500	13,250	14,150	15,050	15,950	
(14)	Taxable Income = (11) − (12) − (13)	$ 26,500	$ 8,850	$ 33,800	$ 47,750	$ 54,700	
(15)	Income Taxes Payable = .40 × (14)	$ 10,600	$ 3,540	$ 13,520	$ 19,100	$ 21,880	

Cash Flow at:							
	End of Year	0	1	2	3	4	5
	Beginning of Year	1	2	3	4	5	6
(16)	Revenues = (10)	—	$105,000	$115,500	$127,050	$139,800	$153,750
(17)	Less Variable Costs = (3)	$ 60,000	48,600	52,500	56,700	40,800	—
(18)	Less Selling Expenses = (13), Lagged	—	12,500	13,250	14,150	15,050	15,950
(19)	Less Income Taxes for Year = (15), Lagged	—	10,600	3,540	13,520	19,100	21,880
(20)	Net Cash Inflow (Outflow) = (16) − (17) − (18) − (19)	$(60,000)	$ 33,300	$ 46,210	$ 42,680	$ 64,850	$115,920
(21)	Present Value at 15 Percent = $126,672	$(60,000)	$ 28,957	$ 34,941	$ 28,063	$ 37,078	$ 57,633

[a]See text for discussion of line-by-line derivation.

and nonoperating cash flows. The calculations for the various lines of Exhibit 10.4 follow:

Line (1) Magee sells 15,000 units each year and produces those amounts each year except in Year 1, when production is 20,000, or 5,000 units more than sales, and in Year 5, when production is 10,000, or 5,000 units fewer.

Exhibit 10.5

MAGEE COMPANY
Analysis of All Cash Flows from Sale of Old Equipment and Purchase of New Equipment

	Present Value at Beginning of Year 1	Undiscounted Cash Flows
Operating Cash Flows (Exhibit 10.4)...	$126,672	$242,960
Cash Outlay for Equipment at Beginning of Year 1	(140,000)	(140,000)
Cash Proceeds from Selling Old Equipment	18,000	18,000
Salvage Proceeds from Selling Equipment at End of Year 5 ($4,406 × .49718)...	2,191	4,406
Taxes at 40 Percent on Salvage Proceeds of $4,406 Paid at the End of Year 6 ($4,406 × .40 × .43233)	(762)	(1,762)
Total	$ 6,101	$123,604

Line (2) Variable cost per unit is $3.00 for Year 1 and $3.24 for Year 2 and increases at the rate of 8 percent per year thereafter to $3.50 in Year 3, $3.78 in Year 4, and $4.08 in Year 5.

Line (3) Total variable costs result from multiplying line **(1)** by line **(2).** Magee pays this amount in cash at the beginning of the year, so transfers it to line **(17)** as a cash outflow at the beginning of each year.

Line (4) Depreciation charge for the year results from multiplying the taxable depreciable basis, $140,000, by the MACRS percentages: 20, 32, 19, 14.5, and 14.5. The financial statement depreciation will be $27,119 [= ($140,000 − $4,406)/5] per year, but this fact is irrelevant for the analysis of cash flows. Tax depreciation is relevant only because of its impact on tax-deductible cost of goods sold, which affects taxable income and income tax payments.

Line (5) Total manufacturing cost is the sum of the preceding two lines.

Line (6) Manufacturing cost per unit is generally irrelevant for decision making in the absence of taxes. Because, however, inventory builds up in Year 1 for sale in Year 5, and because tax rules require full absorption costing, Magee must compute the full cost of the units put into inventory in Year 1. Any firm must compute such unit costs to derive tax effects whenever production volume differs from sales volume.

Line (7) Variable selling costs of $.50 per unit per year increase at the rate of 10 percent per year. The figure affects total selling costs later on line **(13)** and cash outflow for selling costs on line **(18).**

Line (8) Magee has forecast the number of units it will sell.

Line (9) Selling price per unit increases at the rate of 10 percent per year. (The numbers here result from using this formula: Selling price at the end of Year $t = \$7.00 \times 1.10^{t-1}$. One might multiply each year's price by 1.10 to derive the next year's price. These two procedures do not differ significantly, but because of different rounding conventions, analysts may reach differing numbers by the fifth year.)

Line (10) Total revenue results from multiplying the preceding two lines. The product appears on line **(11)** for tax purposes and to line **(16)** for cash flow calculations.

Line (11) See discussion of line **(10)**.

Line (12) Manufacturing cost comes from line **(5)** except for Years 1 and 5. In Year 1, manufacturing cost is the product of manufacturing cost per unit, line **(6),** times number of units sold, line **(8)**: $\$4.40 \times 15,000 = \$66,000$. Magee uses a LIFO cost flow assumption. In Year 5, 10,000 units carry Year 5 manufacturing costs and 5,000 units carry Year 1 manufacturing costs: $\$61,100 + (\$4.40 \times 5,000) = \$83,100$.

Line (13) Selling expenses are variable costs per unit on line **(7)** multiplied by the number of units sold from line **(8)** plus $5,000.

Line (14) Taxable income is revenues, line **(11),** minus expenses on lines **(12)** and **(13).**

Line (15) Income taxes are 40 percent of the amount on line **(14).** Magee pays the amounts at the end of the year of sale.

Line (16) through (20) These lines show all cash flows. Be careful to align the timing of the cash flows. Note that the preceding lines show operations for a period. Magee assumes each cash flow occurs at a specific moment. Because the end of one year is also the beginning of the next, we find it convenient to label these moments with both their end-of-year and beginning-of-year designations to aid analysis. Note, for example, how the cash flows for variable manufacturing costs appear in one column, but the revenues from sale of the items produced appear in the next column.

Line (21) The present values at the beginning of Year 1 result from multiplying the numbers on line **(20)** by the appropriate factor from the 15-percent column in Table 2 at the back of the book. The sum of the numbers on line **(21)** is $126,672.

Analysis of All Cash Flows Exhibit 10.5 shows all the cash flows, operating and nonoperating, with present values at the beginning of Year 1. Magee pays taxes at the end of Year 6 on the salvage proceeds from the end of Year 5. Tax reporting under MACRS ignores salvage value in computing depreciation. The entire depreciable basis of $140,000 becomes deductible through MACRS. Thus, the gain on sale is equal to all the salvage proceeds, $4,406 (= $4,406 − $0).

The net present value of this project is positive, $6,101. Magee should not undertake it, however, without considering the net present value of its mutually exclusive alternative.

c.   If Magee sells the old and quits, the cash flow is $18,000. If Magee acquires the new equipment, the net present value of the estimated cash flows is about $6,000. Because the new equipment does not generate substantial amounts of positive cash flows in the last few years and because the result is worse than selling the old equipment outright, we prefer the outright sale, assuming that is a realistic business alternative. We would not conclude, however, that these data indicate a clear-cut decision either way. Whatever Magee Company does is not likely to be too costly, as compared to the rejected alternative.

Personal Computer Spreadsheet Application to Solving Self-Study Problem 10.2

The text recommends personal computer spreadsheets such as Lotus 1-2-3 and Microsoft Excel for analyzing DCF problems. The discussion here does not teach spreadsheet use. To learn how to use spreadsheets, you need hands-on experience. We hope this short presentation persuades those who do not already know how to use computer spreadsheets to learn to use them. The exhibit may teach users some new techniques. Exhibit 10.6 shows part of the Lotus 1-2-3 file we used to construct Exhibits 10.4 and 10.5. Observe the following:

1.   The exhibit shows only part of the spreadsheet for Exhibit 10.4, the assumptions, called *parameters,* at the top and the calculations at the bottom.
2.   Think of a computer spreadsheet as a chess board, a rectangular grid of squares, called cells. Identify a cell with a column letter and a row number. Every item of data or text in a computer spreadsheet appears in a cell. For example, cell D5 contains the number $3.00, and cell B3 contains the caption "Parameter Section."
3.   The parameters section gathers in one place all of the assumptions needed for Exhibit 10.4.
4.   The calculation section shows the columns for Year 3 and Year 4 in numerical form. We rounded the numbers for Exhibit 10.4.
5.   The calculation section shows also a column of formulas. These are the actual formulas appearing in the cells of the spreadsheet. For example, cell C35 contains the formula +C32*C33, not the number $52,488. When the computer multiplies the contents of cell C32 by the contents of cell C33, the number $52,488 results. Cell C35 shows the number. Cell F35 shows the formula as it would appear in column F.
6.   The formulas in column F use Lotus 1-2-3 (identical to Excel) notation. We do not explain that notation.

Exhibit 10.6

PERSONAL COMPUTER SPREADSHEET EXCERPT

For Exhibit 10.4, Lines (1)–(15): All Parameters and Calculations for Years 3 and 4

	B	C	D E	F	G
1					
2					
3	Parameter Section -----------------------				
4				Tax Depreciation	
5	Variable manufacturing cost in Year 1		$3.00	Rate by Year	
6	Growth rate in variable manufacturing costs per year		8.0%	Year 1 =	20.0%
7	Variable selling cost in Year 1		$0.50	Year 2 =	32.0%
8	Growth rate in variable selling costs per year		10.0%	Year 3 =	19.0%
9	Fixed selling costs per year		$5,000	Year 4 =	14.5%
10	Selling price per unit in Year 1		$7.00	Year 5 =	14.5%
11	Growth rate in selling price per unit		10.0%		
12	Income tax rate		40.0%		
13	New asset tax basis		$140,000		
14	Number of units sold each year		15,000		
15	Number of units produced in Year 1		20,000		
16	Number of units produced in Years 2, 3, and 4		15,000		
17	Number of units produced in Year 5		10,000		
18	Discount rate per year		15.0%		
19					
20	Net present value (calculations not shown here)		$126,672		
21					
22					
23					

Note: Body of exhibit is actual output from Lotus 1-2-3 file. This exhibit omits rows for lines (16)–(21) of Exhibit 10.4.
The spreadsheet carries all data to several more significant digits than appear here. For example, cell C33 is actually $3.49920 in the computer.

Calculation Section

	C	D	E	F	G
	Calculations			Formulas	
Year	3		4	Insert year number as column head	
(1) Production and Selling Costs during Year					
Number of Units Produced	15,000		15,000	+$D$16	
(2) Variable Manufacturing Costs per Unit	$3.50		$3.78	+$D$5*(1+$D$6)^(F29-1)	
(3) Total Variable Manufacturing Costs	$52,488		$56,687	+F32*F33	
(4) Depreciation Charge for Year for Taxes	26,600		20,300	+$G$9*$D$13	
(5) Total Manufacturing Costs for Taxes	$79,088		$76,987	+F35+F36	
(6) Manufacturing Costs per Unit for Taxes	$5.27		$5.13	+F38/F32	
(7) Variable Selling Costs per Unit	$0.61		$0.67	+$D$7*(1+$D$8)^(F29-1)	
Revenues, End of Year					
(8) Number of Units Sold	15,000		15,000	+$D$14	
(9) Selling Price per Unit	$8.47		$9.32	+$D$10*(1+$D$11)^(F29-1)	
(10) Total Revenues	$127,050		$139,755	+F45*F46	
Tax Return for Year					
(11) Total Revenues	$127,050		$139,755	+F45*F46	
(12) Less: Manufacturing Cost of Sales	(79,088)		(76,987)	-F38	
(13) Less: Selling Expenses	(14,075)		(14,983)	-$D$9-F32*F42	
(14) Taxable Income	$33,887		$47,785	@SUM(F51..F53)	
(15) Income Taxes Payable	$13,555		$19,114	+F55*$D$12	

7. The formulas in columns C, D, and F use the parameter cells. Observe that cell D5 contains the variable manufacturing cost per unit, $3 in our example. If you change cell D5 to $4, then the formula for cells C33 and D33 will automatically use the changed number. To see this, note that the formula in cell F33 shows $D$5, which means that the formula does not use $3 every time the program executes, but uses the contents of cell D5, whatever it may be at the time.

Good spreadsheet technique requires discipline and patience. Someone trying to rush through a solution might, for example, not parameterize cell D5. One could just insert the $3 number for variable manufacturing cost for Year 1 in the formula for cell C33. You can construct the spreadsheet faster this way and it will appear simpler. If you do so, you will be unable to test easily the sensitivity of the final result to the assumption about variable manufacturing cost per unit in Year 1.

Key Terms and Concepts

Capital budgeting
Investment decision versus financing
  decision
Discounted cash flow (DCF)
  methods
Net present value of cash flows
Effect of depreciation expense on
  cash flows

Modified accelerated cost recovery
  system (MACRS)
Opportunity cost of capital
Cost of capital
Required rate of return
Mutually exclusive investments

Questions, Exercises, Problems, and Cases

Questions

1. Review the meaning of the concepts or terms given above in Key Terms and Concepts.
2. The capital budgeting process comprises two distinct decisions. Describe these.
3. Assume a margin of error of plus or minus 10 percent in estimating any number required as an input for a capital budgeting decision. Under ordinary conditions, the net present value of a project is most sensitive to the estimate of which of the following?
   (1) Amounts of future cash flows.
   (2) Timing of future cash flows.
   (3) Cost of capital.
4. Financial accounting writers emphasize that ''depreciation is not a source of funds.'' This chapter states that accelerated cost recovery methods result in larger cash flows than does the straight-line depreciation method. Reconcile these two statements.

5. How, if at all, should the amount of inflation incorporated in the cost of capital influence projected future cash flows for a project?

6. In *measuring* the cost of capital, management often measures the cost of the individual equities. A firm has no contractual obligation to pay anything to common shareholders. How can the capital they provide be said to have a cost other than zero?

7. A firm has a choice of three alternative investments:
   (1) Short-term government note promising a return of 8 percent.
   (2) Short-term commercial paper (issued by a blue-chip corporation) promising a return of 10 percent.
   (3) Short-term, lower-grade commercial paper (issued by a less well-established corporation) promising a return of 15 percent.
   How can one define the opportunity cost of capital as the marginal investment available to the firm with at least three such alternatives, each with a different promised rate?

8. Explain how you might analyze a capital budgeting decision where the cash flow data are nominal (including expected inflation of, say, 3 percent per year) but the quoted cost of capital of 10 percent per year is real (excluding anticipated inflation).

9. Assume no change in marginal income tax rates over the life of new equipment about to be acquired. "Whenever the trade-in allowance for an already-owned asset is smaller than its book value for tax purposes, it will always pay to sell that asset rather than trade it in."
   Comment.

10. "Because the Modified Accelerated Cost Recovery System ignores salvage value for tax purposes in computing depreciation charges and the only effect of depreciation on cash flows is for income taxes, the analyst can safely ignore salvage value in capital budgeting."
    Comment.

11. Describe the factors that influence the market rate of interest a company must pay for borrowed funds.

12. Describe the chain of influence, if any, between the rate of anticipated inflation in an economy and the opportunity cost of capital to a firm in that economy.

13. "But, Mr. Miller, you have said that the opportunity cost of capital is the rate of return on alternative investment projects available to the firm. So long as the firm has debt outstanding, one opportunity for idle funds will be to retire debt. Therefore, the cost of capital cannot be higher than the current cost of debt for any firm with debt outstanding."
    How should Mr. Miller reply?

Exercises

Solutions to even-numbered exercises appear at the end of the chapter on page 420.

14. **Computing net present value.** Compute the net present value of
    a. An investment of $15,000 that will yield $1,000 for 28 periods at 4 percent per period.

b. An investment of $100,000 that will yield $250,000 8 years from now at 10 percent compounded semiannually.

15. **Computing net present value.** A firm has an after-tax cost of capital of 10 percent. Compute the net present value of each of the five projects listed in the following exhibit.

| | After-Tax Cash Flow, End of Year | | | |
Project	0	1	2	3
A	$(10,000)	$4,000	$4,000	$4,000
B	(10,000)	6,000	4,000	2,000
C	(10,000)	2,000	4,000	6,000
D	(10,000)	4,400	4,400	4,400
E	(10,000)	3,600	3,600	3,600

16. **Computing net present value.** Hammersmith Homes is considering four possible housing development projects, each requiring an initial investment of $5,000,000. The cash inflows from each of the projects follow:

Year	Project A	Project B	Project C	Project D
1	$2,000,000	$4,000,000	0	$1,000,000
2	2,000,000	2,000,000	0	2,500,000
3	2,000,000	2,000,000	0	3,000,000
4	2,000,000	1,000,000	0	2,500,000
5	2,000,000	1,000,000	$10,000,000	1,000,000

a. Ignoring tax effects, compute the net present value of each of the projects. Hammersmith's cost of capital is 15 percent.

b. Hammersmith can take on only one project; which should it choose? Explain why this project is superior to the others.

17. **Computing net present value.** Westminster Products is considering a project that requires an initial investment of $800,000 and that will generate the following cash inflows for the next 6 years:

Year	Cash Inflow at End of Year
1	$100,000
2	200,000
3	300,000
4	400,000
5	300,000
6	200,000

Ignoring tax effects, calculate the net present value of this project if Westminster's cost of capital is

a. 12 percent.

b. 20 percent.

18. **Computing net present value.** Megatech, a computer software developer, is considering a software development project that requires an initial investment of $200,000 and subsequent investments of $150,000 and $100,000 at the end of the first and second years. Megatech expects this project to yield annual after-tax cash inflows for 6 more years: $90,000 for the third through eighth years. Megatech's after-tax cost of capital is 10 percent.

Calculate the net present value of this project.

19. **Deriving cash flows and computing net present value.** The Eastern States Railroad (ESRR) is considering replacing its power jack tamper, used to maintain track and roadbed, with a new automatic-raising power tamper. ESRR spent $36,000 5 years ago for the present power jack tamper and estimated it to have a total life of 12 years. If ESRR keeps the old tamper, it must overhaul the old tamper 2 years from now at a cost of $10,000. ESRR can sell the old tamper for $5,000 now; the tamper will be worthless 7 years from now.

A new automatic-raising tamper costs $46,000 delivered and has an estimated physical life of 12 years. ESRR anticipates, however, that because of developments in maintenance machines, it should retire the new machine at the end of the seventh year for $10,000. Furthermore, the new machine will require an overhaul costing $14,000 at the end of the fourth year. The new equipment will reduce wages and fringe benefits by $8,000 per year.

Track maintenance work is seasonal, so ESRR normally uses the equipment only from May 1 through October 31 of each year. ESRR transfers track maintenance employees to other work but pays them at the same rate for the rest of the year.

The new machine will require $2,000 per year of maintenance, whereas the old machine requires $2,400 per year. Fuel consumption for the two machines is identical. ESRR's cost of capital is 12 percent per year, and because of operating losses, ESRR pays no income tax.

Should ESRR purchase the new machine?

20. **Observing the effects of using different discount rates.** Refer to the data and analysis developed for the Magee Company in Exhibits 10.4 and 10.5. Evaluate the alternatives using an after-tax cost of capital of 12 percent.

Problems

21. **Deriving cash flows and computing net present value.** The Largay Corporation is contemplating selling a new product. Largay can acquire the equipment necessary to distribute and sell the product for $100,000. The equipment has an estimated life of 10 years and has no salvage value. The following schedule shows the expected sales volume, selling price, and variable cost per unit of production:

Year	Sales Volume	Selling Price	Variable Cost of Production
1	10,000 Units	$5.00	$3.00
2	12,000	5.00	3.10
3	13,000	5.50	3.25
4	15,000	5.75	3.25
5	20,000	6.00	3.30
6	25,000	6.00	3.40
7	20,000	6.10	3.50
8	18,000	6.10	3.50
9	15,000	6.25	3.50
10	15,000	6.30	3.75

Production in each year must be sufficient to meet each year's sales. In addition, Largay will purchase 5,000 extra units in Year 1 to provide a continuing inventory of 5,000 units. Thus production in Year 1 will be 15,000 units but in Year 10 will be only 10,000 units, so that at the end of Year 10, ending inventory will be zero. Largay will use a LIFO (last-in, first-out) cost flow assumption. Largay's income tax rate is 40 percent, and its after-tax cost of capital is 10 percent per year. It receives cash at the end of the year when it makes sales and spends cash at the end of the year when it incurs costs. Largay estimates variable selling expenses at $1 per unit sold. Depreciation on the new distribution equipment is not a product cost but is an expense each period. For tax reporting, depreciation will follow the MACRS percentages: 20 percent in the first, 32 percent in the second, 19.2 percent in the third, 11.5 percent in the fourth, 11.5 percent in the fifth, 5.8 percent in the sixth, and zero thereafter. The Largay Corporation generates sufficient cash flows from other operations so that it can use all depreciation deductions to reduce current taxes otherwise payable.

    a. Prepare a schedule of cash flows for this project.

    b. Verify that the net present value of the project is approximately $7,485.

22. **Analyzing cash flows from alternatives.** Biggart Company is considering replacing some machinery. The old machinery has book value and tax basis of $8,000. Its current market value is $3,000. Biggart does not face the alternative of just selling the old machinery now. It must either use it for another year or replace it. Biggart has been depreciating the old equipment on a straight-line basis at the rate of $8,000 per year. If Biggart retains the machinery it will depreciate the remaining tax basis over 1 year and the financial book value over 3 years. The machinery will have no market value 1 year hence.

    Biggart can acquire new machinery for $30,000, which will produce $10,000 of cash savings at the end of the first year. The new machinery will produce cash savings at the end of Year 2 that is 5 percent greater than at the end of Year 1, and at the end of Year 3 the savings will be 5 percent greater than at the end of Year 2. The new machinery will have a 3-year life. Biggart will depreciate the equipment on a straight-line basis over 3 years for both tax and financial reporting purposes. It will sell the machinery for $5,000 at the end of Year 3 but will ignore salvage value in tax depreciation computations.

Biggart pays income taxes at the rate of 40 percent for both ordinary income and for capital gains. The cost of capital for the new machinery, after taxes, is 15 percent per year. Biggart earns sufficient taxable income that it can deduct from its taxes payable at the beginning of Year 1 (= end of Year 0) the loss from disposition of the old machinery at the beginning of Year 1 (= end of Year 0).

Analyze the present value of the cash flows of the alternatives and make a recommendation to Biggart Company.

23. **Analyzing cash flows from alternatives.** Davis Donuts is considering purchasing a new donut-making machine for $1 million at the end of Year 0 to be put into operation at the beginning of Year 1. The new machine will save $220,000, before taxes, per year from the cash outflows generated by using the old machine. For tax purposes, Davis will depreciate the new machine in the following amounts: $100,000 in Year 1, $300,000 in Year 2, and $200,000 per year thereafter until fully depreciated or sold. The new machine will have no salvage value at the end of Year 5. Davis expects the new machine to have a market value of $400,000 at the end of 3 years.

If Davis acquires the new machine at the end of Year 0, it can sell the old one for $200,000 at that time. The old machine has a tax basis of $300,000 at the end of Year 0. If Davis keeps the old machine, Davis will depreciate it for tax purposes in the amount of $100,000 per year for 3 years, when it will have no market value.

Davis pays taxes at the rate of 40 percent of taxable income and uses a cost of capital of 10 percent in evaluating this possible acquisition. Davis has sufficient otherwise-taxable income in Year 0 to save income taxes for each dollar of loss it may incur if it sells the old machine at the end of Year 0.

a. Compute the net present value of cash flows from each of the alternatives facing Davis.

b. Make a recommendation to Davis.

c. Assume that the cash flows described in the problem for Years 2 through 5 are real, not nominal, amounts, but the 10-percent cost of capital includes an allowance for inflation of 4 percent. Describe how this will affect your analysis. You need not perform new computation.

24. **Net present value graph and indifference cost of capital.** The after-tax net cash flows associated with two mutually exclusive projects, G and H, are as follows:

Project	Cash Flow, End of Year		
	0	1	2
G	$(100)	$125	—
H	(100)	50	$84

a. Calculate the net present value for each project using discount rates of 0, .04, .08, .12, .15, .20, and .25.

b. Prepare a graph as follows. Label the vertical axis "Net Present Value in Dollars" and the horizontal axis "Discount Rate in Percent per Year."

Plot the net present value amounts calculated in part **a** for project G and project H.

c. State the decision rule for choosing between projects G and H as a function of the firm's cost of capital.

d. What generalizations can you draw from this exercise?

25. **Deriving cash flows for asset disposition.** The Wisher Washer Company (WWC) purchased a made-to-order machine tool for grinding washing machine parts. The machine costs $100,000 and WWC installed it yesterday. Today, a vendor offers a machine tool that will do exactly the same work but costs only $50,000. Assume that the cost of capital is 12 percent, that both machines will last for 5 years, that WWC will depreciate both machines on a straight-line basis for tax purposes with no salvage value, that the income tax rate is and will continue to be 40 percent, and that WWC earns sufficient income that it can offset any loss from disposing of or depreciating the "old" machine against other taxable income.

How much, at a minimum, must the "old" machine fetch upon resale at this time to make purchasing the new machine worthwhile?

26. **Deriving cash flows for abandonment decision.** The Ingram Company must decide whether to continue selling a line of children's shoes manufactured on a machine that has no other purpose. The machine has a current book value of $12,000 and Ingram can sell it today for $7,000. Ingram depreciates the machine on a straight-line basis for tax purposes assuming no salvage value and could continue to use it for 4 more years. If Ingram keeps the machine in use, it can sell it at the end of 4 years for $600, although this will not affect the depreciation charge for the next 4 years. The variable cost of producing a pair of shoes on the machine is less than the cash received from customers by $13,000 per year. To produce and sell the children's shoes requires cash outlays of $10,000 per year for administrative and overhead expenditures as well. Ingram Company pays taxes at a rate of 40 percent. The rate applies to any gain or loss on disposal of the machine as well as to other income. From its other activities, Ingram Company earns more income than any losses from the line of children's shoes or from disposal of the machine.

a. Prepare a schedule showing all the cash and cost flows that Ingram Company needs to consider in order to decide whether to keep the machine.

b. Should Ingram Company keep the machine if its after-tax cost of capital is 12 percent?

c. Repeat part **b** assuming an after-tax cost of capital of 15 percent.

27. **Net present value analysis of tax advantages of MACRS.** Assume an after-tax cost of capital of 15 percent per year and an income tax rate of 40 percent. Also assume that all cash flows for taxes occur at year-end.

a. Compute the present values of the tax shield provided by straight-line depreciation over 10 years of an asset costing $10,000.

b. Compute the present value of the tax shield provided by accelerated cost recovery over 6 years using the following percentages: 20, 32, 19.2, 11.5, 11.5, and 5.8.

28. **Outright sale versus trade-in of existing asset** (adapted from problems by D. O. Green). Brogan Company must buy a crane. It can buy a new one from the factory for $150,000. Cromwell Company, a competitor, bought an identi-

cal model last week for $150,000, finds that it needs a larger crane, and offers to sell its crane to Brogan. The new factory crane and the Cromwell crane have economic lives of 5 years with no salvage value.

Cromwell Company can sell its crane to Brogan or can trade in the crane on the larger model, which also has a 5-year life with no salvage value. The cash price of the larger model is $300,000, and the factory will give Cromwell an allowance of $135,000 if Cromwell trades in the ''old'' crane. If Cromwell trades in the old crane it may not recognize the loss for tax purposes, but the depreciable cost of the new asset is the book value of the old asset plus any cash paid for the new asset. Cromwell uses modified accelerated cost recovery for tax purposes with the following percentages of cost claimed in the 5 years: 25, 38, 37, 0, and 0. It has a cost of capital of 12 percent and pays taxes at a marginal rate of 40 percent. If Cromwell sells to Brogan, Cromwell may deduct any loss from taxable income at the time of sale—that is, immediately. Round dollar calculations to the nearest hundred dollars.

a. What is the lowest price Cromwell can get from Brogan and be as well off as by trading in?

b. At what price will the two parties, if they are acting rationally, agree for Cromwell to sell to Brogan?

29. **Deriving cash flows for two mutually exclusive alternatives; no income taxes.** Reinhardt Hospital's director needs a new car. The purchasing agent has narrowed the alternatives to buying one with either a gasoline or diesel engine. The gasoline model costs $18,000, whereas the diesel model costs $22,000. The gasoline model gets 20 miles per gallon of gasoline, whereas the diesel model gets 30 miles per gallon of diesel fuel. Gasoline currently costs $1.40 per gallon. Reinhardt expects gasoline to increase in price at the rate of 12 percent per year. Diesel fuel costs $1.20 per gallon. Reinhardt expects diesel fuel to increase in price at the rate of 8 percent per year. Reinhardt will drive the car for 4 years: 36,000 miles in the first year, 30,000 miles each in the second and third years, and 24,000 miles in the fourth year. The expected salvage value of the gasoline model is $7,000 at the end of the fourth year. Assume that all other operating costs (oil, insurance, and so on) will be the same for the two different kinds of cars.

Assume that all cash flows occur at the start of the year but that receipt of salvage proceeds occurs at the end of the fourth year. Because Reinhardt Hospital is a tax-exempt, nonprofit institution, it need not consider income taxes. The cost of capital to the hospital is 15 percent per year.

You have two mutually exclusive alternatives to analyze. You can subtract the cash flows from acquiring the diesel from those of acquiring the gasoline model to derive the cash flows of an investment project called ''acquisition of diesel rather than gasoline model.''

Using this shortcut, derive the cash flows of acquiring the diesel rather than the gasoline model, compute the net present value of those cash flows, and decide which model car the hospital should acquire.

30. **Computing present value of operating cost savings and replacement cost of used asset.** The Pepper River Electric Company (PREC) produces electricity. Its current oil-burning plant is several years old and can produce electricity for 20 more years. It can produce 15 million kilowatt-hours of electricity per year by burning oil costing $500,000 per year. If PREC were to rebuild a 20-year oil-burning plant today, the costs would be $10 million. Because of drastic increases in oil prices since PREC built the current plant, PREC would not build an oil-burning plant today. Instead, it would build a coal-burning plant. The coal-burning plant would cost $11 million to build, have a 20-year useful life, and produce 15 million kilowatt-hours of electricity per year by burning coal costing $100,000 per year.

Assume a cost of capital of 12 percent per year. Assume also that the fuel cost differential stays constant for 20 years and that all fuel costs are incurred at the beginning of each year. Ignore income tax considerations.

a.   What is the present value of the cash savings from lower fuel costs resulting from operating a coal-burning plant rather than an oil-burning plant?

b.   What is the current replacement cost of the productive capacity owned by PREC? (The chapter does not give guidance on this question, which we ask so that you will consider issues beyond those discussed.)

31.   **Deriving cash flows and performing breakeven analysis; comprehensive sensitivity analysis.** Peugeot once offered its automobile Model 504 in two versions—one with a gasoline engine and one with a diesel engine. The gasoline version had a list price of $716 less than the diesel version. Assume for the purpose of this problem that dealers actually charge the list prices in purchase transactions. According to federal EPA mileage tests and using then-current fuel prices, the operating cost savings for the diesel over the gasoline model amount to $.01108 cent per mile or $133 per year assuming 12,000 miles of use each year. Assume that a purchaser decided to acquire one of these two cars and that the purchaser expected to drive 12,000 miles a year for 5 years before retiring the car. The gasoline version will have a resale value in 5 years of $175 less than the diesel.

Assume that the operating cost differential remains constant over the 5 years. Assume also that the automobile purchase and the first year's fuel payments occur on January 1 of each year, and the owner retires the automobile on January 1 of Year 6.

a.   If the purchaser uses a discount rate of 12 percent per year, which version should the purchaser acquire, and what is the net present value of the savings from buying this version rather than the other?

b.   At what mileage driven each year, assuming equal annual mileage per year for 5 years, constant resale values, and a discount rate of 12 percent, is the purchaser indifferent between the two versions?

c.   Assume that the purchaser drives 12,000 miles each year. At what discount rate is the purchaser indifferent between the two versions? (Find the approximate answer, using the tables at the back of the book.)

Integrative Problems and Cases

32.   **Make-or-buy—Liquid Chemical Co.**[10] The Liquid Chemical Company manufactures and sells a range of high-grade products. Many of these products

---

[10]Adapted from a case by Professor David Solomons, Wharton School, University of Pennsylvania.

require careful packing. The company has a special patented lining made from a material known as GHL, and the firm operates a department to maintain its containers in good condition and to make new ones to replace those beyond repair.

Mr. Walsh, the general manager, has for some time suspected that the firm might save money, and get equally good service, by buying its containers from an outside source. After careful inquiries, he approached a firm specializing in container production, Packages, Inc., and asked for a quotation from it. At the same time, he asked Mr. Dyer, his chief accountant, to let him have an up-to-date statement of the costs of operating the container department.

Within a few days, the quotation from Packages, Inc., arrived. The firm proposed to supply all the new containers required—at that time, running at the rate of 3,000 a year—for $1,250,000 a year, the contract to run for a guaranteed term of 5 years and thereafter to be renewable from year to year. If the number of containers required increased, the contract price would increase proportionally. Also, independent of this contract, Packages, Inc., proposed to carry out purely maintenance work on containers, short of replacement, for a sum of $375,000 a year, on the same contract terms.

Mr. Walsh compared these figures with Mr. Dyer's cost figures, which covered a year's operations of the container department of the Liquid Chemical Company and appear in Exhibit 10.7.

Walsh concluded that he should immediately close the department and sign the contracts offered by Packages, Inc. He felt bound, however, to give the manager of the department, Mr. Duffy, an opportunity to question this conclusion before acting on it. Walsh told Duffy that Duffy's own position was not in jeopardy: even if Walsh closed his department, another managerial position was becoming vacant to which Duffy could move without loss of pay or prospects. The manager Duffy would replace also earns $80,000 a year. More-

---

Exhibit 10.7

LIQUID CHEMICAL
Container Department

Materials		$ 700,000
Labor:		
Supervisor		50,000
Workers		450,000
Department Overheads:		
Manager's Salary	$80,000	
Rent on Container Department	45,000	
Depreciation of Machinery	150,000	
Maintenance of Machinery	36,000	
Other Expenses	157,500	
		468,500
		$1,668,500
Proportion of General Administrative Overheads		225,000
Total Cost of Department for Year		$1,893,500

over, Walsh knew that he was paying $85,000 a year in rent for a warehouse a couple of miles away for other corporate purposes. If he closed Duffy's department, he'd have all the warehouse space he needed without renting.

Duffy gave Walsh a number of considerations to think about before closing the department. "For instance," he said, "what will you do with the machinery? It cost $1,200,000 4 years ago, but you'd be lucky if you got $200,000 for it now, even though it's good for another 5 years. And then there's the stock of GHL (a special chemical) we bought a year ago. That cost us $1,000,000, and at the rate we're using it now, it'll last us another 4 years. We used up about one-fifth of it last year. Dyer's figure of $700,000 for materials includes $200,000 for GHL. But it'll be tricky stuff to handle if we don't use it up. We bought it for $5,000 a ton, and you couldn't buy it today for less than $6,000. But you'd get over $4,000 a ton if you sold it, after you'd covered all the handling expenses."

Walsh worried about the workers if he closed the department. "I don't think we can find room for any of them elsewhere in the firm. I could see whether Packages can take any of them. But some of them are getting on. Walters and Hines, for example, have been with us since they left school 40 years ago. I'd feel bound to give them a pension—$15,000 a year each for 5 years, say."

Duffy showed some relief at this. "But I still don't like Dyer's figures," he said. "What about this $225,000 for general administrative overheads? You surely don't expect to sack anyone in the general office if I'm closed, do you?" Walsh agreed.

"Well, I think we've thrashed this out pretty fully," said Walsh, "but I've been turning over in my mind the possibility of perhaps keeping on the maintenance work ourselves. What are your views on that, Duffy?"

"I don't know," said Duffy, "but it's worth looking into. We shouldn't need any machinery for that, and I could hand the supervision over to the current supervisor who earns $50,000 per year. You'd need only about one-fifth of the workers, but you could keep on the oldest and save the pension costs. You wouldn't save any space, so I suppose the rent would be the same. I don't think the other expenses would be more than $65,000 a year."

"What about materials?" asked Walsh.

"We use 10 percent of the total on maintenance," Duffy replied.

"Well, I've told Packages, Inc., that I'd give them my decision within a week," said Walsh. "I'll let you know what I decide to do before I write to them."

Assume the company has an after-tax cost of capital of 10 percent per year and uses an income tax rate of 40 percent for decisions such as these. Liquid Chemical would pay taxes on any gain or loss on the sale of machinery or the GHL at 40 percent. (Depreciation for book and tax purposes is straight-line over 8 years.) The tax basis of the machinery is $600,000.

Assume the company had a 5-year time horizon for this project. Also assume that any GHL needed for Year 5 is purchased during Year 5.

a.   What are the four alternatives available to Liquid Chemical?

b.   What action should Walsh take? Support your conclusion with a net present value analysis of all the mutually exclusive alternatives.

    c. What, if any, additional information do you think Walsh needs to make a sound decision? Why?

33. Comprehensive review. Demski Company may venture into a new product line. If it does so, it must acquire new equipment at the beginning of Year 1 for $135,000. The equipment, which requires installation expenditures of $15,000, will last for 10 years and will have salvage value then of $2,000 if there is no inflation. Demski expects equipment prices, including prices of used equipment of this sort, to rise at an annual rate of 6 percent, so the actual salvage value expected at the end of the tenth year is $3,582 (= $2,000 $\times$ 1.06^{10}). Demski will pay taxes on any gain on disposal at 40 percent at the end of Year 10.

    Demski Company owns old manufacturing equipment with a book value of $28,000 that it must retire. Demski can sell the old equipment for $28,000 cash.

    Demski will depreciate the new equipment for financial reporting over 10 years using the straight-line method but over 6 years using MACRS for tax purposes. Depreciation deductions on the tax return will equal the following percentages of depreciable basis: 20 percent in the first year, 32 percent in the second, 19.2 percent in the third, 11.5 percent in the fourth, 11.5 percent in the fifth, 5.8 percent in the sixth, and zero thereafter. Recall that Demski does not have to consider salvage value in computing MACRS deductions for tax purposes.

    Demski forecasts sales volume, by year, as follows:

Year 1	10,000 Units
Year 2	12,000
Year 3	15,000
Year 4	18,000
Year 5	20,000
Year 6	25,000
Year 7	28,000
Year 8	23,000
Year 9	19,000
Year 10	15,000

Demski makes the following forecasts and projections:

- Sales price will be $5.50 per unit during Year 1, but will increase by 10 percent per year, to $6.05 in Year 2, $6.66 in Year 3, and so on.
- Variable manufacturing costs are $3.00 per unit in Year 1, but will increase by 8 percent per year, to $3.24 in Year 2, and so on.
- Selling costs are $5,000 per year plus $.50 per unit in Year 1. Variable selling costs per unit will increase by 10 percent per year to $.55 in Year 2, $.61 in Year 3, and so on.
- Income tax rates will remain at 40 percent of taxable income each year.
- The after-tax costs of capital are 15 percent per year.

Demski makes the following assumptions about the timing of cash flows:

- It will pay all variable manufacturing costs in cash at the beginning of each year.
- It will pay all selling costs, fixed and variable, in cash at the end of each year.
- It will collect cash from customers at the end of each year.
- It will pay income taxes for each year's operations at the end of the year.

Demski makes the following assumptions about its operations and accounting:

- Although it may deduct selling costs on the tax return in the year incurred, it may not deduct manufacturing costs until it sells the goods.
- It will have sufficient other taxable income that losses on this project in any period will offset that income, saving $.40 in income taxes for every $1.00 of operating loss.
- It must produce enough each year to meet each year's sales, except that it must produce 15,000 units in Year 1 to provide a continuing supply of inventory of 5,000 units. It need produce only 10,000 units in Year 5, so that ending inventory will be zero.
- It will use a LIFO cost flow assumption for inventories.
- It will charge all depreciation for a year to the cost of units it produces that year.

a. List the mutually exclusive alternatives facing Demski Company.
b. Construct a schedule of cash flows for the alternative of selling the old equipment and acquiring the new equipment.
c. Analyze the alternatives and suggest a decision to the management of Demski Company.

Suggested Solutions to Even-Numbered Exercises

14. **Computing net present value.**
   a. Net Present Value $= -\$15,000 + (\$1,000 \times 16.66306)$
      $= \underline{\underline{\$1,663}}$.

   b. Net Present Value $= -\$100,000 + (\$250,000 \times 0.45811)$
      $= \underline{\underline{\$14,528}}$.

16. Computing net present value.

a.

Year	Present Value Factor	Project A	Project B	Project C	Project D
		Discounted Cash Flows			
0	1.00000	$(5,000,000)	$(5,000,000)	$(5,000,000)	$(5,000,000)
1	.86957	1,739,140	3,478,280	0	869,570
2	.75614	1,512,280	1,512,280	0	1,890,350
3	.65752	1,315,040	1,315,040	0	1,972,560
4	.57175	1,143,500	571,750	0	1,429,375
5	.49718	994,360	497,180	4,971,800	497,180
		$ 1,704,320	$ 2,374,530	$ (28,200)	$ 1,659,035

b. Hammersmith should take Project B, which has the largest net present value. Even though all four projects have similar undiscounted total cash flow streams—that is, $10,000,000—Project B is superior because the bulk of the cash returns come in the earlier years.

18. Computing net present value.

Year (1)	Net Cash Flow (2)	10% Present Value Factor (3)	Present Value (4)[a]
0	$(200,000)	1.00000	$(200,000)
1	(150,000)	.90909	(136,364)
2	(100,000)	.82645	(82,645)
3	90,000	.75131	67,618
4	90,000	.68301	61,471
5	90,000	.62092	55,883
6	90,000	.56447	50,803
7	90,000	.51316	46,184
8	90,000	.46651	41,986
			$ (95,064)

[a](4) = (2) × (3).

20. **Observing the effects of using different discount rates.**

MAGEE COMPANY
Operating Cash Flows, End of Year
(cost of capital, 12 percent)

End of Year (1)	Cash Flow (2)	Present Value Factor at 12 Percent (3)	Present Value at 12 Percent = (2) × (3) (4)
0	$(60,000)	1.00000	$(60,000)
1	33,300	.89286	29,732
2	46,210	.79719	36,838
3	42,680	.71178	30,379
4	64,850	.63552	41,213
5	115,920	.56743	65,776
Total			$143,938

Present Value of All Cash Flows from Sale of
Old Equipment and Purchase of New Equipment

Operating Cash Flow	$143,938
Net Cash Outlay for Equipment (= $140,000 − $18,000)	(122,000)
Salvage Proceeds End of Year 5: $4,406 × .56743	2,500
Taxes on Salvage End of Year 6: $4,406 × .40 × .50663	(893)
Net Present Value	$ 23,545

Present Value of Outright Sale

Sale Proceeds	$ 18,000

Chapter 11

A Closer Look at Capital Budgeting

Learning Objectives

1. Note several alternative methods for evaluating projects with cash flows spread through time—internal rate of return, excess present value index, payback period, discounted payback period, and the accounting rate of return.
2. Understand the shortcomings of each of the alternative methods for decision making; note that circumstances exist where the shortcomings do not matter.
3. Learn not to commit the fundamental error of intermixing the investment and financing decisions: attributing to a specific project the general benefits, if any, from corporate borrowing.
4. Study long-term leases sufficiently to see that they are a form of financing and, as such, subject to the same fundamental error as other forms of financing.

Chapter 10 introduced the fundamentals of capital budgeting: separating the investment decision from the financing decision, analyzing cash flows, and summing the cash flows after discounting them at the firm's opportunity cost of capital. This chapter (1) describes other methods for making capital budgeting decisions, (2) evaluates their strengths and weaknesses, and (3) explores the separation of the investment decision from the financing decision.

Alternative Methods for Evaluating Projects

Managers have used many methods for evaluating projects, but most are inferior to using the net present value (or discounted cash flow) method with a discount rate equal to the cost of capital. Some methods that take the time value of money into account often give the same decision results as the net present value rule. In practice, they prove to be satisfactory. Alternative methods that do not take the time value of money into account are easy to use because they do not involve present value computations. This simplicity is their chief virtue.

The strength of the net present value method for making capital budgeting investment decisions rests on its focus on discounted cash flows. The manager can find the net present value itself, a dollar number with a sign—positive or negative—difficult to compare across alternatives. Some decision makers believe that comparing a project with a net present value of $10,000 to one with a net present value of $100,000 may not be meaningful if the first project requires an initial investment much different from the second's. Decision makers are sometimes uncomfortable with the net present value method because it seems to be independent of the size of the underlying investment. The net present value rule states merely that a positive net present value is good and a negative one is bad.

Practitioners have developed variants of the discounted cash flow method, called internal rate of return analysis and the excess present value index, to take into account the *size* of the projects being considered. We discuss these next, as well as alternative methods often found in practice. We show that these variants can cause other problems and that the net present value method dominates them for decision making.

Internal Rate of Return

The **internal rate of return (IRR),** sometimes called the *time-adjusted rate of return,* of a series of cash flows is the discount rate that equates the net present value of that series to zero. Stated another way, the IRR is the rate that discounts the future cash flows to a present value just equal to the initial investment. The IRR method is another discounted cash flow (DCF) method.

Calculating the Internal Rate of Return   To illustrate the calculation of the internal rate of return, assume that a proposed project requires an initial investment of $11,059 and promises to yield net cash inflows for the next 4 years as follows: Year 1, $5,000; Year 2, $4,000; Year 3, $3,000; Year 4, $2,000. To calculate the internal rate of return, compute the rate that discounts the net cash *inflows* during years 1 to 4 so that they have a present value of $11,059; that is, the net present value of the inflows and outflows is zero. Mathematically, this step involves solving the following equation for r, the discount rate:

$$\$11,059 = \frac{\$5,000}{(1 + r)^1} + \frac{\$4,000}{(1 + r)^2} + \frac{\$3,000}{(1 + r)^3} + \frac{\$2,000}{(1 + r)^4}.$$

Computers and some pocket calculators can compute this discount rate quickly. Whatever device we use, we must try various discount rates until we find the proper

Exhibit 11.1

Calculation of Internal Rate of Return

End of Year (1)	Cash Inflow (Outflow) (2)	Present Value Factor at 10 Percent (3)	Present Value of Cash Flows at 10 Percent (4)	Present Value Factor at 12 Percent (5)	Present Value of Cash Flows at 12 Percent (6)
0	$(11,059)	1.00000	$(11,059)	1.00000	$(11,059)
1	5,000	.90909	4,545	.89286	4,464
2	4,000	.82645	3,306	.79719	3,189
3	3,000	.75131	2,254	.71178	2,135
4	2,000	.68301	1,366	.63552	1,271
Net Present Value			$ 412		$ 0

one. Using trial and error, we begin by trying a discount rate of 10 percent. Columns (3) and (4) of Exhibit 11.1 show that at this discount rate the net present value is positive. This result suggests that the internal rate of return must be larger than 10 percent. So we try 12 percent. Column (6) of Exhibit 11.1 shows that a 12-percent discount rate equates the net present value to zero. Twelve percent therefore is the internal rate of return for this project. (If the net present value for a given trial rate were *negative,* we would try a *smaller* rate at the next trial.) The compound interest appendix at the back of this book provides further illustrations of finding the internal rate of return.

Using the Internal Rate of Return   When using the internal rate of return to evaluate investment alternatives, one specifies a **cutoff rate,** such as 15 percent for the JEP Realty Syndicators example in the previous chapter. The IRR method accepts a project if its internal rate of return exceeds the cutoff rate and rejects if its internal rate of return is less than the cutoff rate. The cutoff rate is sometimes called the **hurdle rate.**

Advocates of the internal rate of return argue that the method does not require knowing the firm's cost of capital and is therefore easier to use than the net present value rule. This assessment is short-sighted, however. For the internal rate of return rule to give the correct answers, the cutoff rate must be the cost of capital. Otherwise, the IRR method will reject some projects that will increase the value of the firm to its owners or accept some projects that will decrease value. The net present value method requires no more data than the internal rate of return method.

Superiority of Net Present Value Method over Internal Rate of Return Method

Single Ranking Measure   The net present value method provides a single net present value amount for each project that the analyst can use to make the accept-reject decision. The internal rate of return method, however, may give more than one internal rate of return for a particular project. This mathematical phenomenon can occur when the pattern of yearly net cash flows contains an intermixing of net cash inflows and outflows. For example, if a project requires cash expenditures at the end of its life to return the plant site to its original condition, then individual cash flows can be negative both at the beginning and at the end of a project's life but positive in between. Projects with intermixing of cash inflows and outflows can have multiple internal rates of return.[1] Examples of multiple internal rates of return have arisen in practice for coal mining companies that use strip mining to generate cash inflows from coal but who must spend cash at the completion of the mining phase to reclaim the stripped land. Problem **19** at the end of this chapter gives an example.

Better Ranking of Alternatives Under the net present value (NPV) rule, projects are either acceptable or unacceptable. When projects are mutually exclusive, the decision maker can choose only one of a set of projects. The NPV rule tells us to choose the project with the largest net present value. The internal rate of return rule ranks projects in the same way as the net present value rule only when the scenario meets each of the four following conditions:

1. The cutoff rate used for the internal rate equals the cost of capital.
2. Projects are not mutually exclusive.
3. Projects have the same life in periods.
4. There is only one internal rate of return.

Otherwise, the internal rate of return leads to incorrect decisions about projects, as demonstrated next.

Mutually Exclusive Projects **Mutually exclusive projects** are a set of alternatives from which the decision maker can choose only one. For example, a firm needing a new truck may prepare a net present value analysis for trucks meeting the firm's specifications from each of four different suppliers. After it selects one of the trucks, it will not consider the other three. The firm needs only one truck. The net present value decision rule for choosing among mutually exclusive projects accepts the project with the largest net present value and rejects the others. The internal rate of return analysis can signal the wrong selection from mutually exclusive projects. Assume that the after-tax cost of capital is 10 percent per year and that a firm can choose only one of the projects, A or B, as shown in Exhibit 11.2. Project A provides a simple illustration for calculating the internal rate of return. The internal rate of return on Proposal A is the rate r such that

$$\$100 = \frac{\$120}{1 + r}.$$

Solving gives $r = .20$. The internal rate of return of .15 for Project B is similarly easy to calculate. The internal rate of return rule prefers Project A to Project B, whereas the net present value rule prefers Project B.

---

[1] Solving for the internal rate of return involves finding the roots of a polynomial. Descartes's rule of signs tells how to determine the limit to the number of roots of such a polynomial. See the Glossary for an explanation of this rule.

Exhibit 11.2
Data for Projects A and B

Project Name	After-Tax Cash Flows by Year, End of Year		Internal Rate of Return	Net Present Value at 10 Percent
	0	1		
A	$(100)	$120	20%	$ 9.09
B	(300)	345	15	13.64

To see that Project B, which requires an investment $200 (= $300 − $100) more than Project A, is better for the firm, consider what the firm must do with the other $200 it will have to invest if the firm chooses Project A. It must invest that $200, by definition, at the after-tax cost of capital of 10 percent and will receive $220, after taxes, at the end of the first year. So the total flows available at the end of the first year from Project A and from the investment of the other funds at 10 percent will be $120 + $220 = $340. This result is less than the $345 available after taxes from Project B. The firm will prefer the results from choosing Project B as the net present value rule signals. A firm choosing Project B will be $5 wealthier at the end of Year 1 than a firm choosing Project A.

To understand better why the net present value ranking is superior, decide whether you would rather invest $.10 today to get $2 a year from now ($r = 1,900$ percent) or invest $1,000 today to get $2,500 a year from now ($r = 150$ percent). You may not do both. We guess that you, as we, would prefer the second alternative even though the internal rate of return on the first is more than 12 times larger than for the second. The internal rate of return rule, applied to mutually exclusive projects, ignores the amount of funds that the firm can invest at that rate. This shortcoming is sometimes called the **scale effect.**[2]

Projects with Different Lifetimes When a project has an initial investment (cash inflow) followed by a series of cash outflows, the analysis must take into account how the firm will use the cash inflows until the project is complete. The major failing of the IRR method is that it assumes that the firm can reinvest all cash outflows from the project at the IRR of the project, rather than at the cost of capital. Consider projects C and D shown in Exhibit 11.3. The internal rate of return on Project D is the rate r that satisfies the equation

$$\$100 = \frac{\$50}{(1 + r)} + \frac{\$84}{(1 + r)^2}.$$

---

[2]The scale effect problem often arises in using the internal rate of return method to evaluate alternatives to existing projects. Refer to Case A (food blenders and processors) on page 393 of Chapter 10. What is the internal rate of return on alternative 2 described there? It is infinite because there is no initial cash outflow. Whenever you must compare a status quo to alternatives requiring initial cash outflows, the internal rate of return analysis is likely to be difficult.

Exhibit 11.3

Data for Projects C and D

Project Name	Cash Flows by Year, End of Year			Internal Rate of Return	Net Present Value at 10 Percent
	0	**1**	**2**		
C	$(100)	$125	—	25%	$13.64
D	(100)	50	$84	20	14.88

You can verify that the internal rate of return is 20 percent by using the 20-percent column of Table 2 at the back of the book. The internal rate of return rule ranks Project C as being better than Project D, whereas the net present value rule ranks Project D as being better than Project C.

To see why Project D is better for the firm, consider what the firm must do during Year 2. If it accepts Project C, it must invest $125 in the average investment project available to the firm. The return from such an average project is, by definition, the cost of capital, 10 percent. At the end of Year 2, the firm will have $125 × 1.10 = $137.50. If the firm accepts Project D, it will invest the $50 cash inflow at the end of the first year at 10 percent to grow to $50 × 1.10 = $55 by the end of Year 2. Thus, the total available at the end of the second year is $55 + $84 = $139, which exceeds the $137.50 if the firm accepts Project C. The internal rate of return rule ignores the fact that the firm must invest the idle funds at the cost of capital.[3]

Excess Present Value Index

Compute the **excess present value index** as follows:

$$\text{Excess Present Value Index} = \frac{\text{Present Value of Future Cash Flows}}{\text{Initial Investment}}.$$

This index indicates the number of present value dollars generated per dollar of investment. For example, if the present value of the *future* cash flows is $17,000 and the initial investment is $12,000, the excess present value index is 1.42 (= $17,000/$12,000). The excess present value (EPV) rule says to accept a project with an index greater than 1.0 and reject it if the index is less than 1.0.

In the absence of mutually exclusive projects, the net present value method and the excess present value method result in the same accept-reject decisions.

When projects are mutually exclusive the net present value and excess present value index methods can give conflicting signals. Consider the data in Exhibit 11.4. The rankings of the four projects differ depending on whether the rankings result from net present values or from excess present value indexes. The difference in the rankings arises because of a scale effect. In Exhibit 11.4 the EPV rule prefers the small Project H to the large Project E. Using the net present value rule will maxi-

---

[3]The firm may invest the idle funds at another rate, which, although different, is equivalent when the analysis takes into account the differential risk.

Exhibit 11.4

Ranking of Projects According to Net Present Value and Excess Present Value Index Methods

Project (1)	Initial Cash Outlay Required (2)	Present Value of Future Cash Inflows (3)	Net Present Value (4)[a]	Ranking by Net Present Value (5)	Excess Present Value Index (6)[b]	Ranking by Excess Present Value Index (7)
E	$120,000	$170,000	$50,000	1	1.42	3
F	110,000	150,000	40,000	2	1.36	4
G	70,000	100,000	30,000	3	1.43	2
H	30,000	55,000	25,000	4	1.83	1

[a]Column **(4)** = column **(3)** − column **(2)**.
[b]Column **(6)** = column **(3)**/column **(2)**.

mize the wealth of the firm because the rule focuses on total dollar return, not the rate of return per dollar. The EPV rule can fail for mutually exclusive projects when the firm must invest other funds at the cost of capital.

Payback Period

Another method for evaluating investment projects involves the payback period. The **payback period** is the length of time that elapses before total cumulative after-tax cash inflows from the project equal the initial cash outlay for the project. Refer to Exhibit 11.1. The proposed project has a payback period of about 2.7 years. By the end of the first year, the firm has recovered $5,000 of the initial investment. By the end of the second year, the cumulative cash inflows total $9,000 (= $5,000 + $4,000). The firm receives the remaining $2,059 (= $11,059 − $9,000) approximately two-thirds of the way through the third year. Hence the payback is 2.7 years. The payback period rule states that the decision maker should accept projects when the payback period is as short as some designated cutoff time period, such as 2 years, and reject them otherwise.

The payback period rule ignores both the time value of money and all cash flows subsequent to the payback date. One project could have a shorter payback period than another but smaller net present value. The payback period rule focuses concern on the firm's liquidity. The net present value rule takes liquidity into account, because the cost of capital is the rate of return required to justify a firm's employing additional assets in the business should a possibility arise.

A mathematical artifact of the payback method follows: When the analyst considers projects not mutually exclusive, each having the same life and uniform cash inflows over its life, the results of using the payback method will be the same as using the net present value method.[4] This fact, plus the fact that in earlier times

---

[4]If the net cash inflows per year from a project are constant and occur for a number of years at least twice as long as the payback period, and when the discount rate is reasonably large—say, 10 percent per year or more—the reciprocal of the payback period is approximately equal to the internal rate of return on the project. Thus the payback period will rank projects in the same way as the internal rate of return and, hence, the net present value method, under the conditions stated.

computing devices were not as accessible and inexpensive as they are today, led to the education of a generation of managers with the techniques of payback analysis. Be aware that some in the business world still use payback methods; they will not necessarily get wrong answers.

Advocates of the payback period rule argue that the net present value rule, even with its discounting of future cash flows, gives too much weight to cash flows more than 3 or 4 years into the future. They point out that many managers have favorite projects they would like the company to undertake. Managers have learned that they can make marginal projects look acceptable under the net present value method by setting some of the distant cash inflows unrealistically large. (They might make optimistic projections of future increases in sales revenues or optimistic estimates of the rate at which production costs will decline as workers learn new skills.) Such managers might figure that they will not be on the same job by the time top management learns that the cash inflows projected for, say, 5 years hence had been too optimistic. Such managers may reasonably expect to have been promoted or fired by the time 5 years elapse. Thus they expect not to be held accountable for their distant projections. Analysts who fear being misled by overly optimistic managers insist on using a payback rule to find out the near-term profitability of a project. Advocates of the net present value method caution about accepting cash flow projections without careful study, but maintain that the net present value method is still conceptually superior. They suggest that the analyst use a higher cost of capital rate for distant years, reflecting increased risk of projections for those years. Although none of the examples so far have illustrated this fact, the discount rate can change from year to year.

Discounted Payback Period

Given the widespread use of the payback period rule and its inability to yield good decisions for the most general case, some accountants have suggested that firms that want a payback rule should use the discounted payback period.[5] The **discounted payback period** resembles the ordinary payback period, but it is defined as the length of time that elapses before the *present value* of the cumulative cash inflows just exceeds the initial cash outlay. The discount rate used in this calculation is most often the cost of capital. The discounted payback period gives some recognition to the time value of funds that flow before payback occurs. The ordinary payback periods of projects J and K in Exhibit 11.5 are the same, 3 years, but the discounted payback criteria will properly prefer K to J.

Either payback rule would improperly prefer both J and K to Project L. Yet analysts sometimes recommend the discounted payback rule to firms that are wary of applying the net present value rule to projects like Project L. As we pointed out previously, the manager who made the original forecast for $50,000 cash inflow for

---

[5]See the results of the following surveys: T. Klammer, "Empirical Evidence of the Adoption of Sophisticated Capital Budgeting Techniques," *Journal of Business* 45 (July 1972), p. 393; L. Schall, G. Sundem, and W. Geijsbeck, "Survey and Analysis of Capital Budgeting Methods," *Journal of Finance* 33 (March 1978), pp. 281–287; and S. H. Kim and E. J. Farragher, "Current Capital Budgeting Practices," *Management Accounting* 62, 12 (June 1981), pp. 26–32.

Exhibit 11.5

Illustrative Data for Payback Rules, Projects J, K, and L

Project	Cash Flow at End of Year					
Name	0	1	2	3	4	5
J.................	$(10,000)	$2,000	$3,000	$5,000	$2,000	—
K.................	(10,000)	5,000	3,000	2,000	2,000	—
L.................	(10,000)	—	—	—	—	$50,000

Year 5 may not be around to be accountable when the firm learns that the forecast was too optimistic.

Accounting Rate of Return

The **accounting rate of return,** sometimes called the "rate of return on investment" or (ROI), for a project is

$$\frac{\text{Average Yearly Income from the Project}}{\text{Average Investment in the Project}}.$$

Assume that a project requiring an investment of $10,000 promises total income of $3,300 over 4 years. The average yearly income is $825. The average investment in the project, assuming straight-line depreciation and no salvage value, is $5,000 [= ($10,000 + $0)/2]. Hence, the accounting rate of return is $825/$5,000 = 16.5 percent. The accounting rate of return pays no attention to the time value of money and uses accounting income, rather than cash flow, data.

Assume that the project results in equal annual after-tax cash flows of $3,325 at the end of each of the 4 years. Net income over the life of the project, then, is $3,300 (= 4 × $3,325 − $10,000). Because the internal rate of return on an investment of $10,000 to yield $3,325 in arrears for 4 years is about 12.5 percent, the net present value of this project will be positive only for discount rates less than 12.5 percent. If the firm has an after-tax cost of capital of 15 percent, this project is not a worthwhile undertaking because it has a negative net present value of about −$500 at that rate. The ROI is 16.5 percent, which may induce the manager making decisions with ROI to think the project is worthwhile.[6]

Because the accounting rate of return ignores the time value of money and uses accounting data rather than cash flow data, analysts should not use it. To see why analysts often use ROI anyway, consider three points. First, ROI is easy to compute. Second, the ROI and the internal rate of return for some projects do not drastically differ, so using ROI for decision making will not always lead to wrong decisions.

---

[6]Furthermore, the ROI will be the same, 16.5 percent, even if all the cash flow from the project occurs at the end of the fourth year, whereas the internal rate of return drops to 7.4 percent in this case. To take another extreme case, assume that $12,300 of cash flows occurred at the end of the first year and $1,000 occurred at the end of the fourth. The ROI would remain 16.5 percent, but the internal rate of return would increase dramatically, to more than 26 percent.

Third, as later chapters discuss, firms often use ROI in performance measurement. Managers who expect to be evaluated by ROI after they make decisions will not always ignore ROI in making decisions.

Thus we see why companies using ROI for *performance measurements* will use ROI to *make decisions.* Chapter 15 shows that a refinement of ROI, residual income, provides better data for performance evaluation than does ROI. Firms need not use ROI for either decision making, before it undertakes plans, or for performance evaluations, after the fact.[7]

Evaluation of Capital Budgeting Decision-Making Tools

The manager must decide whether to undertake some investment project. We have seen that the net present value method applied to cash flow data will lead to maximizing the owners' wealth and that the internal rate of return is almost as good. Sometimes, however, firms use other methods such as payback and ROI, because the computational work may be less burdensome for the analyst. When thousands of dollars are at stake and managers have computer terminals available to them more readily than pencil sharpeners, competent managers will use the computationally more complex discounted cash flow methods. The simple methods can make gross partitions of projects as either (1) clear rejects or (2) those to be considered further with more refined methods.

Problem 11.1 for Self-Study

Comparing Products. Fabco Manufacturing Company considers the purchase of two different types of machines to manufacture rubber gaskets, one of the many products it produces for industrial markets. The two machines are alike in the following ways: Each requires an initial investment of $750,000; lasts 5 years, after which the salvage value is zero; and has sufficient capacity to meet the projected steady demand. The main difference between the two machines is the timing and amount of operating cash flows. Machine A's operating cash costs would start out high and then decrease in subsequent years. Machine B promises constant operating cash costs. The end-of-year incremental net cash flows (revenues minus operating cash costs) for the two machines follow:

	After-Tax Cash Flow per Year, End of Year					
	0	1	2	3	4	5
Machine A	$(750,000)	$100,000	$200,000	$200,000	$300,000	$550,000
Machine B	(750,000)	250,000	250,000	250,000	250,000	250,000

---

[7]Financial accounting, which often requires evaluations of entire businesses after the fact, often uses various ROI measures. See Chapter 18. To summarize, ROI measures are poor for decision making but may be valid for evaluation.

Fabco needs to decide which, if either, of the two machines to buy for manufacturing rubber gaskets. Unsure of which method of evaluation to use, the vice president has asked that calculations be made for the following methods:

(1) Payback period (assume, for this calculation only, that cash flows occur evenly throughout the year).
(2) Accounting rate of return.
(3) Internal rate of return.
(4) Net present value (cost of capital = 10 percent).
(5) Net present value (cost of capital = 12 percent).
  a. Perform these calculations for each machine. (Use discount factors rounded to five decimal places.) For each method, state which machine appears to be the better investment.
  b. Why does the net present value method yield different decisions at the two different discount rates? Does the internal rate of return method exhibit the same phenomenon?
  c. Comment on the usefulness of each of the preceding methods for choosing between the two machines.

The solution to this self-study problem appears at the end of the chapter on page 442.

Separating Investment and Financing Decisions

Make investment decisions independently of financing decisions. If a project can earn a return at least as large as the firm's cost of capital, undertake it. How to raise the specific funds needed for the project is a separate question.

Apparent Net Present Value Benefits to Borrowing

Combining the investment and financing decisions can mislead decision makers into believing that a project financed with debt is worth more than the same project financed with cash on hand. The examples in this section show how the confusion results. Assume that a firm borrows money at the market rate of interest and makes the required debt service payments, both principal and interest, on schedule. Such an undertaking, by itself, can never be worthwhile in the same sense that an investment project with a positive net present value is worthwhile. Such borrowing increases the leverage of the firm, increasing the risk to the owners' equity. Unlike mere leverage, a positive net present value is a favorable gamble, because it promises a rate of return higher than those otherwise available to the firm.

Exhibit 11.6 illustrates the net present values that result from analyzing borrowing activity as though it were an investment project. It assumes a firm with a pretax

---

Exhibit 11.6

Net Present Values from Borrowing at Various Interest Rates, Discounted at 15 Percent Cost of Capital

End of Year (1)	Event (2)	Pretax (3)	From Reduced Income Taxes Caused by Deducting Interest Expense (4)	After-Tax (5)	Present Value at 15 Percent (6)
12 Percent Loan					
0	Borrow	$1,000	—	$1,000	$1,000
1	Interest	(120)	$48	(72)	(63)
2	Interest	(120)	48	(72)	(54)
2	Repayment	(1,000)	—	(1,000)	(756)
	Net Present Value				$ 127
18 Percent Loan					
0	Borrow	$1,000	—	$1,000	$1,000
1	Interest	(180)	$72	(108)	(94)
2	Interest	(180)	72	(108)	(82)
2	Repayment	(1,000)	—	(1,000)	(756)
	Net Present Value				$ 68
25 Percent Loan					
0	Borrow	$1,000	—	$1,000	$1,000
1	Interest	(250)	$100	(150)	(130)
2	Interest	(250)	100	(150)	(114)
2	Repayment	(1,000)	—	(1,000)	(756)
	Net Present Value				$ 0

Column (3): Interest expense determined by terms of loan: 12, 18, or 25 percent.

Column (4): .40 × (3) when column (3) is deductible on tax return.

Column (5): (3) + (4).

Column (6): Amount in column (5) discounted at 15 percent using factors from Table 2.

End of Year 0	1,00000
End of Year 1	.86957
End of Year 2	.75614

---

cost of capital of 25 percent, an income tax rate of 40 percent, and thus an after-tax cost of capital of 15 [= (1.00 − .40) × 25] percent. The firm has sufficient other income that interest expense deducted on the tax return reduces cash outflows for taxes by $.40 for each $1.00 of interest expense.

In Exhibit 11.6, column (3) shows the pretax cash flows from borrowing, and column (5) shows the cash flows after tax effects for the deductibility of interest expense. Column (6) shows the net present values of the cash flows, positive in the top two panels and zero in the third.

The top two panels of Exhibit 11.6 show apparently positive net present value from an outright borrowing. The first two might indicate to a naive analyst that the borrowing is worthwhile.[8]

A net present value analysis of the cash flows from a loan will show a positive net present value whenever the pretax borrowing rate is less than the pretax cost of capital. In this example, the pretax cost of capital is 25 percent $[= .15/(1.00 - .40)]$. Put differently, a loan will show positive net present value whenever the after-tax cost of borrowing is less than the cost of capital. In this case, the after-tax cost of borrowing is the interest rate multiplied by .60 $(= 1.00 - .40$ income tax rate). For example, if the borrowing rate is 12 percent, the after-tax cost of borrowing is 7.2 $[= (1.00 - .40) \times 12]$ percent.

A loan will, as in Exhibit 11.6, show a positive net present value whenever the after-tax cost of capital exceeds the after-tax borrowing rate. This positive net present value appears even though the loan does not improve the borrower's risk-adjusted expected returns. The fact that the present value is positive and the firm is not better off shows the weakness of embedding the financing arrangement in the net present value analysis. Next, we illustrate such an embedding and the misleading signal it causes.

Problem 11.2
for Self-Study

Investment Project. Management of the Antle Company considers an investment project that requires an initial investment of $10,000 and that promises to return $14,641, after taxes, at the end of 4 years. Because the firm's after-tax cost of capital is 10 percent per year, the net present value of the investment is zero. An investment banker points out, however, that if the firm borrows the $10,000 via a 4-year annual coupon bond issue, the annual interest expense (based on 8-percent coupons) will be $800 but will be only $480 after taxes at a 40 percent rate. The net present value of the project will increase from zero to $1,648, and the project will be worthwhile. The banker offers to arrange a $10,000 loan at an 8-percent rate.

a. Verify that the net present value of the project is zero.
b. Reproduce the investment banker's analysis given above; use five-place present value factors.
c. Comment on the investment banker's proposal and advise the Antle Company as to how it should evaluate the project.

The solution to this self-study problem appears at the end of the chapter on page 444.

---

[8]In the top panel of Exhibit 11.6, the market interest rate—12 percent—is lower than the after-tax cost of capital of 15 percent. The other two panels show interest rates—18 percent and 25 percent—higher than the after-tax cost of capital. Twenty-five percent is the breakeven rate—the borrowing rate at which the net present value of the borrowing goes to zero.

Leasing Is a Form of Financing

Types of Leases

Leases are of two broad types. **Cancelable leases,** such as for the use of telephones by the month or of cars by the day or week, are generally short-term and either party in the rental transaction can cancel it. These leases do not present any analytic difficulties because they involve no long-term commitments to making cash payments.

Noncancelable leases, on the other hand, run for longer periods of time. Under these leases, a firm commits itself to payments over the term of the lease whether or not it continues to use the leased asset. The obligation under a noncancelable lease does not, in an economic sense, differ significantly from a loan from a bank or other creditor. These leasing arrangements are, in effect, installment purchases of the property. The noncancelable lease is a means of financing the acquisition of an asset's service for a specified period of time.

Evaluating Leases

Properly evaluating a leasing proposal separates the investment and financial decisions. First, decide if the firm should acquire the asset's services (the investment decision). To do this, calculate the net present value of the cash flows expected to be generated by the asset, assuming that the firm purchases the asset immediately for cash. Use the cost of capital as the discount rate. If the net present value is positive, consider the form of financing. If the net present value is negative, do not consider the proposal further.[9]

Illustration of the Lease Evaluation Procedure

Return to the example of JEP Realty Syndicators discussed in Chapter 10. The company considers acquiring computer hardware that will permit it to market a new investment package. To purchase the computer requires an immediate cash payment of $100,000. Alternatively, the manufacturer will lease the asset to JEP Realty for a rental fee of $29,832 a year for 5 years, after which the lessor will scrap the asset.

Investment Decision   First decide if acquiring the asset's services is a good investment, as in Exhibit 10.2. The analysis appears again in the top panel of Exhibit 11.7. The analysis assumes that JEP purchases the asset outright and that it discounts annual cash flows at the cost of capital of 12 percent per year. If JEP purchases the asset, the net present value of the investment project is $2,208. Acquiring the asset is, therefore, worthwhile.

---

[9]In stating the rule this way, we assume that the lessor has not reduced the implicit purchase price in the lease as compared to the outright purchase price.

Exhibit 11.7

Annual Net Cash Flows and Net Present Values of Alternatives Available to JEP Realty Syndicators for Acquiring Use of Asset[a]

End of Year (1)	Pretax Cash Inflows Minus Cash Outflow Expenses (2)	Depreciation (3)	Lease Payments (4)	Pretax Income (5)	Income Tax Expense (6)	Net Cash Inflows (Outflows) (7)	Present Value of Net Cash Flows at 12% (8)
Purchase Asset Outright; No Borrowing (See Exhibits 10.1 and 10.2)							
0	$(100,000)	—	—	—	—	$(100,000)	$(100,000)
1	50,000	$ 20,000	—	$30,000	$12,000	38,000	33,929
2	40,000	20,000	—	20,000	8,000	32,000	25,510
3	30,000	20,000	—	10,000	4,000	26,000	18,506
4	25,000	20,000	—	5,000	2,000	23,000	14,617
5	15,000	20,000	—	(5,000)	(2,000)	17,000	9,646
	$ 60,000	$100,000		$60,000	$24,000	$ 36,000	$ 2,208
Lease Asset; Lease Payment Made at the End of Each Period							
0	—	—	—	—	—	—	—
1	$ 50,000	—	$ 29,832	$20,168	$ 8,067	$ 12,101	$ 10,804
2	40,000	—	29,832	10,168	4,067	6,101	4,864
3	30,000	—	29,832	168	67	101	72
4	25,000	—	29,832	(4,832)	(1,933)	(2,899)	(1,842)
5	15,000	—	29,829	(14,829)	(5,932)	(8,897)	(5,048)
	$160,000		$149,157	$10,843	$ 4,336	$ 6,507	$ 8,850

[a]Discount rate is 12 percent per year; income taxes are 40 percent of pretax income.

Column (2): Refer to Exhibit 10.2. The amounts shown here are the amounts in column (2) minus the amounts shown in column (3) of Exhibit 10.2. The initial outlay is not an expense.

Column (3): Straight-line method; $100,000 cost/5-year life.

Column (5): Amount in column (2) minus amounts in columns (3) and (4).

Column (6): Forty percent of amount in column (5).

Column (7): Amount in column (2) minus amounts in columns (4) and (6).

Column (8): Amount in column (7) multiplied by present value factor for 12-percent discount rate.

Financing Decision Next we must consider how JEP should finance the investment. We must consider this second question because leasing is a form of financing.

The bottom panel of Exhibit 11.7 shows the calculation of the net present value assuming that JEP acquires the asset by leasing. Instead of a cash outflow of $100,000 at time zero, the cash outflow is $29,832 per year for 4 years for lease payments and $29,829 in the last year. To simplify the illustration, we assume that lease payments occur at the end of each year. Because JEP Realty leases the asset, it will not deduct depreciation expense in calculating taxable income but will deduct rent expense. JEP discounts the net after-tax cash flows using the cost of capital of 12 percent. The net present value of acquiring the asset's services through leasing is $8,850. Notice that the net present value of leasing is four times as large as the net present value of outright purchase.

Some managers would note the much larger net present value for the leasing plan and conclude that leasing is surely better for the firm than buying outright.

Comparing the net present values of buying outright versus leasing is invalid. The analysis has combined the investment decision with the financing decision. A non-cancelable lease is a form of borrowing. In the first case, the firm is not borrowing; in the second case, it is borrowing. To evaluate the leasing plan, the manager should analyze alternative financing plans as well. It will apply the methods of corporate finance.

Why Does Leasing Appear More Attractive Than Outright Purchase?

Leasing has a net present value more than four times as large as the net present value of the outright purchase. Why? We can rephrase this question to make the managerial implications clearer. Suppose that the cash flow in Year 1 were only $45,000, not $50,000. The analysis of the outright purchase then shows a negative net present value, indicating that the project is not worthwhile for the company. The analysis of leasing shows a positive net present value, indicating that the project is worthwhile when leased but not when purchased. What should the manager conclude?

The answers to both questions involve the difference between the after-tax interest cost of debt and the cost of capital used in making investment decisions. In the illustration for JEP Realty, the after-tax cost of capital is 12 percent, whereas the borrowing rate is 15 percent. The net present value analysis of the leasing alternative charges the company with interest on borrowings at 15 percent, with an after-tax cost of 9 percent [= (1.00 − .40) × 15 percent], but discounts the cash flows at 12 percent. Any present value analysis of a series of interest payments discounted at a higher rate than the after-tax rate implied by the loan contract will show the present value of the debt service payments to have a lower present value than the face amount of the borrowing. Recall the discussion of financing methods illustrated in Exhibit 11.6.

The phenomenon of **leverage** occurs when the rate of return on total capital increases because the rate typically earned by the company on its projects exceeds the rate paid to borrow. The difference between the net present values of leasing and outright purchase results from showing the expected returns to leverage as a part of the return to the specific project. But, of course, the firm always has the option to borrow at the current market rate of interest. The returns and risks of leverage accrue to the firm's financing policy as a whole. The analysis should not attribute them to any one investment project.[10]

---

[10]The nature of leasing contracts can be somewhat more complicated than indicated here. For example, the lessee may pay in advance, with the initial lease payment being immediately deductible for tax purposes. It is not usually possible to arrange a straight loan with interest payable in advance that is deductible for tax purposes. (In theory, there is no such thing as interest paid in advance. If a borrower makes payments before interest has accrued, theory says that those payments must be a reduction in the principal amount of the loan, not interest.) Another complication arises when the manufacturer offers a "package deal," where the combined interest payments and asset cost are smaller together than they

Considering Investment and Financing Decisions Simultaneously Can Be Acceptable

Are there conditions under which the analysis in the second panel of Exhibit 11.7 is correct for making an investment decision? In other words, can it ever be correct to consider the net present value of the combined operating and financing cash flows? Yes.

If the lessor allows the lessee to make debt service (lease) payments solely from the cash flows produced by the leased asset, then correct analysis combines the financing plan and the operating cash flows. This is *not* the same thing as saying that the leased asset is collateral for the loan.

Example The Burlington Northern (BN) Railroad leases for 12 years from the General Electric Credit Company a new heavy-duty locomotive for hauling coal from the Powder River Basin in Wyoming to San Antonio. BN promises to pay $2,000,000 per year for 12 years. BN must make the payments whatever use (if any) it makes of the locomotive. If the railroad fails to make payments, the Credit Company may seize the locomotive, which it owns.

Case A The Credit Company expects payments from whatever cash BN has on hand, independent of the business that generated the cash. If BN should go bankrupt, the Credit Company may collect amounts due to it, just as any other creditor. In this case, the decision to acquire the locomotive is independent of the particular financing arrangements offered by the lessor. The railroad ought to make the investment decision on the basis of the cash flows from using the locomotive, assuming that it purchases the locomotive for cash.

Case B The Credit Company agrees to require debt service (lease) payments made solely from the revenues of hauling coal with this particular locomotive. If BN does not use the locomotive for any reason for a given year, BN need not make the $2,000,000 payment for the year. In this case BN can consider the financing decision simultaneously with the investment decision, because BN's acquisition of the debt in becoming the lessee of the locomotive will not affect its ability to borrow funds (or issue new equity shares) to finance other parts of its business. This situation would be unusual, but occasionally arises, particularly in some leveraged leases and oil field product financing arrangements.

---

would be separately. (Automobile dealers often are willing to sell at a lower price when the buyer borrows from the dealer than when the buyer makes an outright purchase.) The advanced questions raised by some leasing contracts are beyond the scope of this introductory, but already sophisticated, discussion. The reader interested in a more advanced discussion can consult Chapter 8 of *Handbook of Modern Accounting,* 2nd ed., Sidney Davidson and Roman L. Weil, eds. (New York: McGraw-Hill, 1977), and S. Basu, *Leasing Arrangements: Managerial Decision Making and Financial Reporting Issues* (Hamilton, Ontario: Society of Management Accountants of Canada, 1980).

Problem 11.3
for Self-Study

The impact of financing on capital budgeting decisions. Only in exceptional cases will a specific financing instrument be tied so closely to a specific investment project that the capital cost of the investment is the cost of the specific financing instrument.

Consider two firms, Company Apple and Company Banana. Both companies operate two lines of business of the same size. The first line of business is owning, and leasing to others, railroad oil tank cars. Their second line of business is owning and leasing vacation homes near recreational lakes. In financing the two businesses, Company Apple and Company Banana borrow funds from local banks to supplement the funds invested by the owners. For purchases of oil tank cars to be put on lease, First National Bank will lend 80 percent of the purchase price through long-term, fixed-interest-rate loans. For purchases of vacation homes, Second National Bank will lend only 40 percent of the purchase price through long-term, fixed-interest-rate loans. First National Bank finances only tank car loans and Second National Bank finances only vacation home loans.

Company Apple First National Bank has agreed that Company Apple need make interest payments on the tank car debt and all tank car debt principal repayments only out of tank car rentals. The only collateral for the loans is the tank cars. Company Apple need not use the proceeds from vacation home rentals in any way to service the tank car debt to First National Bank. The financing of the vacation homes is similar: debt service payments to Second National Bank will come only from rentals of vacation homes, and the only collateral for the loan is the home being financed with a given loan.[11]

Company Banana Company Banana, while identical in its assets and operations to Company Apple, has conventional installment note financing for both its tank car and vacation home purchases. That is, both banks look to all income of the firm—from whatever source—for payment of interest and principal on debt. The banks can receive the payments as they come due from the assets Company Banana has on hand. Thus Company Banana must pay interest due First National Bank, for example, with earnings from vacation homes if tank car rentals are insufficient. Moreover, if Company Banana defaults on its loans to the First National Bank, the bank can expect to receive some of the proceeds of disposing of the vacation homes.

Analyze the differences between Company Apple's and Company Banana's financings. How do the implications of these differences affect capital budgeting decisions?

The solution to this self-study problem appears at the end of the chapter on page 445.

---

[11]These simplified facts highlight the issue. Only in the cases of some leveraged leases, certain loans from the federal Small Business Administration to new businesses and oil field product financing arrangements, have we actually seen financing of this sort. We have, for example, seen such agreements between Amoco and the First National Bank of Chicago.

Summary

The optimal method for evaluating investment projects should take the time value of money into account. All the methods that do take the time value of money into account require a cutoff rate or discount rate, sometimes called a hurdle rate. If the firm wants to make correct economic decisions, it must set the cutoff or discount rate equal to the cost of capital. If the firm uses the cost of capital rate, the net present value rule is no more complex than the others. Using the net present value rule will lead to decisions that will make present value of the firm's wealth equal to or larger than that from using any of the other rules.

Under many circumstances, the net present value method and the internal rate of return method give identical answers. In some circumstances, particularly those involving mutually exclusive projects, the internal rate of return method can give misleading results. Thus the analyst should use the net present value method in making the investment decision.

Analysis should separate the investment decision and the financing decision for investment projects. The use of the present value rule and the differential principle for making decisions will enable the manager to choose between various methods of financing only if the contending financing plans involve equal amounts of borrowing for equal amounts of time. Otherwise, the analysis will combine the benefits of financial leverage with the benefits from a particular investment project.

Solutions to Self-Study Problems

Suggested Solution to Problem 11.1 for Self-Study

Exhibit 11.8 provides data used in various parts of the solution.

a. (1)   Payback period:

> *Machine A:* Cumulative cash inflow at the end of Year 3 = $500,000. Total investment of $750,000 − $500,000 = $250,000 remaining to be recouped in Year 4.

$$\frac{\$250,000}{\$300,000} = .83.$$

Thus payback period = 3.83 years.

> *Machine B:*

$$\text{Payback Period} = \frac{\$750,000}{\$250,000 \text{ per Year}} = 3.0 \text{ Years.}$$

> *Decision:* Purchase Machine B if a payback period of 3 years is acceptable.

Exhibit 11.8

FABCO MANUFACTURING COMPANY
(Problem 11.1 for Self-Study)

	Cash Flow	Discount Factor at 10 Percent	Present Value at 10 Percent	Discount Factor at 12 Percent	Present Value at 12 Percent
Machine A					
Year 0.................	$(750,000)	1.00000	$(750,000)	1.00000	$(750,000)
Year 1.................	100,000	.90909	90,909	.89286	89,286
Year 2.................	200,000	.82645	165,290	.79719	159,438
Year 3.................	200,000	.75131	150,262	.71178	142,356
Year 4.................	300,000	.68301	204,903	.63552	190,656
Year 5.................	550,000	.62092	341,506	.56743	312,087
Net Present Value			$ 202,870		$ 143,823
Machine B					
Year 0.................	$(750,000)	1.00000	$(750,000)	1.00000	$(750,000)
Year 1.................	250,000	.90909	227,273	.89286	223,215
Year 2.................	250,000	.82645	206,613	.79719	199,298
Year 3.................	250,000	.75131	187,828	.71178	177,945
Year 4.................	250,000	.68301	170,753	.63552	158,880
Year 5.................	250,000	.62092	155,230	.56743	141,858
Net Present Value			$ 197,697		$ 151,196

(2) Accounting rate of return (or return on investment):

Machine A:

$$\text{Average Net Income} = \frac{\text{Total Cash Flow} - \text{Total Depreciation}}{5}$$

$$= \frac{\$1,350,000 - \$750,000}{5}$$

$$= \$120,000.$$

$$\text{Average Investment} = \frac{\$750,000}{2}$$

$$= \$375,000.$$

$$\text{ROI} = \frac{\$120,000}{\$375,000} = 32\%.$$

Machine B:

$$\text{Average Net Income} = \frac{\$1,250,000 - \$750,000}{5} = \$100,000.$$

$$\text{Average Investment} = \frac{\$750,000}{2} = \$375,000.$$

$$ROI = \frac{\$100,000}{\$375,000} = 26.7\%$$

Decision: Purchase Machine A if 32 percent is an acceptable ROI.

(3) Internal rate of return:

Machine A:

At 12%, NPV = $143,823,

At 20%, NPV = ($46,330),

calculated using five-decimal-place discount factors.
By interpolation, IRR is approximated as follows:

$$\frac{(\$46,330)}{\$143,823 + \$46,330} \times (20\% - 12\%) = -1.95\%$$

$$20\% - 1.95\% = 18.05\% \text{ IRR.}$$

Or, using a pocket calculator, IRR = 17.78 percent.

Machine B:

At 12%, NPV = $151,195,

At 20%, NPV = ($2,350),

calculated using five-decimal-place discount factors.
Interpolating:

$$\frac{(\$2,350)}{\$151,195 + \$2,350} \times (20\% - 12\%) = -.12\%$$

$$20\% - .12\% = 19.88\% \text{ IRR.}$$

Or, using a pocket calculator, IRR = 19.86 percent.

Decision: Purchase Machine B if 19.86 percent is considered a sufficiently high IRR.

(4) Net present value at 10 percent (see Exhibit 11.9):

Machine A: NPV = $202,870.

Machine B: NPV = $197,697.

Decision: Purchase Machine A. Both have a positive NPV, and the NPV for machine A is higher.

(5) Net present value at 12 percent (see Exhibit 11.9):

Machine A: NPV = $143,823.

Machine B: NPV = $151,196.

Decision: Purchase Machine B. Both have a positive NPV, and Machine B's is higher.

b. Machine A's cash inflows occur later than those of Machine B. Therefore, at higher discount rates, Machine A looks less attractive than Machine B. But because Machine A's total cash inflows are greater, at a sufficiently low discount rate its NPV is greater than that of Machine B. The crossover point occurs somewhere between the discount rates of 10 percent and 12 percent. The internal rate of return is higher than the discount rate at which Machine B becomes more attractive than Machine A; hence, IRR prefers Machine B to Machine A.

c. The payback period and ROI methods both ignore the time value of money. As these two machines differ mainly in the timing of their cash inflows, failure to consider the time value of money results in an incomplete comparison of cash flows.

The internal rate of return method considers all the cash flows and the time value of money, but it still does not always lead to the same decision as the net present value method. As discussed in part **b**, the IRR for each machine is a single number to be compared to the hurdle rate, whereas the relative NPVs for the two machines depend on the firm's cost of capital. The most useful method for making the purchase decision is the net present value method, with careful thought about the firm's measure of its cost of capital.

Suggested Solution to Problem 11.2 for Self-Study

a. Table 2, 4-period row, 10-percent column is .68301; $14,641 × .68301 = $10,000.

b. See Exhibit 11.9.

Exhibit 11.9

ANTLE COMPANY
(Problem 11.2 for Self-Study)

End of Year (1)	Cash Flow If Borrow $10,000 (2)		Present Value Factor at 10 Percent (3)	Amount = (2) × (3) (4)
0	$10,000 − $10,000 = $	0	1.00000	$ 0
1	(800) × (1 − .40) =	(480)	.90909	(436)
2	(800) × (1 − .40) =	(480)	.82645	(397)
3	(800) × (1 − .40) =	(480)	.75131	(361)
4	(800) × (1 − .40) =	(480)	.68301	(328)
4	14,641 − 10,000 =	4,641	.68301	3,170
				$1,648

c. The analysis in Exhibit 11.9 combines the investment and financing decision. Antle should ignore the investment banker's advice unless the only collateral for the loan is the investment project itself *and* the only source of debt service payments for the bond issue is cash flows from the project. (Because the project has cash flows only in the last years, no lender is likely to make such a loan.) Otherwise, this analysis indicates that Antle Company should be indifferent to this project.

Suggested Solution to Problem 11.3 for Self-Study

The risks assumed by the banks in lending to Company Apple differ from the risks assumed in lending to Company Banana. Management of Company Apple would be correct to consider simultaneously the investment and financing decision for a new tank-car debt. The interest rate on the loan is the appropriate cost of funds for management of Company Apple to consider in making decisions about new tank cars. At Company Banana, however, a new loan for a new tank-car deal affects the likelihood of repayment of *all* old loans. Thus management must consider the impact of new loans on the company's entire business. Management of Company Banana must consider more than cost of the new debt used to acquire new assets. Situations like Company Apple's, where specific financing relates to specific assets, are unusual enough that managers who believe they have one ought to be careful to make sure they understand all aspects of the financing.

Key Terms and Concepts

Internal rate of return (IRR)
Cutoff (hurdle) rate
Mutually exclusive projects
Scale effect
Excess present value index
Payback period

Discounted payback period
Accounting rate of return
Cancelable lease contrasted with
 noncancelable lease
Leverage

Questions, Exercises, Problems, and Cases

Questions

1. Review the meaning of the concepts or terms given above in Key Terms and Concepts.
2. a. The internal rate of return rule and the net present value rule both take the time value of money into account and usually give the same decision. When may they give different decisions?

b. "The internal rate of return is more difficult to compute than the net present value of a project. The internal rate of return method can never give a better answer than the net present value method." Why, then, do you suppose that so many people use the internal rate of return method?

3. What are the weaknesses of using the payback period as a device for capital budgeting decisions?

4. For mutually exclusive projects, the project with the lowest net present value of cash inflow per dollar of initial cash outlay can be the best alternative for the firm. How can this be?

5. "Under no conditions should the investment decision be made simultaneously with the financing decision."

Comment.

6. Assume that a firm borrows cash at a fair market interest rate less than its opportunity cost of capital. The net present value of the cash flows from this loan is positive when the cash flows are discounted at the firm's cost of capital.

Why will this loan *not necessarily* increase the wealth of the firm or its owners?

7. Assume that a firm borrows at a fair market interest rate and computes the net present value of the cash flows—proceeds of borrowings and after-tax debt-service payments—using the after-tax cost of capital. Generally, the result will be a positive number, indicating that the borrowing project is a worthwhile undertaking according to the net present value rule.

Comment on this phenomenon.

Exercises

Solutions to even-numbered exercises are at the end of the chapter on page 453.

8. **Net present value and mutually exclusive projects.** The Larson Company must choose between two mutually exclusive projects. The cost of capital is 12 percent. Given the following data, which project should Larson choose, and why?

Project Label	After-Tax Cash Flows, End of Year			
	0	**1**	**2**	**3**
M	$(500,000)	$175,000	$287,500	$400,000
N	(450,000)	477,000	195,000	60,000

9. **Computing internal rate of return.** What is the internal rate of return on the following projects, each of which requires a $10,000 cash outlay now and returns the cash flows indicated?
   a. $5,530.67 at the end of Years 1 and 2.
   b. $1,627.45 at the end of Years 1 through 10.
   c. $1,556.66 at the end of Years 1 through 13.
   d. $2,053.39 at the end of Years 1 through 20.
   e. $2,921.46 at the end of Years 3 through 7.

f. $2,101.77 at the end of Years 2 through 10.

g. $24,883.20 at the end of Year 5 only.

10. **Computing payback.** What is the payback period of the projects in Exercise 9, **a** through **g**?

11. **Relation between internal rate of return and payback period.** Compare the internal rate of return on the projects in Exercise 9, **a** through **d**, with the *reciprocal* of the payback period for those projects computed in Exercise 10. Notice that the internal rate of return on **d** is exactly equal to the reciprocal of its payback period, but this relation does not hold for the other projects. Explain.

12. **Computing payback.** What is the payback period of the projects in Exercise 9, **a** through **g**, assuming that cash flows occur uniformly throughout the year?

13. **Net present value and mutually exclusive projects.** Delta Airlines must choose between two mutually exclusive innovations for improving its computer reservation system—one offered by Digital Equipment (DEC) and the other by IBM. Delta's after-tax cost of capital is 10 percent.

DEC's system costs $1 million and promises after-tax cash flows for 4 years: $400,000 at the end of Year 1 and Year 2, $300,000 at the end of Year 3, and $200,000 at the end of Year 4.

IBM's system costs $1.5 million and promises after-tax cash flows for 3 years: $800,000 at the end of Year 1, $600,000 at the end of Year 2, and $450,000 at the end of Year 3.

a. Compute the net present values of each of the alternatives.

b. Compute the internal rate of return for each of the alternatives.

c. Which alternative, if either, should Delta choose and why?

14. **Computing internal rate of return and payback period.** Compute the internal rate of return and payback period for each of the following projects, each of which requires an initial investment of $100,000 and provides the periodic cash flows indicated.

a. $23,098 per period for 5 periods.

b. $20,336 per period for 6 periods.

c. $17,401 per period for 8 periods.

d. $16,144 per period for 12 periods.

e. $17,102 per period for 15 periods.

15. **Working backward with net present value method.** A manager's favorite project requires an after-tax cash outflow on January 1 of $4,000 and promises to return $1,000 of after-tax cash inflows at the end of each of the next 5 years. The after-tax cost of capital is 10 percent per year.

a. Use the net present value method to decide whether this favorite project is a good investment.

b. How much would the projected cash inflow for the end of Year 5 have to increase for the project to be acceptable?

c. How much would the projected cash inflow for the end of Year 5 have to increase for the project to have a net present value of $100?

16. **Computing internal rate of return.** Carlo Company is considering acquiring a machine that costs $40,000 and that promises to save $8,000 in cash outlays

per year, after taxes, at the end of each of the next 12 years. Carlo expects the new machine to have no salvage value at the end of its useful life. (You may compute the actual return on your calculator or use Table 4 at the back of the book and interpolate.)

a. Compute the internal rate of return for this project.

b. Compute the internal rate of return, assuming that the cash savings were to last only 6, instead of 12, years.

c. Compute the internal rate of return, assuming that the cash savings were to last 20, rather than 12, years.

d. Compute the internal rate of return, assuming that the cash savings would be $6,000 rather than $8,000 per year for 12 years.

17. **Computing net present value of leverage.** Compute the apparent benefits of financial leverage for each of the following annual coupon bond issues. Assume an income tax rate of 40 percent and an after-tax cost of capital of 12 percent.

a. $100,000 borrowed for 5 years at 12 percent.

b. $100,000 borrowed for 10 years at 12 percent.

c. $100,000 borrowed for 5 years at 15 percent.

d. $100,000 borrowed for 5 years at 20 percent.

Problems

18. **Managerial incentives of performance evaluation based on accounting data.** A firm with an opportunity cost of capital of 20 percent faces two mutually exclusive investment projects:

(1) Acquire goods at the start of the year, ship them to Japan, and sell them at the end of the year. The internal rate of return on this project is 25 percent, and it has positive net present value.

(2) Making certain expenditures today that will cause reported earnings for the year to decline. This will result, however, in large cash flows at the ends of the second and third years. The internal rate of return on this project is 35 percent, and it has even larger net present value than the first project. Management observes that for the current year the second project will result in smaller earnings reported to its shareholders than the first.

How might management's observation influence its choice between the two investment projects?

19. **Multiple IRRs.** Consider an investment in a strip-mining operation where the cash flows are negative at the outset, positive during the intermediate years, and negative at the end because of expenditures to restore the mine site to its premining environment. For simplicity, assume that there are only three periodic cash flows: $100,000 initial investment, $225,000 cash inflow from ore at the end of the first period, and a $126,500 cash outflow for restoration at the end of the second period.

a. Demonstrate that this project has two internal rates of return: 10 percent per period and 15 percent per period. Observe that the internal rate of return methodology for capital budgeting as usually stated ("compute the internal rate of return and accept the project if the rate exceeds the hurdle rate'') fails to give clear guidance in this case.

b. Compute the net present value of this project at discount rates of 5 percent, 12 percent, and 20 percent.

c. Using the net present value method, state a decision rule for accepting or rejecting this project as a function of the cost of capital.

20. **Leverage and decision making.** Management of the Xenophon Company is considering an investment project that requires an initial investment of $100,000 and promises to return $176,234, after taxes, at the end of 5 years. Because the after-tax cost of capital of the firm is 12 percent per year, the net present value of this investment is zero. Management finds itself indifferent to the project. A financial analyst points out, however, that if the firm will borrow the $100,000 via a 5-year annual coupon bond issue, the annual interest expense will be $15,000, or $9,000 after taxes, the net present value of the project will increase from zero to $10,814, and it will become worthwhile.

a. Verify that the net present value of the project is zero.

b. Reproduce the analysis that the financial analyst has in mind.

c. Comment on the suggestion of the financial analyst.

21. **Leverage and decision making.** Sony's record distribution department believes that an investment of $675,000 today in a new reggae group (descended from the original Bob Marley group) will lead to an after-tax payoff of $1 million in 3 years. Sony's after-tax cost of capital, adjusted for the risk of such a project, is 15 percent per year. Sony can borrow $675,000 today from Fireman's Fund Insurance Company in return for its promise to pay $850,000 in 3 years—a zero coupon note.

a. Compute the net present value of the investment in the new reggae group.

b. Compute the internal rate of return on the Fireman's Fund borrowing (often called *the interest rate implicit in the note*).

c. Assume that Sony borrows $675,000 from Fireman's Fund and invests in the group. What are the cash flows and the internal rate of return on them?

d. What advice do you give Sony about this investment?

22. **Definition of alternatives to be considered.** Consider two mutually exclusive alternatives facing a manufacturer of food blenders:

(1) Sell the existing blender equipment and get out of the business, netting $1,000 cash proceeds from sale.

(2) Stay in the blender business, generating $200 of net cash inflows per year at the end of each of the next 10 years.

a. Why is there no well-defined internal rate of return on alternative (1)?

b. Why is there no well-defined internal rate of return on alternative (2)?

c. Some who favor the internal rate of return methodology would ''rescue'' that methodology from the difficulty in situations such as this one by defining the *incremental* investment project, which is the algebraic difference between the cash flows of the two alternatives. Consider the incremental project defined as cash flows from alternative (2) minus cash flows from alternative (1), as described previously. Such a project shows an outflow of $1,000 now in return for inflows of $200 at the end of each of the next 10 years. (One may be tempted to say that this incremental project represents the opportunity cost—an investment of $1,000—of staying in business, followed by the actual cash inflows of staying in business—$200 per year. Such intermixing of opportunity costs and actual cash flows can confuse even the experienced analyst.) Demonstrate that such a project has an internal rate of return of about 15 percent and that staying in the blender business is superior to getting out as long as the cost of capital is less than or equal to 15 percent.

d. Consider a third alternative facing the manufacturer of food blenders:

(3) Sell the blender equipment and purchase equipment for manufacturing food processors. This alternative implies cash expenditures of $4,000 currently and cash flows of $900 per year in arrears for 15 years.

How can you compare such an alternative to alternatives (1) and (2) with the internal rate of return methodology?

e. Consider a fourth alternative facing the manufacturer:

(4) Stay in the blender business and add the processor business. This alternative implies cash outflow of $5,000 currently, followed by cash inflows of $1,050 at the end of each of the next 10 years and cash inflows of $900 at the end of each of the 5 years thereafter.

How can you compare such an alternative to (1), (2), and (3) with the internal rate of return methodology?

f. What do you conclude about "rescuing" the internal rate of return method using the technique of constructing incremental investment projects?

23. Analyzing a lease. The Myers Company wonders whether to acquire a computer that has a 3-year life, costs $30,000, and will save $25,000 per year before taxes in cash operating costs as compared to the present data-processing system. Myers Company can borrow for 3 years at 12 percent per year. The computer manufacturer is willing to sell the computer for $30,000 or to lease it for 3 years on a noncancelable basis—that is, on the basis that Myers Company must make payments for the 3 years no matter what happens. The annual lease payment will be $12,490 except in the third year, when it is $12,491. The income tax rate is 40 percent. If Myers purchases the computer, it will depreciate the computer over 3 years, using accelerated cost recovery percentages of 25 percent in the first year, 38 percent in the second, and 37 percent in the third.

Prepare an analysis that will help Myers Company decide what it should do. Round discount factors to two places. The after-tax cost of capital is 10 percent.

Cases

24. Compare lease with borrow/buy. The Carom Company plans to acquire, as of January 1, 19X0, a computerized cash register system that costs $100,000 and that has a 5-year life and no salvage value. The new computerized system will save $35,000 in cash operating costs per year. The company is considering two plans for acquiring the system:

(1) Outright purchase. To finance the purchase, Carom will issue $100,000 of par value, 5-year, 15-percent annual coupon bonds January 1, 19X0, at par.

(2) Lease. The lease requires five annual payments to be made on December 31, 19X0, 19X1, 19X2, 19X3, and 19X4. The lease payments are to be $29,832 and they have a present value of $100,000 on January 1, 19X0, when discounted at 15 percent per year.

The firm's after-tax cost of capital is 12 percent. Carom will use accelerated cost recovery for tax purposes with the following percentages in each of the 5 years, respectively: 25, 38, 37, 0, and 0. The income tax rate is 40 percent.

a. Construct an exhibit similar to Exhibit 11.8. Round discount factors to two decimal places. Use three panels, one for each of the following alternatives.

(i) Outright purchase for cash.

(ii) Outright purchase with borrowing as explained in (1).

(iii) Lease under terms as explained in (2).

b. Should Carom acquire the services of the asset? How did you reach this conclusion?

c. Which of the financing plans, borrowing via a bond issue or leasing, appears preferable? How can one financing plan with an interest cost of 15 percent per year (bond issue) appear to be preferable to another financing plan with an interest cost of 15 percent per year (lease)? What can you conclude from the answers to these two questions?

d. Now assume that the lease contract calls for payments of $28,500 per year (an implicit interest rate of only 13.1 percent). Construct a fourth panel in the exhibit called for in part **a.** Which financing plan, leasing at 13.1 percent or borrowing at 15 percent, appears to be preferable? How can one plan of financing with an interest cost of 15 percent per year (bond issue) appear to be preferable to another plan of financing with an interest cost of 13.1 percent per year (lease)? What can you conclude from the answers to these two questions?

e. Should Carom Company lease the asset or purchase it? How can you tell? If you judge that purchase is preferable, what is the minimum after-tax payment that the lessor could offer to make Carom Company indifferent to leasing?

25. Merits of internal rate of return. A well-known university sponsors a continuing education program for engineers. One of its programs is called ''Evaluating Project Alternatives by Rate of Return.'' The advertising copy for this program says, in part:

> **Why You Should Attend** Traditionally, a large percentage of business decisions have been based solely on payback. Although the payback method has the advantage of computational simplicity, it is not a true measure of life-cycle cost effectiveness and can lead to erroneous accept-reject decisions.

Why Use Rate of Return

(1) Takes into account:

Cash flows beyond the payback period.

Timing of cash flows within the payback period.

(2) Does not discriminate against long-lived projects.

(3) Does not ignore the time value of money.

(4) Differentiates between debt and equity capital.

(5) Does not require stipulation of an interest rate.

(6) Provides for:

Return of and on debt and equity capital.

Income taxes, income tax write-offs.

Inflation.

Costs that escalate at a rate greater than the rate of inflation.

(7) Permits an accurate ranking of alternatives.

(8) Gives correct choice among independent alternatives.

(9) Maximizes return on investment.

Assume that by "rate of return," this advertising means the "internal rate of return."

Comment on the nine numbered points from the copy. Consider these points as they apply to both the internal rate of return method and the net present value method.

26. **Merits of lessee's benefits of leasing.** A well-known company with a financing subsidiary promotes its leasing activities (as lessor) with material containing the following statements. Evaluate these statements.

> **Retain Favorable Tax Advantages** Many companies in capital-intensive industries are not in a position to use accelerated depreciation to full advantage. Yet these companies often need new equipment. Leasing offers a solution to the problem: The lessee can assign tax benefits—benefits it cannot use—to the lessor in exchange for reduced lease payments. No other form of equipment financing provides this important advantage.

> **Conserve Cash** Normally, leasing affords 100-percent financing. There are no down payments or compensating balances. If a company ties up its cash to purchase equipment, the earning power of the cash itself is lost. But if the same company were to lease equipment, it could still put the cash into other profitable investments. For this reason, in the long run, leasing can help maximize the use of a company's resources. Leasing gives a company the opportunity to use more equipment or to spend less for equipment. Leasing, in fact, can often do both.

> **Match Income and Expense, and Stay within Capital Budgets** If a company purchases equipment, it immediately pays for the last day of

production as well as the first. But leasing allows the payment for equipment to be made from the income generated by its use. Furthermore, lease payments can be tailored to fit even the tightest capital equipment budgets. Combined, these attributes make leasing an effective way for companies to sustain rapid growth.

Reduce the Impact of Inflation   If inflation continues, a company that purchases capital equipment will find in the future that the true value of its depreciation allowance has been reduced. But companies that lease equipment will benefit from a reduction in the true value of future lease payments. For this reason leasing can provide an effective hedge against inflation; and to maximize the advantage, many companies choose to lease depreciating assets such as equipment, while purchasing appreciating assets such as property.

Preserve Other Sources of Financing   Growing companies need many sources of financial assistance. When they lease equipment, companies preserve the flexibility to use alternative credit sources in other ways. If a company leases its income-producing equipment, it can still use its bank lines of credit for short-term needs, or it can hold them open in anticipation of future capital requirements.

Control the Use of Equipment   It is the use—not the ownership—of equipment that generates income. A unit of equipment has the same productive capacity regardless of whether it is leased or owned. When equipment is leased, however, its disposition is much easier. At the end of the lease period, the equipment can be leased again, can be purchased, or can be returned to the lessor. The decision is made on the basis of whether the equipment is still profitable, not whether it is owned.

Obtain Favorable Balance Sheet Treatment   When correctly structured, some leases can qualify as operating leases for the purpose of the lessee's accounting treatment. Operating lease payment obligations are not capitalized on the lessee's balance sheet as a liability.

Suggested Solutions to Even-Numbered Exercises

8. **Net present value and mutually exclusive projects.** Choose Project N. See the following table.

End of Year	Discount Factors at 12 Percent	Cash Flows in Thousands		Present Value of Cash Flows in Thousands	
		M	N	M	N
0	1.00000	$(500)	$(450)	$(500.0)	$(450.0)
1	.89286	175	477	156.3	425.9
2	.79719	287.5	195	229.2	155.5
3	.71178	400	60	284.7	42.7
				$170.2	$174.1

Net present value of cash flows discounted at 12 percent is larger for N.

10. **Computing payback.**
    In years: **a.** 2   **e.** 6
    　　　　 b. 7   **f.** 6
    　　　　 c. 7   **g.** 5
    　　　　 d. 5

12. **Computing payback.**
    In years: **a.** 1.81   **e.** 5.42
    　　　　 b. 6.14   **f.** 5.76
    　　　　 c. 6.42   **g.** 4.40
    　　　　 d. 4.87

14. **Computing internal rate of return and payback period.**

	Internal Rate of Return	Payback Period	
a.	5 percent	4.3 years =	$100,000/$23,098 per year
b.	6 percent	4.9 years =	$100,000/$20,336 per year
c.	8 percent	5.7 years =	$100,000/$17,401 per year
d.	12 percent	6.2 years =	$100,000/$16,144 per year
e.	15 percent	5.8 years =	$100,000/$17,102 per year

16. **Computing internal rate of return.**
    Actual internal rate of return:
    a. 16.94%   **b.** 5.47%   **c.** 19.43%   **d.** 10.45%
    Using Table 4 and interpolating:
    a.　　　　　　　　　　$40,000/$8,000 = 5.0
    　　　Present Value of Annuity, 12 periods, 12% = 6.19437
    　　　Present Value of Annuity, 12 periods, 20% = 4.43922
    　　　　　　　　　　　　　　　　　　　　　1.75515

    　　　　　　　　6.19437 − 5.0 = 1.19437
    　　　　　　1.19437/1.75515 = .68049
    　　　　.68049 × (20% − 12%) = 5.44392%
    　　　　　　12% + 5.44392% = 17.44392%.

b.

$$\$40,000/\$8,000 = 5.0$$
Present Value of Annuity, 6 periods, 5% = 5.07569
Present Value of Annuity, 6 periods, 6% = 4.91732
$$0.15837$$

$$5.07569 - 5.0 = .07569$$
$$.07569/.15837 = .47793$$
$$.47793 \times (6.0\% - 5.0\%) = .47793\%$$
$$5\% + .47793\% = 5.47793\%.$$

c.

$$\$40,000/\$8,000 = 5.0$$
Present Value of Annuity, 20 periods, 12% = 7.46944
Present Value of Annuity, 20 periods, 20% = 4.86958
$$2.59986$$

$$7.46944 - 5.0 = 2.46944$$
$$2.46944/2.59986 = .94984$$
$$.94984 \times (20\% - 12\%) = 7.59872\%$$
$$12\% + 7.59872\% = 19.59872\%.$$

d.

$$\$40,000/\$6,000 = 6.66667$$
Present Value of Annuity, 12 periods, 10% = 6.81369
Present Value of Annuity, 12 periods, 12% = 6.19437
$$.61932$$

$$6.81369 - 6.66667 = .14702$$
$$.14702/.61932 = .23739$$
$$.23739 \times (12\% - 10\%) = .47478\%$$
$$10\% + .47478\% = 10.47478\%.$$

PART FOUR

Managerial Planning and Performance Evaluation

This part of the book deals with the use of managerial accounting information for managerial planning and performance evaluation.

Part Three of this book, Chapters 7 through 11, focused on managerial decision making. After making decisions, managers use accounting information to plan their operations and to evaluate performance. Managers use accounting information to address planning and performance evaluation questions such as these:

- What is our projected level of profits for the year?
- How much should budgeted costs go down if the number of customers drops by 10 percent?
- How do we measure the efficiency of production activities?
- How can we design performance measurement systems to encourage employees to act simultaneously in their own best interests and in the best interests of the organization?

Managerial accounting helps managers deal with these issues. Managers use accounting to assign responsibility for actions, primarily through the use of budgets and standards. The accounting system provides information about actual performance that managers can compare with these budgets and standards.

Chapter 12 shows how to develop profit plans. Chapters 13 and 14 give more detail about ways to measure and interpret variances from plans. Chapter 15 considers performance evaluation in decentralized operations and focuses on how to motivate employees.

Planning and Budgeting

1. Understand the use of budgets as tools for planning, performance evaluation, and motivation.
2. Know the different types of responsibility centers.
3. Understand the concept of goal congruence.
4. Know how to develop the master budget profit plan.
5. Understand the importance and difficulty of producing accurate forecasts in the budget.
6. Compare the master budget to the flexible budget and understand the cause of differences between the two.
7. Develop a profit variance analysis and use it as a tool for performance evaluation.
8. Explain the differences between the actual results and the budget.
9. (Appendix 12.1) Develop a comprehensive master budget.
10. (Appendix 12.2) Understand formal incentive models for accurate forecasting.

This chapter focuses on the **short-term operating budget.** This budget states management's plan of action for the coming year in quantitative terms. This budget is a useful tool for planning, performance evaluation, and employee motivation.

Tool for Planning

After management determines the organization's goals, and a strategy for achieving those goals, it develops a formal integrated plan of action, called a *budget*. The budget is like an architect's set of drawings. It presents management with a comprehensive picture of the expected financial effects of its decisions on the firm as a whole. Put another way, budgets are estimates of financial statements prepared before the actual transactions occur.

As **tools for planning,** budgets are generally static; that is, the firm develops budgets for a particular expected level of activity, such as sales or production in units. The budgeting process derives a set of estimates for sales, manufacturing costs, selling and administrative expenses, and profit in the **static budget.**

Tool for Performance Evaluation

Budgets provide estimates of expected performance. As such, they serve as standards for evaluating performance. Comparing budgeted with actual results provides a basis for evaluating past performance and guiding future action. To be effective as **tools for performance evaluation,** the firm must initially develop its budgets for individual responsibility centers.

Responsibility Centers

A **responsibility center** is a division or department in a firm responsible for managing a particular group of activities in the organization. The sportswear manager at Macy's is responsible for the activities of the sportswear department, for example. Accountants classify responsibility centers according to the activities for which the manager is responsible, as follows:

1. **Cost centers,** where management is responsible for costs. Manufacturing departments are examples, because the managers are responsible for the costs of making products.
2. **Revenue centers,** where management is responsible primarily for revenues. Marketing departments are "revenue centers" if the managers are responsible for revenues.
3. **Profit centers,** where management is responsible for both revenues and costs.
4. **Investment centers,** where management is responsible for revenues, costs, and assets. Most corporate divisions are profit centers or investment centers.

There are two categories of cost centers, based on the types of costs incurred in the center. Managers treat most production departments in both service and manufacturing companies as **engineered cost centers.** Input-output relations are sufficiently well established that a particular set of inputs will provide a predictable and measurable set of outputs. Responsibility centers in which input-output relations are not well specified are **discretionary cost centers.** Managers of such centers receive from their superiors a cost budget that provides a ceiling on the center's costs. Most administrative, research, and staff activities are discretionary cost centers.

Flexible Budgets

A **flexible budget** states a fixed cost expected to be incurred regardless of the level of activity, and a variable cost per unit of activity. Total variable costs change *in total* as the level of activity changes. The "flex" in a flexible budget concerns the variable costs (that is, those costs that vary with changes in activity levels). The fixed-cost portion of the budget is static.

Example   Studies of past cost behavior indicate that the Video booth at Thrills Galore amusement park should incur total fixed costs of $100,000 and variable costs of $10 per video made. For planning purposes, management estimates that it will make 50,000 videos. The static cost budget for planning purposes is therefore $600,000 [= $100,000 + ($10 × 50,000)].

Suppose, however, that due to unexpected demand during the period, the department made 70,000 videos. Management will not wish to compare the actual cost of producing 70,000 units with the expected cost of producing 50,000 units for control purposes. The underlying levels of activity differ. To evaluate actual performance, accounting must express the budget or standard in terms of what costs *should have been* to produce 70,000 units. The flexible budget is useful in this situation. It indicates that costs should have been $800,000 [= $100,000 + ($10 × 70,000)] during the period. This is the more appropriate standard for performance evaluation.

Employee Motivation

When you assess the effect of budgets or any other part of a motivation system on people, ask the following two questions:

1. What types of behavior does the system motivate?
2. Is this the right behavior?

Much of managerial accounting has developed to motivate people to behave in particular ways. Accounting reports allow superiors to make decisions about the subordinates' future employment prospects. (For example, should they be promoted? Fired?) In addition, employment contracts use accounting information, such as when an employee receives a bonus based on accounting performance measures.

Thus accounting affects motivation. Subordinates who know managers evaluate them with accounting measures have incentives to make themselves look good with those measures. (Analogously, consider how students may believe employers or graduate school admissions offices use grade-point averages without regard to difficulty of courses. Such students have incentives to take easy courses.)

Goal Congruence

Goal congruence occurs if members of an organization have incentives to perform in the common interest. Although complete goal congruence is rare, we observe team efforts in many cases. Examples include some military units and athletic teams. Many companies attempt to achieve this esprit de corps by carefully selecting employees whom management believes will be loyal, for example. Observers of Japanese industry report that Japanese managers and owners have created team orientations with considerable goal congruence.

Complete goal congruence is, however, unlikely to occur in most business settings. For example, employees may prefer to work less hard than the firm would like. Consequently, firms design performance evaluation and incentive systems to increase goal congruence by encouraging employees to behave more in the firm's interest.

The classroom setting is a good example. Examinations, written assignments, indeed, the entire grading process, is part of a performance evaluation and incentive system to encourage students to learn. Sometimes the system encourages the wrong type of behavior, because students may select easy courses to improve their grades instead of difficult courses in which they will learn more.

Problems of this type occur in all organizations where employees acting in their own best interests do not take actions that serve the best interests of the organization. Consider the case of a plant manager who believes that a promotion and bonus will follow from high plant operating profits. Undertaking a needed maintenance program will cost money and reduce profits in the short run, but the company will benefit in the long run because its product quality will improve. The manager faces a classic trade-off between doing what looks good in the short run and doing what serves the best interests of the company. (This point is analogous to the problem faced by a student in deciding between an easy course that will bolster the grade-point average or a hard course that will have greater long-term benefits.)

The Master Budget

The **master budget** is a complete blueprint of the planned operations of the firm for a period. It requires recognizing the interrelations among the various units of a firm. For example, to prepare a master budget requires knowing how a projected increase in sales of product A affects the producing departments; the selling, general, and administrative effort; and the financial position of the company.

Preparing a master budget requires time and effort by people at all levels. Despite this difficulty, or perhaps because of it, management can effectively use the master budget as an instrument for planning and performance evaluation. Almost all organizations of any size recognize master budget preparation as a vital task of management.

Example We illustrate the budget preparation process for Victoria Corporation for a single period, assumed to be one month. We continue this example in our discussion of performance evaluation in this chapter and in Chapters 13 and 14. An organization chart of Victoria Corporation appears in Exhibit 12.1. Each box in the organization chart is a responsibility center.

Exhibit 12.1

VICTORIA CORPORATION
Organization Chart

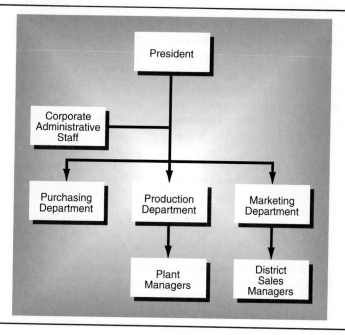

The Sales Budget

The sales budget appears in Exhibit 12.2. The chief marketing executive of the firm usually is responsible for preparing the sales budget. The marketing executive relies on inputs from market research groups as well as from salespeople or district managers in the field. The discussions among sales groups in budget preparation frequently bring out problems in the firm's selling and advertising programs and broadens the participants' thinking about the firm's place in the market.

Previous sales experience is usually the starting point for sales budget estimates. Managers modify these historical data to recognize relevant factors such as market trends, anticipated changes in general economic conditions, and altered advertising

Exhibit 12.2

VICTORIA CORPORATION
Sales Budget for Period 1

Optimistic	90,000 Units at $7 = $630,000
Expected	70,000 Units at $6 = $420,000
Pessimistic	50,000 Units at $5 = $250,000

plans. The marketing executive usually makes the final decision on the precise quantities and dollar amounts to appear in the sales budget for each product.

Example   Victoria Corporation produces one product. It expects to sell 70,000 units at $6 per unit. Market researchers developed an initial sales forecast, estimating pessimistic, optimistic, and expected forecasts of total product sales in the market and Victoria's market share. The company defined optimistic as ''probability of sales this high or higher is .2''; they defined pessimistic as ''probability of sales this low or lower is .2.'' The marketing vice president also had district sales managers prepare optimistic, pessimistic, and expected forecasts for their districts.

According to the marketing vice president, the market researchers and sales managers used two different data bases:

''The market research group uses consumer studies, economic forecasts, and past data about the company. The group provides a good macro-level forecast of economic conditions and consumer preferences for our products, but it explains little about the day-to-day efforts of our sales personnel.

This is where our sales managers' forecasts are most valuable. They know about potential customers, they know which of our present customers we are likely to lose, and they can forecast sales quite accurately for the first few months of the budget year. When I combine the forecasts of the market research group and the sales managers, I have a good idea of both the market conditions affecting the demand for our product and the immediate wishes of our customers.''

The marketing vice president, combining the forecasts from the two groups with personal experience and knowledge of the company, prepared the forecasts shown in Exhibit 12.2. Although we show all three forecasts—optimistic, pessimistic, and expected—we use only the expected in subsequent discussion to keep the example simple.

Production Budget

The sales budget, combined with estimates of beginning inventories and estimates of desired ending inventories, forms the basis of the production budget for the Victoria Corporation shown in the top panel of Exhibit 12.3.

We compute the quantity of each product to be produced from a variant of the basic accounting equation:

Beginning Balance + Transfers In = Transfers Out + Ending Balance,

$$\text{BB} + \text{TI} = \text{TO} + \text{EB}.$$

Expressing the equation in units and relating it to units produced and sold, the basic accounting equation becomes:

$$\text{Units to Be Produced} = \frac{\text{Number of}}{\text{Units to Be Sold}} + \frac{\text{Units in}}{\text{Ending}} - \frac{\text{Units in}}{\text{Beginning}}$$
$$\text{Inventory} \quad \text{Inventory}.$$

The costs to be incurred in producing the desired number of units appear in the lower panel of Exhibit 12.3.

Exhibit 12.3

VICTORIA CORPORATION
Production Budget for Period 1

Units to Be Produced

Budgeted Sales, in Units (see sales budget)	70,000
Desired Ending Inventory (assumed)	8,000
Total Units Needed	78,000
Less Beginning Inventory (assumed)	(8,000)
Units to Be Produced	70,000

Cost Expected to Be Incurred

Direct Materials (2 pounds per unit at $.50 per pound)	$ 70,000
Direct Labor (⅛ hour per unit at $20 per hour)	175,000
Manufacturing Overhead:	
Indirect Labor ($.10 per unit)	7,000
Supplies ($.04 per unit)	2,800
Power ($1,000 per period plus $.03 per unit)	3,100
Maintenance ($13,840 per period)	13,840
Rent ($6,000 per period)	6,000
Insurance ($1,000 per period)	1,000
Depreciation ($10,360 per period)	10,360
Total Production Costs	$289,100

Direct Materials Direct materials are materials traceable to individual units produced. Direct materials costs are almost always variable. Management estimates that each finished unit at Victoria will require 2 pounds of direct materials. The estimates of direct materials requirements result from engineering studies of material usage. The $.50 cost per pound of the direct materials comes from studies of past cost behavior and projected prices of suppliers. Hence, the budgeted or standard direct materials cost per finished unit is $.50 × 2 pounds per finished unit = $1.00 per finished unit.[1]

Direct Labor Direct labor represents work traceable directly to particular units of product. Engineering time and motion studies and studies of past labor time usage behavior indicate that a unit requires about 7.5 minutes of labor time. This estimate allows for normal, periodic rest periods, yet is tight enough to motivate employees to perform efficiently. The standard wage rate, including fringe benefits and payroll taxes (for example, employer's share of Social Security and unemployment taxes), for production workers in Victoria Corporation's plant is $20.00 per hour and is predictable because it results from negotiations with the local labor union.

Direct labor could be fixed, as in high-tech companies having only a few workers, or variable. We assume direct labor is variable in this example.

---

[1]Managers and accountants often use the terms *budgets* and *standards* interchangeably.

Manufacturing Overhead   Variable manufacturing costs vary with units produced. Fixed manufacturing overhead costs give a firm the capacity to produce. As Exhibit 12.3 shows, indirect labor and supplies are variable manufacturing overhead costs. Power is a semivariable, or mixed, cost, having both variable and fixed components. Maintenance, rent, insurance, and depreciation are fixed manufacturing overhead costs.

These estimates result from past experience and projected changes in costs and production methods. One can apply statistical regression methods to overhead to (1) separate fixed from variable overhead and (2) find the relations between variable overhead and a measure of activity (for example, direct labor hours or output). For Victoria Corporation, the measure of activity is output, and we assume variable manufacturing overhead to be $.17 per unit of output.

Summary of Production Budget   The budget in Exhibit 12.3 shows planned production department activity for the period. The production manager must schedule production to manufacture 70,000 units. The production budget can help management evaluate the performance of the production department at the end of the period. If the projected production in units and input costs occurs, the production department should incur costs of $289,100 during the period.

If the level of production differs from the projected amounts, we apply the flexible budget concept to compute the amount of costs that the production department should have incurred. The flexible budget for the production department is

$$\begin{array}{l}\text{Total Budgeted}\\\text{Manufacturing}\\\text{Costs for}\\\text{Production}\\\text{Departments}\end{array} = \$32{,}200 + (\$3.67 \times \text{Units Produced}).$$

Exhibit 12.3 shows the expected fixed costs to be the sum of the estimates for power (fixed cost portion), maintenance, rent, insurance, and depreciation: $32,200 = $1,000 + $13,840 + $6,000 + $1,000 + $10,360. Exhibit 12.3 also shows the expected variable costs to be the estimates for direct materials, direct labor, indirect labor, supplies, and power (variable cost portion): $3.67 = $1.00 + $2.50 + $.10 + $.04 + $.03.

Marketing and Administrative Costs   The budget for marketing costs for the Victoria Corporation's marketing department appears in Exhibit 12.4. Management expects all of the items except commissions and shipping costs to be fixed. Commissions are 2 percent of sales dollars, or $.12 per unit at the budgeted price of $6 per unit ($.12 = 2% × $6). Shipping costs are $.02 per unit shipped. Hence, the variable marketing cost is $.14 per unit sold. Note that variable marketing costs vary with units *sold,* whereas variable manufacturing costs vary with units *produced.*

Management estimates all of the month's central corporate *administrative costs* in Exhibit 12.5 to be fixed.[2]

---

[2]In practice, administrative costs can be fixed or variable.

Exhibit 12.4

VICTORIA CORPORATION
Marketing Cost Budget for Period 1

Variable Costs

Commissions (2 percent of sales; see Exhibit 12.2, sales budget)	$ 8,400[a]	
Shipping Costs ($.02 per unit shipped; see Exhibit 12.2, sales budget)	1,400	
Total Variable Marketing Costs		$ 9,800
Fixed Costs		
Salaries ($25,000 per period)	$25,000	
Advertising ($30,000 per period)	30,000	
Sales Office ($8,400 per period)	8,400	
Travel ($2,000 per period)	2,000	
Total Fixed Marketing Costs		65,400
Total Marketing Cost Budget		$75,200

[a]Also, $.12 per unit sold × 70,000 units sold = $8,400.

Discretionary Fixed Costs   Many of the so-called fixed costs in the production, marketing, and administration budgets are *discretionary costs*. Maintenance, donations, and advertising are examples. Although management budgets them as fixed costs, managers realize that these costs are not committed costs, like rent on a factory building, that are required to run the firm.

When economic conditions make it doubtful that the firm will achieve its budgeted profit goals, management can cut discretionary costs. When managers state that they have reduced their fixed costs, or reduced their breakeven points, they have often cut discretionary costs, not committed costs. For example, IBM, Sears, and General Motors recently made major cuts in expenses that many executives believed were discretionary because the firms survived despite the cost cuts.

Discretionary costs are tempting cost-cutting targets because their reduction does not have serious short-term effects on production and marketing. The long-term

Exhibit 12.5

VICTORIA CORPORATION
Administrative Cost Budget for Period 1

President's Salary	$10,000
Salaries of Other Staff Personnel	17,000
Supplies	2,000
Heat and Light	1,400
Rent	4,000
Donations and Contributions	1,000
General Corporate Taxes	8,000
Depreciation—Staff Office Equipment	1,400
Total Administrative Cost Budget	$44,800

consequences could be disastrous, however, if management cuts maintenance and advertising programs. Slashing the advertising budgets for companies like Nike, Miller Brewing Company, or Procter & Gamble would jeopardize those companies in the long run.

Profit Plan (Budgeted Income Statement) The *profit plan,* or *budgeted income statement,* appears in Exhibit 12.6. The top part presents this statement on a variable costing basis for internal, managerial use at Victoria Corporation. The bottom part shows the income statement prepared using full absorption costing, which generally accepted accounting principles require for external financial reporting and income tax regulations require for tax reporting. As earlier chapters indicated, full absorption costing ''unitizes'' fixed manufacturing costs, which can mislead management in decision making.

Note that although the formats of the two statements differ, the operating profits are the same because *units produced equal units sold.* For the rest of this chapter and the next, we rely on the variable costing profit plan, unless otherwise specified, in discussing the use of accounting for performance evaluation.

After compiling the budget, management projects an operating profit of $10,900. (Recall that this figure is *before taxes* and miscellaneous income and expenses.) If top management is satisfied with this budgeted result and can find adequate cash to

---

Exhibit 12.6

VICTORIA CORPORATION
Master Budget Profit Plan (income statement)

Variable Costing Basis

Sales (70,000 units at $6)	$420,000
Variable Manufacturing Cost of Goods Sold (70,000 units at $3.67)	(256,900)
Variable Marketing Costs (70,000 units at $.14)	(9,800)
Contribution Margin	$153,300
Fixed Manufacturing Costs	(32,200)
Fixed Marketing and Administrative Costs	(110,200)
Operating Profits (variable costing)	$ 10,900

Full Absorption Costing Basis

Sales (70,000 units at $6)	$420,000
Less Cost of Goods Sold (70,000 units at $4.13)[a]	(289,100)
Gross Margin	$130,900
Less Marketing and Administrative Costs	(120,000)
Operating Profits (full absorption costing)	$ 10,900

[a]Full Absorption Manufacturing Cost per Unit

= Total Manufacturing Costs/Total Units Produced

= $289,100/70,000 Units

= $4.13 per Unit.

carry out the operations, it will approve the master budget. If management considers the budgeted results unsatisfactory, it will consider ways to improve the budgeted results using cost reductions or sales increases.

Implementing the Master Budget

The master budget profit plan expresses top management's financial plans for achieving a targeted profit performance for the company. Generally, the board of directors reviews the master budget profit plan and considers it to be an implied or even explicit contract with management about expected results.

The master budget includes a budgeted balance sheet, a cash flow budget, and other relevant budgets, as well as the profit plan developed in the preceding pages. Appendix 12.1 presents a comprehensive master budget including the profit plan, budgeted balance sheets, and the cash flow budget.

Preparing the master budget usually requires the participation of all managerial groups, as discussed in the Managerial Application "Budgeting for New Products at 3M." Once adopted, the budget becomes a major planning and control tool. Further, it becomes the authorization to produce and sell goods and services, to purchase materials, and to hire employees. In governmental units, the budget becomes the *legal* authorization for expenditure.

Incentives for Accurate Forecasts

You can see the importance of the sales forecast to the entire budget process from our Victoria Corporation example. If the sales forecast is too high, for example, and the company produces to meet the forecast, the company will have excess inventory.

If the sales forecast is too low, the firm will likely lose sales opportunities because purchasing and production were planning on lower operating levels and inventory is depleted. Or, to meet unexpected sales demand, employees will work overtime and receive a premium, emergency purchases of materials and supplies will occur at prices above normal, and other costs will increase because production, purchasing, personnel, and other departments were not prepared to meet the sales demand. Yet sales personnel may look good because actual sales exceed the budget.

Rewarding managers only for accurate forecasting could create disincentives for better performance—managers would merely try to meet the forecast, not to beat it. Companies use many different methods of providing incentives for both accurate forecasting *and* good performance. These methods include comparing sales forecasts from year to year and obtaining forecasts from multiple sources.

Probably the most common method of ascertaining the reasonableness of forecasts is for sales managers to know enough about their subordinates' products and territories to have intuitive knowledge of what is reasonable. As indicated in the Managerial Application on page 470, the controllers at 3M watch sales forecasts carefully and let marketing people know if they are consistently too aggressive in their forecasts. Appendix 12.2 discusses formal incentive models that simultaneously motivate accurate forecasts and good performance.

Budgeting for New Products at 3M[a]

Several articles and books in the business press have heralded 3M for its product innovation and entrepreneurship. At the same time, good financial planning and tight cost control are very important to 3M. 3M accomplishes these objectives by using financial targets "to set goals and measure performance rather than to deny expenditures or punish for unmet expectations. For example, an overall corporate goal is to derive 25 percent of total sales each year from products introduced in the last five years."[b]

Many groups are involved in budgeting for new products when the lab develops a new product. Marketing established the market. The laboratory, manufacturing people, and financial people work out the budgeted costs and revenues. If new equipment is involved, manufacturing, engineering, and finance work out the cost of that equipment and how fast it will run.

"From the lab, we will decide how the product is to be made, where it's going to be made, and we will apply some estimated (overhead) rates and costs to try to come up with a projected cost on that particular product. The marketing people then will be looking at the market and projecting volumes and what they think the selling price will be. We try to look at what the market will bear and look at the cost of the product to try to come up with a good return for 3M. Sometimes the controller must keep other division members on track. For example, if marketers tend to be overly aggressive and year after year, quarter after quarter, miss their forecasts, the controller lets them know."[c]

[a]Based on "The Magic of 3M: Management Accounting Excellence," *Management Accounting* (February 1986), pp. 20–27.
[b]Ibid., pp. 20–21.
[c]Ibid., p. 23.

Using the Budget for Performance Evaluation

This section shows how accountants compare actual results achieved with budgets to derive **variances** for performance evaluation.

Comparison of Actual Results with the Flexible and Master Budgets

The following discussion compares the master budget with the flexible budget and with actual results. This comparison ties the results of the planning process (which

Exhibit 12.7

VICTORIA CORPORATION
Flexible Budget and Sales Volume Variance

	Flexible Budget (based on actual sales volume of 80,000)	Sales Volume Variance	Master Budget (based on a prediction of 70,000 units sold)
Sales........................	$480,000[a]	$60,000 F	$420,000[d]
Less:			
Variable Manufacturing Costs ..	293,600[b]	36,700 U	256,900[e]
Variable Marketing Costs	11,200[c]	1,400 U	9,800[f]
Contribution Margin	$175,200	$21,900 F	$153,300
Less:			
Fixed Manufacturing Costs	32,200	—	32,200
Fixed Marketing Costs	65,400	—	65,400
Fixed Administrative Costs	44,800	—	44,800
Operating Profit	$ 32,800	$21,900 F	$ 10,900

[a]80,000 units sold at $6.00.   [e]70,000 units sold at $3.67.

[b]80,000 units sold at $3.67.   [f]70,000 units sold at $.14.

[c]80,000 units sold at $.14.   U denotes unfavorable variance.

[d]70,000 units sold at $6.00.   F denotes favorable variance.

results in the master budget) with flexible budgeting, and forms the basis for analyzing differences between plans and actual results.

Flexible versus Master Budget   Exhibit 12.7 compares the flexible budget with the master budget profit plan for Victoria Corporation. The master budget results from the profit plan shown in Exhibit 12.6. To review, some of the important amounts follow:

Sales Price per Unit	$6.00
Sales Volume per Period	70,000 Units
Variable Manufacturing Costs per Unit	$3.67
Variable Marketing Costs per Unit (2-percent sales commission plus $.02 per-unit shipping costs)	$.14
Fixed Manufacturing Costs per Period	$32,200
Fixed Marketing Costs per Period	$65,400
Fixed Administrative Costs per Period	$44,800

We base the flexible budget in this case on the actual sales and production volume.[3] Variable costs and revenues should change as volume changes. The flexible

---

[3]The relevant activity variable is *sales* volume because this is a profit plan (that is, an income statement). If the objective were to compare the flexible production budget with the master production budget, the relevant activity variable would be *production* volume. Sales and production volumes are assumed to be equal throughout this example so we can avoid allocating fixed manufacturing costs to inventories.

budget indicates expected budgeted revenues and costs at the actual activity level, which is sales volume in this case. You can think of the flexible budget as the cost equation:

$$TC = F + VX,$$

where TC = total budgeted costs, F = budgeted fixed costs, V = budgeted variable cost per unit, and X = actual volume.

Although management predicted sales volume to be 70,000 units, Victoria produced and sold 80,000 units during the period. The **sales volume variance** is the difference in profits caused by the difference between the master budget sales volume and the actual sales volume. In this case, the difference of $21,900 between operating profits in the master budget and the flexible budget is a sales volume variance. It results from the 10,000-unit difference in sales volume from the sales plan of 70,000 units. We can also compute $21,900 by multiplying the 10,000 unit increase times the budgeted contribution margin per unit of $2.19 (= $6.00 − $3.67 − $.14).

What Is the Meaning of Favorable and Unfavorable? Note the use of F (favorable) and U (unfavorable) beside each of the variances in Exhibit 12.7. These terms describe the impact of the variance on the budgeted operating profits. A **favorable variance** means that the variance would *increase* operating profits, holding all other things constant. An **unfavorable variance** would *decrease* operating profits, holding all other things constant.

We do not use these terms in a normative sense. A favorable variance is not *necessarily* good, and an unfavorable variance is not *necessarily* bad. Further note the variable cost variances—they are labeled unfavorable. Does this reflect unfavorable conditions in the company? Unlikely! These variable costs are *expected* to increase because the actual sales volume is higher than planned. In short, the labels favorable or unfavorable do not automatically connote good or bad conditions. Rather, a favorable variance implies that actual profits are higher than budgeted, all other things (for example, other variances) being ignored; conversely, an unfavorable variance implies that actual profits are lower than budgeted, all other things being ignored. Ultimately, the accounting will credit favorable variances and debit unfavorable variances to income statement accounts.

Information Use The information presented in Exhibit 12.7 has a number of uses. First, it shows that the increase in operating profits from the master budget results from the increase in sales volume over the level planned. Sales variances are usually the responsibility of the marketing department, so this information may be useful feedback to personnel in that department, and managers may find it informative for evaluating performance. Second, the resulting flexible budget shows budgeted sales, costs, and operating profits *after* taking into account the volume increase but *before* considering differences in unit selling prices, differences in unit variable costs, and differences in fixed costs from the master budgets.

Problem 12.1
for Self-Study

Comparing the master budget to the flexible budget. Computer Supply, Inc., budgeted production and sales of 40,000 laptop computer cases for the month of April at a selling price of $11 each. The company actually sold 50,000 cases for $10 each. The company budgeted the following costs:

Standard Manufacturing Variable Costs per Unit	$4.00
Fixed Manufacturing Overhead Cost: Monthly Budget	$80,000
Marketing and Administrative Costs:	
Variable (per unit)	$1.00 per unit
Fixed (monthly budget)	$100,000

Prepare a report for management like the one in Exhibit 12.7 showing the master budget, flexible budget, and sales volume variance.

The solution to this self-study problem is at the end of the chapter on page 489.

Actual Results versus Flexible Budget

Assume that actual Victoria Corporation's results for period 1 follow:

Sales Price per Unit	$6.10
Sales Volume for the Period	80,000 Units
Variable Manufacturing Costs per Unit	$3.82
Variable Marketing Costs per Unit	$.16
Fixed Manufacturing Costs for the Period	$34,000
Fixed Marketing Costs for the Period	$64,400
Fixed Administrative Costs for the Period	$44,600

We can now compare these results with both the flexible budget and the master budget, as in Exhibit 12.8. We carry Columns (5), (6), and (7) forward from Exhibit 12.7. We calculate Column (1) in Exhibit 12.8 from the facts presented above.

Overview of the Profit Variance

Exhibit 12.8 shows the source of the total variance from the profit plan, which is $15,700 favorable. The analysis of the causes of the total profit variance (that is, the $15,700 difference between the profit budgeted in the master budget and the profit earned for the period) is known as **profit variance analysis.**

Column (2) in Exhibit 12.8 summarizes purchasing and manufacturing variances, which Chapter 13 discusses in more detail. Columns (3) and (4) show marketing and

Exhibit 12.8

VICTORIA CORPORATION
Profit Variance Analysis: A Comparison of Actual Results with the Profit Plan

	Actual (based on actual sales volume of 80,000 units) (1)	Purchasing and Production Variances (2)	Marketing and Administrative Cost Variances (3)	Sales Price Variance (4)	Flexible Budget (based on actual sales volume of 80,000 units)[f] (5)	Sales Volume Variance[f] (6)	Master Budget (based on a plan of 70,000 units sold)[f] (7)
Sales...........	$488,000[a]	—	—	$8,000 F	$480,000	$60,000 F	$420,000
Less:							
Variable Manufacturing Costs	305,600[b]	$12,000 U			293,600	36,700 U	256,900
Variable Marketing Costs	12,800[c]		$1,440 U[d]	160 U[e]	11,200	1,400 U	9,800
Contribution Margin	$169,600	$12,000 U	$1,440 U	$7,840 F	$175,200	$21,900 F	$153,300
Less:							
Fixed Manufacturing Costs	34,000	1,800 U			32,200	—	32,200
Fixed Marketing Costs	64,400		1,000 F		65,400	—	65,400
Fixed Administrative Costs	44,600		200 F		44,800	—	44,800
Operating Profits	$ 26,600	$13,800 U	$ 240 U	$7,840 F	$ 32,800	$21,900 F	$ 10,900

Total Profit Variance from Flexible Budget = $6,200 U

Total Profit Variance from Master Budget = $15,700 F

[a] 80,000 units sold at $6.10 per unit.
[b] 80,000 units sold at $3.82 per unit.
[c] 80,000 units sold at $.16 per unit.

[d] $1,440 U = ($12,800 − $11,200) − $160.
[e] $160 U = .02 × $8,000 F Sales Price Variance.
[f] Amounts are from Exhibit 12.7.

U denotes unfavorable variance.
F denotes favorable variance.

administrative variances. The increased commissions of $160 (= 2% × $8,000) partly offset the favorable sales price variance of $8,000. The remaining $1,440U marketing and administrative cost variance is the residual: $12,800 actual − $11,200 flexible budget − $160 = $1,440.

Performance Appraisal What is your overall assessment of Victoria Corporation's performance for the period? Clearly the company did better than expected, because sales prices and volume both exceeded expectations. However, costs also exceeded expectations, even after allowing for the increase in volume. The $12,000 unfavorable variable manufacturing cost variance could be of particular concern. Note that the flexible budget has increased the allowance for variable manufacturing costs from $256,900 in the master budget to $293,600 in the flexible budget. However, the actual costs were even higher—$305,600. This implies either that inefficiencies in manufacturing occurred or that the company paid more than expected for variable manufacturing inputs, such as direct materials, direct labor, or variable manufacturing overhead items.

Do Not Get Lost in Details Variance computations and analysis can become detailed, and users of variances (as well as students) sometimes do not see how such detailed computations fit into the "big picture" comparison of achieved results with the master budget. Exhibit 12.8 presents the big picture. Chapters 13 and 14 go into more detailed computations.

Exhibit 12.9 summarizes these results graphically. Note that the flexible budget line shows expected profits for various activity levels for a given level of fixed costs. Any change in fixed costs would *shift* the flexible budget line up or down.

Key Variances

Many top executives receive daily variance reports about a few key items. For example, airline officials receive variance reports on seats sold the previous day; officials in steel companies receive variance reports on the number of tons of steel produced; and officials of merchandising companies receive daily variance reports on sales. As these examples demonstrate, most of these key items deal with *output*. Input variances (that is, cost variances) usually require more detailed data collection. Accounting systems report these weekly or monthly. Accountants prepare "big picture" reports, such as Exhibit 12.8, less frequently, perhaps monthly, quarterly, or yearly.

Problem 12.2 for Self-Study

Preparing the profit variance analysis. This problem continues Problem 12.1 for self-study. Computer Supply, Inc., budgeted production and sales of 40,000 laptop computer cases for the month of April at a selling price of $11 each. The company actually sold 50,000 cases for $10 each. The company budgeted the following costs:

Budget

Standard Variable Manufacturing Costs per Unit	$ 4.00
Fixed Manufacturing Overhead for the Month	$ 80,000
Marketing and Administrative Costs:	
Variable (per unit)	$ 1.00
Fixed (monthly budget)	$100,000

The company incurred the following actual costs in April:

Actual

Actual Manufacturing Costs:	
Variable Costs per Unit	$ 4.88
Fixed Overhead	$83,000
Actual Marketing and Administrative:	
Variable (50,000 at $1.04)	$52,000
Fixed	$96,000

Prepare a profit variance report for management like the one in Exhibit 12.8.

The solution to this self-study problem is at the end of the chapter on page 490.

Budgeting in Nonprofit Organizations

The master budget has added importance in nonprofit organizations because it is usually a document used as a basis for authorizing the expenditure of funds. In many governmental units, *the approved budget is a legal authorization for expenditure,* and the penalties for exceeding the authorized expenditures in the budget could be severe. This partially explains why a balanced budget takes on added importance in nonprofit organizations. The Managerial Application on page 478, "Using Toll Free Hotlines to Solve Budget Problems" discusses attempts to balance the budget in California, governmental organizations need to get serious about balancing their budgets.

Ethical Issues in Budgeting

Budgeting creates serious ethical issues for many people. Much of the information for the budget is provided by managers and employees whose performance is then compared with the budget they helped develop. For example, as a manager, suppose

Exhibit 12.9

VICTORIA CORPORATION
Flexible Budget Line

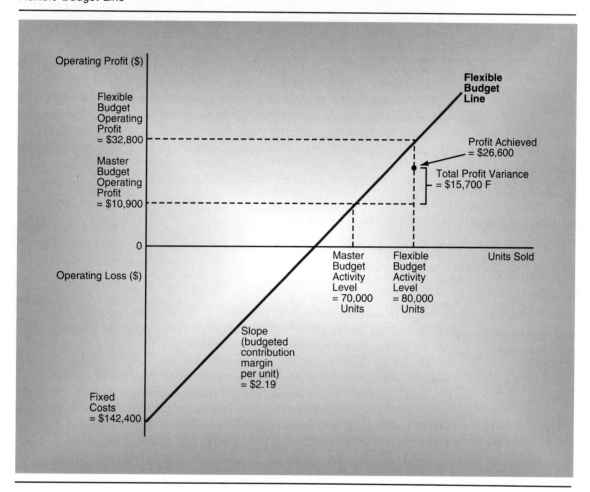

you believe that, while it was possible to achieve a 10-percent increase in your department's sales, a 2-percent increase would be almost certain. If you tell upper management that a 10-percent increase is an appropriate budget, but you fall short of 10 percent, you will lose opportunities for merit pay increases and a promotion. Management may assume the reason you fell short of the 10-percent estimation was not because of market circumstances beyond your control, but because you did not perform well in making sales. On the other hand, if you report that only a 2-percent increase is possible, your performance is likely to exceed expectations, but the company will not provide for enough production capacity to fill the sales orders if the 10-percent increase comes through. What should you do? Should you prepare a budget that is in your best interest or one that presents your best estimate of reality?

> **Managerial Application**
>
> ## Using Toll-Free Hotlines to Solve Budget Problems[a]
>
> After several years of failing to balance the budget, state of California lawmakers installed a toll-free hotline for state employees and the public to call with ideas for balancing the budget. The comments included cost-cutting ideas like auditing and reconciling purchase orders and invoices to avoid double-billing and avoid paying for goods and services never received. Callers also made suggestions for raising revenues, such as raising the fees on toll bridges and charging high school students to park at school. One cost-cutting idea that the lawmakers did not implement was to eliminate the state legislature.
>
> [a]Based on the authors' research.

People in companies face these dilemmas all the time. We hope companies provide incentives for people to report truthfully, which means the company must reward both for honest estimates and good performance. But the reality is that many companies put considerable pressure on employees to achieve continually more difficult targets. Fraudulent financial reporting often occurs because managers cannot meet continually more difficult budgets. The Managerial Application "Conflicts between Meeting Performance Standards and Behaving Ethically" describes General Electric's attempts to instruct employees on ways to deal with conflicts between high standards of ethical conduct and the demands of their jobs.

Summary

This chapter discusses the operating budget, which managers use for planning, performance evaluation, and employee motivation. After management makes decisions about products to produce, pricing, levels of output, production techniques, and so forth, accountants translate the choices into a formal plan of action, known as the master budget profit plan. This plan starts with goals and objectives—a plan is not helpful unless it specifies goals.

The master budget profit plan is fixed; that is, it is based on the *budgeted* sales volume. The flexible budget is based on the *actual* sales volume, however. Whereas the master budget shows budgeted costs at the projected sales volume, the flexible budget shows budgeted costs at the *actual* sales volume.

Managerial Application

Conflicts between Meeting Performance Standards and Behaving Ethically[a]

According to employees at General Electric, "in the frenzy of meeting sales goals, there was little time to scrutinize phony transactions."[b] In attempting to deal with conflicts between meeting performance standards and ethical behavior, General Electric has stated in its personnel manual, "If confronted with apparent conflicts between demands of their jobs and the highest standards of ethical conduct, employees should be guided by their sense of honor until the inconsistency has been resolved."[c] According to a vice-president of the company's aerospace unit, when employees get the message to achieve their performance goals they should also receive the message that they must comply with the company's standards for ethical behavior.

[a]Based on an article in *The Wall Street Journal*, July, 22, 1992.
[b]Ibid, p. A4.
[c]Ibid.

The following diagram summarizes the causes of variances:

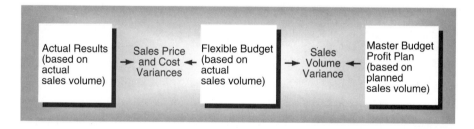

Appendix 12.1: Comprehensive Master Budget—Victoria Corporation

This appendix presents the comprehensive master budget for Victoria Corporation. First, we summarize the profit plan developed in the chapter. Second, we tie the profit plan into the other budgets, such as the cash budget and the capital budget. Finally, we present the budgeted balance sheet. The master budget ties together the financial activities of the firm for the budget period. Hence, it can aid both planning and coordination. For example, planning for cash needs requires knowing cash flows to and from operating activities and also knowing cash needs for the capital budget.

Exhibit 12.10 summarizes the information from the chapter about projected sales and production volumes, revenues, and costs. Exhibit 12.11 presents the master budget profit plan from the chapter.

Exhibit 12.10

VICTORIA CORPORATION
Summary of Sales, Production, and Cost Budgets for Period 1

Sales Budget[a]

70,000 Units at $6	$420,000

Production Budget[b]

Units to Be Produced

Budgeted Sales, in Units (see sales budget)..................	70,000	Units
Desired Ending Inventory (assumed).........................	8,000	
Total Units Needed	78,000	Units
Beginning Inventory (assumed)	(8,000)	
Units to Be Produced	70,000	Units

Cost Expected to Be Incurred

Direct Materials (2 pounds per unit at $.50 per pound)		$ 70,000
Direct Labor (⅛ hour per unit at $20 per hour)		175,000
Manufacturing Overhead:		
Indirect Labor ($.10 per unit).............................	$ 7,000	
Supplies ($.04 per unit)	2,800	
Power ($1,000 per period plus $.03 per unit)	3,100	
Maintenance ($13,840 per period).........................	13,840	
Rent ($6,000 per period)	6,000	
Insurance ($1,000 per period).............................	1,000	
Depreciation ($10,360 per period)	10,360	44,100
Total Production Costs		$289,100

Marketing Cost Budget[c]

Variable Costs

Commissions (2 percent of sales)	$ 8,400	
Shipping Costs ($.02 per unit shipped)......................	1,400	
Total Variable Marketing Costs		$ 9,800

Fixed Costs

Salaries ($25,000 per period)	$25,000	
Advertising ($30,000 per period)	30,000	
Sales Office ($8,400 per period)	8,400	
Travel ($2,000 per period)	2,000	
Total Fixed Marketing Costs		65,400
Total Marketing Cost Budget.............................		$ 75,200

(continued)

Exhibit 12.10 *(continued)*

Administrative Cost Budget[d]

President's Salary	$ 10,000
Salaries of Other Staff Personnel	17,000
Supplies	2,000
Heat and Light	1,400
Rent	4,000
Donations and Contributions	1,000
General Corporate Taxes	8,000
Depreciation—Staff Office Equipment	1,400
Total Administrative Cost Budget	$ 44,800

[a]*Source:* Exhibit 12.2. [c]*Source:* Exhibit 12.4.

[b]*Source:* Exhibit 12.3. [d]*Source:* Exhibit 12.5.

Materials Purchases Budget

The purchasing department is responsible for purchasing materials in Victoria Corporation. Exhibit 12.12 presents the materials purchases budget. The production budget is the basis for the materials purchases budget. For simplicity in presentation, we assume that payments to suppliers equal purchases each period.

Exhibit 12.11

VICTORIA CORPORATION
Master Budget Profit Plan for Period 1

Variable Costing Basis

Sales (70,000 units at $6)	$420,000
Less:	
Variable Manufacturing Cost of Goods Sold (70,000 units at $3.67)	(256,900)
Variable Marketing Costs (70,000 units at $.14)	(9,800)
Contribution Margin	$153,300
Less:	
Fixed Manufacturing Costs	(32,200)
Fixed Marketing and Administrative Costs	(110,200)
Operating Profits (variable costing)	$ 10,900

Full Absorption Costing Basis

Sales (70,000 units at $6)	$420,000
Less:	
Cost of Goods Sold (70,000 units at $4.13)	(289,100)
Gross Margin	$130,900
Less:	
Marketing and Administrative Costs	(120,000)
Operating Profits (full absorption costing)	$ 10,900

Source: Exhibit 12.6.

Exhibit 12.12

VICTORIA CORPORATION
Materials Purchases Budget

Quantities to Be Purchased (in pounds):	
Units to Be Produced (see Exhibit 12.10)	70,000 Units
Purchases Required at 2 Pounds per Unit........................	140,000 Pounds
There are no materials inventories.	

Capital Budget

The capital budget, Exhibit 12.13, shows Victoria Corporation's plan for acquisition of depreciable, long-term assets during the next period. Management plans to purchase major items of equipment, financing part of the cost by issuing notes payable to equipment suppliers in a later period. The capital budget deducts the expected proceeds of the note issuance from the cost of the acquisitions to estimate current cash outlays for equipment. An accepted alternative treatment would have viewed the note issuance as a cash inflow, with the entire cost of the equipment included in cash outflows.

Cash Outlays Budget

Exhibit 12.14 presents a schedule of the planned cash outlays for the budget period. Each period, the Victoria Corporation pays the income taxes accrued in the previous period. Income taxes payable at the start of the budget period appears as $6,200 on the beginning balance sheet (first column of Exhibit 12.18). The firm expects to declare and pay dividends of $5,000 in the budget period.

Receivables and Collections Budget

Victoria collects most of each period's sales in the period of sale, but there is a lag in some collections. The budget for cash collections from customers appears in Exhibit 12.15. Collections for sales of a given period normally occur as follows: 85 percent in the period of sale and 15 percent in the next period. We could introduce

Exhibit 12.13

VICTORIA CORPORATION
Capital Budget for Period 1

	Period 1
Acquisition of New Factory Machinery	$12,000
Miscellaneous Capital Additions	2,000
Total Capital Budget	$14,000
Borrowings for New Machinery—Long-term Notes Payable	(6,000)
Current Cash Outlay	$ 8,000

Exhibit 12.14

VICTORIA CORPORATION
Cash Outflows Budget for Period 1

	Period 1
Materials (Exhibit 12.10)..	$ 70,000
Labor (Exhibit 12.10)...	175,000
Manufacturing Overhead (Exhibit 12.10)[a]................................	33,740
Marketing Costs (Exhibit 12.10)	75,200
Administrative Costs (Exhibit 12.10)[b]	43,400
Capital Expenditures (Exhibit 12.13)	8,000
Payments on Short-term Notes[c]...	13,000
Interest[c]	3,000
Income Taxes[d]	6,200
Dividends[c]	5,000
Total Cash Outflows	$432,540

[a]Manufacturing Overhead Costs − Depreciation = $44,100 − $10,360 = $33,740.

[b]Administrative Costs − Depreciation = $44,800 − $1,400 = $43,400.

[c]Assumed for illustration.

[d]The firm pays income taxes on earnings of previous period in current period. We assume the amount in this case.

sales discounts and estimates of uncollectible accounts into the illustration, but we omit them for simplicity. The estimated accounts receivable at the start of the budget period of $71,400 appears on the beginning balance sheet (first column of Exhibit 12.18). The amount represents 15 percent of the previous period's sales of $476,000; $71,400 = .15 × $476,000. In the budget period, the firm expects to collect 85 percent of sales, leaving $63,000 in Accounts Receivable at the end of the budget period ($63,000 = 15 percent of budget period sales of $420,000).

Exhibit 12.15

VICTORIA CORPORATION
Receivables and Collections Budget for Period 1

	Budget Period
Accounts Receivable, Start of Period:	
From the Period Immediately Preceding the Budget Period (15 percent of $476,000)	$ 71,400
Budget Period Sales	420,000
Total Receivables..	$ 491,400
Less Collections:	
Current Period (85 percent of $420,000)	$(357,000)
Previous Period (15 percent of $476,000)	(71,400)
Total Collections..	$(428,400)
Accounts Receivable, End of Period	$ 63,000

Exhibit 12.16

VICTORIA CORPORATION
Cash Budget for Period 1

	Budget Period
Cash Receipts:	
Collections from Customers (Exhibit 12.15)	$428,400
Other Income[a]	2,000
Total Receipts	$430,400
Cash Outflows (Exhibit 12.14)	(432,540)
Increase (Decrease) in Cash during Period	$ (2,140)
Cash Balance at Start of Period[a]	79,800
Cash Balance at End of Period	$ 77,660

[a]Assumed for illustration.

Cash Budget

Cash flow is important. No budget is more important for financial planning than the cash budget, illustrated in Exhibit 12.16. This budget helps management plan to avoid unnecessary idle cash balances or unneeded, expensive borrowing. Almost all firms prepare a cash budget.

The budgeted amounts for cash outflows and collections from customers come from Exhibits 12.14 and 12.15, respectively. Management estimates the other income, interest and miscellaneous revenues to be $2,000 for the period.

Budgeted (Pro Forma) Income and Retained Earnings Statement

The budgeted income and retained earnings statement and the budgeted balance sheet pull together all of the previous budget information. Exhibit 12.17 illustrates the budgeted income and retained earnings statement. At this stage in the budgeting process, management's attention switches from decision making, planning, and control to external reporting to shareholders. In other words, management becomes interested in how the income statement and balance sheet will reflect the results of its decisions. Accordingly, accountants prepare the budgeted income statement and balance sheet in accordance with generally accepted accounting principles. The statement in Exhibit 12.17 is an *income statement,* rather than a profit plan, and we present it using full absorption costing as required for external reporting.

Compilation of all of the data for the period indicates a budgeted income of $6,039. If top management finds this budgeted result satisfactory, and has available cash adequate to carry out the operations as indicated by Exhibit 12.16, it will approve the master budget. If management does not consider the budgeted results

Exhibit 12.17

VICTORIA CORPORATION
Budgeted (pro forma) Income and Retained Earnings Statement for Period 1

Sales (70,000 units at $6)	$420,000
Less Cost of Goods Sold (70,000 units at $4.13)	(289,100)
Gross Margin	$130,900
Less Marketing Expenses	(75,200)
Less Administrative Expenses	(44,800)
Operating Profits (Exhibit 12.11)	$ 10,900
Other Income (Exhibit 12.16)	2,000
	$ 12,900
Less Interest Expense (Exhibit 12.14)	(3,000)
Pretax Income	$ 9,900
Less Income Taxes[a]	(3,861)
Net Income	$ 6,039
Less Dividends (Exhibit 12.14)	(5,000)
Increase in Retained Earnings	$ 1,039
Retained Earnings at Start of Period (Exhibit 12.18)	56,500
Retained Earnings at End of Period (Exhibit 12.18)	$ 57,539

[a]Income taxes average approximately 39 percent of pretax income. The amount $3,861 is shown as the end-of-period income taxes payable in Exhibit 12.18.

satisfactory, it will consider ways to improve the budgeted results through cost reductions or altered sales plans.

Budgeted Balance Sheet

The final exhibit of this series, Exhibit 12.18, shows the budgeted balance sheets at the start and end of the period. (Accountants prepare the budget before the beginning of the budget period; hence, they must estimate the beginning balance sheet. For example, accountants would prepare a budget for the calendar year during the preceding September through November.)

Here, as in the budgeted income statement, management will have to decide if the budgeted overall results will be acceptable. Will cash balances be satisfactory? Do the receivables meet management's objectives? Will the final capital structure and debt-equity ratio conform to management's desires? If the budgeted balance sheet and income statement are satisfactory, they will become the initial benchmarks against which management will check actual performance in the ensuing period.

Summary of the Master Budget

The master budget summarizes management's plans for the period covered. Preparing the master budget requires the participation of all managerial groups, from local

Exhibit 12.18

VICTORIA CORPORATION
Budgeted Balance Sheet for Period 1

	Start of Budget Period	End of Budget Period
Assets		
Current Assets		
Cash (Exhibit 12.16)	$ 79,800	$ 77,660
Accounts Receivable (Exhibit 12.15)	71,400	63,000
Finished Goods Inventory	33,040[a]	33,040[a]
Total Current Assets	$184,240	$173,700
Plant Assets		
Equipment	460,000[b]	474,000[b]
Less Accumulated Depreciation	(162,000)[b]	(173,760)[b]
Total Assets	$482,240	$473,940
Equities		
Current Liabilities		
Accounts Payable	$ 96,540[b]	$ 96,540[b]
Short-term Notes and Other Payables	41,000[b]	28,000[b]
Income Taxes Payable (Exhibits 12.14 and 12.17)	6,200	3,861
Total Current Liabilities	$143,740	$128,401
Long-term Liabilities		
Long-term Equipment Notes	82,000[b]	88,000[b]
Total Liabilities	$225,740	$216,401
Shareholders' Equity		
Capital Stock ($20 par value)	$200,000[b]	$200,000[b]
Retained Earnings (Exhibit 12.17)	56,500[b]	57,539[b]
Total Shareholders' Equity	$256,500	$257,539
Total Equities	$482,240	$473,940

[a]8,000 units in inventory according to Exhibit 12.10 at $4.13 per unit. $4.13 was given in Exhibit 12.6 as the full absorption manufacturing cost per unit.

[b]Assumed for purposes of illustration.

plant and sales managers to the top executives of the firm and the board of directors. Once management adopts the budget, it becomes the major planning and control instrument.

Master budgets are almost always static budgets; that is, they consider the likely results of operations at the one level of operations specified in the budget. Computerizing the process makes it less costly to develop multiple master budgets that take into account various uncertainties facing the firm, such as market conditions, material prices, labor difficulties, and government regulations.

Appendix 12.2: Incentive Model for Accurate Reporting

How does management provide employees with incentives both for accurate reporting and for high performance?

Example Assume that the Harris Raviv Company solicits sales forecasts from each of its district sales managers. These forecasts become budgets that management compares to actual sales to evaluate performance.

The firm's general manager of marketing wants to provide each district sales manager with a salary and a bonus. Previously sales managers earned a bonus by beating the budget. The sales managers, however, began to ''low-ball'' the forecasts. Management knew this was happening, but it did not know how high the forecasts *should* have been, because it did not have the information the managers had. The general manager of marketing explained:

Managers could always counter our arguments with data that we could not audit. Their low estimates wreaked havoc with our production schedules, purchasing, and hiring decisions.

Next we tried to give them incentives for accurate forecasts. We rewarded them if the actual sales were close to the forecasts, and penalized if actual and forecast deviated a lot. With this system, the managers forecast sales at a level that was sufficiently low to be achievable, then they ''managed'' their sales such that actual was almost right at the forecast. The consequences were that they had disincentives to beat the budget. Also, our internal auditors found numerous cases where managers had delayed sales orders until the following year and even turned down some orders because they did not want the current year's sales to overshoot the forecast.

The incentive plan to deal with this problem has three components.

1. Rewards are positively related to forecasted sales to give managers incentives to forecast high rather than low. Thus, if b_1 is a bonus coefficient that is a percent of forecasted sales, and forecasted sales are $\hat{Y}$, then this component of the bonus is

$$b_1\hat{Y}.$$

2. The plan provides incentives for the sales manager to increase sales beyond the forecast. If b_2 is the bonus coefficient for the excess of Y over $\hat{Y}$, forecast sales, then this component of the bonus is

$$b_2(Y - \hat{Y}), \quad \text{for } Y \geq \hat{Y}.$$

3. When actual sales, Y, are less than the forecast, $\hat{Y}$, the plan penalizes the sales manager. If b_3 is the bonus coefficient for the shortfall, $Y - \hat{Y}$, then this component of the bonus is

$$-b_3(\hat{Y} - Y), \quad \text{for } \hat{Y} > Y.$$

Exhibit 12.19

HARRIS RAVIV COMPANY
Incentives for Accurate Forecasting Bonus Paid to District Sales Managers
(thousands omitted from sales and bonus amounts)

Let $b_1 = 5$ percent, $b_2 = 3$ percent, and $b_3 = 7$ percent

$$B = \begin{cases} .05\hat{Y} + .03(Y - \hat{Y}), & \text{for } Y \geq \hat{Y}; \\ .05\hat{Y} - .07(\hat{Y} - Y), & \text{for } \hat{Y} > Y. \end{cases}$$

		Forecasted Sales, $\hat{Y}$		
		$1,000	**$1,100**	**$1,200**
Actual	**$1,000**	50[a]	48[d]	46[g]
Sales,	**$1,100**	53[b]	55[e]	53[h]
Y	**$1,200**	56[c]	58[f]	60[i]

---

[a]$50 = .05($1,000).
[b]$53 = .05($1,000) + .03($1,100 − $1,000).
[c]$56 = .05($1,000) + .03($1,200 − $1,000).
[d]$48 = .05($1,100) − .07($1,100 − $1,000).
[e]$55 = .05($1,100).

[f]$58 = .05($1,100) + .03($1,200 − $1,100).
[g]$46 = .05($1,200) − .07($1,200 − $1,000).
[h]$53 = .05($1,200) − .07($1,200 − $1,100).
[i]$60 = .05($1,200).

If B is the dollar bonus paid to the manager, the overall bonus plan is

$$B = \begin{cases} b_1\hat{Y} + b_2(Y - \hat{Y}), & \text{for } Y \geq \hat{Y} \text{ (actual sales meet or exceed the forecast);} \\ b_1\hat{Y} - b_3(\hat{Y} - Y), & \text{for } \hat{Y} > Y \text{ (the forecast exceeds actual sales).} \end{cases}$$

The coefficients are set such that

$$b_3 > b_1 > b_2 > 0,$$

and a rule of thumb is that b_3 should be at least 30 percent greater than b_1, and b_1 should be at least 30 percent greater than b_2.[4] Management intends for this incentive plan to reward both accurate forecasts and outstanding performance.

Harris Raviv Company established an incentive system using the methods described here. Exhibit 12.19 shows the bonus that would result from various combinations of forecasted sales and actual sales. For example, if the forecast is $1,100,000 and the actual sales are $1,000,000, the district sales manager receives a bonus of $48,000; if both the forecast and actual sales are $1,100,000, the sales manager receives a bonus of $55,000; and so forth.

Implications

What are the implications of this incentive system? If you read down a column in Exhibit 12.19, you will see that after making the forecast, the manager receives a

---

[4]See M. Weitzman, "The New Soviet Incentive Model," *Bell Journal of Economics* (Spring 1976), pp. 253–254.

larger reward for more sales even if an increase in sales makes the forecast inaccurate. Reading across the rows reveals that the manager receives the highest bonus when the forecast equals actual sales; hence, the manager has an incentive to make accurate forecasts.

This system provides incentives for accurate forecasting and sales output simultaneously. Although our example has dealt with sales forecasts, the method described applies to virtually any type of forecasting (for example, production levels, costs, productivity). At this point, we have little evidence about implementation difficulties. Whereas the method appears to be a clever innovation, we shall have to see it in operation before we pass judgment on it. (Note that top management can adjust the bonus coefficients, b_1, b_2, and b_3, to suit the needs of the particular situation.)

In summary, analysts have developed incentive methods that provide rewards for both accurate forecasts and good performance. Rewards are positively related to forecasted sales to give incentives to forecast high rather than low. Employees receive additional rewards for beating the forecast and penalties for results worse than forecast.

Solutions to Self-Study Problems

Suggested Solution to Problem 12.1 for Self-Study

COMPUTER SUPPLY, INC.
Flexible Budget and Sales Volume Variance
April

	Flexible Budget (based on 50,000 units)	Sales Volume Variance	Master Budget (based on 40,000 units)
Sales Revenue	$550,000[a]	$110,000 F	$440,000
Less:			
Variable Manufacturing Costs	200,000	40,000 U	160,000
Variable Marketing and Administrative Costs	50,000	10,000 U	40,000
Contribution Margin	$300,000	$ 60,000 F	$240,000
Less:			
Fixed Manufacturing Costs	80,000	—	80,000
Fixed Marketing and Administrative Costs	100,000	—	100,000
Operating Profits.	$120,000	$ 60,000 F	$ 60,000

[a]$550,000 = 50,000 × $11. Note the only change is volume, not sales price.

Suggested Solution to Problem 12.2 for Self-Study

COMPUTER SUPPLY, INC.
Profit Variance Analysis
April

	Actual (based on 50,000 units)	Purchasing and Production Variances	Marketing and Administrative Variances	Sales Price Variances	Flexible Budget (based on 50,000 units)	Sales Volume Variance	Master Budget (based on 40,000 units)
Sales Revenue	$500,000	—	—	$50,000 U	$550,000	$110,000 F	$440,000
Less:							
Variable Manufacturing Costs	244,000	$44,000 U	—	—	200,000	40,000 U	160,000
Variable Marketing and Administrative Costs ...	52,000	—	$2,000 U	—	50,000	10,000 U	40,000
Contribution Margin	$204,000	$44,000 U	$2,000 U	$50,000 U	$300,000	$ 60,000 F	$240,000
Less:							
Fixed Manufacturing Costs	83,000	3,000 U	—	—	80,000	—	80,000
Fixed Marketing and Administrative Costs ...	96,000	—	4,000 F	—	100,000	—	100,000
Operating Profits......	$ 25,000	$47,000 U	$2,000 F	$50,000 U	$120,000	$ 60,000 F	$ 60,000

Total Profit Variance from Flexible Budget = $95,000 U

Total Profit Variance from Master Budget = $35,000 U

Key Terms and Concepts

Budgets as tools for planning
Budgets as tools for performance
  evaluation
Static budget
Master budget
Flexible budget
Variances
Sales volume variance
Favorable versus unfavorable
  variance

Profit variance analysis
Incentives for accurate forecasting
Responsibility center
Cost center
Revenue center
Profit center
Investment center
Goal congruence
Discretionary versus engineered cost
  centers

Questions, Exercises, Problems, and Cases

Questions

1. Review the meaning of the concepts or terms discussed above in Key Terms and Concepts.
2. What is the difference between a cost center and a profit center? What is the difference between a profit center and an investment center?
3. Why is it difficult to assess the effectiveness of discretionary cost centers?
4. Who, among university administrators, is most likely to be responsible for each of the following?
   a. Quantity of supplies used in executive education classes that the business school conducts.
   b. Electricity for equipment the university's printing operations use.
   c. Charge for classroom maintenance the business school uses.
   d. Finance professors' salaries.
5. Why is a contribution margin format more useful than a traditional (full absorption) format for performance reporting?
6. A superior criticized a sales manager for selling high-revenue, low-profit items instead of lower-revenue but higher-profit items. The sales manager responded, ''My income is based on commissions that are a percent of revenues. Why should I care about profits? I care about revenues!'' Comment.
7. ''The flexible budget is a poor benchmark. You should develop a budget and stay with it.'' Comment.
8. Why is the sales forecast so important in developing the master budget?
9. When would the master budget profit equal the flexible budget profit?
10. Managers in some companies claim that they do not use flexible budgeting, yet they compute a sales volume variance. How is that different from flexible budgeting?
11. Refer to the Managerial Application about 3M. What departments at 3M are involved in budgeting costs of new products? Why are people from so many different functions involved?

Exercises

Solutions to even-numbered exercises are at the end of the chapter on page 507.

12. **Solving for materials requirements.** Bala Company expects to sell 84,000 units of finished goods over the next 3-month period. The company currently has 44,000 units of finished goods on hand and wishes to have an inventory of 48,000 units at the end of the 3-month period. To produce 1 unit of finished goods requires 4 units of raw materials. The company currently has 200,000 units of raw materials on hand and wishes to have an inventory of 220,000 units of raw materials on hand at the end of the 3-month period. The company does not have, nor does it wish to have, work-in-process inventory.

    How many units of raw materials must the Bala Company purchase during the 3-month period?

13. **Solving for budgeted manufacturing costs.** Candice Candy Company expects to sell 100,000 cases of chocolate bars during the current year. Budgeted costs per case are $150 for direct materials, $120 for direct labor, and $75 (all variable) for manufacturing overhead. Candice Candy began the period with 40,000 cases of finished goods on hand and wants to end the period with 10,000 cases of finished goods on hand.

    Compute the budgeted manufacturing costs of the Candice Candy Company for the current period. Assume no beginning or ending inventory of work in process.

14. **Solving for cash collections** (Appendix 12.1). Jones Corporation normally collects cash from credit customers as follows: 50 percent in the month of sale, 30 percent in the first month after sale, 18 percent in the second month after sale, and 2 percent never collected. Jones Corporation expects its sales, all on credit, to be as follows:

January	$500,000
February	600,000
March	400,000
April	500,000

    a. Calculate the amount of cash Jones Corporation expects to receive from customers during March.
    b. Calculate the amount of cash Jones Corporation expects to receive from customers during April.

15. **Solving for cash payments** (Appendix 12.1). Nguyen Corporation purchases raw materials on account from various suppliers. It normally pays for 50 percent of these in the month purchased, 30 percent in the first month after purchase, and the remaining 20 percent in the second month after purchase. Raw materials purchases during the last 5 months of the year follow:

August	$1,400,000
September	1,800,000
October	2,500,000
November	3,500,000
December	1,500,000

Compute the budgeted amount of cash payments to suppliers for the months of October, November, and December.

16. **Profit variance analysis.** Austin Company prepared a budget last period that called for sales of 7,000 units at a price of $12 each. Variable costs per unit were budgeted to be $5. Fixed costs were budgeted to be $21,000 for the period. During the period, production was exactly equal to actual sales of 7,100 units. The selling price was $12.15 per unit. Variable costs were $5.90 per unit. Fixed costs were $20,000.

    Prepare a profit variance report to show the difference between the master budget and the achieved profits.

17. **Analyzing contribution margin changes.** The Sycamore Sight Center, which sells eyeglasses, provided the following data for years 1 and 2:

	Year 1	Year 2
Sales Volume	7,000 Pairs of Glasses	5,000 Pairs of Glasses
Sales Revenue	$875,000	$750,000
Variable Costs	(735,000)	(525,000)
Contribution Margin	$140,000	$225,000

What impact did the changes in sales volume and in sales price have on the contribution margin? (Hint: Compare the actual, flexible budget, and master budget portion of the profit variance analysis. Use Year 1 as the "Master Budget.")

18. **Graphic comparison of budgeted and actual costs.**

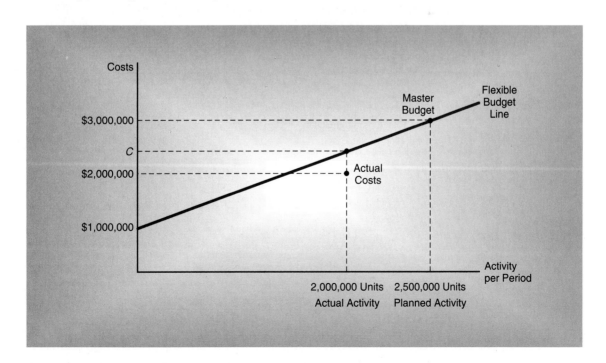

   a. Given the data shown in the graph, what is the budgeted variable cost per unit?

   b. What is the flexible budget cost for an activity level of 2,000,000 units (C on the graph)?

   c. If the actual activity had been 4,000,000 units, what would have been the flexible budget cost amount?

19. Preparing flexible budgets (adapted from CPA exam). Exhibit 12.20 provides information concerning the operations of the Wallace Company for the current period. The firm has no inventories. Prepare a flexible budget for the company.

20. Comparing master budget to actual results. Using the data from Exhibit 12.20 and the flexible budget from Exercise **19,** prepare a profit variance report that will enable Wallace to identify the variances between the master budget and actual results.

Exhibit 12.20

WALLACE COMPANY

	Actual	Master Budget
Sales Volume	85 Units	100 Units
Sales Revenue	$9,200	$10,000
Manufacturing Cost of Goods Sold:		
Variable	3,440	3,900
Fixed.......................................	485	500
Cost of Goods Sold.......................	$3,925	$ 4,400
Gross Profit	$5,275	$ 5,600
Operating Costs:		
Marketing Costs:		
Variable	$1,030	$ 1,100
Fixed....................................	1,040	1,000
Administrative Costs, All Fixed	995	1,000
Total Operating Costs	$3,065	$ 3,100
Operating Profits	$2,210	$ 2,500

21. **Interpreting the flexible budget line.** The graph shows a flexible budget line with some missing data. Fill in the missing amounts for (a) and (b).

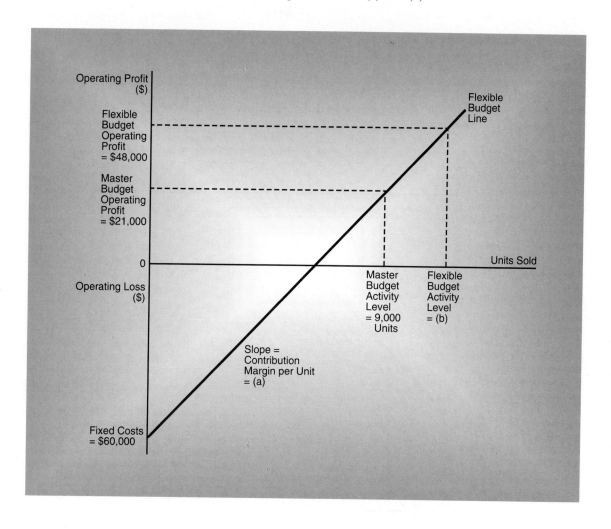

Operating Profit ($)

Flexible Budget Operating Profit = $48,000

Master Budget Operating Profit = $21,000

0

Operating Loss ($)

Fixed Costs = $60,000

Flexible Budget Line

Units Sold

Master Budget Activity Level = 9,000 Units

Flexible Budget Activity Level = (b)

Slope = Contribution Margin per Unit = (a)

22. **Interpreting the flexible budget line.** Label (a) and (b) on the graph and give the number of units sold for each.

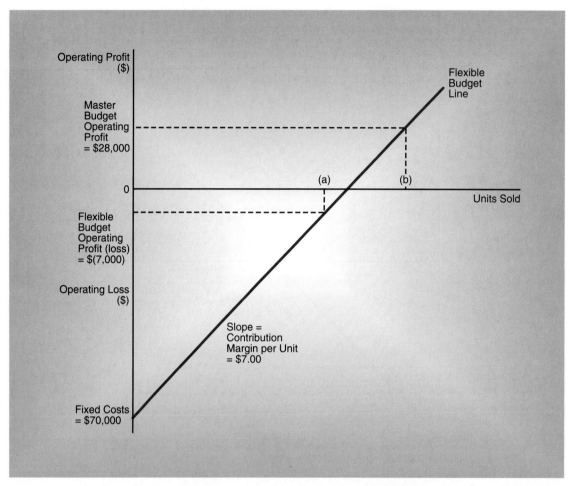

23. **Incentives for accurate forecasting** (Appendix 12.2). Compute the bonus, B, paid to a donut company's franchise managers using the following formulas:

$$B = b_1\hat{Y} + b_2(Y - \hat{Y}), \qquad \text{for } Y \geq \hat{Y}$$

$$B = b_1\hat{Y} - b_3(\hat{Y} - Y), \qquad \text{for } \hat{Y} > Y$$

where

$$b_1 = 5\%$$

$$b_2 = 2\%$$

$$b_3 = 6\%$$

$$\hat{Y} = \text{forecasted sales revenue}$$

$$Y = \text{actual sales revenue.}$$

Let Y and $\hat{Y}$ each have values of $2,500, $3,000, and $3,500.

24. **Incentives for accurate forecasting** (Appendix 12.2). Compute the monthly bonus, B, paid to an automobile dealership using the following formulas:

$$B = b_1\hat{Y} + b_2(Y - \hat{Y}), \qquad \text{for } Y \geq \hat{Y}$$

$$B = b_1\hat{Y} - b_3(\hat{Y} - Y), \qquad \text{for } \hat{Y} > Y$$

where

$b_1 = \$100$ per car

$b_2 = \$70$ per car

$b_3 = \$150$ per car

$\hat{Y} =$ forecasted sales of cars (in units)

$Y =$ actual number of cars sold.

Let Y and $\hat{Y}$ each have values of 20 cars, 21 cars, 22 cars, 23 cars, and 24 cars.

25. **Flexible budgeting—manufacturing costs.** As a result of studying past cost behavior and adjusting for expected price increases in the future, Jordan Corporation estimates that its manufacturing costs will be as follows:

Direct Materials	$2.00 per Unit
Direct Labor	$1.50 per Unit
Manufacturing Overhead:	
Variable	$.75 per Unit
Fixed..	$50,000 per Period

Jordan adopts these estimates for planning and control purposes.

a. Jordan Corporation expects to produce 20,000 units during the next period. Prepare a schedule of the expected manufacturing costs.

b. Suppose that Jordan Corporation produces only 16,000 units during the next period. Prepare a flexible budget of manufacturing costs for the 16,000-unit level of activity.

c. Suppose that Jordan Corporation produces 26,000 units during the next period. Prepare a flexible budget of manufacturing costs for the 26,000 unit level of activity.

26. **Marketing cost budget.** Refer to the marketing cost budget of the Victoria Corporation shown in Exhibit 12.4. Prepare a flexible marketing cost budget for the period, assuming the following levels of sales and shipments and a selling price of $6 per unit.

	Case 1	Case 2	Case 3
Units	60,000	75,000	64,000

27. **Administrative cost budget.** Refer to the central corporate administrative budget of the Victoria Corporation in Exhibit 12.5. Prepare a flexible central corporate administrative cost budget for the period, assuming that production and sales were 70,000 units. Is the term *flexible budget* a misnomer in this case? Explain.

28. **Computing sales price variances.** Budgeted sales of Holt Electronics Merchandisers for 19X0 were as follows:

Product X (5,000 units)	$100,000
Product Y (200 units)	20,000
Product Z (50,000 units)	250,000
Total Budgeted Sales	$370,000

Actual sales for the period were as follows:

Product X (5,300 units)	$111,300
Product Y (240 units)	23,040
Product Z (48,000 units)	192,000
Total Actual Sales	$326,340

Calculate the sales price variances for sales of the three products.

29. **Estimating flexible selling expense budget and computing variances.** Doshi Products, Incorporated, estimates that it will incur the following selling expenses next period:

Salaries (fixed)	$ 20,000
Commissions (.05 of sales revenue)	17,875
Travel (.03 of sales revenue)	10,725
Advertising (fixed)	50,000
Sales Office Costs ($4,000 plus $.05 per unit sold)	7,250
Shipping Cost ($.10 per unit sold)	6,500
Total Selling Expenses	$112,350

a. Estimate the cost equation ($y = a + bx$) for selling expenses.
b. Assume that Doshi sells 50,000 units during the period at an average price of $6 per unit. The company had budgeted sales for the period to be: volume, 65,000 units; price, $5.50. Calculate the sales price and volume variance.
c. The actual selling expenses incurred during the period were $80,000 fixed and $30,000 variable. Prepare a profit variance analysis for sales revenue and selling expenses.

Problems

30. **Profit variance analysis in a service organization.** Wolfson & Scholes (WS) is a CPA firm that gets a large portion of its revenue from tax services. Last year, WS's billable tax hours were up 20 percent from expected levels, but, as the following data shows, profits from the tax department were lower than anticipated.

	Achieved Results	Master Budget
Billable Hours[a]	60,000 Hours	50,000 Hours
Revenue.............................	$3,300,000	$3,000,000
Production Costs:		
Professional Salaries (all variable)......	1,850,000	1,500,000
Other Variable Costs (e.g., supplies, certain computer services)...........	470,000	400,000
General Administrative (all fixed)	580,000	600,000
Tax Department Profit...................	$ 400,000	$ 500,000

[a]These are hours billed to clients. Hours worked exceed this amount because of nonbillable time (e.g., slack periods, time in training sessions) and because WS does not charge all time worked for clients.

Prepare a comparison of the achieved results to the master and flexible budgets. Adapt the approach shown in Exhibit 12.8 to this service organization.

31. **Finding missing data.** Find the values of the missing items (a) through (q).

	Achieved Results, 750 Units	Purchasing and Production Variances	Marketing and Administrative Variances	Sales Price Variance	Flexible Budget (a)	Variance	Master Budget 800 Units
Sales Revenue................	$1,890			(b)	$2,025	(c)	(d)
Variable Manufacturing Costs ..	(f)	$60 F			(e)	$38 F	(g)
Variable Marketing and Administrative	(h)		(j)		(i)	(k)	$216
Contribution Margin	$1,180	(l)	(m)	(n)	(o)	(p)	(q)

32. **Comprehensive problem.** The Micro Company, which makes computer chips, has the following master budget income statement for the month of May:

	Master Budget (based on 8,000 units)
Sales Revenue (8,000 units at $20)	
Less:	
Variable Manufacturing Costs	80,000[a]
Variable Marketing and Administrative Costs..................	8,000[b]
Contribution Margin	$ 72,000
Less:	
Fixed Manufacturing Costs	20,000
Fixed Marketing and Administrative Costs	45,000
Operating Profit	$ 7,000

[a]8,000 budgeted units at $10 per unit.

[b]8,000 budgeted units at $1 per unit.

The company uses the following estimates to prepare the master budget:

Sales Price	$20 per Unit
Sales and Production Volume	8,000 Units
Variable Manufacturing Costs	$10 per Unit
Variable Marketing and Administrative Costs.	$1 per Unit
Fixed Manufacturing Costs	$20,000
Fixed Marketing and Administrative Costs	$45,000

Assume that the actual results for May were as follows:

	Actual
Sales Price	$19 per Unit
Sales and Production Volume	10,000 Units
Variable Manufacturing Costs	$105,440
Variable Marketing and Administrative Costs.	$11,000
Fixed Manufacturing Costs	$21,000
Fixed Marketing and Administrative Costs	$44,000

Compare the master budget, flexible budget, and actual results for the month of May.

33. **Finding missing data.** Find the values of the missing items (a) through (u).

	Achieved Based on Actual Sales Volume	Cost and Sales Price Variances	Flexible Budget Based on Actual Sales Volume	Sales Volume Variance	Master Budget Based on Budgeted Sales Volume
Units	(b)		(a)	2,000 F	10,000
Sales Revenue	(i)	$18,000 F	(h)	(j)	$150,000
Less:					
Variable Manufacturing Costs	(n)	9,000 U	$96,000	(k)	80,000
Variable Marketing and Administrative Costs	$21,600	(o)	24,000	$4,000 U	(c)
Contribution Margin	(p)	(r)	$60,000	(l)	$ 50,000
Less:					
Fixed Manufacturing Costs	(q)	2,000 F	(d)		(e)
Fixed Marketing and Administrative Costs	$18,000	(t)	15,000		(f)
Operating Profits	(s)	(u)	$20,000	(m)	(g)

34. **Assigning responsibility.** Neptune Automobile Company (a competitor of Saturn) is organized into two divisions, Assembling and Finishing. The Assembling Division combines raw materials into a semifinished product. The product then goes to the Finishing Division for painting, polishing, and packing.

During May, the Assembling Division had significantly higher raw materials costs than expected because poor-quality raw materials required extensive rework. As a result of the rework, Assembly transferred fewer units than expected to the Finishing Division. The Finishing Division incurred higher labor costs per unit of finished product because workers had substantial idle time. The president of the company is upset about these events.

a. Who should the firm hold responsible for the raw materials variance in the Assembling Department? Explain.

b. Who should the firm hold responsible for the labor (idle time) variance in the Finishing Department? Explain.

35. **Controls over planning function.** Keating Federal Bank set up an independent planning department at corporate headquarters. This department is responsible for most aspects of budgeting (revenue and expense forecasting, profit planning, capital investment). Planning department personnel are responsible to the vice president for administration. The resulting budgets are incorporated into the control system that the controller's department designed and administered.

Outline an effective control system for the planning department's activities (that is, how the firm should evaluate the performance of the planning department).

36. **Ethical issues** (adapted from CMA exam). Norton Company manufactures infant furniture and carriages. The accounting staff is currently preparing next year's budget. Michelle Jackson is new to the firm and is interested in learning how this process occurs. She has lunch with the sales manager and the production manager to discuss further the planning process. Over the course of lunch, Michelle discovers that the sales manager lowers sales projections 5 to 10 percent before submitting her figures, while the production manager increases cost estimates by 10 percent before submitting his figures. When Michelle asks about why this is done, the response is simply that everyone around here does it.

a. What do the sales and production managers hope to accomplish by their methods?

b. How might this backfire and work against them?

c. Are the actions of the sales and production managers unethical?

37. **Flexible budget** (adapted from CMA exam). The University of Cougars operates a motor pool with 21 vehicles. The motor pool furnishes gasoline, oil, and other supplies for the cars and hires one mechanic who does routine maintenance and minor repairs. A nearby commercial garage does major repairs. A supervisor manages the operations.

Each year, the supervisor prepares a master budget for the motor pool. The accountant records depreciation on the automobiles in the budget to calculate the costs per mile.

The schedule that follows presents the master budget for the year and for the month of March.

The annual budget was based on the following assumptions:

1. 20 automobiles in the pool.
2. 30,000 miles per year per automobile.
3. 30 miles per gallon per automobile.
4. $1.80 per gallon of gas.
5. $0.006 per mile for oil, minor repairs, parts, and supplies.
6. $135 per automobile per year in outside repairs.

UNIVERSITY MOTOR POOL
Budget Report of March

	Annual Master Budget	One-Month Master Budget	March Actual Costs	Over or (Under)
Gasoline.....................	$ 36,000	$ 3,000	$ 3,800	$800
Oil, Minor Repairs, Parts, and Supplies	3,600	300	380	80
Outside Repairs	2,700	225	50	(175)
Insurance....................	6,000	500	525	25
Salaries and Benefits	30,000	2,500	2,500	—
Depreciation	26,400	2,200	2,310	110
	$104,700	$ 8,725	$ 9,565	$840
Total Miles	600,000	50,000	63,000	
Cost per Mile	$0.1745	$0.1745	$0.1518	
Number of Automobiles	20	20	20	

The supervisor claims the report unfairly presents his performance for March. His previous employer used flexible budgeting to compare actual costs to budgeted amounts.

a. What is the monthly flexible budget for gasoline and the resulting amount over or under budget? (Use miles as the activity base.)

b. What is the monthly flexible budget for oil, minor repairs, parts, and supplies and the amount over or under budget? (Use miles as the activity base.)

c. What is the monthly flexible budget for salaries and benefits and the resulting amount over or under budget?

d. What is the *major* reason for the cost per mile to decrease from $0.1745 budgeted to $0.1518 actual?

38. **Computing master budget given actual data.** Consulting Enterprises lost the only copy of the master budget for this period. Management wants to evaluate this period's performance but believes it needs the master budget to do so. Actual results for the period follow:

Sales Volume	12,000 Billable Hours
Sales Revenue....................................	$672,000
Variable Costs	208,600
Contribution Margin	$463,400
Fixed Costs.......................................	318,200
Operating Profit	$145,200

The company planned on 10,800 billable hours at a price of $50 each. At that volume, the contribution margin would have been $380,000. Fixed costs were $272,000 for the period. Management notes, "We budget an operating profit of $10 per billable hour."

a. Construct the master budget for the period.

b. Prepare a profit variance report comparing actual sales to the flexible budget and master budget.

39. Performance evaluation using flexible budgets (adapted from CMA exam). Persons Restaurant-Deli is planning to expand operations and wants to improve its performance reporting system. The budgeted income statement for its Akron facility, which contains a delicatessen and restaurant operations, follows (all dollar amounts in thousands):

	Delicatessen	Restaurant	Total
Gross Sales	$1,000	$2,500	$3,500
Purchases	$ 600	$1,000	$1,600
Hourly Wages	50	875	925
Franchise Fee......................	30	75	105
Advertising........................	100	200	300
Utilities	70	125	195
Depreciation	50	75	125
Lease Cost	30	50	80
Salaries	30	50	80
Total	$ 960	$2,450	$3,410
Operating Profit	$ 40	$ 50	$ 90

The performance report that the company uses for management evaluation follows:

PERSONS RESTAURANT-DELI
Akron, Ohio
Operating Profit for the Year
(all dollar amounts in thousands)

	Actual Results				Over (Under)
	Delicatessen	Restaurant	Total	Budget	Budget
Gross Sales	$1,200	$2,000	$3,200	$3,500	$(300)[a]
Purchases[b]	780	800	1,580	1,600	(20)
Hourly Wages[b]	60	700	760	925	(165)
Franchise Fee[b]......	36	60	96	105	(9)
Advertising.........	100	200	300	300	—
Utilities[b]	76	100	176	195	(19)
Depreciation	50	75	125	125	—
Lease Cost	30	50	80	80	—
Salaries	30	50	80	80	—
Total	$1,162	$2,035	$3,197	$3,410	$(213)
Operating Profit	$ 38	$ (35)	$ 3	$ 90	$ (87)

[a]There is no sales price variance.   [b]Variable costs. All other costs are fixed.

Prepare a profit variance report to indicate the flexible budget and relevant variances for the delicatessen department. (*Hint:* Use gross sales as your measure of volume.)

Cases

40. **Cost data for multiple purposes: Omega Auto Supplies.** Omega Auto Supplies manufactures an automobile safety seat for children that it sells through several retail chains. Omega makes sales exclusively within its five-state region in the Midwest. The cost of manufacturing and marketing children's automobile safety seats at the company's forecasted volume of 15,000 units per month follows:

Variable Materials	$300,000
Variable Labor	150,000
Variable Overhead	30,000
Fixed Overhead	180,200
Total Manufacturing Costs	$660,200
Variable Nonmanufacturing Costs	75,000
Fixed Nonmanufacturing Costs	105,000
Total Nonmanufacturing Costs	180,000
Total Costs	$840,200

Unless otherwise stated, you should assume a regular selling price of $70 per unit. Ignore income taxes and other costs the problem does not mention.

Early in July, the senior management of Omega Auto Supplies met to evaluate the firm on performance for the first half of the year. The following exchange ensued.

Bob Wilson (president): "Our performance for the first half of this year leaves much to be desired. Despite higher unit sales than forecast, our actual profits are $200,000 lower than what we expected."

Sam Brown (sales manager): "I suspect production needs to shape up" (he said smugly). "We in sales have pursued an aggressive marketing strategy and the three-quarters of a million sales revenue higher than forecast is proof enough of our improved performance."

Linda Lampman (production manager): "Wait a minute, now! We managed to bring down unit costs from $44.00 to $43.00—with no help from sales, I must add! What's the use of production plans when sales can change them any time it likes? In February, Sam wanted a rush order for 4,000. In March, it was 8,000 units. Then in April he said to hold off on production; then in June he wanted 6,000. You know what I think . . . ."

Wilson: "Hold on, now! I refuse to let this degenerate into a witch-hunt. We have to examine this problem with more objectivity." (He turned to his assistant, who had been quietly taking notes.) "Do you have any ideas, Smith?"

Suppose you are Smith. Write a report to the President analyzing the company's performance. Include a comparison of the actual results to the flexible budget to the master budget. You also know that planned production and sales for each month of the year is 15,000 units per month. You also know that 108,000 units were produced and sold in the first 6 months of this year, and the income statement was as follows:

Sales Revenue		$7,020,000
Manufacturing Costs:		
Variable Materials	$2,160,000	
Variable Labor	1,134,000	
Variable Overhead	324,000	
Fixed Overhead	1,026,000	(4,644,000)
Gross Margin		$2,376,000
Marketing Costs:		
Variable Marketing	$ 648,000	
Fixed Marketing	650,000	(1,298,000)
Operating Profit		$1,078,000

41. **Solving for unknowns; cost-volume-profit and budget analysis** (adapted from a problem by D. O. Green). A partial income statement of Baines Corporation for 19X0 follows. The company uses just-in-time inventory, so production each year equals sales. Each dollar of finished product produced in 19X0 contained $.50 of direct materials, $.33⅓ of direct labor, and $.16⅔ of overhead costs. During 19X0, fixed overhead costs were $40,000. No changes in production methods or credit policies are anticipated for 19X1.

BAINES CORPORATION
Partial Income Statement for 19X0

Sales (100,000 units at $10)		$1,000,000
Cost of Goods Sold		600,000
Gross Margin		$ 400,000
Selling Costs	$150,000	
Administrative Costs	100,000	250,000
Operating Profit		$ 150,000

Management has estimated the following changes for 19X1:

- 30 percent increase in number of units sold.
- 20 percent increase in unit cost of materials.
- 15 percent increase in direct labor cost per unit.
- 10 percent increase in variable overhead cost per unit.
- 5 percent increase in fixed overhead costs.
- 8 percent increase in selling costs because of increased volume.
- 6 percent increase in administrative costs arising solely because of increased wages.

There are no other changes.

a. What must the unit sales price be in 19X1 for Baines Corporation to earn a $200,000 operating profit?

b. What will be the 19X1 operating profit if selling prices are increased as before, but unit sales increase by 10 percent rather than 30 percent? (Selling costs would go up by only one-third of the amount projected previously.)

    c. If selling price in 19X1 remains at $10 per unit, how many units must be sold in 19X1 for the operating profit to be $200,000?

42. **Incentive plans at McDonald's.** McDonald's Corporation is one of the world's largest and most successful food service companies. As in all service companies, the way the service employees perform their jobs affects the success of the company.

    The performance of managers of McDonald's company-owned restaurants is critical to the quality and efficiency of service provided at McDonald's. Over the past two decades, McDonald's has tried several incentive compensation plans for its company-owned restaurant managers. We describe five of those plans here.

- *Plan 1:* Manager's bonus is a function of the restaurant's sales volume increase over the previous year.
- *Plan 2:* Manager's bonus is based on subjective evaluations by the manager's superiors. Bonuses are not tied explicitly to any quantitative performance measure.
- *Plan 3:* Manager's bonus comprises the following components:

    (1) A bonus of 10 percent of salary is paid if the manager meets the budgeted costs. This budget is based on sales volume and the standard allowed per unit.

    (2) Management visits each restaurant each month and evaluates its performance with regard to quality, cleanliness, and service. Founder Ray Kroc identified these three key success factors for the company. Managers in restaurants receiving an A get a bonus of 10 percent of salary, managers of restaurants receiving a B get a bonus of 5 percent of salary, and managers of restaurants receiving a C receive no bonus for this component of the plan.

    (3) An additional bonus up to 10 percent of salary is earned based on increases in sales volume over the previous year. (The manager can still receive this bonus if volume does not increase because of circumstances beyond the manager's control.)

- *Plan 4:* Superiors evaluate the manager as to the following six performance indicators: quality, service, cleanliness, training ability, volume, and profit. Each indicator is scored 0, 1, or 2. A manager receiving a score of 12 points receives a bonus of 40 percent of salary, a score of 11 points provides a bonus of 35 percent of salary, and so forth.
- *Plan 5:* The manager receives a bonus of 10 percent of the sales volume increase over the previous year plus 20 percent of the restaurant's profit.

    Evaluate each of these incentive plans. Are there better alternatives? Be sure to consider the important things a manager and a restaurant should do to contribute to McDonald's overall company success.

Suggested Solutions to Even-Numbered Exercises

12.   Solving for materials requirements.

$$\begin{array}{l}\text{Finished Units} \\ \text{to Be Produced}\end{array} = \begin{array}{c}84{,}000 \\ \text{Units} \\ \text{to Be Sold}\end{array} + \begin{array}{c}48{,}000\ \text{Units} \\ \text{in Ending} \\ \text{Inventory}\end{array} - \begin{array}{c}44{,}000\ \text{Units} \\ \text{in Beginning} \\ \text{Inventory}\end{array}$$

$$\begin{array}{l}\text{Units to} \\ \text{Be Produced}\end{array} = \underline{\underline{88{,}000.}}$$

$$\begin{array}{l}\text{Units of Raw} \\ \text{Materials to} \\ \text{Be Used}\end{array} = \begin{array}{c}4\ \text{Units of Raw} \\ \text{Materials per} \\ \text{Finished Unit}\end{array} \times 88{,}000\ \text{Finished Units} = 352{,}000.$$

$$\begin{array}{l}\text{Units of Raw} \\ \text{Materials to} \\ \text{Be Purchased}\end{array} = \begin{array}{c}352{,}000\ \text{Units} \\ \text{to Be Used}\end{array} + \begin{array}{c}220{,}000\ \text{Units} \\ \text{Desired Ending} \\ \text{Inventory}\end{array} - \begin{array}{c}200{,}000\ \text{Units} \\ \text{in Beginning} \\ \text{Inventory}\end{array}$$

$$= \underline{\underline{372{,}000.}}$$

14.   Solving for cash collections (Appendix 12.1).

a.   Budgeted cash collections in March:

From January Sales (.18 × $500,000)	$ 90,000
From February Sales (.30 × $600,000)	180,000
From March Sales (.50 × $400,000)	200,000
Total Budgeted Collections in March	$470,000

b.   Budgeted cash collections in April:

From February Sales (.18 × $600,000)	$108,000
From March Sales (.30 × $400,000)	120,000
From April Sales (.50 × $500,000)	250,000
Total Budgeted Collections in April	$478,000

16.   Profit variance analysis.

	Achieved (7,100 units)	Cost Variances	Sales Price Variance	Flexible Budget (7,100 units)	Sales Volume Variance	Master Budget (7,000 units)
Sales Revenue	$86,265[a]		$1,065 F	$85,200[c]	$1,200 F	$84,000[d]
Less Variable						
Costs	41,890[b]	$6,390 U		35,500	500 U	35,000
Contribution Margin	$44,375	$6,390 U	$1,065 F	$49,700	$ 700 F	$49,000
Fixed Costs	20,000	1,000 F	—	21,000	—	21,000
Operating						
Profits	$24,375	$5,390 U	$1,065 F	$28,700	$ 700 F	$28,000

[a]7,100 units × $12.15.   [c]7,100 units × $12.
[b]7,100 units × $5.90.   [d]7,000 units × $12.

18. **Graphic comparison of budgeted and actual costs.**

 a. $\underline{\$.80}$ per Unit

$$V = (TC - F) \div X$$

$$= (\$3,000,000 - \$1,000,000) \div 2,500,000$$

$$= \$.80.$$

 b. $\underline{\$2,600,000}$

$$TC = F + VX$$

$$= \$1,000,000 + (\$.8 \times 2,000,000)$$

$$= \$2,600,000.$$

 c. $\underline{\$4,200,000}$

$$TC = F + VX$$

$$= \$1,000,000 + (\$.8 \times 4,000,000)$$

$$= \$4,200,000.$$

20. **Comparing master budget to actual results.**

	Actual (85 units)	Manufac- turing Variances	Marketing and Administrative Variances	Sales Price Variance	Flexible Budget (85 units)	Sales Volume Variance	Master Budget (100 units)
Sales Revenue	$9,200			$700 F	$8,500	$1,500 U	$10,000
Variable Costs:							
Manufacturing	3,440	$125 U			3,315	585 F	3,900
Marketing	1,030		$ 95 U		935	165 F	1,100
Total Variable Costs	$4,470				$4,250		$ 5,000
Contribution Margin	$4,730	$125 U	$ 95 U	$700 F	$4,250	$ 750 U	$ 5,000
Fixed Costs:							
Manufacturing	485	15 F			500	—	500
Marketing	1,040		40 U		1,000	—	1,000
Administrative	995		5 F		1,000	—	1,000
Operating Profit	$2,210	$110 U	$130 U	$700 F	$1,750	$ 750 U	$ 2,500

22. **Interpreting the flexible budget line.**

 a. Actual Units Sold:

$$\text{Profit} = (P - V)X - F$$

$$\$(7,000) = \$7X - \$70,000$$

$$X = \frac{\$63,000}{7}$$

$$= \underline{9,000 \text{ Units.}}$$

b. Budgeted Units to Be Sold:

$$\$28,000 = \$7X - \$70,000$$

$$X = \frac{\$98,000}{7}$$

$$= \underline{\underline{14,000 \text{ Units.}}}$$

24. **Incentives for accurate forecasting** (Appendix 12.2).

		\multicolumn{5}{c}{Forecasted Sales, $\hat{Y}$}
		20	**21**	**22**	**23**	**24**
	20	$2,000[a]	$1,950[f]	$1,900[i]	$1,850	$1,800
	21	2,070[b]	2,100[g]	2,050[j]	2,000	1,950
Actual Sales, Y	**22**	2,140[c]	2,170[h]	2,200	2,150	2,100
	23	2,210[d]	2,240	2,270	2,300	2,250
	24	2,280[e]	2,310	2,340	2,370	2,400

[a]$2,000 = $100 (20).
[b]$2,070 = $2,000 + $70 (21 − 20).
[c]$2,140 = $2,000 + $70 (22 − 20).
[d]$2,210 = $2,000 + $70 (23 − 20).
[e]$2,280 = $2,000 + $70 (24 − 20).

[f]$1,950 = $100 (21) − $150 (21 − 20).
[g]$2,100 = $100 (21).
[h]$2,170 = $2,100 + $70 (22 − 21), etc.
[i]$1,900 = $100 (22) − $150 (22 − 20).
[j]$2,050 = $2,200 − $150 (22 − 21), etc.

26. **Marketing cost budget.**
Fixed Costs:

Salaries	$25,000
Advertising..	30,000
Sales Office Costs.......................................	8,400
Travel	2,000
Total	$65,400

Variable Costs:

Shipping Costs = $.02 per Unit Sold and Shipped.

Commissions = 2 Percent of Sales, or .02 × Units Sold × Selling Price per Unit.

$$\text{Variable Costs} = \left(\$.02 \times \frac{\text{Units}}{\text{Shipped}}\right) + \left(\$.02 \times \$6 \begin{array}{c}\text{Unit}\\\text{Selling}\\\text{Price}\end{array} \times \frac{\text{Units}}{\text{Sold}}\right).$$

Selling Expense Flexible Budget:

$$\$65,400 + \left(\$.02 \times \frac{\text{Units}}{\text{Shipped}}\right) + \left(\$.12 \times \frac{\text{Units}}{\text{Sold}}\right).$$

Case 1:

$65,400 + ($.02 × 60,000) + ($.12 × 60,000)

= $65,400 + $1,200 + $7,200

= $73,800.

Case 2:

$65,400 + ($.02 × 75,000) + ($.12 × 75,000)

= $65,400 + $1,500 + $9,000

= $75,900.

Case 3:

$65,400 + ($.02 × 64,000) + ($.12 × 64,000)

= $65,400 + $1,280 + $7,680

= $74,360.

28. **Computing sales price variances.**

	Actual Sales	Sales Price Variance	Flexible Budget
Product X Sales	$111,300	$ 5,300 F	$106,000[a]
Product Y Sales	23,040	960 U	24,000[b]
Product Z Sales	192,000	48,000 U	240,000[c]
	$326,340	$43,660 U	$370,000

[a]5,300 Units × $\dfrac{\$100,000}{5,000 \text{ Units}}$ = $106,000.

[b]240 Units × $\dfrac{\$20,000}{200 \text{ Units}}$ = $24,000.

[c]48,000 Units × $\dfrac{\$250,000}{50,000 \text{ Units}}$ = $240,000.

Evaluating Performance

1. Assign responsibility for variances.
2. Separate variances into price and efficiency components.
3. Analyze variances using the variable cost variance model.
4. Know the reasons why variances occur.
5. Understand how the cost variance model in this chapter fits into the profit variance model in Chapter 12.
6. Apply activity-based costing to variance analysis.
7. Apply the cost variance model in service organizations.
8. Use nonfinancial performance measures to evaluate performance.

Chapter 12 presented profit variance analysis, which compares the profits achieved with those budgeted. This chapter presents more detail in analyzing cost variances. As you encounter variance analysis in practice, remember that each organization calculates variances in a unique way, based on the nature of the organization and the needs of its decision makers. We present the fundamental variance analysis model that all types of organizations commonly use in one form or another. Organizations differ in their applications, but the basic concepts underlying the applications are generally the same in all organizations.

Variance Analysis

This chapter continues the Victoria Corporation example discussed in Chapter 12. For convenience, Exhibit 13.1 reproduces Exhibit 12.8, which compares actual results with the budget.

Exhibit 13.1

VICTORIA CORPORATION
Profit Variance Analysis: Comparison of Actual Results to Budgeted Profits for Period 1
(This is Exhibit 12.8, repeated for the reader's convenience.)

	Actual (based on actual sales volume of 80,000 units) (1)	Purchasing and Production Variances (2)	Marketing and Administrative Cost Variances (3)	Sales Price Variance (4)	Flexible Budget (based on actual sales volume of 80,000 units) (5)	Sales Volume Variance (6)	Master Budget (based on a plan of 70,000 units sold) (7)
Sales.................	488,000			8,000 F	480,000	60,000 F	420,000
Less:							
Variable Manufacturing Costs.............	305,600	$12,000 U			293,600	36,700 U	256,900
Variable Marketing Costs...........	12,800		$1,440 U	160 U	11,200	1,400 U	9,800
Contribution Margin........	$169,600	$12,000 U	$1,440 U	$7,840 F	$175,200	$21,900 F	$153,300
Less:							
Fixed Manufacturing Costs.........	34,000	1,800 U			32,200		32,200
Fixed Marketing Costs.........	64,400		1,000 F		65,400		65,400
Fixed Administrative Costs.........	44,600		200 F		44,800		44,800
Operating Profits.........	$ 26,600	$13,800 U	$ 240 U	$7,840 F	$ 32,800	$21,900 F	$ 10,900

Total Profit Variance from Flexible Budget = $6,200 U

Total Profit Variance from Master Budget = $15,700 F

U denotes unfavorable variance.
F denotes favorable variance.

Exhibit 13.1 shows the total variance in operating profits from the original plan, $15,700 favorable. The next step investigates and analyzes the variance to find causes, to ascertain whether the firm needs to take corrective steps, and to reward or penalize employees, where appropriate.

Responsibility for Variances

This section describes variance calculations for each of the major groups responsible for variances in organizations: marketing, administration, purchasing, and production. We calculate each responsibility center's variances, *holding all other things constant*. Hence, we separate marketing variances from production, production variances from purchasing, and so forth. After accountants compute variances, managers investigate the causes of these variances and take corrective action if needed.

Marketing

Management usually assigns responsibility for sales volume, sales price, and marketing cost variances to marketing. Thus the marketing department at Victoria Corporation would be responsible for the variances shown in Exhibit 13.2.

The $21,900 favorable sales volume variance measures the favorable impact on profits of higher-than-expected sales volume as the exhibit shows. The sales volume variance may be a function of factors outside the marketing department's influence, however, such as unexpected or unpredictable changes in the market. The sales volume variance is a contribution margin variance, which equals the budgeted contribution margin times the difference between budgeted and actual sales volume. Chapter 12 stated that each unit sold generates $6.00 of revenue, each unit has a budgeted (or standard) variable manufacturing cost of $3.67, a budgeted shipping cost of $.02 per unit, and a budgeted sales commission of $.12 (= 2 percent × $6.00). Thus the contribution margin expected from each unit is $2.19 (= $6.00 − $3.67 − $.02 − $.12).

Why is the *standard* variable cost used to compute the contribution margin instead of the *actual* cost? Recall that we are calculating the effect of sales *volume* alone. By using standard variable cost in computing contribution margins, we avoid mixing cost variances with the effect of sales volume.

■ Exhibit 13.2

VICTORIA CORPORATION
Marketing Department Variances

Variable Marketing Cost	$ 1,440 U
Fixed Marketing Cost	1,000 F
Sales Volume	21,900 F
Sales Price (net of commissions)	7,840 F[a]

---

[a]$8,000 F price variance − $160 U higher commissions associated with higher-than-expected price = $7,840.

Marketing also may be responsible for the sales price variance. Note that the increase in sales commission (2 percent of $8,000 = $160), a result of the higher-than-budgeted selling price, partially offsets the favorable sales price variance of $8,000.

The $1,440 (unfavorable) variable marketing cost variance investigation should start with sales commissions. Did the firm inappropriately pay commissions—for example, on sales that customers returned? Did the commission rate exceed the 2 percent budgeted? Did the sales staff earn commissions in previous periods reported in the current period? Managers would ask similar questions about shipping costs. Did rates increase, for example?

The accounting staff usually ascertains whether variances resulted from book-keeping adjustments or errors, whereas marketing managers investigate marketing activities that may have caused the variances.

Fixed marketing costs are often discretionary. A favorable variance does not necessarily mean good performance. For example, the $1,000 favorable variance at Victoria Corporation could mean the company did less advertising than intended, which could have a negative effect on future sales.

Administration

The accounting process assigns a $200 favorable variance to administration. Administrative variances are often the hardest to manage because they are not *engineered;* that is, no well-defined causal relation exists between administrative input and administrative output.

Management usually budgets administrative costs with discretion, placing a ceiling on costs for a particular set of tasks. For example, suppose an organization's corporate internal audit staff received a budget of $2,000,000 for 40 people's salaries and an additional $400,000 for travel, supplies, and other costs. The internal audit department may not spend more than those limits without obtaining approvals, which would normally come from top executives (for example, the company president) or the board of directors.

Although discretionary budgets can provide a ceiling for expenditure, they do not provide a norm like a flexible manufacturing cost budget. If you cannot measure output, then you cannot measure the input-output relation, which makes ascertaining the ''proper'' levels of costs difficult. You should take these difficulties into account when you evaluate an administrative cost variance or any other discretionary cost variance.

Purchasing

Purchasing departments are responsible for purchasing the materials to make products and provide services. Monitoring a purchasing department's success in getting a good value for the money is important because materials often make up 50 to 60 percent of a product's cost. Materials are not limited to manufacturing. They comprise a substantial portion of the cost of providing services in many nonmanufacturing businesses, for example, surgical, laboratory, medical supplies in hospitals, and food in restaurants.

In our studies of purchasing departments, we have found virtually all managers using the *materials price variance* to evaluate their purchasing department's performance.[1] This variance measures the difference between the actual and standard prices paid for materials. To demonstrate how accountants compute the materials price variance, assume that Victoria Corporation actually purchased 162,000 pounds of direct materials at an average price of $.525 per pound. Recall that the standard cost was $.50 per pound. The process would charge purchasing with an unfavorable price variance of $4,050 [= ($.525 − $.50) × 162,000 pounds purchased].

Production

The accounting process would charge production departments with the fixed manufacturing cost variance and with the remaining variable manufacturing cost variance that it did not assign to purchasing. For Victoria Corporation, the process would assign variances as follows:

	Total	− Purchasing	= Production
Variable Manufacturing Cost Variance.........	$12,000 U −	$4,050 U	= $7,950 U
Fixed Manufacturing Cost Variance	$ 1,800 U −	0	= $1,800 U

Separating Variances into Price and Efficiency Components

Accountants generally split variable manufacturing cost variances into *price* and *efficiency* components. The price component is the difference between the budgeted (or standard) price and the actual price paid for each unit of input. The efficiency variance measures the efficiency with which the firm uses inputs to produce outputs. To demonstrate, suppose Victoria Corporation's $12,000 unfavorable variable manufacturing cost variance comprises the manufacturing cost variances shown in Exhibit 13.3. Assume that Victoria produced 80,000 units. Note that these total manufacturing variances also appear in column (2) of Exhibit 13.1.

At this point, you should calculate price and efficiency variances without looking ahead. We recommend this exercise because students often make variance calculations by memorizing formulas that they quickly forget. Most organizations incorporate these formulas into computer programs, so you need not memorize formulas.

A **price variance** measures the difference between the price set as the norm— that is, the standard or budgeted price—and the actual price.

An **efficiency variance** measures the difference between the actual quantity of inputs used and those allowed at standard to make a unit of output. Victoria Corpo-

---

[1] A study of internal control practices in U.S. companies found the purchase price variance to be the most common measure used to evaluate a purchasing department's performance. See R. K. Mautz, et al., *Internal Control in U.S. Corporations* (New York: Financial Executives Research Foundation, 1980).

Exhibit 13.3

VICTORIA CORPORATION
Manufacturing Variances

	Actual	**Standard Allowed Based on Actual Production Output of 80,000 Units**	**Variance**
Variable Costs:			
Direct Materials	162,000 Pounds at $.525 = $85,050	160,000 Pounds at $.50 = $80,000	$ 5,050 U
Direct Labor	10,955 Hours at $18.90 = $207,050 (rounded to nearest dollar)	10,000 Hours (= 80,000 Units × ⅛ Hour) at $20 = $200,000	7,050 U
Variable Manufacturing Overhead	$13,500	80,000 Units at $0.17 = $13,600	100 F
Total Variable Manufacturing Costs .	$305,600	$293,600	$12,000 U

	Actual	**Budget**	**Variance**
Fixed Costs:			
Fixed Manufacturing Overhead	$34,000	$32,200	$ 1,800 U

ration allows 2 pounds of direct material for each unit produced. If it used 162,000 pounds to produce 80,000 units, an unfavorable efficiency variance of 2,000 pounds in quantity, or $1,000 (= 2,000 pounds × $.50 standard price per pound), would result.

Problem 13.1 for Self-Study

Price and efficiency variances. Define price and efficiency variances. How might the manager of a coffee house that serves coffee and baked products use price and efficiency variances? *The solution to this self-study problem is at the end of the chapter on page 533.*

Variable Cost Variance Model

A general model for variance calculations appears in Exhibit 13.4. We have divided direct materials and direct labor variances into price and efficiency components. The terms *price* and *efficiency* variances are general categories. Although terminology

Exhibit 13.4

General Model for Variance Analysis: Variable Manufacturing Costs

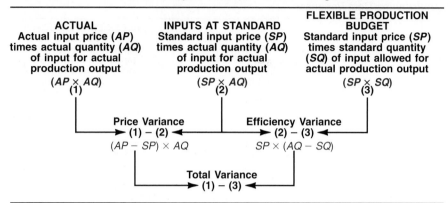

varies from company to company, the following specific variance titles are frequently used:

Input	Price Variance Category	Efficiency Variance Category
Direct Materials	Price (or Purchase Price) Variance	Usage or Quantity Variance
Direct Labor	Rate Variance	Efficiency Variance
Variable Overhead	Spending Variance	Efficiency Variance

We shall avoid unnecessary labeling by simply referring to these variances as either *price* or *efficiency* variances.

We apply the cost variance model to the calculation of direct materials, direct labor, and variable manufacturing overhead variances for Victoria Corporation in Exhibit 13.5. Note that Exhibit 13.5 breaks down the total variable manufacturing cost variance in column (2) of Exhibit 13.1 into more detail. Think of Exhibit 13.1 as the "big picture" and of Exhibit 13.5 as a detailed supporting schedule.

Interpret the computations in column (3) of Exhibit 13.5 carefully. Note that the term SQ refers to the **standard quantity of input allowed to produce the actual output.** SQ is *not* the expected production volume. If each unit of output produced has a standard of $\frac{1}{8}$ hour of direct labor time, and if 80,000 units of output are *actually produced,* then $SQ = 10,000$ hours $(= \frac{1}{8}$ hour $\times$ 80,000 units).

Note that column (3) is also the flexible *production* budget, which you should not confuse with the flexible *sales* budget. Managers use the flexible sales budget to analyze differences between actual and budgeted profits (see column (5) in Exhibit 13.1). In Exhibits 13.4 and 13.5, the activity of interest is production, so production volume drives the budget. In short, column (3) of Exhibits 13.4 and 13.5 shows the **standard cost allowed to produce the actual output,** whereas column (1) of Exhibits 13.4 and 13.5 shows the **actual costs incurred to produce the actual output.** The differences between columns (1) and (3) are the variable manufacturing cost variances, which you can further separate into price and efficiency variances.

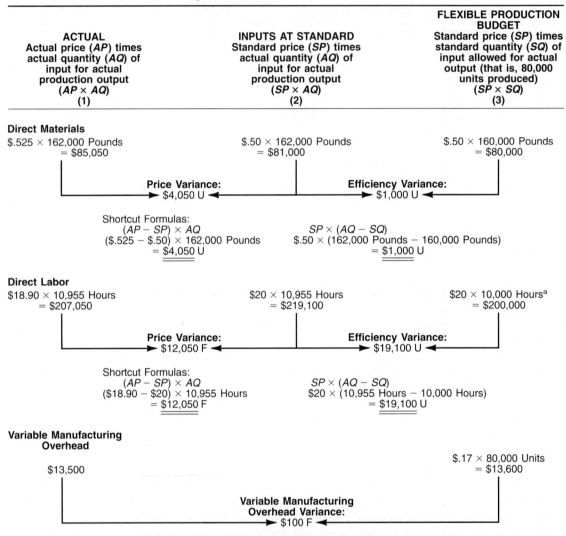

Exhibit 13.5

VICTORIA CORPORATION
Calculation of Variable Manufacturing Cost Variances

| ACTUAL
Actual price (*AP*) times
actual quantity (*AQ*) of
input for actual
production output
(*AP* × *AQ*)
(1) | INPUTS AT STANDARD
Standard price (*SP*) times
actual quantity (*AQ*) of
input for actual
production output
(*SP* × *AQ*)
(2) | FLEXIBLE PRODUCTION
BUDGET
Standard price (*SP*) times
standard quantity (*SQ*) of
input allowed for actual
output (that is, 80,000
units produced)
(*SP* × *SQ*)
(3) |

Direct Materials

$.525 × 162,000 Pounds = $85,050

$.50 × 162,000 Pounds = $81,000

$.50 × 160,000 Pounds = $80,000

Price Variance: $4,050 U

Efficiency Variance: $1,000 U

Shortcut Formulas:
(*AP* − *SP*) × *AQ*
($.525 − $.50) × 162,000 Pounds
= $4,050 U

SP × (*AQ* − *SQ*)
$.50 × (162,000 Pounds − 160,000 Pounds)
= $1,000 U

Direct Labor

$18.90 × 10,955 Hours = $207,050

$20 × 10,955 Hours = $219,100

$20 × 10,000 Hours[a] = $200,000

Price Variance: $12,050 F

Efficiency Variance: $19,100 U

Shortcut Formulas:
(*AP* − *SP*) × *AQ*
($18.90 − $20) × 10,955 Hours
= $12,050 F

SP × (*AQ* − *SQ*)
$20 × (10,955 Hours − 10,000 Hours)
= $19,100 U

Variable Manufacturing Overhead

$13,500

$.17 × 80,000 Units = $13,600

Variable Manufacturing Overhead Variance: $100 F

[a]10,000 hours allowed = 80,000 units produced × $\frac{1}{8}$ hours per unit allowed.
Note: It is sometimes difficult to see intuitively which variances are favorable (F) and which are unfavorable (U). If the amount on the left (the actual) exceeds the amount on the right (the budget or standard), the variance is *unfavorable* because higher costs than budgeted mean lower profits than budgeted. The reverse is true for favorable cost variances: the amounts on the left (actuals) are lower than those on the right. We set up all of the cost variance calculations in this book consistently, with actual costs on the left, standard or budget on the right.

This overview of manufacturing variances provides the essential calculations for management use of variances. Most companies carry out this analysis in much greater detail. Most companies report variances for each type of material, for each category of labor, and for major cost components of variable overhead (for example, power to run machines, indirect materials and supplies, indirect labor).

Problem 13.2 ▓▓▓▓▓▓▓▓▓▓▓
for Self-Study[2]

Computing variable cost variances. During the past month, the following events took place at Computer Supply, Inc.:

1. Produced and sold 50,000 laptop computer cases at a sales price of $10 each. (Budgeted sales were 40,000 units at $11.)
2. Standard variable costs per unit (that is, per case) were as follows:

Direct Materials: 2 Pounds at $1 per Pound	$2.00
Direct Labor: .10 Hours at $15 per Hour	1.50
Variable Manufacturing Overhead: .10 Labor Hours at $5 per Hour	.50
Total	$4.00 per Case

3. Actual production costs were as follows:

Direct Materials Purchased and Used: 110,000 Pounds at $1.20	$132,000
Direct Labor: 6,000 Hours at $14....................................	84,000
Variable Overhead..	28,000

Compute variable manufacturing cost variances in as much detail as possible.

The solution to this self-study problem is at the end of the chapter on page 534.

▓▓▓▓▓▓▓▓▓▓▓▓▓▓▓▓▓▓▓▓▓▓▓▓▓▓▓▓▓▓▓▓▓▓▓▓▓▓

Reasons for Materials and Labor Variances

Variance reports include explanations for the variances. These explanations help managers to ascertain whether they should investigate variances and take corrective action, whether they should reward people responsible for variances, or whether they should take other managerial action.

Variances can occur for many reasons.

1. **A variance is simply the difference between a predetermined norm or standard and the actual results.** Some difference should be expected simply because one measure is expected and the other is actual. For example, if you and several of your friends were each to flip a coin ten times, not all of you would

---

[2]This problem continues the problems for self-study in Chapter 12.

come up with five heads, even though five heads (= 50 percent of ten coin flips) may be the expected value. In short, even when standards are unbiased expected values, and no *systematic* reasons explain variances, some variances will occur anyway.

2. **The standards themselves may be biased.** Sometimes managers set standards intentionally loose or tight. Sometimes they are unintentionally biased, such as when the firm accidentally omits expected labor wage increases or an allowance for waste on direct material usage. The Managerial Application "An Antidote to Biased Standards: How Workers Develop Their Own Standards at NUMMI" demonstrates how a particular plant management dealt with biased standards.

3. **Systematic reasons as discussed next.**

Reasons for Materials Variances

Materials price variances occur for numerous reasons. They may result from failure to take purchase discounts, from using a better (or worse) grade of raw material than expected so that the price paid was higher (or lower) than expected, or from changes in the market supply or demand for the raw material that affected prices. A number of factors cause **materials efficiency variances.** When management, industrial engineers, and others set standards for the amount of direct materials that a unit of output should use, they usually allow for material defects, inexperienced workers who ruin materials, improperly used materials, and so forth. If the firm uses materials more efficiently than these standards, favorable efficiency variances result; usage worse than these standards results in unfavorable variances. Sometimes purchasing, not production, causes a materials efficiency variance. In an effort to reduce prices (and create a favorable price variance), purchasing departments may have bought inferior materials. Purchasing may also be responsible for ordering the wrong materials.

Reasons for Labor Variances

Direct labor price (or wage) **variances** can occur because managers do not correctly anticipate changes in wage rates. Wage rates established by a union contract may differ from the forecasted amount, for example. Also, a wage rate change may occur but the firm will not have adjusted standards to reflect it.

The **direct labor efficiency variance** measures labor productivity. Managers watch this variance because they can usually control it. Many of the things that create variances affect all competitors about the same. Labor wage rates going up dramatically because of a union contract settlement usually affects all companies in an industry, so little competitive advantage or disadvantage results. Labor efficiency is unique to a firm, however, and can lead to competitive advantages or disadvantages.

A financial vice president of a manufacturing company told us:

Raw materials are 57 percent of our product cost; direct labor is only 22 percent. Yet we carry out the labor efficiency variance to the penny. We break it down by product line, by department, and sometimes by specific operation, while we give the raw materials variances only a passing glance. Why? Because there's not much we can do about some of our other variances, like materials price variances, but there's a lot we can do to keep our labor efficiency in line.

Managerial Application

An Antidote to Biased Standards: How Workers Develop Their Own Standards at NUMMI[a]

The Toyota–General Motors joint venture in Fremont, California, known as New United Motor Manufacturing, Inc. (NUMMI), has succeeded in allowing employees to set their own work standards. The NUMMI plant, which makes Toyota Corollas, Geo Prizms, and particular Toyota trucks, was once a General Motors plant notorious for poor quality, low productivity, and morale problems. One worker said he used to be ashamed of the product turned out by the GM Fremont plant, but when he recently saw one of the plant's cars parked at the Monterey Aquarium, he left a business card under the windshield wiper with a note that said, "I helped build this one."[b]

At the old GM Fremont plant, industrial engineers who had little, if any, work experience making cars would shut themselves in a room and ponder how to set standards. The industrial engineers ignored the workers, who in turn ignored the standards. The worker "did the job however he or she was able—except of course when one of [the supervisors or industrial engineers] was looking. If an industrial engineer was actually 'observing'— stopwatch and clipboard in hand—standard practice was to slow down and make the work look harder."[c]

Now, at NUMMI workers themselves hold the stopwatches and set the standards. Worker team members time each other, looking for the most efficient and safest way to do the work. They standardize each task so everyone in the team will do it the same way. The workers compare the standards across shifts and for different tasks, and then they prepare detailed written specifications for each task. The workers are more informed about how to do the work right than industrial engineers. They are more motivated to meet the standards they set, instead of those set by industrial engineers working in an ivory tower.

Involving the workers has had benefits in addition to improved motivation and standards. These include improved safety, higher quality, easier job rotation because tasks are standardized, and more flexibility because workers are both assembly-line workers and industrial engineers. For example, if orders for the product change, NUMMI can change the speed of the assembly line to respond. At the old GM Fremont plant, the assembly line ran at one speed, and responses to changes in orders came either from inventory or from adding or dropping entire shifts.

[a]Based on Paul S. Adler, "Time-and-Motion Regained," *Harvard Business Review* (January-February 1993), pp. 97–108.
[b]Ibid., p. 106.
[c]Ibid., p. 103.

Labor efficiency variances have many causes. The cause may be the workers themselves—poorly motivated or poorly trained workers will be less productive, whereas highly motivated and well-trained workers may generate favorable efficiency variances. Other causes include poor materials, faulty equipment, poor supervision, and scheduling problems.

Although most firms hold production managers responsible for direct labor efficiency variances, they sometimes attribute responsibility to purchasing managers for buying faulty materials. Scheduling problems may result from upstream production departments that have delayed production, from the personnel department that provided the wrong type of worker, or from numerous other sources.

Note the labor price variance in the Victoria Corporation example was favorable, whereas the labor efficiency variance was unfavorable. A manager would probably ask first: ''Did we use workers who were lower paid and not as efficient as expected?'' Although firms go to great lengths to break variances down into small components that they can easily understand and trace to particular responsibility centers, managers should not overlook the fact that variances are usually interrelated.

Variable Overhead Price and Efficiency Variances

Separating variable overhead variances into price and efficiency components helps control overhead costs. For example, energy costs in many firms are both sufficiently large and controllable to warrant special attention.

The manager can use the same method to compute price and efficiency variances for variable overhead as for other variable manufacturing costs. The computation requires a measure of overhead input activity not yet presented in the Victoria Corporation example, however. Suppose the variable overhead at Victoria Corporation consisted of machines' operating costs, such as power and maintenance. The longer the machines ran, the more variable overhead cost is incurred. A **variable overhead price variance** results when the cost per machine hour is either more or less than the standard cost allowed per machine hour. A **variable overhead efficiency variance** results if the machine hours required to make the actual production output exceed the standard machine hours allowed to make that output. For example, suppose the firm makes a large batch of units that consumed several hundred machine hours. Subsequently, the firm found these units to be defective and destroyed them; thus the accounting system did not count them as part of the actual production output. (Managers implicitly assume only good units are counted as part of the actual production output.)

Assume the standard for machine usage was 40 units per machine hour at a standard cost allowed of $6.80 per hour. (This is equivalent to $.17 per unit of output, because $6.80/40 = $.17.) Also assume the actual production output of 80,000 units required 2,100 machine hours, so the efficiency variance was $680 U, as Exhibit 13.6 shows. The actual costs for variable overhead totaled only $13,500, so the favorable variable overhead price variance was $780 F.

Exhibit 13.6

VICTORIA CORPORATION
Variable Manufacturing Overhead Variances

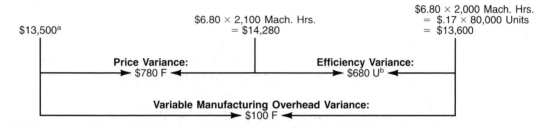

ACTUAL Actual price (*AP*) times actual quantity (*AQ*) of input for actual production output (*AP* × *AQ*) (1)	**INPUTS AT STANDARD** Standard price (*SP*) times actual quantity (*AQ*) of input for actual production output (*SP* × *AQ*) (2)	**FLEXIBLE PRODUCTION BUDGET** Standard price (*SP*) times standard quantity (*SQ*) of input allowed for actual output (i.e., 80,000 units produced) (*SP* × *SQ*) (3)

$13,500[a]

$6.80 × 2,100 Mach. Hrs.
= $14,280

$6.80 × 2,000 Mach. Hrs.
= $.17 × 80,000 Units
= $13,600

Price Variance:
➤ $780 F ◄

Efficiency Variance:
➤ $680 U[b] ◄

Variable Manufacturing Overhead Variance:
➤ $100 F ◄

[a]Because the firm does not typically purchase overhead per machine hour or per unit of some other activity base, the total variable overhead does not contain an actual price (*AP*) component.

[b]Shortcut Formula:

$$SP \times (AQ - SQ)$$
$$\$6.80 \times (2,100 \text{ Hours} - 2,000 \text{ Hours})$$
$$= \$680 \text{ U.}$$

The manager should interpret variable overhead price and efficiency variances with care. The accountant sometimes selects the input activity base (machine hours in our example) without regard for the nature of variable overhead costs. For example, if a company used direct labor hours to apply variable overhead, an unfavorable efficiency variance results when the company inefficiently uses direct labor hours. That variance means nothing if none of the variable overhead costs are associated with direct labor costs. This particular problem occurs in capital-intensive companies in which variable overhead mostly relates to machine usage.

In general, managers are wise to establish a detailed breakdown of variable overhead into cost categories that relate logically to the input activity base. For example, the following variable overhead costs could be applied on the following input activity bases:

Cost	Activity Base
Indirect Labor	Direct Labor Hours
Power to Run Machines	Machine Hours
Materials Inventory Carrying Costs	Materials Inventory

Fixed Manufacturing Cost Variances

The only fixed cost variances computed for managerial purposes are the price variances (also called spending or budget variances). A price variance is the difference between actual and budgeted fixed costs. Because fixed costs do not vary with the measure of activity (such as units), there are no efficiency variances for fixed costs.

Overview of Variances

Exhibit 13.7 presents an overview of variances for Chapters 12 and 13. The top panel reproduces columns 1 through 5 of the profit variance analysis discussed in Chapter 12 and presented in Exhibit 13.1. The bottom panel illustrates the breakdown of variable manufacturing costs into direct materials, direct labor, and variable overhead. This breakdown shows that the cost variance analysis discussed in this chapter simply extends the profit variance analysis discussed in Chapter 12.

Activity-Based Standard Costing

Activity-based costing is commonly used with standard costing. Hewlett-Packard, a pioneer in the development of activity-based costing, uses it to develop standard costs. Using activity-based costing, a company has multiple cost drivers.

For example, assume Mesozoic Company uses activity-based costing to set standard costs for its variable costs of producing wooden crates to ship fruits and vegetables. Assume the company has the following three activity centers: indirect materials, energy costs, and quality testing. (Companies typically have more than three activity centers, but we want to keep the example simple.) Management selects the following cost drivers for these activity centers:

Activity Center	Cost Driver
1. Indirect materials	Board feet of direct materials used
2. Energy......................................	Machine hours
3. Quality testing	Minutes of test time

Variance Analysis for Activity-Based Costing

We use the same approach to variance analysis for activity-based costing as for traditional costing. The price variance is the difference between standard prices and actual prices for the actual quantity of input used for each cost driver. The efficiency variance measures the difference between the actual amount of input, or cost driver units used, and the standard allowed to make the output. We multiply this difference

Exhibit 13.7

VICTORIA CORPORATION
Overview of Variance Analysis

Profit Variance Analysis

	Achieved Profit (based on actual sales volume of 80,000 units) (1)	Purchasing and Production Variances (2)	Marketing and Admin- istrative Cost Variances (3)	Sales Price Variance (4)	Flexible Budget (based on actual sales volume of 80,000 units) (5)
Sales............................	$488,000	—	—	$8,000 F	$480,000
Less:					
Variable Manufacturing					
Costs	**305,600**	**$12,000 U**	—	—	**293,600**
Variable Marketing Costs	12,800	—	$1,440 U	160 U	11,200
Contribution Margin	$169,600	$12,000 U	$1,440 U	$7,840 F	$175,200
Less:					
Fixed Manufacturing Costs	34,000	1,800 U	—	—	32,200
Fixed Marketing Costs	64,400	—	1,000 F	—	65,400
Fixed Administrative Costs	44,600	—	200 F	—	44,800
Operating Profits	$ 26,600	$13,800 U	$ 240 U	$7,840 F	$ 32,800

Total Profit Variance from Flexible
Budget = $6,200 U

Cost Variance Analysis

ACTUAL Actual price (*AP*) times actual quantity (*AQ*) of input for actual production output (*AP* × *AQ*) (1)	INPUTS AT STANDARD Standard price (*SP*) times actual quantity (*AQ*) of input for actual production output (*SP* × *AQ*) (2)	FLEXIBLE PRODUCTION BUDGET Standard price (*SP*) times standard quantity (*SQ*) of input allowed for actual output (that is, 80,000 units produced) (*SP* × *SQ*) (3)

Direct Materials

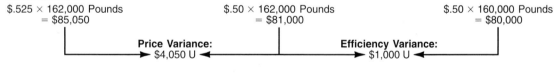

$.525 × 162,000 Pounds = $85,050

$.50 × 162,000 Pounds = $81,000

$.50 × 160,000 Pounds = $80,000

Price Variance: $4,050 U

Efficiency Variance: $1,000 U

Direct Labor

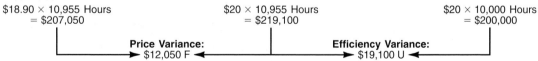

$18.90 × 10,955 Hours = $207,050

$20 × 10,955 Hours = $219,100

$20 × 10,000 Hours = $200,000

Price Variance: $12,050 F

Efficiency Variance: $19,100 U

Variable Manufacturing Overhead

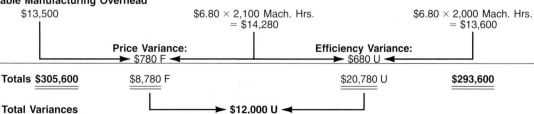

$13,500

$6.80 × 2,100 Mach. Hrs. = $14,280

$6.80 × 2,000 Mach. Hrs. = $13,600

Price Variance: $780 F

Efficiency Variance: $680 U

Totals $305,600	$8,780 F		$20,780 U	$293,600

Total Variances $12,000 U

in quantities by the standard price per cost driver unit to get the dollar value of the variance.

To make this idea concrete, assume the following data for Mesozoic Company for the three activities for the month of June:

		Standard price per unit	Standard quantity of input allowed to produce 10,000 units of output	Actual cost	Actual quantity of input used
1.	Indirect materials	$.05 per board foot	100,000 board feet	$5,180	110,000 board feet
2.	Energy	$.02 per minute of machine time	250,000 minutes of machine time	$5,300	240,000 minutes
3.	Quality testing	$.50 per test minute	30,000 minutes of test time	$16,000	34,000 test minutes

Exhibit 13.8 shows the results of the variance analysis. In effect, we have taken the principle underlying variance computations shown throughout this chapter and ap-

Exhibit 13.8

Activity-Based Costing Variances

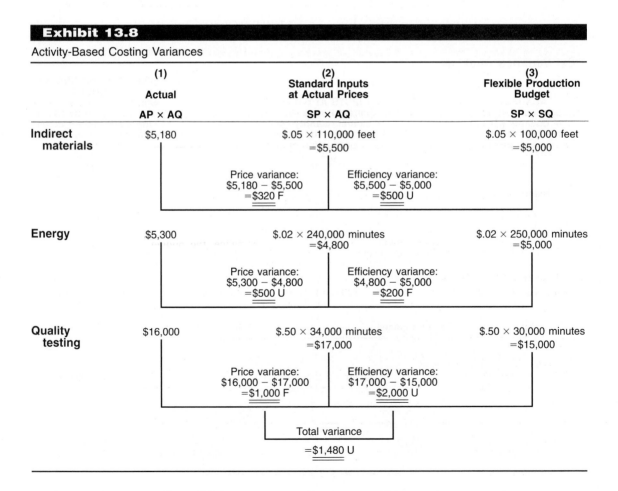

	(1) Actual	(2) Standard Inputs at Actual Prices	(3) Flexible Production Budget
	AP × AQ	SP × AQ	SP × SQ
Indirect materials	$5,180	$.05 × 110,000 feet =$5,500	$.05 × 100,000 feet =$5,000
		Price variance: $5,180 − $5,500 =$320 F	Efficiency variance: $5,500 − $5,000 =$500 U
Energy	$5,300	$.02 × 240,000 minutes =$4,800	$.02 × 250,000 minutes =$5,000
		Price variance: $5,300 − $4,800 =$500 U	Efficiency variance: $4,800 − $5,000 =$200 F
Quality testing	$16,000	$.50 × 34,000 minutes =$17,000	$.50 × 30,000 minutes =$15,000
		Price variance: $16,000 − $17,000 =$1,000 F	Efficiency variance: $17,000 − $15,000 =$2,000 U

Total variance
=$1,480 U

plied it to a situation having three activity centers. If a company had 40 activity centers, the computations would look like Exhibit 13.8, but with 40 computations of price and efficiency variances instead of only three.

Even with just three activity drivers, we think you can see the potential for managers to get a lot more information from activity-based costing than from the traditional approach. For example, the products required 34,000 minutes of quality test time instead of the 30,000 minutes allowed by the standard for 10,000 units produced in June. Does this ''inefficiency'' reflect poorer-quality materials than expected? Does it represent extra concern about putting out a quality product? Is the standard three minutes per crate too low? In short, activity-based costing raises numerous specific questions that managers can address to improve quality and productivity.

Variable Overhead in Service Organizations

Variable overhead often makes up a large portion of the cost of providing services. Next we apply the overhead analysis model to a service organization.

Example American Parcel Delivery, a parcel service, competes with the U.S. Postal Service and United Parcel Service. Each driver is responsible for picking up and delivering parcels in a particular geographic area. One major cost is fuel for the pick-up and delivery vans. The firm uses a fuel efficiency variance to evaluate the performance of drivers. The firm calculates a standard amount of fuel consumption per parcel, whether delivered or picked up, for each territory. These allowances take the population density of the territory into account—allowing more fuel per parcel for sparsely populated territories, less for densely populated territories. Drivers control this variance primarily by scheduling trips to avoid unnecessary driving.

For a particular territory, the standard was .08 gallon of fuel per parcel. The driver assigned to this territory handled 1,100 parcels during March; hence, the budget allows 88 gallons (= 1,100 parcels × .08 gallons per parcel). In all, the driver actually used 93 gallons of fuel. Exhibit 13.9 shows the efficiency variance. Although the driver was not responsible for the fuel price variance, Exhibit 13.9 presents it to complete the comparison of actual with standard. Note the similarity between these calculations and the direct materials and direct labor calculations presented earlier.

Managers often calculate variances for particularly important, controllable overhead items such as power or fuel costs. Computing price and efficiency variances for variable overhead as a total is more difficult. Sometimes managers perform this computation when variable overhead correlates highly with another production input. For example, suppose that variable overhead correlates highly with direct labor hours. The firm could reasonably hold the manager who is responsible for direct labor efficiency variances also responsible for variable overhead efficiency variances.

Exhibit 13.9

AMERICAN PARCEL DELIVERY
Example, Variable Overhead Efficiency Variance—Fuel Costs

Facts

Actual:

Output...	1,100 Parcels Picked Up or Delivered
Fuel Required..	93 Gallons
Cost per Gallon..	$1.58 per Gallon

Standard:

Fuel Allowed...	.08 Gallon per Parcel Picked Up or Delivered
Cost per Gallon..	$1.60 per Gallon

Actual **(AP × AQ)**	**Inputs at Standard** **(SP × AQ)**	**Flexible Production** **Budget** **(SP × SQ)**
$1.58 per Gallon × 93 Gallons = $146.94	$1.60 per Gallon × 93 Gallons = $148.80	$1.60 per Gallon × (.08 Gallon × 1,100 Parcels) = $1.60 × 88 Gallons = $140.80

Price Variance: $1.86 F

Efficiency Variance: $8.00 U

Shortcut Formulas:

$(AP - SP) \times AQ$

($1.58 − $1.60) × 93 Gallons
= $1.86 F

$SP \times (AQ - SQ)$

$1.60 × [93 Gallons − (.08 Gallon
× 1,100 Parcels)]
= $1.60 × 5 Gallons
= $8.00 U

Nonfinancial Performance Measures

Accounting systems provide important measures of performance, but they only capture part of the picture, as demonstrated in the Managerial Application "Texas Instruments' Cost of Quality Program." Nonfinancial performance measures are also important for evaluating quality and customer service. Exhibit 13.10 presents five nonfinancial performance measures that managers use to evaluate performance in customer service and production.

Customer Service Peformance Measures

The first set of measures appearing in Exhibit 13.10 reflect *quality control.* Quality can be measured by the number and type of customer complaints, or by the number of product defects. If we reduce the number of product defects, we likely will reduce the number of customer complaints. The objective is to increase customer satisfaction with our product, reduce costs of dealing with customer complaints, reduce costs of repairing products or providing a new service.

Texas Instruments' Cost of Quality Program[a]

Texas Instruments attempts to measure quality-related costs in the following four categories:

1. **Prevention.** Costs of preventing poor-quality products.
2. **Appraisal.** Costs of detecting poor-quality products.
3. **Internal failure.** Costs of poor quality detected before products are shipped to customers.
4. **External failure.** Costs of poor quality after products are shipped to customers.

The accounting system can measure certain costs of preventing poor quality and appraising quality, such as inspection. Although Texas Instruments has one of the leading programs for measuring quality, it finds the accounting system does not do well at measuring the cost of external failure after a product gets to the customer. Customers who are dissatisfied with the quality of Texas Instruments' products may simply purchase products from a competitor in the future which is a cost that is difficult to quantify.

[a]Based on the case "Texas Instruments: Cost of Quality (A)" (Boston: Harvard Business School, Case 189-029).

Exhibit 13.10

Nonfinancial Performance Measures

Performance Measure	Objective
1. Quality control:	
Number of customer complaints	Customer satisfaction
Number of defects	Quality product
2. Delivery performance:	
Percentage of on-time deliveries.	Increase on-time deliveries
3. Materials waste:	
Scrap and waste as a percentage of total materials used	Decrease scrap and waste
4. Inventory:	
Inventory levels.	Reduce inventory levels
Number of different inventoried items	Decrease number of different items
5. Machine downtime:	
Percentage of machine downtime.	Decrease downtime

Quality-oriented organizations continually monitor the quality of their products and solicit feedback from customers to assess customer satisfaction with goods and services. J. Peterman and Company, a merchandise company, tells its customers to "please hassle us" if customers are not completely satisfied. Nordstrom, Southwest Airlines, and Toyota are among the companies that have built a reputation based on the notion of "hassle us" if you are not completely satisfied. If you visit a manufacturing plant, such as the Nissan plant near Nashville, Tennessee, you will see some of the previous day's production of cars and trucks in the lobby of the plant together with charts showing how many defects were found in the previous day's production. Nissan's display of the product and the performance report gives workers a sense of pride in their work and an incentive to produce quality products.

The second type of nonfinancial measures in Exhibit 13.10 deals with *delivery time*. For some companies, like American Airlines, Amtrak, Washington D.C.'s Metro, and other metropolitan transit systems, and Federal Express, United Parcel Service, and other delivery services, delivery performance is critical to success. The success of companies that sell through catalogs like Lands' End, L.L. Bean, and Territory Beyond is dependent on quick delivery of their merchandise. Bottlers of soft drinks like Pepsi-Cola, and canneries like Campbell's Soup, require the timing of the delivery of cans and bottles to be precise for their production needs; ideally the truck or railroad car load of containers is ready to unload right onto the production line.

Reducing *materials waste,* the third type of nonfinancial measures, can be done by improving the quality of raw materials so there is less waste from defective materials, increasing employee training so workers make fewer mistakes, and improving the production process. Materials waste may show up in the materials efficiency variance. However, standards often allow for some waste, so an unfavorable variance would only be for the excess waste over that allowed in the standard. Workers are generally motivated to find ways to reduce waste if companies keep track of materials waste on the basis of quantity (for example, board feet in the construction of wood products) every day, with immediate feedback to workers the next day, often in the form of large charts. While the report of variances from standard costs is important to department heads and plant managers, workers are more likely to be motivated by immediate feedback in nonfinancial language.

The fourth type of nonfinancial performance measures shown in Exhibit 13.10 deals with *inventory levels.* Companies try to reduce both inventory levels of each item and the number of different items in inventory. A food wholesaler found its inventory contained hundreds of items that were rarely ordered by its convenience store customers. After this discovery, instead of keeping those rare items in inventory, the wholesaler simply ordered them from its supplier when the convenience stores needed them. As a result, the wholesaler reduced its inventory by nearly one-third.

The fifth type of nonfinancial measures, *machine downtime,* is very important in all types of companies. At the NUMMI plant, a joint venture of General Motors and Toyota, assembly-line workers have the authority to stop the assembly line when they see something wrong. It should come as no surprise that such an action brings a lot of attention to the problem from many people in the plant. Stopping production causes a loss of output while people wait for the machine to start up. Machine downtime also can cause customer dissatisfaction and loss of sales, as you may have experienced when your bank teller informs you that you cannot be served because "the computer is down," or when your airline flight has been cancelled because of an airplane's maintenance problems.

Variance Analysis in High-Technology Companies

The variance analysis model in Exhibit 13.4 generally applies to all types of organizations; however, high-technology firms apply the model somewhat differently. Most changes toward high technology involve substituting computerized equipment for direct labor. Examples include automatic teller machines in banks, robots in manufacturing plants, and word processors in various organizations. The result is less direct labor and more overhead.

The substitution of computerized equipment implies that the firm should treat labor more appropriately as a fixed cost than as a variable cost. In high-technology manufacturing companies employees monitor and maintain machines rather than produce output. For these companies, labor efficiency variances may no longer be meaningful because direct labor is a capacity cost, not a cost expected to vary with output. Variable overhead may associate more with machine usage than labor hours. Some high-technology manufacturing organizations have found that the two largest variable costs involve materials and power to operate machines. The model in Exhibit 13.4 would apply to those costs.

Summary

Variances between actual results and norms or standards provide a basis for management to take corrective actions where necessary, penalize and reward employees, and revise goals, plans, and budgets. In this chapter we presented fundamental variance analysis models that are the basis for variance calculations in organizations. Variance analysis is rooted in the philosophy of management by exception, which focuses managerial attention on exceptions, or variances, from the norm.

Management generally assigns responsibility for variances as follows:

	Responsible For
Marketing	Sales Price Variances, Sales Volume Variances, Sales Mix Variances, Marketing Cost Variances
Administration	Administrative Cost Variances
Purchasing	Materials Purchase Price Variances
Production	Direct Materials Usage Variances, Direct Materials Mix Variances, Direct Labor Variances, Manufacturing Overhead Variances

The general model for calculating variable cost variances follows:

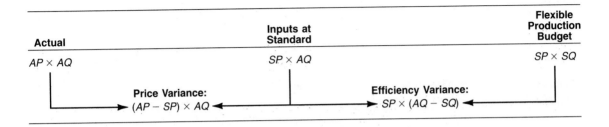

Firms commonly apply this model to direct materials and direct labor costs, but also may apply it to variable marketing costs, variable overhead costs, or any other variable costs.

Why do variances occur? We can classify most reasons for variances as one of the following:

1. Random variation of actual around the standard. Some fluctuation is normal and not worth your concern.
2. Bias in setting the standard (that is, standard is tighter or looser than the expected cost under normal operating conditions). If management intends this bias, it leaves the standard alone; if not, it adjusts the standard to remove the bias.
3. Systematic variance not due to bias in the standard.

Of these three reasons, only the third may require investigation and correction, assuming that the benefits of investigation and correction exceed the costs.

Variable cost variances are often split into price and efficiency components.

1. The price component refers to the difference between the actual price and the standard price allowed per unit. If the price variance is expressed as a total amount, that total is the price variance per unit times the actual units purchased.
2. The efficiency variance is a measure of productivity. It compares the actual input used to make the actual output with the standard allowed to make the actual output. Note that the efficiency variance is based on *actual* output, not budgeted output. If the manufacturing cost efficiency is calculated (for example, efficiency in using labor to manufacture products), the relevant measure of output is production volume.

Exhibit 13.11 diagrams all the variances discussed. It breaks down the $15,700 total favorable variance from Exhibit 13.1 into components and shows their assignment to responsibility centers—marketing, administration, purchasing, and production. Generally, accounting systems report variances in much more detail than we show here. The analysis shows more detailed cost items—by type of direct material, labor, and overhead, for example.

Exhibit 13.11

VICTORIA CORPORATION
Variance Diagram

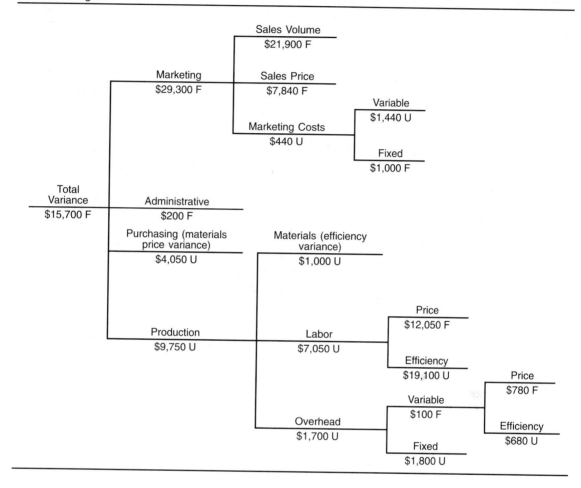

Solutions to Self-Study Problems

Suggested Solution to Problem 13.1 for Self-Study

Definitions. The price variance measures the difference between the actual and standard price per unit times the number of units. This variance measures how well the company is controlling the cost of items purchased. The efficiency variance measures the difference between the actual quantity of inputs and the standard quantity allowed to make the actual output.

Uses. The manager of a coffee shop should monitor the price variance carefully. One can never tell when a revolution or natural disaster might break out in a coffee-producing country that would lead to an increase in the price of coffee beans. Coffee houses are in a competitive business, in general, so failure to pass on the materials (that is, coffee beans) price increase to customers could take the company right out of business. Efficiency variances are more difficult to control because a certain level of staff is needed whether business volume is high or low. If the company has several employees, the manager can use efficiency measures to compare the efficiency of various employees.

Suggested Solution to Problem 13.2 for Self-Study

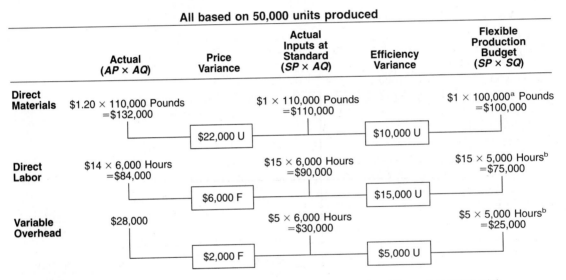

All based on 50,000 units produced

	Actual (AP × AQ)	Price Variance	Actual Inputs at Standard (SP × AQ)	Efficiency Variance	Flexible Production Budget (SP × SQ)
Direct Materials	$1.20 × 110,000 Pounds =$132,000	$22,000 U	$1 × 110,000 Pounds =$110,000	$10,000 U	$1 × 100,000[a] Pounds =$100,000
Direct Labor	$14 × 6,000 Hours =$84,000	$6,000 F	$15 × 6,000 Hours =$90,000	$15,000 U	$15 × 5,000 Hours[b] =$75,000
Variable Overhead	$28,000	$2,000 F	$5 × 6,000 Hours =$30,000	$5,000 U	$5 × 5,000 Hours[b] =$25,000

[a]Standard direct materials pounds allowed in production per unit times actual units produced (2 pounds × 50,000 units).

[b].10 × 50,000 units produced.

Key Terms and Concepts

Price variance
Efficiency variance
Standard quantity of input allowed to produce actual output
Standard cost allowed to produce actual output
Actual costs incurred to produce actual output

Materials price variance
Materials efficiency variance
Direct labor price variance
Direct labor efficiency variance
Variable overhead price variance
Variable overhead efficiency variance

Questions, Exercises, Problems, and Cases

Questions

1. Review the meaning of the concepts or terms given above in Key Terms and Concepts.
2. Why is a materials efficiency variance typically not calculated for the purchasing activity?
3. Refer to the Managerial Application ''An Antidote to Biased Standards: How Workers Develop Their Own Standards at NUMMI.'' What were the benefits of worker involvement in setting the standards at NUMMI?
4. What nonfinancial performance measure could be used to encourage better product quality?
5. What nonfinancial performance measures would encourage better customer service at Amtrak?
6. An airline is considering changing its flight and seat reservation system, enabling customers to make reservations directly using push-button telephones and computer terminals. This innovation would increase the airline's use of computers and almost eliminate the use of reservations agents. What impact would this change have on variances for the department responsible for reservations?
7. Why might the total variable manufacturing overhead variance not be divided into price and efficiency components?
8. For control purposes, why is an efficiency variance not calculated for fixed manufacturing overhead?
9. ''Timely feedback means different things for different types of costs.'' Explain.
10. How would you compute price and efficiency variances for taxicab drivers where the major variable costs are drivers' wages and automobile costs?

Exercises

Solutions to even-numbered exercises are at the end of the chapter on page 545.

11. **Materials and labor variances.** The Fun 4 All Company produces toys. Recently established standard costs are as follows: Materials, 5 pieces per unit at $.20 per piece; Labor, .50 hour per unit at $4.50 per hour. In November, 29,000 pieces of material were purchased for $5,220. These 29,000 pieces of material were used in producing 5,000 units of finished product. Labor costs were $11,880 for 2,700 hours worked.
    a. Compute the materials price variance.
    b. Compute the materials efficiency variance.
    c. Compute the labor price variance.
    d. Compute the labor efficiency variance.
12. **Materials and labor variances.** The Space Invader Company's budget contains these standards for materials and direct labor for a unit:

Material—2 Pounds at $.50 per Pound	....	$1.00
Direct Labor—1 Hour at $9.00	....	9.00

Although the firm budgeted 100,000 units of output for September, it produced only 97,810. It purchased and used 200,000 pounds of materials for $105,500. Direct labor costs were $905,000 for 99,200 hours:

a. Compute the materials price variance.

b. Compute the materials efficiency variance.

c. Compute the labor price variance.

d. Compute the labor efficiency variance.

13. **Materials and labor variances.** Dee's Donuts presents the following data for October:

	Standards per Batch	Actual
Materials	2 Pounds at $5 per Pound	195,000 Pounds
Labor	3 Hours at $6 per Hour	280,000 Hours
Units Produced................		96,000 Batches

During the month, the firm purchased 195,000 pounds of materials for $1,010,000. Wages earned were $1,685,000. Compute all labor and material variances.

14. **Solving for materials quantities and costs.** Crystal Clear Pool Services uses from one to three chemicals to clean swimming pools. Variance data for the month follow (F indicates favorable variance; U indicates unfavorable variance):

	Chemical A	Chemical B	Chemical C
Materials Price Variance...........	$ 42,000 F	$ 25,000 F	$ 21,000 U
Materials Efficiency Variance.......	40,000 U	30,000 U	48,000 U
Net Materials Variance	$ 2,000 F	$ 5,000 U	$ 69,000 U
Pools Cleaned Requiring this Chemical	100,000	110,000	125,000

The budget allowed two pounds of each kind of chemical for each pool cleaning requiring that kind of chemical. For chemical A, the average price paid was $.20 per pound less than standard; for chemical B, $.10 less; for chemical C, $.07 greater. The firm purchased and used all chemicals during the month.

For each of the three types of chemicals, calculate the following:

a. Number of pounds of material purchased.

b. Standard price per pound of material.

15. **Nonmanufacturing variances.** Direct Marketing Company uses standard costs and variances for controlling costs. As a result of studying past cost data, it has established standards as follows: variable costs, $2 per sales call; 9 sales calls per unit sold. Actual data for March, April, and May follow:

	Sales Calls	Units Sold	Actual Costs
March	290,000	30,000	$650,000
April...........................	310,000	40,000	610,000
May	260,000	20,000	530,000

Compute the variable cost price and efficiency variances for each month.

16. **Labor and overhead variances** (adapted from CPA exam). The following data relate to the current month's activities of the Offshore Video Productions:

Actual Total Direct Labor	$43,400
Actual Hours Worked	14,000
Standard Hours Allowed for Actual Output (flexible budget)	15,000
Direct Labor Price Variance.......................................	$1,400 U
Actual Total Overhead	$32,000
Budgeted Fixed Costs	$9,000
Actual Fixed Overhead Costs	$9,100
Standard Variable Overhead Rate per Direct Labor Hour	$1.50
Standard Direct Labor Wages per Hour	$3.00

Compute the following variances:

a. Labor and variable overhead price variances.

b. Labor and variable overhead efficiency variances.

17. **Materials variances.** Information on Medina Company's direct materials costs is as follows:

Actual Quantities of Direct Materials Used............................	21,000
Actual Costs of Direct Materials Used	$40,000
Standard Price per Unit of Direct Materials	$2.05
Flexible Budget for Direct Materials.................................	$41,000

a. What was Medina Company's direct materials price variance?

b. What was the company's direct materials efficiency variance?

18. **Overhead variances.** Hyperspace, Inc., which uses standard costing, shows the following overhead information for the current period:

Actual Overhead Incurred	$12,600 of which $3,500 Is Fixed
Budgeted Fixed Overhead	3,300
Variable Overhead Rate per Machine Hour	$3
Standard Hours Allowed for Actual Production	3,500
Actual Machine Hours Used	3,200

What are the variable overhead price and efficiency variances and the fixed overhead price variance?

19. **Solving for labor hours.** Third National Bank reports the following direct labor information for clerical staff in its commercial lending department:

Month: July	
Standard Rate	$9.00 per Hour
Actual Rate Paid	$9.15 per Hour
Standard Hours Allowed for Actual Production	1,500 Hours
Labor Efficiency Variance.....................................	$540 U

What are the actual hours worked?

20. **Finding purchase price.** Information on Gretzky Softball Company's direct materials cost is as follows:

Standard Price per Materials Unit	$3.60
Actual Quantity Used	1,600
Materials Price Variance...	$240 F

What was the actual purchase price per unit, rounded to the nearest cent?

21. **Variances from activity-based costs.** Assume Future Costing uses activity-based costing for variable overhead costs. For May, it has three cost drivers with the following standard and actual amounts for 5,000 units of output.

Activity center	Cost driver	Standard rate per cost driver unit	Standard input for 5,000 units of output	Actual costs	Actual number of inputs used
Quality testing	Test minutes	$.50	10,000 test minutes	$5,000	9,500 test minutes
Energy	Machine hours	$1.00	10,000 machine hours	$10,000	10,500 machine hours
Indirect labor	Direct labor hours	$.50	15,000 labor hours	$7,100	14,000 hours

Prepare an analysis of the variances like that in Exhibit 13.8.

Problems

22. **Analysis of cost reports** (CMA adapted). Marcia is the production manager of the Bridgton Plant, a division of the larger corporation, Dartmoor, Inc. Marcia has complained several times to the corporate office that their cost reports used to evaluate her plant are misleading. Marcia states, ''I know how to get good quality product out. Over a number of years, I've even cut raw materials used to do it. The cost reports don't show any of this; they're always negative, no matter what I do. There's no way you can win with accounting or the people at headquarters who use these reports.''

A copy of the latest report is shown below.

	Master Budget	Actual Cost	Excess Cost
Bridgton Plant			
Cost Report			
Month of November			
(in thousands)			
Raw Material..............................	$ 400	$ 437	$ 37
Direct Labor	$ 560	$ 540	$(20)
Overhead..................................	$ 100	$ 134	$ 34
Total	$1,060	$1,111	$ 51

Identify and explain changes to the report that would make the cost information more meaningful to the production managers.

23. **Change of policy to improve productivity** (CMA adapted). Brock Toy Company has been experiencing declining profit margins and has been looking for ways to increase operating income. It cannot raise selling prices for fear of losing business to its competitors. It must either cut costs or improve productivity.

Brock uses a standard cost system to evaluate the performance of the assembly department. All negative variances at the end of the month are investigated. The assembly department rarely completes the operations in less time than the standard allows (which would result in a positive variance). Most months the variance is zero or slightly negative. Reasoning that the application of lower standard costs to the products manufactured will result in improved profit margins, the production manager has recommended that all standard times for assembly operations be drastically reduced. The production manager has informed the assembly personnel that she expects them to meet these new standards.

Will the lowering of the standard costs (by reducing the time of the assembly operations) result in improved profit margins and increased productivity?

24. **Ethics and standard costs** (CMA adapted). Quincy Farms is a producer of items made from local farm products that are distributed to supermarkets. Over the years price competition has become increasingly important, so Doug Gilbert, the company's controller, is planning to implement a standard cost system for Quincy Farms. He asked his cost accountant, Joe Adams, to gather cost information on the production of strawberry jam (Quincy Farms' most popular product). Joe reported that strawberries cost $.80 per quart, the price he intends to pay to his good friend who has been operating a strawberry farm in the red for the last couple of years. Due to an oversupply in the market, the prices for strawberries have dropped to $.50 per quart. Joe is sure that the $.80 price will be enough to pull his friend's strawberry farm out of the red and into the black.

Is Joe Adams's behavior regarding the cost information he provided to Doug Gilbert unethical? Explain your answer.

25. **Hospital supply variances.** Healthy Hospital had the following supplies costs for two products used in its operating room. Standard costs for one surgery: Item A, 10 pieces at $100 each; Item B, 20 pieces at $150 each. During August the following data apply to the hospital:

Surgeries Performed	2,000
Supplies Purchased and Used:	
Item A..	22,000 Pieces at $90
Item B..	39,000 Pieces at $152

Compute materials price and efficiency variances.

26. **Labor variances.** Quicki-Burger has two categories of direct labor: unskilled, which costs $8 per hour; and skilled, which costs $12 per hour. Management had established standards per ''equivalent meal,'' which it has defined as a typical meal consisting of a sandwich, a drink, and a side order. Managers set standards as follows: skilled labor, 4 minutes per equivalent meal; unskilled labor, 10 minutes per equivalent meal. During May, Quicki-Burger sold 30,000 equivalent meals and incurred the following labor costs:

Skilled Labor: 1,600 Hours	$19,000
Unskilled Labor: 4,200 Hours	37,000

Compute labor price and efficiency variances.

27. **Comprehensive cost variance.** Here are budget and standard cost data for May for Mike's Pretty Fair Pizza:

Budgeted sales..............................	10,000 pizzas at $10 per pizza
Budgeted production	10,000 pizzas
(Mike's uses just-in-time production methods.)	
Budgeted marketing and administrative costs	$10,000 per month (all fixed)
Standard costs to make one pizza:	
Dough....................................	1/2 pound at $2 per pound
Labor	1/4 hour per pizza at $10 per hour
Production overhead	$20,000 per month (fixed) plus $1 per pizza for toppings, paste, cheese and the like.

For May, the results were as follows:

12,000 pizzas made and sold; revenue was $110,000.
6,100 pounds of dough used at $2.10 per pound.
3,200 labor hours used at $10 per hour.
Production overhead costs were $21,000 fixed and $13,000 variable.
Marketing and administrative costs were $13,000.

a. Prepare a variable cost variance analysis.
b. Write a brief report to the management of Mike's that gives your evaluation of performance and suggests ways management might improve the company's performance.

28. **Labor and overhead variances.** Tsai Company is a producer of handmade wooden chess sets. Direct labor and variable overhead standards per finished unit are as follows: direct labor, 10 hours at $5.00 per hour; variable overhead, 10 hours at $2.00 per hour. During July, the firm produced 5,000 finished units. Direct labor costs were $234,000 (52,000 hours). Actual variable overhead costs were $103,000.

    a. Compute the price and efficiency variances for direct labor.
    b. Compute the price and efficiency variances for variable overhead.
    c. What similar factors might cause both the direct labor price variance and the variable overhead price variance?
    d. What factors might cause both the direct labor efficiency variance and the variable overhead efficiency variance?

29. **Performance evaluation in a service industry.** National Insurance Company estimates that its overhead costs for policy administration should be $72 for each new policy obtained and $2 per year for each $1,000 face amount of insurance outstanding. The company set a budget of 5,000 new policies for the coming period. In addition, the company estimated that the total face amount of insurance outstanding for the period would equal $10,800,000.

    During the period, actual costs related to new policies amounted to $358,400. A total of 4,800 new policies were obtained.

    The cost of maintaining existing policies was $23,200. Had the firm incurred these costs at the same prices as were in effect when it prepared the budget, the costs would have amounted to $22,900. However, $12,100,000 in policies were outstanding during the period.

    Prepare a schedule to indicate the differences between a master production budget and actual costs for this operation.

30. **Manufacturing variances.** Juarez Company manufactures ceramic salad bowls. The company makes two types of bowls, A and B, from the same material. The company has no fixed overhead. The following are the standards and production data for November:

	Bowl A	Bowl B
Standard Costs		
Raw Materials..................	$ .25 (.05 pounds at $5.00)	$ .50 (.10 pounds at $5.00)
Labor	.40 (6 minutes at $4.00)	.45 (6 minutes at $4.50)
Overhead......................	1.60 per Direct Labor Hour	1.50 per Direct Labor Hour
Production Data for November		
Units	5,000	3,000
Pounds of Raw Materials Used........................	250	305
Direct Labor Hours Used	500	299
Labor Costs Incurred	$2,060.00	$1,330.55

Total actual overhead was $1,236. The firm has decided to allocate this amount proportionately to the total costs of the two products on the basis of total standard direct labor hours. The firm purchased one thousand pounds of raw materials for $5,020. The labor efficiency variance for bowl A was zero.

a. Compute the raw materials efficiency variance for bowl A and for bowl B.

b. Compute the direct labor price and efficiency variances for bowl A and for bowl B.

c. Compute the variable overhead price and efficiency variances for bowl A and for bowl B.

31. **Solving for materials and labor.** Sparks 'R Us makes fireplace screens. Under the flexible budget, when the firm uses 60,000 direct labor hours, budgeted variable overhead is $60,000 whereas budgeted direct labor costs are $300,000. All data apply to the month of February.

   The following are some of the variances for February (F denotes favorable; U denotes unfavorable):

Variable Overhead Price Variance	$12,000 U
Variable Overhead Efficiency Variance	10,000 U
Materials Price Variance	15,000 F
Materials Efficiency Variance	8,000 U

During February, the firm incurred $325,500 of direct labor costs. According to the standards, each fireplace screen uses one pound of materials at a standard price of $2.00 per pound. The firm produced 100,000 units in February. The materials price variance was $.20 per pound, whereas the average wage rate exceeded the standard average rate by $.25 per hour.

   Compute the following for February, assuming there are beginning inventories but no ending inventories of materials:

a. Pounds of materials purchased.

b. Pounds of material usage over standard.

c. Standard hourly wage rate.

d. Standard direct labor hours for the total February production.

32. **Manufacturing variances.** The Old Style Company mass-produces children's desks. The standard costs follow:

Wood	25 Pounds at $3.20 per Pound
Trim	8 Pounds at $5.00 per Pound
Direct Labor	5 Hours at $6.00 per Hour
Variable Overhead	$15 per Unit
Fixed Overhead	$62,000 per Period

Transactions during February follow:

(1) The firm purchased 160,000 pounds of wood at $3.25 per pound and issued 160,000 pounds to production.

(2) The firm purchased 25 tons (50,000 pounds) of trim at $4.80 per pound and issued 50,000 pounds to production.

(3) The direct labor payroll was 31,000 hours at $5.75.

(4) Overhead costs were $151,000, of which $60,500 were fixed.

(5) The firm produced 6,000 desks during February.

Calculate all variances to the extent permitted by the data.

33. **Manufacturing cost variances.** The Seasonal Company makes greeting cards. The firm budgets fixed overhead at $6,000 per month. The firm expects variable overhead of $9,500 when it uses 10,000 direct labor hours per month.

The following data are available for April (F denotes favorable; U denotes unfavorable):

Materials Purchased and Used..................................	20,000 Units
Direct Labor Costs Incurred......................................	$36,000
Total Direct Labor Variance	$500 F
Average Actual Wage Rate ($.20 less than the standard wage rate) ..	$4.80
Variable Overhead Costs Incurred	$6,675
Materials Price Variance...	$200 F
Standard Materials Allowed for Actual Output for the Month	$12,810
Price of Purchased Materials	$.60 per Unit
Actual Fixed Overhead	$7,200

Using these data, identify and present computations for all cost variances possible.

34. **Controlling labor costs.** Kellogg Hospital has a contract with its full-time nurses that guarantees a minimum of $2,000 per month to each nurse with at least 12 years of service. One hundred employees currently qualify for coverage. All nurses receive $20 per hour.

The direct labor budget for Year 1 anticipates an annual usage of 400,000 hours at $20 per hour, or a total of $8,000,000. Management believes that, of this amount, $200,000 (100 nurses × $2,000) per month (or $2,400,000 for the year) was fixed. Thus the budgeted labor costs for any given month resulted from the formula Budgeted Labor Costs = $200,000 + $14.00 × direct labor hours worked.

Data on performance for the first 3 months of Year 1 follow:

	January	February	March
Nursing Hours Worked	22,000	32,000	42,000
Nursing Costs Budgeted	$508,000	$648,000	$788,000
Nursing Costs Incurred.............	440,000	640,000	840,000
Variance.........................	68,000 F	8,000 F	52,000 U

The results, which show favorable variances when hours worked were low and unfavorable variances when hours worked were high, perplex a hospital administrator. This administrator had believed the control over nursing costs was consistently good.

a. Why did the variances arise? Explain and illustrate, using amounts and diagrams as necessary.

b. Does this budget provide a basis for controlling nursing costs? Explain, indicating changes that management may make to improve control over nursing costs and to facilitate performance evaluation of nurses.

35. Computing nonmanufacturing cost variances. Rock City Insurance Company estimates that its overhead costs for policy administration should amount to $82 for each new policy obtained and $2 per year for each $1,000 face amount of insurance outstanding. The company set a budget of selling 6,000 new policies during the coming period. In addition, the company estimated that the total face amount of insurance outstanding for the period would equal $12,000,000.

During the period, actual costs related to new policies amounted to $430,000. The firm sold a total of 6,200 new policies.

The cost of maintaining existing policies was $27,000. Had the firm incurred these costs at the same prices as were in effect when it prepared the budget, the costs would have been $26,000. However, some costs changed. Policies worth $13,000,000 were outstanding during the period.

Prepare a schedule to show the variances between the flexible budget and actual costs for this operation.

36. Computing variances for marketing costs. High Pressure Sales, Inc., uses telephone solicitation to sell products. The company has set standards that call for $450 of sales per hour of telephone time. Telephone solicitors receive a commission of 10 percent of dollar sales. The firm expects other variable costs, including costs of sales in the operation, to be 45 percent of sales revenue. It budgets fixed costs at $411,500 per month. The firm computes the number of sales hours per month based on the number of days in a month minus an allowance for idle time, scheduling, and other inefficiencies. This month the firm expected 180 hours of telephone calling time for each of 40 callers.

During the month, the firm earned $2,700,000 of revenues. Marketing and administrative cost data for the period follow:

	Actual	Master Budget
Cost of Sales	$810,000	$972,000
Telephone Time Charges.........................	32,200	32,400
Delivery Services	161,100	194,400
Uncollectible Accounts	121,500	145,800
Other Variable Costs.............................	112,700	113,400
Fixed Costs......................................	409,000	411,500

Using sales dollars as a basis for analysis, compute the variances between actual, flexible budget, and master budget for all costs including cost of sales. (*Hint:* Consider sales volume as an output measure.)

Cases

37. Behavioral impact of implementing standard cost system (CMA adapted). Windsor Healthcare, Inc., a manufacturer of custom-designed home healthcare equipment, has been in business for 15 years. Last year, in an effort to better control the costs of their products, the Controller implemented a standard cost system. Reports are issued monthly for tracking performance, and any negative variances are further investigated.

The production manager complained that the standards are unrealistic, stifle motivation by concentrating only on negative variances, and are out of date too quickly. He noted that his recent switch to titanium for the wheelchairs has resulted in higher material costs but decreased labor times. The net result was no increase in the total cost of producing the wheelchair. The monthly reports continue to show a negative material variance and a positive labor variance, despite the fact that there are indications that the workers are slowing down.

a. Describe several ways that a standard cost system strengthens management cost control.

b. Describe at least two reasons why a standard cost system may negatively impact the motivation of production employees.

38. **Comprehensive problem: Tondamakers, Inc.** Tondamakers produced and sold 1,000 Tonda riding lawnmowers in Year 1, its first year of operation. Actual costs of production appear below:

Actual Results for the Year:	
Direct Materials: 11,000 Pounds at $19	$209,000
Direct Labor: 2,050 Hours at $31	63,550
Manufacturing Overhead ($205,000 fixed)	245,000
Actual Marketing and Administrative	
Costs ($320,000 fixed)	380,000
Total Revenue: 1,000 Units at $940	940,000
Actual Machine Hours Worked	550 Hours
Standard Variable Costs:	
Materials: 10 Pounds at $20	$200
Labor: 2 Hours at $30	60
Variable Overhead: .5 Machine Hours	
at $80	40
Budget Information:	
Budgeted Fixed Manufacturing Costs	$200,000 for Year 1
Master Budget Sales Volume	900 Tondas
Budgeted Marketing and Administrative	
Costs	$350,000 + $50 per Unit Sold
Budgeted Sales Price	$1,000 per Unit

Prepare profit and cost variance analyses such as those in Exhibit 13.7.

Suggested Solutions to Even-Numbered Exercises

12. **Materials and labor variances.**

a. Materials Price Variance = $105,500 − (200,000 pounds × $.50) = $105,500 − $100,000 = $5,500 U.

    b. Materials Efficiency Variance = $.50 × 200,000 pounds actual − (2 standard pounds × 97,810 units produced) = $.50 × (200,000 − 195,620) = $2,190 U.

    c. Labor Price Variance = $905,000 − ($9 × 99,200) = $12,200 U.

    d. Labor Efficiency Variance = (99,200 − 97,810) × $9.00 = $12,510 U.

14. **Solving for materials quantities and costs.**

Chemical A:

    a. Price Variance = $.20 F per Pound.

        Total Price Variance = $42,000 F.

$$\text{Pounds Purchased and Used} = \frac{\$42,000}{\$.20} = 210,000.$$

    b. Standard Pounds Allowed for 100,000 Units = 200,000.

        Pounds Used over Standard = 210,000 − 200,000 = 10,000.

        Efficiency Variance = $40,000 U.

$$\text{Standard Unit Price} = \frac{\$40,000}{10,000} = \$4.00.$$

Chemical B:

    a. $\text{Pounds Purchased and Used} = \dfrac{\$25,000}{\$.10} = 250,000.$

    b. $\text{Standard Unit Price} = \dfrac{\$30,000}{(250,000 - 220,000)} = \dfrac{\$30,000}{30,000} = \$1.00.$

Chemical C:

    a. $\text{Pounds Purchased and Used} = \dfrac{\$21,000}{\$.07} = 300,000.$

    b. $\text{Standard Unit Price} = \dfrac{\$48,000}{(300,000 - 250,000)} = \$.96.$

16. **Labor and overhead variances.**

	Actual Costs	Price Variance	Inputs at Standard Prices	Efficiency Variance	Flexible Production Budget
Direct Labor	$43,400		$43,400 − $1,400 = $42,000		15,000 × $3.00 = $45,000
		$1,400 U		$3,000 F	
Variable Overhead	$32,000 − $9,100 = $22,900		14,000 × $1.50 = $21,000		15,000 × $1.50 = $22,500
		$1,900 U		$1,500 F	
Fixed Overhead	$9,100				$9,000
		$100 U			

18. Overhead variances.

	Actual Costs	Price Variance	Inputs at Standard Prices	Efficiency Variance	Flexible Budget
Variable Overhead.......	$12,600 − $3,500 = $9,100		$3 × 3,200 Hours = $9,600		$3 × 3,500 Hours = $10,500
		$500 F		$900 F	
Fixed Overhead	$3,500				$3,300
		$200 U			

20. Finding purchase price.

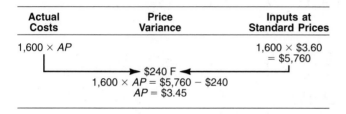

Actual Costs	Price Variance	Inputs at Standard Prices
1,600 × AP		1,600 × $3.60 = $5,760
	$240 F	

$1,600 × AP = \$5,760 − \$240$
$AP = \$3.45$

Variance Analysis: Additional Topics

1. Compute and interpret fixed manufacturing cost variances.
2. Know how to interpret and use materials price variances when the quantity of materials purchased does not equal the quantity used.
3. Use mix variances to evaluate the effects of substitution.
4. Understand how accountants prorate variances to measure actual costs.
5. Decide which variances to investigate for quality control.
6. Understand how variance investigation fits into a total quality improvement program.
7. (Appendix 14.1) Demonstrate how costs flow through accounts using standard costing.

Chapters 12 and 13 presented the fundamental conceptual framework for computing variances that applies to most nonmanufacturing and manufacturing costs and revenues. This chapter expands on those discussions.

Fixed Manufacturing Cost Variances

Chapters 12 and 13 treated fixed costs as lump-sum, period costs in comparing budgeted and actual costs. This practice is appropriate for controlling fixed cost expenditures for managerial purposes. Manufacturing companies, however, use *full absorption costing* to value inventory. Full absorption costing unitizes fixed manufacturing costs and adds these unit fixed costs to unit variable manufacturing costs to compute the cost of a unit of inventory produced.

Companies frequently use a predetermined overhead rate to apply fixed overhead to units produced. For example, assume the following facts for Victoria Corporation:

Estimated (budgeted) Fixed Manufacturing Costs	$32,200
Estimated Production Volume	70,000 Units
Actual Production Volume	80,000 Units
Actual Fixed Manufacturing Costs	$34,000

If Victoria Corporation used full absorption, standard costing, it would apply its fixed manufacturing costs to units as follows:

$$\text{Applied Fixed Manufacturing Cost per Unit} = \frac{\text{Estimated Fixed Manufacturing Cost per Period}}{\text{Estimated Production Volume per Period}}$$

$$= \frac{\$32,200}{70,000 \text{ Units Planned}}$$

$$= \$.46 \text{ per Unit.}$$

Note that we use production, not sales, volumes to unitize fixed manufacturing costs. If you were to unitize fixed marketing costs, you would divide the estimated cost by estimated sales volume.

During the period, the firm produced 80,000 units, so 80,000 units times $.46 per unit equals $36,800 applied to Work-in-Process Inventory. The amount "applied" is the amount of fixed manufacturing overhead debited to Work-in-Process Inventory. The firm could apply fixed manufacturing costs using an input basis such as machine hours. Assume the standard is 40 units per machine hour, or $\frac{1}{40}$ hour per unit. Then you would compute the rate per hour as follows:

$$\text{Fixed Manufacturing Cost Rate per Hour} = \frac{\$32,200}{70,000 \text{ Units} \times \frac{1}{40}} = \frac{\$32,200}{1,750 \text{ Hours}}$$

$$= \$18.40 \text{ per Hour.}$$

The amount applied would still be $36,800 (= $18.40 per Hour $\times \frac{1}{40}$ Hours per Unit $\times$ 80,000 Units = $18.40 per Hour $\times$ 2,000 Hours).

Production Volume Variance

The **production volume variance** is the difference between the budgeted and applied fixed costs. For Victoria Corporation, the production volume variance is:

$$\text{Production Volume Variance} = \text{Budgeted Fixed Manufacturing Costs} - \text{Applied Fixed Manufacturing Costs}$$

$$\$4,600 \text{ F} = \$32,200 - \$36,800.$$

This variance is favorable, as indicated by the F, as explained later.

If management had accurately estimated the production volume to be 80,000 units, the estimated unit cost would have been

$$\frac{\$32,200}{80,000 \text{ Units}} = \$.4025 \text{ per Unit.}$$

Applied fixed manufacturing overhead would have been $32,200 (= $.4025 per unit × 80,000 units actually produced), which equals the budget amount. Thus, if management correctly estimated the production volume, no production volume variance would occur.

The production volume variance applies only to fixed costs, and it emerges because we allocate a fixed period cost to products on a predetermined basis. The production volume variance appears to have little or no benefit for managerial purposes. Some accountants argue that this variance signals a difference between expected and actual production levels, but so does a simple production report comparing actual and planned production volumes.

The production volume variance comes from the use of predetermined fixed-cost rates in full absorption costing, unlike other cost variances that accountants compute to help managers manage the business. Manufacturing firms use predetermined rates and full absorption costing for external reporting, so you will probably encounter production volume variances during your career. Do not assume the production volume variance is useful just because companies compute it, however.

Price (Spending) Variance

Recall from Chapter 13 that the **price variance** (sometimes called the **spending variance**) **for fixed manufacturing costs** is the difference between the actual costs and the budgeted costs. Compute the fixed manufacturing price variance for Victoria Corporation as follows:

Price Variance	=	Actual Fixed Manufacturing Costs	−	Budgeted Fixed Manufacturing Costs
$1,800 U =		$34,000	−	$32,200.

Although we use manufacturing costs for this example, you can compute the price variance this way for any fixed cost.

The fixed manufacturing cost variance used for management and control of fixed manufacturing costs is the price variance, whereas the fixed manufacturing cost production volume variance occurs only when we compute inventory values using full absorption costing and predetermined overhead rates.

Relation of Actual, Budgeted, and Applied Fixed Manufacturing Costs

We summarize the fixed manufacturing cost variances and the relation among actual, budget, and applied fixed manufacturing costs in Exhibit 14.1. Note the price variance is unfavorable because the actual exceeds the budget, but the production volume variance is favorable because the budget is less than the applied. We present a graphic presentation in Exhibit 14.2. Note that the master and flexible budgets for

Exhibit 14.1

VICTORIA CORPORATION
Fixed Manufacturing Cost Variances

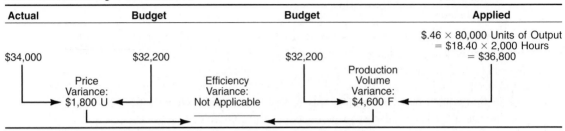

Actual	Budget	Budget	Applied
			$.46 × 80,000 Units of Output = $18.40 × 2,000 Hours = $36,800
$34,000	$32,200	$32,200	
Price Variance: $1,800 U	Efficiency Variance: Not Applicable	Production Volume Variance: $4,600 F	

fixed costs do not differ here because we assume fixed costs do not vary with volume. If fixed costs differed in the flexible budget from the master budget, you would use the flexible budget fixed costs to compute these variances, because we use the flexible budget for performance evaluation and control purposes.

Problem 14.1 for Self-Study

Fixed cost variances. During the past month, the following events took place at Computer Supply, Inc.

(1) The company produces 50,000 computer cases. Actual fixed manufacturing cost was $83,000.
(2) Budgeted fixed manufacturing cost was $80,000. Budgeted direct labor hours worked were 4,000 hours for budgeted production of 40,000 cases. Full absorption costing, if used, applies fixed manufacturing costs to units produced on the basis of direct labor hours. 5,000 standard labor hours were allowed to make 50,000 computer cases.

Compute the fixed manufacturing price and production volume variances.

The solution to this self-study problem is at the end of the chapter on page 572.

Materials Purchased and Used Are Not Equal

In the Victoria Corporation example, the direct materials purchased equalled the amount used. What if they are not equal? Are direct materials variances based on *purchases* or *usage*? Accountants generally base the *price* variance on *purchases,* but base the *efficiency* variance on materials *used.*

Exhibit 14.2

VICTORIA CORPORATION
Graphic Presentation of Fixed Overhead Variances

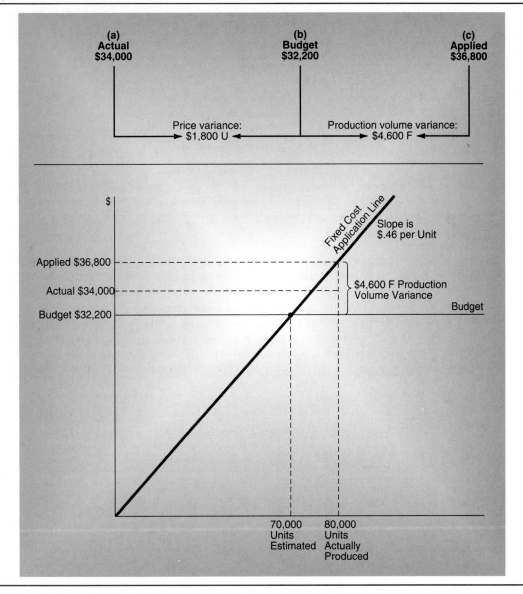

This practice enables managers to spot price variances at the time the firm purchases materials, rather than waiting until they enter into production. In addition, it emphasizes that the purchasing department has responsibility for purchase price variances at the time of purchase, whereas the manufacturing departments have responsibility for efficiency variances.

Exhibit 14.3

VICTORIA CORPORATION
Materials Purchased and Used Are Not Equal

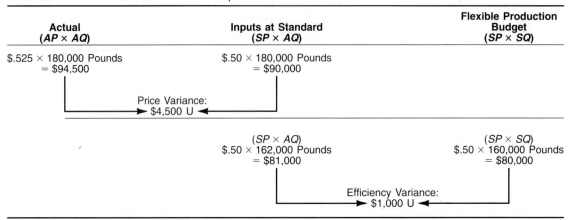

For example, change our example such that Victoria Corporation purchased 180,000 pounds of material at an average price of $.525 per pound, used 162,000 pounds, and had a standard of 160,000 pounds to be used to produce 80,000 units. We would modify the cost variance model presented in Chapter 13 as shown in Exhibit 14.3. The purchase price variance would be $4,500 U [= 180,000 × ($.525 − $.500)]. The efficiency variance would still be $1,000 U [= (162,000 pounds − 160,000 pounds) × $.50]. Materials inventory would increase by $9,000 [= (180,000 pounds − 162,000 pounds) × $.50].

Mix Variances

Most organizations use multiple inputs to produce their output. Massachusetts General Hosptial uses a combination of registered nurses, licensed practical nurses, and nurse's aides to provide nursing care to patients. Bethlehem Steel Company uses a combination of iron ore, coke, and other raw materials to make its product. A **mix variance** shows the impact on profits of using something other than the budgeted mix of inputs.

Example   Engineering Associates, a consulting firm, has bid on a particular job assuming 1,000 hours of partner time at a cost of $100 per hour and 2,000 hours of staff time at $40 per hour. If it gets the job, these hour and cost assumptions become the flexible budget. During the job, scheduling problems arise; the partner spends 2,000 hours because the staff member spends only 1,000 hours. If the cost is actually $100 and $40 for partner and staff time, respectively, no labor price variance occurs. Further, the 3,000 hours required is exactly what was expected. Nevertheless, the job is $60,000 over the flexible budget, as shown in the following calculation:

$$\text{Actual Cost} = (2{,}000 \text{ Hours} \times \$100) + (1{,}000 \text{ Hours} \times \$40)$$
$$= \$200{,}000 + \$40{,}000$$
$$= \underline{\underline{\$240{,}000}}.$$

$$\text{Budgeted Cost} = (1{,}000 \text{ Hours} \times \$100) + (2{,}000 \text{ Hours} \times \$40)$$
$$= \$100{,}000 + \$80{,}000$$
$$= \underline{\underline{\$180{,}000}}.$$

$$\text{Actual Cost} - \text{Budgeted Cost}$$
$$= \$240{,}000 - \$180{,}000$$
$$= \$60{,}000.$$

The $60,000 unfavorable variance results from a mix variance: The substitution of 1,000 hours (= 2,000 hours actual − 1,000 hours budgeted) of partner time at $100 for 1,000 hours of staff time at $40. The mix variance is the difference in labor costs per hour of $60 (= $100 − $40) times the 1,000 hours substituted.

The general model for a mix variance is as follows:

Standard Price of the Inputs × **Actual Proportions** of the Actual Total Quantity × Actual Total Quantity of Inputs	−	Standard Price of the Inputs × **Standard Proportions** of the Actual Total Quantity × Actual Total Quantity of Inputs

Exhibit 14.4 shows the model for computing a mix variance. Columns (2) and (3) in the bottom part of Exhibit 14.4 show the mix variance that we computed above.

This example demonstrates the general concept of a mix variance. You should note two factors always present in a mix variance. First, we assumed that partner time was *substitutable* for staff time. Second, the prices must be different. If the cost per hour were the same for both partner and staff, the substitution of hours would not affect the total cost of the job.

Note that Exhibit 14.4 would have called the mix variance an efficiency variance if we had not calculated a separate mix variance. We call the portion of the efficiency variance that is not a mix variance a **yield variance.** The yield variance measures the input-output relation holding the standard mix of inputs constant.

In this example, we purposefully make the yield variance equal to zero to show that the entire variance results from the mix. Problem 14.2 for Self-Study presents a case in which there is a yield variance.

Managers use mix variances not only to measure performance when inputs are substitutes, as in the preceding example, but also to measure marketing performance with respect to sales mix. Companies with multiple products assume a particular sales mix in constructing their sales budget. If the actual mix of products sold differs from the budgeted mix, and if the products are substitutes, managers often compute a mix variance to measure the impact of the change in mix from the budget.

Exhibit 14.4

ENGINEERING ASSOCIATES
Mix Variance

Cost Variances Ignoring Mix Variance

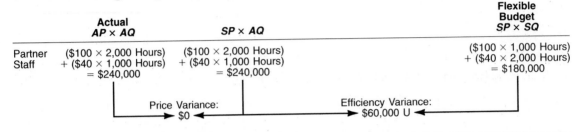

	Actual AP × AQ	SP × AQ	Flexible Budget SP × SQ
Partner Staff	($100 × 2,000 Hours) + ($40 × 1,000 Hours) = $240,000	($100 × 2,000 Hours) + ($40 × 1,000 Hours) = $240,000	($100 × 1,000 Hours) + ($40 × 2,000 Hours) = $180,000

Price Variance: $0

Efficiency Variance: $60,000 U

Cost Variances Considering Mix Variance

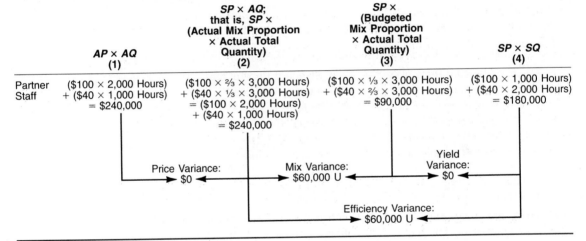

	AP × AQ (1)	SP × AQ; that is, SP × (Actual Mix Proportion × Actual Total Quantity) (2)	SP × (Budgeted Mix Proportion × Actual Total Quantity) (3)	SP × SQ (4)
Partner Staff	($100 × 2,000 Hours) + ($40 × 1,000 Hours) = $240,000	($100 × ⅔ × 3,000 Hours) + ($40 × ⅓ × 3,000 Hours) = ($100 × 2,000 Hours) + ($40 × 1,000 Hours) = $240,000	($100 × ⅓ × 3,000 Hours) + ($40 × ⅔ × 3,000 Hours) = $90,000	($100 × 1,000 Hours) + ($40 × 2,000 Hours) = $180,000

Price Variance: $0

Mix Variance: $60,000 U

Yield Variance: $0

Efficiency Variance: $60,000 U

Problem 14.2 for Self-Study

Mix variance. Alexis Company makes a product, AL, from two materials, ST and EE. The standard prices and quantities follow:

	ST	EE
Price per Pound	$2	$3
Pounds per Unit of AL	10	5

In May, Alexis Company produced 7,000 units of AL, with the following actual prices and quantities of materials used:

	ST	EE
Price per Pound	$1.90	$2.80
Pounds Used	72,000	38,000

Compute materials price, mix, yield and efficiency variances.

The solution to this self-study problem is at the end of the chapter on page 572.

Prorating Variances

Suppose a company produces more than it sells during some period of time, with the excess of production over sales remaining in ending inventory. The company's accountants compute production variances based on the units produced. Should the company expense all of the variances in the period the goods are produced, even though some of those goods are in ending inventory and will not be sold until a future period? In practice, companies typically expense all of the production variances in the period of production.

Common Practice Does Not Prorate Variances

Companies generally do *not* prorate variances for internal reporting purposes. When prorating minimally affects measures of profit and product costs, managers consider it a waste of time.

In addition, accountants may not prorate production variances because managers consider variances to be *period* costs. If a variance results from production in a particular period, managers want it reported that period, not in some future period.

What if variances are sufficiently large that failure to prorate would materially misstate fully absorbed cost of inventories and net income for financial reporting to shareholders? In such a case, accountants would prorate variances.

Example   We use the following example to demonstrate how accountants prorate variances. Suppose a company has beginning inventory of 200 units, it produces 1,200 units, it sells 1,000 units, and it has 400 units in ending inventory. The company uses first-in, first-out (FIFO), so the 400 units in ending inventory all come from the current period's production. Assume the standard cost for each unit is $1.00 and the actual cost of producing the 1,200 units this period was $1,500. These facts indicate a variance of $300 [=$1,500 − ($1.00 × 1,200 units)] for the 1,200 units produced.

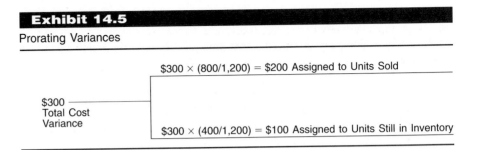

Exhibit 14.5

Prorating Variances

$300 × (800/1,200) = $200 Assigned to Units Sold

$300
Total Cost
Variance

$300 × (400/1,200) = $100 Assigned to Units Still in Inventory

If the company prorates the variance between units sold and units still in ending inventory, it would allocate one-third (= 400/1,200) of the variance to ending inventory and the remaining two-thirds to units sold. As to the allocation of the remaining two-thirds to units sold, recall that using FIFO, the first 200 units sold came from beginning inventory. The remaining 800 units sold came from the current period's production.

The company would allocate the $300 variance as follows: $100 to ending inventory and $200 to units sold, as we show in Exhibit 14.5. The $200 would be expensed on the income statement, either as part of cost of goods sold or as a separate "variance" line item.

By prorating variances, companies convert their inventories from standard cost to actual cost. Note the actual cost of the 1,200 units produced was $1.25 per unit ($1.25 = $1,500/1,200 units). Allocating $100 to ending inventory adds $.25 per unit to each of the 400 units in ending inventory. Adding $.25 per unit converts the standard cost per unit of $1.00 to the actual cost of $1.25 per unit.

Quality Control and Variance Investigation

Managers may receive reports that contain hundreds or even thousands of variances. Managerial time is a scarce resource—following up and investigating variances is costly. When confronted with variance reports, managers ask: Which variances should we investigate?

Managers can deal with the decision of whether to investigate a variance like other decisions—on a cost-benefit basis. Hence they should investigate variances if they expect the benefits from investigation to exceed the costs of investigation. These benefits may include improvements from taking corrective action, such as repairing defective machinery, instructing workers who were performing their tasks incorrectly, or changing a standard purchase order so that the firm can purchase cheaper materials. Further, managers generally believe that periodically investigating or auditing employees improves performances. Because measuring the benefits and costs of investigation is often difficult, decisions about the value of investigating variances rely considerably on managerial judgments.

The major cost of **variance investigation** is the opportunity cost of employees' time. Investigators spend time as do those being investigated. Although measuring costs and benefits of variance investigation is difficult, in many cases the benefits are clearly too low or costs are clearly too high to make investigation worthwhile. In other cases variances are so large that obviously management must do something about them.

Managers use a variety of methods to help them ascertain which variances to investigate, including rules of thumb that have worked well in the past (for example, any variance greater than 10 percent of standard cost, any variance that has been unfavorable for 3 months in a row, and so on). Although we emphasize that managerial experience and good judgment are the most important ingredients for variance investigation decisions, accountants have developed some decision aids to assist managers.

Tolerance Limits

Quality control techniques have long relied on the use of *tolerance limits*. Quality is allowed to fluctuate within predetermined tolerance limits. Applying this concept to variances requires establishing predetermined limits within which variances may fluctuate. These limits may differ for various cost items. For example, managers usually allow greater tolerance for direct materials prices than for labor efficiency, because they have less control over the former due to market fluctuations. Some managers set tighter tolerance limits for unfavorable variances than for favorable variances.

Statistical Significance   Our knowledge about the properties of statistical distributions can help set tolerance limits. Managers can establish tolerance limits based on *statistical confidence limits.*

Example   The manager of a kitchen that makes meals for a college cafeteria wants to set tolerance limits on labor efficiency variances so that variances fall outside the limits less than 5 percent of the time. This analysis assumes that labor efficiency costs are normally distributed. Based on past experience, expected labor time is 58 minutes total labor time to prepare the lunch each day. Estimated standard deviation is 8 minutes.

Exhibit 14.6 presents a control chart of actual observations reported to the kitchen manager for 5 days. A time series of observations allows the manager to see trends and look for cumulative effects of variances. The manager gets this report at 9:00 a.m. each day for the 5 previous working days. The kitchen manager received the report shown in Exhibit 14.6 at 9:00 a.m. Friday. The manager would have investigated the labor efficiency variance for Monday, presumably on Tuesday, because it fell outside the tolerance limits. In addition, the manager would probably investigate this labor variance after receiving the report on Friday because of the trend indicating a shift away from standard.

Decision Models

Although control charts provide data about variances, they do not incorporate the costs and benefits of variance investigation. The simple decision model in the following example shows how to do this.

Exhibit 14.6

Labor Efficiency Variance Report: Friday through Thursday Control Chart[a]

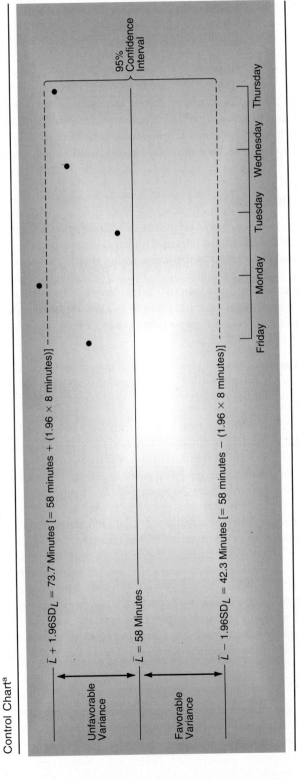

$\bar{L}$ + 1.96SD$_L$ = 73.7 Minutes [= 58 minutes + (1.96 × 8 minutes)]

Unfavorable Variance

$\bar{L}$ = 58 Minutes

Favorable Variance

$\bar{L}$ − 1.96SD$_L$ = 42.3 Minutes [= 58 minutes − (1.96 × 8 minutes)]

95% Confidence Interval

Friday   Monday   Tuesday   Wednesday   Thursday

[a]$\bar{L}$ = expected labor time per unit of output; SD$_L$ = standard deviation of labor time per unit of output.
95 percent of the area in a normal distribution lies between $\bar{L}$ − 1.96SD$_L$ and $\bar{L}$ + 1.96D$_L$, according to tables available in statistics texts.

Example   Electromagnet, Inc., uses a stamping machine to make a product in 10,000-unit batches. An employee adjusts this machine at the beginning of a batch. During the production run, another employee calculates and reports the materials efficiency variances. If the machine is out of adjustment, it will use considerably more materials than needed. Hence, adjusting the machine during a production run could save materials costs. Reported variances may be due to the machine using more materials than needed because of lower-quality materials, variance reporting errors, or other factors that adjusting the machine would not correct. Experience has shown that materials efficiency variances are approximately normally distributed.

Midway through a particular production batch, the stamping department manager receives a report indicating a large negative materials efficiency variance. Based on past experience, the manager estimates a 70-percent chance of the machine's running out of adjustment when the system reports a large negative materials efficiency variance.[1]

The manager faces the decision of whether to investigate. Shutting down the machine would result in idle worker time, loss of materials, and lost managerial time. After computing the opportunity cost of lost time and the cost of lost materials, the department manager estimates the cost of variance investigation, C, to be $1,000. If the machine needs adjustment, making the adjustment will cost $1,200 but the firm will save $3,200 in materials cost. Given the costs, C, and the benefits, B, from investigation, and the probability, P, that the benefits can be obtained, the decision rule is to investigate when expected benefits exceed expected costs:[2] $P \times B > C$.

Expected benefits equal the materials cost savings, $3,200, minus the cost of machine adjustments, $1,200, in this case. Investigating is worthwhile because

$$P \times B > C$$
$$.70 \times (\$3,200 - \$1,200) > \$1,000$$
$$.70 \times \$2,000 > \$1,000$$
$$\$1,400 > \$1,000.$$

This simple example shows how to model the variance investigation decision by applying statistical decision theory tools. In practice, accountants have difficulty applying the model, because they cannot easily estimate C, B, and P. At a minimum, managers should perform sensitivity analysis to see if the decision changes when their estimates of C, B, and P change.

Statistical analysis can provide decision aids to managers. Ultimately, these decision aids are just *aids;* they do not replace managerial judgment and good sense.

---

[1] Readers who have studied statistics will recognize this as the manager's posterior probability that the machine is out of adjustment, given a variance as high as the one reported. Calculation of posterior probabilities relies on Bayes' theorem, which statistics textbooks present.

[2] We have assumed that decision makers are risk-neutral in this example.

Quality Management and the Baldrige Award[a]

Like many of the methods used in the success of the Japanese quality movement, the use of statistical controls in assessing processes originated in the United States. However, Japanese managers applied the concept and had much greater employee involvement in quality improvement than did U.S. companies. Although lagging in implementing quality management programs, many U.S. companies have jumped on the quality management bandwagon.

In 1987, the U.S. Congress created the Malcolm Baldrige National Quality Award in honor of the former secretary of commerce. This award is given to businesses who excel in major aspects of quality, such as quality planning, human resource development, and customer focus. Companies that have won this award include well-known manufacturing companies like Motorola, Westinghouse (Commercial Nuclear Fuel Division), IBM, Texas Instruments (Defense Systems and Electronics Group), and General Motors (Cadillac Division). The award has also been given to service organizations such as Ritz-Carlton Hotels, Federal Express, and AT&T (Network Systems Group) and to small businesses like Granite Rock Co. in Watsonville, California, and Globe Metallurgical in Cleveland. The Baldrige Award is intended to promote sharing of information about effective quality management programs and to identify companies with role-model quality management systems.

[a]Based on George S. Easton, "The 1993 State of U.S. Total Quality Management: A Baldrige Examiner's Perspective," *California Management Reveiw,* vol. 35, no. 3 (Spring 1993), pp. 32–54.

Problem 14.3
for Self-Study

Variance investigation. Pep Seco, the manager of a soft-drink bottling plant, watches the variance reports like a hawk because Pep knows the consequences of the machinery being out of adjustment. Pep just received a variance report indicating a possible problem. Based on years of experience, Pep figures the probability that the machinery is out of adjustment is .40 in light of the variance report. Investigation to learn whether the machinery is out of adjustment would cost $10,000 (mostly Pep's time, which has a high opportunity cost). If the machinery is out of adjustment, it would cost $20,000 to correct the problem but the company would save $50,000. Should Pep investigate? Why or why not?

The solution to this self-study problem is at the end of the chapter on page 573.

Summary

The most common fixed manufacturing overhead variance for performance evaluation is the *price variance* (also called a spending or budget variance), which measures the difference between budgeted and actual fixed costs. If the firm budgets rent costs at $10,000 but actually spends $12,000, the price variance is $2,000 unfavorable. This straightforward calculation has a clear meaning—the firm paid $2,000 more for rent than budgeted. The *production volume variance* occurs only when the analyst unitizes fixed costs, such as when the accountant uses full absorption costing to value inventory and to calculate the cost of goods sold. The production volume variance occurs when the estimate of activity in the denominator of the following equation does not equal actual activity.

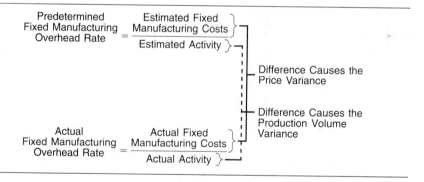

If inventory levels change, companies must decide whether to expense all of the current period purchase and production variances or to prorate them. If prorated, the company expenses variances attributable to goods sold, but the variances attributable to goods still in inventory do not become expensed until the firm sells the inventory.

Managers calculate mix variances when the various inputs (or outputs) can substitute for one another. Mix variances measure the cost of using more expensive material or labor in place of less expensive material or labor, for example.

Managers usually investigate and correct only a small fraction of the variances computed, because investigation and correction is costly—it consumes both managerial and worker time. How do managers select the variances to investigate? Often

Exhibit 14.7

Standard Cost Flows

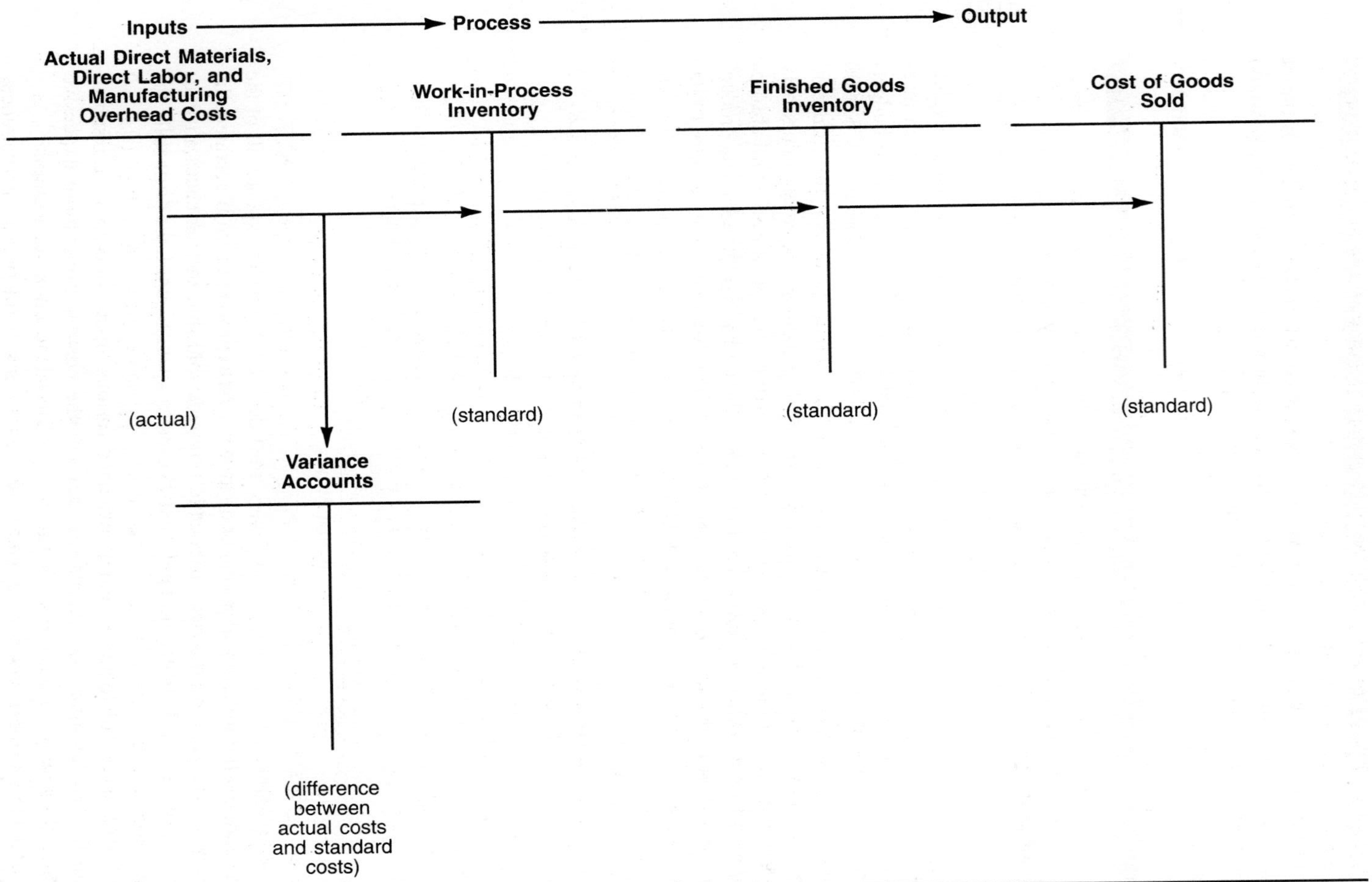

Inputs ⟶ Process ⟶ Output

Actual Direct Materials, Direct Labor, and Manufacturing Overhead Costs

(actual)

Work-in-Process Inventory

(standard)

Finished Goods Inventory

(standard)

Cost of Goods Sold

(standard)

Variance Accounts

(difference between actual costs and standard costs)

they use rules of thumb, such as "investigate if the variance is greater than 10 percent of the standard." If the accountant can estimate properties of frequency distributions, managers can base variance tolerance limits on confidence intervals, as shown in Exhibit 14.6. You may model the variance investigation using statistical decision theory and the following rule:

Investigate if $P \times B > C$,

where B = benefits from investigation

          C = costs of investigation

          P = probability of achieving benefits if variance is investigated.

Whether you use a rule of thumb or a statistical model, you should apply the simple cost-benefit criterion that forms the foundation of all managerial activity: Take action only if the benefits exceed the costs.

Appendix 14.1: Standard Costs

Many organizations use standard costs, but only some use the standards to value inventory and product costs in the accounting records. Manufacturing companies with process systems—for example, steel, chemical, or calculator manufacturers—most commonly use standard costs to value inventory. The published financial statements of both Hewlett-Packard and Intel report these companies use standard costing to value their inventories. The use of standard costs can save significant record-keeping costs, particularly in process manufacturing, where units are homogeneous and not easily identifiable separately.

You may wonder why users of accounting information should study standard cost flows through accounts. First, study of this system will help solidify your understanding of variance measurement and analysis. Our goal is to make your understanding of variances intuitive rather than mechanical. Looking at the way variances emerge from cost flows through the accounting system should help achieve that goal. Second, the better users understand accounting systems, the more input they can have in designing and modifying them.

Standard Cost Flows

The general model for the flow of costs in standard cost accounting systems appears in Exhibit 14.7.

A standard cost system transfers costs through the production process at standard. Process costing values units transferred between departments at standard cost; whereas job costing charges standard costs to the job for its components. Accountants record actual costs in such accounts as Accounts Payable and Wages Payable. The difference between the actual cost assigned to a department and the standard cost of the work done is the variance for the department.

The following sections discuss the flow of costs and demonstrate how the accounting system isolates the variances. These variances will be the same as those calculated in Chapter 13 for Victoria Corporation. Recognize that standard cost systems vary from company to company. We present a typical model, but you may need to modify it to meet the specific needs of a particular company. Our example is based on Victoria Corporation using the data from the case in which materials purchased equalled materials used.

Direct Materials

Materials, whatever their actual cost, usually appear in materials inventory at the standard price per unit of material. The entry for Victoria Corporation for materials purchased follows (numbers in parentheses are the journal entry numbers):

(1) Materials Inventory	81,000	
Materials Price Variance	4,050	
Accounts Payable		85,050
To record the purchase of 162,000 pounds of material at the actual cost of $.525 per pound, and to record the purchase in Materials Inventory at the standard cost of $.50 per pound.		

Note that unfavorable cost variances are always debits and favorable cost variances are always credits. Exhibit 14.8 presents the flow of standard costs through T-accounts. Note that *actual costs* generally appear in the accounts on the left side of Exhibit 14.8 (for example, in Accounts Payable). The costs entered in Work-in-Process are *standard costs*.

The materials price variance appears in the accounting records when the firm purchases materials. As noted in the text, managers may wish to know the materials price variances at the time of purchase so that they can take corrective action if necessary.

We say that direct materials appear at standard cost because the $.50 per pound is the standard allowed per unit of input. But a word of caution: The standard cost recorded is the standard cost per unit of *input* (that is, pounds), *not* standard cost per unit of *output*.

When direct materials enter production, the system assigns each operating department the *actual quantity* of input used at the *standard cost* per input unit. Thus the system assigns the production department at Victoria Corporation the standard cost of $.50 per pound for the actual quantity of 162,000 pounds of materials. Managers do not normally hold production departments responsible for the materials price variances, which are the responsibility of the purchasing department. Managers do hold production departments responsible for materials efficiency variances, however.

The entry charging production for the standard cost of materials used follows:

(2) Work-in-Process Inventory	80,000	
Materials Efficiency Variance	1,000	
Materials Inventory		81,000
To record the requisition of 162,000 pounds of material at the standard cost of $.50 per pound to make 80,000 units of output.		

(Exhibit 14.8 presents this entry in T-accounts.)

Direct Labor

The standard cost system credits the actual direct labor, including fringe benefits and taxes, to various payable accounts. To simplify the presentation, we assume that the credit is just to Wages Payable. The system charges direct labor to Work-in-Process Inventory at the standard direct labor cost allowed for the output produced. This entry for Victoria Corporation follows:

(3) Work-in-Process Inventory	200,000	
Labor Efficiency Variance	19,100	
Labor Price Variance		12,050
Wages Payable		207,050

To charge Production for the standard cost of direct labor at $20 per hour times 10,000 hours allowed (that is, $\frac{1}{8}$ hour per unit of output allowed), to record the actual direct labor cost, and to record direct labor variances.

Variable Manufacturing Overhead

The standard cost system charges standard overhead costs to production based on standard machine hours allowed at the rate of $6.80 per machine hour. This entry can occur before the accountant knows the actual costs as the following sequence of entries demonstrates:

1. The system charges standard overhead costs to production during the period. Debit Work-in-Process Inventory and credit Variable Manufacturing Overhead.
2. The accountant records actual costs in various accounts, then transfers them to Variable Manufacturing Overhead by crediting the various accounts and debiting Variable Manufacturing Overhead. Examples of the accounts credited include Accounts Payable for costs of utilities and Wages Payable for indirect labor costs. The accountant cannot complete this step until after the end of the period.
3. Variances are the difference between the standard costs charged to production and actual costs incurred.

This approach is essentially the same as that used in Chapter 4 for charging production with overhead costs using normal costing. However, variance accounts replace the Under- or Overapplied Overhead accounts used in Chapter 4.

The three entries for Victoria Corporation follow:

(4a) Work-in-Process Inventory	13,600	
Variable Manufacturing Overhead.......................		13,600

To charge Production for the standard variable overhead cost at $6.80 per machine hour times 2,000 machine hours allowed to make 80,000 units actually produced.

(4b) Variable Manufacturing Overhead...........................	13,500	
Various Accounts		13,500
Variable Overhead Price Variance		780

To record actual variable manufacturing overhead costs incurred.

(continued on page 569)

Exhibit 14.8

VICTORIA CORPORATION

Flow of Costs[a]—Full Absorption Costing with Standard Costs

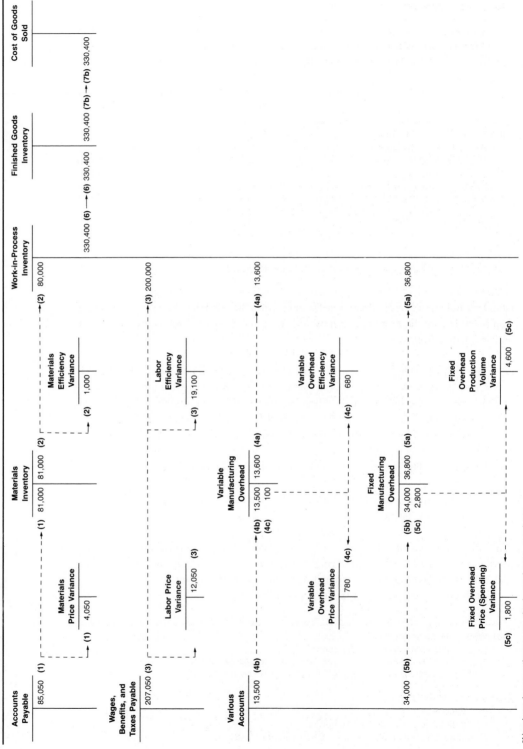

[a]Numbers in parentheses are the journal entry numbers.

(4c) Variable Manufacturing Overhead............................	100	
Variable Overhead Efficiency Variance	680	
Variable Overhead Price Variance		780
To record the variable overhead variances and to close the Variable Manufacturing Overhead account.		

The sequence of events necessitates recording the flow of variable manufacturing overhead costs in the three entries shown. However, if such sequencing is not important, only one entry would be necessary:

Work-in-Process Inventory at Standard............................	13,600	
Variable Overhead Efficiency Variance	680	
Various Accounts at Actual		13,500
Variable Overhead Price Variance		780

Fixed Manufacturing Overhead

Generally accepted accounting principles require accountants to treat fixed manufacturing overhead as a product cost. That is, financial reporting requires full absorption costing. In this book, we treat fixed costs as period costs for managerial decision making, planning, and performance evaluation; that is, we use variable costing. The accountant can design standard cost systems for either full absorption or variable costing. Standard costing systems using variable costing have no special procedures for fixed overhead because fixed overhead is simply expensed as a period expense.

Under full absorption costing, companies unitize fixed manufacturing overhead costs. Each unit produced receives a share of fixed manufacturing overhead.

For Victoria Corporation, we compute the fixed manufacturing overhead rate per machine hour as follows:

$$\text{Fixed Manufacturing Rate} = \frac{\text{Estimated Fixed Manufacturing Cost}}{\text{Estimated Production Volume}}$$

$$= \frac{\$32,200}{70,000 \text{ Units Planned} \times \frac{1}{40} \text{ Hour per Unit}}$$

$$= \frac{\$32,200}{1,750 \text{ Hours}}$$

$$= \$18.40 \text{ per Hour.}$$

We compute the amount charged to production (that is, debited to Work-in-Process Inventory) as follows:

$$\text{Amount Charged to Production} = \text{Fixed Manufacturing Rate} \times \text{Standard Hours Allowed to Produce the Actual Output}$$

$$= \$18.40 \times 2,000 \text{ Hours Allowed to Produce 80,000 Units}$$

$$= \$36,800.$$

Note that $36,800 also equals $.46 per unit times 80,000 units. We could have computed a rate of $.46 per unit, but we computed a rate per hour because that is how you are most likely to see rates computed in practice.

Production Volume Variance In Chapter 13, we showed that the fixed manufacturing price variance is the difference between the actual and budgeted cost. However, the budgeted cost is not the amount charged to production, unless the actual and estimated production volumes are equal. In short, the amount applied, or charged, to production does not equal the budget if the estimated and actual activity levels used in the denominator of the calculation differ.

The following diagram summarizes the relations among actual, budgeted, and applied fixed manufacturing costs for Victoria Corporation:

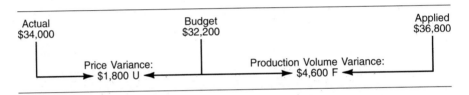

Journal Entries The method of charging fixed manufacturing standard overhead costs to production is similar to the one we used for variable manufacturing costs. For the preceding sequence of events, the three entries for Victoria Corporation follow:

(5a)	Work-in-Process Inventory	36,800	
	Fixed Manufacturing Overhead		36,800
	To charge production with standard fixed manufacturing overhead costs at $18.40 per unit times 2,000 hours.		
(5b)	Fixed Manufacturing Overhead	34,000	
	Various Accounts		34,000
	To record actual fixed manufacturing overhead costs incurred.		
(5c)	Fixed Manufacturing Overhead	2,800	
	Fixed Overhead Price Variance..........................	1,800	
	Fixed Overhead Production Volume Variance		4,600
	To record fixed manufacturing overhead variances and to close the Fixed Manufacturing Overhead account.		

Alternatively, the company could use just one entry:

Work-in-Process Inventory at Standard..........................	36,800	
Fixed Overhead Price Variance	1,800	
Various Accounts at Actual		34,000
Fixed Overhead Production Volume Variance		4,600

Note that both actual and applied fixed overhead show up in the accounts, but budgeted overhead does not.

Transfer Out of Production

The total standard cost per unit follows:

Direct Materials	$1.00
Direct Labor	2.50
Variable Manufacturing Overhead	.17
Fixed Manufacturing Overhead	.46
	$4.13

After manufacturing completes production, the accounting system transfers the standard cost of units completed to Finished Goods Inventory.

(6) Finished Goods Inventory	330,400	
Work-in-Process Inventory		330,400
To transfer 80,000 completed units from Work-in-Process to Finished Goods at a standard cost of $4.13 per unit.		

The following entries record the sale of 80,000 units (selling price = $6.10 per unit):

(7a) Accounts Receivable	488,000	
Sales		488,000
(7b) Cost of Goods Sold	330,400	
Finished Goods Inventory		330,400
To record the sale of 80,000 units at an actual selling price of $6.10 per unit and a standard cost of $4.13 per unit.		

(Entry (7a) is not shown on Exhibit 14.8.)

Closing the Variance Accounts

To complete the accounting cycle, the accountant closes variance accounts to Income Summary or some expense account as appears below:

Income Summary	9,200	
Labor Price Variance	12,050	
Fixed Overhead Production Volume Variance	4,600	
Variable Overhead Price Variance	780	
Materials Price Variance		4,050
Materials Efficiency Variance		1,000
Labor Efficiency Variance		19,100
Variable Overhead Efficiency Variance		680
Fixed Overhead Price Variance		1,800
The amount debited or credited to Income Summary is a plug.		

Debiting the income summary means that the net variance was unfavorable.

Prorating Variances If the accountant has prorated the variance inventories, the amount of the variances shown in the closing entry above would change, but the method of closing variance amounts to the Income Summary would not.

Summary

Exhibit 14.8 shows the complete flow of standard costs through T-accounts. (You should find it helpful to trace each entry in this appendix to the flow of costs in Exhibit 14.8.)

Solutions to Self-Study Problems

Suggested Solution to Problem 14.1 for Self-Study

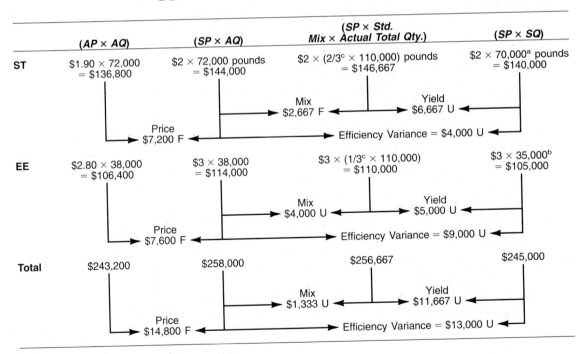

	Actual	Price Variance	Budget	Efficiency Variance	Budget	Production Volume Variance	Applied
Fixed Overhead	$83,000	$3,000 U	$80,000	Not Applicable	$80,000	$20,000 F	$100,000[a]

[a]Fixed overhead rate = $80,000/4,000 = $20 per standard labor hour. 5,000 standard labor hours allowed × $20 = $100,000.

Suggested Solution to Problem 14.2 for Self-Study

	(AP × AQ)	(SP × AQ)	(SP × Std. Mix × Actual Total Qty.)	(SP × SQ)
ST	$1.90 × 72,000 = $136,800	$2 × 72,000 pounds = $144,000	$2 × (2/3[c] × 110,000) pounds = $146,667	$2 × 70,000[a] pounds = $140,000
EE	$2.80 × 38,000 = $106,400	$3 × 38,000 = $114,000	$3 × (1/3[c] × 110,000) = $110,000	$3 × 35,000[b] = $105,000
Total	$243,200	$258,000	$256,667	$245,000

ST: Price $7,200 F; Mix $2,667 F; Yield $6,667 U; Efficiency Variance = $4,000 U

EE: Price $7,600 F; Mix $4,000 U; Yield $5,000 U; Efficiency Variance = $9,000 U

Total: Price $14,800 F; Mix $1,333 U; Yield $11,667 U; Efficiency Variance = $13,000 U

[a]70,000 Pounds = 7,000 Units × 10 Pounds per Unit.

[b]35,000 Pounds = 7,000 Units × 5 Pounds per Unit.

[c]Mix percentage ratio of ST pounds to total and EE pounds to total. For ST, $\frac{10}{10+5} = \frac{2}{3}$. For EE, $\frac{5}{10+5} = \frac{1}{3}$. 110,000 total = 72,000 ST plus 38,000 EE.

Suggested Solution to Problem 14.3 for Self-Study

Pep should figure out whether $P \times B > C$. In this case, $P = .40$, $B = \$50,000 - \$20,000 = \$30,000$, and $C = \$10,000$. We find that $.40 \times \$30,000 > \$10,000$, so Pep should investigate.

Key Terms and Concepts

Production volume variance for fixed
   manufacturing costs
Price (spending) variance for fixed
   manufacturing costs

Mix variance
Yield variance
Variance investigation

Questions, Exercises, Problems, and Cases

Questions

1. Review the meaning of the concepts or terms given above in Key Terms and Concepts.
2. Refer to the Managerial Application "Quality Management and the Baldrige Award." What purpose do you think is served by providing an award limited to only a few companies each year?
3. A firm incurred fixed manufacturing overhead costs of $500,000 for the year. Fixed overhead applied to units produced during the year totaled $600,000. What are some of the reasons for this difference?
4. Why shouldn't management investigate all unfavorable variances?
5. Describe the basic decision that management must make when considering whether to investigate a variance.
6. "The larger the variance, the more likely management is to investigate it." Comment on the rationale for this statement.
7. "Favorable variances should not be investigated." True? Comment.
8. Under what conditions would statistically based quality control charts be useful in responsibility reporting?
9. How could a CPA firm use mix variances to evaluate performance?
10. Why are there no efficiency variances for fixed manufacturing costs?

Exercises

Solutions to even-numbered exercises are at the end of the chapter on page 583.

11. **Overhead variances.** The following facts refer to Mario's Bakery, Inc.:

Actual Fixed Manufacturing Costs	$3,750
Budgeted Fixed Manufacturing Costs	$3,420
Budgeted Labor Hours for 6,000 Pies Planned....................	3,000 Hours
Actual Labor Hours Worked......................................	3,200 Hours
Standard Hours Allowed for Actual Production Output of 7,000 Pies	3,500 Hours

Compute the following amounts:

a. Applied fixed overhead using full absorption, standard costing.

b. Fixed overhead production volume variance.

c. Fixed overhead price variance.

12. **Overhead variances.** Information on Omaha Company's fixed overhead costs follows:

Overhead Applied	$80,000
Actual Overhead	86,000
Flexible Budget Overhead	83,000

a. What is the total amount of the over- or underapplied overhead, assuming that full absorption costing was used?

b. What are the price and production volume variances?

13. **Overhead variances.** Birkett's Brewery Corporation estimated its overhead costs for Year 0 to be as follows: fixed, $450,000; variable, $7 per unit. Birkett expected to produce 100,000 units during the year.

a. Compute the rate to be used to apply overhead costs to products.

b. During Year 0, Birkett incurred overhead costs of $950,000 and produced 90,000 units. Compute overhead costs applied to units produced.

c. Refer to part b. Compute the amount of under- or overapplied overhead for the year.

14. **Overhead variances.** Wyman Company uses a predetermined rate for applying overhead costs to production. The rates for Year 0 follow: variable, $2 per unit; fixed, $1 per unit. Actual overhead costs incurred follow: variable, $95,000; fixed, $45,000. Wyman expected to produce 45,000 units during the year but produced only 40,000 units.

a. What was the amount of budgeted fixed overhead costs for the year?

b. What was the total under- or overapplied overhead for the year?

c. Compute all possible fixed overhead variances.

15. **Graphing overhead variances.** Refer to the data in Exercise 14. Graph the actual, budget, and applied fixed overhead costs like the graph in Exhibit 14.2.

16. **Hospital supply variances.** Refer to Problem 25 in Chapter 13. Compute mix and yield variances for the surgical supplies.

17. **Labor variances.** Refer to Problem 26 in Chapter 13. Compute mix and yield variances for the labor costs.

18. **Variance investigation.** Manhatten Company's production manager is considering whether or not to investigate a computer-integrated manufacturing process. The investigation costs $7,000. If the manager finds that the process is out of control, correcting it costs $20,000. If the process is out of control and is corrected, the company saves $45,000 until the next scheduled investigation.

The probability of the process being in control is .65, and the probability of the process being out of control is .35, given recent variance reports.

Should management investigate the process? Why or why not?

19. **Variance investigation.** The accounting system has reported a large unfavorable variance for Vu Company's food process. Conducting an investigation costs $2,500. If the process is actually out of control, the benefit of correction will be $11,000. The probability is .22 that the large negative variance indicates the process is out of control.

Should management investigate the process?

20. **Recording overhead costs** (Appendix 14.1; adapted from CPA exam). Union Company uses a standard cost accounting system. The following overhead costs and production data are available for August:

Standard Fixed Overhead Rate per Direct Labor Hour	$1
Standard Variable Overhead Rate per Direct Labor Hour	$4
Budgeted Monthly Direct Labor Hours	40,000
Actual Direct Labor Hours Worked.	39,500
Standard Direct Labor Hours Allowed for Actual Production	39,000
Variable Overhead Efficiency Variance, Unfavorable	$2,000
Actual Variable Overhead	$159,500
Actual Fixed Overhead	$33,500
Fixed Overhead Price Variance, Favorable	$6,500

Show the flow of these overhead costs in T-account form.

21. **Recording overhead costs** (Appendix 14.1; adapted from CMA exam). Standard Company has developed standard overhead costs based on a capacity of 190,000 direct labor hours as appears below:

Standard Costs per Unit:	
Variable Portion: 2 Hours at $3	$ 6
Fixed Portion: 2 Hours at $5	10
	$16

During May, the company scheduled 95,000 units for production, but produced only 90,000 units. The following data relate to April:

(1) Actual direct labor cost incurred was $683,000 for 175,000 actual hours of work.

(2) Actual overhead incurred totaled $1,495,000—$575,000 variable and $920,000 fixed.

(3) All inventories are carried at standard cost.

Use T-accounts to show the recording of these overhead costs in Work-in-Process Inventory together with the related variances.

Problems

22. **Comprehensive variance computations.** The following information will assist you in evaluating the performance of the manufacturing operations of the Dartmouth Company:

Units Produced (actual)	21,000
Estimated Units Produced	20,000
Budgeted Fixed Overhead	$80,000
Standard Costs per Unit:	
Direct Materials	$1.65 × 5 Pounds per Unit of Output
Direct Labor	$14 per Hour × ½ Hour per Unit
Variable Overhead	$11.90 per Direct Labor Hour
Actual Costs:	
Direct Materials Purchased and Used	$188,700 (102,000 Pounds)
Direct Labor	$140,000 (10,700 Hours)
Overhead	$204,000 (61% Is Variable)

The company applies variable overhead on the basis of direct labor hours.

Prepare a cost variance analysis to show all variable manufacturing cost price and efficiency variances and fixed manufacturing cost price and production volume variances.

23. **Standard cost flows** (Appendix 14.1). Refer to Problem 22. Prepare journal entries for the transactions and show cost flows through T-accounts, assuming full absorption, standard costing is used.

24. **Comprehensive variance computations.** Lawrence Lawncare fertilizes and applies weed killer to lawns. The company prepared its budgets on the basis of standard costs. Accountants prepare a responsibility report monthly showing the differences between flexible budget and actual. The report analyzes variances separately. The accountants compute materials price variances at the time of purchase.

The following information relates to the current period.

Standard Costs (per average lawn):		
Direct Material (fertilizer and weed killer), 1 kilogram		
@ $1 per kilogram		$ 1
Direct Labor, 2 hours @ $4 per hour		8
Overhead:		
Variable (25% of direct labor cost)		2
Fixed (master budget, 3,600 labor hours)		_1_
Total Standard Cost per Average Lawn Serviced		$12
Actual Costs for the Month:		
Materials Purchased	3,000 Kilograms at $.90 per Kilogram	
Output	1,900 Lawns Serviced Using 2,100 Kilograms of Material	
Actual Labor Costs	3,200 Hours at $5 per Hour	
Actual Overhead:		
Variable	$4,500	
Fixed	1,800	

Prepare a cost variance analysis showing price, efficiency, and fixed overhead production volume variances.

25. **Standard cost flows** (Appendix 14.1). Refer to Problem 24. Prepare journal entries for the transactions and show cost flows through T-accounts, assuming full absorption, standard costing. Use a Work in Process account and a Cost of Services Sold account (assuming all work done has been sold).

26. Prorating variances (adapted from CMA exam). Nashville Company uses a standard cost system for all its products. Nashville carries all inventories at standard cost during the year. The firm adjusts the inventories and cost of goods sold for all variances at the end of the fiscal year for external financial reporting purposes. The accounting system uses a FIFO cost flow assumption for all products moving through the manufacturing process to finished goods and ultimate sale.

The standard cost of one of Nashville's products manufactured in the Dixon Plant, unchanged from the previous year, follows:

Direct Materials	$2
Direct Labor (.5 direct labor hour at $8)	4
Manufacturing Overhead	3
Total Standard Cost	$9

This product has no work-in-process inventory.

The following schedule reports the manufacturing activity and cost of goods sold measured at standard cost for the current fiscal year.

	Units	Dollars
Product Manufactured.....................................	95,000	$855,000
Beginning Finished Goods Inventory (produced last year) ..	15,000	135,000
Goods Available for Sale	110,000	$990,000
Ending Finished Goods Inventory	19,000	171,000
Cost of Goods Sold......................................	91,000	$819,000

The manufacturing performance relative to standard costs was not good, both this year and last year. The balance of the finished goods inventory, $140,800, reported on the balance sheet at the beginning of the year included a $5,800 adjustment for variances from standard cost. The unfavorable standard cost variances for labor for the current fiscal year consisted of a wage rate variance of $32,000 and a labor efficiency variance of $20,000 (2,500 hours at $8). No other variances from standard cost occurred in the company for this year.

Adjust the inventories and cost of goods sold to reflect the actual costs of this year's production.

Integrative Cases

27. Cost and profit analysis; reconciling with full absorption costing. "I just don't understand these financial statements at all!" exclaimed Mr. Elmo Knapp. Mr. Knapp explained that he had turned over management of Racketeer, Inc., division of American Recreation Equipment, Inc., to his son, Otto, the previous month. Racketeer, Inc., manufactures tennis rackets.

"I was really proud of Otto," he beamed. "He was showing us all the tricks he learned in business school and, if I say so myself, I think he was doing a rather good job for us. For example, he put together this budget for Racketeer, which makes it real easy to see how much profit we'll make at any sales volume (Exhibit 14.9). As best as I can figure it, in March we expected to have a volume of 8,000 units and a profit of $14,500 on our rackets. But we did much better than that! We sold 10,000 rackets, so we should have made almost $21,000 on them."

"Another one of Otto's innovations is this standard cost system," said Mr. Knapp proudly. "He sat down with our production people and came up with a standard production cost per unit (see Exhibit 14.10). He tells me this will tell us how well our production people are performing. Also, he claims it will cut down on our clerical work."

Mr. Knapp continued, "But one thing puzzles me. My calculations show that we should have shown a profit of nearly $21,000 in March. However, our

Exhibit 14.9

RACKETEER, INC.
Profit Graph, Rackets

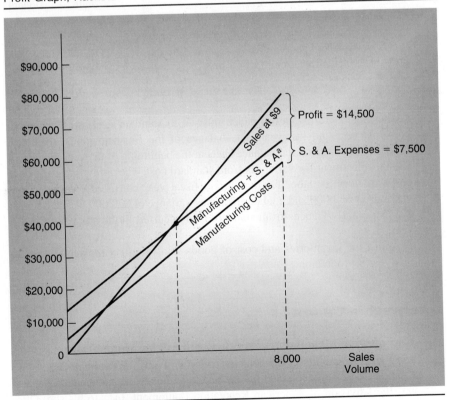

aSelling and administrative expenses.

Exhibit 14.10

RACKETEER, INC.
Standard Costs[a]

	Per Racket
Raw Material:	
Frame (one frame per racket).....................................	$3.15
Stringing Materials: 20 Feet at $.03 per Foot	.60
Direct Labor:	
Skilled ⅛ Hour at $9.60 per Hour	1.20
Unskilled ⅛ Hour at $5.60 per Hour	.70
Plant Overhead:	
Indirect Labor	.10
Power..	.03
Supervision	.12[b]
Depreciation	.20[b]
Other..	.15[b]
Total Standard Cost per Racket	$6.25

[a]Standard costs are calculated for an estimated volume of 8,000 rackets each month.
[b]Fixed costs.

accountants came up with less than $19,000 in the monthly income statement (Exhibit 14.11). This discrepancy bothers me a great deal. Now I'm not sure our accountants are doing their job properly. It appears to me that they're about $2,200 short.''

"As you can probably guess," Mr. Knapp concluded, "we are one big happy family around here. I just wish I knew what those accountants are up to—coming in with a low net income like that.''

Exhibit 14.11

RACKETEER, INC.
Income Statement for March
Actual

Sales: 10,000 Rackets at $9	$90,000
Standard Cost of Goods Sold: 10,000 Rackets at $6.25	62,500
Gross Profit after Standard Costs	$27,500
Variances for the 7,000 rackets produced in March:	
Materials Variance	(490)
Labor Variance	(392)
Overhead Variance	(660)
Gross Profit...	$25,958
Selling and Administrative Expense.................................	7,200
Operating Profit	$18,758

Exhibit 14.12

RACKETEER, INC.
Actual Production Data for March

Production	7,000 Rackets
Costs of Production:	
Direct Materials Purchased and Used:	
Stringing Materials	175,000 Feet at $.025 per Foot
Frames	7,100 at $3.15 per Frame
Labor:	
Skilled ($9.80 per hour)	900 Hours
Unskilled ($8.50 per hour)	840 Hours
Overhead:	
Indirect Labor	$800
Power	$250
Depreciation	$1,600
Supervision	$960
Other....................................	$1.250

Prepare a report for Mr. Elmo Knapp and Mr. Otto Knapp that reconciles the profit graph with the actual results for March. Show the source of each variance from the original plan (8,000 rackets) in as much detail as you can, and evaluate Racketeer's performance in March. (Actual production data for March appear in Exhibit 14.12.) Recommend improvements in Racketeer's profit planning and control methods.

28. **Standard cost flows** (Appendix 14.1). Refer to Problem 27. Present the flow of costs through T-accounts.

29. **Cost and profit variance analysis, variable costing.** The following data are for Tondamakers, which makes Tonda turbo-charged riding lawnmowers. The company has no inventories of any kind at the beginning of Year 2.

Year 2
Tondamakers produced 1,500 Tondas and sold 1,200 Tondas. Actual costs of production follow:

Direct Materials: 14,000 Pounds at $21	$ 294,000
Direct Labor: 3,000 Hours at $29.................................	87,000
Manufacturing Overhead	270,000
Actual Marketing and Administrative Costs	440,000
Total Revenue: 1,200 Tondas at $980	1,176,000
Actual Machine Hours Worked	700 Hours

Year 3
Tondamakers produced 1,200 Tondas and sold 1,500 Tondas. Actual costs of production follow:

Direct Materials: 11,000 Pounds at $22	$ 242,000
Direct Labor: 2,300 Hours at $31.................................	71,300
Manufacturing Overhead	261,000
Actual Marketing and Administrative Costs	460,000
Total Revenue: 1,500 Tondas at $1,050...........................	1,575,000
Actual Machine Hours Worked	600 Hours

Additional information follows.

(1) Here is the division of actual overhead and marketing and administrative costs into variable and fixed components:

	Year 2	Year 3
Overhead:		
Fixed..	$190,000	$195,000
Variable	80,000	66,000
Total	$270,000	$261,000
Marketing and Administrative:		
Fixed..	$360,000	$360,000
Variable	80,000	100,000
Total	$440,000	$460,000

(2) Predetermined overhead rates for machine hours (assume an estimated .5 machine hour per Tonda): Estimated overhead = $200,000 + $80 per hour. Machine hours are used to apply overhead to products. Estimated machine hours were 625 hours per year.

(3) Standard costs per Tonda:

Materials	$200 (= 10 Pounds at $20 per Pound)
Labor	60 (= 2 Hours at $30 per Hour)
Variable Overhead	40
	$300
Fixed Overhead	160 (= $200,000/625 Hours × .5 Hours per Tonda)
	$460

(4) Budgeted sales were 1,300 Tondas each year at $1,000 budgeted price per Tonda.

(5) Tondamakers expenses all production variances in the period of production. Thus, the production variances for the 1,500 Tondas made in Year 2 are expensed in Year 2, even though some of those Tondas were not sold until Year 3.

(6) Budgeted marketing and administrative cost was $350,000 + $50 per Tonda.

(7) Tonda has no beginning or ending materials inventories.

Prepare a profit variance analysis and cost variance analysis. (Do not present the fixed cost production volume variance.)

30. **Reconciling profit variance analysis with full absorption costing.** Reconcile the amounts achieved for Tondamakers (see Problem 29) with the amounts that would be achieved using full absorption costing.

31. **Cost and profit variance analysis; reconciling with full absorption costing.** John Holden, president and general manager of Solartronics, Inc., was confused. Lisa Blocker, the firm's recently hired controller and financial manager, had recently instituted the preparation of a new, summarized income statement. Ms. Blocker was to issue this statement on a monthly basis. Mr. Holden had just received a copy of the statement for January, Year 7 (see Exhibit 14.13).

Exhibit 14.13

SOLARTRONICS, INC.
Income Statement
January, Year 7

Sales....................................			$130,000[a]
Less Cost of Goods Sold (at standard) ..			82,500[a]
Gross Margin			$ 47,500
Less: Selling Expenses ($13,500 fixed) ..		$26,500	
General Corporate Administrative (all fixed)		18,000	
Operating Variances:			
Direct Labor	$ 3,500 U		
Direct Materials	500 F		
Variable Factory Overhead	1,500 U		
Fixed Factory Overhead— Spending	2,000 F		
Fixed Factory Overhead— Volume	17,500 U	20,000 U	64,500
Profit (loss) before Tax			$ (17,000)

[a]Production and sales volume are equal.

Solartronics, Inc., a small, Texas-based manufacturer of solar energy panels, had been in business since Year 2. By the end of Year 6, it had survived some bad years and positioned itself as a reasonably large firm within the industry. As part of a conscious effort to professionalize the firm, Mr. Holden had added Ms. Blocker to the staff in the autumn of Year 6. Previous to that time, Solartronics had employed a full-time, full-charge bookkeeper.

Mr. Holden's confusion arose because he had not expected the firm to report a loss for January. Although he knew that sales had been down, primarily

---

Exhibit 14.14

SOLARTRONICS, INC.
Budgeted Income Statement
Calendar Year, Year 7

Sales...		$3,000,000[a]
Less Cost of Goods Sold (at standard)		1,980,000[b]
Gross Margin		$1,020,000
Less: Selling Expenses	$420,000[c]	
General Corporate Administrative (all fixed)	240,000	660,000
Profit before Tax		$ 360,000

[a]Sales and production volume are budgeted to be equal. Inventories are budgeted to be zero.

[b]The standard cost of goods sold consisted of $420,000 direct labor, $780,000 direct materials, $360,000 variable factory overhead, and $420,000 fixed factory overhead. Ms. Blocker treated direct labor and direct materials as variable costs.

[c]Of this amount, $120,000 was considered to be fixed. The remaining $300,000 represented the 10-percent commission paid on sales.

because of the normal seasonal downturn, and that production had been scaled back to maintain zero levels of inventory, he was still surprised. He wondered if the first month's results were a bad omen in terms of meeting the budgeted results for the year. (See Exhibit 14.14.) Even though the current year's budget represented only a 10-percent increase in sales volume over the previous year, Mr. Holden was concerned that such a poor start to the year might make it difficult to get "back on stream."

Prepare a complete analysis of Solartronics' actual performance compared to budgeted performance. Compute variances in as much detail as possible, using both profit variance and cost variance analyses. In addition, Mr. Holden (a "one-minute manager") would like an explanation for the key factor leading to the loss in 50 words or less. What is it?

Suggested Solutions to Even-Numbered Exercises

12. **Overhead variances.**

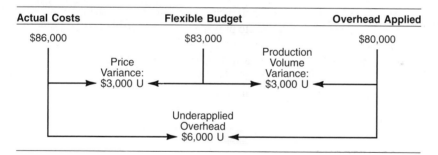

14. **Overhead variances.**

  a. Budgeted Fixed Costs = $1.00 per Unit × 45,000 Units
        = $45,000.

  b. Applied Overhead = ($1.00 × 40,000) + ($2.00 × 40,000)
        = $120,000.
    $140,000 − $120,000 = $20,000 Underapplied.

  c. Fixed overhead variance analysis:

Actual	Price Variance	Budget	Production Volume Variance	Applied
$45,000		$45,000		40,000
	→ 0 ←		→ $5,000 U ←	

16. **Hospital supply variances.** Review price and efficiency variances as given below.

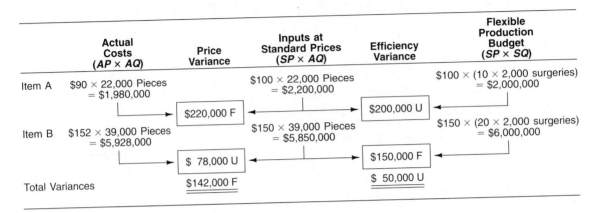

Now extend the analysis to compute mix and yield variances.

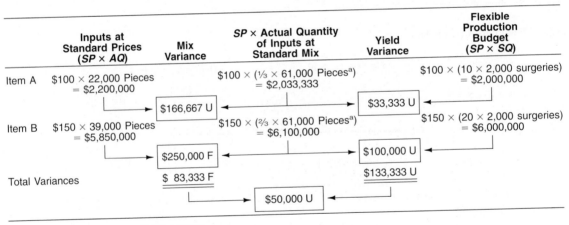

[a]61,000 = Total Pieces Used = 22,000 + 39,000.

18. **Variance investigation.** Is $P \times B > C$? $P = .35$, $B = (\$45,000 - \$20,000)$, and $C = \$7,000$. We find that $.35 \times (\$45,000 - \$20,000) = .35 \times \$25,000 = \$8,750$. $\$8,750 > \$7,000$; therefore, investigate.

20. **Recording overhead costs** (Appendix 14.1).

Variable Overhead		Variable Overhead Price Variance		Variable Overhead Efficiency Variance		Work-in-Process	
159,500	156,000[a]	1,500[d]		2,000[b]		156,000	
	3,500						

Fixed Overhead		Fixed Overhead Price Variance		Fixed Overhead Production Variance			
33,500	39,000[f]		6,500[e]	1,000[c]		39,000	
5,500							

[a]39,000 Direct Labor Hours at $4.00 = $156,000.
[b]Given.
[c](40,000 × $1) − (39,000 × $1) = $1,000.
[d]159,500 − (39,500 × $4) = $1,500.
[e]Given.
[f]39,000 Direct Labor Hours at $1.00 = $39,000.

Chapter 15

Divisional Performance Measures and Incentives

1. Understand the role of accounting in measuring performance and providing incentives in decentralized organizations.
2. Know how to interpret and use return on investment (ROI) as a performance measure.
3. Know the transfer pricing rule.
4. Understand behavioral issues and incentive effects of cost-based, market price-based, and negotiated transfer prices.
5. See the economic consequences of multinational transfer prices.
6. Understand incentive issues in allocating costs to divisions when measuring divisional performance.
7. Understand alternative ways to measure the investment base.
8. Interpret the contribution approach to divisional reporting.
9. Compare ROI to residual income as performance measures.

Companies like Coca-Cola, McDonald's, and IBM have multiple divisions. Central corporate management sets broad corporate policies, establishes long-range plans, raises capital, and conducts other coordinating activities. But corporate management must oversee hundreds of corporate affiliates and divisions. How do companies like these measure and control the performance of their divisions in such widely diverse and geographically dispersed operating environments?

Such firms rely heavily on their accounting systems to measure performance and to help control and coordinate their activities. This chapter discusses concepts and methods of measuring performance and controlling activities in multidivision companies. These concepts and methods are used extensively in both manufacturing and nonmanufacturing organizations.

Divisional Organization and Performance

The term *division* means different things in different companies. Some companies use the term when referring to segments organized according to product groupings, whereas other companies use it when referring to geographic areas served. We use the term **division** to refer to a segment that conducts both production and marketing activities.

A division may be either a **profit center,** responsible for both revenues and operating costs, or an **investment center,** responsible for assets in addition to revenues and operating costs. Many companies treat the division almost as an autonomous company. Headquarters provides funds for its divisions, much as shareholders and bondholders provide funds for the company.

A partial organization chart for Honeywell, Incorporated, appears in Exhibit 15.1. This chart shows how the company's divisions fit into the entire organization. The organization chart in Exhibit 15.1 presents only a small part of this complex organization. Corporate executives hold managers of divisions responsible for revenues, costs, and assets invested in the divisions and groups. Corporate management holds

Exhibit 15.1

HONEYWELL, INCORPORATED
Partial Organization Chart

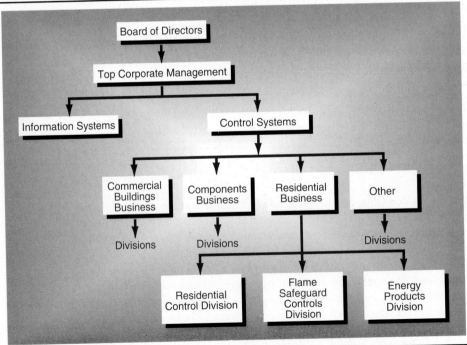

Source: Honeywell annual report.

most operating units below the division level responsible for either revenues or costs alone.

The Nature of Divisionalized Organizations

Top managers delegate or **decentralize** authority and responsibility. The major advantages of decentralization follow:

1. Decentralization allows local personnel to respond quickly to a changing environment.
2. Decentralization frees top management from detailed operating decisions.
3. Decentralization divides large, complex problems into manageable pieces.
4. Decentralization helps train managers and provides a basis for evaluating their decision-making performance.
5. Decentralization motivates: Ambitious managers will be frustrated if they implement only the decisions of others. Delegation allows managers to make their own decisions.

Decentralization has disadvantages, however. Local managers may not act to achieve the overall goals of the organization. For example, a division manager may decide to purchase materials from an outside supplier even though another division of the firm could produce the materials at a lower incremental cost using currently idle facilities. Top management must be alert to situations where the benefits of decentralized authority and the possible conflicts between the goals of a division and those of the organization as a whole require trade-offs. Thus, divisional planning and control systems attempt to create **behavioral congruence** (or **goal congruence**) to encourage division managers to act in ways consistent with organizational goals.[1]

Separating a Manager's Performance from Divisional Performance

In general, managers should distinguish between the measure of an organizational unit's performance and that of the unit manager's performance. Managers often perform well despite the division's poor performance because of factors outside the manager's control.

Consider the following interdivisional conflict. Assume a division purchased materials externally rather than from a division inside the company with idle capacity. By purchasing from an outside source, the company earned lower combined profits from the two divisions than if it purchased the materials from the division inside the company. Should the performance measure for each division reflect the results of its actual transactions? Or should the cost of idle capacity in the one division be

---

[1] For an expanded discussion of these points, see the classic book by David Solomons, *Divisional Performance Measurement and Control* (Homewood, Ill.: Irwin, 1968), or the book by Ken Merchant, *Reward Results: Motivating Profit Center Managers* (Boston, Mass.: Harvard Business School Press, 1989).

charged against the profits of the other division? These questions are not easy to answer. The accounting system needs to inform top management of situations in which actions of individual divisions hurt overall company performance.

Return on Investment as the Performance Measure

Because management expects each division to contribute to the company's profits, managers commonly use divisional operating profit to measure performance. Divisional operating profit by itself, however, does not provide a basis for measuring a division's performance in generating a return on the funds invested in the division. For example, the fact that Division A reported an operating profit of $50,000 does not necessarily mean that it was more successful than Division B, which had an operating profit of $40,000. The difference between these profit levels could be entirely attributable to a difference in the size of the divisions. Management must therefore use some means to relate the division profit measure to the amount of capital invested in the division. Management commonly achieves a comparable statistic by measuring the **division return on investment,** or **ROI,** calculated as follows:

$$\text{Division Return on Investment (ROI)} = \frac{\text{Division Operating Profit}}{\text{Division Investment}}$$
$$= \frac{\text{Division Revenue} - \text{Division Operating Costs}}{\text{Division Investment}}.$$

In the preceding example if management invested $500,000 and $250,000 in Division A and Division B respectively, the ROIs would be 10 percent (= $50,000/ $500,000) and 16 percent (= $40,000/$250,000). Thus Division B earned a higher profit given its investment base than Division A, even though Division A generated a larger absolute amount of profit.

The manager must answer several important questions before applying ROI as a control measure:

1. How does the firm measure revenues, particularly when it transfers part of a division's output to another division rather than selling it externally?
2. Which costs does the firm deduct in measuring divisional operating costs— only those that the division can control, or also a portion of allocated central corporate administration and staff costs?
3. How does the firm measure investment—total assets or net assets, at historical cost or some measure of current cost?

We consider these questions in the following sections.

Transfer Pricing: Measuring Division Revenue

In cases where, because of the nature of the product, a division cannot sell its output to another division and therefore sells all of the output externally, few unique revenue measurement problems will occur beyond those encountered in financial accounting. In other words, accounting policy will address the question whether the firm will recognize revenue (1) as production takes place, (2) at the point of sale, or (3) as it collects cash. It may be of interest to top management to have all divisions follow the same accounting methods, thereby enhancing the comparability of the measures of ROI.

In cases where one division can potentially sell its output to another division, we confront the **transfer pricing problem.** The transfer price accounting assigns to the interdivisional transfer of goods or services represents a revenue for the selling division and a cost to the buying division.[2] Should management set the transfer price equal to the manufacturing cost of the selling division? Or should the transfer price equal the amount at which the selling (buying) division could sell (purchase) the good or service externally? Or should the transfer price equal a negotiated amount somewhere between the selling division's cost of manufacturing and the external market price?

A superficial consideration of the transfer pricing problem may suggest that the selection of a transfer price is inconsequential. After all, what comes out of one corporate pocket goes into another. This simplistic viewpoint ignores the fact that the amount of the transfer price may affect certain divisional decisions, which in turn may affect the overall profitability of the company. For example, suppose that management sets a transfer price at $10 per unit and the product has no external market. If the buying division believes this price is too high, it may take less than it would at a lower price. In this case the buying division may be acting in its own best interests, but the actions of the two divisions together may not optimize the company's interests.

The simplistic view of the transfer pricing problem also ignores the real possibility that a transfer price that corporate headquarters sets arbitrarily may undermine the entire divisional organizational structure. Division managers should, within limits, make decisions freely, as if the divisions were separate companies. If top management imposes a transfer price that determines the return, or profit, from a significant portion of the division's operations, divisional managers will lose some motivational and other benefits of decentralized decision making. The selection of an appropriate transfer price can therefore affect decision making significantly.

We discuss several solutions to the transfer pricing problem in the following sections.

---

[2]Only rarely will cash equal to the transfer price actually change hands. Transfer prices are set at the time of the transfer, so performance of the selling division can be assessed as of the time of the transfer rather than waiting several periods until all manufacturing is completed and the good is sold to someone outside the company.

Direct Intervention

Top management could intervene directly and order a supplying division of the company to produce and transfer products to a buying division. Top management would specify a transfer price that would be incidental to the transaction. In other words, the transfer price would not bear on the decision; rather, management would set it *after* the transaction. For an extraordinarily large order or rare internal product transfers, direct intervention could be the optimal solution because it would virtually ensure that division managers take the "right" actions.

However, when this type of transaction occurs often, direct intervention reduces the value of decentralization.[3] Further, direct intervention uses top management's time that may be better spent elsewhere. To avoid using management's time, the company may set up a transfer pricing *policy* encouraging decentralized managers to make the right decisions without reducing their autonomy.

Management-Established Transfer Pricing Policy

Rather than intervene directly and force a transaction, top management may establish rules for setting transfer prices that encourage division managers to optimize company goals. If division managers establish the transfer price incorrectly, they will not make decisions that are in the best interest of the company. We will discuss some bases for setting these transfer prices. In each case, we assume that one division of the company—the selling division—produces a product that another division of the company—the buying division—could purchase.

Market Prices as Transfer Prices   *Market price* refers to a price in an intermediate market, not the price for the end product the buying division produces. When the transferred product has a competitive external market, market prices work well as transfer prices.[4] Both the selling and buying divisions can sell and buy as much as they want at the market price. Managers of both selling and buying divisions will trade with each other or with outsiders. From a company-wide perspective, using market prices optimizes profits as long as the selling division operates at capacity. Use of a market price also helps ensure profit independence of the divisions. Any gains or losses in the selling division's efficiency do not get passed on to the buying division. Use of competitive market prices also frees managers from arguing over price, thereby saving administrative costs.

A major problem with using market prices can occur when a selling division operates below capacity, as the following example demonstrates.

---

[3]For an expanded discussion, see Joshua Ronen and George McKinney, "Transfer Pricing for Divisional Autonomy," *Journal of Accounting Research* (Spring 1970).

[4]You can find classic work on the economic theory of transfer pricing in Jack Hirschleifer, "On the Economics of Transfer Pricing," *Journal of Business* (July 1956), pp. 172–184. Also see Jack Hirschleifer, "Economics of the Divisionalized Firm," *Journal of Business* (April 1957), pp. 96–108 and David Solomons, *Divisional Performance: Measurement and Control* (Homewood, Ill.: Irwin, 1965), appendix A to chap. 6.

Example The Systems Division of Magna-Products, Incorporated, builds a navigational system that is standard equipment in many commercial and military airplanes. This division—the *selling* division—can make 300 systems per year. Its variable cost per system is $1 million. (Assume differential costs equal variable costs in this example.) The Aircraft Division of Magna-Products, Incorporated—the *buying* division—builds airplanes and uses the selling division's navigational system in those airplanes. The Systems (selling) Division can sell to outside airplane manufacturers, and the Aircraft (buying) Division can buy the system from outside suppliers.

The market for airplanes has temporarily declined so that the Systems Division can sell only 100 systems per year to outside buyers at a price of $2.5 million per system. The Aircraft (buying) Division of Magna-Products could use 50 systems per year in the airplane models it builds. The Aircraft Division also operates below capacity.

If the market price of $2.5 million per navigational system is the transfer price, the Aircraft (buying) Division treats the cost of the system as $2.5 million. Assume that the *other* variable costs of making an airplane are $16 million. From the Aircraft Division's perspective, its variable costs per airplane equal $18.5 million (= $16 million + $2.5 million price paid to the Systems Division). Suppose British Airways has offered to purchase six airplanes for a price of $18 million each.

Given the soft market for airplanes, Magna-Products' company policy is to sell airplanes for any price greater than variable cost. Thus the company serves its best interests if the Aircraft Division sells the airplanes, because the price of $18 million exceeds the variable cost to the company of $17 million (= $16 million + $1 million). The Aircraft Division turns down the order, however, because *its* variable costs are $18.5 million. Clearly, the $2.5 million is not the correct transfer price. Exhibit 15.2 summarizes this analysis.

Exhibit 15.2

Comparison of Total Company Perspective with Buying and Selling Divisions' Perspectives[a]

	Magna-Products: Company Perspective	Aircraft Division: Buying Division Perspective	Systems Division: Selling Division Perspective
Price per Airplane	$18,000,000	$18,000,000	—
Differential (Variable) Cost of Navigational System	(1,000,000)	—	$(1,000,000)
Transfer Price	—	(2,500,000)	2,500,000
Differential (Variable) Cost of Remainder of Airplane	(16,000,000)	(16,000,000)	—
Profit (Loss)	$ 1,000,000	$ (500,000)	$ 1,500,000
Decision	Although the company would make a profit of $1 million per airplane, the buying (Aircraft) division rejects the order because it incurs a loss.		

[a]Costs are in parentheses. The buying division makes airplanes; the selling division makes navigational systems.

Discussion When products transferred between divisions have a competitive market and when the selling division operates at capacity, **market-based transfer prices** are ideal. Division managers who make decisions in response to such transfer prices to maximize division profits also maximize company-wide profits.

Competitive markets for a product being transferred between divisions rarely exist, however. The fact that two responsibility centers belong to one company indicates that they gain some advantages as opposed to dealing with each other as two separate companies in the market. For example, they have more certainty about the internal supplier's product quality or delivery reliability. Or the selling division may make a specialized product with no substitutes in the market. Hence, using market prices may be impossible.

Use of Full Costs and Standard Costs

Measurement Problems When market prices are the appropriate transfer prices and management has information about them readily available, implementing a transfer price policy is not costly. But measurement problems, and costs of implementing a transfer pricing policy, can be substantial when market prices are unknown. Measuring differential costs is often difficult, and measuring implicit opportunity costs may be impossible. Consequently, many companies transfer at full cost, or full cost plus a markup, examples of **cost-based transfer prices.**

Use of Standard Costs Whether transferring at differential cost or full cost, firms often use standard costs (where available) as the basis for the transfer. This practice encourages efficiency in the selling division because they do not pass on inefficiencies or transfer variances to the buying division. Use of standard costs reduces risk to the buyer, because the buyer knows that the seller will transfer at standard costs and the buyer avoids being charged with the supplier's cost overruns.

A General Rule for Transfer Pricing: Differential Cost Plus Opportunity Cost

To set transfer prices so that the buying division makes the optimal economic decisions from the viewpoint of the total company, management follows the general rule of transferring at[5]

$$\text{Differential Cost to the Selling Division} + \text{Implicit Opportunity Cost to Company If It Transfers Goods Internally.}$$

---

[5]Accountants sometimes use *marginal cost, outlay cost,* or *variable cost* instead of differential cost. We use *differential cost* to be consistent with our terminology throughout this book.

Economists will sometimes refer to the general rule as "transfer at marginal opportunity cost." We find it useful to distinguish between the differential cost, which can usually be derived from the accounting records, and implicit opportunity cost, which requires an "off-the-books" calculation.

In the Magna-Products example, the differential cost to the selling division (that is, the Systems Division) was $1 million per unit. What was the implicit opportunity cost to the company if the Systems Division made the systems and transferred them to the buyer (that is, the Aircraft Division)? Recall that both the Systems and Aircraft divisions were operating below capacity. *If the company has no alternative uses for the idle capacity, the implicit opportunity cost to the company is zero.* Thus the transfer price should have been $1 million, and the Aircraft Division's costs would have been the total differential costs of producing an airplane—$17 million.

Selling Division Operates at Capacity If the Systems Division had been operating at capacity, then transferring internally would have created an implicit opportunity cost. The Systems Division would have forgone a sale of a system in the intermediate market to make the internal transfer. The implicit opportunity cost to the company is the lost contribution margin (for example, $2.5 million − $1.0 million = $1.5 million) from not selling the system in the intermediate market.

Thus, if the selling division had sufficient sales in the intermediate market to force it to forgo those sales to transfer internally, the transfer price should have been as follows:

Differential Cost to the Selling Division	+	Implicit Opportunity Cost to Company If Goods Are Transferred Internally
= $1,000,000	+	$1,500,000 lost contribution margin on outside sales
= $2,500,000.		

(Note that this rule is the same as the market price-based transfer price *when the selling division operates at capacity.*)

If the selling division had been operating at capacity, then the buying division would have appropriately treated the $2.5 million as part of *its* differential cost of making and selling airplanes. Now compare how this rule affects each division and the company, both when the selling division operates below and at capacity, as Exhibit 15.3 shows. Note that when the selling division operates at capacity and the transfer price equals $2.5 million, the buying division manager decides not to sell the airplane. The selling division therefore sells the system in the external market for $2.5 million, and the company makes a profit of $1.5 million.

The rule that the transfer price should include the opportunity cost of the transfer applies to any forgone alternative use of resources because the division makes the transfer. For example, suppose that the Systems Division currently operates below capacity, but could rent the idle capacity to an outsider. The opportunity cost of an internal transfer would be the forgone profit or contribution margin from the outsider. In short, the general transfer pricing rule includes any type of opportunity cost.

Exhibit 15.3

MAGNA-PRODUCTS, INCORPORATED
Applying the General Transfer Price Rule
(all dollar amounts in millions)

	Company	Buying (Aircraft) Division	Selling (Systems) Division
Facts			
Price per Airplane	$18.0	$18.0	—
Differential Cost of the System	(1.0)	—	$(1.0)
Differential Cost of the Remainder of the Airplane	(16.0)	(16.0)	—
Case 1: Selling (Systems) Division Operates below Capacity			
Transfer Price	—	(1.0)	1.0
Profit (Loss) to the Company If:			
Airplane Sold and System Purchased Internally	1.0[a]	1.0	0.0
Airplane Sold and System Purchased Externally for $2.5 million	(0.5)[b]	(0.5)	0.0
Airplane Not Sold.	0.0	0.0	0.0
Optimal Decision: Sell Airplane and Purchase System Internally.			
Case 2: Selling (Systems) Division Operates at Capacity			
Transfer Price	—	(2.5)	2.5
Profit (Loss) to the Company If:			
Airplane Sold and System Purchased Internally	1.0[c]	(0.5)	1.5
Airplane Sold and System Purchased Externally . . .	1.0[d]	(0.5)	1.5
Airplane Not Sold.	1.5[e]	0.0	1.5
Optimal Decision: Do Not Sell Airplane, Continue Selling Systems in Outside Market.			

[a]Sales price = $18 million; variable costs = $1 million for the system plus $16 million for the rest of the airplane.

[b]Sales price = $18 million; variable costs = $2.5 million for the system and $16.0 million for the rest of the airplane.

[c]Sales price = $18 million; variable costs = $1 million for the system plus $16 million for the rest of the airplane; forgo the opportunity to sell one system in the external market.

[d]Sales price = $18 million for airplane plus $2.5 million for system sold to external market; variable costs = $1 million for system sold to external market plus $2.5 million for system purchased from external market plus $16 million for rest of airplane. To summarize, $18 + 2.5 − 1 − 2.5 − 16 = $1.

[e]Sales price of system = $2.5 million; variable cost of system = $1 million.

Problem 15.1 for Self-Study

Transfer pricing. The Lee Strauss Company has two divisions, Production and Marketing. Production manufactures designer pants, which it sells to both the Marketing Division and to other retailers (to the latter under a different brand name).

Marketing operates numerous pants stores, and it sells both Lee Strauss pants and other brands. The following facts also pertain to the Lee Strauss Company:

- Sales price to retailers if sold by Production: $38 per pair.
- Variable cost to produce: $19 per pair.
- Fixed costs: $200,000 per month.
- Production currently operates far below its capacity.
- Sales price to customers if sold by Marketing: $50 per pair.
- Variable marketing costs: 5 percent of sales price.

Marketing has decided to reduce the sales price of Lee Strauss pants. The company's variable manufacturing and marketing costs are differential to this decision, whereas fixed manufacturing and marketing costs are not.

a. What is the *minimum* price that Marketing can charge for the pants and still cover differential manufacturing and marketing costs?

b. What is the appropriate transfer price for this decision?

c. What if the transfer price were set at $38? What effect would this have on the minimum price set by the marketing manager?

d. How would your answer to the above questions change if the Production Division had been operating at full capacity?

The solution to this self-study problem is at the end of the chapter on page 611.

Motivational Problems When the Selling Division Receives No Profits

The transfer pricing rule may not give the selling division a profit on the transaction when it makes transfers at actual differential cost. For example, when the selling division operates below capacity and has no opportunity for the use of idle facilities, the selling division receives only a price that equals differential cost. (Note Case 1 in Exhibit 15.3.) Under these circumstances, some criticize the transfer price rule because it does not provide incentives for the selling division to transfer internally. That is, the selling division can seldom, if ever, expect to profit from internal transfers. Firms deal with this situation in several ways.

Use Cost Centers If nearly all of the selling division's transfers are internal, the seller's responsibility center is probably a cost center. As such, management would normally hold the division (if it could be called a division under these circumstances) responsible for costs but not for revenues.

Use Hybrid Centers: Cost and Profit Suppose that the selling division does business with both internal and external customers. Management could set it up as a profit center for the external business, where the manager has some responsibility for setting prices, and as a cost center for the internal business, where the manager does not. Accountants could measure performance for external business as if it were a profit center but measure performance for internal business as if it were a cost center.

Use Dual Transfer Prices The price paid to the selling division does not *have to* equal the price the buying division pays on an internal transaction. With **dual transfer prices,** the accounting system charges the buying division differential costs while crediting the selling division with differential costs plus a markup. Referring to the Magna-Products example, suppose that top management decides to charge the Aircraft (buying) Division with a differential cost (which was $1 million) but to credit the selling division with the intermediate market price of $2.5 million *when the selling division operated below capacity.* This practice enables the Aircraft Division manager to make the correct decision to acquire the system internally and manufacture the airplane. Yet the System Division earned profits on the internal transfer.

Design Incentive Systems to Recognize the Benefits of Internal Transfers We have assumed that firms reward selling division managers based only on their division's profit performance. Selling division managers will have incentives to transfer internally, even if their division earns no profits on the transaction, *if* management also rewards them for internal transfers. Thus many companies recognize internal transfers and incorporate them into the reward system. Other companies base part of the selling managers' rewards on the buying division's performance or the total company's performance. In short, management creates many incentives for managers to trade internally without losing the benefit of the transfer pricing rule.

Negotiated Transfer Prices

Transfer prices based on differential cost represent a lower limit on the price that selling divisions will accept. Transfer prices based on market prices represent an upper limit on the price that buying divisions will pay. The difference between these two prices is the total margin on the transfer. Many firms permit divisional managers to negotiate among themselves about how to split the margin. If both divisions may deal freely either with each other or in the external market, the negotiated price will be close to the external market price. If a selling division cannot sell its total output on the external market (that is, they must sell a portion to the buying division), the negotiated price will be less than the market price and the divisions will share the total margin. The use of **negotiated transfer prices** corresponds with the concept of decentralized decision making in divisionalized firms.

One of the principal disadvantages of negotiated transfer prices is that the divisions may require significant time to carry out the negotiating process. Also, interdivision hostility may result, which could hurt overall company performance.

As we mentioned previously, no particular transfer pricing scheme works best in all circumstances. The choice involves such factors as the extent of external markets, the extent top management chooses to intervene in divisional decisions, the amount of trading among divisions, and other factors.

Current Practices in the United States, Canada, and Japan

What are the current practices in industry regarding transfer prices? The surveys of transfer pricing practices reported in Exhibit 15.4 show that nearly half of the companies surveyed in the United States, Canada, and Japan use cost-based transfer prices. Cost-based transfer prices are usually cost-plus-a-markup. Some companies start with variable costs, which measure short-run differential costs. Others start with full-absorption costs, which measure long-run differential costs. Companies generally use cost-based transfer prices when market price information is not readily available (for example, when the product is custom-made for the buyer).

Approximately one-third of the companies base transfer prices on market prices. Roughly 20 percent of the companies in the three countries let the selling and buying divisions negotiate transfer prices. We generally observe negotiated prices to be between the upper limit of market prices and the lower limit of variable costs.

Multinational Transfer Pricing

In international transactions, transfer prices may affect tax liabilities, royalties, and other payments because of different laws in different countries (or states). Since tax rates are different in different countries, companies have incentives to set transfer prices that will increase revenues (and profits) in low-tax countries and increase costs (thereby reducing profits) in high-tax countries.

To understand the effects of transfer pricing on taxes, consider the case of the Nikbok Shoe Company, which imports shoes from its facility in Lotax Country for sale in Hitax Country. Assume that a pair of shoes cost $50 to make in Lotax Country and cost $10 to market in Hitax Country. The shoes sell for $80 per pair.

Exhibit 15.4
Transfer Pricing Practices

Method Used	United States[a]	Canada[b]	Japan[c]
Cost-based transfer prices	45%	47%	47%
Market-based transfer prices	33	35	34
Negotiated transfer prices	22	18	19
Total	100%	100%	100%

Note: Companies using other methods were omitted from this illustration. These companies were 2 percent or less of the total.

[a]S. Borkowski, "Environmental and Organizational Factors Affecting Transfer Pricing: A Survey," *Journal of Management Accounting Research,* Fall 1990.

[b]R. Tang, "Canadian Transfer Pricing Practices," *CA Magazine,* March 1980.

[c]R. Tang, C. Walter, and R. Raymond, "Transfer Pricing—Japanese Vs. American Style," *Management Accounting,* January 1979.

International Transfer Prices and the Internal Revenue Service[a]

A Japanese manufacturer uses just-in-time production for its manufacturing facility in Japan and ships products to its U.S. subsidiary for sale to dealers. The Japanese facility ships goods at a rate that keeps the Japanese manufacturing facility operating efficiently. Although the Japanese facility does not keep finished good inventories, its U.S. subsidiary does. When demand in the United States for this product dropped, the U.S. subsidiary found itself with lots of inventory. The Japanese manufacturing plant did not want to reduce production below its efficient operating level, however, in order to reduce shipments to the U.S. subsidiary. The Japanese production facility did not stockpile finished goods inventory in Japan because it followed the just-in-time philosophy.

As inventories grew at the U.S. subsidiary, so did expenses to store and sell the mounting inventory of products. At one point, the U.S. subsidiary had more than a year's supply of the product in inventory, when under normal conditions it kept only about 3 months' supply on hand. The U.S. subsidiary's profits declined, and eventually it incurred losses. The United States Internal Revenue Service claimed the transfer price set by the Japanese manufacturer was too high in view of the decreasing demand for the company's product and the increasing costs incurred by the U.S. subsidiary to sell the product.

This case not only demonstrates how tax authorities get involved in transfer pricing, but also how a just-in-time approach by a manufacturer can lead to excessive inventories by its distributors and dealers. The tax issues in this case are still in dispute as this book goes to print.

[a]Based on the authors' research.

Nikbok's company-wide before-tax profit is $20 per pair. The company can use the transfer price to shift before-tax profits from the Hitax Country to the Lotax Country, however.

Assume the tax rate in Lotax Country is 20 percent, while the tax rate in Hitax Country is 50 percent. A transfer price of $70 would give all $20 (=$70 − $50) of Nikbok's profits to its manufacturing facility in Lotax Country. A transfer price of $50 would shift all of the $20 profits to the Hitax Country ($20 profit = $80 sales price − $50 transfer price − $10 selling costs). Nikbok would save $6 per pair in taxes by choosing the $70 transfer price and shifting profits to Lotax Country, calculated as follows:

	Alternative Transfer Prices	
Transfer price	$70	$50
Profits in Lotax Country	20	0
Tax in Lotax Country (20% rate)	4	0
Profits in Hitax Country...	0	20
Tax in Hitax Country (50% rate).......................................	0	10

Net benefit from transferring profits to Lotax Country equals $10 tax paid in Hitax Country minus $4 tax paid in Lotax Country, or $6.

''Tax avoidance'' by foreign companies using inflated transfer prices was a major issue in President Bill Clinton's 1992 presidential campaign. Foreign companies who sell goods to their U.S. subsidiaries at inflated transfer prices artificially reduce the profit of the U.S. subsidiary. According to Clinton advisors, the United States could collect as much as $9 billion to $13 billion per year in additional taxes if transfer pricing had been done according to U.S. tax laws. (The Managerial Application ''International Transfer Prices and the Internal Revenue Service'' presents an example of one of these companies.) Many foreign companies and domestic tax experts dispute the Clinton administration's claim, however.

Interstate Transactions

These same issues apply to interstate transactions. Companies have incentives to transfer profits from high-tax states like Massachusetts and California to low-tax states like New Hampshire and Nevada.

Measuring Division Operating Costs

In measuring divisional operating costs, management must decide how to treat the following costs: (1) controllable, direct operating costs; (2) noncontrollable, direct operating costs; (3) controllable, indirect operating costs; and (4) noncontrollable, indirect operating costs. Direct versus indirect refers to whether the cost associates directly with the division; controllable versus noncontrollable refers to whether the division manager can affect the cost. Exhibit 15.5 shows examples of each.

Exhibit 15.5

Examples of Direct (Indirect) and Controllable (Noncontrollable) Costs

Direct	Indirect
Controllable	
Labor Used in the Division's Production	Costs of Providing Centralized Services, Such as Data Processing and Employee Training, Which the Division's Use Partially Affects
Noncontrollable	
Salary of the Division Manager (controlled by top management)	Company President's Salary

Direct Costs

Management virtually always deducts a division's direct operating costs, whether or not the division manager controls them, from divisional revenues in measuring divisional operating profits. From top management's perspective, any cost necessary for that division to operate is a direct cost, even if the division manager cannot control the cost. If top management believes that division managers should not be held responsible for things outside their control, it can separate the measure of costs assigned to a *division* from the costs assigned to a division *manager*—the latter measure could exclude direct costs of the division that the division manager cannot control (for example, the division manager's salary).

Indirect, Controllable Operating Costs[6]

Divisions can at least partially control indirect, controllable costs. Firms usually centralize these services because of economies of scale in doing so. In some companies, costs would exceed benefits if each division had its own legal staff, research department, data-processing department, and so forth.

For example, many companies have centralized employee training departments. Should management charge divisions for sending their people to these centralized departments? As you may expect, the experiences in most companies follow fundamental laws of economics: The use of centralized services and the price charged for those services are inversely related. When companies charge a high price for employee training, people's attendance from the divisions drops, and vice versa. Top management can use this experience to decide on the desired usage and set the price accordingly. Some companies treat centralized service departments as profit or investment centers; if so, the transfer pricing issues discussed earlier are relevant.

Indirect, Noncontrollable Operating Costs

Indirect, noncontrollable operating costs may be necessary costs to the company (for example, the salaries and staff support of corporate top management). The most frequent arguments against allocating these costs are based on the divisions' inability to control the amount of costs incurred as well as the arbitrary allocation bases that the accountant must use. For example, on what basis should the accountant allocate the president's salary to the divisions—sales, number of employees, square footage of space used? Any allocation base is likely to be meaningless.

One argument advanced for allocation is that, unless the company allocates these costs to the divisions, the divisions will underprice their products and cause the company as a whole to operate at a loss. In other words, the revenues the divisions generate would be insufficient to cover both the direct operating costs of the divisions and the indirect operating costs incurred at central headquarters.

---

[6]Assigning central headquarters' costs to divisions is part of a more general cost allocation problem discussed in Chapter 5.

This argument is not particularly convincing in the short run. Competitive market conditions will determine prices. These prices will be the same whether or not the cost system allocates central corporate operating costs. As a basis for evaluating the month-to-month performance of divisional managers, top management should pay attention to the divisional operating profits before allocation of central corporate operating costs. If divisions seek to optimize this divisional contribution amount, they will also optimize divisional operating profits after allocation of central corporate operating costs, however allocated.

Others argue that allocation keeps division managers aware of the existence of central headquarters costs and the need for the company as a whole to cover those costs. In addition, allocation may stimulate managers to monitor those costs and put pressure on top management if the costs become too great. A top manager of a retail company told us that central headquarters costs were allocated to the stores to keep them aware of these costs. ''We want our store managers to recognize that it's not enough for stores to make a profit for the company to be profitable.'' The corporate manager went on to say that part of a store manager's bonus was based on the store's profit after central headquarter's costs had been allocated to stores. ''This makes them very aware of central headquarter's costs, and it makes us [top management] sensitive to their criticisms about administrative costs'' (that is, central headquarters costs).

Financing Costs and Income Taxes

Some companies do not allocate nonoperating costs, such as interest on debt and income taxes, to divisions. Corporate headquarters nearly always makes decisions about the terms and type of financing—issuing short-term versus long-term bonds, issuing common versus preferred shares, and so forth. Consequently, many companies do not charge divisions with financing costs. Those that do often charge an implicit interest cost to cover both the opportunity cost of equity capital and interest on debt. This implicit interest indicates the minimum desired rate of return that the division should generate.

In the majority of cases, the system assesses income taxes on the taxable income of the company as a whole rather than on each division. Should the company allocate these income taxes to individual divisions?

Those favoring allocating income taxes to divisions argue that managers should be encouraged to make decisions with income tax implications in mind. For example, management should consider the tax savings from depreciation deductions and the tax consequences of selling versus trading in old equipment in capital budgeting decisions.

Those against allocation make arguments similar to those against arbitrary allocation of central headquarters expenses. Divisional managers cannot control the amount of income taxes assessed. In addition, the potential amount of income taxes paid on divisional income if it were a separate taxable entity may differ from the amount actually assessed when it is aggregated with income of other divisions. Thus the income taxes of one division depend on income other divisions generate.

Measuring the Investment in Divisions

Most companies use some measure of capital employed or invested in each division when calculating ROI. In this section we discuss (1) what assets firms include in the investment base and (2) what valuation basis firms use.

Assets Included in the Investment Base

Management obviously should include assets physically located in a division and used only in the division's operations in the investment base. More difficult problems arise with assets shared among divisions and assets that centralized services departments acquire (for example, buildings and equipment used in personnel training). Management may allocate the cost of a shared manufacturing plant between divisions based on square footage used. Where only highly arbitrary allocation bases are possible, wise managers will not allocate the cost of common facilities to divisions.

Valuation of Assets in the Investment Base

Once the firm chooses the assets in the investment base, it must assign them a monetary value. Most firms use acquisition cost as the valuation basis. Management can obtain the necessary amounts directly from the company's accounts.

The use of book values of assets, particularly fixed assets, in the ROI denominator can have undesirable results. The manager of a division with old, low-cost, and almost fully depreciated assets may be reluctant to replace the assets with newer, more efficient, but more costly assets. Replacing old assets with new, more costly ones decreases the numerator—operating profits—of the ROI calculation because of increased depreciation charges. It also increases the denominator—cost of total assets—of the ROI calculation. These two effects combine to reduce calculated ROI.

If use of book values in the investment base affects divisional investment behavior this way, management may deal with the problem in two possible ways. One, they may state all assets at gross book value rather than at net book value. This approach states assets at full acquisition cost regardless of age. Another approach is to state assets at their current replacement cost or net realizable value.

In general, the older the assets, the higher the ROI under net book value compared to gross book value. If replacement cost increases over time, ROI is higher under historical cost compared to current replacement cost.

Contribution Approach to Division Reporting

In previous sections, we discussed some of the factors you should consider in calculating ROI. In this section, we discuss several additional considerations in using and interpreting ROI as a basis for evaluating divisional performance.

We suggest that a firm should decide how it is going to calculate ROI and then use it consistently. Firms tend, however, to overemphasize this single statistic. Exhibit 15.6 presents a divisional performance report in a format that facilitates a variety of uses. For example, management could use the report to evaluate the division and its manager's performance without regard to costs arbitrarily allocated to divisions or to product lines. Further, the report provides data about the division's performance after the firm allocates all central administrative costs. Some corporate managers like to see a bottom line which takes into account all costs, even indirect costs that accounting has arbitrarily allocated to divisions.

Allocation of Headquarters' Costs

We suggested earlier that allocating central headquarters' costs to divisions may not be desirable if the firm wants to obtain a measure for evaluating divisional performance. Divisions do not have control over these costs and, therefore, the firm should not hold them accountable. However, divisional personnel must be conscious of the need to provide a positive contribution margin to the coverage of central corporate expenses and to profits. Top management may communicate this need to divisional personnel by showing on the performance report the relation between the division's contribution and the amount that top management thinks the division should share of central headquarters' costs.

Many divisional performance reports end with "Income before Income Taxes." Some management accountants argue that income taxes are part of controllable costs if they are derived from controllable revenues and controllable costs. Placing income taxes at the bottom of the report compromises between the two positions. This placement recognizes that allocation of income taxes to divisions may be as difficult as allocating central headquarters' costs. However, it emphasizes to division managers the importance of income taxes in decisions and the need to cover them before the division can generate profits for the company's owners.

Components of Return on Investment

The rate of return on investment has two components: profit margin and investment (or asset) turnover.

$$\frac{\text{Return on}}{\text{Investment}} = \frac{\text{Profit Margin}}{\text{Percentage}} \times \frac{\text{Investment}}{\text{Turnover Ratio}}$$

$$\frac{\text{Profit Margin}}{\text{Divisional Investment}} = \frac{\text{Profit Margin}}{\text{Divisional Revenues}} \times \frac{\text{Divisional Revenues}}{\text{Divisional Investment}}.$$

To illustrate the usefulness of dividing ROI into its components, assume the following information about Division A:

Exhibit 15.6

The Contribution Approach to Division Reporting
(all dollar amounts in thousands)

	Company as a Whole	Company Breakdown into Two Divisions		Further Breakdown of Division A into Two Product Lines		
		Division A	Division B	Product 1	Product 2	Not Allocated to Products
Revenues................................	$6,500	$2,500	$4,000	$1,300	$1,200	
Variable Manufacturing Cost of Goods Sold	2,300	800	1,500	500	300	
Manufacturing Contribution Margin ...	4,200	1,700	2,500	800	900	
Variable Selling and Administrative Costs	600	200	400	100	100	
Contribution Margin	3,600	1,500	2,100	700	800	
Fixed Costs Directly Attributable to the Division	2,400	900	1,500	275	200	425[a]
Division Contribution to Unallocated Costs and Profit	$1,200	$ 600	$ 600	$ 425	$ 600	$(425)
Unallocated Costs	800[a]					
Operating Profit	$ 400					

[a]These costs are not direct costs of the division or product line and could be allocated only by an arbitrary allocation method.

Year	Sales	Profit	Investment
1	$1,000,000	$100,000	$ 500,000
2	2,000,000	160,000	1,000,000
3	4,000,000	400,000	2,500,000

The following table shows the ROI for each of the 3 years and the associated profit margin percentages and investment turnover ratios.

Year	ROI =	Profit Margin Percentage	×	Investment Turnover Ratio
1	20% =	10%	×	2.0
2	16 =	8	×	2.0
3	16 =	10	×	1.6

The **profit margin percentage** provides information for assessing divisional management's ability to combine inputs to generate outputs; that is, the accounting system has combined various cost inputs (materials, labor, depreciation) to generate revenue outputs (sales of goods and services). The profit margin percentage indicates the portion of each dollar of revenue that exceeds the costs incurred. Management often uses it as a measure for assessing efficiency in producing and selling goods and services. The profit margin percentage for Division A in this example decreased from 10 percent to 8 percent between Year 1 and Year 2. Because the investment turnover ratio remained the same between the 2 years, it appears that an inability to control costs or an inability to raise selling prices as costs have increased, or both, caused the decrease in ROI.

The **investment turnover ratio** indicates potentially useful information on how effectively the management used the capital invested in the division. Returning to the preceding example, Division A could not increase its ROI between Year 2 and Year 3, despite an increase in its profit margin percentage, because its investment turnover ratio decreased. The division could not generate $2 of revenue for each dollar invested in Year 3, as it had done in previous years.

Studying profit margin percentages and investment turnover ratios for a given division over several periods will provide more useful information than comparing these ratios for all divisions in a particular period. Some divisions, due to the nature of their activities, require more capital than others.

Setting Minimum Desired ROIs

If the ROI is to measure divisional performance effectively, management must set a standard or desired rate each period. Management usually specifies a minimum desired ROI for each division, given its particular operating characteristics. Some divisions are in more risky businesses than others, hence management may have higher expectations for them. Some divisions have a very low investment base (for example, professional services, consulting), thus ROI is sometimes quite high. In short, management should recognize the particular characteristics of a division in setting minimum ROIs.

Residual Income

Critics of ROI argue that managers may turn down investment opportunities that are above the minimum acceptable rate but below the ROI currently being earned. For example, suppose that the division currently earns

$$\text{ROI} = \frac{\$1,000,000}{\$4,000,000} = 25\%.$$

Suppose the manager has an opportunity to make an additional investment. This investment would return $400,000 per year for 5 years for a $2-million investment. At the end of 5 years, the $2-million investment would be returned. Assume that there is no inflation. The ROI each year is

$$\text{ROI} = \frac{\$400,000}{\$2,000,000} = 20\%.$$

The company requires a minimum return of 15 percent for this type of investment. This investment clearly qualifies, but it would lower the investment center ROI to 23.3 percent:

$$\text{ROI} = \frac{\$1,000,000 + \$400,000}{\$4,000,000 + \$2,000,000} = 23.3\%.$$

A comparison of the old (25 percent) and new (23.3 percent) returns would imply performance has worsened; consequently a manager might decide not to make such an investment.

An alternative to ROI is **residual income (RI).** Residual income is defined as

$$\begin{matrix}\text{Residual} \\ \text{Income}\end{matrix} = \begin{matrix}\text{Division} \\ \text{Operating} \\ \text{Profits}\end{matrix} - \left(\begin{matrix}\text{Percent} \\ \text{Capital} \\ \text{Charge}\end{matrix} \times \begin{matrix}\text{Division} \\ \text{Investment}\end{matrix}\right),$$

where the percent capital charge is the minimum acceptable rate of return. The terms *division operating profits* and *division investment* are defined as for ROI. Residual income is similar in concept to economists' definition of profits. If the firm encourages managers to maximize RI, they have incentives to accept all projects above the minimum acceptable rate of return.

Using data from the example just discussed to see the impact of the investment on residual income, we find the following:

Before the investment, the residual income is $400,000.

$$\begin{aligned}\text{RI} &= \$1,000,000 - (.15 \times \$4,000,000) \\ &= \$1,000,000 - \$600,000 \\ &= \$400,000.\end{aligned}$$

The residual income from the additional investment is $100,000.

$$\begin{aligned}\text{RI} &= \$400,000 - (.15 \times \$2,000,000) \\ &= \$400,000 - \$300,000 \\ &= \$100,000.\end{aligned}$$

Hence, *after the additional investment,* the residual income of the division increases to $500,000.

$$RI = (\$1,000,000 + \$400,000) - [.15 \times (\$4,000,000 + \$2,000,000)]$$
$$= \$1,400,000 - (.15 \times \$6,000,000)$$
$$= \$1,400,000 - \$900,000$$
$$= \$500,000.$$

The additional investment *increases* residual income, appropriately improving the measure of performance, whereas the use of ROI worsened the measure of performance.

Managers generally recognize this problem with ROI, and they may take it into account when a new investment lowers the ROI. This practice may explain why residual income does not dominate ROI in practice as a performance measure. Further, ROI is expressed as a percentage that managers can intuitively compare with related percentages—like the cost of capital, the prime interest rate, and the Treasury Bill rate. Most companies use ROI, but many use a combination of RI and ROI.

Problem 15.2 for Self-Study

Return on investment and residual income. The Venus Division of Hyperspace Company has assets of $2.4 billion, operating profits of $.60 billion, and a cost of capital of 20 percent.

Compute return on investment and residual income.

The solution to this self-study problem is at the end of the chapter on page 612.

Summary

Top management must design and implement division performance measures that encourage division managers to act in the best interests of the company as a whole. Fundamentally, top management seeks answers to the following questions: (1) What behavior does the incentive system motivate? (2) What behavior do we *want* the incentive system to motivate? At a minimum, performance measurement methods should show that when division managers take actions in the company's best interests, the managers' own performance also looks good.

The key issues in divisional performance measurement deal with measuring revenues, costs, and investment in the division. For profit centers, the most important measure is

Division Operating Profits = Division Revenues − Division Costs;

for investment centers it is

$$ROI = \frac{\text{Division Revenues} - \text{Division Costs}}{\text{Division Investment}}.$$

(We assume that divisions are investment centers unless otherwise stated.)

When one division can sell its output to another division, management sets a *transfer price* that becomes a revenue to the selling division and a cost to the buying division. Selecting the transfer price can affect decision making significantly. Ideally, management will set the transfer price so that when divisions internally optimize their buy and sell decisions, they also optimize from a company-wide viewpoint.

Transfer pricing choices have numerous alternatives, including direct top management intervention in buy and sell decisions, top management-established transfer pricing policy, and transfer prices negotiated among division managers. You could expect top management's direct intervention to induce managers to make the right decision for the company for a particular transaction. However, direct intervention reduces some of the advantages of decentralization because it overrides delegation of responsibility.

The optimal transfer pricing policy sets the price at the differential cost to the selling division plus the implicit opportunity cost to the company if it transfers the goods internally. When competitive external markets exist for the product being exchanged between divisions and the selling division operates at capacity, the product's external market price satisfies the general rule. The optimal rule requires difficult measures of differential costs and opportunity costs. Consequently, many companies transfer at some measure of cost found in the accounting records—for example, standard full cost or standard variable cost—plus a markup. Many companies carry decentralization to the limit by allowing division managers to set their own prices—so-called negotiated prices.

The issues in measuring the investment of capital in divisions are (1) what assets should the firm include in the investment base and (2) what valuation basis should the firm use. Assets physically located in a division should be included in the investment bases. Firms usually assign assets that divisions or central headquarters share to divisions if the firm can use reasonable allocation bases. Management generally develops a reasonable policy for including assets in the investment base and tries to follow it consistently. Some criticize the use of historical cost and net book value on the grounds that managers of divisions with old, low-cost, and almost fully depreciated assets may be reluctant to replace these with newer, more costly assets that reduce calculated ROI.

Some criticize ROI because if firms encourage managers to have a high ROI, they may turn down investment opportunities that are above the minimum acceptable rate but below the ROI currently being earned. Residual income (RI) is an alternative measure that addresses this problem. Residual income is computed as follows:

$$\begin{matrix} \text{Residual} \\ \text{Income} \end{matrix} = \begin{matrix} \text{Division} \\ \text{Operating} \\ \text{Profits} \end{matrix} - \left(\begin{matrix} \text{Percent} \\ \text{Capital} \\ \text{Charge} \end{matrix} \times \begin{matrix} \text{Division} \\ \text{Investment} \end{matrix} \right).$$

Any project accepted with a return above the minimum acceptable rate (that is, the percent capital charge) will increase residual income. Hence, projects that will profit the company also improve the division manager's performance measure.

Solutions to Self-Study Problems

Suggested Solution to Problem 15.1 for Self-Study

a. From the company's perspective, the minimum price would be the variable cost of producing and marketing the goods. It would solve for this minimum price, P_C (the subscript C means that the minimum price in the *company's* best interest), as follows:

$$P_C = \$19 + .05\,P_C$$
$$P_C - .05P_C = \$19$$
$$.95P_C = \$19$$
$$P_C = \underline{\underline{\$20}}.$$

The *minimum* price the company should accept is $20. If the company were centralized, we would expect the information system to convey this information to the manager of Marketing, who would be instructed not to set a price below $20.

b. The transfer price that correctly informs the marketing manager about the differential costs of manufacturing is $19. Since Production operates below capacity, the opportunity cost of transferring internally equals zero.

c. If the production manager set the price at $38, the marketing manager would solve for the minimum price (which we call P_M for *Marketing's* solution):

$$P_M = \$38 + .05\,P_M$$
$$P_M - .05P_M = \$38$$
$$.95P_M = \$38$$
$$P_M = \underline{\underline{\$40}}.$$

So the marketing manager sets the price in excess of $40 per pair, when, in fact, prices exceeding $20 would have generated a positive contribution margin from the production and sale of pants.

d. If the Production Division had been operating at capacity, an internal transfer would have had an implicit opportunity cost. Production would have forgone a sale in the wholesale market to make the internal transfer. The implicit opportunity cost to the company is the lost contribution margin ($38 − $19 = $19) from not selling in the wholesale market.

   Thus, if Production had sufficient sales in the wholesale market to force it to forego those sales to transfer internally, the transfer price should have been

$$\begin{array}{c}\text{Differential Cost} \\ \text{to Production}\end{array} + \begin{array}{c}\text{Implicit Opportunity Cost} \\ \text{to Company If Goods Are} \\ \text{Transferred Internally}\end{array} = \$19 + \$19$$
$$= \underline{\underline{\$38}}.$$

Marketing would have appropriately treated the $38 as part of *its* differential cost of buying and selling the pants.

Suggested Solution to Problem 15.2 for Self-Study

$$ROI = \frac{\$.60\ \text{Billion}}{2.4\ \text{Billion}} = \underline{\underline{25\%.}}$$

Residual Income = \$.60 Billion − (.20 × \$2.4 Billion)

= \$.60 Billion − \$.48 Billion

= \$.12 Billion (that is, residual income of \$120 million).

Key Terms and Concepts

Division
Profit center
Investment center
Decentralized decision making
Behavioral or goal congruence
Division return on investment (ROI)
Transfer pricing problem

Market-based transfer price
Cost-based transfer price
Dual transfer price
Negotiated transfer price
Profit margin percentage
Investment turnover ratio
Residual income (RI)

Questions, Exercises, Problems, and Cases

Questions

1. Review the meaning of the concepts or terms given above in Key Terms and Concepts.

2. "It may be desirable to use a different ROI measure for evaluating the performance of a division and the performance of the division's manager." Explain.

3. "An action that is optimal for a division may not be optimal for the company as a whole." Explain.

4. Why are transfer prices necessary?

5. In what sense is the word "price" in the term *transfer price* a misnomer?

6. "The case for allocating central service department costs is stronger than the case for allocating central administration costs to divisions." Explain.

7. "The return on investment measure may be biased in favor of divisions with older plant and equipment." Explain.

8. What are the advantages of using the ROI measure rather than the value of division profits as a performance evaluation technique?

9. Under what conditions would the use of ROI measures inhibit goal-congruent decision making by a division manager?

10. What are the advantages of using residual income instead of ROI?
11. Refer to this chapter's Managerial Application, "International Transfer Prices and the Internal Revenue Service." Why did the Internal Revenue Service dispute the transfer prices? Did the IRS want the prices set higher or lower? Why?
12. What factors should companies consider when setting transfer prices for products sold from a division in one country to a division in another country?
13. Why may transfer prices exist even in highly centralized organizations?
14. Why do some consider market-based transfer prices optimal under many circumstances?
15. What are the limitations to market-based transfer prices?
16. What are the advantages of a centrally administered transfer price (that is, direct intervention)? What are the disadvantages of such a transfer price?
17. Why do companies often use prices other than market prices for interdivisional transfers?
18. Division A has no external markets. It produces a product that Division B uses. Division B cannot purchase this product from any other source. What transfer pricing system would you recommend for the interdivisional sale of the product? Why?
19. What are the disadvantages of a negotiated transfer price system?
20. Describe the economic basis for transfer pricing systems.

Exercises

Solutions to even-numbered exercises are at the end of this chapter on page 627.

21. **Transfer pricing.** Fizz-it, Inc., produces bottled drinks. The New England Division acquires the water, adds carbonation, and sells it in bulk quantities to the California Division of Fizz-it and to outside buyers. The California Division buys carbonated water in bulk, adds flavoring, bottles it, and sells it.

    Last year, the New England Division produced 1,500,000 gallons, of which it sold 1,300,000 gallons to the California Division and the remaining 200,000 gallons to outsiders for $.20 per gallon. The California Division processed the 1,300,000 gallons which it sold for $750,000. New England's variable costs were $220,000 and its fixed costs were $40,000. The California Division incurred an additional variable cost of $160,000 and $80,000 fixed costs. Both divisions operated below capacity.
    a. Prepare division income statements assuming the transfer price is at the external market price of $.20 per gallon.
    b. Repeat part **a** assuming a negotiated transfer price of $.15 per gallon is used.
    c. Respond to the statement: "The choice of a particular transfer price is immaterial to the company as a whole."
22. **Return on investment computations.** The following information relates to the operating performance of three divisions of Langston Retail Corporation for 19X0.

	New York Division	Philadelphia Division	Los Angeles Division
Divisional Contribution Margin before Allocating Central Corporate Expenses to Divisions...........	$500,000	$500,000	$500,000
Divisional Investment	$4,000,000	$5,000,000	$6,000,000
Divisional Sales	$24,000,000	$20,000,000	$16,000,000
Divisional Employees	22,500	12,000	10,500

Langston evaluates divisional performance using rate of return on investment (ROI) after allocating a portion of the central corporate expenses to each division. Central corporate expenses for 19X0 were $900,000.

a. Compute the ROI of each division before allocation of central corporate expenses.

b. Compute the ROI of each division assuming central corporate expenses are allocated based on divisional investments (that is, allocate 4/15 to the New York Division, 5/15 to the Philadelphia Division, and 6/15 to the Los Angeles Division).

c. Repeat part **b,** allocating central corporate expenses based on divisional sales.

d. Repeat part **b,** assuming that management allocates central corporate expenses based on the number of employees.

23. **ROI computations with a capital charge.** The following information relates to the operating performance of three divisions of Tobias Trucking for 19X0.

	Local Moving Division	Intercity Division	Interstate Division
Operating Profit	$ 750,000	$ 3,000,000	$ 5,250,000
Investment....................	9,375,000	12,000,000	37,500,000

a. Compute the rate of return on investment (ROI) of each division for 19X0.

b. Assume that the firm levies a charge on each division for the use of capital. The charge is 10 percent on investment, and the accounting system deducts it in measuring divisional net income. Recalculate ROI using divisional net income after deduction of the use-of-capital charge in the numerator.

c. Which of these two measures do you think gives the better indication of operating performance? Explain your reasoning.

24. **ROI computations with replacement costs.** The following information relates to the operating performance of two divisions of Pratt Electronics Corporation for 19X0.

	Boston Division	Mexico City Division
Operating Profit	$ 400,000	$ 600,000
Total Assets (based on acquisition cost)	4,000,000	7,500,000
Total Assets (based on current replacement costs) ...	6,000,000	8,000,000

a. Compute the return on investment (ROI) of each division, using total assets stated at acquisition cost as the investment base.

b. Compute the ROI of each division, using total assets based on current replacement cost as the investment base.

c. Which of the two measures do you think gives the better indication of operating performance? Explain your reasoning.

25. **ROI computations comparing net and gross book value.** The following information relates to the operating performance of two divisions of the Hardrock Quarry for last year.

	Eastern Division	Western Division
Operating Profit	$ 600,000	$ 900,000
Total Assets (at gross acquisition cost)	6,250,000	20,000,000
Total Assets (net of accumulated depreciation)	5,000,000	5,000,000

a. Compute the return on investment (ROI) of each division, using total assets at gross book value as the investment base.

b. Compute the ROI of each division, using total assets net of accumulated depreciation (net book value) as the investment base.

c. Which of the two measures do you think gives the better indication of operating performance? Explain your reasoning.

26. **Comparing profit margin and ROI as performance measures.** Cafe Italia operates coffeehouses on college campuses in three districts. The operating performance for each district follows.

	District		
	New Hampshire	Illinois	California
Sales	$3,800,000	$17,000,000	$20,000,000
Operating Profit	200,000	500,000	1,000,000
Investment	2,000,000	6,250,000	8,000,000

a. Using the operating profit margin percentage as the criterion, which is the most profitable district?

b. Using the rate of return on investment as the criterion, which is the most profitable district?

c. Which of the two measures better indicates operating performance? Explain your reasoning.

27. **Profit margin and investment turnover ratio computations.** The Bronco Division of the Mile High Company had a rate of return on investment (ROI) of 15 percent (= $300,000/$2,000,000) during 19X0, based on sales of $4,000,000. In an effort to improve its performance during 19X1, the company instituted several cost-saving programs, including the substitution of automatic equipment for work previously done by workers and the purchase of raw materials in large quantities to obtain quantity discounts. Despite these cost-

saving programs, the company's ROI for 19X1 was 12 percent (= $330,000/ $2,750,000), based on sales of $4,000,000.

a. Break down the ROI for 19X0 and 19X1 into profit margin and investment turnover ratios.

b. Explain the reason for the decrease in ROI between the 2 years, using results from part **a.**

28. **ROI and residual income computations.** A bank considers acquiring new computer equipment. The computer will cost $160,000 and result in a cash savings of $70,000 per year (excluding depreciation) for each of the 5 years of the asset life. It will have no salvage value after 5 years. Assume straight-line depreciation.

a. What is the ROI for each year of the asset's life if the division uses beginning-of-year net book value asset balances for the computation?

b. What is the residual income each year if the capital costs 25 percent?

29. **Transfer pricing** (adapted from CPA exam). E-Z Computing has two decentralized divisions, Hardware and Computers. Computers has always purchased certain units from Hardware at $55 per unit. Because Hardware plans to raise the price to $70 per unit, Computers desires to purchase these units from outside suppliers for $55 per unit. Hardware's costs follow: variable costs per unit, $50; annual fixed costs, $15,000. Annual production of these units for Computers is 1,500 units.

   If Computers buys from an outside supplier, the facilities Hardware uses to manufacture these units would remain idle. What would be the result if E-Z Computing management enforces a transfer price of $70 per unit between Hardware and Computers?

30. **Transfer pricing.** The consulting group in an accounting firm offers its products to outside clients at a price of $200 per hour. Last month, the consultants billed 10,000 hours to outside clients, incurred variable costs of $70 per hour billed to outside clients, and incurred $500,000 in fixed costs.

   The firm's auditing group can acquire consulting services from outsiders or from the firm's own consultants. If it acquires the services from outsiders, it must pay $180 per hour. It would pay $200 for consulting services from the internal group.

a. What are the costs and benefits of the alternatives available to these two groups, the consultants and the auditors, and to the accounting firm as a whole, with respect to consulting services? Assume the consulting group operates at capacity.

b. How would your answer change if the accounting firm's consulting group had sufficient idle capacity to handle all of the auditors' needs?

Problems

31. **Transfer pricing.** Technology Plus Company produces computers and computer components. The company is organized into several divisions that operate essentially as autonomous companies. The firm permits division managers to make capital investment and production-level decisions. The division managers can also decide whether to sell to other divisions or to outside customers.

Networks Division produces a critical component for computers manufactured by Computers Division. It has been selling this component to Computers for $1,500 per unit. Networks recently purchased new equipment for producing the component. To offset its higher depreciation charges, Networks increased its price to $1,600 per unit. The manager of Networks has asked the president to instruct Computers to purchase the component for the $1,600 price rather than to permit Computers to purchase externally for $1,500 per unit. The following information is obtained from the company's records: Computers' annual purchases of the component, 100 units; Networks' variable costs per unit, $1,200; Networks' fixed costs per unit, $300.

a. Assume that the firm has no alternative uses for Networks' idle capacity. Will the company as a whole benefit if Computers purchases the component externally for $1,500? Explain.

b. Assume that the firm can use the idle capacity of Networks for other purposes, resulting in cash operating savings of $20,000. Will the company as a whole benefit if Computers purchases the component externally for $1,500? Explain.

c. Assume the same facts as in part **b** except that the outside market price drops to $1,350 per unit. Will the company as a whole benefit if Computers purchases the component externally for $1,350? Explain.

d. As president, how would you respond to the manager of Networks? Discuss each scenario described in parts **a, b,** and **c.**

32. **Biases in ROI computations.** Champion Sports Products uses rate of return on investment (ROI) as a basis for determining the annual bonus of divisional managers. Before calculating ROI at year-end, the accounting system assigns all manufacturing cost variances to units produced, whether sold or in ending inventory, so that standard costs become actual costs. The firm allocates central corporate expenses to the divisions based on total sales. The calculation of ROI for 19X0 for two of its divisions follows:

	Tennis Products Division	Golf Products Division
Division Contribution to Central Corporate Expenses and Operating Profit..................	$100,000	$ 500,000
Share of Central Corporate Expenses	(10,000)	(25,000)
Divisional Operating Profit	$ 90,000	$ 475,000
Divisional Investment (assets).....................	$600,000	$4,750,000
ROI	15 Percent	10 Percent

Indicate several factors that, if present, would bias the ROI measure as Champion has calculated and lead to possible inequities in determining the annual bonus.

33. **Issues in designing ROI measures.** The Domestic Corporation manufactures and sells a patented electronic device for detecting burglaries. The firm uses return on investment as a measure for the control of operations for each of its sixteen U.S. divisions.

Recently the firm has organized a new division in Brazil. Domestic contributed the necessary capital for the construction of manufacturing and sales facilities in Brazil, whereas it obtained debt financing locally for working capital requirements. The new division will remit annually the following amounts to the U.S. central corporate office: (1) a royalty of $10 for each burglary device sold in Brazil, (2) a fee of $40 per hour plus traveling expenses for central corporate engineering services used by the division, and (3) a dividend equal to 10 percent of the capital Domestic committed. The division will retain for its own use the remaining funds that operation generates. The division will receive the right to produce and market in Brazil any future electronic devices the central corporate research and development staff develops.

List some of the questions that the firm must address in designing an ROI measure for this division.

34. **Evaluating profit impact of alternative transfer decisions** (adapted from CMA exam). A. R. Oma, Inc., manufactures a line of men's colognes and after-shave lotions. The firm manufactures the products through a series of mixing operations with the addition of certain aromatic and coloring ingredients; the firm packages the finished product in a company-produced glass bottle and packs it in cases containing six bottles.

Management of A. R. Oma believes appearance of the bottle heavily influences the sale of its product. Management has developed a unique bottle of which it is quite proud.

Cologne production and bottle manufacturing have evolved over the years in an almost independent manner; in fact, a rivalry has developed between management personnel as to which division is the more important to A. R. Oma. This attitude is probably intensified because the bottle manufacturing plant was purchased intact 10 years ago, and no real interchange of management personnel or ideas (except at the top corporate level) has taken place.

Since the acquisition, the cologne manufacturing plant has absorbed all bottle production. Management considers each area a separate profit center and evaluates each area as a separate profit center. As the new corporate controller, you are responsible for the definition of a proper transfer value to use in crediting the bottle production profit center and in debiting the packaging profit center.

At your request, the bottle division general manager has asked certain other bottle manufacturers to quote a price for the quantity and sizes the cologne division demands. These competitive prices follow:

Volume	Total Price	Price per Case
2,000,000 Cases[a]	$ 4,000,000	$2.00
4,000,000 Cases	7,000,000	1.75
6,000,000 Cases	10,000,000	1.67 (rounded)

A cost analysis of the internal bottle plant indicates that it can produce bottles at these costs:

Volume	Total Price	Cost per Case
2,000,000 Cases	$3,200,000	$1.60
4,000,000 Cases	5,200,000	1.30
6,000,000 Cases	7,200,000	1.20

These costs include fixed costs of $1,200,000 and variable costs of $1 per case.

These figures resulted in discussion about the proper value to use in the transfer of bottles to the cologne division. Corporate executives are interested because a significant portion of a division manager's income is an incentive bonus based on profit center results.

The cologne production division incurred the following costs in addition to the bottle costs:

Volume	Total Cost	Cost per Case
2,000,000 Cases	$16,400,000	$8.20
4,000,000 Cases	32,400,000	8.10
6,000,000 Cases	48,400,000	8.07

After considerable analysis, the marketing research department furnishes you with the following price-demand relation for the finished product:

Sales Volume	Total Sales Revenue	Sales Price per Case
2,000,000 Cases	$25,000,000	$12.50
4,000,000 Cases	45,600,000	11.40
6,000,000 Cases	63,900,000	10.65

a. The A. R. Oma Company has used market-based price transfer prices in the past. Using the current market prices and costs, and assuming a volume of 6,000,000 cases, calculate the income for
   (1) The bottle division.
   (2) The cologne division.
   (3) The corporation.
b. Is this production and sales level the most profitable volume for
   (1) The bottle division?
   (2) The cologne division?
   (3) The corporation?
Explain your answer.

Cases

35. Transfer pricing and organizational structure.[7] "If I were to price these boxes any lower than $480 a thousand, I'd be countermanding my order of last

---

[7]Copyright © 1957, 1985 by the President and Fellows of Harvard College. W. Rotch prepared this case under the direction of Neil E. Harlan as the basis for class discussion rather than to illustrate either effective or ineffective handling of an administrative situation. Reprinted by permission of Harvard Business School. From Harvard Business School case 158-001.

month for our salespeople to stop shaving their bids and to bid full cost quotations. I've been trying for weeks to improve the quality of our business, and if I turn around now and accept this job at $430 or $450 or something less than $480, I'll be tearing down this program I've been working so hard to build up. The division can't very well show a profit by putting in bids that don't even cover a fair share of overhead costs, let alone give us a profit.''

James Brunner, Manager of Thompson Division

Birch Paper Company was a medium-sized, partly integrated paper company, producing white and kraft papers and paperboard. A portion of its paperboard output was converted into corrugated boxes by the Thompson division, which also printed and colored the outside surface of the boxes. Including Thompson, the company had four producing divisions and a timberland division, which supplied part of the company's pulp requirements.

For several years, each division had been judged independently on the basis of its profit and return on investment. Top management had been working to gain effective results from a policy of decentralizing responsibility and authority for all decisions except those relating to overall company policy. The company's top officials believed that in the past few years they had applied the concept of decentralization successfully and that the company's profits and competitive position had definitely improved.

Early in 1975 the Northern division designed a special display box for one of its papers in conjunction with the Thompson division, which was equipped to make the box. Thompson's staff for package design and development spent several months perfecting the design, production methods, and materials that were to be used. Because of the box's unusual color and shape, these were far from standard. According to an agreement between the two divisions, the Thompson division was reimbursed by the Northern division for the cost of its design and development work.

When the specifications were all prepared, the Northern division asked for bids on the box from the Thompson division and from two outside companies, West Paper Company and Erie Papers, Ltd. Each division manager normally was free to buy from whichever supplier he or she wished; on intercompany sales, divisions selling to other divisions were expected to meet the going market price.

In 1975, the profit margins of converters such as the Thompson division were being squeezed. Thompson, as did many other similar converters, bought its board, liner, or paper, and its function was to print, cut, and shape the material into boxes.[8] Though it bought most of its materials from other Birch divisions, most of its sales were made to outside customers. If Thompson got the order from Northern, it probably would buy its liner board and corrugating medium from the Southern division of Birch. Thus, before giving its bid to Northern, Thompson got a quote for materials from the Southern Division.

Though Southern division had been running below capacity and had excess inventory, it quoted the market price, which had not noticeably weakened as a

---

[8]The walls of a corrugated box consist of outside and inside sheets of linerboard and a center layer of fluted corrugating medium.

result of the oversupply. Its out-of-pocket costs on both liner and corrugating medium were about 60 percent of the selling price. About 70 percent of Thompson's out-of-pocket cost of $400 a thousand for the order represented the cost of linerboard and corrugating medium.

The Northern division received bids on the boxes of $480 a thousand from the Thompson division, $430 a thousand from West Paper Company, and $432 a thousand from Erie Papers, Ltd. Erie Papers offered to buy from Birch the outside linerboard with the special printing already on it, but it would supply its own liner and corrugating medium. The outsider liner would be supplied by the Southern division at a price equivalent to $90 a thousand boxes, and the Thompson division would print it for $30 a thousand. Of the $30, about $25 would be out-of-pocket costs.

Since the bidding results appeared to be a little unusual, William Kenton, manager of the Northern division, discussed the wide discrepancy of bids with Birch's commercial vice president. She told the commercial vice president, ''We sell in a very competitive market, where higher costs cannot be passed on. How can we be expected to show a decent profit and return on investment if we have to buy our supplies at more than 10 percent over the going market?''

Knowing that Mr. Brunner had been unable to operate the Thompson division at capacity on occasion in the past few months, it seemed odd to the vice-president that Mr. Brunner would add the full 20 percent overhead and profit charge to his out-of-pocket costs. When he asked Mr. Brunner about this over the telephone, his answer was the statement that appears at the beginning of the case. Mr. Brunner continued saying that since they did the developmental work on the box and received no profit on that, he felt entitled to a good markup on the production of the box itself.

The vice president explored further the cost structures of the various divisions. He remembered a comment the controller had made at a meeting the week before to the effect that costs that for one division were variable could be largely fixed for the company as a whole. He knew that in the absence of specific orders from top management, Mr. Kenton would accept the lowest bid, which was that of the West Paper Company, for $430. However, it would be possible for top management to order the acceptance of another bid if the situation warranted such action. And although the volume represented by the transactions in question was less than 5 percent of the volume of any of the divisions involved, future transactions could conceivably raise similar problems.

a. Does the system motivate Mr. Brunner in such a way that actions he takes in the best interest of the Thompson division are also in the best interest of the Birch Paper Company? If your answer is no, give some specific instances related as closely as possible to the type of situation described in the case. Would the system correctly motivate managers of *other* divisions?

b. What should the vice president do?

36. **Impact of division performance measures on management incentives.** The home office staff of The Nomram Group evaluates managers of the Nomram divisions by keeping track of the rate of return each division earns on the average level of assets invested at the division. The home office staff considers 20 percent, which is The Nomram Group's after-tax cost of capital, to be the minimum acceptable annual rate of return on average investment. When a division's rate of return drops below 20 percent, division management can expect an unpleasant investigation by the home office and perhaps some firings. When the rate of return exceeds 20 percent and grows through time, the home office staff is invariably pleased and rewards division management. When the rate of return exceeds 20 percent but declines over time, the home office staff sends out unpleasant memorandums and cuts the profit-sharing bonuses of the division managers.

In Division A, average assets employed during the year amount to $60,000. Division A has been earning 40 percent per year on its average investment for several years. Management of Division A is proud of its extraordinary record—earning a steady 40 percent per year.

In Division B, average assets employed during the year also amount to $60,000. Division B has been earning 25 percent per year on its average investment. In the preceding 3 years, the rate of return on investment was 20 percent, 22 percent, and 23 percent, respectively. Management of Division B is proud of its record of steadily boosting earnings.

New investment opportunities have arisen at both Division A and Division B. In both cases, the new investment opportunity will require a cash outlay today of $30,000 and will provide a rate of return on investment of 30 percent for each of the next 8 years. The average amount of assets invested in the project will be $30,000 for each of the next 8 years. Both new investment opportunities have positive net present value when the discount rate is 20 percent per year (the after-tax cost of capital of The Nomram Group).

When word of the new opportunities reached the home office staff, the prospects of the two new investments pleased the staff, because both investments would yield a better-than-average return for The Nomram Group.

Management of Division A computed its rate of return on investment both with and without the new investment project and decided not to undertake the project. Management of Division B computed its rate of return on investment both with and without the new investment project and decided to undertake it.

When word of the two divisions' actions reached the home office staff, it was perplexed. Why did Division A's management turn down such a good opportunity? What in the behavior of the home office staff induced Division A's management to reject the new project? Is management of Division B doing a better job than management of Division A? What may the home office do to give Division A an incentive to act in a way more consistent with the well-being of The Nomram Group?

37. **Capital investment analysis and decentralized performance measurement—a comprehensive case.**[8] The following exchange occurred just after Diversified Electronics rejected a capital investment proposal.

---

[8]J. M. Lim, M. W. Maher, and J. S. Reece, copyright © 1993. This case requires knowledge of discounted cash flow methods.

Ralph Browning (Product Development): I just don't understand why you have rejected my proposal. This new investment is going to be a sure money maker for the Residential Products division. No matter how we price this new product, we can expect to make $230,000 on it before tax.

Sue Gold (Finance): I am sorry that you are upset with our decision, but this product proposal just does not meet our short-term ROI target of 15 percent after tax.

Browning: I'm not so sure about the ROI target, but it goes a long way toward meeting our earnings-per-share growth target of 20 cents per share after tax.

Phil Carlson (Executive Vice President): Ralph, you are right, of course, about the importance of earnings per share. However, we view our three divisions as investment centers. Proposals like yours must meet our ROI targets. It is not enough that you show an earnings-per-share increase.

Gold: We believe that a company like Diversified Electronics should have a return on investment of 12 percent after tax, especially given the interest rates we have had to pay recently. This is why we have targeted 12 percent as the appropriate minimum ROI for each division to earn next year.

Carlson: If it were not for the high interest rates and poor current economic outlook, Ralph, we would not be taking such a conservative position in evaluating new projects. This past year has been particularly rough for our industry. Our two major competitors had ROIs of 10.8 and 12.3 percent. Though our ROI of about 9 percent after tax was reasonable (see Exhibit 15.9), performance varied from division to division. Professional Services did very well with 15 percent ROI, while the Residential Products division managed just 10 percent. The performance of the Aerospace Products division was especially dismal, with an ROI of only 6 percent. We expect divisions in the future to carry their share of the load.

Chris McGregor (Aerospace Products): My division would be showing much higher ROI if we had a lot of old equipment like the Residential Products or relied heavily on human labor like Professional Services.

Carlson: I don't really see the point you are trying to make, Chris.

Diversified Electronics, a growing company in the electronics industry, had grown to its present size of more than $140 million in sales. (See Exhibits 15.7, 15.8, and 15.9 for financial data.) Diversified Electronics has three divisions, Residential Products, Aerospace Products, and Professional Services, each of which accounts for about one-third of Diversified Electronics' sales. Residential Products, the oldest division, produces furnace thermostats and similar products. The Aerospace Products division is a large job shop that builds electronic devices to customer specifications. A typical job or batch takes several months to complete. About one-half of Aerospace Products' sales are to the U.S. Defense Department. The newest of the three divisions, Professional Services, provides consulting engineering services. This division has grown tremendously since Diversified Electronics acquired it 7 years ago.

Each division operates independently of the others and corporate management treats each as a separate entity. Division managers make many of the operating decisions. Corporate management coordinates the activities of the

---

Exhibit 15.7

DIVERSIFIED ELECTRONICS
Income Statement for 1992 and 1993
(all dollar amounts in thousands, except earnings-per-share figures)

	Year Ended December 31	
	1992	**1993**
Sales..	$141,462	$148,220
Cost of Goods Sold................................	108,118	113,115
Gross Margin	$ 33,344	$ 35,105
Selling and General................................	13,014	13,692
Profit before Taxes and Interest	$ 20,330	$ 21,413
Interest Expense	1,190	1,952
Profit before Taxes	$ 19,140	$ 19,461
Income Tax Expense	7,886	7,454
Net Income	$ 11,254	$ 12,007
Earnings per Share (2,000 shares outstanding in 1992 and 1993)	$5.63	$6.00

---

various divisions, which includes review of all investment proposals over $400,000.

Diversified Electronics measures return on investment as the division's Net Income divided by total assets. Each division's expenses includes the allocated portion of corporate administrative expenses.

Exhibit 15.8

DIVERSIFIED ELECTRONICS
Balance Sheets for 1992 and 1993
(all dollar amounts in thousands)

	December 31	
	1992	**1993**
Assets		
Cash and Temporary Investments	$ 1,404	$ 1,469
Accounts Receivable................................	13,688	15,607
Inventories..	42,162	45,467
Total Current Assets	$ 57,254	$ 62,543
Plant and Equipment:		
Original Cost.....................................	107,326	115,736
Accumulated Depreciation	42,691	45,979
Net	$ 64,635	$ 69,757
Investments and Other Assets	3,143	3,119
Total Assets	$125,032	$135,419

(continued)

Exhibit 15.8 *(continued)*

	December 31	
	1992	**1993**
Liabilities and Owners' Equity		
Accounts Payable	$ 10,720	$ 12,286
Taxes Payable	1,210	1,045
Current Portion of Long-Term Debt	—	1,634
Total Current Liabilities	$ 11,930	$ 14,965
Deferred Income Taxes	559	985
Long-Term Debt	12,622	15,448
Total Liabilities	$ 25,111	$ 31,398
Common Stock.	47,368	47,368
Retained Earnings	52,553	56,653
Total Owners' Equity	$ 99,921	$104,021
Total Liabilities and Owners' Equity	$125,032	$135,419

Since each of Diversified Electronics' divisions is located in a separate facility, management can easily attribute most assets, including receivables, to specific divisions. Management allocates the corporate office assets, including the centrally controlled cash account, to the divisions on the basis of divisional revenues.

Exhibit 15.10 shows the details of Ralph Browning's rejected product proposal.

a. Why did corporate headquarters reject Ralph Browning's product proposal? Was their decision the right one? If top management used the discounted cash flow (DCF) method instead, what would the results be? The company uses a 15-percent cost of capital (i.e., hurdle rate) in evaluating projects such as these.

b. Evaluate the manner in which Diversified Electronics has implemented the investment center concept. What pitfalls did they apparently not anticipate? What, if anything, should be done with regard to the investment center approach and the use of ROI as a measure of performance?

c. What conflicting incentives for managers can occur between the use of a yearly ROI performance measure and DCF for capital budgeting?

Exhibit 15.9

DIVERSIFIED ELECTRONICS
Ratio Analysis

	1992	1993
ROI = Net Income/Total Assets	$\dfrac{\$11,254}{\$125,032} = 9.0\%$	$\dfrac{\$12,007}{\$135,419} = 8.9\%$

Exhibit 15.10

DIVERSIFIED ELECTRONICS
Financial Data for New Product Proposal

---

1. Projected Asset Investment:[a]

Land Purchase	$ 200,000
Plant and Equipment[b]	800,000
Total	$1,000,000

2. Cost Data, before Taxes (first year):

Variable Cost per Unit	$3.00
Differential Fixed Costs[c]	$170,000

3. Price/Market Estimate (first year):

Unit Price	$7.00
Sales	100,000 Units

4. Taxes: The company assumes a 40-percent tax rate for investment analyses. Depreciation of plant and equipment according to tax law is as follows: Year 1, 20 percent; Year 2, 32 percent; Year 3, 19 percent; Year 4, 14.5 percent; Year 5, 14.5 percent. Taxes are paid for taxable income in Year 1 at the end of Year 1, taxes for Year 2 at the end of Year 2, etc.

5. Inflation is assumed to be 10 percent per year and applies to revenues and all costs except depreciation.

6. The project has an 8-year life. Land will be sold at the end of Year 8. The nominal land price is expected to increase with inflation.

---

[a]Assumes sales of 100,000 units.

[b]Annual capacity of 120,000 units.

[c]Includes straight-line depreciation on new plant and equipment, depreciated for 8 years with no net salvage value at the end of 8 years.

---

38. **Honeywell, Inc.: relative performance evaluation.**[9] A major issue in divisional performance evaluation is the process companies use to separate performance results that division managers can control from those that outside environmental factors cause. For instance, firms could hold division managers accountable for achieving a fixed target, independent of the performance of other divisions operating in similar product markets, or evaluate their performance relative to the performance of other divisions. The latter approach, known as *relative performance evaluation,* is analogous to ''grading on the curve.''

The Aerospace and Defense Business at Honeywell, Inc., experimented with relative performance evaluation. Honeywell is a technology-oriented company, particularly in the Aerospace and Defense Business. They historically emphasize growth, customer satisfaction, and new product development. As the Aerospace and Defense Business has become more cost competitive, with less cost-plus contracting, in recent years top management has become more interested in providing incentives to reduce costs. Honeywell has also increased its emphasis on financial measures of performance. The firm changed incentive contracts for top management and division managers to

---

[9]Based on the authors' research.

emphasize return on investment. Aerospace and Defense, in particular, experimented with a "peer company analysis" to create a self-reassessment of the status quo.

The strategic planning group that performed the peer group analysis first identified the business segments of 22 competitors in the aerospace and defense industry. Of these 22 competitors, 9 are prime contractors (e.g., Boeing and Lockheed), who are in aerospace and defense but do not face the same market environment. Of the remaining 13 competitors, public data were not available for two competitors, leaving 11 competitors that Aerospace and Defense managers believed face the same market environment as they did.

Honeywell used these results initially to identify highly ranked competitors and to examine their characteristics to see what Aerospace and Defense could do to improve its financial performance. Over time, the firm will incorporate these comparisons with peer companies into the evaluation of division managers' performance.

a. What are the advantages to Honeywell of using relative performance evaluation?

b. As a division manager, would you rather have your performance evaluated using relative performance evaluation ("grading on the curve") or without regard to your competitors?

Suggested Solutions to Even-Numbered Exercises

22. **Return on investment computations.**

a. New York Division: $\dfrac{\$500,000}{\$4,000,000} = 12.5\%$

Philadelphia Division: $\dfrac{\$500,000}{\$5,000,000} = 10\%$

Los Angeles Division: $\dfrac{\$500,000}{\$6,000,000} = 8.33\%$

b. New York Division:

$$\dfrac{\$500,000 - (\$4,000,000/\$15,000,000)(\$900,000)}{\$4,000,000} = 6.5\%$$

Philadelphia Division:

$$\dfrac{\$500,000 - (\$5,000,000/\$15,000,000)(\$900,000)}{\$5,000,000} = 4.0\%$$

Los Angeles Division:

$$\dfrac{\$500,000 - (\$6,000,000/\$15,000,000)(\$900,000)}{\$6,000,000} = 2.33\%$$

c. New York Division:

$$\dfrac{\$500,000 - (\$24,000,000/\$60,000,000)(\$900,000)}{\$4,000,000} = 3.5\%$$

Philadelphia Division:
$$\frac{\$500,000 - (\$20,000,000/\$60,000,000)(\$900,000)}{\$5,000,000} = 4.0\%$$

Los Angeles Division:
$$\frac{\$500,000 - (\$16,000,000/\$60,000,000)(\$900,000)}{\$6,000,000} = 4.33\%.$$

d. New York Division:
$$\frac{\$500,000 - (22,500/45,000)(\$900,000)}{\$4,000,000} = 1.25\%$$

Philadelphia Division:
$$\frac{\$500,000 - (12,000/45,000)(\$900,000)}{\$5,000,000} = 5.2\%$$

Los Angeles Division:
$$\frac{\$500,000 - (10,500/45,000)(\$900,000)}{\$6,000,000} = 4.83\%.$$

24. ROI computations with replacement costs.

a. Boston Division: $\dfrac{\$400,000}{\$4,000,000} = 10\%;$ Mexico City Division: $\dfrac{\$600,000}{\$7,500,000} = 8\%.$

b. Boston Division: $\dfrac{\$400,000}{\$6,000,000} = 6.67\%;$ Mexico City Division: $\dfrac{\$600,000}{\$8,000,000} = 7.5\%.$

c. Analysts make two principal arguments for using acquisition cost in the denominator as in part **a.** First, firms can easily obtain it from their records and it does not require estimates of current replacement costs. Second, it is consistent with the measurement of net income in the numerator (that is, depreciation expense is based on acquisition cost, and unrealized holding gains are excluded). Analysts also make two principal arguments for using current replacement cost in the denominator as in part **b.** First, it eliminates the effects of price changes and permits the division that can use the depreciable assets most efficiently to show a better ROI. Second, as discussed in the chapter, it may lead division managers to make better equipment-replacement decisions. If firms use acquisition cost as the valuation basis in calculating ROI, divisions with older, more fully depreciated assets may be reluctant to replace them and thereby introduce higher, current amounts in the denominator. If firms use current replacement cost in the denominator, the asset base will be the same regardless of whether or not the assets are replaced. Thus the replacement decision can be made properly (that is, based on net present value), independent of any effects on ROI.

26. Comparing profit margin and ROI as performance measures. The return on investment (ROI), profit margin percentage, and asset turnover ratio of the three divisions follow. (Asset turnover is not required, but we include it to show the relation between ROI and its components.)

	Return on Investment	=	Profit Margin Percentage	×	Asset Turnover Ratio

New Hampshire District:	$\dfrac{\$200,000}{\$2,000,000}$	$=$	$\dfrac{\$200,000}{\$3,800,000}$	$\times$	$\dfrac{\$3,800,000}{\$2,000,000}$
	10%	=	5.26%	×	1.9.
Illinois District:	$\dfrac{\$500,000}{\$6,250,000}$	$=$	$\dfrac{\$500,000}{\$17,000,000}$	$\times$	$\dfrac{\$17,000,000}{\$6,250,000}$
	8%	=	2.94%	×	2.72.
California District	$\dfrac{\$1,000,000}{\$8,000,000}$	$=$	$\dfrac{\$1,000,000}{\$20,000,000}$	$\times$	$\dfrac{\$20,000,000}{\$8,000,000}$
	12.5%	=	5%	×	2.5.

a. Using the profit margin percentage, the ranking of the divisions is (1) New Hampshire, (2) California, and (3) Illinois.

b. Using ROI, the ranking of divisions is (1) California, (2) New Hampshire, and (3) Illinois.

c. The ROI is a better measure of overall performance because it relates profits to the investment, or capital, required to generate those profits. New Hampshire had the largest profit margin percentage. It required more capital to generate a dollar of sales than did California. Thus its overall profitability is less. Illinois had the largest asset turnover ratio. However, it generated the smallest amount of net income per dollar of sales, resulting in the lowest ROI of the three divisions.

28. ROI and residual income computations.

$$\text{Annual Income} = \$70,000 - \dfrac{\$160,000}{5} = \$38,000.$$

Year	Investment Base	a. ROI $38,000/Base	b. Residual Income $38,000 − 25 Percent × Base
1	$160,000	23.8 Percent	$ (2,000)
2	128,000[a]	29.7	6,000
3	96,000	39.6	14,000
4	64,000	59.4	22,000
5	32,000	118.8	30,000

[a]Base decreases by annual depreciation of $32,000.

30. **Transfer pricing.**

a.

	Auditors	Consultants	Accounting Firm	
Transfer Internally ...	Pay $200	Receive $200	Pays	$ 70
		Pay 70	Pays	$ 70
Transfer Externally ..	Pay $180	Receive $200	Receives	$ 20 (net)
		Pay 70	Pays	$ 70
			Pays	$ 50

It is advantageous to transfer externally.

b.

	Auditors	Consultants	Accounting Firm
Transfer Internally	Pay $200	Receive $200	Pays $ 70
		Pay 70	Pays $ 70
Transfer Externally ...	Pays $180	Receives	Pays $180
		and Pays 0	

It is advantageous to transfer internally.

PART FIVE

Special Topics

Chapter 16

Getting the Most from Managerial Accounting

1. See how financial reports can be misleading.

2. Understand the need for different accounting information for different decisions.

3. Understand how accounting information developed for external reporting is often not appropriate for managerial use.

4. Know key characteristics of divisional incentive compensation plans.

5. Explain the nature of fraudulent financial reporting.

6. Understand motives and situations that are conducive to fraudulent financial reporting.

7. Know methods of reducing opportunities for fraudulent reporting.

This book focuses on three principal uses of accounting information: (1) decision making; (2) planning and internal performance evaluation; and (3) external financial reporting. Data useful for one of these purposes may be inappropriate for another. This chapter reviews the data needed for each of these purposes and provides examples of how errors can result when managers use data designed for one purpose for a different purpose. We also discuss incentive and ethical issues in managerial accounting.

We present the material in this chapter in a format different from previous chapters. This chapter synthesizes concepts discussed in previous chapters. We use case studies, both in the chapter and in the end-of-chapter materials, to bring out the key issues. We intend to raise these issues here so that you will be aware of them and be prepared to deal with them in your career.

Managerial Decision Making Meets Financial Reporting

This section contains an illustration based on discussions between a firm's president (John Presley), its controller (Jill Contreras), and the manager of a division (Tom Divito). The initial setting takes place during January, Year 2, at a meeting of the three.

Presley (President): Tom, I have just received a report on the first year of operations for your division (Exhibit 16.1), and the results look bad. You show a loss of $2,000 for the year. Our shareholders want to see increasing net income and earnings per share each year. We can't afford to have one division pulling down the rest of the company.

Divito (Division Manager): But Mr. Presley, we operated exactly according to plan during Year 1. We anticipated producing 12,000 units, and we were right on the mark. At this production level, we projected a unit production cost of $4.50, and that's right where we came out.

Presley: I'm still not happy. I've received an offer from a competitor to purchase your inventory and plant assets for $17,000, and I'm inclined to accept.

Contreras (Controller): I think such a decision would be unwise until we analyze the situation further. Basing such a decision on the divisional profit report for Year 1 could lead to a bad decision. For one thing, Exhibit 16.1 reports the results for last year. That's history now; we can't do anything about the loss incurred. What's important for decision making is what we expect to happen in the future.

Presley: Okay, Jill. You've just finished the budget for Year 2. What do you show for Tom's division this year?

Exhibit 16.1

Divisional Performance Report for Year 1

Sales (10,000 × $5)		$50,000
Cost of Goods Sold:		
Beginning Inventory	$ 0	
Direct Materials (12,000 × $2.00)	24,000	
Direct Labor (12,000 × $1.50)	18,000	
Overhead:		
Variable (12,000 units × $.75 per unit)	9,000	
Fixed (12,000 units × $.25[a] per unit)	3,000	
Total	$54,000	
Less Ending Inventory (2,000 × $4.50)	(9,000)	
Cost of Goods Sold		(45,000)
Gross Margin		$ 5,000
Selling Expenses (.04 × $50,000)		(2,000)
Share of Corporate Administrative Costs (.10 × $50,000)		(5,000)
Divisional Net Loss		$ (2,000)

[a] $\dfrac{\text{Budgeted and Actual Fixed Overhead Costs}}{\text{Budgeted and Actual Production in Units}} = \dfrac{\$3,000}{12,000} = \$.25$ per unit.

Exhibit 16.2

Divisional Budget for Year 2

Sales (12,000 × $5)		$60,000
Cost of Goods Sold:		
Beginning Inventory (2,000 × $4.50)	$ 9,000	
Direct Materials (12,000 × $2.00)	24,000	
Direct Labor (12,000 × $1.50)	18,000	
Overhead:		
Variable (12,000 units × $.75 per unit)	9,000	
Fixed (12,000 units × $.25[a] per unit)	3,000	
Total	$63,000	
Less Ending Inventory (2,000 × $4.50)	(9,000)	
Cost of Goods Sold		(54,000)
Gross Margin		$ 6,000
Selling Expenses (.04 × $60,000)		(2,400)
Share of Corporate Administrative Costs (.10 × $60,000)		(6,000)
Divisional Net Loss		$ (2,400)

[a] $\dfrac{\text{Budgeted Fixed Overhead Costs}}{\text{Budgeted Production}} = \dfrac{\$3,000}{12,000} = \$.25$ per unit.

Contreras: Exhibit 16.2 presents the expected results for Year 2. We expect sales to increase to 12,000 units, which should improve things a bit. Tom expects to produce 12,000 units again at a unit cost of $4.50. The higher sales level, however, will mean that Tom's division must absorb a higher portion of central corporate costs. Thus we project a loss of $2,400 for next year.

Presley: You mean with an increase in sales of $10,000, we expect an even *bigger* loss next year? That about does it for me. How much loss will I report to shareholders if I sell the division for $17,000?

Contreras: The inventory on hand at the beginning of Year 2 costs us $9,000 (= 2,000 × $4.50) to produce. We acquired the plant assets at the beginning of Year 1 for $10,000. Based on straight-line depreciation and a 10-year life, they now have a book value of $9,000. Thus we would lose $1,000 (= $17,000 − $9,000 − $9,000) on the sale before taxes.

Presley: I am inclined to cut my losses and get rid of the division. I'll report a loss of $1,000 instead of $2,400 for Year 2, and I won't have to worry about the division dragging down my profits in future years.

Contreras: That may be the correct decision, but I think we should think this thing through more clearly. Exhibit 16.2 does show the expected divisional profit for Year 2 instead of actual for Year 1, but you should not base your decision on this analysis alone.

First, we prepared Exhibit 16.2 using generally accepted accounting principles (GAAP). Although we must follow GAAP for external reporting, we're not constrained to do so for internal managerial purposes. We should be looking at the future cash flows under each of our alternatives, not accounting profits.

Presley: Because we sell most of our products for cash or on short-term credit and pay most of our expenses soon after purchase, can't we assume that the revenues and expenses in Exhibit 16.2 are essentially the same as cash receipts and disbursements?

Contreras: That's okay for most items, but not for all. For example, fixed manufacturing overhead includes a $1,000 depreciation charge, which is not a cash flow. Furthermore, we should focus primarily on those future cash flows that differ between alternatives.

Presley: Jill, why don't you show me what Exhibit 16.2 would look like if it focused just on those cash flows for Year 2 that would differ between alternatives?

Contreras: I thought you might want such analysis. Exhibit 16.3 shows what I came up with. As you can see, cash outflows for fixed manufacturing overhead will equal $2,000 if we operate the division; depreciation of $1,000 does not require a cash outflow. The $2,000 includes property taxes and insurance on the division's inventory and plant assets. Also, I have left out the $6,000 share of central corporate expenses.

Presley: Wait a minute! Your salary and my salary will require cash next year. I don't intend to work for nothing. The division's fair share of central corporate expenses is $6,000. Thus you must change the net cash inflow from operating the division of $4,600 in your analysis to a net cash outflow of $1,400.

Contreras: Mr. Presley, I don't intend to work for nothing any more than you do. I left the $6,000 out of the analysis because the firm will incur that cost whether we continue to operate the division or whether we sell it off. We can safely ignore future cash flows that will not differ between alternatives because they are the same in either case.

Presley: I'm not totally convinced yet, but let's see where we stand. If I sell the division outright, I will get $17,000 in cash. If I operate the division next year, I will receive $4,600. I am inclined to stick by my earlier inclination to sell the division for the $12,400 differential cash flow. Jill, is this right, or am I missing some other point?

Contreras: Possibly. You have compared the two alternatives over different time periods. The plant assets in the division have a remaining useful life of 9 years, not

Exhibit 16.3

Cash Flows Comparison:
Keep Division versus Sell Division

	Keep Division (1)	Sell Division (2)	Keep − Sell Differential Cash Flows = (1) − (2) (3)
Sales Revenue (12,000 × $5.00)	$60,000	$ —	$ 60,000
Direct Materials (12,000 × $2.00)	(24,000)	—	(24,000)
Direct Labor (12,000 × $1.50)	(18,000)	—	(18,000)
Variable Overhead (12,000 × $.75)	(9,000)	—	(9,000)
Fixed Overhead ($3,000 − $1,000)	(2,000)	—	(2,000)
Selling Expense ($60,000 × .04)	(2,400)	—	(2,400)
Selling Price of Division	—	17,000	(17,000)
Net Cash Flows	$ 4,600	$17,000	$(12,400)

just 1 year. We have to look at the cash flows that the division would generate over the next 9 years to see the benefit of keeping the division.

Presley: Assuming that the division will generate a net cash inflow of $4,600 each year during the next 9 years, we will generate $41,400 of cash flow. But I know that we cannot compare the $41,400 to the $17,000 cash we would get from selling the division, because the $41,400 inflows are spread out more. To make the two sets of cash flows comparable, I must discount the annual $4,600 cash flows back for 9 years at our cost of capital of 12 percent. That results in a net present value of $24,510.[1] The present value of selling the division is, of course, $17,000. Maybe we shouldn't sell the division.

Divito: That's what I like to hear. I was beginning to wonder where I would be working next year.

Presley: Jill, as I understand it, we've calculated the present value of the future cash flows that will differ between the alternatives. I think I understand now why this is the correct basis for making managerial decisions. Before bringing important nonquantitative factors into the decision, have we left out anything?

Contreras: Unfortunately, yes. We have not considered income taxes. Because 12 percent is the after-tax cost of capital, we must compute the income tax ramifications of this decision.

Presley: But Jill, you know that we have centralized our income tax planning and strategy function in central corporate headquarters. We don't hold the divisions responsible for the impact of income taxes on their decisions. We report divisional profit performance on a before-tax basis.

Contreras: Our treatment of income taxes may or may not be appropriate for internal performance reporting. But for decision making, income taxes affect cash flows and we must consider them. At our tax rate of 40 percent, income taxes can affect the decision greatly.

Presley: Well, Jill, let's see the analysis.

Contreras: Exhibit 16.4 gives the figures. The top panel shows the present value of the cash inflows and outflows along with the related tax effects, assuming that we continue to operate the division. While depreciation is itself not a cash flow, we can subtract depreciation in calculating taxable income. Thus it indirectly affects cash flows. The amounts reported as depreciation for tax purposes are the accelerated cost recovery amounts. Depreciation for tax purposes follows: Year 1, $1,500; Year 2, $2,200; Year 3, $2,100; Year 4, $2,100; Year 5, $2,100. The net present value if the division continues to operate is $17,292.

If we sell the division, we'll lose on the disposal of the inventory and equipment. As I indicated earlier, the inventory has a book value of $9,000 for both tax and financial reporting. We depreciated the plant assets, however, during Year 1 at $1,000 for financial reporting and $1,500 for tax reporting. In calculating the tax consequences of the sale, the *tax* basis of the plant assets of $8,500 (= $10,000 − $1,500) is relevant. The loss on the sale for tax purposes is $500 (= $17,000 − $9,000 − $8,500) and the tax savings are $200 (= .40 × $500).

---

[1]$24,510 = $4,600 × 5.32825, the factor for the present value of an annuity in arrears for nine periods at twelve percent.

Exhibit 16.4

After-Tax Cash Flow Comparison:
Keep Division versus Sell Division

	Present Value at 12 Percent	End of Period								
		2	3	4	5	6	7	8	9	10
Keep Division										
Cash Receipts from Sales	$319,695[a]	$60,000	$60,000	$60,000	$60,000	$60,000	$60,000	$60,000	$60,000	$60,000
Cash Expenditures for Variable Manufacturing Costs	(271,741)[a]	(51,000)	(51,000)	(51,000)	(51,000)	(51,000)	(51,000)	(51,000)	(51,000)	(51,000)
Cash Expenditures for Fixed Manufacturing Costs	(10,657)[a]	(2,000)	(2,000)	(2,000)	(2,000)	(2,000)	(2,000)	(2,000)	(2,000)	(2,000)
Cash Expenditures for Selling Expenses	(12,788)[a]	(2,400)	(2,400)	(2,400)	(2,400)	(2,400)	(2,400)	(2,400)	(2,400)	(2,400)
Depreciation for Tax Purposes		(2,200)	(2,100)	(2,100)	(2,100)	—	—	—	—	—
Taxable Income		$ 2,400	$ 2,500	$ 2,500	$ 2,500	$ 4,600	$ 4,600	$ 4,600	$ 4,600	$ 4,600
Cash Expenditures for Income Taxes at 40 Percent	(7,217)	(960)	(1,000)	(1,000)	(1,000)	(1,840)	(1,840)	(1,840)	(1,840)	(1,840)
Net Present Value	$ 17,292									
Sell Division										
Selling Price	$ 17,000									
Tax Effect of Loss on Sale	200[b]									
Net Present Value	$ 17,200									

[a]Based on a factor of 5.32825, the present value of an annuity in arrears for nine periods at twelve percent.

[b]Cash inflow is 40 percent of loss at $500 = $17,000 − $9,000 − $8,500; 40 × $500 loss is $200.

Presley: As I see it, the net present value of the after-tax cash flows favors keeping the division, but it's so close that I think selling is more prudent—''a bird in the hand,'' you know.

Divito: Before you make up your mind, Mr. Presley, I would like to put in my two cents about delaying such a sale for a while. The market for our products is expanding. With aggressive promotion, I believe that we can increase our market share. Given this potential for growth, I think that we can cover not only our own costs but provide for coverage of central corporate costs as well. We also anticipate that through more efficient purchasing of raw materials and better training of our workers, we can reduce our direct manufacturing costs.

Presley: OK, Tom, I'll let you have a go at it for another year. Perhaps one year of operation is not enough to form a judgment on the profit-generating ability of your division. Good luck.

One Year Later

John Presley (President), Jill Contreras (Controller), and Tom Divito (Division Manager) meet to review the performance of Tom's division for Year 2.

Presley: Well, Tom, now you face the time of reckoning. I've kept a copy of the budget for your division for Year 2 (Exhibit 16.2) in my desk for the last year. I have asked Jill to show your actual results for Year 2 side by side with your budget so that I can see clearly how you've done. Jill, have you prepared the analysis?

Contreras: Yes; Exhibit 16.5 presents the results.

Presley: Well, I like your actual bottom line for Year 2—a profit of $1,400 instead of a loss of $2,400. I'm not happy, though, with the large production cost

---

Exhibit 16.5

Comparison of Budgeted and Actual Performance for Year 2

	Budget	Actual	Variance
Sales.....................................	$ 60,000	$ 61,200	$ 1,200
Cost of Goods Sold:			
Beginning Inventory.........................	$ 9,000	$ 9,000	—
Direct Materials	24,000	28,500	$ (4,500)
Direct Labor	18,000	21,750	(3,750)
Overhead:			
Variable	9,000	10,500	(1,500)
Fixed....................................	3,000	3,750	(750)
Total	$ 63,000	$ 73,500	$(10,500)
Less Ending Inventory	(9,000)	(21,500)	12,500
Cost of Goods Sold.........................	$ 54,000	$ 52,000	$ 2,000
Gross Margin	$ 6,000	$ 9,200	$ 3,200
Fixed Overhead Variance......................	—	750	750
Selling Expenses	(2,400)	(2,520)	(120)
Share of Corporate Administrative Costs	(6,000)	(6,030)	(30)
Division Net Profit (Loss)	$ (2,400)	$ 1,400	$ 3,800

variances. In contrast to the promises made a year ago, your production costs have been much larger than expected. It looks to me like you have been grossly inefficient. I don't understand two things about this performance report. What do the $12,500 variance relating to ending inventory and the $750 fixed overhead variance mean?

Contreras: In Exhibit 16.5, we base the budget amounts on a production level of 12,000 units. But the division actually produced 15,000 units. The unfavorable manufacturing cost variances and the ending inventory variance result from the fact you are comparing the manufactured costs expected to be incurred in producing 12,000 units with the actual costs of producing 15,000 units.

Presley: I read the other day about something called a "flexible budget." It seemed to apply when you produced or sold a different number of units than you expected.

Contreras: That's right. We know what the manufacturing costs should have been to produce 12,000 units. We can now see what they should have been to produce the 15,000 units actually produced. Exhibit 16.6 presents the analysis. As you can see, the actual manufacturing costs for direct material, direct labor, and variable manufacturing overhead were less than they should have been for 15,000 units. Thus the firm realized the efficiencies that Tom promised you.

Divito: I'm glad to see that they show up in my performance report. I increased production this year because I anticipate that we will capture a larger market share in Year 3. I was concerned, though, about how the increase in costs required for these additional units would show up in my performance report, because the budgeted costs based on 12,000 units were so much less. I like this flexible budget report.

Exhibit 16.6

Comparison of Flexible Budget and Actual Performance for Year 2

	Flexible Budget	Actual	Variance
Sales	$ 60,000	$ 61,200	$ 1,200
Costs of Goods Sold:			
Beginning Inventory	$ 9,000	$ 9,000	$ —
Direct Materials	30,000	28,500	1,500
Direct Labor	22,500	21,750	750
Overhead:			
Variable	11,250	10,500	750
Fixed	3,000	3,750	(750)
Total	$ 75,750	$ 73,500	$ 2,250
Less Ending Inventory	(21,500)	(21,500)	—
Cost of Goods Sold	$ 54,250	$ 52,000	$ 2,250
Gross Margin	$ 5,750	$ 9,200	$ 3,450
Fixed Overhead Variance	—	750	750
Selling Expenses	(2,400)	(2,520)	(120)
Share of Corporate Administrative Costs	(6,000)	(6,030)	(30)
Division Net Profit	$ (2,650)	$ 1,400	$ 4,050

Presley: You have answered my question about the large variable manufacturing cost variances and about the ending inventory variance. I can see now that they relate to the larger production volume achieved. But what about the $750 fixed overhead variance? What's that?

Contreras: That variance results from producing more units than anticipated. We budgeted fixed overhead costs for Year 2 to be $3,000. With anticipated production of 12,000 units, we set the fixed overhead rate at $.25 per unit. By producing 15,000 units, the division applied $3,750 (= 15,000 × $.25) to units produced. The difference of $750 is not really a variance at all. We should not give the division manager any credits for such a variance.

Divito: Now wait a minute. I used my plant assets more efficiently this year, producing 15,000 units instead of 12,000 units. The $750 fixed overhead variance measures the benefits of this more efficient utilization, and I should get credit for it.

Contreras: The practice under full absorption costing of treating fixed costs like variable costs caused the variance. We prepared Exhibit 16.6 in accordance with full absorption costing as required under GAAP for financial reporting. We divided fixed manufacturing costs for the year by the expected level of production to obtain a rate per unit, $.25 in this case. We allocated each unit produced a share of the fixed cost using this rate. Because you produced 3,000 more units than anticipated, you applied $750 (= 3,000 × $.25) more fixed overhead to production than you would have *had you anticipated that you would produce 15,000 units during Year 2.* Note that the $750 favorable variance in the lower portion offsets the unfavorable variance of $750 for fixed overhead in the upper portion of Exhibit 16.6. Full absorption costing can do some crazy things to your performance report when expected and actual production differ.

Presley: What you say makes sense, but we've little choice. We must use full absorption costing in our external financial statements.

Contreras: Yes, but GAAP do not constrain our internal reports. With some modifications, we can adapt our accounting system to generate data both on a full absorption costing basis for external reporting and on another basis for internal performance evaluation.

Presley: What do you suggest we should do?

Contreras: We should classify our costs according to their behavior, either variable or fixed. Raw materials and direct labor are variable. Except for a few easily identifiable overhead items (depreciation, insurance, property taxes), our overhead costs are essentially variable as well. Selling costs are also variable. The performance report would then distinguish costs by their behavior rather than by their nature (that is, production, selling). Exhibit 16.7 shows what I mean. Product costs include only variable material, labor, and overhead costs. Fixed costs are treated as an expense of the period. I prepared this report on a variable costing, instead of absorption costing, basis. The report shows no overapplied fixed overhead nor a favorable overhead variance resulting from producing more than expected. This format has the added advantage of classifying data in a form useful for decisions. For many decisions, incremental costs will be the variable costs. If the time horizon is short enough, fixed costs often do not change. Of course, in the long run decisions can alter even the fixed costs.

Exhibit 16.7

Comparison of Flexible Budget and Actual Performance for Year 2 Using Variable Costing

	Flexible Budget		Actual		
	Per Unit	Total	Per Unit	Total	Variance
Sales......................	$5.00	$60,000	$5.10	$61,200	$1,200
Variable Costs:					
Manufacturing:					
Beginning Inventory.......		$ 8,500		$ 8,500	
Direct Materials	$2.00	30,000	$1.90	28,500	$1,500
Direct Labor	1.50	22,500	1.45	21,750	750
Variable Overhead........	.75	11,250	.70	10,500	750
Total	$4.25	$72,250	$4.05	$69,250	$3,000
Less Ending Inventory		(21,250)		(20,250)	(1,000)
Goods Sold		$51,000		$49,000	$2,000
Selling.....................	.20	2,400	.21	2,520	(120)
Total Variable Costs	$4.45	$53,400	$4.26	$51,520	$1,880
Contribution Margin	$ .55	$ 6,600	$ .84	$ 9,680	$3,080
Fixed Costs:					
Manufacturing..............	—	(3,000)	—	(3,000)	—
Contribution to Corporate Administrative Costs and Corporate Profits		$ 3,600		$ 6,680	

Presley: The only thing that bothers me with the performance report you have prepared in Exhibit 16.7 is that you have deleted the division's share of central costs. I can buy the fact that our decision to continue running the division or to sell it does not affect these costs and, therefore, they are irrelevant to that decision. However, someone must cover these costs if the company is to survive in the long run.

Divito: This is a good place for me to sound off. It really bothers me that my division can operate at a positive divisional profit before allocation of central corporate costs, but my bottom line really gets hit by costs over which I have no control. Not only can't I control these costs, but I get penalized when my sales go up. Central corporate headquarters provides us with little or no marketing support. So why should they get a bigger piece of the action when my division increases its sales?

Contreras: You have both made legitimate points. Mr. Presley, you are correct that revenues from the operating divisions must cover these costs if the firm is to survive. Tom, you have grounds for complaining that these costs are not under your control. The decentralized, divisional corporate structure makes each operating unit feel that it is running its own separate company. If the allocation of central corporate costs to the division motivates you to hold back on sales increases, we must do something about the allocation. We either have to stop allocating or else find a more appropriate allocation method. We will judge your performance primarily on your division's contribution to central corporate expenses and net income.

Divito: This seems reasonable to me.

Presley: Good, then we have developed a new basis for internal performance evaluation. We will break out costs by responsibility center according to their behavior (variable or fixed). We will design the performance report in a variable costing format. Jill, at the end of each year, you can make the necessary adjustments to convert to an absorption costing basis for external reporting.

Contreras: Now we see the three different uses of accounting data and the appropriate model for each one. In managerial decision making, we are concerned with the differential future cash flows between alternatives. The three key words are (1) future, (2) cash flows, and (3) differential. In many cases, variable costs will differ and fixed costs will not. However, some fixed costs may also differ if we can eliminate or alter them even in the short run. In the long run, we can change all costs, which makes all costs differential. If the decision horizon extends beyond 1 year, we should discount the differential cash flows to their present value when comparing alternatives.

In planning, control, and internal performance evaluation, we focus on individual responsibility centers. We want to attribute revenues and costs to those units within a firm that control the amounts. Because unitizing fixed manufacturing overhead under absorption costing can lead to confusing results, the firm should prepare the performance report on a variable costing basis. Each division should subtract variable costs from revenue to obtain the contribution margin. Then it should subtract fixed costs of the responsibility center to obtain the center's contribution to coverage of central corporate expenses and to corporate profits.

For external reporting, we are required to follow generally accepted accounting principles (GAAP). The main point to keep in mind is that we do not and, in general, should not use these same reports for managerial decision making, planning, and control. While GAAP theoretically should also be concerned primarily with economic effects, standard setters set accounting for financial reporting based on objectivity, practicability, and political pressure.

Different Data for Different Purposes

We use accounting data for several different purposes: decision making, managerial planning, control, internal performance evaluation, external financial reporting, income tax reporting, and reporting to various regulatory agencies. Data appropriate for one of these purposes is sometimes inappropriate for another.

Exhibit 16.8 summarizes some of the uses of accounting information and contrasts the data necessary for different uses. If you read across the exhibit from left to right, you will see how accounting requirements change as you move from decision making to planning to performance evaluation.

Exhibit 16.8

Different Data for Different Purposes

	Purpose			
	Internal			External
	Decision Making	Planning (budgeting)	Performance Evaluation	Financial Reporting
Activity	Differential Analysis; Selecting from Alternatives for Action	Expressing Expectations for Alternatives Selected	Comparing Actual Results with Expectations	Reporting Actual Results to Owners and Other External Entities
Accounting Reports	Differential Cash Flows	Static Budgets; Profit Plans and Capital Budgets	Flexible Budgets; Performance Reports; Variances	Financial Statements
Time Orientation........	Future	Future	Past and Current (input to future)	Past and Current
Focus of Accounting............	Particular Decision Specifics	Responsibility Centers	Responsibility Centers	Company-Wide plus Segments
Model	Short-Run: Differential Cash Flows; Long-Run: Net Present Value	Short-Run: Profit Plan, Operating Budget; Long-Run: Capital Budgets	ROI, Residual Income	Earnings, ROI, Earnings per share
Variables in the Model	Differential Future Cash Flows	Revenues, Variable Costs, Fixed Costs	Revenues, Variable Costs, Fixed Costs, Investment in Division	Revenues Matched with Expenses in Compliance with GAAP

Consistent with Variable Costing

Full-Absorption Costing

Problem 16.1 for Self-Study

Different accounting information for different purposes. Answer the following two questions based on Exhibit 16.8.

a. What internal purposes of accounting focus on responsibility centers?
b. What purposes of accounting focus on the future? What purposes focus on the current and past?

The solution to this self-study problem is at the end of the chapter on page 654.

Incentive Compensation Plans

The method of rewarding managers for their performance is an important part of the total planning and control process. Firms design incentive compensation plans to provide incentives for managers to achieve organizational objectives. For top managers, incentive compensation plans usually include rewards both for current performance based on accounting numbers and for increasing stockholder share values. The latter is often in the form of stock options that can be quite lucrative if the value of the company's shares increases substantially over time.[2] For example, most of Chrysler Corporation chairperson Lee Iacocca's compensation from Chrysler came from exercising stock options.

Some critics point out that rewarding executives for performance reflected in annual accounting numbers gives managers incentives to take actions that improve short-run performance but not actions that benefit organizations in the long run. A classic example would be a firm's failure to develop new production methods and new products that may substantially increase expenses in the short run but provide more value for shareholders in the long run. General Motors, for example, is concerned about this issue. It recently replaced a bonus plan based on short-run profit growth with a system that focuses more managerial attention on long-run increases in value to stockholders.

Using accounting numbers in performance measurement may give managers incentives to make accounting choices and otherwise manipulate accounting data to put their performance in the most favorable light.

Divisional Incentive Compensation Plans

Effective incentive compensation schemes must induce individual behavior compatible with increasing the firm's wealth. Management can evaluate a company's performance using both accounting numbers and returns to stockholders, the latter reflecting a market assessment of how well the company is doing. Divisions normally do not have their own shares trading in capital markets, and the impact of one division's performance on the total company's share value would typically be small. Consequently, stock market assessments of performance are less useful at the divisional level than at the company level.

A study of **divisional incentive compensation plans** found that most of these plans have the following characteristics.[3]

1. Cash bonuses and profit sharing plans reward managers for short-term performance.
2. Deferred compensation, such as stock and stock options, are available to managers several years after they earn the compensation. Deferring receipt of pro-

---

[2]Stock options give an individual the right to purchase a certain number of shares of the company's stock at a specified price within a certain time period.

[3]See M. Maher and S. Butler, *Management Incentive Compensation Plans* (Montvale, N.J.: National Association of Accountants, 1986).

Conflicts in an Incentive Compensation Plan[a]

A large, multidivision manufacturer of industrial and consumer electrical products is organized into divisional profit centers. The firm rewards each division manager, at least in part, on the basis of the accounting profits and rate of return on assets that the division earned. Each division has its own controller, who reports directly to the central corporate controller. This direct reporting line, bypassing the division president, gives division controllers a feeling of independence from the division presidents, who would otherwise be their bosses. Central corporate management wants independent scorekeepers providing unbiased reports about ongoing operations.

In spite of this organizational design, the division controllers' compensation results in part from the same formula as that of the division presidents—a function of accounting profits and the rate of return on assets. Thus, division controllers have a financial stake in the reported profits of their divisions, giving them an incentive, at the margin, to boost reported profits.

The division controllers are aware of the potential conflict between their charge from central corporate management and their compensation packages. They feel conflict. At periodic meetings of controllers, they express their dissatisfaction to top management but so far have not been able to persuade top management to change the compensation plan.

[a]This example comes from a study by the authors. We do not reveal the company's name at management's request.

ceeds from stock gives managers incentives to take actions that increase long-run share value.

3. Firms give special awards for particular actions or extraordinary performance. For example, Johnson & Johnson presents a special stock award to employees responsible for developing new products. Top management and the board of directors believe new product development is critical to the future success of the company.

When designing incentive systems, management must ascertain the behavior the system motivates and the behavior management desires. Although incentive plans universally attempt to motivate good performance, each organization has its own particular set of problems that affect incentive system design.

For example, when Pillsbury acquired Burger King, Pillsbury's managers had little experience in managing fast-food restaurants. The company wanted to provide incentives for Burger King's managers to remain with the company. Consequently, the incentive system provided for lucrative deferred compensation that the hamburger chain's managers would forgo if they quit.

Each company's top management and board of directors must match its incentive system to its particular set of circumstances in deciding what type of behavior is desired. The goal is to design an incentive-compatible compensation scheme.

Problem 16.2 for Self-Study

Divisional incentive systems. What two key questions must management answer in designing incentive systems?

The solution to this self-study problem is at the end of the chapter on page 654.

Fraudulent Financial Reporting

Fraudulent financial reporting is intentional conduct resulting in materially misleading financial statements. Common examples of fraudulent financial reporting occur when companies recognize revenue before making the sale and when companies do not write down obsolete inventory. Stealing is not the same as financial fraud, but falsifying financial reports to cover up a theft could be financial fraud. Unintentional errors in preparing financial statements do not constitute fraudulent financial reporting.

For financial reporting to be fraudulent,

(1) it must result from intentional or reckless conduct, and

(2) the resulting misstatements must be material to the financial statements.

To be *material,* the misstatement must be large enough to affect the judgment of a responsible person relying on the information. Simply stated, to be *material,* the misstatement must be important.

For a law enforcement agency, such as the Securities and Exchange Commission (SEC), to prove fraud requires the agency to prove either intent to commit fraud or reckless conduct, a difficult task. Consequently, when the SEC brings charges against people for violating the antifraud provisions of the securities laws, it often settles the cases by having the accused sign ''consent'' documents. The signer of such a document agrees to certain restrictions without admitting or denying the commission of fraud. The cases we discuss below involve *alleged* fraud because the SEC has generally not proved financial fraud.

Who Commits Fraud?

Employees at all levels in the organization, from top management to low-level employees, might participate in fraudulent financial reporting. Enforcement agencies sometimes find the company's external auditors responsible for their clients' fraudulent financial reporting.

We focus on the use of accounting information by managers inside organizations. Department and division managers may commit fraud reporting to their superiors. For example, managers at certain PepsiCo bottling plants misled their superiors at corporate headquarters in Purchase, New York, by failing to write off obsolete or unusable bottle inventories.

Fraudulent reporting inside a company misleads top management and the board of directors as well as stockholders and other outsiders who rely on the company's financial information. Top managers sometimes commit fraud by misleading outsiders. Most cases reported by the media involve top management.

In many cases, management or the board of directors cure the problem involving potential fraud before financial reporting occurs and the firm files fraudulent financial statements with the Securities and Exchange Commission. In many cases, people started out bending the rules a little, only to find themselves in deep trouble after bending the rules for a long time.

Types of Fraud

People have tried many types of fraud, including omitting liabilities from financial statements, overstating assets on the balance sheet, and preparing false appraisals or other documents to support loans. Subsequent investigation showed that many of the savings and loan companies that failed in the 1980s had relied on fraudulent loan documentation. Our research indicates the two most common types of fraud involve improper revenue recognition and overstating inventory.

Improper Revenue Recognition

Over long-enough time spans, total revenue will equal total cash (or other assets) received from customers. Improper revenue recognition occurs when the firm reports the profit-increasing effects of revenue in the wrong accounting period—typically, but not always, too early. Improper revenue recognition results if a firm backdates sales to report revenue on December 30, Year 1, when the firm should have reported the sales as having occurred in January of Year 2. Such a firm shows both the revenue and the cost of goods sold in Year 1 instead of Year 2.

For example, MiniScribe, a Denver-based computer disk drive manufacturer, backdated invoices for sales made on the first day of the year to the last day of the previous year.[4] The company also had shipped bricks to distributors and booked them as sales of disk-drives. In other cases, companies have shipped products to company-owned warehouses but claimed the shipments were sales.

To compensate for the effects of previous fraud, perpetrators must continue to commit fraud. Note that early revenue recognition, resulting from backdating invoices or prematurely recording a sale, has only a temporary effect on reported revenues and profits. Pulling a sale out of Period 2 to report it in Period 1 improves profits for Period 1, but reduces sales to be reported in Period 2. Now Period 2 does not look as good as it should, so the perpetrator moves sales from Period 3 back to Period 2 to cover for the sales previously moved from Period 2 to Period 1. The perpetrator must continue this practice or else the most current period will show a revenue shortfall.

Overstating Inventory

Overstated ending inventory leads to overstated earnings. Recall the inventory equation:

Cost of Goods Sold = Beginning Inventory + Purchases − Ending Inventory.

The higher Ending Inventory, the lower Cost of Goods Sold, and the higher reported earnings. Overstated inventory results, for example, when managers or accountants fail to write down obsolete inventory. Department or division managers may not want to "take a hit" (reduce reported earnings) on the financial reports in the current period, so they postpone the write-off until later. In other cases, people falsify the ending inventory numbers during physical inventory counts or on audit papers.

For example, investigators of the MiniScribe case said that senior company officials " . . . apparently broke into locked trunks containing the auditors' workpapers" during the audit and inflated inventory values by approximately $1 million. In addition, employees created a computer program they called "Cook Book" to inflate inventory figures.[5]

Overstating ending inventory will increase reported earnings in the period of overstatement, but in the absence of continuing overstatement must result in reduced earnings reported in the next period. Refer again to the inventory equation. Higher Beginning Inventory increases Cost of Goods Sold and decreases reported earnings. To continue to appear successful, the perpetrator of frauds must continue to overstate ending inventory, just to keep reported earnings from decreasing.

Effect on Taxes   Fraudulent financial reporting which results in higher reported earnings sometimes also overstates taxable income. Because over long-enough time spans, reported earnings must equal operating cash inflows less operat-

---

[4]"How MiniScribe Got Its Auditor's Blessing on Questionable Sales," *The Wall Street Journal,* May 14, 1992, p. A5.

[5]"Coopers & Lybrand Agrees to Payment of $95 Million in the MiniScribe Case," *The Wall Street Journal,* October 30, 1992, p. A2.

ing cash outflows, lower taxable income in some future period must offset any overstated taxable income in earlier periods. Nevertheless, overstating taxable income in early periods likely increases the present value of a company's tax payments. Financial fraud might not affect the total taxes paid, but does change the timing of tax payments and, therefore, their present value.

Causes of Financial Fraud

Short-Term Orientation

Many firms use accounting numbers to grade, or evaluate, managers. Bonuses, merit pay increases, and promotions often depend on reported accounting numbers.

Why would a manager backdate sales from one year to an earlier year, which merely shifts profits, but does not create them? Managers given a short-term perspective by their employment and pay arrangements will have an incentive to "manage earnings" this way. Department and division managers may believe they have an opportunity to be promoted to a new position or transferred to another part of the company if they perform well in the current year. If so, they have incentives to look good in their current year, not caring about the subsequent shortfall on their unit's reported performance.

Some companies reward managers for achieving a performance threshold, providing large and discontinuous, or lumpy, rewards for meeting specified targets. For example, a company may offer a bonus of 50 percent of salary if the manager's division achieves its target return on investment (ROI), but only 25 percent of the manager's salary if the division achieves 95 to 100 percent of the target ROI, and no bonus if the division reports an ROI less than 95 percent of the target. A manager who finds the ROI just below the threshold, say just under 95 percent of the target ROI, has a personal financial stake on reporting ROI at the 95-percent level. The manager may hope that moving a few sales forward from next year to this year will not hurt next year's rewards as much as it helps this year's rewards.

Do Performance Evaluation Systems Create Incentives to Commit Fraud?

Management sometimes correctly believes that high-pressure performance evaluation systems effectively motivate employees. If so, management must also realize that putting pressure on people to perform well also creates incentives to commit fraud. The pressure to perform can affect top executives as well as middle managers and employees. Top executives in a company often feel pressured to perform because of the demands of stockholders, the expectations of financial analysts, or simply their own egos.

In 1987, the Treadway Commission, a federal commission on fraudulent financial reporting, reported the results of its study of financial fraud involving top management and fraudulent reporting to stockholders. The Commission concluded that fraudulent financial reporting occurred because of a combination of pressures, incentives, opportunities, and environment. According to the Commission, the forces that seemed to give rise to financial fraud " . . . are present to some degree in all companies. If the right combustible mixture of forces and opportunities is present, fraudulent financial reporting may occur."[6]

The Commission went on to say fraud in financial reporting sometimes results from a manager's wish to improve a company's financial appearance to obtain a higher stock price or to escape penalty for poor performance. The Commission listed examples of pressures to perform that may lead to financial fraud, including the following:

- "Unrealistic budget pressures, particularly for short-term results. These pressures occur when headquarters arbitrarily determines profit objectives and budgets without taking actual conditions into account.
- "Financial pressure resulting from bonus plans that depend on short-term economic performance. This pressure is particularly acute when the bonus is a significant component of the individual's total compensation."[7]

Note the Treadway Commission's reference to companies' emphasis on *short-term* performance. Most cases of financial fraud involve a timing adjustment. Management will take chances on the future to make the current period look good. One department manager told us, "Of course I'm more concerned about the short-run than the long-run. If I don't look good now, I won't be around in the long-run."

The Treadway Commission concluded that unrealistic profit objectives in budgets can cause financial fraud. Top management in large and widely dispersed companies have difficulty setting reasonable expectations for their far-flung divisions. That companies decentralize their operations reflects the reality that top management of large and disperse companies cannot involve themselves in the details of local operations. Consequently, top management may mistakenly expect unrealistically good performance.

The MiniScribe case involved pressure from top management. According to investigators of the fraud at MiniScribe, MiniScribe's chief executive's " . . . unrealistic sales targets and abusive management style created a pressure cooker that drove managers to cook the books or perish. And cook they did—booking shipments as sales, manipulating reserves, and simply fabricating figures—to maintain the illusion of unbounded growth even after the computer industry was hit by a severe slump."[8]

---

[6]*Report of the National Commission on Fraudulent Financial Reporting* (Treadway Commission) (Washington, D.C: National Commission on Fraudulent Financial Reporting, 1987), p. 23.

[7]Ibid., p. 24.

[8]"How Pressure to Raise Sales Led MiniScribe to Falsify Numbers," *The Wall Street Journal,* September 11, 1989, p. A1.

Environmental Conditions

In our opinion, the tone at the top most strongly influences fraudulent financial reporting. The tone at the top refers to the environment top management sets for dealing with ethical issues. No matter how extensive management's list of rules, no matter the clarity of a company code of conduct employees must read and sign, top management's own behavior sends the most important signal about how to do things. Just looking the other way when subordinates act unethically sets a tone that encourages fraudulent reporting.

In a "Dateline" news story, NBC employees rigged a General Motors truck to explode on impact to demonstrate that General Motors had improperly placed gas tanks on the trucks. Although this case does not involve fraudulent financial reporting, it demonstrates the tone at the top of NBC because its president " . . . told employees that the problem with the 'Dateline' incident wasn't so much that it happened, but that NBC got caught."[9]

During your careers, you will almost certainly sense the tone at the top in companies you work with or for. If top management looks away from unethical behavior, the chances increase that employees will commit fraud. You will less likely find financial fraud when top managers set firm guidelines and follow those guidelines themselves.

Controls to Prevent Fraud

Enough clever people working together to commit fraud will succeed. Companies establish internal controls to help prevent fraud. **Internal controls** are policies and procedures designed to provide top management with reasonable assurances that actions undertaken by employees will meet organizational goals. Internal controls help assure top management that the data it relies on for decision making do not result from fraudulent reports by lower-level employees. Because top management can override internal controls, such controls do not necessarily assure stockholders and other readers of companies' financial statements that top management reports accurately.

A fundamental principle of internal control to prevent fraud separates duties where a single person carrying out a series of tasks could commit fraud and take steps to hide it. For example, separation of duties in a department store requires that the person making the sale be different from the person who records it in the financial records. For the sale to be fraudulently reported, the sales clerk and the recorder would have to work together, or collude. **Collusion** is the cooperative effort of employees to commit fraud or other unethical acts.

Internal controls that separate duties make fraud more difficult because with separation of duties, fraud requires collusion. As the number of people colluding increases, so does the chance of whistle blowing to higher authorities, such as

---

[9] "NBC News President, Burned by Staged Fire and GM, Will Resign," *The Wall Street Journal,* March 2, 1993, p. A8.

auditors, the Securities and Exchange Commission, and the media. Thus, the separation-of-duties doctrine of internal control prefers more, rather than fewer, people to handle a series of functions.

Internal Auditing

Firms hire internal auditors to help management or the board of directors, or both. They often report to the audit committee of a company's board of directors. Internal auditors can both deter and detect fraud. They can deter fraud by reviewing and testing internal controls and ensuring controls are in place and working well.

Independent Auditors

Firms hire independent auditors primarily to express an opinion on published financial statements, not to detect fraud. Nevertheless, the presence of the independent auditors and their review of a company's internal controls help to prevent fraud. Further, independent auditors increasingly attempt to detect fraud, which should help deter it. The board of directors, management, or stockholders can also hire independent auditors to do examinations for fraud.

Problem 16.3 for Self-Study

Fraudulent financial reporting. Why is the "tone at the top" of a company important in preventing fraudulent financial reporting?

The solution to this self-study problem is at the end of the chapter on page 654.

Summary

This chapter illustrates the importance of using appropriate data for the particular task at hand. It also indicates areas where sound management decisions and financial reporting may conflict. Managerial decisions must rely on estimates of current and future cash flows. Financial reporting focuses on past cash flows and the allocation of those cash flows to periods in accordance with generally accepted accounting principles.

The potential uses of accounting data lead to some important implications for accounting system design. In designing a home, ideally we start with the major uses and activities, then design the structure. Similarly, in accounting we start with uses of data and work back to the appropriate system. We make the decisions keeping both the costs and benefits in mind.

Intentional conduct that results in materially misleading financial statements constitutes fraudulent financial reporting. Fraudulent financial reporting results most often from management's failure to write down obsolete inventory or its recognition of revenue before the firm has made the sale.

Financial fraud usually results from a combustible mixture of motives and opportunities. The motives result from compensation arrangements or other forms of employment contracts which give managers incentives to misreport. The opportunities arise in firms with inadequate internal controls, such as inadequate separation of duties. While no one factor necessarily leads to fraud, the likelihood of fraud increases with the appropriate combination of motives and opportunities.

Solutions to Self-Study Problems

Suggested Solution to Problem 16.1 for Self-Study

a. The internal purposes of accounting that focus on responsibility centers are planning and performance evaluation.
b. Future: Decision making and planning.
   Past and current: Internal performance evaluation and external financial reporting.

Suggested Solution to Problem 16.2 for Self-Study

First, what behavior does the incentive system motivate?
Second, what behavior does management desire?

Suggested Solution to Problem 16.3 for Self-Study

The ''tone at the top'' is important because top management influences the morale and behavior of all employees. Top management can override or circumvent an internal control system, and can circumvent the formal performance evaluation and reward system, to encourage fraudulent reporting.

Key Terms and Concepts

Divisional incentive compensation plans
Fraudulent financial reporting

Internal controls
Collusion

Questions, Problems, and Cases

Questions

Note: Because of the nature of this chapter, we have not included exercises. The questions, problems, and cases are intended to synthesize concepts discussed in prior chapters and encourage critical thought about accounting issues.

1. Review the meaning of the concepts or terms discussed above in Key Terms and Concepts.
2. Each of the following terms contains the word *cost*. Accounting, business, and economics use these terms in various ways. We explain the terms in the glossary at the back of the book under the heading *cost terminology*. Review the meaning and usage of each of these terms.

a.	Avoidable cost.	**k.**	Marginal cost.
b.	Common cost.	**l.**	Opportunity cost.
c.	Controllable cost.	**m.**	Out-of-pocket cost.
d.	Current cost.	**n.**	Product cost.
e.	Differential cost.	**o.**	Standard cost.
f.	Direct cost.	**p.**	Sunk cost.
g.	Fixed cost.	**q.**	Traceable cost.
h.	Historical cost.	**r.**	Unavoidable cost.
i.	Incremental cost.	**s.**	Variable cost.
j.	Indirect cost.		

3. Assume 2 years of constant production quantities, decreasing sales, and, hence, rising end-of-year inventory quantities. In Year 2, fixed costs are substantially higher than in Year 1. Compare the differences in reported income resulting from using full absorption costing on the one hand and variable costing on the other in Years 1 and 2.
4. Under what circumstances would the shift from full absorption costing to variable costing negligibly affect the balance sheet and income statement?
5. Inventory valuations appear only on the balance sheet. How, then, do inventory valuations affect net income for the period?
6. Meals in restaurants are not inventoriable (usually); that is, once it's prepared, a restaurant cannot save a meal until the next accounting period. Yet some restaurants compute the cost of meals using full absorption, whereas others use variable costing methods.

   Explain how the full absorption costing versus variable costing accounting methods could be relevant for analysis of such noninventoriable items.
7. Over sufficiently long time periods, income is cash in minus cash out. Eventually the entire book value of an owned asset will be written off through depreciation or on disposal of the asset, regardless of the depreciation method accountants use.

   What difference could it possibly make whether accountants use straight-line or accelerated depreciation methods for external financial reporting?

8. "Because the FASB generally does not allow a firm to capitalize its research and development (R&D) costs, internal financial statements will not be consistent with external financial reports unless the firm expenses R&D costs internally. Therefore, accounting should expense R&D costs for internal evaluation of managerial performance."

   Comment.

9. What are the major characteristics of divisional incentive compensation plans?

10. Refer to the Managerial Application, "Conflicts in an Incentive Compensation Plan." What were the conflicting incentives facing the divisional controllers?

11. What is fraudulent financial reporting? What are the two key concepts in the definition of fraudulent financial reporting?

12. What are common types of fraudulent financial reporting?

13. An employee has been stealing some of the company's merchandise and selling it. Is this behavior financial fraud?

14. Suppose the employee in question **13** covers up the theft by accounting for it as spoilage. Would accounting for the stolen items as spoilage be financial fraud?

15. Suppose an accounting clerk who knows nothing about the theft in question **13** erroneously records the "lost" parts as spoilage. Would that be fraudulent financial reporting?

16. Suppose an accounting clerk fails to write off $5 million of obsolete inventory at a large department store. The amount is material. Suppose the Securities and Exchange Commission filed a charge against the clerk alleging financial fraud. Do you believe the clerk's failure to write off the inventory, which resulted in misstated financial statements, could be considered unintentional? Explain your answer.

17. A large company hired your friend. She confides in you about a problem with her boss. Her boss is asking customers to sign a sales agreement just before the end of the year, which indicates a sale has been made. Her boss then tells these customers that he will give them 30 days, which is well into next year, to change their minds. If they do not change their minds, then he sends the merchandise to them. If they change their minds, her boss agrees to cancel the orders, take back the merchandise, and cancel the invoices. Her boss gives the sales agreements to the accounting department, which prepares an invoice and records the sale. One of the people in accounting keeps the invoices and shipping documents for these customers in a desk drawer until the customers either change their minds, in which case the sale is canceled, or until the merchandise is sent at the end of the 30-day waiting period.

    Your friend likes the company, and she wants to keep her job. What would you advise her to do?

18. The Treadway Commission indicated that bonus plans based on achieving short-run financial results have been a factor in financial frauds, particularly when the bonus is a large component of an individual's compensation. Why do these bonus plans affect fraud?

19. How does the separation of duties help prevent financial fraud?

20. How do internal auditors deter or detect financial fraud?

Integrative Problems and Cases

21. **Inventory costing.**[10] The All Fixed Costs Company is so named because it has no variable costs—all of its costs are fixed and vary with time rather than with output. The All Fixed Costs Company is located on the bank of a river and has its own hydroelectric plant to supply power, light, and heat. The company manufactures a synthetic material from air and river water, and it sells its product on a long-term, fixed-price contract. It has a small staff of employees, all hired on an annual salary basis. The output of the plant can be increased or decreased by adjusting a few dials on the control panel. Exhibit 16.9 presents data on production, sales, and cost information for the first 2 months of operations.
   a. Prepare income statements for each of the 2 months, using full absorption costing.
   b. Prepare income statements for each of the 2 months, using variable costing.
   c. Which costing method is management likely to prefer? Why?

22. **Inventory costing.** The Semi-Fixed Costs Company is just like the All Fixed Costs Company (see the preceding problem) except that its fixed production costs are $210,000 per month and variable production costs are $7 per ton. The production, sales, and general and administrative cost data for Months 1 and 2 for the All Fixed Costs Company apply to the Semi-Fixed Costs Company as well.
   a. Prepare income statements for each of the 2 months, using full absorption costing.
   b. Prepare income statements for each of the 2 months, using variable costing.
   c. Which costing method is management likely to prefer? Why?

23. **Divisional performance reports.** A company that assembles and sells cordless telephones has operations in two divisions for internal performance evaluation. The Anselmo Division assembles the firm's product, and the Ramos

Exhibit 16.9		
ALL FIXED COSTS COMPANY		
	Month 1	**Month 2**
Production	20,000 Tons	0 Tons
Sales..	10,000 Tons	10,000 Tons
Selling Price per Ton...........................	$30	$30
Costs (all fixed):		
Production	$280,000	$280,000
General and Administrative	$40,000	$40,000

[10]Problems 21 and 22 are adapted from Raymond P. Marple, "Try This on Your Class, Professor," *The Accounting Review,* vol. 31.

Division conducts the finishing, packing, and selling activities. Management expects quarterly sales during the first year of operations to be seasonal in the following percentages: 20 percent, 30 percent, 30 percent, 20 percent.

The Anselmo Division plans to produce units at a reasonably uniform rate throughout the year. Anselmo immediately transfers its completed units to Ramos on the basis of cost of manufacturing plus a 25-percent markup on cost. A representative market price for the product at this stage is $22. The firm allocates divisional fixed selling and administrative expenses equally to each quarter during the year. It also allocates central corporate expenses to divisions on the basis of total sales.

A performance report for the first quarter appears in Exhibit 16.10.

a. What strengths and weaknesses do you see in this divisional performance report?

b. Making whatever changes you believe are appropriate, prepare a divisional performance report for these two divisions for the first quarter. Describe briefly the justification for your treatment of the transfer price, fixed manufacturing expenses, fixed selling and administrative expenses, and central corporate expenses.

24. **Financial accounting and decision making.** Biogenetics, Inc., uses a cost of capital rate of 12 percent in making investment decisions. It currently is considering two mutually exclusive projects, each requiring an initial investment of $10 million. The first project has a net present value of $21 million and an internal rate of return of 20 percent. The firm will complete this project within 1 year. It will raise accounting income and earnings per share almost immediately thereafter. The second project has a net present value of $51 million and an internal rate of return of 30 percent. The second project requires incurring large, noncapitalizable expenses over the next few years before net cash in-

---

Exhibit 16.10

Performance Report for Critique in Problem 23

	Anselmo Division	Ramos Division
Annual Budgeted Production (units)	48,000	40,000
Budgeted Production—First Quarter (units)	12,000	8,000
Units Produced	10,000	8,000
Units Sold	10,000	5,000
Sales...	$250,000	$500,000
Cost of Goods Sold:		
Variable Expenses	(150,000)	(375,000)
Fixed Expenses[a]	(50,000)	(50,000)
Gross Profit	$ 50,000	$ 75,000
Divisional Fixed Selling and Administrative		
Expenses	(12,000)	(50,000)
Central Corporate Expenses	(25,000)	(50,000)
Divisional Income (Loss)	$ 13,000	$ (25,000)

[a]Exclusive of any adjustment for under- or overapplied expenses.

flows from sales revenue result. Thus accounting income and earnings per share for the next few years will not only be lower than if the first project is accepted but will also be lower than earnings currently reported.

a. Should the short-run effects on accounting income and earnings per share influence the decision about the choice of projects? Explain.

b. Should either of the projects be accepted? If so, which one? Why?

25. **Accounting for advertising.** Equilibrium Company spends $30,000 advertising the company's brand names and trademarks. Gross margin on sales after taxes is up $33,000 each year because of these advertising expenditures. For the purposes of this problem, assume that the firm makes all advertising expenditures on the first day of each year and that the $33,000 extra after-tax gross margin on sales occurs on the first day of the next year. Excluding any advertising assets or profits, Equilibrium Company has $100,000 of other assets that have produced an after-tax income of $10,000 per year. Equilibrium Company follows a policy of declaring dividends each year equal to net income, and it has a cost of capital of 10 percent per year.

a. Is the advertising policy a sensible one? Explain.

b. How should accounting report the expenditures for advertising in Equilibrium Company's financial statements to reflect accurately the managerial decision of advertising at the rate of $30,000 per year? In other words, how can the firm account for the advertising expenditures in such a way that the accounting rate of return for the advertising project and the rate of return on assets for the firm reflect the 10-percent return from advertising?

26. **Management incentives and accounting for research and development.** The Eager Division has $300,000 of total assets, earns $45,000 per year, and generates $45,000 per year of cash flow. The cost of capital is 15 percent. Each year, Eager pays cash of $45,000 to its parent company, Greed Enterprises. Eager's management has discovered a project requiring research and development costs now that will lead to new products. The anticipated cash flows for this project follow: beginning of Year 1, outflow of $24,000; beginning of years 2, 3, and 4, inflows of $10,000 each.

Assume that Greed undertakes the project, that cash flows are as planned, and Eager pays $45,000 to Greed at the end of the first year and $47,000 at the end of each of the next 3 years.

a. Compute Eager's rate of return on assets for each year of the project, assuming that accounting expenses R&D expenditures as they occur. Use the year-end balance of total assets in the denominator.

b. Compute Eager's rate of return on assets for each year of the project, assuming that accounting capitalizes and then amortizes R&D costs on a straight-line basis over the last 3 years of the project. Use the year-end balance of total assets in the denominator.

c. Compute the new project's accounting rate of return, independent of the other assets and of the income of Eager assuming that accounting capitalizes and then amortizes R&D costs on a straight-line basis over the entire 4 years of the project.

d. How well has the management of the Eager Division carried out its responsibility to its owners? On what basis do you make this judgment?

27. **Explain premature revenue recognition.** You have been asked to advise a manufacturing company how to detect fraudulent financial reporting. Management does not understand how early revenue recognition by backdating invoices from next year to this year would affect financial statements. Further, management wants to know which accounts could be audited for evidence of fraud in the case of early revenue recognition.

    a. Using your own numbers, make up an example to show management the effect of early revenue recognition.

    b. Prepare a short report to management explaining the accounts that early revenue recognition would affect. Suggest some ways management could find errors in those accounts.

28. **Explain inventory overstatement.** A merchandising company has asked you to advise it how to detect fraudulent financial reporting. Management wants your help in detecting inventory overstatement. Further, management wants to know how to find evidence of inventory overstatement.

    a. Using your own numbers, make up an example to show management the effect of overstating inventory. Show how inventory overstatement at the end of Year 1 carries through to the beginning inventory overstatement.

    b. Prepare a brief report to management suggesting ways management could detect inventory overstatement.

29. **Top management's awareness of fraud.** The chief executive of Leslie Fay, the dressmaking company charged with committing financial fraud, was dismayed that the controller and other employees had committed fraud. He said the company could have taken steps to improve the situation if senior management had known the poor financial results. Financial analysts who follow the company had noted, however, that the company had marked down its clothing line in sales to retail stores such as May Department Stores and Federated Department Stores.

    After the company cut prices 20 percent across the board, retail executives who were customers of Leslie Fay wondered how Leslie Fay could continue to be profitable. "'When you cut 20% out, you must get dramatically large orders to make up for it,' says one. 'We were wondering how they could continue to make a profit.'" [11]

    One analyst wondered how top management could not have known about the company's financial difficulties in view of the 20-percent markdown.

    For your information, top management is located in New York City, and the fraud occurred at the financial offices in Wilkes-Barre, Pennsylvania. The line of reporting is as follows: the controller reports to the chief financial officer and the chief financial officer reports to the chief executive of the company. Both the controller and chief financial officer work in Wilkes-Barre. The chief financial officer reportedly has considerable autonomy.

    Write a short report indicating whether you think top management of the company is responsible for the fraud and state why (or why not).

---

[11]"Loose Threads: Dressmaker Leslie Fay Is an Old-Style Firm That's in a Modern Fix," *Wall Street Journal*, February 23, 1993, p. A20.

30. **Motives and opportunities for fraud.** A report on the "income transferal" activities at the H. J. Heinz Company made the following statements.[12] First, decentralized authority is a central principle of the company's operations. Second, the company expected its divisions to generate an annual growth in profits of approximately 10 to 12 percent per year. Third, it was not unusual nor undesirable for management to put pressure on the division managers and employees to produce improved results.

The report noted that putting pressure on the divisions to produce improved results coupled with the company's philosophy of autonomy, which it extended to financial and accounting controls, provided both an incentive and opportunity for division managers to misstate financial results. The report further stated, "the autonomous nature of the (divisions) combined with the relatively small World Headquarters financial staff permitted the conception of what at best can be described as a communications gap . . . In its simplest form, there seems to have been a tendency to issue an order or set a standard with respect to achieving a financial result without regard to whether complete attainment was possible." [13] "In the managements of certain of the [divisions], there was a feeling of 'us versus them' towards World Headquarters." [14]

The report indicated there was an effort in certain divisions to transfer income from one fiscal period to another to provide a "financial cushion" for achieving the goal for the succeeding year. For example, divisions would overpay expenses so they could get a credit or refund in a subsequent year. Or they would pay an expense such as insurance or advertising early, but instead of charging the amount to a prepaid expense account, they would charge the amount to expense. In good years, this practice would keep profits down and provide a cushion to meet the company's target for constantly increasing profits.

a. Using your own numbers, construct an example to demonstrate the kind of income transferal that was done at H. J. Heinz.

b. What was the motive to transfer income from one period to the other? What were the opportunities to transfer income?

c. Comment on how the communications gap and the "us versus them" attitude contributed to the fraud.

d. Refer to **c.** Have you seen communications gaps in organizations that have resulted in an "us versus them" attitude on the part of employees? If so, briefly describe the circumstances and the cause of the "us versus them" attitude. What could have been done (or be done) to change the "us versus them" attitude in your example?

31. **Puzzling accounting reports including inventory costing.** Lucius Green runs a distillery under the corporate name Green's Distillery. Each year Green

---

[12]This problem is based on the "Report of Audit Committee to the Board of Directors, Income Transferal and Other Practices," H. J. Heinz Company, May 6, 1980.

[13]Ibid., p. 9.

[14]Ibid., p. 14.

distills 10,000 barrels of whiskey, puts the product in barrels, and stores the barrels for 4 years. Each year Green sells 10,000 barrels of 4-year-old whiskey to a retail chain, which bottles the whiskey and puts its own label on the product. The retailer has a long-term, fixed-price contract with Green. The retailer is so pleased with Green's product that it is willing to buy the whiskey at any age. The contract specifies that the retailer will buy a barrel of newly distilled whiskey for $100, a barrel of 1-year-old whiskey for $118, a barrel of 2-year-old whiskey for $140, a barrel of 3-year-old whiskey for $168, and a barrel of 4-year-old whiskey for $200. In the past, Green has always sold only 4-year-old whiskey. Prices and costs have been stable for several years and are expected to remain so. An income statement for Green's Distillery for a typical year, when it distills 10,000 barrels and sells 10,000 barrels of 4-year-old whiskey, appears in Exhibit 16.11.

During Year 0, the retailer suggested to Lucius Green that he double the capacity of the distillery and that they rewrite the contract so that the retailer could promise to buy as much as Green wanted to produce.

Assume that Green doubled capacity and, starting in Year 1, distilled 20,000 barrels of whiskey each year to be aged. All costs shown on the income statement for 10,000 barrels doubled (that is, *unit costs* including depreciation remained constant) except for general and administrative expenses, which increased $100,000 a year to $300,000 a year. By Year 5, the first batch of extra product was fully aged, and, starting in Year 5, Green sold 20,000 barrels of 4-year-old whiskey to the retail chain. During Year 1 through Year 4, he sold 10,000 barrels.

a. Prepare income statements for each of the Years 1 through 5, using full absorption costing.

b. Prepare income statements for each of the Years 1 through 5, using variable costing.

c. Which of the costing methods appears to give a better picture of the results of Green's Distillery for Years 2 through 4?

d. You will probably judge in part **c** that full absorption costing better reflects the situation. Why does variable costing appear to fail in this case, and what should we conclude from this result?

Exhibit 16.11

GREEN'S DISTILLERY
Income Statement for Typical Year When 10,000 Barrels
Are Produced and 10,000 Barrels Are Sold

Sales (10,000 barrels at $200)		$2,000,000
Cost of Goods Sold:		
Variable Costs ($50 per barrel, 10,000 barrels)	$500,000	
Depreciation of Distilling Equipment	100,000	
Storage Costs of Aging Whiskey ($20 per barrel		
per year, 40,000 barrels)	800,000	(1,400,000)
General and Administrative Expenses..............		(200,000)
Income before Taxes		$ 400,000

32. **Measuring managerial performance: new challenges.** Many commentators about North American business have argued that the relative deterioration in manufacturing productivity compared to Japanese manufacturers results from a preoccupation with short-term financial performance measures. Many firms base bonus plans for senior executives on annual accounting income. This method provides incentives to take actions that enhance short-term earnings performance that may not serve the best long-term interests of the firm. By contrast, Japanese firms give executives incentives to ensure the long-run viability of their companies. Consequently, they are more concerned than their North American counterparts with long-run productivity, quality control, and managing the company's physical assets.

Not everyone agrees with the observation that North American business executives are preoccupied with short-term financial performance to the extent that they would take actions contrary to the best long-run economic interests of the organization just to make themselves look good on the performance measures. But suppose that an executive faces a choice between an action with a positive short-run effect on performance measures and another that has better long-run consequences for the organization but that will not affect short-run performance measures positively. We cannot fault a rational executive for taking the action that looks good in the short run. As the saying goes, "you have to look good in the short run to be around in the long run."

How would you design a control system that encourages top-level managers to be concerned about long-run productivity, quality of products, and long-run economic well being of the company? Assume that these managers have previously focused on maximizing quarterly and annual earnings numbers to the detriment of these other factors.

33. **Management decisions and external financial reports.** "Squeezing oranges in your idle time is not a by-product," said the Big Six partner in charge of the audit of Regent Company, disapprovingly.

"But," replied the president of Regent, "squeezing oranges is not our usual business, and your accounting plan will make us show a substantial decline in income. We all know that our decision this year to squeeze oranges was a good one that is paying off handsomely."

The argument concerned the accounting for income during the year 1983 by Regent Company.

Background The Alcoholic Control Board (ACB) of Georgia, a state not known for its production of grapes and wines, wanted to encourage the production of wine within the state. The executives formed the Regent Company in response to the encouragement of the ACB. The production process for wine involves aging the product. The company commenced production in 1987, but did not sell its first batch of wine until 1989. At the start of 1987, Regent made a cash investment of $4,400,000 in grape-pressing equipment and a facility to house that equipment. The ACB has promised to buy Regent Company's output for 10 years, starting with the first batch in 1989. Regent Company decided to account for its operations by including in the cost of the wine all depreciation on the grape-pressing equipment and on the facility to house it. The firm judged the economic life of the equipment to be 10 years, the life of the contract with the ACB. Regent Company reported general and administrative expenses of $100,000 per year in external financial reports for both 1987 and 1988.

Regent Company's contract with the ACB promised payments of $1.8 million per year. The direct costs of labor and materials for each year's batch of wine were $130,000 each year. Accounting charges depreciation on a straight-line basis over a 10-year life. The income taxes were 40 percent of pretax income.

The wine sales began in 1989 and operations proceeded as planned. The income statements for the years 1989 through 1992 appear in Exhibit 16.12.

Management of Regent Company was delighted with the offer from a manufacturer of frozen orange juice to put its idle capacity to work. It contracted with the manufacturer to perform the services. At the end of 1993, it compiled the income statement shown in Exhibit 16.12 as "Management's View."

The Accounting Issue Management of Regent Company suggested that the revenues from squeezing oranges are an incremental by-product of owning the wine-making machinery. The wine-making process was undertaken on its own merits and has paid off according to schedule. The revenues from squeezing

Exhibit 16.12

REGENT COMPANY
Income Statements
(all dollar amounts in thousands)

	1989 to 1992 Each Year, Actual	For 1993	
		Management's View	Auditor's View
Revenues:			
From Wine Put into Production 2 Years Previously.............	$1,800	$1,800	$1,800
From Orange Juice Squeezed in Current Year	—	100[a]	100[a]
Total Revenues	$1,800	$1,900	$1,900
Cost of Goods Sold:			
Direct Costs of Wine Put into Production 2 Years Previously	$ 300	$ 300	$ 300
Depreciation of Buildings and Equipment:			
From 2 Years Prior, Carried in Inventory until Wine Is Sold.....	440	440	440
From Current Year, Allocated to Orange Juice	—	100	352
Selling, General, and Administrative Expenses......................	130	130[a]	130[a]
Income Taxes at 40 Percent	372	372	271
Total Expenses...................	$1,242	$1,342	$1,493
Net Income	$ 558	$ 558	$ 407

[a]Manufacturer of orange juice pays out-of-pocket costs directly. These items are not shown here.

oranges are a by-product of the main purpose of the business. Ordinarily, the accounting for by-products assigns to them costs equal to their net realizable value; that is, accounting assigns costs in exactly the amount that will make the sale of the by-products show neither gain nor loss. In this case, because the incremental revenue of squeezing oranges was $100,000, Regent Company assigned $100,000 of the overhead to this process, reducing from $440,000 to $340,000 the overhead assigned to the main product. This will make the main product appear more profitable when it is sold.

Management of Regent Company was aware that its income for 1993 would appear no different from that of the preceding year. Management knew that the benefits from squeezing oranges began to occur in 1993 but allowed the benefits to appear on the financial statements later.

The Big Six auditor who saw management's proposed income statement disapproved. The partner in charge of the audit spoke as quoted at the beginning of this case.

The auditor argued that squeezing oranges under these circumstances was not a by-product and that by-product accounting was inappropriate. Regent Company must allocate the overhead costs between the two processes of grape pressing and orange squeezing according to some reasonable basis. The most reasonable basis, the auditor thought, was the time devoted to each of the processes. Because grape pressing used about 20 percent of the year, whereas orange squeezing used 80 percent of the year, the auditor assigned $352,000, or 80 percent, of the overhead costs to orange squeezing and $88,000, or 20 percent, to the wine production. Exhibit 16.12 shows the auditor's income statement.

This statement upset the president of Regent Company. Reported net income in 1993 is down almost 30 percent from 1992, yet things have improved. The president fears the reaction of the board of directors and the shareholders. The president wonders what has happened and what to do.

a. Assuming that the Regent Company faces an after-tax cost of capital of 10 percent, did the company in fact make a good decision in 1986 to enter into an agreement with the state to produce wine? Explain.

b. Did the company in fact make a good decision in 1992 to enter into the agreement with the manufacturer of frozen orange juice?

c. Using management's view of the proper accounting practices, construct financial statements for the years 1994, 1995, and 1996, assuming that events occur as planned and in the same way as in 1993. Generalize these statements to later years.

d. Are management's statements correct given its interpretation of by-product accounting? If not, construct an income statement for 1993 that is consistent with by-product accounting.

e. Is management correct in its interpretation that the orange juice is a by-product?

f. Using the auditor's view of the situation and assuming the same facts as in part c, construct income statements for the years 1994, 1995, and 1996. Generalize these statements to later years.

g. Assuming that the auditor is right, what may management of Regent Company do to solve its problem?

Overview of Financial Statements

1. Understand four principal activities of business firms: (a) establishing goals and strategies, (b) obtaining financing, (c) making investments, and (d) conducting operations.

2. Understand the purpose and content of the three principal financial statements that firms prepare to measure and report the results of their business activities: (a) the balance sheet, (b) the income statement, and (c) the statement of cash flows.

3. Understand the concepts of assets, liabilities, and shareholders' equity, including when firms recognize such items (recognition issues), the amounts at which firms report them (valuation issues), and how firms disclose them in the balance sheet (classification issues).

4. Understand the accrual basis of accounting that underlies the income statement, including when firms recognize revenues and expenses (recognition issues), the amount at which firms report them (measurement issues), and how firms disclose them in the income statement.

5. Understand why using the accrual basis of accounting to prepare the balance sheet and income statement creates the need for a statement of cash flows.

6. Understand the relation between cash flows from operating, investing, and financing activities for various types of businesses.

Accounting *measures* the results of business activities and *communicates* those measurements to interested users. Previous chapters explored the measurements made to assist managers in making decisions, planning operations, and evaluating performance. We also considered the appropriate formats of various managerial accounting reports (for example, income statement in contribution format). In designing accounting systems for internal, or managerial, uses, accountants have considerable flexibility in the manner in which they measure and report business activities.

A firm also reports the results of its business activities to individuals and entities outside the firm: owners, creditors, governmental agencies, labor unions, and others. This variety of users and the uses they make of financial accounting reports generate a need for some standardization in both measurement methods and reporting formats. This chapter and the next explore the content of the principal financial statements prepared for external users and the techniques used to analyze and interpret them. Understanding the external reporting process helps the manager to see how the principal financial statements communicate the results of various financing, investing, and operating decisions to owners, creditors, and others. It also provides insights about how a firm ''manages'' the external reporting process.

This chapter examines the purpose and content of the principal financial statements included in annual reports to owners and other external users. Chapter 18 explores techniques for analyzing these financial statements.

Overview of Business Activities

Financial statements for external users attempt to present in a meaningful way the results of a firm's business activities. Understanding these financial statements requires an understanding of the business activities they attempt to portray. A firm's business activities include (1) establishing goals and strategies, (2) obtaining financing, (3) making investments, and (4) conducting operations.

Example 1   Bill Marsh and Janet Nelson, while working toward degrees in engineering, develop a computerized mechanism for monitoring automobile engine performance. They receive a patent on the device and want to set up their own firm to manufacture and sell it. They will call the firm Marnel Corporation.

The *goals* of any firm are the targets, or end results, toward which the firm directs its energies. The *strategies* of the firm are the means for achieving these goals. The firm sets goals and strategies in light of the economic, institutional, and cultural environment in which it intends to operate. Marnel Corporation's goal is to develop a continuing stream of quality electronic products that it can manufacture and market profitably, thereby increasing the value of the firm and the wealth of its owners. Its strategies to accomplish this goal include the following:

1. Manufacturing all electronic devices internally to ensure quality and provide some protection against competitors' attempts to imitate the devices.
2. Using the firm's sales staff to sell and service the devices and to provide close working relations with customers.

3. Investing in research and development to promote the ongoing creation of new products.

Marnel Corporation will need funds, or *financing,* for its activities. Two primary sources of capital are a firm's creditors and its owners. Creditors provide funds but require that the firm repay the funds, usually with interest, at some date in the future. Owners also provide funds. In return, they receive some evidence of their ownership in the firm. When a firm organizes as a corporation, shares of capital stock evidence the ownership. Unlike the demands creditors make in return for lending funds, owners generally do not require repayment at a particular future date. All firms must decide the amount of capital to obtain from creditors and the amount from owners. Chapter 18 explores some of the more important factors in such financing decisions.

Once a firm obtains funds, it must *invest* them. The firm will invest some of the funds in land, buildings, and equipment. These resources provide a firm with a capacity to manufacture and sell products for many years. Chapters 10 and 11 discussed techniques for making these capital budgeting, or capacity investment, decisions. Firms must also invest in raw materials, employee training, and other goods and services to carry out operating activities.

Operating activities involve the creation and delivery of goods or services to customers. Firms strive to receive more funds from customers than it costs the firm to create and deliver the good or service, thereby generating a profit.

Exhibit 17.1 depicts these four dimensions of business activity.

Exhibit 17.1

Overview of Business Activities

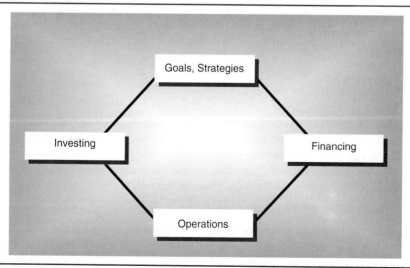

Overview of Principal Financial Statements

Periodic reports to external users include three principal financial statements:

1. Balance sheet.
2. Income statement.
3. Statement of cash flows.

The remainder of this chapter discusses the purpose and content of each of these three financial statements.

The Balance Sheet: Measuring Financial Position

The **balance sheet** presents a snapshot of the investments of a firm (assets) and financing on those investments (liabilities and shareholders' equity, or total equities) as of a specific time. Exhibit 17.2 presents a balance sheet for Marnel Corporation as of December 31, Year 1, and December 31, Year 2. The assets portion of the balance sheet reports as of a specific time the effects of all of a firm's past investment decisions. In this case, Marnel Corporation has invested in accounts receivable, merchandise inventory, land, buildings, and equipment. The equities portion of the balance sheet reports as of a specific time the effects of all of a firm's past financing decisions. Both short- and long-term creditors and owners have provided capital.

The balance sheet shows the following balance, or equality:

$$\text{Assets} = \text{Liabilities} + \text{Shareholders' Equity.}$$

This equation shows that a firm's assets balance with, or equal, the financing of those assets by creditors and owners. In the balance sheet, we view resources from two angles: a listing of the specific forms in which the firm holds them (for example, cash, inventory, equipment) and a listing of the persons or interests that provided the financing and therefore have a claim on them (for example, suppliers, employees, governments, shareholders).

We now address several questions regarding the balance sheet:

1. Which resources does a firm recognize as assets?
2. What valuations does it place on these assets?
3. How does it classify, or group, assets within the balance sheet?
4. Which claims against a firm's assets appear on the balance sheet as liabilities?
5. What valuations does a firm place on these liabilities?
6. How does a firm classify liabilities within the balance sheet?
7. What valuation does a firm place on shareholders' equity, and how does it disclose the shareholders' equity within the balance sheet?

To answer these questions, one must consider several accounting concepts underlying the balance sheet. This discussion not only provides a background for understanding the statement as currently prepared, but also permits the reader to assess alternative methods of measuring financial position.

MARNEL CORPORATION
Comparative Balance Sheets for December 31, Year 1 and Year 2

	December 31	
	Year 1	Year 2
Assets		
Current Assets		
Cash	$ 30,000	$ 3,000
Accounts Receivable	20,000	55,000
Merchandise Inventory	40,000	50,000
Total Current Assets	$ 90,000	$108,000
Noncurrent Assets		
Buildings and Equipment (cost)	$100,000	$225,000
Accumulated Depreciation	(30,000)	(40,000)
Total Noncurrent Assets	$ 70,000	$185,000
Total Assets	$160,000	$293,000
Equities		
Current Liabilities		
Accounts Payable—Merchandise Suppliers	$ 30,000	$ 50,000
Accounts Payable—Other Suppliers	10,000	12,000
Salaries Payable	5,000	6,000
Total Current Liabilities	$ 45,000	$ 68,000
Noncurrent Liabilities		
Bonds Payable	0	100,000
Total Liabilities	$ 45,000	$168,000
Shareholders' Equity		
Capital Stock ($10 par value)	$100,000	$100,000
Retained Earnings	15,000	25,000
Total Shareholders' Equity	$115,000	$125,000
Total Equities	$160,000	$293,000

Asset Recognition

Assets are resources with the potential for providing a firm with a future economic benefit. That benefit is the ability to generate future cash inflows or to reduce future cash outflows. Accounting recognizes the resources as assets when (1) the firm has acquired rights to their use in the future as a result of a past transaction or exchange and (2) the firm can measure or quantify the future benefits with a reasonable degree of precision.[1] All assets are future benefits; not all future benefits, however, are assets.

---

[1]Financial Accounting Standards Board, *Statement of Financial Accounting Concepts No. 6,* ''Elements of Financial Statements,'' 1985, par. 25. See the Glossary for the Board's definition of an asset.

Example 2 Miller Corporation sold merchandise and received a note from the customer, who agreed to pay $2,000 within 4 months. This note receivable is an asset of Miller Corporation because Miller has a right to receive a definite amount of cash in the future as a result of the previous sale of merchandise.

Example 3 Miller Corporation acquired manufacturing equipment costing $40,000 and agreed to pay the seller over 3 years. After the final payment, legal title to the equipment will transfer to Miller Corporation. Even though Miller Corporation does not possess legal title, the equipment is Miller's asset because Miller has obtained the rights and responsibilities of ownership and can maintain those rights as long as it makes payments on schedule.

Example 4 Miller Corporation has developed a good reputation with its employees, customers, and citizens of the community. The firm expects this good reputation to provide benefits in future business activities. A good reputation, however, is generally *not* an accounting asset. Although Miller Corporation has made various expenditures in the past to develop the reputation, the future benefits are too difficult to quantify with a sufficient degree of precision to allow Miller to recognize an asset.

Example 5 Miller Corporation plans to acquire a fleet of new trucks next year to replace those wearing out. These new trucks are not assets now because Miller Corporation has made no exchange with a supplier, and, therefore, has not established a right to the future use of the trucks.

Most of the difficulties accountants have in deciding which items to recognize as assets relate to unexecuted or partially executed contracts. In Example 5, suppose that Miller Corporation entered into a contract with a local truck dealer to acquire the trucks next year at a cash price of $60,000. Miller Corporation had acquired rights to future benefits, but the contract remains unexecuted. Accounting does not generally recognize unexecuted contracts of this nature, sometimes called executory contracts. Miller Corporation will recognize an asset for the trucks when it receives them next year.

To take the illustration one step further, assume that Miller Corporation advances the truck dealer $15,000 of the purchase price upon signing the contract. Miller Corporation has acquired rights to future benefits and has exchanged cash. Current accounting practice treats the $15,000 as an advance on the purchase of equipment and reports it as an asset under a title such as Advances to Suppliers. The trucks are not assets at this time, however, because Miller Corporation has not received sufficient future rights to justify their inclusion in the balance sheet. Similar asset recognition questions arise when a firm leases buildings and equipment for its own use under long-term leases or contracts with a transport company to deliver all of the firm's products to customers for some period of years.

Asset Valuation Bases

Accounting must assign a monetary amount to each asset in the balance sheet. Accountants might use several methods of computing this amount.

Acquisition or Historical Cost   The amount of cash payment (or cash equivalent value of other forms of payment) made in acquiring an asset is the acquisition, or historical, cost of the asset. The accountant can typically ascertain this amount by referring to contracts, invoices, and canceled checks. Because a firm need not acquire a given asset, the firm must expect the future benefits from an asset that it does acquire to be at least as large as the acquisition cost. Historical cost, then, is a lower limit on the amount that a firm considered the future benefits of the asset to be worth at the time of acquisition.

Current Replacement Cost   Each asset might appear on the balance sheet at the current cost of replacing it. Current replacement cost is often referred to as an entry value, because it represents the amount currently required to acquire, or enter into, the rights to receive future benefits from the asset.

For assets purchased frequently, such as merchandise inventory, the accountant can often calculate current replacement cost by consulting suppliers' catalogs or price lists. The replacement cost of assets purchased less frequently, such as land, buildings, and equipment, is more difficult to ascertain. A major obstacle to using current replacement cost as the valuation basis is the absence of well-organized secondhand markets for many used assets. Ascertaining current replacement cost in these cases requires finding the cost of a similar new asset and then adjusting that amount downward somehow for the services of the asset already used. Difficulties can arise, however, in finding a similar asset. With technological improvements and other quality changes, equipment purchased currently will likely differ from equipment that the firm acquired 10 years previously but still uses. Thus the accountant may be unable to find similar equipment on the market to measure replacement cost. Alternatively, the accountant might substitute the current replacement cost of an asset capable of rendering equivalent services when the replacement cost of the specific asset is not readily available. This approach, however, requires subjectivity in identifying assets with equivalent service potential.

Current Net Realizable Value   The net amount of cash (selling price less selling costs) that the firm would receive currently if it sold each asset separately is the current net realizable value. This amount is an exit value, because it reflects the amount the firm would receive currently if it disposed of the asset, or exited ownership. In measuring net realizable value, one generally assumes that the firm sells the asset in an orderly fashion rather than through a forced sale at some distress price.

Measuring net realizable value entails difficulties similar to those in measuring current replacement cost. A well-organized secondhand market may not exist for used equipment, particularly equipment specially designed for a firm's needs. In this case, the current selling price of the asset (value in exchange) may be substantially less than the value of the future benefits to the firm from using the asset (value in use).

Present Value of Future Net Cash Flows   Another possible valuation basis is the present value of future net cash flows. An asset is a resource that provides a future benefit. This future benefit is the ability of an asset either to generate future net cash receipts or to reduce future cash expenditures. For example, accounts receivable from customers will lead directly to future cash receipts. The firm can sell merchandise inventory for cash or promises to pay cash. The firm can use equipment to manufacture products that it can sell for cash. A building that the firm owns reduces future cash outflows for rental payments. Because these cash flows represent the future services, or benefits, of assets, the accountant might base asset valuations on them.

Because cash can earn interest over time, today's value of a stream of future cash flows, called the present value, is worth less than the sum of the cash amounts a firm will receive or save over time. The accountant prepares the balance sheet as of a current date. If future cash flows are to measure an asset's value, then accountants might discount the future net cash flows to find their present value as of the date of the balance sheet.

Using discounted cash flows in the valuation of individual assets requires solving several problems. The uncertainty of the amounts of future cash flows is one. The amounts a firm will receive can depend on whether competitors introduce new products, the rate of inflation, and other factors. A second problem is allocating the cash receipts from the sale of a single item of merchandise inventory to all of the assets involved in its production and distribution (for example, equipment, buildings, sales staff's automobiles). A third problem is selecting the appropriate rate to use in discounting the future cash flows to the present. Is the interest rate at which the firm could borrow the appropriate one? Or is the rate at which the firm could invest excess cash the one that it should use? Or is the appropriate rate the firm's cost of capital?

Selecting the Appropriate Valuation Basis

The valuation basis selected depends on the purpose of the financial report.

Example 6 Miller Corporation prepares its income tax return for the current year. The Internal Revenue Code and Regulations specify that firms must use acquisition or adjusted acquisition cost valuation in most instances.

Example 7 A fire recently destroyed the manufacturing plant, equipment, and inventory of Miller Corporation. The firm's fire insurance policy provides coverage in an amount equal to the cost of replacing the assets that were destroyed. Current replacement cost at the time of the fire is appropriate for supporting the insurance claim.

Example 8 Miller Corporation plans to sell a manufacturing division that it has operated unprofitably. In deciding on the lowest price to accept for the division, the firm considers the net realizable value of each asset.

Example 9 Brown Corporation considers purchasing Miller Corporation. The highest price Brown Corporation should pay is the present value of the future net cash flows to be realized from owning Miller Corporation.

Generally Accepted Accounting Asset Valuation Bases

The asset valuation basis appropriate for financial statements issued to shareholders and other investors is perhaps less obvious. The financial statements currently prepared by publicly held firms use one of two valuation bases—one for monetary assets and one for nonmonetary assets.

Monetary assets, such as cash and accounts receivable, generally appear on the balance sheet at their net present value—their current cash, or cash equivalent, value. Cash appears at the amount of cash on hand or in the bank. Accounts receivable from customers appear at the amount of cash the firm expects to collect in the future. If the time until a firm collects a receivable spans more than 1 year, the firm discounts the expected future cash to a present value. Most firms collect their accounts receivable within 1 to 3 months. The amount of future cash flows approximately equals the present value of these flows, and thus accounting ignores the discounting process.

Nonmonetary assets, such as merchandise inventory, land, buildings, and equipment, appear at acquisition cost, in some cases adjusted downward to reflect the services of the assets that the firm has consumed.

The acquisition cost of an asset includes more than its invoice price. Cost includes all expenditures made or obligations incurred in order to put the asset into usable condition. Transportation cost, costs of installation, handling charges, and any other necessary and reasonable costs incurred until the firm puts the asset into service are part of the total cost assigned to the asset. For example, the accountant might calculate the cost of an item of equipment as follows:

Invoice Price of Equipment	$12,000
Less: 2-Percent Discount for Prompt Cash Payment	(240)
Net Invoice Price	$11,760
Transportation Cost	326
Installation Costs	735
Total Cost of Equipment	$12,821

Accountants record the acquisition cost of this equipment as $12,821.

Instead of disbursing cash or incurring a liability, the firm might give other forms of consideration (for example, common stock, merchandise inventory, land) in acquiring an asset. In these cases, the accountant measures acquisition cost by the market value of the consideration given or the market value of the asset received, whichever market value the accountant can more reliably measure.

Foundations for Acquisition Cost   Accounting's use of acquisition cost valuations for nonmonetary assets rests on three important concepts or conventions. First, accounting assumes that a firm is a going concern. In other words, accounting assumes a firm will remain in operation long enough to carry out all of its current plans. The firm will realize any increases in the market value of assets in the normal course of business when the firm receives higher prices for its products. Second, acquisition cost valuations are more objective than the other valuations.

Objectivity in accounting refers to the ability of several independent measurers to come to the same conclusion about the valuation of an asset. Obtaining consensus on the acquisition cost of an asset is relatively easy. Differences among measurers can arise in ascertaining an asset's current replacement cost, current net realizable value, or present value of future cash flows. Objectivity is necessary if independent accountants are to audit the financial statements. Third, acquisition cost generally provides more conservative valuations of assets (and measures of earnings) relative to the other valuation methods. Many accountants believe that financial statements will less likely mislead users if balance sheets report assets at lower rather than higher amounts. Thus, conservatism has evolved as a convention to justify acquisition cost valuations.

The general acceptance of these valuation bases does not justify them. The valuation basis most relevant to users—acquisition cost, current replacement cost, current net realizable value, or present value of future cash flows—is an empirical issue for which research has not yet provided convincing evidence.

Asset Classification

The classification of assets within the balance sheet varies widely in published annual reports. The following discussion gives the principal asset categories.

Current Assets Cash and other assets a firm expects to realize in cash or sell or consume during the normal operating cycle of the business, usually 1 year, are **current assets.** The operating cycle refers to the period of time that elapses for a given firm during which it converts cash into salable goods and services, sells goods and services to customers, and customers pay for their purchases with cash. Current assets include cash, marketable securities held for the short term, accounts and notes receivable, inventories of merchandise, raw materials, supplies, work in process, and finished goods and prepaid operating costs, such as prepaid insurance and prepaid rent. Prepaid costs, or prepayments, are current assets because if the firm had not paid in advance, it would use current assets within the next operating cycle to acquire those services.

Investments A second section of the balance sheet, investments, includes long-term investments in securities of other firms. For example, a firm might purchase shares of common stock of a supplier to help ensure continued availability of raw materials. Or it might acquire shares of common stock of a firm in another area of business activity to permit the acquiring firm to diversify its operations. When one corporation (the parent) owns more than 50 percent of the voting stock in another corporation (the subsidiary), it usually prepares a single set of consolidated financial statements. That is, the accounting merges, or consolidates, the specific assets, liabilities, revenues, and expenses of the subsidiary with those of the parent corporation. The investments section of the balance sheet therefore shows investments where the parent or investor has not consolidated the subsidiary's assets and liabilities.

Property, Plant, and Equipment Property, plant, and equipment (sometimes called plant assets or fixed assets) designates the tangible, long-lived assets a firm uses in its operations over a period of years and which the firm generally does not acquire for resale. This category includes land, buildings, machinery, automobiles, furniture, fixtures, computers, and other equipment. The balance sheet shows these items at acquisition cost less accumulated depreciation, if any, since the firm acquired the asset. Frequently, only the net balance, or book value, appears on the balance sheet. Land appears at acquisition cost.

Intangible Assets Intangible assets include such items as patents, trademarks, franchises, and goodwill. Accountants generally do not recognize expenditures a firm makes in developing intangibles as assets because of the difficulty of ascertaining the existence of future benefits. Accounting does, however, recognize specifically identifiable intangible assets acquired in market exchanges from other entities, such as a patent acquired from its holder, as assets.

Problem 17.1 for Self-Study

Asset recognition and valuation. The transactions listed below relate to the Coca-Cola Company. Indicate whether or not each transaction immediately gives rise to an asset of the company under generally accepted accounting principles. If accounting recognizes an asset, state the account title and amount.

a. The Coca-Cola Company spends $10 million to develop a new soft drink. No commercially feasible product has yet evolved, but the company hopes that such a product will evolve in the near future.

b. The company signs a contract with United Can Corporation for the purchase of $4 million of soft-drink cans. It makes a deposit of $400,000 upon signing the contract.

c. The company spends $2 million for advertisements that appeared during the past month: $500,000 to advertise the Coca-Cola name and $1,500,000 for specific brand advertisements, such as for Diet Coke.

d. The company issues 50,000 shares of its common stock valued on the market at $2.5 million in the acquisition of all the outstanding stock of Coring Glass Company, a supplier of soft-drink bottles.

e. The company spends $800,000 on educational assistance programs for its middle-level managers to obtain MBAs. Historically, 80 percent of the employees involved in the program receive their MBAs and remain with the company 10 years or more thereafter.

f. The company acquires land and a building by signing a mortgage payable for $150 million. Because the company has not yet paid the mortgage, the title document for the land and building remains in the vault of the holder of the mortgage note.

The solution to this self-study problem is at the end of the chapter on page 710.

Liability Recognition

A **liability** arises when a firm receives benefits or services and in exchange promises to pay the provider of those goods or services a reasonably definite amount at a reasonably definite future time. The firm usually promises to pay cash but may promise goods or services.[2] All liabilities are obligations; not all obligations, however, are liabilities.

Example 10 Miller Corporation purchased merchandise inventory and agreed to pay the supplier $8,000 within 30 days. This obligation is a liability because Miller Corporation received the goods and must pay a definite amount at a reasonably definite future time.

Example 11 Miller Corporation borrowed $4 million by issuing long-term bonds. It must make annual interest payments of 10 percent of the amount borrowed on December 31 of each year, and must repay the $4 million principal in 20 years. This obligation is a liability because Miller Corporation received the cash and must repay the debt in a definite amount at a definite future time.

Example 12 Miller Corporation provides a 3-year warranty on its products. The obligation to maintain the products under warranty plans creates a liability. The selling price for its products implicitly includes a charge for future warranty services. As customers pay the selling price, Miller Corporation receives a benefit (that is, the cash collected). Past experience provides a basis for estimating the amount of the liability. Miller Corporation can estimate the proportion of customers who will seek services under the warranty agreement and the expected cost of providing warranty services. Thus, Miller Corporation can measure the amount of the obligation with a reasonable degree of accuracy and will show it as a liability.

Example 13 Miller Corporation signed an agreement with its employees' labor union, promising to increase wages by 6 percent and to provide for medical and life insurance. Although this agreement creates an obligation, it does *not* immediately create a liability. Employees have not yet provided labor services that require the firm to make payments for wages and insurance. As employees work, a liability arises.

The most troublesome questions of liability recognition relate to obligations under unexecuted contracts. The labor union agreement in Example 13 is an unexecuted contract. Other examples include some leases, purchase order commitments, and employment contracts. Accounting does not currently recognize as liabilities the obligations created by unexecuted contracts, but the issue continues to be controversial.

Liability Valuation

Most liabilities are monetary, requiring payments of specific amounts of cash. Those due within 1 year or less appear at the amount of cash the firm expects to pay to

---

[2]Financial Accounting Standards Board, *Statement of Financial Accounting Concepts No. 6,* "Elements of Financial Statements," 1985, par. 35. See the glossary for the Board's definition of a liability.

discharge the obligation. If the payment dates extend more than 1 year into the future (for example, as in the case of the bonds in Example 11), the liability appears at the present value of the future cash outflows. The discount rate in the present value calculations throughout the life of the liability is the borrower's interest rate at the time it incurs the obligation.

A liability that requires delivering goods or rendering services, rather than paying cash, is nonmonetary. For example, magazine publishers typically collect cash for subscriptions, promising delivery of magazines over many months. The firm receives cash currently, whereas it discharges the obligation under the subscription by delivering magazines in the future. Theaters and football teams receive cash for season tickets and promise to admit the ticket holder to future events. Landlords receive cash payment in advance and promise to let the tenant use the property. Such nonmonetary obligations are liabilities. The amount at which they appear, however, is the amount of cash received, rather than at the expected cost of publishing the magazines or of providing the theatrical or sporting entertainment. The title frequently used for nonmonetary liabilities is Advances from Customers.

Liability Classification

The balance sheet typically classifies liabilities in one of the following categories.

Current Liabilities Obligations that a firm expects to pay during the normal operating cycle of the firm, usually 1 year, are **current liabilities.** In general, the firm uses current assets to pay current liabilities. This category includes liabilities to merchandise suppliers, employees, and governmental units. It also includes notes and bonds payable to the extent that they will require the use of current assets within the next year.

Long-Term Debt Obligations having due dates, or maturities, more than 1 year after the balance sheet date appear as long-term debt. Long-term debt includes bonds, mortgages, and similar debts, as well as some obligations under long-term leases.

Other Long-Term Liabilities Obligations not properly considered as current liabilities or long-term debt appear as other long-term liabilities, which include such items as deferred income taxes, some pension obligations, and advances from customers for goods to be delivered more than one year from the balance sheet date.

Problem 17.2
for Self-Study

Liability recognition and valuation. The transactions listed below relate to the New York Times Company. Indicate whether or not each transaction immediately gives rise to a liability of the company under generally accepted accounting principles. If the New York Times Company recognizes a liability, state the account title and amount.

a. The company receives $10 million for newspaper subscriptions covering the 1-year period beginning next month.

b. The company receives an invoice for $4 million from its advertising agency for television advertisements that appeared last month.

c. The company signs a 1-year lease for rental of new delivery vehicles. It pays $40,000 of the annual rental of $80,000 upon signing.

d. Attorneys have notified the company that a New York City resident, seriously injured by one of the company's delivery vehicles, has sued the New York Times Company for $10 million. Although the court is likely to find the company liable in the lawsuit, the company carries sufficient insurance to cover any losses.

e. Refer to part **d** above. Assume now that the company carries no insurance against such losses.

f. A 2-week strike by employees has closed down newspaper publishing operations. As a result, the company could not deliver subscriptions totaling $2 million.

The solution to this self-study problem is at the end of the chapter on page 710.

Shareholders' Equity Valuation and Disclosure

The **shareholders' equity** in a firm is a residual interest.[3] That is, the owners have a claim on all assets not required to meet the claims of creditors.[4] The valuation of the assets and liabilities included in the balance sheet therefore determines the valuation of total shareholders' equity.

The remaining question concerns the manner of disclosing this total shareholders' equity. Accounting distinguishes between contributed capital and earnings retained by a firm. The balance sheet for a corporation generally separates the amount shareholders contribute directly for an interest in the firm (that is, common stock) from earnings the firm subsequently realizes in excess of dividends declared (that is, retained earnings).

In addition, the balance sheet usually further separates the amount received from shareholders into the par or stated value of the shares and amounts contributed in excess of par value or stated value. A corporation's charter assigns the par or stated value of a share of stock to comply with corporation laws of each state. The amount

---

[3]Although shareholders' equity is equal to assets minus liabilities, accounting record-keeping procedures provide an independent method for computing the amount.

[4]Financial Accounting Standards Board, *Statement of Financial Accounting Concepts No. 6,* "Elements of Financial Statements," 1985, par. 49.

will rarely equal the market price of the shares at the time the firm issues them. As a result, the distinction between par or stated value and amounts contributed in excess of par or stated value contains little information.

Example 14 Stephens Corporation legally incorporated on January 1, Year 1. It issued 15,000 shares of $10 par value common stock for $10 cash per share. During Year 1, Stephens Corporation generated net income of $30,000 and paid dividends of $10,000 to shareholders. The shareholders' equity section of the balance sheet of Stephens Corporation on December 31, Year 1, is as follows:

Common Stock (par value of $10 per share, 15,000 shares issued and outstanding)	$150,000
Retained Earnings	20,000
Total Shareholders' Equity	$170,000

Example 15 Instead of issuing $10 par value common stock as in Example 14, assume that Stephens Corporation issued 15,000 shares of $1 par value common stock for $10 cash per share. (The market price of a share of common stock depends on the economic value of the firm, not on the par value of the shares.) The shareholders' equity section of the balance sheet of Stephens Corporation on December 31, Year 1, is as follows:

Common Stock (par value of $1 per share, 15,000 shares issued and outstanding)	$ 15,000
Capital Contributed in Excess of Par Value	135,000
Retained Earnings	20,000
Total Shareholders' Equity	$170,000

Balance Sheet Account Titles

This section describes balance sheet account titles commonly used. The descriptions should help you understand the nature of various assets, liabilities, and shareholders' equities as well as to select appropriate account names when solving problems. One can use alternative account titles. The list does not show all the account titles used in this book or in the financial statements of publicly held firms.

Assets

Cash Coins and currency and items such as bank checks and money orders. (The latter items are merely claims against individuals or institutions but by custom are called cash.) Bank deposits against which the firm can draw checks, and time deposits, usually savings accounts and certificates of deposit.

Marketable Securities Government bonds, or stocks and bonds of corporations, which the firm plans to hold for a relatively short time. The word *marketable* implies that their owner can buy and sell them readily through a security exchange such as the New York Stock Exchange.

Accounts Receivable Amounts due from customers of a business from the sale of goods or services. The collection of cash occurs some time after the sale. These accounts are also known as charge accounts or open accounts. The general term Accounts Receivable used in financial statements describes the figure representing the total amount the firm expects to receive from all customers. The firm, of course, keeps a separate record for each customer.

Notes Receivable Amounts due from customers or from others to whom the firm has made loans or extended credit. The customer or other borrower has put the claim into writing in the form of a formal note (which distinguishes it from an open account receivable).

Interest Receivable Interest on assets such as promissory notes or bonds that has accrued (or come into existence) through the passing of time but that the firm has not yet collected as of the date of the balance sheet.

Merchandise Inventory Goods on hand purchased for resale, such as canned goods on the shelves of a grocery store or suits on the racks of a clothing store.

Raw Materials Inventory Unused materials for manufacturing products.

Supplies Inventory Lubricants, abrasives, and other incidental materials used in manufacturing operations. Stationery, computer disks, pens, and other office supplies. Bags, tape, boxes, and other store supplies. Gasoline, oil, spare parts, and other delivery supplies.

Work-in-Process Inventory Partially completed manufactured products.

Finished Goods Inventory Completed but unsold manufactured products.

Prepaid Insurance Insurance premiums paid for future coverage.

Advances to Suppliers The general name used to indicate payments made in advance for goods or services the firm will receive at a later date. If the firm does not make a cash payment when it places an order, it does not recognize an asset.

Prepaid Rent Rent paid in advance for future use of land, buildings, or equipment. In parallel with the account title above, could also be called ''Advances to Landlord.''

Investment in Securities   Bonds or shares of common or preferred stock in other companies where the firm plans to hold the securities for a relatively long time, typically longer than one year.

Land   Land occupied by buildings or used in operations.

Buildings   Factory buildings, store buildings, garages, warehouses, and so forth.

Equipment   Lathes, ovens, tools, boilers, computers, bins, cranes, conveyors, automobiles, and so forth.

Furniture and Fixtures   Desks, tables, chairs, counters, showcases, scales, and other store and office equipment.

Accumulated Depreciation   The cumulative amount of the cost of long-term assets (such as buildings and equipment) allocated to the costs of production or to current and prior periods in measuring net income. The amount in this account reduces the acquisition cost of the long-term asset to which it relates when measuring the net book value of the asset shown in the balance sheet.

Leasehold   The right to use property owned by someone else.

Organization Costs   Amounts paid for legal and incorporation fees, for printing the certificates for shares of stock, and for accounting and other costs incurred in organizing a business so that it can function.

Patents   Rights granted for up to 17 years by the federal government to exclude others from manufacturing, using, or selling certain processes or devices. Generally accepted accounting principles require the firm to expense research and development costs in the year incurred rather than recognize them as assets with future benefits.[5] As a result, a firm that develops a patent will not normally show it as an asset. On the other hand, a firm that purchases a patent from another will recognize the patent as an asset.

Goodwill   An amount paid by one firm in acquiring another business enterprise that exceeds the sum of the then-current values assignable to individual identifiable assets and liabilities. A good reputation and other desirable attributes are generally not accounting assets for the firm that creates or develops them. However, when one firm acquires another firm, these desirable attributes become recognized as assets insofar as they cause the amount paid for the acquired firm to exceed the values assigned to the individual identifiable assets and liabilities.

---

[5]Financial Accounting Standards Board, *Statement of Financial Accounting Standards No. 2*, ''Accounting for Research and Development Costs,'' 1974.

Liabilities

Accounts Payable Amounts owed for goods or services acquired under an informal credit agreement. The firm must pay these accounts usually within 1 or 2 months. The same items appear as Accounts Receivable on the creditor's books.

Notes Payable The face amount of promissory notes given in connection with loans from a bank or the purchase of goods or services. The same items appear as Notes Receivable on the creditor's (lender's) books.

Interest Payable Interest on obligations that has accrued or accumulated with the passage of time but that the firm has not yet paid as of the date of the balance sheet. The liability for interest customarily appears separately from the face amount of the obligation.

Income Taxes Payable The estimated liability for income taxes, accumulated and unpaid, based on the taxable income of the business from the beginning of the taxable year to the date of the balance sheet.

Advances from Customers The general name used to indicate payments received in advance for goods or services a firm will furnish to customers in the future; a nonmonetary liability. If the firm does not receive cash when a customer places an order, it does not record a liability.

Advances from Tenants or Rent Received in Advance Another example of a nonmonetary liability. For example, a firm owns a building that it rents to a tenant. The tenant prepays the rental charge for several months in advance. The firm cannot include the amount applicable to future months as a component of income until the landlord renders rental services with the passage of time. Meanwhile the advance payment results in a liability payable in services (that is, in the use of the building). On the records of the tenant, the same amount appears as an asset, Prepaid Rent or Advances to Landlord.

Mortgage Payable Long-term promissory notes that the borrower has protected by pledging specific pieces of property as security for payment. If the borrower does not pay the loan or interest according to the agreement, the lender can require the sale of the property to generate funds to repay the loan.

Bonds Payable Amounts borrowed by a business for a relatively long period of time under a formal written contract or indenture. The borrower usually obtains the loan from a number of lenders, all of whom receive written evidence of the share of the loan.

Convertible Bonds Payable Bonds that the holder can convert into, or trade in, for shares of common stock. The bond indenture specifies the number of shares the lenders will receive when they convert their bonds into stock, the date when conversion can occur, and other details.

Capitalized Lease Obligations The present value of the commitment to make future cash payments in return for the right to use property owned by someone else.

Deferred Income Taxes Particular income tax amounts that are delayed beyond the current accounting period.

Shareholders' Equity

Common Stock Amounts received equal to the par or stated value of a firm's principal class of voting stock.

Preferred Stock Amounts received for the par value of a class of a firm's stock that has some preference relative to the common stock. This preference is usually with respect to dividends and to assets in the event of corporate liquidation. Sometimes the holder of preferred stock may convert it into common stock.

Capital Contributed in Excess of Par or Stated Value Amounts received from the issuance of common or preferred stock in excess of such shares' par value or stated value. Other titles for this account are Additional Paid-in Capital and Premium on Preferred (or Common) Stock.

Retained Earnings The increase in net assets since a business began operations, which results from its generating earnings in excess of dividend declarations. When a firm declares dividends, the accounting decreases net assets and retained earnings by equal amounts.

Treasury Shares The cost of shares of stock that a firm originally issued but subsequently reacquires. Treasury shares do not receive dividends and accounting does not identify them as outstanding shares. The cost of treasury shares is almost always shown on the balance sheet as a deduction from the total of the other shareholders' equity accounts.

Summary of Balance Sheet Concepts

The balance sheet comprises three major classes of items—assets, liabilities, and shareholders' equity.

Resources become accounting assets when a firm has acquired rights to their future use as a result of a past transaction or exchange and when it can measure the value of the future benefits with reasonable precision. Monetary assets appear, in general, at their current cash, or cash equivalent, values. Nonmonetary assets appear at acquisition cost, in some cases adjusted downward for the cost of services that the firm has consumed. Liabilities represent obligations of a firm to make payments of a reasonably definite amount at a reasonably definite future time for benefits already received. Shareholders' equity, the difference between total assets and total liabilities, is typically split for corporations into contributed capital and retained earnings.

Analysis of Balance Sheet

The balance sheet reflects the effects of a firm's investing and financing decisions. In general, firms attempt to balance the term structure of their financing with the term structure of their investments (that is, short-term financing for current assets and long-term financing for noncurrent assets). *Term structure* refers to the length of time that must elapse before an asset becomes cash or a liability or shareholders' equity requires cash. One tool for studying the term structure of a firm's assets and the term structure of its financing is a **common size balance sheet.** In a common size balance sheet, the analyst expresses each balance sheet item as a percentage of either total assets or total liabilities plus shareholders' equity. Exhibit 17.3 presents common size balance sheets for Wal-Mart Stores, discount stores and warehouse clubs, American Airlines, an airline, Merck, a pharmaceuticals company, and Interpublic Group of Companies, an advertising services company.

Wal-Mart Stores maintains a large percentage of its assets in merchandise inventories, which it expects to sell within a period of 1 to 2 months. It therefore uses a high proportion of short-term financing (that is, accounts payable).

Exhibit 17.3

Common Size Balance Sheets for Selected Companies

	Wal-Mart Stores	American Airlines	Merck	Interpublic Group
Assets				
Current Assets:				
Cash	.2%	7.7%	14.9%	9.9%
Accounts Receivable	2.7	5.0	16.3	61.2
Inventories	47.8	3.8	10.4	—
Prepayments	4.8	.8	3.8	1.9
Total Current Assets	55.5%	17.3%	45.4%	73.0%
Investments in Securities	—	—	11.0	1.0
Property, Plant, and Equipment	41.6	68.2	36.9	6.8
Intangible Assets	2.9	14.5	6.7	19.2
Total Assets	100.0%	100.0%	100.0%	100.0%
Liabilities and Shareholders' Equity				
Current Liabilities:				
Accounts Payable	22.4%	6.2%	14.7%	52.3%
Notes Payable	3.2	6.4	3.6	5.6
Other Current Liabilities	6.8	16.7	11.3	8.7
Total Current Liabilities	32.4%	29.3%	29.6%	66.6%
Long-term Debt	21.2	36.3	5.2	6.1
Other Noncurrent Liabilities	1.1	11.0	13.4	6.2
Total Liabilities	54.7%	76.6%	48.2%	78.9%
Shareholders' Equity	45.3	23.4	51.8	21.1
Total Liabilities and Shareholders' Equity	100.0%	100.0%	100.0%	100.0%

American Airlines, on the other hand, invests a large percentage of its assets in property, plant, and equipment. It finances these assets with long-term sources of financing (long-term debt plus shareholders' equity). Airlines tend to use more long-term debt than shareholders' equity to finance the acquisition of equipment because (1) the equipment serves as collateral for the borrowing (that is, the lender can repossess or confiscate the equipment if the airline fails to make debt payments on time) and (2) long-term debt usually has a lower explicit cost to the firm than funds provided by shareholders.

Merck also invests a high proportion of its assets in property, plant, and equipment. Pharmaceutical companies tend to maintain capital-intensive, automated manufacturing facilities to ensure quality control of their products. Unlike airlines, however, pharmaceutical companies tend not to carry much long-term debt. One reason for not using debt relates to the nature of the ''assets'' of a pharmaceutical company. One key resource is its research scientists, who could leave the firm at any time. Another key resource is its patents on pharmaceutical products, which competitors could render worthless by developing new, superior products. Given the risk inherent in these off-balance sheet ''assets,'' pharmaceutical firms tend not to add risk on the financing side of their balance sheets by taking on debt, which requires fixed interest and principal payments. A second reason for not using debt is that pharmaceutical companies have historically generated the highest ratios of profitability and operating cash flow of any industry group. Such companies therefore do not need to borrow to finance operating and investing activities.

The Interpublic Group of Companies provides advertising services for clients. It purchases time or space in various media (television, newspapers, magazines), for which it incurs an obligation (Accounts Payable). It develops advertising copy for clients and sells them media time or space to promote their products, resulting in a receivable from the clients (Accounts Receivable). Service firms such as Interpublic Group have few assets other than their employees, which accounting does not recognize as an asset. Thus, current receivables dominate the asset side of the balance sheet and current payables dominate the financing side of the balance sheet.

A potential cause for concern occurs when the percentage of short-term financing begins to exceed the percentage of current assets. In this case, the firm uses short-term financing for noncurrent assets. Like savings and loan associations during the early 1990s, such firms may face difficulties obtaining sufficient cash from these assets to meet short-term commitments to creditors.

The Income Statement: Measuring Operating Performance

The total assets of a firm may change over time because of financing and investment activities. For example, a firm may issue common stock for cash or acquire a building and assume a mortgage for part or all of the purchase price. Holders of convertible bonds may exchange them for shares of common stock. These financing and investment activities affect the amount and structure of a firm's assets and equities.

Exhibit 17.4	
MARNEL CORPORATION	
Income Statement for Year 2	

Sales Revenue...	$125,000
Less Expenses:	
Cost of Goods Sold..	$ 60,000
Salaries	19,667
Depreciation	10,000
Interest..	2,000
Income Taxes	13,333
Total Expenses...	$105,000
Net Income	$ 20,000

The total assets of a firm may also change over time because of operating activities. Firms sell goods or services to customers for an amount that the firm hopes is larger than the cost of acquiring or producing the goods and services. Creditors and owners provide funds to a firm with the expectation that the firm will use the funds to generate a profit and provide an adequate return to the suppliers of the funds. The second principal financial statement, the **income statement**, provides information about the operating performance of a firm for some particular period of time.

Exhibit 17.4 presents an income statement for Marnel Corporation for Year 2. **Net income** equals revenues minus expenses. **Revenues** measure the net assets (assets less liabilities) that flow into a firm when it sells goods or renders services. **Expenses** measure the net assets used up in the process of generating revenues. As a measure of operating performance, revenues reflect the services rendered by a firm, and expenses indicate the efforts required.

Accounting Methods for Measuring Performance

Some operating activities both start and finish within a given accounting period. For example, a firm might purchase merchandise from a supplier, sell it to a customer on account, and collect the cash, all within a particular accounting period. These cases present few difficulties in measuring performance. The difference between the cash received from customers and the cash disbursed to acquire, sell, and deliver the merchandise represents earnings from this series of transactions.

Many operating activities, however, start in one accounting period and finish in another. A firm uses buildings and equipment acquired in one period over several years. Firms purchase merchandise in one accounting period and sell it during the next period, collecting cash from customers during a third period. To measure performance for a specific accounting period requires measuring the amount of revenues and expenses from operating activities that are in process at the beginning or end of the period. Two approaches to measuring operating performance are (1) the cash basis of accounting and (2) the accrual basis of accounting.

Cash Basis of Accounting

Under the **cash basis of accounting**, a firm recognizes revenues from selling goods and providing services in the period when it receives cash from customers. It reports expenses in the period when it makes cash expenditures for merchandise, salaries, insurance, taxes, and similar items. To illustrate the measurement of performance under the cash basis of accounting, consider the following example.

Donald and Joanne Ace open a hardware store on January 1, Year 1. The firm receives $20,000 in cash from the Aces and borrows $12,000 from a local bank. The firm must repay the loan on June 30, Year 1, with interest at the rate of 12 percent per year. The firm rents a store building on January 1, and pays 2 months' rent of $4,000 in advance. On January 1, it also pays the premium of $2,400 for property and liability insurance coverage for the year ending December 31, Year 1. During January it acquires merchandise costing $40,000, of which it purchases $26,000 for cash and $14,000 on account. Sales to customers during January total $50,000, of which $34,000 is for cash and $16,000 is on account. The acquisition cost of the merchandise sold during January is $32,000, and various employees receive $5,000 in salaries.

Exhibit 17.5 presents a performance report for Ace Hardware Store for the month of January, Year 1, using the cash basis of accounting. Cash receipts from sales of merchandise of $34,000 represent the portion of the total sales of $50,000 made during January that the firm collects in cash. Whereas the firm acquires merchandise costing $40,000 during January, it disburses only $26,000 cash to suppliers, and therefore subtracts only this amount in measuring performance under the cash basis. The firm also subtracts the amounts of cash expenditures made during January for salaries, rent, and insurance in measuring performance, without regard to whether the firm fully consumes the services by the end of the month. Cash expenditures for merchandise and services exceeded cash receipts from customers during January by $3,400.[6]

As a basis for measuring performance for a particular accounting period (for example, January, Year 1, for Ace Hardware Store), the cash basis of accounting has two weaknesses. First, it does not adequately match the cost of the efforts required in generating revenues with those revenues. The performance of one period mixes with the performance of preceding and succeeding periods. The store rental payment of $4,000 provides rental services for both January and February, but the cash basis subtracts the full amount in measuring performance during January. Likewise, the annual insurance premium provides coverage for the full year, whereas the cash basis of accounting subtracts none of this insurance cost in measuring performance during February through December.

The longer the period over which a firm receives future benefits, the more serious is this criticism of the cash basis of accounting. Consider, for example, the investments of a capital-intensive firm in buildings and equipment which it will use for 20 or more years. The length of time between the purchase of these assets and the collection of cash for goods produced and sold can span many years.

---

[6]Note that, under the cash basis, the performance report does not include cash received from owners and through borrowing (financing transactions).

Exhibit 17.5

ACE HARDWARE STORE
Performance Measurement on a Cash Basis for the Month of January, Year 1

Cash Receipts from Sales of Merchandise		$34,000
Less Cash Expenditures for Merchandise and Services:		
Merchandise	$26,000	
Salaries	5,000	
Rental...	4,000	
Insurance..	2,400	
Total Cash Expenditures		37,400
Excess of Cash Expenditures over Cash Receipts		$(3,400)

Second, the cash basis of accounting postpones unnecessarily the time when firms recognize revenue. In most cases, the sale (delivery) of goods or rendering of services is the important event in generating revenue. Collecting cash is relatively routine or at least highly predictable. In these cases, recognizing revenue at the time of cash collection may result in reporting the effects of operating activities one or more periods after the critical revenue-generating activity has occurred. For example, sales to customers during January by Ace Hardware Store totaled $50,000. Under the cash basis of accounting, the firm will not recognize $16,000 of this amount until it collects the cash, during February or even later. If the firm checks the creditworthiness of customers prior to making the sales on account, it will probably collect a predictable amount of cash and will have little reason to postpone recognition of the revenue.

Lawyers, accountants, and other professionals are the principal users of the cash basis of accounting. These professionals have relatively small investments in multi-period assets such as buildings and equipment, and usually collect cash from clients soon after they render services. Most of these firms actually use a modified cash basis of accounting, under which they treat the costs of buildings, equipment, and similar items as assets when purchased. They then recognize a portion of the acquisition cost as an expense when they consume services of these assets. Except for the treatment of these long-lived assets, such firms recognize revenues at the time they receive cash and recognize expenses when they disburse cash.

Most individuals use the cash basis of accounting for the purpose of computing personal income and personal income taxes. Where inventories are an important factor in generating revenues, such as for a merchandising or manufacturing firm, the Internal Revenue Code prohibits a firm from using the cash basis of accounting in its income tax returns.

Accrual Basis of Accounting

The **accrual basis of accounting** typically recognizes revenue when a firm sells goods or renders services. Costs incurred lead to expenses in the period when the firm recognizes the revenues that the costs helped produce. Thus accrual accounting

Exhibit 17.6

ACE HARDWARE STORE
Income Statement for January, Year 1
(accrual basis of accounting)

Sales Revenue		$50,000
Less Expenses:		
Cost of Goods Sold	$32,000	
Salaries Expense	5,000	
Rent Expense	2,000	
Insurance Expense	200	
Interest Expense	120	
Total Expenses		39,320
Net Income		$10,680

attempts to match expenses with associated revenues. Costs incurred that a firm cannot closely identify with specific revenue streams become expenses of the period in which the firm consumes the services of an asset and the future benefits of the asset disappear.

Exhibit 17.6 presents an income statement for Ace Hardware Store for January of Year 1 using the accrual basis of accounting. The firm recognizes the entire $50,000 of sales during January as revenue, even though it has not yet received cash in that amount. Because the firm will probably collect the outstanding accounts receivable, the sale of the goods, rather than the collection of cash from customers, triggers the recognition of revenue. The merchandise sold during January costs $32,000. Recognizing this amount as an expense (cost of goods sold) matches the cost of the merchandise sold with revenue from sales. Of the advance rental payment of $4,000, only $2,000 applies to the cost of services consumed during January. The remaining rental of $2,000 applies to the month of February. Likewise, only $200 of the $2,400 insurance premium represents coverage used up during January. The remaining $2,200 of the insurance premium provides coverage for February through December and will become an expense during those months. The interest expense of $120 represents 1 month's interest on the $12,000 bank loan at an annual rate of 12 percent ($= \$12,000 \times .12 \times 1/12$). Although the firm will not pay this interest until the loan comes due on June 30, Year 1, the firm benefited from having the funds available for its use during January; it should therefore recognize an appropriate portion of the total interest cost on the loan as an expense of January. The salaries, rental, insurance, and interest expenses, unlike the cost of merchandise sold, do not associate directly with revenues recognized during the period. These costs therefore become expenses of January to the extent that the firm consumed services during the month.

The accrual basis of accounting provides a better measure of operating performance for Ace Hardware Store for the month of January than does the cash basis for two reasons:

1. Revenues more accurately reflect the results of sales activity during January.
2. Expenses more closely match reported revenues.

Likewise, the accrual basis will provide a superior measure of performance for future periods, because activities of those periods will bear their share of the costs of rental, insurance, and other services the firm will consume. Thus the accrual basis focuses on inflows of net assets from operations (revenues) and the use of net assets in operations (expenses), regardless of whether those inflows and outflows currently produce or use cash.

Most business firms, particularly those involved in merchandising and manufacturing activities, use the accrual basis of accounting. The next section examines the measurement principles of accrual accounting.

Problem 17.3 for Self-Study

Cash versus accrual basis of accounting. Thompson Hardware Store commences operations on January 1, Year 5. J. Thompson invests $10,000 and the firm borrows $8,000 from a local bank. The firm must repay the loan on June 30, Year 5, with interest at the rate of 9 percent per year.

The firm rents a building on January 1 and pays 2 months' rent in advance in the amount of $2,000. On January 1, it also pays the $1,200 premium for property and liability insurance coverage for the year ending December 31, Year 5.

The firm purchases $28,000 of merchandise inventory on account on January 2 and pays $10,000 of this amount on January 25. A physical inventory indicates that the cost of merchandise on hand on January 31 is $15,000.

During January, the firm makes cash sales to customers totaling $20,000 and sales on account totaling $9,000. The firm collects $2,000 from these credit sales by the end of January.

The firm pays other costs during January as follows: utilities, $400; salaries, $650; and taxes, $350.

a. Prepare an income statement for January, assuming that Thompson uses the accrual basis of accounting and recognizes revenue at the time goods are sold (delivered).
b. Prepare an income statement for January, assuming that Thompson uses the cash basis of accounting.
c. Which basis of accounting do you believe provides a better indication of the operating performance of the firm during January? Why?

The solution to this self-study problem is at the end of the chapter on page 710.

Measurement Principles of Accrual Accounting

Under the accrual basis of accounting, one must consider *when* a firm recognizes revenues and expenses (timing questions) and *how much* it recognizes (measurement questions).

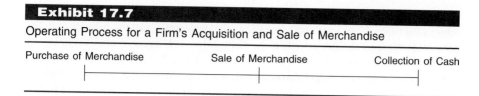

Exhibit 17.7

Operating Process for a Firm's Acquisition and Sale of Merchandise

Purchase of Merchandise   Sale of Merchandise   Collection of Cash

Timing of Revenue Recognition

Exhibit 17.7 depicts the operating process for the acquisition and sale of merchandise. A firm could recognize revenue, a measure of the increase in net assets from selling goods or providing services, at the time of purchase, sale, or cash collection, at some point between these events, or even continually. Answering the timing question requires a set of criteria for revenue recognition.

Criteria for Revenue Recognition   The accrual basis of accounting recognizes revenue when both of the following have occurred:

1. A firm has performed all, or a substantial portion, of the services it expects to provide.
2. The firm has received either cash, a receivable, or some other asset susceptible to reasonably precise measurement.

The majority of firms involved in selling goods and services recognize revenue at the time of sale (delivery). The firm has transferred the goods to a buyer or has performed the services. Future services, such as for warranties, are either insignificant or, if significant, the firm can estimate their cost with reasonable precision. An exchange between an independent buyer and seller provides an objective measure of the amount of revenue. If the firm sells on account, past experience and an assessment of credit standings of customers provide a basis for predicting the amount of cash that the firm will collect. Thus the time of sale usually meets the criteria for revenue recognition.

Measurement of Revenue

A firm measures the amount of revenue by the cash or cash-equivalent value of other assets it receives from customers. As a starting point, this amount is the agreed-upon price between buyer and seller at the time of sale. If a firm recognizes revenue in a period before the collection of cash, however, it may need to make adjustments to the agreed-upon price in measuring revenue.

Uncollectible Accounts   If a firm does not expect to collect some portion of the sales for a period, it must adjust the amount of revenue recognized for that period for estimated uncollectible accounts arising from those sales. This adjustment of revenue occurs in the period when the firm recognizes revenue, not in a later period when it identifies specific customers' accounts as uncollectible. If the firm postpones the adjustment, the earlier decision to extend credit to customers will affect income of subsequent periods. A failure to recognize anticipated uncollectibles at the time of sale incorrectly measures the performance of the firm for both the period of sale and the period when the firm judges the account uncollectible.

Sales Discounts and Allowances Customers may take advantage of discounts for prompt payment, and the seller may grant allowances for unsatisfactory merchandise. In these cases, the stated selling price will exceed the amount of cash a firm eventually receives. It must estimate these amounts and make appropriate reductions in measuring the amount of revenue it recognizes at the time of sale.

Delayed Payments Firms sometimes permit customers to delay payment for purchases of goods or services, but make no provision for explicit interest charges. In such cases, accountants assume the selling price includes an implicit interest charge for the right to delay payment. The accrual basis of accounting should recognize this interest element as interest revenue during the periods between sale and collection. Recognizing all revenue entirely in the period of sale results in recognizing too soon the return for services rendered over time in lending money. When a firm delays cash collection beyond 1 year, generally accepted accounting principles require it to report revenue for the current period at an amount less than the selling price. The reduction accounts for interest between sale and cash collection. At the time of sale, the firm recognizes as revenue only the present value of the amount it expects to receive.

For most accounts receivable, the period between sale and collection spans only 2 to 3 months. The interest element is usually insignificant in these cases. As a result, accounting practice makes no reduction for interest on delayed payments for receivables a firm expects to collect within 1 year or less. This practical procedure does not strictly follow the underlying accounting theory.

Timing of Expense Recognition Assets provide future benefits to the firm. Expenses measure the assets consumed in generating revenue. Assets are unexpired costs, and expenses are expired costs or ''gone assets.'' Our attention focuses on *when* the asset expiration takes place. The critical question is ''When do the benefits of an asset expire (leaving the balance sheet) and become expenses (entering the income statement as reductions in shareholders' equity)?'' Thus:

Balance Sheet	Income Statement
Assets or Unexpired Costs $\longrightarrow$	Expenses or Expired Costs

Expense Recognition Criteria Asset expirations become expenses as follows:

1. Asset expirations associated directly with particular types of revenues are expenses in the period when a firm recognizes revenues. This treatment, called the matching convention, matches cost expirations with revenues.
2. Asset expirations not clearly associated with revenues become expenses of the period when a firm consumes services in operations.

Product Costs The expense for the cost of goods or merchandise sold most easily associates with revenue. At the time of sale, the asset physically changes hands. The firm recognizes revenue, and the cost of the merchandise sold becomes an expense.

A merchandising firm purchases inventory and later sells it without changing its physical form. The inventory appears as an asset stated at acquisition cost on the balance sheet. Later, when the firm sells the inventory, the same amount of acquisition cost appears as an expense (cost of goods sold) on the income statement.

A manufacturing firm, on the other hand, incurs various costs in changing the physical form of the goods it produces. Three types of costs are (1) direct material, (2) direct labor, and (3) manufacturing overhead (sometimes called indirect manufacturing costs). Direct material and direct labor costs associate with particular products manufactured. Manufacturing overhead includes a mixture of costs that provide a firm with a capacity to produce. Examples of manufacturing overhead costs are expenditures for supervisors' salaries, utilities, property taxes, and insurance on the factory, as well as depreciation on the manufacturing plant and equipment. The firm uses the services of each of these items during a period when it creates new assets—the inventory of goods it works on or holds for sale.

Benefits from direct material, direct labor, and manufacturing overhead transfer to, or become embodied in, the asset represented by units of inventory. Because the inventory items are assets until the firm sells to customers, the various direct material, direct labor, and manufacturing overhead costs incurred in producing the goods remain in the manufacturing inventory under the titles Work-in-Process Inventory and Finished Goods Inventory. Such costs, called **product costs,** are assets transformed from one form to another. Product costs are assets; they become expenses only when the firm sells the produced goods.

Selling Costs In most cases, the costs incurred in selling or marketing a firm's products relate to the units sold during the period. For example, a firm incurs costs for salaries and commissions of the sales staff, sales literature used, and advertising in generating revenue. Because these selling costs associate with the revenues of the period, accounting reports them as expenses in the period when the firm uses their services. One might argue that some selling costs, such as advertising and other sales promotions, provide future-period benefits for a firm and therefore the firm should continue to treat them as assets. Distinguishing the portion of the cost relating to the current period (an expense) from the portion relating to future periods (an asset) can, however, be difficult. Accountants, therefore, treat most selling and other marketing activity costs as expenses of the period when the firm uses the services. Even though such costs may enhance the future marketability of a firm's products, these selling costs are **period expenses** rather than assets.

Administrative Costs The costs incurred in administering the activities of a firm do not closely associate with units produced or sold and, like selling costs, are period expenses. Examples include the president's salary, accounting and data-processing costs, and the costs of conducting various supportive activities, such as legal services, employee training, and corporate planning.

Measurement of Expenses

Expenses represent assets consumed during the period. The amount of an expense is therefore the cost of the expired asset. Thus the basis for expense measurement is the same as for asset valuation. Because accounting reports assets primarily at acquisition cost on the balance sheet, it measures expenses by the acquisition cost of the assets sold or used during the period.

Problem 17.4 for Self-Study

Revenue and expense recognition. A firm uses the accrual basis of accounting and recognizes revenues at the time it sells goods or renders services. Indicate the amount of revenue or expense that the firm recognizes during April in each of the following transactions:

a. Collects cash from customers during April for merchandise sold and delivered in March, $4,970.
b. Sells merchandise to customers during April for cash, $14,980.
c. Sells merchandise to customers during April that the firm expects to collect in cash during May, $5,820.
d. Pays suppliers during April for merchandise received by the firm and sold to customers during March, $2,610.
e. Pays suppliers during April for merchandise received and sold to customers during April, $5,440.
f. Receives from suppliers and sells to customers during April merchandise costing $2,010 that the firm expects to pay for during May.
g. Receives from suppliers during April merchandise costing $1,570 that the firm expects to sell to customers and to pay for during May.

The solution to this self-study problem is at the end of the chapter on page 711.

Format and Classification within the Income Statement

Income Statement Format

Firms use different reporting formats in their income statements. Most firms use a multiple-step format that presents several subtotals before reporting the amount of net income for the period. One common multiple-step format separates income from operating activities and revenues and expenses relating to investment and financing activities. The upper panel of Exhibit 17.8 presents an income statement for May Department Stores in this multiple-step format. Note that this format nets revenues

Exhibit 17.8

MAY DEPARTMENT STORES
Income Statement for Year 6, Year 7, and Year 8
(amounts in millions)

	Year 6	Year 7	Year 8
Multiple-Step Format			
Sales.....................................	$10,376	$10,581	$11,742
Cost of Goods Sold............................	(7,533)	(7,706)	(8,453)
Selling and Administrative Expenses..............	(2,048)	(2,019)	(2,279)
Operating Income	$ 795	$ 856	$ 1,010
Interest Revenue	26	22	18
Interest Expense	(153)	(135)	(247)
Income before Income Taxes	$ 668	$ 743	$ 781
Income Tax Expense	(287)	(299)	(278)
Net Income	$ 381	$ 444	$ 503

	Year 6	Year 7	Year 8
Single-Step Format			
Sales.....................................	$10,376	$10,581	$11,742
Interest Revenue	26	22	18
Total Revenues	$10,402	$10,603	$11,760
Cost of Goods Sold...........................	$ 7,533	$ 7,706	$ 8,453
Selling and Administrative Expenses..............	2,048	2,019	2,279
Interest Expense	153	135	247
Income Tax Expense	287	299	278
Total Expenses.............................	$10,021	$10,159	$11,257
Net Income	$ 381	$ 444	$ 503

from sales of merchandise and expenses related to generating these revenues to obtain operating income. Then it adds interest revenues from investments and subtracts interest expenses on debt to derive income before income taxes. This reporting format attempts to capture in the income statement the distinction made earlier in this chapter between operating, investing, and financing activities. Other multiple-step income statement formats are common.

The lower panel of Exhibit 17.8 presents an income statement for May Department Stores in a single-step format. The format presents and totals all revenue items followed by all expense items. The computation of net income results from a "single arithmetic step"—a subtraction of total expenses from total revenues. This income statement format classifies neither revenues nor expenses as operating, investing, and financing activities.

Income Statement Classification

Income statements provide information used both for evaluating the past operating performance of a firm and for projecting the amount of future net income. The income statement can help the statement user achieve these purposes when the income statement distinguishes between (1) revenues and expenses that comprise the ongoing operating activities that the firm expects to recur, and (2) unusual, nonrecurring revenues and expenses. To provide such information, income statements contain some or all of the following sections or categories, depending on the nature of the firm's income for the period:

1. Income from continuing operations.
2. Income, gains, and losses from discontinued operations.
3. Extraordinary gains and losses.
4. Adjustments for changes in accounting principles.

Most income statements include only the first section (see, for example, the income statements for May Department Stores in Exhibit 17.8). The other sections appear only if necessary.

Income from Continuing Operations Revenues, gains, expenses, and losses from the continuing areas of business activity of a firm appear in the first section of the income statement, titled **Income from Continuing Operations**. Firms without nonrecurring categories of income need not use the title Income from Continuing Operations in their income statements. In this case, absence of nonrecurring types of income implies that all reported revenues and expenses relate to continuing operations.

Income, Gains, and Losses from Discontinued Operations Sometimes a firm sells a major division or segment of its business during the year or expects to sell it within a short time after the end of the accounting period. If so, the income statement must disclose separately any income, gains, and losses related to that segment. The separate disclosure appears in a section titled **Income, Gains, and Losses from Discontinued Operations**.[7] This section follows the section presenting Income from Continuing Operations.

Extraordinary Gains and Losses A separate section of the income statement presents **Extraordinary Gains and Losses**. For an item to be extraordinary, it must generally meet both of the following criteria:

1. It is unusual in nature.
2. It is infrequent in occurrence.[8]

An example of an item likely to be extraordinary for most firms would be a loss from an earthquake or confiscation of assets by a foreign government. Such items are likely to be rare. Since 1973, when the Accounting Principles Board issued

---

[7]Accounting Principles Board, *Opinion No. 30,* "Reporting the Results of Operations," 1973.

[8]Accounting Principles Board, *Opinion No. 30.*

Opinion No. 30, extraordinary items seldom appear in published annual reports (except for gains or losses on bond retirements).[9]

Adjustments for Changes in Accounting Principles A firm that changes its principles (or methods) of accounting during the period must in some cases disclose the effects of the change on current and previous years' net income.[10] This information appears in a separate section, titled Adjustments for Changes in Accounting Principles, after Extraordinary Gains and Losses.

Earnings per Share Publicly held firms must show earnings-per-share data in the income statement.[11] Earnings per common share results from dividing net income minus preferred stock dividends by the average number of outstanding common shares during the accounting period. For example, assume that a firm had net income of $500,000 during the year. It declared and paid dividends on outstanding preferred stock of $100,000. The average number of shares of outstanding common stock during the year was 1 million shares. The firm would report earnings per common share of $.40 [= ($500,000 − $100,000)/1,000,000].

If a firm has securities outstanding that the holder can convert into common stock (for example, convertible bonds) or exchange for common stock (for example, stock options), it may need to present two sets of earnings-per-share amounts—primary earnings per share and fully diluted earnings per share.[12]

Summary of Income Statement Concepts

Over sufficiently long time periods, income equals cash inflows minus cash outflows from operating and investing activities; that is, the *amount* of income from operating activities equals the difference between the cash received from customers and the amount of cash paid to suppliers, employees, and other providers of goods and services.[13] Cash receipts from customers do not, however, always occur in the same accounting period as the related cash expenditures to the providers of goods and services. The accrual basis of accounting provides a measure of operating performance in which outflows more closely match inflows than is the case under the cash basis.

The accrual basis determines the *timing* of income recognition. The accrual basis typically recognizes revenue at the time of sale (delivery). Costs that associate directly with particular revenues become expenses in the period when a firm recognizes the revenues. A firm treats the cost of acquiring or manufacturing inventory items in this manner. Costs that do not closely associate with particular revenue

---

[9]Financial Accounting Standards Board, *Statement of Financial Accounting Standards No. 4,* "Reporting Gains and Losses from Extinguishment of Debt," 1975.

[10]Accounting Principles Board, *Opinion No. 20,* "Accounting Changes," 1971.

[11]Accounting Principles Board, *Opinion No. 15,* "Earnings per Share," 1969.

[12]Accounting Principles Board, *Opinion No. 15.*

[13]The general rule that over sufficiently long time periods income equals cash inflows minus cash outflows excludes cash transactions with owners, such as capital contributions and dividends.

streams become expenses of the period when a firm consumes the goods or services in operations. Most selling and administrative costs receive this treatment.

Analyzing the Income Statement

The income statement provides information for assessing the operating profitability of a firm. A starting point for this analysis examines the **quality of earnings.** Does the measurement of revenues or expenses require significant estimates? Does net income include nonrecurring or unusual items? Previous sections of this chapter discussed several issues related to the quality of earnings.

A second step prepares a **common size income statement,** which expresses each expense and net income as a percentage of revenues. A common size income statement permits an analysis of changes or differences in the relation between revenues, expenses, and net income and identifies relations which the analyst should explore further.

Time Series Analysis

Exhibit 17.9 presents a common size income statement for Boise Cascade Corporation, a forest products company, for a recent 3-year period. The changes in sales from the preceding year were as follows: Year 9, +5.9 percent; Year 10, −3.5 percent; Year 11, −5.6 percent.

Boise Cascade experienced substantially decreased profitability during this 3-year period. The most important contributing cause of the decline was an increase in the cost of goods sold percentage. Forest products companies use capital-intensive manufacturing facilities. As a consequence, depreciation and other costs of maintaining these manufacturing facilities do not change significantly as the level of output changes. Boise Cascade Corporation experienced decreased sales in Year 10 and Year 11 as a result of recessionary conditions in the economy. Its cost of goods sold percentage increased because of decreased use of its plant facilities.

The percentage for selling and administrative expenses also increased, probably because of the presence of certain costs that remained fixed despite the decreased level of sales (for example, salaries of selling and administrative staff, depreciation on selling and administrative facilities). The percentage for interest expense in-

---

Exhibit 17.9

Common Size Income Statement for Boise Cascade Corporation

	Year 9	Year 10	Year 11
Sales...	100.0%	100.0%	100.0%
Cost of Goods Sold..............................	(78.8)	(84.4)	(90.9)
Selling and Administrative Expenses.................	(9.4)	(10.0)	(10.4)
Interest Expense	(2.2)	(2.8)	(4.4)
Income Tax Expense	(3.8)	(1.0)	1.2
Net Income	5.8%	1.8%	(4.5)%

Exhibit 17.10
Income Statement for Three Retailers

	The Limited	May Department Stores	Wal-Mart
Sales...............................	100.0%	100.0%	100.0%
Cost of Goods Sold.................	(70.9)	(69.0)	(79.2)
Selling and Administrative Expenses...	(17.4)	(20.4)	(14.3)
Interest Expense	(1.0)	(3.0)	(.6)
Income Tax Expense	(4.1)	(2.7)	(2.2)
Net Income	6.6%	4.9%	3.7%

creased because the firm did not decrease its level of debt, despite the decrease in sales. The income tax percentage decreased because of a decreased pre-tax profit margin.

Cross Section Analysis

A common size income statement also provides information about differences in company strategies. Exhibit 17.10 presents a common size income statement for The Limited (specialty retailer), May Department Stores (department stores), and Wal-Mart Stores (discount stores and warehouse clubs).

The Limited has the highest net income to sales percentage. The Limited has a lower cost of goods sold percentage than Wal-Mart, reflecting its specialty, fashion-oriented product line. May Department Stores ranks second on the net income to sales percentage. Its cost of goods sold percentage is similar to The Limited, reflecting the movement of department stores to a multiple mini-boutiques merchandising strategy. May Department Stores, however, has a higher selling and administrative expense percentage than The Limited, arising from the overhead cost of maintaining and staffing its comparatively larger retail stores. Wal-Mart's high cost of goods sold percentage results from its low-price strategy. It gains an advantage on the selling and administrative expense percentage, however, from lower overhead in its stores.

Statement of Cash Flows

The third principal financial statement is the **statement of cash flows.** This statement reports the net **cash flows** relating to operating, investing, and financing activities for a period of time. Exhibit 17.11 presents a statement of cash flows for Marnel Corporation for Year 2. Operations lead to an increase in cash of $8,000. (Recall that not all revenues result in an immediate increase in cash and that not all expenses result in an immediate decrease in cash.) Acquiring noncurrent assets used cash of $125,000. Financing activities led to a $90,000 net increase in cash. Of what significance is a statement explaining or analyzing the change in cash during a period of time? Consider the following example.

Exhibit 17.11

MARNEL CORPORATION
Statement of Cash Flows for Year 2

Operations:		
Net Income	$ 20,000	
Plus Expenses Not Using Cash:		
Depreciation	10,000	
Plus Increases in Current Liabilities:		
Accounts Payable—Merchandise Suppliers	20,000	
Accounts Payable—Other Suppliers	2,000	
Salaries Payable	1,000	
Less Increases in Current Assets Other Than Cash:		
Accounts Receivable	(35,000)	
Merchandise Inventory	(10,000)	
Cash Flow from Operations		$ 8,000
Investing:		
Acquisition of Equipment		(125,000)
Financing:		
Issue of Long-Term Bonds	$100,000	
Dividends	(10,000)	
Cash Flow from Financing		90,000
Net Change in Cash		$ (27,000)

Example 16 Diversified Technologies Corporation began business 4 years ago. In its first 4 years of operations, net income was $100,000, $300,000, $800,000, and $1,500,000, respectively. The company retained all of its earnings for growth. Early in the fifth year, the company learned that despite the retention of all of its earnings, it was running out of cash. A careful study of the problem revealed the company was expanding accounts receivable, inventories, buildings, and equipment so fast that operations and external financing were not generating funds quickly enough to keep pace with the growth.

This example illustrates a common phenomenon for business firms. Firms may not generate cash in sufficient amounts or at the proper times to finance all ongoing or growing operations. If a firm is to continue operating successfully, it must generate more funds than it spends. In some cases the firm can borrow from creditors to replenish its cash, but future operations must generate funds to repay these loans.

Classification of Items in the Statement of Cash Flows

Exhibit 17.11 classifies the inflows and outflows of cash in parallel with the three principal business activities described earlier in the chapter. Exhibit 17.12 depicts these various sources and uses graphically.

1. Operations: The excess of cash received from customers over the amount of cash paid to suppliers, employees, and others in carrying out a firm's operating activities is a primary source of cash for most firms.

2. Investing: Firms that expect either to maintain current operating levels or to grow must continually acquire buildings, equipment, and other noncurrent as-

Exhibit 17.12

Components of Statement of Cash Flows

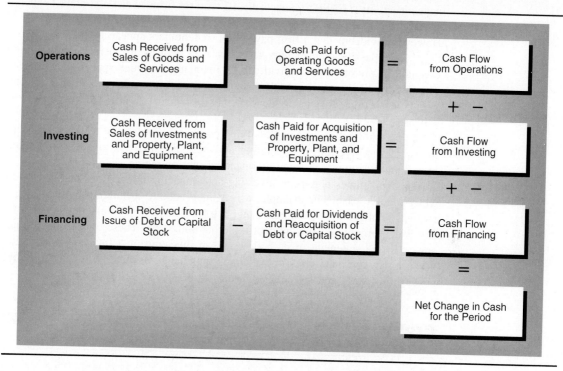

sets. Firms obtain some of the cash needed from selling existing land, buildings, and equipment. The cash proceeds, however, are seldom sufficient to replace the assets sold.

3. Financing: Firms obtain additional financing to support operating and investing activities by issuing bonds or common stock. The firm uses cash for dividends and retiring old financing.

Certain cash flows do not fit unambiguously into one of these three categories of cash flows. For example, the accountant might conceivably classify cash received from interest and dividend revenues from investments in securities as an operating activity (the logic for this treatment is that interest and dividends appear as revenues in the income statement, the financial statement that reports the results of a firm's operations) or as an investing activity (the logic for this treatment is that cash flows related to the purchase and sale of investments in securities appear as investing activities). FASB *Statement No. 95* requires firms to classify interest and dividend revenues as an operating activity but the purchase and sale of investments in securities as an investing activity.[14]

Similar ambiguities arise with interest expense on debt. Should a cash outflow for interest expense appear as an operating activity (to achieve consistency with its

---

[14]*Statement of Financial Accounting Standards No. 95*, "Statement of Cash Flows," para. 16, 17, 22.

inclusion in the income statement as an expense) or as a financing activity (to achieve consistency with the classification of debt issues and retirements as a financing activity)? FASB *Statement No. 95* requires firms to classify interest expense as an operating activity but the issue or redemption of debt as a financing activity.[15] However, dividends that a firm pays to its shareholders appear as financing activities.[16] The classification of interest expense on debt as an operating activity and common or preferred stock dividends as financing activities appears inconsistent. The FASB's likely rationale is that accountants treat interest as an expense in computing net income whereas dividends represent a distribution of net income, not an expense.

Similar ambiguities arise in classifying purchases and sales of marketable securities (treated as investing, not operating, activities) and increases and decreases short-term bank borrowings (treated as financing, not operating, activities).

Firms sometimes engage in investing and financing transactions that do not directly involve cash. For example, a firm may acquire a building by assuming a mortgage obligation or might exchange a tract of land for equipment. Holders of a firm's debt might convert the debt into common stock. These transactions do not appear in the statement of cash flows as an investing or a financing transaction because they are not factors in explaining the change in cash. Firms must disclose noncash investing and financing activities in a separate schedule or note.[17]

Problem 17.5 for Self-Study

Classifying cash flows by type of activity. Classify each of the following cash flows of the current period as either an operating, investing, or financing activity.

1. Disbursement of $96,900 to merchandise suppliers.
2. Receipt of $200,000 from issuing common stock.
3. Receipt of $49,200 from customers for sales made this period.
4. Receipt of $22,700 from customers this period for sales made last period.
5. Receipt of $1,800 from a customer for goods the firm will deliver next period.
6. Disbursement of $16,000 for interest expense on debt.
7. Disbursement of $40,000 to acquire land.
8. Disbursement of $25,300 as compensation to employees for services rendered this period.
9. Disbursement of $7,900 to employees for services rendered but not paid last period.

---

[15]*Statement of Financial Accounting Standards No. 95,* op. cit., para. 19, 20, 23.

[16]*Statement of Financial Accounting Standards No. 95,* op. cit., para. 20.

[17]*Statement of Financial Accounting Standards No. 95,* op. cit., para. 32.

10. Disbursement of $53,800 for a patent.
11. Disbursement of $19,300 as a dividend to shareholders.
12. Receipt of $12,000 from the sale of equipment that originally cost $20,000 and had $8,000 of accumulated depreciation at the time of sale.
13. Disbursement of $100,000 to redeem bonds at maturity.
14. Disbursement of $40,000 to acquire shares of IBM common stock.
15. Receipt of $200 dividend from IBM relating to the shares of common stock acquired in transaction 14 above.

The solution to this self-study problem is at the end of the chapter on page 711.

Using Information in the Statement of Cash Flows

The statement of cash flows provides information that helps the reader in

1. assessing the impact of operations on liquidity, and
2. assessing the relations among cash flows from operating, investing, and financing activities.

Impact of Operations on Liquidity Perhaps the most important factor not reported on either the balance sheet or the income statement is how the operations of a period affected cash flows. Increased earnings do not always generate increased cash flow. A growing, successful firm may find that its accounts receivable and inventories are increasing, resulting in a lag between earnings and cash flows. On the other hand, increased cash flow can accompany reduced earnings. Consider, for example, a firm that is experiencing operating problems and reduces the scope of its activities. Such a firm likely will report reduced net income or even losses. However, it might experience positive cash flow from operations because it collects accounts receivable from prior periods but it does not replace inventories, thus saving cash.

Relations among Cash Flows from Operations, Investing, and Financing Activities The relations among the cash flows from each of the three principal business activities likely differ depending on the characteristics of the firm's products and the maturity of its industry. Consider each of the four following patterns of cash flows.

Cash Flows from:	A	B	C	D
Operations	$ (3)	$ 7	$15	$ 8
Investing	(15)	(12)	(8)	(2)
Financing	18	5	(7)	(3)
Net Cash Flow	$ 0	$ 0	$ 0	$ 3

Case A is typical of a new, rapidly growing firm. It is not yet operating profitably, and it experiences buildups of its accounts receivable and inventories. Thus its cash flow from operations is negative. To sustain its rapid growth, the firm must invest heavily in plant and equipment. During this stage, the firm must rely on external sources of cash to finance both its operating and investing activities.

Case B illustrates a firm somewhat more seasoned than in Case A, but still growing. It operates profitably, but because its rapid growth is beginning to slow, it generates positive cash flow from operations. However, this cash flow from operations is not sufficient to finance acquisitions of plant and equipment. The firm therefore requires external financing.

Case C illustrates the cash flow pattern of a mature, stable firm. It generates a healthy cash flow from operations—more than enough to acquire new plant and equipment. It uses the excess cash flow to repay financing from earlier periods.

Case D illustrates a firm in the early stages of decline. Its cash from operations begins to decrease but is still positive because of decreases in accounts receivable and inventories. It cuts back significantly on capital expenditures because it is in a declining industry. It uses some of its excess cash flow to repay any outstanding financing, and the remainder is available for investment in new products or other industries.

These four cases do not, of course, cover all of the patterns of cash flows found in corporate annual reports. They do illustrate, however, how the characteristics of a firm's products and industry can affect the interpretation of information in the statement of cash flows.

Problem 17.6 for Self-Study

Interpreting the statement of cash flows. Exhibit 17.13 presents a statement of cash flows for Sun Microsystems. Comment on the pattern of cash flows from operating, investing, and financing activities and the relation of net income to cash flow from operations.

Exhibit 17.13

SUN MICROSYSTEMS
Statement of Cash Flows

	Year 5	Year 6	Year 7	Year 8
Operations				
Net Income	$ 6	$ 12	$ 36	$ 66
Depreciation	4	6	25	51
Working Capital Provided by Operations..............................	$ 10	$ 18	$ 61	$ 117

(continued)

Exhibit 17.13 *(continued)*

	Year 5	Year 6	Year 7	Year 8
(Inc.) Decr. in Receivables..................	−18	−24	−58	−117
(Inc.) Decr. in Inventories..................	−16	−21	−32	−77
(Inc.) Decr. in Other Current Assets..................................	−1	−18	−31	−30
Inc. (Decr.) in Accounts Payable —Trade	4	21	33	58
Inc. (Decr.) in Other Current Liabilities	9	6	35	52
Cash Flow from Operations.............................	$−12	$−18	$ 8	$ 3

Investing

Fixed Assets Acquired	$−15	$−36	$−76	$−117
Other Investing Transactions...............	−2	−2	−23	−32
Cash Flow from Investing..............................	$−17	$−38	$−99	$−149

Financing

Incr. Short-term Borrowing..................	$ 3	$ 11	$ 21	$ 0
Incr. Long-term Borrowing	5	1	121	0
Issue of Capital Stock......................	45	47	96	63
Decr. Short-term Borrowing.................	0	0	0	−6
Decr. Long-term Borrowing	−1	−2	0	0
Other Financing Transactions	3	3	0	0
Cash Flow from Financing.............................	$ 55	$ 60	$238	$ 57
Change in Cash...........................	$ 26	$ 4	$147	$ −89
Cash, January 1...........................	4	30	34	181
Cash, December 31	$ 30	$ 34	$181	$ 92

The solution to this self-study problem is at the end of the chapter on page 712.

Other Items in Annual Reports

Supporting Schedules and Notes

The balance sheet, income statement, and statement of cash flows condense information to ease comprehension by the average reader. Some readers desire additional details omitted from these condensed versions. Firms therefore include with their financial statements schedules which provide more detail for some of the items reported in the three main statements. For example, most firms present separate schedules to explain the change in contributed capital and retained earnings.

Every set of published financial statements also contains explanatory notes as an integral part of the statements. In preparing their financial statements, firms select accounting methods from a set of generally accepted methods. The notes indicate the actual accounting methods the firm uses and also disclose additional information that elaborates on items presented in the three principal statements. To understand fully a firm's balance sheet, income statement, and statement of cash flows requires a careful reading of the notes.

Auditor's Opinion

The annual report to the shareholders contains the opinion of the independent auditor, or certified public accountant, on the financial statements, supporting schedules, and notes.

The **auditor's opinion** generally follows a standard format, with some variations to meet specific circumstances. An auditor's opinion on the financial statements of Marnel Corporation might be as follows:

We have audited the accompanying balance sheet of Marnel Company as of January 1 and December 31, Year 1, and the related statements of income, retained earnings, and cash flows for the year then ended. These financial statements are the responsibility of the Company's management. Our responsibility is to express an opinion on these financial statements based on our audits.

We conducted our audits in accordance with generally accepted auditing standards. Those standards require that we plan and perform the audit to obtain reasonable assurance about whether the financial statements are free of material misstatement. An audit includes examining, on a test basis, evidence supporting the amounts and disclosures in the financial statements. An audit also includes assessing the accounting principles used and significant estimates made by management, as well as evaluating the overall financial statement presentation. We believe that our audits provide a reasonable basis for our opinion.

In our opinion, the financial statements referred to above present fairly, in all material respects, the financial position of Marnel Company as of January 1 and December 31, Year 1, and the results of its operations and its cash flows for the years then ended in conformity with generally accepted accounting principles.

The opinion usually contains three paragraphs. The first paragraph indicates the financial presentations covered by the opinion and indicates that the responsibility for the financial statements rests with management. The second paragraph affirms that the auditor has followed auditing standards and practices generally accepted by the accounting profession unless it notes otherwise. Exceptions to the statement that the auditor's examination was conducted ''in accordance with generally accepted auditing standards'' are rare. The auditor may make occasional reference to having relied on financial statements examined by other auditors, particularly for subsidiaries or for data from prior periods.

The opinion expressed by the auditor in the third paragraph is the heart of the report. It may be an **unqualified** or **qualified opinion**. The great majority of opinions are unqualified; that is, there are no exceptions or qualifications to the auditor's opinion that the statements ''present fairly . . . the financial position . . . and the results of its operations and its cash flows . . . in conformity with generally accepted accounting principles.'' Qualifications to the opinion result primarily from material uncertainties regarding realization or valuation of assets, outstanding litigation or tax liabilities, or accounting inconsistencies between periods caused by changes in the application of accounting principles.

A qualification so material that the auditor cannot express an opinion on the fairness of the financial statements as a whole must result in either a disclaimer of opinion or an adverse opinion. Adverse opinions and disclaimers of opinion rarely appear in published reports.

Management's Discussion and Analysis of Operations and Financial Position

The annual report to shareholders must include a discussion by management of the reasons for important changes in a firm's profitability, liquidity, and capital structure. Management must also comment on the impact of inflation on the firm.[18]

Summary

This chapter describes how accounting measures and discloses the results of a firm's activities in published accounting reports. The relation among the three principal financial statements may be depicted as follows:

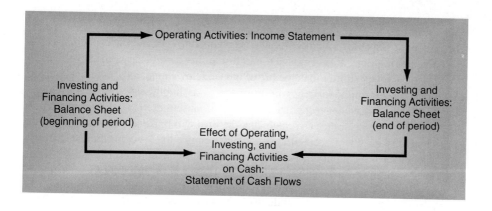

Perhaps the most effective overview of external financial reporting results from reading and studying the annual reports of several publicly held corporations.

---

[18]Securities and Exchange Commission, *Accounting Series Release No. 279,* 1980.

Solutions to Self-Study Problems

Suggested Solution to Problem 17.1 for Self-Study

a. Accounting does not recognize research and development expenditures as assets under generally accepted accounting principles because of the uncertainty of future benefits that a firm can measure with reasonable precision.

b. Deposit on Containers, $400,000. This is a partially executed contract that accountants recognize as an asset to the extent of the partial performance.

c. Accounting does not recognize an asset for the same reason as in part **a** above. Accounting makes no distinction in this regard between institutional advertising and specific product advertising.

d. Investment in Common Stock, $2.5 million. As financial accounting courses discuss more fully, this corporate acquisition may qualify as a pooling of interests, in which case the valuation would likely differ from $2.5 million.

e. Accounting does not recognize an asset for the same reasons as in part **a** above.

f. Land and Building, $150 million. It is necessary to allocate the aggregate purchase price between the land and the building because the building is depreciable and the land is not.

Suggested Solution to Problem 17.2 for Self-Study

a. Subscription Fees Received in Advance, $10 million.

b. Account Payable, $4 million. Other account titles are also acceptable.

c. Accounting does not recognize a liability in this case because the 1-year rental period is much shorter than the life of the vehicles. Financial accounting courses discuss the criteria for recognition of leases as liabilities.

d. Accounting does not recognize a liability because there is a very low probability, given the insurance coverage, that the firm will make a future cash payment.

e. Generally accepted accounting principles require the recognition of a liability when a cash payment is ''probable.'' GAAP provides no specific guidelines as to how high the probability needs to be to recognize a liability.

f. It is likely that the $2 million was previously recorded in the account, Subscription Fees Received in Advance. The strike will probably extend the subscription period by 2 weeks. Thus, the firm has already recognized a liability.

Suggested Solution to Problem 17.3 for Self-Study

a and b.

	a. Accrual Basis	b. Cash Basis
Sales Revenue	$29,000	$22,000
Less Expenses:		
Cost of Merchandise Sold	$13,000	—
Payments on Merchandise Purchased	—	$10,000
Rental Expense	1,000	2,000
Insurance Expense	100	1,200
Interest Expense	60	—
Utilities Expense.	400	400
Salaries Expense	650	650
Taxes Expense.	350	350
Total Expenses.	$15,560	$14,600
Net Income	$13,440	$ 7,400

c. The accrual basis gives a better measure of operating performance because it matches revenues generated during January with costs incurred in generating that revenue. The cash basis mixes operating and financing activities together, principally with regard to sales and purchases on account. Note that the capital contributed by Thompson and the bank loan received do not give rise to revenue under either basis of accounting because they are financing, not operating, activities.

Suggested Solution to Problem 17.4 for Self-Study

a. None
b. $14,980
c. $5,820
d. None
e. $5,440
f. $2,010
g. None

Suggested Solution to Problem 17.5 for Self-Study

1. Operating
2. Financing
3. Operating

4. Operating
5. Operating
6. Operating
7. Investing
8. Operating
9. Operating
10. Investing
11. Financing
12. Investing
13. Financing
14. Investing
15. Operating

Suggested Solution to Problem 17.6 for Self-Study

The rapid increase in net income and fixed assets acquired suggests that the firm operates in high-growth markets. That depreciation expense comprises such a high proportion of net income suggests that the firm is relatively capital intensive. During Year 5 and Year 6 the firm experienced negative cash flow from operations. Even though net income was positive in these years, increases in accounts receivable and inventories caused a negative cash flow from operations. Cash flow from operations turned positive in Year 7 and Year 8. In none of the 4 years, however, was cash flow from operations sufficient to finance acquisitions of fixed assets. Sun Microsystems relied on additional common stock and long-term debt to finance those investing activities.

Key Terms and Concepts

Balance sheet
Assets
Monetary and nonmonetary assets
Current assets
Liability
Monetary and nonmonetary liabilities
Current liability
Shareholders' equity
Common size balance sheet
Income statement
Net income
Revenues
Expenses
Cash basis of accounting

Accrual basis of accounting
Product costs
Period expenses
Income from continuing operations
Income, gains, and losses from
  discontinued operations
Extraordinary gains and losses
Quality of earnings
Common size income statement
Statement of cash flows
Cash flows
Auditor's opinion
Unqualified or qualified opinion

Questions, Exercises, Problems, and Cases

Questions

1. Review the meaning of the concepts or terms given above in Key Terms and Concepts.
2. The chapter describes four activities common to all entities: setting goals and strategies, financing activities, investing activities, and operating activities. How would these four activities likely differ for a charitable organization versus a business firm?
3. "The photographic analogy for the balance sheet is a snapshot and for the income statement and statement of cash flows is a motion picture." Explain.
4. "Asset valuation and income measurement are closely related." Explain.
5. If the total net income from a particular business activity equals the difference between cash inflows and cash outflows, why don't accountants use the cash basis of accounting rather than the accrual basis?
6. "The use of the accrual basis of accounting for measuring operating performance gives rise to the need for a statement of cash flows." Explain.
7. A student states: "It is inconceivable to me that a firm could report increasing net income yet run out of cash." Clarify this student's confusion.
8. Does an unqualified, or "clean," opinion of an independent auditor indicate that the financial statements are free of errors and misrepresentations? Explain.
9. Suggest reasons why the format and content of financial accounting reports tend to be more standardized than accounting reports that firms prepare for their internal decision-making, planning, and control purposes.

Exercises

Solutions to even-numbered exercises are at the end of this chapter on page 727.

10. **Balance sheet relations.** Selected balance sheet amounts for Georgia-Pacific Corporation, a forest products company, for 4 recent years appear below (amounts in millions):

	Year 8	Year 9	Year 10	Year 11
Noncurrent Assets	$5,223	$5,227	$10,294	?
Shareholders' Equity	?	2,717	2,975	$2,736
Total Assets	?	?	12,060	?
Current Liabilities	1,013	924	?*	?**
Current Assets	1,892	?	?*	?**
Noncurrent Liabilities	3,467	?	?	5,164
Total Liabilities and Shareholders' Equity	?	7,056	?	10,622

*Current Assets − Current Liabilities = $−769.
**Current Assets − Current Liabilities = $−1,160.

  a. Compute the missing balance sheet amounts for each of the 4 years.
  b. How did the structure of total assets (that is, the proportion of current versus noncurrent assets) change over the 4-year period? What might account for such a change?
  c. How did the structure of total liabilities plus shareholders' equity change over the 4-year period? What might account for such a change?
  d. What factors might explain the change in total assets between Year 9 and Year 10?
  e. What factors might explain the change in total assets between Year 10 and Year 11?

11. **Balance sheet relations.** Selected balance sheet amounts for Nissan Motor Cars, Ltd., a Japanese automobile manufacturer, for 4 recent years appear below (amounts in billions):

	Year 6	Year 7	Year 8	Year 9
Current Assets	¥2,456	?	¥3,358	?
Noncurrent Assets	?	¥1,911	2,387	¥3,059
Total Assets	4,174	?	?	?
Current Liabilities	1,949	?	?	3,196
Noncurrent Liabilities	780	876	?	?
Contributed Capital	?	574	598	600
Retained Earnings	1,003	1,075	?	1,180
Total Liabilities and Shareholders' Equity	?	4,742	?	?
Net Income	65	?	135	?
Dividends	31	33	35	35
Current Assets/Current Liabilities	?	?	1.20	1.06

  a. Compute the missing amounts for each of the 4 years.
  b. Identify changes in the component structure of total assets and in the component structure of total liabilities plus shareholders' equity over the 4-year period. Suggest the events or transactions that might explain these changes.

12. **Asset recognition and valuation.** The transactions listed below relate to Eli Lilly and Company, a pharmaceutical company. Indicate whether or not each transaction immediately gives rise to an asset of the company under generally accepted accounting principles. If accounting recognizes an asset, state the account title and amount.
  a. The firm sends a check for $12,000,000 to an insurance company for liability insurance. The period of coverage begins next month.
  b. The firm issues a check for $500,000 as a deposit on specially designed scientific equipment. The equipment will have a total purchase price of $2,000,000 and will be completed and delivered next year.
  c. The firm acquires shares of common stock in Genetic Engineering, Inc. a leading firm in genetics research, for $325,000. Eli Lilly holds these shares with the expectation of developing long-term relations with this genetic engineering firm.

d. The firm acquires chemicals used as raw materials in its pharmaceutical products with a list price of $800,000, with payment in time to secure a 2-percent discount for prompt payment. Eli Lilly treats cash discounts as a reduction in the acquisition cost of inventory.

e. The firm hires a well-known scientist to manage its research and development activities. Employment begins next month. One-twelfth of the annual salary of $480,000 is payable at the end of each month worked.

f. The firm purchases bonds with a face value of $3,000,000 for $3,200,000. The bonds mature in 20 years and require interest payments of 8 percent annually. Eli Lilly made the investment with temporarily excess cash and intends to sell the bonds when it needs cash.

g. The firm receives an order from Revco Drug Stores for $15,000 of pharmaceutical products.

h. The firm receives notice from a supplier that has shipped by freight raw materials billed at $200,000, with payment due in 30 days. Eli Lilly obtains title to the raw materials as soon as the supplier ships them to the seller.

13. **Asset recognition and valuation.** The transactions listed below relate to General Mills, Inc., a consumer foods company. Indicate whether or not each transaction immediately gives rise to an asset under generally accepted accounting principles. If accounting recognizes an asset, state the account title and amount.

a. The firm spends $3,400,000 to develop and test market a new breakfast cereal. It intends to launch the new product nationally next month.

b. The firm spends $2,800,000 to acquire rights to manufacture and sell a new low-cholesterol, salt-free cake mix developed by a local Minneapolis resident.

c. The firm spends $1,800,000 to obtain options to purchase land as future sites for its Red Lobster and Olive Garden restaurant chains.

d. The firm spends $760,000 for television advertisements that appeared last month.

e. The firm issues shares of its common stock currently selling on the market for $3,500,000 for 30 percent of the shares of Pizza-To-Go Restaurants, Inc., a regional, family-owned pizza chain. Recent appraisals suggest that a 30-percent share of Pizza-To-Go, Inc., is worth between $3,200,000 and $4,000,000. General Mills intends to hold these shares as a long-term investment.

f. The firm acquires land and an old building costing $2,000,000 by paying $800,000 in cash and signing a promissory note for the remaining $1,200,000 of the purchase price. General Mills expends $60,000 for a title search and other legal fees, $8,000 in recording fees with the state of Minnesota, and $120,000 to destroy the building. General Mills intends to use the land for a parking lot.

14. **Liability recognition and valuation.** The transactions listed below relate to Travelers Insurance Company. Indicate whether or not each transaction immediately gives rise to a liability of the company under generally accepted accounting principles. If accounting recognizes a liability, state the account title and amount.

a. The firm receives $6,500,000 from customers for insurance coverage beginning next month.
b. The firm hires its president under a 3-year contract beginning next month. The contract calls for $750,000 of compensation each year.
c. The firm receives a bill from its attorneys for $1,200,000 to cover services rendered in defending the company in a successful lawsuit.
d. The firm issues additional common stock with a par value of $3,000,000 for $7,600,000.
e. The firm has not yet paid employees who earned salaries and commissions totaling $950,000 during the most recent pay period. The employer must also pay payroll taxes of 8 percent of the compensation earned.
f. The firm received a legal notice that it is subject to a lawsuit by a group of customers who allege that the company improperly canceled its insurance. The suit claims damages of $6,000,000.

15. **Liability recognition and valuation.** The transactions below relate to Kansas City Royals, Inc., owner of a professional baseball team and Royals Stadium. Indicate whether or not each of the following transactions immediately gives rise to a liability of the firm under generally accepted accounting principles. If accounting recognizes a liability, state the account title and amount.
a. The firms signs a 5-year contract with Joe Superstar for $1,400,000 per year. The contract period begins on February 1 of next year.
b. The firm receives $2,700,000 from sales of season tickets for the baseball season starting April 1 of next year.
c. The firm issues bonds in the principal amount of $8,000,000 for $8,400,000. The bonds mature in 20 years and bear interest at 8 percent per year. The firm intends to use the proceeds to expand Royals Stadium.
d. The firm receives a bill for utility services received last month totaling $3,400.
e. The firm receives notice that a former player has filed suit against Kansas City Royals, Inc., alleging nonperformance of contractual terms. The player claims $10,000,000 in damages.
f. The firm orders new uniforms for the team for the baseball season beginning next spring. The contract calls for a $10,000 deposit upon signing the contract and a $10,000 payment upon delivery of the uniforms in February of next year.

16. **Retained earnings relations.** Selected data affecting retained earnings for Volvo Group, a Swedish automobile manufacturer, for 4 recent years appear below (amounts in millions of Swedish kronor):

	Year 3	Year 4	Year 5	Year 6
Retained Earnings, January 1.........	25,634	?	?	37,922
Net Income	5,665	4,940	?	?
Dividends Declared and Paid	815	?	1,203	1,203
Retained Earnings, December 31	?	34,338	37,922	35,699

a. Compute the missing amounts for each of the 4 years.
b. Retained earnings increased but at a decreasing rate between Year 3 and

Year 5 and declined between Year 5 and Year 6. What is the apparent explanation for these changes?

17. **Revenue recognition.** J.C. Penney uses the accrual basis of accounting and recognizes revenue at the time it sells goods or renders services. Indicate the amount of revenue the firm recognizes during the month of May in each of the following transactions:

    a. Collects cash from customers during May for merchandise sold and delivered in April, $2,450,000.

    b. Sells merchandise during May for cash, $16,940,000.

    c. Sells merchandise to customers during May for which the firm will collect cash from customers in June, $2,925,000.

    d. Collects cash from customers during May for merchandise the firm will sell and deliver in June, $18,000.

    e. Rents a store building to a toy shop for $8,000 a month, effective May 1. J.C. Penney receives a check for $16,000 for 2 months' rent on May 1.

    f. Data in part **e,** except that it receives the check from the tenant in June.

18. **Expense recognition.** Assume that Hewlett Packard (HP) uses the accrual basis of accounting and recognizes revenue at the time it sells goods or renders services. Indicate the amount of expense recognized during March (if any) from each of the following transactions or events.

    a. HP pays an insurance premium of $18,000 on March 1 for 1 year's coverage beginning on that date.

    b. On April 3, HP receives a utilities bill totaling $4,600 for services during March.

    c. HP purchases on account office supplies costing $7,000 during March. It makes payment for $5,000 of these purchases on account in March and pays the remainder in April. On March 1, supplies were on hand that cost $3,000. On March 31, supplies that cost $3,500 were still on hand.

    d. Data in part **c,** except that $2,000 of supplies were on hand March 1.

    e. In January, HP paid property taxes of $48,000 on an office building for the year.

    f. On March 29, HP paid an advance of $250 on the April salary to an employee.

19. **Income statement relations.** Selected income statement information for Wal-Mart Stores, a discount store and warehouse club chain, for 3 recent years appears below (amounts in millions):

	Year 6	Year 7	Year 8
Sales.....................................	$25,986	?	$44,289
Cost of Goods Sold.........................	20,070	$25,500	?
Selling and Administrative Expenses...........	4,070	5,152	6,684
Interest Expense	138	169	266
Income Tax Expense	632	752	945
Net Income	?	1,291	1,608

    a. Compute the missing amounts for each of the 3 years.

    b. Prepare a common size income statement for each year where sales equals

100 percent and each expense and net income is expressed as a percentage of sales. What factors appear to explain the change in the ratio of net income to sales?

20. **Statement of cash flows relations.** Selected data from the statement of cash flows for Sun Microsystems, a computer manufacturer, for 3 recent years appear below (amounts in millions):

	Year 8	Year 9	Year 10
Inflows of Cash			
Proceeds from Bank Borrowings	$ 11	$ 21	—
Revenues from Operations Increasing Cash	1,046	1,258	$1,515
Issue of Common Stock........................	47	96	63
Issue of Long-term Debt.......................	4	121	—
Total Inflows	$1,108	$1,496	$1,578
Outflows of Cash			
Acquisition of Property, Plant, and Equipment	$ 38	$ 99	$ 149
Repayment of Bank Borrowings	—	—	6
Repayment of Long-term Debt	2	—	—
Expenses for Operations Decreasing Cash	1,064	1,250	1,512
Total Outflows.....................	$1,104	$1,349	$1,667
Change in Cash	$ 4	$ 147	$ (89)

a. Prepare a statement of cash flows for Sun Microsystems for each of the 3 years using the format in Exhibit 17.11.

b. Net income was $12 in Year 8, $36 in Year 9, and $66 in Year 10. Why do the amounts for cash flow from operations computed in **a** above differ from these net income amounts?

c. In what sense is the pattern of cash flows from operating, investing, and financing activities for Sun Microsystems during the 3 years typical of a growing company?

21. **Statement of cash flows relations.** Selected data from the statement of cash flows for Humana, Inc., a hospital management company, for Year 2, Year 3, and Year 4 appear below (amounts in millions):

	Year 2	Year 3	Year 4
Inflows of Cash			
Sale of Property, Plant, and Equipment	$ 13	$ 73	$ 36
Issue of Long-term Debt.........................	131	188	182
Revenues from Operations Increasing Cash	2,653	2,903	3,260
Issue of Common Stock..........................	0	0	0

(continued)

	Year 2	Year 3	Year 4
Outflows of Cash			
Dividends	$ 72	$ 75	$ 81
Repurchase of Common Stock	0	0	0
Expenses for Operations			
Decreasing Cash	2,188	?	2,780
Acquisition of Property,			
Plant, and Equipment	?	398	295
Redemption of Long-term			
Debt	87	170	?
Change in Cash	−22	27	66

a. Compute the amount of each of the missing items above. Prepare a statement of cash flows for Humana, Inc., for each of the 3 years using the format in Exhibit 17.11.

b. What major changes do you observe in the pattern of cash flows from operating, investing, and financing activities over the 3 years? Net income for the 3 years was Year 2, $54; Year 3, $183; Year 4, $227.

Problems

22. **Preparing a balance sheet and income statement.** The accounting records of Ben and Jerry's Homemade Ice Cream, Inc., reveal the following for a recent year (amounts in thousands):

	December 31:	
	Year 6	Year 7
Balance Sheet Items		
Accounts Payable	$ 5,219	$ 7,873
Accounts Receivable.......................	5,044	6,940
Bonds Payable (due Year 20)	10,313	4,602
Cash	796	6,704
Common Stock............................	6,532	12,959
Inventories................................	10,083	9,000
Other Current Assets	518	1,091
Other Current Liabilities	2,623	4,249
Other Noncurrent Assets	559	21
Property, Plant, and Equipment	17,299	19,300
Retained Earnings	9,570	13,310
Salaries Payable	42	63

	Year 7
Income Statement Items	
Administrative Expense	$ 4,798
Cost of Goods Sold.........................	68,500
Income Tax Expense	2,765
Interest Expense	736
Sales Revenue.............................	97,005
Selling Expense	16,466

    a. Prepare a comparative balance sheet for Ben and Jerry's as of December 31, Year 6 and Year 7. Classify each balance sheet item into one of the following categories: current assets, noncurrent assets, current liabilities, noncurrent liabilities, and shareholders' equity.

    b. Prepare an income statement for Ben and Jerry's for Year 7. Separate income items into revenues and expenses.

    c. Prepare a schedule explaining the change in retained earnings between the beginning and end of Year 7.

    d. Compare the amounts on Ben and Jerry's balance sheet on December 31, Year 6, and December 31, Year 7. Identify the major changes and suggest possible explanations for these changes.

23. **Interpreting balance sheet changes.** Exhibit 17.14 presents a common size balance sheet for Humana, Inc., a hospital chain, for 3 recent years.

    a. Identify the ways in which the structure of Humana's assets and the structure of its financing correspond to that which one would expect of a hospital chain.

    b. Identify the major changes in the structure of Humana's assets and its financing over the 3-year period and suggest possible reasons for the changes.

    c. "An increase in the common size balance sheet percentage between 2 year-ends for a particular balance sheet item (for example, cash) does not necessarily mean that its dollar amount increased." Explain.

Exhibit 17.14

Common Size Balance Sheet for Humana, Inc.
(Problem 23)

| | August 31 | | |
	Year 6	Year 7	Year 8
Assets			
Current Assets			
Cash	5.9%	6.6%	7.2%
Accounts Receivable	14.5	15.4	14.8
Inventories	1.9	1.8	2.0
Other Current Assets	.8	2.9	3.1
Total Current Assets	23.1%	26.7%	27.1%
Investments	4.3	8.3	9.2
Property, Plant, and Equipment	68.4	61.3	58.1
Other Assets	4.2	3.7	5.6
Total Assets	100.0%	100.0%	100.0%
Liabilities and Shareholders' Equity			
Current Liabilities			
Accounts Payable	2.8%	2.6%	3.2%
Notes Payable	2.4	1.7	1.0
Other Current Liabilities	12.9	13.9	14.4
Total Current Liabilities	18.1%	18.2%	18.6%

(continued)

Exhibit 17.14 (continued)

	August 31		
	Year 6	Year 7	Year 8
Noncurrent Liabilities			
Bonds Payable	41.7	38.5	35.4
Other Noncurrent Liabilities	9.5	11.8	12.3
Total Noncurrent Liabilities.	51.2%	50.3%	47.7%
Total Liabilities	69.3%	68.5%	66.3%
Shareholders' Equity			
Common stock	.5%	.5%	.5%
Additional Paid-in Capital	7.8	7.0	6.8
Retained Earnings	22.4	24.0	26.4
Total Shareholders' Equity	30.7%	31.5%	33.7%
Total Liabilities and			
Shareholders' Equity	100.0%	100.0%	100.0%

24. **Cash versus accrual basis of accounting.** Argenti Corporation commenced operations on January 1, Year 6. The firm's cash account revealed the following transactions for the month of January.

Date	Transaction	Amount
Cash Receipts		
Jan. 1	Investment by Mary Argenti for 100 percent of Argenti Corporation's Common Stock	$50,000
Jan. 1	Loan from Upper Valley Bank, due June 30, Year 6, with interest at 6 percent per year	20,000
Jan. 15	Advance from a customer for merchandise scheduled for delivery in February, Year 6	800
Jan. 1–31	Sales to customers	40,000
Cash Disbursements		
Jan. 1	Rental of retail space at a monthly rental of $2,500	(5,000)
Jan. 1	Purchase of display equipment (5-year life, zero salvage value)	(30,000)
Jan. 1	Premium on property and liability insurance for coverage from January 1 to December 31, Year 5 .	(2,400)
Jan. 15	Payment of utility bills	(850)
Jan. 16	Payment of salaries	(2,250)
Jan. 1–31	Purchases of merchandise	(34,900)
	Balance, January 31, Year 6	$35,400

The following information relates to Argenti Corporation as of January 31, Year 6.

1. Customers owe the firm $7,500 from sales made during January.
2. The firm owes suppliers $4,400 for merchandise purchased during January.

3. Unpaid utility bills total $760 and unpaid salaries total $2,590.
4. Merchandise inventory on hand totals $7,200.
    a. Prepare an income statement for January, assuming that Argenti Corporation uses the accrual basis of accounting and recognizes revenue at the time it sells goods to customers.
    b. Prepare an income statement for January, assuming that Argenti Corporation uses a cash basis of accounting.
    c. Which basis of accounting do you believe provides a better indication of the operating performance of the firm during January? Why?

25. **Cash versus accrual basis of accounting.** Management Consultants, Inc., opens a consulting business on July 1, Year 2. Roy Bean and Sarah Bower each contribute $5,000 cash for shares of the firm's common stock. The corporation borrows $6,000 from a local bank on August 1, Year 2. The loan is repayable on July 31, Year 3, with interest at the rate of 9 percent per year.

    The firm rents office space on August 1, paying 2 months' rent in advance. It pays the remaining monthly rental fees of $1,600 per month on the first of each month, beginning October 1. The firm purchases office equipment with a 4-year life for cash on August 1 for $12,000.

    The firm renders consulting services for clients between August 1 and December 31, Year 2, totaling $45,000. It collects $39,000 of this amount by year-end.

    It incurs and pays other costs by the end of the year as follows: utilities, $350; salaries, $28,200; supplies, $650. It has unpaid bills at year-end as follows: utilities, $50; salaries, $1,800; supplies, $40. The firm used all the supplies it had acquired.

    a. Prepare an income statement for the 5 months ended December 31, Year 2, assuming that the corporation uses the accrual basis of accounting and recognizes revenue at the time services are rendered.
    b. Prepare an income statement for the 5 months ended December 31, Year 2, assuming that the corporation uses the cash basis of accounting.
    c. Which basis of accounting do you believe provides a better indication of operating performance of the consulting firm for the period? Why?

26. **Interpreting a common size income statement.** Merck, Inc., develops, manufactures, and sells prescription pharmaceutical products. The time required to develop, patent, and gain Federal Drug Administration approval of a new drug can span 10 or more years. The manufacturing process relies heavily on automation, which minimizes human involvement and helps maintain strict quality controls. The marketing of pharmaceutical products involves personal selling efforts to physicians, hospitals, and pharmacies. Federal government efforts to constrain medical cost price increases have led to increased competition in the industry. Exhibit 17.15 presents a common size income statement for Merck for 3 recent years. Sales increased as follows relative to the preceding year: Year 4, 10.3 percent; Year 5, 14.2 percent; Year 6, 12.1 percent.
    a. Pharmaceutical companies tend to exhibit among the lowest cost of goods sold percentages (20 percent to 30 percent of sales) of any industry group in the United States. What factors might explain this low cost of goods sold percentage?

Exhibit 17.15

MERCK, INC.
Common Size Income Statement
(Problem 26)

	Year 4	Year 5	Year 6
Sales.....................................	100.0%	100.0%	100.0%
Cost of Goods Sold..........................	(23.7)	(23.2)	(22.5)
Selling and Administrative Expenses.............	(30.7)	(31.1)	(31.6)
Research and Development Expenses...........	(11.5)	(11.1)	(11.0)
Operating Income	34.1%	34.6%	34.9%
Interest Revenue	2.1	1.9	1.7
Interest Expense	(.8)	(.8)	(.8)
Net Income before Taxes.....................	35.4%	35.7%	35.8%
Income Tax Expense	(12.0)	(12.0)	(12.0)
Net Income	23.4%	23.7%	23.8%

b. What factors might explain the decreasing cost of good sold percentage over the 3-year period?

c. What factors might explain the increasing selling and administrative expense percentage?

d. Does the decreasing research and development expense percentage indicate that Merck has reduced its expenditures on this critical cost item?

e. What factors might explain the common size percentages for interest revenue and interest expense?

f. How has the income tax position of Merck changed over the 3-year period?

27. **Interpreting the statement of cash flows.** Exhibit 17.16 presents a statement of cash flows for NIKE, Inc., an athletic shoes company, for 3 recent years.

a. Why did NIKE experience increasing net income but decreasing cash flow from operations during this 3-year period?

b. What is the likely explanation for the changes in NIKE's cash flow from investing during the 3-year period?

c. How did NIKE finance its investing activities during the 3-year period?

d. Evaluate the appropriateness of NIKE's use of short-term borrowing during Year 9.

28. **Relations between net income and cash flows.** The ABC Company starts the year in fine shape. The firm makes widgets—just what the customer wants. It makes them for $0.75 each and sells them for $1.00. The ABC Company keeps an inventory equal to shipments of the past 30 days, pays its bills promptly, and collects cash from customers within 30 days after the sale. The sales manager predicts a steady increase of 500 widgets each month beginning in February. It looks like a great year, and it begins that way.

Exhibit 17.16

NIKE, INC.
Statement of Cash Flows
(all dollar amounts in millions)
(Problem 27)

	Year 7	Year 8	Year 9
Operations			
Net Income	$ 167	$ 243	$ 287
Depreciation and Amortization	15	17	34
Other Addbacks and Subtractions	(5)	5	3
Working Capital Provided by Operations	$ 177	$ 265	$ 324
(Inc.) Dec. in Accounts Receivable	(38)	(105)	(120)
(Inc.) Dec. in Inventories	(25)	(86)	(275)
(Inc.) Dec. in Other Operating Current Assets	(2)	(5)	(6)
Inc. (Dec.) in Accounts Payable	21	36	59
Inc. (Dec.) in Other Current Operating Liabilities . .	36	22	32
Cash Flow from Operations	$ 169	$ 127	$ 14
Investing			
Sale of Property, Plant, and Equipment	$ 3	$ 1	$ 2
Acquisition of Property, Plant, and Equipment	(42)	(87)	(165)
Acquisition of Investments	(1)	(3)	(48)
Cash Flow from Investing	$ (40)	$ (89)	$(211)
Financing			
Increase in Short-term Debt	—	—	$ 269
Increase in Long-term Debt	—	$ 1	5
Issue of Common Stock	$ 3	2	3
Decrease in Short-term Debt	(96)	(8)	—
Decrease in Long-term Debt	(4)	(2)	(10)
Dividends	(22)	(26)	(41)
Cash Flow from Financing	$(119)	$ (33)	$ 226
Change in Cash	$ 10	$ 5	$ 29
Cash, Beginning of Year	74	84	89
Cash, End of Year	$ 84	$ 89	$ 118

(Problem 28)

January 1	Cash, $875; receivables, $1,000; inventory, $750.
January	In January, the firm sells on account for $1,000, 1,000 widgets costing $750. The firm collects receivables outstanding at the beginning of the month. Production equals 1,000 units at a total cost of $750. Net income for the month is $250. The books at the end of January show:
February 1	Cash, $1,125; receivables, $1,000; inventory, $750.
February	This month's sales jump, as predicted, to 1,500 units. With a corresponding step-up in production to maintain the 30-day inventory, ABC Company makes 2,000 units at a cost of $1,500. All receivables from January sales are collected. Net income so far, $625. Now the books look like this:

(continued)

March 1	Cash, $625; receivables, $1,500; inventory, $1,125.
March	March sales are even better—2,000 units. Collections, on time; Production, to adhere to the inventory policy, 2,500 units; Operating results for the month, net income of $500; Net income to date, $1,125. The books:
April 1	Cash, $250; receivables, $2,000; inventory, $1,500.
April	In April, sales jump another 500 units to 2,500, and the manager of ABC Company pats the sales manager on the back. Customers are paying right on time. Production increases to 3,000 units, and the month's business nets $625 for a net income to date of $1,750. The manager of ABC Company takes off for Miami before the accountant issues a report. Suddenly a phone call comes from the treasurer: "Come home! We need money!"
May 1	Cash, $0; receivables, $2,500; inventory, $1,875.

a. Prepare an analysis that explains what happened to ABC Company. (*Hint:* Compute the amount of cash receipts and cash disbursements for each month during the period January 1 to May 1.)

b. How can a firm show increasing net income but a decreasing amount of cash?

c. What insights are provided by the problem about the need for all three financial statements—balance sheet, income statement, and statement of cash flows?

29. **Relation between income and cash flows** (adapted from a problem by Professor Leonard Morrissey). RV Suppliers, Incorporated, founded in July, Year 1, manufactures "Kaps." A Kap is a relatively low-cost camping unit attached to a pickup truck. Most units consist of an extruded aluminum frame and a fiberglass skin.

After a loss in Years 1 through 2, the company was barely profitable in fiscal Year 3 and Year 4. It realized more substantial profits in fiscal Year 5 and Year 6, as indicated in the financial statements shown in Exhibits 17.17 and 17.18.

Exhibit 17.17

RV SUPPLIERS, INCORPORATED
Income Statements
(all dollar amounts in thousands)
(Problem 29)

	Fiscal Years Ended June 30		
	Year 5	Year 6	Year 7
Net Sales.....................................	$266.4	$424.0	$247.4
Cost of Goods Sold...........................	191.4	314.6	210.6
Gross Margin	$ 75.0	$109.4	$ 36.8
Operating Expenses[a]	35.5	58.4	55.2
Income (Loss) before Income Taxes	$ 39.5	$ 51.0	$ (18.4)
Income Taxes	12.3	16.4	(5.0)
Net Income (Loss)	$ 27.2	$ 34.6	$ (13.4)

[a]Includes depreciation expense of $1.7 in Year 5, $4.8 in Year 6, and $7.6 in Year 7.

Exhibit 17.18

RV SUPPLIERS, INCORPORATED
Balance Sheet
(all dollar amounts in thousands)
(Problem 29)

	June 30		
	Year 5	Year 6	Year 7
Assets			
Current Assets			
Cash	$ 14.0	$ 12.0	$ 5.2
Accounts Receivable	28.8	55.6	24.2
Inventories	54.0	85.6	81.0
Tax Refund Receivable	0	0	5.0
Prepayments	4.8	7.4	5.6
Total Current Assets	$101.6	$160.6	$121.0
Property, Plant, Equipment—Net[a]	30.2	73.4	72.2
Total Assets	$131.8	$234.0	$193.2
Liabilities and Shareholders' Equity			
Current Liabilities			
Bank Notes Payable	$ 10.0	$ 52.0	$ 70.0
Accounts Payable	31.6	53.4	17.4
Income Taxes Payable	5.8	7.0	0
Other Current Liabilities	4.2	6.8	4.4
Total Current Liabilities	$ 51.6	$119.2	$ 91.8
Shareholders' Equity			
Capital Stock	$ 44.6	$ 44.6	$ 44.6
Retained Earnings	35.6	70.2	56.8
Total Shareholders' Equity	$ 80.2	$114.8	$101.4
Total Liabilities and Shareholders' Equity	$131.8	$234.0	$193.2

[a]Details of Property, Plant, and Equipment

	Year 5	Year 6	Year 7
Acquisitions	$ 13.4	$ 48.4	$ 11.8
Depreciation Expense	(1.7)	(4.8)	(7.6)
Book Value and Sales Proceeds from Retirements	(.4)	(.4)	(5.4)
Net Change in Property, Plant, and Equipment . . .	$ 11.3	$ 43.2	$ (1.2)

However, in fiscal Year 7, ended just last month, the company suffered a loss of $13,400. Sales dropped from $424,000 in fiscal Year 6 to $247,400 in fiscal Year 7. The outlook for fiscal Year 8 is not encouraging. Potential buyers continue to shun pickup trucks in preference to more energy-efficient small foreign and domestic automobiles.

How did the company finance its rapid growth during the year ended

June 30, Year 6? What were the inflows and outflows of cash during the year? Similarly, how did the company manage its financial affairs during the abrupt contraction in business during the year just ended last month?

Suggested Solutions to Even-Numbered Exercises

10. **Balance sheet relations.**

    a. The following equation characterizes the balance sheet:

$$\frac{\text{Current}}{\text{Assets}} + \frac{\text{Noncurrent}}{\text{Assets}} = \frac{\text{Current}}{\text{Liabilities}} + \frac{\text{Noncurrent}}{\text{Liabilities}} + \frac{\text{Shareholders'}}{\text{Equity}}$$

$$\text{Total Assets} = \text{Total Liabilities} + \frac{\text{Shareholders'}}{\text{Equity}}$$

    The missing information is (amounts in millions):

Year 8	
Shareholders' Equity	$ 2,635
Total Assets	7,115
Total Liabilities and Shareholders' Equity	7,115

Year 9	
Total Assets	$ 7,056
Current Assets	1,829
Noncurrent Liabilities	3,415

Year 10	
Current Liabilities	$ 2,535
Current Assets	1,766
Noncurrent Liabilities	6,550
Total Liabilities and Shareholders' Equity	12,060

Year 11	
Noncurrent Assets	$ 9,060
Total Assets	10,622
Current Liabilities	2,722
Current Assets	1,562

    b. Noncurrent assets increased as a proportion of total assets, suggesting major new investments in property, plant, and equipment or the acquisition of a firm with heavy investments in property, plant, and equipment. The latter is the actual explanation in that Georgia-Pacific Corporation acquired Great Northern Nekoosa Corporation, a pulp and paper manufacturer.

    c. The proportion of liabilities (both current and noncurrent) increased while the proportion of shareholders' equity decreased. Georgia-Pacific Corporation used debt to finance the acquisition of Great Northern Nekoosa.

    d. The acquisition of Great Northern Nekoosa Corporation.

    e. Possible explanations include the following:

        (1) The sale of a portion of the assets acquired from Great Northern Nekoosa Corporation and the reduction in debt with the proceeds.

        (2) Same as (1) above but common stock repurchased with the proceeds.

        (3) The firm operated at a net loss for Year 11, so that net asset outflows for expenses exceeded net asset inflows from revenues.

12. **Asset recognition and valuation.**

    a. Prepaid Insurance, $12,000,000.

    b. Deposit on Equipment, $500,000.

    c. Investment in Securities, $325,000.

    d. Raw Materials Inventory, $784,000.

    e. Accounting does not recognize the employment contract, a mutually unexecuted contract, as an asset.

    f. Marketable Securities, $3,200,000.

    g. Accounting does not recognize the customer's order as an asset because no exchange between buyer and seller has occurred.

    h. Raw Materials Inventory, $200,000. Legal rights to use the raw material have passed to Eli Lilly, creating a legal obligation to make payment.

14. **Liability recognition and valuation.**

    a. Insurance Premiums Received in Advance or Advances from Customers, $6,500,000.

    b. Accounting normally does not recognize a liability for mutually unexecuted contracts. When the president renders services, a liability arises.

    c. Legal Fees Payable, $1,200,000.

    d. Common stock does not meet the definition of a liability because the firm need not repay the funds in a particular amount at a particular time.

    e. Salaries and Commissions Payable, $950,000; Payroll Taxes Payable, $76,000 (=.08 × $950,000).

    f. The treatment of this item depends on the probability of having to make a cash payment in the future, whose amount and timing of payment the company can estimate with reasonable accuracy. Most firms do not recognize unsettled lawsuits as liabilities because it is not clear (1) that the firm received benefits in the past and (2) that the lawsuit will require a future cash payment.

16. **Retained earnings relations.**

    a. The changes in retained earnings appear below. Given amounts appear in boldface (amounts in millions of Swedish kronor).

	Year 3	Year 4	Year 5	Year 6
Retained Earnings, January 1.........	**25,634**	30,484	34,338	**37,922**
Net Income	**5,665**	**4,940**	4,787	(1,020)[a]
Dividends.........................	815	1,086	1,203	**1,203**
Retained Earnings, December 31	30,484	**34,338**	**37,922**	**35,699**

[a]Net loss.

b. Volvo Group experienced decreasing amounts of net income over the 4 years, even operating at a net loss in Year 6. The firm, however, increased or at least maintained its dividends during this period of declining profitability. Thus, retained earnings grew at a declining rate (Year 3 to Year 5) or decreased (Year 6).

18. **Expense recognition.**
   a. $1,500.
   b. $4,600.
   c. $6,500 (=$3,000 + $7,000 − $3,500).
   d. $5,500 (=$2,000 + $7,000 − $3,500).
   e. $4,000 (=$48,000/12).
   f. Zero (an expense of April).

20. **Statement of cash flows relations.**

SUN MICROSYSTEMS
Statement of Cash Flows
(dollar amounts in millions)

a.

	Year 8	Year 9	Year 10
Operations			
Revenues from Operations Increasing Cash	$ 1,046	$ 1,258	$ 1,515
Expenses for Operations Decreasing Cash	(1,064)	(1,250)	(1,512)
Cash Flow from Operations	$ (18)	$ 8	$ 3
Investing			
Acquisition of Property, Plant, and Equipment	$ (38)	$ (99)	$ (149)
Cash Flow from Investing	$ (38)	$ (99)	$ (149)
Financing			
Proceeds from Bank Borrowings	$ 11	$ 21	—
Issue of Long-term Debt	4	121	—
Issue of Common Stock	47	96	$ 63
Repayment of Bank Borrowing	—	—	(6)
Repayment of Long-term Debt	(2)	—	—
Cash Flow from Financing	$ 60	$ 238	$ 57
Change in Cash	$ 4	$ 147	$ (89)

b. Sun Microsystems makes a larger amount of sales on account each period than it collects from customers from sales on account of prior periods (that is, accounts receivable increases). Likewise, Sun Microsystem manufactures more computers each period than it sells in order to meet growing demand. Thus, cash inflows are less than sales revenues, and cash outflows for operations exceed expenses. The net result is that net income exceeds cash flow from operations.

c. A growing firm typically experiences an excess of net income over cash flow from operations as the preceding answer explains. Also, Sun Microsystems made significant expenditures on property, plant, and equipment to build production capacity. Because cash flow from operations was not sufficient to finance these acquisitions, Sun Microsystems relied on bank borrowing, long-term borrowing, and common stock issues.

Chapter 18

Introduction to Financial Statement Analysis

1. Understand the relation between the expected return and risk of investment alternatives and the role financial statement analysis can play in providing information about returns and risk.
2. Understand the usefulness of the rate of return on assets (ROA) as a measure of a firm's operating profitability independent of financing and the insights gained by disaggregating ROA into profit margin and assets turnover components.
3. Understand the usefulness of the rate of return on common shareholders' equity (ROCE) as a measure of profitability that incorporates a firm's particular mix of financing and the insights gained by disaggregating ROCE into profit margin, assets turnover, and leverage ratio components.
4. Understand the strengths and weaknesses of earnings per common share as a measure of profitability.
5. Understand the distinction between short-term liquidity risk and long-term liquidity (solvency) risk and the financial statement ratios used to assess these two dimensions of risk.
6. Develop skills to interpret effectively the results of an analysis of profitability and risk.

Investors, bankers, and others analyze the financial statements firms prepare for external users in making investment, credit, and similar decisions. Management also analyzes these financial statements, either for a firm as a whole or for segments thereof, in evaluating the performance of the firm and its various operating units.

This chapter describes some of the techniques commonly used by investors and other external users in analyzing financial statements. Management can use many of the same techniques in evaluating performance internally.

Objectives of Financial Statement Analysis

The first question the analyst asks in analyzing a set of financial statements is "What do I look for?" The response to this question requires an understanding of investment decisions.

To illustrate, assume that you recently inherited $25,000 and must decide what to do with the bequest. You narrow the investment decision to purchasing either a certificate of deposit at a local bank or shares of common stock of Horrigan Corporation, currently selling for $50 per share. You will base your decision on the **return** you anticipate from each investment and the **risk** associated with that return.

The bank currently pays interest at the rate of 6 percent annually on certificates of deposit. Because the bank is unlikely to go out of business, you are virtually certain of earning 6 percent each year.

The return from investing in the shares of Horrigan Corporation's common stock has two components. First, the firm paid a cash dividend in its most recent year of $.625 per share, and you anticipate that it will continue paying this dividend in the future. Also, the market price of the stock will likely change between the date you purchase the shares and the date in the future when you sell them. The difference between the eventual selling price and the purchase price, often called a *capital gain* (or *loss*), is a second component of the return from buying the stock.

The return from the common stock investment is riskier than the interest on the certificate of deposit. The future profitability of the firm will likely affect future dividends and market price changes. Future income might be less than you currently anticipate if competitors introduce new products that erode Horrigan Corporation's share of its sales market. Future income might be greater than you currently anticipate if Horrigan Corporation makes important discoveries or introduces successful new products.

Economy-wide factors such as inflation and changes in international tensions will also affect the market price of Horrigan Corporation's shares. Also, specific industry factors, such as raw materials shortages or government regulatory actions, may influence the market price of the shares. Because most individuals prefer less risk to more risk, you will probably demand a higher expected return if you purchase the Horrigan Corporation's shares than if you invest in a certificate of deposit.

Theoretical and empirical research has shown that the expected return from investing in a firm relates, in part, to the expected profitability of the firm.[1] The

---

[1] Ray Ball and Phillip Brown, "An Empirical Evaluation of Accounting Income Numbers," *Journal of Accounting Research* (Autumn 1968): 159–78; Jane A. Ou and Stephen H. Penman, "Financial Statement Analysis and the Prediction of Stock Returns," *Journal of Accounting and Economics* (November (1989): 295–329.

Exhibit 18.1

Relation Between Financial Statement Analysis and Investment Decisions

	Time Dimension	
Past	**Present**	**Future**

Financial Statement Analysis of:

- Profitability
- Risk (Short-term and Long-term Liquidity)

$\longrightarrow$ Expected Return

$\longrightarrow$ Risk

$\uparrow$

Investment Decision

analyst studies a firm's past operating, or earnings, performance to help forecast its future profitability.

Investment decisions also require that the analyst assess the risk associated with the expected return.[2] A firm may find itself short of cash and unable to repay a short-term loan coming due. Or the amount of long-term debt in the capital structure may be so large that the firm has difficulty meeting the required interest and principal payments. The financial statements provide information for assessing how these and other elements of risk affect expected return.

Most financial statement analysis, therefore, explores some aspect of a firm's profitability or its risk, or both. Exhibit 18.1 summarizes the relation between financial statement analysis and investment decisions.

Usefulness of Ratios

The reader may have difficulty interpreting the various items in financial statements in the form presented. For example, assessing the profitability of a firm by looking at the amount of net income alone may be difficult. Comparing earnings with the assets or capital required to generate those earnings can help. The analyst can express this relation, and other important ones between various items in the financial statements, in the form of ratios. Some ratios compare items within the income statement; some use only balance sheet data; others relate items from more than one of the three principal financial statements. Ratios are useful tools of financial statement analysis because they conveniently summarize data in a form easy to understand, interpret, and compare.

Ratios are, by themselves, difficult to interpret. For example, does a rate of return on common shareholders' equity of 8.6 percent reflect satisfactory performance?

---

[2]Modern finance makes a distinction between systematic (market) risk and nonsystematic (firm-specific) risk. The discussion in this chapter makes no distinction between these two dimensions of risk.

Exhibit 18.2

HORRIGAN CORPORATION
Comparative Income Statements
(all dollar amounts in millions)

	Years Ended December 31		
	Year 2	Year 3	Year 4
Sales Revenue	$210	$310	$475
Less Expenses:			
Cost of Goods Sold.	$119	$179	$280
Selling.	36	42	53
Administrative	15	17	22
Depreciation	12	14	18
Interest	5	10	16
Total	$187	$262	$389
Net Income before Taxes.	$ 23	$ 48	$ 86
Income Tax Expense	7	14	26
Net Income	$ 16	$ 34	$ 60

Once calculated, the analyst must compare the ratios with some standard. Several possible standards are

1. The planned ratio for the period.
2. The corresponding ratio during the preceding period for the same firm.
3. The corresponding ratio for a similar firm in the same industry.
4. The average ratio for other firms in the same industry.

Exhibit 18.3

HORRIGAN CORPORATION
Comparative Balance Sheets
(all dollar amounts in millions)

	December 31			
	Year 1	Year 2	Year 3	Year 4
Assets				
Cash	$ 10	$ 14	$ ·8	$ 12
Accounts Receivable (net)	26	36	46	76
Inventories	14	30	46	83
Total Current Assets	$ 50	$ 80	$100	$171
Land	$ 20	$ 30	$ 60	$ 60
Building	150	150	150	190
Equipment	70	192	276	313
Less Accumulated Depreciation	(40)	(52)	(66)	(84)
Total Noncurrent Assets.	$200	$320	$420	$479
Total Assets	$250	$400	$520	$650

(continued)

Exhibit 18.3 *(continued)*

	December 31			
	Year 1	Year 2	Year 3	Year 4
Liabilities and Shareholders' Equity				
Accounts Payable	$ 25	$ 30	$ 35	$ 50
Salaries Payable	10	13	15	20
Income Taxes Payable	5	7	10	20
Total Current Liabilities	$ 40	$ 50	$ 60	$ 90
Bonds Payable	50	50	100	150
Total Liabilities	$ 90	$100	$160	$240
Common Stock ($10 par value)	$100	$150	$160	$160
Additional Paid-in Capital	20	100	120	120
Retained Earnings	40	50	80	130
Total Shareholders' Equity	$160	$300	$360	$410
Total Liabilities and Shareholders' Equity	$250	$400	$520	$650

Later sections of this chapter discuss difficulties encountered in using each of these bases for comparison.

The sections that follow describe several ratios useful for assessing profitability and various dimensions of risk. To demonstrate the calculation of various ratios, we use data for Horrigan Corporation for Years 2 through 4 appearing in Exhibit 18.2 (comparative income statements), Exhibit 18.3 (comparative balance sheets), and Exhibit 18.4 (comparative statements of cash flows). Our analysis for Horrigan

Exhibit 18.4

HORRIGAN CORPORATION
Comparative Statements of Cash Flows
(all dollar amounts in millions)

	For the Year Ended December 31		
	Year 2	Year 3	Year 4
Operations:			
Net Income	$ 16	$ 34	$ 60
Additions:			
Depreciation Expense	12	14	18
Increase in Accounts Payable......................	5	5	15
Increase in Salaries Payable.......................	3	2	5
Increase in Income Taxes Payable	2	3	10
Subtractions:			
Increase in Accounts Receivable	(10)	(10)	(30)
Increase in Inventories	(16)	(16)	(37)
Cash Flow from Operations........................	$ 12	$ 32	$ 41

(continued)

Exhibit 18.4 (continued)

	For the Year Ended December 31		
	Year 2	Year 3	Year 4
Investing:			
Purchase of Land	$ (10)	$ (30)	—
Purchase of Building	—	—	$(40)
Purchase of Equipment	(122)	(84)	(37)
Cash Flow from Investing	$(132)	$(114)	$(77)
Financing:			
Issuance of Bonds.....................................	—	$ 50	$ 50
Issuance of Common Stock........................	$ 130	30	—
Dividends...	(6)	(4)	(10)
Cash Flow from Financing...........................	$ 124	$ 76	$ 40
Net Change in Cash	$ 4	$ (6)	$ 4

Corporation studies changes in its various ratios over the 3-year period. We refer to such an analysis as a **time-series analysis. Cross-section analysis** involves comparing a given firm's ratios with those of other firms for a particular period. Several problems at the end of the chapter involve cross-section analysis (problems **11, 12, 13,** and **28**).

Analysis of Profitability

A firm engages in operations to generate net income. This section discusses three measures of **profitability:**

1. Rate of return on assets.
2. Rate of return on common shareholders' equity.
3. Earnings per common share.

Rate of Return on Assets

The **rate of return on assets (ROA)** measures a firm's performance in using assets to generate earnings independent of the financing of those assets. Previous chapters described three principal business activities: investing, financing, and operating. The rate of return on assets relates the results of *operating* performance to the *investments* of a firm without regard to how the firm *financed* the acquisition of those investments. Thus, ROA attempts to measure the success of a firm in creating and selling goods and services to customers, activities that fall primarily within the responsibility of production and marketing personnel. The rate of return on assets excludes consideration of the particular mix of financing used (debt versus share-holders' equity), an activity that falls within the responsibility of finance personnel.

The calculation of the rate of return on assets is as follows:

$$\frac{\text{Net Income plus Interest Expense Net of Income Tax Savings}}{\text{Average Total Assets}}.$$

ROA uses an earnings figure in the numerator that excludes any payments or distri-butions to the suppliers of capital. Because firms recognize interest on debt as an expense in computing net income, the analyst must add back the interest expense to net income if the numerator is to exclude the effect of financing. Firms, however, can deduct interest expense in calculating taxable income. Thus, interest expense does not reduce *aftertax* net income by the full amount of interest expense. The analyst, therefore, adds back interest expense reduced by the income taxes that interest deductions save to calculate the numerator of ROA.

For example, interest expense for Horrigan Corporation for Year 4, appearing in Exhibit 18.2, is $16 million. The income tax rate is 30 percent of pretax income. The income taxes saved, because Horrigan can deduct interest in computing taxable income, equals $4.8 million (= .30 × $16 million). The amount of interest expense net of income tax savings added back to net income is therefore $11.2 million (= $16 million −$4.8 million). The analyst need not add back dividends paid to shareholders, because the firm does not deduct them as an expense in calculating net income.

Because we are computing the earnings rate *for a year,* the measure of investment should reflect the average amount of assets in use during the year. A crude but usually satisfactory figure for average total assets is one-half the sum of total assets at the beginning and at the end of the year.[3]

The calculation of rate of return on assets for Horrigan Corporation for Year 4 is as follows:[4]

$$\frac{\begin{array}{c}\text{Net Income plus}\\ \text{Interest Expense}\\ \text{Net of Income Tax}\\ \text{Savings}\end{array}}{\text{Average Total Assets}} = \frac{\$60 + (\$16 - \$4.8)}{\frac{1}{2}(\$520 + \$650)} = 12.2 \text{ percent.}$$

---

[3]Most financial economists would subtract average, noninterest-bearing liabilities (for example, accounts payable, salaries payable) from average total assets in the denominator. Economists realize that when liabilities do not provide for explicit interest charges, the creditor adjusts the terms of the contract, such as setting a higher selling price or lower discount, for those who do not pay cash immediately. This ratio requires in the numerator the income amount before a firm accrues any charges to suppliers of funds. We cannot measure the interest charges implicit in the noninterest-bearing liabilities; items such as cost of goods sold and salary expense are somewhat larger because of these charges. Thus, implicit interest charges reduce the measure of operating income in the numerator. Subtracting average noninterest-bearing liabilities from average total assets likewise reduces the denominator for assets financed with such liabilities. The examples and problems in this book use average total assets in the denominator of the rate of return on assets, making no adjustment for noninterest-bearing liabilities.

[4]Throughout the remainder of this chapter, we omit reference to the fact that the amounts for Horrigan Corporation are in millions of dollars.

Thus, for each dollar of assets used, the management of Horrigan Corporation earned $.122 during Year 4 before payments to the suppliers of capital. The rate of return on assets was 8.9 percent in Year 3 and 6.0 percent in Year 2. Thus the rate of return increased steadily during this 3-year period.

One might question the rationale for a measure of return that excludes the costs of financing. After all, the firm must finance the assets and must cover the cost of the financing if it is to be profitable.

The rate of return on assets has particular relevance for lenders, or creditors, of a firm. These creditors have a senior claim on earnings and assets relative to common shareholders. Creditors receive their return in the form of interest. This return typically comes from earnings generated from assets before any other suppliers of capital receive a return (for example, dividends). When extending credit or providing debt capital to a firm, creditors want to be sure that the return generated by the firm on that capital (assets) exceeds its cost.

Common shareholders find the rate of return on assets useful in assessing financial leverage. A later section of this chapter discusses financial leverage.

Disaggregating the Rate of Return on Assets

To study changes in the rate of return on assets, the analyst can disaggregate ROA into two other ratios, as follows:

$$\begin{array}{c} \text{Rate of} \\ \text{Return} \\ \text{on Assets} \end{array} = \begin{array}{c} \text{Profit Margin Ratio} \\ \text{(before interest expense} \\ \text{and related income tax effects)} \end{array} \times \begin{array}{c} \text{Total Assets} \\ \text{Turnover} \\ \text{Ratio} \end{array}$$

or

$$\frac{\begin{array}{c}\text{Net Income plus}\\\text{Interest Expense}\\\text{Net of Income}\\\text{Tax Savings}\end{array}}{\begin{array}{c}\text{Average Total}\\\text{Assets}\end{array}} = \frac{\begin{array}{c}\text{Net Income plus}\\\text{Interest Expense}\\\text{Net of Income}\\\text{Tax Savings}\end{array}}{\text{Sales}} \times \frac{\text{Sales}}{\begin{array}{c}\text{Average Total}\\\text{Assets}\end{array}}.$$

The **profit margin ratio** measures a firm's ability to control the level of expenses relative to sales. By holding down costs, a firm can increase the profits from a given amount of sales and thereby improve its profit margin ratio. The **total assets turnover ratio** measures a firm's ability to generate sales from a particular level of investment in assets. To put it another way, the total assets turnover measures a firm's ability to control the level of investment in assets for a particular level of sales.

Exhibit 18.5 disaggregates the rate of return on assets for Horrigan Corporation into profit margin and total assets turnover ratios for Year 2, Year 3, and Year 4. Much of the improvement in the rate of return on assets between Year 2 and Year 3 resulted from an increase in the profit margin ratio from 9.3 percent to 13.2 percent. The total assets turnover ratio remained relatively stable between these 2 years. On the other hand, one can attribute most of the improvement in the rate of return on assets between Year 3 and Year 4 to the increased total assets turnover. The firm

Exhibit 18.5

HORRIGAN CORPORATION

Disaggregation of Rate of Return on Assets for Year 2, Year 3, and Year 4

	Net Income plus Interest Expense Net of Income Tax Savings / Average Total Assets		Net Income plus Interest Expense Net of Income Tax Savings / Sales	×	Sales / Average Total Assets

Year 2: $\dfrac{\$16 + (\$5 - \$1.5)}{\frac{1}{2}(\$250 + \$400)} = \dfrac{\$16 + (\$5 - \$1.5)}{\$210} \times \dfrac{\$210}{\frac{1}{2}(\$250 + \$400)}$

$\quad 6.0\% \qquad = \qquad 9.3\% \qquad \times \qquad .65$

Year 3: $\dfrac{\$34 + (\$10 - \$3)}{\frac{1}{2}(\$400 + \$520)} = \dfrac{\$34 + (\$10 - \$3)}{\$310} \times \dfrac{\$310}{\frac{1}{2}(\$400 + \$520)}$

$\quad 8.9\% \qquad = \qquad 13.2\% \qquad \times \qquad .67$

Year 4: $\dfrac{\$60 + (\$16 - \$4.8)}{\frac{1}{2}(\$520 + \$650)} = \dfrac{\$60 + (\$16 - \$4.8)}{\$475} \times \dfrac{\$475}{\frac{1}{2}(\$520 + \$650)}$

$\quad 12.2\% \qquad = \qquad 15.0\% \qquad \times \qquad .81$

generated $.81 of sales from each dollar invested in assets during Year 4 as compared with $.67 of sales per dollar of assets in Year 3. The increased total assets turnover, coupled with an improvement in the profit margin ratio, permitted Horrigan Corporation to increase its rate of return on assets during Year 4. We must analyze the changes in the profit margin ratio and total assets turnover ratio further to pinpoint the causes of the changes in Horrigan Corporation's profitability over this 3-year period. We return to this analysis shortly.

Firms improve their rate of return on assets by increasing the profit margin ratio, the rate of assets turnover, or both. Some firms, however, have limited flexibility to alter one or the other of these components. For example, a firm selling commodity products in a highly competitive market may have little opportunity to increase its profit margin. Such a firm would likely take actions to improve its assets turnover (for example, institute improved inventory controls to shorten the holding period for inventories) when attempting to increase its rate of return on assets. The activities of other firms might require substantial investments in property, plant, and equipment. The need for such investment might constrain the firm's ability to increase its rate of return on assets by increasing its assets turnover. Such a firm might have more flexibility to take actions that increase the profit margin (for example, creating brand loyalty for its products).

Analyzing Changes in the Profit Margin Ratio

The analyst studies changes in the profit margin ratio by examining changes in a firm's expenses relative to sales. One approach expresses individual expenses and net income as a percentage of sales. Exhibit 18.6 presents such an analysis, which

Exhibit 18.6

HORRIGAN CORPORATION
Common Size Income Statements for Year 2, Year 3, and Year 4

	Years Ended December 31		
	Year 2	Year 3	Year 4
Sales Revenue	100.0%	100.0%	100.0%
Less Operating Expenses:			
Cost of Goods Sold	56.7%	57.7%	58.9%
Selling	17.1	13.6	11.2
Administrative	7.1	5.5	4.6
Depreciation	5.7	4.5	3.8
Total	86.6%	81.3%	78.5%
Income before Income Taxes and Interest	13.4%	18.7%	21.5%
Income Taxes at 30 Percent	4.1	5.5	6.5
Income before Interest and Related Income Tax Effect	9.3%	13.2%	15.0%
Interest Expense Net of Income Tax Effect	1.7	2.2	2.4
Net Income	7.6%	11.0%	12.6%

analysts characterize as a common size income statement, for Horrigan Corporation. Note that this analysis alters somewhat the conventional income statement format by subtracting interest expense (net of its related income tax effects) as the last expense item. The percentages on the line titled Income before Interest and Related Income Tax Effect correspond to the profit margin ratios (before interest and related tax effects) in Exhibit 18.5.

The analysis in Exhibit 18.6 indicates that the improvement in Horrigan Corporation's profit margin ratio over the 3 years relates primarily to decreased selling, administrative, and depreciation expenses as a percentage of sales. The analyst should explore further with management the reasons for these decreasing percentages. Does the decrease in selling expenses as a percentage of sales reflect a reduction in advertising expenditures that could hurt future sales? Does the decrease in depreciation expense as a percentage of sales reflect a failure to expand plant and equipment as sales increased? On the other hand, do these decreasing percentages merely reflect the realization of economies of scale as the firm spreads fixed selling, administrative, and depreciation expenses over a larger number of units?[5] Neither the amount nor the trend in a particular ratio can, by itself, convince the analyst to invest in a firm. Ratios indicate areas requiring additional analysis. For example, the analyst should explore further the increasing percentage of cost of goods sold to sales. The increase may reflect a successful, planned pricing policy of reducing gross margin (selling price less cost of goods sold) to increase the volume of sales. On the other hand, the replacement cost of inventory items may be increasing

---

[5]*Operating leverage* is the term used to describe this phenomenon, which previous chapters and managerial economics textbooks discuss more fully.

without corresponding increases being made in selling prices. Or the firm may be accumulating excess inventories that are physically deteriorating or are becoming obsolete.

Analyzing Changes in the Total Assets Turnover Ratio

The total assets turnover ratio depends on the turnover ratios for its individual asset components. The analyst generally calculates three turnover ratios: accounts receivable turnover, inventory turnover, and fixed asset turnover.

Accounts Receivable Turnover The rate at which accounts receivable turn over indicates how soon the firm will collect cash. **Accounts receivable turnover ratio** equals net sales on account divided by average accounts receivable. Most firms, except some retailers that deal directly with final consumers, sell their goods and services on account. For Horrigan Corporation, the accounts receivable turnover for Year 4, assuming that all sales are on account (that is, none are for immediate cash), is as follows:

$$\frac{\text{Net Sales on Account}}{\text{Average Accounts Receivable}} = \frac{\$475}{\frac{1}{2}(\$46 + \$76)} = 7.8 \text{ times per year.}$$

The analyst often expresses the accounts receivable turnover in terms of the average number of days that receivables are outstanding before the firm collects cash. To calculate this ratio, divide 365 days by the accounts receivable turnover ratio. The average number of days that accounts receivable are outstanding for Horrigan Corporation for Year 4 is 46.8 days (= 365 days/7.8 times per year). Thus, on average, it collects accounts receivable approximately $1\frac{1}{2}$ months after the date of sale. Interpreting this average collection period depends on the terms of sale. If the terms of sale are "net 30 days," the accounts receivable turnover indicates that collections do not accord with the stated terms. Such a ratio would warrant a review of the credit and collection activity for an explanation and for possible corrective action. If the firm offers terms of "net 60 days," the results indicate that the firm handles accounts receivable well.

Inventory Turnover The **inventory turnover ratio** indicates how frequently firms sell inventory items. Inventory turnover equals cost of goods sold divided by the average inventory during the period. The inventory turnover for Horrigan Corporation for Year 4 is as follows:

$$\frac{\text{Cost of Goods Sold}}{\text{Average Inventory}} = \frac{\$280}{\frac{1}{2}(\$46 + \$83)} = 4.3 \text{ times per year.}$$

This inventory is typically on hand an average of 84.9 days (= 365 days/4.3 times per year) before sale.

   Interpreting the inventory turnover figure involves two opposing considerations. Firms prefer to sell as many goods as possible with a minimum of capital tied up in inventories. An increase in the rate of inventory turnover between periods may indicate more profitable use of the investment in inventory. On the other hand, management does not want to have so little inventory on hand that shortages result. An increase in the rate of inventory turnover in this case may mean a loss of customers, thereby offsetting any advantage gained by decreased investment in inventory. Firms must make trade-offs in deciding the optimum level of inventory and, thus, the desirable rate of inventory turnover.

Some analysts calculate the inventory turnover ratio by dividing sales, rather than cost of goods sold, by the average inventory. As long as selling prices have a relatively constant relation with cost of goods sold, either measure will identify changes in the *trend* of the inventory holding period. Using sales in the numerator is inappropriate if the analyst wishes to use the inventory turnover ratio to calculate the average number of days inventory is on hand until sale.

Plant Asset Turnover The **plant asset turnover ratio** measures the relation between sales and the investment in plant assets such as property, plant, and equipment. The plant asset turnover ratio for Horrigan Corporation for Year 4 is

$$\frac{\text{Sales}}{\text{Average Plant Assets}} = \frac{\$475}{\frac{1}{2}(\$420 + \$479)} = 1.1 \text{ times per year.}$$

Thus each dollar invested in plant assets during Year 4 generated $1.10 in sales.

The analyst must interpret changes in the plant asset turnover ratio carefully. Firms often invest in plant assets (for example, production facilities) several periods before they generate sales from products manufactured in their plants. Thus a low or decreasing rate of plant asset turnover may indicate an expanding firm preparing for future growth. On the other hand, a firm may cut back its capital expenditures if it foresees a poor near-term outlook for its products. Such an action could lead to an increase in the plant asset turnover ratio.

Summary of Asset Turnovers We noted earlier that the total assets turnover for Horrigan Corporation was relatively stable between Year 2 and Year 3 but increased dramatically in Year 4. Exhibit 18.7 presents the four turnover ratios discussed for Horrigan Corporation over this 3-year period. The accounts receivable turnover ratio increased steadily over the 3 years, indicating either more careful screening of credit applications or more effective collection efforts. The inventory turnover ratio decreased during the 3 years. Coupling this result with the increasing percentage of cost of goods sold to sales shown in Exhibit 18.6 indicates that there

Exhibit 18.7

HORRIGAN CORPORATION
Asset Turnover Ratios for Year 2, Year 3, and Year 4

	Year 2	Year 3	Year 4
Total Assets Turnover	.65	.67	.81
Accounts Receivable Turnover	6.8	7.6	7.8
Inventory Turnover	5.4	4.7	4.3
Plant Asset Turnover	.8	.8	1.1

may be excessive investments in inventories that are physically deteriorating or becoming obsolete.

Most of the increase in the total assets turnover between Year 3 and Year 4 relates to an increase in the plant asset turnover. We note in the statement of cash flows for Horrigan Corporation in Exhibit 18.4 that total capital expenditures on land, buildings, and equipment decreased over the 3-year period, possibly accounting for the increase in the plant asset turnover.

Summary of the Analysis of the Rate of Return on Assets

This section began by stating that the rate of return on assets helps assess a firm's performance in using assets to generate earnings independent of the financing of those assets. We then disaggregated the rate of return on assets into profit margin and total assets turnover components. We analyzed the profit margin ratio further by relating various expenses and net income to sales. We gained better understanding of the total assets turnover by calculating turnover ratios for accounts receivable, inventory, and plant assets.

The analysis for Horrigan Corporation revealed the following:

1. The rate of return on assets increased steadily over the 3-year period from Year 2 to Year 4.
2. An increasing profit margin over all 3 years and an improved total asset turnover during Year 4 help to explain the improved rate of return on assets.
3. Decreases in the percentages of selling, administrative and depreciation expenses to sales largely explain the improved profit margin. The analyst should explore further the reasons for these decreases to ascertain whether the firm is curtailing selling and administrative efforts that might unfavorably affect future sales and operations.
4. The changes in the total assets turnover reflect the effects of increasing accounts receivable and plant asset turnover ratios and a decreasing inventory turnover. The increasing plant asset turnover coupled with the decreased depreciation expense percentage might relate to a reduced level of investment in new property, plant, and equipment that could hurt future productive capacity. The decreasing rate of inventory turnover coupled with the increasing percentage of cost of goods sold to sales may indicate inventory control problems (buildup of obsolete inventory).

Problem 18.1 for Self-Study

Analyzing the rate of return on assets. Exhibit 18.8 presents profitability ratios for Abbott Corporation for 3 recent years.

Exhibit 18.8

ABBOTT CORPORATION
Profitability Ratios
(Problem 18.1 for Self-Study)

Rate of Return on Assets

	Year 1	Year 2	Year 3
	10.0%	9.6%	9.2%

Profit Margin (before interest expense and related tax effects)				Total Assets Turnover		
Year 1	**Year 2**	**Year 3**		**Year 1**	**Year 2**	**Year 3**
6.0%	6.1%	6.1%		1.7	1.6	1.5

Common Size Income Statements				**Individual Asset Turnovers**		
	Year 1	Year 2	Year 3		Year 1	Year 2	Year 3
Sales............	100.0%	100.0%	100.0%	Accounts Receivable			
Cost of Goods Sold	(79.7)	(79.6)	(79.4)	Turnover..	4.3	4.3	4.2
Selling and Administrative	(10.3)	(10.2)	(10.4)	Inventory Turnover..	3.2	3.4	3.6
Income Taxes	(4.0)	(4.1)	(4.1)	Plant Asset Turnover..	.8	.7	.6
Profit Margin	6.0%	6.1%	6.1%				

a. Identify the likely reason for the decreasing rate of return on assets. Analyze the financial statement ratios to the maximum depth possible.

b. What is the likely explanation for the decreasing cost of goods sold to sales percentage coupled with the increasing inventory turnover ratio?

The solution to this self-study problem is at the end of this chapter on page 767.

Rate of Return on Common Shareholders' Equity

The **rate of return on common shareholders' equity** measures a firm's performance in using assets to generate earnings. Unlike the rate of return on assets, the rate of return on common shareholders' equity explicitly considers the financing of those assets. Thus this measure of profitability incorporates the results of operating, investing, and financing decisions. The rate of return on common shareholders' equity is of primary interest to investors in a firm's common stock. The calculation of the rate of return on common shareholders' equity is as follows:

$$\frac{\text{Net Income} - \text{Dividends on Preferred Stock}}{\text{Average Common Shareholders' Equity}}.$$

To calculate the amount of earnings assignable to common shareholders' equity, the analyst subtracts all amounts allocable to other providers of capital. Accountants subtract interest expense in computing net income so the analyst need not adjust for interest. The analyst must subtract from net income any earnings allocable to preferred stock equity, usually the dividends on preferred stock declared during the period. The capital provided by common shareholders during the period equals the average par value of common stock, capital contributed in excess of par value on common stock, and retained earnings for the period. (Alternatively, subtract average preferred shareholders' equity from average total shareholders' equity.)

The rate of return on common shareholders' equity of Horrigan Corporation for Year 4 is as follows:

$$\frac{\text{Net Income} - \text{Dividends on Preferred Stock}}{\text{Average Common Shareholders' Equity}} = \frac{\$60 - \$0}{\frac{1}{2}(\$360 + \$410)} = 15.6 \text{ percent.}$$

The rate of return on common shareholders' equity was 7.0 percent in Year 2 and 10.3 percent in Year 3. Thus, like the rate of return on assets, the rate of return on common shareholders' equity increased dramatically over the 3 years.

Relation between Return on Assets and Return on Common Shareholders' Equity

Exhibit 18.9 graphs the two measures of rate of return discussed thus far for Horrigan Corporation for Year 2, Year 3, and Year 4. In each year, the rate of return on common shareholders' equity exceeded the rate of return on assets. What accounts for this relation?

Recall that the rate of return on assets measures the profitability of a firm before any payments to the suppliers of capital. Each of the various providers of capital receives an allocated share of this return on assets. The allocated share for creditors equals any contractual interest to which they have a claim (net of tax savings the firm realizes from deducting interest for tax purposes). The allocated share for preferred shareholders, if any, equals the stated dividend rate on the preferred stock. Any remaining return belongs to the common shareholders; that is, common shareholders have a residual claim on all earnings after creditors and preferred shareholders receive amounts contractually owed them. Thus,

$$\begin{array}{c}\text{Rate of Return} \\ \text{on Assets}\end{array} \rightarrow \begin{array}{c}\text{Return to} \\ \text{Creditors} + \\ \text{(interest)}\end{array} \begin{array}{c}\text{Return to} \\ \text{Preferred} \\ \text{Shareholders} \\ \text{(dividends)}\end{array} + \begin{array}{c}\text{Return to} \\ \text{Common} \\ \text{Shareholders} \\ \text{(residual).}\end{array}$$

We can now see how the rate of return on common shareholders' equity can exceed the rate of return on assets: the rate of return on assets must exceed the

Exhibit 18.10

Effects of Financial Leverage on Rate of Return on Common Shareholders' Equity
(income tax rate is 30 percent of pretax income)

	Long-Term Equities		Income after Taxes but before Interest Charges[a]	After-Tax Interest Charges[b]	Net Income	Rate of Return on Total Assets[c] (percent)	Rate of Return on Common Shareholders' Equity (percent)
	Long-Term Borrowing at 10 Percent per Year	Shareholders' Equity					
Good Earnings Year							
Leveraged Company...............	$40,000	$ 60,000	$10,000	$2,800	$ 7,200	10.0%	12.0%
No-Debt Company...........	—	100,000	10,000	—	10,000	10.0	10.0
Neutral Earnings Year							
Leveraged Company.........	40,000	60,000	7,000	2,800	4,200	7.0	7.0
No-Debt Company.........	—	100,000	7,000	—	7,000	7.0	7.0
Bad Earnings Year							
Leveraged Company.........	40,000	60,000	4,000	2,800	1,200	4.0	2.0
No-Debt Company.........	—	100,000	4,000	—	4,000	4.0	4.0

[a]Not including any income tax savings caused by interest charges. Income before taxes and interest for *good* year is $14,286; for *neutral* year is $10,000; for *bad* year is $5,714.

[b]$40,000 (borrowed) × .10 (interest rate) × [1 − .30 (income tax rate)]. The numbers shown in the preceding column for after-tax income do not include the effects of interest charges on taxes.

[c]In each year, the rate of return on assets is the same for both companies as the rate of return on common shareholders' equity for No-Debt Company: 10 percent, 7 percent, and 4 percent, respectively.

Exhibit 18.9

Rates of Return for Horrigan Corporation

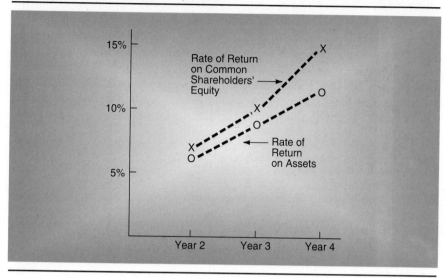

after-tax cost of debt (Horrigan Corporation has no preferred stock outstanding). For Year 4, the rate of return on assets was 12.2 percent and the after-tax cost of liabilities was 5.6 percent [= (1 − .3)($16)/.5($160 + $240); see Exhibits 18.2 and 18.3]. This excess return belongs to the common shareholders.

The common shareholders earned a higher return only because they undertook more risk in their investment. The riskier position results from the firm's incurring debt obligations with fixed payment dates. The phenomenon of common shareholders trading extra risk for a potentially higher return is called *financial leverage.*

Financial Leverage: Trading on the Equity

Financing with debt and preferred stock to increase the potential return to the residual common shareholders' equity is referred to as **financial leverage.** As long as a firm earns a rate of return on assets higher than the rate it paid for the capital used to acquire those assets, the rate of return to common shareholders will increase.

Exhibit 18.10 explores this phenomenon. Leveraged Company and No-Debt Company both have $100,000 in assets. Leveraged Company borrows $40,000 at a 10-percent annual rate. No-Debt Company raises all its capital from common shareholders. Both companies pay income taxes at the rate of 30 percent.

Consider first a good earnings year. Both companies earn $10,000 before interest charges (but after taxes, except for tax effects of interest charges).[6] This represents a rate of return on assets for both companies of 10 percent (= $10,000/$100,000).

---

[6]Income before taxes and before interest charges is $14,286; $10,000 = (1 − .30) × $14,286.

Leveraged Company's net income is $7,200 [= $10,000 − (1 − .30 tax rate) × (.10 interest rate × $40,000 borrowed)], representing a rate of return on common shareholders' equity of 12.0 percent (= $7,200/$60,000). Net income of No-Debt Company is $10,000, representing a rate of return on shareholders' equity of 10 percent. Leverage increased the rate of return to shareholders of Leveraged Company, because the capital contributed by the long-term debtors earned 10 percent but required an after-tax interest payment of only 7 percent [= (1 − .30 tax rate) × (.10 interest rate)]. This additional 3-percent return on each dollar of assets financed by creditors increased the return to the common shareholders, as the following analysis shows:

Rate of Return to Common Shareholders

Excess Return on Assets Financed with Debt:	
(.10 − .07) × ($40,000)	$ 1,200
Return on Assets Financed by Common Shareholders:	
(.10) × ($60,000)	6,000
Total Return to Common Shareholders	$ 7,200
Common Shareholders' Equity	$60,000
Rate of Return on Common Shareholders' Equity:	
$7,200/$60,000	12%

Although leverage increased the return to common stock equity during the good earnings year, a larger increase would occur if the firm financed a greater proportion of its assets with long-term borrowing and the firm's risk level increased. For example, assume that the firm financed its assets of $100,000 with $50,000 of long-term borrowing and $50,000 of shareholders' equity. Net income of Leveraged Company in this case would be $6,500 [= $10,000 − (1 − .30 tax rate) × (.10 × $50,000 borrowed)]. The rate of return on common stock equity would be 13 percent (= $6,500/$50,000). This compares with a rate of return on common stock equity of 12 percent when long-term debt was only 40 percent of the total capital provided.

The components of this 13-percent rate of return on common stock equity are as follows:

Rate of Return to Common Shareholders

Excess Return on Assets Financed with Debt:	
(.10 − .07) × ($50,000)	$ 1,500
Return on Assets Financed by Common Shareholders:	
(.10) × ($50,000)	5,000
Total Return to Common Shareholders	$ 6,500
Common Shareholders' Equity	$50,000
Rate of Return on Common Shareholders' Equity:	
$6,500/$50,000	13%

Financial leverage increases the rate of return on common stock equity when the rate of return on assets is higher than the after-tax cost of debt. The greater the proportion of debt in the capital structure, however, the greater the risk the common shareholders bear. Of course, a firm cannot increase debt without limit; as it adds more debt to the capital structure, the risk of default or insolvency becomes greater. Lenders, including investors in a firm's bonds, require a higher and higher return (interest rate) to compensate for this additional risk. At some point, the after-tax cost of debt will exceed the rate of return earned on assets. At this point, leverage no longer increases the potential rate of return to common stock equity. For most large manufacturing firms, liabilities represent between 30 percent and 60 percent of total capital.

Exhibit 18.10 also demonstrates the effect of leverage in a neutral earnings year and in a bad earnings year. In the neutral earnings year, leverage neither increases nor decreases the rate of return to common shareholders, because the return on assets is 7 percent and the after-tax cost of long-term debt is also 7 percent. In the bad earnings year, the return on assets of 4 percent is less than the after-tax cost of debt of 7 percent. The return on common stock equity therefore drops below the rate of return on assets to only 2 percent. Clearly, financial leverage can work in two ways. It can enhance owners' rate of return in good years, but owners run the risk that bad earnings years will be even worse than they would be without the borrowing.

Disaggregating the Rate of Return on Common Shareholders' Equity

The analyst can disaggregate the rate of return on common shareholders' equity into several components (in a manner similar to the disaggregation of the rate of return on assets) as follows:

$$
\begin{array}{c}
\text{Rate of Return} \\
\text{on Common} \\
\text{Shareholders'} \\
\text{Equity}
\end{array}
=
\begin{array}{c}
\text{Profit Margin Ratio} \\
\text{(after interest} \\
\text{expense and} \\
\text{preferred dividends)}
\end{array}
\times
\begin{array}{c}
\text{Total} \\
\text{Assets} \\
\text{Turnover} \\
\text{Ratio}
\end{array}
\times
\begin{array}{c}
\text{Leverage} \\
\text{Ratio.}
\end{array}
$$

The profit margin percentage indicates the portion of the sales dollar left over for the common shareholders after covering all operating costs and subtracting all claims of creditors and preferred shareholders. The total assets turnover, as discussed earlier, indicates the sales generated from each dollar of assets. The **leverage ratio** indicates the extent to which common shareholders versus creditors and preferred shareholders provide capital. The larger the leverage ratio, the smaller the portion of capital common shareholders provide and the larger the proportion creditors and preferred shareholders provide. Thus, the larger the leverage ratio, the greater the extent of financial leverage.

The disaggregation of the rate of return on common shareholders' equity ratio for Horrigan Corporation for Year 4 is as follows:

$$
\frac{\$60}{\frac{1}{2}(\$360 + \$410)} = \frac{\$\ 60}{\$475} \times \frac{\$475}{\frac{1}{2}(\$520 + \$650)} \times \frac{\frac{1}{2}(\$520 + \$650)}{\frac{1}{2}(\$360 + \$410)}
$$

$$
15.6 \text{ percent} = 12.6 \text{ percent} \times \quad .81 \quad \times \quad 1.5.
$$

Exhibit 18.11 shows the disaggregation of the rate of return on common shareholders' equity for Horrigan Corporation for Year 2, Year 3, and Year 4. Most of the

Exhibit 18.11

HORRIGAN CORPORATION
Disaggregation of Rate of Return on Common Shareholders' Equity

	Rate of Return on Common Shareholders' Equity =	Profit Margin ×	Total Assets Turnover ×	Leverage Ratio
Year 2.....................	7.0%	= 7.6% ×	.65 ×	1.4
Year 3.....................	10.3	= 11.0 ×	.67 ×	1.4
Year 4.....................	15.6	= 12.6 ×	.81 ×	1.5

increase in the rate of return on common shareholders' equity relates to an increasing profit margin over the 3-year period plus an increase in total assets turnover in Year 4. The leverage ratio remained reasonably stable over this period.

Problem 18.2 for Self-Study

Analyzing the rate of return on common shareholders' equity. Refer to the profitability analysis for Abbott Corporation in Problem 18.1 for Self-Study. Consider the following additional data:

	Year 1	Year 2	Year 3
Profit Margin (after subtracting financing costs)	5.1%	4.9%	4.6%
Total Assets Turnover.................................	1.7	1.6	1.5
Leverage Ratio......................................	1.6	1.8	2.1
Rate of Return on Common Shareholders' Equity[a]	14.0%	14.2%	14.2%

[a]Amounts may not equal the product of the three preceding ratios due to rounding.

a. What is the likely explanation for the increasing rate of return on common shareholders' equity?
b. Is financial leverage working to the advantage of the common shareholders in each year?

The solution to this self-study problem is at the end of this chapter on page 767.

Earnings per Share of Common Stock

A third measure of profitability is **earnings per share** of common stock. Earnings per share equals net income attributable to common stock divided by the average number of common shares outstanding during the period.

The calculation of earnings per share for Horrigan Corporation for Year 4 is as follows:

$$\frac{\text{Net Income} - \text{Preferred Stock Dividend}}{\substack{\text{Weighted Average}\\ \text{Number of Common Shares}\\ \text{Outstanding}\\ \text{during the Period}^7}} = \frac{\$60 - \$0}{16 \text{ shares}} = \$3.75 \text{ per share.}$$

Earnings per share were \$1.28 (= \$16/12.5) for Year 2 and \$2.19 (= \$34/15.5) for Year 3.

If a firm has securities outstanding that holders can convert into or exchange for shares of common stock, the firm might report two earnings-per-share amounts: **primary earnings per share** and **fully diluted earnings per share.** Convertible bonds and convertible preferred stock permit their holders to exchange these securities directly for shares of common stock. Many firms have employee stock option plans which allow employees to acquire shares of the company's common stock. Assuming holders convert their securities or employees exercise their options, the firm will issue additional shares of common stock. Then, the amount otherwise shown as earnings per share will probably decrease, or become diluted. When a firm has securities outstanding that, if exchanged for shares of common stock, would decrease earnings per share by 3 percent or more, generally accepted accounting principles require a dual presentation of primary and fully diluted earnings per share.[8]

Primary Earnings per Share Calculations of earnings per share adjust the denominator for securities that are nearly the same as common stock. The principal value of these common stock equivalents arises from their owners' right to exchange them for, or convert them into, common stock, rather than from the securities' own periodic cash yields. Stock options and warrants are always common stock equivalents. Convertible bonds and convertible preferred stock may or may not be common stock equivalents. If the return from these convertible securities at the date of their issue is substantially below the return available from other debt or preferred stock investments, generally accepted accounting principles presume that the securities derive their value primarily from their conversion privileges and are therefore common stock equivalents. Calculations of primary earnings per share adjust for the dilutive effects of these securities.

Fully Diluted Earnings per Share As the name implies, fully diluted earnings per share indicates the maximum possible dilution that would occur if the owners of all options, warrants, and convertible securities outstanding at the end of the accounting period exchanged them for common stock. Therefore, this amount represents the maximum limit of possible dilution that could take place on the date of the balance sheet. All securities convertible into or exchangeable for common

---

[7]Exhibit 18.3 indicates that the par value of a common share is \$10 and that the common stock account has a balance of \$160 million throughout Year 4. The shares outstanding were therefore 16 million.

[8]Accounting Principles Board, *Opinion No. 15,* "Earnings per Share," 1969.

stock, whether or not classified as common stock equivalents, enter into the calculation of fully diluted earnings per share if they dilute earnings per share.

Firms that do not have convertible or other potentially dilutive securities outstanding compute earnings per share in the conventional manner. Firms with outstanding securities that have the potential for materially diluting earnings per share as conventionally computed must present dual earnings-per-share amounts. Problem **29** at the end of this chapter explores more fully the calculation of earnings per share.

Interpreting Earnings per Share   Some accountants and financial analysts criticize earnings per share as a measure of profitability because it does not consider the amount of assets or capital required to generate that level of earnings. Two firms with the same earnings and earnings per share will not be equally profitable if one of the firms requires twice the amount of assets or capital to generate those earnings as does the other firm.

In comparing firms, earnings-per-share amounts are of limited use. For example, assume that two firms have identical earnings, common shareholders' equity, and rates of return on common shareholders' equity. One firm may have a lower earnings per share simply because it has a larger number of shares outstanding (perhaps due to the use of a lower par value for its shares or to different earnings retention policies; see Problem **20** at the end of this chapter).

Price-Earnings Ratio   Financial analysts often compare earnings-per-share amounts with the market price of the stock. They usually express this comparison as a **price-earnings ratio** (= market price per share/earnings per share). For example, the common stock of Horrigan Corporation sells for $50 per share at the end of Year 4. The price-earnings ratio, often called the P/E ratio, is 13.3 to 1 (= $50/$3.75). The analyst often expresses the relation by saying that "the stock sells at 13.3 times earnings."

Tables of stock prices and financial periodicals often present price-earnings ratios. The analyst must interpret these published P/E ratios cautiously, however. In cases in which a firm has discontinued operations or extraordinary gains and losses, the reader must ascertain whether the published ratio uses only income from continuing operations or final net income in the numerator. Also, the published P/E ratios for firms operating at a net loss for the most recent year are sometimes reported as positive numbers. This occurs because the publisher (for example, Value Line) converts the net loss for the year to a longer-run expected profit amount to calculate the P/E ratio. To serve their intended purpose, P/E ratios should use normal, ongoing earnings data in the denominator (that is, earnings from continuing operations).

Summary of Profitability Analysis

This chapter has discussed three broad measures for assessing a firm's profitability. Because the rate of return on assets and rate of return on common shareholders' equity relate earnings to some measure of the capital required to generate those earnings, we have focused most of our attention on these two profitability measures.

Exhibit 18.12

Profitability Ratios

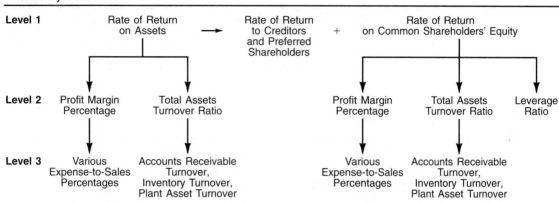

Exhibit 18.12 summarizes the analysis discussed. On the most general level (Level 1), the concern is with overall measures of profitability and the effectiveness of financial leverage. On the next level (Level 2), we disaggregate the overall measures of profitability into profit margin, asset turnover, and leverage components. On the third level (Level 3), we further disaggregate the profit margin and assets turnover ratios to gain additional insights into reasons for changes in profitability. The depth of analysis required in any particular case depends on the relative size of the observed differences or changes in profitability.

Analysis of Risk

The second parameter in investment decision making is risk. Various factors affect the risk of business firms:

1. Economy-wide factors, such as increased inflation or interest rates, unemployment, or recessions.
2. Industry-wide factors, such as increased competition, lack of availability of raw materials, changes in technology, or increased government antitrust actions.
3. Firm-specific factors, such as labor strikes, loss of facilities due to fire or other casualty, or poor health of key managerial personnel.

The ultimate risk is that a firm will become bankrupt; then, creditors and investors may lose the capital they provided to the firm.

Analysts assessing risk generally focus on the relative liquidity of a firm. Cash and near-cash assets provide a firm with the resources needed to adapt to the various types of risk; that is, liquid resources provide a firm with financial flexibility. Cash is also the connecting link that permits the operating, investing, and financing activities of a firm to run smoothly and effectively.

When assessing liquidity, time is critical. Consider the three questions that follow:

1. Does a firm have sufficient cash to repay a loan due tomorrow?
2. Will the firm have sufficient cash to repay a note due in 6 months?
3. Will the firm have sufficient cash to repay bonds due in 5 years?

In answering the first question, the analyst probably focuses on the amount of cash on hand and in the bank relative to the obligation coming due tomorrow. In answering the second question, the analyst compares the amount of cash expected from operations during the next 6 months, as well as from any new borrowing, with the obligations maturing during that period. In answering the third question, the focus shifts to the longer-run cash-generating ability of a firm relative to the amount of long-term debt maturing.

Measures of Short-Term Liquidity Risk

This section discusses four measures for assessing **short-term liquidity risk:** (1) the current ratio, (2) the quick ratio, (3) the operating cash flow to current liabilities ratio, and (4) working capital turnover ratios.

Current Ratio

The **current ratio** equals current assets divided by current liabilities. Recall that current assets comprise cash and assets that a firm expects to turn into cash, sell, or consume within approximately 1 year of the balance sheet date. Current liabilities include obligations that will require cash (or the rendering of services) within approximately 1 year. Thus, the current ratio indicates a firm's ability to meet its short-term obligations. The current ratio of Horrigan Corporation on December 31, Year 1, Year 2, Year 3, and Year 4, is as follows:

	$\dfrac{\text{Current}}{\text{Ratio}} = \dfrac{\text{Current Assets}}{\text{Current Liabilities}}$	
December 31, Year 1	$\dfrac{\$\,50}{\$\,40}$ =	1.25 to 1.0
December 31, Year 2	$\dfrac{\$\,80}{\$\,50}$ =	1.60 to 1.0
December 31, Year 3	$\dfrac{\$100}{\$\,60}$ =	1.67 to 1.0
December 31, Year 4	$\dfrac{\$171}{\$\,90}$ =	1.90 to 1.0

Although the analyst generally prefers an excess of current assets over current liabilities, changes in the trend of the ratio can mislead. For example, when the current ratio is larger than 1 to 1, an increase of equal amount in both current assets and current liabilities (acquiring inventory on account) results in a decline in the ratio, whereas equal decreases (paying an accounts payable) result in an increased current ratio.

In a recessionary period, a business may contract and pay its current liabilities, and even though current assets may be at a low point, the current ratio may go to high levels. In a boom period, just the reverse effect may occur. In other words, a high current ratio may accompany unsatisfactory business conditions, whereas a falling ratio may accompany profitable operations.

Furthermore, firms can manipulate the current ratio. Management can take deliberate steps to produce a financial statement that presents a better current ratio at the balance sheet date than the average or normal current ratio. For example, a firm might delay normal purchases on account toward the close of a fiscal year. Or it might collect loans to officers, classified as noncurrent assets, and use the proceeds to reduce current liabilities. These actions produce a current ratio that is as favorable as possible in the annual financial statements at the balance sheet date. Such manipulation is sometimes known as "window dressing."

Although analysts commonly use the current ratio in statement analysis, its trends may not indicate substantial changes, and management can easily manipulate it.

Quick Ratio

A variation of the current ratio is the **quick ratio** (sometimes called the **acid-test ratio**). The quick ratio includes in the numerator only those current assets that a firm could convert quickly into cash. The numerator customarily includes cash, marketable securities, and receivables. Some businesses can convert their inventory of merchandise into cash more quickly than other businesses can convert their receivables. The facts in each case will indicate whether the analyst should include receivables or exclude inventories.

Assuming that the quick ratios of Horrigan Corporation include accounts receivable but exclude inventory, the quick ratios on December 31, Year 1, Year 2, Year 3, and Year 4, are as follows:

	Quick Ratio $=$	Cash, Marketable Securities, Accounts Receivable
		Current Liabilities
December 31, Year 1	$\dfrac{\$36}{\$40} =$	.90 to 1.0
December 31, Year 2	$\dfrac{\$50}{\$50} =$	1.0 to 1.0
December 31, Year 3	$\dfrac{\$54}{\$60} =$	.90 to 1.0
December 31, Year 4	$\dfrac{\$88}{\$90} =$	.98 to 1.0

Whereas the current ratio increased steadily over the period, the quick ratio remained relatively constant. The increase in the current ratio resulted primarily from a buildup of inventories.

Cash Flow from Operations to Current Liabilities Ratio

One might criticize the current ratio and quick ratio because they use amounts at a specific point in time. If financial statement amounts at that particular time are unusually large or small, the resulting ratios will not reflect normal conditions.

The **cash flow from operations to current liabilities ratio** overcomes these deficiencies. The numerator of this ratio is cash flows from operations for the year. The denominator is average current liabilities for the year. The cash flow from operations to current liabilities ratios for Horrigan Corporation for Year 2, Year 3, and Year 4 are as follows:

	Cash Flow from Operations to Current Liabilities =	$\dfrac{\text{Cash Flow from Operations}}{\text{Average Current Liabilities}}$
Year 2................	$\dfrac{\$12}{\frac{1}{2}(\$40 + \$50)} \quad =$	26.7 percent
Year 3................	$\dfrac{\$32}{\frac{1}{2}(\$50 + \$60)} \quad =$	58.2 percent
Year 4................	$\dfrac{\$41}{\frac{1}{2}(\$60 + \$90)} \quad =$	54.7 percent

A healthy firm typically has a ratio of 40 percent or more.[9] Thus the liquidity of Horrigan Corporation improved dramatically between Year 2 and Year 3.

Working Capital Turnover Ratios

During the *operating cycle,* a firm completes the following activities:

1. Purchases inventory on account from suppliers.
2. Sells inventory on account to customers.
3. Collects amounts due from customers.
4. Pays amounts due to suppliers.

This cycle occurs continually for most businesses. The number of days that a firm holds inventories (that is, 365 days/inventory turnover ratio) indicates the length of the period between the purchase and sale of inventory during each operating cycle. The number of days that a firm's receivables remain outstanding (that is, 365 days/ accounts receivable turnover ratio) indicates the length of the period between the sale of inventory and the collection of cash from customers during each operating cycle.

Firms must finance their investments in inventories and accounts receivable. Suppliers typically provide a portion of the needed financing. The number of days that a firm's accounts payable remain outstanding (that is, 365 days/accounts payable

---

[9]Cornelius Casey and Norman Bartczak, ''Using Operating Cash Flow Data to Predict Financial Distress: Some Extensions,'' *Journal of Accounting Research* (Spring 1985): 384–401.

turnover ratio) indicates the length of the period between the purchase of inventory on account and the payment of cash to suppliers during each operating cycle. The **accounts payable turnover ratio** equals purchases on account divided by average accounts payable. Although firms do not disclose their purchases, the analyst can approximate the amounts as follows:

$$\text{Purchases} = \text{Cost of Goods Sold} + \text{Ending Inventory} - \text{Beginning Inventory.}$$

The purchases of Horrigan Corporation appear below:

	Purchases =	Cost of Goods Sold	+	Ending Inventory	−	Beginning Inventory.
Year 2.........................	$135 =	$119	+	$30	−	$14
Year 3.........................	$195 =	$179	+	$46	−	$30
Year 4.........................	$317 =	$280	+	$83	−	$46

The accounts payable for Year 4 is:

$$\frac{\text{Purchases}}{\text{Average Accounts Payable}} = \frac{\$317}{\frac{1}{2}(\$35 + \$50)} = 7.5.$$

The accounts payable turnover was 4.3 for Year 2 and 5.5 for Year 3. The average number of days payables were outstanding was 84.9 days for Year 2, 66.4 days for Year 3, and 48.7 days for Year 4. Thus, the days payables declined sharply during the three years.

Interpreting the accounts payable turnover ratio involves opposing considerations. An increase in the accounts payable turnover ratio indicates that a firm pays its obligations to suppliers more quickly, requiring cash. On the other hand, a faster accounts payable turnover means a smaller relative amount of accounts payable that the firm must pay in the near future.

A comparison of the days outstanding for inventories, accounts receivable, and accounts payable reveals the following:

Year	Days Inventory Held	Days Accounts Receivable Outstanding	Days Accounts Payable Outstanding
Year 2...................	67.6	53.7	84.9
Year 3...................	77.7	48.0	66.4
Year 4...................	84.9	46.8	48.7

The increased number of days the firm held inventories suggests increased short-term liquidity risk. However, a reduction in the number of days accounts receivable remain outstanding reduced short-term liquidity risk. Interpreting the decreased number of days accounts payable remain outstanding involves the opposing considerations discussed above. Clearly, however, Horrigan Corporation must obtain more short-term financing for its investments in inventories and accounts receivable in Year 4 than in Year 2. The operating cash flow to current liabilities ratio discussed in the preceding section suggests that operations have provided more than sufficient cash flow to finance this increased financing need.

Summary of Short-Term Liquidity Analysis

The current and quick ratios measure liquidity at particular points in time. These ratios for Horrigan Corporation indicate satisfactory conditions at the end of each year, although they show a buildup of inventories.

The cash flow from operations and working capital turnover ratios measure short-term liquidity for a period of time. The increase in the number of days the firm held inventory coupled with a decrease in the number of days it delays paying its accounts payables suggests an increased need for short-term financing. However, Horrigan Corporation's increased profitability and accounts receivable turnover ratio resulted in an increasing cash flow from operations to current liabilities ratio, well above the 40 percent typically found for a financially healthy firm.

Problem 18.3 for Self-Study

Analyzing short-term liquidity risk. Refer to the profitability ratios for Abbott Corporation in Problems 18.1 and 18.2 for Self-Study. Consider the following additional data.

	Year 1	Year 2	Year 3
Current Ratio	1.4	1.3	1.2
Quick Ratio	1.0	.9	1.0
Cash Flow from Operations to Current Liabilities	38.2%	37.3%	36.4%
Days Accounts Receivable Outstanding	84.9	84.9	86.9
Days Inventories Held...............................	114.1	107.4	101.4
Days Accounts Payable Outstanding.................	58.6	59.1	58.8

a. What is the likely explanation for the decreasing current ratio coupled with the stable quick ratio?
b. What is the likely explanation for the decline in the cash flow from operations to current liabilities ratio?
c. What is your assessment of the short-term liquidity risk of Abbott Corporation at the end of Year 3?

The solution to this self-study problem is at the end of this chapter on page 767.

Measures of Long-Term Liquidity Risk

Analysts use measures of **long-term liquidity risk** to evaluate a firm's ability to meet interest and principal payments on long-term debt and similar obligations as they come due. If a firm cannot make the payments on time, it becomes insolvent and may have to reorganize or liquidate.

Perhaps the best indicator of a firm's long-term liquidity risk is its ability to generate profits over a period of years. If a firm is profitable, it will either generate sufficient cash from operations or obtain needed capital from creditors and owners. The measures of profitability discussed previously therefore apply for this purpose as well. Three other measures of long-term liquidity risk are debt ratios, the cash flow from operations to total liabilities ratio, and the interest coverage ratio.

Debt Ratios

The debt ratio has several variations, but one most commonly encounters the **long-term debt ratio** in financial analysis. It reports the portion of the firm's long-term capital that debtholders furnish. To calculate this ratio, divide total long-term debt by the sum of total long-term debt and total shareholders' equity.

Another form of the debt ratio is the **debt-equity ratio**. To calculate the debt-equity ratio, divide total liabilities (current and noncurrent) by total equities (= liabilities plus shareholders' equity = total assets).

Exhibit 18.13 shows the two forms of the debt ratio for Horrigan Corporation on December 31, Year 1, Year 2, Year 3, and Year 4. In general, the higher these ratios, the higher the likelihood that the firm may be unable to meet fixed interest and principal payments in the future. The decision for most firms is how much financial leverage, with its attendant risk, they can afford to take on. Funds obtained from issuing bonds or borrowing from a bank have a relatively low interest cost but require fixed, periodic payments that increase the likelihood of bankruptcy.

In assessing the debt ratios, analysts customarily vary the standard in relation to the stability of the firm's earnings and cash flows from operations. The more stable the earnings and cash flows, the higher the debt ratio considered acceptable or safe. The debt ratios of public utilities are customarily high, frequently on the order of 60 to 70 percent. The stability of public utility earnings and cash flows makes these ratios acceptable to many investors. These investors might find such high leverage

Exhibit 18.13

HORRIGAN CORPORATION
Debt Ratios

Long-Term Debt Ratio = $\dfrac{\text{Total Long-Term Debt}}{\substack{\text{Total Long-Term Debt} \\ \text{plus Shareholders'} \\ \text{Equity}}}$		Debt-Equity Ratio = $\dfrac{\text{Total Liabilities}}{\substack{\text{Total Liabilities plus} \\ \text{Shareholders'} \\ \text{Equity}}}$	
Dec. 31, Year 1 ...	$\dfrac{\$\,50}{\$210} = 24$ percent	Dec. 31, Year 1 ...	$\dfrac{\$\,90}{\$250} = 36$ percent
Dec. 31, Year 2 ...	$\dfrac{\$\,50}{\$350} = 14$ percent	Dec. 31, Year 2 ...	$\dfrac{\$100}{\$400} = 25$ percent
Dec. 31, Year 3 ...	$\dfrac{\$100}{\$460} = 22$ percent	Dec. 31, Year 3 ...	$\dfrac{\$160}{\$520} = 31$ percent
Dec. 31, Year 4 ...	$\dfrac{\$150}{\$560} = 27$ percent	Dec. 31, Year 4 ...	$\dfrac{\$240}{\$650} = 37$ percent

unacceptable for firms with less stable earnings and cash flows, such as a computer software developer or biotechnology firm. The debt ratios of Horrigan Corporation are about average for an industrial firm.

Because several variations of the debt ratio appear in corporate annual reports, the analyst should take care when comparing debt ratios among firms.

Cash Flow from Operations to Total Liabilities Ratio

The debt ratios do not consider the availability of liquid assets to cover various levels of debt. The **cash flow from operations to total liabilities ratio** overcomes this deficiency. This cash flow ratio resembles the one for assessing short-term liquidity risk, but here the denominator includes *all* liabilities (both current and noncurrent). The cash flow from operations to debt ratios for Horrigan Corporation follow:

	Cash Flow from Operations to Total Liabilities Ratio	=	Cash Flow from Operations / Average Total Liabilities
Year 2.	$\dfrac{\$12}{\frac{1}{2}(\$90 + \$100)}$	=	12.6 percent
Year 3.	$\dfrac{\$32}{\frac{1}{2}(\$100 + \$160)}$	=	24.6 percent
Year 4.	$\dfrac{\$41}{\frac{1}{2}(\$160 + \$240)}$	=	20.5 percent

A financially healthy company normally has a cash flow from operations to total liabilities ratio of 20 percent or more. Thus the long-term liquidity risk decreased significantly between Year 2 and Year 3 but increased again in Year 4.

Interest Coverage Ratio

Another measure of long-term liquidity risk is the number of times that earnings cover interest charges. The **interest coverage ratio** equals net income before interest and income tax expenses divided by interest expense. For Horrigan Corporation, the interest coverage ratios for Year 2, Year 3, and Year 4 are as follows:

	Interest Coverage Ratio	=	Net Income before Interest and Income Taxes / Interest Expense
Year 2.	$\dfrac{\$16 + \$5 + \$7}{\$5}$	=	5.6 times
Year 3.	$\dfrac{\$34 + \$10 + \$14}{\$10}$	=	5.8 times
Year 4.	$\dfrac{\$60 + \$16 + \$26}{\$16}$	=	6.4 times

Thus, whereas the bonded indebtedness increased sharply during the 3-year period, the growth in net income before interest and income taxes provided increasing coverage of the fixed interest charges.

This ratio attempts to indicate the relative protection that operating profitability provides bondholders, permitting them to assess the probability of a firm's failing to meet required interest payments. If bond indentures require periodic repayments of principal on long-term liabilities, the denominator of the ratio might include such repayments. The ratio would then be called the *fixed charges coverage ratio.*

One can criticize the interest or fixed charges coverage ratios as measures for assessing long-term liquidity risk because they use earnings rather than cash flows in the numerator. Firms pay interest and other fixed payment obligations with cash, not with earnings. When the value of the ratio is relatively low (for example, two to three times), the analyst should use some measure of cash flows, such as cash flow from operations, in the numerator.

Summary of Long-Term Liquidity Analysis

Long-term liquidity analysis focuses on the amount of debt (particularly long-term debt) in the capital structure and the adequacy of earnings and cash flows to service debt (that is, to provide interest and principal payments as they mature). Although both short- and long-term debt of Horrigan Corporation increased over the 3-year period, increases in sales, earnings, and cash flows from operations all appear to be increasing sufficiently to cover the current levels of debt.

Problem 18.4 for Self-Study

Analyzing long-term liquidity risk. Refer to the profitability and short-term liquidity risk ratios for Abbott Corporation in Problems 18.1, 18.2, and 18.3 for Self-Study. Consider the following additional data.

	Year 1	Year 2	Year 3
Long-term Debt Ratio	37.5%	33.8%	43.3%
Debt-Equity Ratio.....................................	37.5%	44.4%	52.4%
Cash Flow from Operations to Total Liabilities Ratio	16.3%	13.4%	11.1%
Interest Coverage Ratio	6.7	5.1	4.1

a.   What is the likely explanation for the decrease in the cash flow from operations to total liabilities ratio?
b.   What is the likely explanation for the decrease in the interest coverage ratio?
c.   What is your assessment of the long-term liquidity risk of Abbott Corporation at the end of Year 3?

The solution to this self-study problem is at the end of this chapter on page 768.

Limitations of Ratio Analysis

The analytical computations discussed in this chapter have a number of limitations that the analyst should keep in mind when preparing or using them. Several of the more important limitations are the following:

1. Because ratios use financial statement data as inputs, the ratios have shortcomings similar to the financial statements (for example, use of acquisition cost for assets rather than current replacement cost or net realizable value, the latitude permitted firms in selecting from among various generally accepted accounting principles).
2. Changes in many ratios strongly correlate with each other. For example, the changes in the current ratio and quick ratio between different times are often in the same direction and approximately proportional. The analyst need not compute all the ratios to assess a particular dimension of profitability or risk.
3. When comparing the size of a ratio between periods for the same firm, one must recognize conditions that have changed between the periods (for example, different product lines or geographic markets served, changes in economic conditions, changes in prices, changes in accounting principles, corporate acquisitions).
4. When comparing ratios of a particular firm with those of similar firms, one must recognize differences between the firms (for example, use of different methods of accounting, differences in the method of operations, type of financing, and so on).

The analyst cannot use financial statement ratios as direct indicators of good or poor management. Such ratios indicate areas that the analyst should investigate further. For example, a decrease in the turnover of raw materials inventory, ordinarily considered an undesirable trend, may reflect the accumulation of scarce materials to keep the plant operating at full capacity during shortages. Such shortages may force competitors to restrict operations or to close down. The analyst must combine ratios derived from financial statements with an investigation of other facts before drawing valid conclusions.

Summary

For convenient reference, Exhibit 18.14 summarizes the calculation of the financial statement ratios discussed in this chapter.

This chapter began with the question, ''Should you invest your inheritance in a certificate of deposit or in the shares of common stock of Horrigan Corporation?'' Analysis of Horrigan Corporation's financial statements indicates that it has been a growing, profitable company with few indications of either short-term or long-term liquidity problems. You need at least three additional inputs before making the investment decision. First, you should consult sources of information other than the financial statements (for example, articles in the financial press, capital spending plans, and new product introduction plans by competitors) to improve projections of

Exhibit 18.14

Summary of Financial Statement Ratios

Ratio	Numerator	Denominator
Profitability Ratios		
Rate of Return on Assets	Net Income + Interest Expense (net of tax effects)[a]	Average Total Assets during the Period[b]
Profit Margin Ratio (before interest effects)	Net Income + Interest Expense (net of tax effects)[a]	Sales
Various Expense Ratios	Various Expenses	Sales
Total Assets Turnover Ratio	Sales	Average Total Assets during the Period
Accounts Receivable Turnover Ratio	Net Sales on Account	Average Accounts Receivable during the Period
Inventory Turnover Ratio	Cost of Goods Sold	Average Inventory during the Period
Plant Asset Turnover Ratio	Sales	Average Plant Assets during the Period
Rate of Return on Common Shareholders' Equity	Net Income − Preferred Stock Dividends	Average Common Shareholders' Equity during the Period
Profit Margin Ratio (after interest expense and preferred dividends)	Net Income − Preferred Stock Dividends	Sales
Leverage Ratio	Average Total Assets during the Period	Average Common Shareholders' Equity during the Period
Earnings per Share of Stock[c]	Net Income − Preferred Stock Dividends	Weighted-Average Number of Common Shares Outstanding during the Period
Short-term Liquidity Ratios		
Current Ratio	Current Assets	Current Liabilities
Quick or Acid-Test Ratio	Highly Liquid Assets (ordinarily cash, marketable securities, and receivables)[d]	Current Liabilities
Cash Flow from Operations to Current Liabilities Ratio	Cash Flow from Operations	Average Current Liabilities during the Period
Accounts Payable Turnover Ratio	Purchases[e]	Average Accounts Payable during the Period
Days Accounts Receivable Outstanding	365 days	Accounts Receivable Turnover Ratio
Days Inventories Held	365 days	Inventory Turnover Ratio

(continued)

Exhibit 18.14 (continued)

Ratio	Numerator	Denominator
Days Accounts Payable Outstanding	365 days	Accounts Payable Turnover Ratio
Long-term Liquidity Ratios		
Long-term Debt Ratio	Total Long-term Debt	Total Long-term Debt Plus Shareholders' Equity
Debt-Equity Ratio	Total Liabilities	Total Equities (total liabilities plus shareholders' equity)
Cash Flow from Operations to Total Liabilities Ratio	Cash Flow from Operations	Average Total Liabilities during the Period
Interest Covered Ratio	Net Income before Interest and Income Taxes	Interest Expense

[a]If the parent company does not own all of a consolidated subsidiary, the calculation also adds back to net income the minority interest share of earnings.

[b]See footnote 3 on page 737.

[c]This calculation is more complicated when there are convertible securities, options, or warrants outstanding.

[d]The calculation could conceivably exclude receivables for some firms and include inventories for others.

[e]Purchases = Cost of Goods Sold + Ending Inventories − Beginning Inventories.

a firm's future profitability and risk. Second, you must decide your attitude toward, or willingness to assume, risk. Third, you must decide if you think the stock market price of the shares makes them an attractive current purchase.[10] Before making buy/sell recommendations to investors, analysts compare their assessment of the firm's profitability and risk to the firm's share price. Analysts might recommend purchasing the shares of a poorly run company whose shares they judge underpriced rather than recommend shares of a well-run company whose shares they judge overpriced in the market. It is at this stage in the investment decision that the analysis becomes particularly subjective.

Problem 18.5 for Self-Study

Computing profitability and risk ratios. Exhibit 18.15 presents an income statement for Year 2, and Exhibit 18.16 presents a comparative balance sheet for Cox Corporation as of December 31, Year 1 and Year 2. Using information from these financial statements, compute the following ratios. The income tax rate is 30 percent. Cash flow from operations totals $3,300.

---

[10]Finance texts discuss other important factors in the investment decision. Perhaps the most important question of all is how a particular investment fits in with the investor's entire portfolio. Modern research suggests that the suitability of a potential investment depends more on the attributes of the other components of an investment portfolio and the risk attitude of the investor than it does on the attributes of the potential investment itself.

Exhibit 18.15

COX CORPORATION
Income and Retained Earnings Statement for Year 2
(Problem 18.5 for Self-Study)

Sales Revenue		$30,000
Less Expenses:		
Cost of Goods Sold	$18,000	
Selling	4,500	
Administrative	2,500	
Interest	700	
Income Taxes	1,300	
Total Expenses		27,000
Net Income		$ 3,000
Less Dividends:		
Preferred	$ 100	
Common	700	800
Increase in Retained Earnings for Year 2		$ 2,200
Retained Earnings, December 31, Year 1		4,500
Retained Earnings, December 31, Year 2		$ 6,700

Exhibit 18.16

COX CORPORATION
Comparative Balance Sheet
December 31, Year 1 and Year 2
(Problem 18.5 for Self-Study)

	December 31	
	Year 1	Year 2
Assets		
Current Assets:		
Cash	$ 600	$ 750
Accounts Receivable	3,600	4,300
Merchandise Inventories	5,600	7,900
Prepayments	300	380
Total Current Assets	$10,100	$13,330
Property, Plant, and Equipment:		
Land	$ 500	$ 600
Buildings and Equipment (net)	9,400	10,070
Total Property, Plant, and Equipment	$ 9,900	$10,670
Total Assets	$20,000	$24,000

(continued)

Exhibit 18.16 *(continued)*

	December 31	
	Year 1	Year 2
Liabilities and Shareholders' Equity		
Current Liabilities:		
Notes Payable	$ 2,000	$ 4,000
Accounts Payable	3,500	3,300
Other Current Liabilities	1,500	1,900
Total Current Liabilities	$ 7,000	$ 9,200
Noncurrent Liabilities:		
Bonds Payable	4,000	2,800
Total Liabilities	$11,000	$12,000
Shareholders' Equity:		
Preferred Stock	$ 1,000	$ 1,000
Common Stock...	2,000	2,500
Additional Paid-in Capital	1,500	1,800
Retained Earnings	4,500	6,700
Total Shareholders' Equity	$ 9,000	$12,000
Total Liabilities and Shareholders' Equity	$20,000	$24,000

a. Rate of return on assets.
b. Profit margin ratio (before interest and related tax effects).
c. Cost of goods sold to sales percentage.
d. Selling expense to sales percentage.
e. Total assets turnover.
f. Accounts receivable turnover.
g. Inventory turnover.
h. Plant asset turnover.
i. Rate of return on common shareholders' equity.
j. Profit margin (after interest).
k. Leverage ratio.
l. Current ratio (both dates).
m. Quick ratio (both dates).
n. Cash flow from operations to current liabilities.
o. Accounts payable turnover.
p. Long-term debt ratio (both dates).
q. Debt-equity ratio (both dates).
r. Cash flow from operations to total liabilities.
s. Interest coverage ratio.

Solutions to Self-Study Problems

Suggested Solution to Problem 18.1 for Self-Study

a. The declining rate of return on assets results from a decreasing total assets turnover. The profit margin ratio (before interest expense and related tax effects) was stable. The declining total assets turnover results primarily from a decreasing plant assets turnover. Abbott Corporation has probably added productive capacity in recent years, anticipating higher sales in the future, which causes the plant asset turnover to decline.

b. Abbott Corporation has probably implemented more effective inventory control systems, resulting in an increasing inventory turnover ratio. The more rapid inventory turnover results in fewer writedowns of inventory items for product obsolescence and physical deterioration, thereby decreasing the cost of goods sold to sales percentage.

Suggested Solution to Problem 18.2 for Self-Study

a. The increasing rate of return on common shareholders' equity results from an increasing proportion of debt in the capital structure. Although the rate of return on assets declined, the increase in the leverage ratio more than offset the declining operating profitability.

b. The rate of return on common shareholders' equity exceeds the rate of return on assets, suggesting that the firm earned more on assets financed by creditors than the cost of creditors' capital. The excess return benefited the common shareholders.

Suggested Solution to Problem 18.3 for Self-Study

a. Inventories are the principal asset that appears in the current ratio but not in the quick ratio. The declining current ratio indicates that inventories are not growing as rapidly as the overall level of operations. Note the decrease in the number of days inventory items are held, suggesting the firm exerts more effective control over the level of inventories.

b. Abbott Corporation experienced a slight increase in the number of days receivables are outstanding, which tends to decrease cash flow from operations. The decrease in the number of days a firm holds inventories increases cash flow from operations and more than offsets the effect of accounts receivable on cash flow from operations. The stable accounts payable turnover also indicates that an acceleration or delay in paying accounts payable does not explain the decline in the cash flow from operations to current liabilities ratio. Most likely, declining profitability, which results in operations throwing off less cash with each revolution of the operating cycle, caused the decline. Note that the profit margin ratio excluding financing costs remained stable over the 3 years (see Problem 18.1 for Self-Study), whereas the profit margin ratio including financing costs, declined (see Problem 18.2 for Self-Study). Thus, the declining profitability results from increased financing costs, probably related to the level of debt in the capital structure.

c. Abbott Corporation's cash flow operations to current liabilities ratio is marginally less than the 40 percent considered desirable for a healthy firm. Its declining current ratio results from more effective inventory control systems, reducing short-term liquidity risk. A quick ratio around 1.0 indicates that the most liquid current assets are sufficient to pay current liabilities. These signals suggest a satisfactory level of short-term liquidity risk.

Suggested Solution to Problem 18.4 for Self-Study

a. The response to question **b** in Problem 18.3 for Self-Study indicates that declining profitability helps explain the decrease in the cash flow from operations to total liabilities ratio. So does the increase in borrowing. This increased borrowing is both short-term and long-term, as the two debt ratios indicate.

b. The declining interest coverage ratio results primarily from increased interest expense or the increased debt loads. (Note from Problem 18.1 for Self-Study that the profit margin ratio excluding financing costs was stable during the last 3 years.)

c. The cash flows from operations to total liabilities ratio is marginally below the 20 percent considered desirable for a healthy firm. Its interest coverage ratio remains four times earnings before interest and taxes. The growth in debt appears related to increases in plant assets (see the response to question **a** in Problem 18.1 for Self-Study). If Abbott Corporation experienced difficulty servicing its debt, it could perhaps sell some of these plant assets to obtain funds. Thus, the overall long-term liquidity risk level appears reasonable.

Suggested Solution to Problem 18.5 for Self-Study

a. Rate of return on assets $= \dfrac{\$3,000 + (1 - .30)(\$700)}{.5(\$20,000 + \$24,000)} = 15.9$ percent.

b. Profit margin ratio $= \dfrac{\$3,000 + (1 - .30)(\$700)}{\$30,000} = 11.6$ percent.

c. Cost of goods sold to sales percentage $= \dfrac{\$18,000}{\$30,000} = 60.0$ percent.

d. Selling expense to sales percentage $= \dfrac{\$4,500}{\$30,000} = 15.0$ percent.

e. Total assets turnover $= \dfrac{\$30,000}{.5(\$20,000 + \$24,000)} = 1.4$ times per year.

f. Accounts receivable turnover $= \dfrac{\$30,000}{.5(\$3,600 + \$4,300)} = 7.6$ times per year.

g. Inventory turnover $= \dfrac{\$18,000}{.5(\$5,600 + \$7,900)} = 2.7$ times per year.

h. Plant asset turnover $= \dfrac{\$30,000}{.5(\$9,900 + \$10,670)} = 2.9$ times per year.

i. Rate of return on common shareholders' equity $= \dfrac{\$3,000 - \$100}{.5(\$8,000 + \$11,000)} =$ 30.5 percent.

j. Profit margin (after interest) $= \dfrac{\$3,000 - \$100}{\$30,000} = 9.7$ percent.

k. Leverage ratio $= \dfrac{.5(\$20,000 + \$24,000)}{.5(\$8,000 + \$11,000)} = 2.3$.

l. Current ratio

December 31, Year 1: $\dfrac{\$10,100}{\$7,000} = 1.4:1$.

December 31, Year 2: $\dfrac{\$13,330}{\$9,200} = 1.4:1$.

m. Quick ratio

December 31, Year 1: $\dfrac{\$4,200}{\$7,000} = .6:1$.

December 31, Year 2: $\dfrac{\$5,050}{\$9,200} = .5:1$.

n. Cash flow from operations to current liabilities $= \dfrac{\$3,300}{.5(\$7,000 + \$9,200)} = 40.7$ percent.

o. Accounts payable turnover $= \dfrac{\$18,000 + \$7,900 - \$5,600}{.5(\$3,500 + \$3,300)} = 6.0$ times per year.

p. Long-term debt ratio

December 31, Year 1: $\dfrac{\$4,000}{\$13,000} = 30.8$ percent.

December 31, Year 2: $\dfrac{\$2,800}{\$14,800} = 18.9$ percent.

q. Debt-equity ratio

December 31, Year 1: $\dfrac{\$11,000}{\$20,000} = 55.0$ percent.

December 31, Year 2: $\dfrac{\$12,000}{\$24,000} = 50.0$ percent.

r. Cash flow from operations to total liabilities $= \dfrac{\$3,300}{.5(\$11,000 + \$12,000)} = 28.7$ percent.

s. Interest coverage ratio $= \dfrac{\$3,000 + \$1,300 + \$700}{\$700} = 7.1$ times.

Key Terms and Concepts

Return and risk
Time-series analysis
Cross-section analysis
Profitability
Rate of return on assets (ROA)
Profit margin ratio
Total assets turnover ratio
Accounts receivable turnover ratio
Inventory turnover ratio
Plant asset turnover ratio
Rate of return on common
  shareholders' equity
Financial leverage
Leverage ratio
Earnings per share

Primary and fully diluted earnings
  per share
Price-earnings ratio
Short-term liquidity risk
Current ratio
Quick ratio or acid-test
Cash flow from operations to current
  liabilities ratio
Accounts payable turnover ratio
Long-term liquidity risk
Long-term debt ratio
Debt-equity ratio
Cash flow from operations to total
  liabilities ratio
Interest coverage ratio

Questions, Exercises, Problems, and Cases

Questions

1. Review the meaning of the terms and concepts listed above in Key Terms and Concepts.
2. Describe several factors that might limit the comparability of a firm's financial statement ratios over several periods.
3. Describe several factors that might limit the comparability of one firm's financial statement ratios with those of another firm in the same industry.
4. "I can understand why the analyst adds back interest expense to net income in the numerator of the rate of return on assets, but I don't see why an adjustment is made for income taxes." Provide an explanation.
5. One company president stated, "The operations of our company are such that we must turn inventory over once every 4 weeks." Another company president in a similar industry stated, "The operations of our company are such that we can live comfortably with a turnover of four times each year." Explain what these two company presidents probably had in mind.

6. Some have argued that for any given firm at a particular time there is an optimal inventory turnover ratio. Explain.

7. Under what circumstances will the rate of return on common shareholders' equity exceed the rate of return on assets? Under what circumstances will it be less?

8. A company president stated, "The operations of our company are such that we can effectively use only a small amount of financial leverage." Explain.

9. Define financial leverage. As long as a firm's rate of return on assets exceeds its aftertax cost of borrowing, why doesn't the firm increase borrowing to as close to 100 percent of financing as possible?

10. Illustrate with amounts how a decrease in working capital can accompany an increase in the current ratio.

Exercises

Solutions to even-numbered exercises are at the end of the chapter on page 791.

11. **Calculating and disaggregating rate of return on assets.** Recent annual reports of The Coca-Cola Company and PepsiCo, Inc., reveal the following for Year 8 (amounts in millions):

	Coca-Cola	PepsiCo
Revenues..	$10,236	$17,803
Interest Expense	231	689
Net Income	1,382	1,091
Average Total Assets	8,780	10,135

The Coca-Cola Company engages primarily in soft drinks, while PepsiCo's involvements include soft drinks, food snacks, and restaurants (Pizza Hut, KFC, Taco Bell). The income tax rate for Year 8 is 34 percent.

a. Calculate the rate of return on assets for each company.

b. Disaggregate the rate of return on assets in part **a** into profit margin and total assets turnover components.

c. Comment on the relative profitability of the two companies for Year 8.

12. **Profitability analysis for two types of retailers.** Information taken from recent annual reports of two retailers appears below (amounts in millions). One of these companies is Wal-Mart, a discount store chain, and the other is The Limited, a specialty retailer of women's clothing. The income tax rate is 34 percent. Indicate which of these companies is Wal-Mart and which is The Limited. Explain.

	Company A	Company B
Sales..	$6,149	$43,887
Interest Expense	257	266
Net Income	403	1,608
Average Total Assets	3,145	13,416

13. **Analyzing accounts receivable for two companies.** The annual reports of Campbell Soup Company and Heinz, two consumer foods companies, reveal the following for the current year (amounts in millions):

	Campbell Soup	Heinz
Sales..	$6,204	$6,647
Accounts Receivable, January 1	625	641
Accounts Receivable, December 31	527	678

   a. Compute the accounts receivable turnover for each company.
   b. Compute the average number of days that accounts receivable are outstanding for each company.
   c. Which company is managing its accounts receivable more efficiently?

14. **Analyzing inventories over 4 years.** The following information relates to the activities of Bristol-Myers Squibb, a manufacturer of prescription drugs as well as household cleaning products and toiletries (amounts in millions):

	Year 5	Year 6	Year 7	Year 8
Sales.............................	$8,558	$9,189	$10,300	$11,159
Cost of Goods Sold.................	2,484	2,656	2,874	2,930
Average Inventory	989	1,092	1,252	1,408

   a. Compute the inventory turnover for each year.
   b. Compute the average number of days that inventories are held each year.
   c. Compute the cost of goods sold to sales percentage for each year.
   d. How well has Bristol-Myers Squibb managed its inventories over the 4 years?

15. **Analyzing plant asset turnover over 4 years.** The following information relates to Boise Cascade, a forest products company (amounts in millions):

	Year 2	Year 3	Year 4	Year 5
Sales..............................	$4,095	$4,338	$4,186	$3,950
Average Plant Assets	2,495	2,791	3,282	3,550
Expenditures on Plant Assets	430	699	758	299

   a. Compute the plant asset turnover for each year.
   b. How well has Boise Cascade managed its investment in plant assets over the 4 years?

16. **Calculating and disaggregating rate of return on common shareholders' equity.** Information taken from the annual reports of Glaxo, a pharmaceutical

company headquartered in the United Kingdom, for 3 recent years appears below (amounts in millions):

	Year 4	Year 5	Year 6
Revenues.....................................	£1,741	£2,059	£2,570
Net Income	495	574	634
Average Total Assets	2,099	2,630	3,184
Average Common Shareholders' Equity	1,282	1,638	2,090

   a. Compute the rate of return on common shareholders' equity for each year.
   b. Disaggregate the rate of return on common shareholders' equity into profit margin, total assets turnover, and leverage ratio components.
   c. How has the profitability changed over the 3 years?

17. **Profitability analyses for three companies.** The following data show five items from the financial statements of three companies for a recent year (amounts in millions):

	Company A	Company B	Company C
For Year			
Revenues......................	$5,739	$5,787	$10,615
Income before Interest and Related Taxes[a]...............	739	644	724
Net Income to Common Shareholders[b].................	534	606	515
Average during Year			
Total Assets	10,518	3,838	8,512
Common Shareholders' Equity.......................	4,472	2,031	2,635

[a]Net Income + Interest Expense × (1 − Tax Rate).
[b]Net Income − Preferred Stock Dividends.

   a. Compute the rate of return on assets for each company. Disaggregate the rate of return on assets into profit margin and total assets turnover components.
   b. Compute the rate of return on common shareholders' equity for each company. Disaggregate the rate of return on common shareholders' equity into profit margin, total assets turnover, and leverage ratio components.
   c. The three companies are May Department Stores, Kellogg's (breakfast cereals), and Consolidated Edison (electric utility). Which of the companies corresponds to A, B, and C? What clues did you use in reaching your conclusions?

18. **Relating profitability to financial leverage.**
   a. Compute the ratio of return on common shareholders' equity in each of the following independent cases.

Case	Average Total Assets	Average Interest-Bearing Debt	Average Common Share-holders' Equity	Rate of Return on Assets	After-tax Cost of Interest-Bearing Debt
A	$200	$100	$100	6%	6%
B	200	100	100	8	6
C	200	120	80	8	6
D	200	100	100	4	6
E	200	50	100	6	6
F	200	50	100	5	6

    b. In which cases is leverage working to the advantage of the common share-holders?

19. **Analyzing financial leverage.** The Borrowing Company has total assets of $100,000 during the year. The firm's borrowings total $20,000 at a 10-percent annual rate, and it pays income taxes at a rate of 30 percent of pretax income. Shareholders' equity is $80,000.

    a. Calculate the amount of net income needed for the rate of return on share-holders' equity to equal the rate of return on assets.

    b. Compute the rate of return on common shareholders' equity for the net income determined in part **a.**

    c. Calculate the amount of income before interest and income taxes needed to achieve this net income.

    d. Repeat parts **a, b,** and **c,** assuming borrowing of $80,000 and common shareholders' equity of $20,000.

    e. Compare the results from the two different debt-equity relations, making generalizations where possible.

20. **Interpreting changes in earnings per share.** Company A and Company B both start Year 1 with $1 million of shareholders' equity and 100,000 shares of common stock outstanding. During Year 1, both companies earn net income of $100,000, a rate of return of 10 percent on common shareholders' equity at the beginning of the year. Company A declares and pays $100,000 of dividends to common shareholders at the end of Year 1, whereas Company B retains all its earnings and declares no dividends. During Year 2, both companies earn net income equal to 10 percent of shareholders' equity at the beginning of Year 2.

    a. Compute earnings per share for Company A and for Company B for Year 1 and for Year 2.

    b. Compute the rate of growth in earnings per share for Company A and Company B, comparing earnings per share in Year 2 with earnings per share in Year 1.

    c. Using the rate of growth in earnings per share as the criterion, which company's management appears to be doing a better job for its sharehold-ers? Comment on this result.

21. **Calculating and interpreting short-term liquidity ratios.** Data taken from the financial statement of Digital Equipment Corporation, a computer manu-facturer, appear as follows (amounts in millions):

For the Year	Year 6	Year 7	Year 8
Revenues....................................	$12,742	$12,943	$13,911
Cost of Goods Sold.........................	6,242	6,795	7,278
Net Income	1,073	74	(617)
Cash Flow from Operations..................	1,479	1,434	1,041

On December 31	Year 5	Year 6	Year 7	Year 8
Cash	$2,164	$1,655	$2,009	$1,924
Accounts Receivable.................	2,592	2,966	3,207	3,317
Inventories.........................	1,575	1,638	1,538	1,595
Prepayments........................	59	636	868	818
Total Current Assets	$6,390	$6,895	$7,622	$7,654
Accounts Payable	$ 523	$ 554	$ 661	$ 773
Bank Loans.........................	155	30	13	23
Other Current Liabilities	1,736	1,810	2,616	3,295
Total Current Liabilities	$2,414	$2,394	$3,290	$4,091

a. Compute the current and quick ratios on December 31 of each year.
b. Compute the cash flow from operations to current liabilities ratio and the accounts receivable, inventory, and accounts payable ratios for Year 6, Year 7, and Year 8.
c. How has the short-term liquidity risk of Digital Equipment Corporation changed during the 3-year period?

22. **Relating profitability to short-term liquidity.** Following is a schedule of the current assets and current liabilities of the Lewis Company.

	December 31	
	Year 2	Year 1
Current Assets:		
Cash	$ 355,890	$ 212,790
Accounts Receivable...........................	389,210	646,010
Inventories.....................................	799,100	1,118,200
Prepayments...................................	21,600	30,000
Total Current Assets	$1,565,800	$2,007,000
Current Liabilities:		
Accounts Payable	$ 152,760	$ 217,240
Accrued Payroll, Taxes, etc.	126,340	318,760
Notes Payable	69,500	330,000
Total Current Liabilities	$ 348,600	$ 866,000

During Year 2, the Lewis Company operated at a loss of $100,000. Depreciation expense during year 2 was $30,000.
a. Calculate the current ratio for each date.
b. Calculate the amount of cash provided by operations for Year 2.
c. Explain how the improved current ratio is possible under the Year 2 operating conditions.

23. **Calculating and interpreting long-term liquidity ratios.** Data taken from the financial statement of Humana, Inc., a hospital management company, appear below (amounts in millions):

For the Year	Year 2	Year 3	Year 4
Net Income before Interest and Income Taxes	$475	$484	$499
Cash Flow from Operations.	365	409	480
Interest Expense	164	154	146

On December 31	Year 1	Year 2	Year 3	Year 4
Long-Term Debt	$1,206	$1,216	$1,237	$1,211
Total Liabilities	1,817	2,020	2,197	2,268
Total Shareholders' Equity	902	896	1,012	1,154

   a. Compute the long-term debt ratio and the debt-equity ratio at the end of Year 2, Year 3, and Year 4.
   b. Compute the cash flow from operations to total liabilities ratio and the interest coverage ratio for Year 2 through Year 4.
   c. How has the long-term liquidity risk of Humana, Inc., changed over this 3-year period?

24. **Calculating and interpreting long-term liquidity ratios.** Data taken from the financial statements of Scott Paper Company (forest products company) appear below (amounts in millions):

For the Year	Year 5	Year 6	Year 7
Net Income before Interest Expense and Income Taxes	$699	$355	$131
Cash Flow from Operations.	496	566	582
Interest Expense	158	199	221

On December 31	Year 4	Year 5	Year 6	Year 7
Long-Term Debt	$1,450	$1,678	$2,455	$2,333
Total Liabilities	3,204	3,678	4,718	4,504
Shareholders' Equity	1,952	2,068	2,182	1,989

   a. Compute the long-term debt ratio and the debt-equity ratio at the end of each year.
   b. Compute the cash flow from operations to total liabilities ratio and the interest coverage ratio for Year 5 through Year 7.
   c. How has the long-term liquidity risk of Scott Paper Company changed over this period?

25. **Effect of various transactions on financial statement ratios.** Indicate the immediate effects (increase, decrease, no effect) of each of the following independent transactions on (1) the rate of return on common shareholders' equity, (2) the current ratio, and (3) the debt-equity ratio. State any necessary assumptions.

a. A firm purchases merchandise inventory costing $205,000 on account.

b. A firm sells for $150,000 on account merchandise inventory costing $120,000.

c. A firm collects $100,000 from customers on accounts receivable.

d. A firm pays $160,000 to suppliers on accounts payable.

e. A firm sells for $10,000 a machine costing $40,000 and with accumulated depreciation of $30,000.

f. A firm declares dividends of $80,000. It will pay the dividends during the next accounting period.

g. A firm issues common stock for $75,000.

h. A firm acquires a machine costing $60,000. It gives $10,000 cash and signs a note for $50,000 payable 5 years from now for the balance of the purchase price.

26. **Effect of various transactions on financial statement ratios.** Indicate the effects (increase, decrease, no effect) of the following independent transactions on (1) earnings per share, (2) working capital, and (3) the quick ratio, where accounts receivable are *included* but merchandise inventory is *excluded* from quick assets. State any necessary assumptions.

a. A firm sells on account for $300,000 merchandise inventory costing $240,000.

b. A firm declares dividends of $160,000. It will pay the dividends during the next accounting period.

c. A firm purchases merchandise inventory costing $410,000 on account.

d. A firm sells for $20,000 a machine costing $80,000 and with accumulated depreciation of $60,000.

e. Because of defects, a firm returns to the supplier merchandise inventory purchased for $7,000 cash. The firm receives a cash reimbursement.

f. A firm issues 10,000 shares of $10 par value common stock on the last day of the accounting period for $15 per share. It uses the proceeds to acquire the assets of another firm composed of the following: accounts receivable, $30,000; merchandise inventory, $60,000; plant and equipment, $100,000. The acquiring firm also agrees to assume current liabilities of $40,000 of the acquired company.

Problems

27. **Calculating and interpreting profitability and risk ratios.** Wal-Mart Stores, Inc., is the largest retailing company in the United States. It maintains a chain of discount stores primarily in the southern and eastern sections of the United States. In recent years, it has expanded operations into warehouse clubs. Exhibit 18.17 presents comparative balance sheets, Exhibit 18.18 presents comparative income statements, and Exhibit 18.19 presents comparative statements of cash flows for Wal-Mart Stores for 3 recent years. Exhibit 18.20 presents a financial statement ratio analysis for Wal-Mart Stores for Year 10 and Year 11. The income tax rate is 34 percent.

a. Compute the amounts of the ratios listed in Exhibit 18.20 for Year 12.

Exhibit 18.17

WAL-MART STORES, INC.
Comparative Balance Sheets
(amounts in millions)

	Year 9	Year 10	Year 11	Year 12
Assets				
Cash	$ 13	$ 13	$ 13	$ 31
Accounts Receivable	127	156	305	419
Inventories	3,351	4,428	5,809	7,384
Prepayments	140	116	288	741
Total Current Assets	$3,631	$4,713	$ 6,415	$ 8,575
Property, Plant, and Equipment				
(net)	2,662	3,430	4,711	6,434
Other Assets	67	56	262	434
Total Assets	$6,360	$8,199	$11,388	$15,443
Liabilities and Shareholders' Equity				
Accounts Payable	$1,390	$1,827	$ 2,651	$ 3,454
Notes Payable	40	209	425	494
Other Current Liabilities	636	810	913	1,056
Total Current Liabilities	$2,066	$2,846	$ 3,989	$ 5,004
Long-term Debt	1,194	1,273	1,899	3,278
Other Noncurrent Liabilities	92	115	134	172
Total Liabilities	$3,352	$4,234	$ 6,022	$ 8,454
Common Stock	$ 57	$ 57	$ 114	$ 115
Additional Paid-in Capital	174	180	416	625
Retained Earnings	2,777	3,728	4,836	6,249
Total Shareholders' Equity	$3,008	$3,965	$ 5,366	$ 6,989
Total Liabilities and Shareholders'				
Equity	$6,360	$8,199	$11,388	$15,443

Exhibit 18.18

WAL-MART STORES, INC.
Comparative Income Statements
(amounts in millions)
(Problem 27)

	Year 10	Year 11	Year 12
Sales Revenue	$25,986	$32,864	$44,289
Expenses:			
Cost of Goods Sold	$20,070	$25,500	$34,786
Selling and Administrative	4,070	5,152	6,684
Interest	138	169	266
Income Taxes	632	752	945
Total Expenses	$24,910	$31,573	$42,681
Net Income	$ 1,076	$ 1,291	$ 1,608

Exhibit 18.19

WAL-MART STORES, INC.
Comparative Statements of Cash Flows
(amounts in millions)
(Problem 27)

	Year 10	Year 11	Year 12
Operations			
Net Income	$ 1,076	$ 1,291	$ 1,608
Depreciation Expense	269	347	475
Other.......................................	5	3	(8)
(Increase) in Accounts Receivable............	(29)	(58)	(114)
(Increase) in Inventories.....................	(1,077)	(1,088)	(1,460)
(Increase) Decrease in Prepayments	(11)	12	(10)
Increase in Accounts Payable.................	437	689	710
Increase in Other Current Liabilities	197	100	156
Cash Flow from Operations.................	$ 867	$ 1,296	$ 1,357
Investing			
Acquisition of Property, Plant, and			
Equipment	$(1,086)	$(1,533)	$(2,142)
Other.......................................	7	7	(8)
Cash Flow from Investing	$(1,079)	$(1,526)	$(2,150)
Financing			
Increase in Short-term Borrowing..............	$ 166	$ 30	$ 58
Increase in Long-term Borrowing	189	500	1,010
Increase in Common Stock	6	5	13
Decrease in Long-term Borrowing	(25)	(134)	(75)
Acquisition of Common Stock	—	(26)	—
Dividends	(124)	(159)	(195)
Other.......................................	—	14	—
Cash Flow from Financing.................	$ 212	$ 230	$ 811
Change in Cash	$ 0	$ 0	$ 18
Cash, Beginning of Year	13	13	13
Cash, End of Year...........................	$ 13	$ 13	$ 31

b. What is the likely reason for the changes in Wal-Mart's rate of return on assets during the 3-year period? Analyze the financial ratios to the maximum depth possible.

c. What is the likely reason for the changes in Wal-Mart's rate of return on common shareholders' equity during the 3-year period?

d. How has the short-term liquidity risk of Wal-Mart changed during the 3-year period?

e. How has the long-term liquidity risk of Wal-Mart changed during the 3-year period?

28. Calculating and interpreting profitability and risk ratios. NIKE and Reebok maintain dominant market shares in the athletic footwear market. NIKE places somewhat greater emphasis on the performance characteristics of its footwear, while Reebok places somewhat greater emphasis on the fashion

---

Exhibit 18.20

WAL-MART STORES, INC.
Financial Ratio Analysis
(Problem 27)

	Year 10	Year 11
Rate of Return on Assets	16.0%	14.3%
Profit Margin for Rate of Return on Assets	4.5%	4.3%
Total Assets Turnover	3.6	3.4
Cost of Goods Sold/Sales	77.2%	77.6%
Selling and Administrative Expense/Sales	15.7%	15.7%
Interest Expense/Sales	.5%	.5%
Income Tax Expense/Sales	2.4%	2.3%
Accounts Receivable Turnover Ratio	183.6	142.6
Inventory Turnover Ratio	5.2	5.0
Plant Assets Turnover Ratio	8.5	8.1
Rate of Return on Common Shareholders' Equity	30.9%	27.7%
Profit Margin for Return on Common Shareholders' Equity	4.1%	3.9%
Leverage Ratio	2.09	2.10
Current Ratio	1.66	1.61
Quick Ratio	.06	.08
Cash Flow from Operations to Current Liabilities Ratio	35.3%	37.9%
Accounts Payable Turnover Ratio	13.1	12.0
Long-term Debt Ratio	24.3%	26.1%
Debt-Equity Ratio	51.6%	52.9%
Cash Flow from Operations to Total Liabilities Ratio	22.9%	25.3%
Interest Coverage Ratio	13.4	13.1

Exhibit 18.21

NIKE AND REEBOK
Comparative Balance Sheets
(amounts in millions)
(Problem 28)

	NIKE		Reebok	
	Year 10	Year 11	Year 10	Year 11
Assets				
Cash	$ 90	$ 120	$ 227	$ 85
Accounts Receivable	401	522	391	425
Inventories	309	587	367	437
Prepayments	38	51	45	80
Total Current Assets	$ 838	$1,280	$1,030	$1,027
Property, Plant, and Equipment (net)	160	292	111	146
Other Assets	97	136	262	258
Total Assets	$1,095	$1,708	$1,403	$1,431

(continued)

Exhibit 18.21 *(continued)*

	NIKE		Reebok	
	Year 10	Year 11	Year 10	Year 11
Liabilities and Shareholders' Equity				
Accounts Payable	$ 107	$ 166	$ 166	$ 308
Bank Loans	39	301	70	40
Other Current Liabilities	127	161	58	76
Total Current Liabilities	$ 273	$ 628	$ 294	$ 424
Long-term Debt	26	30	106	170
Other Noncurrent Liabilities	11	18	6	13
Total Liabilities	$ 310	$ 676	$ 406	$ 607
Common Stock	$ 3	$ 3	$ 1	$ 1
Additional Paid-in Capital	79	85	281	503
Retained Earnings	703	944	715	924
Treasury Stock	—	—	—	(604)
Total Shareholders' Equity	$ 785	$1,032	$ 997	$ 824
Total Liabilities and Shareholders' Equity	$1,095	$1,708	$1,403	$1,431

characteristics of its footwear. Exhibit 18.21 presents comparative balance sheets for NIKE and Reebok at the end of Year 10 and Year 11. Exhibit 18.22 presents an income statement for each firm for Year 11. Cash flow from operations for Year 11 were $14 million for NIKE and $339 million for Reebok. The income tax rate is 34 percent. On the basis of this information and appropriate financial statement ratios, which company is

a. More profitable?
b. Less risky in terms of short-term liquidity?
c. Less risky in terms of long-term solvency?

Exhibit 18.22

NIKE AND REEBOK
Comparative Income Statements
(amounts in millions)
(Problem 28)

	For Year 11	
	NIKE	Reebok
Sales Revenues	$3,004	$2,746
Expenses:		
Cost of Goods Sold	$1,851	$1,645
Selling and Administrative	664	683
Interest	27	29
Income Taxes	175	154
Total Expenses	$2,717	$2,511
Net Income	$ 287	$ 235

Cases

29. **Case introducing earnings-per-share calculations for a complex capital structure.** The Layton Ball Corporation has a relatively complicated capital structure. In addition to common shares, it has issued stock options, warrants, and convertible bonds. Exhibit 18.23 summarizes some pertinent information about these items. Net income for the year is $9,500, and the income tax rate used in computing income tax expense is 40 percent of pretax income.

a. First, ignore all items of capital except for the common shares. Calculate earnings per common share.

b. In past years, employees have been issued options to purchase shares of stock. Exhibit 18.23 indicates that the price of the common stock throughout the year was $25 but that the stock options could be exercised at any time for $15 each. The option allows the holder to surrender it along with $15 cash and receive one share in return. Thus the number of shares would increase, which would decrease the earnings-per-share figure. The company would, however, have more cash. Assume that the holders of options tender them, along with $15 each, to purchase shares. Assume that the company uses the cash to purchase shares for the treasury at a price of $25 each. Compute a new earnings-per-share figure. (Treasury shares are *not* counted in the denominator of the earnings-per-share calculation.)

c. Exhibit 18.23 indicates that there were also warrants outstanding in the hands of the public. The warrant allows the holder to turn in that warrant, along with $30 cash, to purchase one share of stock. If holders exercised the warrants, the number of outstanding shares would increase, which would reduce earnings per share. However, the company would have more cash, which it could use to purchase shares for the treasury, reducing the number of shares outstanding. Assume that all holders of warrants exercise them. Assume that the company uses the cash to purchase out-

Exhibit 18.23

LAYTON BALL CORPORATION
Information on Capital Structure for Earnings-per-Share Calculation
(Problem 29)

Assume the following data about the capital structure and earnings for the Layton Ball Corporation for the year:	
Number of Common Shares Outstanding throughout the Year . . .	2,500 shares
Market Price per Common Share throughout the Year	$25
Options Outstanding during the Year:	
Number of Shares Issuable on Exercise of Options	1,000 shares
Exercise Price per Share	$15
Warrants Outstanding during the Year:	
Number of Shares Issuable on Exercise of Warrants	2,000 shares
Exercise Price per Share	$30
Convertible Bonds Outstanding:	
Number (issued 15 years ago)	100 bonds
Proceeds per Bond at Time of Issue (= par value)	$1,000
Shares of Common Issuable on Conversion (per bond)	10 shares
Coupon Rate (per year)	$4\frac{1}{8}$ percent

standing shares for the treasury. Compute a new earnings-per-share figure. (Ignore the information about options and the calculations in part **b** at this point.) Note that a rational warrant holder would *not* exercise his or her warrants for $30 when a share could be purchased for $25.

d. There were also convertible bonds outstanding. The convertible bond entitles the holder to trade in that bond for 10 shares. If holders convert the bonds, the number of shares would increase, which would tend to reduce earnings per share. On the other hand, the company would not have to pay interest and thus would have no interest expense on the bond, because it would no longer be outstanding. This would tend to increase income and earnings per share. Assume that all holders of convertible bonds convert their bonds into shares. Compute a new net income figure (do not forget income tax effects on income of the interest saved) and a new earnings-per-share figure. (Ignore the information about options and warrants and the calculations in parts **b** and **c** at this point.)

e. Now consider all the previous calculations. Which sets of assumptions from parts **b, c,** and **d** lead to the lowest possible earnings per share when they are all made simultaneously? Compute a new earnings per share under the most restrictive set of assumptions about reductions in earnings per share.

f. Accountants publish several earnings-per-share figures for companies with complicated capital structures and complicated events during the year. *The Wall Street Journal,* however, publishes only one figure in its daily columns (where it reports the price-earnings ratio—the price of a share of stock divided by its earnings per share). Which of the figures computed previously for earnings per share do you think *The Wall Street Journal* should report as *the* earnings-per-share figure? Why?

30. **Detective analysis: identify the company.** In this problem, you become a financial analyst/detective. Exhibit 18.24 expresses condensed financial statements for 13 companies on a percentage basis. In all cases, total sales revenues appear as 100.00%. All other numbers were divided by sales revenue for the year. The 13 companies (all corporations except for the accounting firm) shown on the next page represent the following industries:

(1) Advertising agency.
(2) Computer manufacturer.
(3) Department store chain (that carries its own receivables).
(4) Distiller of hard liquor.
(5) Electric utility.
(6) Finance company (lends money to consumers).
(7) Grocery store chain.
(8) Insurance company.
(9) Pharmaceutical company.
(10) Public accounting (CPA) partnership.
(11) Soft drink company.
(12) Steel manufacturer.
(13) Tobacco products company.

Exhibit 18.24

Data for Ratio Detective Exercise
(Problem 30)

	Company Numbers						
	(1)	(2)	(3)	(4)	(5)	(6)	(7)
Balance Sheet at End of Year:							
Current Receivables	1.20%	29.11%	15.80%	13.70%	22.65%	14.11%	8.38%
Inventories.....................	9.18	0.00	6.87	23.19	16.40	14.02	8.54
Net Plant and Equipment*	5.12	9.63	10.77	16.01	29.68	17.62	24.97
All Other Assets	3.64	7.02	37.91	25.63	13.49	38.18	46.45
Total Assets	19.14%	45.76%	71.35%	78.53%	82.22%	83.93%	88.34%
*Cost of Plant and Equipment (gross)	17.71%	14.80%	21.50%	29.47%	42.79%	27.07%	38.41%
Current Liabilities	7.87%	9.82%	21.87%	14.09%	14.34%	22.39%	35.58%
Long-term Liabilities	2.06	7.96	12.30	16.07	41.56	39.38	14.51
Owners' Equity	9.21	27.98	37.18	48.37	26.32	22.16	38.25
Total Equities	19.14%	45.76%	71.35%	78.53%	82.22%	83.93%	88.34%
Income Statement for Year:							
Revenues......................	100.00%	100.00%	100.00%	100.00%	100.00%	100.00%	100.00%
Cost of Goods Sold (excluding depreciation) or Operating Expenses[a]	77.17%	53.77%	53.93%	33.99%	69.14%	45.37%	40.17%
Depreciation	1.23	1.39	7.55	1.95	3.01	2.65	2.26
Interest Expense	2.44	0.52	2.88	.91	2.98	2.92	1.66
Advertising Expense	.89	0.00	0.00	1.38	2.53	4.29	8.54
Research and Development Expense....................	0.00	1.00	10.95	0.00	0.00	0.70	0.00
Income Taxes	1.08	0.53	2.88	5.09	2.65	5.39	6.61
All Other Items (net)	15.29	18.87	15.98	47.05	14.84	31.72	26.78
Total Expenses...............	98.10%	76.08%	94.17%	90.37%	95.15%	93.04%	86.02%
Net Income	1.90%	23.92%	5.83%	9.63%	4.85%	6.96%	13.98%

(continued)

Use whatever clues you can to match the companies in Exhibit 18.24 with the industries listed above. You may find it useful to refer to average industry ratios compiled by Dun & Bradstreet, Prentice-Hall, Robert Morris Associates, and the Federal Trade Commission. Most libraries carry copies of these documents.

31. **Interpreting profitability and risk ratios.** The BF Goodrich Company manufactures a broad range of specialty chemical products, with an emphasis on products with a petroleum base. Its manufacturing facilities are capital intensive (property, plant, and equipment comprise approximately 50 percent of total assets). Exhibit 18.25 presents financial statement ratios for BF Goodrich Company for 3 recent years.

   a. What are the likely reasons for the declining profit margin for rate of return on assets?

Exhibit 18.24 *(continued)*

Data for Ratio Detective Exercise
(Problem 30)

	Company Numbers					
	(8)	**(9)**	**(10)**	**(11)**	**(12)**	**(13)**
Balance Sheet at End of Year:						
Current Receivables	9.22%	14.58%	6.89%	113.30%	48.15%	295.65%
Inventories................................	7.81	13.92	7.72	0.00	0.00	0.00
Net Plant and Equipment*	55.55	66.06	152.60	13.07	8.97	10.95
All Other Assets..........................	18.71	50.38	18.99	62.50	241.21	647.73
Total Assets	91.29%	144.94%	186.20%	188.87%	298.33%	954.33%
*Cost of Plant and Equipment (gross)	146.54%	92.26%	207.74%	17.81%	15.12%	12.21%
Current Liabilities	15.96%	39.68%	16.73%	129.32%	228.94%	515.13%
Long-term Liabilities	37.18	18.53	79.94	22.30	11.19	320.34
Owners' Equity	38.15	86.73	89.53	37.25	58.20	118.86
Total Equities	91.29%	144.94%	186.20%	188.87%	298.33%	954.33%
Income Statement for Year:						
Revenues................................	100.00%	100.00%	100.00%	100.00%	100.00%	100.00%
Cost of Goods Sold (excluding depreciation) or Operating Expenses[a]	83.78%	28.89%	75.03%	87.69%	87.78%	26.86%
Depreciation	6.20	5.23	5.97	2.02	0.08	0.00
Interest Expense	1.23	.70	4.45	1.38	0.00	55.48
Advertising Expense	0.00	.37	0.00	0.00	0.00	0.00
Research and Development Expense...............................	.55	13.39	0.00	0.00	0.00	0.00
Income Taxes	.23	9.86	5.04	5.23	2.83	7.82
All Other Items (net)	3.33	18.60	(.45)	(2.17)	0.00	(2.01)
Total Expenses.........................	95.32%	77.04%	90.04%	94.15%	90.69%	88.15%
Net Income	4.68%	22.96%	9.96%	5.85%	9.31%	11.85%

[a]Represents operating expenses for the following companies: advertising agency, insurance company, finance company, and the public accounting partnership.

   b. What are the likely reasons for the declining total assets turnover?
   c. What are the likely reasons for the declining rate of return on common shareholders' equity?
   d. BF Goodrich's current ratio increased between Year 5 and Year 6, yet its quick ratio remained constant. What explanation might account for the difference in the trend of these ratios between these 2 years?
   e. What are the likely reasons for the decrease in the current and quick ratios between Year 6 and Year 7?
   f. What are the likely explanations for the decrease in the two cash flow from operations to liabilities ratios between Year 6 and Year 7?
32. Interpreting profitability and risk ratios. Digital Equipment Company (DEC) manufactures and services a broad line of computer hardware and

Exhibit 18.25

BF GOODRICH COMPANY
Financial Statement Ratios
(Problem 31)

	Year 5	Year 6	Year 7
Rate of Return on Assets	11.9%	9.0%	5.7%
Profit Margin for Rate of Return on Assets	9.9%	8.0%	5.5%
Total Assets Turnover	1.2	1.1	1.0
Cost of Goods Sold/Sales	70.1%	70.2%	74.2%
Selling and Administrative Expense/Sales	17.5%	19.5%	19.6%
Income Tax Expense on Operating Income/ Sales	2.5%	3.5%	1.1%
Interest Expense/Sales	1.8%	1.5%	1.1%
Income Tax Savings on Interest Expense/Sales	.6	.5	.4
Accounts Receivable Turnover Ratio	8.8	8.0	7.6
Inventory Turnover Ratio	5.0	4.7	5.0
Plant Assets Turnover Ratio	2.6	2.5	2.3
Rate of Return on Common Shareholders' Equity	20.9%	14.6%	8.9%
Profit Margin for Return on Common Shareholders' Equity	8.8%	7.1%	4.8%
Leverage Ratio	2.1	2.0	1.9
Current Ratio	2.04	2.14	1.40
Quick Ratio	1.22	1.22	.78
Cash Flow from Operations to Current Liabilities Ratio	53.0%	56.3%	29.0%
Accounts Payable Turnover Ratio	7.6	7.3	7.9
Long-term Debt Ratio	19.6%	18.4%	13.2%
Debt-Equity Ratio	43.8%	43.3%	42.2%
Cash Flow from Operations to Total Liabilities Ratio	28.4%	29.1%	16.0%
Interest Coverage Ratio	6.82	7.78	6.12

Trend Ratios (Year 4 = 100)

Sales	115	120	120
Net Income	98	82	55
Total Assets	107	117	122
Capital Expenditures	127	169	170

software. DEC's sales mix and gross margins for Year 7, Year 8, and Year 9 are as follows:

	Year 7	Year 8	Year 9
Sales Mix			
Product Sales	67%	66%	64%
Services	33	34	36
	100%	100%	100%
Gross Margin			
Product Sales	59.5%	59.7%	57.7%
Services	36.8%	38.3%	39.1%

Exhibit 18.26 presents profitability and risk ratios for DEC for these 3 years.

a. What are the likely explanations for the decreased rate of return on assets between Year 8 (14.4 percent) and Year 9 (10.6 percent)?

b. How does one reconcile a constant total assets turnover in light of the changes in the individual assets turnovers for accounts receivable, inventories, and plant assets?

c. The rate of return on assets decreased between Year 7 and Year 8, yet the rate of return on common shareholders' equity remained the same. Explain this apparent paradox.

d. What are the likely explanations for the decrease in the current ratio and quick ratio between Year 7 and Year 8?

e. What is the likely explanation for the decrease in the two cash flow from operations to liabilities ratios between Year 7 and Year 9?

Exhibit 18.26

DIGITAL EQUIPMENT CORPORATION
Financial Statement Ratios
(Problem 32)

	Year 7	Year 8	Year 9
Rate of Return on Assets	15.3%	14.4%	10.6%
Profit Margin for Rate of Return on Assets	12.7%	11.6%	8.6%
Total Assets Turnover	1.2	1.2	1.2
Cost of Goods and Services Sold/Sales	48.1%	47.6%	49.0%
Selling and Administrative Expense/Sales	23.4%	26.7%	28.6%
Research and Development Expense/Sales	10.8%	11.4%	12.0%
Interest Expense/Sales	1.1%	.3%	.3%
Income Tax Expense/Sales	5.9%	3.8%	2.7%
Accounts Receivable Turnover Ratio	4.5	4.7	4.6
Inventory Turnover Ratio	3.4	3.6	3.9
Plant Assets Turnover Ratio	4.7	4.4	3.8
Rate of Return on Common Shareholders' Equity	18.9%	18.9%	13.8%
Profit Margin for Return on Common Shareholders' Equity	12.1%	11.4%	8.4%
Leverage Ratio	1.3	1.3	1.3
Current Ratio	3.40	2.87	2.88
Quick Ratio	2.43	1.97	1.93
Cash Flow from Operations to Current Liabilities Ratio	114.0%	80.0%	62.0%
Accounts Payable Turnover Ratio	13.8	11.7	11.7
Long-term Debt Ratio	4.1%	1.6%	1.7%
Debt-Equity Ratio	25.1%	25.7%	24.7%
Cash Flow from Operations to Total Liabilities Ratio	93.0%	72.0%	57.0%
Interest Coverage Ratio	17.6	46.8	37.4
Interperiod Percentage Changes			
Sales	23.7%	22.2%	11.0%
Net Income	84.2%	14.7%	−17.8%
Total Assets	17.2%	20.3%	5.5%
Capital Expenditures	33.7%	202.8%	−19.4%

33. **Case analysis of bankruptcy.** On October 2, 1975, W. T. Grant Company filed for bankruptcy protection under Chapter XI of the Bankruptcy Act. At that time, assets totaled $1.02 billion and liabilities totaled $1.03 billion. The company operated at a profit for most years prior to 1974, but reported an operating loss of $177 million for its fiscal year January 31, 1974, to January 31, 1975.

The accompanying Exhibits 18.27 through 18.30 contain the following:
1. Balance sheets, income statements, and statements of cash flows for W. T. Grant Company for the 1971 through 1975 fiscal periods.

Exhibit 18.27

W. T. GRANT COMPANY
Comparative Balance Sheets
(Problem 33)

	January 31				
	1971	**1972**	**1973**	**1974**	**1975**
Assets:					
Cash and Marketable Securities.............	$ 34,009	$ 49,851	$ 30,943	$ 45,951	$ 79,642
Accounts Receivable.......................	419,731	477,324	542,751	598,799	431,201
Inventories................................	260,492	298,676	399,533	450,637	407,357
Other Current Assets	5,246	5,378	6,649	7,299	6,581
Total Current Assets	$719,478	$831,229	$ 979,876	$1,102,686	$ 924,781
Investments...............................	23,936	32,367	35,581	45,451	49,764
Property, Plant, and Equipment (net)	61,832	77,173	91,420	100,984	101,932
Other Assets..............................	2,382	3,901	3,821	3,862	5,790
Total Assets	$807,628	$944,670	$1,110,698	$1,252,983	$1,082,267
Equities:					
Short-term Debt	$246,420	$237,741	$ 390,034	$ 453,097	$ 600,695
Accounts Payable	118,091	124,990	112,896	103,910	147,211
Current Deferred Taxes	94,489	112,846	130,137	133,057	2,000
Total Current Liabilities	$459,000	$475,577	$ 633,067	$ 690,064	$ 749,906
Long-term Debt	32,301	128,432	126,672	220,336	216,341
Noncurrent Deferred Taxes	8,518	9,664	11,926	14,649	—
Other Long-term Liabilities................	5,773	5,252	4,694	4,195	2,183
Total Liabilities	$505,592	$618,925	$ 776,359	$ 929,244	$ 968,430
Preferred Stock	$ 9,600	$ 9,053	$ 8,600	$ 7,465	$ 7,465
Common Stock............................	18,180	18,529	18,588	18,599	18,599
Additional Paid-in Capital..................	78,116	85,195	86,146	85,910	83,914
Retained Earnings	230,435	244,508	261,154	248,461	37,674
Total	$336,331	$357,285	$ 374,488	$ 360,435	$ 147,652
Less Cost of Treasury Stock...............	(34,295)	(31,540)	(40,149)	(36,696)	(33,815)
Total Shareholders' Equity................	$302,036	$325,745	$ 334,339	$ 323,739	$ 113,837
Total Equities	$807,628	$944,670	$1,110,698	$1,252,983	$1,082,267

Exhibit 18.28

W. T. GRANT COMPANY
Statement of Income and Retained Earnings
(Problem 33)

	Years Ended January 31				
	1971	**1972**	**1973**	**1974**	**1975**
Sales.................................	$1,254,131	$1,374,811	$1,644,747	$1,849,802	$1,761,952
Concessions	4,986	3,439	3,753	3,971	4,238
Equity in Earnings	2,777	2,383	5,116	4,651	3,086
Other Income	2,874	3,102	1,188	3,063	3,376
Total Revenues	$1,264,768	$1,383,735	$1,654,804	$1,861,487	$1,772,652
Cost of Goods Sold...................	$ 843,192	$ 931,237	$1,125,261	$1,282,945	$1,303,267
Selling, General, and Administration......................	329,768	373,816	444,377	518,280	540,953
Interest..............................	18,874	16,452	21,127	51,047	199,238
Taxes: Current	21,140	13,487	9,588	(6,021)	(19,439)
Deferred	11,660	13,013	16,162	6,807	(98,027)
Other Expenses	557	518	502	—	24,000
Total Expenses....................	$1,225,191	$1,348,523	$1,617,017	$1,853,058	$1,949,992
Net Income	$ 39,577	$ 35,212	$ 37,787	$ 8,429	$ (177,340)
Dividends...........................	(20,821)	(21,139)	(21,141)	(21,122)	(4,457)
Other...............................	—	—	—	—	(28,990)
Change in Retained Earnings	$ 18,756	$ 14,073	$ 16,646	$ (12,693)	$ (210,787)
Retained Earnings— Beg. of Period	211,679	230,435	244,508	261,154	248,461
Retained Earnings— End of Period......................	$ 230,435	$ 244,508	$ 261,154	$ 248,461	$ 37,674

2. Additional financial information about W. T. Grant Company, the retail industry, and the economy for the same period.

Prepare an analysis that explains the major causes of Grant's collapse. You may find it useful to refer to financial and nonfinancial data presented in other sources, such as *The Wall Street Journal,* in addition to that presented here. Assume an income tax rate of 48 percent.

Exhibit 18.29

W. T. GRANT COMPANY
Statement of Cash Flows
(Problem 33)

	Years Ended January 31				
	1971	**1972**	**1973**	**1974**	**1975**
Operations					
Net Income	$39,577	$ 35,212	$ 37,787	$ 8,429	$(177,340)
Additions:					
Depreciation and Other	9,619	10,577	12,004	13,579	14,587
Decrease in Accounts Receivable	—	—	—	—	121,351
Decrease in Inventories	—	—	—	—	43,280
Increase in Accounts Payable................	13,947	6,900	—	—	42,028
Increase in Deferred Taxes	14,046	18,357	17,291	2,920	—
Subtractions:					
Equity in Earnings and Other	(2,470)	(1,758)	(1,699)	(1,344)	(16,993)
Increase in Accounts Receivable	(51,464)	(57,593)	(65,427)	(56,047)	—
Increase in Inventories	(38,365)	(38,184)	(100,857)	(51,104)	—
Increase in Prepayments	(209)	(428)	(1,271)	(651)	(11,032)
Decrease in Accounts Payable..............	—	—	(12,093)	(8,987)	—
Decrease in Deferred Taxes	—	—	—	—	(101,078)
Cash Flow from Operations...................	($15,319)	($ 26,917)	($114,265)	($ 93,205)	($ 85,197)
Investing					
Acquisitions:					
Property, Plant, and Equipment	($16,141)	($ 25,918)	($ 26,250)	($ 23,143)	($ 15,535)
Investments in Securities	(436)	(5,951)	(2,040)	(5,700)	(5,182)
Cash Flow from Investing	($16,577)	($ 31,869)	($ 28,290)	($ 28,843)	($ 20,717)
Financing					
New Financing:					
Short-Term Bank Borrowing	$64,288	—	$152,293	$ 63,063	$147,898
Issue of Long-Term Debt	—	$100,000	—	100,000	—
Sale of Common Stock:					
To Employees...........................	5,218	7,715	3,492	2,584	886
On Open Market	—	2,229	174	260	—
Reduction in Financing:					
Repayment of Short-Term Borrowing (net)	—	(8,680)	—	—	—
Retirement of Long-Term Debt	(1,538)	(5,143)	(1,760)	(6,336)	(3,995)
Reacquisition of Preferred Stock	(948)	(308)	(252)	(618)	—
Reacquisition of Common Stock..............	(13,224)	—	(11,466)	(133)	—
Dividends.................................	(20,821)	(21,138)	(21,141)	(21,122)	(4,457)
Cash Flow from Financing....................	$32,975	$ 74,675	$121,340	$137,698	$140,332
Other.......................................	(47)	(47)	2,307	(642)	(727)
Net Change in Cash	$ 1,032	$ 15,842	$(18,908)	$ 15,008	$ 33,691

Exhibit 18.30

Additional Information
(Problem 33)

	Fiscal Years Ending January 31				
	1971	1972	1973	1974	1975
W. T. Grant Company					
Range of Stock Price, Dollar per Share[a]	$41\frac{7}{8}$–$70\frac{5}{8}$	$34\frac{3}{4}$–$48\frac{3}{4}$	$9\frac{7}{8}$–$44\frac{3}{8}$	$9\frac{5}{8}$–41	$1\frac{1}{2}$–12
Earnings per Share in Dollars	$2.64	$2.25	$2.49	$0.76	$(12.74)
Dividends per Share in Dollars	$1.50	$1.50	$1.50	$1.50	$ 0.30
Number of Stores	1,116	1,168	1,208	1,189	1,152
Total Store Area, Thousands of Square Feet	38,157	44,718	50,619	53,719	54,770

	Calendar Year Ending December 31				
	1970	1971	1972	1973	1974
Retail Industry[b]					
Total Chain Store Industry Sales in Millions of Dollars	$6,969	$6,972	$7,498	$8,212	$8,714

	Calendar Year Ending December 31				
	1970	1971	1972	1973	1974
Aggregate Economy[c]					
Gross National Product in Billions of Dollars	$1,075.3	$1,107.5	$1,171.1	$1,233.4	$1,210
Bank Short-term Lending Rate	8.48%	6.32%	5.82%	8.30%	11.28%

[a]Source: *Standard and Poor's Stock Reports.*
[b]Source: *Standard Industry Surveys.*
[c]Source: *Survey of Current Business.*

Suggested Solutions to Even-Numbered Exercises

12. **Profitability analysis for two types of retailers.** Company A is the specialty retailer (The Limited) because of its higher profit margin and lower total assets turnover, relative to Company B (Wal-Mart).

$$\frac{\text{Rate of Return on Assets}}{} = \frac{\text{Profit Margin Ratio}}{} \times \frac{\text{Total Assets Turnover Ratio}}{}$$

Company A: $\dfrac{\$403 + (1 - .34)(\$257)}{\$3,145} = \dfrac{\$403 + (1 - .34)(\$257)}{\$6,149} \times \dfrac{\$6,149}{\$3,145}$

 18.2 percent = 9.3 percent × 1.96

Company B: $\dfrac{\$1,608 + (1 - .34)(\$266)}{\$13,416} = \dfrac{\$1,608 + (1 - .34)(\$266)}{\$43,887} \times \dfrac{\$43,887}{\$13,416}$

 13.3 percent = 4.1 percent × 3.27

14. **Analyzing inventories over 4 years.**

a.

Year		Numerator	Denominator	Inventory Turnover
5	....	$2,484	$ 989	2.5
6	....	2,656	1,092	2.4
7	....	2,874	1,252	2.3
8	....	2,930	1,408	2.1

b.

Year		Numerator	Denominator	Days Inventory Held
5	....	365	2.5	146
6	....	365	2.4	152
7	....	365	2.3	159
8	....	365	2.1	174

c.

Year		Numerator	Denominator	Cost of Goods Sold Percentage
5	....	$2,484	$ 8,558	29.0%
6	....	2,656	9,189	28.9
7	....	2,874	10,300	27.9
8	....	2,930	11,159	26.3

d. The decreasing inventory turnover coupled with the decreased cost of goods sold percentage suggests a shift in product mix toward slower-moving, higher-margin products. A shift in sales mix toward prescription drugs is consistent with slower inventory turnover and higher gross margin.

16. **Calculating and disaggregating rate of return on common shareholders' equity.**

a.

Year		Numerator	Denominator	Rate of Return on Common Shareholders' Equity
4	....	£ 495	£1,282	38.6%
5	....	574	1,638	35.0
6	....	634	2,090	30.3

b. **Profit Margin**

Year		Numerator	Denominator	Profit Margin
4	....	£ 495	£1,741	28.4%
5	....	574	2,059	27.9
6	....	634	2,570	24.7

Total Assets Turnover

Year	Numerator	Denominator	Total Assets Turnover
4	£1,741	£2,099	.83
5	2,059	2,630	.78
6	2,570	3,184	.81

Leverage Ratio

Year	Numerator	Denominator	Leverage Ratio
4	£2,099	£1,282	1.64
5	2,630	1,638	1.61
6	3,184	2,090	1.52

c. The rate of return on common shareholders' equity declined during the 3 years, the result of decreased profitability and decreased financial leverage. The decreased profitability results primarily from a decreased profit margin. Given the reduced proportion of debt in the capital structure, the declining profitability probably results from lower operating profitability rather than substantially increased interest expense. Average common shareholders' equity increased faster than sales, net income, and assets, suggesting the issuance of additional common stock and/or the retention of earnings.

18. Relating profitability to financial leverage.

a.

Case	Net Income Plus After-tax Interest Expense[a]	After-tax Interest Expense[b]	Net Income[c]	Rate of Return on Common Shareholders' Equity
A	$12	$6.0	$ 6	$ 6/$100 = 6%
B	$16	$6.0	$10	$10/$100 = 10%
C	$16	$7.2	$ 8.8	$ 8.8/$80 = 11%
D	$ 8	$6.0	$ 2	$ 2/$100 = 2%
E	$12	$3.0	$ 9	$ 9/$100 = 9%
F	$10	$3.0	$ 7	$ 7/$100 = 7%

[a]Numerator of the rate of return on assets. In Case A, $12 = .06 × $200.

[b]After-tax cost of borrowing times interest-bearing debt. In Case A, $6.0 = .06 × $100.

[c]Net income plus after-tax interest expense minus after-tax interest expense. In Case A, $6 = $12 − $6.

b. Leverage works successfully in Cases B, C, E, and F with respect to total debt. With respect to interest-bearing debt, leverage works successfully in Cases B and C.

20. **Interpreting changes in earnings per share.**
    a. **Company A Earnings per Share:**

    Year 1 $\dfrac{\$100,000}{100,000\ \text{Shares}} = \$1$ per Share.

    Year 2 $\dfrac{\$100,000}{100,000\ \text{Shares}} = \$1$ per Share.

    Compare B Earnings per Share:

    Year 1 $\dfrac{\$100,000}{100,000\ \text{Shares}} = \$1$ per Share.

    Year 2 $\dfrac{.10 \times (\$1,000,000 + \$100,000)}{100,000\ \text{Shares}} = \$1.10$ per Share.

    b. Company A: No growth.
       Company B: 10 percent annual growth.
    c. Company B: This result is misleading. Comparisons of growth in earnings per share are valid only if firms employ equal amounts of assets in the business. Both the rate of return on assets and on shareholders' equity are better measures of growth performance. Earnings per share results do not, in general (as in this problem), take earnings retention into account.

22. **Relating profitability to short-term liquidity.**
    a.

December 31, Year 1	December 31, Year 2
$\dfrac{\$2,007,000}{\$866,000} = 2.32\!:\!1$	$\dfrac{\$1,565,800}{\$348,600} = 4.49\!:\!1$

    b.

Net Loss	$(100,000)
Additions:	
Depreciation Expense	30,000
Decrease in Accounts Receivable	256,800
Decrease in Inventories	319,100
Decrease in Prepayments	8,400
Subtractions:	
Decrease in Accounts Payable	(64,480)
Decrease in Accrued Payroll, Taxes, etc.	(192,420)
Cash Flow from Operations	$ 257,400

    c. The reduction in both current assets and current liabilities appears to be largely the result of a retrenchment program. The proceeds from reductions in inventories and collections of receivables reduced current indebtedness. The working capital increased slightly, probably through the sale of noncurrent assets. The cash from operations is not reduced by the full amount of the operating loss, but rather by the operating loss less expenses not requiring the use of cash, such as depreciation.

24. Calculating and interpreting long-term liquidity ratios.

a. Long-term Debt Ratio

Year	Numerator	Denominator	Long-Term Debt Ratio
4	$1,450	$1,450 + $1,952	42.6%
5	1,678	1,678 + 2,068	44.8
6	2,455	2,455 + 2,182	52.9
7	2,333	2,333 + 1,989	54.0

Debit-Equity Ratio

Year	Numerator	Denominator	Debt-Equity Ratio
4	$3,204	$3,204 + $1,952	62.1%
5	3,678	3,678 + 2,068	64.0
6	4,718	4,718 + 2,182	68.4
7	4,504	4,504 + 1,989	69.4

b. Cash Flow from Operations to Total Liabilities Ratio

Year	Numerator	Denominator	Cash Flow from Operations to Total Liabilities Ratio
2	$496	.5($3,204 + $3,678)	14.4%
3	566	.5($3,678 + $4,718)	13.5
4	582	.5($4,718 + $4,504)	12.6

Interest Coverage Ratio

Year	Numerator	Denominator	Times Interest Charges Earned
2	$699	$158	4.42
3	355	199	1.78
4	131	221	.59

c. The long-term solvency risk of Scott Paper Company increased during the 3-year period. The debt ratios increased while the cash flow from operations to total liabilities and interest coverage ratios decreased. Increasing amounts of debt coupled with decreased profitability account for the increased long-term solvency risk.

26. **Effect of various transactions on financial statement ratios.**

Transaction	Earnings per Common Share	Working Capital	Quick Ratio
a.	Increase	Increase	Increase
b.	No Effect	Decrease	Decrease
c.	No Effect	No Effect	Decrease
d.	No Effect	Increase	Increase
e.	No Effect	No Effect	Increase
f.	Decrease	Increase	Decrease

Compound Interest Examples and Applications

Learning Objectives

1. Understand why accountants and financial managers need to master compound interest methods.
2. Distinguish between future and present value and between single payments and annuities.
3. Begin practice converting written problem descriptions into a form suitable for analytic solution.
4. Practice finding internal rate of return on a series of equally spaced cash flows.

Managerial accountants and managers deal with interest calculations because expenditures for an asset most often precede the receipts for services that asset produces. Money received sooner is more valuable than money received later. The difference in timing can affect whether or not acquiring an asset is profitable. Amounts of money received at different times are different commodities. Managers use interest calculations to make valid comparisons among amounts of money their firm will pay or receive at different times.

Managers evaluate a series of money payments over time, such as from an investment project, by finding the present value of the series of payments. The *present value* of a series of payments is a single amount of money at the present time that is the economic equivalent of the entire series.

This appendix illustrates the use of compound interest techniques with a comprehensive series of examples, which use the tables appearing after this appendix. Hand-held calculators can do the same computations.

Future Value

If you invest $1 today at 10 percent compounded annually, it will grow to $1.10000 at the end of 1 year, $1.21000 at the end of 2 years, $1.33100 at the end of 3 years, and so on, according to the formula

$$F_n = P(1 + r)^n,$$

where

$$F_n = \text{accumulation or future value}$$
$$P = \text{one-time investment today}$$
$$r = \text{interest rate per period}$$
$$n = \text{number of periods from today.}$$

The amount F_n is the future value of the present payment, P, compounded at r percent per period for n periods. Table 1, at the end of this appendix, shows the future values of $P = \$1$ for various periods and for various interest rates.

Example 1   How much will $1,000 deposited today at 8 percent compounded annually be worth 10 years from now?

One dollar deposited today at 8 percent will grow to $2.15892; therefore $1,000 will grow to $1,000(1.08)^{10} = \$1,000 \times 2.15892 = \$2,158.92$.

Present Value

This section deals with the problems of calculating how much principal, P, you must invest today to have a specified amount, F_n, at the end of n periods. You know the future amount, F_n, the interest rate, r, and the number of periods, n; you want to find P. To have $1 one year from today when deposits earn 8 percent, you must invest P of $.92593 today. That is, $F_1 = P(1.08)^1$ or $\$1 = \$.92593 \times 1.08$. Because $F_n = P(1 + r)^n$, dividing both sides of the equation by $(1 + r)^n$ yields

$$\frac{F_n}{(1 + r)^n} = P,$$

or

$$P = \frac{F_n}{(1 + r)^n} = F_n(1 + r)^{-n}.$$

Table 2 at the end of this appendix shows discount factors or, equivalently, present values of $1 for various interest (or discount) rates for various periods.

Example 2   What is the present value of $1 due 10 years from now if the interest rate (or, equivalently, the discount rate) r is 12 percent per year?

From Table 2, 12-percent column, 10-period row, the present value of $1 to be received 10 periods hence at 12 percent is $.32197.

Exhibit A.1

Verification of Net Present Value of $10,717
Single Cash Flow of $13,500 at the End of Year 3
Discounted at 8 Percent per Year

Year	Beginning Amount	+	Interest at 8 Percent	=	Ending Amount
1	$10,717		$ 857		$11,574
2	11,574		926		12,500
3	12,500		1,000		13,500

Example 3   You project that an investment will generate cash of $13,500 three years from today. What is the net present value of this cash receipt today if the discount rate is 8 percent per year?

One dollar received 3 years hence discounted at 8 percent has a present value of $.79383. See Table 2, 3-period row, 8-percent column. Thus the project has a present value of $13,500 × .79383 = $10,717. Exhibit A.1 shows how $10,717 grows to $13,500 in 3 years.

Changing the Compounding Period: Nominal and Effective Rates

"Twelve percent, compounded annually" is the price for a loan; this price means interest increases, or converts to, principal once a year at the rate of 12 percent. Often, however, the price for a loan states that compounding will take place more than once a year. A savings bank may advertise that it pays interest of 6 percent, compounded quarterly. This kind of payment means that at the end of each quarter the bank credits savings accounts with interest calculated at the rate 1.5 percent (= 6 percent/4). The investor can withdraw the interest payment or leave it on deposit to earn more interest.

If you invest $10,000 today at 12 percent compounded annually, it will grow to a future value 1 year later of $11,200. If the rate of interest is 12 percent compounded semiannually, the bank adds 6-percent interest to the principal every 6 months. At the end of the first 6 months, $10,000 will have grown to $10,600; that amount will grow to $10,600 × 1.06 = $11,236 by the end of the year. Notice that 12 percent compounded semiannually results in the same amount as 12.36 percent compounded annually.

Suppose that the bank quotes interest as 12 percent, compounded quarterly. It will add an additional 3 percent of the principal every 3 months. By the end of the year, $10,000 will grow to $10,000 × $(1.03)^4$ = $10,000 × 1.12551 = $11,255. Twelve percent compounded quarterly is equivalent to 12.55 percent compounded annually. At 12 percent compounded monthly, $1 will grow to $1 × $(1.01)^{12}$ = $1.12683, and $10,000 will grow to $11,268. Thus, 12 percent compounded monthly is equivalent to 12.68 percent compounded annually.

For a given *nominal* rate, such as the 12 percent in the examples above, the more often interest compounds, the higher the *effective* rate of interest paid. If a nominal rate, r, compounds m times per year, the effective rate is equal to $(1 + r/m)^m - 1$.

In practice, to solve problems that require computation of interest quoted at a nominal rate r percent per period compounded m times per period for n periods, use the tables for rate r/m and $m \times n$ periods. For example, 12 percent compounded quarterly for 5 years is equivalent to the rate found in the interest tables for $r = 12/4 = 3$ percent for $m \times n = 4 \times 5 = 20$ periods.

Example 4 What is the future value 5 years hence of $600 invested at 8 percent compounded quarterly?

Eight percent compounded four times per year for 5 years is equivalent to 2 percent per period compounded for 20 periods. Table 1 shows the value of $F_{20} = (1.02)^{20}$ to be 1.48595. Six hundred dollars, then, would grow to $600 \times 1.48595 = \$891.57$.

Example 5 How much money must you invest today at 12 percent compounded semiannually to have $1,000 four years from today?

Twelve percent compounded two times a year for 4 years is equivalent to 6 percent per period compounded for 8 periods. The *present value,* Table 2, of $1 received 8 periods hence at 6 percent per period is $.62741; that is, $.62741 invested today for 8 periods at an interest rate of 6 percent per period will grow to $1. To have $1,000 in 8 periods (4 years), you must invest $627.41 ($= \$1,000 \times \$.62741$) today.

Example 6 A local department store offers its customers credit and advertises its interest rate at 18 percent per year, compounded monthly at the rate of $1\frac{1}{2}$ percent per month. What is the effective annual interest rate?

One and one-half percent per month for 12 months is equivalent to $(1.015)^{12} - 1 = 19.562$ percent per year. See Table 1, 12-period row, $1\frac{1}{2}$-percent column, where the factor is 1.19562.

Example 7 If prices increased at the rate of 6 percent during each of two consecutive 6-month periods, how much did prices increase during the entire year?

If a price index is 100.00 at the start of the year, it will be $100.00 \times (1.06)^2 = 112.36$ at the end of the year. The price change for the entire year is $(112.36/100.00) - 1 = 12.36$ percent.

Annuities

An *annuity* is a series of equal payments, one per equally spaced period of time. Examples of annuities include monthly rental payments, semiannual corporate bond coupon (or interest) payments, and annual payments to a lessor under a lease contract. Armed with an understanding of the tables for future and present values, you can solve any annuity problem. Annuities arise so often, however, and their solution is so tedious without special tables or calculator functions that annuity problems merit special study and the use of special tables or functions.

Terminology for Annuities

Annuity terminology can confuse you because not all writers use the same terms.

An annuity with payments occurring at the end of each period is an *ordinary annuity* or an *annuity in arrears*. Semiannual corporate bonds usually promise coupon payments paid in arrears or, equivalently, the first payment does not occur until after the bond has been outstanding for 6 months.

An annuity with payments occurring at the beginning of each period is an *annuity due* or an *annuity in advance*. Rent paid at the beginning of each month is an annuity due.

In a *deferred annuity,* the first payment occurs some time later than the end of the first period.

Annuities payments can go on forever. Such annuities are *perpetuities*. Bonds that promise payments forever are *consols*. The British and Canadian governments have issued consols from time to time. A perpetuity can be in arrears or in advance. The two differ only in the timing of the first payment.

Annuities may confuse you. Studying them is easier with a time line such as the one shown below.

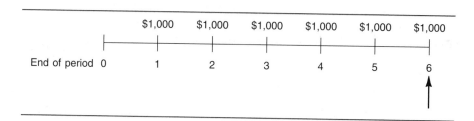

A time line marks the end of each period, numbers the period, shows the payments the investor receives or pays, and shows the time in which the accountant wants to value the annuity. The time line above represents an ordinary annuity (in arrears) for six periods of $1,000 to be valued at the end of period 6. The end of period 0 is "now." The first payment occurs one period from now. The arrow points to the valuation date.

Ordinary Annuities (Annuities in Arrears)

The future values of ordinary annuities appear in Table 3 at the end of this appendix.

Consider an ordinary annuity for three periods at 12 percent. The time line for the future value of such an annuity is

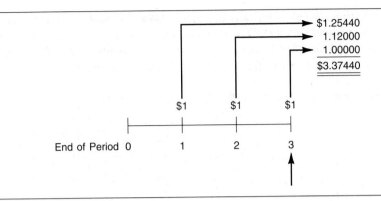

The $1 received at the end of the first period earns interest for two periods, so it is worth $1.25440 at the end of period 3. (See Table 1.) The $1 received at the end of the second period grows to $1.12000 by the end of period 3, and the $1 received at the end of period 3 is, of course, worth $1.00000 at the end of period 3. The entire annuity is worth $3.37440 at the end of period 3. This amount appears in Table 3 for the future value of an ordinary annuity for three periods at 12 percent. Factors for the future value of an annuity for a particular number of periods sum the factors for the future value of $1 for each of the periods. The future value of an ordinary annuity is

$$\frac{\text{Future Value of}}{\text{Ordinary Annuity}} = \frac{\text{Periodic}}{\text{Payment}} \times \frac{\text{Factor for the Future}}{\text{Value of an Ordinary}}_{\text{Annuity.}}$$

Thus,

$$\$3.37440 \quad = \quad \$1 \quad \times \quad 3.37440.$$

Table 4 at the end of this appendix shows the present value of ordinary annuities.

The time line for the present value of an ordinary annuity of $1 per period for three periods, discounted at 12 percent, is

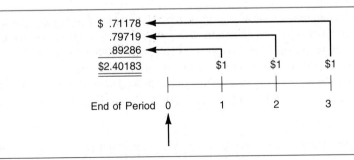

The $1 the investor receives at the end of period 1 has a present value of $.89286, the $1 the investor receives at the end of period 2 has a present value of $.79719, and the $1 the investor receives at the end of the third period has a present value of

$.71178. Each of these numbers comes from Table 2. The present value of the annuity is the sum of these individual present values, $2.40183, shown in Table 4.

The present value of an ordinary annuity for n periods is the sum of the present value of $1 received one period from now plus the present value of $1 received two periods from now, and so on until we add on the present value of $1 received n periods from now. The present value of an ordinary annuity is

$$\begin{matrix} \text{Present Value} \\ \text{of an} \\ \text{Ordinary Annuity} \end{matrix} = \begin{matrix} \text{Periodic} \\ \text{Payment} \end{matrix} \times \begin{matrix} \text{Factor for the} \\ \text{Present} \\ \text{Value of an Ordinary} \\ \text{Annuity.} \end{matrix}$$

Thus,

$$\$2.40183 \;=\; \$1 \;\times\; 2.40183.$$

Example 8 Accountants project an investment to generate $1,000 at the end of each of the next 20 years. If the interest rate is 8 percent compounded annually, what will the future value of these flows be at the end of 20 years?

The time line for this problem is

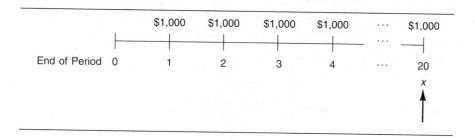

The symbol x denotes the amount you must calculate. Table 3 indicates that the factor for the future value of an annuity at 8 percent for 20 periods is 45.76196. Thus,

$$\begin{matrix} \text{Future Value} \\ \text{of an} \\ \text{Ordinary Annuity} \end{matrix} = \text{Periodic Payment} \times \begin{matrix} \text{Factor for} \\ \text{the Future} \\ \text{Value of an} \\ \text{Ordinary Annuity} \end{matrix}$$

$$\begin{aligned} x &= \$1,000 \times 45.76196 \\ x &= \$45,762. \end{aligned}$$

The cash flows have future value of $45,762.

Example 9 Parents want to accumulate a fund to send their child to college. The parents will invest a fixed amount at the end of each calendar quarter for the next 10 years. The funds will accumulate in a savings certificate that promises to pay 8-percent interest compounded quarterly. What amount must the parents invest to accumulate a fund of $50,000?

The time line for this problem is

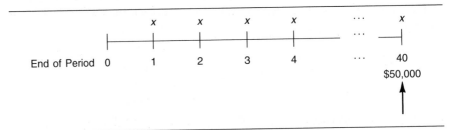

This problem is similar to Example 8 because both involve periodic investments of cash that accumulate interest over time until a specific time in the future. In Example 8, you know the periodic investment and compute the future value. In Example 9, you know the future value and compute the periodic investment. Table 3 indicates that the future value of an annuity at 2 percent (= 8 percent per year/4 quarters per year) per period for 40 (= 4 quarters per year × 10 years) periods is 60.40198. Thus,

$$
\begin{aligned}
\text{Future Value of an Ordinary Annuity} &= \text{Periodic Payment} \times \text{Factor for the Future Value of an Ordinary Annuity} \\
\$50,000 &= X \times 60.40198 \\
X &= \frac{\$50,000}{60.40198} \\
X &= \$828.
\end{aligned}
$$

Because you want to find the periodic payment, you divide the future value amount of $50,000 by the future value factor.

Example 10 A firm borrows $30,000 from an insurance company. The interest rate on the loan is 8 percent compounded semiannually. The firm agrees to repay the loan in equal semiannual installments over the next 5 years and make the first payment 6 months from now. What is the amount of the required semiannual payment?

The time line is

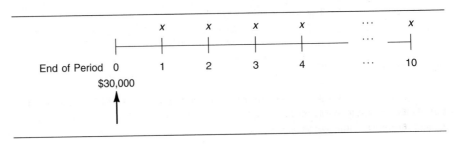

You know the present value and must compute the periodic payment. Table 4 indicates that the present value of an annuity at 4 percent (= 8 percent per year/2 semiannual periods per year) for 10 periods (= 2 periods per year × 5 years) is 8.11090. Thus,

$$
\begin{array}{ccc}
\text{Present Value} & & \text{Factor for} \\
\text{of an} & = \text{Periodic Payment} \times & \text{the Present} \\
\text{Ordinary Annuity} & & \text{Value of an} \\
& & \text{Ordinary Annuity}
\end{array}
$$

$$\$30,000 = x \times 8.11090$$

$$x = \frac{\$30,000}{8.11090}$$

$$x = \$3,699.$$

Because you are finding the periodic payment, you divide the present value amount of $30,000 by the present value factor. Exhibit A.2 shows how periodic payments of $3,700 amortize the loan. We call such a schedule an *amortization schedule.* If the periodic payments were $3,699, not $3,700, the "error" in the final payment would be even smaller.

Example 11 A company signs a lease acquiring the right to use property for 3 years. The company promises to make lease payments of $19,709 annually at the

Exhibit A.2

Amortization Schedule for $30,000 Mortgage, Repaid in 10 Semiannual Installments of $3,700, Interest Rate of 8 Percent, Compounded Semiannually

6-Month Period (1)	Mortgage Principal Start of Period (2)	Interest Expense for Period (3)	Payment (4)	Portion of Payment Reducing Principal (5)	Mortgage Principal End of Period (6)
0					$30,000
1	$30,000	$1,200	$3,700	$2,500	27,500
2	27,500	1,100	3,700	2,600	24,900
3	24,900	996	3,700	2,704	22,196
4	22,196	888	3,700	2,812	19,384
5	19,384	775	3,700	2,925	16,459
6	16,459	658	3,700	3,042	13,417
7	13,417	537	3,700	3,163	10,254
8	10,254	410	3,700	3,290	6,964
9	6,964	279	3,700	3,421	3,543
10	3,543	142	3,685	3,543	0

Column **(2)** = column **(6)** from previous period.
Column **(3)** = .04 × column **(2)**.
Column **(4)** is given, except row 10, where it is the amount such that column **(4)** = column **(2)** + column **(3)**.
Column **(5)** = column **(4)** − column **(3)**.
Column **(6)** = column **(2)** − column **(5)**.

Managerial Application

Present Value of Cost Savings Guides Pricing Decision

In the 1970s, Robert Mendenhall discovered a process that enables highway and road builders to reuse asphalt pavement in constructing rebuilt or new roads. He patented the process. Mendenhall's discovery promised large cost savings in road building. Mendenhall licensed his patent to CMI Corp. CMI began to produce and sell recycling plants capable of producing high-quality road surface materials from recycled asphalt.

In the 1980s, competitors, such as Barber-Greene (BG), approached CMI about obtaining licenses to use the patent. Management at CMI wanted some method for thinking about the license fees it might reasonably expect to collect from others' use of the patent. Management believed that the cost savings from incorporating the new process into asphalt plants justified prices at least 25 percent larger than prices for equipment using the old processes.

Data pertinent to the analysis:

- Prices for the asphalt plant using the old processes averaged $735,000.
- The new recycling plants had a capacity to produce 150,000 to 300,000 tons of new road surfaces per year.
- Contractors expect the recycling plants to last for 15 to 18 years but depreciate them over 10 years on a straight-line basis for tax reporting.
- Because of air pollution problems, a contractor cannot use 100-percent recycled asphalt in producing new paving materials. Instead, the contractor must use a mixture of recycled and new, virgin asphalt. Depending on the application, the ratio of recycled to virgin asphalt ranges from 70/30 to 50/50.
- To produce a ton of paving materials from virgin asphalt costs the contractors from $14 to $17 per ton in materials and plant operating costs, not counting the cost of the plant itself.
- Various industry studies indicate a costs savings from using recycled asphalt of $0.50 to $11.40 per ton of new pavings materials produced from recycled asphalt.
- The risk of the contracting processes for road builders suggests a discount rate for plant acquisitions of 15 to 20 percent per year before taxes.

CMI's financial analysts constructed the analysis of two examples appearing in Exhibit A.3 to help management think about its opportunity. These examples helped management understand that cost savings justify price increases for asphalt plants of even larger than 25 percent and license fees in excess of $100,000 per plant.

Exhibit A.3

Derivation of Price Increase for Recycling Asphalt Drum Plant Justified by Cost Savings

First Illustration: Worst-case assumptions
Second Illustration: Best-case assumptions

Price (List) of New Asphalt Plant	$735,000	
Capacity of New Plant to Produce Output		
In tons per year		
First Illustration	150,000	
Second Illustration	300,000	
Life of New Asphalt Plant in Years		
First Illustration	10	
Second Illustration	15	
Savings per Ton of Output Produced [Note A]		
First Illustration	$1.50	
Second Illustration	$2.50	
Dollar Savings per Year		
First Illustration	$225,000	= 150,000 tons × $1.50 per ton
Second Illustration	$750,000	= 300,000 tons × $2.50 per ton
Annual Discount Rate for Owner of Plant		
First Illustration	20.0%	
Second Illustration	15.0%	
Present Value of Dollar Savings		
Over Life of Plant		
First Illustration	$943,306	= present value of $225,000 per year for 10 years discounted at 20 percent per year.
		= $225,000 × 4.19247
Second Illustration	$4,385,528	= present value of $750,000 per year for 15 years discounted at 15 percent per year.
		= $750,000 × 5.84737
Percentage Increase in Selling Price		
of New Asphalt Plant Justified by		
Cost Savings		
First Illustration	128%	= $943,306/$735,000
Second Illustration	597%	= $4,385,528/$735,000

Note A. If each ton of output requires as much as 70 percent, or as little as 50 percent, of new material, then the savings per ton of output ranges from $1.50 (= .30 × $5.00) to $2.50 (= .50 × $5.00) per ton of output.

end of this and the next 2 years. The discount, or interest, rate is 15 percent per year. What is the present value of the lease payments, which is the equivalent cash purchase price for this property?

The time line is

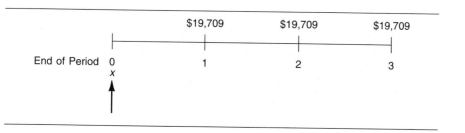

The factor from Table 4 for the present value of an annuity at 15 percent for 3 periods is 2.28323. Thus,

Present Value of an Ordinary Annuity		= Periodic Payment ×	Factor for the Present Value of an Ordinary Annuity
x	=	$19,709	× 2.28323
x	=	$45,000.	

Example 12 Mr. Mason is 62 years old. He wishes to invest equal amounts on his sixty-third, sixty-fourth, and sixty-fifth birthdays so that starting on his sixty-sixth birthday he can withdraw $50,000 on each birthday for 10 years. His investments will earn 8 percent per year. How much should he invest on the sixty-third through sixty-fifth birthdays?

The time line for this problem is

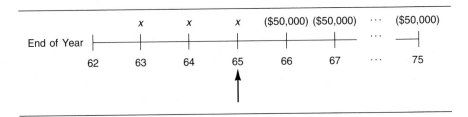

At 65, Mr. Mason needs to have accumulated a fund equal to the present value of an annuity of $50,000 per period for 10 periods, discounted at 8 percent per period. The factor from Table 4 for 8 percent and 10 periods is 6.71008. Thus,

Present Value of an Ordinary Annuity		= Periodic Payment ×	Factor for the Present Value of an Ordinary Annuity
x	=	$50,000	× 6.71008
x	=	$335,504.	

The time line now appears as follows:

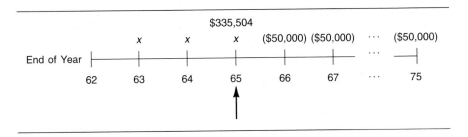

The question now becomes: How much must Mr. Mason invest on his sixty-third, sixty-fourth, and sixty-fifth birthdays to accumulate a fund of $335,504 on his sixty-fifth birthday? The factor for the future value of an annuity for three periods at 8 percent is 3.24640. Thus,

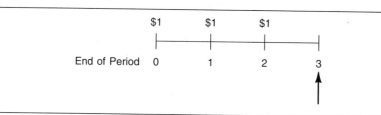

$$\text{Future Value of an Ordinary Annuity} = \text{Periodic Payment} \times \text{Factor for the Future Value of an Ordinary Annuity}$$

$$\$335,504 = x \times 3.24640$$

$$x = \frac{\$335,504}{3.24640}$$

$$x = \$103,346.$$

Annuities in Advance (Annuities Due)

The time line for the future value of a three-period annuity in advance is

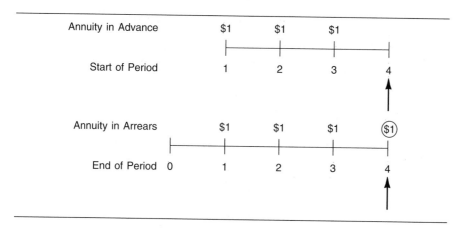

Notice that we calculated the future value for the *end* of the period in which the last payment occurs. When you have tables of ordinary annuities, tables for annuities due are unnecessary.

To see this, compare the time line for the future value of an annuity in advance for three periods with the time axis relabeled to show the start of the period and the time line for the future value of an ordinary annuity (in arrears) for four periods.

A $1 annuity in advance for *n* periods has a future value equal to the future value of a $1 annuity in arrears for *n* + 1 periods *minus* $1. The $1 circled in the time line for the annuity in arrears is the $1 that you must subtract to calculate the future value of an annuity in advance. Note that no annuity payment occurs at the end of period 3. The note at the foot of Table 3 states: "To convert from this table to values of an annuity in advance, find the annuity in arrears above for one more period and subtract 1.00000."

Example Problem Involving Future Value of Annuity Due

Example 13 A student plans to invest $1,000 a year at the beginning of each of the next 10 years in certificates of deposit paying interest of 12 percent per year, making the first payment today. What will be the amount of the certificates at the end of the tenth year?

The time line is

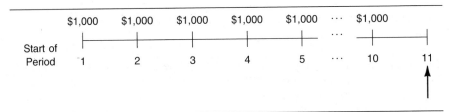

The factor for the future value of an annuity for 11 (= 10 + 1) periods is 20.65458. Because a $1,000 investment does not occur at the end of the tenth year, you subtract 1.000000 from 20.65458 to obtain the factor for the annuity in advance of 19.65458. The future value of the annuity in advance is

$$
\begin{array}{ccc}
\text{Future Value} & & \text{Factor for} \\
\text{of an} & = \text{Periodic Payment} \times & \text{the Future Value} \\
\text{Annuity} & & \text{of an} \\
\text{in Advance} & & \text{Annuity} \\
& & \text{in Advance}
\end{array}
$$

$$
\begin{array}{ccccc}
X & = & \$1,000 & \times & 19.65458 \\
X & = & \$19,655. & &
\end{array}
$$

Present Value of Annuity Due

The time line for the present value of an annuity in advance for three periods is

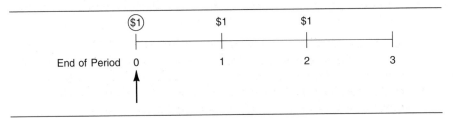

Notice that except for the first, circled payment, it looks just like the present value of an ordinary annuity for two periods. A $1 annuity in advance for n periods has a present value equal to the present value of a $1 annuity in arrears for $n - 1$ periods *plus* $1. The note at the foot of Table 4 states: "To convert from this table to values of an annuity in advance, find the annuity in arrears above for one fewer period and add 1.00000."

Example 14 What is the present value of rents of $350 paid monthly, in advance, for 1 year when the discount rate is 1 percent per month?

The present value of $1 per period *in arrears* for 11 periods at 1 percent per period is $10.36763; the present value of $1 per period in advance for 12 periods is $10.36763 + $1.00 = $11.36763, and the present value of this year's rent is $350 × 11.36763 = $3,979.

Deferred Annuities

When the first payment of an annuity occurs some time after the end of the first period, the annuity is *deferred*. The time line for an ordinary annuity of $1 per period for four periods deferred for two periods is

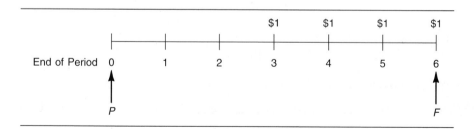

The arrow marked P shows the time of the present value calculation; the arrow marked F shows the future value calculation. The deferral does not affect the future value, which equals the future value of an ordinary annuity for four periods.

Notice that the time line for the present value looks like one for an ordinary annuity for six periods *minus* an ordinary annuity for two periods:

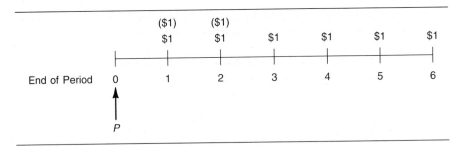

Calculate the present value of an annuity of n payments deferred for d periods by subtracting the present value of an annuity for d periods from the present value of an annuity for $n + d$ periods.

Example 15   Refer to the data in Example 12. Recall that Mr. Mason wants to withdraw $50,000 per year on his sixty-sixth through his seventy-fifth birthdays. He wishes to invest a sufficient amount on his sixty-third, sixty-fourth, and sixty-fifth birthdays to provide a fund for the later withdrawals.

The time line is

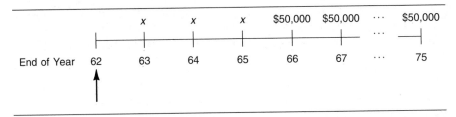

As of his sixty-second birthday, the $50,000 series of payments on Mr. Mason's sixty-sixth through seventy-fifth birthdays is a deferred annuity. The interest rate is 8 percent per year.

You can find the present value using the factor for the present value of an annuity for 13 periods (10 payments deferred for three periods) of 7.90378 and subtracting the factor for the present value of an annuity for three periods of 2.57710. The net amount is 5.32668 (= 7.90378 − 2.57710). Multiplying by the $50,000 payment amount, you find the present value of the deferred annuity on Mr. Mason's sixty-second birthday ($266,334 = $50,000 × 5.32668).

Perpetuities

A periodic payment to be received forever is a *perpetuity*. Future values of perpetuities are undefined. One dollar to be received at the end of every period discounted at rate r percent has present value of $1/r$. Observe what happens in the expression for the present value of an ordinary annuity of $A per payment as n, the number of payments, approaches infinity:

$$P_A = \frac{A[1 - (1 + r)^{-n}]}{r}.$$

As n approaches infinity, $(1 + r)^{-n}$ approaches zero, so P_A approaches $A(1/r)$. If the first payment of the perpetuity occurs now, the present value is $A[1 + (1/r)]$.

Example 16 The Canadian government offers to pay $30 every 6 months forever in the form of a perpetual bond. What is that bond worth if the discount rate is 10 percent compounded semiannually?

Ten percent compounded semiannually is equivalent to 5 percent per 6-month period. If the first payment occurs 6 months from now, the present value is $30/.05 = $600. If the first payment occurs today, the present value is $30 + $600 = $630.

Implicit Interest Rates: Finding Internal Rates of Return

The preceding examples computed a future value or a present value given the interest rate and stated cash payments. Or, they computed the required payments given their known future value or their known present value. In some calculations, we know the present or future value and the periodic payments; we must find the implicit interest rate. Assume, for example, a case in which we know that a cash investment of $10,500 will grow to $13,500 in 3 years. What is the implicit interest rate, or market rate of return, on this investment? The time line for this problem is

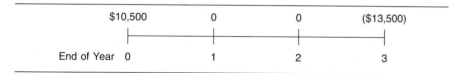

The implicit interest rate is r, such that

(A.1)
$$\$10,500 = \frac{\$13,500}{(1 + r)^3}.$$

(A.2)
$$0 = \$10,500 - \frac{\$13,500}{(1 + r)^3}.$$

In other words, the present value of $13,500 discounted three periods at r percent per period is $10,500. The present value of all current and future cash flows nets to zero when future flows are discounted at r percent per period. In general, the only way to find such an r is a trial-and-error procedure.[1] The procedure is finding the internal rate of return of a series of cash flows. The *internal rate of return* of a series of cash flows is the discount rate that equates the net present value of that series of cash flows to zero. Follow these steps to find the internal rate of return:

1.   Make an educated guess, called the "trial rate," at the internal rate of return. If you have no idea what to guess, try zero.

---

[1] In cases where r appears in only one term, as here, you can find r analytically. Here, $r = (\$13,500/\$10,500)^{1/3} - 1 = .087380$.

2. Calculate the present value of all the cash flows (including the one at the end of year 0).
3. If the present value of the cash flows is zero, stop. The current trial rate is the internal rate of return.
4. If the amount found in step 2 is less than zero, try a larger interest rate as the trial rate and go back to step 2.
5. If the amount found in step 2 is greater than zero, try a smaller interest rate as the new trial rate and go back to step 2.

The following iterations illustrate the process for the example in Equation A.1.

Iteration Number	Trial Rate = r	Net Present Values: Right-Hand Side of A.2
1	0.00%	($3,000)
2	10.00	357
3	5.00	(1,162)
4	7.50	(367)
5	8.75	3

With a trial rate of 8.75 percent, the right-hand side is close enough to zero so that you can use 8.75 percent as the implicit interest rate. Continued iterations would find trial rates even closer to the true rate, which is about 8.7380 percent.

You may find calculating the internal rate of return for a series of cash flows tedious, and you should not attempt it unless you have at least a desk calculator. An exponential feature, the feature that allows the computation of $(1 + r)$ raised to various powers, helps.[2] Computer spreadsheets, such as Lotus 1-2-3, have a built-in function to find the internal rate of return.

Example 17 The Alexis Company acquires a machine with a cash price of $10,500. It pays for the machine by giving a note for $12,000 promising to make payments equal to 7 percent of the face value, $840 (= .07 × $12,000), at the end of each of the next 3 years and a single payment of $12,000 in 3 years. What is the implicit interest rate in the loan?

The time line for this problem is

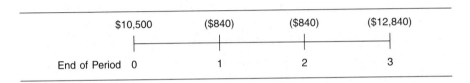

	$10,500	($840)	($840)	($12,840)
End of Period	0	1	2	3

---

[2]You may use other methods to guess the trial rate that will approximate the true rate in fewer iterations than the method described here. If you want to find internal rates of return efficiently with successive trial rates, refer to a mathematical reference book to learn about the "Newton search" method, sometimes called the "method of false position."

The implicit interest rate is r, such that[3]

(A.3)
$$\$10,500 = \frac{\$840}{(1 + r)} + \frac{\$840}{(1 + r)^2} + \frac{\$12,840}{(1 + r)^3}.$$

The iteration process finds internal rate of return of 12.2 percent to the nearest tenth of 1 percent:

Iteration Number	Trial Rate	Right-Hand Side of A.3
1	7.0%	$12,000
2	15.0	9,808
3	11.0	10,827
4	13.0	10,300
5	12.0	10,559
6	12.5	10,428
7	12.3	10,480
8	12.2	10,506
9	12.1	10,533

Example 18   In some contexts, such as mortgages or leases, one knows the amount of a series of future periodic payments, which are identical in all periods, and the present value of those future payments. For example, a firm may borrow $100,000 and agree to repay the loan, in 20 payments of $11,746 each, at the end of each of the next 20 years. To calculate interest expense each period, you must find the interest rate implicit in the loan.

You have the following information:

Present Value of an Ordinary Annuity		Periodic Payment $\times$	Factor for the Present Value of an Ordinary Annuity
$100,000	=	$11,746 $\times$	X
X	=	$\dfrac{\$100,000}{\$11,746}$	
X	=	8.51354.	

The factor to discount 20 payments of $11,746 to a present value of $100,000 is 8.51354. To find the interest rate implicit in the discounting, scan the 20-payment row of Table 4 to find the factor 8.51354. The interest rate at the head of the column is the implicit interest rate, approximately 10 percent in the example.

---

[3]Compare this formulation to that in Equation A.2. Note that the left-hand side is zero in one case but not in the other. The left-hand side can be either nonzero or zero, depending on what seems convenient for the particular context.

Example 19   An investment costing $11,400 today provides the following after-tax cash inflows at the ends of each of the next five periods: $5,000, $4,000, $3,000, $2,000, $1,000. What is the internal rate of return on these flows? That is, find r such that

(A.4) $$0 = (\$11,400) + \frac{\$5,000}{(1 + r)} + \frac{\$4,000}{(1 + r)^2} + \frac{\$3,000}{(1 + r)^3} + \frac{\$2,000}{(1 + r)^4} + \frac{\$1,000}{(1 + r)^5}.$$

Trial rates r produced the following sequence of estimates of the internal rate of return:

Iteration Number	Trial Rate	Right-Hand Side of A.4
1	0.00%	$3,600
2	10.00	692
3	15.00	(414)
4	12.50	115
5	13.50	(102)
6	13.00	6
7	13.10	(16)
8	13.01	4
9	13.02	2
10	13.03	(1)

The estimating process proceeds several steps further than necessary. To the nearest whole percentage point, the internal rate of return is 13 percent.

To the nearest one-hundredth of a percent, the internal rate of return is 13.03 percent. Futher trials find an even more precise answer, $r = 13.027$ percent. Physical scientists learn early in their training not to use more significant digits in calculations than the accuracy of the measuring devices merits. Accountants, too, should not carry calculations beyond the point of accuracy. Given the likely uncertainty in the estimates of cash flows, an estimate of the internal rate of return accurate to the nearest whole percentage point will serve its intended purpose.

Compound Interest and Annuity Tables

Table 1

Future Value of $1

$$F_n = P(1 + r)^n$$

r = interest rate; n = number of periods until valuation; $P = \$1$

Periods = n	½%	1%	1½%	2%	3%	4%	5%	6%	7%	8%	10%	12%	15%	20%	25%
1	1.00500	1.01000	1.01500	1.02000	1.03000	1.04000	1.05000	1.06000	1.07000	1.08000	1.10000	1.12000	1.15000	1.20000	1.25000
2	1.01003	1.02010	1.03023	1.04040	1.06090	1.08160	1.10250	1.12360	1.14490	1.16640	1.21000	1.25440	1.32250	1.44000	1.56250
3	1.01508	1.03030	1.04568	1.06121	1.09273	1.12486	1.15763	1.19102	1.22504	1.25971	1.33100	1.40493	1.52088	1.72800	1.95313
4	1.02015	1.04060	1.06136	1.08243	1.12551	1.16986	1.21551	1.26248	1.31080	1.36049	1.46410	1.57352	1.74901	2.07360	2.44141
5	1.02525	1.05101	1.07728	1.10408	1.15927	1.21665	1.27628	1.33823	1.40255	1.46933	1.61051	1.76234	2.01136	2.48832	3.05176
6	1.03038	1.06152	1.09344	1.12616	1.19405	1.26532	1.34010	1.41852	1.50073	1.58687	1.77156	1.97382	2.31306	2.98598	3.81470
7	1.03553	1.07214	1.10984	1.14869	1.22987	1.31593	1.40710	1.50363	1.60578	1.71382	1.94872	2.21068	2.66002	3.58318	4.76837
8	1.04071	1.08286	1.12649	1.17166	1.26677	1.36857	1.47746	1.59385	1.71819	1.85093	2.14359	2.47596	3.05902	4.29982	5.96046
9	1.04591	1.09369	1.14339	1.19509	1.30477	1.42331	1.55133	1.68948	1.83846	1.99900	2.35795	2.77308	3.51788	5.15978	7.45058
10	1.05114	1.10462	1.16054	1.21899	1.34392	1.48024	1.62889	1.79085	1.96715	2.15892	2.59374	3.10585	4.04556	6.19174	9.31323
11	1.05640	1.11567	1.17795	1.24337	1.38423	1.53945	1.71034	1.89830	2.10485	2.33164	2.85312	3.47855	4.65239	7.43008	11.64153
12	1.06168	1.12683	1.19562	1.26824	1.42576	1.60103	1.79586	2.01220	2.25219	2.51817	3.13843	3.89598	5.35025	8.91610	14.55192
13	1.06699	1.13809	1.21355	1.29361	1.46853	1.66507	1.88565	2.13293	2.40985	2.71962	3.45227	4.36349	6.15279	10.69932	18.18989
14	1.07232	1.14947	1.23176	1.31948	1.51259	1.73168	1.97993	2.26090	2.57853	2.93719	3.79750	4.88711	7.07571	12.83918	22.73737
15	1.07768	1.16097	1.25023	1.34587	1.55797	1.80094	2.07893	2.39656	2.75903	3.17217	4.17725	5.47357	8.13706	15.40702	28.42171
16	1.08307	1.17258	1.26899	1.37279	1.60471	1.87298	2.18287	2.54035	2.95216	3.42594	4.59497	6.13039	9.35762	18.48843	35.52714
17	1.08849	1.18430	1.28802	1.40024	1.65285	1.94790	2.29202	2.69277	3.15882	3.70002	5.05447	6.86604	10.76126	22.18611	44.40892
18	1.09393	1.19615	1.30734	1.42825	1.70243	2.02582	2.40662	2.85434	3.37993	3.99602	5.55992	7.68997	12.37545	26.62333	55.51115
19	1.09940	1.20811	1.32695	1.45681	1.75351	2.10685	2.52695	3.02560	3.61653	4.31570	6.11591	8.61276	14.23177	31.94800	69.38894
20	1.10490	1.22019	1.34686	1.48595	1.80611	2.19112	2.65330	3.20714	3.86968	4.66096	6.72750	9.64629	16.36654	38.33760	86.73617
22	1.11597	1.24472	1.38756	1.54598	1.91610	2.36992	2.92526	3.60354	4.43040	5.43654	8.14027	12.10031	21.64475	55.20614	135.5253
24	1.12716	1.26973	1.42950	1.60844	2.03279	2.56330	3.22510	4.04893	5.07237	6.34118	9.84973	15.17863	28.62518	79.49685	211.7582
26	1.13846	1.29526	1.47271	1.67342	2.15659	2.77247	3.55567	4.54938	5.80735	7.39635	11.91818	19.04007	37.85680	114.4755	330.8722
28	1.14987	1.32129	1.51722	1.74102	2.28793	2.99870	3.92013	5.11169	6.64884	8.62711	14.42099	23.88387	50.06561	164.8447	516.9879
30	1.16140	1.34785	1.56308	1.81136	2.42726	3.24340	4.32194	5.74349	7.61226	10.06266	17.44940	29.95992	66.21177	237.3763	807.7936
32	1.17304	1.37494	1.61032	1.88454	2.57508	3.50806	4.76494	6.45339	8.71527	11.73708	21.11378	37.58173	87.56507	341.8219	1262.177
34	1.18480	1.40258	1.65900	1.96068	2.73191	3.79432	5.25335	7.25103	9.97811	13.69013	25.54767	47.14252	115.80480	492.2235	1972.152
36	1.19668	1.43077	1.70914	2.03989	2.89828	4.10393	5.79182	8.14725	11.42394	15.96811	30.91268	59.13557	153.15185	708.8019	3081.488
38	1.20868	1.45953	1.76080	2.12230	3.07478	4.43881	6.38548	9.15425	13.07927	18.62528	37.40434	74.17966	202.54332	1020.675	4814.825
40	1.22079	1.48886	1.81402	2.20804	3.26204	4.80102	7.03999	10.28572	14.97446	21.72452	45.25926	93.05097	267.86355	1469.772	7523.164
45	1.25162	1.56481	1.95421	2.43785	3.78160	5.84118	8.98501	13.76461	21.00245	31.92045	72.89048	163.9876	538.76927	3657.262	22958.87
50	1.28323	1.64463	2.10524	2.69159	4.38391	7.10668	11.46740	18.42015	29.45703	46.90161	117.3909	289.0022	1083.65744	9100.438	70064.92
100	1.64667	2.70481	4.43205	7.24465	19.21863	50.50495	131.5013	339.3021	867.7163	2199.761	13780.61	83522.27	117×10^4	828×10^5	491×10^7

Table 2

Present Value of $1

$$P = F_n(1 + r)^{-n}$$

r = discount rate; n = number of periods until payment; F = $1

Periods = n	½%	1%	1½%	2%	3%	4%	5%	6%	7%	8%	10%	12%	15%	20%	25%
1	.99502	.99010	.98522	.98039	.97087	.96154	.95238	.94340	.93458	.92593	.90909	.89286	.86957	.83333	.80000
2	.99007	.98030	.97066	.96117	.94260	.92456	.90703	.89000	.87344	.85734	.82645	.79719	.75614	.69444	.64000
3	.98515	.97059	.95632	.94232	.91514	.88900	.86384	.83962	.81630	.79383	.75131	.71178	.65752	.57870	.51200
4	.98025	.96098	.94218	.92385	.88849	.85480	.82270	.79209	.76290	.73503	.68301	.63552	.57175	.48225	.40960
5	.97537	.95147	.92826	.90573	.86261	.82193	.78353	.74726	.71299	.68058	.62092	.56743	.49718	.40188	.32768
6	.97052	.94205	.91454	.88797	.83748	.79031	.74622	.70496	.66634	.63017	.56447	.50663	.43233	.33490	.26214
7	.96569	.93272	.90103	.87056	.81309	.75992	.71068	.66506	.62275	.58349	.51316	.45235	.37594	.27908	.20972
8	.96089	.92348	.88771	.85349	.78941	.73069	.67684	.62741	.58201	.54027	.46651	.40388	.32690	.23257	.16777
9	.95610	.91434	.87459	.83676	.76642	.70259	.64461	.59190	.54393	.50025	.42410	.36061	.28426	.19381	.13422
10	.95135	.90529	.86167	.82035	.74409	.67556	.61391	.55839	.50835	.46319	.38554	.32197	.24718	.16151	.10737
11	.94661	.89632	.84893	.80426	.72242	.64958	.58468	.52679	.47509	.42888	.35049	.28748	.21494	.13459	.08590
12	.94191	.88745	.83639	.78849	.70138	.62460	.55684	.49697	.44401	.39711	.31863	.25668	.18691	.11216	.06872
13	.93722	.87866	.82403	.77303	.68095	.60057	.53032	.46884	.41496	.36770	.28966	.22917	.16253	.09346	.05498
14	.93256	.86996	.81185	.75788	.66112	.57748	.50507	.44230	.38782	.34046	.26333	.20462	.14133	.07789	.04398
15	.92792	.86135	.79985	.74301	.64186	.55526	.48102	.41727	.36245	.31524	.23939	.18270	.12289	.06491	.03518
16	.92330	.85282	.78803	.72845	.62317	.53391	.45811	.39365	.33873	.29189	.21763	.16312	.10686	.05409	.02815
17	.91871	.84438	.77639	.71416	.60502	.51337	.43630	.37136	.31657	.27027	.19784	.14564	.09293	.04507	.02252
18	.91414	.83602	.76491	.70016	.58739	.49363	.41552	.35034	.29586	.25025	.17986	.13004	.08081	.03756	.01801
19	.90959	.82774	.75361	.68643	.57029	.47464	.39573	.33051	.27651	.23171	.16351	.11611	.07027	.03130	.01441
20	.90506	.81954	.74247	.67297	.55368	.45639	.37689	.31180	.25842	.21455	.14864	.10367	.06110	.02608	.01153
22	.89608	.80340	.72069	.64684	.52189	.42196	.34185	.27751	.22571	.18394	.12285	.08264	.04620	.01811	.00738
24	.88719	.78757	.69954	.62172	.49193	.39012	.31007	.24698	.19715	.15770	.10153	.06588	.03493	.01258	.00472
26	.87838	.77205	.67902	.59758	.46369	.36069	.28124	.21981	.17220	.13520	.08391	.05252	.02642	.00874	.00302
28	.86966	.75684	.65910	.57437	.43708	.33348	.25509	.19563	.15040	.11591	.06934	.04187	.01997	.00607	.00193
30	.86103	.74192	.63976	.55207	.41199	.30832	.23138	.17411	.13137	.09938	.05731	.03338	.01510	.00421	.00124
32	.85248	.72730	.62099	.53063	.38834	.28506	.20987	.15496	.11474	.08520	.04736	.02661	.01142	.00293	.00079
34	.84402	.71297	.60577	.51003	.36604	.26355	.19035	.13791	.10022	.07305	.03914	.02121	.00864	.00203	.00051
36	.83564	.69892	.58509	.49022	.34503	.24367	.17266	.12274	.08754	.06262	.03235	.01691	.00653	.00141	.00032
38	.82735	.68515	.56792	.47119	.32523	.22529	.15661	.10924	.07646	.05369	.02673	.01348	.00494	.00098	.00021
40	.81914	.67165	.55126	.45289	.30656	.20829	.14205	.09722	.06678	.04603	.02209	.01075	.00373	.00068	.00013
45	.79896	.63905	.51171	.41020	.26444	.17120	.11130	.07265	.04761	.03133	.01372	.00610	.00186	.00027	.00004
50	.77929	.60804	.47500	.37153	.22811	.14071	.08720	.05429	.03395	.02132	.00852	.00346	.00092	.00011	.00001
100	.60729	.36971	.22563	.13803	.05203	.01980	.00760	.00295	.00115	.00045	.00007	.00001	.00000	.00000	.00000

Table 3

Future Value of Annuity of $1 in Arrears

$$F = \frac{(1 + r)^n - 1}{r}$$

r = interest rate; n = number of payments

No. of Payments = n	½%	1%	1½%	2%	3%	4%	5%	6%	7%	8%	10%	12%	15%	20%	25%
1	1.00000	1.00000	1.00000	1.00000	1.00000	1.00000	1.00000	1.00000	1.00000	1.00000	1.00000	1.00000	1.00000	1.00000	1.00000
2	2.00500	2.01000	2.01500	2.02000	2.03000	2.04000	2.05000	2.06000	2.07000	2.08000	2.10000	2.12000	2.15000	2.20000	2.25000
3	3.01503	3.03010	3.04523	3.06040	3.09090	3.12160	3.15250	3.18360	3.21490	3.24640	3.31000	3.37440	3.47250	3.64000	3.81250
4	4.03010	4.06040	4.09090	4.12161	4.18363	4.24646	4.31013	4.37462	4.43994	4.50611	4.64100	4.77933	4.99338	5.36800	5.76563
5	5.05025	5.10101	5.15227	5.20404	5.30914	5.41632	5.52563	5.63709	5.75074	5.86660	6.10510	6.35285	6.74238	7.44160	8.20703
6	6.07550	6.15202	6.22955	6.30812	6.46841	6.63298	6.80191	6.97532	7.15329	7.33593	7.71561	8.11519	8.75374	9.92992	11.25879
7	7.10588	7.21354	7.32299	7.43428	7.66246	7.89829	8.14201	8.39384	8.65402	8.92280	9.48717	10.08901	11.06680	12.91590	15.07349
8	8.14141	8.28567	8.43284	8.58297	8.89234	9.21423	9.54911	9.89747	10.25980	10.63663	11.43589	12.29969	13.72682	16.49908	19.84186
9	9.18212	9.36853	9.55933	9.75463	10.15911	10.58280	11.02656	11.49132	11.97799	12.48756	13.57948	14.77566	16.78584	20.79890	25.80232
10	10.22803	10.46221	10.70272	10.94972	11.46388	12.00611	12.57789	13.18079	13.81645	14.48656	15.93742	17.54874	20.30372	25.95868	33.25290
11	11.27917	11.56683	11.86326	12.16872	12.80780	13.48635	14.20679	14.97164	15.78360	16.64549	18.53117	20.65458	24.34928	32.15042	42.56613
12	12.33556	12.68250	13.04121	13.41209	14.19203	15.02581	15.91713	16.86994	17.88845	18.97713	21.38428	24.13313	29.00167	39.58050	54.20766
13	13.39724	13.80933	14.23683	14.68033	15.61779	16.62684	17.71298	18.88214	20.14064	21.49530	24.52271	28.02911	34.35192	48.49660	68.75958
14	14.46423	14.94742	15.45038	15.97394	17.08632	18.29191	19.59863	21.01507	22.55049	24.21492	27.97498	32.39260	40.50471	59.19592	86.94947
15	15.53655	16.09690	16.68214	17.29342	18.59891	20.02359	21.57856	23.27597	25.12902	27.15211	31.72248	37.27971	47.58041	72.03511	109.6868
16	16.61423	17.25786	17.93237	18.63929	20.15688	21.82453	23.65749	25.67253	27.88805	30.32428	35.94973	42.75328	55.71747	87.44213	138.1085
17	17.69730	18.43044	19.20136	20.01207	21.76159	23.69751	25.84037	28.21288	30.84022	33.75023	40.54470	48.88367	65.07509	105.9306	173.6357
18	18.78579	19.61475	20.48938	21.41231	23.41444	25.64541	28.13238	30.90565	33.99903	37.45024	45.59917	55.74971	75.83636	128.1167	218.0446
19	19.87972	20.81090	21.79672	22.84056	25.11687	27.67123	30.53900	33.75999	37.37896	41.44626	51.15909	63.43968	88.21181	154.7400	273.5558
20	20.97912	22.01900	23.12367	24.29737	26.87037	29.77808	33.06595	36.78559	40.99549	45.76196	57.27500	72.05244	102.44358	186.6880	342.9447
22	23.19443	24.47159	25.83758	27.29898	30.53678	34.24797	38.50521	43.39229	49.00574	55.45676	71.40275	92.50258	137.63164	271.0307	538.1011
24	25.43196	26.97346	28.63352	30.42186	34.42647	39.08260	44.50200	50.81558	58.17667	66.76476	88.49733	118.1552	184.16784	392.4842	843.0329
26	27.69191	29.52563	31.51397	33.67091	38.55304	44.31174	51.11345	59.15638	68.67647	79.95442	109.1818	150.3339	245.71197	567.3773	1319.489
28	29.97452	32.12910	34.48148	37.05121	42.93092	49.96758	58.40258	68.52811	80.69769	95.33883	134.2099	190.6989	327.10408	819.2233	2063.952
30	32.28002	34.78489	37.53868	40.56808	47.57542	56.08494	66.43885	79.05819	94.46079	113.2832	164.4940	241.3327	434.74515	1181.881	3227.174
32	34.60862	37.49407	40.68829	44.22703	52.50276	62.70147	75.29883	90.88978	110.2181	134.2135	201.1378	304.8477	577.10046	1704.109	5044.710
34	36.96058	40.25770	43.93309	48.03380	57.73018	69.85791	85.06696	104.1838	128.2588	158.6267	245.4767	384.5210	765.36535	2456.118	7884.609
36	39.33610	43.07688	47.27597	51.99437	63.27594	77.59831	95.83632	119.1209	148.9135	187.1022	299.1268	484.4631	1014.34568	3539.009	12321.95
38	41.73545	45.95272	50.71989	56.11494	69.15945	85.97034	107.7095	135.9042	172.5610	220.3159	364.0434	609.8305	1343.62216	5098.373	19255.30
40	44.15885	48.88637	54.26789	60.40198	75.40126	95.02552	120.7998	154.7620	199.6351	259.0565	442.5926	767.0914	1779.09031	7343.858	30088.66
45	50.32416	56.48107	63.61420	71.89271	92.71986	121.0294	159.7002	212.7435	285.7493	386.5056	718.9048	1358.230	3585.12846	18281.31	91831.50
50	56.64516	64.46318	73.68283	84.57940	112.7969	152.6671	209.3480	290.3359	406.5289	573.7702	1163.909	2400.018	7217.71628	45497.19	280255.7
100	129.33370	170.4814	228.8030	312.2323	607.2877	1237.624	2610.025	5638.368	12381.66	27484.52	137796.1	696010.5	783×10^4	414×10^6	196×10^8

Note: To convert from this table to values of an annuity in advance, find the annuity in arrears above for one more period and subtract 1.00000.

Table 4

Present Value of an Annuity of $1 in Arrears

$$P_A = \frac{1 - (1 + r)^{-n}}{r}$$

r = discount rate; n = number of payments

n Periods = Payments — Payments in Arrears

$$P_A \; \text{(Value in Table 4)} = \sum \text{(Individual Values from Table 2)}$$

No. of Payments = n	½%	1%	1½%	2%	3%	4%	5%	6%	7%	8%	10%	12%	15%	20%	25%
1	.99502	.99010	.98522	.98039	.97087	.96154	.95238	.94340	.93458	.92593	.90909	.89286	.86957	.83333	.80000
2	1.98510	1.97040	1.95588	1.94156	1.91347	1.88609	1.85941	1.83339	1.80802	1.78326	1.73554	1.69005	1.62571	1.52778	1.44000
3	2.97025	2.94099	2.91220	2.88388	2.82861	2.77509	2.72325	2.67301	2.62432	2.57710	2.48685	2.40183	2.28323	2.10648	1.95200
4	3.95050	3.90197	3.85438	3.80773	3.71710	3.62990	3.54595	3.46511	3.38721	3.31213	3.16987	3.03735	2.85498	2.58873	2.36160
5	4.92587	4.85343	4.78264	4.71346	4.57971	4.45182	4.32948	4.21236	4.10020	3.99271	3.79079	3.60478	3.35216	2.99061	2.68928
6	5.89638	5.79548	5.69719	5.60143	5.41719	5.24212	5.07569	4.91732	4.76654	4.62288	4.35526	4.11141	3.78448	3.32551	2.95142
7	6.86207	6.72819	6.59821	6.47199	6.23028	6.00205	5.78637	5.58238	5.38929	5.20637	4.86842	4.56376	4.16042	3.60459	3.16114
8	7.82296	7.65168	7.48593	7.32548	7.01969	6.73274	6.46321	6.20979	5.97130	5.74664	5.33493	4.96764	4.48732	3.83716	3.32891
9	8.77906	8.56602	8.36052	8.16224	7.78611	7.43533	7.10782	6.80169	6.51523	6.24689	5.75902	5.32825	4.77158	4.03097	3.46313
10	9.73041	9.47130	9.22218	8.98259	8.53020	8.11090	7.72173	7.36009	7.02358	6.71008	6.14457	5.65022	5.01877	4.19247	3.57050
11	10.67703	10.36763	10.07112	9.78685	9.25262	8.76048	8.30641	7.88687	7.49867	7.13896	6.49506	5.93770	5.23371	4.32706	3.65640
12	11.61893	11.25508	10.90751	10.57534	9.95400	9.38507	8.86325	8.38384	7.94269	7.53608	6.81369	6.19437	5.42062	4.43922	3.72512
13	12.55615	12.13374	11.73153	11.34837	10.63496	9.98565	9.39357	8.85268	8.35765	7.90378	7.10336	6.42355	5.58315	4.53268	3.78010
14	13.48871	13.00370	12.54338	12.10625	11.29607	10.56312	9.89864	9.29498	8.74547	8.24424	7.36669	6.62817	5.72448	4.61057	3.82408
15	14.41662	13.86505	13.34323	12.84926	11.93794	11.11839	10.37966	9.71225	9.10791	8.55948	7.60608	6.81086	5.84737	4.67547	3.85926
16	15.33993	14.71787	14.13126	13.57771	12.56110	11.65230	10.83777	10.10590	9.44665	8.85137	7.82371	6.97399	5.95423	4.72956	3.88741
17	16.25863	15.56225	14.90765	14.29187	13.16612	12.16567	11.27407	10.47726	9.76322	9.12164	8.02155	7.11963	6.04716	4.77463	3.90993
18	17.17277	16.39827	15.67256	14.99203	13.75351	12.65930	11.68959	10.82760	10.05909	9.37189	8.20141	7.24967	6.12797	4.81219	3.92794
19	18.08236	17.22601	16.42617	15.67846	14.32380	13.13394	12.08532	11.15812	10.33560	9.60360	8.36492	7.36578	6.19823	4.84350	3.94235
20	18.98742	18.04555	17.16864	16.35143	14.87747	13.59033	12.46221	11.46992	10.59401	9.81815	8.51356	7.46944	6.25933	4.86958	3.95388
22	20.78406	19.66038	18.62082	17.65805	15.93692	14.45112	13.16300	12.04158	11.06124	10.20074	8.77154	7.64465	6.35866	4.90943	3.97049
24	22.56287	21.24339	20.03041	18.91393	16.93554	15.24696	13.79864	12.55036	11.46933	10.52876	8.98474	7.78432	6.43377	4.93710	3.98111
26	24.32402	22.79520	21.39863	20.12104	17.87684	15.98277	14.37519	13.00317	11.82578	10.80998	9.16095	7.89566	6.49056	4.95632	3.98791
28	26.06769	24.31644	22.72672	21.28127	18.76411	16.66306	14.89813	13.40616	12.13711	11.05108	9.30657	7.98442	6.53351	4.96967	3.99226
30	27.79405	25.80771	24.01584	22.39646	19.60044	17.29203	15.37245	13.76483	12.40904	11.25778	9.42691	8.05518	6.56598	4.97894	3.99505
32	29.50328	27.26959	25.26714	23.46833	20.38877	17.87355	15.80268	14.08404	12.64656	11.43500	9.52638	8.11159	6.59053	4.98537	3.99683
34	31.19555	28.70267	26.48173	24.49859	21.13184	18.41120	16.19290	14.36814	12.85401	11.58693	9.60857	8.15656	6.60910	4.98984	3.99797
36	32.87102	30.10751	27.66068	25.48884	21.83225	18.90828	16.54685	14.62099	13.03521	11.71719	9.67651	8.19241	6.62314	4.99295	3.99870
38	34.52985	31.48466	28.80505	26.44064	22.49246	19.36786	16.86789	14.84602	13.19347	11.82887	9.73265	8.22099	6.63375	4.99510	3.99917
40	36.17223	32.83469	29.91585	27.35548	23.11477	19.79277	17.15909	15.04630	13.33171	11.92461	9.77905	8.24378	6.64178	4.99660	3.99947
45	40.20720	36.09451	32.55234	29.49016	24.51871	20.72004	17.77407	15.45583	13.60552	12.10840	9.86281	8.28252	6.65429	4.99863	3.99983
50	44.14279	39.19612	34.99969	31.42361	25.72976	21.48218	18.25593	15.76186	13.80075	12.23348	9.91481	8.30450	6.66051	4.99945	3.99994
100	78.54264	63.02888	51.62470	43.09835	31.59891	24.50500	19.84791	16.61755	14.26925	12.49432	9.99927	8.33323	6.66666	5.00000	4.00000

Note: To convert from this table to values of an annuity in advance, find the annuity in arrears above for one less period and add 1.00000.

A

ABC. Activity-based costing.

abnormal spoilage. Actual spoilage exceeding that expected when operations are normally efficient. Usual practice treats this cost as an expense of the period rather than as a product cost. Contrast with normal spoilage.

absorbed overhead. Overhead costs allocated to individual products at some overhead rate. Also called applied overhead.

absorption costing. See full absorption costing.

Accelerated Cost Recovery System. ACRS. A form of accelerated depreciation that Congress enacted in 1981 and amended in 1986. The system provides percentages of the asset's cost that a firm depreciates each year for tax purposes. ACRS ignores salvage value. We do not generally use these amounts for financial accounting.

accelerated depreciation. Any method of calculating depreciation charges where the charges become progressively smaller each period. Examples are double-declining-balance and sum-of-the-years'-digits methods.

account. Any device for accumulating additions and subtractions relating to a single asset, liability, or owners' equity item, including revenues and expenses.

account analysis method. A method of separating fixed from variable costs involving the classification of the various product cost accounts. For example, we classify direct materials as variable and depreciation on a factory building as fixed.

account payable. A liability representing an amount owed to a creditor, usually arising from purchase of merchandise or materials and supplies; not necessarily due or past due. Normally, a current liability.

account receivable. A claim against a debtor usually arising from sales or services rendered, not necessarily due or past due. Normally, a current asset.

accountability center. Responsibility center.

accounting. A system conveying information about a specific entity. The information is in financial terms and

appears only if it is reasonably precise. The AICPA defines accounting as a service activity whose "function is to provide quantitative information, primarily financial in nature, about economic entities that is intended to be useful in making economic decisions."

accounting cycle. The sequence of accounting procedures starting with journal entries for various transactions and events and ending with the financial statements or, perhaps, the post-closing trial balance.

accounting equation. Assets = Equities. Assets = Liabilities + Owners' Equity.

accounting period. The time period between two consecutive balance sheets. The time period for which financial statements that measure flows, such as the income statement and the statement of cash flows, are prepared. Should be clearly identified on the financial statements.

accounting principles. The methods or procedures used in accounting for events reported in the financial statements. We tend to use this term when the method or procedure has received official authoritative sanction from a pronouncement of a group such as the FASB or SEC. Contrast with accounting conventions and conceptual framework.

accounting rate of return. Income for a period divided by average investment during the period. Based on income, rather than discounted cash flows and, hence, is a poor decision making aid or tool. See ratio.

accounting system. The procedures for collecting and summarizing financial data in a firm.

accrual. Recognition of an expense (or revenue) and the related liability (or asset) that is caused by an accounting event, frequently by the passage of time, and that is not signaled by an explicit cash transaction. For example, the recognition of interest expense or revenue (or wages, salaries, or rent) at the end of a period even though no explicit cash transaction is made at that time. Cash flow follows accounting recognition; contrast with deferral.

accrual basis of accounting. The method of recognizing revenues as a firm sells goods (or delivers them) and as it renders services, independent of the time when it receives cash. This systems recognizes expenses in the period when it recognizes the related revenue independent of the time when it pays out cash. *SFAC No. 1* says ''accrual accounting attempts to record the financial effects on an enterprise of transactions and other events and circumstances that have cash consequences for the enterprise in the periods in which those transactions, events, and circumstances occur rather than only in the periods in which cash is received or paid by the enterprise.'' Contrast with the cash basis of accounting. See accrual and deferral. We could more correctly call the basis ''accrual/deferral'' accounting.

acquisition cost. Of an asset, the net invoice price plus all expenditures to place and ready the asset for its intended use. The other expenditures might include legal fees, transportation charges, and installation costs.

ACRS. Accelerated Cost Recovery System.

activity accounting. Responsibility accounting.

activity-based costing. ABC. Method of assigning indirect costs, including non-manufacturing overhead, to products and services. ABC assumes that almost all overhead costs associate with activities within the firm and vary with respect to the drivers of those activities. Some practitioners suggest that ABC attempts to find the drivers for all indirect costs; these people note that in the long run, all costs are variable, so fixed indirect costs do not occur. The method first assigns costs to activities and then to products based on the products' usages of the activities.

activity-based depreciation. Production method of depreciation.

activity basis. Costs are variable or fixed (incremental or unavoidable) with respect to some activity, such as production of units (or the undertaking of some new project). Usage calls this activity the ''activity basis.''

activity center. Unit of the organization that performs a set of tasks.

activity variance. Sales volume variance.

actual cost (basis). Acquisition or historical cost. Also contrast with standard cost.

actual costing (system). Method of allocating costs to products using actual direct materials, actual direct labor, and actual factory overhead. Contrast with normal costing and standard costing.

additional processing cost. Costs incurred in processing joint products after the splitoff point.

administrative costs (expenses). Costs (expenses) incurred for the firm as a whole, in contrast with specific functions such as manufacturing or selling. Includes items such as salaries of top executives, general office rent, legal fees, and auditing fees.

after cost. Said of expenditures to be made subsequent to revenue recognition. For example, expenditures for repairs under warranty are after costs. Proper recognition of after costs involves a debit to expense at the time of the sale and a credit to an estimated liability. When the liability is discharged, the debit is to the estimated liability and the credit is to the assets consumed.

agency theory. A branch of economics relating the behavior of principals (such as owner non-managers or bosses) and their agents (such as non-owner managers or subordinates). The principal assigns responsibility and authority to the agent but the agent's own risks and preferences differ from those of the principal. The principal cannot observe all activities of the agent. Both the principal and the agent must consider the differing risks and preferences in designing incentive contracts.

agent. One authorized to transact business, including executing contracts, for another.

allocate. To spread a cost from one account to several accounts, to several products or activities, or to several periods.

allocation base. Accounting often assigns joint costs to cost objectives with some systematic method. The allocation base specifies the method. For example, a firm might assign the cost of a truck to periods based on miles driven during the period; the allocation base is miles. Or, the firm might assign the cost of a factory supervisor to a product based on direct labor hours; the allocation base is direct labor hours.

analysis of variances. See variance analysis.

annuity. A series of payments of equal amount, usually made at equally spaced time intervals.

annuity certain. An annuity payable for a definite number of periods. Contrast with contingent annuity.

annuity due. An annuity whose first payment is made at the start of period 1 (or at the end of period 0). Contrast with annuity in arrears.

annuity in advance. An annuity due.

annuity in arrears. An ordinary annuity whose first payment occurs at the end of the first period.

applied cost. A cost that a firm has allocated to a department, product, or activity; it is not necessarily based on actual costs incurred.

applied overhead. Overhead costs charged to departments, products, or activities. Also called absorbed overhead.

approximate net realizable value method. A method of assigning joint costs to joint products based on revenues minus additional processing costs of the end products.

asset. *SFAC No. 6* defines assets as ''probable future economic benefits obtained or controlled by a particular entity as a result of past transactions. . . . An asset has three essential characteristics: (a) it embodies a probable future benefit that involves a capacity, singly or in combination with other assets, to contribute directly or indirectly to future net cash inflows, (b) a particular entity can obtain the benefit and control others' access to it, and (c) the transaction or other event giving rise to the entity's right to or control of the benefit has already occurred.'' A footnote points out that ''probable'' means that which we can reasonably expect or believe but that is not certain or proved. May be tangible or intangible, short-term (current) or long-term (noncurrent).

audit. Systematic inspection of accounting records involving analyses, tests, and confirmations.

audit committee. A committee of the board of directors of a corporation usually consisting of outside directors who nominate the independent auditors and discuss the auditors' work with them. If the auditors believe the shareholders should know about certain matters, the auditors first bring these matters to the attention of the audit committee.

auditor's opinion. Auditor's report.

auditor's report. The auditor's statement of the work done and an opinion of the financial statements. The auditor usually gives unqualified (''clean'') opinions, but may qualify them, or the auditor may disclaim an opinion in the report. Often called the ''accountant's report.''

average. The arithmetic mean of a set of numbers; obtained by summing the items and dividing by the number of items.

average collection period of receivables. See ratio.

average-cost flow assumption. An inventory flow assumption where the cost of units equals the weighted average cost of the beginning inventory and purchases.

avoidable cost. A cost that ceases if a firm discontinues an activity. An incremental or variable cost. See programmed cost.

B

backlog. Orders for which a firm has insufficient inventory on hand for current delivery and will fill in a later period.

bailout period. In a capital budgeting context, the total time that must elapse before net accumulated cash inflows from a project including potential salvage value of assets at various times equal or exceed the accumulated cash outflows. Contrast with payback period, which assumes completion of the project and uses terminal salvage value. Bailout is superior to payback because bailout takes into account, at least to some degree, the present value of the cash flows after termination date being considered. The potential salvage value at any time includes some estimate of the flows that can occur after that time.

balance. As a noun, the sum of debit entries minus the sum of credit entries in an account. If positive, we call the difference a debit balance; if negative, a credit balance. As a verb, to find the difference described above.

balance sheet. Statement of financial position that shows Total Assets = Total Liabilities + Owners' Equity. The balance sheet accounts comprising Total Assets are usually classified under the headings (1) current assets, (2) investments, (3) property, plant, and equipment, or (4) intangible assets. The balance sheet accounts comprising Total Liabilities are usually classified under the heading current liabilities or long-term liabilities.

basic accounting equation. Accounting equation.

basic cost-flow equation. Cost flow equation.

beginning inventory. Valuation of inventory on hand at the beginning of the accounting period.

behavioral congruence. Goal congruence.

betterment. An improvement, usually capitalized.

Big Six. The six largest U.S. public accounting (CPA) partnerships; in alphabetical order: Arthur Andersen & Co.; Coopers & Lybrand; Deloitte & Touche; Ernst & Young; KPMG Peat Marwick; and Price Waterhouse.

bill of materials. A specification of the quantities of direct materials a firm expects to use to produce a given job or quantity of output.

book. As a verb, to record a transaction. As a noun, usually plural, the journals and ledgers. As an adjective, see book value.

book inventory. An inventory amount that results, not from physical count, but from the amount of beginning inventory plus invoice amounts of net purchases less invoice amounts of requisitions or withdrawals; implies a perpetual method.

book value. The amount shown in the books or in the accounts for an asset, liability, or owners' equity item. Generally used to refer to the net amount of an asset or group of assets shown in the account that records the asset and reductions, such as for amortization, in its cost. Of a firm, the excess of total assets over total liabilities. Net assets.

breakeven point. The volume of sales required so that total revenues and total costs are equal. May be expressed in units (fixed costs/contribution per unit) or in sales dollars [selling price per unit × (fixed costs/contribution per unit)].

budget. A financial plan that a firm uses to estimate the results of future operations. Frequently used to help control future operations. In governmental operations, budgets often become the law.

budgetary control. Management of governmental (nongovernmental) unit in accordance with an official (approved) budget in order to keep total expenditures within authorized (planned) limits.

budgeted cost. See standard cost for definition and contrast.

budgeted statements. Pro forma statements prepared before the event or period occurs.

burden. See overhead costs.

by-product. A joint product whose sales value is so small relative to the sales value of the other joint product(s) that it does not receive normal accounting treatment. The costs assigned to by-products reduce the costs of the main product(s). Accounting allocates by-products a share of joint costs such that the expected gain or loss upon their sale is zero. Thus, by-products appear in the accounts at net realizable value.

C

cancelable lease. See lease.

capacity. Stated in units of product, the amount that a firm can produce per unit of time. Stated in units of input, such as direct labor hours, the amount of input that a firm can use in production per unit of time. A firm uses this measure of output or input in allocating fixed costs if the amounts producible are normal, rather than maximum, amounts.

capacity cost. A fixed cost incurred to provide a firm with the capacity to produce or to sell. Consists of standby costs and enabling costs. Contrast with programmed costs.

capacity variance. Production volume variance.

capital budget. Plan of proposed outlays for acquiring long-term assets and the means of financing the acquisition.

capital budgeting. The process of choosing investment projects for an enterprise by considering the present value of cash flows and deciding how to raise the funds the investment requires.

capital lease. A lease treated by the lessee as both the borrowing of funds and the acquisition of an asset to be amortized. Both the liability and the asset are recognized on the balance sheet. Expenses consist of interest on the debt and amortization of the asset. The lessor treats the lease as the sale of the asset in return for a series of future cash receipts. Contrast with operating lease.

capital rationing. In a capital budgeting context, the imposing of constraints on the amounts of total capital expenditures in each period.

capitalization of earnings. The process of estimating the economic worth of a firm by computing the net present value of the predicted net income (not cash flows) of the firm for the future.

capitalization rate. An interest rate used to convert a series of payments or receipts or earnings into a single present value.

CASB. Cost Accounting Standards Board. A board authorized by the U.S. Congress to ''promulgate cost-accounting standards designed to achieve uniformity and consistency in the cost-accounting principles followed by defense contractors and subcontractors under federal contracts.'' The principles the CASB promulgated since 1970 have considerable weight in practice where the FASB has not established a standard. Congress allowed the CASB to go out of existence in 1980 but reinstated it in 1990.

cash basis of accounting. In contrast to the accrual basis of accounting, a system of accounting in which a firm recognizes revenues when it receives cash and recognizes expenses as it makes disbursements. The firm makes no attempt to match revenues and expenses in measuring income.

cash budget. A schedule of expected cash receipts and disbursements.

cash flow. Cash receipts minus disbursements from a given asset, or group of assets, for a given period. Financial analysts sometimes use this term to mean net income + depreciation + depletion + amortization.

central corporate expenses. General overhead expenses incurred in running the corporate headquarters and related supporting activities of a corporation. Accounting treats these expenses as period expenses. Contrast with manufacturing overhead. A major problem in line of business reporting is the treatment of these expenses.

central processing unit (CPU). The component of a computer system carrying out the arithmetic, logic, and data transfer.

certified internal auditor. See CIA.

certified management accountant. See CMA.

certified public accountant. CPA. An accountant who has satisfied the statutory and administrative requirements of his or her jurisdiction to be registered or licensed as a public accountant. In addition to passing the Uniform CPA Examination administered by the AICPA, the CPA must meet certain educational, experience, and moral requirements that differ from jurisdiction to jurisdiction. The jurisdictions are the 50 states, the District of Columbia, Guam, Puerto Rico, and the Virgin Islands.

CGA. Canada. Certified General Accountant. An accountant who has satisfied the experience, education, and examination requirements of the Certified General Accountants' Association.

charge. As a noun, a debit to an account; as a verb, to debit.

CIA. Certified Internal Auditor. One who has satisfied certain requirements of the Institute of Internal Auditors including experience, ethics, education, and passing examinations.

CICA. Canadian Institute of Chartered Accountants.

closing inventory. Ending inventory.

CMA. Certified Management Accountant certificate. Awarded by the Institute of Management Accountants of the Institute of Management to those who pass a set of examinations and meet certain experience and continuing education requirements.

collusion. Cooperative effort by employees to commit fraud or other unethical acts.

common cost. Cost resulting from use of raw materials, a facility (for example, plant or machines), or a service (for example, fire insurance) that benefits several products or departments and that a firm must allocate to those products or departments. Common costs result when two or more departments produce multiple products together although the departments could produce them separately; joint costs occur when two or more departments must produce multiple products together. Many writers use common costs and joint costs synonymously. See joint costs, indirect costs, and overhead. See sterilized allocation.

company-wide control. See control system.

compound interest. Interest calculated on principal plus previously undistributed interest.

compounding period. The time period for which a firm calculates interest. At the end of the period, the borrower may pay interest to the lender or may add the interest (that is, convert it) to principal for the next interest-earning period, which is usually a year or some portion of a year.

comptroller. Same meaning and pronunciation as controller.

confidence level. The measure of probability that the actual characteristics of the population lie within the stated precision of the estimate derived from a sampling process. A sample estimate may be expressed in the following terms: ''Based on the sample, we are 95% sure [confidence level] that the true population value is within the range of X to Y [precision].'' See precision.

conservatism. A reporting objective that calls for anticipation of all losses and expenses but defers recognition of gains or profits until they are realized in arm's-length transactions. In the absence of certainty, events are to be reported in a way that tends to minimize cumulative income. Conservatism does not mean reporting low income in every period. Over long-enough time spans, income is cash-in less cash-out. If a reporting method shows low income in early periods, it must show higher income in some later period.

contingent annuity. An annuity whose number of payments depends upon the outcome of an event whose timing is uncertain at the time the annuity is set up; for example, an annuity payable until death of the annuitant. Contrast with annuity certain.

continuous budget. A budget that perpetually adds a period in the future as the period just ended is dropped.

continuous compounding. Compound interest where the compounding period is every instant of time. See *e* for the computation of the equivalent annual or periodic rate.

contra account. An account, such as accumulated depreciation, that accumulates subtractions from another account, such as machinery.

contribution approach. Method of preparing income statements that separates variable costs from fixed costs in order to emphasize the importance of cost behavior patterns for purposes of planning and control.

contribution margin. Revenue from sales less all variable expenses. Contrast with gross margin.

contribution margin ratio. Contribution margin divided by net sales; usually measured from the price and cost of a single unit, but sometimes in total for companies with multiple products.

contribution per unit. Selling price less variable costs per unit.

control (controlling) account. A summary account with totals equal to those of entries and balances that appear in individual accounts in a subsidiary ledger. Accounts Receivable is a control account backed up with an account for each customer. The balance in a control account should not be changed unless a corresponding change is made in one of the subsidiary accounts.

control system. A device top management uses to ensure that lower-level management carries out its plans or to safeguard assets. Control designed for a single function within the firm is "operational control;" control designed for autonomous segments within the firm that generally have responsibility for both revenues and costs is "divisional control;" control designed for activities of the firm as a whole is "company-wide control." Systems designed for safeguarding assets are "internal control" systems.

controllable cost. A cost influenced by the way a firm carries out operations. For example, marketing executives control advertising costs. These costs are fixed or variable. See programmed costs and managed costs.

controller. The title often used for the chief accountant of an organization. Often spelled comptroller.

conversion cost. Direct labor costs plus factory overhead costs incurred in producing a product. That is, the cost to convert raw materials to finished products. Manufacturing cost.

co-product. A product sharing production facilities with another product. For example, if an apparel manufacturer produces shirts and jeans on the same line, these are co-products. Distinguish co-products from joint products and by-products that, by their very nature, a firm must produce together, such as the various grades of wood a lumber factory produces.

cost. The sacrifice, measured by the price paid or required to be paid, to acquire goods or services. Terminology often uses the term "cost" when referring to the valuation of a good or service acquired. When writers use the word in this sense, a cost is an asset. When the benefits of the acquisition (the goods or services acquired) expire, the cost becomes an expense or loss. Some writers, however, use cost and expense as synonyms. Contrast with expense.

cost accounting. Classifying, summarizing, recording, reporting, and allocating current or predicted costs. A subset of managerial accounting.

Cost Accounting Standards Board. See CASB.

cost accumulation. Bringing together, usually in a single account, all costs of a specified activity. Contrast with cost allocation.

cost allocation. Assigning costs to individual products or time periods. Contrast with cost accumulation.

cost-based transfer price. A transfer price based on historical costs.

cost behavior. The functional relation between changes in activity and changes in cost. For example, fixed versus variable costs; linear versus curvilinear cost.

cost/benefit criterion. Some measure of costs compared to some measure of benefits for a proposed undertaking. If the costs exceed the benefits, then the analyst judges the undertaking not worthwhile. This criterion will not yield good decisions unless the analyst estimates all costs and benefits flowing from the undertaking.

cost center. A unit of activity for which a firm accumulates expenditures and expenses.

cost driver. A factor that causes an activity's costs. See activity basis.

cost effective. Among alternatives, the one whose benefit, or payoff, per unit of cost is highest. Sometimes said of an action whose expected benefits exceed expected costs whether or not other alternatives exist with larger benefit/cost ratios.

cost estimation. The process of measuring the functional relation between changes in activity levels and changes in cost.

cost flow equation. Beginning Balance + Transfers In = Transfers Out + Ending Balance; BB + TI = TO + EB.

cost flows. Costs passing through various classifications within an entity. See flow of costs for a diagram.

cost objective. Any activity for which management desires a separate measurement of costs. Examples include departments, products, and territories.

cost of capital. Opportunity cost of funds invested in a business. The rate of return rational owners require an asset to earn before they will devote that asset to a particular purpose. Sometimes measured as the average rate per year a company must pay for its equities. In efficient capital markets, the discount rate that equates the expected present value of all future cash flows to common shareholders with the market value of common stock at a given time.

Analysts often measure the cost of capital by taking a weighted average of the firm's debt and various equity securities. We sometimes call the measurement so derived the "composite cost of capital," and some analysts confuse this measurement of the cost of capital with the cost of capital itself. For example, if the equities of a firm include substantial amounts for the deferred income tax liability, the composite cost of capital will underestimate the true cost of capital, the required rate of return on a firm's assets, because the deferred income tax liability has no explicit cost.

cost of goods manufactured. The sum of all costs allocated to products completed during a period, including materials, labor, and overhead.

cost of goods purchased. Net purchase price of goods acquired plus costs of storage and delivery to the place where the items can be productively used.

cost of goods sold. Inventoriable costs that firms expense because they sold the units; equals beginning inventory plus cost of goods purchased or manufactured minus ending inventory.

cost of sales. Generally refers to cost of goods sold; occasionally, to selling expenses.

cost pool. Indirect cost pool. Groupings or aggregations of costs, usually for subsequent analysis.

cost sheet. Statement that shows all the elements comprising the total cost of an item.

cost terminology. The word "cost" appears in many accounting terms. The accompanying exhibit classifies some of these terms according to the distinctions between the terms in accounting usage. Joel Dean was, to our knowledge, the first to attempt such distinctions; we have used some of his ideas here. We discuss some of the terms in more detail under their own listings.

Cost Terminology Chart: Distinctions among Terms Containing the Word "Cost"

Terms (Synonyms Given in Parentheses)	Distinctions and Comments
1. The following pairs of terms distinguish the basis measured in accounting.	
Historical cost v. Current Cost (Acquisition Cost)	A distinction used in financial accounting. Current cost can be used more specifically to mean replacement cost, net realizable value, or present value of cash flows. "Current cost" is often used narrowly to mean replacement cost.
Historical Cost v. Standard Cost (Actual Cost)	The distinction between historical and standard costs arises in product costing for inventory valuation. Some systems record actual costs while others record the standard costs.
2. The following pairs of terms denote various distinctions among historical costs. For each pair of terms, the sum of the two kinds of costs equals total historical cost used in financial reporting.	
Variable Cost v. Fixed Cost (Constant Cost)	Distinction used in breakeven analysis and in designing cost accounting systems, particularly for product costing. See (4), below, for a further subdivision of fixed costs and (5), below, for an economic distinction closely paralleling this one.

(continued)

Terms (Synonyms Given in Parentheses)			Distinctions and Comments
Traceable Cost	v.	Common Cost (Joint Cost)	Distinction arises in allocating manufacturing costs to product. Common costs are allocated to product, but the allocations are more-or-less arbitrary. The distinction also arises in segment reporting and in separating manufacturing from nonmanufacturing costs.
Direct Cost	v.	Indirect Cost	Distinction arises in designing cost accounting systems and in product costing. Direct costs can be traced directly to a cost object, (e.g., a product, a responsibility center) whereas indirect costs cannot.
Out-of-Pocket Cost (Outlay Cost; Cash Cost)	v.	Book Cost	Virtually all costs recorded in financial statements require a cash outlay at one time or another. The distinction here separates expenditures to occur in the future from those already made and is used in making decisions. Book costs, such as for depreciation, reduce income without requiring a future outlay of cash. The cash has already been spent. See future v. past costs in (5), below.
Incremental Cost (Marginal Cost; Differential Cost)	v.	Unavoidable Cost (Inescapable Cost; Sunk Cost)	Distinction used in making decisions. Incremental costs will be incurred (or saved) if a decision is made to go ahead (or to stop) some activity, but not otherwise. Unavoidable costs will be reported in financial statements whether the decision is made to go ahead or not, because cash has already been spent or committed. Not all unavoidable costs are book costs, as, for example, a salary promised but not yet earned, that will be paid even if a no-go decision is made.
			The economist restricts the term marginal cost to the cost of producing one more unit. Thus the next unit has a marginal cost; the next week's output has an incremental cost. If a firm produces and sells a new product, the related new costs would properly be called incremental, not marginal. If a factory is closed, the costs saved are incremental, not marginal.
Escapable Cost	v.	Inescapable Cost (Unavoidable Cost)	Same distinction as incremental v. sunk costs, but this pair is used only when the decision maker is considering stopping something—ceasing to produce a product, closing a factory, or the like. See next pair.
Avoidable Cost	v.	Unavoidable Cost	A distinction sometimes used in discussing the merits of variable and absorption costing. Avoidable costs are treated as product cost and unavoidable costs are treated as period expenses under variable costing.
Controllable Cost	v.	Uncontrollable Cost	The distinction here is used in assigning responsibility and in setting bonus or incentive plans. All costs can be affected by someone in the entity; those who design incentive schemes attempt to hold a person responsible for a cost only if that person can influence the amount of the cost.

3. In each of the following pairs, used in historical cost accounting, the word "cost" appears in one of the terms where "expense" is meant.

Expired Cost	v.	Unexpired Cost	The distinction is between *expense* and *asset*.
Product Cost	v.	Period Cost	The terms distinguish product cost from period expense. When a given asset is used, is its cost converted into work in process and then into finished goods on the balance sheet until the goods are sold, or is it an expense shown on this period's income statement? Product costs appear on the income statement as part of cost of goods sold in the period when the goods are sold. Period expenses appear on the income statement with an appropriate caption for the item in the period when the cost is incurred or recognized.

(continued)

Terms (Synonyms Given in Parentheses) | **Distinctions and Comments**

4. The following subdivisions of fixed (historical) costs are used in analyzing operations. The relation between the components of fixed costs is:

$$\text{Fixed Costs} = \text{Capacity Costs} + \text{Programmed Costs}$$

$$\underbrace{\text{Semifixed Costs} + \text{``Pure'' Fixed Costs}\quad +\quad \text{Fixed Portions of Semivariable Costs}}_{} \quad \underbrace{\text{Standby Costs} + \text{Enabling Costs}}_{}$$

Terms			Distinctions and Comments
Capacity Cost (Committed Cost)	v.	Programmed Cost (Managed Cost; Discretionary Cost)	Capacity costs give a firm the capability to produce or to sell. Programmed costs, such as for advertising or research and development, may not be essential, but once a decision to incur them is made, they become fixed costs.
Standby Cost	v.	Enabling Cost	Standby costs will be incurred whether capacity, once acquired, is used or not, such as property taxes and depreciation on a factory. Enabling costs, such as for security force, can be avoided if the capacity is unused.
Semifixed Cost	v.	Semivariable Cost	A cost fixed over a wide range but that can change at various levels is a semifixed cost or "step cost." An example is the cost of rail lines from the factory to the main rail line where fixed cost depends on whether there are one or two parallel lines, but are independent of the number of trains run per day. Semivariable costs combine a strictly fixed component cost plus a variable component. Telephone charges usually have a fixed monthly component plus a charge related to usage.

5. The following pairs of terms distinguish among economic uses or decision making uses or regulatory uses of cost terms.

Terms			Distinctions and Comments
Fully Absorbed Cost	v.	Variable Cost (Direct Cost)	Fully absorbed costs refer to costs where fixed costs have been allocated to units or departments as required by generally accepted accounting principles. Variable costs, in contrast, may be more relevant for making decisions, such as in setting prices.
Fully Absorbed Cost	v.	Full Cost	In full costing, all costs, manufacturing costs as well as central corporate express (including financing expenses) are allocated to product or divisions. In full absorption costing, only manufacturing costs are allocated to product. Only in full costing will revenues, expenses, and income summed over all products or divisions equal corporate revenues, expenses, and income.
Opportunity Cost	v.	Outlay Cost (Out-of-Pocket Cost)	Opportunity cost refers to the economic benefit foregone by using a resource for one purpose instead of for another. The outlay cost of the resource will be recorded in financial records. The distinction arises because a resource is already in the possession of the entity with a recorded historical cost. Its economic value to the firm, opportunity cost, generally differs from the historical cost; it can be either larger or smaller.
Future Cost	v.	Past Cost	Effective decision making analyzes only present and future outlay costs, or out-of-pocket costs. Opportunity costs are relevant for profit maximizing; past costs are used in financial reporting.
Short-Run Cost	v.	Long-Run Cost	Short-run costs vary as output is varied for a given configuration of plant and equipment. Long-run costs can be incurred to change that configuration. This pair of terms is the economic analog of the accounting pair, see

(continued)

Terms (Synonyms Given in Parentheses)			Distinctions and Comments
			(2) above, variable and fixed costs. The analogy is not perfect because some short-run costs are fixed, such as property taxes on the factory, from the point of view of breakeven analysis.
Inputed Cost	v.	Book Cost	In a regulatory setting some costs, for example the cost of owners' equity capital, are calculated and used for various purposes; these are imputed costs. Imputed costs are not recorded in the historical costs accounting records for financial reporting. Book costs are recorded.
Average Cost	v.	Marginal Cost	The economic distinction equivalent to fully absorbed cost of product and variable cost of product. Average cost is total cost divided by number of units. Marginal cost is the cost to produce the next unit (or the last unit).
Differential Cost (Incremental Cost)	v.	Variable Cost	Whether a cost changes or remains fixed depends on the activity basis being considered. Typically, but not invariably, costs are said to be variable or fixed with respect to an activity basis such as changes in production levels. Typically, but not invariably, costs are said to be differential or not with respect to an activity basis such as the undertaking of some new venture. For example, consider the decision to undertake the production of food processors, rather than food blenders, which the manufacturer has been making. To produce processors requires the acquisition of a new machine tool. The cost of the new machine tool is incremental with respect to a decision to produce food processors instead of food blenders, but, once acquired, becomes a fixed cost of producing food processors. If costs of direct labor hours are going to be incurred for the production of food processors or food blenders, whichever is produced (in a scenario when not both are to be produced), such costs are variable with respect to production measured in units, but not incremental with respect to the decision to produce processors rather than blenders. This distinction is often blurred in practice, so a careful understanding of the activity basis being considered is necessary for an understanding of the concepts being used in a particular application.

cost-volume-profit analysis. A study of the sensitivity of profits to changes in units sold (or produced) or costs or prices.

cost-volume-profit graph (chart). A graph that shows the relation between fixed costs, contribution per unit, breakeven point, and sales. See breakeven chart.

costing. The process of calculating the cost of activities, products, or services. The British word for cost accounting.

Critical Path Method. A method of network analysis in which normal duration time is estimated for each activity within a project. The critical path identifies the shortest completion period based on the most time-consuming sequence of activities from the beginning to the end of the network. Compare PERT.

cross-section analysis. Analysis of financial statements of various firms for a single period of time; contrast with time-series analysis where accountants analyze statements of a given firm for several periods of time.

current assets. Cash and other assets that a firm expects to turn into cash, sell, or exchange within the normal operating cycle of the firm or one year, whichever is longer. One year is the usual period for classifying asset balances on the balance sheet. Current assets include cash, marketable securities, receivables, inventory, and current prepayments.

current cost. Cost stated in terms of current values (of productive capacity) rather than in terms of acquisition cost.

current liability. A debt or other obligation that a firm must discharge within a short time, usually the earnings cycle or one year, normally by expending current assets.

current ratio. Sum of current assets divided by sum of current liabilities. See ratio.

curvilinear (variable) cost. A continuous, but not necessarily linear (straight-line), functional relation between activity levels and costs.

D

DCF. Discounted cash flow.

debt-equity ratio. Total liabilities divided by total equities. See ratio. Sometimes the denominator is merely total shareholders' equity. Sometimes the numerator is restricted to long-term debt.

decentralized decision making. A firm gives a manager of a business unit responsibility for that unit's revenues and costs, freeing the manager to make decisions about prices, sources of supply, and the like, as though the unit were a separate business that the manager owns. See responsibility accounting and transfer price.

deferral. The accounting process concerned with past cash receipts and payments; in contrast to accrual. Recognizing a liability resulting from a current cash receipt (as for magazines to be delivered) or recognizing an asset from a current cash payment (or for prepaid insurance or a long-term depreciable asset).

deferred annuity. An annuity whose first payment is made sometime after the end of the first period.

denominator volume. Capacity measured in the number of units the firm expects to produce this period; divided into budgeted fixed costs to obtain fixed costs applied per unit of product.

department(al) allocation. First, accumulate costs in cost pools for each department. Then, using separate rates, or sets of rates, for each department, allocate from each cost pool to products produced in that department.

dependent variable. See regression analysis.

depreciation. Amortization of plant assets; the process of allocating the cost of an asset to the periods of benefit—the depreciable life. Classified as a production cost or a period expense, depending on the asset and whether the firm uses absorption or variable costing.

Descartes' rule of signs. In a capital budgeting context, the rule says that a series of cash flows will have a nonnegative number of internal rates of return. The number equals the number of variations in the sign of the cash flow series or is less than that number by an even integer. Consider the following series of cash flows, the first occurring now and the others at subsequent yearly intervals:

$-100, -100, +50, +175, -50, +100$. The internal rates of return are the numbers for r that satisfy the equation

$$-100 - \frac{100}{(1 + r)} + \frac{50}{(1 + r)^2} + \frac{175}{(1 + r)^3} - \frac{50}{(1 + r)^4} + \frac{100}{(1 + r)^5} = 0.$$

The series of cash flows has three variations in sign: a change from minus to plus, a change from plus to minus, and a change from minus to plus. The rule says that this series must have either one or three internal rates of return; in fact, it has only one, about 12 percent. But also see reinvestment rate.

determination. See determine.

determine. Accountants and those who describe the accounting process often use (in our opinion, overuse) the verb "determine" and the noun "determination." A leading dictionary associates the following meanings with the verb "determine": settle, decide, conclude, ascertain, cause, affect, control, impel, terminate, and decide upon. In addition, accounting writers can mean any one of the following: measure, allocate, report, calculate, compute, observe, choose, and legislate. In accounting, there are two distinct sets of meanings—those encompassed by the synonym "cause or legislate" and those encompassed by the synonym "measure." The first set of uses conveys the active notion of causing something to happen and the second set of uses conveys the more passive notion of observing something that someone else has caused to happen. An accountant who speaks of cost or income "determination" generally means measurement or observation, not causation; management and economic conditions cause costs and income to be what they are. One who speaks of accounting principles "determination" can mean choosing or applying (as in "determining depreciation charges" from an allowable set) or causing to be acceptable (as in the FASB "determining" the accounting for leases). In the long run, income is cash in less cash out, so management and economic conditions "determine" (cause) income to be what it is. In the short run, reported income is a function of accounting principles chosen and applied, so the accountant "determines" (measures) income. A question such as "Who determines income?" has, therefore, no unambiguous answer. The meaning of "an accountant determining acceptable accounting principles" is also vague. Does the clause mean merely choosing one from the set of generally acceptable principles, or does it mean using professional judgment to decide that some of the generally accepted principles are not correct under the current circumstances? We try never to use "determine" unless we mean "cause." Otherwise we use "measure," "report," "calculate," "compute," or whatever specific verb seems appropriate. We suggest that careful writers will always "determine" to use the most specific verb to convey meaning. "Determine" is seldom the best choice of words to describe a process where those who make decisions often differ from those who apply technique.

differentiable cost. If a total cost curve is smooth (in mathematical terms, differentiable), then we say that the curve graphing the derivative of the total cost curve shows differentiable costs, the cost increments associated with infinitesimal changes in volume.

differential. An adjective used to describe the change (increase or decrease) in a cost, expense, investment, cash flow, revenue, profit, and the like as the firm produces or sells one or more additional (or fewer) units or undertakes (or ceases) an activity.

differential analysis. Analysis of differential costs, revenues, profits, investment, cash flow, and the like.

differential cost. See differential.

direct cost. Cost of direct material and direct labor incurred in producing a product. In some accounting literature, writers use this term to mean the same thing as variable cost.

direct costing. Another, less-preferred, term for variable costing.

direct labor (material) cost. Cost of labor (material) applied and assigned directly to a product; contrast with indirect labor (material).

direct labor variance. Difference between actual direct labor costs and standard direct labor costs allowed.

discount factor. The reciprocal of one plus the discount rate. If the discount rate is 10 percent per period, the discount factor for three periods is $1/(1.10)^3 = (1.10)^{-3} = 0.75131$.

discount rate. Interest rate used to convert future payments to present values.

discounted bailout period. In a capital budgeting context, the total time that must elapse before discounted value of net accumulated cash flows from a project, including potential salvage value at various times of assets, equals or exceeds the present value of net accumulated cash outflows. Contrast with discounted payback period.

discounted cash flow. DCF. Using either the net present value or the internal rate of return in an analysis to measure the value of future expected cash expenditures and receipts at a common date. In discounted cash flow analysis, choosing the alternative with the largest internal rate of return may yield wrong answers given mutually exclusive projects with differing amounts of initial investment for two of the projects. Consider, to take an unrealistic example to illustrate the point, a project involving an initial investment of $1, with an IRR of 60 percent and another project involving an initial investment of $1 million with an IRR of 40 percent. Under most conditions, most firms will prefer the second project to the first, but choosing the project with the larger IRR will lead to undertaking the first, not the second. Usage calls this shortcoming of choosing between alternatives based on the magnitude of the internal rate or return, rather than based on the magnitude of the net present value of the cash flows, the "scale effect."

discounted payback period. The shortest amount of time which must elapse before the discounted present value of cash inflows from a project, excluding potential salvage value, equals the discounted present value of the cash outflows.

discretionary costs. Programmed costs.

distributed processing. Processing in a complex computer information network, in which data relevant only to individual locations is processed locally, while information required elsewhere is transmitted either to the central computer or to a local computer for further processing.

division. A more or less self-contained business unit which is part of a larger family of business units under common control.

driver. A cause of costs incurred. Examples include order processing, issuing an engineering change order, changing the production schedule, and stopping production to change machine settings. The notion arises primarily in product costing, particularly activity-based costing.

dual transfer prices. The transfer price charged to the buying division differs from that credited to the selling division. Such prices make sense when the selling division has excess capacity and, as usual, the fair market value exceeds the incremental cost to produce the goods or services being transferred.

E

e. The base of natural logarithms; 2.71828. . . . If interest compounds continuously during a period at stated rate of r

per period, then the effective interest rate is equivalent to interest compounded once per period at rate i where $i = e^r - 1$. Tables of e^r are widely available. If 12 percent annual interest compounds continuously, the effective annual rate is $e^{.12} - 1 = 12.75$ percent. Interest compounded continuously at rate r for d days is $e^{rd/365} - 1$. For example, interest compounded for 92 days at 12 percent is $e^{.12 \times 92/365} - 1 = 3.07$ percent.

earnings per share (of common stock). Net income to common shareholders (net income minus preferred dividends) divided by the average number of common shares outstanding. See ratio.

economic order quantity. In mathematical inventory analysis, the optimal amount of stock to order when demand reduces inventory to a level called the "reorder point." If K_o represents the incremental cost of placing a single order, D represents the total demand for a period of time in units, and K_c represents the incremental holding cost during the period per unit of inventory, then the economic order quantity $Q = \sqrt{2K_oD/K_c}$. Usage sometimes calls Q the "optimal lot size."

effective (interest) rate. Of a bond, the internal rate of return or yield to maturity at the time of issue. Contrast with coupon rate. If the bond is issued for a price below par, the effective rate is higher than the coupon rate; if it is issued for a price greater than par, then the effective rate is lower than the coupon rate. In the context of compound interest, when the compounding period on a loan is different from one year, such as a nominal interest rate of 12 percent compounded monthly. The effective interest is the single rate that one could use at the end of the year to multiply the principal at the beginning of the year and give the same amount as results from compounding interest each period during the year. For example, if 12 percent per year is compounded monthly, the effective annual interest rate is 12.683 percent. That is, if you compound $100 each month at 1 percent per month, the $100 will grow to $112.68 at the end of the year. In general, if the nominal rate is r percent per year and is compounded m times per year, then the effective rate is $(1 + r/m)^m - 1$.

efficiency variance. A term used for the quantity variance for materials, labor, or variable overhead in a standard costing system.

efficient market hypothesis. The supposition in finance that securities' prices reflect all available information and react nearly instantaneously and in an unbiased fashion to new information.

enabling costs. A type of capacity cost that a firm will stop incurring if it shuts down operations completely but will incur in full if it carries out operations at any level. Costs of a security force or of a quality control inspector for an assembly line might be examples. Contrast with standby costs.

ending inventory. The cost of inventory on hand at the end of the accounting period, often called "closing inventory." The dollar amount of inventory is carried to the subsequent period.

engineering method (of cost estimation). Estimates of unit costs of product built up from study of the materials, labor, and overhead components of the production process.

EOQ. Economic order quantity.

EPS. Earnings per share.

EPVI. Excess present value index.

equities. Liabilities plus owners' equity. See equity.

equity. A claim to assets; a source of assets. *SFAS No. 3* defines equity as "the residual interest in the assets of an entity that remains after deducting its liabilities." Usage may be changing so that "equity" will exclude liabilities. We prefer to keep the broader definition, including liabilities, because there is no other single word that serves this useful purpose.

equivalent production. Equivalent units.

equivalent units (of work). The number of units of completed output that would require the same costs as a firm would actually incur for production of completed and partially completed units during a period. Used primarily in process costing calculations to measure in uniform terms the output of a continuous process.

escapable cost. Avoidable costs.

excess present value. In a capital budgeting context, present value of (anticipated net cash inflows minus cash outflows including initial cash outflow) for a project.

excess present value index. Present value of future cash inflows divided by initial cash outlay.

expected value. The mean or arithmetic average of a statistical distribution or series of numbers.

expected value of (perfect) information. Expected net benefits from an undertaking with (perfect) information minus expected net benefits of the undertaking without (perfect) information.

expense. As a noun, a decrease in owners' equity caused by using up assets in producing revenue or carrying out other activities that comprise a part of the entity's

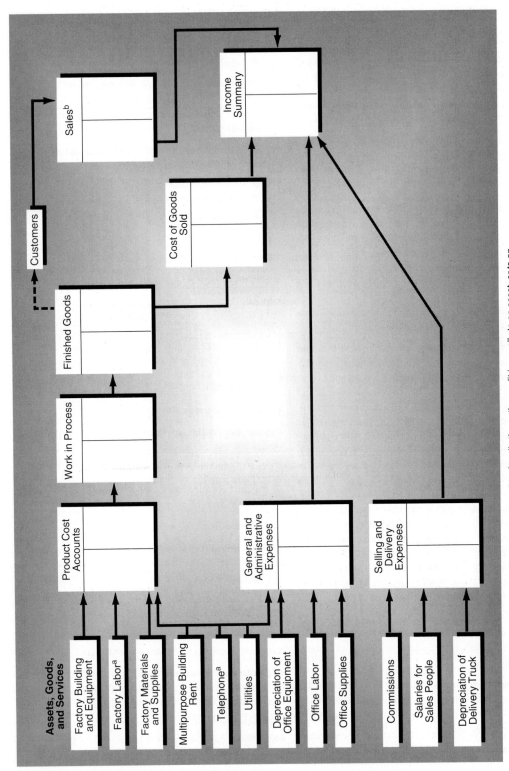

Assets, Goods, and Services

Factory Building and Equipment

Factory Labor[a]

Factory Materials and Supplies

Multipurpose Building Rent

Telephone[a]

Utilities

Depreciation of Office Equipment

Office Labor

Office Supplies

Commissions

Salaries for Sales People

Depreciation of Delivery Truck

Product Cost Accounts

Work in Process

Finished Goods

Customers

Sales[b]

Cost of Goods Sold

General and Administrative Expenses

Selling and Delivery Expenses

Income Summary

a   The credit in the entry to record these items is usually to a payable, for all others, the credit is usually to an asset, or to an asset contra account.

b   When the firm records sales to customers, it credits the Sales account. The debit is usually Cash or Accounts Receivable.

G-14

operations. A "gone" asset or net asset; an expired cost. The amount is the cost of the assets used. Do not confuse with expenditure or disbursement, which may occur before, when, or after the firm recognizes the related expense. Use the word "cost" to refer to an item that still has service potential and is an asset. Use the word "expense" after the firm has used the asset's service potential. As a verb, to designate a past or current expenditure as a current expense.

extraordinary item. A material expense or revenue item characterized both by its unusual nature and infrequency of occurrence that appears along with its income tax effects separately from ordinary income and income from discontinued operations on the income statement. Accountants would probably classify a loss from an earthquake as an extraordinary item. Accountants treat gain (or loss) on retirement of bonds as an extraordinary item under the terms of *SFAS No. 4*.

F

factory. Used synonymously with manufacturing as an adjective.

factory burden. Manufacturing overhead.

factory cost. Manufacturing cost.

factory expense. Manufacturing overhead. Expense is a poor term in this context because the item is a product cost.

factory overhead. Usually an item of manufacturing cost other than direct labor or direct materials.

FASB. Financial Accounting Standards Board. An independent board responsible, since 1973, for establishing generally accepted accounting principles. Its official pronouncements are *"Statements of Financial Accounting Concepts" ("SFAC"), "Statements of Financial Accounting Standards" ("SFAS"),* and *"Interpretations."*

favorable variance. An excess of actual revenues over expected revenues. An excess of standard cost over actual cost.

feedback. The process of informing employees about how their actual performance compares with the expected or desired level of performance in the hope that the information will reinforce desired behavior and reduce unproductive behavior.

FIFO. First-in, first-out; the inventory flow assumption which firms use to compute ending inventory cost from most recent purchases and cost of goods sold from oldest purchases including beginning inventory. Contrast with LIFO.

financial accounting. The accounting for assets, equities, revenues, and expenses of a business. Primarily concerned with the historical reporting of the financial position and operations of an entity to external users on a regular, periodic basis. Contrast with managerial accounting.

financial leverage. See leverage.

finished goods (inventory account). Manufactured product ready for sale; a current asset (inventory) account.

first in, first out. See FIFO.

fixed budget. A plan that provides for specified amounts of expenditures and receipts that do not vary with activity levels. Sometimes called a "static budget." Contrast with flexible budget.

fixed cost (expense). An expenditure or expense that does not vary with volume of activity, at least in the short run. See capacity costs, which include enabling costs and standby costs, and programmed costs for various subdivisions of fixed costs. See cost terminology.

fixed manufacturing overhead applied. The portion of fixed manufacturing overhead cost allocated to units produced during a period.

fixed overhead variance. Difference between actual fixed manufacturing costs and fixed manufacturing costs applied to production in a standard costing system.

flexible budget. Budget that projects receipts and expenditures as a function of activity levels. Contrast with fixed budget.

flexible budget allowance. With respect to manufacturing overhead, the total cost that a firm should have incurred at the level of activity actually experienced during the period.

flow. The change in the amount of an item over time.

flow of costs. Costs passing through various classifications within an entity. See the accompanying diagram for a summary of product and period cost flows.

fraudulent financial reporting. Intentional or reckless conduct that results in materially misleading financial statements.

full absorption costing. The method of costing which assigns all types of manufacturing costs (direct material, direct labor, fixed and variable overhead) to units produced; required by GAAP. Also called "absorption costing." Contrast with variable costing.

full costing. full costs. The total cost of producing and selling a unit. Full cost per unit equals full absorption cost per unit plus marketing, administrative, interest, and other central corporate expenses, per unit. The sum of full costs for all units equals total costs of the firm. Often used in long-term profitability and pricing decisions.

future value. Value at a specified future date of a sum increased at a specified interest rate.

G

GAAP. Generally accepted accounting principles. A plural noun.

GAAS. Generally accepted auditing standards. A plural noun. Not to be confused with GAS.

GAS. Goods available for sale. Not to be confused with GAAS.

GASB. Governmental Accounting Standards Board. An independent body responsible, since 1984, for establishing accounting standards for state and local government units. It is part of the Financial Accounting Foundation, parallel to the FASB, and currently consists of five members.

generally accepted accounting principles. GAAP. As previously defined by the APB and now by the FASB, the conventions, rules, and procedures necessary to define accepted accounting practice at a particular time; includes both broad guidelines and relatively detailed practices and procedures.

generally accepted auditing standards. GAAS. The standards, as opposed to particular procedures, promulgated by the AICPA (in *Statements on Auditing Standards*) that concern "the auditor's professional quantities" and "the judgment exercised by him in the performance of his examination and in his report." Currently, there are ten such standards: three general ones (concerned with proficiency, independence, and degree of care to be exercised), three standards of field work, and four standards of reporting. The first standard of reporting requires that the auditor's report state whether or not the financial statements are prepared in accordance with generally accepted accounting principles. Thus the typical auditor's report says that the examination was conducted in accordance with generally accepted auditing standards and that the statements are prepared in accordance with generally accepted accounting principles.

goal congruence. All members of an organization have incentives to perform for a common interest, such as shareholder wealth maximization for a corporation.

going-concern assumption. For accounting purposes, accountants assume a business will remain in operation long enough to carry out all its current plans. This assumption partially justifies the acquisition cost basis, rather than a liquidation or exit value basis, of accounting.

goods available for sale. The sum of beginning inventory plus all acquisitions of merchandise or finished goods during an accounting period.

Governmental Accounting Standards Advisory Council. A group that consults with the GASB on agenda, technical issues, and the assignment of priorities to projects. It comprises more than a dozen members representing various areas of expertise.

Governmental Accounting Standards Board. GASB.

gross margin. Net sales minus cost of goods sold.

H

historical cost. Acquisition cost; original cost; a sunk cost.

hurdle rate. Required rate of return in a discounted cash flow analysis.

I

I. Identity matrix.

ICMA. Institute of Certified Management Accountants. Overseas administration of the CMA program. Its parent organization is the IMA, the Institute of Management Accountants.

ideal standard costs. Standard costs set equal to those that a firm would incur under the best-possible conditions.

identity matrix. A square matrix with ones on the main diagonal and zeros elsewhere; a matrix $\mathbf{I}$ such that for any other matrix $\mathbf{A}$, $\mathbf{IA} = \mathbf{AI} = \mathbf{A}$. The matrix equivalent to the number one.

implicit interest. Interest not paid or received. All transactions involving the deferred payment or receipt of cash involve interest, whether explicitly stated or not. The implicit interest on a single-payment note is the difference between the amount collected at maturity less the amount lent at the start of the loan. The implicit interest rate per year can be computed from

$$\left[\frac{\text{Cash Received at Maturity}}{\text{Cash Lent}} \right]^{(1/t)} - 1,$$

where t is the term of the loan in years; t need not be an integer.

imputed cost. A cost that does not appear in accounting records, such as the interest that could be earned on cash spent to acquire inventories rather than, say, government bonds. Or, consider a firm that owns the buildings it occupies. This firm has an imputed cost for rent in an amount equal to what it would have to pay to use similar buildings owned by another. Opportunity cost.

incentive compatible compensation. Said of a compensation plan for managers that induces them to act for the interests of owners while acting in their own interests. For example, a time of rising prices and increasing inventories when using a LIFO cost flow assumption implies paying lower income taxes than using FIFO. A bonus scheme for managers based on accounting net income would not be incentive compatible, because the owners benefit more under LIFO, while managers benefit more if they report using FIFO. See goal congruence.

income. Excess of revenues and gains over expenses and losses for a period; net income. Sometimes used with an appropriate modifier to refer to the various intermediate amounts shown in a multiple-step income statement. Sometimes used to refer to revenues, as in "rental income."

income from continuing operations. As defined by *APB Opinion No. 30,* all *revenues* less all expenses except for the following: results of operations (including income tax effects) that a firm has discontinued or will discontinue; gains or losses, including income tax effects, on disposal of segments of the business; gains or losses, including income tax effects, from extraordinary items; and the cumulative effect of accounting changes.

income from discontinued operations. Income, net of tax effects, from parts of the business that it has discontinued during the period or will discontinue in the near future. Accountants report such items on a separate line of the income statement after income from continuing operations but before extraordinary items.

income statement. The statement of revenues, expenses, gains, and losses for the period ending with net income for the period. Accountants usually show the earnings-per-share amount on the income statement; the recon-

ciliation of beginning and ending balances of retained earnings may also appear in a combined statement of income and retained earnings.

incremental. See differential. An adjective used to describe the increase in cost, expense, investment, cash flow, revenue, profit, and the like if the firm produces or sells one or more units or if it undertakes an activity.

incremental cost. See incremental.

indirect cost pool. Any grouping of individual costs that a firm does not identify with a cost objective.

indirect costs. Costs of production not easily associated with the production of specific goods and services; overhead costs. Accountants may allocate them on some arbitrary basis to specific products or departments.

indirect labor (material) cost. An indirect cost for labor (material) such as for supervisors (supplies).

inescapable cost. A cost that is not avoidable because of an action. For example, if two operating rooms in a hospital are closed, but security is still employed, the security costs are "inescapable" with respect to the decision to close the operating rooms.

Institute of Management Accountants. See IMA. Oversees administration the CMA examination.

Institute of Internal Auditors. IIA. The national association of accountants who are engaged in internal auditing and are employed by business firms. Administers a comprehensive professional examination; those who pass qualify to be designated CIA, certified internal auditor.

intangible asset. A nonphysical, noncurrent right that gives a firm an exclusive or preferred position in the marketplace. Examples are a copyright, patent, trademark, goodwill, organization costs, capitalized advertising cost, computer programs, licenses for any of the preceding, government licenses (e.g., broadcasting or the right to sell liquor), leases, franchises, mailing lists, exploration permits, import and export permits, construction permits, and marketing quotas.

interest. The charge or cost for using money, usually borrowed funds. Interest on own money used is an opportunity cost, imputed interest. The amount of interest for a loan is the total amount paid by borrower to lender less the amount paid by lender to borrower. See interest rate for discussion of quoted amount. See effective interest rate and nominal interest rate.

interest rate. See interest. A basis used for computing the cost of borrowing funds usually expressed as a ratio per period of time between the number of currency units (e.g., dollars) charged per number of currency units borrowed for that same period of time. See simple interest, compound interest, effective (interest) rate, nominal interest rate.

internal audit. An audit conducted by employees to ascertain whether internal control procedures are working, as opposed to an external audit conducted by a CPA.

internal control. See control system.

internal controls. Policies and procedures designed to provide management with reasonable assurance that employees behave in a way that enables the firm to meet its organizational goals.

internal rate of return. IRR. The discount rate that equates the net present value of a stream of cash outflows and inflows to zero.

inventory. As a noun, the balance in an asset account such as raw materials, supplies, work in process, and finished goods. As a verb, to calculate the cost of goods on hand at a given time or to count items on hand physically.

investment center. A responsibility center, with control over revenues, costs, and assets.

investment decision. The decision whether to undertake an action involving production of goods or services; contrast with the financing decision.

IRR. Internal rate of return.

isoprofit line. On a graph delimiting feasible production possibilities of two products that require the use of the same, limited resources, a line showing all feasible production possibility combinations with the same profit or, perhaps, contribution margin.

J

JIT. See just-in-time inventory.

job cost sheet. A schedule showing actual or budgeted inputs for a special order.

job (-order) costing. Accumulation of costs for a particular identifiable batch of product, known as a job, as it moves through production.

joint cost. Cost of simultaneously producing or otherwise acquiring two or more products, called joint products, that a firm must, by the nature of the process, produce or acquire together, such as the cost of beef and hides

of cattle. Generally, accounting allocates the joint costs of production to the individual products in proportion to their respective sales value (or, sometimes physical quantities) at the splitoff point. Other examples include central corporate expenses and overhead of a department when it manufactures several products.

joint cost allocation. See joint cost.

joint product. One of two or more outputs with significant value produced by a process that a firm must produce or acquire simultaneously. See by-product and joint cost.

journal. The place where transactions are recorded as they occur. The book of original entry.

journal entry. A dated recording in a journal, showing the accounts affected, of equal debits and credits, with an explanation of the transaction, if necessary.

just-in-time inventory (production). JIT. System of managing inventory for manufacturing where a firm purchases or manufactures each component just before the firm uses it. Contrast with systems where firms acquire or manufacture many parts in advance of needs. JIT systems have much smaller, ideally no, carrying costs for inventory, but run higher risks of incurring stockout costs.

K

K. Two to the tenth power (2^{10} or 1,024), when referring to computer storage capacity. It derives from the prefix ''kilo'' which represents 1,000 in decimal notation.

know-how. Technical or business information of the type defined under trade secret, but that a firm does not maintain as a secret. The rules of accounting for this asset are the same as for other intangibles.

L

labor variances. The price (or rate) and quantity (or usage) variances for direct labor inputs in a standard costing system.

lead time. The time that elapses between placing an order and receipt of the goods or services ordered.

learning curve. A mathematical expression of the phenomenon that incremental unit costs to produce decrease as managers and labor gain experience from practice.

lease. A contract calling for the lessee (user) to pay the lessor (owner) for the use of an asset. A cancelable lease allows the lessee to cancel at any time. A noncancelable lease requires payments from the lessee for the life of the lease and usually shares many of the economic characteristics of debt financing. Most long-term noncancelable leases meet the usual criteria classifying them as liabilities but the firm need not show some leases entered into before 1977 as liabilities. *SFAS No. 13* and the SEC require disclosure in notes to the financial statements of the commitments for long-term noncancelable leases.

least and latest rule. Pay the least amount of taxes as late as possible within the law to minimize the present value of tax payments for a given set of operations.

leverage. "Operating leverage" refers to the tendency of net income to rise at a faster rate than sales when fixed costs are present. A doubling of sales, for example, usually implies a more than doubling of net income. "Financial leverage" (or "capital leverage") refers to the increased rate of return on owners' equity (see ratio) when an investment earns a return larger than the after-tax interest rate paid for debt financing. Because the interest charges on debt are usually fixed, any incremental income benefits owners and none benefits debtors. When writers use the term "leverage" without a qualifying adjective, the term usually refers to financial leverage, the use of long-term debt in securing funds for the entity.

liability. An obligation to pay a definite (or reasonably definite) amount at a definite (or reasonably definite) time in return for a past or current benefit. That is, the obligation arises from other than an executory contract. A probable future sacrifice of economic benefits arising from present obligations of a particular entity to transfer assets or to provide services to other entities in the future as a result of past transactions or events. *SFAC No. 6* says that "probable" refers to that which we can reasonably expect or believe but that is neither certain nor proved. A liability has three essential characteristics: (1) an obligation to transfer assets or services at a specified or knowable date, (2) the entity has little or no discretion to avoid the transfer, and (3) the event causing the obligation has already happened; that is, it is not executory.

life annuity. A contingent annuity in which payments cease at death of a specified person(s), usually the annuitant(s).

LIFO. Last-in, first-out. An inventory flow assumption where the cost of goods sold equals the cost of the most recently acquired units and a firm computes the ending inventory cost from costs of the oldest units; contrast with FIFO. In periods of rising prices and increasing inventories, LIFO leads to higher reported expenses and therefore lower reported income and lower balance sheet inventories than does FIFO.

linear programming. A mathematical tool for finding profit maximizing (or cost minimizing) combinations of products to produce when a firm has several products that it can produce but faces linear constraints on the resources available in the production processes or on maximum and minimum production requirements.

long-run. long-term. A term denoting a time or time periods in the future. How far in the future depends on context. For some securities traders, "long-term" can mean anything beyond the next hour or two. For most managers, it means anything beyond the next year or two. For government policy makers, it can mean anything beyond the next decade or two. For geologists, it can mean millions of years.

long-term debt ratio. Noncurrent liabilities divided by total assets.

long-term solvency risk. The risk that a firm will not have sufficient cash to pay its debts sometime in the long run.

loophole. Imprecise term meaning a technicality allowing a taxpayer (or financial statements) to circumvent a law's (or GAAP's) intent without violating its letter.

M

make-or-buy decision. A managerial decision about whether the firm should produce a product internally or purchase it from others. Proper make-or-buy decisions in the short run result when a firm considers only incremental costs in decision making.

management. Executive authority that operates a business.

management accounting. See managerial accounting.

management audit. An audit conducted to ascertain whether a firm or one of its operating units properly carries out its objectives, policies, and procedures. Generally applies only to activities for which accountants can specify qualitative standards.

management by exception. A principle of management where managers focus attention on performance only if it differs significantly from that expected.

management by objective. A management approach designed to focus on the definition and attainment of overall and individual objectives with the participation of all levels of management.

management information system. A system designed to provide all levels of management with timely and reliable information required for planning, control and evaluation of performance.

managerial (management) accounting. Reporting designed to enhance the ability of management to do its job of decision making, planning, and control; contrast with financial accounting.

manufacturing cost. Cost of producing goods, usually in a factory.

manufacturing expense. An imprecise, and generally incorrect, alternative title for manufacturing overhead.

manufacturing overhead. General manufacturing costs incurred in providing a capacity to carry on productive activities not directly associated with identifiable units of product. Accounting treats fixed manufacturing overhead cost as a product cost under full absorption costing but as an expense of the period under variable costing.

margin of safety. Excess of actual, or budgeted, sales over breakeven sales. Expressed in dollars or in units of product.

marginal cost. The incremental cost or differential cost of the last unit added to production or the first unit subtracted from production. See cost terminology.

marginal costing. Direct costing.

marginal revenue. The increment in revenue from sale of one additional unit of product.

market-based transfer price. A transfer price based on external market data, rather than internal company data.

marketing costs. Costs incurred to sell; includes locating customers, persuading them to buy, delivering the goods or services, and collecting the sales proceeds.

master budget. A budget projecting all financial statements and their components.

material. As an adjective, it means relatively important. See materiality. Currently, no operational definition exists. As a noun, raw material.

materials variances. Price and quantity variances for direct materials in standard costing systems. Difference between actual cost and standard cost.

materiality. The concept that accounting should disclose separately only those events that are relatively important (no operable definition yet exists) for the business or for understanding its statements. *SFAC No. 2* suggests that accounting information is material if "the judgment of a reasonable person relying on the information would have been changed or influenced by the omission or misstatement."

matrix. A rectangular array of numbers or mathematical symbols.

matrix inverse. For a given square matrix $\mathbf{A}$, the square matrix inverse is the matrix, $\mathbf{A}^{-1}$, such that $\mathbf{AA}^{-1} = \mathbf{A}^{-1}\mathbf{A} = \mathbf{I}$, the identity matrix. Not all square matrices have inverses. Those that do not we call "singular"; those that do are nonsingular.

mix variance. Many standard cost systems specify combinations of inputs, for example, labor of a certain skill and materials of a certain quality grade. Sometimes combinations of inputs used differ from those contemplated by the standard. The mix variance attempts to report the cost difference that changing the combination of inputs causes.

mixed cost. A semifixed or a semivariable cost.

monetary items. Amounts fixed in terms of dollars by statute or contract. Cash, accounts receivable, accounts payable, and debt. The distinction between monetary and nonmonetary items is important for constant dollar accounting and for foreign exchange gain or loss computations. In the foreign exchange context, account amounts denominated in dollars are not monetary items, whereas amounts denominated in any other currency are monetary.

moving average. An average computed on observations over time. As a new observation becomes available, analysts drop the oldest one so that they always compute the average for the same number of observations and only the most recent ones. Some, however, use this term synonymously with weighted average.

mutually exclusive projects. Competing investment projects, where accepting one project eliminates the possibility of undertaking the remaining projects.

N

NASDAQ. National Association of Securities Dealers Automated Quotation System; a computerized system to provide brokers and dealers with price quotations for securities traded over the counter as well as for some NYSE securities.

National Association of Accountants. NAA. Former name for the national society open to all engaged in activities closely associated with managerial accounting. Now called the Institute of Management Accountants.

National Automated Accounting Research System. NAARS. A computer-based information retrieval system containing, among other things, the complete text of most public corporate annual reports and *Forms 10-K*. The system is available to users through the AICPA.

negotiated transfer price. A transfer price set jointly by the buying and selling divisions.

net. Reduced by all relevant deductions.

net income. The excess of all revenues and gains for a period over all expenses and losses of the period.

net present value. Discounted or present value of all cash inflows and outflows of a project or from an investment at a given discount rate.

net realizable (sales) value. A method for allocating joint costs in proportion to realizable values of the joint products. For example, joint products A and B together cost $100 and A sells for $60 whereas B sells for $90. Then a firm would allocate to A ($60/$150) × $100 = .40 × $100 = $40 of cost while it would allocate to B ($90/$150) × $100 = $60 of cost.

network analysis. A method of planning and scheduling a project, usually displayed in diagrammatic form, in order to identify the interrelated sequences that must be accomplished to complete the project.

New York Stock Exchange. NYSE. A public market where various corporate securities are traded.

NIFO. Next in, first out. In making decisions, many managers consider replacement costs (rather than historical costs) and refer to them as NIFO costs.

noncontrollable cost. A cost that a particular manager cannot control.

nonmanufacturing costs. All costs incurred other than those to produce goods.

normal costing. Method of charging costs to products using actual direct materials, actual direct labor, and predetermined factory overhead rates.

normal costing system. Costing based on actual material and labor costs, but using predetermined overhead rates per unit of some activity basis (such as direct labor hours or machine hours) to apply overhead to production. Management decides the rate to charge to production for overhead at the start of the period. During, or at the end of, the period the accountant multiplies this rate by the actual number of units of the base activity (such as actual direct labor hours worked or actual machine hours used during the period) to apply overhead to production.

normal spoilage. Costs incurred because of ordinary amounts of spoilage; accounting prorates such costs to units produced as product costs; contrast with abnormal spoilage.

normal standard cost. normal standards. The cost a firm expects to incur under reasonably efficient operating conditions with adequate provision for an average amount of rework, spoilage, and the like.

normal volume. The level of production over a time span, usually 1 year, that will satisfy purchasers' demands and provide for reasonable inventory levels.

O

objective function. In linear programming, the name of the profit or cost criterion the analyst wants to optimize.

operating budget. A formal budget for the operating cycle or for a year.

operating cash flow. Financial statement analysts use this term to mean cash flow − capital expenditures − dividends.

operating leverage. Usually said of a firm with a large proportion of fixed costs in its total costs. Consider a book publisher or a railroad: the incremental costs of producing another book or transporting another freight car are much less than average cost, so the gross margin upon sale of the unit is relatively large. Contrast, for example, a grocery store, where the contribution margin is usually less than 5 percent of the selling price. For firms with equal profitability, however defined, we say the one with the larger percentage increase in income from a given percentage increase in unit sales has the larger operating leverage. See leverage for contrast of this term with ''financial leverage.'' See cost terminology for definition of terms involving the word ''cost.''

operational control. See control system.

opportunity cost. The present value of the income (or costs) that a firm could earn (or save) from using an asset in its best alternative use to the one under consideration.

opportunity cost of capital. Cost of capital.

ordinary annuity. An annuity in arrears.

outlier. Said of an observation (or data point) which appears to differ significantly in some regard from other observations (or data points) of supposedly the same phenomenon. Often used in describing the results of a regression analysis when an observation is not "near" the fitted regression equation.

out-of-stock cost. The estimated decrease in future profit as a result of losing customers because a firm has insufficient quantities of inventory currently on hand to meet customers' demands.

output. Physical quantity or monetary measurement of goods and services produced.

overapplied (overabsorbed) overhead. An excess of costs applied, or charged, to product for a period over actual overhead costs during the period. A credit balance in an overhead account after overhead is assigned to product.

overhead costs. Any cost not directly associated with the production or sale of identifiable goods and services. Sometimes called "burden" or "indirect costs" and, in Britain, "oncosts." Frequently limited to manufacturing overhead.

overhead rate. Standard, or other predetermined rate, at which a firm applies overhead costs to products or to services.

owners' equity. Proprietorship; assets minus liabilities; paid-in capital plus retained earnings of a corporation; partners' capital accounts in a partnership; owner's capital account in a sole proprietorship.

P

payback period. Amount of time that must elapse before the cash inflows from a project equal the cash outflows.

payback reciprocal. One divided by the payback period. This number approximates the internal rate of return on a project when the project life exceeds twice the payback period and the cash inflows are identical in every period after the initial period.

percent. Any number, expressed as a decimal, multiplied by 100.

period cost. An inferior term for period expense.

period expense (charge). Expenditure, usually based upon the passage of time, charged to operations of the accounting period rather than capitalized as an asset; contrast with product cost.

perpetuity. An annuity whose payments continue forever. The present value of a perpetuity in arrears is p/r where p is the periodic payment and r is the interest rate per period. If \$100 is promised each year, in arrears, forever and the interest rate is 8 percent per year, then the value of the perpetuity is $\$1,250 = \$100/.08$.

PERT. *P*rogram *e*valuation and *r*eview *t*echnique. A method of network analysis in which three time estimates are made for each activity—the optimistic time, the most likely time, and the pessimistic time—and which gives an expected completion date for the project within a probability range.

physical units method. A method of allocating a joint cost to the joint products based on a physical measure of the joint products. For example, allocating the cost of a cow to sirloin steak and to hamburger, based on the weight of the meat. This method usually provides nonsensical (see sterilized allocation) results unless the physical units of the joint products tend to have the same value.

planning and control process. General name for the techniques of management comprising the setting of organizational goals and strategic plans, capital budgeting, operations budgeting, comparison of plans with actual results, performance evaluation and corrective action, and revisions of goals, plans, and budgets.

plantwide allocation method. First, use one cost pool for the entire plant. Then, allocate all costs from that pool to product using a single overhead allocation rate, or one set of rates, to all of the products of the plant, independent of the number of departments in the plant.

practical capacity. Maximum level at which the plant or department can operate efficiently.

precision. The degree of accuracy with which the estimate derived from sampling process is stated, usually expressed as a range of values around the estimate. A sample estimate may be expressed in the following terms: "Based on the sample, we are 95% sure [confidence level] that the true population value is within the range of X to Y [precision]." See confidence level.

predetermined (factory) overhead rate. Rate used in applying overhead to products or departments developed at the start of a period by dividing estimated overhead cost by the estimated number of units of the overhead allocation base (or denominator volume) activity. See normal costing.

present value. Value today (or at some specific date) of an amount or amounts to be paid or received later (or at other, different dates), discounted at some interest or discount rate.

price-earnings ratio. At a given time, the market value of a company's common stock, per share, divided by the earnings per common share for the past year. The denominator is usually based on income from continuing operations or, if the analyst thinks the current figure for that amount is not representative—such as when the number is negative—on some estimate of the number. See ratio.

price variance. In accounting for standard costs, (actual cost per unit − standard cost per unit) times actual quantity.

prime cost. Sum of direct materials plus direct labor costs assigned to product.

principal. An amount in which interest is charged or earned. The face amount of a loan. Also, the absent owner (principal) who hires the manager (agent) in a ''principal-agent'' relationship.

process costing. A method of cost accounting based on average costs (total cost divided by the equivalent units of work done in a period). Typically used for assembly lines or for products that are produced in a series of steps that are more continuous than discrete.

product. Goods or services produced.

product cost. Any manufacturing cost that can be inventoried. See flow of costs for example and contrast with period expenses.

production cost. Manufacturing cost.

production cost account. A temporary account for accumulating manufacturing costs during a period.

production department. A department producing salable goods or services; contrast with service department.

production volume variance. Standard fixed overhead rate per unit of normal capacity (or base activity) times (units of base activity budgeted or planned for a period minus actual units of base activity worked or assigned to product during the period). Often called a ''volume variance.''

profit center. A responsibility center for which a firm accumulates both revenue and expenses; contrast with cost center.

profit margin. Sales minus all expenses as a single amount. Frequently used to mean ratio of sales minus all operating expenses divided by sales.

profit margin percentage. Profit margin divided by net sales.

profit variance analysis. Analysis of the causes of the difference between budgeted profit in the master budget and the profits earned.

profit-volume analysis (equation). Analysis of changes in volume or contribution margin per unit or fixed costs on profit. See breakeven point.

program budgeting. Specification and analysis of inputs, outputs, costs, and alternatives that link plans to budgets.

programmed costs. A fixed cost not essential for carrying out operations. A firm can control research and development and advertising costs designed to generate new business, but once it commits to incur them, they become fixed costs. Sometimes called managed costs or discretionary costs; contrast with capacity costs.

prorate. To allocate in proportion to some base; for example, allocate service department costs in proportion to hours of service used by the benefitted department. Or, to allocate manufacturing variances to product sold and to product added to ending inventory.

prorating variances. See prorate.

Q

quantitative performance measure. A measure of output based on an objectively observable quantity, like units produced or direct costs incurred, rather than on an unobservable quantity or one observable only non-objectively, like quality of service provided.

quantity variance. Efficiency variance. In standard cost systems, the standard price per unit times (actual quantity used minus standard quantity that should be used).

quick ratio. Sum of (cash, current marketable securities, and receivables) divided by current liabilities. The analyst may exclude some nonliquid receivables from the numerator. Often called the ''acid test ratio.'' See ratio.

R

R^2. The proportion of the statistical variance of a dependent variable explained by the equation fit to independent variable(s) in a regression analysis.

rate of return on assets. Return on assets.

rate variance. Price variance, usually for direct labor costs.

ratio. The number resulting when one number is divided by another. Analysts generally use ratios to assess aspects of profitability, solvency, and liquidity. The commonly used financial ratios fall in three categories: (1) those that summarize some aspect of operations for a period, usually a year, (2) those that summarize some aspect of financial position at a given moment—the moment for which a balance sheet has been prepared, and (3) those that relate some aspect of operations to some aspect of financial position.

Exhibit 18.14 lists the most common financial ratios and shows separately both the numerator and denominator used to calculate each ratio.

For all ratios that require an average balance during the period, the analyst often derives the average as one half the sum of the beginning and ending balances. Sophisticated analysts recognize, however, that particularly when companies use a fiscal year different from the calendar year, this averaging of beginning and ending balances may be misleading. Consider, for example, the rate of return on assets of Sears, Roebuck & Company whose fiscal year ends on January 31. Sears chooses a January 31 closing date at least in part because inventories are at a low level and are therefore easy to count—it has sold the Christmas merchandise and the Easter merchandise has not yet all arrived. Furthermore, by January 31, Sears has collected for most Christmas sales, so receivable amounts are not unusually large. Thus at January 31, the amount of total assets is lower than at many other times during the year. Consequently, the denominator of the rate of return on assets, total assets, for Sears is more likely to represent the smallest amount of total assets on hand during the year than the average amount. The return on assets rate for Sears and other companies who choose a fiscal year-end to coincide with low points in the inventory cycle is likely to be larger than if a more accurate estimate of the average amounts of total assets were used.

raw material. Goods purchased for use in manufacturing a product.

regression analysis. A method of cost estimation based on statistical techniques for fitting a line (or its equivalent in higher mathematical dimensions) to an observed series of data points, usually by minimizing the sum of squared deviations of the observed data from the fitted line. Common usage calls the cost the analysis explains the "dependent variable"; it calls the variable(s) we use to estimate cost behavior "independent variable(s)." If we use more than one independent variable, the term for the analysis is "multiple regression analysis." See R^2, standard error, t-value.

reinvestment rate. In a capital budgeting context, the rate at which cash inflows from a project occurring before the project's completion are invested. Once such a rate is assumed, there will never be multiple internal rates of return. See Descartes' rule of signs.

relative performance evaluation. Setting performance targets and, sometimes, compensation in relation to performance of others, perhaps in different firms or divisions, facing a similar environment.

relevant cost. Incremental cost. Opportunity cost. The proper cost to use for making a decision.

relevant range. Activity levels over which costs are linear or for which flexible budget estimates and break-even charts will remain valid.

relative sales value method. Net realizable (sales) value method.

replacement cost. For an asset, the current fair market price to purchase another, similar asset (with the same future benefit or service potential).

required rate of return. Cost of capital.

research and development. Firms engage in research in hopes of discovering new knowledge that will create a new product, process, or service or improving a present product, process, or service. Development translates research findings or other knowledge into a new or improved product, process, or service. *SFAS No.2* requires that firms expense costs of such activities as incurred on the grounds that the future benefits are too uncertain to warrant capitalization as an asset. This treatment seems questionable to us because we wonder why firms would continue to undertake R&D if there were no expectation of future benefit; if future benefits exist, then its costs should be assets.

residual income. In an external reporting context, this term refers to net income to common shares (= net income less preferred stock dividends). In managerial accounting, this term refers to the excess of income for a division or segment of a company over the product of the cost of capital for the company multiplied by the average amount of capital invested in the division during the period over which the income was earned.

responsibility accounting. Accounting for a business by considering various units as separate entities, or profit centers, giving management of each unit responsibility for the unit's revenues and expenses. See transfer price.

responsibility center. Part or segment of an organization that top management holds accountable for a specified set of activities. Also called "accountability center." See cost center, investment center, profit center, revenue center.

return. A schedule of information required by governmental bodies, such as the tax return required by the Internal Revenue Service. Also the physical return of merchandise. See also return on investment.

return on assets. Net income plus after-tax interest charges plus minority interest in income divided by average total assets. Perhaps the single most useful ratio for assessing management's overall operating performance. Most financial economists would subtract average non-interest bearing liabilities from the denominator. Economists realize that when liabilities do not provide for explicit interest charges, the creditor adjusts the terms of contract, such as setting a higher selling price or lower discount, to those who do not pay cash immediately. (To take an extreme example, consider how much higher salary a worker who receives salary once per year, rather than once per month, would demand.) This ratio requires in the numerator the income amount before the firm accrues any charges to suppliers of funds. We cannot measure the interest charges implicit in the non-interest bearing liabilities, because items such as cost of goods sold and salary expense are somewhat larger because of these charges. Subtracting their amount from the denominator adjusts for their implicit cost. Such subtraction assumes that assets financed with non-interest bearing liabilities have the same rate of return as all the other assets.

return of investment. return on capital. Income (before distributions to suppliers of capital) for a period. As a rate, this amount divided by average total assets. Interest, net of tax effects, should be added back to net income for the numerator. See ratio.

revenue. The increase in owners' equity caused by a service rendered or the sale of goods. Sales of products, merchandise, and services, and earnings from interest, dividends, rents, and the like. The amount of revenue is the expected net present value of the net assets received.

Do not confuse with receipt of funds, which may occur before, when, or after revenue is recognized. Contrast with gain and income. Some writers use the term gross income synonymously with revenue; avoid such usage.

revenue center. A responsibility center within a firm that has control only over revenues generated; contrast with cost center. See profit center.

risk. A measure of the variability of the return on investment. For a given expected amount of return, most people prefer less risk to more risk. Therefore, in rational markets, investments with more risk usually promise, or investors are expected to yield, a higher rate of return than investments with lower risk. Most people use "risk" and "uncertainty" as synonyms. In technical language, however, these terms have different meanings. We use "risk" when we know the probabilities attached to the various outcomes are known, such as the probabilities of heads or tails in the flip of a fair coin. "Uncertainty" refers to an event where the probabilities of the outcomes, such as winning or losing a lawsuit, can only be estimated.

risk-adjusted discount rate. In a capital budgeting context, a decision maker compares projects by comparing their net present values for a given interest rate, usually the cost of capital. If a given project's outcome is considered to be much more or much less risky than the normal undertakings of the company, then the interest rate used in discounting will be increased (if the project is more risky) or decreased (if less risky) and the rate used is said to be "risk-adjusted."

ROI. Return on investment, but usually used to refer to a single project and expressed as a ratio: income divided by average cost of assets devoted to the project.

S

safety stock. Extra items of inventory kept on hand to protect against running out.

sales activity variance. Sales volume variance.

sales value method. Relative sales value method. See net realizable value method.

sales volume variance. Budgeted contribution margin per unit times (planned sales volume minus actual sales volume).

scale effect. See discounted cash flow.

scatter diagram. A graphic representation of the relation between two or more variables within a population.

SEC. Securities and Exchange Commission, an agency authorized by the U.S. Congress to regulate, among other things, the financial reporting practices of most public corporations. The SEC has indicated that it will usually allow the FASB to set accounting principles but it often requires more disclosure than required by the FASB. The SEC's accounting requirements are stated in its *Accounting Series Releases (ASR), Financial Reporting Releases (FRR), Accounting and Auditing Enforcement Releases, Staff Accounting Bulletins* (these are, strictly speaking, interpretations by the accounting staff, not rules of the Commissioners themselves), and *Regulation S-X.*

Securities and Exchange Commission. SEC.

semifixed costs. Costs that increase with activity as a step function.

semivariable costs. Costs that increase strictly linearly with activity but that are positive at zero activity level. Royalty fees of 2 percent of sales are variable; royalty fees of $1,000 per year plus 2 percent of sales are semivariable.

sensitivity analysis. Most decision making requires the use of assumptions. Sensitivity analysis is the study of how the outcome of a decision-making process changes as one or more of the assumptions change.

service cost. (current) service cost. Pension plan expenses incurred during an accounting period for employment services performed during that period; contrast with prior service cost.

service department. A department, such as the personnel or computer department, that provides services to other departments, rather than direct work on a salable product; contrast with production department. A firm must allocate costs of service departments whose services benefit manufacturing operations to product costs under full absorption costing.

setup. The time or costs required to prepare production equipment for doing a job.

SFAC. *Statement of Financial Accounting Concepts* of the FASB.

SFAS. *Statement of Financial Accounting Standards* of the FASB.

shadow price. One output of a linear programming analysis is the potential value of having available more of the scarce resources that constrain the production process; for example, the value of having more time available on a machine tool critical to the production of two products.

Common terminology refers to this value as "shadow price" or the "dual value" of the scarce resource.

short-run. short-term. The opposite of long-run or long-term. This pair of terms is equally imprecise.

shutdown cost. Those fixed costs which continue to be incurred after production has ceased. The costs of closing down a particular production facility.

simple interest. Interest calculated on principal where interest earned during periods before maturity of the loan is neither added to the principal nor paid to the lender. Interest = principal × interest rate × time, where the rate is a rate per period (typically a year) and time is expressed in units of that period. For example, if the rate is annual and the time is two months, then in the formula, use 2/12 for time. Seldom used in economic calculations except for periods less than one year and then only for computational convenience; contrast with compound interest.

spending variance. In standard cost systems, the rate or price variance for overhead costs.

splitoff point. The point where all costs are no longer joint costs but an analyst can identify costs associated with individual products or perhaps with a smaller number of joint products.

spoilage. See abnormal spoilage and normal spoilage.

standard cost. Anticipated cost of producing a unit of output; a predetermined cost to be assigned to products produced. Standard cost implies a norm: what costs should be. Budgeted cost implies a forecast, something likely, but not necessarily a "should," as implied by a norm. Firms use standard costs as the benchmark for gauging good and bad performance. While a firm may similarly use a budget, it need not. A budget may simply be a planning document, subject to changes whenever plans change, whereas standard costs usually change annually or when technology significantly changes or costs of labor and materials significantly change.

standard costing. Costing based on standard costs.

standard costing system. Product costing using standard costs rather than actual costs. May be based on either full absorption or variable costing principles.

standard error (of regression coefficients). A measure of the uncertainty about the magnitude of the estimated parameters of an equation fit with a regression analysis.

standard manufacturing overhead. Overhead costs expected to be incurred per unit of time and per unit produced.

standard price (rate). Unit price established for materials or labor used in standard cost systems.

standard quantity allowed. The quantity of direct material or direct labor (inputs) that production should have used if it produced the units of output in accordance with preset standards.

standby costs. A type of capacity cost, such as property taxes, incurred even if a firm shuts down operations completely. Contrast with enabling costs.

statement of cash flows. The FASB requires that all for-profit companies present a schedule of cash receipts and payments, classified by investing, financing, and operating activities. Companies may report operating activities with either the direct method (where only receipts and payments of cash appear) or the indirect method (which starts with net income and shows adjustments for revenues not currently producing cash and for expenses not currently using cash). ''Cash'' includes cash equivalents such as Treasury bills, commercial paper, and marketable securities held as current assets. Sometimes called the ''funds statement.'' Before 1987, the FASB required the presentation of a similar statement called the statement of changes in financial position, which tended to emphasize working capital, not cash.

static budget. Fixed budget.

status quo. Events or costs incurrences that will happen or a firm expects to happen in the absence of taking some contemplated action.

step allocation method. Step-down method.

step cost. Semifixed cost.

step-down method. The method for allocating service department costs that starts by allocating one service department's costs to production departments and to all other service departments. Then the firm allocates a second service department's costs, including costs allocated from the first, to production departments and to all other service departments except the first one. In this fashion, a firm may allocate the costs of all service departments, including previous allocations, to production departments and to those service departments whose costs it has not yet allocated.

stepped cost. Semifixed cost.

sterilized allocation. Optimal decisions result from considering incremental costs, only. Allocations of joint or common costs are never required for optimal decisions. An allocation of these costs that causes the optimal decision choice not to differ from the one that occurs when joint or common costs are unallocated is ''sterilized'' with respect to that decision. The term was first used in this context by Arthur L. Thomas. Because absorption costing requires that all manufacturing costs be allocated to product, and because some allocations can lead to bad decisions, Thomas (and we) advocate that the allocation scheme chosen lead to sterilized allocations that do not alter the otherwise optimal decision. There is, however, no single allocation scheme that is always sterilized with respect to all decisions. Thus, Thomas (and we) advocate that decisions be made on the basis of incremental costs before any allocations.

stockout. A firm needs a unit of inventory in production or to sell to a customer but it is unavailable.

stock-out costs. Contribution margin or other measure of profits not earned because a seller has run out of inventory and cannot fill a customer's order. A firm may incur an extra cost because of delay in filling an order.

summary of significant accounting principles. *APB Opinion No. 22* requires that every annual report summarize the significant accounting principles used in compiling the annual report. A firm may present this summary as a separate exhibit or as the first note to the financial statements.

sunk cost. Costs incurred in the past that current and future decisions cannot affect, and hence are irrelevant for decision making aside from income tax effects; contrast with incremental costs and imputed costs. For example, the acquisition cost of machinery is irrelevant to a decision of whether or not to scrap the machinery. The current exit value of the machine is the opportunity cost of continuing to own it and the cost of, say, electricity to run the machine is an incremental cost of its operation. Sunk costs become relevant for decision making when the analysis requires taking income taxes (gain or loss on disposal of asset) into account because the cash payment for income taxes depends on the tax basis of the asset. Avoid the term in careful writing because it is ambiguous. Consider, for example, a machine costing $100,000 with current salvage value of $20,000. Some (including us) would say that $100,000 is ''sunk''; others would say that only $80,000 is ''sunk.''

T

t-statistic. t-value. For an estimated regression coefficient, the estimated coefficient divided by the standard error of the estimate.

10-K. The name of the annual report required by the SEC of nearly all publicly held corporations.

time-adjusted rate of return. Internal rate of return.

time-series analysis. See cross-section analysis for definition and contrast.

traceable cost. A cost that a firm can identify with or assign to a specific product; contrast with a joint cost.

trade secret. Technical or business information such as formulas, recipes, computer programs, and marketing data not generally known by competitors and maintained by the firm as a secret. A famous example is the secret formula for Coca-Cola (a registered trademark of the company). Compare with know-how. Theoretically capable of having an infinite life, this intangible asset is capitalized only if purchased and then amortized over a period not to exceed 40 years. If the firm develops it internally, then it shows no asset.

transfer price. A substitute for a market, or arm's length, price used in profit, or responsibility center, accounting when one segment of the business "sells" to another segment. Incentives of profit center managers will not coincide with the best interests of the entire business unless a firm sets transfer prices properly.

transfer pricing problem. The problem of setting transfer prices so that both buyer and seller have goal congruence with respect to the parent organization's goals.

treasurer. The name sometimes given to the financial officer of a business in charge of managing cash and raising funds for investment.

20-F. Form required by the SEC for foreign companies issuing or trading their securities in the U.S. This form reconciles the foreign accounting results using foreign GAAP to amounts resulting from using U.S. GAAP.

U

unavoidable cost. A cost that is not an avoidable cost.

uncertainty. See risk for definition and contrast.

underapplied (underabsorbed) overhead. An excess of actual overhead costs for a period over costs applied, or charged, to products produced during the period. A debit balance remaining in an overhead account after the accountant assigns overhead to product.

unfavorable variance. In standard cost accounting, an excess of expected revenue over actual revenue or an excess of actual cost over standard cost.

usage variance. Efficiency variance.

V

value. Monetary worth; the term is usually so subjective that you should not use it without a modifying adjective unless most people would agree on the amount. Do not confuse with cost.

value added. Cost of a product or work in process, minus the cost of the material purchased for the product or work in process.

value variance. Price variance.

variable annuity. An annuity whose periodic payments depend on some uncertain outcome, such as stock market prices.

variable budget. Flexible budget.

variable costing. This method of allocating costs assigns only variable manufacturing costs to products and treats fixed manufacturing costs as period expenses. Contrast with full absorption costing.

variable costs. Costs that change as activity levels change. Strictly speaking, variable costs are zero when the activity level is zero. See semivariable costs. In accounting this term most often means the sum of direct costs and variable overhead.

variable overhead variance. Difference between actual and standard variable overhead costs.

variance. Difference between actual and standard costs or between budgeted and actual expenditures or, sometimes, expenses. The word has completely different meanings in accounting and statistics, where it means a measure of dispersion of a distribution.

variance analysis. Variance computation and investigation. This term's meaning differs in statistics.

variance investigation. Standard cost systems produce variance numbers of various sorts. These numbers are seldom exactly equal to zero. Management must decide when a variance differs sufficiently from zero to study its cause. This terms refers to deciding when to study the cause and the study itself.

visual curve fitting method. Sometimes, when a firm needs only rough approximations to the amounts of fixed and variable costs, management need not perform a formal regression analysis, but merely plot the data and draw in a line by hand that seems to fit the data, using the parameters of that line for the rough approximations.

volume variance. Production volume variance. Less often, used to mean sales volume variance.

W

waste. Residue of material from manufacturing operations with no sale value. Frequently, it has negative value because a firm must incur additional costs for disposal.

weighted average. An average computed by counting each occurrence of each value, not merely a single occurrence of each value. For example, if a firm purchases one unit for $1 and two units for $2 each, then the simple average of the purchase prices is $1.50 but the weighted average price per unit is $5/3 = $1.67. Contrast with moving average.

work in process (inventory account). Partially completed product; appears on the balance sheet as inventory.

working capital. Current assets minus current liabilities.

Y

yield. Internal rate of return of a stream of cash flows. Cash yield is cash flow divided by book value. Dividend yield.

yield variance. Measures the input-output relation holding the standard mix of inputs constant. It is the part of the efficiency variance not called the mix variance. It is (standard price multiplied by actual amount of input used in the standard mix) − (standard price multiplied by standard quantity allowed for the actual output).

Z

zero-base(d) budgeting. ZBB. In preparing an ordinary budget for the next period, a manager starts with the budget for the current period and makes adjustments as seem necessary, because of changed conditions for the next period. Because most managers like to increase the scope of the activities managed and since most prices increase most of the time, amounts in budgets prepared in the ordinary, incremental way seem to increase period after period. The authority approving the budget assumes operations will be carried out in the same way as in the past and that next period's expenditures will have to be at least as large as the current period's. Thus, this authority tends to study only the increments to the current period's budget. In ZBB, the authority questions the process for carrying out a program and the entire budget for next period. The authority studies every dollar in the budget, not just the dollars incremental to the previous period's amounts. The advocates of ZBB claim that in this way: (1) management will more likely delete programs or divisions of marginal benefit to the business or governmental unit, rather than continuing with costs at least as large as the present ones and (2) management may discover and implement alternative, more cost-effective, ways of carrying out programs. ZBB implies questioning the existence of programs, and the fundamental nature of the way firms carry them out, not merely the amounts used to fund them. Experts appear to be evenly divided as to whether the middle word should be ''base'' or ''based.''

NOTE: Companies and entities in **bold** represent real companies and entities.